The Family, Law and Society
Cases and Materials

The Family, Law and Society Cases and Materials

Fourth edition

Brenda M Hoggett MA (Cantab)
formerly a Law Commissioner, now The Hon
Mrs Justice Hale DBE
Judge of the High Court (Family Division);
Visiting Professor of Law, King's College, London

Judge David Pearl MA, LLM, PhD (Cantab)
Circuit Judge, Chief Adjudicator, Immigration Appeals;
Visiting Professor, King's College, London;
Honorary Professor, University of East Anglia;
Life Fellow, Fitzwilliam College, Cambridge

Elizabeth J Cooke MA (Oxon), LLM (Reading)
Solicitor; Lecturer in Law, University of Reading

Philip D Bates LLB, MA (Sheffield)
Lecturer in Law, University of Reading

Butterworths
London, Edinburgh, Dublin
1996

United Kingdom	Butterworths, a Division of Reed Elsevier (UK) Ltd, Halsbury House, 35 Chancery Lane, LONDON WC2A 1EL and 4 Hill Street, EDINBURGH EH2 3JZ
Australia	Butterworths, SYDNEY, MELBOURNE, BRISBANE, ADELAIDE, PERTH, CANBERRA and HOBART
Canada	Butterworths Canada Ltd, TORONTO and VANCOUVER
Ireland	Butterworth (Ireland) Ltd, DUBLIN
Malaysia	Malayan Law Journal Sdn Bhd, KUALA LUMPUR
New Zealand	Butterworths of New Zealand Ltd, WELLINGTON and AUCKLAND
Singapore	Reed Elsevier (Singapore) Pte Ltd, SINGAPORE
South Africa	Butterworths Publishers (Pty) Ltd, DURBAN
USA	Michie, CHARLOTTESVILLE, Virginia

A CIP Catalogue record for this book is available from the British Library.

First edition 1983
Second edition 1987
Third edition 1991

ISBN 0 406 04588 7

Typeset by Columns Design Ltd, Reading
Printed by Mackays of Chatham PLC, Chatham, Kent

Preface

The aim of this book has always been to introduce the student of family law, at whatever level, to a wider range of materials than can be found in the statutes and law reports. Family lawyers need to know about the Law Commission and other official reports which led or even did not lead to the present law. They also need to know about current demographic and social trends and about some of the research which is relevant to how the law works or how it might be improved. It can be very hard to track these down in a library when so many other students may be looking for exactly the same thing at the same time.

When they compiled the first edition in 1982, Brenda Hoggett and David Pearl were both law teachers who knew something of what their students needed. Since the third edition was published in 1991, they have both become judges who know more about legal practice but less about legal education. They are delighted therefore to welcome two new authors, Lizzie Cooke and Philip Bates, who are members of a new generation of law teachers and can take the book on towards the next century.

As always there is no shortage of new developments to think about. It is hard to remember what life was like before the Children Act 1989; but many of the old debates have been replaced with others. The Family Law Act 1996 will bring the same sort of change not only to divorce law but also the remedies for domestic violence and occupation of the family home. The Adoption Bill is likely to bring further radical changes within the lifetime of this edition. Above all, no family law student can ignore the developing impact of our international obligations, particularly on child abduction, human rights and the respect for family life, and the rights of the child. We have therefore devoted a new chapter to these.

We are always grateful to the many authors who allow us to reproduce their work and to the many other people who have helped us in our own work. The uncertain passage of the Family Law Bill has made compiling this edition particularly difficult. Staff at Butterworths have done a magnificent job in producing it in time for the coming academic year. Our own families have been especially helpful and supportive – particularly their youngest member, Gillian Cooke, whose lively presence at editorial meetings almost since the day she was born has reminded us what this is all about.

15 July 1996

Brenda Hale
David Pearl
Lizzie Cooke
Philip Bates

Contents

Table of statutes

References in this Table to *Statutes* are to Halsbury's Statutes of England (Fourth Edition) showing the volume and page at which the annotated text of the Act may be found. References in **bold** type indicate where the section of an Act is set out in part or in full.

List of cases

Pages on which cases are principally treated are indicated by the use of **bold** figures.

Bibliography

[Asterisks indicate works from which extracts have been quoted.]

Chapter 1

- * M. Anderson, *Approaches to the History of the Western Family (1500–1914)* (1980) London and Basingstoke, Macmillan, pp. 40, 51, 69.
- * M. Anderson (ed.), *Sociology of the Family* (1980) Harmondsworth, Penguin Books, p. 81.
- R. Bailey, 'Decree of Nullity of Marriage of True Hermaphrodite who has Undergone Sex-change Surgery' (1979) 53 Australian Law Journal 659.
- R. Ballard, 'South Asian Families' in R.N. Rapoport, M. Fogarty and R. Rapoport (eds) *Families in Britain* (1982) London, Routledge.
- J. Barrow, 'West Indian Families: An Insider's Perspective' in R.N. Rapoport, M. Fogarty and R. Rapoport (eds) *Families in Britain* (1982) London, Routledge.
- C. Barton, 'Weddings To Go – The Marriage Act 1994' (1995) 25 Family Law 153.
- L.K. Berkner, 'Peasant Household Organization and Demographic Change in Lower Saxony (1689–1766)' in R.D. Lee (ed.), *Population Patterns in the Past* (1977) New York and London, Academic Press.
- M. Bovey, 'Out and Out: UK Immigration Law and the Homosexual' (1994) 8 I&NL&P 61
- A. Bradney, 'The Family in Family Law' (1979) 9 Family Law 244.
- A. Bradney, 'How Not to Marry People' (1989) 19 Family Law 408.
- A. Dickey, 'The Nature of Family in Law' (1982) 14 West Aust L Rev 417.
- G. Driver 'West Indian Families: An Anthropological Perspective' in R.N. Rapoport, M. Fogarty and R. Rapoport (eds) *Families in Britain* (1982) London, Routledge.
- * *Efficiency Scrutiny of the Registration Service* (1985) London, HMSO, para. 46.2.
- * F. Engels, *Origins of the Family, Private Property and the State* (1st edn., 1884) New York, Lawrence and Wishart, p. 244.
- * R. Fletcher, *The Family and Marriage in Britain* (1966) Harmondsworth, Pelican Books, pp. 26–27, 128 (3rd edn., 1973).
- * R. Fletcher, *The Shaking of the Foundations* (1988) London and New York, Routledge, p. 43.
- R. Fletcher, *The Abolitionists: The Family and Marriage under Attack* (1988) London and New York, Routledge.
- M.A. Glendon, *State, Law and Family* (1977) Amsterdam, North Holland.
- J. Goody, *The Development of the Family and Marriage in Europe* (1983) Cambridge, Cambridge University Press.
- * E.K. Gough, 'The Nayars and the Definition of Marriage' (1959) 89 Journal of the Royal Anthropological Institute, pp. 23, 32.
- * W.J. Goode, *World Revolution and Family Patterns* (1963) The Free Press, a Division of Macmillan Publishing Company, p. 41.

* C.C. Harris, *The Family: an Introduction* (1979) London, Allen and Unwin, p. 49.

J. Jackson, *The Formation and Annulment of Marriage* (2nd edn., 1969) London, Butterworths.

* T.E. James, 'The English Law of Marriage' in R.H. Graveson and F.R. Crane (eds.), *A Century of Family Law* (1957) London, Sweet and Maxwell, pp. 32–33.

* Judicial Studies Board, *Handbook on Ethnic Minority Issues* (1994, now 1995) Chapter 6, paras 3.1–3.2.

* P. Laslett and R. Wall, *Household and Family in Past Time* (1972) Cambridge, Cambridge University Press, pp. 28–30, 63, 64.

* E.R. Leach, 'Polyandry, Inheritance, and the Definition of Marriage' (1955) Man, no. 199, p. 183.

* Law Commission, *Report on Nullity of Marriage,* Law Com. No. 33 (1970) London, HMSO, paras. 24, 25, 52.

* Law Commission, *Report on Solemnisation of Marriage,* Law Com. No. 53 (1973) London, HMSO, paras. 14–16.

C. Lind, 'Time for Lesbian and Gay Marriages' (1995) vol 145 New Law Journal 1553.

A. MacFarlane, *Origins of English Individualism: the Family, Property and Social* Transition (1978) Oxford, Blackwell.

* A. MacFarlane, *Marriage and Love in England 1300–1840* (1986) Oxford, Basil Blackwell, pp. 246–247.

K. Meselman, *Incest* (1979) New York, Jessey Bross.

* L. Mair, *Marriage* (1971) Harmondsworth, Pelican Books; (1977) London, Scolar Press, p. 19.

M. Mullally, 'Decrees of Nullity in the Catholic Church' (1996) 26 Family Law 115.

* K. O'Donovan, *Sexual Divisions in Law* (1985) London, Weidenfeld and Nicholson, pp. 45ff.

* A. Oakley, *Housewife* (1974) London, Allen Lane; (1976) Harmondsworth, Pelican Books, pp. 236–237.

R. Oakley, 'Cypriot Families' in R.N. Rapoport, M. Fogarty and R. Rapoport (eds) *Families in Britain* (1982) London, Routledge.

* Population Trends 'A Review of the 1980s' (1990) 62 Population Trends I at p. 11 (Table H) London, HMSO.

S. Parker, 'Informal Marriage, Cohabitation and the Law, 1750–1989' (1990) Basingstoke, Macmillan.

S. Poulter, *English Law and Ethnic Minority Customs* (1986) London, Butterworths.

J. Priest, 'Child of the Family' (1984) 14 Family Law 134.

Registration: A Modern Service (Cm 531) (1988) London, HMSO.

Registration: Proposals for Change (Cm 939) (1990) London, HMSO.

* E. Shorter, *The Making of the Modern Family* (1975) New York, Basic Books; (1977) London, Fontana, p. 38.

* L. Stone, *The Family, Sex, and Marriage in England 1500–1800* (1977) London, Weidenfeld and Nicholson, pp. 26–27, 102–104.

L. Stone, *Road to Divorce; England 1530–1987 (*1990) Oxford, Oxford University Press.

L.A. Tilly, 'Individual Lives and Family Strategies in the French Proletariat' (1979) Journal of Family History (IV).

L.D. Wardle, 'International Marriage and Divorce Regulation and Recognition: A Survey' (1995) vol 29 Family Law Quarterly, p. 497.

* A. Wilson, *Family* (1985) London and New York, Tavistock Publications, pp. 78–81.

C. Winberg, 'Population Growth and Proletarianization' in S. Akerman et al. (eds.), *Chance and Change* (Odense University Studies in History and Social Sciences, Vol. 52) (1978) Odense, Odense University Press.

R. Wall (ed.), *Family Forms in Historic Europe* (1983) London, Edward Arnold.

S. Whittle, 'An Association for as Noble a Purpose as Any' (1996) vol 146 New Law Journal 366.

* K. Wrightson, *English Society 1580–1680* (1982) London, Hutchinson, pp. 71, 103, 104.

Chapter 2

H. Astor and J. Nothdurft, 'Report of the New South Wales Law Reform Commission on De Facto Relationships' (1985) 48 Modern Law Review at 61.

C. Barton, *Cohabitation Contracts, Extra Marital Partnerships and Law Reform* (1985) Aldershot, Gower, Coventry.

W. Blackstone, *Commentaries on the Laws of England* (1765) 17th edition by Edward Christian and others (1830) London, Tegg.

J. Bradshaw and J. Millar, 'Lone Parent Families in the UK', Department of Social Security Research Report No. 6, p. 98 (HMSO, 1991).

J. Bowlber, J. Jackson and E. Longbridge, *Living Together* (1991) London, Century.

C. Bruch, 'Non-marital Cohabitation in the Common Law Countries: A Study in Judicial-Legislative Interaction' (1981) 29 American Journal of Comparative Law, p. 217.

S. Brownmiller, *Against our Will* (1975) London, Secker and Warburg.

E.H. Butler, *Traditional Marriage and Emerging Alternatives* (1979) Harper and Row, London.

Central Statistical Office, *Social Trends 21* (1991) London, HMSO, Table 2.16.

Central Statistical Office, *Social Trends* 26 (1996) London HMSO, Tables 2.12, 2.13, 2.14, 2.15.

* E.M. Clive, 'Marriage: An Unnecessary Legal Concept' in J .M. Eekelaar and S.M. Katz (eds.), *Marriage and Cohabitation in Contemporary Societies: Areas of Legal, Social and Ethical Change* (1980) Toronto, Butterworths, p. 72.

* Criminal Law Revision Committee, *11th Report* (Cmnd. 4991) (1972) London, HMSO, para. 147.

Criminal Law Revision Committee, *Working Paper on Sexual Offences* (1980) London, HMSO.

Criminal Law Revision Committee, *15th Report on Sexual Offences* (Cmnd. 9213) (1984) London, HMSO.

S. Danielson, 'Unmarried Partners and their Children: Scandinavian Law in the Making' (1983) 3 Oxford Journal of Legal Studies 59.

* R. Deech, 'The Case Against Legal Recognition of Cohabitation' in J.M. Eekelaar and S.M. Katz (eds.), *Marriage and Cohabitation in Contemporary Societies: Areas of Legal, Social and Ethical Change* (1980) Toronto, Butterworths, pp. 309–310.

J. de Montmorency, 'The Changing Status of a Married Woman' (1897) 13 Law Quarterly Review 187.

* Equal Opportunities Commission, *The Taxation of Husband and Wife: Response* of the Equal Opportunities Commission to the Government Green Paper (1981) Manchester, Equal Opportunities Commission, paras. 10 et seq.

H.A. Finley, A.J. Bradbrook and R.J. Bailey-Harris, *Family Law: Cases and Commentary* (1985) Sydney, Butterworths.

M.D.A. Freeman and C.M. Lyon, *Cohabitation Without Marriage* (1983) Aldershot, Gower,

* M.D.A. Freeman, 'Doing his Best to Sustain the Sanctity of Marriage' in N. Johnson (ed.) *Marital Violence* (1985) London, Routledge and Kegan Paul, p. 124 at 136–139.

* M.A. Glendon, 'Withering Away of Marriage' (1976) 62 Virginia Law Review 663, p. 686.

* R. Graveson, 'The Background of the Century' in R.H. Graveson and F.R. Crane (eds.), *A Century of Family Law* (1957) London, Sweet & Maxwell, pp. 2–3.

Sir Matthew Hale, *History of the Pleas of the Crown* (1736) vol. I, p. 629 ed. by George Wilson (1778) London, Sollom Emlyn.

Hansard, House of Lords, vol. 429 (4 May 1982) col. 1104.

* C. Harpum, 'Adjusting Property Rights Between Unmarried Cohabitees' (1982) 2 Oxford Journal of Legal Studies 287.

* J. Haskey and K. Kiernan, 'Cohabitation in Great Britain – Characteristics and Estimated Number of Cohabiting Partners' (1989) 58 Population Trends, p. 23, table 5.6, figs 1, 2, 4, 5, 9, 10.

* J. Haskey 'Trends in Marriage and Cohabitation: the Decline in Marriage and the Changing Pattern of Living in Partnerships' (1995) 80 Population Trends, p. 5, figs 7, 8, 9.

* Inland Revenue, *The Taxation of Husband and Wife* (Cmnd. 8093) (1980) London, HMSO, paras. 14 et seq., 31–41, 83–85.

* Inland Revenue, *The Reform of Personal Taxation* (Cmnd. 9756) (1986) London, HMSO, paras. 3.10–3.21.

Institute of Law Research and Reform, Alberta, *Towards Reform of the Law Relating to Cohabitation Outside Marriage* (1987) Issues Paper No. 2; (1989) Report No. 53.

* International Association of Young Lawyers, Conference in Philadelphia (1980), *an Example of a Cohabitation Contract.*

* *International Social Attitudes* (1993–1994), J. Scott, M. Braun and D. Alwyn, Aldershot, Gower, Tables 1, 2, 3.

R. Johnson, 'Cohabitation Without Formal Marriage in England and Wales' (1986) 16 Family Law 47.

K. Kiernan, V. Estaugh, 'Cohabitation: Extra-Marital Childbearing and Social Policy', (1993) London, Family Policy Studies Centre.

* H.D. Krause, *Family Law* (3rd edn) (1990) St Paul, Minnesota, West Publishing Company, p. 248.

* Law Commission, Working Paper no. 116, *Rape within Marriage* (1990) London, HMSO, paras. 4.20–4.24.

D. Lush, *Cohabitation and Co-ownership Precedents* (1993) Bristol, Family Law.

A. MacFarlane, *Marriage and Love in England 1300–1840* (1986) Oxford, Basil Blackwell.

* S. McRae, *Cohabiting Mothers* (1993), London, Policy Studies Institute, table 5.2.

* D. Meade, 'Consortium Rights of the Unmarried – Time for a Reappraisal' (1981) 12 Family Law Quarterly 213.

J.G. Miller, 'Provision for a Surviving Spouse' (1986) 102 Law Quarterly Review 445.

* C.A. Morrison, 'Tort' in R.H. Graveson and F.R. Crane (eds.), *A Century of Family Law* (1957) London, Sweet and Maxwell, pp. 91–93.

New South Wales Law Reform Commission (1983), *Report on De Facto Relationships* (LRC 36).

D. Oliver, 'The Mistress in Law' [1978] Current Legal Problems 81.

D. Oliver, 'Why Do People Live Together?' [1982] Journal of Social Welfare Law, p. 209.

One Plus One, *Cohabitation*, (1994) London.

* H. Oppenheimer, *Marriage* (1990) London, Mowbray, pp. 32–34.

S. Parker, *Cohabitees* (1987) London, Kluwer Law Publishers.

M.L. Parry, *The Law Relating to Cohabitation* (1988) London, Sweet & Maxwell.

J. Priest, *Families Outside Marriage* (1990) Bristol, Family Law.

* *Report of the Committee on One-Parent Families* (Chairman: The Hon. Sir Morris Finer) (Cmnd. 5629) (1974) London, HMSO, paras. 6.88–6.90.

* The Scottish Law Commission, *The Effects of Cohabitation in Private Law* (1990) Scot. Law Com. Discussion Paper No. 86, Edinburgh, HMSO, paras. 5.2, 5.5.

O. Stone, *Family Law* (1977) London, Macmillan.

J. Temkin, 'Towards a Modern Law of Rape' (1982) 45 Modern Law Review 405.

* L.A. Tilly and J.W. Scott, *Women, Work and Family* (1987) New York and London, Methuen, pp. 4, 220, 253.

E.L. Van Deuson, *Contract Cohabitation: An Alternative to Marriage* (1975) New York, Avon Books.

* L. Weitzman, *The Marriage Contract: Spouses, Lovers, and the Law* (1981) London, Collier MacMillan, p. 361.

* L. Weitzman et al, 'Contracts for Intimate Relationships' (1978) Alternative Lifestyles, vol. I, no. 3, August, figure I (p. 303).

M. Welstead, 'Truly a Charter for Mistresses' (1990) Denning Law Journal, p. 117.

* W. Weyrauch, 'Metamorphoses of Marriage' (1980) 13 Family Law Quarterly 436.

* W. Weyrauch, S. Katz, and F. Olsen, *Cases and Materials on Family Law* (1994) St. Paul, Minnesota, West Publishing Company, pp. 304–306.

G.L. Williams, 'The Legal Unity of Husband and Wife' (1947) 10 Modern Law Review 16.

* O.P. Wylie, *Taxation of Husband and Wife* (1990) London, Butterworths, pp. 4, 253.

A. Zuckerman, 'Formality and the Family – Reform and Status Quo' (1980) 96 Law Quarterly Review 248.

A.A. Zuckerman, *The Principles of Criminal Evidence* (1989) Oxford, Oxford University Press.

Chapter 3

M. Anderson, 'Family, Household and the Industrial Revolution' in M. Anderson (ed.), *Sociology of the Family* (1980) Harmondsworth, Penguin Books.

Association of Market Survey Organisations, *Men and Domestic Work* (1987).

L. Baillyn, 'Career and Family Orientation of Husband and Wife' (1971) Human Relations 23, pp. 97 et seq.

M. Barrett and M. McIntosh, *The Anti-Social Family* (1982) London, Verso Editions.

J. Bernard, *The Future of the Family* (1972) New York, World.

J. Burgoyne, R. Ormrod, M. Richards, *Divorce Matters* (1987) Harmondsworth, Penguin Books.

* Central Statistical Office, *Social Trends 21* (1991) London, HMSO, table 4.2.

E. Clive, 'Marriage: An Unnecessary Legal Concept' in J.M. Eekelaar and S.N. Katz (eds.), *Marriage and Cohabitation in Contemporary Societies: Areas of Legal, Social and Ethical Change* (1980) Toronto, Butterworths.

L. Colley, *Britons* (1992), London, Pimlico (Chapter 6: Womenpower).

L. Comer, *Wedlocked Women* (1974) Leeds, Feminist Books.

W.B. Creighton, *Working Women and the Law* (1979) London, Mansell.

R. Deech, 'The Work of the Law Commission in Family Law: The First Twenty Years' in M.D.A. Freeman (ed.) *Essays in Family Law 1985* (1986) London, Stevens.

* Sir M. Finer and O.R. McGregor, 'The History of the Obligation to Maintain'. App. 5, *Report of the Committee on One-Parent Families* (Cmnd. 5629–1) (1974) London, HMSO, para. 36.

* D. Gittins, *The Family in Question* (1985) Basingstoke, Macmillan, pp. 27, 28, 131.

H. Gavron, *The Captive Wife* (1966) London, Routledge and Kegan Paul; Harmondsworth, Penguin Books.

* M.A. Glendon, *State, Law and Family* (1977) Amsterdam, North Holland, p. 75.

C. Glendinning and J. Millar, *Women and Poverty in Britain* (1987) Brighton, Wheatsheaf Books.

G. Gorer, *Sex and Marriage in England Today* (1971) London, Nelson.

D. Gowler and K. Legge, 'Dual Worker Families' in R.N. Rapoport, M.P. Fogarty, and R. Rapoport (eds.), *Families in Britain* (1982) London, Routledge and Kegan Paul.

E. Granseth, 'Work Sharing: a Norwegian Experience' in R.N. Rapoport and R. Rapoport (eds.), *Working Couples* (1978) London, Routledge and Kegan Paul.

* K. Gray, *Reallocation of Property on Divorce* (1977) Abingdon, Professional Books, p. 176.

M.W. Gray, 'Prescriptions for Productive Female Domesticity in a Transitional Era: Germany's Hausmutterliteratur 1780–1840', (1987) 8 History of European Ideas, p. 413.

C. Hakim, *Key Issues in Women's Work* (1996), London , Athlone.

H. Harman, *The Century Gap* (1993) London, Vermilion.

E. Hobsbaum and G. Ride, *Captain Swing* (1973) Harmondsworth, Penguin.

L. Hoffman and F. Nye, *Working Mothers* (2nd edn., 1978) New York, Jossey Bass.

* *Home Office Statistical Bulletin 26/1993* Map 1.

* A. Honore, *The Quest for Security: Employees, Tenants, Wives* (1982) London, Stevens, p. 62.

* P. Hudson and W.R. Lee 'Women's Work and the Family Economy in Historical Perspective' in P. Hudson and W.R. Lee (eds), *Women's Work and the Family Economy in Historical Perspective* (1990) Manchester and New York, Manchester University Press, pp. 26, 27, 28, 31, 32.

* Inland Revenue, *The Taxation of Husband and Wife* (Cmnd. 8093) (1980) London, HMSO, tables 1–3.

* Inland Revenue, *The Reform of Personal Taxation* (Cmnd. 9756) (1986) London, HMSO, Charts 2.2, 2.3.

J. Jephcott, N. Seear and J. Smith, *Married Women Working* (1962) London.

H. Land, 'Women: Supporters or Supported?' in D.L. Baker and S. Allen (eds.) *Sexual Divisions and Society: Process and Change* (1976), London, Tavistock.

H. Land, *Large Families in London* (1969) London, G. Bell & Sons.

P. Laslett, *The World We Have Lost* (2nd edn., 1971) London, Methuen.

* Law Commission, Working Paper No. 53, *Matrimonial Proceedings in Magistrates' Courts* (1973) London, HMSO, paras. 7–11, 24, 35, 42, 43.

* Law Commission, *Report on Matrimonial Proceedings in Magistrates' Courts*, Law Com No. 77 (1976) London, HMSO, paras. 2.8–2.11, 2.15, 2.60–2.61.

Law Commission, Working Paper No. 90, *Transfer of Money Between Spouses*.

* Law Commission, *Report on Family Law: Matrimonial Property*, Law Com. No. 175 (1988) London, HMSO, paras. 5.1–5.4.

* Law Commission *Report on Family Law: The Ground for Divorce*, Law Com. No. 192 (1990) London, HMSO, paras. 4.22–4.28.

J. Lewis and D. Piachaud, 'Women and Poverty in the Twentieth Century' in C. Glendinning and J. Millar (eds) *Women and Poverty in Britain* (1987) Brighton, Wheatsheaf Books.

O.R. McGregor, *Social History and Law Reform* (1981) London, Stevens.

J. Martin and C. Roberts, *Women and Employment: A Lifetime Perspective* (1984) London, HMSO.

* S. McRae, *Cohabiting Mothers* (1993) London, Policy Studies Institute, tables 6.5, 6.6.

J. Mortimore, 'Dual-career Families – A Sociological Perspective' (1977) Conference Papers, Minnesota.

P. Morton, *Women's Work is Never Done* (1970) London, Leviathan.

P. Moss and I.P. Lewis, *Young Children in the Inner City* (1979) London, HMSO (T. Coram Research Unit – Pre-school project).

K. O'Donovan, 'Should All Maintenance of Spouses be Abolished?' (1982) 45 Modern Law Review 4311.

* A. Oakley, *The Sociology of Housework* (1974) London, Martin Robertson & Co. pp. 122, 124.

A. Oakley, *Subject Women* (1981) London, Martin Robertson & Co., (1982) Harmondsworth, Penguin Books.

A. Oakley, 'Conventional Families' in R.N. Rapoport, M. Fogarty and R. Rapoport (eds.), *Families in Britain* (1982) London, Routledge and Kegan Paul.

* Office of Population Censuses and Surveys, *Family Formation Survey* (1979) London, HMSO.

S. Orden and M. Bradburn, 'Dimensions of Marriage Happiness' (18) 74 Journal of Sociology 715.

J. Pahl, 'Patterns of Money Management Within Marriage' (1980) 9 Journal of Social Policy 313.

* J. Pahl, 'The Allocation of Money Within the Household' in M.D.A. Freeman (ed.) *State, Law and the Family* (1984) London and New York, Tavistock Publications, p. 36 at pp. 40–42, 44, 45.

* J. Pahl, *Money and Marriage* (1989) Basingstoke and London, Macmillan, pp. 94, 108, 178.

R.N. Rapoport, R. Rapoport and Z. Strelitz, *Fathers, Mothers and Others* (1977) London, Routledge and Kegan Paul.

R.N. Rapoport and R. Rapoport (eds.), *Working Couples* (1978) London Routledge and Kegan Paul.

* R.N. Rapoport and R. Rapoport, 'The Impact of Work on the Family' in P. Moss and N. Fonda (eds.), *Work and the Family* (1980) London, Temple Smith, pp. 172 et seq., 177.

R.N. Rapoport and R. Rapoport, 'Dual Career Families: Progress and Prospect' (1978) Marriage and Family Review.

* *Report of the Committee on One-Parent Families* (Chairman: The Hon Sir Morris Finer) (Cmnd. 5629) (1974) London, HMSO, paras. 4.386, 4.67–68.

* *Report of the Royal Commission on Marriage and Divorce* (Chairman: Lord Morton of Henryton) (Cmd. 9678) (1956) London, HMSO, paras. 1042, 1046.

L. Rimmer, *Employment Trends and the Family* (1981) London, Study Commission on the Family.

H. Ross and I. Sawhill, *Time of Transition: the Growth of Families headed by Women* (1975) Washington, Urban Institute.

M. Rutter, *Maternal Deprivation Reassessed* (1972) Harmondsworth, Penguin Books.

S. Rowbotham, *Women's Consciousness, Man's World* (1973) Harmondsworth, Penguin Books.

H. Scott, *Working Your Way to the Bottom: the Feminisation of Poverty* (1984) London, Pandora Press.

* J. Todd and L. Jones, *Matrimonial Property* (1972) London, HMSO, paras. 4.0, 4.2.

* L. Tilly and J. Scott, *Woman, Work and Family* (1987) New York and London, Methuen, pp. 21 et seq. 105, 123, 124, 176.

M. Weissman and E. Paykel, *The Depressed Woman* (1974) Chicago, University of Chicago Press.

* L. Weitzman, 'Legal Regulation of Marriage: Tradition and Change' (1974) 62 California Law Review 1169.

A. Wilensky, 'Women's Work, Economic Growth, Ideology and Structure' (1968) 7 Industrial Relations 235.

* E. Wilson, *Women and the Welfare State* (1977) London, Tavistock, p. 176.

M. Young, 'Distribution of Income Within the Family' (1952) 3 British Journal of Sociology 303.

* M. Young and P. Willmott *The Symmetrical Family* (1973) London, Routledge and Kegan Paul (1980) Harmondsworth, Penguin Books, pp. 28 et seq.

F. Zweig, *The Workers in the Affluent Society* (1961) London, Heineman.

Chapter 4

G. Ashton, *Elderly People and the Law* (1995), Butterworths.

* Sir William Beveridge, *Social Insurance and Allied Services* (Cmd. 6404) (1942) London, HMSO, para. 347.

R. Bird, *Child Support Calculation Pack 1996/97* (1996), Family Law.

* J. Bradshaw and J. Millar, *Lone Parent Families in the UK* (1991) Social Security Research Report, no. 6, London, HMSO, p. 18.

* Central Statistical Office, *Social Trends 20* (1990) London, HMSO, table 1.20.

* Central Statistical Office, *Social Trends 25* (1991) London, HMSO, table 8.22; p. 146.

* Central Statistical Office, *Social Trends 26* (1996) London, HMSO, tables 1.1, 1.5, 2.4, 2.11, 5.10, 5.15.

* *Children Come First: (Cm 1264)* (1990) London, HMSO, The Government's proposals on the maintenance of children, vol. 1:1/16; Appendix C; vol. 2. 1.3.2.; 1.4.; 1.5.

DHSS/SBC, *Low Incomes* (1979) London, HMSO.

G. Douglas, 'Individual Economic Security for the Elderly and the Divorced: A Consideration of the Position in England and Wales' in M.T. Meulders-Klein and J. Eekelaar (eds) *Family, State and Individual Economic Security* (1988) Brussels, Story-Scientia, p. 491.

* J.M. Eekelaar, 'Public Law and Private Rights: the Finer Proposals' [1976] Public Law 64, pp. 70–77.

J. Eekelaar and D. Pearl (eds.) *An Aging World* (1989) Oxford, Oxford University Press.

Equal Opportunities Commission, *The Taxation of Husband and Wife: Response of the Equal Opportunities Commission to the Government Green Paper* (1981) Manchester, Equal Opportunities Commission.

F. Field, *Fair Shares for Families – the Need for a Family Impact Statement* (1981) London, Study Commission on the Family.

V. George, *Social Security and Society* (1973) London, Routledge and Kegan Paul.

H. Green, *Informal Carers* (1988) OPCS (Social Survey Division) Series GH 5 no. 15 supp A, London, HMSO.

A. Griffiths and G. Roberts (eds), *The Law and Elderly People* (1995), London, Routledge.

* *Guidelines on the Application of the Requirement to Co-operation* (1993) Department of Social Security, pp. 5, 9–10.

* *Hansard,* House of Commons, vol. 192 (4 June 1991) cols 178–249.

* *Hansard,* House of Lords, vol. 526 (25 February 1991) cols 779, 781–782, 830.

J. Haskey, 'One-Parent Families and Their Children in Great Britain: Numbers and Characteristics' (1989) 55 Population Trends 27.

House of Commons Social Security Committee, *Second Report,* (Session 1990–91) (HC 277–1) para. 11.

House of Commons Social Security Committee, *First Report,* (Session 1993–94) (HC 69).

* House of Commons Social Security Committee, *Fifth Report,* (Session 1993–94) (HC 470) paras. 21, 23, 53, 57, 65, 67.

* Improving Child Support (Cm 2745) (1995) London, HMSO, p. 8.

* J. Leigh, 'Child Maintenance: A View from the Law Society' [1991] Journal of Child Law.

P. Lewis, 'Cutting Poverty in Half' One-Parent Times, Spring 1979.

R. Lister, *Patching Up the Safety Net* (1977) London, Child Poverty Action Group.

R. Lister, *The No-Cost, No-Benefit Review* (1979) London, Child Poverty Action Group.

* R. Lister, 'Income Maintenance for Families with Children' in R.N. Rapoport, M.P. Fogarty and R. Rapoport (eds.), *Families in Britain* (1982) London, Routledge and Kegan Paul, p. 432.

* M. Maclean and J. Eekelaar, *Children and Divorce: Economic Factors* (1983) Oxford, SSRC, p. 10.

A.J. Manners and I. Rauta, *Family Property in Scotland* (1981), Edinburgh, HMSO.

J.E. Meade, *The Structure and Reform of Direct Taxation* (1978) London, George Allen and Unwin.

M.T. Meulders-Klein and J. Eekelaar (eds) *Family, State and Individual Economic Security* (1988) Brussels, Story-Scientia.

S. Monk, 'Child Support: the View from the National Council for One-Parent Families' (1991) Journal of Child Law.

S. Parker, 'Child Support in Australia: Children's Rights or Public Interest' (1991) vol. 5 Int Journal of Law and the Family, p. 24.

D. Piachaud, *The Cost of a Child* (1979) London, Child Poverty Action Group.

C. Pond, *The Poverty Trap* (1978) Milton Keynes, Open University Press.

* P. Paillat, 'Recent and Predictable Population Trends in Developed Countries' in J. Eekelaar and D. Pearl (eds.), *An Aging World* (1989) Oxford, Oxford University Press, p. 25 at p. 35.

Reform of Social Security vol. I (1985) (Cmnd. 9517) London, HMSO.

* *Reform of Social Security* (Programme for Change) vol. 11 (1985) (Cmnd. 9518) London, HMSO paras. 4.44–4.48.

Reform of Social Security (Programme for Action) (1985) (Cmnd. 9691) London, HMSO.

* *Report of the Committee on One-Parent Families* (Chairman: The Hon. Sir Morris Finer) (Cmnd. 5629) (1974) London, HMSO, paras. 4.179–4.183, 4.193, 4.207, 4.188–4.189, 5.104, 5.81–5.86.

Royal Commission on the Taxation of Profits and Income, *Second Report* (Cmd. 9105) (1954) London, HMSO.

Supplementary Benefits Commission, *Cohabitation* (1971) London, HMSO.

J.E. Todd and C.M. Jones, *Matrimonial Property* (1972) London, HMSO.

P. Townsend, *Poverty in the United Kingdom* (1981) Harmondsworth, Penguin Books.

Supplementary Benefits Commission, *Response of the Supplementary Benefits Commission to Social Assistance* (1979) London, HMSO.

* The Independent Newspaper, November 2nd 1990 (comment by J. Eekelaar).

* The Independent Newspaper, April 25th 1991 (letter).

J. Walley, *Social Security: Another British Failure?* (1972) London, Charles Knight.

M. Wynn, *Family Policy* (1972) Harmondsworth, Penguin Books.

Chapter 5

* L. Clarke and R. Edmunds, 'H v M: Equity and the Essex Cohabitant' (1992) 22 Family Law 523.

P. Clarke, 'The Family Home, Intention and Agreement' (1992) 22 Fam Law 72.

E.J. Cooke, 'Property Adjustment Orders for Children' (1994) 6 Journal of Child Law 156.

E.J. Cooke, 'Reliance and Estoppel' (1995) 111 Law Quarterly Review 389.

K. Gray, *Reallocation of Property on Divorce* (1977) Abingdon, Professional Books.

* P. Ferguson, 'Constructive Trusts – A Note of Caution' (1993) 109 Law Quarterly Review 114; 124–5.

* S. Gardiner, 'Rethinking Family Property' (1993) 109 Law Quarterly Review 263, pp. 264–5.

D. Hayton, 'The Equitable Rights of Cohabitees' [1990] Conveyancer 370.

D. Hayton, 'Constructive Trusts of Homes – A Bold Approach' 109 Law Quarterly Review 485.

* B. Hale, *Family Law Reform: Wither or Whither* (1995) Current Legal Problems 217, pp. 228–229.

* C. Harpum, 'Adjusting Property Rights Between Unmarried Cohabitees' (1982) 2 Oxford Journal of Legal Studies 287.

C. Harpum, 'Cohabitation Consultation' (1995) 25 Family Law 657.

* *Insolvency Law and Practice* (Report of the Review Committee chaired by Sir Kenneth Cork) (Cmnd 8558) (1982) London, HMSO, para. 1118.

* O. Kahn-Freund, *Matrimonial Property: where do we go from here?* Joseph Unger Memorial Lecture, University of Birmingham, (1974) pp. 11, 20–21, 22, 23, 25, 46–47.

* Law Reform Commission of Canada, *Family Property,* Working Paper No. 8 (1975) Ottowa, Information Canada, pp. 9–10, 18, 19–22, 27.

* Law Commission, Working Paper No. 42, *Family Property Law* (1971) London, HMSO paras. 0.12, 0.13, 0.15, 0.16, 0.25–0.29, 0.37–0.41, 4.65, 4.71.

* Law Commission, *First Report on Family Property: A New Approach,* Law Com. No. 52 (1973) London, HMSO, paras. 21–24, 38, 39, 41, 44, 47–59.

Law Commission, *Second Report on Family Property: Family Provision on Death*, Law Com. No. 61 (1974) London, HMSO.

* Law Commission, *Third Report on Family Property: The Matrimonial Home (Co-ownership and Occupation Rights) and Household Goods,* Law Com. No. 86 (1978) London, HMSO, paras. 1.113–1.119.

Law Commission, *Property Law: The implications of Williams and Glyn's Bank Ltd v Boland,* Law Com. No. 115 (1982) London, HMSO.

Law Commission, *Report on Illegitimacy,* Law Com. No. 118 (1982) London, HMSO.

* Law Commission, Working Paper No. 90, *Transfer of Money Between Spouses – the Married Women's Property Act 1964* (1985) London, HMSO, paras. 5.5–5.6.

* Law Commission, *Matrimonial Property: Second Consultation Paper* (1986) London, HMSO, paras. 1.1–1.6; 2.1, 2.2.

* Law Commission, *Property Law: 3rd Report on Land Registration,* Law Com. No. 158 (1987) London, HMSO paras. 2.6, 2.12.

* Law Commission, *Family Law, Matrimonial Property,* Law Com. No. 175 (1988) London, HMSO, para 1.4, footnote 21.

Law Commission, *Distribution on Intestacy,* Law Com. No. 187 (1989) London, HMSO.

Law Commission, *Transfer of Land: Land Registration, First Report of a Joint Working Group on the Implementation of the Law Commission's Third and Fourth Reports on Land Registration,* Law Com. No. 235 (1995) London, HMSO.

A.J. Manners and I. Rauta, *Family Property in Scotland* (1981) Edinburgh, HMSO.

J. Masson, 'A New Approach to Matrimonial Property' (1988) 18 Family Law 327.

J.G. Miller, *Family Property and Financial Provision* (1974) (3rd edn. 1983) London, Sweet and Maxwell.

J. Montgomery, 'A Question of Intention' (1987), Conveyancer 86, p. 16.

P. Parkinson, 'The Property Rights of Cohabitees – Is Statutory Reform the Answer?' in A. Bainham, D. Pearl and R. Pickford (eds) *Frontiers of Family Law,* (1995) Chichester, John Wiley and Sons.

Report of the Committee on One-Parent Families (Chairman: The Hon Sir Morris Finer) (Cmnd. 5629) (1974) London, HMSO.
M. Rheinstein and M. Glendon, 'Interspousal Relations' (1980) International Encyclopedia of Comparative Law, vol. IV.
* The Scottish Law Commission, *Family Law: Report on Matrimonial Property* (1984) Scot. Law Com. No. 86 HC 467, Edinburgh, HMSO, para. 3.
* The Scottish Law Commission, *The Effects of Cohabitation in Private Law* (1990) Scot. Law Com. Discussion Paper No. 86, Edinburgh, HMSO, paras. 5.2, 5.3.
The Scottish Law Commission, *Report on Family Law* (1992) Scot. Law Com. No. 135 Edinburgh, HMSO.
* Sir Jocelyn Simon, *With All My Worldly Goods*, Holdsworth Club, Presidential Address, University of Birmingham (1964), pp. 1–4, 8–9, 10–13, 14–17, 100, 101, 102, 103.

Chapter 6

S. Anderson, 'Legislative Divorce – Law for the Aristocracy' in G.R. Rubin and N. Sugarman (eds.) *Law, Society and Economy: Essays in Legal History* (1984), Abingdon, Professional Books.
* G. Alpern, *Rights of Passage* (1982) Aspen, Colorado, Psychological Development Publications, p. 19.
A. Alvarez, *Life after Marriage: Love in an Age of Divorce* (1981) New York, Simon and Schuster.
A. Bainham, 'Divorce and the Lord Chancellor: Looking to the Future or Getting Back to Basics?' (1994) 53 Cambridge Law Journal 253, p. 256.
J. Burgoyne, R. Ormrod, M. Richards, *Divorce Matters* (1987) Harmondsworth, Penguin Books.
* Central Statistical Office, *Social Trends 21* (1991) London, HMSO, chart 2.15.
A.J. Cherlin, *Marriage, Divorce and Remarriage* (1981) Cambridge, Massachusetts, Harvard University Press.
R. Chester (ed.), *Divorce in Europe* (1978) Leiden, Martin Nijhoff.
R. Chester and J. Streather, 'Cruelty in English Divorce: Some Empirical Findings' (1972) 34 Journal of Marriage and the Family, 706.
* J. Cleese and R. Skynner, *Families and How to Survive Them* (1993) London, Cedar, pp. 15, 16.
E. Clive, *The Divorce (Scotland) Act 1976* (1976) Edinburgh, Green.
* H. Conway, 'Divorce and Religion' (1995) New Law Journal, p. 1618.
* S. Cretney, 'The Divorce White Paper – Some Reflections' (1995) Family Law 302, p. 304.
* G. Davis, A. Macleod and M. Murch, 'Special Procedure in Divorce and the Solicitor's Role' (1982) 12 Family Law 39, pp. 39, 43–44.
* G. Davis and M. Murch, *Grounds for Divorce* (1988) Oxford, Clarendon Press, pp. 78–85.
* R. Deech, 'Marriage as a Short-term Option' (1990) The Independent Newspaper, 2nd November 1990.
* R. Deech, *Divorce Dissent – Dangers in Divorce Reform* (1994) London, Centre for Policy Studies, pp. 14, 20–21.
J. Dominian, 'Families in Divorce' in R.N. Rapoport, M.P. Fogarty and R. Rapoport (eds.), *Families in Britain* (1982) London, Routledge and Kegan Paul.
J. Eekelaar, *Family Law and Social Policy* (2nd edn.) (1984) London, Weidenfeld and Nicolson.
J. Eekelaar, *Regulating Divorce* (1991) Oxford, Clarendon.

J. Eekelaar, 'The Family Law Bill: The Politics of Family Law' (1996) 26 Family Law 46.

E. Elston, J. Fuller and M. Murch, 'Judicial Hearings of Undefended Divorce Petitions' (1975) 38 Modern Law Review 609.

* Sir Morris Finer and O.R. McGregor, 'The History of the Obligation to Maintain' App. 5, *Report of the Committee on One-Parent Families* (Cmnd. 5629–1) (1974) London, HMSO, paras. 1, 2, 4, 5, 6, 13, 14, 17, 18, 30, 31, 34, 42, 43.

T. Fisher, 'Impressions of the Family Law Bill in the House of Lords' (1996) Family Mediation vol. 6 no. 1, p. 3.

M.D.A. Freeman, 'Divorce without Legal Aid' (1976) 6 Family Law 255.

C. Gibson, 'The Effect of Legal Aid on Divorce in England and Wales, Part 1: Before 1950' (1971) 1 Family Law 90.

C. Gibson and A. Beer, 'The Effect of Legal Aid on Divorce in England and Wales, Part 11: Since 1950' (1971) 1 Family Law 122.

C. Gibson, 'The Association between Divorce and Social Class in England and Wales' (1974) 25 British Journal of Sociology 79.

C. Gibson, 'Divorce and the Recourse to Legal Aid' (1980) 43 Modern Law Review 609.

* M.A. Glendon, *Abortion and Divorce in Western Law* (1987) Cambridge (Mass) and London, Harvard University Press, pp. 63–64, 66–68.

* *Hansard*, House of Commons, vol. 276 (24 April 1996) cols 502, 505.

J. Haskey, 'The Proportion of Marriages ending in Divorce' (1982) 27 Population Trends 4.

* J. Haskey, 'Social Class and Socio-economic Differentials in Divorce in England and Wales' (1984) Population Studies, p. 38.

J. Haskey, 'Grounds for Divorce in England and Wales – a Social and Demographic Analysis' (1986) 18 J. Biosoc. Sci., p. 127, Fig. 2, Table 3.

J. Haskey, 'Recent Trends in Divorce in England and Wales: the Effects of Legislative Changes' (1986) 44 Population Trends, p. 9.

* J. Haskey, 'Trends in Marriage and Divorce 1837–1987' (1987) 48 Population Trends, p. 11, figure 6 (at p. 17).

* J. Haskey, 'Regional Patterns of Divorce in England and Wales' (1988) 52 Population Trends, p. 5, table 6 (at p. 13).

* J. Haskey, 'Children in Families Broken by Divorce' (1990) 61 Population Trends, p. 34, figure I (p. 35), table I (p. 35).

* J. Haskey, 'Pre-marital Cohabitation and the Probability of Subsequent Divorce' (1982) 68 Population Trends 10, pp. 17–18 and fig. 3.

* J. Haskey, 'Patterns of Marriage, Divorce, and Cohabitation in the Different Countries of Europe' (1992) 69 Population Trends 26, pp. 29–31, figs 2(a) and 2(b).

* J. Haskey, 'Formulation and dissolution of unions in the different countries of Europe' in A. Blum and J.-L. Rallu (eds) *European Population, vol. II: Demographic Dynamics* (1993) Paris, John Libbey Eurotext, Figures 2a and 2b.

* J. Haskey, 'Divorce Statistics' (1996) 26 Family Law 301, table 2.

Cardinal B. Hume, 'Why We Need a Change of Heart on Divorce Law' (1996) The Times, 20th January 1996, p. 20.

* Law Commission, *Reform of the Grounds of Divorce – The Field of Choice* (Cmnd. 3123) (1966) London, HMSO, paras. 11, 15, 19, 52, 120.

Law Commission, Working Paper No. 76, *Time Restrictions on Presentation of Divorce and Nullity Petitions* (1980) London, HMSO.

* Law Commission, *Report on Time Restrictions of Presentation of Divorce and Nullity Petitions,* Law Com. No. 116 (1982) London, HMSO, paras. 2.14, 2.15, 2.27, 2.30, 2.31, 2.33.

Law Commission, *Facing the Future – A Discussion Paper on the Ground for Divorce,* Law Com. No. 170 (1988) London, HMSO.

★ Law Commission, *The Ground for Divorce,* Law Com. No. 192 (1990) London, HMSO, paras. 1.5–1.8; 2.8–2.21; 3.29–3.48; 5.25; 5.27; 5.28; 5.75–5.77.

★ Law Commission, *Court Record Study* Appendix C to *The Ground for Divorce,* Law Com. No. 192 (1990) London, HMSO, paras. 26, 31, 32, 44, 51.

Law Reform Commission of Canada, Working Paper No. 13, *Divorce* (1975) Ottowa, Information Canada, pp. 31, 34, 35.

Law Society, Family Law Sub-Committee, *A Better Way Out: Suggestions for the Reform of the Law of Divorce and Other Forms of Matrimonial Relief; for the Setting Up of a Family Court; and for its Procedure* (1979) London, The Law Society, paras. 33, 35–38, 40, 42, 44, 46–52, 58, 69, 70.

Law Society, Standing Committee on Family Law, *A Better Way Out Reviewed* (1982) London, The Law Society, paras. 27, 28.

B.H. Lee, *Divorce Law Reform in England* (1974) London, Peter Owen.

★ R. Leete, *Changing Patterns of Family Formation and Dissolution in England and Wales 1964–1976,* OPCS Studies on Medical and Population Subjects No. 39 (1979) London, HMSO, tables 36, 38, figures 19, 20.

Legal Aid – Targeting Need. The future of publicly funded help in solving legal problems and disputes in England and Wales. A consultation paper issued by the Lord Chancellor's Department. (Cm 1854) (1995) London, HMSO, pp. 66–67.

★ *Looking to the Future: Mediation and the Ground for Divorce. A consultation paper.* (Cm 2424) (1993) London, HMSO, paras. 9.28–9.30.

Looking to the Future: Mediation and the Ground for Divorce. The Government's proposals. (Cm 2799) (1995) London, HMSO.

★ Lord Chancellor's Department, *Judicial Statistics – Annual Reports* 1994 (Cmnd. 2891) table 5.5.

O.R. McGregor, *Divorce in England – A Centenary Study* (1957) London, Heinemann.

M. Maclean and R.E.J. Wadsworth, 'The Interests of Children after Parental Divorce: A Long-term Perspective' (1988) 2 Int. J. of Law and the Family 155.

S. Maidment, *Judicial Separation – A Research Study* (1982) Oxford, Centre for Socio-Legal Studies.

M. Mears, 'Getting it Wrong Again? Divorce and the Law Commission' (1991) 21 Family Law 231.

B. Mortlock, *The Inside of Divorce* (1972) London, Constable.

★ National Family Mediation, 'The Mediation Process', in *Briefing for the Family Law Bill,* 1996.

★ Office of Population Censuses and Surveys, *Updates* No. 11, November 1995, tables 1, 2 and 3.

★ Office of Population Censuses and Surveys, *Updates* No. 14, February 1996, tables 1 and 2.

F. Pollock and F.W. Maitland, *The History of English Law Before the Time of Edward I* (2nd edn., 1898) Cambridge, Cambridge University Press.

★ Report of a Group appointed by the Archbishop of Canterbury (Chairman: The Rt Rev. R.C. Mortimer, Lord Bishop of Exeter), *Putting Asunder – A Divorce Law for Contemporary Society* (1966) London, Society for Promoting Christian Knowledge, paras. 17, 18, 45(f), 55, 69.

★ *Report of the Committee on One-Parent Families* (Chairman: The Hon. Sir Morris Finer) (Cmnd. 5629) (1974) London, HMSO, paras. 4.29–4.32.

★ *Report of the Matrimonial Causes Procedure Committee* (Chairman: The Hon. Mrs. Justice Booth, D.B.E.) (1985) London, HMSO, paras. 2.9, 2.10.

Report of the Royal Commission on Divorce (Chairman: Lord Gorell), (Cd. 6478) (1912) London, HMSO.

Report of the Royal Commission on Marriage and Divorce (Chairman: Lord Morton of Henryton) (Cmd. 9678) (1956) London, HMSO.

M. Rheinstein, *Marriage Stability, Divorce and the Law* (1972) Chicago, University of Chicago Press.

* M.P.M. Richards, 'Divorce Research Today' (1991) 21 Family Law, pp. 70–72.

* M.P.M. Richards, 'Private Worlds and Public Intentions – The Role of the State in Divorce' in A. Bainham, D. Pearl and R. Pickford (eds) *Frontiers of Family Law*, (1995) Chichester, John Wiley and Sons.

M.P.M. Richards and M. Dyson, *Separation, Divorce and the Development of Children: a Review* (1982) London, DHSS.

L. Rimmer, *Families in Focus* (1981) London, Study Commission on the Family.

* St. Mark, 'Gospel according to St. Mark' *Holy Bible* Authorised King James version, ch. 10.

Sir Jocelyn Simon, 'Recent Developments in the Matrimonial Law' Riddell lecture, 1970. Printed in *Rayden on Divorce* (11th edn., 1971) London, Butterworths.

'So What's Unreasonable Behaviour?', *The Times*, 15th February 1996, p. 15.

Society of Conservative Lawyers, *The Future of Marriage – A Report by a Research Sub-Committee* (1981) London, Conservative Political Centre.

* L. Stone, *Road to Divorce: England 1530–1987* (1990) Oxford, Oxford University Press, pp. 27, 310.

S.D. Sugarman and H.H. Kay, *Divorce Reform at the Crossroads* (1990) New Haven and London, Yale University Press.

B. Thornes and J. Collard, *Who Divorces?* (1979) London, Routledge and Kegan Paul.

The Scottish Law Commission, *Report on Reform of the Ground for Divorce* (1989) Scot. Law Com. No. 116, Edinburgh, HMSO.

L. Tottie, 'The Elimination of Fault in Swedish Divorce Law' in J.M. Eekelaar and S.N. Katz (eds.), *Marriage and Cohabitation in Contemporary Societies: Areas of Legal, Social and Ethical Change* (1980) Toronto, Butterworths.

United States National Conference of Commissioners on Uniform State Laws, *Uniform Marriage and Divorce Act* (1970), s. 305.

W. Wadlington, 'Divorce Without Fault Without Perjury' (1966) 52 Virginia Law Review 32.

J. Walker, 'Divorce – Whose Fault?' (1991) 21 Family Law 234.

* J. Walker, P. McCarthy, N. Timms, *Mediation: the Making and Remaking of Co-operative Relationships. An evaluation of the effectiveness of comprehensive mediation* (1994) Newcastle upon Tyne, Relate Centre for Family Studies (the *Rowntree Report*).

J.S. Wallerstein and J.B. Kelly, *Surviving the Breakup* (1980) New York, Basic Books Inc.

J.S. Wallerstein and S. Blakeslee, *Second Chances* (1989) London, Bantam.

L. Weitzman and R.B. Dixon, 'The Transformation of Marriage through No Fault Divorce – The Case of the United States' in J.M. Eekelaar and S.N. Katz (eds.), *Marriage and Cohabitation in Contemporary Societies: Areas of Legal, Social and Ethical Change* (1980) Toronto, Butterworths.

S. Wolfram, 'Divorce in England 1700–1857' (1984) 5 Oxford Journal of Legal Studies 156.

Chapter 7

ACAS, The Advisory, Conciliation and Arbitration Service, *The ACAS Role in Conciliation, Arbitration and Mediation* (1979) London, HMSO.

Dame Margaret Booth, 'The UK College of Family Mediators' (1996) 26 Family Law 67.

Booth Committee, see Report of the Matrimonial Causes Procedure Committee.

* A. Bottomley, 'Resolving family disputes – a critical view in M.D.A. Freeman (ed.), *The State, the Law and the Family: Critical Perspectives* (1984) London, Stevens, pp. 294–298.

* British Agencies for Adoption and Fostering and Association of Directors of Social Services, *Family justice – a structure for the family court,* The Report of the BAAF/ADSS Family Courts Working Party (Denis Allen, ed.) (1986) London, BAAF, para. 30.

British Association of Social Workers, *Family Courts – A Discussion Document* (1984) Birmingham, BASW.

* L. Neville Brown, 'The Legal Background to the Family Court' [1966] British Journal of Criminology 139, p. 149.

Central Statistical Office, *Family Expenditure Survey 1989,* (1990) London, HMSO.

* S. Cretney, 'The Divorce White Paper – Some Reflections' [1995] 25 Fam Law 302, p. 304.

* S. Cretney, *Family Law – 'A Bit of a Racket',* the Joseph Jackson Memorial Lecture 1996, published in (1996) New Law Journal 91.

G. Davis, *Partisans and Mediators* (1988) Oxford, Oxford University Press.

G. Davis and K. Bader, *In Court Mediation on Custody and Access Issues – The Files Study* (1983a) Bristol, Department of Social Administration, University of Bristol.

G. Davis and K. Bader, *In Court Mediation on Custody and Access Issues at Bristol County Court – The Observation Study* (1983b) Bristol, Department of Social Administration, University of Bristol.

G. Davis with K. Bader, *Research Report on the Pre-trial Review Scheme at the Principal Registry* (1982) Bristol, University of Bristol.

G. Davis and K. Bader, 'In-court Mediation: the Consumer View' (1985) 15 Family Law 42.

* G. Davis and M. Murch, *Grounds for Divorce* (1988) Oxford, Clarendon Press, pp. 53–56.

* Department of Health, *An Introduction to the Children Act 1989* (1989) London, HMSO, para. 3.4.

* Department of Health, Guidance and Regulations on the Children Act 1989, vol.1, *Court Orders* (1991) London, HMSO, paras. 1.13–1.15.

Department of Health and Social Security, *Low Income Families 1985* (1988) London, DHSS.

Department of Health and Social Security, *Households Below Average Income* (1988) London, DHSS.

R. Dingwall and J.M. Eekelaar (eds.), *Divorce Mediation and the Legal Process* (1988) Oxford, Clarendon Press.

J.M. Eekelaar and R. Dingwall, 'The development of conciliation in England' in R. Dingwall and J.M. Eekalaar (eds.), *Divorce Mediation and the Legal Process* (1988) Oxford, Clarendon Press.

Eisenberg, 'The Bargain Principle and its Limits' (1982) 95 Harvard Law Review 741.

Family Courts Campaign, *A Court Fit For Families* (1986) London, Family Courts Campaign.

T. Fisher (ed.), *Family Conciliation within the UK* (1990) Bristol, Family Law.

M.A. Glendon, *State, Law and Family* (1977) London, North Holland.

The Right Reverend Lord Habgood, letter to The Times, 6th April 1996.

B.M. Hoggett, 'Family courts or family law reform – which should come first?' (1986) 6 Legal Studies 1.

Home Office, *Marriage Matters. A Consultative Document by the Working Party on Marriage Guidance set up by the Home Office in consultation with the DHSS* (1979) London, HMSO.

Interdepartmental Review of Family and Domestic Jurisdiction, *A Consultation Paper* (1986) London, Lord Chancellor's Department.

M. King and C. Piper, *How the Law Thinks About Children* (1990), Gower.

* Law Commission, *Court Record Study,* Appendix C to the Report on the Ground for Divorce, Law Com. No. 192 (1990) London, HMSO, paras. 13–15, 21–22.

Law Commission, *Reform of the Grounds of Divorce – The Field of Choice,* Cmnd. 3123 (1966) London, HMSO.

* Law Commission, *Report on the Ground for Divorce,* Law Com. No. 192 (1990) London, HMSO, paras. 5.29–5.30, 5.33–5.39.

Law Reform Commission of Canada, *The Family Court,* Working Paper 1 (1974) Ottowa Information Canada.

Law Society Family Law Sub-Committee, *A Better Way Out: suggestions for the reform of the Law of Divorce and Other Forms of Matrimonial Relief; for the Setting-up of a Family Court; and for its Procedure* (1979) London, The Law Society.

Law Society, Standing Committee on Family Law, *A Better Way Out Reviewed* (1982) London, The Law Society.

Law Society, Standing Committee on Family Law, *A Family Court – Consultation Paper* (1985) London, The Law Society.

Law Society, Standing Committee on Family Law, *A Suggested Model for the Family Court* (1986) London, The Law Society.

* *Looking to the Future: Mediation and the Ground for Divorce. The Government's proposals.* (Cm 2799) (1995) London, HMSO, para. 7.39.

Lord Chancellor's Department, *Family Jurisdiction of the High Court and County Courts,* Consultation Paper (1983) London, Lord Chancellor's Department.

* P. McCarthy and I. Walker, *Involvement of Lawyers in the Mediation Process* (1996) 26 Family Law 154, pp. 157–8.

J.S. Mill, *On Liberty* (1859), London.

R.H. Mnookin, 'Bargaining in the Shadow of the Law: The Case of Divorce' [1979] Current Legal Problems 65, p. 65.

* R.H. Mnookin, 'Divorce Bargaining: the Limits on Private Ordering' in J.M. Eekelaar and S.N. Katz (eds.), *The Resolution of Family Conflict: Comparative Legal Perspectives* (1984), Toronto, Butterworths, pp. 366–372, 376–379.

* M. Murch, *Justice and Welfare in Divorce* (1980) London, Sweet and Maxwell, p. 223.

* M. Murch, 'The Cross-Disciplinary Approach to Family Law', in A. Bainham, D. Pearl and R. Pickford (eds) *Frontiers of Family Law* (1995) Chichester, John Wiley and Sons.

Newcastle Report, see University of Newcastle.

L. Parkinson, 'Bristol Courts Family Conciliation Service' (1982) 12 Family Law 13.

L. Parkinson, 'Conciliation: Pros and Cons' (1983) 13 Family Law 22.

L. Parkinson, 'Conciliation: A New Approach to Family Conflict Resolution' (1983) 13 British Journal of Social Work 19.

L. Parkinson, *Conciliation in Separation and Divorce: Finding common ground* (1986) London, Croom Helm, pp. 52, 65.

G.M. Parmiter, 'Bristol In-Court Conciliation Procedure' Law Society's Gazette, 25 February 1981.

J. Pugsley et al, 'Conciliation and Report Writing: Tasks for One Officer' (1986) 16 Family Law 169.

* *Report of the Committee on One-Parent Families* (Chairman: The Hon. Sir Morris Finer) (Cmnd. 5629) (1974) London, HMSO, paras. 4.282–3, 4.285–6, 4.288–9, 4.290, 4.298–4.300, 4.404–5.

Report of the Committee on Procedure in Matrimonial Causes (Chairman: The Hon. Mr. Justice Denning) (Cmd. 7024) (1947) London, HMSO.

* *Report of the Children Act Advisory Committee 1993/94* (1994) London, HMSO, pp. 13–14.

* *Report of the Expert Witness Group,* chaired by Dr. Eileen Vizard: quoted in the *Report of the Children Act Advisory Committee 1993/94.*

Report of the Inter-departmental Committee on Conciliation (1983) London, HMSO.

* *Report of the Matrimonial Causes Procedure Committee* (Chairman: The Hon. Mrs. Justice Booth D.B.E.) (1985) London, HMSO, paras. 3.11–3.12.

Report of the Royal Commission on Marriage and Divorce (Chairman: Lord Morton of Henryton) (Cmd. 9678) (1956) London, HMSO.

I. Ricci, *Mom's House/Dad's House* (1980).

* M. Roberts, letter at (1995) 25 Fam Law 271.

S. Roberts, 'Mediation in Family Law Disputes' (1983) 46 Modern Law Review 537.

S. Roberts, 'The Location and Occasion of Mediation' in *The Role of Mediation in Divorce Proceedings: A Comparative Perspective* (1987) University of Vermont.

Society of Conservative Lawyers, *The Case for Family Courts* (1978) London, Conservative Political Centre.

* Solicitors' Family Law Association Code of Practice.

* F. Szwed, 'The Family Court' in M.D.A. Freeman (ed.), *The State, the Law and the Family: Critical Perspectives* (1984) London, Stevens, p. 272.

G. Teubner, *Law as an Autopoietic System* (1993) Oxford, Basil Blackwell.

* University of Newcastle Conciliation Project Unit, *Report to the Lord Chancellor on the Costs and Effectiveness of Conciliation in England and Wales* (1989) Newcastle, University of Newcastle upon Tyne, paras. 2.21–2.35, 20.1, 20.19.

J.A. Walker, 'Divorce Mediation – Is it a Better Way?' in J. McRory (ed.), *The Role of Mediation in Divorce Proceedings: A Comparative Perspective* (1987) University of Vermont.

J.A. Walker, 'Conciliation Research' in T. Fisher (ed.), *Family Conciliation within the UK* (1990) Bristol, Family Law, p. 156.

* J. Walker, P. McCarthy, N. Timms, *Mediation: the Making and Remaking of Co-operative Relationships. An evaluation of the affectiveness of comprehensive mediation* (1994) Newcastle upon Tyne, Relate Centre for Family Studies (the *Rowntree Report),* pp. iii, 8, 81–84, 160.

M. Wilkinson, *Children and Divorce* (1981) Oxford, Basil Blackwell.

E. Wilson, *Women and the Welfare State* (1977) London, Tavistock.

Chapter 8

* Australian Law Reform Commission, *'Matrimonial Property',* Report no. 39 (1987) Sydney, Australian Law Reform Commission, pp. 41, 65, 68, 73–75, 80, 85, 86, 106.

F.A.R. Bennion, 'First Consideration: A Cautionary Tale' (1976) 126 New Law Journal 2237.

* J. Bispham, 'Pension Reform – Tilting at Windmills' (1994) 24 Fam Law 332.

* J. Black, J. Bridge and T Bond, *A Practical Approach to Family Law* (3rd edn.) (1994) London, Blackstone.

P. Bohannan (ed.), *Divorce and After* (1970) Garden City, New York, Doubleday.

Dame Margaret Booth, Nicholas Wall, G.I. Maple, A.K. Biggs, *Rayden and Jackson on Divorce and Family Matters* (16th ed) (1991) London, Butterworths, para. 29.84.

* J. Bradshaw and J. Millar, *Lone Parent Families in the UK* (1991) Social Security Research Report, no. 6, London, HMSO, p. 98.

J. Burgoyne, R. Ormrod and M. Richards, *Divorce Matters* (1987) Harmondsworth, Penguin Books.

E. Clive, 'The Financial Consequences of Divorce: Reform from the Scottish

Perspective' in M.D.A. Freeman (ed.), *State, Law, and the Family* (1984) London, Tavistock.

S. Cretney, 'Money After Divorce – The Mistakes We Have Made?' in M.D.A. Freeman (ed.), *Essays in Family Law 1985* (1986) London, Stevens.

* G. Davis, S. Cretney and J. Collins, *Simple Quarrels* (1994), Oxford, Clarendon Press, pp. 105–6.

G. Davis, A. MacLeod and M. Murch 'Divorce: Who Supports the Family' (1983) 13 Fam Law 217.

* R. Deech, 'The Principles of Maintenance' (1977) 7 Family Law 229, pp. 230–232.

R. Deech, 'Financial Relief: the Retreat from Precedent and Principle' (1982) 98 Law Quarterly Review 621.

* R. Deech, 'Divorce Studies and Empirical Studies' (1990) 106 Law Quarterly Review 229 at p. 237.

J. Dewar, 'Reforming Financial Provision: The Alternatives' [1984] Journal of Social Welfare Law 1.

A.R. Dewar, 'The Family Law (Scotland) Act 1985 in practice' (1989) Journal of the Law Society of Scotland (February 42).

G. Douglas, 'The Clean Break on Divorce' (1981) 11 Family Law, pp. 42–53, 45, 48.

J.M. Eekelaar, 'Commission Reports on the Financial Consequences of Divorce' (1982) 45 Modern Law Review 420.

J.M. Eekelaar, *Family Law and Social Policy* (2nd edn., 1984) London, Weidenfeld and Nicholson.

Eekelaar and Maclean, 'Financial Provision on Divorce: A Reappraisal', in M.D.A. Freeman (ed) *State, Law and Family: Critical Perspectives* (1984) London, Tavistock, Chap 13.

* J.M. Eekelaar and M. Maclean, *Maintenance After Divorce* (1986) Clarendon Press, p. 62, table 10 (p. 25), table 11 (p. 27).

* J.M. Eekelaar and M. MacLean, 'Divorce Law and Empirical Studies – A Reply' (1990) 106 Law Quarterly Review 621.

* Sir Morris Finer and O.R. McGregor, 'The History of the Obligation to Maintain', App. 5, *Report of the Committee on One-Parent Families* (Cmnd. 5629–1) (1974) London, HMSO, paras. 26–27, 32–33, 35–38.

D. Freed and H. Foster 'Divorce in the Fifty States: an Overview as of August 1st 1979' (1979) 5 Family Law Reporter.

J. Freedman, *Property and Marriage: An Integrated Approach* (IFS Report Series No. 29) (1988) London, Institute of Fiscal Studies.

M.A. Glendon, *The New Family and the New Property* (1981) Toronto, Butterworths.

K. Gray, *Reallocation of Property on Divorce* (1977) Abingdon, Professional Books.

* *Hansard*, House of Lords, vol 561 (20 February 1995), cols 922–923.

W.M. Harper, *Divorce and Your Money* (1979) London, Allen and Unwin.

M. Harrison, P. MacDonald and R. Weston, 'Payment of Child Maintenance in Australia: the Current Position. Research Findings and Reform Proposals' (1987) 1 International Journal of Law and the Family 92.

* J. Haynes, *The Fundamentals of Family Mediation* (1993) Tonbridge, Old Bailey Press, pp. 6–7, 11.

S. Hoffman and G. Duncan, 'What Are The Economic Consequences of Divorce?' (1988) 25 Demography 641.

* E. Jackson, F. Wasoff, M. Maclean and R.E. Dobash, 'Financial Support on Divorce: the Right Mixture of Rules and Discretion?' (1993) 7 International Journal of Law and the Family 230, p. 245.

H. Joshi and H. Davies, *The Pension Consequences of Divorce* (1991) (Discussion Paper No. 550) London, Joseph Rowntree Foundation.

H. Land, 'Poverty and Gender, The Distribution of Resources within the

Family' in M. Brown (ed.), *The Structure of Disadvantage* (1983) London, Heinemann.

* Law Commission, *The Financial Consequences of Divorce: the Basic Policy: a Discussion Paper* (Cmnd. 8041) (1980) London, HMSO, paras. 24–27, 59, 66, 70, 73, 75, 77, 80, 84, 86.

* Law Commission, *The Financial Consequences of Divorce* (Law Com. No. 112) (1982) London, HMSO, para. 17.

* The Law Society, *Maintenance and Capital Provision on Divorce* (1991), the Law Society, London, 2.17–2.25; 3.3.

Looking to the Future: Mediation and the Ground for Divorce. A consultation paper. (Cm 2424) (1993) London, HMSO.

Looking to the Future: Mediation and the Ground for Divorce. The Government's proposals. (Cm 2799) (1995) London, HMSO.

P. McDonald (ed.), *Settling Up; Property and Income Distribution on Divorce in Australia* (1986) Institute of Family Studies' Family Reformation Project, Sydney, Prentice-Hall of Australia.

P. McDonald, *The Economic Consequences of Marriage Breakdown in Australia (A Summary)* (1985) Melbourne, Institute of Family Studies, pp. 33–36.

M. Maclean and J.M. Eekelaar, *Children and Divorce: Economic Factors* (1983) Oxford, S.S.R.C.

R. Malone, letter to The Times, 26th August 1995.

M.M. Marvin, *Divorced Man's Guide through Pain and Misery* (1981, 4th ed. 1984) Stilwell, Kansas, Deej Publishing Company.

A.C. Martin, 'Actuaries, Pensions and Divorce' (1991) 21 Family Law 258.

J.G. Miller, 'Trusts and Financial Provision on Divorce' (1990) Trusts Law and Practice (May 42).

R. Mnookin, et al., 'Private Ordering Revisited: What Custodial Arrangements are Parents Negotiating?' in S. Sugarman and H.H. Kaye (eds) *Divorce Reform at the Cross Roads* (1990) New Haven and London, Yale University Press.

* K. O'Donovan, 'The Principle of Maintenance: an Alternative View' (1978) 8 Family Law 180–184.

* Office of Population Censuses and Surveys, *General Household Survey 1993* (1995) London, HMSO; figure 3A and text; tables 3.23, 3.26.

Pensions and Law Reform, The Report of the Pensions Law Reform Committee, Chaired by Sir Roy Goode (Cm 2342) (1993) London, HMSO.

Pensions Management Institute, *Pensions and Divorce* (May 1993) London, Pensions Management Institute.

* M. Rae, *Pensions and Divorce – Time for Change* (1995) New Law Journal 310.

Report of the Committee on One-Parent Families (Chairman: The Hon. Sir Morris Finer) (Cmnd. 5629) (1974) London, HMSO.

Report (Final) of the Royal Commission on Legal Services (Cmnd. 7648) (1979) London, HMSO, vol. 1.

* The Scottish Law Commission, *Report on Aliment and Financial Provision,* Scot. Law Com. No. 67 (1981) Edinburgh, HMSO, paras. 3.18–3.22, 3.62, 3.65–3.68, 3.92–3.94, 3.107–3.110.

* *Security, Equality, Choice: The Future for Pensions* (Cm 2594-I & II) (1994) London, HMSO, para. 1.45.

* C. Smart, *The Ties that Bind* (1984) London, Routledge and Kegan Paul, pp. 223, 224, 227, 228.

S. Sugarman, 'Dividing Financial Interests on Divorce', in S. Sugarman and H.H. Kaye (eds) *Divorce Reform at the Cross Roads* (1990) New Haven and London, Yale University Press.

* P. Symes, 'Indissolubility and the Clean Break' (1985) 48 Modern Law Review 44 at pp. 46, 47, 51, 52, 53, 57, 59, 60.

R. Thornton, 'Homelessness Through Relationship Breakdown: The Local Authorities' Response' [1989] Journal of Social Welfare Law 67.

E. Wasoff, R.E. Dobash and Harcus, *The Impact of the Family Law Scotland Act 1985 on Solicitors' Divorce Practice* (1990) Scottish Office, Central Research Unit Papers.

* L. Weitzman, *The Divorce Revolution* (1985) New York, The Free Press, table 12 (p. 152), figure 3 (p. 338), p. 362.

L. Weitzman and R. Dixon, 'The Alimony Myth: Does No Fault Divorce Make a Difference?' (1980) 14 Family Law Quarterly 142.

Chapter 9

J. Barron, *Not worth the paper? ... the effectiveness of legal protection for women and children experiencing domestic violence* (1990) London, Women's Aid Federation, England.

M. Borkowski, M. Murch and V. Walker, *Marital Violence – the community response* (1983) London, Tavistock.

A. Bourlet, *Police Involvement in Marital Violence* (1990) Milton Keynes, Open University Press.

British Association of Social Workers, *Working Party on Home Violence* (1975) 6 Social Work Today 409.

I. Browniee, 'Compellability and Contempt in Domestic Violence Cases' (1990) Journal of Social Welfare Law 107.

B. Cade, 'Family Violence: An Interactional View' (1978) 9 Social Work Today, no. 26, p. 15.

J.R. Chapman and M. Gates (eds.) *The Victimisation of Women* (1978) Beverley Hills, Cailfornia, Sage.

* I. Clifton, 'Factors Predisposing Family Members to Violence', in Social Work Services Group, Scottish Education Department, *Violence in the Family – Theory and Practice in Social Work* (1982) Edinburgh, HMSO, p. 31.

* A. Cretney and G. Davis 'Prosecuting "Domestic" Assault' [1996] Criminal Law Review 162, pp.173–174.

B. Dawson and T. Faragher, *Battered Women's Project: Interim Report* (1977) Keele, University of Keele, Department of Sociology.

Department of Health, Social Services Inspectorate, *Domestic Violence and Social Care* (1996) London, Department of Health.

R. Dobash and R. Dobash, 'Wives: the Appropriate Victims of Marital Violence' and (with C. Cavanagh and M. Wilson) 'Wife Beating: the Victims Speak' (1978) 2 Victimology.

R. Dobash and R. Dobash, *Violence Against Wives: A Case Against the Patriarchy* (1980) London, Open Books.

R.E. Dobash and R.P. Dobash, 'Community response to violence against wives: charivari, abstract justice and patriarchy' (1981) 28 Social Problems 563.

R.E. Dobash and R.P. Dobash, 'The Nature and Antecedents of Violent Events' (1984) 24 British Journal of Criminology 269.

* R.E. Dobash and R.P. Dobash, *Women, Violence and Social Change* (1992) London, Routledge, pp. 208–209, 231.

* M. Dow, 'Police Involvement' in M. Borland (ed.), *Violence in the Family* (1976) Manchester, Manchester University Press, pp. 132–133.

S.M. Edwards, 'A sociolegal evaluation of gender ideologies in domestic violence, assault and spousal homicides' (1985)10 Victimology 186.

S.M. Edwards and A. Halpern, 'Conflicting interests: protecting children or protecting title to property' [1988] Journal of Social Welfare Law 110.

S.M. Edwards, 'What shall we do with a frightened witness?' [1989] New Law Journal 1740.

S.M. Edwards and A. Halpern, 'Protection for the victim of domestic violence: time for radical revision?' [1991] Journal of Social Welfare and Family Law 94.

* S.M. Edwards, *Sex and Gender in the Legal Process* (1996) London, Blackstone, pp. 182–183.

J.M. Eekelaar and S.N. Katz (eds.) *Family Violence: An International and Interdisciplinary Study* (1978) Toronto, Butterworths.

E. Evason, *Hidden Violence* (1982) Belfast, Farset Press.

Family and Civil Committees of the Council of Her Majesty's Circuit Judges, 'Domestic Violence and Occupation of the Family Home' (1990) 20 Family Law 225.

* T. Faragher, 'The Police Response to Violence Against Women in the Home', in J. Palil (1985) op. cit., p. 117.

M.D.A. Freeman, *Violence in the Home* (1979) Farnborough, Saxon House (now Aldershot, Gower).

M.D.A. Freeman, 'Violence Against Women: Does the Legal System Provide Solutions or Itself Constitute the Problem?' (1980) 7 British Journal of Law and Society 215.

M.D.A. Freeman, 'Legal ideologies, patriarchal precedents and domestic violence' in M.D.A. Freeman (ed.), *The State, the Law and the Family: Critical Perspectives* (1984) London, Stevens.

M.D.A. Freeman, *Dealing with Domestic Violence* (1987) Oxford, CCH.

* Judge Fricker QC, *Evidence to the Special Public Bill Committee on the Family Homes and Domestic Violence Bill,* HL Paper 55 (1994–95), pp. 73–74.

* S. Grace, *Policing Domestic Violence in the 1990s,* Home Office Research Study 139 (1995) London, HMSO, pp. 53–54, 56.

* G. Hague and E. Malos, *Domestic Violence: Action for Change* (1993) Cheltenham, New Clarion Press, pp. 54–56, 58, 61–62.

* G. Hague and E. Malos, 'Children, Domestic Violence and Housing' in Morley and Mullender (1994) op cit, pp. 131–132.

M. Hayes, 'The Law Commission and the Family Home' (1990) 53 Modern Law Review 222.

* M. Hayes, 'Non-molestation Protection: Only Associated Persons Need Apply' (1996) 26 Family Law 134, p. 136.

Home Office, Domestic Proceedings, England and Wales 1992 (1993) Home Office Statistical Bulletin 26/93.

* Home Office Circular (60/90), *Domestic Violence,* London, Home Office, paras. 2, 4, 11–18, 21, 24.

Home Office and Lord Chancellor's Department, *Stalking – The Solutions: A Consultation Paper* (1996) London, Home Office and Lord Chancellor's Department.

M. Homer, et al., 'The burden of dependency' in N. Johnson (ed.), *Marital Violence* (1985) London, Routledge and Kegan Paul.

M. Horton, 'The Family Law Bill – Domestic Violence' (1996) 26 Family Law 49.

* House of Commons Select Committee on Violence in Marriage, *Report,* Minutes of Evidence and Appendices HC 553-11 (1974–75) (1975) London, HMSO, paras. 73, 74, 634; p. 366.

* House of Commons Home Affairs Committee, Third Report, *Domestic Violence,* HC 245-I (1992–93) (1993), paras 9, 109.

* House of Commons Home Affairs Committee, *Domestic Violence, Evidence and Appendices* HC 245-11 (1992–93) (1993), pp. 21–22, 26, 87–88, 104.

G. Jones, D. Lockton, R. Ward and E. Kashefi 'Domestic Violence Applications: An empirical study of one court' (1995) 17 Journal of Social Welfare and Family Law 67.

D.S. Kalmuss and M.A. Straus, 'A wife's marital dependency and wife abuse' [1981] Journal of Marriage and the Family 277.

G. Kaufman Kantor and M.A. Straus, *Stopping the Violence: Battered Women,* Police Utilisation and Police Response (1987) Paper presented to the American Society of Criminology Meeting, Montreal.

L. Kelly, 'The Interconnectedness of Domestic Violence and Child Abuse: Challenges from Research, Policy and Practice' in Morley and Mullender (eds.), (1994) op cit.

D. Klein, 'Battered wives and the domination of women' in N.H. Rafter and E. Stanko (eds.), *Judge, Lawyer, Victim, Thief: Women, Gender Roles and Criminal Justice* (1982) Boston, Mass., Northeastern University Press.

Law Commission, *Report on Matrimonial Proceedings in Magistrates' Courts,* Law Com No.77, (1976) London, HMSO.

Law Commission, Working Paper No. 113, *Domestic Violence and Occupation of the Family Home* (1989) London, HMSO.

* Law Commission, *Domestic Violence and Occupation of the Family Home,* Law Com No. 207, (1992) London, HMSO, paras. 2.3, 2.8, 2.21–2.25, 2.48, 3.19, 4.6, 4.7, 4.23, 4.34.

Lord Chancellor's Department, *Judicial Statistics: England and Wales for the Year 1995* (Cm 3290) (1996).

S. Maidment, 'The Law's Response to Marital Violence in England and the U.S.A.' (1977) 26 International and Comparative Law Quarterly 403.

* S. Maidment, 'The Relevance of the Criminal Law to Domestic Violence' [1980] Journal of Social Welfare Law 26, pp. 30–31.

E. Malos and G. Hague, 'Domestic Violence and Housing: Local Authority Responses to Women and Children Escaping from Violence in the Home' (1993) Bristol, Women's Aid Federation England, and University of Bristol School of Applied Social Studies.

D. Marsden, 'Sociological Perspectives on Family Violence' in J.P. Martin (ed.), *Violence and the Family* (1978) Chichester, Wiley.

D. Martin, *Battered Wives* (1976) San Francisco, Glide Publications.

D. Martin, 'Battered women: society's problem' in J.R. Chapman and M. Gates, *The Victimisation of Women* (1978) Beverley Hills, California, Sage.

J.S. Mill, *The Subjection of Women* (1869); reprinted in Everyman's Library (1929) London, Dent.

* J. Mooney, *The Hidden Figure: Domestic Violence in North London* (1993) London, School of Sociology and Social Policy, Middlesex University, p. 26, Table 5.

M. Morash, 'Wife Battering' [1986] Criminal Justice Abstracts 252.

* R. Morley and A. Mullender, 'Hype or hope? The importation of pro-arrest policies and batterers' programmes from North America to Britain as key measures for preventing violence against women in the home' (1992) 6 International Journal of Law and the Family 265, p. 268.

R. Morley and A. Mullender (eds.), *Children Living with Domestic Violence* (1994) London, Whiting & Birch.

R. Morley and A. Mullender, 'Domestic Violence and Children: What do we know from research?' in Morley and Mullender (eds.), (1994) op cit.

New York Task Force Report, 'Domestic Violence' (1987) 15 Fordham Urban Law Journal 28.

J. Pahl, 'Police Response to Battered Women' [1982] Journal of Social Welfare Law 337.

J. Pahl (ed.) *Private Violence and Public Policy. The needs of battered women and the response of the public services* (1985) London, Routledge and Kegan Paul.

S. Parker, 'The Legal Background' in J. Pahl (1985) op cit.

E. Pence, *Criminal Justice Response to Domestic Assault Cases* (1985) Duluth, Minnesota, Domestic Abuse Intervention Project, Minnesota Program Development Inc.

* E. Pizzey, *Scream Quietly or the Neighbours Will Hear* (1974) Harmondsworth, Penguin Books, pp. 98, 119–121.

M. Roy (ed.), *Battered Women* (1977) New York, Van Nostrand Reinhold.
A. Sanders, 'Personal Violence and Public Order: The prosecution of domestic violence in England and Wales' (1988) 16 International Journal of the Sociology of Law 359.
S. Schechter, *Women and Male Violence* (1982) Boston, South End Press.
* L. Smith, *Domestic Violence: an overview of the literature,* Home Office Research Study 107 (1989) London, HMSO, pp. 27–29.
M.A. Straus, 'A sociological perspective on the prevention and treatment of wifebeating' in M. Roy (ed.), *Battered Women* (1977) New York, Van Nostrand Reinhold.
H.I. Subin, *Criminal Justice in a Metropolitan Court; the Processing of Serious Criminal Cases in the District of Columbia Court of General Sessions* (1966) Washington, Office of Criminal Justice, US Department of Justice.
R. Thornton, 'Homelessness through relationship breakdown: the local authorities' response' [1989] Journal of Social Welfare Law 67.
United Nations Centre for Social Development and Humanitarian Affairs, *Violence Against Women in the Family* (1989) New York, United Nations.
Victim Support, *Domestic Violence: Report of a National Inter-Agency Working Party* (1992) London, Victim Support.
L.E. Walker, *The Battered Woman Syndrome* (1984) New York, Springer.
F. Wasoff, 'Legal Protection from Wife Beating: The Processing of Domestic Assaults by Scottish Prosecutors and Criminal Courts' (1982) 10 International Journal of the Sociology of Law 187.
E. Wilson, *The Existing Research into Battered Women* (1976) London, National Women's Aid Federation (now Women's Aid Federation, England).
E. Wilson, *What is to be done about Violence against Women?* (1983) Harmondsworth, Penguin.
* Women's National Commission, *Violence Against Women,* Report of an ad hoc Working Group (1985) London, Cabinet Office, paras. 108, 111, 113, 115.

Chapter 10

R. Adler and A. Dearling, 'Children's Rights: A Scottish Perspective' in B. Franklin (ed.), *The Rights of Children* (1986) Oxford, Basil Blackwell.
* Anon., 'Mental Hospitalisation of Children and the Limits of Parental Authority' (1978) 88 Yale Law Journal 186, pp. 194–208.
Jasmine Beckford, see Brent Council.
* Sir William Blackstone, *Commentaries on the Laws of England* (1st edn., 1765) Oxford, Clarendon Press, book 1, pp. 434–435, 440–441.
Brent Council, *A Child in Trust – The Report of the Panel of Inquiry into the Circumstances Surrounding the Death of Jasmine Beckford* (Chairman: L. Blom-Cooper Q.C.) (1985) London, London Borough of Brent.
J.E. Coons and R.H. Mnookin, 'Toward a Theory of Children's Rights' in L.F.G. Baxter and M.A. Eberts (eds.), *The Child and the Courts* (1978) London, Sweet and Maxwell.
Council of Europe, European Convention for the Protection of Human Rights and Fundamental Freedoms (1950).
* Department of Health, *An Introduction to the Children Act 1989* (1989) London, HMSO, paras. 1.4–1.5.
DHSS, Health Circular HC (86) 1, Family Planning Services for Young People (1986) London, DHSS.
* DHSS, Review of Child Care Law – Report to Ministers of an Interdepartmental Working Party (1985) London, HMSO, paras. 2.12–2.13, 15.11.

B.M. Dickens, 'The Modern Function and Limits of Parental Rights' (1981) 97 Law Quarterly Review 462.

* J. Eekelaar, 'Parental Responsibility: State of Nature or Nature of the State?' [1991] Journal of Social Welfare and Family Law 37, pp. 38–39.

J.M. Eekelaar, *Family Law and Social Policy* (2nd edn., 1984) London, Weidenfeld and Nicholson.

* J. M. Eekelaar, 'The Emergence of Children's Rights' (1986) 6 Oxford Journal of Legal Studies 161, pp. 169–174, 176, 180–182.

R. Farson, *Birthrights* (1978) Harmondsworth, Penguin Books.

R. Frank, 'Family Law and the Federal Republic of Germany's Basic Law' (1990) 4 International Journal of Law and the Family 214.

B. Franklin (ed.), *The Rights of Children* (1986) Oxford, Basil Blackwell.

M.D.A. Freeman, 'The Rights of Children in the International Year of the Child' [1980] Current Legal Problems 1.

M.D.A. Freeman, *The Rights and Wrongs of Children* (1983) London, Frances Pinter.

* J. Goldstein, A. Freud and A.J. Solnit, *Before the Best Interests of the Child* (1980) London, Burnett Books, pp. 8–10, 11–12, 16–17, 92, 93–94.

Tyra Henry, see Lambeth London Borough Council.

J. Holt, *Escape from Childhood* (1974) New York, Dutton.

House of Commons Social Services Committee, Second Report Session 1983–84, Children in Care HC 360 (1984) London, HMSO.

I. Kennedy, 'The Karen Quinlan Case: Problems and Proposals' (1976) 2(3) Journal of Medical Ethics 6.

Lambeth London Borough Council, Whose Child ? The Report of the Inquiry into the Death of Tyra Henry (1987) London, London Borough of Lambeth.

Law Commission, *Report on Illegitimacy*, Law Com. No. 118 (1982) London, HMSO.

Law Commission, Working Paper No. 91, *Review of Child Law: Guardianship* (1985) London, HMSO.

* Law Commission, Working Paper No. 91, *Review of Child Law: Custody* (1986) London, HMSO, paras. 6.20–6.22.

* Law Commission, *Report on Guardianship and Custody*, Law Com. No. 172 (1988) London, HMSO, paras. 2.4–2.16.

N. MacCormick, 'Children's Rights: A Test Case for Theories of Right' (1976) 62: Archiv für Rechts und Sozialphilosophie 305.

J.S. Mill, *On Liberty* (first published 1859) (1985) Harmondsworth, Penguin Classics.

P.H. Pettitt, 'Parental Control and Guardianship' in R.H. Graveson and F.R. Crane (eds.), *A Century of Family Law* (1957) London, Sweet and Maxwell.

Report of the Committee on the Age of Majority (Chairman: Mr. Justice Latey) Cmnd. 3342 (1967) London, HMSO.

Review of Child Care Law, see DHSS.

M. Richards, 'Developmental Psychology and Family Law: A Discussion Paper' (1986) British Journal of Developmental Psychology.

C.M. Rogers and L.S. Wrightsman, 'Attitudes towards Children's Rights: Nurturance or Self-Determination' (1978) 34 Journal of Social Issues, no. 2, p. 59.

R.M. Rolfe and A.D. MacClintock, 'The Due Process Rights of Minors "Voluntarily admitted" to Mental Institutions' (1976) 4 Journal of Psychiatry and Law 333.

United Nations, Convention on the Rights of the Child (1989).

C.A. Wringe, *Children's rights – A philosophical study* (1981) London, Routledge and Kegan Paul.

Chapter 11

D. Barber, *Unmarried Fathers* (1975) London, Hutchinson.

P. Bean (ed.), *Adoption: Essays in Social Policy, Law and Sociology* (1984) London, Tavistock.

* Sir William Blackstone, *Commentaries on the Laws of England* (1st edn., 1765) Oxford, Clarendon Press, book 1, p. 447.

* E. Blyth, 'Assisted reproduction: what's in it for the children?' (1990) 4 Children and Society 167, pp. 174–177.

P. Braidwood, 'Artificial choices' (1989) The Observer, 23 July.

British Medical Association, *Changing Conceptions of Motherhood – the Practice of Surrogacy in Britain* (1996) London, British Medical Association.

* N. Bruce, 'On the Importance of Genetic Knowledge' (1990) 4 Children and Society 183, pp. 191–192.

* Cellmark Diagnostics, DNA Fingerprinting Information and Procedures Guide.

* Central Statistical Office, Social Trends 24 (1994) London, HMSO, Graph 2.21.

* Central Statistical Office, Social Trends 25 (1995) London, HMSO, Graphs 2.25 and 2.29.

* Central Statistical Office, Social Trends 26 (1996) London, HMSO, Graph 1.11, Table 2.26.

* Children Act Advisory Committee, Annual Report 1994/95 (1995), London, Lord Chancellor's Department, Table 4.

Children Come First, Cm. 1263 (1990) London, HMSO.

* Ciba Foundation Symposium, No. 17 (new series), G.E.W. Wolstenholme and D.W. Fitzsimmons (eds.), Law and Ethics of A.I.D. and Embryo Transfer (1973) Amsterdam, Associated Scientific Publishers, pp. 63, 66.

R. Collins and A. Macleod, 'Denials of paternity: the impact of DNA tests on court proceedings' [1991] Journal of Social Welfare and Family Law 209.

R. Collins and A. Macleod, *The End of Illegitimacy, Research Report* (1990) British, University of Bristol.

Council for Science and Society, Human Procreation: Ethical Aspects of the New Techniques (1984) Oxford, Oxford University Press.

* Council of Europe, European Convention on the Legal Status of Children born out of Wedlock (1981).

E. Crellin, M.L. Kellmer Pringle and P. West, *Born Illegitimate: Social and Educational Implications* (1971) Windsor, National Foundation for Educational Research.

K.R. Daniels, 'Semen donors in New Zealand: their characteristics and attitudes' (1987) 5 Clinical Reproduction and Fertility 177.

K.R. Daniels, 'Semen donors: their motivations and attitudes to their offspring' (1989) 7 Journal of Reproductive and Infant Psychology 121.

* K. Davis, 'Illegitimacy and the Social Structure' (1939) 45 American Journal of Sociology 215, pp. 215, 216, 219, 221, 223.

C. Day, 'Access to Birth Records: General Register Office Study' (1979) 3(4) Adoption and Fostering 17.

R. Deech, 'The Reform of Illegitimacy Law' (1980) 10 Family Law 101.

D. Derrick (ed.), *Illegitimate – the Experience of People Born Outside Marriage* (1986) London, National Council for One-Parent Families.

* DHSS, Legislation on Human Infertility Services and Embryo Research, A Consultation Paper, Cm 46 (1986) London, HMSO, paras. 8–13.

R.J. Edelmann and K.J. Connelly, 'Psychological aspects of infertility' (1986) 59 British Journal of Medical Psychology 209.

* H. Elisofon, 'A Historical and Comparative Study of Bastardy' (1973) 2 Anglo-American Law Review 306, p. 318.

F. Engels, *The Origin of the Family, Private Property and the State* (1st edn., 1884) New York, Lawrence and Wishart.

* Sir Morris Finer and O.R. McGregor, 'The History of the Obligation to Maintain' App. 5, Report of the Committee on One-Parent Families (Cmnd. 5629–1) (1974) London, HMSO, paras. 56, 57, 59–62, 64.

R. Fox, *Kinship and Marriage* (1967) Harmondsworth, Penguin Books.

J. Fratter, 'How adoptive parents feel about contact with birth parents after adoption' (1989) 13 (4) Adoption and Fostering 18.

D. Gill, *Illegitimacy, Sexuality and the Status of Women* (1977) Oxford, Basil Blackwell.

J. Glover, *Fertility and the Family: The Glover Report on Reproductive Technologies to the European Commission* (1989) London, Fourth Estate.

E. Goffman, *Stigma: notes on the management of spoiled identity* (1963) Harmondsworth, Penguin Books.

S. Golombek, A. Spencer and M. Rutter, 'Children in single parent and lesbian households: psychosexual and psychiatric appraisal' (1983) 24(4) Journal of Psychiatry and Psychology 551.

E. Haimes and N. Timms, *Adoption, Identity and Social Policy – The search for distant relatives* (1985) Aldershot, Gower.

* Hansard (House of Lords), Vol. 516, cols. 1097–1098.

J. Harris, *The Value of Life: An Introduction to Medical Ethics* (1985) London, Routledge.

* M. Hayes, 'Law Commission Working Paper No. 74: Illegitimacy' (1980) 43 Modern Law Review 299, p. 299.

U.R.Q. Henriques, 'Bastardy and the New Poor Law' (1967) 37 Past and Present.

* J. Heywood, *Children in Care: The Development of the Service for the Deprived Child* (3rd edn., 1978) London, Routledge and Kegan Paul, pp. 173–174.

D. Howell and M. Ryburn, 'New Zealand: new ways to choose adopters' (1987) 11(4) Adoption and Fostering 38.

* Human Fertilisation and Embryology Authority, Code of Practice (Second Revision 1995) London, Human Fertilisation and Embryology Authority, paras. 3.13, 3.14, 3.16–3.19, 3.20.

* L. Lambert and J . Streather, *Children in Changing Families: A Study of Adoption and Illegitimacy* (1980) London and Basingstoke, Macmillan, pp. 55–57, 136, 140–142.

* P. Laslett, *The World We Have Lost* (2nd edn., 1971) London, Methuen, pp. 137, 140–141.

P. Laslett, *Family Life and Illicit Love in Earlier Generations* (1977) Cambridge, Cambridge University Press.

P. Laslett, K. Oosterven and R.M. Smith (eds.), *Bastardy and Its Comparative History* (1980) London, Arnold.

Law Commission, Working Paper No. 91, *Review of Child Law: Guardianship* (1985) London, HMSO.

* Law Commission, Working Paper No. 74, *Illegitimacy* (1979) London, HMSO, paras. 2.10–2.12, 3.2–3.6, 3.8–3.9, 3.14–3.16, 9.12, 9.18, 9.23, 9.24, 9.27, 9.28, 9.33, 9.40, 10.9, 10.11, 10.17, 10.25, 10.26.

* Law Commission, *Report on Guardianship and Custody*, Law Com. No. 172 (1988) London, HMSO, paras. 2.18–2.20.

* Law Commission, *Report on Illegitimacy*, Law Com. No. 118, (1982) London, HMSO, paras. 4.26, 4.39, 4.44, 4.49, 4.51.

Law Commission, *Report on Declarations in Family Matters*, Law Com. No. 132 (1984) London, HMSO.

* Law Commission, *Illegitimacy* (*Second Report*), Law Com. No. 157 (1986) London, HMSO, paras. 3.1–3.3, 3.4, 3.18–3.19.

* R. Leete, 'Adoption Trends and Illegitimate Births' (1978) 14 Population Trends 9, pp. 11, 13, 14, 15.

* L. Mair, *Marriage* (1971) Harmondsworth, Pelican Books, pp. 11–14, 16.

A. McWhinnie, 'The case for greater openness concerning AID' in *AID and After* (1984) London, British Agencies for Adoption and Fostering.

* National Council for One-Parent Families, An Accident of Birth – A Response to the Law Commission's Working Paper on Illegitimacy (1980) London, One-Parent Families, pp. 2–4, 9, 11–12.

S. Pollock and J. Sutton, 'Father's Rights, Women's Losses' (1985) 8 Women's Studies International Forum 593.

G.R. Quaife, *Wanton Wenches and Wayward Wives* (1979) London, Croom Helm.

S. Reid, *Labour of Love: Story of the World's first Surrogate Grandmother* (1988) Oxford, Bodley Head.

* *Report (first) of the Child Adoption Committee* (Chairman: Mr Justice Tomlin) (Cmd. 2401) (1925) London, HMSO, paras. 4, 9, 11, 15, 18, 19, 28.

Report of the Committee on Child Adoption (Chairman: Sir Alfred Hopkinson K.C.) (Cmd. 1254) (1921) London, HMSO.

* *Report of the Committee of Inquiry into Human Fertilisation and Embryology* (Chairman: Dame Mary Warnock) (Cmnd. 9314) (1984) London, HMSO, paras. 4.19–4.22, 6.8, 8.10–8.16.

* *Report of the Committee on the Law of Succession in relation to Illegitimate Persons* (Chairman: The Rt. Hon. Lord Justice Russell) (Cmnd. 3051) (1966) London, HMSO, para. 19.

Report of the Departmental Committee on Adoption Societies and Agencies (Chairman: Miss Florence Horsbrugh M.P.) (Cmd. 5499) (1937) London, HMSO.

Report of the Departmental Committee on the Adoption of Children (Chairman: His Honour Sir Gerald Hurst Q.C.) (Cmd. 9248) (1954) London, HMSO.

* *Report of the Departmental Committee on the Adoption of Children* (Chairman: Sir William Houghton, later Judge F.A. Stockdale) (Cmnd. 5107) (1972) London, HMSO, paras. 33–36, 38, 83–88, 93–94, 116, 120–122, 125–127, 144, 146, 168, 170, 221, 223–224, 237, 244, 252, 253, 301–303, 326, 327.

Report of the Departmental Committee on Human Artificial Insemination (Chairman: The Earl of Feversham) (Cmnd. 1105) (1960) London, HMSO.

* *Review of Adoption Law – Report to Ministers of an Interdepartmental Working Group* (1992), London, Department of Health and Welsh Office, paras. 26.4, 26.7–26.16.

L. Ripple, 'A Follow-up Study of Adopted Children' (1968) 42 Social Service Review, no. 4, p. 479.

D. Saunders, 'Assessment of the infertile couple for AID' in C. Wood, J. Leeton and G. Kovacs (eds.), *Artificial Insemination by Donor* (1980) Melbourne, Brown, Prior Anderson Property Ltd.

H.R. Schaffer, 'Family structure or interpersonal relationships' (1988) 2(2) Children and Society 91.

* Scottish Law Commission, *Family Law – Illegitimacy*, Consultative Memorandum No. 53 (1982) Edinburgh, Scottish Law Commission, paras. 1.15, 1.16.

* Scottish Law Commission, *Report on Illegitimacy*, Scot. Law Com. No. 82 (1984) Edinburgh, HMSO, paras. 9.2, 9.3.11.

* Scottish Law Commission, *Report on Family Law*, Scot. Law Com. No 135 (1992), Edinburgh, HMSO, para. 2.48.

* J. Seglow, M.L. Kellmer Pringle and P. Wedge, *Growing Up Adopted* (1972) London, National Foundation for Educational Research, pp. 9–10, 157, 170, 176.

C. Smith, *Adoption and Fostering* (1984) London, Macmillan.

R. Snowden and G.D. Mitchell, *The Artificial Family – A Consideration of Artificial Intermination by Donor* (1981) London, George Allen and Unwin.

R. Snowden and E.M. Snowden, *The Gift of a Child* (1984) London, George Allen and Unwin.

M.T. Sverne, 'The Swedish view of artificial insemination by donor' in *Artificial procreation, genetics and the Law* (1986) Proceedings of the Lausanne Colloquium.

* B. Tizard, *Adoption: A Second Chance* (1977) London, Open Books, pp. 1, 3–8.

J. Triseliotis, 'Identity and Adoption' (1974) 78 Child Adoption.

* J. Triseliotis, *In Search of Origins: The Experiences of Adopted People* (1973) London, Routledge and Kegan Paul, pp. 84, 85, 101.

J. Triseliotis, 'Foster care outcomes: a review of key research findings' (1989) 13(3) Adoption and Fostering 5.

* J. Triseliotis, 'Obtaining birth certificates' in P. Bean (ed.), *Adoption: Essays in social policy, law and sociology* (1984) London, Tavistock, pp. 51–52.

United Nations, *Convention on the Rights of the Child* (1989).

United Nations, *Declaration on the Rights of the Child* (1959).

* C. Walby and B. Symons, *Who am I? Identity, adoption and human fertilisation, Discussion Series No. 12* (1990) London, British Agencies for Adoption and Fostering, pp. 39–41, 68.

V. Wimperis, *The Unmarried Mother and Her Child* (1960) London, Allen and Unwin.

Chapter 12

C.R. Albiston, E.E. Maccoby and R.H. Mnookin, 'Joint Legal Custody: Does it Affect Non-Residential Fathers' Contact, Coparenting and Compliance after Divorce?' (1990) 1(2) Stanford Law and Policy Review.

P.R. Amato and B. Keith, 'Parental Divorce and the Well-being of Children: a meta-analysis' (1991) 110(1) Psychological Bulletin 26.

* Anon, 'Saturday Parent' (1980) 144 Justice of the Peace 353.

F.R. Bennion, 'First consideration: a cautionary tale' (1976) 126 New Law Journal 1237.

Booth Committee, see *Report of the Matrimonial Causes Procedure Committee.*

* J. Bowlby, *Child Care and the Growth of Love* (2nd edn., 1965) Harmondsworth, Pelican Books, pp. 13–15.

* J. Bradshaw and J. Millar, *Lone Parent Families in the UK*, Department of Social Security Research Report No. 6 (1991), London, HMSO, Tables 2.8, 2.10.

J. Brophy, 'Child Care and the Growth of Power: the status of mothers in custody disputes' in J. Brophy and C. Smart (eds.) *Women in Law* (1985) London, Routledge and Kegan Paul.

J. Brophy, 'Custody Law, Childcare and Parenthood in Thatcher's Britain', in C. Smart and S. Sevenhuijsen (eds.), op. cit.

* L. Burghes, *Lone Parenthood and Family Disruption: The Outcomes for Children* (1994) London, Family Policy Studies Centre, pp. 22–23.

* J. Burgoyne and D. Clark, 'Reconstituted Families' in R.N. Rapoport, M.P. Fogarty and R. Rapoport (eds.), *Families in Britain* (1982) London, Routledge and Kegan Paul, pp. 299–301.

* J. Burgoyne and D. Clark, *Making a go of it – A study of stepfamilies in Sheffield* (1984) London, Routledge and Kegan Paul, Table 6.1.

J. Burgoyne, R. Ormrod and M. Richards, *Divorce Matters* (1987) Harmondsworth, Penguin.

* Central Statistical Office, *Social Trends 25* (1995) London, HMSO, Graph 2.10.

* Central Statistical Office, *Social Trends 26* (1996) London, HMSO, Graph 2.11.

P.L. Chase-Langdale and E.M. Hetherington, 'The Impact of Divorce on Life-

Span Development: Short and Long Term Effects,' in D.L. Featherman and R.M. Lerner (eds.), *Life Span Development and Behavior* (1990) Hillsdale, New Jersey, Lawrence Erlbaum Associates.

A.J. Cherlin *et al.*, 'Longitudinal Studies of Effects of Divorce on Children in Great Britain and the United States' (1991) 252 Science 1386.

A.J. Cherlin, K.E. Kiernan and P.L. Chase-Langdale, 'Parental Divorce in Childhood and Demographic Outcomes in Young Adulthood' (forthcoming in 1996).

C. Clulow and C . Vincent, *In the Child's Best Interests? Divorce court welfare and the search for a settlement* (1987) London, Tavistock.

M. Cockett and J. Tripp, *The Exeter Family Study – Family breakdown and its impact on children* (1995), Exeter, University of Exeter Press.

E. Crellin *et al.*, *Born Illegitimate, a Report by the National Children's Bureau* (1971) London, National Foundation for Educational Research.

G. Davis, A. Macleod and M. Murch, 'Undefended Divorce: Should Section 41 of the Matrimonial Causes Act 1973 be Repealed?' (1983) 46 Modern Law Review 121.

Department of Health, *The Children Act 1989. Guidance and Regulations. Vol. 1: Court Orders* (1991) London, HMSO.

Department of Health and others, *Adoption: The Future,* Cm 2288 (1993) London, HMSO.

Department of Health and Welsh Office, *Adoption – A Service for Children, Adoption Bill – A Consultative Document* (1996) London, Department of Health.

* Departmental Committee on the Adoption of Children (Chairman: Sir William Houghton), *Working Paper* (1970) London, HMSO, paras. 93–94.

N. Dennis and G. Erdos, *Families without Fatherhood* (1992), London, Institute of Economic Affairs.

R. Dingwall and J. Eekelaar, 'Judgements of Soloman: psychology and family law' in M. Richards and P. Light (eds.) (1986) *op cit.*

M. Dodds, 'Children and Divorce' [1983] Journal of Social Welfare Law 228.

J.W.B. Douglas, 'Broken Families and Child Behaviour' (1970) 4 Journal of the Royal College of Physicians 203.

J.M. Eekelaar, 'What Are Parental Rights?' (1973) 89 Law Quarterly Review 210.

J.M. Eekelaar, 'Children in Divorce: Some Further Data' (1982) 2 Oxford Journal of Legal Studies 62.

* J.M. Eekelaar, 'Custody appeals' (1985) 48 Modern Law Review 704, p. 705.

* J.M. Eekelaar and E. Clive with K. Clarke and S. Raikes, *Custody After Divorce: The Disposition of Custody in Divorce Cases in Great Britain* (1977) Oxford, Centre for Socio-legal Studies, paras. 3.6, 13.7, 13.29, table 34.

B.J. Elliott and M. Richards, 'Children and Divorce. Educational Performance and behaviour before and after parental separation' (1991) 5 International Journal of Law and the Family 258.

R.E. Emery, *Marriage, Divorce and Children's Adjustment* (1988) Beverley Hills, California, Sage Publications.

E. Fern, *Growing Up in a One-Parent Family* (1976) Windsor, NFER Publishing.

E. Fern, *Step Children: A National Study* (1984) London, NFER Nelson.

K. Funder, S. Kinsella and P. Courtney, 'Step fathers in Children's Lives' (1992) Family Matters No. 30.

F.F. Furstenberg, *Renegotiating Parenthood After Divorce and Remarriage* (1981) Paper presented at Biennial Meeting of the Society for Research in Child Development, Boston, USA.

F.F. Furstenberg, C. Winquist Nord, J.L. Peterson and N. Zill, 'The Life Course of Children of Divorce: Marital Disruption and Parental Contact' (1983) 48 American Sociological Review 656.

F.F. Furstenberg, S.P. Morgan and P.D. Allason, 'Paternal Participation and Children's well-being after Marital Dissolution' (1987) 52 American Sociological Review 695.

* F.F. Furstenberg and A.J. Cherlin, *Divided Families: What happens* to *children when parents part* (1991), Harvard University Press, pp. 71–76.

* J. Goldstein, A. Freud and A.J. Solnit, *Beyond the Best Interests of the Child* (1973) London, Collier Macmillan, pp. 31–34, 37, 40–41, 49–50, 51, 53, 62–63.

W.J. Goode, *After Divorce* (1956) New York, Free Press.

J. Haskey, 'Widowhood, Widowerhood and Remarriage' (1982) 30 Population Trends 15.

J. Haskey, 'Social class differentials in remarriage after divorce: results from a forward linkage study' (1987) 47 Population Trends 34.

J. Haskey, 'Children of Families broken by Divorce' (1990) 61 Population Trends 34, pp. 41–42.

J. Haskey, 'Estimated numbers of One-Parent Families and their Prevalence in Britain in 1991' (1994) 76 Population Trends.

* A. Heath-Jones, 'Divorce and the Reluctant Father' (1980) 10 Family Law 75, p. 75.

M. Hestor and L. Radford, 'Domestic Violence and Access Arrangements for Children in Denmark in Britain' [1992] 1 Journal of Social Welfare and Family Law 57.

E.M. Hetherington, 'Effects of Father's Absence on Personality Development in Adolescent Daughters' (1972) 1 Developmental Psychology 313.

E.M. Hetherington, 'Family Relations Six Years after Divorce,' in K. Pasley and M. Ihinger-Tallman (eds.), *Remarriage and Step-parenting: Current Research and Theory* (1987), New York, Guilford Press.

E.M. Hetherington, 'Coping with Family Transitions: Winners, Losers and Survivors' (1989) 60 Child Development 1.

E.M. Hetherington and W.G. Clingempeel, *Coping with Marital Transitions. A Family Systems Perspective* (1992) Child Development Research Monograph Vol. 57.

* K. Hewitt, 'Divorce and Parental Disagreement' (1996) 26 Family Law 368, p. 370.

Houghton, Working Paper – see Departmental Committee on the Adoption of Children.

Houghton, Report – see *Report of the Departmental Committee on the Adoption of Children.*

* Inter-departmental Review of Adoption Law, *The Nature and Effects of Adoption,* Discussion Paper No. 1 (1990) London, Department of Health, paras. 131–134.

* C. Itzin, *Splitting Up: Single Parent Liberation* (1980) London, Virago, pp. 130, 138.

* A. James, 'Social Work in Divorce: Mediation, Welfare and Justice' (1995) 9 International Journal of Law and Society 256, pp. 263–267.

A. James and W. Hay, *Court Welfare in Action: Practice and Theory* (1993) London, Harvester Wheatsheaf.

A. James and W. Hay, with D. Greatbatch and C. Walker, *Court Welfare Work: Research, Practice and Development* (1992) Hull, Centre for Criminology and Criminal Justice, University of Hull.

* Justice, *Report on Parental Rights and Duties and Custody Suits* (1975) London, Stevens, paras. 89(h), 91.

H.F. Keshet and K.M. Rosenthal, *Father Presence: Four Types of Post-marital Separation Fathering Arrangements* (1978) Paper presented at N.L.M.H. Symposium on Mental Health Consequences of Divorce on Children, Washington D.C.

K.E. Kiernan, 'The Impact of Family Disruption in Childhood on Transitions made in Young Adult Life' (1992) 46 Population Studies 213.

M. King, 'Playing the Symbols – Custody and the Law Commission' (1987) 17 Family Law 186.

M. King and J. Trowell, *Children's Welfare and the Law: The Limits of Legal Intervention* (1992) London, Sage Publications.

M. Kline, J.M. Tschann, J.R. Johnston and J.S. Wallerstein, 'Children's Adjustment in Joint and Sole Physical Custody Families' (1989) 25 Developmental Psychology 430.

D. Kuh and M. Maclean, 'Women's Childhood Experience of Parental Separation and their subsequent Health and Status in Adulthood' (1990) 22 Journal of Biosocial Science 121.

* Law Commission, *Report on Guardianship and Custody,* Law Com. No. 172 (1988) London, HMSO, paras 3.2–3.9, 3.13–3.14, 3.18–3.19, 3.22–3.25, 4.2–4.21, 4.55–4.57.

Law Commission, Working Paper No. 91, *Review of Child Law: Guardianship* (1985) London, HMSO.

* Law Commission, Working Paper No. 96, *Review of Child Law: Custody* (1986) London, HMSO, paras. 4.8–4.10, 4.35–4.38, 4.40–4.45, 6.40–6.43.

Law Commission, Working Paper No. 100, *Care, Supervision and Interim Orders in Custody Proceedings* (1987) London, HMSO.

C. Lewis, *Becoming a Father* (1986) Milton Keynes, Open University Press.

Lord Chancellor's Department, *Judicial Statistics 1995* (1996) London, HMSO.

N. Lowe, 'The Legal Status of Fathers – Past and Present' in L. McKee and M. O'Brien (eds.), *The Father Figure* (1982) London, Tavistock.

D.A. Luepnitz, *Child Custody: A Study of Families After Divorce* (1982) Lexington, Mass., Lexington Books.

M. Lund, 'The non-custodial father', in C. Lewis and M. O'Brien (eds.), *Reassessing Fatherhood* (1987) London, Sage.

E.E. Maccoby, C.E. Depner and R.H. Mnookin, 'Coparenting in the Second Year after Divorce' (1990) 52 Journal of Marriage and the Family 141.

M. Maclean and M. Wadsworth, 'The Interests of Children after Parental Divorce: a long term Perspective' (1988) 2 International Journal of Law and the Family 155.

A. Macleod with M. Borkowski, *Access after Divorce: The Follow-Up to the Special Procedure in Divorce Project* (1985) Bristol, University of Bristol.

* B. Maddox, *Step-parenting* (1980) London, Unwin Paperbacks, pp. 37–39.

S. Maidment, 'Access Conditions in Custody Orders' (1975) 2 British Journal of Law and Society 182.

S. Maidment, 'A Study in Child Custody' (1976) 6 Family Law 195 and 236.

S. Maidment, *Child Custody and Divorce* (1984) London, Croom Helm.

S. Maidment, 'Step-parent and Step-children: Legal Relationships in Serial Unions' in J.M. Eekelaar and S.N. Katz (eds.), *Marriage and Cohabitation in Contemporary Societies: Areas of Legal, Social and Ethical Change* (1980) Toronto, Butterworths.

* J. Masson, D. Norbury and S. Chatterton, *Mine, Yours or Ours? A study of stepparent adoption* (1984) London, HMSO, pp. 84, 103–105.

A. Mitchell, *Children in the Middle: Living through Divorce* (1985) London, Tavistock.

* R.H. Mnookin, 'Child Custody Adjudication: Judicial Functions in the Face of Indeterminacy' (1975) 39 Law and Contemporary Problems 226, pp. 286–287 (Duke University School of Law).

R.H. Mnookin, 'Bargaining in the Shadow of the Law: The Case of Divorce' [1979] Current Legal Problems 65.

P. Morgan, *Child Care: Sense and Fable* (1975) London, Temple Smith.

N. Murch, *Justice and Welfare in Divorce* (1980) London, Sweet and Maxwell.

NCH – Action for Children, *The Hidden Victims – Children and Domestic Violence* (1994).

* *New English Bible* (1972) The Bible Societies, I Kings 3, vs. 22–27.

F. Olsen, 'The Politics of Family Law' (1984) 2(1) Law and Inequality.

J.L. Peterson and N. Zill, 'Marital disruption, parent-child relationships and behavior problems in children' (1986) 49 Journal of Marriage and the Family 295.

* J.A. Priest and J.C. Whybrow, *Custody Law in Practice in the Divorce and Domestic Courts.* Supplement to Law Commission W.P. No. 96, *Review of Child Law: Custody* (1986) London, HMSO, Table 6.

* Probation and Aftercare Service, *Specimen Welfare Officer's Report* (1981).

R.N. Rapoport, R. Rapoport and Z. Strelitz, *Fathers, Mothers and Others* (1977) London, Routledge and Kegan Paul.

Report of the Committee on One-Parent Families (Chairman: The Hon. Sir Morris Finer) (Cmnd. 5629) (1974) London, HMSO.

* *Report of the Departmental Committee on the Adoption of Children* (Chairman: Sir William Houghton, later Judge F.A. Stockdale) (Cmnd. 5107) (1972) London, HMSO, para. 108.

Report of the Matrimonial Causes Procedure Committee (Chairman: The Hon. Mrs. Justice Booth D.B.E.) (1985) London, HMSO.

Report of the Royal Commission on Marriage and Divorce (Chairman: Lord Morton of Henryton) (Cmd. 9678) (1956) London, HMSO.

* *Review of Adoption Law – Report to Ministers of an Interdepartmental Working Group* (1992) London, Department of Health, paras. 19.2–19.9.

* M. Richards, 'Post Divorce Arrangements for Children: A Psychological Perspective' [1982] Journal of Social Welfare Law 133, pp. 135–136, 142–149.

* M. Richards, 'Private Worlds and Public Intentions – The Role of the State at Divorce' in A. Bainham and D. Pearl (eds.), *Frontiers of Family Law* (1993) London, Chancery Law Publishing, pp. 26–27.

M. Richards, *The Interests of Children on Divorce,* paper presented to an international conference on 'Families and Justice', Brussels (1994).

M. Richards and M. Dyson, *Separation, Divorce and the Development of Children: A Review* (1982) Child Care and Development Group, University of Cambridge.

M. Richards and P. Light (eds.), *Children of Social Worlds* (1986) Cambridge, Polity Press.

N. Richards, 'Behind the Best Interests of the Child: An Examination of the Arguments of Goldstein, Freud and Solnit Concerning Custody and Access at Divorce' [1986] Journal of Social Welfare Law 77.

Rights of Women, *Lesbian Mothers on Trial. A report on Lesbian mothers and child custody* (1985) London, Rights of Women.

N. Roman and W. Haddad, *The Disposable Parent: The Case for Joint Custody* (1978) New York, Penguin Books.

* N. Rutter, *Maternal Deprivation Reassessed* (1972; 2nd edn. 1981; rep. 1986) Harmondsworth, Penguin Books, pp. 126–127.

H.R. Shaffer and P.E. Emerson, 'The Development of Social Attachments in Infancy' (1964) 29 Monograph Soc. Res. Child Development, no. 3, p. 1.

J. Shulman and V. Pitt, 'Second Thoughts on Joint Custody: Analysis of Legislation and Its Impact for Women and Children' (1982) 12 Golden Gate University Law Review 539.

B. Simpson, P. McCarthy and J. Walker, *Being There: Fathers After Divorce* (1995) Newcastle, Relate Centre for Family Studies.

C. Smart, *The Ties that Bind* (1984) London, Routledge and Kegan Paul.

* C. Smart, *The Legal and Moral Ordering of Child Custody* (1990) University of Warwick, Department of Sociology, pp. 82–85, 91–92, 9–12.

C. Smart and S. Sevenhuijsen (eds.), *Child Custody and the Politics of Gender* (1989) London, Routledge.

S. Steinman, 'The Experience of Children in a Joint Custody Arrangement' (1981) 51 American Journal of Orthopsychiatry 403.

J. Tronto, 'Women and Caring: What can Feminists Learn about Morality from Caring?', in A. Jaggar and S. Bordo (eds.), *Gender/Body/Knowledge* (1989) London, Rutgers University Press.

* D. Utting, *Family and Parenthood – Supporting Families, Preventing Breakdown* (1995), York, Joseph Rowntree Foundation, Figure 12, pp. 45–47, pp. 22, 24.

D. Utting, J. Bright and C. Henricson, *Crime and the Family: improving child-rearing and preventing delinquency* (1993) London, Family Policy Studies Centre.

N. Wadsworth, 'Parenting Skills and their Transmission through Generations' (1985) 9 (1) Adoption and Fostering 28.

N. Wadsworth, 'Evidence from Three Birth Cohort Studies for Long Term and Cross Generational Effects on the Development of Children' in N. Richards and P. Light (1986) op. cit.

Y. Walczak with S. Burns, *Divorce: The Child's Point of View* (1984) London, Harper and Row.

J.S. Wallerstein and J.B. Kelly, *Surviving the Breakup: How Children and Parents Cope with Divorce* (1980) London, Grant Mcintyre.

J.S. Wallerstein and S. Blakeslee, *Second Chances* (1989) London, Bantam.

R.S. Weiss, *Marital Separation* (1975) New York, Basic Books.

R.S. Weiss, *Going It Alone: The Family Life and Social Situation of the Single Parent* (1979) New York, Basic Books.

L.J. Weitzman and R.B. Dixon, 'Child Custody Awards: Legal Standards and Empirical Patterns for Child Custody, Support and Visitation after Divorce' (1979) 12 UC Davis Law Review 473.

D.J. West, *Delinquency: its roots, careers and prospects* (1982) London, Heinemann.

Chapter 13

* Lady Allen of Hurtwood, 'Whose Children? Wards of State or Charity' *The Times*, 15 July 1944.

Susan Auckland, see under Reports.

Jasmine Beckford, see Brent Council.

J. Bowlby, *Child Care and the Growth of Love* (1953; 2nd edn., 1965) Harmondsworth, Penguin Books.

* Brent Council, *A Child in Trust – The Report of the Panel of Inquiry into the Circumstances surrounding the Death of Jasmine Beckford* (Chairman: L. Blom-Cooper Q.C.) (1985) London, London Borough of Brent.

Wayne Brewer, see Somerset Area Review Committee.

Kimberley Carlile, see Greenwich London Borough Council.

* Children Act Advisory Committee, *Annual Report 1994/5* (1996) London, Lord Chancellor's Department, pp. 51–52.

Ciba Foundation (R. Porter, ed.), *Child Sexual Abuse within the Family* (1984) London, Tavistock.

H. Cleaver and P. Freeman, *Parental Perspectives in Cases of Suspected Child Abuse* (1995) London, HMSO.

Cleveland Report, see Report of the Inquiry into Child Abuse in Cleveland 1987.

Maria Colwell, see under Reports.

Curtis Committee, see Report of the Care of Children Committee.

Dartington, see S. Miliham *et al*, op. cit.

* Department of Health, *Working Together – A guide to arrangements for inter agency*

co-operation for the protection of children from abuse (1991) London, HMSO, paras. 1.4, 3.8, 5.11.1–5.11.2, 5.14.7, 6.1, 6.3, 6.10, 6.13, 6.15, 6.18, 6.24–6.28, 6.36–6.40, 6.44, 6.52–6.54.

* Department of Health, Guidance and Regulations on the Children Act 1989, vol.1, *Court Orders* (1991) London, HMSO, paras. 3.77, 4.6, 4.9, 4.12, 4.15, 4.28, 4.29, 4.31, 4.44.

Department of Health, *Child Abuse – A Study of Inquiry Reports 1980–1989* (1991) London, HMSO.

* Department of Health and others, *Child Protection – Medical Responsibilities* (1994) London, Department of Health, paras. 6.1, 4.5–4.6.

* Department of Health, *Child Protection – Messages From Research* (1995) London, HMSO, pp. 15, 25–29, 32, 54–55.

* Department of Health, *Children Looked After by Local Authorities Year Ending 31 March 1994 England, A/F* 94/12 (1996) London, Department of Health, p. 33, table I.

DHSS, *Child Abuse – A Study of Inquiry Reports, 1973–1981* (1982) London, HMSO.

* DHSS, *Review of Child Care Law – Report to Ministers of an Interdepartmental Working Party* (1985) London, HMSO, paras. 2.20–2.25, 15.12–15.24, 18.5–18.15.

DHSS, *Social Work Decisions in Child Care – Recent Research Findings and their Implications* (1985) London, HMSO.

* DHSS and others, *The Law on Child Care and Family Services,* Cm. 62 (1987) London, HMSO, paras. 16–18, 20–22, 42–43.

R. Dingwall, J.M. Eekelaar and T. Murray, *Care or Control? Decision-Making in the Care of Children Thought to have been Abused or Neglected. A Summary of the Final Report* (1981) Oxford, Centre for Socio-legal Studies, pp. 40–42.

R. Dingwall, J.M. Eekelaar and T. Murray, *The Protection of Children: State Intervention and Family Life* (1983) Oxford, Basil Blackwell.

R. Dingwall, 'The Jasmine Beckford Affair' (1986) 49 Modern Law Review 489, pp. 493–495, 497–501.

* J.M. Eekelaar, R. Dingwall and T. Murray, 'Victims or Threats? Children in Care Proceedings' [1982] Journal of Social Welfare Law 67, pp. 71–78.

J Gibbons, S. Conroy and C. Bell, *Operating the Child Protection System* (1995) London, HMSO.

Greenwich London Borough Council and Greenwich Health Authority, A *Child in Mind – the Report of the Commission of Inquiry into the Circumstances Surrounding the Death of Kimberley Carlile* (Chairman: L. Blom-Cooper Q.C.) London, London Borough of Greenwich.

M. Hayes, *'R v Devon County Council ex parte L:* Bad practice, bad law and a breach of human rights?' (1992) 22 Family Law 245.

Tyra Henry, see Lambeth London Borough Council.

* J.S. Heywood, *Children in Care: The Development of the Service for the Deprived Child* (3rd edn., 1978) London, Routledge and Kegan Paul, pp. 7–10, 92–93.

Hillingdon Council, Area Review Committee on Child Abuse, *Report of the Review Panel into the Death of Heidi Koseda* (1986) London, London Borough of Hillingdon.

A.S. Holden, *Children in Care* (1980) London, Comyn.

Home Office, *The Child, the Family and the Young Offender* (Cmnd. 2742) (1965) London, HMSO.

Home Office, *Children in Trouble* (Cmnd. 3061) (1968) London, HMSO.

Home Office, *Memorandum of Good Practice on Video Recorded Interviews with Child Witnesses for Criminal Proceedings* (1992) London, HMSO.

House of Commons Select Committee on Violence in the Family, *Violence to*

Children. Vol. 1: Report (together with the Proceedings of the Committee) HC 329-i (1976–77) (1977) London, HMSO.

House of Commons Social Services Committee, *Children in Care, Minutes of Evidence,* HC 26-i and ii (1982–83) (1982) London, HMSO.

House of Commons Social Services Committee, Second Report Session 1983–84, *Children in Care,* HC 360 (1984) London, HMSO.

Ingleby Committee, see Report of the Committee on Children and Young Persons.

Kimberley Carlile, see Greenwich London Borough Council.

Heidi Koseda, see Hillingdon Council.

Lambeth London Borough Council, *Whose Child? The Report of the Public Inquiry into the Death of Tyra Henry* (1987) London, London Borough of Lambeth.

Law Commission, Working Paper No. 101, *Wards of Court* (1987) London, HMSO, para. 3.30.

Law Commission, *Domestic Violence and Occupation of the Family Home,* Law Com. No. 207 (1992) London, HMSO.

S. Millham, R. Bullock, K. Hosie and M. Haak (Dartington Social Research Unit), *Lost in Care – The problems of maintaining links between children in care and their families* (1986) Aldershot, Gower.

* J. Packman, *The Child's Generation: Child Care Policy in Britain* (2nd edn., 1981) Oxford, Basil Blackwell, pp. 57–59, 156, 161.

* J. Packman, with J. Randall and N. Jacques, *Who Needs Care? Social-Work Decisions about Children* (1986) Oxford, Basil Blackwell, pp. 194–197.

* *The Pindown Experience and the Protection of Children: The Report of the Staffordshire Child Care Inquiry* (Allan Levy Q.C. and Barbara Kahan) (1991) London, HMSO, paras. 11.17–11.35.

* J. Renvoize, *Children in Danger* (1974) London, Routledge and Kegan Paul; (1975) Harmondsworth, Penguine Books, pp. 20, 24.

* *Report by Sir Walter Monckton, KCMC, KCVO, MC, KC, on the circumstances which led to the boarding-out of Denis and Terence O'Neill at Bank Farm, Minsterley, and the steps taken to supervise their welfare* (Cmd. 6636) (1945) London, HMSO, paras. 2, 3 and 54.

* *Report of the Care of Children Committee* (Chairman: Miss M. Curtis) (Cmd. 6922) (1946) London, HMSO, paras. 10, 138, 140, 144, 154, 171, 193, 370, 427, 441, 443, 447.

Report of the Committee on Children and Young Persons (Chairman: Viscount Ingleby) (Cmnd. 1191) (1960) London, HMSO.

Report of the Committee of Inquiry into the Care and Supervision provided in relation to Maria Colwell (Chairman: T.G. Field-Fisher Q.C.) (1974) London, HMSO.

Report of the Committee of Inquiry into the Provision and Co-ordination of Services to the Family of John George Auckland (Chairman: P.J.M. Kennedy Q.C.) (1975) London, HMSO.

Report of the Committee on Local Authority and Allied Personal Social Services (Chairman: F. Seebohm) (Cmnd. 3703) (1968) London, HMSO.

* *Report of the Inquiry into Child Abuse in Cleveland 1987* (Chairman: The Hon. Mrs. Justice Butler-Sloss D.B.E.) (Cm. 412) (1988), London, HMSO pp. 4–9; paras. 10.6–10.13, 12.1–12.42.

Review of Child Care Law, see DHSS *(1985).*

J. Rowe and L. Lambert, *Children Who Wait* (1973) London, Association of British Adoption Agencies (now British Agencies for Adoption and Fostering).

E. Sharland, H. Seal, M. Croucher, J. Aldgate and D. Jones, *Professional Intervention in Child Sexual Abuse* (1996) London, HMSO.

M. Smith, P. Bee, A. Heverin and G. Nobes, *Parental Control within the Family: The Nature and Extent of Parental Violence to Children* (1996), papers forthcoming from the Thomas Coram Research Unit, University of London.

Somerset Area Review Committee of Non-Accidental Injury to Children, *Wayne Brewer – Report of the Review Panel* (1977).

J. Thoburn, A. Lewis and D. Shemmings, *Paternalism or Partnership? Family Involvement in the Child Protection Process* (1995) London, HMSO.

White Paper, see DHSS and others (1987).

Working Together, see Department of Health (1991).

Chapter 14

M. Adcock and R. White (eds.), *Terminating Parental Contact* (1980) London, Association of British Adoption and Fostering Agencies (now British Agencies for Adoption and Fostering).

J. Aldgate, 'Identification of Factors Influencing Children's Length of Stay in Care' in J. Triseliotis (ed.), *New Developments in Foster Care and Adoption* (1980) London, Routledge and Kegan Paul.

C. Bagley, 'Adjustment, Achievement and Social Circumstances of Adopted Children in a National Survey' (1980) 102 Adoption and Fostering 47.

P. Bean (ed.), *Adoption: Essays in Social Policy, Law and Sociology* (1984) London, Tavistock.

Jasmine Beckford, see Brent Council.

D. Berridge and H. Cleaver, *Foster Home Breakdown* (1987) Oxford, Blackwell.

Brent Council, *A Child in Trust – The Report of the Panel of Inquiry into the Circumstances Surrounding the Death of Jasmine Beckford* (Chairman: L. Blom-Cooper Q.C.) London, London Borough of Brent.

* E. Bullard and E. Malos, with R.A. Parker, *Custodianship – A Report to the Department of Health on the Implementation of Part II of the Children Act 1975 in England and Wales from December 1985 to December 1988* (1990) Bristol, Department of Social Policy and Social Planning, University of Bristol, paras. 9.31–9.40.

* J. Dare, *The Advantages and Disadvantages of Open Adoption and the Merits of Subsequent Contact with Natural Parents,* paper presented at a Judicial Studies Board seminar, May 1995.

* Department of Health, *Patterns and Outcomes in Child Care* (1991) London. HMSO, pp. 26–34, 36–37.

Department of Health and others, *Adoption: The Future,* Cm 2288 (1993) London, HMSO.

* Department of Health and Welsh Office, *Adoption – A Service for Children, Adoption Bill – A Consultative Document* (1996) London, Department of Health and Welsh Office, paras. 4.4–4.14, clauses 1, 46.

DHSS, *Report of the Committee of Inquiry into the Care and Supervision provided in relation to Maria Colwell* (Chairman: T.G. Field-Fisher Q.C.) (1974) London, HMSO.

DHSS, *Review of Child Care Law – Report to Ministers of an Interdepartmental Working Party* (1985) London, HMSO.

J. Dunn, 'Sibling influences on childhood development' (1988) 29(2) Journal of Child Psychology and Psychiatry.

D. Fanshel and E.B. Shinn, *Children in Foster Care: A Longitudinal Study* (1978) New York, Columbia University Press.

E. Farmer and R. Parker, *Trials and Tribulations: Returning Children From Care to Their Families* (1991) London, HMSO.

M. Fisher et al., *In and Out of Care: The Experiences of Children, Parents and Social Workers* (1986) London, Batsford.

M.D.A. Freeman, 'Subsidised adoption' in P. Bean (ed.), op. cit.

V. George, *Foster Care: Theory and Practice* (1970) London, Routledge and Kegan Paul.

* J. Gibbons, B. Gallagher, C. Bell and D. Gordon, *Development after Physical Abuse in Early Childhood* (1993) London, HMSO, pp. 88–90.

J. Goldstein, A. Freud and A.J. Solnit, *Beyond the Best Interests of the Child* (1973) London, Collier Macmillan.

M. Hill, L. Lambert and J. Triseliotis, *Achieving Adoption with Love and Money* (1989) London, National Children's Bureau.

R. Holman, *Trading in Children: A Study of Private Fostering* (1973) London, Routledge and Kegan Paul.

R. Holman, 'The Place of Fostering in Social Work' (1975) 5 British Journal of Social Work 3, pp. 8–14.

D. Howe, 'Assessing adoptions in difficulty' (1992) 22 British Journal of Social Work 1.

* Inter-departmental Review of Adoption Law, Discussion Paper No.1, *The Nature and Effects of Adoption* (1990) London, Department of Health, paras. 97–98, 100, 102–108.

House of Commons Social Services Committee, Second Report Session 1983–84, *Children in Care,* HC 360 (1984) London, HMSO.

L. Lambert, M. Buist, J. Triseliotis and M. Hill, *Freeing Children for Adoption: Final Report to the Social Work Services Croup* (1989) Edinburgh, Scottish Office; see also *Freeing for Adoption,* Research Series 7 (1990) London, British Agencies for Adoption and Fostering.

* Law Commission, Working Paper No. 96, *Review of Child Law: Custody* (1986) London, HMSO, paras. 5.15, 5.17, 5.19, 5.37, 5.39, 5.41, 5.42, 5.46.

* M. Little, *Research on Open Adoption,* paper presented at a Judicial Studies Board seminar, May 1995.

N. Lowe, 'Freeing for Adoption – the Experience of the 1980s' [1990] Journal of Social Welfare Law 220.

A. McWhinnie, *Adopted Children, how they grow up* (1966) London, Routledge and Kegan Paul.

A.N. Maluccio, B. Fein and K.A. Olmstead, *Permanency Planning for Children: Concepts and Methods* (1986) London, Tavistock.

B. Maugham and A. Pickles, 'Adopted and illegitimate children growing up,' in L.N. Robins and M. Rutter, *Straight and Devious Pathways from Childhood to Adulthood* (1990) Cambridge, Cambridge University Press.

S. Millham, R. Bullock, K. Hosie and M. Haak, *Lost in Care – The problems of maintaining links between children in care and their families* (1986) Aldershot, Gower.

S. Millham, R. Bullock, K. Hosie and M. Haak, *Access Disputes in Child Care* (1989) Aldershot, Gower.

S. Millham, R. Bullock and M. Little, *Going Home* (1993) Dartmouth.

C. Morris, *The Permanency Principle in Child Care Social Work,* Social Work Monograph 21 (1984) Norwich, University of East Anglia.

A. Mullender (ed.), *Open Adoption – the philosophy and the practice,* BAAF Practice Series 19 (1991) London, British Agencies for Adoption and Fostering.

* J. Packman, *The Child's Generation: Child Care Policy in Britain* (2nd edn. 1981) Oxford, Basil Blackwell, pp. 137–138.

L. Raynor, *The Adopted Child Comes of Age* (1980) London, George Allen and Unwin.

Report (first) of the Child Adoption Committee (Chairman: Mr Justice Tomlin) (Cmd. 2401) (1925) London, HMSO.

* *Report of the Adoption Practices Review Committee* (1990) New Zealand Ministry of Social Welfare, pp. 39–43.

* *Report of the Departmental Committee on the Adoption of Children* (Chairman: Sir William Houghton, later Judge F.A. Stockdale) (Cmnd. 5107) (1972) London, HMSO, paras. 93–94, 168–170, 221, 223–224.

* *Review of Adoption Law, Report to Ministers of an Interdepartmental Working Group, A Consultation Document* (1992) London, Department of Health and Welsh Office, paras. 6.2–6.5, 7.1, 7.2, 12.4–12.6, 14.1–14.5, 20.4, 21.1–21.3, 22.1.

Review of Child Care Law, see DHSS.

J. Rowe, 'Fostering in the 1970s' (1977) Adoption and Fostering, no. 4, p. 15.

J. Rowe, *Fostering in the Eighties* (1983), London, British Agencies for Adoption and Fostering.

J. Rowe and L. Lambert, *Children Who Wait* (1973) London, Association of British Adoption Agencies (now British Agencies for Adoption and Fostering).

* J. Rowe, H. Cain, M. Hundleby and A. Keane, *Long-Term Foster Care* (1984) London Batsford and BAAF, pp. 225–226.

J. Rowe, H. Cain, M. Hundleby and A. Keane, *Long-term fostering and the Children Act – a study of foster parents who went on to adopt* (1984) London, British Agencies for Adoption and Fostering.

J. Rowe, M. Hundleby and L. Garnett, *Child Care Now – a survey of placement patterns,* BAAF Research Series 6 (1989) London, British Agencies for Adoption and Fostering.

A. Rushton, J. Treseder and D. Quinton, *New Parents for Older Children,* BAAF Discussion Series 10 (1988), London, British Agencies for Adoption and Fostering.

A. Rushton, J. Treseder and D. Quinton, 'Sibling groups in permanent placements' (1989) 13(4) Adoption and Fostering 5.

* J. Stone, *Making Positive Moves – Developing Short-term Fostering Services* (1995) London, British Agencies for Adoption and Fostering, pp. 52–61.

J. Thoburn, *Review of Research Relating to Adoption,* Interdepartmental Review of Adoption Law, Background Paper No. 2 (1990) London, Department of Health.

J. Thoburn, *Success and Failure in Permanent Family Placement* (1990) Avebury, Gower.

* J. Thoburn, 'Survey findings and conclusions,' in J. Fratter, J. Rowe, D. Sapsford and J. Thoburn, *Permanent family placement – a decade of experience,* BAAF Research Series 8 (1991) London, British Agencies for Adoption and Fostering, pp. 37, 51–56.

J. Thoburn, A. Murdoch and A. O'Brien, *Permanence in Child Care* (1986) Oxford, Basil Blackwell.

J. Thoburn and J. Rowe, 'Research: A Snapshot of Permanent Family Placement' (1988) 12(3) Adoption and Fostering 29.

R. Thorpe, 'The Experience of Children and Parents Living Apart' in J. Triseliotis (ed.), *New Developments in Foster Care and Adoption* (1980) London, Routledge and Kegan Paul.

* B. Tizard, *Adoption: A Second Chance* (1977) London, Open Books, pp. 7–8, 206–209.

G. Trasler, *In Place of Parents* (1960) London, Routledge and Kegan Paul.

J. Trent, *Homeward Bound* (1989), London, Barnardo's.

* J. Triseliotis, 'Growing Up in Foster Care and After' in J. Triseliotis (ed.), *New Developments in Foster Care and Adoption* (1980) London, Routledge and Kegan Paul, pp. 138 and 148.

J. Triseliotis, 'Identity and Security in Adoption and Long-Term Fostering' (1983) 7(1) Adoption and Fostering 22.

J. Triseliotis and J. Russell, *Hard to Place: The Outcome of Late Adoption and Residential Care* (1984) London, Heinemann.

J. Triseliotis, 'Foster care outcomes: a review of key research findings' (1989) 13(3) Adoption and Fostering 5, pp. 12–15.

P. Wedge and G. Mantle, *Sibling Groups and Social Work* (1991) Avebury, Gower.

Chapter 15

M. Agopian, 'The Impact on Children of Abduction by Parents' (1984) 63 Child Welfare 511.

★ P. Alston and S. Parker, 'Introduction' in P. Alston, S. Parker and J. Seymour (eds.), *Children, Rights and the Law* (1992) Oxford, Clarendon Press, p. viii.

P. Alston (ed), *The Best Interests of the Child: Reconciling Culture and Human Rights* (1994) Oxford, Clarendon Press.

C. Barton and A. Bissett-Johnson, 'The European Convention and Parental Rights' (1995) 25 Family Law 507.

C. Bruch, 'Child Abduction and the English Courts' in A. Bainham and D. Pearl (eds) *Frontiers of Family Law* (1993) London, Chancery Law Publishing, reprinted in A. Bainham, D. Pearl and R. Pickford (eds) *Frontiers of Family Law*, 2nd edn. (1995) Chichester, John Wiley and Co.

B. Cass, 'The Limits of the Public/Private Dichotomy: A Comment on Coady & Coady' in P. Alston, S. Parker and J. Seymour (eds.), *Children, Rights and the Law* (1992) Oxford, Clarendon Press, p. 140.

D. Cheney, 'Valued Judgements: A Reading of Immigration Cases' in A. Bottomley and J. Conaghan (eds.), *Feminist Theory and Legal Strategy* (1993) Oxford, Basil Blackwell Ltd.

C.P. Cohen, 'The United Nations Convention on the Rights of the Child: Implications for Change in the Care and Protection of Refugee Children' (1992) 3 International Journal of Refugee Law p. 675.

★ Council of Europe, *European Convention for the Protection of Human Rights and Fundamental Freedoms* (1950), Seventh Protocol (1984).

★ Department of Health, Circular Cl(90)17, *Adoption of Children from Overseas*, London, Department of Health, paras. 1, 2, 7–8.

★ Department of Health *et al.*, *Adoption: The Future* (Cm 2288) (1993) London, HMSO, paras 6.1–6.10, 6.16–6.36.

★ Department of Health and Welsh Office, *Adoption – A Service for Children, Adoption Bill – A Consultative Document* (1996) London, Department of Health and Welsh Office.

★ W. Duncan, 'Regulating Intercountry Adoption – An International Perspective' in A. Bainham and D. Pearl (eds.), *Frontiers of Family Law* (1993) London, Chancery Law Publishing, pp. 49–50, reprinted in A. Bainham, D. Pearl and R. Pickford (eds.), Frontiers of Family Law, 2nd edn. (1995) Chichester, John Wiley and Co.

D. Evans, *International Families and the Law* (1988) Bristol, Jordan and Sons.

M. Freeman and P. Veerman (eds), *The Ideologies of Children's Rights* (1992) Dordrecht, Kluwer Academic Publishers.

D. Freestone, 'The United Nations Convention on the Rights of the Child' in D. Freestone (ed.), *Children and the Law (Essays in Honour of Professor H.K. Bevan)* (1990) Hull, Hull University Press.

R. Hegar and G. Greif, 'Abduction of Children by their Parents: A Survey of the Problem' (1991) 36 Social Work 421.

The Home Office, DP/3/96; DP/4/96; DP/5/96.

★ M. King, 'Children's Rights as Communication: Reflections on Autopoietic Theory and the United Nations Convention' (1994) 57 Modern Law Review p 385 at pp. 388–389, 392, 400–401.

★ Lord Chancellor's Department in consultation with the Foreign and

Commonwealth Office, Home Office and Reunite, *Child Abduction* (1992) London, Lord Chancellor's Department.

D. McClean and K. Beevers, 'International Child Abduction – Back to Common Law Principles' (1995) 7 Child and Family Law Quarterly 128.

C. Mortimore, *Immigration and Adoption* (1994) Stoke on Trent, Trentham Books.

D. Ngabonziza, 'Moral and Political Issues facing Relinquishing Countries' (1991) 15 Adoption and Fostering 75.

R. O'Grady, *The Child and the Tourist* (1992) Auckland, Pace Publishing.

* F. Olsen, 'Children's Rights: Some Feminist Approaches to the United Nations Convention on the Rights of the Child' in P. Alston, S. Parker and J. Seymour (eds.), *Children, Rights and the Law* (1992) Oxford, Clarendon Press pp. 195–216.

O. O'Neill, 'Children's Rights and Children's Lives' in P. Alston, S. Parker and J. Seymour (eds.), *Children, Rights and the Law* (1992) Oxford, Clarendon Press.

* Parliamentary Working Party on Abduction, *Home and Away – Child Abduction in the Nineties* (1993) London, Reunite, pp. 4–5.

* D. Rosettenstein, 'Transracial Adoption in the United States and the Impact of Considerations relating to Minority Population Groups on International Adoptions in the United States' (1995) 9 International Journal of Law and the Family 131, pp. 139–140, 142–143, 149.

R.J. Simon and H. Altstein, *Transracial Adoptees and Their Families* (1987), UNICEF, The State of the World's Children (1991).

* United Nations, *Convention on the Rights of the Child* (1989).

United Nations, *Declaration on the Rights of the Child* (1951).

* G. Van Bueren, 'The Challenges for the International Protection of Family Members' Rights as the 21st Century Approaches' in N. Lowe and G. Douglas (eds.), *Frontiers of Family Law* (1996) The Hague, Martinus Nijhoff Publishers (forthcoming).

G. Van Bueren, 'The Struggle for Empowerment: the Emerging Civil and Political Rights of Children' in *Selected Essays on International Children's Rights* (1993) Geneva, Defence for Children International.

Chapter 1

The family and marriage

1 Definitions of 'household' and 'family'

Most people understand that the word *family* refers to a group of persons related to each other by blood and/or marriage. The introduction of an additional word, such as 'immediate', suggests that the members of the family probably live together within a single household, and (although to a variable extent) pool their resources for the common well-being of the unit. However, many important questions are immediately raised by this series of assumptions. Is it necessary for the members of the family to be related in the manner described? Is it a prerequisite that there be a single household? Why should members pool resources?

The family's structure will vary from culture to culture. Most are based on monogamous marriages although there are still some cultures which tolerate polygamous marriages. In the England of the 1990s, we must not assume that the answer to the question 'What is a family?' is necessarily going to produce a simple and straightforward response. In the context of a traditional Indian family, or a Chinese family, the familial group may be much larger than a simple household; there may be a pooling of certain resources only, financial obligations may be extended to a wider kinship group than the familial nexus.

The following extract comes from the Judicial Studies Board's *Handbook on Ethnic Minority Issues* (1994):

3. COMPOSITION OF FAMILIES

There are a number of common stereotypes about the composition of ethnic minority families in Britain, the accuracy of which it is important to ascertain. These include that ethnic minority families are larger in size than those of the indigenous majority; that South Asian families take the form of 'extended families'; and that Afro-Caribbean families consist typically of a single mother bringing up children on her own.

Despite the fact that these images may have some basis in reality, as rigid stereotypes they can be misleading and dangerous. They over-generalise certain tendencies, and conceal the existence of considerable diversity in family composition among Britain's minority ethnic communities. They also do nothing to help with understanding why there may be differences in family patterns between ethnic groups.

3.1 Family Size

By 'family size' is normally meant 'size of household'. Statistics for the size of households do in fact show some quite substantial differences between ethnic groups. For example, both Indian and Pakistani/Bangladeshi households – averaging 3.8 and 4.8 persons respectively – tend to be considerably larger than households classified as 'white', which average at 2.5. Households classified as 'West Indian' on the other hand are on average almost identical in size to white households with an average of 2.6 (Labour Force Survey).

It is important to bear in mind that when overall averages differ in this way, they tend to highlight – and thus perhaps exaggerate – the differences. Not only do averages of this kind conceal substantial variation within each group, but they conceal also a great deal of overlap in the distribution of family size between the groups. Thus 60% of Pakistani/Bangladeshi families, and 84% of Indian families, are of between 1 and 5 persons in size, the range that accounts for almost all of the white families.

On the other hand, the fact that 41% of Pakistani/Bangladeshi households include 6 persons or more, as compared with 2% in the white group, is clearly a very substantial difference. Further statistical breakdown shows that part of this difference can be attributed to the larger numbers of children in such households. The other part is explained by the much more frequent presence of more than two adults than in 'white' homes.

To some extent these differences may be explained by cultural factors, which include marriage and child-bearing practices, and the greater strength of obligations to elderly parents and other kin. The differences, however, should not be presumed to be due to cultural factors alone. Economic circumstances are also important, as are the age profiles of minority ethnic communities, which tend (especially within the Bangladeshi community) to be relatively youthful due to their immigration being more recent.

3.2 Extended families

One of the cultural factors which explains the larger size of South Asian households in Britain is undoubtedly the greater significance of what is often referred to as the 'extended family'. This term, however, may refer to various features and can sometimes be misleading, and it is important to clarify the respects in which this applies to South Asian communities.

In the white British context, the 'extended family' usually means one of two things: a household which consists of three generations (i.e. including grandparents/grandchildren), or a wider network of relatives who are felt to belong to one another and cooperate in certain ways. Generally speaking, the former is usually viewed as a temporary arrangement when it occurs: a married child is waiting to be able to obtain a home of its own, or a widowed grandparent is taken in so that he or she does not have to live alone. The latter is most often observed and referred to at temporary gatherings such as weddings or funerals, though in some circles (e.g. established working-class or rural communities, or among Travellers) this network may be of much greater significance in people's social and economic lives.

In all these examples, however, it remains the case that the primary unit is seen as the 'nuclear family', and the 'extension' is relative to this nucleus which is in control of its own affairs. In the white British context, therefore, the 'extended family' is precisely what the word implies: an extension of a nuclear unit of parents and children which is assumed to be the appropriate and basic core.

At first sight, there may appear to be no difficulty about applying this term also to families from the Indian sub-continent, and to those from other parts of the world. For example, the term may be presumed to apply to their tendency to form larger households, due to the presence of a wider range of relatives than that of parent and child alone. Likewise, it may be applied to the commonly observed tendency for such families to maintain a greater degree of social contact than the white British, and to use family ties commonly as the basis for business partnerships as well.

Care needs to be taken, however, over whether this term (and the thinking behind it) captures the distinctive character of these cultural patterns, and whether it is in danger of misleading us as to why these patterns occur. The important point to appreciate, here, is that not all family systems operate on the same principles as the white British one, and that misunderstanding can arise by assuming this is so.

Unlike the white British family system, most Asian and African systems traditionally have not operated on the basis that there is a 'nuclear unit' of parents and children that should be autonomous and sovereign. Their view, on the contrary, has tended to be that the interests of individual parents and children should be seen as subordinate to the wider group of kin as a whole. The membership of this group is most commonly defined in terms of shared patrilineal descent (i.e. in the male line), although matrilineal descent is used in some areas, notably in parts of West Africa. This larger group will act corporately in dealing with a wide range of affairs – certainly most economic and property matters, and often marriage and domestic affairs as well.

In family systems of the above kind, the 'nuclear family' as a biologically related group is usually given some degree of recognition, and in most cases would co-reside. However, it would be a mistake to view the group as a whole as 'made up' of such units in terms of how it organises its affairs: such families are not 'extended' in the British sense, but function traditionally as enduring corporate units of persons related through the male (or in some cases female) line.

On the Indian sub-continent, this family pattern has generally been known as the 'joint-family' system. The term 'joint-family' refers to the common situation that, following the death of the father as head of the family, the sons jointly inherit and manage the family property, forming a single corporate kinship group together with their wives and children. In China, those sharing descent in the male line would similarly own and manage property corporately, the ethos of solidarity among patrilineal kin being especially strong due to belief in the spiritual powers of dead ancestors over the living.

Family systems of this kind are probably far older and certainly have been far more extensive across the world than the fragmented 'nuclear' British/European forms. Early urban civilisations were built upon them – but they tend to break down in the face of the more aggressive kinds of urbanisation and change in the modern era. For migrants, however, they often continue to provide a framework within which life can be organised, even if this may need to be modified and adapted to circumstances for which such traditional family patterns were not devised. Features such as corporate family enterprises, and 'arranged marriages', should therefore be expected to be maintained to some degree within migrant communities (perhaps even for several generations), and they need to be understood in terms of their original context and not solely as departures from their host country's norms.

If the term 'extended family' is used to refer to Asian and African families, therefore, it is important that the distinctive character of such family traditions is appreciated. This does not imply that such traditions will be always maintained: some people may not wish to do so anyway, whilst others in attempting to do so may find practical problems in their way. The effects of migration and of immigration controls can be very divisive for such families, and the small size of housing units in Britain also constrains the establishment of traditional corporate family groups.

Nonetheless, the higher degree of family cooperation (especially among the migrant generation) often found among Asian and African as compared with the white British population is witness to the strength of such cultural traditions. For example, a married son with his wife and children may readily continue to live under the same roof as his father, even in a relatively small home, as it is not traditionally the norm to move away on marriage as among white British families. On the other hand, some South Asian households recorded in the statistics as 'nuclear-family households' will be socially autonomous units as the term implies; but many may, despite their spatial separation, be extremely closely linked with other households in the traditional way. Localised settlement, and activities such as weekend visiting and use of the telephone, are examples of ways in which the physical obstacles to family unity can be overcome.

It is important to be clear about the difference in meaning between household and family.

A *household* according to Stone, writing about the family in England from 1500–1800, consists of persons 'living under one roof'. In *The Family, Sex and Marriage* (1977), he says:

> The core of any household is clearly the family, namely members related by blood or marriage, usually the conjugal pair and their unmarried children, but sometimes including grandparents, the married children, or occasionally kin relatives. But most households also included non-kin inmates, sojourners, boarders or lodgers, occupying rooms vacated by children or kin, as well as indentured apprentices and resident servants, employed either for domestic work about the house or as an additional resident labour force for the fields or the shop.

Laslett and Wall, in their seminal work published in 1972 entitled *Household and Family in Past Time,* define the two words 'household' and 'family' in the context of the historical demographic data which they collect and analyse:

It must be strongly stressed that in this vocabulary the word *family* does not denote a complete coresident domestic group, though it may appear as an abbreviated title. The word *household* particularly indicates the fact of shared location, kinship and activity. Hence all solitaries have to be taken to be households, for they are living with themselves, and this is the case when they have servants with them, since servants are taken as household members. …

The expression *simple family is* used to cover what is variously described as the *nuclear family*, the *elementary family* or (not very logically, since spouses are not physiologically connected) the *biological family*. It consists of a married couple, or a married couple with offspring, or of a widowed person with offspring. The concept is of the conjugal link as the structural principle. … For a simple family to appear then, it is necessary for at least two individuals connected by that link or arising from that link to be coresident: *conjugal family unit* (CFU) is a preciser term employed to describe all possible groups so structured.

No solitary can form a conjugal family unit and for such a group to subsist it is necessary for at least two immediate partners (spouses and/or offspring) to be present. More remotely connected persons, whose existence implies more than one conjugal link, do not constitute a conjugal family unit if they reside together with no one else except servants. Nor do brothers and sisters. Hence a widow with a child forms a conjugal family unit, but a widow with a grandchild does not, nor does an aunt with a nephew. Whenever a conjugal family unit is found on its own, it is always taken to be a household, just as solitaries are, and such a coresident domestic group is called a *simple family household*. …

An *extended family household* [or stem family] consists of a conjugal family unit with the addition of one or more relatives other than offspring, the whole group living together on its own or with servants. It is thus identical with the simple family household except for the additional item or items.

Multiple family households comprise all forms of domestic group which include two or more conjugal family units connected by kinship or by marriage. The disposition of a secondary unit, that is of a constituent unit which does not contain the head of the whole household, is said to be UP if its conjugal link involves a generation earlier than that of the head, as for example when his father and mother live with him. Such a secondary unit can include offspring of the head's parents other than the head himself, that is his resident unmarried brothers or sisters, and the presence of such persons keeps this secondary unit in being if one or other of the head's parents dies. A secondary unit is disposed DOWN if, for example, a head's married son lives with him along with his wife and perhaps offspring, with similar implications about siblings and widowhood. …

If conjugal family units within households of the multiple kind are all disposed laterally, as when married brothers and/or sisters live together, the overall arrangement is the one often referred to as the 'fraternal joint family' by social anthropologists.

Questions

(i) Is your family a simple family household, an extended family household or a multiple family household?
(ii) What about your grandparents' family?

It is necessary to consider another introductory matter, namely the difference between *familial experience* and *familial ideology*. There may be a correspondence between experience and ideology; however, it has been argued by Laslett and Wall that although the nuclear monogamous family has a claim to universality, it has never possessed a normative and ideological force:

There must be few behavioural institutions of which it can be said that ideology and experience are entirely congruent. No one would question that the English society of our day is correctly described as monogamous, because monogamous behaviour is nearly universal amongst a people whose belief in monogamy as a value is very widespread, and whose conduct is consistent with monogamy as the norm. It could be called the marital institution under which the English live, for no other distinct practice-with-belief exists alongside it as an alternative. Yet divorce is now quite frequent, scepticism about single spouse unions often encountered, and sexual intercourse outside marriage a commonplace. Indeed we know that children have been begotten illegitimately in appreciable numbers in England during the whole period for which figures can be recovered. …

Departure from the monogamous ideal of behaviour, amongst English people nowadays, and perhaps amongst their ancestors, has been particularly conspicuous within the elite, and rejection of the beliefs associated with monogamy especially common with the intellectuals, the makers of opinions and of norms. Monogamy as an institution, then, has been underwritten by a general correspondence of ideology and experience, but is consistent with an appreciable degree of disharmony between the two. We do not find ourselves enquiring how much they could diverge before a practice ceased to be *the* institution, and became one amongst others, *an* institution. We do not easily contemplate a situation where plural institutions, or highly variable behaviour, exist in one society at one time in such matters as sexual behaviour and marriage.

Yet if we turn to the question of how far any of the forms of the coresident domestic group, … could be called *the* institution, or *an* institution, of the societies where examples of them are found, this issue becomes inescapable. Glancing again at England as it is today, it seems safe enough to claim that the nuclear family, the simple family household, is *the* familial institution, and that again because experience of it, belief in it, willingness to obey its norms, are in fact all congruent with each other. The nuclear family, of course, complements the English institution of monogamy in a particular way. But it has, and has had for hundreds of years as far as we can yet see, a markedly better claim to universality in behaviour and experience than monogamous marriage with exclusively marital sexual intercourse. Yet the nuclear family never seems to have possessed the normative force, certainly not the ideological potential of monogamy, in England or indeed in Western culture.

The hiatus, therefore, between familial experience and familial ideology is of a somewhat different character than that which divides the two in the matter of monogamy. The intellectuals and opinion makers who deal in the ideology of our world, have a tendency to deplore the circumstance that the complex family household is not sufficiently established as a norm in our society. Extended and even multiple households exist amongst us, but not in anything like enough numbers to ensure that the widowed and the elderly unmarried have a family to live in, or our children the emotional advantage of the presence of the extended kin in the households where they grow up.

[Bear this last sentence in mind when you consider the issues raised in Chapter 4.]

Laslett and Wall's definition of monogamy may be contrasted with the following extract from Engels, *Origins of the Family, Private Property and the State* (1884):

Sex love in the relation of husband and wife is and can become the rule only among the oppressed classes, that is, at the present day, among the proletariat, no matter whether this relationship is officially sanctioned or not. But all the foundations of classical monogamy are removed. Here there is a complete absence of all property, for the safeguarding and inheritance of which monogamy and male domination were established. Therefore, there is no stimulus whatever here to assert male domination. …

Moreover, since large-scale industry has transferred the woman from the house to the labour market and the factory, and makes her, often enough, the bread winner of the family, the last remnants of male domination in the proletarian home have lost all foundation – except, perhaps, for some of that brutality towards women which became firmly rooted with the establishment of monogamy. Thus, the proletarian family is no longer monogamian in the strict sense, even in cases of the most passionate love and strictest faithfulness of the two parties, and despite all spiritual and worldly benedictions which may have been received. …

Questions

(i) Polygamy is permitted in some cultures; for example, in classical Islamic law a man is permitted four wives; the husband inherits a large slice of his wife's property, but she does have rights of ownership while she is alive and can inherit a share of the estate of her deceased father. Do you think that polygamy has anything to do with: (*a*) control of property and (*b*) male domination?

(ii) Do you think that a male worker has a vested interest in the domination of his wife and children?

(iii) Section 8(3) of the Immigration Act 1971 states that the provisions introduced under the Act for immigration control shall not apply to any person so long as he is a member of a mission, or 'a person who is a member of the family and forms part of the household of such a member'. Are the following exempt from control:

(*a*) the distant cousin of a Pakistani diplomat who has been looked after by this diplomat and his wife after the death of the parents;
(*b*) the fourth wife of a Yemeni diplomat who has been provided with separate accommodation by her husband in Yemen in accordance with Islamic law; and
(*c*) the young brother of an Indian diplomat who has equal rights with the diplomat in the joint property they have both inherited from their father?

See *Re Wirdestedt,* reported as a note [1990] Imm AR 20 where the Court of Appeal held that a 'firm, stable and lasting homosexual relationship' was not a relationship which was capable of recognition within the Immigration Rules. A homosexual partner was not a 'close relative' and thus was not qualified for admission for settlement on the application of the sponsor. (Although his case was unsuccessful, Mr Wirdestedt was subsequently allowed to remain in the UK. See Bovey 'Out and Out: UK Immigration Law and the Homosexual' (1994) Imm and Nat LP vol. 8 p. 61.)

(iv) Private sector tenancies: the Housing Act 1988, s. 17(4) defines a tenant's spouse, who can succeed to a periodic assured tenancy, as including 'a person who was living with the tenant as his or her wife or husband'. Does this rule apply to the following: (*a*) a close friend of the original tenant, where both had for many years lived together in a platonic association; (*b*) the survivor of two old cronies who had shared a house; (*c*) a lady of 'independence' who had lived with the deceased for many years as his cohabitant but who had deliberatedly remained unmarried?

(v) In *Carega Properties SA v Sharratt* [1979] 2 All ER 1084, [1979] 1 WLR 928, the House of Lords emphasised that the relevant question under the Rent Act 1977 (then in force) is whether the 'ordinary man' would regard the relationship in question as establishing 'a broadly recognisable familial nexus'. Historically, is this phrase restricted to a biological or marital connection?

(vi) Public sector tenancies: Section 113(1) of the Housing Act 1985 states:

'A person is a member of another's family … if–
(*a*) he is the spouse of that person, or he and that person live together as husband or wife, or
(*b*) he is that person's parent, grandparent, child, grandchild, brother, sister, uncle, aunt, nephew or niece.'

In *Harrogate Borough Council v Simpson* [1986] 2 FLR 91, [1986] Fam Law 359, the Court of Appeal held that a woman who lived in council accommodation with another woman, a secured tenant, and who shared a 'committed, monogamous, homosexual relationship' with her, was not a 'member of the tenant's family' within the meaning of s. 113(1), (2) of the Housing Act 1985, and accordingly was not entitled to succeed to the tenancy on the death of the tenant (s. 87 of the 1985 Act).

Would you be prepared to make a case in favour of extending the section so as to include monogamous yet homosexual relationships? And what of cousins or other collaterals who live together in an extended family which operates a system of joint property?

In *M v M* (1981) 2 FLR 39, the Court of Appeal refused an application of a wife for a maintenance order against her husband in favour of a child of hers. The court decided that the husband had not treated the child as a child of the family (s. 52(1) of the Matrimonial Causes Act 1973; see now s. 105(1) of the Children Act 1989). The parties were married in September 1970. They separated in April 1971. After the separation the wife became pregnant by another man. The wife did not want her family to know that the husband was not the father. The husband acquiesced in this state of affairs and allowed the wife's family to think the child was his.

Ormrod LJ: In my judgment the first question the learned judge had to ask himself was, 'Could there possibly be said to have been at any time during this child's life a family of which he could be treated as part?' In my judgment, the answer to that must be 'No'. These two parties, husband and wife, had been living apart in the full sense of the phrase ever since April 1971. There had been nothing whatsoever in their relationship which bore any relation to that of husband and wife. The learned judge himself put it that they were, if anything, friends, still on friendly terms. ...

Here the husband has filed his petition (he has not got his decree yet) on the ground that the parties had been living apart in that sense for five years, and the one thing that emerges perfectly clearly from the facts of this case is that neither of them regarded the marriage as subsisting. Once you get to that stage, it seems to me wholly artificial to say that the family as a social unit continued to exist. It must, as a family, using the language in ordinary sense, come to an end when the parties regard their marriage as at an end. These two parties plainly regarded their marriage as at an end from April 1971 onwards. ...

They were living apart, held together only by the empty shell of this marriage which could have been dissolved at any time. ...

My conclusions on the facts of this case are, firstly, that there was in fact at no time during this child's life a family. Therefore, it was not possible to treat the child as a child of this (non-existent) family; secondly on the question of 'treatment', it is a matter of fact to be judged by looking at and carefully considering what the husband in this case did and how he behaved towards the child. The difficulty in this case is that the husband, if he did anything, behaved towards this child not as if the child were a child of the family but as if, for certain purposes, the child was his own natural child. That is, he took part in the pretence without protesting. I do not think the evidence goes any further than that. The fact that he put the word 'Dad' on some Christmas cards and presents does not, in my judgment, amount to anything more than following the line he had taken up at the request of the wife, which was to cover up for her to all intents and purposes. He, as he said himself, was quite fond of the child as a child. He was kind to the boy and was quite pleased to see him on the rare occasions when he visited the mother. It goes no further than that.

Questions

(i) Is 'child of the family' the same thing as 'child of the household'? (See the article by Jacqueline Priest 'Child of the Family' in (1984) 14 Fam Law p. 134 where other cases are discussed; in particular *W v W* [1984] FLR 796, CA and *Teeling v Teeling* [1984] FLR 808, CA.)

(ii) Does a 'household' include a man who has been committed to prison for nine months? (See *Taylor v Supplementary Benefit Officer* [1986] 1 FLR 16, [1986] Fam Law 16, CA.)

Read what Lord Langdale MR said in 1836 in relation to wills in *Blackwell v Bull* (1836) 1 Keen 176, 5 LJ Ch 251:

It is evident that the word 'family' is capable of so many applications that if any one particular construction were attributed to it in wills, the intention of testators would be more frequently defeated than carried into effect. Under different circumstances it means a man's household, consisting of himself, his wife, children and servants; it may mean his wife and children, or his children excluding his wife; in the absence of wife and children, it may mean his brother and sisters or his next of kin, or it may mean the genealogical stock from which he may have sprung. All these applications of the word and some others are found in common parlance.

In the case of a will we must endeavour to ascertain the meaning in which the testator employed the word, by considering the circumstances and situations in which he was placed, the object he had in view, and the context of the will.

(See also *Re Barlow's Will Trusts* [1979] 1 All ER 296, [1979] 1 WLR 278. For an interesting article see A. Dickey, 'The Notion of Family in Law' (1982) 14 U West Aust L Rev 417.)

The United States Supreme Court has had to consider the definition of 'family' and 'household' on a number of occasions. In *Department of Agriculture v Moreno* 413 US 528 (1973) the court declared unconstitutional a provision of the Food Stamp Act which failed to provide assistance to households containing any unrelated individuals.

The second case is *Belle Terre v Boraas* 416 US 1 (1973). This concerned a so-called 'zoning' Ordinance which restricted occupancy to one-family units with 'family' as 'one or more persons related by blood, adoption, or marriage, living or cooking together as a single housekeeping unit, exclusive of household servants'. There was a proviso to this definition which permitted two unrelated persons to constitute a family, but no more than two such persons in any housekeeping unit. Belle Terre enforced the Ordinance against a property owner who had rented his home to six students. The Supreme Court held the Ordinance to be constitutional.

The third US case is *Moore v City of Cleveland* 431 US 494 (1977) which also concerned a Housing Ordinance. East Cleveland's Ordinance limits occupancy of dwelling units to single families, and by s. 1341.08 defines 'family' in this way:

'Family' means a number of individuals related to the nominal head of the household or to the spouse of the nominal head of the household living as a single housekeeping unit in a single dwelling unit, but limited to the following:

(*a*) Husband or wife of the nominal head of the household.

(*b*) Unmarried children of the nominal head of the household or of the spouse of the nominal head of the household, *provided,* however, that *such unmarried children have no children residing with them.*

(*c*) Father or mother of the nominal head of the household or of the spouse of the nominal head of the household.

(*d*) *Nothwithstanding* the provisions of subsection (*b*) hereof, a family may include not more than one dependent married or unmarried child of the nominal head of the household or of the spouse of the nominal head of the household and the spouse and dependent children of such dependent child. For the purpose of this subsection, a dependent person

is one who has more than fifty per cent of his total support furnished for him by the nominal head of the household and the spouse of the nominal head of the household.
(*e*) A family may consist of one individual. [Italics added]

The Supreme Court declared this provision unconstitutional in the following circumstances. The appellant, Mrs Moore, lived in her home with her son and two grandsons, one of whom was the child of the son living with her, and the other who was the child of her deceased daughter. Mrs Moore was charged with a criminal offence in violation of the Ordinance. The Supreme Court distinguished *Belle Terre*.

Powell J: But one overriding factor sets this case apart from *Belle Terre.* The ordinance there *affected only unrelated individuals.* It expressly allowed all who were related by 'blood, adoption, or marriage' to live together, and in sustaining the ordinance we were careful to note that it promoted 'family needs' and 'family values', 416 US at 9. *East Cleveland*, in contrast, has chosen to regulate the occupancy of its housing by *slicing deeply into the family itself.* This is no mere incidental result of the ordinance. On its face *it selects certain categories of relatives who may live together and declares that others may not.* In particular, it makes a crime of a grandmother's choice to live with her grandson in circumstances like those presented here.

When thus examined, this ordinance cannot survive. The city seeks to justify it as a means of preventing overcrowding, minimizing traffic and parking congestion, and avoiding an undue financial burden on East Cleveland's school system. Although these are legitimate goals, the ordinance before us serves them marginally, at best. For example, the ordinance permits any family consisting only of husband, wife and unmarried children to live together, even if the family contains a half dozen licensed drivers, each with his or her own car. At the same time it *forbids an adult brother and sister to share a household,* even if both faithfully use public transportation. The ordinance would permit a grandmother to live with a single dependent son and children, even if his school-age children number a dozen, yet it forces Mrs. Moore to find another dwelling for her grandson John, simply because of the presence of his uncle and cousin in the same household. [Italics added]

Questions

(i) Do you find attractive the distinction suggested in *Moore* between that case and *Belle Terre*?
(ii) Is the legal meaning of family different according to the functional context in which it is used? If so, should it be?

2 Approaches to the history of the family

In *Approaches to the History of the Western Family* (1980) Anderson distinguishes three approaches to family history: the demographic approach, the sentiments approach, and the household economic approach. These three schools of thought emphasise different aspects of the available source material. The extracts in this section have been selected to provide illustrations of the debate upon which family historians remain engaged.

(a) THE DEMOGRAPHIC APPROACH

Peter Laslett and his co-workers at the Cambridge ESRC group for the History of Population and Social Structure are the major writers who adhere to this approach.

A particular matter which must be of considerable interest for the policymakers of the present time is the historical evidence relating to the size of households, and whether this information has a bearing on the size, type and function of the family. It is to this question that the Laslett team has directed its gaze. Laslett suggests that the 'mean household size' (including servants in England) 'has remained more or less constant at about 4.75 from the sixteenth century right through the industrialisation period until the end of the nineteenth century when a steady decline set in to a figure of about three in contemporary censuses.' The work of the Group is based on 100 English communities at dates between 1574 and 1821. 70% of households are classed as two-generational and 24% as one generational. Only 6% contain relatives of three different generations and less than 1% of four generations. The major conclusion is that a nuclear familial form 'may have been one of the enduring and fundamental characteristics of the Western family system.' Indeed, Alan MacFarlane in *Origins of English Individualism* (1978) has argued that the nuclear family as a behavioural fact has existed in England since 1200.

However, other research has tended to suggest that this view is a gross exaggeration and overgeneralisation. In Southern and Eastern Europe, households were of a more complex type (see Berkner, 1977). Indeed even in relation to England, Laslett's conclusions have been doubted, as Anderson (1980) explains:

> If we imagine a household where land is transferred to a son on his marriage and the son subsequently has children of his own, then, if this occurs before his father's death, a three-generation family will appear in a census listing. A few years later, when the father has died, only a widow, married child and grandchildren will be left and the evidence for a stem household becomes ambiguous. On the widow's death, a nuclear household will result and the census listing will reveal no evidence of any extension at all. Nevertheless – and this is the crucial point – while no stem-family[1] *household* is present, a stem-family *organisation* remains since, in due course, the same process will be repeated by the next generation. Indeed, even where no stem-family system is in operation the availability of data on ages frequently shows a marked life-cycle effect in household data which is not apparent in aggregate data.

What is at issue is the life cycle of the family: first, newly-married couple; second, nuclear family with children; third, extended family; and fourth, back again to nuclear family. Static listings of households conceal this pattern.

The conclusions of Laslett and other members of the group are also criticised by Edward Shorter, in *The Making of the Modern Family* (1975):

> In earlier writings on the history of the family, sociologists acquired the bad habit of assuming that families before the Industrial Revolution were organized in clans or were at least highly 'extended'. Because any historian with even a passing familiarity with Europe's social history would realize at once the inaccuracy of that assumption, a revisionist reaction developed in the 1960s: the nuclear family was 'unearthed' time and again in history, to the accompaniment of loud shouts of discovery. As often happens to revisionists, these writers fell over backwards attempting to overturn the conventional wisdom; instead of merely correcting the sociologists' fantasies about clans and sprawling patriarchies, they tended to proclaim that at most times and places it was the conjugal family – mother, father, children, and servants – that had prevailed. The revisionists thus proceeded to create a little fantasy of their own; the nuclear family as a historical constant.

1. Extended.

Now, many kinless families did exist; indeed, they often represented a majority of all households. But to get a sense of the typical experience of the average person, we must ask what kind of household a child would most likely have been socialized in: extended (stem), or nuclear? And there is a good chance that in better-off households as opposed to poorer ones, and in east Europe as opposed to west Europe, the average child was raised in a dwelling that contained many relatives besides his mother and father. ...

Conjugal groups *minus* kin also turned up frequently enough in rural Europe. There were, for example, the pastoral regions of the Netherlands, where the grandparents seldom lived with the farmer and his wife. In Norwegian villages relatives co-resided with propertied peasants only about a fifth of the time, and the percentage was even lower among the cottagers. Across much of Lower Austria and in at least two well-documented villages in Salzburg province, three-generation households were unusual. ...

Yet we must still consider the possibility that in such communities many households might, at some point in time, have contained several generations, but that death snatched away the grandparents before the census-taker arrived. Thus in the census they appeared as single-family units, whereas they might actually have been, for a period of years, stem families.

However, in many other areas of western and central Europe, the stem family was commonplace and the kinless family an anomaly. Frédéric Le Play, the nineteenth-century French sociologist, coined the term *famille souche* to denote families that passed on a given farm undivided from one generation to the next over long periods of time.

(b) THE ECONOMIC APPROACH

A question often asked is why a detailed knowledge of household composition should necessarily tell us much about familial behaviour? Indeed, there are many who see household composition as a by-product of more fundamental economic processes. There is a group of writers who seek to interpret the historical data relating both to households and to families in the context of the economic realities of the period and of the region. The major question is based around the value of the household as a means of production. Anderson summarises these writings for us, in the context of the family economy of the Western peasant, in *Approaches to the History of the Western Family* (1980):

This approach has taken as its central concept the often unconscious 'strategies' employed by family members to maintain a customary standard of living, both for themselves in the present and, under certain circumstances, for themselves and their descendants in the future. The types of strategies available are constrained in a number of ways: by the family's resource-generating potential (particularly its age/sex composition); by the mode of production in which the family is involved; by the income-generating relationships which are implied by that mode; by law and custom regarding property acquisition (including inheritance); by the possibilities of access to alternative resource-generating activities (including wage-labour or domestic manufacturing) or resource-providing rights (including, for example, both customary rights to pasture animals on common land and social welfare provision); by the intervention of powerful groups external to the family (landlords, employers and others with power in the local community); by customs limiting the range of resource-generating options which individuals see as practically available at a point in time (for example, ideas over what is appropriate work for women) (Tilly, 1979).

For the Western peasant or yeoman farmer, the principal scarce resource was land, so family strategies were constrained by the conditions under which land could be obtained and by the labour inputs required to work it. The literature on continental Europe, on Ireland, and on some areas of England even in the early nineteenth century, portrays the dominant peasant/yeoman pattern as one where the family's subsistence needs could be met only through the continual application of the labour of all its members to productive tasks in agriculture or, to a greater or lesser extent, in certain craft or other domestically organised productive activities. Almost all production was intended either for family use or for local and known markets.

One of the central problems of the peasant family, from this perspective, was the need to ensure that enough labour was available to meet current and future needs while yet not having too many mouths to feed for the resource-generating capacity of the means of production

(Winberg, 1978). On the one hand it was necessary to avoid childless marriages, which gave no security for old age (hence perhaps norms encouraging premarital intercourse to ensure marriage only to fertile girls). On the other hand too many children threatened current subsistence. This problem could, however, in some places be solved by one or more strategic responses. For example: one could acquire more productive resources as children grew ..., one could expand non-agricultural activities and devote more effort to domestic craft production (but this was not always available) ..., one could restrict family size by marriage to older women ..., by some form of contraception (found in seventeenth-century England, eighteenth- and early-nineteenth-century Sweden and many other places) ... or by some other strategy such as prolonging breast feeding. Finally, as in England, Scandinavia and elsewhere, poor households could regulate their numbers by sending 'surplus' children into service at an early age.

(c) THE SENTIMENTS APPROACH

There is another group of writers which is not prepared either to see household composition as a by-product of fundamental economic processes, or to deduce the historical development of the Western family from demographic sources. Shorter (1975) and Stone (1977, 1990) in particular have emphasised what has been termed 'the tale of sentiments.' Anderson illustrates the difference in the approach between Laslett, and the work of Shorter and Stone: 'The demographic approach started from a particular set of documents, by which their questions and conclusions have been constrained. The sentiments writers began with a set of questions about the ideas associated with family behaviour and were then faced with the problem of finding suitable source material to throw light on such ideas.'

The following extract is taken from Stone's chapter on family characteristics, in *The Family, Sex and Marriage* (1977):

In the sixteenth century, relations between spouses in rich families were often fairly remote. Living in big houses, each with his or her own bedroom and servants, husband and wife were primarily members of a functioning social universe of a large household and were rarely in private together. ... Their marriage was usually arranged rather than consensual, in essence the outcome of an economic deal or a political alliance between two families. The transaction was sealed by the wedding and by the physical union of two individuals, while the emotional ties were left to develop at a later date. If they did not take place, and if the husband could find sexual alternatives through casual liaisons, the emotional outlet through marriage was largely non-existent for either husband or wife.

In any case, the expectations of felicity from marriage were pragmatically low, and there were many reasons why disappointment was minimal. The first is that the pair did not need to see very much of one another, either in elite circles, where they could go their own way, or among the plebs, where leisure activities were segregated, with the men resorting to the ale-house, and the women to each other's houses. ...

The second reason why such a system was so readily accepted was the high adult mortality rates, which severely reduced the companionship element in marriage and increased its purely reproductive and nurturance functions. There was a less than fifty-fifty chance that the husband and wife would both remain alive more than a year or two after the departure from the home of the last child, so that friendship was hardly necessary. William Stout's comment on a marriage in 1699 could stand as an epitaph for many sixteenth- and seventeenth-century couples: 'they lived very disagreeably but had many children.'

Nor was the position very different amongst the lower classes in pre-nineteenth century France:

Eighteenth-century middle-class observers of social relations among the labouring classes, peasants and urban *petite bourgeoisie* in France could find no trace of affection in the marital relationship.

Their observations may be biased by class and background, but if they are at all accurate, they must reflect a permanent feature of the traditional European society. All over France, 'If the horse and the wife fall sick at the same time, the ... peasant rushes to the blacksmith to care for the animal, and leaves the task of healing his wife to nature.' If necessary, the wife could be replaced very cheaply, while the family economy depended on the health of the animal. This peasant pragmatism was confirmed by traditional proverbs, such as 'rich is the man whose wife is dead and horse alive.' The same lack of marital sentiment was evident in the towns. '*L'amitié*, that delicious sentiment, is scarcely known. There are in these little towns only marriages of convenience; nobody appreciates that true happiness consists in making others happy, who always reward us in kind.'

This bleak portrait is modified in a number of ways by Stone himself:

This rather pessimistic view of a society with little love and generally low and widely diffused affect needs to be modified if it is accurately to reflect the truth. Romantic love and sexual intrigue were certainly the subject of much poetry of the sixteenth and early seventeenth centuries, and of many of Shakespeare's plays. It was also a reality which existed in one very restricted social group: the one in which it had always existed since the twelfth century, that is the households of the prince and the great nobles. Here, and here alone, well-born young persons of both sexes were thrown together away from parental supervision and in a situation of considerable freedom as they performed their duties as courtiers, ladies and gentlemen in waiting, tutors and governesses to the children. They also had a great deal of leisure, and in the enclosed hot-house atmosphere of these great houses, love intrigues flourished as nowhere else.

The second modification of the pessimistic general description of affective relations concerns a far wider group, including many who were subjected to the loveless arranged marriage, which was normal among the propertied classes. It is clear from correspondence and wills that in a considerable number of cases, some degree of affection, or at least a good working partnership, developed after the marriage. In practice, as anthropologists have everywhere discovered, the arranged marriage works far less badly than those educated in a romantic culture would suppose, partly because the expectations of happiness from it are not set unrealistically high, and partly because it is a fact that sentiment can fairly easily adapt to social command. In any case, love is rarely blind, in the sense that it tends to be channelled along socially acceptable lines, towards persons of the other sex of similar background. This greatly increases the probability that an arranged marriage, provided it is not undertaken purely for mercenary considerations and that there is not too great a discrepancy in age, physical attractiveness or temperament, may well work out not too badly. This is especially the case where leisure is segregated, so that the pair are not thrown together too much, and where both have a multitude of outside interests and companions to divert them. In a 'low affect' society, a 'low affect' marriage is often perfectly satisfactory.

The final modification to be made to the bleak affective picture is that, owing to the high adult death rate and the late age of marriage, by no means all marriages among persons of property in the sixteenth century were arranged by the parents, since many of them were dead: marriages by choice certainly occurred, although freedom of choice was far more difficult to achieve for women other than widows.

Similar considerations are the basis of Shorter's work. Here he describes the change to 'domesticity', in *The Making of the Modern Family* (1975):

The 'companionate' marriage is customarily seen as the hallmark of contemporary family life, the husband and wife being friends rather than superordinate and subordinate, sharing tasks and affection. Perhaps that is correct. But the emotional cement of the modern family binds more than the husband and wife; it fixes the children, as well, into this sentimental unit. The notion of companionship doesn't necessarily say anything about the relationship between the couple and their children. Also, 'companionship' implies incorrectly that some form of intense romantic attachment continues to unite the couple. Both ideas are incomplete, and for that reason I prefer the expression 'domesticity' in demarcating the modern family from the traditional.

Domesticity, or the family's awareness of itself as a precious emotional unit that must be protected with privacy and isolation from outside intrusion, was the third spearhead of the great onrush of sentiment in modern times. Romantic love detached the couple from communal sexual supervision and turned them towards affection. Maternal love created a sentimental nest within which the modern family would ensconce itself, and it removed many women from involvement with community life. Domesticity, beyond that, sealed off the family as a whole from its traditional interaction with the surrounding world. The members of the family came to feel far more solidarity with one another than they did with their various age and sex peer groups.

Stone's thesis has been commented on critically by other historians. For example, Keith Wrightson in *English Society 1580–1680* (1982) writes:

Stone's powerful arguments and adventurous hypotheses constitute the most ambitious attempt yet undertaken to interpret the development of the English family over time. Nevertheless they are seriously open to question in both their characterization of family life in later sixteenth and seventeenth century England and in their account of change within this period. Although he is undoubtedly aware of the major distinctions which may have existed between social groups in England, Stone has devoted insufficient care to the exploration of the experience of the mass of the population. As a result his interpretation has been elaborated on the basis of the historical experience of the aristocracy, upper gentry and urban plutocracy with which he is primarily concerned and retains at its heart the tacit assumption that analytical categories derived from their experience can somehow be extended to encapsulate phases in the history of the English family. This is a mistaken assumption. For whatever their historical prominence, the familial behaviour of the English elite was very far from representative of that of their countrymen. Nor can shifts in their behaviour be asserted to have been significant advances in familial development when set in the full context of the already established and persisting characteristics of the family life of their social inferiors.

In a later extract, Wrightson continues:

Of marital relations in late sixteenth- and seventeenth-century England, much remains obscure. The weight of the evidence reviewed here, however, suggests that, despite the inevitable counter-examples and the individual and social variation which is to be expected, there is little reason to follow Professor Stone in regarding the rise of the companionate marriage as a new phenomenon for the later seventeenth and eighteenth centuries. It seems to have been already well established. It is true that the best of our evidence is derived from the diaries of deeply religious people, puritans who had especial cause to follow the advice of moral teachers on the subject of mutuality. Yet such supplementary evidence as can be gathered does not suggest that they were unusual in their marital relations, while the teachings of the moralists themselves were neither new, nor distinctively Puritan. They represented for the most part the mainstream of opinion on the best practice in marriage. In the present state of our knowledge it would seem unwise to make too sharp a dichotomy between the 'patriarchal' and the 'companionate' marriage, and to erect these qualities into a typology of successive stages of family development. It may well be that these are less evolutionary stages of familial progress, than the poles of an enduring continuum in marital relations in a society which accepted both the primacy of male authority and the ideal of marriage as a practical and emotional partnership. Most people established their roles within marriage somewhere between the two, with the emphasis, for the most part, on the latter.

Given these wide differences of perspective, it is appropriate to pause and to ask what relevance is there for a lawyer in the last few years of the twentieth century to have answers to the questions raised by the historians. It is to this matter that we now turn.

(d) THE RELEVANCE OF THE HISTORY OF THE FAMILY

Anderson asks the question whether family history can 'justify itself', in *Sociology of the Family* (now 1980):

... It can do so above all by drawing out the implications of these changes for the kind of family life which is possible today and, above all, by demonstrating that old moralities and old behaviours cannot meet new situations and that, accordingly, present problems require new and not obsolete solutions.

Perhaps the most significant, and certainly analytically the most difficult of these changes have been in the family's relation to production. The peasant household was the focus of production with head and spouse organizing production using the household's own labour and exploiting and co-ordinating the contribution of all household members. Each class of individual had a clearly prescribed role and each member was dependent on the activities of all the others. In this situation there is a high degree of role interdependence both between spouses and between generations. … Not merely was production a joint activity but almost all consumption was either shared or was undertaken in some way or other on behalf of the household.

By contrast, under our kind of capitalist system of production, work for the mass of the population becomes directed by others who select and reward labour on an individualistic basis. One or more household members leaves the domestic arena and each is remunerated by outsiders on a basis which normally takes no account of his or her family situation. The wage received is the personal property of the individual, is dependent on the individual's own level of activity and achievement, and is paid to the individual in private leaving him or her to negotiate with the rest of the family over how and to what extent the money is to be distributed in order to satisfy their wants.

The contrast between the jointness of income generation in the peasant family and its individualistic basis under capitalism was, to a considerable extent, concealed under early capitalist production by the continued participation of all except the youngest family members in income-generating activities. Even after legislation had removed children from full time factory employment there remained within local communities significant opportunities for children to add to family resources through cash or goods in kind obtained in return for odd jobs done outside school hours. In addition, the substantial levels of labour input required to process food and other materials for domestic consumption, together with the significant amount of domestic productive activity for both home production and for the market, allowed those who remained in the domestic arena to contribute significantly to family resource generation processes. Thus, in as far as the husband earned income outside the home on behalf of the family, the children (and particularly the male children) sought odd jobs on behalf of the family, and the wife (aided by the female children) produced domestically on behalf of the family, all resources being pooled together, the role interdependence remained and there was little analytical difference between this situation and the peasant system where the husband and male children worked in the outfield producing in part marketable products to pay the rent, while wife and female children worked in the infield and the home on the production and reproduction of labour power. Of course, because wages were the private property of the individual there was no guarantee that wages were in fact pooled – as the harrowing descriptions of the wives of nineteenth-century factory workers trying to extract their husbands from public houses on pay day testify. …

Models which assume that family-based decision making took place over how necessary income should be generated and over who should work in which sectors of production, have a clear empirical fit with data from most nineteenth- and early twentieth-century working-class communities.

However, developments of the last fifty years have moved most families significantly away from this position. Children have become almost totally dependent. They leave the home daily for education which is oriented far more to their individual futures than to their current family roles and subsequently enter the labour force to receive pay much of which is again retained for their own use even in the very few years that now typically remain between starting work and marriage. In this way children have almost totally ceased to be part of an interdependent resource-generating system. Similarly, in as far as both spouses enter the labour force and each receives a private reward for labour (and particularly as in many dual career families where outside workers come in to perform most of the domestic work, which anyway can now if desired require a much smaller labour input), the work of the spouses can no longer so easily be seen as a co-operative productive activity or even as involving a complementary division of labour where each performs different but interrelated tasks on behalf of the family unit. … The ties between family members thus become based not on an interdependence rooted in co-operative productive activity essential for survival, but on personal interdependence oriented towards the joint attainment of essentially intrinsic 'projects' of highly diverse kinds.

However, these aspirations are much more susceptible to change over time than are the basic survival objectives of pre-industrial European societies, and their interpersonal basis is much more fragile. … Thus it is not surprising that wherever we see communities moving from family groups based on property and co-operative production, so we also see a decline in parental involvement in mate selection and, usually, a fall in the age of marriage and a rise in marital instability.

These changes are further facilitated by the parallel changes in the roles of children in the family, which involve both a drastic reduction in the power of parents over their children and in their 'interests' in their children's future welfare. ...

Viewed in a historical perspective, therefore, there is in the contemporary capitalist world a marked lack of structural support for familial bonds. In addition, demographic changes have increased the emphasis on intrinsic functions of marriage through the reduction in the period of the family life cycle which is devoted to the bearing and rearing of small children. Marriage at a younger age and an increase in life expectancy among adults have combined roughly to double the average duration of marriages unbroken by social dissolution; the median duration of such marriages is rapidly appoaching fifty years. At the same time, the fall in family size and the concentration of childbirth into the earlier years of marriage has led for the first time to a situation where the majority of the life span of marriages does not involve the bearing of and caring for, small children; far from being a brief interval in old age, the 'empty nest' situation, with all its attendant problems of role reallocation, is fast coming to comprise a majority of the marital cycle. Increased leisure has only come to extend still further the time and the energy available for interpersonal relationships between spouses and thus, by inference at least, to make more problematical a lack of success in them. ...

Equally importantly, the other main prop to traditional family morality – close community supervision – has also been undermined and, indeed, in a comparative perspective, family behaviour has become the most private and personal of all areas of behaviour, almost totally free from external supervision and control.

Anderson concludes his review:

The study of the history of the Western family shows quite clearly that we cannot go back to a strict conformity to the family morality that we have inherited from the past without also – which is clearly impossible – reverting to the economic and social relations of the past. We are not peasants any more and thus cannot sustain a peasant morality. We have to develop new institutions and new behaviours to cope with new situations.

One aspect of family forms which is often overlooked when discussing the history of the family is the fact that the UK has a history of population migration, and immigration has necessarily brought with it a number of family forms different from traditional patterns. Adrian Wilson summarises this trend for us in *Family Forms* (1985).

Such families put a much greater emphasis on the demands and duties of kinship. Asian families are a clear example of this. Family members feel that they have obligations both to their kin in Britain and also to the rest of their family, who are still resident in the home village. Many Indian families in Britain continue to provide financial support for their relatives in India.

The family structure of many ethnic groups tends to be both hierarchical and patriarchal. Ballard (1982) argues that the basic pattern of the south Asian family consists of a man, his sons and grandsons, together with their wives and unmarried daughters. This family has been transferred into a British setting. The man is clearly the head of the household, controlling the family finances, and negotiating the major family decisions. R. Oakley (1982) suggests that a similar pattern is true for Greek Cypriot families living in London. The Cypriot husband is an authoritarian figure, the source of family discipline. It is the husband who handles all the external dealings of the family with the wider society. Conjugal roles are essentially segregated, although complementary to each other.

The male-dominated nature of family life creates a very different experience for women within the ethnic minorities. In the early years of immigration, many women found themselves cut off from outside society. Social and language barriers kept them trapped in the domestic setting. Some Asian families created a state of purdah for their womenfolk, setting them apart from society at large. Oakley contrasts the social isolation of Cypriot women in England with the physical openness and outdoor character of life in Cyprus.

The reason for the attempt by ethnic minorities to control the lives of women lies in the need to maintain family honour. It is important that family members do not bring shame on the family name. Every member should be seen to behave properly. Inevitably, life in a British environment has thrown up major challenges to this traditional view of family life.

Serious problems have been created with the second generation, the immigrants' children, who were born and have been brought up in the United Kingdom. School teaches these children to want more independence. The socializing influence of the family stresses loyalty and obedience. It must also be remembered that many of the first-generation immigrants grew up in societies where there was no such thing as adolescence or youth culture, so conflict is inevitable when their children act like British teenagers. However, ethnic minority families have proved to be more flexible than was at first expected. An example of this flexibility can be seen in the way that the traditional arranged marriage is being modified to allow young people some say in the process.

West Indian families in Britain present a further distinct family pattern that reflects their culture of origin. The colonial system that was based on slavery weakened the bonds between men and women. The lack of a stable employment system left the man unable to support a family by his own efforts. The mother-child relationship became the central structure of the family.

Driver (1982) and Barrow (1982) use studies of family structures in the West Indies to suggest three models of family life. The first type is the conventional nuclear family household. Such a family form was most typical of the respectable and more affluent section of the community. The second type was a common-law household, where a man and a woman lived together with their children, but without a formal marriage. Third, there was the female-dominated household, where women had to care for their children and provide an income, without the presence of a man. Studies conducted in the West Indies suggested that each type accounted for about a third of all households in the West Indies.

Driver suggests that these family forms have been transplanted into the British West Indian community. He suggests that there are two types of black family structure in Britain. There is the nuclear family, where both partners share the full range of domestic roles. But there is also the mother-centred family. Driver says this is again associated with the lack of stable employment for men. The black mother is left to bring up the children, run the home, and provide an income. She must do this in England without the range of support that she could have obtained from female relatives in the West Indies. This kind of family might even be growing in Britain, providing a clear contrast to both Asian and traditional English family patterns.

It is hard to predict how ethnic minority families will develop with the third and subsequent generations. The size of minority families is dropping rapidly. Young couples seem to be more sceptical about the need to maintain such a wide family network. But the young Asians, Chinese, and Cypriots are well aware of their different cultural heritages. For many of these young people, their family life will be a compromise between the two cultures they inhabit.

Question

Does a possibly false view of family history in this country prevent us from accepting that families fall today and have always fallen into different types?

3 The family as a social group

The historical strands – the nuclear unit, the rise of domesticity, the economic inter-relationship – are viewed, as we have seen, in different ways by the scholars who have looked at the evidence. Similarly, the modern family has been described by sociologists in many variations. Two extremes are Fletcher (1966) and Oakley (1974). The following extract is from Ronald Fletcher's *The Family and Marriage in Britain* (1966) and emphasises the sense of 'belonging' which is, for him, so important:

The family is, in fact, a community in itself: a small, relatively permanent group of people, related to each other in the most intimate way, bound together by the most personal aspects of life; who experience amongst themselves the whole range of human emotions; who have to strive continually to resolve those claims and counter-claims which stem from mutual but often conflicting needs; who experience continual responsibilities and obligations towards each other;

who experience the sense of 'belonging' to each other in the most intimately felt sense of that word. The members of a family share the same name, the same collective reputation, the same home, the same intricate, peculiar tradition of their own making, the same neighbourhood. They share the same sources of pleasure, the same joys, the same sources of profound conflict. The same vagaries of fortune are encountered and overcome together. Degrees of agreement and degrees of violent disagreement are worked out amongst them. The same losses and the same griefs are shared. Hence the family is that group within which the most fundamental appreciation of human qualities and values takes place – 'for better for worse': the qualities of truth and honesty, of falsehood and deceit; of kindliness and sympathy, of indifference and cruelty; of cooperation and forbearance, of egotism and antagonism; of tolerance, justice, and impartiality, of bias, dogmatism, and obstinacy; of generous concern for the freedom and fulfilment of others, of the mean desire to dominate – whether in overt bullying or in psychologically more subtle ways. All those values, and all those discriminations and assessments of value, which are of the most fundamental importance for the formation of adult character are first experienced and exercised by children in the context of the family. Furthermore, these qualities are not 'taught' or 'learned' in any straightforward or altogether rational way; they are actually embodied in people and their behaviour.

Later, Fletcher offers a definition of the contemporary British family summarising the points developed in the book. He asserts that the modern British family is:

1. contracted or founded at an early age, and therefore of long duration,
2. consciously planned,
3. small in size,
4. to a great extent separately housed, and in an improved material environment,
5. economically self-responsible, self-providing, and therefore (*a*) relatively independent of wider kindred, and (*b*) living at a 'distance' from wider kindred, sometimes geographically, but also in terms of a diminished degree of close and intimate social life shared with them,
6. entered into and maintained on a completely voluntary basis by partners of equal status, and therefore entailing a marital relationship based upon mutuality of consideration,
7. democratically managed, in that husband and wife (and frequently children) discuss family affairs together when decisions have to be taken, and
8. centrally concerned with the care and upbringing of children – to such an extent that it is frequently called 'child-centred'.
Finally, we might add:
9. that the importance of the modern family is widely recognized by government and by the whole range of social services, and is therefore aided in achieving health and stability by a wide range of public provisions.

When these points are considered, there can surely be little doubt that the characteristics of the family in contemporary Britain manifest considerable moral improvements upon the family types of the past. How, then, does it come about that the modern family is said to be in a condition of 'instability'? Why is it said that the family is 'declining in importance as a social institution'? On what grounds can it be argued that there is evidence of 'moral decline'?

Questions

(i) Do you agree with each of these nine points?
(ii) Is Fletcher correct in saying that the contemporary British family manifests a considerable 'moral improvement'?
(iii) What answers can you give to Fletcher's final three questions? (Remember that the book was published in 1966.)
(iv) It often happens that members of a family do not share the same name, sometimes by choice, sometimes as a result of death or divorce. Do you think that the lack of a common name weakens the sense of belonging?

Fletcher writes with passion in defence of the family in *The Shaking of the Foundations* (1988):

> I can only confess that the more I reconsider these relatively recent condemnations of the family, the more absurd, the more lacking in any serious sense of perspective, they seem to be. If a grave and restless disorder, a profound disorientation, a decline of conviction in beliefs, principles and morality, assailed – and continues to assail – our society, it does not seem to me at all surprising. During a time in which every secure foundation of every society in the world has been thrown into a vast vortex of war and social change, when the entire order of civilized thought in the world is undergoing a process of rapid transformation the outcome of which we cannot yet foresee, how can it be even remotely sensible to make *the family* the butt of our criticisms? The very highest levels of supposed authority – in international affairs, in other societies, and in our own society – rock with uncertainty, indecision, and unprincipled manipulation. The doctrines of all religions, including those of our own national church, are riddled with doubts, cleavages, illogicalities, and even downright simple-mindedness. The realities of public corruption are only occasionally and partially glimpsed (though now with increasing frequency), but none the less very revealingly so, in the pages of the press and the procedures of the courts. And yet, for some curious reason, it is *the family* which is the scapegoat. It is '*the breakdown of the family*' within the supposed '*laxities of the Welfare State*' – or it is '*the reactionary strength of the family*' and the pernicious influences of '*the intensity of its too-private world*' – which is blamed for our bad behaviour! But surely, if anything seems true in all this, it is that the family in society, and all its members, have been the *victims* of society's disasters, not their *causes*?

Ann Oakley in her book *Housewife* (1974) presents a very different picture:

> A greater equality may characterize the relationships between husband and wife in some areas – legal rights for instance – but mother and father roles, husband and wife roles, remain distinct, and – conspicuous of all – the allocation to women of the housewife role endures. Apparent changes, such as the increasing likelihood of a wife's employment, may not be changes at all, and we should not be taken in by surface appearances, nor by that pseudoegalitarian phrase the 'dual-career' marriage. ...
>
> The capacity of the housewife's employment to affect fundamentally and permanently the structure of marital roles is undermined by the ideology of non-interchangeability, of role-segregation, subscribed to by the married couple – the ideology of gender differentiation which is basic to marriage as an institution.

Question

Ann Oakley is talking about marriage as an institution; and what is more, it is the nuclear arrangement which is the object of her scorn. But would an extended family household make the structure of personal relationships and sex differentiation any different?

4 The definition of marriage

We turn our attention to the definition of the conjugal unit or marriage. This is not as easy to describe as may at first appear. Harris (1979) expressed the problem in the following way: 'The inhabitants of Europe and America have an idea which they call marriage. People in other cultures have other ideas which are similar to, but not the same as, our ideas. Traditionally the argument has been about how dissimilar the ideas have to get to force us to stop describing their ideas as "marriage".' Leach (1955) argues that no definition can be found which applies to all institutions which ethnographers and anthropologists commonly refer to as marriage. Therefore he submits for consideration a definition based on a 'bundle of rights'. At least one part of the bundle must be present before the term 'marriage' can be used. The list, which according to Leach is not closed, is as follows:

A. To establish the legal father of a woman's children.
B. To establish a legal mother of a man's children.
C. To give the husband a monopoly in the wife's sexuality.
D. To give the wife a monopoly in the husband's sexuality.
E. To give the husband partial or monopolistic rights to the wife's domestic and other labor services.
F. To give the wife partial or monopolistic rights to the husband's labor services.
G. To give the husband partial or total rights over property belonging or potentially accruing to the wife.
H. To give the wife partial or total rights over property belonging or potentially accruing to the husband.
I. To establish a joint fund of property – a partnership – for the benefit of the children of the marriage.
J. To establish a socially significant 'relationship of affinity' between the husband and his wife's brothers.

In contrast with Leach, there are other scholars, of whom E. Kathleen Gough, in *The Nayars and the Definition of Marriage* (1959), is representative, who argue that 'the status of children born to various types of union (is) critical for decisions as to which of these unions constitute marriage.' As a tentative definition that would have cross-cultural validity, and will fit the unusual cases such as that of the Nayar,[2] Gough suggests: 'Marriage is a relationship established between a woman and one or more other persons which provides that a child born to the woman under circumstances not prohibited by the rules of the relationship, is accorded full birth-status rights common to normal members of his society or social stratum.'

A slightly different way of looking at the problem is suggested by Harris (1979). He says that the major question is to consider *tasks*. The only significant question is the following: 'How do societies arrange for the orderly procreation and rearing of future generations and the transmission of material and cultural possessions?' Harris emphasises child rearing. We shall see later in Chapter 11, below, how judges in English courts have been preoccupied by similar considerations.

If nothing else, then, marriage is about the licence to beget children. There are therefore three questions which assume importance in legal terms. First, who is entitled to marry so as to produce these children? Second, when if at all, should society step in to prevent a marriage from being solemnised or pronounce a decree of nullity? Third, how is such a relationship formalised? We deal with these matters in turn.

---

2. In a period before the British took control of India, Nayar women customarily had a small but not a fixed number of husbands. When a woman became pregnant, it was essential for one of those men to acknowledge probable paternity. The genitor, however, had no economic, social, legal or ritual rights in nor obligations to his children once he had paid the fees of their births. Their guardianship, care and discipline were entirely the concern of their matrilineal kinsfolk.

5 Who can marry?

In *Corbett v Corbett (otherwise Ashley)* [1971] P 83, [1970] 2 All ER 33, Ormrod J said: 'on the other hand, sex is clearly an essential determinant of the relationship called marriage, because it is and always has been recognised as the union of man and woman. It is the institution on which the family is built, and of which the capacity for natural heterosexual intercourse is an essential element'. Ormrod J defined a person's sex according to his birth, regardless of any sex change operation.

In *Rees v UK* (1986) 9 EHRR 56, [1993] 2 FCR 49, the applicant, who was born with all the physical and biological characteristics of the female sex, applied to the European Court of Human Rights contending that the UK Government was in breach of his right to respect for his private life under article 8 (see p. 714, below) and article 12 of the European Convention for the Protection of Human Rights and Fundamental Freedoms, in that the Registrar General refused to amend the birth certificate notwithstanding surgical sexual conversion under the National Health Service. Article 12 provides that 'Men and women of marriageable age have the right to marry and to found a family, according to the national laws governing the exercise of this right'. The Court held that there was no violation of article 12 because that provision referred to the traditional marriage between persons of opposite biological sex.

Rees v UK was endorsed by the European Court of Human Rights in *Cossey v UK* (1990) 13 EHRR 622, [1991] 2 FLR 492 which was a male to female transsexual case. Having determined that there was no violation of article 8, the majority turned to article 12:

> 44. Miss Cossey placed considerable reliance, as did the Delegate of the Commission, on the fact that she could not marry at all: as a woman, she could not realistically marry another woman and English law prevented her from marrying a man.
>
> In the latter connection, Miss Cossey accepted that Article 12 referred to marriage between a man and a woman and she did not dispute that she had not acquired all the biological characteristics of a woman. She challenged, however, the adoption in English law of exclusively biological criteria for determining a person's sex for the purposes of marriage and the Court's endorsement of that situation in the *Rees* judgment, despite the absence from Article 12 of any indication of the criteria to be applied for this purpose. In her submission, there was no good reason for not allowing her to marry a man.
>
> 45. As to the applicant's inability to marry a woman, this does not stem from any legal impediment and in this respect it cannot be said that the right to marry has been impaired as a consequence of the provisions of domestic law.
>
> As to her inability to marry a man, the criteria adopted by English law are in this respect in conformity with the concept of marriage to which the right guaranteed by Article 12 refers.
>
> 46. Although some Contracting States would now regard as valid a marriage between a person in Miss Cossey's situation and a man, the developments which have occurred to date cannot be said to evidence any general abandonment of the traditional concept of marriage. In these circumstances, the Court does not consider that it is open to it to take a new approach to the interpretation of Article 12 on the point at issue. It finds, furthermore, that attachment to thc traditional concept of marriage provides sufficient reason for the continued adoption of biological criteria for determining a person's sex for the purposes of marriage, this being a matter encompassed within the power of the Contracting States to regulate by national law the exercise of the right to marry.

There were however strong dissenting opinions, in particular the joint dissent of Judges Palm, Foignel and Pekkanen:

5. When drafting Article 12 of the Convention the craftsmen probably had in mind the traditional marriage between persons of opposite biological sex as the Court stated in *Rees*. However, transsexualism was not at that time a legal problem, so that it cannot be assumed that the intention was to deny transsexuals the right to marry. Moreover, as we have tried to show above, there have been significant changes in public opinion as regards the full legal recognition of transsexualism. In view of the dynamic interpretation of the Convention followed by the Court, these social and moral developments should also be taken into account in the interpretation of Article 12.

Gender reassignment surgery does not change a person's biological sex. It is impossible for Miss Cossey to bear a child. Yet, in all other respects, both psychological and physical, she is a woman and has lived as such for years.

The fact that a transsexual is unable to procreate cannot, however, be decisive. There are many men and women who cannot have children but, in spite of this, they unquestionably have the right to marry. Ability to procreate is not and cannot be a prerequisite for marriage.

The only argument left against allowing Miss Cossey to marry a man is the fact that biologically she is considered not to be a woman. But neither is she a man, after the medical treatment and surgery. She falls somewhere between the sexes. In this situation a choice must be made and the only humane solution is to respect the objective fact that, after the surgical and medical treatment which Miss Cossey has undergone and which was based on her firm conviction that she is a woman, Miss Cossey is psychologically and physically a member of the female sex and socially accepted as such.

It should also be borne in mind that Miss Cossey has no possibility of marrying unless she is allowed to marry a man as she wishes. It would be impossible, both psychologically and physically, for her to marry a woman. There would certainly also be doubts as to the legality of a marriage of this kind.

6. For these reasons we are of the opinion that in the present case there is a violation of Articles 8 and 12 of the Convention.

Questions

(i) Is it only a matter of time before the European Court of Human Rights changes its mind about transsexuals (Read *B v France* [1993] 2 FCR 145)?
(ii) And what do you think the Court would say about homosexuals having the right to marry?
(iii) Can transsexuals who are lesbian or gay after gender realignment marry? Should this be? (See C. Lind 'Time for Lesbian and Gay Marriages' (1995 New Law Journal p. 1553) and S. Whittle 'An Association for as Noble a Purpose As Any' (1996 New Law Journal p. 366)).

We turn our attention now to prohibitions based on affinity and consanguinity. The Marriage Acts 1949–94 state that marriages between certain relatives are void.

Schedule 1 to the Marriage Act 1949 (as amended) lists the following prohibitions based on consanguinity:

Male	*Female*
Mother	Father
Adoptive mother or former adoptive mother	Adoptive father or former adoptive father
Daughter	Son
Adoptive daughter or former adoptive daughter	Adoptive son or former adoptive son
Father's mother	Father's father
Mother's mother	Mother's father
Son's daughter	Son's son

Male	*Female*
Daughter's daughter	Daughter's son
Sister	Brother
Father's sister	Father's brother
Mother's sister	Mother's brother
Brother's daughter	Brother's son
Sister's daughter	Sister's son

The surviving prohibitions based on affinity are laid down in the Marriage (Prohibited Degrees of Relationship) Act 1986, s. 1 and Sch. 1 as follows:

1.–(1) A marriage solemnized after the commencement of this Act between a man and a woman who is the daughter or granddaughter of a former spouse of his (whether the former spouse is living or not) or who is the former spouse of his father or grandfather (whether his father or grandfather is living or not) shall not be void by reason only of that relationship if both the parties have attained the age of twenty-one at the time of the marriage and the younger party has not at any time before attaining the age of eighteen been a child of the family in relation to the other party.

(2) A marriage solemnized after the commencement of this Act between a man and a woman who is the grandmother of a former spouse of his (whether the former spouse is living or not) or is a former spouse of his grandson (whether his grandson is living or not) shall not be void by reason only of that relationship.

(3) A marriage solemnized after the commencement of this Act between a man and a woman who is the mother of a former spouse of his shall not be void by reason only of that relationship if the marriage is solemnized after the death of both that spouse and the father of that spouse and after both the parties to the marriage have attained the age of twenty-one.

(4) A marriage solemnized after the commencement of this Act between a man and a woman who is a former spouse of his son shall not be void by reason only of that relationship if the marriage is solemnized after the death of both his son and the mother of his son and after both the parties to the marriage have attained the age of twenty-one.

(5) In this section 'child of the family' in relation to any person, means a child who has lived in the same household as that person and been treated by that person as a child of his family.

Part II

Degrees of affinity referred to in section 1(2) *and* (3) *of this Act*

Daughter of former wife	Son of former husband
Former wife of father	Former husband of mother
Former wife of father's father	Former husband of father's mother
Former wife of mother's father	Former husband of mother's mother
Daughter of son of former wife	Son of son of former husband
Daughter of daughter of former wife	Son of daughter of former husband

Part III

Degrees of affinity referred to in section 1(4) *and* (5) *of this Act*

Mother of former wife	Father of former husband
Former wife of son	Former husband of daughter

But most people do not marry their kin.

MacFarlane in *Marriage and Love in England 1300–1840* (1986) provides historical background to the move from kinship marriages to what he refers to as 'free-floating' marriages:

... We may wonder when and how it originated. Is there any evidence in the period from the fifteenth to the nineteenth century of a transformation from the marriage system based on kinship rules, to the free-floating marriages based on psychology and economics which exist today? In answering the questions concerning the curious link between economics and demography raised by Malthus and Wrigley, we need to pursue this further. A marriage system embedded in kinship is close to biological restraints: marriage for women will very often be at or near puberty. Marriages will not adjust sensitively to economic changes, since they are mainly determined by kinship. Nor will there be space for personal psychological pressures. Likes and dislikes, love and passion, have no formal place where the decision about whom to marry is encoded in the kinship structure. ...

... Essentially one may marry all except members of the nuclear family and all those, including uncles and aunts, nephews and nieces, in the ascending and descending generations. First cousin marriage is now, as it was from 1540, legal, if often disapproved of. At marriage the couple became 'one blood'. Thus a man was forbidden from marrying the same range of wife's kin as of his own blood relatives. For instance, he could not marry his wife's aunt even though she was not a blood relative. The prohibitions continued after the spouse's death. Hence marriage with a deceased wife's sister was forbidden.

In the three centuries before 1540 the prohibitions were wider. By the decision of the Fourth Lateran Council of 1215, impediments of consanguinity and affinity were set at the fourth degree, according to the canonical computation. Thus a person could not marry his own or his wife's third cousin, or any nearer relative. Furthermore, wide rules of spiritual affinity prevented those related by godparenthood from marrying. On the other hand, dispensations were easily available, for a price, from the Church. There was a very limited prohibition in early Anglo-Saxon England, then a widening of the ring of prohibited persons, and then a narrowing again, so that England in 1540 returned to the situation that had prevailed in the seventh century. The change at the Reformation was important, but it was neither unprecedented nor indicative of a shift from 'elementary' to 'complex' structures. Indeed, by allowing all to marry first and second cousins without dispensation, the Reformers, if anything, encouraged a move towards the possibility of an elementary system. It is difficult to see how preferential kin marriages can have been enormously attractive and common when the whole weight of the Church forbade them.

More important in assessing the presence of kinship pressures are the positive rules. To prevent estates going out of the family, or to consolidate social, political and other ties, most societies are organized so that strong pressures are put on the individual stating which kin he should marry. To find a person standing in the right kinship relationship is one of the central tasks of an elaborate kinship vocabulary, as well as of the 'marriage brokers' who exist in many societies.

Questions

(i) What do you see as the advantages of a preferential kin system?

(ii) The criminal law prohibits only sexual intercourse between direct ascendants and descendants and brothers and sisters (Sexual Offences Act 1956, ss. 10 and 11): how would you account for the difference?

(iii) Why should both parties to a marriage involving a step relationship have to be over 21 at the time of the marriage?

(iv) 'Child of the family' is defined as a child who has lived in the same household as that person and been treated by that person as a child of his family. Do you think that this restriction serves any useful purpose, and, if so, what purpose? Would it be possible for the child in *M v M* (see p. 7, above) to marry a former wife of his father?

(v) Do you agree that a marriage should only be possible between a man and his mother-in-law after the death of both the former wife and the father of the former wife? The father of the former wife may not necessarily have been married to the mother. Should this make a difference?

(vi) Do you believe that the changes which have been made to the bars based on affinity undermine the integrity of family life?

(vii) What justification is there for retaining any bars based on consanguinity or affinity?

The Law Commission, in their Report on *Nullity of Marriage* (1970), saw no need to change the law relating to consanguinity:

52 (*a*) In so far as the question is biological, the answer depends on an evaluation of scientific evidence. The marriage of uncle and niece, or nephew and aunt is permitted in some countries and by some religions and it may well be that there is no such biological objection to these marriages as to justify legal prohibition. They may well be no more objectionable biologically than the marriage of a man with his grandparent's sister or of a woman with her grandparent's brother, which is not within the prohibited degrees.

(*b*) Nevertheless, the question raises social and moral problems, the answer to which must depend on public opinion. Would public opinion tolerate or object to marriages between uncle and niece or nephew and aunt and, if it objects to such unions, does it wish to extend the prohibition to great-uncle and great-niece and great-nephew and great-aunt? Many people would no doubt instinctively hold the view that such marriages are unnatural and wrong, just as they would view with revulsion a marriage between brother and sister, even if there were no biological reasons against such a union. There are some matters of conviction on which men hold strong feelings of right and wrong though they cannot place their fingers on any particular reason for this conviction. It may be that such unions would be generally regarded as just as wrong as a marriage between adopter and adopted child – a union which is clearly considered objectionable although there cannot be any biological ground for this.

Question

Are there any objections to amending the law still further so as to permit marriages between uncle and niece or aunt and nephew?

6 Age at marriage

W.J. Goode in *World Revolution and Family Patterns* (1963) describes the history of attitudes to the proper age to marry thus:

It seems likely that toward the end of the nineteenth century Western attitudes did alter toward a belief that very young girls should not marry. Prior to the twentieth century, marriages of girls aged 15–17 were not disapproved of providing that the man was sufficiently well-to-do. In the absence of sufficient data my hypothesis is that chronological maturity as a prerequisite for marriage was not an important focus of social attention in the West until about the turn of the century.

Let us consider this point. Prior to the French Revolution, the legal minimum age for marriage in France was 14 years for boys and 12 years for girls. These were also the legal minimum marriage ages accepted under both the older English law and Roman law. In most cases these minimum ages – the assumed ages of puberty for each sex – probably permitted parents to arrange the marriages of their children whenever it seemed suitable. Children of so young an age could not marry independently, and marriage in many Western nations without the consent of parents is even now forbidden to young people under 21 years of age. In the West, there has generally been a substantial difference between the legal minimum age for marriage and the minimum age at which young people might marry *without* parental consent. Since one youngster may be forbidden to marry because of parental refusal, and another of the same age may marry *with* parental consent, it is clear that Western laws concerning minimum ages at marriage were aimed at maintaining the power of the parent, *not* at enforcing a 'right' age at marriage. Over the past generation, a typical legal change has been to narrow the gap between the two age minimums by raising the age at marriage *with* parental consent, or establishing a lower age at marriage without consent.

Since marriage was not thought in the West to be properly based on free courtship until late in the nineteenth century, 'maturity' as measured by years was given no great weight. If a good match could be made for a girl of 15 or 16 years, her age was no barrier, and there were indeed many youthful marriages. Within noble or well-to-do rural families, a young couple could be married precisely because they did *not* have to support themselves or assume the responsibility of a profession.

In contrast to upper-class families, farming families in regions without free land did not ordinarily permit their children to marry until much later, when the parents were ready to relinquish control of the property, or had accumulated sufficient money to afford the marriage. Without land, marriage was not possible. And, of course, servants and apprentices might not marry at all, since their status was viewed as a semi-familial one, and they had no right to introduce a spouse into the family circle. However, a 'proper' age was not the question. Instead, it was whether there was adequate land or income available. Until the end of the nineteenth century the couple had either to wait for land or, if the productive unit was large enough, to become part of a larger kin group, taking part in its economic activities and sharing from the common store. Thus, age in itself was of little importance.

We must therefore conclude that in most parts of the West, until some time in the nineteenth century, marriage came relatively late for the bulk of the population, and the myth that marriages occurred extremely early as we go back in time comes from the fact that the many marriages at very young ages occurred among the most conspicuous classes. ...

In the contemporary West, however, a 'proper' age (varying from country to country and from class to class – higher in the upper strata) has now come to be accepted, since, under the conjugal family system, a couple must be self-sufficient. The young couple cannot be extremely young, since they have to take care of themselves; on the other hand, they do not have to be very old, because they can be independent.

Here, we encounter an empirical puzzle. It seems likely that in the early period of England's industrialization, the age of marriage would not have changed greatly because, although they did work in the factories, for the most part children were given their jobs through relatives and often were supervised by their own male parents. They were not independent workers, and the traditions of the times dictated that they should give their pay to their parents. It was only when they obtained jobs on their own, without the intervention of parents or relatives, that they could make their own decision about choice of spouse or age at which to marry. However, the age at marriage did not change substantially until still later, i.e., in this century, and now seems to be tied at least in part to the independent participation of *females* in the labor force. The job becomes the young girl's 'dowry' in the unskilled and semiskilled white- and blue-collar strata, where, in fact, the highest proportion of women are to be found in the labor force.

The author continues by giving the figures of the median age at marriage for men and women (i.e. the age below which 50% of persons married in any one year):

Marriage age for spinsters and bachelors and number of minors married per thousand marriages in England and Wales, 1876–1956

	Median age of marrying		*Number of minors (under 21 years of age) per thousand marriages*	
Year	*M*	*F*	*M*	*F*
1881–1885	25.9	24.4	73.0	215.0
1891–1895	26.6	25.0	56.2	182.6
1901–1905	26.9	25.4	48.3	153.1
1911–1915	27.5	25.8	39.2	136.6
1921–1925	27.5	25.6	48.2	149.2
1931–1935	27.4	25.5		
1941–1945	26.8	24.6	33.8	163.8
1951–1955	26.6	24.2	65.0	271.1
1956	26.2	23.7		

The median age at marriage increased during the 1970s and 1980s following a drop in the 1960s. We give opposite a table taken from *Population Trends* (Spring 1995).

Questions

(i) (*a*) Why do you think the median age dropped in the 1950s and 1960s? (*b*) Why do you think it increased in the 1970s and 1980s? (*c*) What do you think will happen in the latter part of the 1990s?

(ii) Bearing in mind the association between the age at marriage and divorce (p. 235, below), should there be any changes in the law?
(iii) Should the minimum age of marriage be the same as the age of consent to sexual intercourse?

Table F Marriages by previous marital status and median age of marriage, England and Wales

	Total number of marriages (thousands)	*Percentage of marriages which were:*			*Median age at marriage (years)*					
		First for both	*First for one*	*Second or subsequent*	*Bachelors*	*Divorced men*	*Widowers*	*Spinsters*	*Divorced women*	*Widows*
1972	426	73	15	11	23.5	38.3	60.2	21.5	33.8	54.0
1978	368	65	19	16	23.8	35.7	60.4	21.6	32.7	55.0
1982	342	64	19	16	24.3	36.3	61.0	22.1	33.8	55.7
1988	348	63	20	17	25.6	38.4	61.9	23.6	35.1	55.3
1991	307	63	21	17	26.5	39.0	62.0	24.6	35.7	55.6
1992	312	62	21	17	26.8	39.2	62.1	25.0	35.8	55.3

7 Void and voidable marriages

Grounds on which a marriage is voidable under the Matrimonial Causes Act 1973 are as follows:

12. A marriage celebrated after 31st July 1971 shall be voidable on the following grounds only, that is to say –

(*a*) that the marriage has not been consummated owing to the incapacity of either party to consummate it;
(*b*) that the marriage has not been consummated owing to the wilful refusal of the respondent to consummate it;
(*c*) that either party to the marriage did not validly consent to it, whether in consequence of duress, mistake, unsoundness of mind or otherwise;
(*d*) that at the time of the marriage either party, though capable of giving a valid consent, was suffering (whether continuously or intermittently) from mental disorder within the meaning of the [Mental Health Act 1983] of such a kind or to such an extent as to be unfitted for marriage;
(*e*) that at the time of the marriage the respondent was suffering from venereal disease in a communicable form;
(*f*) that at the time of the marriage the respondent was pregnant by some person other than the petitioner.

Singh v Singh
[1971] P 226, [1971] 2 All ER 828, [1971] 2 WLR 963, 115 Sol Jo 205, CA.

The wife was a 17 year-old girl from an orthodox Sikh family. She went through a ceremony of marriage in a Register Office with a 21 year-old Sikh boy. The marriage was arranged by her parents, and the bride had never seen the bridegroom before the actual ceremony of marriage. The plan was that there would be a religious ceremony of marriage and then the parties would commence living together. When the wife saw the husband at the Register

Office, she did not like what she saw, and although she participated in the civil ceremony, she refused to go through with the religious ceremony or to live with the husband. She petitioned for a decree of nullity on two grounds, namely, duress and incapacity to consummate due to her invincible repugnance. Her petition was dismissed. Karminski LJ dealt with the issue of duress and continued:

There is the alternative matter of repugnance. It is true that the wife never submitted herself to the physical embraces of the husband, because after the ceremony of marriage before the registrar it does not appear that she saw him again or went near him. Having taken the view which she did, that she did not want to be married to him, it is understandable that she did not want to have sexual intercourse with him; but that again seems to be a very long way from an invincible repugnance. True, as counsel for the wife argued, invincible repugnance can have a number of forms; and he reminded us of a decided case where the wife refused to undress when she went to bed so that the husband could not have intercourse with her. But here the wife abandoned the idea of her marriage altogether, and there is nothing of a psychiatric or sexual aversion on her part which is in any way established. In my view that ground of nullity fails completely.
Appeal dismissed.

In *Kaur v Singh* [1972] 1 All ER 292, the parties – both Sikhs – solemnised a civil ceremony of marriage which, in accordance with the custom of their community, was an arranged marriage. It was clearly understood by all that the civil ceremony would be followed by a religious ceremony, and that the parties would not cohabit prior to the religious ceremony. The husband failed to make arrangements for the religious ceremony, and the wife succeeded in obtaining a decree of nullity based on s. 12(*b*) of the Matrimonial Causes Act 1973, in that the husband's action (or inaction) amounted to wilful refusal to consummate the marriage.

Question

(i) In *Kaur v Singh*, if the husband had attempted to consummate the marriage, would the wife have had a valid excuse?
(ii) Can you really see the difference between the wife who refuses to undress because of a repugnance to her husband and the wife who refuses to comply with the requirements of contracting a marriage according to her religious beliefs because of a repugnance to the man she married in a civil form? (See *A v J (Nullity Proceedings)* [1989] 1 FLR 110 where it was held that a wife's insistence on the postponement of a religious ceremony because she was 'disappointed by the husband's cool and inconsiderate behaviour to her' amounted to wilful refusal on her part to consummate the marriage.)

Hirani v Hirani
(1982) 4 FLR 232, CA.

The wife was 19 and she was living with her parents. The family is Hindu. The girl became friendly with a young Indian Muslim, a Mr Husain. When the parents discovered this relationship, they immediately made arrangements for her to marry a Mr Hirani, who like them was a Hindu of the same caste and linguistic background. She had never seen this man nor had her parents.

The Judge recalled the pressure which was put on her by her parents to marry in this way: 'You want to marry somebody who is strictly against our religion; he is a Muslim, you are a Hindu. You had better marry somebody we want you to – otherwise pick up your belongings and go.' She married him, lived with him for six weeks and then left her husband and went to Mr Husain's house. Her petition for a decree of nullity on the ground of duress was dismissed. On appeal:

Ormrod LJ: The crucial question in these cases ... is whether the threats, pressure or whatever it is is such as to destroy the reality of consent and overbears the will of the individual. It seems to me that this case ... is a classic case of a young girl, wholly dependent on her parents being forced into a marriage with a man she has never seen in order to prevent her (reasonably from her parents' point of view) continuing in an association with a Muslim which they would regard with abhorrence. But it is as clear a case as one could want of the overbearing of the will of the petitioner and thus invalidating or vitiating her consent.
Appeal allowed.

In *MK (otherwise M McC) v F McC* [1982] ILR 277, an Irish case, the petitioner became pregnant. Her parents threatened her with expulsion from the family home unless she married the respondent. For his part, he was told by his mother that he could no longer remain at home. His father stopped speaking to him. The young couple, aged 19 and 21, went through a ceremony of marriage, but after three years' cohabitation they separated. The judge granted the wife a decree of nullity based on duress:

I am satisfied that the will, not merely of one partner but of both husband and wife, was overborne by the compulsion of their respective parents and that they were driven unwillingly into a union which neither of them desired, or gave real consent to, in the true sense of the word, and which was doomed to failure from the outset ... An unwilling bride and resentful husband were dragged to the altar and went through a ceremony of marriage which neither of them wanted, and without any genuine feelings of attraction or affection which might have led on to a happy union in the course of time.

Questions

(i) Is it necessary to have genuine feelings of attraction or affection for a marriage to be valid in English law? What about arranged marriages?
(ii) Do you think the absence of divorce in Ireland makes a difference in the way judges in that jurisdiction consider nullity petitions? Should it?
(iii) Is there a difference between saying 'I can't' and 'I won't'?
(iv) Does the decision in *Hirani v Hirani* open the floodgates to large numbers of nullity petitions on this ground?
(v) What is the point of keeping alive, even for a short time longer, a marriage such as the one contracted in the *Singh v Singh* litigation?
(vi) It is clear that inability to consummate does not render the marriage void. Should it?
(vii) Why should 'mistake' render a marriage merely voidable rather than void?
(viii) Should English law retain the concept of a voidable marriage in relation to ss. 12(*a*) and 12(*b*) of the Matrimonial Causes Act 1973?

The Law Commission Report on *Nullity of Marriage* (1970) provides the following four reasons for retaining nullity of a voidable marriage:

24 (*a*) It is not true to say that the difference between a nullity decree of a voidable marriage and a decree of divorce is a mere matter of form. It may be that the consequences of the two decrees are substantially similar, but the concepts giving rise to the two decrees are quite different: the decree of nullity recognises the existence of an impediment which prevents the marriage from initially becoming effective, while the decree of divorce records that some cause for terminating the marriage has arisen since the marriage. This distinction may be of little weight to the lawyer, but is a matter of essence in the jurisprudence of the Christian Church.

(*b*) The Church attaches considerable importance to consent as a pre-requisite to marriage. Consent to marriage includes consent to sexual relations and, hence, impotence can be regarded as having the effect of vitiating consent. Likewise, the grounds under section 9(1)(*b*), (*c*) and (*d*) of the Act of 1965 (mental disorder, epilepsy, pregnancy by another or venereal disease) can be considered to fall under the head of conditional consent [see now s. 12(*d*)(*e*)(*f*) Matrimonial Causes Act 1973] and are acceptable to the Church. Except with regard to wilful refusal to consummate, which the Church of England considers should cease to be a ground for nullity and be a ground for divorce, the Church is satisfied with the existing law of nullity. Therefore, so radical a change as is involved in the substitution of a decree of divorce for a decree of nullity in respect of matters which the Church regards as relevant to the formation of marriage and irrelevant to divorce, is likely to be unwelcome to the Church. It is also likely to be resented by people not necessarily belonging to the Church who associate a stigma with divorce and who would therefore prefer to see such matters as impotence and mental disorder, which are illnesses, remain grounds for annulling the marriage rather than causes for dissolving it.

(*c*) It may be that many people do not appreciate the distinction between divorce and nullity. They, presumably, would not oppose turning a nullity of a voidable marriage into a divorce. If, however, such a change is likely to cause offence to a substantial minority, then the proposal cannot be recommended unless some worthwhile advantage is to be gained from the change. The only advantage to be gained would be that one of the present voidable marriages (*i.e.*, one voidable for wilful refusal to consummate), might be thought by some to fit in more 'neatly' among divorces than among nullities.

(*d*) The assimilation of voidable marriages and dissolvable marriages could not be complete so long as we retained the bar on divorce within three years of the marriage. [This has now been changed: see later p. 230.] Such a bar would be wholly inappropriate to nullity cases.

25. We are therefore, opposed to the abolition of the class of voidable marriages and think that it should be retained. But the effect of the decrees of nullity of a voidable marriage should be modified so as to make it clear that the marriage is to be treated in every respect as a valid marriage until it is annulled and as a nullity only from the date when it is annulled.

On wilful refusal, in particular, they said:

(*a*) Wilful refusal to consummate is in most cases the alternative allegation to impotence as it is often uncertain whether the respondent's failure to consummate is due to one cause or the other; the petitioner may not know whether the respondent refuses to consummate the marriage because he is unable to have sexual intercourse or because, though able to have sexual intercourse, he does not want to have it; in such cases the court must draw an inference from the evidence before it and it seems unreal that the relief granted to the petitioner – nullity or divorce – should depend in any given case on the court's view as to which of the two reasons prevented the consummation of the marriage.

(*b*) Failure to consummate, whether it be because the respondent is unable or because he is unwilling to have sexual intercourse, deprives the marriage of what is normally regarded as one of its essential purposes. Parties would think it strange that the nature of the relief should depend on the court's decision whether non-consummation was due to the respondent's inability or whether it was due to his unwillingness. From the parties' point of view the relevant fact would be that the marriage had never become a complete one. To tell them that, in the eyes of the law, failure to complete it due to one cause results in their marriage being annulled, whereas such failure due to another cause results in their marriage being dissolved, would seem to them to be a strange result.

Questions

(i) What advantages, other than those mentioned by the Law Commission, can you see for retaining the concept of nullity in this context?
(ii) Do you agree with the four arguments referred to in the Law Commission Report generally?
(iii) Are the two arguments in relation to wilful refusal sufficient reasons by themselves to justify the retention of the present state of the law?

8 The formalities of marriage

As Lucy Mair explains in *Marriage* (1971):

There are some societies in which it is possible to get married almost without any formalities at all, and some in which a marriage without formality is a permitted alternative for people who cannot afford the formalities or do not attach importance to them. ...

There is a correlation between the amount of formality and display and the importance of the alliance that is being created. There are also in some societies – but these are different ones – ways of circumventing parental choice and forcing the consent of elders to a marriage agreed on by a young couple.

Informal Marriages
It is possible for a marriage to be created and announced in one breath by the simple fact that a couple are seen to be eating together. This is what happens in the Trobriand Islands in the Pacific, as they were described by Malinowski (in the *Sexual Life of Savages* (1929)) in the first ethnographic account to clothe formal statements of rules with the reality of actual behaviour. Since a marriage is concluded in such a simple way, a couple can marry in defiance of parental opposition. ...

England is not the Trobriand Islands, although prior to the Council of Trent (1545–1563) all that was necessary to constitute a valid marriage according to the canon law was the free consent of the parties expressed in any way so as to provide evidence that they contemplated a permanent and lawful union. Even after the Council, 'informal' marriages were recognised by the ecclesiastical courts. Lord Hardwicke's Marriage Act of 1753 was designed primarily to prevent these informal and often clandestine marriages from being performed although the reasons for this may not have been entirely altruistic. As K. O'Donovan (1985) states:

The proponents of the new Act were not concerned about popular common law marriage but about the threat to the propertied classes and to patriarchy of clandestine marriage:

> 'How often have we known the heir of a good family seduced, and engaged in a clandestine marriage, perhaps with a common strumpet? How often have we known a rich heiress carried off by a man of low birth, or perhaps by an infamous sharper? What distress some of our best families have been brought into what ruin some of their sons or daughters have been involved in, by such means, every gentleman may from his own knowledge recollect.' (Parliamentary History of England, vol. 13 (1813) col. 3)

Not all the Members of Parliament were convinced that the legislature had the power to declare null and void a conjugal promise. Robert Nugent pointed out:

> '... the most pernicious consequence of this Bill will be, its preventing marriage among the most useful, I will not scruple to say, the best sort of our people. The healthy, the strong, the laborious and the brave, I may justly call so. ... Shall we for the sake of preventing a few

misfortunes to the rich and great amongst us, make any law which will be a bar to the lawful procreation of such sort of men in this country?' (Ibid. col. 17)

Several speakers suggested that the cost of a licence deterred many of the poor from marrying in church and that those labourers mobile by trade would be prevented from marrying at all. Parental failure to control marriage among the rich might result in 'a great disappointment to the avarice or ambition of the parents'; but now the poor would be prevented from marriage.

The arguments of patriarchy carried the day: 'It is not only the interest but the duty of every parent to take care that his child shall not contract a scandalous or infamous marriage, and if he cannot do this by paternal authority the laws ought to assist him,' said Lord Barrington. 'I cannot suppose that any gentleman who has ever known what it is to be a father, will be against it,' was the view of the Solicitor-General.

A short description of the present English law is given by T.E. James, 'The English Law of Marriage' in *A Century of Family Law* (1957):

From 1753 until 1836 the formalities required for a valid marriage had all to be in accordance with the rites of the Church of England.[3] After 1836 civil marriages were permitted. ... There have been a large number of statutes modifying and extending the formal requirements; but now the matter is governed by the Marriage Act, 1949, which consolidated existing legislation and modified it to some extent.

Marriage according to the rites of the Church of England can be solemnised in four ways, that is, after due publication of banns,[4] by special licence,[5] by common licence[6] or by the certificate issued by a Superintendent Registrar without a licence. The resulting ceremonies, according to the rites of the Church of England, require the presence of at least two witnesses and of a clergyman in holy orders. ...

The distinction between the superintendent registrar's certificate with and without a licence lies in the procedure to be followed which affects the time of residence and the display of the notice of marriage prior to the granting of the certificate.

Marriages by virtue of the superintendent registrar's certificate may be solemnised in the appropriate parish church or authorised chapel, if according to the rites of the Church of England; if they are in accordance with other rites, then in a registered building[7] or the office of the Superintendent Registrar,[8] or according to the usages of the Society of Friends or of the Jews.

As a result of the Marriage (Registrar General's Licence) Act 1970, there is power for the civil authorities to authorise a marriage to be solemnised at any convenient time or place. The Registrar General has to be satisfied, inter alia, that one of the persons to be married is seriously ill and is not expected to recover. In addition, the Marriage Act 1983 enables a marriage to be solemnised on the authority of a Superintendent Registrar's Certificate of a person who is housebound or is a detained person at a place where that person usually resides.

---

3. Except for Quakers and Jews.
4. The banns must be published on three Sundays preceding the marriage. If the parties reside in the same parish, the banns must be published in the parish church. If they reside in separate parishes, then the banns must be published in both parishes. A clergyman is not obliged to publish banns unless the parties deliver or cause to be delivered seven days' notice in writing with their full names, place of residence and the period during which each has resided there.
5. These are special dispensations granted by the Archbishop of Canterbury enabling marriages to be solemnised according to the rites of the Church of England at any convenient time or place.
6. The common licence is issued under the authority of the bishop of the diocese. It can be granted only for the marriage in a church or chapel of an ecclesiastical district in which one of the parties has had his usual place of residence for 15 days immediately before the grant of the licence, or a parish church or chapel which is the usual place of worship of one or both of the parties.
7. This is defined as a 'separate building of public religious worship'.
8. Or premises which have been approved as a venue for a wedding (Marriage Act 1994 s. 1).

The Law Commission's Report on *Solemnisation of Marriage* (1973) presents a powerful case for uniform civil preliminaries:

The need for compulsory civil preliminaries

14. We have said that the primary objectives of preliminaries are to ensure that 'there should be proper opportunity for the investigation of capacity (and, in the case of minors, parental consent) before the marriage, and that the investigation should be carried out, uniformly for parties to all marriages, by persons trained to perform this function,' and that 'there should be proper opportunity for those who may know of a lawful impediment to a marriage to declare it'. In fact it is difficult to imagine a system less calculated to achieve these objectives. It is not uniform. It does not ensure that there is always a proper opportunity for investigation or that the investigation is carried out by those who have been trained for that role. Nor does it ensure that those whose consents are required or who may know of impediments have an adequate opportunity of stopping the marriage. These strictures are least justified in the case of marriages after a superintendent registrar's certificate. There, at any rate, there is a three-week waiting period, an opportunity of investigation by trained personnel, and some information on which to base an investigation and a right to demand some further evidence. But, even there, there is no method whereby those who wish to object can be sure of doing so effectively. Potential objectors may in practice have no idea where the couple propose to marry. It is impracticable to search every marriage notice book in the country; and a search will be ineffective if the couple choose to marry in Church after ecclesiastical preliminaries. Nor will there be time to make searches if the couple have paid a little extra in order to cut down the waiting period from 21 days to one day. The outstanding absurdity of the present position is, perhaps, that the payment of an extra fee enables the major safeguard of a waiting period to be by-passed.

15. Although in the case of banns there is generally an equally long waiting period it is a less effective safeguard. ... there is no legal requirement that the parties shall make any declaration about capacity, nor is there any legal duty upon the person to whom application is made for the publication of banns (who is not necessarily the incumbent himself) to satisfy himself on these matters although many clergymen do so. The historical justification for banns is, of course, that their publication will give adequate advance public notice of the couple's intention to marry which will enable anyone knowing of an impediment to come forward. In social conditions which prevailed in this country before the present century this may have been sound. To-day, with the growth and increased mobility of the population and the increase in urban living, it clearly is not. Unless the banns happen to be published in a church regularly attended by the parties and their friends and relations the chances of any impropriety coming to light are remote.

16. In our view, it is impossible adequately to reform the present system unless uniform civil preliminaries are made compulsory in the case of all marriages and unless the civil preliminaries are themselves reformed. Only then will it be possible to ensure that there is adequate investigation and to provide an effective system of raising objections. This is far from being a novel or revolutionary suggestion. When the Marriage Bill was introduced in 1836 it in fact provided for civil preliminaries to all marriages. The clauses which required this in the case of Church of England marriages were removed during the course of the Bill's passage in order to hasten the enactment of the Bill's major reforms. But the Government of the day then expressed the view that it would be necessary on a future occasion to carry the whole of the original plan into effect. Such preliminary enquiries as we have made suggest that the Church of England would not now oppose this rationalisation. It will not, of course, prevent the Church requiring publication of banns as an ecclesiastical preliminary to a Church wedding. All that we are proposing is that the publication of banns should cease to be a requirement of the civil law. This could, if desired by the Church, be coupled with the removal of the present obligation on incumbents to marry any of their parishioners (even though they have never set foot in the Church before), affording them the same freedom as ministers of the Roman Catholic and Free Churches to decide whether or not they will perform a particular marriage. Marriage by common licence would necessarily disappear. We would see no objection to the retention of the Archbishop's special licence but this would not be essential if the legislation were amended so that the Registrar General's licence could be used as a preliminary to a marriage according to the rites of the Church of England.

Questions

(i) Were the Law Commission correct in their view that the Church authorities would not oppose universal preliminaries? (There is certainly some opinion in

the Church, referred to in the Report, which feels that there would be a reduction of 'pastoral opportunities' and that 'universal civil preliminaries might lead to the eventual introduction of a compulsory civil ceremony'.)
(ii) The *Efficiency Scrutiny of the Registration Service* (1985) considered that universal civil preliminaries would assist the efficiency of the Registration Service. It made a number of detailed comments on the non-Church of England procedures primarily designed to cut costs and increase choice, for example that 'authorised persons' (who solemnise and register marriages) be registered without reference to a building, that there be no limitation on the register office a couple can choose to be married in, that the marriage notice book be discontinued and that marriage notices no longer be displayed on public notice boards.

These ideas were taken up by the Government in its White Paper, *Registration: Proposals for Change* (1990). The Marriage Act 1994 s. 1 introduces (s. 46A of the Marriage Act 1949) a procedure whereby the Secretary of State can make regulations permitting local authorities to approve, for a fee, premises other than their own register offices. As of August 1995, some 465 premises had been approved. The list includes Woburn Abbey, Ripley Castle, Cheltenham and Epsom Race Courses, several football grounds, and terminal 4 at Heathrow airport!

The ceremony cannot be religious (Marriage Act 1949 s. 46B(4)). Why not? [Note also that by the Marriage Act 1994 s. 2 (Marriage Act 1949 s. 35(2A)) a couple may choose to marry in a register office in a district other than one where either is resident.]
(iii) There are two other models different from the one which exists at present – whether it further be modified or not by the Law Commission recommendations. One model would be to have universal civil procedures followed by a ceremony of marriage anywhere. Marriages would not be confined to Churches, places of public religious worship, register offices or approved premises. Another model, moving the other way, would be to impose compulsory civil ceremonies of marriage, which could be followed by religious blessings if the parties so desired. Do you favour either of these reforms? Why shouldn't people be able to marry wherever they like?

Mary Ann Glendon (1977) distinguishes compulsory pre-marital procedures from compulsory ceremonies necessary for the actual creation of a contract of marriage. As to the first, she states: 'the preliminaries required by modern States before a marriage can take place are revealing as indications of the degree to which the State is actively involved in regulation of marriage formation, as opposed to contenting itself with the promulgation of rules which describe ideal behaviour in the area but which have no real sanction.'

In commenting on the English law of marriage preliminaries, Glendon states that: 'the apparent complexity of the system. ... masks the fact that the system as a whole exercises little control over the formation of marriage and that the English State takes little advantage of the occasion of marriage to promote any particular social policies.'

Questions

(i) What social policies do you think that the State should promote? In particular do you think that the State should impose longer waiting periods,

greater publicity, compulsory counselling, compulsory medical tests (for instance for HIV antibodies), or evidence of financial or residential security? Or are all these impositions contrary to the basic freedom to marry?
(ii) Do you think that State intervention in marriage formalities will lead to more people simply living together in informal arrangements?

Chapter 2

The legal structure of marriage and cohabitation

1 The factual background

Previous editions of this book have had separate chapters on the legal structure of marriage and on the issue of cohabitation. However, it would seem that the time has now come for us to treat cohabitation and marriage in a single chapter, echoing as it does the reality of how most people now run their lives.

By 1993, the total number of marriages had fallen to just under 300,000 and the number of marriages which were the first for both partners had become the lowest recorded at 182,000. In 1979, the number of all marriages was 426,000 and the number of first marriages was 340,000. In contrast, the number of cohabiting couples had increased very substantially. The cohabitation rate for non-married women aged 18–49 rose from 11% in 1979 to 22% in 1993, and for single women (i.e. those who have never married) the corresponding rate increased from 9% in 1979 to 23% in 1993. There is a very clear link between marriage and cohabitation, and the evidence suggests that seven out of ten first marriages in the early 1990s were preceded by cohabitation. Twenty years ago the figure was closer to one in ten, and thirty years ago it was probably no higher than one in twenty. Interestingly, the period of premarital cohabitation has also increased from a median of one year in the 1970s to about two years in the 1990s.

'Cohabitation' is defined in *Social Trends 21* (1991) as 'living together as husband and wife without having legally married'. A similar definition is adopted by the Scottish Law Commission in their discussion paper *The Effects of Cohabitation in Private Law* (1990) but they add that it matters not whether the couple pretend to others that they are married to each other. The first two editions of this book refer to 'cohabitees'. This, as Stephen Parker in *Cohabitees* (1987) points out, is an ugly irregular form of 'cohabitant'. We have abandoned the irregular form.

Until recently, 'informal' arrangements have been confined to a large extent to intellectual elites and the sub-cultures of the poor for whom the structures of traditional marriage and divorce law have been to a large extent irrelevant. This is no longer the case.

Mary Ann Glendon, in *Withering Away of Marriage* (1976), reflects on some of the reasons for the acceptance by society of informal arrangements:

> Today, however, informal marriage is increasingly common among other social groups and, perhaps more significant, increasingly accepted. These two facts interact. The more persons in a particular group 'live together,' the more such behaviour becomes accepted. The more acceptance this alternative to formal marriage gains, the more people employ it. Thus, informal marriage has

become a recurring subject in popular songs and cartoons and was discussed in the 1972 federal government report on population. Cohabitation is favored among young people, among pensioners and others receiving benefits terminable or reducible upon formal marriage, and increasingly among other diverse social groups. …

Motivations to enter informal rather than legal marriage include economic advantages as in the case of many elderly people, inability to enter a legal marriage, unwillingness to be subject to the legal effects of marriage, desire for a 'trial marriage,' and lack of concern with the legal institution. This lack of concern is nothing new among groups accustomed to forming and dissolving informal unions without coming into contact with legal institutions. Among these groups legal marriage is but an aspect of the irrelevance of traditional American family law, law that is viewed as being property-oriented and organized around the ideals of a dominant social group. Lack of concern with marriage law has been growing, however, among many who definitely are not outside the mainstream of American life. Until recently these converts accepted unquestioningly the traditional structures of the enacted law, but they now find that on balance the enacted law offers no advantages over informal arrangements.

Helen Oppenheimer in *Marriage* (1990) presents a thoughtful message from the liberal Christian viewpoint.

The harder moral argument is about relationships which are physical, emotional, social and even high-minded, but decline to be irrevocable. Once it is granted that sexuality is not as such unclean, why must it be confined so rigidly to matrimony? Why talk about 'fornication' at all, except perhaps for relationships which are irresponsibly ephemeral? Of course faithfulness is a good and life-enhancing thing, but must it be the only consideration? To answer these questions satisfactorily in a still traditional way one must keep one's head and consider the real good and the real harm in the partial commitments.

Sometimes what is missing is fairly clear: the relationship is simply one-sided and means more to one partner than to the other. Then we do well to wonder, though not triumphantly, whether somebody is being exploited or is presently going to be hurt. It is not moralistic to be convinced that such liberty to be unshackled does not constitute a moral breakthrough.

Nor is it moralistic still to look rather suspiciously for lopsidedness when the claim is made that options are being kept open: 'It would be nice if it lasted but if we get tired of one another it is nobody's else's business. So long as we are not irresponsible or inefficient enough to have a child, there is no question of blame or "immorality" if we live together for a while and then split up. Much better that than all the miserable struggle of divorce. We can try it out without getting too involved and see how we get on.' There is not much safeguard here for the emotionally weaker party against misery and bitterness not easily distinguishable from the misery and bitterness of divorce. To ask them how sure they really can be that they are totally at one in the degree of commitment is like asking a polygamist whether he can be quite sure of loving his wives equally. Practical experience is not altogether on their side.

Lovers sometimes part 'good friends'. They sometimes do after a broken marriage. But an advance promise of mature detachment is no more likely to be easy to keep in the end than an advance promise of faithfulness. How many people truly like it when their partners take care to keep their options open? This is the sort of freedom that is not so happy in the claiming as in the propounding. How many middle-aged women would want to allow the lovers of their youth to feel quite free to leave them, with no ill-feelings? Indeed how many fairly young women will go on being content with the condition they thought they could accept: no child?

Traditionalists who have taken the old morality for granted and lived contentedly by it all their lives torment themselves nowadays with the idea that this generation, maybe their own sons and daughters, are badly brought up and indeed immoral. They would be justified in forgetting the word 'fornication' but remembering these real questions about human happiness.

It is only fair to add, and even insist, that sometimes when people live together unmarried the commitment really is there, or is beginning to be there, and all that is lacking is the wedding ceremony. Instead of bandying about the idea of 'living in sin' a Christian would do well to consider honestly whether what we have here truly is a kind of marriage.

The standard way to make a marriage is a wedding. The couple take each other as husband and wife before witnesses. It is their consent that makes the marriage, not the ministrations of registrar or even priest. The wedding ceremony is a solemn way of making that consent public, and to ask for the blessing of family and friends and especially, for religious people, the blessing of God. But if what makes the marriage is consent, to dispense with the ceremony may not invalidate the consent.

There are a good many couples today who have seen the previous generation's notions about marriage and their ensuing ups and downs as hindrance rather than help. When people try to work out a different and more humanly satisfying way for themselves, it must be recognized that what they are engaged upon is a moral enterprise. At least in all seriousness let it not be nipped in the bud for the sake of respectability.

If we think, as well we may, that people who avoid formal commitment are living dangerously, we ought not to wash our hands of them but stand by to help pick up the pieces if necessary, which does not mean being ready to say 'I told you so'.

Question

Is this an argument in favour of providing cohabitation with the legal consequences of marriage?

Some cohabitants remain so simply because they do *not* want to become trapped with the legal implications of a marriage. But this is not the case for all.

Meade, in *Consortium Rights of the Unmarried – Time for a Reappraisal* (1981), tends towards the view that there are a large number of interrelated reasons why couples opt out of traditional marriage. They include the following:

(1) a desire to avoid the sex-stereotyped allocation of roles associated with marriage;
(2) a belief that marriage is unnecessary or irrelevant if no children are involved;
(3) a reluctance to enter a supposedly permanent marriage;
(4) bohemian philosophy;
(5) a conscientious objection to state regulation of marriage;
(6) a desire to avoid the expense and trauma of a possible divorce;
(7) an insouciant outlook on legally sanctioned relationships;
(8) the desire for various forms of companionship;
(9) a trial period to test suitability for marriage;
(10) the need to share expenses in the face of long-lasting inflation.

One reason left out of Meade's list which will be relevant in some cases is simply that the parties are *unable* to marry because previous legal ties have not yet been broken.

Question

Do you think any of the reasons given by Meade to be more important than any other?

Jacqueline Scott, Michael Braun and Duane Alwin in their contribution to International Social Attitudes (1993–1994) asked their respondents from four different countries what advice they would give – first to a young woman, then to a young man – as to whether to live alone, live with a steady partner without marrying, live together and then marry, or marry without living together first. They identify the fact that older women in particular might adopt the 'role of protector of traditional family values and urge marriage' while younger men might be the most favourable to cohabitation. Finally, they asked the question whether the respondents agreed with the proposition that married people are generally happier than unmarried people. Their results are as follows:

Table 1: Advice would give to a young woman*

	Britain %	*Irish Republic* %	*USA* %	*West Germany* %
Live alone without a steady partner	4	3	9	5
Live with steady partner, without marrying	4	1	3	11
Live with steady partner and then marry	43	32	26	50
Marry without living together first	37	59	46	19

*Advice for a young man is substantially the same.

Table 2: % advising marriage without living together first (by birth cohorts)

		Men born in ...			*Women born in ...*		
	Total	*1950–1970*	*1930–1949*	*Pre-1930*	*1950–1970*	*1930–1949*	*Pre-1930*
Britain	37	17	41	64	17	46	61
Irish Republic	59	38	68	86	44	69	86
USA	46	32	46	65	36	49	65
West Germany	19	6	18	39	8	22	40

Table 3: % agreeing that married people are generally happier than unmarried people

		Men born in ...			*Women born in ...*		
	Total	*1950–1970*	*1930–1949*	*Pre-1930*	*1950–1970*	*1930–1949*	*Pre-1930*
Britain	33	19	40	59	15	33	56
Irish Republic	46	40	61	64	30	43	61
USA	51	43	59	71	36	48	67
West Germany	38	23	49	59	21	40	54

Questions

(i) Do you think that these results teach us anything which you think you did not already suspect?
(ii) Susan McRae in her book *Cohabiting Mothers* (1993) brings together the various factors influencing women's decisions *to* marry.

Table 5.2: Factors influencing decision to marry

Column percentages

	Cohabited pre-maritally: Married after baby	Cohabited pre-maritally: Married before baby	Non-cohabiting married mothers
Own security	41	33	41
Children's security	69	28	14
Fell in love	12	39	65
Parents wanted us to marry	10	18	17
Religious reasons	2	7	15
To make a commitment	57	53	62
Could afford a house	0	10	17
Pregnancy	8	16	11
Wanted a child*	10	40	26
Children wanted us to marry	8	2	1
She/he became legally free to marry	18	19	1
Base:	*51*	*57*	*92*

* Excluding women who indicated that pregnancy was precipitating factor in decision to marry.

Do you think that men's decisions to marry would be substantially different, and if you do think so, why do you?

Figure 9: Percentages of all men and all women who were married, cohabiting or living alone or not in a family, for each age group separately, 1986–93, Great Britain

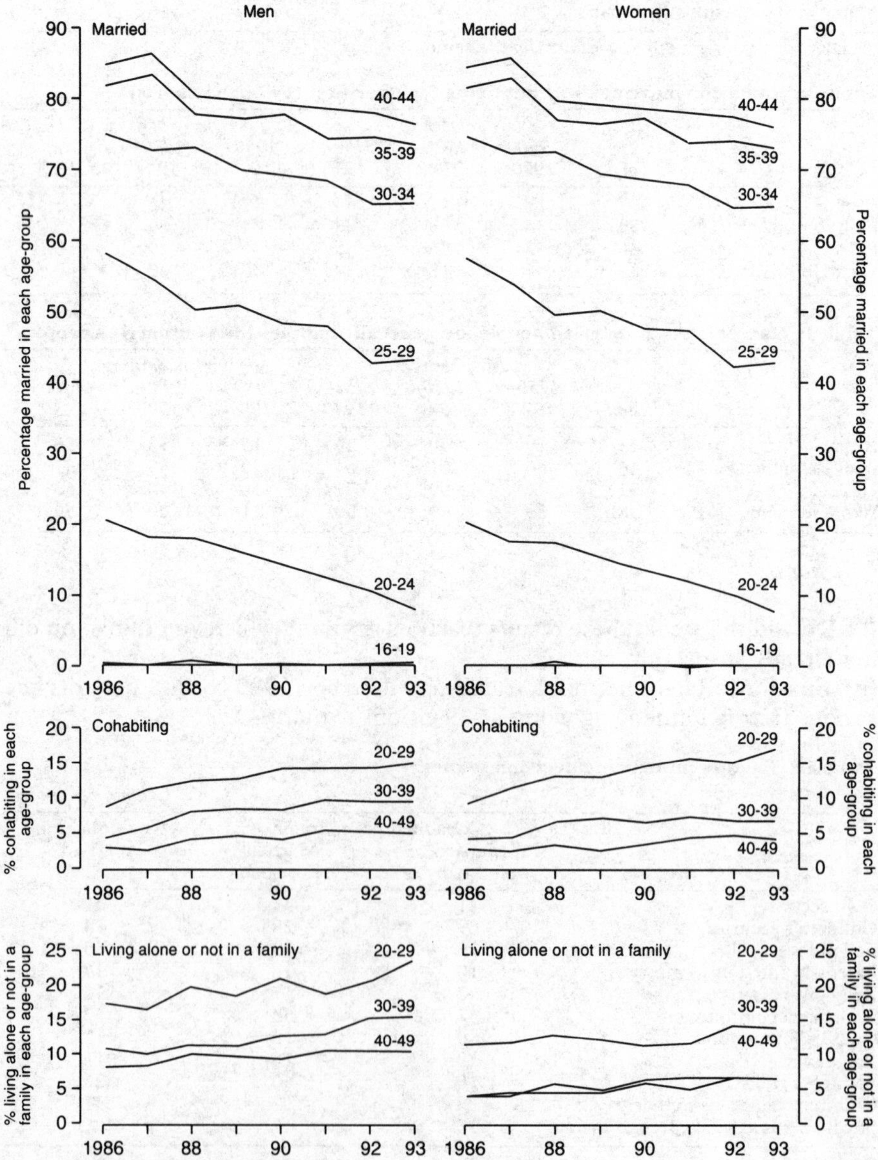

Source: General Household Surveys

Figure 7: Distribution by age of cohabiting men and women aged 16–59, 1990–93, Great Britain

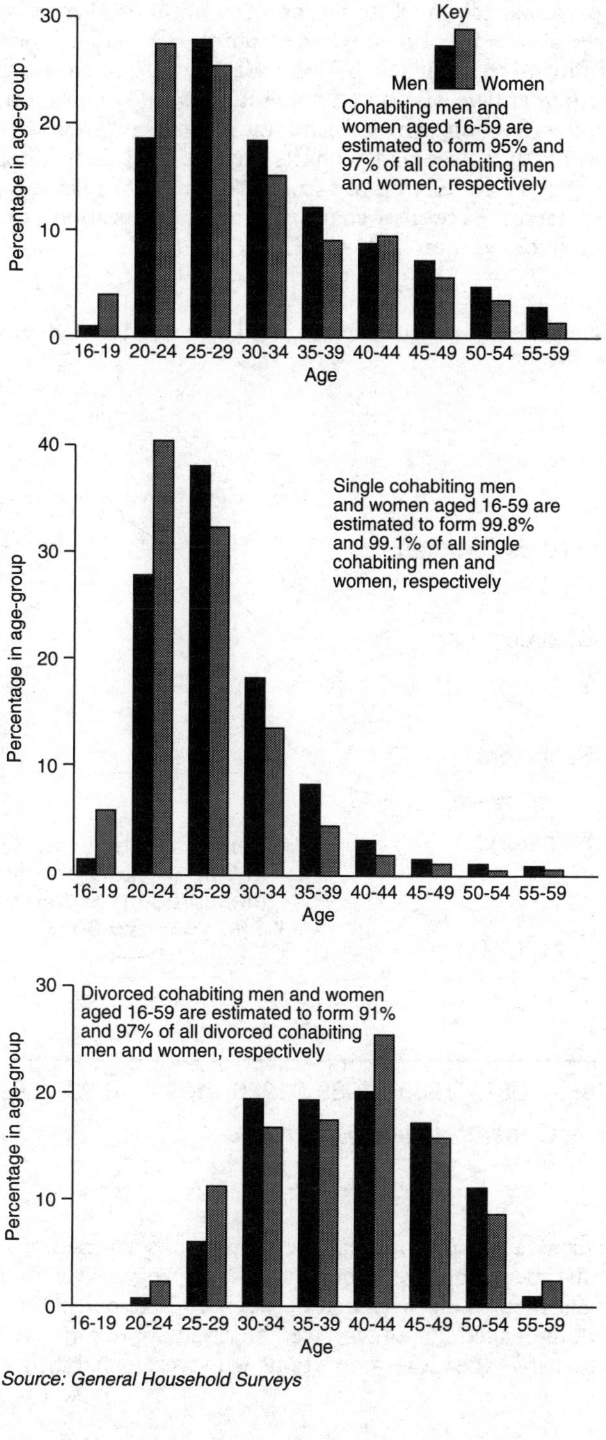

Source: General Household Surveys

Statistical information obtained from the General Household Surveys in Great Britain since 1979 traces the recent trends and gives an indication of the level of extramarital cohabitation and the number of marriages. Our first two tables (see above, pp. 40, 41) come from the General Household Surveys and are reproduced in an article by John Haskey (1995) from which it can be seen that the percentage of women cohabiting is most common amongst the 20–24 year old age group, whilst for men it is most common 25–29.

John Haskey (1995) (see p. 40) charts the trends in the proportions of men and women aged 16 to 59 who are (*a*) cohabiting, (*b*) married and (*c*) living outside a partnership. He also charts the median durations of cohabitation for single and divorced men and women.

Figure 8: Median durations of cohabitation* for single and divorced† men and women, 1986–93, Great Britain

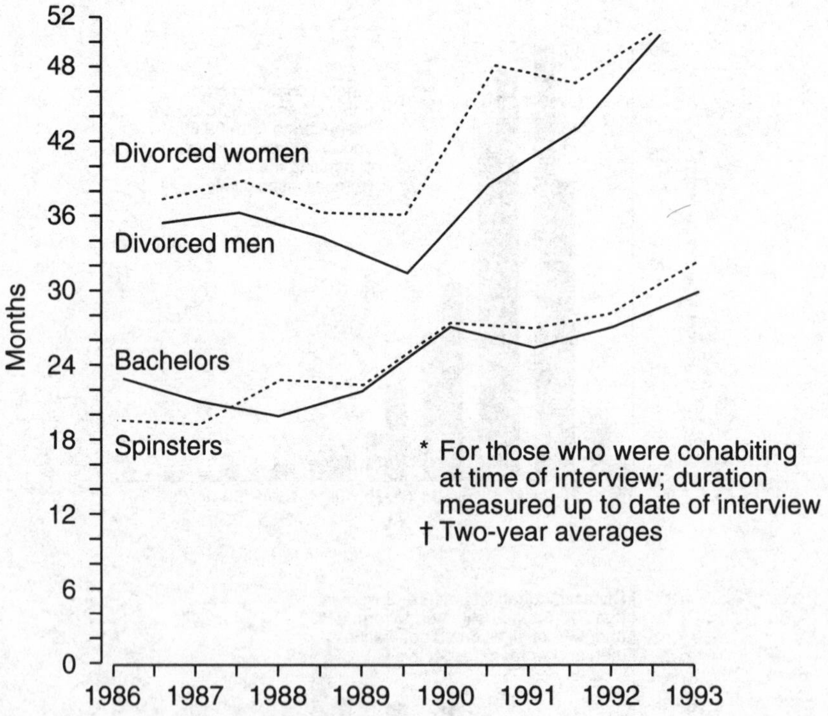

Source: General Household Surveys

Questions

(i) Does it surprise you to note that the proportions married have consistently declined, whilst the proportions cohabiting have progressively increased?
(ii) Are you alarmed to discover that between 1986 and 1993, the proportions of men and women aged 20–24 who were married approximately halved, whilst for those in their twenties, the proportions who were cohabiting approximately doubled?

(iii) Is it important for the lawyer to ask whether cohabitation is becoming: (*a*) institutionalised as an alternative to marriage; or (*b*) a new phase in a courtship process in which couples set up home before, rather than after, the 'paperwork'?
(iv) If you think it important, why do you think so?

Haskey and Kiernan (1989) (see below, pp. 44, 45 and 46) provide us with information on the socio-economic divisions, educational levels, and regional variations.

Questions

(i) Does any of this surprise you?
(ii) Do you think that there is likely to be any substantial change in the next five years to the information which is illustrated by these three tables?

2 Cohabitation contracts

Weyrauch, *Metamorphoses of Marriage* (1980) writes:

The legal device of contract is particularly useful for women from the middle classes and of high educational attainment who are self-assertive and competitive in their relations with men. It is less adequate for parties of the lower classes and those who, because of continued differential treatment of the sexes, lack equal bargaining power. The courts may then fall back on traditional conceptions of marriage as status and emphasize the conjugal obligations of the husband. If there is no marriage, the courts may surreptitiously apply public policy by reading into a supposedly implied contract provisions that never occurred to the parties. A host of legal theories, equitable in nature, may also affect the obligations of parties to quasi-marital relationships. Thus, the courts may develop remedies akin to those in modern contract law when dealing with terms that are manifestly unfair and oppressive, and may borrow the reasoning from commercial litigation when deciding marital and quasi-marital disputes. They may refuse to enforce unconscionable terms that have been found to exist between the parties, married or not, and imply a duty of good faith and fair dealing.

This is a contract drawn up by a firm of Philadelphia lawyers:

1. The parties desire to maintain their relationship as independent persons and to have their relationship be a natural consequence of their mutual love and affection without material or economic considerations. Each of the parties has, prior to the date hereof, achieved a measure of material independence and by the execution hereof, each party expresses his or her intention not to claim any interest whatsoever in the property accumulated by the other party prior or subsequent hereto, or in any of the income or appreciation derived therefrom except as expressly provided herein.
2. The parties intend and desire to hereby define and clarify their respective rights in the property of the other and in any jointly owned property they might accumulate after the date hereof and to avoid such interests, which, except for the operation of this agreement, they might otherwise acquire in the property of the other as a consequence of their relationship.
3. The parties desire that all property presently owned by either of them of whatsoever nature and wheresoever located and all income derived therefrom and all increases in the value thereof, shall be and remain their respective separate property. The parties agree that in no time during their relationship shall there be any transmutation of any of their separate property interests into jointly

Table 5: Proportions of men and women, aged 20–39, who were cohabiting, by educational level, 1986–87, Great Britain

Educational level (highest qualification*)	Single				Divorced and separated			
	Men		Women		Men		Women	
	Percentage	*Sample number*	Percentage	*Sample number*	Percentage	*Sample number*	Percentage	*Sample number*
Degree (first or higher)	17	*342*	26	*200*	29	*17*	40	*25*
Higher education below degree level	18	*261*	22	*185*	16	*37*	20	*49*
GCE 'A' level†	13	*476*	13	*326*	30	*47*	33	*43*
GCE 'O' level†	14	*526*	20	*529*	50	*64*	21	*145*
CSE* and commercial	14	*274*	22	*245*	40	*10*	23	*105*
No qualifications	18	*532*	20	*349*	37	*107*	22	*284*
All educational levels‡	15	*2,480*	20	*1,932*	36	*302*	24	*672*

* CSE grade 1 is equivalent to GCE 'O' level, and is *not* included under CSE and commercial qualifications.
† Or equivalent(s).
‡ Includes other qualifications: foreign and other qualifications, and apprenticeships.

Table 6: Proportions of men and women, aged 20–39, who were cohabiting, by socio-economic group, 1986–87, Great Britain

Educational level	Single				Divorced and separated			
	Men		Women		Men		Women	
	Percentage	*Sample number*	Percentage	*Sample number*	Percentage	*Sample number*	Percentage	*Sample number*
Professional	18	*154*	25	*55*	30	*10*	56	*9*
Employers and managers	20	*271*	28	*154*	47	*47*	32	*56*
Intermediate non-manual	17	*313*	22	*411*	17	*29*	24	*105*
Junior non-manual	9	*266*	18	*669*	37	*27*	21	*192*
Skilled manual	17	*768*	19	*119*	35	*130*	25	*68*
Semi-skilled manual and personal service	15	*466*	19	*411*	44	*45*	20	*189*
Unskilled manual	12	*146*	31	*26*	25	*12*	28	*39*
All socio-economic groups	16	*2,395*	20	*1,845*	36	*302*	23	*658*

Regional variations in the proportions of single, separated and divorced persons* who were cohabiting 1986-87, Great Britain

*aged 16-59

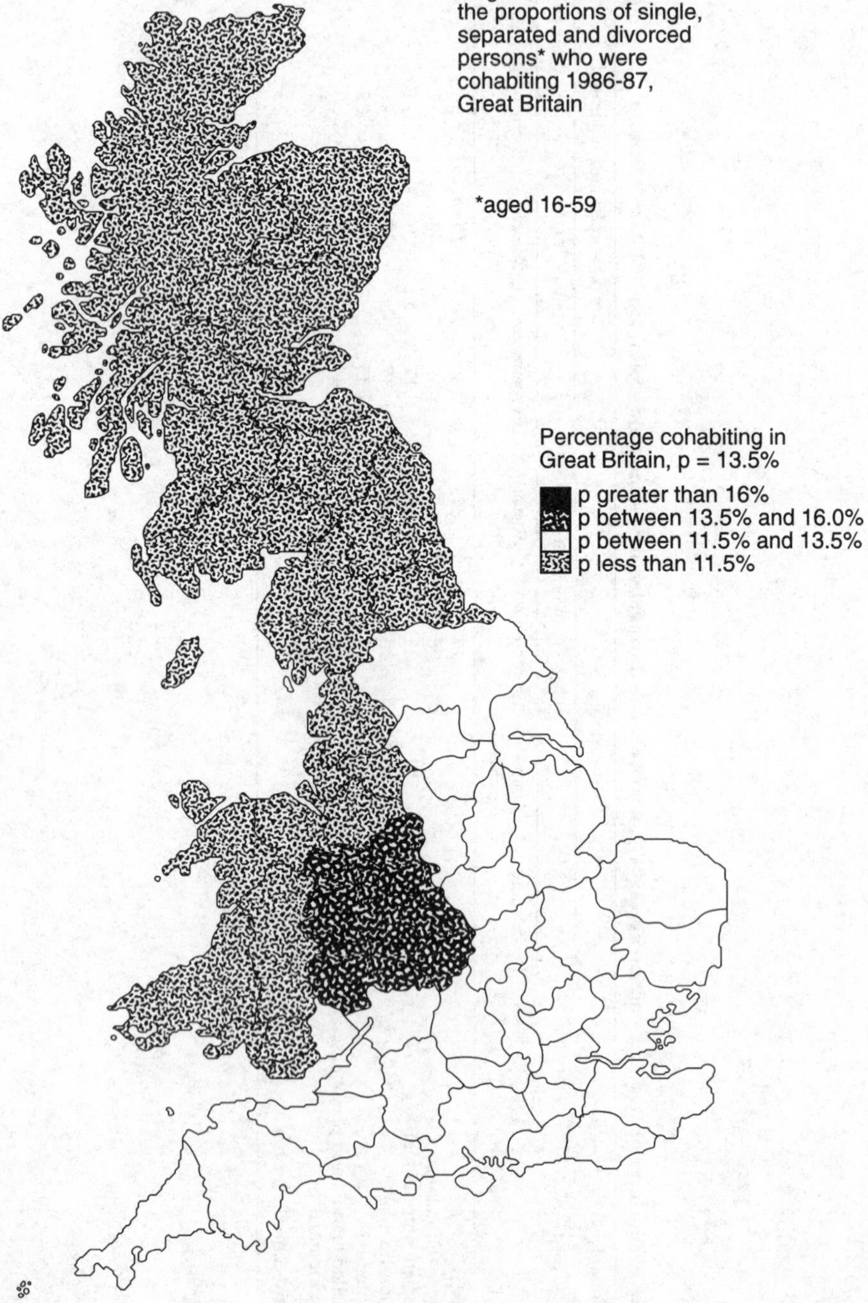

owned property, except by an express written agreement. The following events shall, under no circumstances, be evidence of any intention by either party of an agreement between the parties to transmute their separate property interests into jointly owned property or to transmute their separate income into joint income:

(*a*) The filing of joint tax returns;
(*b*) The designation of one party by the other as a beneficiary of his or her estate;
(*c*) The co-mingling by one party of his or her separate funds or property with jointly owned funds or property or with the separate funds or property of the other party;
(*d*) Any oral statement by either party;
(*e*) Any written statement by either party other than the express written agreement of transmutation;
(*f*) The payment from jointly held funds of any separate obligation, including but not limited to the payment of mortgage, interest or real property taxes on a separately owned residence or other separately owned real estate;
(*g*) The joint occupation of a separately owned or leased residence.

4. Both parties to this Agreement have made to each other a full and complete disclosure of the nature, extent and probable value of all their property and estate. Attached hereto as Exhibit 'A' is a statement of the separate property of the parties as of the date hereof. It is understood that as a result of income from or increases in the value of their presently existing separate property, each party may acquire other and different separate property in the future.

5. Except as otherwise provided herein with regard to the income and appreciation of the parties' separate property, and except as the parties may otherwise agree in writing, property heretofore acquired by the parties or hereafter acquired by the parties, and the earnings themselves, shall remain separate property.

Each of the parties covenants and agrees that all property now owned by either of the parties of whatsoever nature and wheresoever located and any property which he or she may hereafter acquire, whether real, personal or mixed, including but not limited to any earnings, salaries, commissions, or income resulting from his or her personal services, skills and efforts shall be and remain the sole and separate property of the party acquiring same and each party may dispose of said property as said party sees fit. ...

8. In full settlement of any and all claims by either party to the property of the other of whatsoever nature and wheresoever located and any property which might be hereafter acquired, whether real, personal or mixed, including but not limited to any earnings, salaries, commissions, or income heretofore or hereafter earned, [A] agrees that upon separation or the acquiring of separate living quarters by the parties, [B] shall receive as follows:

(*a*) Ten Thousand ($10,000.00) Dollars;
(*b*) payment of the premiums for Blue Cross, Blue Shield for a period of one (1) year from the date of separation;
(*c*) all right, title and interest to the property as set forth in Schedule 'B' attached hereto and made a part hereof.

9. This Agreement shall continue in force until it is modified by a writing executed by both parties.

10. This Agreement shall be construed under the laws of the Commonwealth of Pennsylvania.

11. The terms, provisions and conditions of this Agreement shall be binding upon any and all of the heirs, executors, administrators, successors or assigns of either of the respective parties hereto.

Some English precedents are reproduced in Lush *Cohabitation and Co-ownership Precedents* (1993).

Questions

(i) Lord Wright in *Fender v St John-Mildmay* [1938] AC 1, [1937] 3 All ER 402 said: 'the law will not enforce an immoral promise, such as a promise between a man and a woman to live together without being married or to pay a sum of money or to give some other consideration in return for an immoral association.' Scarman LJ in *Horrocks v Forray* [1976] 1 All ER 737, [1976] 1 WLR 230 said: 'When an illegitimate child has been born, there is certainly nothing contrary to public policy in the parents coming to an agreement, which they intend to be binding in law, for the maintenance of the child and the mother.' Do you think that a contract similar to the Philadelphia contract would be enforceable in English law?

(ii) Would Mrs Burns, Miss Layton, Mrs Grant, and Miss Windeler have been in a better or a worse position if they had signed a document similar to this? (See p. 167, below.)

In *Contracts for Intimate Relationships* (1978), four researchers from the University of California (Weitzman et al) looked at a sample of contracts. Included in the group were contracts written by married couples, as those identified as pursuing a 'trial marriage', and those who seek an alternative to marriage (cohabitants).

Aims and expectations for the relationship

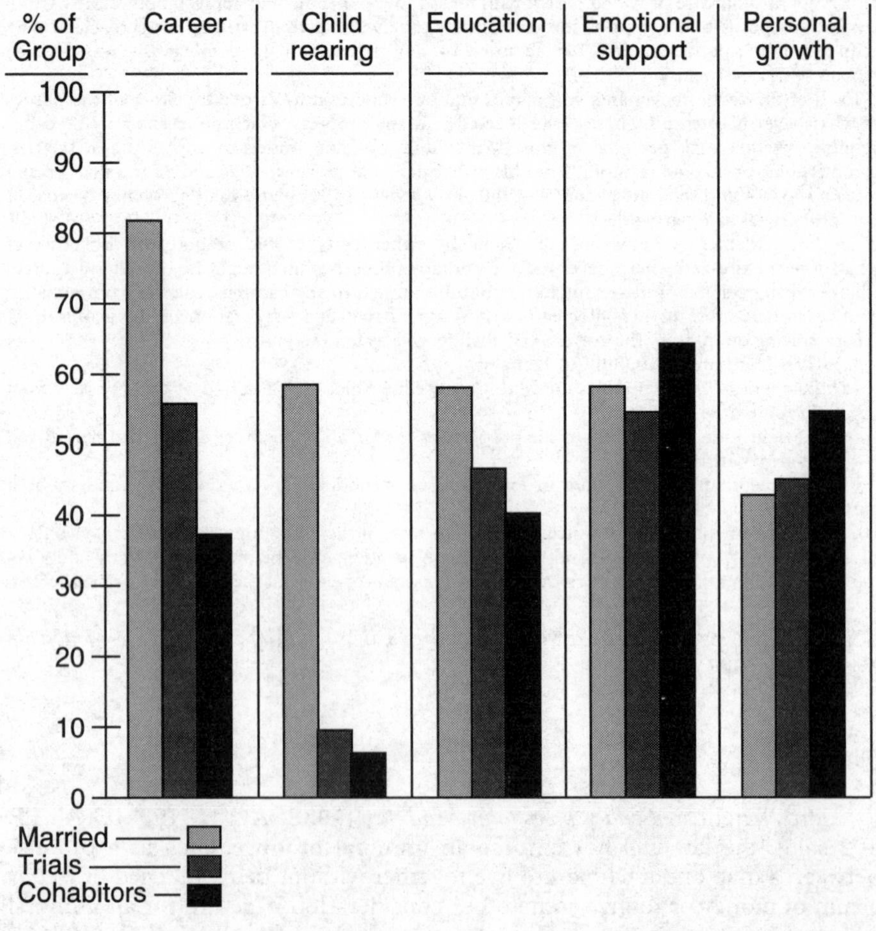

But perhaps California is not really typical of the rest of the world. For instance there is in force in San Francisco a 'Recognition of Domestic Partners Law'.

SAN FRANCISCO RECOGNITION OF DOMESTIC PARTNERS LAW
Section 121

SEC. 121.1 PURPOSE. The purpose of this ordinance is to create a way to recognize intimate committed relationships, including those of lesbians and gay men who otherwise are denied the right to identify partners with whom they share their lives. All costs of registration must be covered by fees to be established by ordinance. (Add by Proposition K, 11/6/90)

SEC. 121.2 DEFINITIONS.

(*a*) Domestic Partnership. Domestic Partners are two adults who have chosen to share one another's lives in an intimate and committed relationship of mutual caring, who live together, and who have agreed to be jointly responsible for basic living expenses incurred during the Domestic Partnership. They must sign a Declaration of Domestic Partnership, and establish the partnership under Section 121.3 of this chapter.

(*b*) 'Live Together.' 'Live together' means that two people share the same living quarters. It is not necessary that the legal right to possess the quarters be in both of their names. Two people may live together even if one or both have additional living quarters. Domestic Partners do not cease to live together if one leaves the shared quarters but intends to return.

(*c*) 'Basic Living Expenses.' 'Basic living expenses' means the cost of basic food and shelter. It also includes the expenses which are paid at least in part by a program or benefit for which the partner qualified because of the domestic partnership. The individuals need not contribute equally or jointly to the cost of these expenses as long as they agree that both are responsible for the costs.

(*d*) 'Declaration of Domestic Partnership.' A 'Declaration of Domestic Partnership' is a form provided by the County Clerk. By signing it, two people agree to be jointly responsible for basic living expenses which they incur during the domestic partnership and that this agreement can be enforced by anyone to whom those expenses are owed. They also state under penalty of perjury that they met the definition of domestic partnership when they signed the statement that neither is married, that they are not related to each other in a way which would bar marriage in California, and that neither had a different domestic partner less than six months before they signed. This last condition does not apply if the previous domestic partner died. The form will also require each partner to provide a mailing address. (Added by Proposition K, 11/6/90)

SEC. 121.3 ESTABLISHING A DOMESTIC PARTNERSHIP.

(*a*) Methods.
Two persons may establish a Domestic Partnership by either:
(1) Presenting a signed Declaration of Domestic Partnership to the County Clerk, who will file it and give the partners a certificate showing that the Declaration was filed; or
(2) Having a Declaration of Domestic Partnership notarized and giving a copy to the persons who witnessed the signing (who may or may not be the notary).

(*b*) Time Limitation. A person cannot become a member of a Domestic Partnership until at least six months after any other Domestic Partnership of which he or she was a member ended. This does not apply if the earlier domestic partnership ended because one of the members died.

(*c*) Residence Limitation. The County Clerk will only file Declaration of Partnership if:
(1) The partners have a residence in San Francisco; or
(2) At least one of the partners works in San Francisco. (Added by Proposition K, 11/6/90)

SEC. 121.4 ENDING DOMESTIC PARTNERSHIPS.

(*a*) When the Partnership Ends. A Domestic Partnership ends when:
(1) One partner sends the other a written notice that he or she has ended the partnership; or
(2) One of the partners dies; or
(3) One of the partners marries or the partners no longer live together.

(*b*) Notice the Partnership Has Ended.

(1) To Domestic Partners. When a Domestic Partnership ends, at least one of the partners must sign a notice saying that the partnership has ended. The notice must be dated and signed under penalty of perjury. If the Declaration of Domestic Partnership was filed with the County Clerk, the notice must be filed with the clerk; otherwise, the notice must be notarized. The partner who signs the notice must send a copy to the other partner.

(2) To Third Parties. When a Domestic Partnership ends, a Domestic Partner who has given a copy of a Declaration of Domestic Partnership to any third party (or, if that partner has died, the surviving member of a domestic partnership) must give that third party a notice signed under penalty of perjury stating the partnership has ended. The notice must be sent within 60 days of the end of the domestic partnership.

(3) Failure to Give Notice. Failure to give either of the notices required by this subsection will neither prevent nor delay termination of the Domestic Partnership. Anyone who suffers any loss as a result of failure to send either of these notices may sue for actual losses. (Added by Proposition K, 11/6/90)

SEC. 121.5 COUNTY CLERK'S RECORDS.

(*a*) Amendments to Declarations. A Partner may amend a Declaration of Domestic Partnership filed with County Clerk at any time to show a change in his or her mailing address.

(*b*) New Declarations of Domestic Partnership. No person who has filed a Declaration of Domestic Partnership with the County Clerk may file another Declaration of Domestic Partnership until six months after a notice the partnership has ended has been filed. However, if the Domestic Partnership ended because one of the partners died, a new Declaration may be filed anytime after the notice the partnership ended is filed.

(*c*) Maintenance of County Clerk's Records. The County Clerk will keep a record of all Declarations of Domestic Partnership, amendments to Declarations of Domestic Partnership and all notices that a partnership has ended. The records will be maintained so that amendments and notices a partnership has ended, are filed with the Declaration of Domestic Partnership to which they apply.

(*d*) Filing Fees. The Board of Supervisors will set the filing fee for Declarations of Domestic Partnership and Amendments. No fee will be charged for notice that a partnership has ended. The fees charged must cover the city's cost of administering this ordinance. (Added by Proposition K, 11/6/90)

SEC. 121.6 LEGAL EFFECT OF DECLARATION OF DOMESTIC PARTNERSHIP.

(*a*) Obligations. The obligations of domestic partners to each other are those described by the definition.

(*b*) During the Rights and Duties. If a domestic partnership ends, the partners incur no further obligations to each other. (Added by Proposition K, 11/6/90)

SEC. 121.7 CODIFICATION. Upon adoption, the Clerk of the Board shall codify this amendment into the San Francisco Administrative Code. (Added by Proposition K, 11/6/90)

Question

If a proposal similar to this law was suggested in the UK, would you (*a*) welcome it, (*b*) fight against it, or (*c*) do nothing at all on the ground that it will make little difference?

3 The treatment of marriage by the common law

It may be a coincidence, but nonetheless true that the dramatic increase in cohabitation and corresponding decline in marriage has occurred at the same time as the death throes of the pre-eminent legal position of the man in the marital context. Indeed, at common law the wife had no legal position.

Blackstone's *Commentaries on the Laws of England* (1765):

. … By marriage, the husband and wife are one person in law: that is, the very being or legal existence of the woman is suspended during the marriage, or at least is incorporated and consolidated into that of the husband: under whose wing, protection, and *cover*, she performs every thing; and is therefore called in our law-french a *feme-covert*, *foemina viro co-operta*; is said to be *covert-baron*, or under the protection and influence of her husband, her *baron*, or lord; and her condition during her marriage is called her *coverture*. Upon this principle, of a union of person in husband and wife, depend almost all the legal rights, duties and disabilities, that either of them acquire by the marriage. …

William Cobbett, *Advice to Young Men and (incidentally) to Young Women* (1837) [quoted in A. MacFarlane, *Marriage and Love in England 1300–1840* (1986)]

[She] makes a surrender, an absolute surrender, of her liberty, for the joint lives of the parties: she gives the husband the absolute right of causing her to live in what place, and in what manner and what society, he pleases; she gives him the power to take from her, and to use, for his own purposes, all her goods, unless reserved by some legal instrument; and, above all, she surrenders to him her *person*.

As we can see from the quotations above, the common law 'incorporated and consolidated' the wife's legal existence into that of her husband. In *A Century of Family Law* (1957), Ronald Graveson sketched the legal position at common law in his introductory essay, 'The Background of the Century':

The English family in the years following Waterloo differed in many ways from the family of today. The husband was in a real sense the authoritarian head of the family, with very extensive powers over both person and property of his wife and children. But his right to inflict personal chastisement on his wife had greatly declined in importance since Blackstone had described it half a century before as one which the lower orders took seriously and cherished dearly. On marriage husband and wife became for many purposes one person in law, a doctrine of common law of great antiquity. In the words of a late nineteenth-century lawyer, 'The Creator took from Adam a rib and made it Eve; the common law of England endeavoured to reverse the process, to replace the rib and to remerge the personalities.' [de Montmorency (1897)]. On marriage all the wife's personal chattels became the absolute property of the husband, while the husband could dispose of the wife's leasehold property during his life and enjoyed for his own benefit her freehold estate during her life. Subject to the institution by the Court of Chancery of what was known as the wife's separate estate in equity, the married woman, both physically and economically, was very much in the position of a chattel of her husband. But her position was not completely black. The doctrine of the legal identity of husband and wife was never applied to its extreme limit. In the words of de Montmorency, 'The English judges were too reasonable to be logical, if they could possibly help it.'

In criminal law a presumption existed that a wife who committed a felony (other than the most serious ones) had been coerced by her husband. Civilly the husband was liable for torts, such as slander, committed by his wife, while rules of evidence prevented husband and wife bearing witness against one another in all but the most exceptional circumstances. Each of these aspects of the nineteenth-century relationship of husband and wife … reflect the general position in the early nineteenth century when the relations of society were largely relations of status, that is, a legal position imposed by rules of general law by virtue of persons being in certain relationship with one another, such as husband and wife, parent and child, master and servant. The dominant character of these relationships was one of an often profitable guardianship to the person to whom the law gave control. But the idea of guardianship carried with it one of responsibility for the acts and defaults of what we may call the junior member of the relationship. Thus, while the husband obtained great economic advantages from marriage, he was liable to a great extent, both criminally and civilly, to suffer for the misdeeds of his wife, in a somewhat similar manner to that in which a master was and still is liable for the wrongful acts of his servant committed in the course of his employment.

It is clear that so far as the law is concerned, one spouse no longer automatically predominates. However, the movement towards equality and joint responsibility has by no means been a simple process:

(a) SEXUAL RELATIONS

R v Clarence
(1888) 22 QBD 23, 58 LJMC 10, 59 LT 780, 53 JP 149, 37 WR 166, 5 TLR 61, 16 Cox CC 511, High Court

Mr Clarence had been convicted of an assault upon his wife occasioning 'actual bodily harm' and of unlawfully and maliciously inflicting upon her 'grievous bodily harm.' It appears that Mr Clarence, to his knowledge, was suffering from a form of gonorrhoea yet he nevertheless had marital intercourse with his wife without informing her of this fact. He infected her, and from this infection, it was claimed that his wife suffered grievous bodily harm. He was convicted, but he appealed successfully to the Queen's Bench Division against conviction. The case was considered by all of the thirteen judges: nine quashed the conviction and four dissented.

Hawkins J: ... The wife *submits* to her husband's embraces because at the time of marriage she gave him an irrevocable right to her person. The intercourse which takes place between husband and wife after marriage is not by virtue of any special consent on her part, but is mere submission to an obligation imposed upon her by law. Consent is immaterial.

A. L. Smith J: ... At marriage the wife consents to the husband exercising the marital right. The consent then given is not confined to a husband when sound in body, for I suppose no one would assert that a husband was guilty of an offence because he exercised such right when afflicted with some complaint of which he was then ignorant. Until the consent given at marriage be revoked, how can it be said that the husband in exercising his marital right has assaulted his wife? In the present case at the time the incriminated act was committed, the consent given at marriage stood unrevoked. Then how is it an assault?

The utmost the Crown can say is that the wife would have withdrawn her consent if she had known what her husband knew, or, in other words, that the husband is guilty of a crime, viz., an assault because he did not inform the wife of what he then knew. In my judgment in this case, the consent given at marriage still existing and unrevoked, the prisoner has not assaulted his wife.

Question

Would Mrs Clarence have been guilty of the offence charged against Mr Clarence if she had been suffering from venereal disease, or the AIDS virus, undisclosed to her husband?

But the so-called 'marital immunity' to rape caused the greatest controversy. This immunity is allegedly based on the pronouncement of Sir Matthew Hale in *History of the Pleas of the Crown* (vol 1 1736, p. 629) where he said:

But the husband cannot be guilty of a rape committed by himself upon his lawful wife, for by their mutual matrimonial consent and contract the wife hath given up herself in this kind unto her husband, which she cannot retract.

In the Supreme Court of New Jersey in 1981, *State v Smith* (85 NJ 193, 426 A 2d 38 (1981)). Pashman J commented on the issue of 'implied consent' in the following way:

... this implied consent rationale, besides being offensive to our valued ideals of personal liberty, is not sound where the marriage itself is not irrevocable. If a wife can exercise a legal right to separate from her husband and eventually terminate the marriage 'contract', may she not also revoke a 'term' of that contract, namely, consent to intercourse? Just as a husband has no right to imprison his wife because of her marriage vow to him, he has no right to force sexual relations upon her against her will. If her repeated refusals are a 'breach' of the marriage 'contract', his remedy is in a matrimonial court, not in violent or forceful self-help.

However, the Criminal Law Revision Committee, which produced its Report on *Sexual Offences* (15th Report) in 1984, recommended by a majority to retain the immunity in all cases except where the parties are living apart:

Arguments for retaining the present law in relation to married couples cohabiting at the time of the act of sexual intercourse

2.64 The majority of us, who would not extend the offence of rape to married couples cohabiting at the time of the act of sexual intercourse, believe that rape cannot be considered in the abstract as merely 'sexual intercourse without consent'. The circumstances of rape may be peculiarly grave. This feature is not present in the case of a husband and wife cohabiting with each other when an act of sexual intercourse occurs without the wife's consent. They may well have had sexual intercourse regularly before the act in question and, because a sexual relationship may involve a degree of compromise, she may sometimes have agreed only with some reluctance to such intercourse. Should he go further and force her to have sexual intercourse without her consent, this may evidence a failure of the marital relationship. ...

2.65 ... At present a person convicted of rape is usually sentenced to immediate imprisonment, often for a substantial period. ... For rape between cohabiting spouses, however, immediate imprisonment might not be appropriate; where no physical injury was caused to the wife, imprisonment would be most unlikely. A category of rape that was dealt with leniently might lead to all rape cases being regarded less seriously. ...

2.66 There are also several grave practical consequences which would flow from an extension of the offence to all marriages and which might be detrimental to marriage as an institution. It is the common experience of practitioners in domestic violence cases that allegations of violence made by a wife against her husband are often withdrawn some days later or not pursued. Violence occurs in some marriages but the wives do not always wish the marital tie to be severed, whatever their initial reaction to the violence. Once, however, a wife placed the facts of an alleged rape by her husband before the police she might not be able to stop the investigation process if she wanted to. ... All of this, more likely than not, would be detrimental to the interests of any children of the family.

2.67 This would be unfortunate enough if it was the wife on her own who made the decision to go to the police in full knowledge of the consequences. This degree of foresight is likely to be rare; moreover she may not always be left to make up her own mind. She might be persuaded by others to embark upon a course of action which she might later regret and from which she might find difficulty in withdrawing.

2.68 Nor would the actual investigation of the offence be easy. The fact of sexual intercourse having occurred would prove little unless it was allied to other evidence. ...

2.69 There are also other considerations ... Some of us consider that the criminal law should keep out of marital relationships between cohabiting partners – especially the marriage bed – except where injury arises, when there are other offences which can be charged.

The Law Commission, Working Paper 116, *Rape Within Marriage* (1990) find the view of the CLRC hard to accept.

4.20 First, and most fundamentally, if the rights of the married and the non-married woman are in this respect the same, those rights should be protected in the same way, unless there are cogent reasons of policy for taking a different course.

4.21 Second, it is by no means necessarily the case that non-consensual intercourse between spouses has less serious consequences for the woman, or is physically less damaging or disturbing for her, than in the case of non-consensual intercourse with a stranger. Depending on the circumstances the wife whose husband thrusts intercourse upon her may suffer pain from the act of intercourse itself; or the fear or the actuality of venereal or other disease; or the fear or the actuality of an unwanted pregnancy if because of the suddenness of the attack she has taken no contraceptive precautions or such precautions are unacceptable or impossible for medical reasons; and in the event of actual pregnancy a termination may be unavailable or morally offensive to her. All of these hazards may apply equally in the case of marital as of non-marital rape.

4.22 Third, we think that there is a danger that the CLRC underestimated the emotional and psychological harm that a wife may suffer by being subjected by her husband to intercourse against her will, even though on previous occasions she has willingly participated in the same act with the same partner. In *Kowalski*[1] the Court of Appeal approved the trial judge's ruling, in respect of an act of fellatio that the husband compelled the wife to perform on him, that she was entitled to say –

> 'I agree I have done that with you before. I agree I did not find it indecent when we did it as an act of love, but I now find it indecent; I find it repell[e]nt; I find it abhorrent.'

It is well recognised that unwanted sexual intercourse can be a particularly repellent and abhorrent experience for a woman: that is one main justification for the existence of the offence of rape. We see no reason why a wife cannot say that she feels that abhorrence for such intercourse with her husband, whether or not she has willingly participated on previous occasions.

4.23 Fourth, for a man to oblige his wife to have intercourse without her consent may be equally, or even more, 'grave' or serious as when that conduct takes place between non-spouses. In the case of the husband, he abuses not merely an act to which, as a matter of abstract principle, society attaches values, but the act that has been or should have been his means of expressing his love for his wife. There seems every reason to think that that abuse can be quite as serious on the part of the husband, and quite as traumatic for the wife, as is rape by a stranger or casual acquaintance.

4.24 Fifth, in many cases where the husband forces intercourse on his wife they will be living in the same household, or at least she will be in some sort of dependent relationship with him. It is likely to be harder, rather than easier, for such a woman to avoid her husband's insistence on intercourse, since to do so she may for instance have to leave the matrimonial home. That is a further respect in which non-consensual intercourse by a husband may be a particular abuse.

The House of Lords eventually came to the rescue in *R v R* [1992] 1 AC 599. In this case, the appellant married his wife in 1984 and they had one son born in 1985. The wife left the matrimonial home in 1989 with their son as a result of matrimonial difficulties and went to her own parents' house. Three weeks later, the husband forced his way into his parents-in-law's house and attempted to have sexual intercourse with his wife against her will.

The husband pleaded guilty to attempted rape following the ruling by the trial judge that a man may rape his wife when the consent to intercourse has been revoked. His conviction was upheld by the Court of Appeal but he was granted leave to appeal to the House of Lords.

Lord Keith of Kinkel [After reviewing earlier case law, *R v Clarke* [1949] 2 All ER 448, *R v Miller* [1954] 2 QB 282, *R v O'Brien (Edward)* [1974] 3 All ER 663, *R v Steele* (1976) 65 Cr App R 22, *R v Roberts* [1986] Crim LR 188, and *R v Sharples* [1990] Crim LR 198, he concluded]: The foregoing represent all the decisions in the field prior to the ruling by Owen J. in the present case. In all of them lip service, at least, was paid to Hale's proposition. Since then there have been three further decisions by single judges. The first of them is *R v C (Rape: Marital Exemption)* [1991] 1 All ER 755. There were nine counts in an indictment against a husband and a co-defendant charging various offences of a sexual nature against an estranged wife. One of these was of rape as a principal. Simon Brown J. followed the decision in *S v HM Advocate* 1989 SLT 469 and held that the whole concept of a marital exemption in rape was misconceived. He said, at p. 758:

---

1. [1988] 1 FLR 447, [1988] Fam Law 259.

'Were it not for the deeply unsatisfactory consequences of reaching any other conclusion on the point, I would shrink, if sadly, from adopting this radical view of the true position in law. But adopt it I do. Logically, I regard it as the only defensible stance, certainly now as the law has developed and arrived in the late 20th century. In my judgment, the position in law today is, as already declared in Scotland, that there is no marital exemption to the law of rape. That is the ruling I give. Count seven accordingly remains and will be left to the jury without any specific direction founded on the concept of marital exemption.'

A different view was taken in the other two cases, by reason principally of the terms in which rape is defined in section 1(1) of the Sexual Offences (Amendment) Act 1976, viz:

'For the purposes of section 1 of the Sexual Offences Act 1956 (which relates to rape) a man commits rape if – (a) he has unlawful sexual intercourse with a woman who at the time of the intercourse does not consent to it; and (b) at that time he knows that she does not consent to the intercourse or he is reckless as to whether she consents to it: ...'

In *R v J. (Rape: Marital Exemption)* [1991] 1 All ER 759 a husband was charged with having raped his wife, from whom he was living apart at the time. Rougier J. ruled that the charge was bad, holding that the effect of section 1(1)(*a*) of the Act of 1976 was that the marital exemption embodied in Hale's proposition was preserved, subject to those exceptions established by cases decided before the Act was passed. He took the view that the word 'unlawful' in the subsection meant 'illicit,' i.e. outside marriage, that being the meaning which in *R v Chapman* [1959] 1 QB 100 it had been held to bear in section 19 of the Sexual Offences Act 1956. Then in *R v S* (15 January 1991, unreported), Swinton-Thomas J. followed Rougier J. in holding that section 1(1) of the Act of 1976 preserved the marital exemption subject to the established common law exceptions. Differing, however, from Rougier J., he took the view that it remained open to judges to define further exceptions. In the case before him the wife had obtained a family protection order in similar terms to that in *R v Sharples* [1990] Crim LR 198. Differing from Judge Fawcus in that case, Swinton-Thomas J. held that the existence of the family protection order created an exception to the marital exemption. It is noteworthy that both Rougier J. and Swinton-Thomas J. expressed themselves as being regretful that section 1(1) of the Act of 1976 precluded them from taking the same line as Simon Brown J. in *R v C (Rape: Marital Exemption)* [1991] 1 All ER 755.

The position then is that that part of Hale's proposition which asserts that a wife cannot retract the consent to sexual intercourse which she gives on marriage has been departed from in a series of decided cases. On grounds of principle there is no good reason why the whole proposition should not be held inapplicable in modern times. The only question is whether section 1(1) of the Act of 1976 presents an insuperable obstacle to that sensible course. The argument is that 'unlawful' in the subsection means outside the bond of marriage. That is not the most natural meaning of the word, which normally describes something which is contrary to some law or enactment or is done without lawful justification or excuse. Certainly in modern times sexual intercourse outside marriage would not ordinarily be described as unlawful. If the subsection proceeds on the basis that a woman on marriage gives a general consent to sexual intercourse, there can never be any question of intercourse with her by her husband being without her consent. There would thus be no point in enacting that only intercourse without consent outside marriage is to constitute rape. ...

I am therefore of the opinion that section 1(1) of the Act of 1976 presents no obstacle to this House declaring that in modern times the supposed marital exception in rape forms no part of the law of England. The Court of Appeal (Criminal Division) took a similar view. Towards the end of the judgment of that court Lord Lane C.J. said, at p. 1074:

'The remaining and no less difficult question is whether, despite that view, this is an area where the court should step aside to leave the matter to the Parliamentary process. This is not the creation of a new offence, it is the removal of a common law fiction which has become anachronistic and offensive and we consider that it is our duty having reached that conclusion to act upon it.'

I respectfully agree.

My Lords, for these reasons I would dismiss this appeal, and answer the certified question in the affirmative.

An attempt to take matters further to Europe spectacularly failed (*SW v UK*; *CR v UK* [1996] 1 FLR 434, [1996] Fam Law 275, ECtHR).

In the European Court of Human Rights, the issue was made crystal clear:

... the abandonment of the unacceptable idea of a husband being immune against prosecution for rape of his wife was in conformity not only with a civilised concept of marriage but also, and above all, with the fundamental objectives of the Convention, the very essence of which is respect for human dignity and human freedom.

Questions

(i) What, if anything, do you think is meant by the phrase 'civilised concept of marriage'?
(ii) Section 142 of the Criminal Justice and Public Order Act (1994) amends s. 1 of the Sexual Offences Act 1956 in the following way:

1. Rape of woman or man
(1) It is an offence for a man to rape a woman or another man.
(2) A man commits rape if –
(*a*) he has sexual intercourse with a person (whether vaginal or anal) who at the time of the intercourse does not consent to it; and
(*b*) at the time he knows that the person does not consent to the intercourse or is reckless as to whether that person consents to it.
(3) A man also commits rape if he induces a married woman to have sexual intercourse with him by impersonating her husband.
(4) Subsection (2) applies for the purpose of any enactment.

Now that the House of Lords has spoken, why was there need for legislation?
(iii) Do you believe there is any strength in the argument advanced by some that if a category of rape ends up being dealt with leniently this might lead to all rape cases being regarded less seriously?

(b) HAVING A BABY

There is one particular matter on which the law grants the casting vote to the woman, and this is the decision whether to abort a foetus or to give birth to the child already in the womb. So far as a possible abortion is concerned, the law clearly excludes the man from any right to demand or to refuse such an operation for his partner.

Paton v British Pregnancy Advisory Service Trustees
[1979] QB 276, [1978] 2 All ER 987, [1978] 3 WLR 687, 122 Sol Jo 744, High Court, Queen's Bench Division

The plaintiff, William Paton, was the husband of the second defendant, Joan Mary Paton. On 8 May 1978, the wife's general practitioner confirmed that she was pregnant. The wife thereafter applied for and obtained the necessary medical certificate entitling her to an abortion within the terms of the Abortion Act 1967. On 16 May 1978, the wife left the matrimonial home.

On 17 May 1978, the husband applied for an injunction to restrain the first defendants, the trustees of the British Pregnancy Advisory Service, and the wife from causing or permitting an abortion to be carried out on the wife. Sir George Baker P adjourned the case for one week to 24 May 1978, to enable all the parties to be represented. Also on 17 May the wife filed her petition for divorce.

The husband originally put his case on the basis that the wife had no proper legal grounds for seeking the termination of her pregnancy and that she was being spiteful, vindictive and utterly unreasonable in so doing. At the resumed hearing on 24 May it was accepted by all the parties that the provisions of the Abortion Act 1967 had been correctly complied with. The husband contended that he had the right to have a say in the destiny of the child he had conceived.

Sir George Baker P: By a specially endorsed writ the plaintiff, who is the husband of the second defendant, seeks an injunction in effect to restrain the first defendants, a charitable organisation, and particularly his wife, the second defendant, from causing or permitting an abortion to be carried out upon his wife without his consent.

Such action, of course, arouses great emotions, and vigorous opposing views as was recently pointed out in 1972 in the Supreme Court of the United States by Blackmun J in *Roe v Wade* 93 S Ct 705 (1973), 708–709. In the discussion of human affairs and especially of abortion, controversy can rage over the moral rights, duties, interests, standards and religious views of the parties. Moral values are in issue. I am, in fact, concerned with none of these matters. I am concerned, and concerned only, with the law of England as it applies to this claim. My task is to apply the law free of emotion or predilection.

Nobody suggests that there has ever been such a claim litigated before the courts in this country. Indeed, the only case of which I have ever heard was in Ontario. It was unreported because the husband's claim for an injunction was never tried.

In considering the law the first and basic principle is that there must be a legal right enforceable in law or in equity before the applicant can obtain an injunction from the court to restrain an infringement of that right. That has long been the law.

The law is that the court cannot and would not seek to enforce or restrain by injunction matrimonial obligations, if they be obligations, such as sexual intercourse or contraception (a non-molestation injunction given during the pendency of divorce proceedings could, of course, cover attempted intercourse). No court would ever grant an injunction to stop sterilisation or vasectomy. Personal family relationships in marriage cannot be enforced by the order of a court. An injunction in such circumstances was described by Judge Mager in *Jones v Smith* 278 So 2d 339 (1973) in the District Court of Appeal of Florida as 'ludicrous'.

I ask the question, 'If an injunction were ordered, what could be the remedy?' and I do not think I need say any more than that no judge could even consider sending a husband or wife to prison for breaking such an order. That, of itself, seems to me to cover the application here; this husband cannot by law stop his wife by injunction from having what is now accepted to be a lawful abortion within the terms of the Abortion Act 1967. ...

The Abortion Act 1967 gives no right to a father to be consulted in respect of a termination of a pregnancy. True, it gives no right to the mother either, but obviously the mother is going to be right at the heart of the matter consulting with the doctors if they are to arrive at a decision in good faith, unless, of course, she is mentally incapacitated or physically incapacitated (unable to make any decision or give any help) as, for example, in consequence of an accident. The husband, therefore, in my view, has no legal right enforceable in law or in equity to stop his wife having this abortion or to stop the doctors from carrying out the abortion.

In *C v S* [1988] QB 135, [1987] 1 All ER 1230 a similar case was heard in connection with the application by the father to prevent his former girlfriend from having an abortion. The argument primarily was centred around the meaning of 'capable of being born alive' as defined in the Infant Life (Preservation) Act 1929, and whether the termination of the girl's pregnancy was a potential criminal abortion.[2]

2. See now *Rance v Mid-Downs Health Authority* [1991] 1 QB 587, [1991] 1 All ER 801.

Heilbron J agreed with Sir George Baker P in *Paton v BPAST* that the Abortion Act 1967 had not given the father the right to be consulted in respect of a termination of pregnancy. The point was not considered by the Court of Appeal.

Missouri in the United States once had a spousal consent provision:

Section 3. No abortion shall be performed prior to the end of the first twelve weeks of pregnancy except:

(1) By a duly licensed, consenting physician in the exercise of his best clinical medical judgment;

(2) After the woman, prior to submitting to the abortion, certifies in writing her consent to the abortion and that her consent is informed and freely given and is not the result of coercion;

(3) With the written consent of the woman's spouse, unless the abortion is certified by a licensed physician to be necessary in order to preserve the life of the mother;

(4) With the written consent of one parent or person in loco parentis of the woman if the woman is unmarried and under the age of eighteen years, unless the abortion is certified by a licensed physician as necessary in order to preserve the life of the mother.

Planned Parenthood of Missouri v Danforth
428 US 52, 49 L Ed 2d 788, 96 S Ct 2831 (1976), Supreme Court

The plaintiffs, a non-profit-making organisation which maintains a facility in Missouri for the performance of abortions, brought proceedings to obtain declaratory relief on the grounds, amongst others, that certain provisions of the Act deprived the organisation and its doctors and their patients of various constitutional rights; the right to privacy in the physician-patient relationship, the female patients' right to determine whether to bear children and other constitutional rights.

The Supreme Court concluded that both s. 3(3) and 3(4) were unconstitutional: we report here their *opinion* relating to s. 3(3) (for a discussion of parental control over their children, see Chapter 10):

The appellees defend § 3(3) on the ground that it was enacted in the light of the General Assembly's 'perception of marriage as an institution,' Brief for Appellee Danforth 34, and that any major change in family status is a decision to be made jointly by the marriage partners. Reference is made to an abortion's possible effect on the woman's childbearing potential. It is said that marriage always has entailed some legislatively imposed limitations: reference is made to adultery and bigamy as criminal offences; to Missouri's general requirement, Mo Rev Stat § 453.030.3 (1969), that for an adoption of a child born in wedlock the consent of both parents is necessary; to similar joint-consent requirements imposed by a number of States with respect to artificial insemination and the legitimacy of children so conceived; to the laws of two States requiring spousal consent for voluntary sterilization; and to the long-established requirement of spousal consent for the effective disposition of an interest in real property. It is argued that '[r]ecognizing that the consent of both parties is generally necessary ... to begin a family, the legislature has determined that a change in the family structure set in motion by mutual consent should be terminated only by mutual consent,' Brief for Appellee Danforth 38, and that what the legislature did was to exercise its inherent policymaking power 'for what was believed to be in the best interests of all the people of Missouri.' Id., at 40.

The appellants, on the other hand, contend that § 3(3) obviously is designed to afford the husband the right unilaterally to prevent or veto an abortion, whether or not he is the father of the fetus, and that this not only violates *Roe v Wade* 410 US 113, 93 S Ct 705 (1973) but is also in conflict with other decided cases. See, e.g. *Poe v Gerstein* 517 F 2d 787, 794–796 (CA5 1975), appeal docketed, No. 75–713; *Wolfe v Schroering* 388 F Supp, at 636–637; *Doe v Rampton* 366 F Supp 189, 193 (Utah 1973). They also refer to the situation where the husband's consent cannot be obtained because he cannot be located. And they assert that § 3(3) is vague and overbroad.

In *Roe [v Wade]* we specifically reserved decision on the question whether a requirement for consent by the father of the fetus, by the spouse, or by the parents, or a parent, of an unmarried minor, may be constitutionally imposed, 410 US, at 165 n 67, 35 L Ed 2d 147, 93 S Ct 705. We now hold that the State may not constitutionally require the consent of the spouse, as is specified under § 3(3) of the Missouri Act, as a condition for abortion during the first 12 weeks of pregnancy. We thus agree with the dissenting judge in the present case, and with the courts whose decisions are cited above, that the State cannot 'delegate to a spouse a veto power which the state itself is absolutely and totally prohibited from exercising during the first trimester of pregnancy.' 392 F Supp, at 1375. Clearly, since the State cannot regulate or proscribe abortion during the first stage, when the physician and his patient make that decision, the State cannot delegate authority to any particular person, even the spouse, to prevent abortion during that same period.

We are not unaware of the deep and proper concern and interest that a devoted and protective husband has in his wife's pregnancy and in the growth and development of the fetus she is carrying. Neither has this Court failed to appreciate the importance of the marital relationship in our society. See, e.g., *Griswold v Connecticut* 381 US 479, 486, 14 L Ed 2d 510, 85 S Ct 1678 (1965); *Maynard v Hill* 125 US 190, 211, 31 L Ed 654, 8 S Ct 723 (1888). Moreover, we recognize that the decision whether to undergo or to forgo an abortion may have profound effects on the future of any marriage, effects that are both physical and mental, and possibly deleterious. Notwithstanding these factors, we cannot hold that the State has the constitutional authority to give the spouse unilaterally the ability to prohibit the wife from terminating her pregnancy, when the State itself lacks that right. See *Eisenstadt v Baird* 405 US 438, 453, 31 L Ed 2d 349, 92 S Ct 1029 (1972).

It seems manifest that, ideally, the decision to terminate a pregnancy should be one concurred in by both the wife and her husband. No marriage may be viewed as harmonious or successful if the marriage partners are fundamentally divided on so important and vital an issue. But it is difficult to believe that the goal of fostering mutuality and trust in a marriage, and of strengthening the marital relationship and the marriage institution, will be achieved by giving the husband a veto power exercisable for any reason whatsoever or for no reason at all. Even if the State had the ability to delegate to the husband a power it itself could not exercise, it is not at all likely that such action would further, as the District Court majority phrased it, the 'interest of the state in protecting the mutuality of decisions vital to the marriage relationship.' 392 F Supp, at 1370.

We recognize, of course, that when a woman, with the approval of her physician but without the approval of her husband, decides to terminate her pregnancy, it could be said that she is acting unilaterally. The obvious fact is that when the wife and the husband disagree on this decision, the view of only one of the two marriage partners can prevail. Inasmuch as it is the woman who physically bears the child and who is the more directly and immediately affected by the pregnancy, as between the two, the balance weighs in her favor. Cf. *Roe v Wade* 410 US, at 153, 35 L Ed 2d 147, 93 S Ct 705.

We conclude that § 3(3) of the Missouri Act is ... unconstitutional.

Questions

(i) Are these cases examples of the judiciary: (*a*) being reluctant to interfere in domestic relations; (*b*) championing the rights of women; or (*c*) suppressing the rights of men?

(ii) If you think these cases suppress the rights of men, do you consider that a man should be able to compel his partner to have an abortion, or be relieved from maintenance if she does not have the abortion and goes ahead with the birth? Would your answer be different depending on whether the man and woman were married to each other?

(iii) If a father cannot obtain an injunction what else can he do?

(iv) Can you think of any decisions taken by husband and wife in their marriage or by partners in their relationship which the courts would actually force the parties to make jointly, by way of injunction if need be?

Jones v Smith
278 So 2d 339 (1973), District Court of Appeal of Florida

The case turned upon the constitutional provision relating to the right of privacy. The court decided that the decision to terminate a pregnancy is one that is purely personal to the mother and a matter between her and the attending physician. The court held further that 'any unreasonable governmental interference must yield to the mother's right of privacy.' The facts of the case are set out in the judgment.

Mager J: ... This is an appeal from an order denying a claim for injunctive relief seeking to restrain the 'obtaining or aiding in the obtaining of an abortion'. Although pseudonyms are used the parties are real persons.

The primary question presented is whether a potential putative father has the right to restrain the natural mother from terminating a pregnancy resulting from their cohabitation. The appellant, who acknowledges that he is the father of the unborn child, is twenty-seven years old, was formerly married and is the father of a six-year-old daughter by such previous marriage. The appellee-mother is nineteen years old and unmarried and had been dating the appellant for approximately six months during which time the parties were frequently intimate. The appellant in seeking injunctive relief has indicated his desire to marry the appellee and to assume all the obligations financial and otherwise for the care and support of the unborn child; that, notwithstanding such affirmations, the appellee-mother, who has expressed her desire not to marry the appellant, has sought to terminate the pregnancy.

Although the appellant alleged in his complaint below 'that the mother's mental and physical health will not be endangered by bringing the child to term in allowing its natural birth' there is no allegation and proof that the proposed termination of pregnancy does not comply with Florida's newly enacted 'Termination of Pregnancy' law (Chapter 72–196, Laws of Florida, numbered as Section 458.22, Florida Statutes, F.S.A.). It is interesting to note a suggestion by the appellant that his own health would be affected if the pregnancy is terminated; testimony from a psychiatrist examining the appellant suggested 'the possibility of him suffering depressive symptoms and depressive reactions in the future'.

The main thrust of the appellant's position is that as a potential putative father he has the 'right' to participate in the decision to terminate the pregnancy.

Because of the time factors involved and in particular the fact that the mother is reaching the end of the first trimester of pregnancy this court has granted an emergency hearing and has expedited its review.

The appellant contends that whatever right of privacy that the mother might have enjoyed, such right was 'waived' by virtue of her consent to and participation in the sex act. This argument is somewhat tenuous. The right of privacy of the mother with respect to a termination of pregnancy as delineated by the decisions of the United States Supreme Court is a right separate and apart from any act of conception. The determination of whether to carry the child the full term is not 'controlled' or 'waived' by virtue of the act of conception no more so than the fact that were the child conceived in the State of Florida would give the State the right to interfere with the termination of pregnancy during the first trimester. Moreover, whatever purported 'waiver' might have occurred as a result of the conception, the interest or 'right' of the natural father must remain subservient to 'the life or health of the female' (see F.S. Section 458.22(2)(*a*), F.S.A.).

Questions

(i) In the course of his judgment, Judge Mager asked the following question: 'Could a potential putative father (or for that matter a husband) seek an injunction to restrain the woman from using contraceptives or compel the woman to bear children?' What would be your answer to this question? Do you think there should be a different answer depending on whether the father is or is not married to the mother? (Judge Mager's answer is referred to in the

judgment of Baker P in *Paton v British Pregnancy Advisory Service Trustees* [1979] QB 276, [1978] 2 All ER 987 – see p. 57, above.)
(ii) If English law introduced a paternal veto, would it be contrary to article 8 of the European Convention of Human Rights (set out on p. 714, below)?

Krause (1990) reports the following story:

New York Times, Nov. 14, 1968, p. 36, col. 1. Hempstead, L.I., Nov. 13 (AP) – A 24-year-old mother of three children, who was injured in an automobile crash, died today after her husband had refused on religious grounds to allow doctors to give her a blood transfusion.

The police said the victim, Betty Jackson, was pinned in her car when it struck a utility pole at Wellsley Street and Rumsem Avenue near her home. She was admitted to Hempstead General Hospital at about 11:30 A.M.

Doctors said examination showed Mrs. Jackson was suffering from multiple injuries and bleeding internally. They sought permission from her husband, Clemons Jackson, to administer a transfusion.

Mr. Jackson, a follower of Jehovah's Witnesses, refused. He remained adamant, despite the pleading of several doctors, and at 4:30 P.M. the hospital administrator appealed to State Supreme Court Judge William Sullivan.

'If I allow blood to be given into her and if she lived, she wouldn't be considered my wife,' the Nassau County police said Mr. Jackson had told the doctors.

Judge Sullivan refused to order the transfusion. Mrs. Jackson died at 6:30 P.M. Her three children, who were with her when the car struck the utility pole, were also in the hospital and reported in fair condition.

Questions

(i) What do you think an English judge would do in this situation? See *Re S (a minor) (medical treatment)* [1993] 1 FLR 376; *Re F* [1990] 2 AC 1; *Re T (adult: refusal of treatment)* [1993] Fam 95, [1992] 4 All ER 649, CA.
(ii) If the doctor failed to obtain the consent of a judge, would he be guilty of any crime?
(iii) What difference would it make that Mrs Jackson was or was not herself a Jehovah's Witness?

(c) TORT

Under the common law, as the husband and wife became 'one person in law' neither could sue the other and the wife could not be sued directly by a third party; all proceedings were brought against her husband. The common law position together with the amendments made to it by the legislation of the nineteenth century is summarised in the following extracts from C.A. Morrison's essay on Tort, in *A Century of Family Law* (1957):

At common law
(1) The wife still retained sufficient separate identity to be able to commit a tort or to have torts inflicted upon her. She might sue or be sued for these, but she had no procedural existence alone and her husband had to be joined with her in the action, and might thereupon become liable.
(2) The husband thus found himself under a liability for torts committed by his wife whether before or during marriage, but it was a joint liability with her. His liability might be justified on the legal ground that she had no procedural personality without him and he had to be joined as co-defendant; on the moral ground that he had her property, and that if his wife brought an action, he would acquire any damages she obtained.
(3) Husband and wife could not sue each other in tort.

As a result of statutory changes in the nineteenth century

In the second half of the nineteenth century there came a period of twelve years of reform by a series of Married Women's Property Acts which greatly altered the picture. The effects of the French and the Industrial Revolutions and perhaps the example of the Queen herself all aided in this feverish period of reform, which in little more than a decade changed the law of centuries. The 1870 [Married Women's Property] Act, designed primarily to protect the earnings of the married woman, did not affect the position in tort. The 1874 Act affected the position only of torts committed by the wife before marriage and reduced the husband's liability for these so that he was liable only to the extent of certain specified assets which he had acquired from or through his wife on marriage.

Judgment was to be a joint one to the extent to which the husband was liable and a separate one against the wife for the residue, if any. The main reform however came with the Act of 1882, which affected torts committed before or during marriage. This Act deprived the husband of all the interest he acquired by marriage in his wife's property and earnings, then, having recognised the married woman's capacity to acquire and dispose of property, it went on to regularise and protect that new position by altering the law in tort and contract. It was necessary that the separate property now recognised by statute should be protected against her husband and against outsiders. This meant, first, that against outsiders she needed the right to sue in her own name, for it would appear that she could not have compelled her husband to join with her to protect her property. This was achieved by dispensing with the need to join her husband in actions by or against her. It meant, secondly, that her property might need protection against even her husband. The Act recognised this by permitting an exception to the rule that husband and wife could not sue each other in tort. By section 12 the wife was given civil and criminal rights of action against her husband for the protection and security of her property. To these two main reforms was added a further which made the married woman herself liable to the extent of her separate property for her torts, whether committed before or during marriage, and liable to be sued alone for these torts. But she could be made bankrupt to the extent of her separate property only if she were carrying on a trade separately from her husband.

The doctrine of unity still prevailed into the twentieth century. There were criticisms of this state of the law as early as 1930. In *Gottliffe v Edelston* [1930] 2 KB 378 McCardie J said: '... wives however wealthy of purse or independent of character, possess powers and privileges which are wholly denied to husbands. Husbands are placed under burdens from which wives are free. ... Upon the husband there has fallen one injustice after another.'

Question

Would you criticise the common law in this way?

In 1935, five years after this judgment was delivered, the Law Reform (Married Women and Tortfeasors) Act abolished the rule which prevented wives from being sued by third parties. By s. 1, a married woman may sue or be sued in all respects as if she were a feme sole and is made subject to the law relating to bankruptcy and to the enforcement of judgments and orders. Section 3 provides that a husband shall not, by reason only of his being her husband, be liable in respect of any tort committed by his wife whether before or during the marriage. Finally, the Law Reform (Husband and Wife) Act 1962 abolished the common law prohibition preventing one party to the marriage from suing the other.

The common law fiction that husband and wife are in law one person was described by Oliver J in *Midland Bank v Green (No 3)* [1979] Ch 496, [1979] 2 All ER 193; in the following way: 'It is a useful instrument for the furtherance of the policy of the law to protect the institution of marriage, but as an exposition in itself of the living law it is as real as the skeleton of the brontosaurus in a museum of natural history.' Oliver J was concerned in that case with the question of whether a husband and wife who agree with one another to injure a third person, and by their concerted action do injure him, are liable in damages for the tort of conspiracy. Oliver J's affirmative response to that question was the subject of an appeal.

Midland Bank Trust Co Ltd v Green (No 3)
[1982] Ch 529, [1981] 3 All ER 744, [1982] 2 WLR 1, 125 Sol Jo 554, Court of Appeal

Lord Denning MR: The point of principle raised by Mr Munby for the appellant is this. He says that the doctrine of unity between husband and wife is an established doctrine in English law. So well established that the doctrine and its ramifications are still part of our law today: and must still be applied by the courts except in so far as it has been altered by statute. One of the ramifications of the doctrine (that husband and wife are one) is that they cannot be guilty as conspirators together. So they cannot be made liable in damages for a conspiracy.

The authorities cited by Mr Munby show clearly enough that mediaeval lawyers held that husband and wife were one person in law: and that the husband was that one. It was a fiction then. It is a fiction now. It has been eroded by the judges who have created exception after exception to it. It has been cut down by statute after statute until little of it remains. It has been so much eroded and cut down in law, it has so long ceased to be true in fact, that I would reject Mr Munby's principle.

I would put it in this way. Nowadays, both in law and in fact, husband and wife are two persons, not one. They are partners – equal partners – in a joint enterprise, the enterprise of maintaining a home and bringing up children. Outside that joint enterprise they live their own lives and go their own ways – always, we hope, in consultation one with the other, in complete loyalty one with the other, each maintaining and deserving the trust and confidence of the other. They can and do own property jointly or severally or jointly and severally, with all the consequences that ownership entails. They can and do enter into contracts with others jointly or severally or jointly and severally, and can be made liable for breaches just as any other contractors can be. They can and do commit crimes jointly or severally and can be punished severally for them. They can and do commit wrongs jointly or severally and can be made liable jointly or severally just as any other wrong-doers. The severance in all respects is so complete that I would say that the doctrine of unity and its ramifications should be discarded altogether, except in so far as it is retained by judicial decision or by Act of Parliament.

I turn now to our particular case – conspiracy. So far as criminal conspiracy is concerned, a husband and wife cannot be found guilty of conspiring with one another. That is now statutory in section 2(2)(*a*) of the Criminal Law Act 1977. But they can be found guilty if the two of them jointly conspire with a third person.

Mr Munby says that the tort of conspiracy should be treated in the same way as the crime of conspiracy. He says that husband and wife cannot be made liable in tort for conspiracy with one another. But they can, he admits, be made liable if the two of them jointly conspire with a third person. For instance, he agrees that if the conspiracy charged in this case was between Walter (the husband) and Evelyne (the wife) and their other son Derek, and it was found that all three conspired together, all could be made liable in damages. But as the only conspiracy charged is against Walter and Evelyne alone, they cannot be made liable at all. That seems to me a most illogical and unreasonable state of the law, not to be accepted unless covered by authority, and there is none to cover it, no decision and really no statement of authority as far as I can discover. ...

I see no good reason for applying the doctrine of unity to the modern tort of conspiracy. It is clear that in a like case father and son could be made liable in conspiracy; so mother and daughter; so man and mistress. Why then should not husband and wife be made liable? If the allegations against Walter and Evelyne are correct, they did a grievous wrong to Geoffrey. Together with their son Derek they deprived Geoffrey of his birth right, just as Jacob deprived Esau. Both are now dead, but their estates can be made liable in conspiracy, or at any rate Walter's estate which is the only one now before the court. It seems to me that Mrs Kemp [Walter's executrix] would be liable in full if the conspiracy were established which is alleged.

And if she were held liable for the conspiracy and the damages which flow from it after giving any credit from the solicitors' action she would be liable for it, and then her only recourse would be against the lawyers who failed on her behalf to plead plene administravit, if she could prove that they were in any way at fault.

For these reasons I agree with the decision of Oliver J and would dismiss the appeals.

(d) EVIDENCE

At common law, as a general rule, a party's spouse was incompetent as a witness both for or against him. It is also suggested that there was a prohibition on disclosure of marital communications by any witness.

The Evidence Amendment Act 1853 allowed a husband or a wife of a party in a civil case to be a permissible witness for that party and also to give evidence on the other side. A competent witness is normally obliged to give evidence at the instance of either party; thus in this sense the husband or the wife are compellable witnesses in civil actions. Section 3 of that Act gave a privilege in civil proceedings to the spouse to whom a statement was made not to be compelled to disclose this statement. The privilege was abolished by the Civil Evidence Act 1968, s. 16(3) although s. 14(1)(*b*) confers on the witness in a civil trial 'a right to refuse to answer any question or produce any document or thing if to do so would tend to expose the husband or the wife of that person to proceedings for any ... criminal offence or for the recovery of ... a penalty'.

So far as criminal trials are concerned, s. 80 of the Police and Criminal Evidence Act 1984 has now swept away the previous unsatisfactory position.

(1) In any proceedings the wife or husband of the accused shall be competent to give evidence –
(*a*) subject to subsection (4) below, for the prosecution; and
(*b*) on behalf of the accused or any person jointly charged with the accused.

(2) In any proceedings the wife or husband of the accused shall, subject to subsection (4) below, be compellable to give evidence on behalf of the accused.

(3) In any proceedings the wife or husband of the accused shall, subject to subsection (4) below, be compellable to give evidence for the prosecution or on behalf of any person jointly charged with the accused if and only if –
(*a*) the offence charged involves an assault on, or injury or a threat of injury to, the wife or husband of the accused or a person who was at the material time under the age of sixteen; or
(*b*) the offence charged is a sexual offence alleged to have been committed in respect of a person who was at the material time under that age; or
(*c*) the offence charged consists of attempting or conspiring to commit, or of aiding, abetting, counselling, procuring or inciting the commission of, an offence falling within paragraph (*a*) or (*b*) above.

(4) Where an information or indictment charges a husband and his wife jointly with an offence neither spouse shall at the trial of the information or indictment be competent or compellable by virtue of subsection (1)(*a*), (2) or (3) above to give evidence in respect of that offence unless that spouse is not, or is no longer, liable to be convicted of that offence at the trial as a result of pleading guilty or for any other reason.

The policy which lay behind the Act is identified in the following extract from the Criminal Law Revision Committee's 11th Report (1972):

147. How far the wife of the accused should be competent and compellable for the prosecution, for the accused and for a co-accused is in these days essentially a question of balancing the

desirability that all available evidence which might conduce to the right verdict should be before the court against (i) the objection on social grounds to disturbing marital harmony more than is absolutely necessary and (ii) what many regard as the harshness of compelling a wife to give evidence against her husband. Older objections, even to competence, based on the theoretical unity of the spouses or on the interest of the accused's wife in the outcome of the proceedings, and in particular on the likelihood that his wife will be biased in favour of the accused, can have no place in the decisions as to the extent of competence and compellability nowadays. But the question of the right balance between the considerations of policy mentioned is one on which different opinions are inevitably – and sometimes strongly – held. The arguments relate mostly to compellability for the prosecution but, as will be seen, not entirely so. The argument for more compellability for the prosecution is the straightforward one that, if it is left to the wife to choose whether to give evidence against her husband, the result may be that a dangerous criminal will go free. The argument to the contrary is that, if the wife is not willing to give the evidence, the state should not expose her to the pitiful clash between the duty to aid the prosecution by giving evidence, however unwillingly, and the natural duty to protect her husband whatever the circumstances. It has been argued strongly in support of this view that the law ought to recognize that, as between spouses, conviction and punishment may have consequences of the most serious economic and social kind for their future and that neither of them should in any circumstances be compelled, against his or her will, to contribute to bringing this about. It is also pointed out that there is at least a considerable likelihood that the result of more compellability will be either perjury or contempt by silence. The particular provisions which we recommend are intended (in addition to simplifying the law) as a compromise between these views.

Questions

(i) Note that the Act does not make the spouse compellable for the prosecution in all cases. Should it have done so?
(ii) Is the accused's wife compellable against him if he kisses a fifteen-year-old? Is the accused's wife compellable against him if he rapes and murders a sixteen-year-old? [See Zuckerman (1990) p. 294.]
Can you justify the different answers you give to these questions?
(iii) Section 14(1)(*b*) of the Civil Evidence Act 1968 (see p. 64) has no corresponding provision in criminal law. When a witness testifies in a criminal trial, he or she has no right to refuse to answer a question on the ground that to answer would incriminate his or her spouse. However, the privilege of communication between spouses still exists in criminal law although it has now been abolished in a civil action. Are these rules consistent?
(iv) Section 98 of the Children Act 1989 states:

Self Incrimination

(1) In any proceedings in which a court is hearing an application for an order under Part IV or V, no person shall be excused from –

(*a*) giving evidence on any matter; or
(*b*) answering any question put to him in the course of his giving evidence, on the ground that doing so might incriminate him or his spouse of an offence.

(2) A statement or admission made in such proceedings shall not be admissible in evidence against the person making it or his spouse in proceedings for an offence other than perjury.

What would happen if a person simply refused to answer a question put to him or her in these proceedings? Should there be protection for a cohabitant? Does s. 98 extend to protecting admissions made in advance of care proceedings to a social worker? (See *Re G (Minor) (Social Worker Disclosure)* [1996] 2 All ER 65, [1996] 1 FLR 276, CA.)

(e) TAXATION

Income tax law once aggregated the resources of husband and wife and treated them as those of the husband. A married man received an allowance higher than that given to a single person. In addition, the husband whose wife went out to work, received an additional earned income allowance. These allowances were not transferable. In recent years, the Government has produced two Green Papers, one in 1980 and the other in 1986.

The 1986 Green paper, entitled *The Reform of Personal Taxation*, moved towards a fully transferable allowance:

Husband and wife

3.10 If transferable allowances were introduced, married women would be treated as independent taxpayers; they would be responsible for their own tax affairs, be able to fill in their own tax returns, and to pay their own tax. It follows that the legislation which deems a married woman's income to be her husband's for tax purposes would be abolished.

3.11 Transferable allowances would give married women an opportunity for complete privacy in tax matters. Couples where the husband and wife both had income above the tax threshold would be treated, in effect, wholly independently. For other couples, any transfer of allowances would be wholly voluntary: people would not have to make any transfer, or they could transfer an amount less than the whole of their unused allowances if they so chose (accepting that their partner would be entitled to less tax relief in consequence of their choice).

3.12 A system of transferable allowances would thus reflect the Government's belief that a married woman should have the same right to deal with her own tax affairs as any other taxpayer. ...

The family

3.14 Transferable allowances would provide a means for recognising through the tax system that, at different times and for different reasons, one partner in a marriage may be financially dependent on the other. The Government reject the view that the tax system should pay no regard to the special relationship and responsibilities that exist within marriage. The aim is to recognise these in a way that is straightforward, flexible, and does not seek to make invidious distinctions between couples in different circumstances.

3.15 With transferable allowances there would no longer be discrimination against couples where, for whatever reason, the wife was not in paid employment. And since transferability could operate both ways between a husband and wife, the system would give equal recognition to circumstances where the husband did not have income but his wife did.

3.16 Transferable allowances would ensure that a couple's total allowances remained the same and did not fall when one partner left paid work. This is often at a time when the couple may be under financial pressure, for example when they start a family. ...

3.18 The Government believe that the tax system should not discriminate against families where the wife wishes to remain at home to care for young children. Transferable allowances would direct more tax relief to such families.

3.19 The effect of transferable allowances on the willingness of married women to go out to work would need to be carefully considered. Since it would give everybody the same tax allowance, the system would treat married men and married women in exactly the same way. What it would remove is the present special incentive for two-earner couples, introduced in the war-time conditions of 1942. Such positive discrimination is neither necessary nor economically desirable at a time of high unemployment, particularly among the young (of both sexes). In principle, transferable allowances are neither an incentive nor a deterrent for married women seeking work.

3.20 It is sometimes argued that transferable allowances would deter married women from seeking work because they would suffer tax on every pound that they earned. That would not be the position: a married woman would be entitled to a single allowance against her earnings or other income, in precisely the same way as any man or single woman. A variant of this argument is that, in practice, the husband would regard both allowances as a married man's allowance, and would not want his wife to go back to work because he would lose the benefit of her tax allowance. There can be no direct evidence for or against this view. But it is interesting to note that Denmark, which has operated a form of transferable tax allowance for some time, has the highest proportion of married women working of any country in the European Community.

3.21 By taxing a husband and wife separately and giving a married woman her own allowance and tax rate bands in the same way as any other taxpayer, transferable allowances could remove the tax penalty which arises for married couples where the wife has more than a modest amount of savings income. ...

The law was altered by the Finance Act 1988 as from April 1990.

Income tax law no longer aggregates all resources and treats them as that of the husband. Husbands and wives are treated as independent tax payers with separate incomes. However, tax law still contains within it certain vestiges of the former system, as the following extract from Wylie, *The Taxation of Husband and Wife* (1990), makes clear:

... apart from choosing the individual as the unit of taxation, the Government had opted for two basic principles. First, independent taxation should operate with non-transferable personal allowances; and, second, there should be no losers as a result of the change from aggregate taxation to independent taxation. One consequence of this latter decision is that the married man's allowance has been retained in another guise, the married couple's allowance. ...[3]

... However the balance of taxation has swung against cohabitation and, if anything, is now in favour of marriage. Virtually all the tax disadvantages of marriage have been removed. Spouses now have their incomes and gains taxed as if they were unmarried rather than have them aggregated, and cohabitees no longer have the ability to claim double mortgage interest relief, or double additional personal allowance if they have two or more children. Indeed a married couple without children are now significantly better off than their unmarried counterpart. The husband is entitled to claim married couple's allowance, and assets can be freely transferred from one spouse to the other with no capital gains tax or inheritance tax penalty.

Of these concessions in favour of marriage perhaps the most anomalous is the married couple's allowance. This was retained mainly to ensure that married men did not suffer a significant drop in their take home pay following the introduction of independent taxation.

Questions

(i) Married couples' allowances still continue. Why?
(ii) Would some people object that the abolition of the married couple's allowance and the use of the revenue to increase child benefit: (*a*) discriminates in favour of families with children; (*b*) discriminates in favour of high-income two worker families; and (*c*) does nothing to help the low paid – especially if only one works and there is only one child, or no child?
(iii) If a system of wholly independent taxation is introduced, do you think that more people would decide that there is no point in getting married?
(iv) Do you think that the present system 'is a compromise which seems to be broadly acceptable to many people'?
(v) Do you agree with the view expressed in the Green Paper (1986) that transferable allowances do not deter married women from seeking work?

---

3. Income and Corporation Taxes Act 1988, s. 251(1). From April 1996, relief is restricted to 15%.

Chapter 3

Family economics – income

The economic arrangements of a married or cohabiting couple do not exist in isolation. There is a need for a body of flexible rules within which the couple are free to regulate their affairs. These rules exist in all relationships; whether they be created by the parties themselves, by the society and the culture within which they live, or imposed upon them by judicial or other external intervention. The concern of the lawyer in this area tends to be expressed most often in terms of making a sensible allocation of the economic assets of the parties after the relationship has broken down. However, no legal solution to this particular problem can reflect a logical and realistic readjustment of the tangled affairs unless there is a clear understanding of the economic expectations of the parties during their relationship. Thus, the question 'what happens to property after divorce?' is closely interlinked with the question 'what were the economic arrangements of the husband and the wife when they were married?' Increasingly, a similar question must be asked in the context of a non-marital union. Thus although most of the material in this chapter concerns married couples, there is an underlying theme as to how relevant these issues are to the resolution of financial affairs. There are also two important ideological questions to be raised relating to support obligations of spouses or partners for one another and the state involvement in the support of the family.

Professor Tony Honoré is fully aware of the link which we have just made between the dynamic and subsisting marriage and what has been described as the 'pathology of family law', when he categorises marriage ideologically into three distinct groups - as a partnership, as a contract, and thirdly as an arrangement by which a husband assumes the role of provider. The following extract is taken from *The Quest for Security: Employees, Tenants, Wives* (1982).

> There are three main ways of viewing marriage. Some see it as a *partnership*. On a traditional view, it is a partnership, come what may, for life. In that case, after divorce the partnership notionally continues, and the wife is entitled to the support she would have received had the marriage not broken up, or at any rate to a standard of living which continues to be the equal of her husband's. ... More often, marriage is now seen as an equal partnership which lasts, like other partnerships, until it is dissolved. On that view there must on divorce be a fair division of the profits of the partnership, including property acquired during the marriage. ...
>
> Another conception of marriage is that of an *arrangement* (a collateral contract?) *by which a husband induces his wife to change her career*. Had it not been for the marriage she might, for example, have had good earning prospects. She gives these up to marry. On divorce she must now retrain, sometimes late in life, with diminished prospects. If so, her husband must compensate her by keeping her, during a transitional period, while she brings up the children, if she wants to, and redeploys. If, after a long time together, she has become emotionally attached to her status as a wife, her husband may also be required to compensate her for the wrench.

Yet another conception views marriage not as a contract but *as an arrangement by which a husband assumes the role of providing for his wife's needs and those of their children.* This idea, more ancient and deeply rooted in genetics than the contractual ones, makes the husband to some extent the wife's insurer. If she is in need, it is to him, rather than the state, that she turns in the first instance. It is he who must see to her subsistence, and perhaps more, in ill-health, old age or disablement. It is only in this framework of anticipated security that childbearing and childrearing can flourish. But how far does the husband's responsibility extend? How far, in modern conditions does that of the state or community? [italics added]

These three categories must be borne in mind when we consider the historical evidence from both an economic and a sociological perspective.

1 The economic evidence

It is argued that the economic process of change in the family has proceeded through three stages, as explained by M. Young and P. Wilmot in *The Symmetrical Family* (1973):

Even though there is so much in common between family life at each stage, and even though the boundaries between one stage and another are somewhat arbitrary, the rough-and-ready division seems to us useful, as does the generalization, even though it cannot any more than most generalizations do justice to all the evidence. In the first stage, the pre-industrial, the family was usually the unit of production. For the most part, men, women and children worked together in home and field. This type of economic partnership was, for working-class people, supplanted after a bitter struggle by the Stage 2 family, whose members were caught up in the new economy as individual wage-earners. The collective was undermined. Stage 2 was the stage of disruption. One historian has pointed the contrast in this way (E.P. Thompson 1963).

> 'Women became more dependent upon the employer or the labour market, and they looked back to a "golden" period in which home earnings from spinning, poultry and the like, could be gained around their own door. In good times the domestic economy, like the peasant economy, supported a way of life centred upon the home, in which inner whims and compulsions were more obvious than external discipline. Each stage in industrial differentiation and specialisation struck also at the family economy, disturbing customary relations between man and wife, parents and children, and differentiating more sharply between "work" and "life". It was to be a full hundred years before this differentiation was to bring returns, in the form of labour-saving devices, back into the working woman's home. Meanwhile, the family was roughly torn apart each morning by the factory bell.'

The process affected most the families of manual workers (and not all of these by any means). The trends were different in the middle class family, where the contrasts for both husbands and wives were somewhat less sharp than they had been in the past. But as working-class people were preponderant most families were probably 'torn apart' by the new economic system. In the third stage the unity of the family has been restored around its functions as the unit not of production but of consumption.

It is clearly not possible, since social history is unlike political or military history, to do more by way of dating than to indicate a rough manner when the successive waves of change started going through the social structure. The Stage 1 family lasted until the new industry overran it in a rolling advance which went on from the eighteenth well into the nineteenth century. The development of the new industry was uneven as between different parts of the country, coming much later to London than to the industrial north. It also outmoded the old techniques of production more slowly in some occupations than in others. But come it did, eventually, along with many other forms of employment which shared one vital feature, that the employees worked for wages. This led to the Stage 2 family. The third stage started early in the twentieth century and is still working its way downwards. At any one period there were, and still are, families representing all three stages. But as first one wave and then another has been set in motion, the proportions in Stage 2 increased in the nineteenth century and in Stage 3 in the twentieth.

The new kind of family has three main characteristics which differentiate it from the sort which prevailed in Stage 2. The first is that the couple, and their children, are very much centred on the home, especially when the children are young. They can be so much together, and share so much together, because they spend so much of their time together in the same space. Life has, to use another term, become more 'privatized'. ... This trend has been supported by the form taken by technological change.

The second characteristic is that the extended family (consisting of relatives of several different degrees to some extent sharing a common life) counts for less and the immediate, or nuclear, family for more. ...

The third and most vital characteristic is that inside the family of marriage the roles of the sexes have become less segregated.

Social historians, Louise Tilly and Joan Scott, describe each of these three stages in *Women, Work and Family* (1987). They speak first of the family as the labour and consumption unit:

In both England and France, in city and country, people worked in small settings, which often overlapped with households. Productivity was low, the differentiation of tasks was limited. And many workers were needed. The demand for labor extended to women as well as men, to everyone but the youngest children and the infirm. Jobs were differentiated by age and by sex, as well as by training and skill. But, among the popular classes, some kind of work was expected of all able-bodied family members. ... But whether or not they actually worked together, family members worked in the economic interest of the family. In peasant and artisan households, and in proletarian families, the household allocated the labor of family members. In all cases, decisions were made in the interest of the group, not the individual. This is reflected in wills and marriage contracts which spelled out the obligation of siblings or elderly parents who were housed and fed on the family property, now owned by the oldest son. They must work 'to the best of their ability' for 'the prosperity of the family' and 'for the interest of the designated heir.' Among property-owning families the land or the shop defined the tasks of family members and whether or not their labor was needed. People who controlled their means of production adjusted household composition to production needs. For the propertyless, the need for wages – the subsistence of the family itself – sent men, women, and children out to work. These people adjusted household composition to consumption needs. The bonds holding the proletarian family together, bonds of expediency and necessity, were often less permanent than the property interest (or the inheritable skill) which united peasants and craftsmen. The composition of propertied and propertyless households also differed. Nevertheless, the line between the propertied and propertyless was blurred on the question of commitment to work in the family interest.

One of the goals of work was to provide for the needs of family members. Both property owning and proletarian households were consumption units, though all rural households were far more self-sufficient than urban households. Rural families usually produced their own food, clothing, and tools, while urban families bought them at the market. These differences affected the work roles of family members. Women in urban families, for example, spent more time marketing and less time in home manufacture. And there were fewer domestic chores for children to assist with in the city. In the urban family, work was oriented more to the production of specific goods for sale, or it involved the sale of one's labor. For the peasant family, there were a multiplicity of tasks involved in working the land and running the household. The manner of satisfying consumption needs thus varied and so affected the kinds of work family members did.

When the number of household members exceeded the resources available to feed them, and when those resources could not be obtained, the family often adjusted its size. Non-kin left to work elsewhere when children were old enough to work. Then children migrated. Inheritance systems led non-heirs to move away in search of jobs, limited positions as artisans forced children out of the family craftshop, while the need for wages led the children of the propertyless many miles from home. People migrated from farm to farm, farm to village, village to town, and country to city in this period. Although much migration was local and rural in this period, some migrants moved to cities, and most of these tended to be young and single when they migrated. Indeed, in this period cities grew primarily by migration; for urban death rates were high and deaths often outnumbered births, a result largely of the crowded and unsanitary conditions that prevailed.

In the second stage, the family wage economy, we enter a distributive period. As Kevin Gray (1977) says: 'In the distributive stage, production occurs outside the family, and the family merely distributes among the family members the economic product of the labour performed by the provider husband, the house-maker wife of course playing a vital role in this secondary process of distribution.'

Tilly and Scott emphasise that this distributive period (the 'family wage economy', as they call it) developed gradually during the mid-nineteenth century:

Under the family wage economy married women performed several roles for their families. They often contributed wages to the family fund, they managed the household, and they bore and cared for children. With industrialization, however, the demands of wage labor increasingly conflicted with women's domestic activities. The terms of labor and the price paid for it were a function of employers' interest, which took little account of household needs under most circumstances. Industrial jobs required specialization and a full-time commitment to work, usually in a specific location away from home. While under the domestic mode of production women combined market-oriented activities and domestic work, the industrial mode of production precluded an easy reconciliation of married women's activities. The resolution of the conflict was for married women not to work unless family finances urgently required it, and then to try to find that work which conflicted least with their domestic responsibilities ... .

In general, married women tended to be found in largest numbers in the least industrialized sectors of the labor force, in those areas where the least separation existed between home and workplace and where women could control the rhythm of their work.

Question

The authors concentrate on working class families. Do you think that their comments might need modifying for the middle classes in the nineteenth century?

The authors then describe how the third stage, the consumer economy, developed:

By the early twentieth century the higher wages of men particularly and the availability of cheap consumer goods raised the target income of working-class families. Necessities now included not only food and clothing, but also other items that once had been considered luxuries. What we have termed the family consumer economy then was a wage earning unit which increasingly emphasized family consumption needs.

The organization of the family consumer economy was not dramatically different from that of the family wage economy. The management of money and of family affairs in an increasingly complex urban environment did, however, require additional time and a certain expertise. As a result, the household division of labor tended to distinguish even more sharply than in the past between the roles of husband and wife and of daughters and wives. Husbands and unmarried children were family wage earners, while wives devoted most of their time to child care and household management. Wives continued, however, to work sporadically in order to earn wages to help raise the family's level of consumption.

Tilly and Scott inform us that women who worked chose to do so not simply from individualistic motives and certainly hardly ever for financial independence. Rather the prime motive was to improve the financial position of the family and to raise its standard of living. The mother's work was a supplement to her domestic responsibilities.

The three models of family organisation described by Tilly and Scott and by Young and Wilmot have been criticised by Hudson and Lee in their introductory essay to *Women's Work and the Family Economy* (1990):

The temporal sequence of organisational change from the traditional family economy to the family wage economy, and finally to the family consumer economy based on a 'symmetrical' marriage structure is of only limited usefulness. It is also problematic to view work at home for pay as constituting a 'transitional model', given both its traditional and contemporary prevalence. Even within the middle class, adherence to the Victorian cult of domesticity was not always translated into the reality of separate spheres of activity and maintaining the 'paraphernalia of gentility' was often financially impossible. With changing economic conditions participation by middle-class women in the public sphere became 'both respectable and necessary', and there is increasing evidence of their role in decision-making in relation to their husbands' careers and family businesses. To this extent nineteenth-century middle-class practice was not too dissimilar from the joint responsibility for financial matters enshrined in the earlier German tradition of *Hausmutterliteratur.*[1] Furthermore, despite the apparent pervasiveness of patriarchy in the later nineteenth century, there were certain industries, such as pottery, where the male breadwinner ethos failed to take root, and where women retained a strong presence, even in trade union organisations. A joint contribution to the family economy could also encourage mutuality in dealing with domestic responsibilities.

Pottery was an exception.

Diana Gittins in *The Family in Question* (1985) describes how the ideology of a single male breadwinner per family developed during the nineteenth century:

Although never an entirely secure institution, marriage in pre-industrial society had provided women with a reasonable means of economic survival involving both production and domestic work in and around the home, with a good chance of some minimal security in the event of widowhood. The growth of wage labour and the increasing separation of home from work put women more than ever before at the mercy of two increasingly unstable markets: the marriage market and the labour market. In both their position was weak, and economic survival was precarious whether a woman entered one or both.

In other areas the response to mechanisation, de-skilling and proletarianisation was different. Sometimes machine breaking was an immediate response, as in the Luddite and Captain Swing riots (Hobsbaum and Rude, 1973). More often, men in skilled crafts or industries formed themselves into associations or unions. Their general purpose was to defend their members against further capitalist exploitation, mechanisation and wage cuts, and to protect themselves from cheap labour. Since most cheap labour was made up of women and children, the unions tended to contribute further to the already disadvantaged position of women. Until the second half of the nineteenth century, however, the majority of unions were made up of men from only the most skilled trades and crafts, and one of their main aims was to procure a 'family wage' – a single wage that was adequate to support a man and dependent wife and children on his work alone. This new emphasis on the father/husband as sole earner was a powerful factor in the development of modern notions of 'masculinity'. While the concept of a single male breadwinner had started with the rise of the middle classes in the late eighteenth century, this was the first time a sector of the working class – and a very small sector at that – did so.

As Hilary Land (1976) points out, it is hard to know whether their argument for wanting to keep their wives and children out of the workforce was more a matter of conviction or a rationale for higher wages that they knew would appeal to middle-class ears. Whatever the rationale, the ideal of a family wage became increasingly important as an ideal of the organised trade union movement, and it was an ideal which coincided with the new middle-class ideology of women and children as dependants of the husband/father.

During the nineteenth century, however, the proportion of working-class families who could survive on the basis of the man's wage alone was very small. Nevertheless, the objective of a single male breadwinner per family was one of the most radical changes in family ideology of the modern era, and one that had dramatic effects on notions of fatherhood, masculinity, motherhood, femininity, family life and family policy, and still has. The ideal, then as now, was often very far removed from the reality, and the majority of working-class families in the

1. M.W. Gray 'Prescriptions for Productive Female Domesticity in a Transitional Era: Germany's *Hausmutterliteratur* 1780–1840', History of European Ideas 8 (1987) pp. 413–26.

nineteenth century still relied heavily on a household economy based on several wages. Working-class men and women, but women in particular, were therefore dependent on both wage labour in the labour market and a partner through the marriage market in order to survive economically. Both markets were insecure and in fact many individuals had to find extra economic support through children's or other kin's labour.

Questions

(i) Do you feel that this campaign was one worth winning?
(ii) Think of your parents and of your grandparents. Do their household economies fit into the descriptions, so far as you know, provided by the previous extracts?

2 The sociological evidence

In *Legal Regulation of Marriage: Tradition and Change* (1974), Lenore Weitzman writes:

The sociological data ... are closely related to the economic data ..., for in large part it is the changing position of women with respect to men in the larger society which has influenced and altered the position of the two sexes within the family. Thus the increased labor force participation of married women has probably been instrumental in causing a decline in the absolute authority of the husband, with a consequent growth in the wife's role in the family decision-making. With an expansion in women's roles, especially economic roles, outside the family, roles within the family have also become less strongly differentiated. Wives are assuming more responsibility for financial and domicile decisions, and husbands are assuming a greater share of the responsibility for housework and child care. In general, there is a strong trend toward egalitarian family patterns, those in which authority is shared and decisions are made jointly by the husband and the wife.

The spread in egalitarian family patterns may be briefly noted in several areas. First, there is an increase in the sharing of financial decisions within the family. As the wife's contribution to the total family budget assumes greater relative importance, financial responsibilities within the family are more equally shared. Decisions on family expenditures, savings, and the general 'struggle for financial security' are now made jointly or apportioned on a less sex-stereotyped basis. Second, the determination of the family domicile and the decision of when and where to move has become more of a family decision, with the needs and interests of the wife and children assuming a much greater importance than in the past. Although both of these trends represent a decline in the traditional authority of the husband, there is also a significant decline in the traditional authority of the wife as the husband assumes a more important role in household decisions and in household tasks. ...

A third area in which there is a significant trend toward more egalitarian patterns is that of sexuality. The current sexual revolution has focused increased attention and emphasis on the wife's participation and satisfaction in sexual relations, and consequently on more mutual and egalitarian sexual relationships. ...

A fourth and closely related trend is in the increased sharing of responsibility for birth control. Knowledge and use of some form of contraception has become nearly universal in the United States today. The most recently introduced and most highly effective methods of contraception, the pill and the I.U.D., are the first to give women independent control over their reproductive decisions, and the first to allow couples a real choice about the number and timing of children. With technological advances in effective methods of female contraception, the decision of when to have children, as well as the decision of when to have sexual relations, may be increasingly decided by the husband and wife together.

Fifth, and most important, is an extended range of family roles which are now being shared or alternated between husbands and wives.

Question

Is Weitzman saying that industrialisation and changes in women's labour force participation are responsible for changes in family patterns?

Although between the end of the Second World War and the 1990s, the proportion of economically active women has risen dramatically (see p. 88, below), the evidence all points to the fact that women still bear the primary burden of domestic labour in the household. The table on p. 75 is taken from *Social Trends* 17 (1987).

Questions

(i) Is it not true that 'most women still regard family and domestic roles and responsibilities as their chief source of personal worth and fulfilment'? (Burgoyne, Ormrod and Richards, 1987).
(ii) Would it surprise you to be told that a larger percentage of working-class couples shared the housework between them than do middle-class couples?
(iii) The Labour party politician, Harriet Harman MP in *The Century Gap* (1993) asks: 'What must men do to narrow the century gap in marriage?' She answers her own question thus: 'They will have to relinquish the position of breadwinner in fantasy as they have done in fact.' (The evidence which has been collected by Hakim in *Key Issues in Women's Work* (1996) suggests that all the net increase in employment in Britain in the past half century has come from female part-time work, and in contrast in the 1980s alone, some two million full-time male jobs were lost.)

Do you think that the continuing increase in economically inactive men will lead to any change in male responsibility for housework and child rearing?

Todd and Jones' survey of *Matrimonial Property* (1972) provides additional evidence of the general financial management of household affairs. It was carried out in early 1971 on behalf of the Law Commission:

4.1 Household duties involving regular expenditure

We wanted to have some picture of how the couple organised their roles with regard to handling their money, and we also wanted to lead up to asking the wife how interested she was in financial matters. In the first series of questions we asked the couple who usually bought the food, paid the gas or electricity bills, paid the rates, rent or mortgage and who, if there was any money left, dealt with the surplus. In these questions we were asking who carried out the tasks, not who provided the money for them.

Who usually dealt with:–	**Buying food** %	**Paying for gas or electricity** %	**Paying rates, rent, mortgage** %	**Dealing with any surplus** %
Husband	3	38	45	20
Wife	89	49	45	36
Either or both	7	10	8	43
Other answer	1	3	2	1
	100	100	100	100
Base	(1877)	(1877)	(1877)	(1877)

Table A.2: Household division of labour: by marital status, 1984
Great Britain

Percentages

	Married people[1]						Never-married people[2]		
	Actual allocation of tasks			Tasks should be allocated to			Tasks should be allocated to		
	Mainly man	Mainly woman	Shared equally	Mainly man	Mainly woman	Shared equally	Mainly man	Mainly woman	Shared equally
Household tasks (percentage[3] allocation)									
Washing and ironing	1	88	9	–	77	21	–	68	30
Preparation of evening meal	5	77	16	1	61	35	1	49	49
Household cleaning	3	72	23	–	51	45	1	42	56
Household shopping	6	54	39	–	35	62	–	31	68
Evening dishes	18	37	41	12	21	64	13	15	71
Organisation of household money and bills	32	38	28	23	15	58	19	16	63
Repairs of household equipment	83	6	8	79	2	17	74	–	24
Child-rearing (percentage[3] allocation)									
Looks after children when they are sick	1	63	35	–	49	47	–	48	50
Teaches the children discipline	10	12	77	12	5	80	16	4	80

1 1,120 married respondents, except for the questions on actual allocation of child-rearing tasks which were answered by 479 respondents with children under 16

2 283 never-married respondents. The table excludes results of the formerly married (widowed, divorced, or separated) respondents.

3 'Don't know' and non-response to the question mean that some categories do not sum to 100 per cent.

Source: British Social Attitudes Survey, 1984, Social and Community Planning Research

In some cases someone other than one of the spouses carried out the duties, or there was some special method of payment, for example, payment by standing order. The wife was predominantly the person responsible for buying the food but in the other matters there was a fairly even split of responsibility between the couple. We examined in more detail whether the housing and earnings situation of the couple were associated with the sharing of responsibilities for paying bills for heating and lighting, and rates, rent or mortgage.

Who usually deals with:–	**Paying for gas or electricity**		**Paying rates, rent, mortgage**	
	Method of payment from husband's employment			
	cash	not cash	cash	not cash
	%	%	%	%
Husband	26	58	30	65
Wife	61	31	60	23
Either or both	9	10	7	10
Other answers	4	1	3	2
	100	100	100	100
Base	(1099)	(534)	(1099)	(534)

The method by which the husband is paid is closely associated with which spouse pays both types of bills, fuel and rates, rent or mortgage. Where the husband is paid in cash there is a much greater likelihood that the wife carries out these duties. Where the husband is not paid in cash it is most likely that he has responsibility for these bills.

We next examine whether these duties are associated at all with whether the matrimonial home is owned by the couple or not.

Who usually deals with:–	**Paying for gas or electricity**		**Paying rates, rent, mortgage**	
	Ownership of the matrimonial home			
	Couple do not own the home	Couple own the home	Couple do not own the home	Couple own the home
	%	%	%	%
Husband	27	49	29	59
Wife	58	40	61	30
Either or both	10	10	6	11
Other answers	5	1	4	–
	100	100	100	100
Base	(896)	(978)	(896)	(978)

The variation here is similar to that in the previous table. Where the couple own their own home the husband is more likely to take the responsibility for paying the bills for fuel and housing. Where the couple do not own their home these duties are more frequently carried out by the wife.

Thus the duties that the spouses carry out in relation to these particular household responsibilities are associated with other factors in their domestic situation.

4.2 Wife's interest in money matters

After the series of questions about household management we asked wives whether they liked to know about money matters or whether they preferred to leave such things to their husbands. We first classified separately those wives who said they received the whole pay packet and were obviously responsible themselves for domestic financial management.

Wife's interest in money matters

	%
Is given the whole pay packet	5
Likes to know about money matters	76
Prefers to leave such things to husband	19
	100
Base	(1877)

Giving the whole pay packet to the wife is often talked of as a regional phenomenon so we examined to what extent the 5% of wives in this position varied in the different economic planning regions.

Region	**Proportion of wives who receive pay packet**	Base
North	15%	(122)
East Midlands	8%	(142)
South West	8%	(152)
Wales	8%	(99)
Yorkshire and Humberside	5%	(199)
West Midlands	4%	(201)
East Anglia	3%	(62)
North West	3%	(275)
South East	2%	(391)
Greater London	2%	(234)
England and Wales	5%	(1877)

It is thus a way of life occurring most frequently in the North but also occurring more than average in the East Midlands, the South West and Wales.

Susan McRae (1993) obtained the following information from her female sample.

Table 6.5 Household division of labour (I): Proportion who reported tasks shared equally

Column percentages

	Long-term cohabiting mothers	Cohabited pre-maritally Married after baby	Cohabited pre-maritally Married before baby	Non-cohab. married mothers
Cleaning	22	18	14	7
Washing up	34	33	35	29
Cooking	20	29	27	14
Washing clothes	12	6	4	1
Taking children to doctor	31	26	28	34
Painting/decorating	26	31	25	34
Car maintenance	8	14	10	5
Gardening	48	48	46	39
Helping children with homework	60	47	62	61
Base:	77	51	57	92

Question

If she had asked their male companions the same questions, how do you think they would have responded?

Table 6.6 Household division of labour (II): Proportion who reported tasks done entirely or mainly by women

Column percentages

	Long-term cohabiting mothers	Cohabited pre-maritally Married after baby	Cohabited pre-maritally Married before baby	Non-cohab. married mothers
Cleaning	77	74	81	90
Washing up	57	50	51	60
Cooking	75	63	72	84
Washing clothes	87	94	96	97
Taking children to doctor	65	74	70	64
Painting/decorating	13	28	19	12
Car maintenance	5	11	4	4
Gardening	23	29	25	22
Helping children with homework	40	43	36	33
Base:	77	51	56	92

Distribution of family income between its members is a difficult research field. Notwithstanding the difficulties, Jan Pahl in *Money and Marriage* (1984, 1990) attempts a structure for the research she and others have conducted in this field:

Patterns of allocation of money

There is an infinite variety of different allocative systems within the great variety of types of households. ... In reality, the proposed typology represents points on a continuum of allocative systems, but previous research suggests that the typology has considerable validity both within Britain and in other parts of the world. Two criteria are central in distinguishing one system from another: these are, first, each individual's responsibility for expenditure between and within expenditure categories, and second, each individual's access to household funds, other than those for which he or she is responsible.

The whole wage system

In this system one partner, usually the wife, is responsible for managing all the finances of the household and is also responsible for all expenditure, except for the personal spending money of the other partner. The personal spending money of the other partner is either taken out by him before the pay packet is handed over, or is returned to him from collective funds. If both partners earn, both pay packets are administered by the partner who manages the money. Where a whole wage system is managed by a husband, his wife may have no personal spending money of her own and no access to household funds.

The allowance system

In the most common form of this system the husband gives his wife a set amount, which she adds to her own earnings if she has any; she is responsible for paying for specific items of household expenditure. The rest of the money remains in the control of the husband and he pays for other specific items. Thus each partner has a sphere of responsibility in terms of household expenditure. If a wife does not earn she only has access to the 'housekeeping' allowance and, since this is allocated for household expenditure, she may feel that she has no personal spending money of her own: the same phenomenon can also be seen in the case of the whole wage system where the wife is responsible for all family expenditure but has no personal spending money. The allowance system has many variations, mainly because of the varying patterns of responsibility. At one extreme a wife may only be responsible for expenditure on food; at the other extreme she may be responsible for everything except the running of the car and the system may come close to resembling the whole wage system. The allowance system is also known as the 'wife's wage' and the 'spheres of responsibility' system, while the whole wage system is sometimes called the 'tipping up' system (Barrett and Mcintosh 1982).

The shared management or pooling system
The essential characteristic of this system is that both partners have access to all or almost all the household money and both have responsibility for management of the common pool and for expenditure out of that pool. The partners may take their personal spending money out of the pool. On the other hand one or both of them may retain a sum for personal spending; when this sum becomes substantial the system begins to acquire some characteristics of the independent management system. ...

The independent management system
The essential characteristic of this system is that both partners have an income and that neither has access to all the household funds. Each partner is responsible for specific items of expenditure, and though these responsibilities may change over time, the principle of keeping flows of money separate within the household is retained.

The political economy of the household
Distinguishing different types of allocative system is, however, only a beginning. What are the variables which determine the allocative system adopted by any one couple at any one time? What are the implications for the couple as a whole, and for individuals, of adopting one system rather than another?

Pahl (1990) provides interesting information regarding the reasons given by her sample of wives and husbands for their system of money management.

Table 6.1 Reasons given by wives and husbands for their system of money management

		Number mentioning each reason	
		Wives	*Husbands*
	'Ideological' reasons		
1	System seemed natural/right/fair	41	53
	'Practical' reasons		
2	Seemed more efficient/'it just works for us'	27	22
3	Response to way in which wages/salaries paid	22	19
4	More convenient/one partner able to get to bank	19	15
	'Psychological' reasons		
5	Wife 'better manager' so she manages money	23	15
6	Husband 'better manager' so he manages money	10	9
	'Generational' reasons		
7	Tried to avoid parents' mistakes	5	2
8	Money management similar to parents' system	4	1

Note: Numbers add up to more than sample because some individuals gave more than one reason.

Questions

(i) Are you impressed by the 'ideological' reasons given, or do you think that people simply drift into particular arrangements?
(ii) Is it more or less likely that parties to a marriage where one or both of them have been married before will opt for an independent management system?
(iii) Is it more or less likely that cohabitants will opt for an independent management system?

Pahl (1990) moves the debate along by writing:

... It has become clear that, far from protecting them, women's assumed and actual dependence on men constitutes a major cause of their poverty (Glendinning and Millar, 1987). Women carry the burden of scarcity, not just because they are more likely than men to be poor, but also because when a household is poor it is women who are usually responsible for seeing that the money goes round; when money is short it is typically women who go without. The recent idea of the 'feminisation of poverty' implies that women are now at greater risk of poverty than men (Scott, 1984). However, evidence from Britain suggests that throughout the twentieth century women have been more likely to fall into poverty than men (Lewis and Piachaud, 1987).

Question

What should politicians do with this information?

3 An ideological basis?

Mary Ann Glendon, in *State, Law and Family: Family Law in Transition in the United States and Western Europe* (1977), emphasises the difficulties which appear when this question is explored.

The prevailing ideologies of marriage have never been alike for all groups of any large population. In Western society, however, one ideology has been dominant and until modern times has found universal expression in the law. The family law of Western legal systems has traditionally embodied ideas of separate spheres of activity appropriate for women and men. It has carried the image of the woman as principal caretaker of the home and children, the man as principal provider, and of a family authority structure dominated by the husband and father. This should not be understood as meaning that the woman's *exclusive* task has been to care for home and children. In pre-industrial society, the wife was often a co-worker with the husband on the farm, in the craft and in the shop. The exclusively housewife-marriage seems to be a phenomenon of the 20th century. Already this period is beginning to appear to have been a brief interlude in history. Today, as more and more women engage in economic activity outside the home, housewife-marriage is only one of many current marriage patterns. Where housewife-marriage exists, it is now more apt to be a phase of a marriage than a description of the marriage from beginning to end.

Organized around a hierarchical model, with a clear division of roles between the sexes, traditional family law placed primary responsibility for support of the family on the male partner and vested authority in him to determine the place and mode of family life and to deal with all the family property, including that of the wife. Among the wealthy, property matters could to some extent be arranged so that the interests of the wife (and her family of origin) could be protected. The law paid little attention to the needs of the poor, even when large numbers of women began to be employed outside the home in the early 19th century in England, and later in France and Germany. The set of legal rules organized along these traditional lines persisted in England, France, the United States and Germany well into the 20th century, long after behavior of many married people had ceased to correspond to the image enshrined in the laws.

This model was constantly adjusted, beginning in the late 19th century and in the first half of the 20th century, but at last the center could not hold. Laws which might have been appropriate for the family production community, or for the housewife-marriage when divorce was rare, no longer worked when many women's economic activity had been transferred to the marketplace and when divorce had become pandemic.

Although Glendon's point is a necessary reminder of the shift in emphasis of the women's economic activity, it is appropriate to recall the material contained at p. 75 that housework and child care continue to a great extent to be the responsibility of women. Elizabeth Wilson, in *Women and the Welfare State* (1977), asks the question why:

Because more and more married women are going out to work, and because, although there has been a rise in the number of women who bear a child or children at some point in their lives maternity has become quantitatively less and less absorbing, the importance, drudgery, and significance of domestic work in the home has become more and more clear (Gardiner 1975). Why then is it retained? Why has it not been socialized when in the industrial sphere capitalism constantly seeks to transform and revolutionize its technology? The economic significance of domestic labour has been discussed for some years in the Women's Movement (e.g. Benston 1969; Morton 1970; Rowbotham 1973) and more recently the subject has been taken up by a number of socialist and Marxist economists (Harrison 1974; Secombe 1974). Whatever the precise nature of its relationship to surplus value it is clear that the domestic unpaid work of the housewife helps to keep costs down for the employer by making it possible for the worker to be cared for much more cheaply than would otherwise be possible. The socialized care of the worker – canteens, living accommodation, laundry – alone would be likely in this country to cost the capitalist more than the efforts of the housewife who takes pride in making do. Where it is cheaper for the workman to be separated from his family – as is the case in South Africa where black workers can be compelled to live in barracks – that is what happens. The strength of the working class has also much to do with the achievement of more tolerable living conditions.

There is a second reason for the retention of domestic work: the supportive emotional functions of the family. The intensity of the parental-child relationships within the family make for the vulnerability of the child and therefore the family is a highly functional ideological institution for the upbringing of children in such a manner that they conform, as adults, to authoritarian/submissive social relationships. Then there is the marriage relationship. It is pleasanter for workers to be married. The marriage relationship may have its problems, men may feel henpecked or hamstrung; the sexual relationship may have its inhibitions and disappointments, especially for the woman; yet State brothels could hardly provide an adequate substitute. ...

A third reason for the retention of the unwaged housewife and her children as the dependants of the individual worker is that this arrangement reinforces the incentive of the father to work regularly and hard. The ability to support a family is early equated in the male child's mind as an essential part of his manhood. Much value is attached to virility and loss of his job can lead to the man losing also his sense of identity in his own and his wife's eyes. ... The male role thus reinforces the work ethic quite directly.

Elizabeth Wilson's thesis is that even though women are now increasingly available to seek employment, there is an ideology which continues to define them narrowly as wives and mothers, responsible for the domestic work within the nuclear family.

Ann Oakley, in *The Sociology of Housework* (1974), provides an interesting table of self-assessment. She states that asking women to describe themselves is likely to yield the following:

I am a housewife	I am a good housewife
I am a mother	I am good to my children
I am ordinary	I am good at housework
I am a wife	I am good to my husband
I am happy	I am good at washing
I am reasonably attractive	I am fed up at times
I am a sister	I am bad tempered at times
I am a neighbour	I am very happy with my work
I am a friend	I am happy with my children
I am sociable	I am seldom unhappy

Question

Would you add to the list, or delete anything from it?

Diana Gittins, in *The Family in Question* (1985), places the debate in a feminist framework:

Understanding why 'a woman's work is never done' means first of all accepting the dual nature of the 'work' for women. For a very long time the idea of womanhood – and increasingly wifehood – has been synonymous with a women's 'natural' responsibility for child-care and domestic work. However a society or household is organised, there has always been the assumption that a certain core of domestic work is by definition woman's work. This regardless of whether she engages in paid work, whether she is totally or partly dependent on a husband or father, regardless of whether she is single, married, widowed or divorced, young or old. There is no equivalent assumption for men. A man *may* empty the rubbish, bath the baby, wash the dishes or sweep the floor, but if he elects not to do so – as many have and do – he is in no way socially or economically ostracised or penalised. His domestic participation is totally and always voluntary.

If a woman chooses not to keep the house clean, not to supervise the children adequately, she is in danger of being labelled as a 'bad' mother or a bad wife – she can be divorced, she can have her children taken away from her by the State. Housework and child-care are not voluntary for married women in contemporary society, unless their class position is such that they have the financial resources to pay others to carry out their responsibilities. But they remain their responsibilities.

Domestic labour does have more than just a use value. It can be bought, exchanged and sold, and frequently is. Although domestic labour is an integral and implicit part of the marriage contract, it is not specific to married women only – single mothers are equally held responsible for carrying out domestic work for their children.

Questions

(i) Do you believe that society in the 1990s in the UK is ordered on a gender role basis, legitimising patriarchal power?
(ii) If you do believe this, should the law leave people free to arrange their lives thus, or should it encourage some different pattern?
(iii) If the latter, what and how?

4 Women and employment

Hudson and Lee, in *Women's Work and the Family Economy in Historical Perspective* (1990), describe the scale of married women's involvement in the formal labour market, which has altered dramatically in the twentieth century:

... The post-1945 period in particular witnessed a rapid development in women's employment in advanced industrial economies despite the resurgence of a 'back to the kitchen ideology' in the 1970s fuelled by official concern about male unemployment. The abolition of the marriage bar in public-sector employment in Britain aided this trend. There were significant changes in a variety of areas, with women increasingly dominating such occupations as clerical work, retail sales, elementary teaching and nursing. The increasing importance of 'new industries' in the 1920s and 1930s, including rayon manufacture, light engineering, food processing, and white goods provided a boost for female employment in the formal sector, although on a regionally selective basis and with an emphasis on 'semi-skilled' and 'unskilled' work. Furthermore, the inter-war period generally was characterised by official restrictions on married women's employment as a reaction to male unemployment.

'New' female occupations in the service sector continued to expand after 1945, particularly in retailing, banking, public administration and other forms of clerical work. This trend was assisted by a variety of factors, including improved levels of female pay in certain sectors, shorter working hours, lower fertility, and the gradual provision of suitable, if still inadequate welfare support. ... Technological innovations in the production and conception of household consumer durables such as vacuum cleaners, cookers and electric irons were potentially a source of reduction of domestic burdens as they slowly percolated down the social scale, especially from the 1960s, but new higher standards of domestic cleanliness and decor put pressure on women to spend as much time as in the past on homemaking.

Despite growth in the employment of married women in the formal economy in the twentieth century, many of the factors which determined female labour force participation in the early stages of capitalist development continue to affect occupation choice, gender segregation and women's overall subordination in work. Married women frequently choose jobs which do not directly challenge the prevailing concept of a 'woman's proper place', and many people still 'view it unseemly and inappropriate for wives to work'. Women's occupational choices are clearly influenced by a variety of factors, both work and non-work related. The nature of the labour-market is important but persistently negative facets of women's employment, such as sex-typed jobs, low-ranking position and low comparative earnings, reflect the continued operation of more long-term and deep-seated factors. Married women are still not expected to express any dissatisfaction with their domestic status, so that a return to formal employment frequently has to be legitimised in a socially accepted fashion, with hours tailored to suit child care (for example, mothers' evening shifts in factories) and with earnings treated as 'pin money', or with work portrayed as an emergency measure. As important is the assertion that women have a different relationship to money and wages from men, a notion which has helped to cement the social construction of gender dependency.

Just as women's wage labour in the early phases of capitalist development was frequently an extension of home-based skills, so the general expansion of the service sector, particularly in the twentieth century, has tended to replicate a similar bond between the domestic and work environments. There has been an unprecedented expansion in nursing services since the nineteenth century, accompanied by the formation of professional nursing associations, but these have been based on women's 'traditional' role as carer. Moreover, gender segregation in the health sector as a whole has been associated with persistent low pay for nurses in comparison with other sections of the medical profession. Librarianship has also provided a fast-growing demand for low-paid, but educated, female recruits. Women librarians have frequently been employed because of their submissive attitudes or, as in Tsarist Russia, because of their function as 'guardians of traditional culture'. Even in the retail trades women have been employed not just because they were cheaper than men but because they had such positive virtues as 'politeness' and 'sobriety'. They could also function effectively in a 'world of women', linking women as workers with women as consumers.

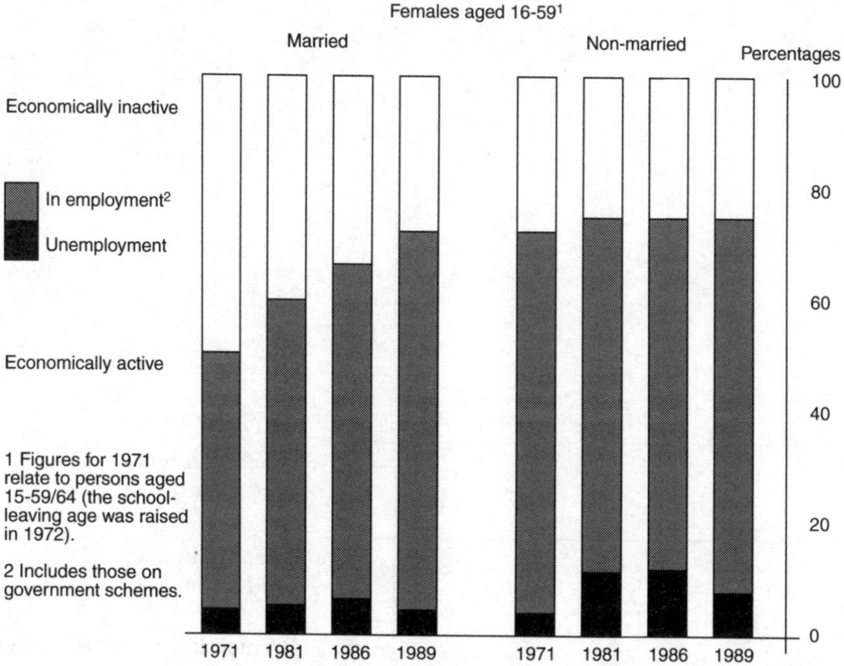

Source: Population Census 1971, Office of Population Censuses and Surveys: Labour Force Survey, Employment Department

In the long term, therefore, despite an unprecedented expansion in the employment of married women in the formal economy, many of the earlier facets of women's work have been retained, particularly in relation to economic marginalisation, pay discrimination, occupational segregation and trade union participation.

Question

Is there gender segregation in the legal profession?

Social Trends 21 (1991) (above, p. 83) provides a useful chart illustrating the economic activity of married and unmarried women. Whereas the position of unmarried women has been constant, the position of married women has changed a great deal. Why?

Evidence of why women seek employment is available from the OPCS *Family Formation Survey* (1979) (see below, p. 86):

Reasons given by married women for being economically inactive

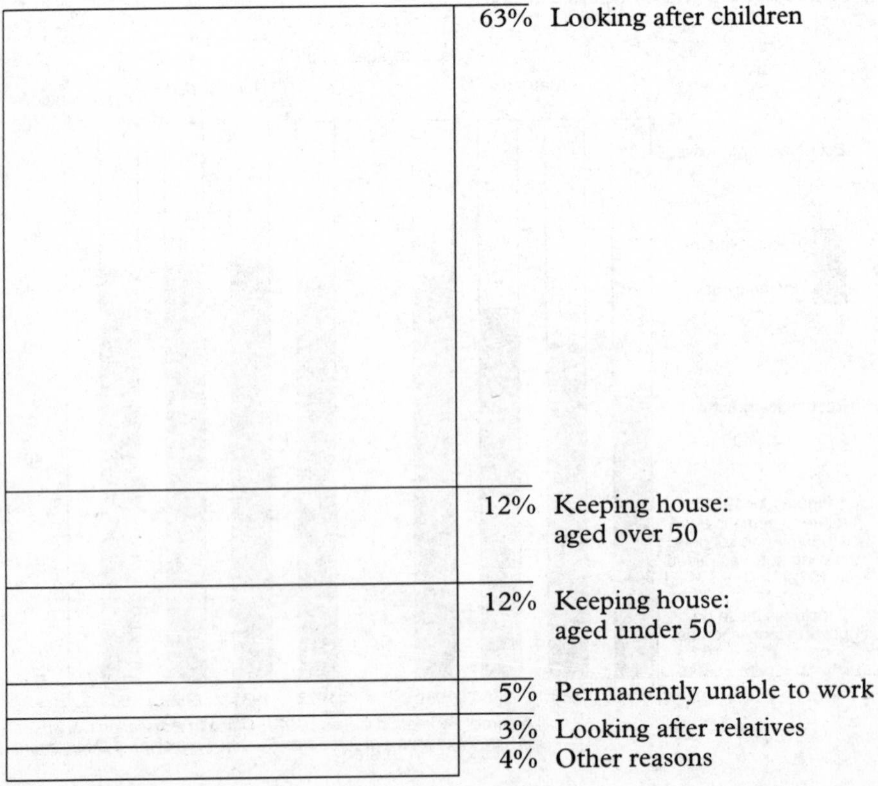

Schematic diagram showing percentage of women employed by life/family cycle stage, England

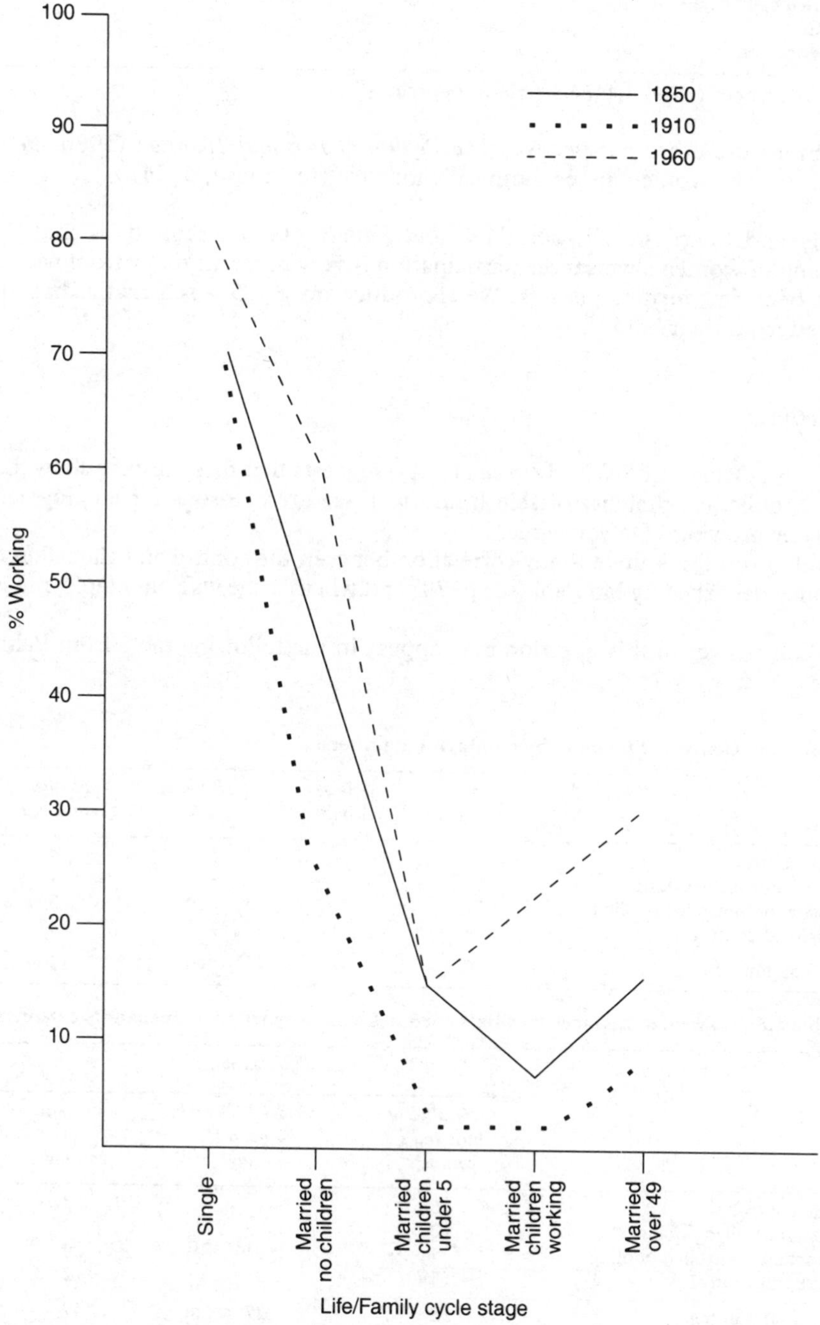

Reason for working between first and second live births in four different time periods

Worked because:	1956–60	1961–65	1966–70	1971–5
Really needed the money	52	51	48	47
Wanted extra things	27	25	27	27
Liked it	16	19	20	22
Other reason	5	5	5	4

Source: Dunnell (1979) Table 6.5. Crown copyright.

From the other perspective, *The Reform of Personal Taxation* (1986) gives reasons why women are economically inactive (see above, p. 84):

Tilly and Scott, in *Women, Work and Family* (1987), remind us that the timing of women's workforce participation is very different today from what it has been in previous periods. We reproduce on p. 85 a schematic diagram taken from their book:

Questions

(i) Ann Oakley, in *Subject Women* (1981), suggests that these surveys show that the 'public acceptability of selfish and work-centred reasons for employment may be growing.' Do you agree?
(ii) Do you think there is any correlation between the control and allocation of money described by Jan Pahl (see p. 79) and whether the wife has employment?

The answer to this question may appear in the following table from Pahl's (1990) study:

Table 6.5: Control of finances by employment pattern

	Both employed	*Wife only*	*Husband only*	*Neither employed*
Wife control	5	–	5	4
Wife-controlled pooling	19	–	7	1
Husband-controlled pooling	17	–	19	3
Husband control	9	1	9	3
Total number	50	1	40	11

Table 6.6: Control of finances by wife's earnings as a proportion of husband's earnings

	Wife's earnings		
	Over 30% of husband's earnings	*Under 30% of husband's earnings*	*Wife had no earnings*
Wife control	6	–	8
Wife-controlled pooling	12	8	7
Husband-controlled pooling	5	14	20
Husband control	5	5	12
Total number	28	27	47

Table 6.7: Control of finances by social class

	Both middle class	*Husband middle class wife working class*	*Wife middle class husband working class*	*Both working class*
Wife control	3	2	2	7
Wife-controlled pooling	10	0	10	7
Husband-controlled pooling	18	6	1	14
Husband control	7	2	3	10
Total number	38	10	16	38

(iii) Do you think that those who are 'keeping house' or 'looking after children' actually consider themselves as being 'economically inactive'? Isn't the word 'inactive' emotive?

We must now consider 'dual career' families. A dramatic chart reproduced in *The Reform of Personal Taxation* (1986) illustrates the place of married women in the work force over the last 50 years (see below, p. 88).

Questions

(i) What type of allocative system exists, do you think, in families from South Asia and from the West Indies?
(ii) In *Women and Employment: A Lifetime Perspective* (1984) it was found: 'amongst the mothers who were interviewed, there were marked differences in the types of occupational changes made by them before and after having their first child. Before childbirth, only 18 per cent of mothers who worked had experienced downward occupational mobility when they changed jobs, while 62 per cent had maintained a level occupational status (as defined by the classification used). On returning to work after childbirth the first job found by 37 per cent of mothers was lower down the occupational scale than their previous job, while only about half (49 per cent) of them found a job which was of the same occupational status. Much of this downward movement was associated with mothers entering part-time employment on return to the labour market; 45 per cent of those who took part-time employment had gone to a lower level occupation, and only 42 per cent retained their occupational status. Many of those who chose part-time employment did so because of the need to combine domestic responsibilities with paid work; the convenient hours of a part-time job were a priority. However, because part-time employment tends to be concentrated in occupations with low skill content, the opportunities available do not generally provide the range of occupations required for higher proportions of working mothers to retain their occupational status on returning to work after having children'. Is this another illustration that 'women cannot at one and the same time be married as we understand marriage, and independent?' (Wilson, 1977).
(iii) Women are mainly economically inactive in a period in their lives when their husbands may be most economically productive. Should this be relevant in determining what sort of distribution of family wealth our legal system should aspire towards?

The proportion of married women working or looking for work

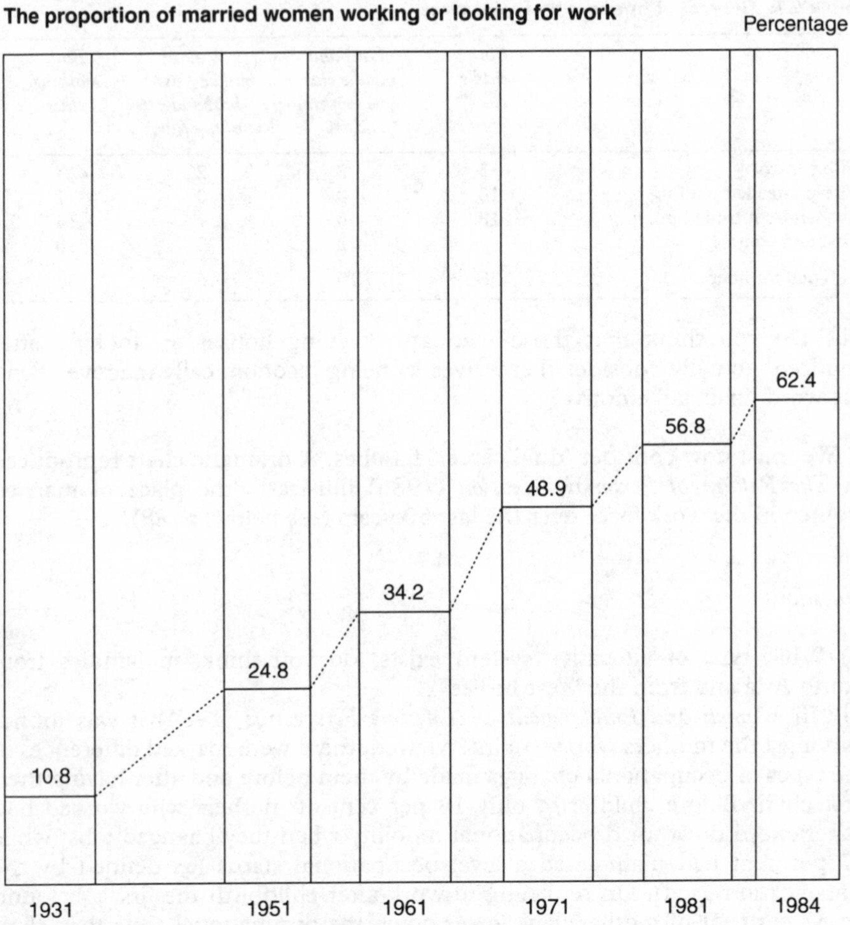

Source: Censuses of Population and Labour Survey 1984

In 'The Impact of Work on the Family' (*Work and the Family*, ed. by P. Moss and N. Fonda (1980)) Rhona and Robert Rapoport identify some of the economic issues associated with the 'dual career' model of family and employment:

Dual-worker families

There have always been families in which both husbands and wives have worked regularly. Shopkeeping families like the baker's family described by Peter Laslett (1971) in *The World We Have Lost* persist to the present day; and shiftworking couples like those described by Michael Anderson (1973) from nineteenth-century Lancashire may actually be on the increase. There are many small businesses – pubs, inns, boarding schools, restaurants and the like – which rely on the team effort of a working couple.

But the modern pattern of dual-worker families, while somewhat similar to these long-standing patterns, is in many ways a new phenomenon. It arises through the increase in the number of married women choosing to work on a regular basis, and at the same time to have a family. As there are many motivations for the choice and many conditions under which it can operate, it is not surprising that there are various forms it can take. These affect the impact of the pattern on parents and children. We now have three generations of research on aspects of this pattern (Rapoport and Rapoport, 1978); with all the variations there are some generic issues that occur, and some characteristic ways of resolving them (Gowler and Legge, 1981).

Peter Moss has indicated some of the *economic* issues associated with the pattern. The consequences, if not the intentions, of operating the pattern are very different for those at the lower end of the social-class scale than for those higher up. At the lower end, it has the effect of keeping families above the poverty line. Higher up the scale, it enables families to increase their standard of living, taking holidays abroad, making home extensions or buying second homes and so on. It also has the effect of providing security against rapid downward mobility in the event of unemployment or career reversals of a breadwinner.

Another general feature of the pattern, also mentioned above, is that though there is a substantial basis in social values, particularly middle-class values, to support the pattern as an expression of an egalitarian orientation, the observed behaviour of husbands leads to the conclusion that this is often lip-service. Generally speaking, husbands do not replace the time by which their wives reduce household work. Sometimes, as Ann Oakley (1974) has shown, part of the husband's replacement takes the form of skimming off more enjoyable elements like playing with the children, leaving his wife with a more unremitting portion of drudgery. One writer on 'dual-career' families (Mortimer, 1977) noted that husbands in such families are often not aware of the discrepancy between what they say and what they do.

Nor is work outside the home a panacea, even when freely chosen. Weissman and Paykel (1974) noted that employed wives who are mismatched with their jobs are prone to depression in a way not dissimilar to 'captive housewives'. If a married woman, for example, takes a job for which she is over-qualified in order to escape the loneliness and boredom of being a housewife, she may come to feel that she has jumped from the frying pan into the fire, as regards the degree of personal stress she has to endure. This highlights the importance of 'fit' between person and role as an important intervening variable.

Just as there is a sub-group of conventional housewives who are reluctant in their role and would prefer to be at work, there is a sub-group of reluctant working wives. A recent study (Moss and Lewis, 1979) suggests that these women are more prevalent in the lower income groups, and that most of them would not like to stop work altogether but would rather work a little less in order to achieve a better balance between what a recent Russian study with similar findings called their functions as 'toilers, mothers, child-rearers and home-makers' (reported in *New Society*, 30 August 1979). Though this is a statistical tendency, reflecting the strains on women who have low income, ungratifying jobs and unsupportive husbands, it probably has wider validity.

However, for various reasons and in various ways, increasing proportions of families are adopting a dual-worker pattern. It is not, as some early commentators on research on dual-career families held, a freakish pattern tenable in peacetime only by a privileged minority. It is being chosen by increasing numbers of families because of its appeal to ordinary people – and its demonstrated feasibility. But, as with other patterns of work/family interrelationship, it has both gains and strains.

We are now able to define the issues with a fair degree of precision. Research on dual-worker families has now reached a state where it is possible to say that many of the early 'doomwatcher' hypotheses are 'unproven', and many of the 'advocacy' hypotheses can now be placed in perspective for further investigation. To illustrate this, there are two 'doomwatcher' hypotheses which can be examined:

(*a*) that dual-worker marriages will produce marital conflict;

(*b*) that dual-worker marriages will produce a poor environment for parenthood, leading to neglected 'latchkey' children who will swell the ranks of the delinquent, retarded and mentally disordered.

Impact on parents. Most of the reviews of literature that could help us to assess the hypothesis are inconclusive. Either they relate to overlapping but not identical populations (e.g. Hoffman and Nye's (1974) review of literature on working mothers; and Michael Rutter's (1972) review of literature on maternal deprivation); or they show no statistically significant relationship (which does not, of course, mean that there are never any negative consequences of the pattern). There are, however, some useful studies which contribute insight into the issues involved.

One American study by Orden and Bradburn (1968) of the National Opinion Research Center in Chicago suggests that marital happiness depends less on whether or not both partners work than on whether their choice was freely entered into. This work highlights the importance of the *meaning of work* (as well as the fact of working) as part of assessing work's impact on family life.

A study of British graduate couples by Lotte Bailyn (1971) indicates that while conventional families show a slightly higher proportion stating that their marriage is 'very happy', the proportions are not significantly less for working couples. Moreover, the latter are less likely to give stereotyped 'happiness' responses. But the subgroup which are markedly *low* on marital satisfaction are those in which the husband is extremely 'career-oriented' – i.e. seeks his major life satisfactions from his work and not at all from his family life (as distinct from men who place career first but also rate family as an important source of satisfaction). This circumstance occurs in conventional families, as well as dual-worker families.

Heather Ross and Isabel Sawhill (1975) of the Urban Research Institute in Washington note an association between the rising divorce rate and the rising rate of wives at work. They observe that the economic benefits of marriage are less decisive for wives who are independent earners, and that divorce has a different sub-cultural meaning among secular urban couples than in more conventional settings. The whole issue of the significance of divorce, and its occurrence at different points in the family and career cycles is involved here, but research to date provides more questions than answers.

On the other side of the coin is the body of literature from case studies of dual-worker families in which wives who hold satisfying jobs by choice express the view that they are more fulfilled: while husbands view them as more interesting marital partners. They emphasise the idea that both as spouses and parents, it is 'quality' rather than 'quantity' that counts, and that though the pattern is stressful they prefer it to the alternatives that they see for themselves, e.g. operating the conventional pattern and feeling bored and resentful.

Question

What do you think of the *second* hypothesis as a statement? Do *you* think it is unproven?

5 The duty to support

(a) AT COMMON LAW

Manby v Scott
(1663) 1 Keb 482, 1 Lev 4, 1 Mod Rep 124, O Bridg 229, 1 Sid 109, King's Bench Division

Hyde J: ... In the beginning, when God created woman as helpmate for man, he said, 'They twain shall be one flesh'; and thereupon our law says, that husband and wife are but one person in law: presently after the Fall, the judgment of God upon woman was, 'Thy desire shall be to thy husband, for thy will shall be subject to thy husband, and he shall rule over thee' (Gen iii, 16). Hereupon our law put the wife *sub potestate viri* ...

[His wife] was bone of his bone, flesh of his flesh, and no man did ever hate his own flesh so far as not to preserve it.

Question

Has the duty of support at common law anything to do with the law relating to unity of property? (See p. 51, above.)

(b) MAINTENANCE AND 'HOUSEKEEPING'

Even after the Married Women's Property Act 1882 allowed the wife to keep anything she acquired by gift or purchase, money received for housekeeping remained the property of the husband. She simply had custody of it and any savings belonged to him. (See *Hoddinott v Hoddinott* [1949] 2 KB 406 at p. 92, below.) Further, the statutes under which she could apply for a maintenance order only permitted her to enforce any order after the parties had separated. This restriction was discussed in the Report of the Royal Commission on *Marriage and Divorce* (1956):

The husband's liability where the wife is cohabiting with her husband

1042. Some witnesses suggested that if a wife's only complaint against her husband is that of wilful neglect to provide reasonable maintenance for her or her children, she should be able to obtain an order which should be fully effective notwithstanding that she and her husband continue to live together as man and wife. They pointed out that a husband's neglect to provide for his wife may not be deliberate or malicious but may be due rather to thoughtlessness or improvidence and that the existence of an effective court order may then be sufficient to keep him up to the mark. ...

1043. Against this proposal it was argued that the existence of an effective order could only further exacerbate relations which were already strained, to the point where the final breakdown of the marriage would be inevitable. Moreover, it was said that the proposal would be impracticable. The amount of the order is based on what the wife requires to keep herself when living apart from her husband. If husband and wife were in fact living together then the husband could argue that he was being asked to pay too much since he was providing her with a home; on the other hand, she might say that she was not getting enough under the order since she was expected to make all the housekeeping expenses out of a sum intended for her own needs.

1044. Other witnesses were concerned more with the status of the wife in the home. It was said that a wife should not be dependent on the whim of her husband for the amount which he allows her for housekeeping; every wife should have a right to a housekeeping allowance. Some of these witnesses proposed that the amount should be fixed by law as a certain proportion of the family income; others considered that the wife should be able to apply to the court for an order fixing the amount. These proposals we are unable to accept. The first would be clearly impracticable. The second would require the court in effect to determine the standard of living of the family.

1045. We are impressed, however, by the argument that the present law fails to make any provision for the case where the wife has constant difficulty in getting money from her husband but at the same time does not want to break up the home. We have been told that in fact quite often a wife who has obtained a maintenance order does not leave her husband and that the situation improves because he, not realising that her order is unenforceable, makes her regular payments. We therefore think that it would be desirable to allow a wife who has obtained a maintenance order solely on the ground of her husband's wilful neglect to provide reasonable maintenance for her (or for the children) to be able to enforce that order without leaving her husband.

1046. We have carefully considered the arguments advanced against the proposal but in our opinion their force has been exaggerated. If relations between husband and wife are already seriously strained, we think it unlikely that the fact that the wife has obtained a court order which is enforceable will make matters any worse. But where the situation has not gone so far we believe that in some cases at least there is reasonable hope that the making of an order may bring the husband to his senses. Moreover, the very fact that the court has power to make such an order may in itself have a salutary effect on those husbands who are apt to be careless of their financial responsibility for their families. ...

1047. As to the practical difficulty referred to in paragraph 1043, we feel confident that it is not insuperable. If the wife wishes to go on living with her husband we see no reason why the court, when assessing the amount of the order, should not take into account the fact that the husband is paying the rent. At the same time the court could point out to the husband that if he expects his wife to run his household he must pay her a sum over and above that specified in the order. If the wife subsequently left her husband she could apply for an increase in the amount of the order to meet the cost of providing accommodation for herself.

The Law Commission in their Working Paper on *Matrimonial Proceedings in Magistrates' Courts* (1973) agreed with the Royal Commission. The Law Commission felt that there might be advantages if an order which is made on the ground of failure to provide reasonable maintenance (see p. 96, below) could be enforceable for the period of six months whilst the parties continued to live together. If the parties continued to live together for more than six months the order would become unenforceable. In their subsequent Report (1976), the Law Commission commented on the evidence submitted on this topic:

2.60 This tentative proposal by the Working Party, not unnaturally, aroused strong feelings amongst those commenting on the working paper. The feeling of the majority was that such a provision would be useful, but it was pointed out that there would be practical difficulties. How, for example, would payments be made under such an order? Would a husband who had failed to maintain his wife be required to send payments to the court each week for collection by his wife? Or would he be expected to make payments direct to her? Neither course would be free of difficulty. Another significant criticism of this proposal was that it might lead to a number of wives asking the court to 'fix the housekeeping'.
2.61 We have no doubt that cases occur in which the sole cause, or the real cause, of matrimonial difficulties is the husband's carelessness of his financial responsibilities. Where the parties are still living together in such cases, it seems to us to be wrong that the court should be unable to make an immediately enforceable financial order in favour of the wife. The result is that a wife who stays with her husband is worse off financially than she would be by leaving him. While the law is in such a state it may be argued that it is providing an inducement for the wife to leave her husband and is thus favouring the break down of the marriage instead of its repair. We, therefore, think that a maintenance order made in favour of a spouse while the parties are cohabiting should be enforceable notwithstanding the cohabitation.

The recommendation of the Law Commission is contained in s. 25(1) of the Domestic Proceedings and Magistrates' Courts Act 1978 (as amended by the Children Act 1989):

25. – (1) Where –

(*a*) periodical payments are required to be made to one of the parties to a marriage (whether for his own benefit or for the benefit of a child of the family) by an order made under section 2 or 6 of this Act or by an interim maintenance order made under section 19 of this Act (otherwise than on an application under section 7 of this Act), ...

the order shall be enforceable notwithstanding that the parties to the marriage are living with each other at the date of the making of the order or that, although they are not living with each other at that date, they subsequently resume living with each other; but the order shall cease to have effect if after that date the parties continue to live with each other, or resume living with each other, for a continuous period exceeding six months.

Questions

(i) Is an order for maintenance of the wife and/or the children the same thing as an order for a housekeeping allowance?
(ii) When the wife obtains a maintenance order, whom should she spend it on?
(iii) At the end of six months, the wife will have to decide either to leave with an order, or stay without one. Does this rule make matters worse?

At common law, any savings which the wife was able to accumulate from housekeeping allowances from the husband, and any property which she purchased out of such savings, belonged to the husband:

Hoddinott v Hoddinott
[1949] 2 KB 406, 65 TLR 266, 93 Sol Jo 296, Court of Appeal

A husband and wife regularly invested in football pools, in the husband's name, the savings on housekeeping moneys. Forecasting was the result of their joint effort. Their forecast won a prize of £138. 7s which was paid into the husband's bank account. Part of the money was used to purchase furniture in the home. The parties quarrelled and separated and the wife claimed the furniture or at least part of it.

Bucknill LJ: ... I am not at all satisfied that she had got any legal interest in the housekeeping money as such. The money belonged to the husband, and I should have thought she held it in trust for him for keeping them both, and if the husband decides to take some of it away from the purchase of food and such things to invest it in football pools, it seems to me that the money still remained his, and that in the absence of any contract between them the proceeds or winnings on that housekeeping money also belong to him.

Questions

(i) If the wife holds the housekeeping money in trust for the husband, for keeping them both, might she not at least be entitled to retain sufficient of the money to maintain herself at their standard of living?
(ii) The husband decides the standard of living. What can a wife do about this if the standard of living is not appropriate to his means?
(iii) The Married Women's Property Act 1964 provides:

1. If any question arises as to the right of a husband or wife to money derived from any allowance made by the husband for the expenses of the matrimonial home or for similar purposes, or to any property acquired out of such money, the money or property shall, in the absence of any agreement between them to the contrary, be treated as belonging to the husband and the wife in equal shares.

Husband and wife are both earning similar amounts. The wife does the household shopping one week and the husband does it the next week. In one week, when it is the wife's turn, she gives the husband her purse and asks him to do the shopping. There is more than enough in the purse. Will she be entitled to the change? Would it make a difference to your answer if the parties were not married?

The Law Commission's Working Paper, *Transfer of Money Between Spouses* (1985) recommended reform in part so that the sexually discriminatory aspect of the 1964 Act be removed. The responses to the Working Paper persuaded the Law Commission to look at the whole issue in a much broader context. The recommendations in *Family Law: Matrimonial Property* are as follows:

5.1 We *recommend* that in future the purchase of property (with some exclusions) by one or both spouses for their joint use or benefit should give rise to joint ownership of that property subject to a contrary intention on the part of the purchasing spouse, known to the other spouse.

5.2 We further *recommend* that transfer of property by one spouse to the other for their joint use or benefit should give rise to joint ownership of that property subject to a contrary intention on the part of the transferring spouse, known to the other spouse. If the transferred property is not for joint use or benefit it should become the sole beneficial property of the spouse to whom it is transferred, subject to a contrary intention on the part of the transferring spouse, known to the other spouse.

5.3 These recommendations do *not* extend to property purchased or transferred for business purposes.

5.[4] We *recommend* that the Married Women's Property Act 1964 be repealed.

(We discuss these recommendations in detail in Chapter 5.)

6 The enforcement of the duty of support

The history of the magistrates' matrimonial jurisdiction is not free from controversy. The Law Commission Working Paper (1973) describes the development in the following way:

7. The Matrimonial Causes Act 1857 established a secular court to hear and determine matrimonial causes. Named 'the Court for Divorce and Matrimonial Causes', it was empowered to dissolve marriages (a power previously exercisable only by Act of Parliament) and to grant judicial separation (a remedy previously available only in the ecclesiastical courts). The remedies provided in the 1857 Act (divorce, judicial separation, nullity and restitution of conjugal rights) dealt with breakdown of marriage but had little or no relevance save in the context of breakdown induced by grievous matrimonial offence, and the Act made no provision, except in one respect, for the exercise of any matrimonial jurisdiction by magistrates. The provision it did make was really directed towards a situation of irretrievable breakdown – the 'protection order' which magistrates were empowered to make to protect 'any money or property [a deserted wife] may acquire by her lawful industry' or otherwise against the claims of her husband and his creditors.

8. The 1857 Act was of very little value to anyone outside the propertied classes. The great majority of wives whom their husbands abandoned or maltreated had to make do with such relief as they could find in the poor law or the criminal law. The first help to the ill-treated woman was given by section 4 of the Matrimonial Causes Act 1878, which brought together the strands of the criminal and the poor law for her benefit. It provided that, if a husband was convicted summarily or otherwise of an aggravated assault upon his wife, the court or magistrate before whom he was convicted, if satisfied that the wife's future safety was in peril, should have power to order that she should no longer be bound to cohabit with her husband (such order to have the force and effect in all respects of [sic] a decree of judicial separation on the grounds of cruelty). The order might further provide for:

(i) the husband to pay the wife weekly maintenance, and
(ii) the legal custody of any children under 10 to be given to the wife.

9. The 1878 Act was followed by a wider ranging reform in 1886, when the Married Women (Maintenance in Case of Desertion) Act gave a more direct and economically useful remedy to wives. Under this Act if a married woman could establish that her husband was able to support her and his children but had refused or neglected to do so and had deserted her, a magistrates' court could award her maintenance of up to £2 a week. Powers under the 1878 Act were unaffected. The Summary Jurisdiction (Married Women) Act 1895 gave magistrates' courts their general matrimonial jurisdiction.

10. The 1895 Act was a major advance. It empowered magistrates to order the payment of a weekly sum of money where the husband's only offence was 'wilful neglect to provide reasonable maintenance'. Thus, it constituted a code of matrimonial relief designed to deal with the situation where matrimonial breakdown had occurred but was not irretrievable, and to provide relief before it became irretrievable. This code remained the basis of the magistrates' law until 1960. ... The Matrimonial Proceedings (Magistrates' Courts) Act 1960 attempted to rationalise and modernise the law in the light of the recommendations of the Morton Commission on Marriage and Divorce (1956) and of the Arthian Davies Committee (1959). The major advance was that the Act made relief generally available to husbands as well as wives (though the husband had to prove impairment of earning capacity to obtain a money order) and gave power to make orders providing for the custody and support of children, even when the wife (or husband) failed to prove her (or his) ground of complaint.

11. Over the years Parliament has raised the limits of financial relief that the magistrates can order (there has never been a limit on the powers of the divorce court in this respect). ... Finally, the Maintenance Orders Act 1968, on the recommendation of the Departmental Committee on Statutory Maintenance Limits, abolished the upper limit for the maintenance of both spouse and child.

The Finer Report on *One-Parent Families* (1974) suggested that the Law Commission was guilty of a 'seriously mistaken interpretation of history' in asserting that the magistrates' jurisdiction was designed to deal with situations where matrimonial breakdown had occurred but was not irretrievable. The view of the Finer Report is as follows:

36. The creation, ... of a matrimonial jurisdiction to be exercised in the magistrates' courts was to have a profound and lasting effect on the arrangements, both substantive and procedural, which English law makes for regulating the consequences of matrimonial breakdown. All of the following characteristics were implanted into this part of our legal system. First, two separate jurisdictions, High Court and summary, existing side by side, but administering different and overlapping rules and remedies, came into being for the purpose of dealing with the same human predicament. Secondly, while the reforms of 1857 were designed to remove matrimonial disputes to the arbitrament of a superior and civil court of record, the jurisdiction created in 1878 was vested in inferior tribunals, given over to the criminal process, and universally known, because of their close association with the police, as 'police courts.' Thirdly, whereas the 1857 reformers regarded legal intervention into matrimony, maintenance and the custody of children as so delicate and important that the jurisdiction had to be entrusted to professional judges of the highest rank, the 1878 jurisdiction was to be exercised by a magistracy overwhelmingly lay in its composition. Finally, the concern for extending to a larger population the benefits which the 1857 reforms had afforded to the wealthy bore fruit in the creation of a secondary system designed for what were considered to be the special and cruder requirements of the poor.

The different treatment of the history led the two bodies to formulate different principles upon which the law and procedure should be based. The Law Commission's Working Paper suggested:

24. There is a clear contrast between the magistrates' jurisdiction and that exercised by the divorce court under the 1969 and 1970 Acts. The magistrates' jurisdiction is normally exercised at a stage earlier than irretrievable breakdown and is not concerned with change of status. Indeed, the marriage may only temporarily have run into difficulties. There is evidence that many orders made by the magistrates come to an end because the parties are reconciled. The role of the magistrates' court in dealing with those involved in matrimonial breakdown may perhaps be illustrated by comparing it with a casualty clearing station. All the casualties of marriage can be brought to the magistrates' court. Some are clearly mortal; they should go on to be laid to rest by proceedings in the divorce court; some are serious, being more likely than not to end in final breakdown; some however will respond to local treatment and may well recover completely; others are trivial, requiring no more than sympathetic handling and encouragement. It is the duty of those who work in a casualty clearing station to give attention and interim or substantive treatment to all, to do nothing which might turn a minor case into a major one, and to refrain from attempting to treat those whom they have not the competence or equipment to treat. So too the magistrates in their matrimonial jurisdictions. They must look to the possibility that no more may be needed than sympathy and the opportunity for reconciliation. But they must also have the means of treating the more serious casualties of marriage. Turning away from the language of metaphor, we suggest therefore that the role of the magistrates – the principle and objectives of their matrimonial jurisdiction – should be to enable them to intervene on the application of either party to a marriage:

(i) to deal with family relations during a period of breakdown which is not necessarily permanent or irretrievable
   (*a*) by relieving the financial need which breakdown can bring to the parties,
   (*b*) by giving such protection to one or other of the parties as may be necessary, and
   (*c*) by providing for the welfare and support of the children; and

(ii) to preserve the marriage in existence, where possible.

The Finer Report refuted the 'casualty clearing station' approach:

4.383 We think the working party has allowed itself to be misled concerning the actual role of magistrates' courts in matrimonial breakdown by the attractions of a medico-military analogy. We have assembled compelling evidence to demonstrate that the very existence and persistence of the dual jurisdiction, and of the attitudes and institutions stemming from it, account for the presence in magistrates' courts of many very poor folk who possess neither knowledge nor expectation of any other legal cure for their marital ills. Nor is the analogy compelling when we find that two thirds of the casualties on the books in January 1966 were to be found there in July 1971, that nearly half of the discharges during this period had been patients for ten years or more at the time of their discharge, and that on 1 July 1971 there were some 58,000 magistrates' orders in force which were ten years old, or older. We doubt whether many clearing stations would find this a satisfactory work record.

The Finer Report argued strongly that the matrimonial jurisdiction of the magistrates' court used, as it is, by only one section of the community, serves to highlight the social divisions within the community.

Questions

(i) Now that the law applied by the magistrates' courts has been reformed into Family Proceedings Courts along the lines advanced by the Law Commission in their Report and Working Paper (see p. 271, below), is there any force left in the Finer Report's criticism?
(ii) One of the most important aspects of the magisterial jurisdiction in the present dual system is as a registration and enforcement agency of county court orders. Many of the applications to the magistrates' courts seek variation of these orders and/or remission of arrears which have accrued. Is the effect of a refusal to remit arrears as serious to a paying party as a decision on a successful application by the payee to vary an order?

Under the 1960 Act, in order to obtain a matrimonial order in the magistrates' court, the applicant had to prove that the respondent had committed a matrimonial offence. The Working Paper fully accepted that the time had come for the obligation of each spouse to maintain the other to be recognised as the cornerstone to the new grounds. The obligation of support should be seen to be fully reciprocal. Given this general principle the Working Paper went on to consider the possible new grounds:

35. If the obligation to maintain were to be recognised in the general matrimonial law as fully reciprocal, in what circumstances should magistrates have power to order maintenance and what facts should they take into account in doing so? For the purpose of discussion we tentatively put forward the proposition that the principal ground upon which a court should have power to order maintenance should be failure by one of the parties to the marriage to provide such maintenance for the other party or for any children as is reasonable in all the circumstances. We recognise that such a formulation, which relies upon the concept of 'reasonable in all the circumstances', leaves a very wide discretion to the court. But we think this is a good starting point, particularly for the lay magistracy.

Questions

(i) Do you think it a good idea for the lay magistracy to have such a wide discretion?
(ii) Do you think it a good idea for anyone to have such a wide discretion?

The amended Domestic Proceedings and Magistrates' Courts Act 1978 now reads:

1. Either party to a marriage may apply to a magistrates' court for an order under section 2 of this Act on the ground that the other party to the marriage (in this Part of this Act referred to as 'the respondent') –
   (*a*) has failed to provide reasonable maintenance for the applicant; or
   (*b*) has failed to provide, or to make a proper contribution towards, reasonable maintenance for any child of the family ...

Questions

(i) Is there an argument for abolishing the magistrates' courts jurisdiction in these matters outright? What if anything would you exchange for magistrates' courts jurisdiction? (See Chapter 7.)
(ii) Is there anything left of the husband's common law duty to maintain?
(iii) Is an earning wife under any duty to provide housekeeping money (*a*) to a non-earning husband or (*b*) to an earning husband?
(iv) Section 6 of the 1978 Act as amended states:

6. – (1) Either party to a marriage may apply to a magistrates' court for an order under this section on the ground that *either the party making the application* or the other party to the marriage has agreed to make such financial provision as may be specified in the application and, subject to subsection (3) below, the court on such an application may, if –

(*a*) it is satisfied that the applicant or the respondent, as the case may be, has agreed to make that provision, and
(*b*) it has no reason to think that it would be contrary to the interests of justice to exercise its powers hereunder,

order that the *applicant* or the respondent, as the case may be, shall make the financial provision specified in the application.

What advantages are there, for a payee and a payer in obtaining an order under s. 6?
(v) In *Simister v Simister* [1987] 1 All ER 233, [1986] 1 WLR 1463, Waite J said that 'maintenance is normally very much a dunning process, with one side pressing for as much, and the other side holding out for as little, as each can fairly get or give.' (*a*) Is such a process desirable? (*b*) If you think that it is not desirable, how would you change the law to lessen this effect?

Three cases on the Act are the following. In the first case there were no children.

Robinson v Robinson
[1983] Fam 42, [1983] 1 All ER 391, [1983] 2 WLR 146, 4 FLR 521, 13 Fam Law 48, Court of Appeal

The parties were married in 1976. The husband was a soldier and the wife ceased her employment after she married him. They lived in married quarters. In late 1980, the husband was posted to Belize, and the wife returned to her parents. When the husband returned from overseas duty in March 1981, the wife decided that she was not going back to him, although she did not tell him of her decision until August 1981. The wife applied for maintenance under s. 2 of the Domestic Proceedings and Magistrates' Courts Act 1978. The magistrates' found that the wife had deserted her husband and that this behaviour was 'gross and obvious'. The magistrates' court said 'the wife's desertion of her husband, he not having committed any misconduct, was a matter of the gravest importance in relation to this marriage and was a matter to be taken into account together with all the other matters set out in section 3 of the 1978 Act when deciding what financial provision order, if any, should be made in favour of the applicant.' The magistrates' court awarded her periodical payments of £15 per week, one-tenth of the joint income, for a period of five years from the date of the order. The wife appealed unsuccessfully to the Divisional Court and on further appeal to the Court of Appeal.

Waller LJ: The magistrates held that (the conduct of the wife) was 'gross and obvious misconduct' and in so doing were referring to the test applied by Lord Denning MR and Ormrod J (in *Wachtel v Wachtel* [1973] Fam 72, [1973] 1 All ER 829). The words 'gross and obvious misconduct' can be somewhat misleading, but as I understand it they were referring to the fact that this was an unusual case far removed from those where much blame could be put on both sides and it was a case where it would have been unjust to give the financial support which would normally be given. In answer to the question would it offend a reasonable man's sense of justice that this wife's conduct should be left out of account in deciding the financial provision which the husband should make, the magistrates were answering 'Yes it would' when they said: 'The wife's desertion of her husband, he not having committed any misconduct was a matter of the gravest importance in relation to the marriage ...'. On the facts found the behaviour of the wife was quite capable of being within the terms I have outlined above. In my opinion it is quite impossible to interfere with the decision of the magistrates.
Appeal dismissed.

In the second case, there was a child.

Vasey v Vasey
[1985] FLR 596, [1985] Fam Law 158, Court of Appeal.

The magistrates' court granted the custody of the child of the family to the wife with access to the husband. They ordered that the husband pay £15 a week for the child but refused to make an order for the maintenance of the wife because she had deserted her husband. The wife appealed unsuccessfully to the Divisional Court and then to the Court of Appeal.

Dunn LJ: In *Robinson v Robinson* the magistrates had found, as in this case, that conduct was a relevant consideration and, accordingly, they made a substantial reduction in the maintenance order as compared with the order they would have made in the absence of such a finding. ...

In this case there is no appeal against the finding of the magistrates that conduct was relevant. Indeed, there could have been no such appeal since the wife left the husband after less than 9 months of marriage and did not attempt to justify her leaving. But what is said in this court by Mr Lightwing (counsel for the wife) is that the magistrates failed to take into account matters which they were required to take into account by reason of the provisions of s. 3 of the Act; that, accordingly, they failed to carry out the balancing exercise required by that section and consequently, by reason of the decision of this court in *Dicocco v Milne* (1982) 4 FLR 247, an appellate court was free to carry out the balancing exercise since there was sufficient evidence to enable it to do so. ... The proper approach for magistrates in considering any application under s. 2 of the Act is therefore to make findings seriatim upon each of the matters set out in [s. 3(2)] and then to balance the factors against one another so as to arrive at an order which is just and reasonable. The weight to be attached to any particular matter is for the magistrates, but they must take account of all of them. The most important function of magistrates is usually to balance needs and responsibilities against financial resources; and if, in an exceptional case, the magistrates decide that conduct is relevant, that must be put into the balance. I say 'an exceptional case' because experience has shown that it is dangerous to make judgments about the cause of the breakdown of a marriage without full inquiry, since the conduct of the one spouse can only be measured against the conduct of the other, and marriages seldom break down without faults on both sides.

In this case the magistrates do not appear to have considered either para. (*a*) or (*b*) of [s. 3(2),] the most important paragraphs dealing with financial resources and needs, and they carried out apparently no balancing exercise at all. With respect to the Divisional Court, the fact that they may have considered the alternative of a reduction of maintenance for the wife is, in my judgment, no indication that they took into account any factor save conduct.

[Dunn LJ then dealt with the various matters relating to the needs and resources of the parties, and continued ...]

Mr Lightwing submitted that were it not for the relevant conduct, the wife in this case could have expected to receive an order in excess of £5,000 a year less tax, if the conventional one-third approach was applied as a starting figure. But because of the finding as to conduct he conceded that there should be a substantial reduction. He submitted that the wife should at least be put into the position in which she now is on social security, which I should emphasize is, by definition, to put her at subsistence level. That would involve, said Mr Lightwing, an order of between £30 and £40 a week for her, in addition to £15 a week for the child. That would still leave her below the tax belt.

In my view this proposal by Mr Lightwing is by no means an excessive one, and Mr Briggs (counsel for the husband) accepted that if we were to come to the conclusion that it was open to us to review the magistrates' order his proposal was a reasonable one – indeed, I would say that it is a modest one. It would give the wife about £55 a week for herself and the child under the terms of the order and, in addition, she would be entitled to £10.55 a week child allowance and single parent allowance. Of course the wife, out of those moneys, would have to pay her own rent of £20 or £25 a week. ...

I would only add that I would make these orders on the basis that the wife is not working. If and when she is able to work, it would be open to the husband to apply for an appropriate reduction having regard to the means of the parties at that time.

Appeal allowed: £33 p.w. for wife, £20 p.w. expenses to be paid direct to the child.

Questions

(i) Are you relieved by the approach taken by the Court of Appeal in *Vasey v Vasey?*

(ii) Do you think this case is affected by the introduction of the Child Support Act 1991 (see p. 116, below).

In the third case, there were step-children.

Day v Day

[1988] FCR 470, [1988] 1 FLR 278, High Court, Family Division

The marriage had lasted only six weeks. Nevertheless, the husband married the wife after a long relationship and both treated and accepted the children as children of the family. He had in effect 'taken on a commitment'. The magistrates' court made an order for the husband to pay £15 per week to the wife and £5 per week to each of the children on the basis of his admitted desertion. On appeal, the husband contended that the court should have made a nominal order for five reasons: (i) the wife, now on social security benefits, was in fact better off financially without her husband than with him; (ii) she was of an age to go out to work; (iii) the husband had no means to pay such amounts to his wife because of his outgoings; (iv) the marriage had been a short one; and (v) although the husband's desertion could be criticised it did not entitle any payment to be increased.

Wood J: This is an appeal from a decision of the justices sitting at Tottenham on 23 September 1985. ...

The justices found that this husband knew what he was doing in accepting these two children as children of the family; that he did so, and that he provided subsistence and maintenance for them during the short duration of the cohabitation.

Having found those general facts, the justices looked at the means of the wife, namely, the receipts that she had from the DHSS and her outgoings.

Prior to the marriage, the wife and children had been on social security and after the departure of the husband they returned to remain on social security and, to a substantial extent, they are still reliant upon social security. It is right to point out that any money paid by this husband towards the maintenance of his wife and the children of the family will reduce the liability of the taxpayer, but that is conceded not to be a relevant factor.

Mr Marks [for the husband] submits that, based upon those factors which I have mentioned [the five factors above], the justices really did not take into consideration the various factors set out in s. 3 of the 1978 Act, the financial resources, the need and obligations, the standard of living, the ages and duration. They ignored the amendment [in 1984] and ignored the fact that somebody else, namely the natural father, should have been maintaining these children. Looking at the reasons it is quite clear that the justices, in their reasons, expressly referred to s. 3 and the amendment. It is quite apparent that the many factors which are mentioned by Mr Marks are taken into account in their findings of fact and their reasoning if one looks at the document as a whole, and, in my judgment, it would not be right to seek to look upon the reasons given by justices as one would a carefully reserved judgment and to search with too fine a toothcomb for the phraseology and the criticisms which are possible. I have no doubt here that these justices took the very greatest care, as one can see from their reasons in this case. They saw and heard the witnesses, they have indicated whose evidence they preferred and they have referred to the correct statutory provisions which they must have had before them. They also had the assistance of Mr Marks who, I am sure, presented the case before them with the skill and determination with which he has presented this appeal.

I am satisfied here that there are no reasons for this appeal to succeed and it is dismissed.

Question

Can you find any common thread which runs through the judgments?

The statistics for domestic proceedings in magistrates' courts suggest a dramatic drop in applications for 'married women maintenance orders' – from 28,004 in 1968 to 6,851 in 1978. Applications increased during the early 1980s to 13,900 in 1984, but then dropped again to 11,070 in 1985. There has been a continuing fall, and there were only 8,590 applications in 1989 and no more than 3,600 in 1992. Applications under s. 6 (agreed payments orders) show a similar drop from 8,340 in 1986 to 5,190 in 1989 and only 1,110 in 1992. Applications under s. 7 have always been low; in 1992 there were just 20. The magistrates' courts are often used to register orders made elsewhere, and in 1992, some 7,900 orders made by other courts were registered. There were also 32,500 applications for variation, revival or revocation of financial provision orders. Both these figures, however, represent significant falls from the figures in earlier years (Home Office Statistical Bulletin 26/1993).

Questions

(i) Which of the following do you consider the most likely explanation for the fall: (*a*) the reform of the law of divorce which came into force in 1971; (*b*) a fall in the number of married women needing support from their husbands; (*c*) the decision of the supplementary benefit authorities at the time, following the Finer Report (1974) no longer to advise married women who claimed benefit to take action against their husbands; (*d*) some other reason or combination of reasons?

Domestic proceedings per 100,000 population at magistrates' courts England and Wales 1992

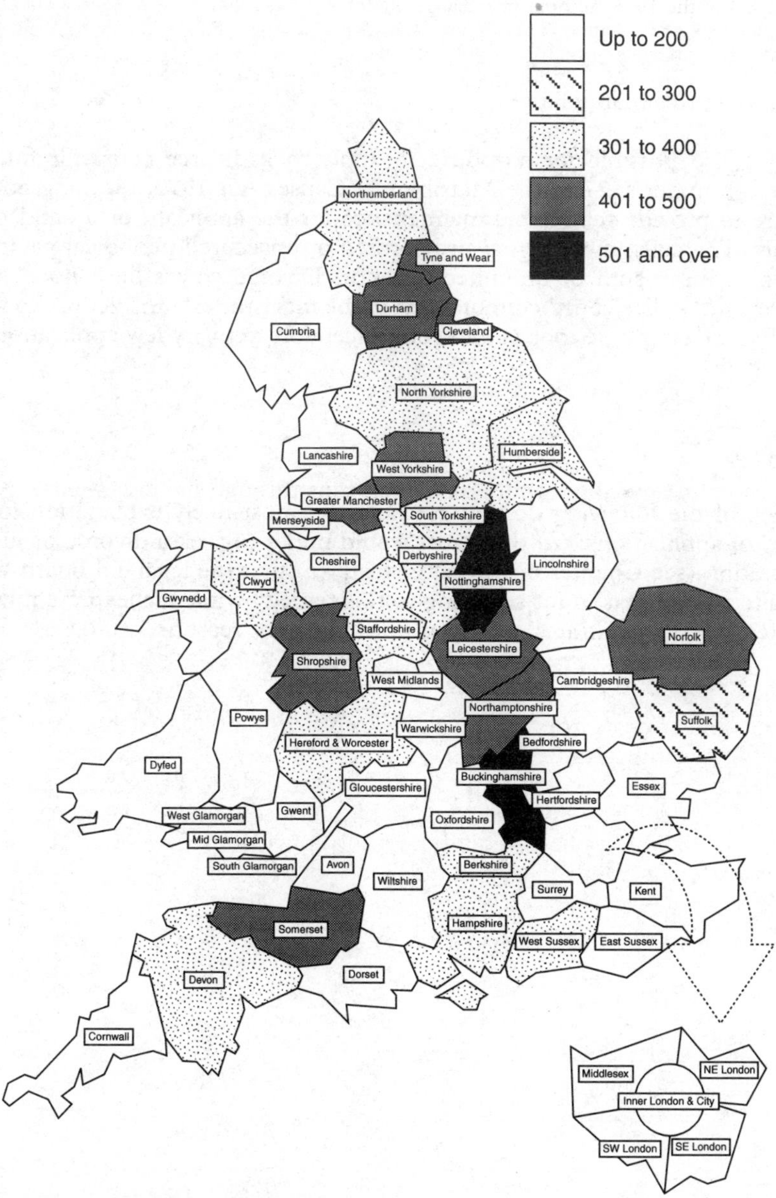

Source: HO Statistical Bulletin, 26/93

(ii) Do you think that the changes brought about by the Child Support Act (1991) (see Chapter 4, below) will result in an increase or further decrease in 'married women maintenance orders'?

The map above (p. 101) illustrates the distribution of domestic proceedings in magistrates' courts in 1992.

Question

What does this map tell us?

It is also possible for a spouse to apply to a divorce court for financial provision under s. 27 of the Matrimonial Causes Act 1973, on the ground of failure to provide reasonable maintenance for the applicant or a child of the family. The court may then award secured or unsecured periodical payments, and/or a lump sum of unlimited amount. Divorce courts have none of the unpleasant 'police court' connotations of the magistrates' jurisdiction, to which the Finer Committee took such strong exception, yet very few applications are ever made.

Question

Which of the following do you consider the most likely explanation for the rarity of applications: (*a*) that most would prefer to seek a divorce or judicial separation (see Chapter 6, below) instead; (*b*) that the legal aid board would require a good reason for resorting to this remedy while a cheaper equivalent existed in the magistrates' court; or (*c*) some other reason?

Chapter 4

State support and private support

This chapter considers the complex questions which surround the question of state involvement in family income support. Of necessity, the chapter is concerned with priorities and with parity of treatment. It looks at lone-parent families, some of whom may well have forms of support other than the state; it looks at poor two-parent families, who may well have no other means of support; and it looks at those families where there is a dependent elderly adult living in the household.

We consider first the financial position of lone parents and their children. This question necessarily links up with the section in the previous chapter on maintenance claims in the domestic court. An examination of this area is also important in an appreciation of parity with other families when it comes to considering competing claims to state funds.

1 Poverty and the lone-parent family

The growth in the number of lone-parent families in Great Britain is apparent from the following table from *Social Trends* 26 (1996).

Families headed by lone parents as a percentage[1] of all families with dependant children

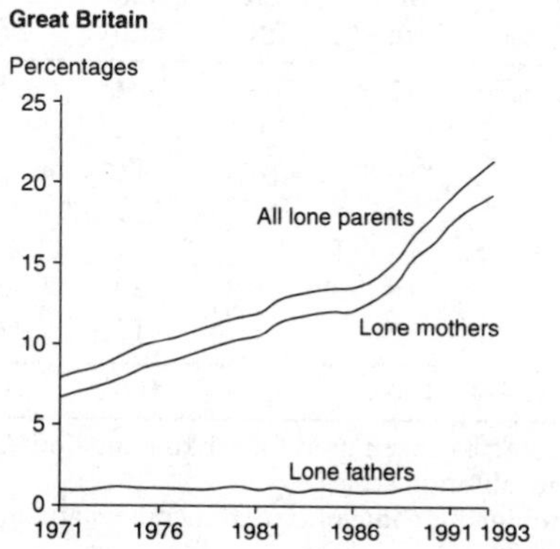

1 Three year moving averages used (apart from 1993).

Source: General Household Survey, Office of Population Censuses and Surveys

In 1993 lone parents comprised 22% of all households in Great Britain with dependent children; in 1971, the figure was about 7½%.

To place the numbers in perspective, we print below the following two tables from *Social Trends* 26 (1996).

Households[1]: by type of household and family

Great Britain — Percentages

	1961	1971	1981	1991	1994–95
One person					
Under pensionable age	4	6	8	11	12
Over pensionable age	7	12	14	16	15
Two or more unrelated adults	5	4	5	3	6
One family					
Married couple[2]					
No children	26	27	26	28	25
1–2 dependent children[3]	30	26	25	20	20
3 or more dependent children	8	9	6	5	5
Non-dependent children only	10	8	8	8	6
Lone parent[2]					
Dependent children[3]	2	3	5	6	7
Non-dependent children only	4	4	4	4	3
Two or more families	3	1	1	1	1
All households (=100%)(millions)	16.2	18.2	19.5	22.4	23.1

1 See Appendix, Part 2: Households.
2 Other individuals who were not family members may also be included.
3 May also include non-dependent children.

Source: Office of Population Censuses and Surveys; Department of the Environment

Household disposable income: by quintile grouping and household type, 1994–95

United Kingdom — Percentages

	Quintile groups of households[1]					
	Bottom fifth	Next fifth	Middle fifth	Next fifth	Top fifth	All households
Retired households[2]	41	45	24	14	10	27
Non-retired households						
1 adult	12	10	11	14	21	14
2 adults	9	11	19	25	36	20
1 adult with children	14	8	4	2	1	6
2 adults with children	18	18	29	27	22	23
3 or more adults[3]	6	8	13	18	10	11
All households	100	100	100	100	100	100

1 Equivalised disposable income has been used for ranking the households into quintile groups. See Appendix, Part 5: Equivalisation scales.
2 Households where the combined income of retired members amounts to at least half the total gross income of the household.
3 With or without children.

Source: Central Statistical Office

Thus a substantial proportion of lone parent families form a part of the lower income group of households on whom the bulk of state benefits are targeted. Bradshaw and Millar, in *Lone Parent Families in the UK* (1991) explain:

Lone parents are very different from other families with children in terms of both the sources and the level of their incomes. Unlike other (non-retired) households where earnings typically form the largest component of income, lone parents more often combine income from a variety of other sources, and benefits play a much larger role in the total. According to the 1989 Family Expenditure Survey the average gross weekly incomes of lone parent households were made up 49 per cent from earnings, 35 per cent from benefits and 29 per cent from other sources. By contrast the average gross weekly incomes of couples with two children were made up 81 per cent from earnings, five per cent from benefits and one per cent from other sources. Thus while benefits usually form a small addition to earnings for married couples, for lone parents they are often the major or sole source of income ...

The official statistics on 'low income' families and the new series on 'households below average income' also show lone parents significantly over-represented among the poorest families. In 1985 there were 540,000 lone parent families in receipt of supplementary benefit and a further 100,000 with incomes no higher than 40 per cent above supplementary benefit level – giving a total of 640,000 families (1.7 million adults and children) or 73 per cent of those in lone parent families at that time. This represents an increase of 40 per cent in the numbers of lone parents with incomes at that sort of level since 1979. The number of persons in lone-parent families with incomes below 110 per cent of supplementary benefit level increased by 67 per cent between 1979 and 1987. The 'households below average income' also show lone parents at the bottom end of the income distribution.

Maclean and Eekelaar in *Children and Divorce: Economic Factors* (1983) speaking of children of divorced parents, emphasise the importance of relating the problems of the poverty level for dependent children of lone-parent families to other children in comparable situations:

... but these children have potential sources of support not available to children of sick or unemployed fathers, or children in large families. On divorce there are essentially four sources from which support might be found to arrest the decline in the economic circumstances of the former family. The first comprises *the resources of the former family* as they stood at the moment of the dissolution. However, as most studies have shown, these are generally meagre (Todd and Jones, 1972; Manners and Rauta, 1981). But where an independent household existed, a dwelling, either owner-occupied or rented, is likely to be the most significant item. The second is *the earning capacity of the custodial parent* (which we assume for simplicity to be the mother). The third is *the earning capacity of the non-custodial parent* (the father). And the last resource is to be found in *State provisions*.

Questions

(i) In spite of the overall growth in the number of lone-parent families, the number of widowed mothers has actually declined since the early 1970s. Why do you think this is?
(ii) Maclean and Eekelaar actually identify in their examination of potential sources of support for children of divorced parents a 'fifth and powerful economic resource'. What do you think they are referring to?

In her chapter on 'Income Maintenance for Families with Children', in *Families in Britain* (1982), Ruth Lister described the framework of the system of state support up until the reforms in the Social Security Act 1986.

The basic framework for today's income maintenance provisions was laid down in the Beveridge Report of 1942. The Beveridge Plan envisaged a comprehensive 'scheme of social insurance against interruption and destruction of earning power' combined with a 'general system of children's allowances, sufficient to meet the subsistence needs' of children. Family allowances (for all children but the first) and contributory national insurance benefits (such as unemployment and widows' benefits) were introduced after the war. The Beveridge Plan also included the safety-net of a means-tested national assistance scheme designed to protect the minority who fell through the meshes of the insurance scheme. It was intended that this safety-net would wither away until it was catering for only a tiny minority. Instead, because of the failure to pay adequate national insurance benefits, as recommended by Beveridge, the numbers claiming means-tested assistance (renamed supplementary benefit in 1966) trebled from one to three million between 1948 and 1978. Further, governments have attempted to bolster up inadequate income maintenance provisions for both those in and out of work through the introduction of a range of means-tested benefits, which have been much criticised. A classic example was the introduction, in 1971, of Family Income Supplement for poor working families, as an alternative to fulfilling an election pledge to increase family allowances. The failure to pay high enough national insurance benefits and family allowances was one reason for the growing dependence on means-tested benefits. The other was the exclusion from the Beveridge Plan of people such as the congenitally disabled who could not meet the contribution conditions attached to the insurance benefits. During the 1970s a number of non-contributory benefits were, therefore, introduced to help the disabled and those at home to care for disabled relatives.

The overall picture today is, thus, one of a confusing patchwork of contributory, non-contributory and means-tested benefits. Much of this patchwork has grown up in isolation from the other main element in our income maintenance provisions: the tax system. ... The system of personal tax allowances was supposed to ensure that 'there should be no income tax levied upon any income which is insufficient to provide the owner with what he requires for subsistence' (Royal Commission on the Taxation of Profits and Income, 1954). [However] the personal tax allowances patently no longer perform this function. The value of the tax allowances has been so eroded since the war that people can now start to pay tax at incomes which are below the poverty line. ... When you take the growing dependence on means-tested benefits and add to it the growing numbers of low income working families drawn into the tax net, the result is one of the more ludicrous aspects of the income maintenance scheme: 'the poverty trap'. The 'poverty trap' is a term 'used to describe the situation in which a family loses more in terms of extra tax paid and reduced benefits received than it gains from a pay increase which brought them about' (Pond, 1978). It is families with children who are most vulnerable to the poverty trap.

The most recent development in income maintenance provision for families has been the introduction of the child benefit scheme. This represented the fusion of two hitherto separate strands of financial support for children: family allowances and child tax allowances.

The Social Security Act 1986 replaced the supplementary benefit with a system known as income support. A claimant is entitled to income support if he or she is aged 18 or over and available for employment although not engaged in 'remunerative work'. There are certain categories of claimant exempt from the requirement of having to show evidence of availability for employment. Lone parents may qualify for income support at 16. The income of the claimant must not exceed an 'applicable amount'. Likewise the capital must not exceed a 'prescribed level'. The amount which is paid by way of income support is based on a complicated formula of allowances and premiums, described in this way in Appendix C to *Children Come First* (1990) (we have amended the figures to show the benefit rates from April 1996):

The personal allowance is the basic element of the Income Support payment and is intended to cover all normal living expenses. Premiums are additions to Income Support allowances for groups of people with extra needs. Normally, a person who qualifies for more than one premium will only get the one that gives them the most money. However, a person entitled to the family, disabled child, severe disability or carer premium can get them as well as any other premiums they qualify for.

	Weekly Personal Allowances [as from April 1996]	
Single People		
18–24 years old	£37.90	
18 years and over and bringing up a child	£47.90	
25 years old and over	£47.90	
Couples		
both under 18	£57.20	
[both] 18 or over	£75.20	
And for each child		
under 11	£16.45	
11 to 15 years old	£24.10	
16 to 17 years old, doing a full-time course not above A level, Scottish Certificate of Education (Higher Grade) or equivalent	£28.85	
18 years old, doing a full-time course not above A level, Scottish Certificate of Education (Higher Grade) or equivalent	£37.90	
Weekly Premiums		
Premiums for people with children		
Family Premium		
for people with at least one child	£10.55	
Disabled Child Premium		
for people with a child who is getting Attendance Allowance or Mobility Allowance or who is registered blind	£20.40	
Lone Parent Premium		
for people bringing up one or more children on their own	£5.20	
Premiums for long term sick or disabled people		
	Single Person	**Couple**
Disability Premium		
for people getting Invalidity Benefit, Severe Disablement Allowance, Mobility Allowance, Attendance Allowance, registered blind or who are sick and cannot work and have been sending doctor's statements for at least 28 weeks	£20.40	£29.15
Severe Disability Premium		
for people getting Attendance Allowance and living alone and no-one gets Invalid Care Allowance for looking after them.		
Single person	£36.40	
Couple both partners get Attendance Allowance but someone gets Invalid Care Allowance for looking after them		£36.40
Couple, both partners get Attendance Allowance, no-one gets Invalid Care Allowance for looking after either of them		£72.80
Premiums for Carers		
Carer Premium		
	Single Person	**Couple**
for people getting Invalid Care Allowance	£13.00	£13.00 (for each person on ICA)

There are also premiums for people aged 60 or over.

Help with Housing and Community Charge Costs

Income Support can include money to help people to meet interest charges on a mortage or home loan.

The Social Security Act 1986 also made two other changes in terminology. First, Single Payments were replaced by a scheme known as the Social Fund which provides Social Fund Officers with a wide discretion to meet needs, albeit often by loans. Secondly, Family Credit (see p. 127, below) is introduced to replace FIS so as to provide some limited assistance for low income families where the claimant or partner is responsible for a child member of the household.

The two reports which are still of profound importance are Sir William Beveridge's Report on *Social Insurance and Allied Services* (1942) and Sir Maurice Finer's *Report of the Committee on One-Parent Families* (1974).

Sir William Beveridge's Report on *Social Insurance and Allied Services* (1942) had this to say of the divorced and separated:

347. **End of marriage otherwise than by widowhood**
Divorce, legal separation, desertion and voluntary separation may cause needs similar to those caused by widowhood. They differ from widowhood in two respects: that they may occur through the fault or with the consent of the wife, and that except where they occur through the fault of the wife they leave the husband's liability for maintenance unchanged. If they are regarded from the point of view of the husband, they may not appear to be insurable risks; a man cannot insure against events which occur only through his fault or with his consent, and if they occur through the fault or with the consent of the wife she should not have a claim to benefit. But from the point of view of the woman, loss of her maintenance as housewife without her consent and not through her fault is one of the risks of marriage against which she should be insured; she should not depend on assistance. Recognition of housewives as a distinct insurance class, performing necessary service not for pay, implies that, if the marriage ends otherwise than by widowhood, she is entitled to the same provision as for widowhood, unless the marriage maintenance has ended through her fault or voluntary action without just cause. That is to say, subject to the practical considerations mentioned in the note below she should get temporary separation benefit (on the same lines as widow's benefit), and guardian or training benefit where appropriate.

NOTE. – The principle that a married woman who without fault of her own loses the maintenance to which she is entitled from her husband should get benefit is clear. It is obvious, however, that except where the maintenance has ended through divorce or other form of legal separation establishing that the default is not that of the wife, considerable practical difficulties may arise in determining whether a claim to benefit, as distinct from assistance, has arisen. There will often be difficulty in determining responsibility for the break-up of the marriage. There will in cases of desertion be difficulty in establishing the fact or the permanence of desertion. There will in all cases be the problem of alternative remedies open to the wife. The point to which the principle of compensating a housewife for the loss of her maintenance otherwise than by widowhood can be carried in practice calls for further examination. It may for practical reasons be found necessary to limit the widow's insurance benefit to cases of formal separation, while making it clear that she can in all cases of need get assistance and that the Ministry of Social Security will then proceed against the husband for recoupment of its expenditure.

The proposal was not adopted. A major reason why the idea did not meet with approval, apart from the practical difficulties noted above, may lie in the need to reconcile the collective security involved in an insurance scheme with the concept of individual responsibility. In a welfare state, the moral virtue of contributing to a scheme which will provide relief against, for example, sickness and unemployment – both your own and your neighbours' – is, one hopes, self-evident. Contributing to a scheme which provides relief for the wives in other people's broken marriages, however, is not so easy to justify.

Question

Do you consider that the state has a responsibility to ensure that children do not spend most of their childhood living at the officially-defined subsistence level? If you do think this way should state resources be directed at (*a*) enforcing the 'liable relative' obligation (see p. 115, below) or (*b*) helping to alleviate the poverty of children and others in comparable situations?

The Finer Committee looked for an alternative state benefit to resolve the lone parent's problems, and opted for a 'guaranteed maintenance allowance' (GMA).

The ten main features of the proposed benefit are summarised in the Finer Report:

> (1) The allowance would normally, in the hands of the lone parent, be a substitute for maintenance payments; maintenance payments would be assessed and collected by the authority administering the allowance; they would be offset against the allowance paid and any excess paid to the mother; the need for lone mothers to go to court to sue for maintenance awards would be largely eliminated;
> (2) the level of the benefit would be fixed in relation to supplementary benefit payments, and, like them, would be reviewed regularly, so that, taken in conjunction with whatever family support was generally available (family allowances or tax credits) it would normally be sufficient to bring one-parent families off supplementary benefit even if they had no earnings;
> (3) all one-parent families would be eligible for the benefit, including motherless families;
> (4) the benefit would be non-contributory;
> (5) the benefit would consist of a child-care allowance for the adult and a separate allowance for each child;
> (6) the benefit would not be adjusted to the particular needs of individual families, except in so far as it would reflect the size of the family;
> (7) for lone parents who are working or have other income the benefit would be tapered, after an initial disregard, so that it fell by considerably less than the amount by which income increased;
> (8) the adult benefit would be extinguished by the time income reached about the level of average male earnings, but the child benefit would continue to be payable to all lone parents, whatever their income;
> (9) once awarded, benefit would be fixed at that level for three months at a time, without in the normal way being affected by changes in circumstances. There would thus normally be no need for changes, including the beginning of a cohabitation, to be reported, until a fresh claim to benefit was made. Taken in conjunction with subparagraph (6) above this should much reduce the need for detailed enquiries;
> (10) the benefit would be administered by post, on the lines of the family income supplements scheme.

Questions

(i) The Finer proposals have not been adopted: besides the obvious economic reasons, why do you think the Conservative and the Labour parties, for their differing reasons, have both been slow to support the scheme?
(ii) Do you think that public opinion nowadays would object to a *contributory* scheme for lone-parent families?

It is noteworthy that only a very small proportion of lone-parent families headed by widows are obliged to rely upon income support. This is because widowed mothers are entitled to a widowed mother's allowance if the deceased husband has paid the necessary contributions (and the contribution conditions are not very severe). The parent is entitled to a flat-rate benefit and an addition for each child. There is no reduction for earnings, or indeed for any other income, such as a pension from her deceased husband's occupational pension scheme, or from life insurance.

Question

Are there any arguments against extending this benefit to include unmarried, divorced and separated mothers? Or separated fathers?

2 The private law obligation and the state – maintenance and income support

Section 78 of the Social Security Administration Act 1992 states:

(*a*) a man shall be liable to maintain his wife and any children of whom he is the father, and
(*b*) a woman shall be liable to maintain her husband and any children of whom she is the mother.

Section 107 of that Act extends this duty, so that unmarried or divorced parents of children under 16 are liable to make payments to maintain each other as well as their children. Yet the state, as we have seen, has an obligation to provide income support in the case of need.

Can a departing partner morally argue that his new responsibility is with a new liaison, leaving the state to provide support for his former partner and the children by that relationship? It is this question which lies at the heart of the *Report of the Committee on One-Parent Families*, the Finer Report (1974):

The dilemma of liable relatives

4.179 At this stage, it will be helpful to create the characters in an everyday drama. John, let it be supposed, contracted a marriage by which there are children of school age, or younger. He earns an average wage in a semi-skilled occupation. His marriage has broken down, and he has left home. He may or may not be divorced. Mary is John's former or deserted wife. Her lack of training, or the demands of the children, or both, prevent her from taking employment, or, at any rate, from earning more than a small amount in part-time work, insufficient for the needs of herself and the children. John is living with his second wife, or with his mistress. She and John have children of their own, or, it may be, she has children by a former marriage or association whom John looks after as his own. This woman also earns little or nothing. …

4.181 … Given John's earning capacity, however, it is clear that he cannot, when in work, earn enough money to maintain both the families. If he elects to do his duty by Mary's family, he will to that extent relieve the Supplementary Benefits Commission [now the DSS] from paying money to Mary, but the inevitable effect will be to deprive the family of which he is a current member of the means of subsistence in circumstances where, since he is in work, they will not themselves be eligible for benefit. If, on the other hand, he elects to maintain the latter family, then, with equal inevitability, he has to break his obligations towards Mary's family. But she, in that case, can claim supplementary benefit; in such circumstances neither family starves.

4.182 When a man is put in such a dilemma the solution he will lean towards is tolerably clear. He will feed, clothe and house those with whom he is living, knowing that the State will provide for the others.

This view of the dilemma and its solution is illustrated by the following cases.

Delaney v Delaney
[1991] FCR 161, [1990] 2 FLR 457, [1991] Fam Law 22, Court of Appeal

The parties married in January 1978. They separated in February 1987 and were divorced in March 1989. There were three children of the marriage – a boy aged eleven, a girl aged ten and another boy aged five. In February 1989 the wife applied for periodical payments for herself and the three children. On September 8, 1989 the deputy district judge ordered that the husband should pay £10 a week in respect of each child. He further made a nominal order for the wife of 5p a year. The husband appealed to the circuit judge. The husband and his girl friend had acquired a three bedroomed semi-detached house in conjunction with a housing association. They were paying a mixture of mortgage repayments and rent, amounting to £40.28 per week each. The judge found that this exceeded their needs and the husband had deliberately taken on unnecessary and excessive obligations after he had an obligation to the children. He dismissed the appeal.

The husband appealed. On appeal, Ward J noted that the wife's income, including the various state benefits to which she was entitled, amounted to £152 a week. He commented:

The Circuit Judge said this of her income and her need: 'After paying her rent and rates, she has left £50, with which to feed and clothe herself and her three children. This patently is not enough', and quite clearly it is not. …

Ward J then considered the husband's outgoings, and reached this conclusion:

The real issue, therefore, is the extent to which the husband can meet that need for this wife and this family. …

In my judgment the approach of this court in this case must be, firstly, to have regard to the need of the wife and the children for proper support. Having assessed that need, the court should then consider the ability of the husband to meet it. Whilst this court deprecates any notion that a former husband and extant father may slough off the tight skin of familial responsibility and may slither into and lose himself in the greener grass on the other side, nonetheless this court has proclaimed and will proclaim that it looks to the realities of the real world in which we live, and that among the realities of life is that there is a life after divorce. The respondent husband is entitled to order his life in such a way as will hold in reasonable balance the responsibilities to his existing family which he carries into his new life, as well as his proper aspirations for that new future. In all life, for those who are divorced as well as for those who are not divorced, indulging one's whims or even one's reasonable desires must be held in check by the constraints imposed by limited resources and compelling obligations. But this husband's resources, even when one adds to them the contribution made by his girl friend, are very limited indeed. He brings in £115 a week net and she brings in £97 a week net. Their joint income is £212 per week. Their expressed outgoings, as found by the Judge, … were £179.39, and that took no account of food, clothing, entertainment, holidays, house repairs, car repairs, servicing, the television licence or the road fund tax. … After meeting those expenses their joint income is then reduced to something in the region of £25 a week on which this man and his girl friend have to feed and clothe themselves and maintain the first family.

In my judgment this father was reasonably entitled to say that for the welfare of his children, … he should have accommodation sufficient for proper access and so suitable to be able to offer them staying access. Two bedrooms may have been sufficient, but three bedrooms does not far exceed his need having regard to the fact that the wife herself lives in a three-bedroomed house. … I find it difficult to say that this husband, in incurring these liabilities, was behaving in an extravagant fashion. That was the test applied in the case of *Furniss v Furniss* (1981) 3 FLR 46.

The approach in *Barnes v Barnes* [1972] 1 WLR 1381 was to permit expenditure to a proper standard. The approach in *Preston v Preston* [1982] Fam 17 was to look at need within the context of s. 25 of the Matrimonial Causes Act in terms of what was reasonably required. So whether one judges this man by a standard of extravagant expenditure or of living to an improper standard or of behaving unreasonably, I do not find it possible to judge him to have gone beyond the limit of what is permissible. His share of £40.28 per week is not out of proportion to the wife's rental of £33 per week. Consequently, I find that this expenditure as set out is reasonably incurred by him and I find, as a result, that the £25 a week or thereabouts left for himself and the girl friend to feed and clothe themselves is barely adequate to sustain any reasonable way of life.

In my judgment, therefore, this father would find it extremely difficult, if not impossible, to meet the obligation he has and which ordinarily he should honour to maintain his children. In paying him due credit, I observe that he has paid £10 a week to the children, being the most that he felt he could afford.

This court is entitled, as the authority of *Stockford v Stockford* (1981) 3 FLR 58 makes clear, to approach the case upon a basis that if, having regard to the reasonable financial commitments undertaken by the husband with due regard to the contribution properly made by the lady with whom he lives, there is insufficient left properly and fully to maintain the former wife and children, then the court may have regard to the fact that in proper cases social security benefits are available to the wife and children of the marriage; that having such regard, the court is enabled to avoid making orders which would be financially crippling to the husband. Benefits are available to this family of which the Judge was not made aware, and I have come to the conclusion that the husband cannot reasonably be expected to contribute at all to the maintenance of his previous family without financially crippling himself. In my judgment, it is far better that the spirit of effecting a clean break and starting with a fresh slate be implemented in this case, not by dismissing the claims of the wife and the children, but by acknowledging that now and, it is likely, in the foreseeable future he will not be able to honour the obligations he has recognised towards his children, and in my judgment the appeal should be allowed and I would substitute a nominal order to each of the children for the order of £10 which each of them is currently ordered to receive.

Appeal allowed; an order of £0.50 per annum per child substituted for the order made by the judge in the court below.

Ward J in *Delaney v Delaney* referred to the case of *Barnes v Barnes*:

Barnes v Barnes
[1972] 3 All ER 872, [1972] 1 WLR 1381, 116 Sol Jo 801, Court of Appeal

The parties were married in 1960. They had four children – aged eleven, ten, eight and seven. In March 1971, the wife obtained a decree nisi of divorce, the decree being made absolute in June 1971. In July 1971, the husband remarried. The second child, Peter, remained with his father until May 1971, then went to his mother, returned for a short time to his father, and at the time of the appeal in this case was in a residential home.

The other children remained with their mother. In March 1971, the county court judge made an order in favour of each of the three children who were with their mother in the sum of £2.50 per week. He made no order for the wife. By the order of 30 June 1971, the judge reduced the weekly payments to the three children to £2.00 each and made an order with respect to Peter for £2.00. He made a nominal order of 5p per annum in respect of the wife. On 13 March 1972, the judge ordered that the husband should pay only £1.50 for each of the children and the payment of 5p for the wife should continue. The wife appealed against the orders of 30 June 1971 and 13 March 1972 on the ground that the judge erred in making only nominal orders for periodical payments for herself.

Edmund Davies LJ: [referred to the order made on 30 June 1971 and continued]: ..., the conclusion to which I have come is that in the first place when the court is seeking to arrive at what would be a proper order, it is desirable that regard should not be had to social security benefits but that one should, looking at all the features of the case, ... seek to arrive at a fair figure. But if the case is one in which the income of the parties is of modest proportions, and if the total available resources of both parties are so modest that an adjustment of that totality would result in the husband's being left with a sum quite inadequate to enable him to meet his own financial commitments, then the court may have regard to the fact that in proper cases social security benefits will be available to the wife and the children of the marriage. Having such regard, the court is enabled to avoid making such an order as would be financially crippling to the husband if it considered only the combined income, earning capacity and property of the parties. It would be, I am persuaded, unrealistic to take any other course, ...

I think the time has come when the wife should have an order made in her favour. How much better off she is going to be is extremely open to doubt; nevertheless, I would be for allowing the appeal against this second order to this extent and to this extent only: while leaving the four children to have the sum of £1.50 a week each, I would be in favour of ordering that the wife receive the sum of £2, making a totality of £8. That would mean that the husband would have something in the region of £12 weekly for himself and his wife. I hope and believe that that would meet the justice of the case; beyond that I would not be prepared to go. To that extent I would allow the appeal against the second order.

Maintenance payments made to a partner who is in receipt of income support (or supplementary benefit, at the time of these cases) will, of course, reduce her benefit pound for pound. In *Berry v Berry* [1987] Fam 1, [1986] 2 All ER 948, [1986] 3 WLR 257, [1987] 1 FLR 105, [1986] Fam Law 304, CA, one of the husband's grounds for appeal from an order made in the magistrates' court was that the order failed to take into account the fact that the former wife would not benefit from his payments, because she was in receipt of supplementary benefit. Arnold P, with whom Bush and Booth JJ agreed, had this to say:

As regards that ... ground, it seems to me to be wholly unjustified. It is perfectly true that the respondent to this appeal is in receipt of supplementary benefit, and will continue to be in receipt of supplementary benefit irrespective of the order which the court makes on this appeal, or indeed irrespective of any order which the justices could have made. But that is not a ground for allowing the appeal. Supplementary benefit is available under the relevant statutes for those whose means are insufficient to enable them to live without the payment of social security benefits: and the proper level of those benefits has to be determined after the means of the claimant have been assessed, and if the claimant is able to obtain a larger sum by means of a maintenance order, then plainly the amount of the supplementary benefit would be reduced. So that the mere circumstance that the claimant is in receipt of supplementary benefit does not by itself reduce the proper level of maintenance which should be ordered.

Nevertheless, the husband's appeal was allowed on the grounds that, being in receipt of supplementary benefit himself, he had no means to pay; and that the magistrates' order appeared to require the husband to make payments to his former wife from his new wife's earnings. Arnold P explained:

In so far as it was right for [the magistrates] to consider (as of course they must consider) how far the husband's ability to pay was reduced by any maintenance for his present wife which he was compelled to find, it would be relevant for them to consider her earnings and their combined funds. But in so far as they were assessing what he could afford to pay to his former wife, it would be quite wrong to take the present wife's earnings into account; and it does appear to me in the circumstances of this case that it was in relation to the latter matter that the justices must have taken the present wife's earnings into account.

Questions

(i) Do you agree with the proposition that a court should strive to avoid making orders that are financially crippling to the husband? Does not this approach encourage irresponsibility on the part of the husband? Or do you think that an order is justified so as to impress upon fathers that their primary obligation is to their own children and their first wives?
(ii) Is there any principle at all which comes over to you from an examination of these cases?
(iii) Do you think that s. 78 of the 1992 Act (see p. 110, above) helps or hinders solving the problems which arise?
(iv) Can you think of *any* advantages from the point of view of the wife for obtaining a court order in her favour in a case such as *Barnes v Barnes* [1972] 3 All ER 872, [1972] 1 WLR 1381?
(v) As a tax payer, can you see any justification for the legal aid fund being used in this case on behalf of the wife's applications?
(vi) Do you see any value at all in sending a man to prison for non-payment of maintenance payments?
(vii) *Is* there a difference between failure to pay 'wife support' and failure to pay 'child support'?
(viii) Bradshaw/Millar (1991) found that only 30% of lone mothers received regular payments of maintenance. They also found that maintenance formed less than 10% of lone parents' total net income compared with 45% for income support and 22% for net earnings. *Children Come First* (1990), complains: 'The contribution made by maintenance to the income of lone-parent families therefore remains too low.' Do you agree with this statement?

The Finer Report discusses the practice of the supplementary benefit authority, as it then was, in relation to private support claims:

The allegations of pressure

4.193 Several of the organisations which gave evidence showed concern that women who are reluctant to institute legal proceedings for maintenance against liable relatives are, or at least feel themselves to be, subjected to pressure from officials to do so. We quote from some of the representations we have received:

> '... health visitors have noted with concern the distress of some deserted or unmarried mothers when social security officers insist that legal proceedings be instituted ... undue pressure is sometimes brought to bear at a time when the mother is already under considerable stress (Health Visitors' Association).'

If a woman eligible for income support applies for and obtains a maintenance order in her favour which is less than the full rate of her benefit entitlement, she may authorise the magistrates' clerk to divert any payments which are received to the DSS, provided the order was made or registered in the magistrates' court:

4.207 . . . When such a transfer is effected, the wife receives an order book entitling her to supplementary benefit (calculated on the basis that there is no maintenance order) which she can cash at the post office: and the clerk of the court transmits to the Department whatever is paid in to the collecting office under the maintenance order. (The procedure is also available in the much rarer case where the amount of the maintenance order exceeds the supplementary benefit entitlement; but here no invitation to transfer the maintenance order is made until the circumstances, such as repeated failure to pay on the order, show this to be desirable.) The effect is that the wife receives her full entitlement regularly, whether the maintenance order is paid in full, intermittently or not at all. She is relieved of the anxiety of irregular payments and the harassment and indignity of commuting between different officials and different procedures.

Section 24B of the Social Security Act 1986 (inserted by the Social Security Act 1990) permitted the DSS to enforce a lone parent's private maintenance order where the parent is on income support. In addition, the DSS will accept an offer of payment from a liable relative if it forms the view that the offer is reasonable.

But this was clearly not enough.

It is put in this way in *Children Come First* (1990) 'The Government's Proposals on the Maintenance of Children: The Background':

1.3.2 When a lone parent claims Income Support the DSS tries to ensure that the absent parent pays enough maintenance to remove his dependants' need for Income Support, or as much towards that amount as he can reasonably afford. A separated parent is asked to pay enough to support the claimant and the children fully so that payment of Income Support can stop. Divorced parents and parents who were never married who are not liable to maintain each other are currently asked to pay an amount equal to the personal benefit rates for the children they are liable to maintain plus the family and lone parent premiums payable under Income Support because there are children in the household. The Social Security Act 1990 has provided for courts to be able to include the amount to be recovered from the absent parent in recognition that it is responsibility for the care of the children which prevents the claimant working.

Children Come First proposed a major change in approach both by the courts and the DSS:

2.1 The Government proposes to establish a system of child maintenance which will be equally available to any person seeking maintenance for the benefit of a child and which will:

- ensure that parents honour their legal and moral responsibility to maintain their own children whenever they can afford to do so. It is right that other taxpayers should help to maintain children when the children's own parents, despite their own best efforts, do not have enough resources to do so themselves. That will continue to be the case. But it is not right that taxpayers, who include other families, should shoulder that responsibility instead of parents who are able to do it themselves;
- recognise that where a liable parent has formed a second family and has further natural children, he is liable to maintain all his own children. A fair and reasonable balance has to be struck between the interests of the children of a first family and the children of a second;
- produce consistent and predictable results so that people in similar financial circumstances will pay similar amounts of maintenance, and so that people will know in advance what their maintenance obligations are going to be;
- enable maintenance to be decided in a fair and reasonable way which reduces the scope for its becoming a contest between the parents to the detriment of the interests of the children;
- produce maintenance payments which are realistically related to the costs of caring for a child;
- allow for maintenance payments to be reviewed regularly so that changes in circumstances can be taken into account automatically;
- recognise that both parents have a legal responsibility to maintain their children;
- ensure that parents meet the cost of their children's maintenance whenever they can without removing the parents' own incentives to work, and to go on working;
- enable caring parents who wish to work to do so as soon as they feel ready and able;
- provide an efficient and effective service to the public which ensures that:
  (*a*) maintenance is paid regularly and on time so that it provides a reliable income for the caring parent and the children and
  (*b*) produces maintenance quickly so that the habit of payment is established early and is not compromised by early arrears;
- avoid the children and their caring parent becoming dependent on Income Support whenever this is possible and, where it is not possible, to minimise the period of dependence.

The proposal, put into effect in the Child Support Act 1991, was for an 'integrated package' involving a formula for the assessment of how much maintenance should be paid, a child support agency which has responsibility for tracing absent parents and for the assessment, collection and enforcement of maintenance payments, and changes in the rules of Social Security to encourage caring parents to go to work if they wish to do so.

Lord Mackay, in moving that the Child Support Bill be read a second time in the House of Lords stated that the Bill provided a firm foundation for assessing what people can afford to pay in a coherent and equitable way. He said this:

> ... There are four basic elements.
>
> First, there is the maintenance requirement. This is an amount, which will be calculated with reference to the income support rates, which represents the basic costs of maintaining the children who qualify for a formula award. Secondly, there is the assessable income. This is derived by deducting an exempt income from the parents' net income, that is, income after tax and national insurance. This exempt income represents the weekly amount which it is considered parents need for their own essential day-to-day expenses. It will be based on income support allowances, and will include reasonable housing costs and the costs of any children for whom they are liable. The remaining income is the assessable income, such income of both parents will be taken into account.
>
> Thirdly, there is the deduction rate. A percentage of the assessable income of each parent will be taken into account in order to meet the maintenance requirement, where possible. We intend that, until the maintenance requirement is met, assessable income should be shared equally between the absent parent and his children who qualify under the Bill. A smaller percentage will apply in individual cases after the maintenance requirement has been met. Beyond that, there will be an upper limit to the operation of the formula and, as I indicated earlier, in high income cases above that limit the parties will be able to seek additional maintenance for the child from the courts.
>
> Fourthly and lastly, there is the protected income. This is the income level below which no family of a person liable to maintain a child will be allowed to fall as a result of his meeting his maintenance obligations and his essential living expenses. It will protect those who are working, or who have other sources of income, from being left with an income less than a level set on the basis of income support levels.

Something of the flavour of the Child Support Act 1991 can be gathered from the following examples of the expressions which make up the formula, in Sch. 1:

> 1.—(1) In this Schedule the 'maintenance requirement' means the amount, calculated in accordance with the formula set out in sub-paragraph (2), which is to be taken as the minimum amount necessary for the maintenance of the qualifying child ...
>
> (2) The formula is—
>
> $$MR = AG - CB$$
>
> ...
>
> 3. (2) The value of G shall be determined by applying the formula—
>
> $$G = \frac{MR}{(A + C) \times P}$$
>
> ...
>
> 4.—(1) ... the additional element shall be calculated by applying the formula—
>
> $$AE = (1 - G) \times A \times R$$
>
> ...
>
> (3) The alternative formula is—
>
> $$AE = Z \times Q \times \frac{A}{(A + C)}$$

That extract is obviously incomplete, as it omits the definitions of the expressions 'MR', 'AG', etc. But it indicates the complexity of the formula, which is further elaborated in numerous statutory instruments. Consider by contrast the method of calculation in Australia and New Zealand, upon whose child support systems ours is to some extent modelled. There, the maintenance requirement is a proportion of gross income, after a deduction for exempt income based upon current family commitments, based upon the number of children for whom child support is being assessed:

In Australia the percentages used are:

1 child: 18 per cent
2 children: 27 per cent
3 children: 32 per cent
4 children: 34 per cent
5 or more children: 36 per cent

In New Zealand the percentages used are:

1 child: 18 per cent
2 children: 24 per cent
3 children: 27 per cent
4 or more children: 30 per cent

(From the Fifth Report of the House of Commons Social Security Select Committee, October 1994, para. 57, summing up the evidence of the Chief Executive of the New Zealand Child Support Agency.)

The following illustration of the operation of the formula has been adapted from the worked example given in Roger Bird's *Child Support Calculation Pack 1996/97*. It is based on the fictitious case of Denis and Margaret who have two chldren, Mark aged 8 and Carol aged 13. The children live with Margaret.

Stage One: The Maintenance Requirement

	Scale allowance for qualifying children	
Add	Child under 11	£16.45
	Child 11–15	£24.10
	Total scale allowances	**Subtotal = £40.55**
Add	Allowance for parent as carer where there is one child under 11	£47.90
	Family premium	£10.55
	Lone parent premium	£5.20
		Subtotal = £104.20
Deduct	Child benefit for first child	£10.80
	Child benefit for second child	£8.80
		MAINTENANCE REQUIREMENT (MR) = £84.60

Stage Two: Assessable Incomes

MOTHER'S ASSESSABLE INCOME (C)

Mother is receiving income support.
Therefore mother's assessable income is nil.

MOTHER'S ASSESSABLE INCOME (C) = £NIL

FATHER'S ASSESSABLE INCOME

	Father's net income (N)	
	Father's net income = gross income less income tax, national insurance and 50% pension contributions	
		Father's net income (N) = £250.00
	Father's exempt income (E)	
	Adult single allowance	£47.90
	Housing costs	£60.00
		Father's exempt income (E) = £107.90
	Father's net income (N)	£250.00
Deduct	Father's exempt income (E)	£107.90
		FATHER'S ASSESSABLE INCOME (A) = £142.10

Stage Three: The Assessment

Add	Mother's assessable income (C)	NIL
and	Father's assessable income (A)	£142.10
		A + C = **£142.10**
Divide	this figure by 2	$\frac{A + C}{2}$ = £71.05

The Maintenance requirement (MR) is £84.60 $\frac{A + C}{2}$ does not exceed MR, so the maintenance assessment is half the father's assessable income $\left(\frac{A}{2}\right)$.

MAINTENANCE ASSESSMENT = £71.05

Stage Four is the calcualtion of the father's protected income, which in this case does not affect the maintenance requirement; *Stage Five* is the calculation of 30% of the father's net income, as the maintenance assessment must not exceed that figure. Again, in this instance the assessment is unaffected so that the final maintenance assessment is £71.05.

The enactment of the Child Support Act 1991 gave rise to various expressions of concern.

John Eekelaar was clearly suspicious that the main reason for the Child Support Act 1991 is to reduce the level of expenditure if at all possible (The Independent, Friday 2 November 1990):

Readers of the Government's White Paper, *Children Come First*, may believe it would have been better entitled *Taxpayers Come First*.

It points out that lone parents cost the taxpayer £3.6bn, compared with £1.75bn in 1981/82. It then sets out a formula that the proposed child support agency would apply to recover this cost.

The formula is based unashamedly on a 'maintenance bill' that reflects the state benefits many lone parents and their children receive. The absent father will be required to pay the Exchequer 50 per cent of his disposable income after allowances – the highest rate the Government believes it can collect without driving him to give up work – until this 'bill' is met.

Courts may be stopped from making property settlements that favour children if the taxpayer suffers because of any resulting reliance on benefits.

There is a suspicion that the Government's claims about benefiting children are a cover for cutting public spending.

For some, this is confirmed by plans for the agency's first customers to be those solely dependent on income support. In fact, it is these people who will least need the agency's enforcement services because many absent parents are unlikely to pay more than a lone parent receives in benefits.

Where they do pay more, however, the Department of Social Security will be able to reduce income support pound for pound.

That it is the state, not the single-parent family, that has most to gain from maintenance payments is implicitly recognised in the proposal that lone parents who failed, without good reason, to take action through the agency to make the absent parent pay risk a cut in their benefits of up to 20 per cent.

Another concern is that the Act is contrary to the principle of the clean break developed by the divorce court (see p. 343, below), as Lord Mishcon states in the Parliamentary debate on 25 February 1991:

At the moment the family home is usually the only asset that a family in the middle and lower income groups possesses – possibly the upper end of the lower income group, but nevertheless, in spite of the difficulties occasioned by mortgages and high interest rates in these latter days, it is more and more the pride of the family to have a family home. What happens now – in fulfilment of an aim of our recent divorce legislation, of which the noble and learned Lord is a great supporter – is that it is the rule and the desirability in many cases to achieve a clean break. That means that the husband or father, as a rule, does not have round his neck a millstone of unceasing maintenance for the years ahead. It means providing the ability to create new lives; to write new chapters when the old ones are unhappy. The way that the courts achieve the clean break is often by suggesting – and certainly agreeing to any consent order – that the father transfers the family home over to the mother. Often the mother will thereupon get income support, the idea being that spouse maintenance ceases when the father or husband does that, and the child maintenance order is a pretty low one.

... Faced with a maintenance order under the statutory provisions that we are now looking at, the court will be unable to make an order transferring the house to the wife for the benefit of the children and their security.

The husband will say, 'Goodness gracious me, I face a continuing liability'. There is no question now of the ability to carry out the provisions of the divorce legislation which has pertained until now, and which cut off the liability and allowed such a settlement to be made.

Question

In his evidence to the House of Commons Social Security Committee (Session 1990/91), Eekelaar outlined a further concern:
'when circumstances allow it, the main objective of courts, and also of most caregiving parents, is to retain the house for the children [see Chapter 8, below]. The rest of the package is fashioned to achieve that purpose. Under the [Child Support Act 1991] the child support element is fixed; it may not then be possible to fashion the package so as to prevent the homelessness of the children'.

Is this (*a*) a real or (*b*) an acceptable risk?

The House of Commons Social Security Committee was so concerned by these aspects that they issued an interim report:

Effect of the new system on divorce settlements

11. ... The Law Society expressed particular anxieties about the effect that legislation is already having on divorce settlements involving children in the courts, as well as doubts about the new system for child support. They told us that, as a result of the provisions in the Social Security Act 1990, it was possible that a fresh claim for maintenance could be made in cases where 'the matrimonial home was conveyed to the wife as part of the clean break'. Mr David Salter, of the Law Society, explained how this might occur in the future:

> 'The husband will refer back to the court saying that there has been a fundamental change in the underlying circumstances which govern that order and invite the court to effectively appeal out of time to set the order aside because he will have given up far more capital in the expectation that he was not going to face a future claim for maintenance'.

Mr Henry Hodge, also of the Law Society, told us that solicitors were already drafting clauses in clean break divorce agreements to the effect that a clean break would be overturned if the husband was approached by the DSS or the Agency with a claim for maintenance. As we note above in paragraph 7 a clause in the Child Support Bill will render such arrangements void, but we believe that, in cases where a substantial amount of capital has been foregone in the expectation of a clean break, it is not reasonable to return to the case to pursue a further claim for the financial security of the child. ...

Questions

(i) Do you prefer the approach of this arithmetical formula or the judicial discretion for (*a*) those families on or close to income support and (*b*) those families a long way away from income support?
(ii) Liable relatives on low incomes pay a much larger proportion of their income as maintenance than those with above average incomes (Monk, 1991). Is it harmful for children (*a*) in the former case to operate a deduction rate of 50% (above the exempt slice of income), (*b*) in the latter case to operate an additional deduction rate of 15% from the paying parent's 'assessable' income?
(iii) Do you think that there should be a residual discretion to allow courts to vary the formula (*a*) upwards and/or (*b*) downwards?
(iv) When assessing the father's exempt income, the presence of step-children is overlooked except in exceptional cases. Is this approach reconcilable with the philosophy underlying the Children Act 1989?
(v) Is it an exceptional case that a step-father has assumed responsibility for looking after the children of his new partner and treated them as children of the family?
(vi) Eight academic observers wrote to The Independent on 25 April 1991:

Shortcomings of the Child Support Bill

From Mrs R. Deech and others
Sir: As university law teachers, we wish to express our concern over the Government's opposition to amendments to the Child Support Bill designed to give a parent the option to seek child support through the proposed agency or in the courts.

The Bill, which will be at report stage this week, contains the power to order child support to the agency, using a formula, with the following consequences:

1. Parties in disagreement over their divorce settlement will need to have child support liability and other aspects of the settlement (property, capital, school fees, children's residence) determined by separate institutions using different procedures and at different times, adding to costs and delay; if a court makes a property settlement after child support is ordered, they may need to return to the agency for adjustment to the child support order.
2. Child support will become non-negotiable. A financial settlement, even if approved by a court, in which child support liability as dictated by the formula is modified in favour of other benefits will not prevent the agency later making a full child support order. This could inhibit people from reaching sensible agreements.

Views differ over the merits of the agency and the formula. But it makes no sense to introduce them in such a way as to undermine the policies of reducing legal costs and delay and encouraging negotiated settlement and consumer choice.
Your sincerely,

R. DEECH (Principal, St Anne's College, Oxford), G. DOUGLAS (Lecturer, Cardiff), J. EEKELAAR (Reader, Oxford), M. FREEMAN (Professor, London), M. HAYES (Reader, Sheffield), N. LOWE (Professor, Cardiff), J. MASSON (Professor, Warwick), D. PEARL (Professor, East Anglia)

Do you believe that child support should be non-negotiable?
(vii) Do you think that the money spent on establishing and running the Child Support Agency would have been better spent on placing resources at the courts' disposal?
(viii) Do you think that a mother should have a reduction in her income support or family credit if she fails to provide information which will allow maintenance to be recovered from an absent parent where there is a risk of her or of any child living with her suffering harm or undue distress as a result (s. 6(2)(*a*); s. 46, Child Support Act 1991)?
(ix) The Spastics Society had this to say as quoted by Lord Prys-Davies in the Debate in the House of Lords on 25 February 1991:

> The possibility that there should be sanctions to ensure the naming of an absent parent so that maintenance can be collected by the Agency is a cause of grave concern to the Spastics Society. Where a relationship has foundered on the birth of a disabled child, such measures might put unnecessary and regrettable pressure on the caring parent who might prefer to severe connections with as little pain as possible.

What do you think 'undue distress' means, and would it cover this example?

The Secretary of State's Guidelines on the Application of the Requirement to Co-operate (Department of Social Security, 1993) states that: 'the PWC [parent with care] has a right to be believed unless what she says is inherently contradictory or implausible' and stresses the need for interviews to be 'handled with care and sensitivity' (para. 13). The Guidance lists as examples circumstances where it would be reasonable to conclude that a PWC had good cause not to co-operate in seeking maintenance:

- PWC fears violence;
- PWC a rape victim;
- the AP (absent parent) has sexually abused one of her children;
- child conceived as a result of sexual abuse (including incest).

It then lists, again as examples, 'circumstances in which the PWC will say that she or her children would suffer harm or undue distress, where there may be less of a *prima facie* case that this would be so', including:

- fears that the AP will want to see the child;
- PWC wishes to sever links with the AP;
- PWC wishes to protect the AP, 'usually because he is living in a stable relationship with someone else who is unaware of the child he shares with the AP';
- PWC wanted the child; AP did not.

One possible escape route is handled with a very straight face:

> *Naming unlikely fathers*
> 37. There may be some instances where the PWC names as the AP someone who, the balance of probability suggests, is unlikely to be the AP. Examples might include entertainment or sports personalities or other well-known individuals.
> 38. Although the allegation may seem improbable, sufficient detail should be obtained of the circumstances to enable a judgment to be made about its validity.
> 39. If the claim is judged to be improbable, the PWC may have good cause not to name the real AP. She should be reminded of the advantages to her of getting maintenance, and encouraged to be open with the CSA about her real fears.

Question

Would you mind being labelled an 'absent parent'?

The Child Support Act 1991 came into force in April 1993. Since then, a number of the concerns expressed at the time it was enacted have come home to roost. In particular, it was not long before the issue of whether or not a past clean break could be 'unscrambled' in the light of a new demand for maintenance was tested.

Crozier v Crozier
[1994] Fam 114, [1994] 2 All ER 362, [1994] 2 WLR 444, [1994] 1 FLR 126

In 1989 a consent order was made in divorce proceedings between Mr. and Mrs. Crozier, to the effect that the husband should transfer to the wife absolutely his share in the matrimonial home in full and final settlement of all her financial claims against him. The house had been held in joint names, and was agreed to be worth £28,000 with an equity of £16,000; so the order represented a transfer of the husband's interest worth £8,000. At the same time, an order was made for nominal maintenance payments by Mr. Crozier for the one child of the family, a boy then aged five. Subsequently, Mrs. Crozier received income support. Mr. Crozier remained, of course, a liable relative, and in 1993 an order was made pursuant to the Social Security Administration Act 1992 that he pay £4 per week towards the boy's maintenance. However, he had now received documents from the Child Support Agency, and it was anticipated that his liability would be increased to £29 per week. At the same time, Mrs. Crozier was about to marry her new partner; the former matrimonial home had been sold and the proceeds, about £20,000, had been placed on deposit. Accordingly Mr. Crozier applied for the original consent order to be set aside or varied, so that his half share, now amounting to around £10,000, could be invested to pay the maintenance in the future. In order to succeed, Mr. Crozier had to establish the grounds set out in *Barder v Caluori* [1988] AC 20, HL, among them that 'new events have occurred since the making of the order which invalidate the basis, or fundamental assumption, upon which the order was made'. Booth J held that the application could not succeed:

I am unable to accept that submission. The fact that Parliament has chosen a new administrative method by which the state may intervene to compel a parent to contribute towards the maintenance of a child, by-passing the jurisdiction of the courts, does not fundamentally alter the position as it was in law in February 1989. The parties were then unable to achieve a clean financial break in respect of their son. The legal liability to maintain him remained on them both as his parents. While the wife was prepared to assume that responsibility as between herself and the husband, she could not in fact fulfil that obligation without the assistance of state moneys. The state was never bound by the agreement or the order. At any time it could have intervened, through the Secretary of State, to seek an order through the courts and the parties were not entitled to assume for the purposes of their agreement that it would not do so. I consider that it is immaterial for this purpose that that same parental liability will now be enforced through an agency outside the courts. That is a difference only in the means by which the state may proceed to relieve itself of the obligation which it is the duty of the parents to discharge. The fact that the sum required of a parent may be greater under the new procedure than under the old is a consequence of the procedural change and not of any new and unforeseen power vested in the state. In my judgment, neither the existing order made in March 1993 under the statutory machinery which existed in February 1989 nor any anticipated liability which may be levied under the new machinery introduced by the Act of 1991 constitutes a new event, in fact or in law, sufficient to invalidate the basis of the consent order.

Questions

(i) How do you react to the fact that the maintenance ordered by a magistrates' court in 1993 in this case was £4 per week, while the maintenance calculated by the formula under the Child Support Act 1991 was over seven times that amount?
(ii) Do you agree that the new level of payments did not undermine the basis of the original consent order?

Following the First Report of the Social Security Select Committee on the operation of the Child Support Act, a number of changes were made in February 1994. The formula was made a little more generous to the paying parent, and his 'protected income' raised; and provision was made to enable absent parents who had been paying lower rates of maintenance in the past to phase in their now increased payments over 18 months. Nevertheless, the level of concern about the Act prompted the Select Committee to report again on the same subject, in its Fifth Report of the session in October 1994. Its report began by endorsing the principles and aims of the Act. Nevertheless, it went on to list a number of recommendations made in the light of detailed evidence given to the Committee. Examples of issues raised include the inefficiency of the agency:

21. ... One non-custodial parent wrote of his prolonged troubles caused by the Agency's inefficiency; this case is described in some detail as it illustrates well the points raised by many parents.

> 'I have had dealings with the Child Support Agency [over the past year] and it has been nothing but a catalogue of errors and incompetence. Recently I have been getting threats of Deduction From Earnings Orders being served on my employers because the CSA say I am in arrears. I have always paid their demands on time and in full and I have receipts to prove that I have paid on time and in full. I have also had telephone conversations with the CSA when they have verbally agreed that no arrears exist and that no further action would be taken, only to receive another Deduction From Earnings Order a few weeks later. I have also found out that because the CSA say I am in arrears, which I am not, they have not been sending the money I have paid them for the maintenance of my son to his mother. The result is that she has had to go to the DSS and ask for emergency help. ...'

The stringency of the formula:

53. From the inception of the Child Support Act, the Government has maintained that the formula is fair and leaves the non-custodial parent with adequate income after assessment. In earlier evidence the Parliamentary Under Secretary of State for Social Security, Mr. Alistair Burt, had told the Committee,

> 'What we have sought to do in the formula is to provide ... that there is sufficient net income left available, typically 70–85 per cent (of net income) to allow that individual ... to make choices about how that income is spent. ...'

Therefore we were very surprised to be informed by the Chief Executive of the Child Support Agency that 'one in five [are left] with less than 70 per cent. ... Most [of these] fall into the band 65–70 per cent and virtually no absent parent is left with less than 60 per cent.'

The disclosure that 20 per cent of non-custodial parents were having more than 30 per cent of their net income taken in maintenance assessment helped account for some of the cases being submitted to the Committee where the non-custodial parent was clearly encountering financial difficulty.

The inevitability of arrears because of the way the assessment is dated:

23. ... Virtually every assessment is made after the effective date of liability (two weeks from issue of the Maintenance Enquiry Form (MEF)). Arrears of maintenance have therefore built up before the non-custodial parent even knows his assessment. ... The current situation ensures that the Agency's relationship with almost all non-custodial parents gets off to a bad start.

The failure of the formula to leave the non-custodial parent with funds for travel to work or to see his children:

65. Many of the submissions to the Committee have advocated adding new categories to exempt income. The most common ones requested are travel to work costs, costs of access to children plus the costs of presents, clothes etc. on these visits, various insurance charges and council tax liability.

and the treatment by the formula of the needs of the non-custodial parent's new partner and step-children:

67. ... Rightly or wrongly, most people believe that their primary responsibility is with the present, not with the past. The Child Support Act in its entirety correctly aims to ensure adequate responsibility is taken for past children but the provisions concerning step-children take this principle to an unfair extreme.

Several paragraphs of the Report are devoted to the difficulties arising from past capital settlements.

The Report also commented upon the way public concern had been expressed:

The case of those wishing to see reform of the Child Support Act has been weakened by the behaviour and wilder claims of certain groups, especially some purporting to represent the non-custodial parent. The Committee has been appalled by reports of abuse and harassment of Child Support Agency staff and by some of the offensive literature circulated. Nothing in the reforms recommended should be seen to exonerate any of this behaviour. This Report aims to provide recommendations that will ensure balance between all the parties involved and will therefore lead to greater acceptance of the Act and the principles on which it is based.

As a result of the Committee's recommendations a White Paper, 'Improving Child Support', was published in January 1995 announcing the following changes:

a. The introduction during 1996/7, following primary legislation, of some discretion to depart from the maintenance formula assessment in cases where the absent parent would otherwise face hardship or where certain property or capital transfers took place before April 1993. There will be closely specified grounds for the special circumstances that will be considered, and limits on the extent of the departure. Either parent will be able to apply for a departure, and both will be entitled to make representations.

b. Changes to the maintenance formula from April 1995:

- no absent parent will be assessed to pay more than 30 per cent of his normal net income in current child maintenance, or more than 33 per cent in a combination of current maintenance and start-up arrears;

- a broad-brush adjustment will be provided in the maintenance formula to take account of property and capital settlements;
- an allowance will be made towards high travel-to-work costs;
- housing costs will be allowed for a new partner or step-children;
- the maximum level of maintenance payable under the formula will be reduced.

c. From April 1997, parents with care in receipt of Income Support or Jobseeker's Allowance will be able to build up a maintenance credit which will be paid as a lump sum when the recipient starts work of at least 16 hours a week.

d. Family Credit and Disability Working Allowance recipients will receive some compensation for loss of maintenance where the changes in b. above result in a reduction in their assessment during an award of benefit.

e. Fees will be suspended for a period of two years until April 1997; and interest payments will also be suspended, to be replaced after two years with a penalty for late payment.

f. Changes will also be made to improve the administration of the scheme. ...

These changes have been put into effect, partly by Statutory Instruments and partly by the Child Support Act 1995, which substantially amends the Child Support Act 1991. Schedule 4B of the 1991 Act now makes provision for circumstances where a 'departure direction' may be given, that is, where discretion may be exercised and the formula departed from. Among them are:

2.—(1) A departure direction may be given with respect to special expenses of the applicant which were not, and could not have been, taken into account in determining the current assessment in accordance with the provisions of, or made under, Part I of Schedule 1.

(2) In this paragraph 'special expenses' means the whole, or any prescribed part, of expenses which fall within a prescribed description of expenses.

(3) In prescribing descriptions of expenses for the purposes of this paragraph, the Secretary of State may, in particular, make provision with respect to—

(*a*) costs incurred in travelling to work;

(*b*) costs incurred by an absent parent in maintaining contact with the child, or with any of the children, with respect to whom he is liable to pay child support maintenance under the current assessment;

(*c*) costs attributable to a long-term illness or disability of the applicant or of a dependant of the applicant;

(*d*) debts incurred, before the absent parent became an absent parent in relation to a child with respect to whom the current assessment was made—

(i) for the joint benefit of both parents;

(ii) for the benefit of any child with respect to whom the current assessment was made; or

(iii) for the benefit of any other child falling within a prescribed category;

(*e*) pre-1993 financial commitments from which it is impossible for the parent concerned to withdraw or from which it would be unreasonable to expect that parent to have to withdraw;

(*f*) costs incurred by a parent in supporting a child who is not his child but who is part of his family.

(4) For the purposes of sub-paragraph (3)(*c*)—

(*a*) the question whether one person is a dependant of another shall be determined in accordance with regulations made by the Secretary of State;

(*b*) 'disability' and 'illness' have such meaning as may be prescribed; and

(*c*) the question whether an illness or disability is long-term shall be determined in accordance with regulations made by the Secretary of State.

(5) For the purposes of sub-paragraph (3)(*e*), 'pre-1993 financial commitments' means financial commitments of a prescribed kind entered into before 5th April 1993 in any case where—

(*a*) a court order of a prescribed kind was in force with respect to the absent parent and the person with care concerned at the time when they were entered into; or

(*b*) an agreement between them of a prescribed kind was in force at that time.

(6) For the purposes of sub-paragraph (3)(*f*), a child who is not the child of a particular person is a part of that person's family in such circumstances as may be prescribed.

Paragraphs 3 and 4 deal with circumstances where property or capital transfers have been made before April 1993. Finally:

5.—(1) The Secretary of State may by regulations prescribe other cases in which a departure direction may be given.

(2) Regulations under this paragraph may, for example, make provision with respect to cases where—

(*a*) assets which do not produce income are capable of producing income;
(*b*) a person's life-style is inconsistent with the level of his income;
(*c*) housing costs are unreasonably high;
(*d*) housing costs are in part attributable to housing persons whose circumstances are such as to justify disregarding a part of those costs;
(*e*) travel costs are unreasonably high; or
(*f*) travel costs should be disregarded.

Questions

(i) Can you think of cases other than those mentioned in para 5(2) where departure directions should be given?
(ii) Have the changes made to the child support system now resolved all the initial difficulties with the Child Support Act 1991?

3 Support for other families with children and families with elderly and/or disabled dependants

There has been some attempt to allocate resources towards families with children. From 1945, there was in existence a system of family allowances. The philosophy behind this scheme was that the state should not meet the whole cost of the needs of children. The amount of the allowance therefore was based on the estimates of the cost of meeting physical needs only, for example, for food, clothing and housing. There was no notional account taken of items such as toys or books.

In particular, allowances were not payable for the first child of the family. Family allowances were subject to a tax 'claw-back'. But, under a child tax allowance scheme, tax payers could obtain exemption from a certain amount of their income from taxation for each dependent child. Tax allowances of course only benefited those subject to tax, and would hardly be of any value to those categories of persons who fall within or close to the poverty trap. Child benefit was phased in as from 1977, and provides a merger of child tax allowances and family allowances. Child benefit is a universal, non-means tested and tax-free cash benefit for all children. There is an additional payment, known as the one-parent benefit, for a lone parent. The benefit was seen by politicians from all parties as a way 'to put cash into the hands of mothers and to give a measure of independence to mothers' (Patrick Jenkin MP on 9 February 1977, in a debate on the Child Benefit Scheme in the House of Commons). In the same debate the then Minister, Mr Stan Orme MP said:

Child Benefit is non-means tested and non-taxable. The scheme has two big advantages over the present method of family support which relies on child tax allowances and family allowances. The child benefit will be paid to the mother, as it is typically the mother who is responsible for the housekeeping in raising the children. This contrasts with the child tax allowances, which typically go to the father. Thus, income is transferred within the family from father to mother. Wage earners who earn under the tax threshold do not get the benefit of the child tax allowances, but they will get the child benefit.

However, another MP present during this debate, Mr John Ovenden MP said:

Successive Governments have a pretty shameful record of support for families. They have an even worse record if we attempt to make international comparisons. There are few European and non-European countries with which we stand any comparison in this league. That is why it is important to talk about the whole level of family support and why we should commit ourselves to policies aimed at relieving the problem of family poverty.

The Government has responded to these criticisms by introducing the system of family credit. The argument in favour of these changes is contained in Volume II of *Reform of Social Security (Programme for Change)* (1985):

Child benefit and one-parent benefit

4.44 As we have made clear the Government accept the case for continuing the system of child benefit. It is right that families with children at all income levels should receive some recognition for the additional costs of bringing up children and that the tax/benefit system should allow for some general redistribution of resources from those without children to those who have responsibility for caring for them. Child benefit is simple, well understood and popular. ...

A new family credit system

4.45 Although the general principle of providing support to families through child benefit is important, the greatest priority for additional resources in the area of family support is to provide better targeted help for those on low incomes. The proposals for the new income support scheme have been designed to give greater relative priority to families with children. But it is clear that the present arrangements for assisting low-income working families with children must be improved. The existing family income supplement is not effective in meeting this need. It will, therefore, be abolished and a new family credit system will be introduced.

4.46 The objectives of the new family credit will be:

first, to provide an effective bridge between the higher level of support for children available to those in the income support scheme (which is intended to cover the full costs of caring for children) and the general recognition of family costs implied by child benefit;

second, to ensure that families do not find themselves worse off in work than they would be if they were not working;

third, to provide such extra help as is required as part of income from work rather than as a separate payment through the benefit system;

fourth, to avoid the position, which can occur now where net family income can be reduced as earnings rise over significant ranges of earnings;

fifth, to give greater freedom of choice to the families concerned by providing assistance in cash rather than in kind;

4.47 The new family credit scheme will use the same basic structure as the income support scheme. Maximum entitlement to benefit at the lowest income levels will comprise a substantial premium payable to all families (including one-parent families) augmented by allowances for each child which, when taken together with child benefit, will exceed the allowances within the income support scheme. The aim will be to ensure that at earnings above the income support level for a couple, a family with children should not be worse off in work. Entitlement will be assessed by the Department of Health and Social Security but the benefit will be paid by employers as an offset to tax and national insurance or, where appropriate, as an addition to gross pay. Above the lowest income levels, the benefit entitlement will be reduced proportionately as income rises. But the assessment will be based on net income so that the reduction in benefit resulting cannot exceed any increase in earnings. The benefit will also be treated as income for the assessment of housing benefit so that the combined effect of the two benefits cannot lead to a marginal tax rate above 100 per cent.

4.48 A key feature of the scheme will be its impact on the poverty and unemployment traps. By adopting a similar structure to income support, and a similar net income test to both income support and housing benefit, it should be possible both to ensure that those in work are better off than if they were not working and that the worst effects of the poverty trap are eliminated.

The number of families with children who were receiving FIS fell from about 89,000 in December 1977 to an average of about 77,000 in 1979. From

1979, there was a marked increase, and in December 1981, the number of families on FIS had increased to 132,000. By September 1986, this figure had further increased to 210,000. Family credit then replaced FIS; in 1991–92 the family credit case load was 352,000, in 1993–94 it was 513,000.

The following table, from *Social Trends* 26 (1996), shows the effect of increased earnings upon spending power, taking into account the effect of taxation and benefits. The accompanying text claims (at p. 90) that 'the poverty trap has been removed by social security reforms and, in general, net income increases with gross income'.

Net weekly spending power[1]: by gross weekly earnings[2] and type of family, July 1995

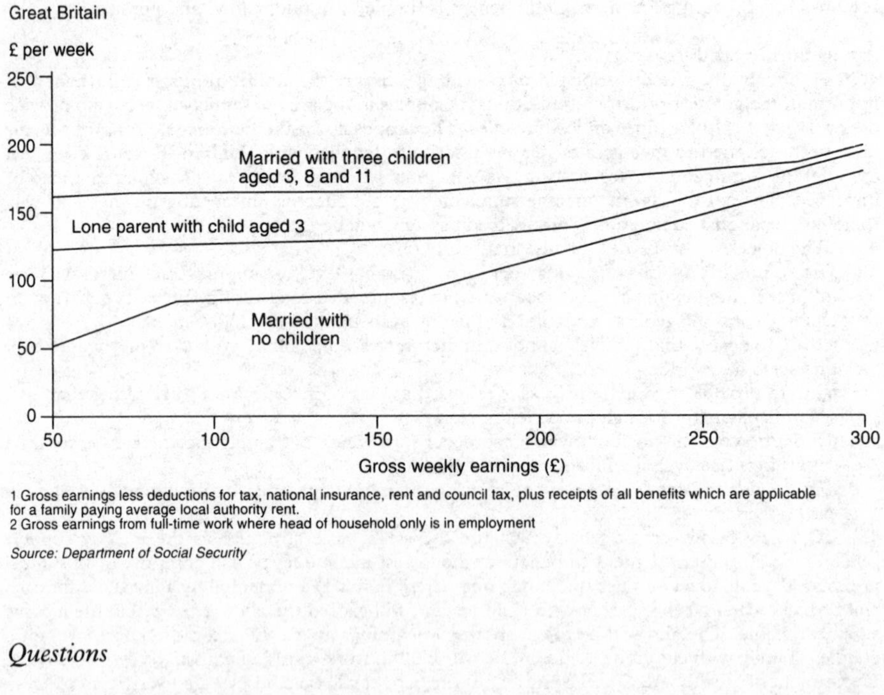

1 Gross earnings less deductions for tax, national insurance, rent and council tax, plus receipts of all benefits which are applicable for a family paying average local authority rent.
2 Gross earnings from full-time work where head of household only is in employment

Source: Department of Social Security

Questions

(i) Might family credit be a palliative? Would the introduction of a national minimum wage eliminate the need for family credit, and/or put more people on unemployment benefit and income support?
(ii) Is there any merit in abolishing child benefit and using the money to target more help to more people through the mechanism of family credit?
(iii) Has the poverty trap really been removed? What about the single mother who receives just enough maintenance for her children from their father to take her off income support, but insufficient to compensate her for the loss of benefits that go with income support such as free school meals, free milk, etc?
(iv) How much help should the state be giving to single teenage mothers?

We must now return to the question of priorities. The age structure of the population has changed in recent years. The proportion of children aged under 16 is falling, and the proportion over 60 is rising and projected to increase further as the tables from *Social Trends* 26 (1996) illustrate.

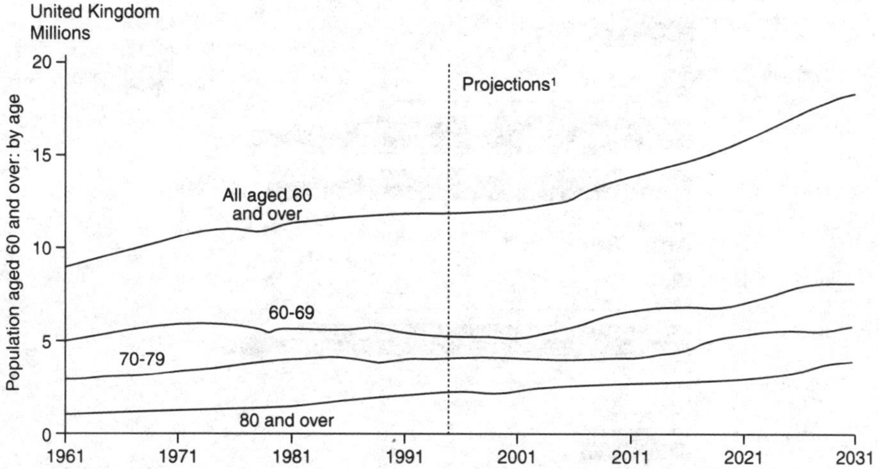

1 1992-based projections

Source: Office of Population Censuses and Surveys; Government Actuary's Department; General Register Office (Scotland); General Register Office (Northern Ireland)

Population[1]: by age and gender

United Kingdom Percentages

	Under 16	16–39	40–64	65–79	80 and over	All ages (= 100%) (millions)
Mid-year estimates						
1961	25	31	32	10	2	52.8
1971	25	31	30	11	2	55.9
1981	22	35	28	12	3	56.4
1991	20	35	29	12	4	57.8
1994	21	35	29	12	4	58.4
Males	22	36	29	11	2	28.6
Females	20	33	29	13	5	29.8
Mid-year projections[2]						
2001	21	33	31	11	4	59.8
2011	19	30	34	12	5	61.3
2021	18	30	33	14	5	62.1
2031	18	28	30	16	7	62.2
Males	19	29	31	16	5	30.9
Females	18	28	30	17	8	31.3

1 See Appendix, Part 1: Population and population projections.
2 1992-based projections.

Source: Office of Population Censuses and Surveys; Government Actuary's Department; General Register Office (Scotland); General Register Office (Northern Ireland)

Another table from *Social Trends* 20 (1990) shows that all EC countries project a similar growth.

Population aged 70 and over : EC comparison

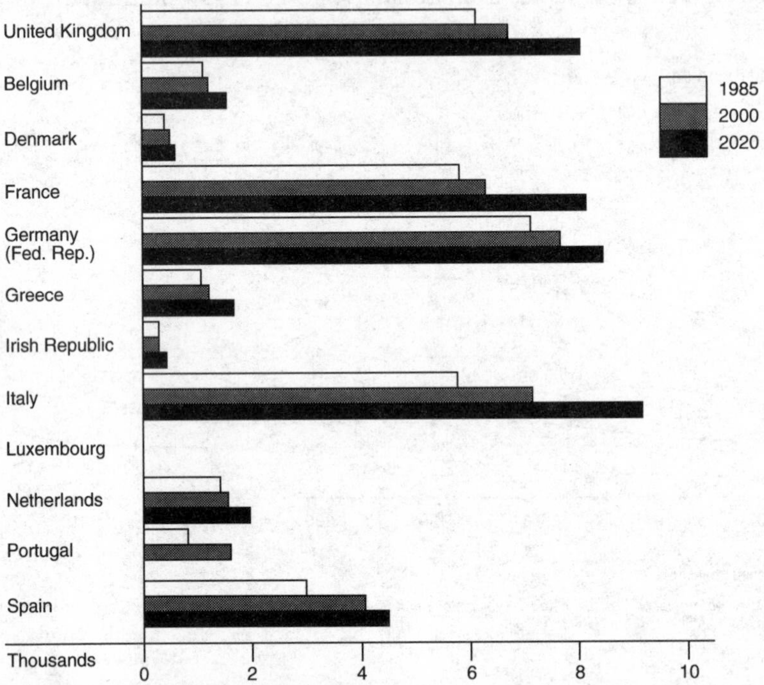

Source: EUROSTAT Demographic Statistics

These figures suggest that many more people than at present are likely to be involved in caring for dependent relatives. The following table in *Social Trends* 25 (1995) records information obtained by the General Household Survey in 1990; the accompanying text (at p. 146) explains that caring includes 'helping with personal care (such as washing), giving medicine, physical help, paperwork, providing company and keeping an eye on a dependant'.

Carers: by relationship with dependant, 1990

Great Britain — Percentages

	In the same household	In another private household	All
Dependant			
Parent	23	39	35
Friend/neighbour	2	25	19
Other relative	10	20	18
Parent-in-law	6	15	13
Spouse	41	0	10
Child over 16	10	10	3
Child under 16	8	0	2
All carers (= 100%) (millions)	1.6	5.2	6.8

Source: Office of Population Censuses and Surveys

Questions

(i) Before 23 June 1986, the invalid care allowance (ICA), which is made available to the carers of the severely disabled, was not available to any married or cohabiting woman. In *Drake v Chief Adjudication Officer* 150/85 [1987] QB 166, [1986] 3 All ER 65, the European Court of Justice held that the original provision in s. 37(3)(*a*)(i) of the Social Security Act 1975 contravened the principle of equality of treatment set out in Council Directive 79/7 EEC. The Government changed the law (a day before the judgment!) so that the benefit is made available to such women. The rules for ICA state that a carer must provide care for at least 35 hours a week. The 'disregard' for part-time work is now £50 per week. These rules exclude many people, especially those who look after relatives who live in residential homes during the week and go to the carer's home at weekends. Why should these people be excluded from benefiting?
(ii) If you do not think that they should be excluded, would you welcome a universal non-means tested benefit such as child benefit, or would you prefer to see the introduction of a means-tested benefit? How about zero-rating VAT for the supply and delivery of goods and services for home carers?
(iii) What is the justification for the part-time earnings 'disregard' operated at present? Should it be abolished?

In *An Aging World* (ed Eekelaar and Pearl) (1989) P. Paillat concluded his remarks on 'Recent and Predictable Population Trends in Developed Countries' as follows:

Population trends in developed countries at the end of the [twentieth] century can be summarized in the following way:

– A low fertility, much lower than the replacement level and including a generalized aging process, expressed on the one hand by an increase of the proportion of old people, and on the other hand by internal aging of the working age population;

– A lengthening of life after age 50, without anyone being able to state that quality of life after 80 will also improve.

This latter issue is worth paying attention to. Problems in very old age are not the same and cannot be solved the same way in a young population or in an aging one. 60-year-old 'children' cannot provide as good a care for old dependent parents aged 85, as a 40-year-old child with a father or mother, aged 65 and in good health. The scattering of families all over the national territory is limiting exchanges of services between generations.

... [P]opulation aging will be the socially central issue of the coming century, associated with disrupting population balance all over the world.

Questions

(i) Do you consider Paillat alarmist?
(ii) Does poverty in old age involve different issues from those raised by poverty among younger adults?
(iii) Would you agree with the view that we 'may make more fruitful efforts in tackling poverty [of various groups] if we look at the common factors which unite them rather than the more superficial aspects which distinguish their problems. In this way, we could perhaps develop strategies which encompass all who live in poverty, rather than seeking to exclude or differentiate by means of formal marital status or the accident of age.' (Douglas, 1985)?

Maybe there are no priorities after all!

Chapter 5

Family property

In the last two chapters we have concentrated on income. In this chapter, we turn our attention to a discussion of family property. For many families, until comparatively recently, only the former question had much relevance. However, there has always been a substantial group who have enjoyed capital assets in the form of land, chattels, and stocks and shares. Rules have developed to regulate and administer this property during the lives and after the deaths of its owners. In contrast to the modern concern for what has been termed by the Finer Report 'the pathology of the family', traditional property law has been regarded as a law 'which fortifies and regulates an institution central to society'. Accordingly, the law's priorities in dealing with family property have shifted somewhat during recent years. Another change during the last quarter of the twentieth century has been the growth of the 'property owning democracy' and the spread of ownership of capital assets, so that the number of people owning their homes – not to mention other forms of wealth such as shares, pensions, annuities, life policies, etc – has expanded considerably. Thus although property law was developed in a different age by the land owners and the bourgeoisie who in effect made their own laws by contracts, trusts and wills, there has been a 'proletarianisation' during the present century. The only restraint on this expansion is the ever present shadow of state involvement (interference?) through taxation, social security law and death duties. Traditional property law was mainly concerned with devolution rules within the kinship group. Modern commercial activity now involves third parties: banks, building societies and other creditors. Courts are increasingly asked to adjudicate between competing claims.

We begin our examination of family property by considering one of the earlier issues the law had to tackle, namely the ownership of property by married persons.

1 Separate property for spouses

(a) HISTORICAL BACKGROUND

The law which at present governs the property of married persons is based on the principle of separate property: 'each spouse may acquire and deal with his or her property as if he or she were single.' (Law Commission Working Paper on *Family Property Law* 1971.) But this was not always the case, as Sir Jocelyn Simon explains in *With all my Worldly Goods* (1964):

I invite you to accompany me to a village church where a wedding is in progress. The mellifluous cadences of the vicar's voice fall hypnotically on the ear – '... honourable estate ... mutual society, help and comfort ... comfort her, honour and keep her. ...' Now he has reached the ceremony of the ring. The bridegroom bends a gaze of ineffable tenderness on his bride – ... with this ring ... with my body ... and with all my worldly goods I thee endow.' I hold my breath, aghast. Will the vicar rend his cassock? Will he sprinkle on his head ashes from the ancient coke stove? Will he hurl the bridegroom from the chancel steps with imprecation and anathema? For the man has committed the most horrible blasphemy. In that holy place, at this most solemn moment, actually invoking the names of the Deity, he has made a declaration which is utterly false. He is not endowing the bride with a penny, a stick, a clod. Nor does he intend ever to do so. And yet the service proceeds as if nothing untoward has happened. How does this come about?

The phrase originates in the ancient Use of Sarum, where it is almost unique in liturgy. It reflects a mediaeval custom, the endowment of the bride at the church door, dower *ad ostium ecclesiae* itself a relic, I surmise, of a still more archaic usage, the payment of the brideprice negotiated between the families of bride and bridegroom.

Dower *ad ostium ecclesiae*, however, gave way to common law dower, where the law itself determined what interest the wife should have in her husband's property. That was a life estate after the death of her husband in one third of any land of which the husband had ever been solely seised at any time during the marriage for an estate of inheritance to which issue of the wife by the husband might possibly succeed.

But this was small compensation for the proprietary and personal rights that the wife lost at Common Law on her marriage.

In this country the feudal theory was, under the Norman kings, applied in all its rigour. The proper purpose of a tenement – and wealth at that time was largely to be measured in land – was the maintenance of a vassal in such a state that he could suitably perform his feudal services to his lord – not least military service. A married woman was considered to be generally incapable of performing the feudal services. Any freehold estate of which the wife was seised was therefore vested in the husband as well as the wife during coverture, and it was under his sole management and care. If there was any issue of the marriage born alive, the husband immediately gained an estate in the wife's freeholds corresponding to her dower in his lands, but extending to the whole estate, not merely to one third: this was significantly called the husband's estate by the courtesy of England. As soon as issue was born alive, he had therefore a life estate in his wife's land which he could charge to the full. Chattels being more evanescent than land, the Common Law took the simple course of letting the husband have them as his. Any goods, including money, in the wife's actual possession, came under his absolute ownership forthwith. Any property to which the wife might be entitled by bringing an action at law – her 'chose in action'; for example, any debt due to her – became the husband's if during coverture he recovered it or otherwise reduced it into possession. When leasehold interests began to be created, for the investment of money rather than for the enjoyment of land, the Common Law treated them largely as chattels: though they did not in theory become the husband's property, he might nevertheless sell them and take the proceeds as his own. During coverture the husband was entitled to the whole of the wife's income from any source, including her own earnings or the rent from her leasehold or freehold property. She could only bequeath her personal property with the consent of her husband; and such consent might be revoked by him at any time. On the wife dying intestate by virtue of this rule, all her personal property, including her leaseholds and her choses in action, passed to her husband. In such circumstances, it was a real triumph for 18th century self-satisfaction that Blackstone could write: 'Even the disabilities which the wife lies under are for the most part intended for her protection and benefit: so great a favourite is the female sex of the laws of England.' It could have been little less inconvenient to have been a favourite of Haroun-al-Raschid.

However, in mediaeval England, the wife did enjoy some limited rights. As Sir Jocelyn Simon says:

It is almost certain that in the 12th and 13th centuries our own law recognised, ... a reserved portion of a man's chattels of which he might not dispose by will if he left wife or child. After payment of debts the estate was divided into 'wife's part','bairns' part', and 'dead's part' (the two former were also called 'the reasonable parts'). Only over the 'dead's part' was there freedom of disposition.

Why did they not lead the lawyers to adopt a system of Community of Goods similar to that of our continental neighbours? Why, indeed, did it not survive in England, as it has in Scotland to this day? I think there were two reasons. First, with the invention of the English system of heirship in land, the heir took the whole of the freehold estate, the widow only a life interest and only in a third. Furthermore, she did not automatically enter the land as of right at the death of her husband: she had to wait to be assigned her portion by the heir. In the field of devolution which remained firmly within the view of the common lawyers, the widow, therefore, looked like a pensioner of the heir rather than a partner of the ancestor.

Secondly, in the eyes of the mediaeval Church intestacy was almost a sin: the 'dead's part' must be suitably devoted to such pious uses (especially ecclesiastic benefaction) as would mitigate the transcendental pains and penalties which would otherwise be the reward for the deceased's terrestrial shortcomings. In order to make sure that nothing went wrong about this, the Church – in this country alone – secured jurisdiction over probate of wills. The common lawyers became intensely jealous. Moreover, the interference of the Church courts with morals made them highly unpopular with laymen too. Thus neither common lawyers nor laymen were in the least disposed to follow the Church courts or their law. So it came about that in Edward III's reign the Lords in Parliament expressly disapproved the custom of the 'reasonable part' of the personal estate reserved from disposition by will – it was an intolerable interference with freedom. Under such disapprobation the custom had died out in the province of Canterbury by the end of the 15th century. In the northern province it lasted until 1692, but was then abolished by Act of Parliament. The excuse was that a system of jointuring widows had been invented, and if they enjoyed both jointure and 'wife's part' there would be too little left for the younger children; so it was helpfully arranged that a testator could thenceforward leave his children with nothing at all.

It is well known that equity intervened. Simon puts it in the following way:

During the Middle Ages the influence of the Church and the cults of chivalry and courtly love had brought about a steady rise in the status of women. ... But others besides the wife were interested in what happened to her property, not least her kinsfolk. They will wish to make suitable provision for her on her marriage, to ensure in particular that the children of the marriage, who will be their own blood relations, are properly advanced. But if there is no issue of the marriage the primary interest of the wife's kinsfolk is that the property which they have put into the marriage should return to them, rather than pass to the husband's family. This consideration was until quite modern times particularly potent among the ruling classes, where marriages were to be considered, at least partly, as political and economic alliances. But by the end of the Middle Ages ... the Common Law was too far committed to the interest of the husband to be able to recognise the claims of the wife and her kinship group. It had lost the flexibility to provide new remedies for new needs as they arose. ...

[But] a woman about to enter matrimony, or her kinsfolk, could transfer property to a trustee: at Common Law it was in his ownership; but in Chancery he was bound to deal with it according to the terms of the trust – which could, simply, be according to the married woman's wishes. Or the trust could provide that, in the absence of any issue of the marriage to take a vested interest in the property, it should after the wife's death or that of her husband revert to her kinsfolk. Moreover, if the husband had recourse to the Court of Chancery, with its superior remedies, for the purpose of asserting his common law rights over the wife's property, that Court would as a condition of its aid compel the husband to settle on his wife and children part of any such property; and ultimately the wife herself or the children could initiate the claim. Over the wife's interest acquired in these two ways Equity at last gave her nearly all the rights of a single woman: she could give it away or sell it, or leave it by will to whoever she wished, or charge it with her contracts. A married woman could thus possess separate property over which her husband had no control whatever, and against which neither he nor his creditors had any claim. But in safeguarding in this peculiar way the interests of the married woman and of her kinship group, Equity took a further and decisive step away from any system of Community of Goods between married people.

Equity created a regime of separate property for married women. This regime was limited, however, to the investment property of the wealthy. Simon explains how the doctrines of Equity were used in the late nineteenth century to deal with the needs of 'middle and lower middle classes':

First, the proponents of reform, led by John Stuart Mill, were principally interested in abrogating the subjection of women and in giving them equal political and civil rights with men. Men owned their own property, virtually untrammelled by any claims by their spouses. So women must be given similar rights. To entrench, say, the married woman's right to occupation of her husband's house would be to treat her as an unequal. ... Secondly, Mill was at this time in the full tide of his individualism. Indeed, there was as yet no significant movement of thought orientated towards the foundation of society on small voluntary groupings, such as the family, of which the law of property should take specific cognizance. Thirdly, together with Mill there was a vociferous group of emancipated women writers, who were acutely conscious that the Common Law delivered over to their husbands the fruits of their professional activities, but who were understandably less concerned with the claims of all the housewives and mothers whose real needs were security in the matrimonial home and the right to participate in the proprietary benefits which their husbands enjoyed through their own economic self-abnegation. Fourthly, comparative jurisprudence was virtually unstudied at this time; and there was in any event a tendency to regard French political and social institutions with a well-bred distaste. Lastly, and most important, legal reform proceeds largely on the principle of inertia, not least in countries where the rule of precedent colours legal thinking. A movement once started continues of its own momentum. We have already seen the Common Law operate in that way in this very field. And now Parliament. Equity had permitted married women of the wealthier classes to own their separate property: how could it be denied to the generality of married women? So the Married Women's Property Acts did not attempt to remove married women's incapacities in any general way; still less in their interests to put restriction on the freedom of disposition of married men. Statute merely followed Equity in permitting married women to hold and handle and bind themselves with regard to any property which might come to them.

Questions

(i) Do you see similarities between the individualism of the nineteenth century and trends in the present generation which have led to the introduction of a system of independent taxation?
(ii) Modern feminists would regard chivalry and courtly love as the reverse of equalising the status of women. Why?
(iii) Do you think that a major reason why the Married Women's Property Acts were enacted could have been the tradesmen's difficulties in enforcing their debts?

(b) CRITICISMS AND SURVIVAL OF SEPARATION OF PROPERTY

Sir Jocelyn Simon made the following observation in his 1964 lecture:

But men can only earn their incomes and accumulate capital by virtue of the division of labour between themselves and their wives. The wife spends her youth and early middle age in bearing and rearing children and in tending the home; the husband is thus freed for his economic activities. Unless the wife plays her part the husband cannot play his. The cock bird can feather his nest precisely because he is not required to spend most of his time sitting on it.

In such a state of affairs a system of Separation of Goods between married people is singularly ill adapted to do justice. Community of Goods, or at the least community in acquisitions and accumulations, is far more appropriate. And as one leaves the sphere of those who enjoy investment property for that of those whose property largely consists of the home and its contents a régime of Separation is utterly remote from social needs.

The difficulties are taken up by the English Law Commission in 1971 in a Working Paper on *Family Property Law*:

0.12 It is said that equality of power, which separation of property achieves, does not of itself lead to equal opportunity to exercise that power; it ignores the fact that a married woman, especially if she has young children, does not in practice have the same opportunity as her husband or as an unmarried woman to acquire property; it takes no account of the fact that marriage is a form of partnership to which both spouses contribute, each in a different way, and that the contribution of each is equally important to the family welfare and to society.

The Law Commission give an example of how the principle works unfairly. This is what strict separation of property used to mean:

0.13 Mr Brown earns the family income. The home is in his name and he is responsible for the mortgage repayments and outgoings. Mrs Brown has given up her employment and earnings to attend to domestic affairs and to look after the family. She has no savings or private income, and cannot contribute in cash to the acquisition of property. If the marriage breaks down, the law regards the home, its contents, and any other property or savings acquired by Mr Brown in his name, as his sole property. Mrs Brown has a right to occupy the home and to be maintained, but she does not own the home or any other property acquired out of Mr Brown's earnings. On a decree of divorce, nullity or judicial separation she may apply to the court for property to be transferred to or settled on her [see Chapter 8, below]. If Mr Brown dies leaving a will which disinherits her (though this is relatively uncommon) she has a limited right of support, available only on application to a court and at its discretion: she has no right other than to ask for what is normally needed for her support. In short, she has no right of property in her dead husband's estate if he has made a will which disinherits her.

There are three reasons given for dissatisfaction with the principle of separation: (i) unfairness, (ii) uncertainty, particularly in relation to the matrimonial home, and (iii) that even when adjustments can be made, these adjustments depend on the discretion of the court after the termination of the marriage. As Sir Otto Kahn-Freund explains in *Matrimonial Property: Where do we go from here?* (1971):

0.15 Mr and Mrs Jones have been married for ten years and have three children. When they married they bought a house on mortgage. The deposit was paid partly from Mrs Jones' savings and partly from a loan from Mr Jones' employer. The mortgage instalments have usually been paid by Mr Jones. At the beginning Mrs Jones had a job; she went back to part-time work when the children were older. From her wages she paid a large part of the household expenses and bought some of the furniture. Occasionally she paid the mortgage instalments. A car and a washing machine were bought on hire-purchase in Mr Jones' name, but the instalments were sometimes paid by him and sometimes by her. Mr Jones has now left his wife and children and is living with another woman.

0.16 If, in the above situation, Mrs Jones asks what her property rights are so that she can make arrangements, she will receive no clear answer. In effect, the law will ask her what intentions she and her husband had about the allocation of their property, and to this she would only be able to reply that they had no clear intention.

Question

Which of the three reasons for dissatisfaction do you consider the most powerful reason for reform?

It is necessary to discuss the alleged uncertainty of the law in detail. Lord Denning had attempted to introduce an element of discretion, both through his interpretation of the courts' powers under s. 17 of the Married Women's Property Act 1882 (see below) and through his approach to the ownership of 'family assets'. This may have made the law even more uncertain, but in his view it certainly made it more fair. In the event, the House of Lords, in *Pettitt v Pettitt* [1970] AC 777, [1969] 2 All ER 385 and *Gissing v Gissing* [1971] AC 886, [1970] 2 All ER 780 overruled his interpretation of s. 17 and emphasised that the interests of husband and wife in property must be determined in accordance with the ordinary rules of property law (as to which, see pp. 163ff, below).

Pettitt v Pettitt
[1970] AC 777, [1969] 2 All ER 385, [1969] 2 WLR 966, 113 Sol Jo 344, House of Lords

The case was concerned with work carried out by a husband upon a matrimonial home which was owned by his wife. The facts appear in the speech of Lord Reid.

Lord Reid: My Lords, the appellant was married in 1952. For about nine years she and her husband lived in a house which she had inherited. During that time her husband carried out a number of improvements, largely redecorating, on which he says he spent some £80. In 1961 this house was sold and she acquired another. After this had been paid for there was a surplus of a few hundred pounds and he used this money, apparently with the consent of the appellant, in paying for his car. The spouses lived for about four years in the new house. Then the appellant left her husband, alleging cruelty, and she obtained a divorce in 1967. The husband then left the house and raised the present proceedings. He said that during those four years he carried out a considerable number of improvements to the house and garden and estimated that in doing so he performed work and supplied material to a value of £723. He sought a declaration that he was beneficially interested in the proceeds of sale of the house in the sum of £1,000 and an order on the appellant to pay. Then an order was made that she should pay him £300. The Court of Appeal reluctantly dismissed her appeal, holding that they were bound by the decision in *Appleton v Appleton* [1965] 1 All ER 44, [1965] 1 WLR 25. They gave leave to appeal.

For the last twenty years the law regarding what are sometimes called family assets has been in an unsatisfactory state. There have been many cases showing acute differences of opinion in the Court of Appeal. Various questions have arisen, generally after the break-up of a marriage. Sometimes both spouses have contributed in money to the purchase of a house; sometimes the contribution of one spouse has been otherwise than money: sometimes one spouse owned the house and the other spent money or did work in improving it: and there have been a variety of other circumstances. ...

Many of the cases have been brought by virtue of the provisions of section 17 of the Married Women's Property Act 1882. That is a long and complicated section: the relevant part is as follows:

> 'In any question between husband and wife as to the title to or possession of property, either party ... may apply by summons or otherwise in a summary way to any judge of the High Court of Justice ... and the judge ... may make such order with respect to the property in dispute ... as he thinks fit.'

The main dispute has been as to the meaning of the latter words authorising the judge ... to make such order with respect to the property in dispute as he thinks fit. They are words normally used to confer a discretion on the court: where discretion is limited, the limitations are generally expressed: but here no limitation is expressed. So it has been said that here these words confer on the court an unfettered discretion to override existing rights in the property and to dispose of it in whatever manner the judge may think to be just and equitable in the whole circumstances of the case. On the other hand it has been said that these words do not entitle the court to disregard any existing property right, but merely confer a power to regulate possession or the exercise of property rights, or, more narrowly, merely confer a power to exercise in proceedings under section 17 any discretion with regard to the property in dispute which has already been conferred by some other enactment. And other intermediate views have also been expressed.

I would approach the question in this way. The meaning of the section cannot have altered since it was passed in 1882. At that time the certainty and security of rights of property were still generally regarded as of paramount importance and I find it incredible that any Parliament of that era could have intended to put a husband's property at the hazard of the unfettered discretion of a judge (including a county court judge) if the wife raised a dispute about it. Moreover, this discretion, if it exists, can only be exercised in proceedings under section 17: the same dispute could arise in other forms of action; and I find it even more incredible that it could have been intended that such a discretion should be given to a judge in summary proceedings but denied to the judge if the proceedings were of the ordinary character. So are the words so unequivocal that we are forced to give them a meaning which cannot have been intended? I do not think so. It is perfectly possible to construe the words as having a much more restricted meaning and in my judgment they should be so construed. I do not think that a judge has any more right to disregard property rights in section 17 proceedings than he has in any other form of proceedings. ...

I would therefore refuse to consider whether property belonging to either spouse ought to be regarded as family property for that would be introducing a new conception into English law and not merely developing existing principles. There are systems of law which recognise joint family property or communio bonorum. I am not sure that those principles are very highly regarded in countries where they are in force, but in any case it would be going far beyond the functions of the court to attempt to give effect to them here.

As a result of this case, Parliament enacted s. 37 of the Matrimonial Proceedings and Property Act 1970:

It is hereby declared that where a husband or wife contributes in money or money's worth to the improvement of real or personal property in which or in the proceeds of sale of which either or both of them has or have a beneficial interest, the husband or wife so contributing shall, if the contribution is of a substantial nature and subject to any agreement between them to the contrary express or implied, be treated as having then acquired by virtue of his or her contribution a share or an enlarged share, as the case may be, in that beneficial interest of such an extent as may have been then agreed or, in default of such agreement, as may seem in all the circumstances just to any court before which the question of the existence or extent of the beneficial interest of the husband or wife arises (whether in proceedings between them or in other proceedings).

Questions

(i) Mr Pettitt lost his case: would s. 37 have made any difference?
(ii) What interest would Mr Pettitt have acquired if he had spent his money on a new roof or on rewiring?

In *Gissing v Gissing* the House of Lords considered the mechanisms available in the law of trusts to assist the spouse who has no legal estate in the property and no formally created equitable interest.

Gissing v Gissing
[1971] AC 886, [1970] 2 All ER 780, [1970] 3 WLR 255, 114 Sol Jo 550, House of Lords

The facts are set out in the speech of Lord Diplock:

In the instant appeal the matrimonial home was purchased in 1951 for £2,695 and conveyed into the sole name of the husband. The parties had by then been married for some 16 years and both were in employment with the same firm, the husband earning £1,000 and the wife £500, per annum. The purchase price was raised as to £2,150 on mortgage repayable by instalments, as to £500 by a loan to the husband from his employers, and as to the balance of £45 and the legal charges was paid by the husband out of his own moneys. The wife made no direct contribution to the initial deposit or legal charges, nor to the repayment of the loan of £500 nor to the mortgage instalments. She continued earning at the rate of £500 per annum until the marriage broke down in 1961. During this period the husband's salary increased to £3,000 per annum. The husband repaid the loan of £500 and paid the mortgage instalments. He also paid the outgoings on the house, gave to his wife a housekeeping allowance of £8 to £10 a week out of which she paid the running expenses of the household and he paid for holidays. The only contribution which the wife made out of her earnings to the household expenses was that she paid for her own clothes and those of the son of the marriage and for some extras. No change in this arrangement was made when the house was acquired. Each spouse had a separate banking account, the wife's in the Post Office Savings Bank, and each made savings out of their respective earnings. There was no joint bank account and there were no joint savings. There was no express agreement at the time of the purchase or thereafter as to how the beneficial interest in the house should be held. The learned judge was prepared to accept that after the marriage had broken down the husband said to the wife: 'Don't worry about the house – it's yours'; but this has not been relied upon, at any rate in your Lordships' House, as an acknowledgment of a pre-existing agreement on which the wife had acted to her detriment so as to give rise to a resulting, implied or constructive trust, nor can it be relied upon as an express declaration of trust as it was oral only.

On what then is the wife's claim based? In 1951 when the house was purchased she spent about £190 on buying furniture and a cooker and refrigerator for it. She also paid about £30 for improving the lawn. As furniture and household durables are depreciating assets whereas houses have turned out to be appreciating assets it may be that she would have been wise to have devoted her savings to acquiring an interest in the freehold; but this may not have been so apparent in 1951 as it has now become. The court is not entitled to infer a common intention to this effect from the mere fact that she provided chattels for joint use in the new matrimonial home; and there is nothing else in the conduct of the parties at the time of the purchase or thereafter which supports such an inference. There is no suggestion that the wife's efforts or her earnings made it possible for the husband to raise the initial loan or the mortgage or that her relieving her husband from the expense of buying clothing for herself and for their son was undertaken in order to enable him the better to meet the mortgage instalments or to repay the loan. The picture presented by the evidence is one of husband and wife retaining their separate proprietary interests in property whether real or personal purchased with their separate savings and is inconsistent with any common intention at the time of the purchase of the matrimonial home that the wife, who neither then nor thereafter contributed anything to its purchase price or assumed any liability for it, should nevertheless be entitled to a beneficial interest in it.

Earlier in his speech, Lord Diplock looked at the role of the agreement in the creation of an equitable interest in real property.

Any claim to a beneficial interest in land by a person, whether spouse or stranger, in whom the legal estate in the land is not vested must be based upon the proposition that the person in whom the legal estate is vested holds it as trustee upon trust to give effect to the beneficial interest of the claimant as cestui que trust. The legal principles applicable to the claim are those of the English law of trusts and in particular, in the kind of dispute between spouses that comes before the courts, the law relating to the creation and operation of 'resulting, implied or constructive trusts.' Where the trust is expressly declared in the instrument by which the legal estate is transferred to the trustee or by a written declaration of trust by the trustee, the court must give effect to it. But to constitute a valid declaration of trust by way of gift of a beneficial interest in land to a cestui que trust the declaration is required by section 53(1) of the Law of Property Act 1925, to be in writing. If it is not in writing it can only take effect as a resulting, implied or constructive trust to which that section has no application.

A resulting, implied or constructive trust – and it is unnecessary for present purposes to distinguish between these three classes of trust – is created by a transaction between the trustee and the cestui que trust in connection with the acquisition by the trustee of a legal estate in land, whenever the trustee has so conducted himself that it would be inequitable to allow him to deny to the cestui que trust a beneficial interest in the land acquired. And he will be held so to have conducted himself if by his words or conduct he has induced the cestui que trust to act to his own detriment in the reasonable belief that by so acting he was acquiring a beneficial interest in the land.

This is why it has been repeatedly said in the context of disputes between spouses as to their respective beneficial interests in the matrimonial home, that if at the time of its acquisition and transfer of the legal estate into the name of one or other of them an express agreement has been made between them as to the way in which the beneficial interest shall be held, the court will give effect to it – notwithstanding the absence of any written declaration of trust. Strictly speaking this states the principle too widely, for if the agreement did not provide for anything to be done by the spouse in whom the legal estate was not to be vested, it would be a merely voluntary declaration of trust and unenforceable for want of writing. But ... [w]hat the court gives effect to is the trust resulting or implied from the common intention expressed in the oral agreement between the spouses that if each acts in the manner provided for in the agreement the beneficial interests in the matrimonial home shall be held as they have agreed.

An express agreement between spouses as to their respective beneficial interests in land conveyed into the name of one of them obviates the need for showing that the conduct of the spouse into whose name the land was conveyed was intended to induce the other spouse to act to his or her detriment upon the faith of the promise of a specified beneficial interest in the land and that the other spouse so acted with the intention of acquiring that beneficial interest. The agreement itself discloses the common intention required to create a resulting, implied or constructive trust.

But parties to a transaction in connection with the acquisition of land may well have formed a common intention that the beneficial interest in the land shall be vested in them jointly without having used express words to communicate this intention to one another; or their recollections of the words used may be imperfect or conflicting by the time any dispute arises. In such a case – a common one where the parties are spouses whose marriage has broken down – it may be possible to infer their common intention from their conduct.

As in so many branches of English law in which legal rights and obligations depend upon the intentions of the parties to a transaction, the relevant intention of each party is the intention which was reasonably understood by the other party to be manifested by that party's words or conduct notwithstanding that he did not consciously formulate that intention in his own mind or even acted with some different intention which he did not communicate to the other party. ... It is in this sense that ... effect is given to the inferences as to the intentions of parties to a transaction which a reasonable man would draw from their words or conduct and not to any subjective intention or absence of intention which was not made manifest at the time of the transaction itself. It is for the court to determine what those inferences are.

In drawing such an inference, what spouses said and did which led up to the acquisition of a matrimonial home and what they said and did while the acquisition was being carried through is on a different footing from what they said and did after the acquisition was completed. Unless it is alleged that there was some subsequent fresh agreement, acted upon by the parties, to vary the original beneficial interests created when the matrimonial home was acquired, what they said and did after the acquisition was completed is relevant if it is explicable only upon the basis of their having manifested to one another at the time of the acquisition some particular common intention as to how the beneficial interests should be held. ... The conduct of the spouses in relation to the payment of the mortgage instalments may be no less relevant to their common intention as to the beneficial interests in a matrimonial home acquired in this way than their conduct in relation to the payment of the cash deposit.

It is this feature of the transaction by means of which most matrimonial homes have been acquired in recent years that makes difficult the task of the court in inferring from the conduct of the spouses a common intention as to how the beneficial interest in it should be held. Each case must depend upon its own facts but there are a number of factual situations which often recur in the cases.

Where a matrimonial home has been purchased outright without the aid of an advance on mortgage it is not difficult to ascertain what part, if any, of the purchase price has been provided by each spouse. If the land is conveyed into the name of a spouse who has not provided the whole of the purchase price, ... the prima facie inference is that their common intention was that the contributing spouse should acquire a share in the beneficial interest in the land in the same proportion as the sum contributed bore to the total purchase price. This prima facie inference is more easily rebutted in favour of a gift where the land is conveyed into the name of the wife: but as I understand the speeches in *Pettitt v Pettitt* [1970] AC 777, [1969] 2 All ER 385 four of the members of your Lordships' House who were parties to that decision took the view that even if the 'presumption of advancement' as between husband and wife still survived today, it could seldom have any decisive part to play in disputes between living spouses in which some evidence would be available in addition to the mere fact that the husband had provided part of the purchase price of property conveyed into the name of the wife.

Similarly when a matrimonial home is not purchased outright but partly out of moneys advanced on mortgage repayable by instalments, and the land is conveyed into the name of the husband alone, the fact that the wife made a cash contribution to the deposit and legal charges not borrowed on mortgage gives rise, in the absence of evidence which makes some other explanation more probable, to the inference that their common intention was that she should share in the beneficial interest in the land conveyed. But it would not be reasonable to infer a common intention as to what her share should be without taking account also of the sources from which the mortgage instalments were provided. If the wife also makes a substantial direct contribution to the mortgage instalments out of her own earnings or unearned income ... [the] likely inference is that her contributions to the mortgage instalments were intended by the spouses to have some effect upon her share.

Where there has been an initial contribution by the wife to the cash deposit and legal charges which points to a common intention at the time of the conveyance that she should have a beneficial interest in the land conveyed to her husband, it would be unrealistic to regard the wife's subsequent contributions to the mortgage instalments as without significance unless she pays them directly herself. It may be no more than a matter of convenience which spouse pays particular household accounts particularly when both are earning, and if the wife goes out to work and devotes part of her earnings or uses her private income to meet joint expenses of the household which would otherwise be met by the husband, so as to enable him to pay the mortgage instalments out of his moneys this would be consistent with and might be corroborative of an original common intention that she should share in the beneficial interest in the matrimonial home and that her payments of other household expenses were intended by both spouses to be treated as including a contribution by the wife to the purchase price of the matrimonial home.

Even where there has been no initial contribution by the wife to the cash deposit and legal charges but she makes a regular and substantial direct contribution to the mortgage instalments it may be reasonable to infer a common intention of the spouses from the outset that she should share in the beneficial interest or to infer a fresh agreement reached after the original conveyance that she should acquire a share. But it is unlikely that the mere fact that the wife made direct contributions to the mortgage instalments would be the only evidence available to assist the court in ascertaining the common intention of the spouses.

Where in any of the circumstances described the above contributions, direct or indirect, have been made to the mortgage instalments by the spouse into whose name the matrimonial home has not been conveyed, and the court can infer from their conduct a common intention that the contributing spouse should be entitled to *some* beneficial interest in the matrimonial home, what effect is to be given to that intention if there is no evidence that they in fact reached any express agreement as to what the respective share of each spouse should be? ...

In such a case the court must first do its best to discover from the conduct of the spouses whether any inference can reasonably be drawn as to the probable common understanding about the amount of the share of the contributing spouse upon which each must have acted in doing what each did, even though that understanding was never expressly stated by one spouse to the other or even consciously formulated in words by either of them independently. It is only if no such inference can be drawn that the court is driven to apply as a rule of law, and not as an inference of fact, the maxim 'equality is equity,' and to hold that the beneficial interest belongs to the spouses in equal shares.

The same result however may often be reached as an inference of fact. The instalments of a mortgage to a building society are generally repayable over a period of many years. During that period, as both must be aware, the ability of each spouse to contribute to the instalments out of their separate earnings is likely to alter, particularly in the case of the wife if any children are born of the marriage. If the contribution of the wife in the early part of the period of repayment is substantial but is not an identifiable and uniform proportion of each instalment, because her contributions are indirect or, if direct, are made irregularly, it may well be a reasonable inference that their common intention at the time of acquisition of the matrimonial home was that the beneficial interest should be held by them in equal shares and that each should contribute to the cost of its acquisition whatever amounts each could afford in the varying exigencies of family life to be expected during the period of repayment. In the social conditions of today this would be a natural enough common intention of a young couple who were both earning when the house was acquired but who contemplated having children whose birth and rearing in their infancy would necessarily affect the future earning capacity of the wife.

The relative size of their respective contributions to the instalments in the early part of the period of repayment, or later if a subsequent reduction in the wife's contribution is not to be accounted for by a reduction in her earnings due to motherhood or some other cause from which the husband benefits as well, may make it a more probable inference that the wife's share in the beneficial interest was intended to be in some proportion other than one-half. And there is nothing inherently improbable in their acting on the understanding that the wife should be entitled to a share which was not to be quantified immediately upon the acquisition of the home but should be left to be determined when the mortgage was repaid or the property disposed of, on the basis of what would be fair having regard to the total contributions, direct or indirect, which each spouse had made by that date. Where this was the most likely inference from their conduct it would be for the court to give effect to that common intention of the parties by determining what in all the circumstances was a fair share.

Difficult as they are to solve, however, these problems as to the amount of the share of a spouse in the beneficial interest in a matrimonial home where the legal estate is vested solely in the other spouse, only arise in cases where the court is satisfied by the words or conduct of the parties that it was their common intention that the beneficial interest was not to belong solely to the spouse in whom the legal estate was vested but was to be shared between them in some proportion or other.

Where the wife has made no initial contribution to the cash deposit and legal charges and no direct contribution to the mortgage instalments nor any adjustment to her contribution to other expenses of the household which it can be inferred was referable to the acquisition of the house, there is in the absence of evidence of an express agreement between the parties no material to justify the court in inferring that it was the common intention of the parties that she should have any beneficial interest in a matrimonial home conveyed into the sole name of the husband, merely because she continued to contribute out of her own earnings or private income to other expenses of the household. For such conduct is no less consistent with a common intention to share the day-to-day expenses of the household, while each spouse retains a separate interest in capital assets acquired with their own moneys or obtained by inheritance or gift. There is nothing here to rebut the prima facie inference that a purchaser of land who pays the purchase price and takes a conveyance and grants a mortgage in his own name intends to acquire the sole beneficial interest as well as the legal estate: and the difficult question of the quantum of the wife's share does not arise.

Lord Diplock concluded that he was unable to draw an inference that there was any common intention that the wife should have any beneficial interest in the matrimonial home.

Lord Dilhorne and Lord Morris were against indirect contributions entitling a spouse to some beneficial interest in the matrimonial home. Lord Reid and Lord Pearson would appear to permit a beneficial interest to be acquired through indirect contributions but do not elaborate this concept.

Thus, the separation of property principle survived the attempt by Lord Denning and others to sweep it away. However, Parliament stepped in to grant discretionary powers to courts to re-allocate property after the termination of marriage. Such discretionary powers can take into account non-financial contributions. These provisions, now contained in the Matrimonial Causes Act 1973, are looked at in detail in Chapter 8, below.

Question

If Lord Diplock had drawn an inference that there was a common intention that the wife should have a beneficial interest in the matrimonial property, would this have been sufficient *without more* to have decided the case in her favour?

Strict property law is still important as we can see from:

Lloyds Bank plc v Rosset
[1991] 1 AC 107, [1990] 1 All ER 1111, House of Lords

The husband and wife bought a semi-derelict property as a family home. The acquisition was in the husband's sole name, apparently because of the insistence by the Swiss trustees of the husband's family trust. However, the wife carried out a considerable amount of the decorating work and generally supervised the builders. A lot of this work was done prior to exchange of contracts. The cost of the renovation was met by an overdraft on the husband's account. The husband signed the bank's form of legal charge. The husband left the house in 1984, and the loan was not repaid. In a claim by the bank for possession and an order for sale, the wife resisted the claim on the basis that she had a beneficial interest in the property under a constructive trust that qualified as an overriding interest under s. 70(1)(*g*) of the Land Registration Act 1925 (see p. 157, below) because she had been in actual occupation at the relevant date. The House of Lords, in following *Abbey National Building Society v Cann* [1991] 1 AC 56, [1990] 1 All ER 1085, held that the relevant date for ascertaining whether an interest in registered land was protected by actual occupation so as to prevail against the holder of a legal estate as a overriding interest under s. 70(1)(*g*) was that of the transfer or creation of the estate rather than its registration. However, it was not necessary to determine whether she was in actual occupation at the relevant date, because the House was of the unanimous view that she did not possess a beneficial interest.

Lord Bridge of Harwich: The first and fundamental question which must always be resolved is whether, independently of any inference to be drawn from the conduct of the parties in the course of sharing the house as their home and managing their joint affairs, there has at any time prior to acquisition, or exceptionally at some later date, been any agreement, arrangement or understanding reached between them that the property is to be shared beneficially. The finding of an agreement or arrangement to share in this sense can only, I think, be based on evidence of express discussions between the partners, however imperfectly remembered and however imprecise their terms may have been. Once a finding to this effect is made it will only be necessary for the partner asserting a claim to a beneficial interest against the partner entitled to the legal estate to show that he or she has acted to his or her detriment or significantly altered his or her position in reliance on the agreement in order to give rise to a constructive trust or a proprietary estoppel.

In sharp contrast with this situation is the very different one where there is no evidence to support a finding of an agreement or arrangement to share, however reasonable it might have been for the parties to reach such an arrangement if they had applied their minds to the question, and where the court must rely entirely on the conduct of the parties both as the basis from which to infer a common intention to share the property beneficially and as the conduct relied on to give rise to a constructive trust. In this situation direct contributions to the purchase price by the partner who is not the legal owner, whether initially or by payment of mortgage instalments, will readily justify the inference necessary to the creation of a constructive trust. But, as I read the authorities, it is at least extremely doubtful whether anything less will do.

The leading cases in your Lordships' House are *Pettitt v Pettitt* [1970] AC 777 and *Gissing v Gissing* [1971] AC 886 [see pp. 137, 138, above]. Both demonstrate situations in the second category to which I have referred and their Lordships discuss at great length the difficulties to which these situations give rise.

...

Outstanding examples on the other hand of cases giving rise to situations in the first category are *Eves v Eves* [1975] 1 WLR 1338 and *Grant v Edwards* [1986] Ch 638 [see Chapter 8, below]. In both these cases, where the parties who had cohabited were unmarried, the female partner had been clearly led by the male partner to believe, when they set up home together, that the property would belong to them jointly. In *Eves v Eves* the male partner had told the female partner that the only reason why the property was to be acquired in his name alone was because she was under 21 and that, but for her age, he would have had the house put into their joint names. He admitted in evidence that this was simply an 'excuse'. Similarly in *Grant v Edwards* the female partner was told by the male partner that the only reason for not acquiring the property in joint names was because she was involved in divorce proceedings and that, if the property were acquired jointly, this might operate to her prejudice in those proceedings. As Nourse LJ put it, at p. 649:

> 'Just as in *Eves v Eves* [1975] 1 WLR 1338, these facts appear to me to raise a clear inference that there was an understanding between the plaintiff and the defendant, or a common intention, that the plaintiff was to have some sort of proprietary interest in the house; otherwise no excuse for not putting her name on to the title would have been needed.'

The subsequent conduct of the female partner in each of these cases, which the court rightly held sufficient to give rise to a constructive trust or proprietary estoppel supporting her claim to an interest in the property, fell far short of such conduct as would by itself have supported the claim in the absence of an express representation by the male partner that she was to have such an interest. It is significant to note that the share to which the female partners in *Eves v Eves* and *Grant v Edwards* were held entitled were one quarter and one half respectively. In no sense could these shares have been regarded as proportionate to what the judge in the instant case described as a 'qualifying contribution' in terms of the indirect contributions to the acquisition or enhancement of the value of the houses made by the female partners.

I cannot help thinking that the judge in the instant case would not have fallen into error if he had kept clearly in mind the distinction between the effect of evidence on the one hand which was capable of establishing an express agreement or an express representation that Mrs. Rosset was to have an interest in the property and evidence on the other hand of conduct alone as a basis for an inference of the necessary common intention.

Appeal allowed.

Question

Is Lord Bridge saying the same as Lord Diplock in *Gissing v Gissing*? (See p. 139, above.)

Bankruptcy is another example where there can be conflict between the rights of the spouse to occupy the matrimonial home and the rights of third parties to realise their interest. This is now regulated by ss. 336 and 337 of the Insolvency Act 1986.

336.(2) – Where a spouse's matrimonial home rights under Part IV of the Family Law Act 1996 are a charge on the estate or interest of the other spouse, or of trustees for the other spouse, and the other spouse is adjudged bankrupt –

(*a*) the charge continues to subsist notwithstanding the bankruptcy and … binds the trustee of the bankrupt's estate and persons deriving title under that trustee; and

(*b*) any application for an order under section 1 of that Act shall be made to the court having jurisdiction in relation to the bankruptcy.

(3) Where a person and his spouse or former spouse are trustees for sale of a dwelling house and that person is adjudged bankrupt, any application by the trustee of the bankrupt's estate for an order under section 30 of the Law of Property Act … shall be made to the court having jurisdiction in relation to the bankruptcy.

(4) On such an application as is mentioned under subsection (2) or (3) the court shall make such order under section 33 of the Act of 1996 or section 30 of the Act of 1925 as it thinks just and reasonable having regard to –

(*a*) the interests of the bankrupt's creditors,

(*b*) the conduct of the spouse or former spouse, so far as contributing to the bankruptcy,

(*c*) the needs and financial resources of the spouse or former spouse,

(*d*) the needs of any children, and

(*e*) all the circumstances of the case other than the needs of the bankrupt.

(5) Where such an application is made after the end of the period of one year beginning with the first vesting … of the bankrupt's estate in a trustee, the court shall assume, unless the circumstances of the case are exceptional, that the interests of the bankrupt's creditors outweigh all other considerations.

(Section 337 applies the principles of s. 336 to the situation where the bankrupt has no spouse with occupational rights, and children under 18 'had their home' with him. The needs of the children are to be taken into account but not the needs of the bankrupt himself. Section 337(6) is to the same effect as s. 336(5).)

These provisions have their origin in *Insolvency Law and Practice* (The Cork Committee) (1982) which states:

1118: It would be consistent with present social attitudes to alleviate the personal hardships of those who are dependent on the debtor but not responsible for his insolvency, if this can be achieved by delaying for an acceptable time the sale of the family home.

Question

Would Mrs Rossett have fared better if her husband had been declared bankrupt?

In *Re Holliday (a bankrupt), ex p Trustee of the Bankrupt v Bankrupt* [1981] Ch 405, [1980] 3 All ER 385, the Court of Appeal decided that the interests of the wife and her children should prevail over the interests of the creditors to the extent that the sale of the house should be deferred for a substantial period.

Sir David Cairns: I reach that view because I am satisfied that it would at present be very difficult, if not impossible, for the wife to secure another suitable home for the family in or near Thorpe Bay; because it would be upsetting for the children's education if they had to move far away from their present schools, even if it were practicable, having regard to the wife's means, to find an alternative home at some more distant place; because it is highly unlikely that postponement of the payment of the debts would cause any great hardship to any of the creditors ...

However, in *Re Citro (a bankrupt)* [1991] Ch 142, [1990] 3 All ER 952, involving two bankrupts and their wives, the majority of the Court of Appeal distinguished the earlier case. At first instance, Hoffmann J imposed a provision for postponement of sale on the application of the trustee in bankruptcy until the youngest child in each case reached 16 years of age. He was of the opinion that if immediate orders for sale were made, the half shares to which each of the wives were entitled would be insufficient for them to acquire other accommodation in the area which would inevitably disturb the education of the children. In reversing the decision of Hoffmann J at first instance, Nourse LJ said:

Did Hoffmann J correctly apply [the law] to the facts which were before him? I respectfully think that he did not. First, for the reasons already stated, the personal circumstances of the two wives and their children, although distressing, are not by themselves exceptional. Secondly, I think that the judge erred in fashioning his orders by reference to those which might have been made in the Family Division in a case where bankruptcy had not supervened. ... Thirdly, and perhaps most significantly, he did not ask himself the critical question whether a further postponement of payment of their debts would cause hardship to the creditors. ...

Finally, I refer to section 336 of the Insolvency Act 1986 which, although it does not apply to either of these cases, will apply to such cases in the future. In subsection (5) of that section the court is required, in the circumstances there mentioned, to 'assume, unless the circumstances of the case are exceptional, that the interests of the bankrupt's creditors outweigh all other considerations'. I have no doubt that that section was intended to apply the same test as that which has been evolved in the previous bankruptcy decisions, and it is satisfactory to find that it has. I say that not least because section 336 only applies to the rights of occupation of those who are or have been married. The case law will continue to apply to unmarried couples, who nowadays set up house together in steadily increasing numbers. A difference in the basic tests applicable to the two classes of case would have been most undesirable.

Question

Both of these cases were decided under the old law. Suppose that Harry is declared bankrupt, and he lives with his wife, Wendy, and their three children in a house which they jointly own. The eldest child is physically handicapped and the house has been adapted for her purposes. The other two children are gifted twins and attend a local school for gifted children. Harry is a self-employed builder and many of his creditors are local traders with families. Do you think that the court would (*a*) make an immediate order for sale? (*b*) if the application for sale is made after the end of one year beginning with the first vesting of the estate in Harry's trustee, postpone the sale for a further period? (*c*) in either (*a*) or (*b*) would it make any difference if Harry has the sole legal and beneficial interest? (*d*) in either (*a*) or (*b*) would it make any difference if Harry and Wendy were not married? (*e*) in either (*a*) or (*b*) would it make any difference if Harry and Wendy were not married and if Harry has the sole legal and beneficial interest?

The family home can be – and frequently is – used as security for a loan to the family business, or, indeed, to a business in which only one of the parties is involved. In this latter case, of course, it may be that only one party benefits from the loan, while the home of both is put at risk.

We have seen in the bankruptcy cases that, generally, creditors are in a stronger position than the bankrupt's family. One exception to this trend is the case where a spouse has been misled or pressurised into agreeing to the use of the family home as security for a loan to the other spouse. The law recognises that this is particularly likely to happen in the context of family relationships. As Lord Browne-Wilkinson put it in *Barclays Bank plc v O'Brien* [1994] 1 AC 180, HL:

... even today, many wives repose confidence and trust in their husbands in relation to their financial affairs. ... Moreover the informality of business dealings between spouses raises a substantial risk that the husband has not accurately stated to the wife the nature of the liability she is undertaking. ...

At first sight, the wife in such a case is in difficulties because her husband's misrepresentation or undue influence would not normally affect her position vis-à-vis the creditor, where the latter was not involved in the husband's wrongdoing. The House of Lords' decision in *O'Brien* establishes that the creditor may nevertheless be unable to enforce its security against the wife if it had constructive notice of the husband's wrong. The creditor will have constructive notice where the transaction is one that would only benefit one party, because of the 'substantial risk' in these domestic circumstances that such a wrong has been committed. However, the creditor can ensure that it does not have constructive notice by warning the wife, at a meeting not attended by the husband, of the amount of the potential liability and the risks involved, and advising her to take independent legal advice.

Lord Browne-Wilkinson stressed that although his judgment referred throughout to a wife being misled by her husband, the principle applied to 'all other cases where there is an emotional relationship between cohabitees', whether heterosexual or homosexual. The subsequent decision of the House of Lords in *CIBC Mortgages plc v Pitt* [1994] 1 AC 200 made it clear that the creditor does not have constructive notice of undue influence or misrepresentation when a loan is made to the two joint owners of the property charged in circumstances where there is nothing to indicate that the two are not to benefit equally from the loan.

Questions

(i) Should there be any restriction on the availability of the family home for use as security for a loan to one spouse (or cohabitant) alone?
(ii) How is the creditor to know whether the joint owners of a property offered as security are in an 'emotional relationship' or are merely 'mortgage-mates'?

(c) THE SPOUSE'S RIGHT OF OCCUPATION

At common law, each spouse had a personal right, as against the other spouse, to occupy a matrimonial home to which that other was entitled. But this gave no rights against third parties to whom the owning spouse might seek to dispose of his interest. By selling the property, or defaulting on mortgage payments, he was therefore free to leave the other spouse homeless. This caused concern, and there were judicial attempts to create a 'deserted wife's equity', a right which she could enforce against, say, a mortgagee who was entitled to take possession of and sell the property. Such attempts were finally frustrated by the House of Lords' decision in *National Provincial Bank Ltd v Ainsworth* [1965] AC 1175, which reiterated the principle that a wife had only a personal right against her husband. To remedy the hardship to non-owning spouses, the Matrimonial Homes Act 1967 (later 1983) was passed. The relevant provisions are now to be found in Part IV of the Family Law Act 1996.

Section 30 defines the rights of the parties between themselves:

30. – (1) This section applies if
- (*a*) one spouse is entitled to occupy a dwelling-house by virtue of
  - (i) a beneficial estate or interest or contract; or
  - (ii) any enactment giving that spouse the right to remain in occupation; and
- (*b*) the other spouse is not so entitled.

(2) Subject to the provisions of this Part, the spouse not so entitled has the following rights ('matrimonial home rights') –
- (*a*) if in occupation, a right not to be evicted or excluded from the dwelling-house or any part of it by the other spouse except with the leave of the court given by an order under section 33;
- (*b*) if not in occupation, a right with the leave of the court so given to enter into and occupy the dwelling-house.

An important part of the Act's function is to make available orders regulating the occupation of the home as between the spouses themselves, (whether their right to occupy the home arises from their legal or beneficial ownership of it, or from s. 30). We shall have to consider these rights further in connection with protection from domestic violence and harassment in Chapter 9. Insofar as that protection is extended to cohabitants, we can say that they too have occupation rights of a purely personal nature in the house where the couple have lived together – and that includes, albeit on a temporary basis, cohabitants who have no property rights in that home (that has been the case since the enactment of the Domestic Violence and Family Proceedings Act 1976; *Davis v Johnson* [1979] AC 264). However, for spouses only, the Family Law Act 1996 enables the rights in s. 30(2) to be enforced against third parties, by providing that it shall be a charge on the other's estate or interest. The charge is registrable as a class F land charge in unregistered land, or as a notice in registered land (Land Charges Act 1972 s. 2(7), Family Law Act 1996 s. 31(10)); it cannot be an overriding interest in registered land.

The potential practical effects of the registrable right can be seen in one of the earliest cases following the 1967 Act:

Wroth v Tyler
[1974] Ch 30, [1973] 1 All ER 897, [1973] 2 WLR 405, 117 Sol Jo 90, 25 P & CR 138, High Court, Chancery Division

The wife registered a charge under the Matrimonial Homes Act 1967 after her husband, who was the sole legal and beneficial owner of the house, had signed a contract for the sale of the house. The registration of the charge meant that the sale with vacant possession could not be completed, and the husband was thus held liable in damages. It is not immediately apparent from the facts of the case why the husband did not seek an order under s. 1(3) of the Matrimonial Homes Act 1967, as it then was, for the wife's right of occupation to be terminated so as to allow the completion to go ahead. It certainly appears on the face of it that the wife had led both the husband and the prospective purchasers, a newly married couple, reasonably to believe that she was not actively dissenting from the wish of the husband to move from Kent, where they had previously lived, so as to set up home in a cottage in Norfolk. Megarry J commented on the facts in the following manner:

> Let me add that I would certainly not regard proceedings under the Act by the defendant against his wife as being without prospect of success. As the evidence stands (and of course I have not heard the defendant's wife) there is at least a real prospect of success for the defendant. He does not in any way seek to deprive his wife of a home; the difference between them is a difference as to where the matrimonial home is to be. In that, the conduct of the wife towards the plaintiffs and the defendant must play a substantial part.

Megarry J was not prepared to order specific performance of the contract, for to do so would be indirectly to force the husband to take proceedings under the Matrimonial Homes Act against his wife. This was a decision which only he could take. Perhaps therefore, one should not feel too concerned about the fate of the husband – who had to pay damages amounting to £5,500 – for after all the remedy was in his own hands. Certainly, on the result of *Wroth v Tyler,* the wife had the 'casting vote'.

Megarry J in *Wroth v Tyler* called the statutory right of occupation 'a weapon of great power and flexibility':

I can now say something about the nature of the charge and the mode of operation of the Act. First, for a spouse in occupation, the right seems to be a mere statutory right for the spouse not to be evicted. There appears to be nothing to stay the eviction of others. For example, if a wife is living in her husband's house with their children and her parents, her charge, even if registered, appears to give no protection against eviction to the children or parents. ... Nor if the wife takes in lodgers does there seem to be anything to prevent the husband from evicting them. If, for example, the husband is himself living in the house, it would be remarkable if the Act gives the wife the right to insist upon having other occupants in the home against his will. The statutory right appears in essence to be a purely personal right for the wife not to be evicted; and it seems wholly inconsistent with the Act that this right should be assignable or otherwise disposable. I may add that there is nothing to require the wife to make any payment to the husband for her occupation, unless ordered by the court under section 1(3), though if she is in occupation against his will and by virtue of her statutory rights, it may be that she will be in rateable occupation.

Second, although the right given to an occupying wife by section 1(1) is merely a right not to be evicted or excluded 'by the other spouse,' and so at first sight does not appear to be effective against anyone except that other spouse, section 2(1) makes the right 'a charge' on the husband's estate or interest; and it is this, rather than the provisions for registration, which makes the right binding on successors in title. The operation of the provision for registration seems to be essentially negative; the right is a charge which, if not duly protected by registration, will become void against subsequent purchasers, or fail to bind them. In this, the right seems not to differ from other registrable charges, such as general equitable charges or puisne mortgages. Yet there is this difference. For other charges, the expectation of the statute is plainly that they will all be protected by registration, whereas under the Act of 1967 there does not seem to be the same expectation.

Questions

(i) If statutory co-ownership were to be introduced (see p. 154, below), will the protection afforded under s. 30 of the Family Law Act 1996 be of any value?
(ii) What are the practical effects of the requirement of registration?

Another important third party to be reckoned with when the occupation of the home is in issue is the landlord, in the case of rented property.

Section 30(3), (4) of the Family Law Act 1996 is an important provision regarding rented property. If the tenancy is a protected or a statutory tenancy under the Rent Act 1977 or a periodic assured tenancy under the Housing Act 1988 (private tenancies) or a secure tenancy under the Housing Act 1985 (council tenancies), an occupying spouse may keep the tenancy of the other spouse 'alive', even though the latter spouse is not living in the accommodation. In addition, Sch. 7 of the Family Law Act 1996 gives a spouse a right to seek transfer of a protected, statutory or secure tenancy or assured tenancy on the granting of a decree of divorce etc., or at any time thereafter. (Unlike its predecessors the Matrimonial Homes Acts, the 1996 Act gives similar rights to cohabitants; see p. 185, below.)

Questions

(i) Does this mean that the tenant spouse cannot defeat the occupation rights of the wife by purporting to surrender the tenancy to the landlord? (See *Middleton v Baldock* [1950] 1 KB 657, [1950] 1 All ER 708, CA.)

(ii) Do you think that the local authority should be under an obligation to provide alternative accommodation for the ex-tenant?
(iii) In the case of a periodic joint tenancy, when one of the tenants gives notice to quit, it seems that the tenancy terminates (see *Greenwich London Borough Council v McGrady* (1982) 81 LGR 288, 6 HLR 36, CA; *Hammersmith and Fulham London Borough Council v Monk* [1992] 1 AC 478). Is this a sufficient protection for a wife who has the support of a housing authority? Consider *Harrow London Borough Council v Johnstone* [1995] 2 FLR 191, [1995] Fam Law 550, CA.

Such 'secure' tenancies were originally confined to private tenancies. The *Report of the Committee on One-Parent Families* (the Finer Report) discussed this in 1974:

> 6.88 The reasons for the exclusion of council tenancies from the statutory protection appear to be that the landlord in these cases is a democratically elected public body which can be trusted to behave reasonably in dealing with its tenants, and which also may find itself in a position where its duty to the tenant conflicts with some other public duty, to resolve which it has to retain a free hand. ...
> 6.90 ... we can see no continuing good reason for depriving local authority or New Town tenants of the basic protection in security of tenure which the Rent Acts give to the tenants of private landlords. ...
> Our recommendation in principle is that security of tenure similar to the Rent Acts protection be extended to tenancies in the public sector. It should be noted that one effect would be always to interpose the court between an authority wanting possession and a tenant unwilling to go – a safeguard that we think would be of special value when the dispute with the authority was connected with or happened to coincide with some breakdown of marital relations within the home.

This recommendation was accepted, and council house tenancies are in most cases secure tenancies within the meaning given to that phrase under the Housing Act 1985. In particular the s. 1(5) protection applies to secure council tenancies. Further, if proceedings are brought against the tenant and as a result of those proceedings the tenancy is ended as against the tenant then in certain cases at least, the spouse in occupation has the right to ask the court to adjourn the proceedings, postpone the date of possession, and stay or suspend execution of the order.

Questions

(i) The Finer Report (1974) stated that 'the protection which the wife and children may require when the family live in rented accommodation is protection in occupancy, which may be achieved irrespective of rights of ownership.' In the context of council housing, (*a*) do you think that it is appropriate that this protection should be exercised by the courts rather than by the local authorities, and if so, (*b*) why do you have this view?
(ii) A number of authorities have introduced clauses into their tenancy agreements which state that violence or threats of violence constitute a breach of the tenancy agreement and can thus be grounds for possession giving the local authority the power to determine the tenancy. Do you feel that such clauses are appropriate, or would you deal with the problem of domestic violence in some other way (see further, pp. 388ff).

2 The field of choice

(a) THE ISSUES

There are three possibilities: a complete freedom of choice for the parties with little or no judicial discretion available to the judges; a system of fixed property rights; and a freedom of choice but with a power for the courts to readjust the parties' rights either during the marriage or at the end of the marriage.

The distinction between the fixed and discretionary system is highlighted in the First Report on *Family Property – A New Approach* (1973) where the Law Commission acknowledge that there is a body of opinion that would oppose the introduction of any form of fixed property rights between husband and wife on the ground that this is unnecessary and in itself objectionable:

10 ... They believed that in so far as the existing law led to any injustice, the proper remedy was to allow the court to exercise its discretionary powers in matrimonial or family provision proceedings. It was claimed that all necessary reforms could be achieved by developing the traditional discretionary systems, which ensured great flexibility. The principal reasons for considering any form of fixed property rights undesirable were as follows:

(*a*) fixed property rights would cause more dissension and injustice than they would alleviate;
(*b*) the state should not interfere in the relations between spouses by imposing automatic rules regulating their property rights;
(*c*) fixed property rights would deter marriage and compel people to take advice before marrying.

Question

Is advice before marriage a good thing which should be encouraged?

By contrast, the Canadian Law Reform Commission (1975) put the alternative point of view:

Another drawback to a discretionary system lies in its lack of fixed legal rights. Even were equality to be stated as a general legislative policy, the essential nature of judicial discretion would leave the court free to make whatever sort of property disposition seemed to be appropriate in any given case. A married person would not have a *right* to equality, but only a *hope* to obtain it. If no concept of equality were contained in the law establishing a discretionary system, then it would be accurate to say that a married person would have no property rights at all at the time of divorce. Our concern here is not limited to the way things would work out in practice, since the courts would do their best to ensure that arbitrary dispossession did not occur. Rather, it includes the psychological advantage that accrues to a person who knows he or she has a positive right that is guaranteed and protected by law.

But if there is to be a fixed system, what would it mean?

The following extract is taken from the Canadian Law Reform Commission (1975):

The community property concept of marital property rights is based upon the assumption that marriage, among other things, is an economic partnership. As such, the partnership, or community, owns the respective talents and efforts of each of the spouses. Whatever is acquired as a result of their talents and efforts is shared by and belongs to both of them equally, as *community property*.

Community property regimes exist in Quebec, in many European countries and in eight of the United States. Quebec's community property regime, like the separate property regime in that province, is an option available to married persons who choose not to be governed by the basic regime providing for separate ownership of property during a marriage, with fixed sharing upon divorce.

The essential idea of community property is very simple: the earnings, and property purchased with the earnings, of either spouse become community property in which each spouse has a present equal legal interest. Where the community is terminated – for example by divorce – the community property, after payment of community debts, is divided equally between the spouses. The community is also terminated by the death of a spouse, and in some jurisdictions, including Quebec, by an agreement between the spouses to switch to some other regime or to regulate their property relations by a contract. This simple formula conceals some rather complex rules. We can do no more in this paper than touch upon the general principles and a few of the major problem areas involved in community property systems without dealing with finer points in any great detail.

Under community regimes, there are three kinds of property: the separate property of the husband, the separate property of the wife, and community property. Typically, the property owned by either spouse before marriage is the separate property of that spouse, along with property acquired after marriage by a spouse by way of gift or inheritance. Separate property is not shared at the time of divorce, but rather is retained by the owner-spouse. All other property, however acquired, becomes community property, in which each spouse has a present interest as soon as it is purchased or obtained, and an equal share in its division upon divorce. In some jurisdictions, someone giving property to a married person must specify that the property is to be the separate property of the recipient. Otherwise it will be treated as a gift to both spouses, even though it is only given to one, and will become community property. In the Province of Quebec, some types of property owned before marriage become community property, but it is possible for persons giving such types of property to a single person to make the gift on the condition that it remain the separate property of the recipient should he or she thereafter marry under the regime of community property.

Under a community property regime, all property owned by either spouse at the time of a divorce is generally presumed in law to be community property unless it can be proved to be separate. In many marriages the spouses will not have adequate records of ownership or the source of funds used to acquire property. This produces the legal phenomenon of 'commingling' – that is, the separate property of each spouse eventually becomes mixed with that of the other spouse and with the community property, resulting in all the property being treated as sharable community property at the time of divorce. Commingling makes it impossible for the spouses to establish that certain items of property were owned before marriage, or otherwise fall into the classification of separate property. …

Even assuming that the separate property of a spouse can in fact be kept identifiable, it is necessary to have rules governing the situation where community funds are expended with respect to such property. If, for example, a husband owns a house as separate property and has it repaired, using community funds, the community property is entitled to reimbursement at the time of divorce to the extent of the value of the repairs. Or if he sells the house and buys another, using for the purchase some community funds plus proceeds of the sale, the rule might be that if more than fifty per cent of the price of the second house came from the first house, it remains separate property subject to an appropriate compensation to the community upon divorce. If more than fifty per cent of the price of the second house came from community funds, then it loses its character as separate property and becomes community property. In the latter case there would be a compensation paid from the community at the time of divorce to the husband's separate property equal to the amount realized on the sale of the first house. When it is recognized that most families only have available the earnings of one spouse, which belong to the community, and that many items of separate property over the course of a marriage would be maintained and repaired out of these earnings, or sold and 'traded up' for newer property using the proceeds of the sale of the separate property plus community funds, then some of the practical difficulties in accounting during the marriage and sorting out community and separate property at its termination become readily apparent.

Deferred Community is described in detail in the Canadian Law Reform Commission's Working Paper (1975).

Deferred sharing, or deferred community of property as it is sometimes called, is based on the idea that there should be separate ownership of property during marriage, and an equal distribution of property on divorce. Deferred sharing, therefore, lies somewhere between the extremes of separate property on the one hand and full community of property on the other. Deferred sharing regimes exist in Denmark, Sweden, Norway, Findland, West Germany and Holland. In Canada, Quebec adopted a deferred sharing regime in 1970 – the 'partnership of acquests' – as its basic family property law, applicable to all married persons who did not make a positive choice of community property or separate property. ...

The basic theory of the deferred sharing system is simple. In general terms, all property acquired by either spouse during marriage is to be shared equally when the marriage partnership is dissolved.

The possibility of a deferred community regime was raised in the English Law Commission Working Paper (1971), and the Law Commission commented on the results of the consultation in the First Report (1973):

47. The proposals relating to such a system of 'deferred community' attracted far more interest and comment than did those relating to legal rights of inheritance. No clear view, however, emerged from the consultation. ... On balance, the majority did not support deferred community. Some thought that community would give effect to the partnership element in marriage and create definite property rights without the need to depend upon the exercise of the court's discretion; it was seen as a natural extension of the principle of co-ownership of the home into a wider field. Others thought that community could be unfair if applied arbitrarily without regard to the circumstances and to conduct, that it would be a cause of dissension and that it would be inconsistent with the independence of the spouses. ...

49. Very few took the extreme view that fixed principles of deferred community should replace the present discretionary powers exercisable on divorce or in family provision proceedings. The vast majority thought that existing discretionary powers should be retained.

53. The principle of deferred community should be considered in the light of the conclusions we have already reached in this Report, namely that the principle of co-ownership of the home is a necessary measure which would be widely accepted as better achieving justice than the present law, and that a system of fixed legal rights of inheritance is neither necessary nor desirable. Assuming, for the moment, that the principle of co-ownership of the home will be implemented, is the further step of introducing a system of community needed in order to attain the proper balance of justice?

54. The Working Paper pointed out that anomalies could arise if a fixed principle of sharing were limited to just one asset. It would apply only where there was a matrimonial home. Further, the spouse who acquired an interest in the matrimonial home under the co-ownership principle might own other assets of similar or greater value which did not have to be shared. It was suggested that a wider principle of sharing might appear fairer. The results of the Social Survey throw some light on both these points. The Survey confirms that spouses who do not own their home seldom have assets of any substantial value. It also indicates that where a home is owned, it represents a substantial proportion of the total value of the spouses' assets. For the majority of home-owners, sharing the home would, in effect, be sharing the most substantial asset of the family. How far is deferred community necessary as a means of eliminating the anomalies in other cases? ...

59. *Our conclusion* is that if the principle of co-ownership of the matrimonial home were introduced into English law much of what is now regarded as unsatisfactory or unfair would be eliminated, and the marriage partnership would be recognised by family property law in this very important context. Having regard to our conclusions regarding co-ownership of the matrimonial home, to the broad interpretation by the court of its powers to order financial provision on divorce, and to our conclusion that the court should have similar powers in family provision proceedings, we do not consider that there is at present any need to introduce a system of deferred community.

A system similar to deferred community has been introduced in Scotland by s. 10 of the Family Law (Scotland) Act 1985 (see Chapter 8, below) and to be honest with ourselves, in England as a result of case law developments (see Chapter 8, below).

Question

Is the introduction of deferred community good enough (*a*) for women in the higher paid sectors of the employment market (*b*) for women who do not work, or who work only part time? (See Chapter 8, below.)

(b) THE MATRIMONIAL HOME

The two areas which feature predominantly in Law Commission reports in England are the matrimonial home and household goods. We discuss each in turn. It is natural that discussions should centre around the home.

As we have seen (p. 147, above), problems invariably involve third party creditors.

The English Law Commission Working Paper, *Family Property Law* (1971) discussed the topic in detail, and formed the conclusion that a system of co-ownership should be introduced to meet many of the objections to the present law:

0.25 The matrimonial home is often the principal, if not the only, family asset. Where this is the case, if satisfactory provision could be made for sharing the home, the problem of matrimonial property would be largely solved. Under present rules, apart from any question of gift or agreement, ownership is decided on the basis of: (1) the documents of title, and (2) the financial contribution of each spouse. Part 1 of the Paper considers whether there should be alternative ways or additional considerations for determining ownership.

0.26 One possibility would be to allow the court to decide ownership of the home on discretionary grounds whenever a dispute arose between the spouses, taking into account various factors, including the contribution of each spouse to the family. ...

0.27 Another possibility would be to introduce a presumption that the matrimonial home is owned by both spouses equally. ...

0.28 A third possibility would be to go further than a presumption, which could be rebutted, and to provide that, subject to any agreement to the contrary, the beneficial interest in the matrimonial home should be shared equally by the spouses. We refer to this as the principle of co-ownership. There are advantages in this solution: it would in the absence of agreement to the contrary apply universally; it would acknowledge the partnership element in marriage by providing that the ownership of the principal family asset should be shared by the spouses; it would provide a large measure of security and certainty for a spouse in case of breakdown of marriage or on the death of the other spouse; and it would help to avoid protracted disputes and litigation.

0.29 ... The Paper proposes that a new form of matrimonial home trust should apply whenever the beneficial interest in the home is shared between the spouses, in order that they should have a direct interest in the property.

In their First Report on *Family Property – A New Approach* (1973) the Law Commission stated that the principle of co-ownership was widely supported.

21. It emerged clearly from the consultation that the principle of co-ownership of the matrimonial home is widely supported both as the best means of reforming the law relating to the home, and as the main principle of family property law. The great majority who supported co-ownership included legal practitioners, academic lawyers, women's organisations and members of the public. Those who opposed co-ownership were those who were opposed to any form of fixed property rights, and they were relatively few in number.

23. The opinions expressed favouring the co-ownership principle are supported by a change in the pattern of ownership of the matrimonial home in recent years. The Social Survey [Todd and Jones, 1972] analysed the pattern and found that 52% of couples owned their home; among the

home owners 52% had their home in joint names. However, when the figures were broken down by the year of purchase of the home it was clear that a marked increase in the rate of joint ownership began in the middle 1960s and is continuing. ... In cases where the wife had made some financial contribution to the home the proportion of homes put into joint names was higher than in cases where there had been no such contribution. The rate of joint ownership was also very high in cases where the couple had owned more than one home.

Having examined this evidence, the Law Commission arrived at the conclusion that, subject to the proviso that a husband and wife remain free to make any arrangements they choose, the principle of automatic co-ownership of the matrimonial home should be introduced.

The Scottish Law Commission in their Report on *Matrimonial Property* (1984) disagreed with the English proposals.

(i) Statutory co-ownership of the matrimonial home would not be a good way of giving expression to the idea of marriage as an equal partnership. In some cases it would go too far, particularly if it applied to a home owned before marriage, or acquired by gift or inheritance during the marriage. These are not the results of the spouses' joint efforts. In other cases it would not go far enough and could produce results which were unfair as between one spouse and another. If the wife, say, owned the home and the husband owned other property, he could acquire a half share in the home without having to share any of his property. A spouse with investments worth thousands of pounds could allow the other to buy a home and then claim half of it without contributing a penny. The scheme would also work very unevenly as between different couples. If Mr A had invested all his money in the matrimonial home while his next-door neighbour Mr B had mortgaged his home to its full value in order to finance his business, the law would operate very unevenly for the benefit of Mrs A and Mrs B. It would, in short, be a hit or miss way of giving effect to the partnership ideal.
(ii) Statutory co-ownership of the matrimonial home would not be a good way of recognising contributions in unpaid work by a non-earning spouse. It would benefit the undeserving as well as the deserving. Extreme cases can be imagined. A man might marry a wealthy widow, encourage her to buy an expensive house, claim half of her house and leave her. Even in less extreme cases statutory co-ownership would be a poor way of rewarding unpaid work. Most housewives would get nothing from the new law because its effects would be confined to owner-occupiers. Only about 37% of married couples in Scotland live in owner-occupied accommodation.[1] Even where the new law did apply, its effects would be totally arbitrary. Not only would the net value of the home vary enormously from case to case, and from time to time, but so too would the respective values of the spouses' contributions.
(iii) Statutory co-ownership of the matrimonial home would not necessarily bring the law into line with the views of most married people. We know that most married owner-occupiers in Scotland favour voluntary co-ownership of the matrimonial home.[2] We do not know that most married people in Scotland would favour forcing co-ownership on an unwilling owner regardless of the circumstances of the particular case.
(iv) It is not self-evident that property which is used in common should be owned in common. Even if this proposition were accepted, it would lead further than co-ownership between spouses. It would lead to co-ownership between the members of a household, including for example, children and parents.
(v) A scheme for statutory co-ownership of the matrimonial home would be very complex. The scheme we outlined in our consultative memorandum was as simple as we could make it, but even so it raised many difficult questions. Should, for example, co-ownership come about automatically by operation of law (in which case how would third parties, such as people who have bought the house in good faith, be protected) or should it come about only, say, on registration of a notice by the non-owner spouse (in which case would non-owner spouses bother to register before it was too late)? Should co-ownership apply to a house owned by one spouse before the marriage? Should it apply to a home which is part of commercial or agricultural property? Should it apply to

---

1. In Great Britain as a whole, 69% of married men are owner-occupiers (GHS, 1984).
2. A.J. Manners and I. Rauta *Family Property in Scotland* (1981).

a home bought by one spouse after the couple have separated? If not, should it make any difference if the spouses resume cohabitation for a short period? Should the spouses become jointly liable for any debts secured on the home? When should it be possible for one spouse, or both, to opt out of co-ownership and how should this be done? Should a spouse be able to claim half of the sale proceeds of one home, refuse to contribute to the purchase price of a new home, and then claim half of that one too? If not, how can this be remedied without forcing one spouse to invest in a home he or she does not want to invest in? These are just some of the less technical questions which would have to be answered.

(vi) Statutory co-ownership of the matrimonial home would not benefit many people. ... The majority of ... owner-occupier couples already have their home in joint names. Of those owner-occupiers who have their home in the sole name of one spouse, a number will have a good reason for this and would presumably opt out of a statutory scheme. In many cases a co-ownership scheme would confer no long-term benefit on the non-owner spouse because he or she would succeed to the house on the death of the other in any event, or would receive as much by way of financial provision on divorce as he or she would have received if the scheme had applied.

(vii) A scheme for statutory co-ownership of the matrimonial home would have to co-exist with the law on financial provision on divorce. It would make little sense, it might be said, to introduce a complicated scheme for fixed co-ownership rights in the home during the marriage if the whole financial circumstances of the spouses were to be thrown into the melting-pot on divorce. The supposed benefit of fixed rights would be illusory. It would be most useless when most needed.

(viii) Finally, a scheme for forced co-ownership could exacerbate matrimonial disputes. If co-ownership came about only when the non-owner spouse registered a notice, the act of registration might well be seen as a deliberate raising of the level of a domestic dispute. An intimation by one spouse that he or she was opting out of co-ownership would also be unlikely to promote good domestic relations.

Questions

(i) Which if any of these criticisms do you agree with, and why?

(ii) The Law Commission proposal was that the legal estate would remain in the sole name of the spouse whose name was on the title. The spouses would therefore become equitable joint tenants. Why did the Law Commission not recommend joint legal ownership?

(iii) Why do you think the Law Commission's proposal has not been enacted?

Brenda Hale, in *Family Law Reform: Wither or Whither?* (1995) comments:

The Commission's 1973 proposals for automatic joint ownership of the matrimonial home might have caught the same tide of public opinion which led to the Sex Discrimination Act 1975 and the Domestic Violence and Matrimonial Proceedings Act 1976. But by the time that the Commission's conveyancers had worked out a solution which satisfied them that tide had been missed. The experience of our later proposals on savings and chattels indicates the depth of opposition at official and political level to any alteration of the current rules on the acquisition of property rights, no matter how limited or subject to the contrary intentions of the parties. This seems particularly to occur with proposals [that] are thought to reflect a slightly different balance between the various interests and will be applicable to all couples rather than to those who separate or divorce. ... Continued examination and reform of the discretionary remedies on marital or family breakdown is more likely to bear fruit than attempts to introduce new rules of substantive law which will affect [the] whole population – especially in the property law area where, however misguidedly, this may be seen as benefiting certain (usually less powerful) groups at the expense of others (usually more powerful).

The Law Commission in their Third Report on *Family Property* (1978) recommended that statutory co-ownership should only give protection against third parties if the interest is registered, and that it would not be an overriding interest. However, the House of Lords decided that beneficial interests in registered land were overriding in certain circumstances:

Williams and Glyn's Bank Ltd v Boland
[1981] AC 487, [1980] 2 All ER 408, [1980] 3 WLR 138, 124 Sol Jo 443, [1980] RVR 204, 40 P & CR 451, House of Lords

In 1969 Michael Boland bought a house in his sole name (the land was registered land) and went to live there with his wife and son. The wife made a substantial contribution to the purchase price. A loan was subsequently guaranteed to the husband by the bank to whom he charged the house as security. The bank made no enquiries about the wife's interest. Subsequently, the bank brought proceedings for possession, with a view to its sale with vacant possession and the recovery, from the proceeds, of so much of the loan as remained due. Mrs Boland maintained that she had rights which prevailed against those of the bank. She claimed that she was entitled to a property interest in the house by reason of her contribution to the purchase; that she occupied the house and was entitled to continue to occupy it; and that her rights constituted an 'overriding interest' under s. 70(1)(*g*) of the Law Registration Act 1925 which prevailed against the bank. The bank succeeded at first instance, but the judgment was reversed by the Court of Appeal whose decision was unanimously upheld by the House of Lords. (The case was heard together with a similar appeal in *Williams and Glyn's Bank Ltd v Brown*.)

Lord Wilberforce: There was physical presence with all the rights that occupiers have, including the right to exclude all others except those having similar rights. The house was a matrimonial home, intended to be occupied, and in fact occupied by both spouses, both of whom have an interest in it: it would require some special doctrine of law to avoid the result that each is in occupation. ... It was suggested that the wife's occupation was nothing but the shadow of the husband's – a version I suppose of the doctrine of unity of husband and wife. This expression and the argument flowing from it was used by Templeman J in *Bird v Syme-Thomson* [1978] 3 All ER 1027, [1979] 1 WLR 440, a decision preceding and which he followed in the present case. The argument was also inherent in the judgment in *Caunce v Caunce* [1969] 1 All ER 722, [1969] 1 WLR 286 which influenced the decisions of Templeman J. It somewhat faded from the arguments in the present case and appears to me to be heavily obsolete. The appellant's main and final position became in the end this: that, to come within the paragraph, the occupation in question must be apparently inconsistent with the title of the vendor. This, it was suggested, would exclude the wife of a husband-vendor because her apparent occupation would be satisfactorily accounted for by his. But, apart from the rewriting of the paragraph which this would involve, the suggestion is unacceptable. Consistency, or inconsistency, involves the absence, or presence, of an independent right to occupy, though I must observe that 'inconsistency' in this context is an inappropriate word. But how can either quality be predicated of a wife, simply qua wife? A wife may, and everyone knows this, have rights of her own; particularly, many wives have a share in a matrimonial home. How can it be said that the presence of a wife in the house, as occupier, is consistent or inconsistent with the husband's rights until one knows what rights she has? And if she has rights, why, just because she is a wife (or in the converse case, just because an occupier is the husband), should these rights be denied protection under the paragraph? If one looks beyond the case of husband and wife, the difficulty of all these arguments stands out if one considers the case of a man living with a mistress, or of a man and a woman – or for that matter two persons of the same sex – living in a house in separate or partially shared rooms. Are these cases of apparently consistent occupation, so that the rights of the other person (other than the vendor) can be disregarded? The only solution which is consistent with the Act (section 70(1)(*g*)) and with common sense is to read the paragraph for what it says. Occupation, existing as a fact, may protect rights if the person in occupation has rights. On this part of the case I have no difficulty in concluding that a spouse, living in a house, has an actual occupation capable of conferring protection, as an overriding interest, upon rights of that spouse.

Lord Wilberforce goes on to consider whether such rights as a spouse has under a trust for sale are capable of recognition as overriding interests. He examines the structure of the Land Registration Act 1925, and reaches the conclusion that such rights are indeed capable of recognition.

In *Boland* the land was registered. In *Kingsnorth Trust Ltd v Tizard* [1986] 2 All ER 54, [1986] 1 WLR 783, the court was faced with a case where the disputed property was unregistered title. The question was whether the plaintiff's legal mortgage was subject to the wife's agreed equitable rights in the house. In the course of his judgment the judge said: 'if the purchaser or mortgagee carries out such inspections "as ought reasonably to be made" and does not either find the claimant in occupation or find evidence of that occupation reasonably sufficient to give notice of the occupation, then I am not persuaded that the purchaser or mortgagee is in such circumstances fixed with notice of the claimant's rights'. On the facts, the plaintiffs should have been alerted to make further inquiries, they did not do so, and accordingly they were fixed with notice of her interest.

Questions

(i) In the light of these cases, do you think that there is any substantial difference between the situation of registered land compared with unregistered land?
(ii) Surely not all married women have beneficial interests in the matrimonial home? (See p. 138, above.)
(iii) As a result of the *Boland* decision, it was said that the cost of conveyancing has increased, and new sources of delay and complication have been created (see for instance *Winkworth v Edward Baron Development Co Ltd* [1987] 1 All ER 114, [1986] 1 WLR 1512, HL). Is this a reasonable price to pay for the additional protection accorded to those, especially married women, who have equitable interests in the family home?
(iv) If Mrs Boland had been asked to agree to the charge, in order to secure her husband's business and source of income, do you think that she would have done so? (See *Bristol and West Building Society v Henning* [1985] 2 All ER 606, [1985] 1 WLR 778, CA.)
(v) What would have been the position if Mrs Boland had then claimed that her consent had been obtained by her husband's misrepresentation or undue influence? (See p. 146, above.)
(vi) What would have been the position if the bank had advanced capital moneys to two trustees? (See *City of London Building Society v Flegg* [1988] AC 54, [1987] 3 All ER 435, HL.)

The Law Commission, in their paper, *The Implications of Williams and Glyn's Bank Ltd v Boland* (1982) still considered that registration was the solution, provided that this was accompanied by a requirement for spouses to consent to dispositions *and* the implementation of their earlier co-ownership scheme. This proposal was not widely welcomed. Instead, the Land Registration and Law of Property Bill was introduced in 1985. This Bill would have retained the entitlement to automatic protection enjoyed by spouses who occupied dwelling houses, whilst at the same time removing from others the 'overriding interest' status who would be protected only by notice or caution. Similar provisions were proposed for unregistered land. The Bill was withdrawn owing to lack of parliamentary time when aspects of the Bill proved controversial.

In looking afresh at the whole question, the Law Commission in the *Third Report on Land Registration* (1987) state:

2.6 ... The ideal of a complete register of title is certainly compatible with the policy of the law for over one hundred and fifty years of both simplifying conveyancing and maintaining the security of property interests on the one hand and the marketability of land on the other. But the longevity of a policy hardly guarantees its acceptability to-day in the light of modern developments affecting land ownership. Plainly no policy should be followed blindly which works against rather than for 'rights conferred by Parliament or recognised by judicial decision, as being necessary for the achievement of social justice'. Put simply, it may be unjust to require that a particular interest be protected by registration on pain of deprivation. Apart from this basic aspect, also militating against the ideal of a complete register are the various matters the nature of which is such that recording them on the register would be 'unnecessary, impracticable or undesirable'. Thus there are self-evident difficulties in reproducing in verbal form on the register rights which are acquired or arise without any express grant or other provision in writing. Again some rights may seem so transient as to be not worth the trouble of recording. Beyond this, other rights may be so readily discoverable by any purchaser without recourse to the register that no greater protection would be conferred by recording them. Similarly, perhaps, there is clearly common-sense behind the general rule relieving the registrar from the necessity of entering on the register notice of any liability, right, or interest appearing to him to be 'of a trivial or obvious character, or the entry of which on the register is likely to cause confusion or inconvenience'. In addition, requiring an entry on the register to protect a right or interest otherwise accepted and exercised may be to provoke litigation unnecessarily soon: neighbours as well as spouses may see a notice or caution as a hostile act. Finally to be borne fully in mind is the point that, as the law now stands, any reduction in the list of overriding interests inevitably involves a corresponding increase in the number of potential claims for indemnity (these provisions are not at present available where losses are in respect of overriding interests). These considerations persuade us to adopt two principles, with the first being subject to the second: (1) 'in the interests of certainty and of simplifying conveyancing, the class of right which may bind a purchaser otherwise than as the result of an entry in the register should be as narrow as possible' *but* (2) interests should be overriding where protection against purchasers is needed, yet it is either not reasonable to expect or not sensible to require any entry on the register. Thus far the welfare of the conveyancer, or rather his client, is our first but not our paramount consideration. However, particularly perturbed by thoughts of honest and careful purchasers suffering losses because of principle (2), we will proceed to propose that the ordinary indemnity provisions should become available for claims occasioned by overriding interests. ...

Principle (2) deals with the implication of *Williams and Glyn's Bank v Boland.* The Law Commission (1987) then go on to propose that in order to protect the 'honest and careful purchaser' who could suffer loss as a result of principle (2), the ordinary indemnity provisions should become available for claims occasioned by overriding interests, so as to 'go some way to enabling an acceptable balance to be achieved between competing innocent interests' (para. 2.12).

Questions

(i) Do you consider that this proposal will solve the problems?
(ii) This idea is not mentioned in Law Com No 235, *Transfer of Land: Land Registration, First Report of a Joint Working Group on the Implementation of the*

Law Commission's Third and Fourth Reports on Land Registration, published in 1995. Why do you suppose that such an innovative way of reconciling the claims of occupiers with overriding interests and of lenders who were ignorant of them has apparently been abandoned?
(iii) If practitioners have now come to terms with the implications of the *Boland* decision, why worry?
(iv) The Law Commission take the ascertainment of beneficial interests a stage further in *Matrimonial Property* (1988) (see p. 161, below). The Law Commission exclude land and hence the matrimonial home. Should they have done?

The Law Commission propose that the co-ownership principle should be extended to the rented sector. Local authorities increasingly use joint tenancy agreements in the case of husband and wife. If the tenancy is a joint one, the Housing Act 1985 provides that in general the tenancy is 'secure' so long as at least one of them occupies the dwelling house as his or her only or principal home (s. 81). The two major components of secure tenancies are the right of succession on the death of the first tenant and the security from eviction. Whether the tenancy is sole or joint, there is provision for only *one* succession on the death of the first tenant. Succession will be in favour, first of the tenant's spouse provided that that person 'occupied the dwelling house as his only or principal home at the time of the tenant's death,' or secondly, failing this, of any other member of the tenant's family who has resided with the tenant throughout the period of 12 months ending with the tenant's death. The other major element of the security of tenure conferred by the Housing Act 1985 relates to the circumstances in which possession of a dwelling house let on a secure tenancy may be recovered. A landlord cannot get possession from a secure tenant without a court order and the court cannot make such an order except on the grounds specified in detail in Sch. 2 to the Housing Act 1985. These include non-payment of rent, deterioration in the condition of the dwelling house, nuisance or annoyance and so on.

Questions

(i) It is often argued that joint tenancies have a psychological effect. However, where there is a joint tenancy, each partner is jointly and severally liable for the rent even if the arrears were due purely to the 'fault' of one of them. Is this too high a price to pay for the alleged psychological advantage of joint tenancies?
(ii) Why restrict rights of succession to one?
(iii) If the husband dies in 1996 and the wife dies in 1997, what then happens to the children?
(iv) Is the position of the children in (iii) the same under the scheme for succession to a Rent Act 1977 tenancy?

(c) THE FAMILY ASSETS OTHER THAN THE MATRIMONIAL HOME

Professor Sir Otto Kahn-Freund was a strong advocate of an introduction of 'community' in the family assets, and we quote the following extracts from his Unger Memorial Lecture (1971):

What I suggest is a general rule that such assets as form the matrimonial aggregate – 'family assets' – should, in the absence of special circumstances, be shared by the spouses half and half. The special circumstances would have to be found by the court in the light of the facts of the case. It is here that the court should have a wide discretion, especially in assessing the significance in each case of various conflicting considerations. Some of the considerations enumerated in section 5 of the Matrimonial Proceedings and Property Act 1970 [now s. 25(1) of the Matrimonial Causes Act 1973 as amended; see Chapter 8, below] would be relevant, including above all, the value of pensions expectations which either spouse – in most cases the wife – stands to lose as a result of the termination of a marriage. Occasionally the court may also have to assess the value of the contributions made by either spouse to the welfare of the family, 'including any contribution made by looking after the home and caring for the family'. But this should only be done in exceptional cases – and normally the value of the contributions should be deemed to be equal. ...

But, of course, this leaves us with two fundamental problems: how should the assets which make up the aggregate be identified? And, equally important, is all this to affect the spouses themselves only, or also third parties?

Kahn-Freund answers his first question in the following manner;

I should identify the assets which are to constitute the aggregate not by reason of how, when, by whom and with whose resources they were acquired. My criterion of selection would not be their origin, but their purpose.

... An asset is a family asset if, at any given time it is by consent of the spouses, dedicated to the common use of the household family, irrespective of whether it was acquired before or after the marriage, or through the spouses' work or thrift or through inheritance or gift. It comprises the family home and its contents (furniture and equipment), but also a family car and other implements intended to be enjoyed by the family. It also includes such funds, however invested, as are, by the spouses' consent, at any given moment dedicated to future family expenditure, including expenditure for the benefit of a child of the family, or as have been saved by either spouse without the knowledge of the other and been dedicated by him for future family expenditure. In the absence of proof to the contrary any house or flat used as a matrimonial home is presumed to be a family asset, and so are all chattels in common use. No other asset belonging to either spouse is presumed to be a family asset.

The major problem relating to family assets is whether any principle of co-ownership should affect third parties. The Law Commission, possibly aware of this difficulty, state that in their view the primary consideration should be to devise a scheme which protects the 'occupation rights' of the spouses (see p. 147, above). In the First Report (1973), they say:

... It is more important at this stage to protect the use and enjoyment of those goods than to change the ownership rules. The reason for this is that such goods usually have a rapidly diminishing realisable value; in most cases a spouse's share in the proceeds of sale of secondhand furniture would not go far towards the cost of its replacement (save in the case of antiques). Because of this a spouse's main concern is to retain the use and enjoyment of the goods and we propose that the spouse in occupation of the home should have this right. This would be essentially a support right supplementing the rights of occupation which are protected under the Matrimonial Homes Act 1967 [now 1983].

However, the Law Commission's Working Paper, *Transfer of Money Between Spouses* (1985) recommended more extensive reform, as did the Second Consultation Paper (1986).

Finally, in the Law Commission Report on *Matrimonial Property* (1988) (see Chapter 3, above) they reviewed their earlier work:

1.4 There were two consistent themes running through all the Commission's earlier work. The first was the persistent observation that the present rules for determining the ownership of property during marriage were arbitrary, uncertain and unfair. The second was that the ownership of property while a marriage continues is important and that it is not right to consider marital property only in relation to what happens when a marriage ends. There are those who have said, and no doubt will continue to say, that since English law now provides for the discretionary re-allocation of property between spouses on various events, for example death or divorce, the precise detail of the ownership of property during marriage does not matter. It has also been said that in their attitudes to, and arrangements for, ownership of their property, married couples vary so greatly that it is impossible to generalise about the way in which such property would or should be regarded. If the parties did give thought to the ownership of property which they acquired for their joint use and benefit, they would not do so on any consistent or common basis. We cannot, however, accept these arguments, for the following main reasons:

(i) To a partner who is the sole or main wage earner in the family, the present rules for determining ownership may seem as unimportant during the marriage as they are important when the marriage has broken down; to the partner who has no separate income, on the other hand, they may appear as unfair during the marriage as they do when it ends. Respondents to our Working Paper who represented the latter were unanimously of this view. …

(ii) It is a false dichotomy to split marriages into the happy and the unhappy, and to say that while the couple are happy, property ownership does not matter and that, if they are not, they will get divorced and that the court will reallocate the property. Most marriages do not end in divorce. There may be occasions during a marriage when knowledge of who owns what property is important to either or both spouses. We believe that a law which aims to reduce uncertainty and to reflect the intentions of both parties is more likely to further stability in the relationship of marriage than one which does not.

(iii) Although it is undoubtedly true that the attitude of the spouses to family property will vary enormously and will depend upon individual expectations, nevertheless the law already provides an extensive body of rules affecting the property rights of the spouses. Changes in the principles upon which these rules are based will not alter the fact that the law finds it necessary to make provision for such rules, which are just as much an intrusion into the private lives of the parties whether they are made by Parliament or by judges.

(iv) It is clear that in some cases property rights during marriage are important when either spouse becomes bankrupt or dies. Even when the court has to reallocate property on divorce, rules which have become common knowledge and which clarify the ownership of property acquired for joint use and benefit during the marriage could provide a more satisfactory basis for reallocation and could reduce the arguments, acrimony and delay in reaching a settlement of property rights.

The proposal made was as follows:

3.9 … where money is paid by either spouse to the other or to buy property and the payment or purchase is for common purposes, the money or property will be jointly owned, subject to a contrary intention on the part of the purchasing spouse known to the other spouse.
… To expand a little, the purchase of property for common purposes would give rise to joint ownership, even though there had been no transfer of money to the other spouse and no expenditure on common purposes by the other spouse. This avoids the likely difficulties of the 'notional pool'. It might be thought that it would go too far and produce more joint ownership than is warranted. However, it would give way to a contrary intention which need not be communicated to the other spouse, so a spouse who wishes to retain sole ownership can do so. The main effect would be to produce co-ownership in household assets even though there was no thought given to it at the time and/or the formalities technically required for a transfer to the other spouse (such as delivery of goods or a declaration of trust) had not been complied with. It might be thought that this proposal alone is sufficient. However, it makes no provision for ownership of money that is not spent, … Hence we would retain the idea of making money paid by one spouse to the other for common purposes into jointly owned money.

However, the Law Commission do not speak with one voice on the question.

B. Davenport QC: I do not share the view of my colleagues that to give effect to the policy expressed in this report by enactment of the draft Bill in Appendix A would bring about an improvement in English Law. Some of my principal reasons are, in summary, as follows:-

(*a*) Apart from making technical changes to the Married Women's Property Act 1964, I am not persuaded that there is any real need for reform in that area of the law. The reform suggested is as likely to lead to matrimonial quarrelling as to matrimonial concord.
(*b*) Having regard to the almost infinite variety in relations between husbands and wives, the law should be very cautious before imposing any statutory regime of property rights upon them. The policy recommended in this report ... is to provide a series of rules which are intended positively to lay down when property is to be jointly owned. These rules are, I consider, too inflexible to be applied satisfactorily to every marriage. Indeed, it is not difficult to think of situations where an application of the rules can lead to consequences which many might regard as unjust.
(*c*) Assumptions made about household goods, generally of limited value, cannot safely be extrapolated to motor vehicles or to securities (both of which are excluded from the Scottish Act [see below]). The title to both vehicles and securities is likely to pass from person to person and claims for damages for wrongful interference or conversion by a spouse who had not consented to the sale would seem an almost inevitable consequence of giving effect to the draft Bill. Indeed, the sale of 'family' motor vehicles might become significantly more difficult, as might the sale of securities, unless special protection is given to *bona fide* purchasers.

Questions

(i) What situations can you think of which might lead to unjust consequences?
(ii) Who do you agree with – Mr Davenport or his colleagues?
(iii) The Law Commission decided to exclude life insurance policies and to include motor cars. Why?
(iv) Why do you think the Law Commission's proposals have not been enacted?
(v) The Family Law (Scotland) Act 1985, s. 25 states:

Presumption of equal shares in household goods

25. – (1) If any question arises (whether during or after a marriage) as to the respective rights of ownership of the parties to a marriage in any household goods obtained in prospect of or during the marriage other than by gift or succession from a third party, it shall be presumed, unless the contrary is proved, that each has a right to an equal share in the goods in question.

(2) For the purposes of subsection (1) above, the contrary shall not be treated as proved by reason only that while the parties were married and living together the goods in question were purchased from a third party by either party alone or by both in unequal shares.

(3) In this section 'household goods' means any goods (including decorative or ornamental goods) kept or used at any time during the marriage in any matrimonial home for the joint domestic purposes of the parties to the marriage, other than –
(*a*) money or securities;
(*b*) any motor car, caravan or other road vehicle;
(*c*) any domestic animal.

What about the pet Boxer? The Scottish Law Commission suspect that animals would often be regarded by the spouses as belonging fairly definitely to one of them. Are they right?

3 Property claims

We revert now to the general law of property. We have remarked that this governs the property rights of married persons except where the Matrimonial

Causes Act 1973 applies; as this is rather a large exception, most of the cases relating to family property have involved unmarried persons (who might be cohabitants, or other family members). It is therefore in this section that we look at the way the law has dealt with the property of such persons.

We have seen that the law's stance on the separate property of married couples was emphasised in the context of the constructive trust, in particular the 'common intention constructive trust' expounded in *Gissing v Gissing* [1971] AC 886 (p. 138). In the years following that decision, its implications were explored further by the courts.

Cooke v Head
[1972] 2 All ER 38, [1972] 1 WLR 518, 116 Sol Jo 298, Court of Appeal

The plaintiff formed a relationship with the defendant, a married man, in 1962. In 1964, they decided to acquire land in order to build a bungalow for their use. It was their hope that the defendant would obtain a divorce from his wife. The conveyance was taken in the defendant's name, and he paid a deposit and raised a mortgage from a building society. The plaintiff helped in the construction of the bungalow. To adopt the words used by Lord Denning MR in his judgment: 'She used a sledge hammer to demolish some old buildings. She filled the wheelbarrow with rubble and hard core and wheeled it up the bank. She worked the cement mixer, which was out of order and difficult to work. She did painting and so forth. The plaintiff did much more than most women would do.' The bungalow was nearing completion when, in 1966, the couple separated. The defendant sold the bungalow, and the plaintiff issued a writ to determine the way in which the proceeds of sale were to be divided. The trial judge held that she should have one-twelfth of the proceeds. She appealed against that decision to the Court of Appeal:

Lord Denning MR: ... I do not think it is right to approach this case by looking at the money contributions of each and dividing up the beneficial interest according to those contributions. The matter should be looked at more broadly, just as we do in husband and wife cases. We look to see what the equity is worth at the time when the parties separate. We assess the shares as at that time. If the property has been sold, we look at the amount which it has realised, and say how it is to be divided between them. Lord Diplock in *Gissing v Gissing* [1971] AC 886 at 909 intimated that it is quite legitimate to infer that:

> 'the wife should be entitled to a share which was not to be quantified immediately upon the acquisition of the home but should be left to be determined when the mortgage was repaid or the property disposed of.'

Likewise with a mistress.

The court decided that the plaintiff's share of the net proceeds of sale should be one-third.

Eves v Eves
[1975] 3 All ER 768, [1975] 1 WLR 1338, 119 Sol Jo 394, Court of Appeal

The plaintiff (referred to in the judgment of Lord Denning MR as 'Janet' because 'she has had four surnames already') met the defendant in 1968. The relationship lasted four and a half years and during this time she took his surname and had two children by him. He was a married man and they lived together initially in his house. In 1969, they moved to another house which was conveyed into the defendant's name, paid for in part by the sale of the former house and in part by a mortgage raised by the defendant. As in *Cooke v Head,* the plaintiff put in a lot of initial work on the renovation of the house. The couple separated in 1972, and she applied to the county court for a declaration of an interest in the house. On appeal to the Court of Appeal:

Lord Denning MR: ... Although Janet did not make any financial contribution, it seems to me that this property was acquired and maintained both by their joint efforts with the intention that it should be used for their joint benefit until they were married and thereafter as long as the marriage continued. At any rate, Stuart Eves cannot be heard to say to the contrary. He told her that it was to be their home for them and their children. He gained her confidence by telling her that he intended to put it in their joint names (just as married couples often do) but that it was not possible until she was 21. The judge described this as a 'trick,' and said that it 'did not do him much credit as a man of honour.' The man never intended to put it in joint names but always determined to have it in his own name. It seems to me that he should be judged by what he told her – by what he led her to believe – and not by his own intent which he kept to himself. Lord Diplock made this clear in *Gissing v Gissing* [1971] AC 886 at 906. It seems to me that this conduct by Mr Eves amounted to a recognition by him that, in all fairness, she was entitled to a share in the house, equivalent in some way to a declaration of trust; not for a particular share, but for such share as was fair in view of all she had done and was doing for him and the children and would thereafter do. By so doing he gained her confidence. She trusted him. She did not make any financial contribution but she contributed in many other ways. She did much work in the house and garden. She looked after him and cared for the children. It is clear that her contribution was such that if she had been a wife she could have had a good claim to have a share in it on a divorce: see *Wachtel v Wachtel* [1973] Fam 72 at 92–94.

Brightman J: The defendant clearly led the plaintiff to believe that she was to have some undefined interest in the property, and that her name was only omitted from the conveyance because of her age. This, of course, is not enough by itself to create a beneficial interest in her favour; there would at best be a mere 'voluntary declaration of trust' which would be 'unenforceable for want of writing': *per* Lord Diplock in *Gissing v Gissing* [1971] AC 886 at 905. If, however, it was part of the bargain between the parties, expressed or to be implied, that the plaintiff should contribute her labour towards the reparation of a house in which she was to have some beneficial interest, then I think that the arrangement becomes one to which the law can give effect. This seems to be consistent with the reasoning of the speeches in *Gissing v Gissing.*

The Court of Appeal decided that the defendant held the legal estate on trust for sale in the proportion one-quarter to the plaintiff and three-quarters to the defendant.

Similar reasoning is seen in the following case.

Bernard v Josephs
[1982] Ch 391, [1982] 3 All ER 162, [1982] 2 WLR 1052, 126 Sol Jo 361, Court of Appeal

Lord Denning explained:

The law
In our time the concept of marriage – I am sorry to say – is being eroded. Nowadays many couples live together as if they were husband and wife, but they are not married. They hope and expect that their relationship will be permanent. They acquire a house in their joint names. Most

of the purchase price is obtained on mortgage in both their names. They are both responsible for payment of the instalments. Both go out to work. They pay the outgoings out of their joint resources. One paying for the food and housekeeping. The other paying the mortgage instalments. And so forth. Just as husband and wife do. But later on, for some reason or other, they fall out. They go their own separate ways. One or other leaves the house. The other stays behind in it. There is no need to divorce. They just separate. What is to happen to the house? Is it to be sold? If so, are the proceeds to be divided? And, if so, in what proportion? Or is one of them to be allowed to stay in it? If so, on what terms? If they had been husband and wife, our matrimonial property legislation would give the Family Division a very wide discretion to deal with all these problems. It is contained in sections 23 to 25 of the Matrimonial Causes Act 1973. But there is no such legislation for couples like these. ...

In my opinion in ascertaining the respective shares, the courts should normally apply the same considerations to couples living together (as if married) as they do to couples who are truly married. The shares may be half-and-half, or any such other proportion as in the circumstances of the case appears to be fair and just.

In this case the plaintiff, Miss Bernard, was awarded a one-half share in the value of the house. By the time of the Court of Appeal's decision the defendant was living in the house with his new wife, and Lord Denning described the calculation required to ascertain Miss Bernard's entitlement:

It would be unduly harsh to turn Mr Josephs and his wife out of this house – simply in order to provide funds for Miss Bernard. But, seeing that he has the use of her share, it would only be fair that he should pay an occupation rent in respect of it: see *Dennis v McDonald* [1982] Fam 63, [1982] 1 All ER 590. No doubt, however, he has been paying the whole of the mortgage instalments and this should be taken into account as well. It may relieve him of paying any occupation rent for her half-share.

The problem is to calculate the sum which Mr Josephs should pay to Miss Bernard to buy her out. This is to be done by taking the price obtainable for the house if it were sold now with vacant possession. Then deduct the sum payable to redeem the mortgage. Then deduct one-half of the amount paid by Mr Josephs since the separation for mortgage instalments (deducting, of course, the amount received from the tenants). He should only get credit for one-half, because he has had the benefit of her half-share. Then make any other special adjustments.

One of the problems in Lord Denning's approach is that some couples remain unmarried because they do not wish to make the commitment of marriage. As Griffiths LJ said, in his judgment in *Bernard v Josephs*:

... There are many reasons why a man and a woman may decide to live together without marrying, and one of them is that each values his independence and does not wish to make the commitment of marriage; in such a case it will be misleading to make the same assumptions and to draw the same inferences from their behaviour as in the case of a married couple. The judge must look most carefully at the nature of the relationship, and only if satisfied that it was intended to involve the same degree of commitment as marriage will it be legitimate to regard them as no different from a married couple.

Questions

(i) Reread *Gissing v Gissing* [1971] AC 886, [1970] 2 All ER 780, HL and *Pettitt v Pettitt* [1970] AC 777, [1969] 2 All ER 385, HL. (See pp. 137, 138, above). Is there any justification for Lord Denning MR's views given the speeches of Lord Diplock in those two cases?

(ii) Applying the principles you know from *Gissing v Gissing* [1971] AC 886, [1970] 2 All ER 780 (p. 138, above), if the litigants in each of these cases had been married, and the issues arose in the context, for instance, of the bankruptcy of the men, do you think that the women would have been entitled to the shares they were given?

Perhaps it comes as no surprise that the opportunity was taken to limit the extent of the 'Lord Denning approach' at the first available opportunity.

Burns v Burns
[1984] Ch 317, [1984] 1 All ER 244, [1984] 2 WLR 582, [1984] FLR 216, [1984] Fam Law 244, Court of Appeal

The plaintiff and the defendant set up house together in 1961. In 1963, when the plaintiff was expecting their second child, the defendant decided to buy a house. This was purchased, and conveyed in the sole name of the defendant. He financed the purchase price out of his own money and paid the mortgage. The plaintiff remained at home in order to look after the two children and maintain the home. She did not go out to work until 1975. Subsequent to that date she used some of her earnings to pay for the rates and telephone bills and buy certain items for the house. She also redecorated the interior of the house. The relationship deteriorated, and the plaintiff left the home in 1980. She claimed that she was entitled to a beneficial interest in the house by reason of her contributions to the household over the 17 years she had lived in the house with him. The judge dismissed her claim and she appealed.

Fox LJ rejected the proposition that there was any evidence of a payment or payments by the plaintiff which it can be inferred was referable to the acquisition of the house. He also felt that the redecoration gave no indication of a common intention that she had a beneficial interest. (*Pettitt v Pettitt* [1970] AC 777, [1969] 2 All ER 385, HL. See p. 137, above.) He then turned to the question of housekeeping and domestic duties.

There remains the question of housekeeping and domestic duties. So far as housekeeping expenses are concerned, I do not doubt that (the house being in the man's name) if the woman goes out to work in order to provide money for the family expenses, as a result of which she spends her earnings on the housekeeping and the man is thus able to pay the mortgage instalments and other expenses out of his earnings, it can be inferred that there was a common intention that the woman should have an interest in the house – since she will have made an indirect financial contribution to the mortgage instalments. But that is not this case

During the greater part of the period when the plaintiff and the defendant were living together she was not in employment or, if she was, she was not earning amounts of any consequence and provided no money towards the family expenses. Nor is it suggested that the defendant ever asked her to. He provided, and was always ready to provide, all the money that she wanted for housekeeping. The house was not bought in the contemplation that the plaintiff would, at some time, contribute to the cost of its acquisition. She worked to suit herself. And if towards the very end of the relationship she had money to spare she spent it entirely as she chose. It was in no sense 'joint' money. It was her own; she was not expected and was not asked to spend it on the household.

I think it would be quite unreal to say that, overall, she made a substantial financial contribution towards the family expenses. That is not in any way a criticism of her; it is simply the factual position.

But, one asks, can the fact that the plaintiff performed domestic duties in the house and looked after the children be taken into account? I think it is necessary to keep in mind the nature of the right which is being asserted. The court has no jurisdiction to make such order as it might think fair; the powers conferred by the Matrimonial Causes Act 1973 in relation to the property of married persons do not apply to unmarried couples. The house was bought by the defendant in his own name and, prima facie, he is the absolute beneficial owner. If the plaintiff, or anybody else, claims to take it from him, it must be proved the claimant has, by some process of law, acquired an interest in the house. What is asserted here is the creation of a trust arising by common intention of the parties. That common intention may be inferred where there has been a financial contribution, direct or indirect, to the acquisition of the house. But the mere fact that parties live together and do the ordinary domestic tasks is, in my view, no indication at all that they thereby intended to alter the existing property rights of either of them. As to that I refer to the passage from the speech of Lord Diplock in *Pettitt v Pettitt* [1970] AC 777, 826 which I have already mentioned; and also to the observations of Lord Hodson in *Pettitt v Pettitt* at p. 811 and of Lord Reid at p. 796. The undertaking of such work is, I think, what Lord Denning MR in *Button v Button* [1968] 1 WLR 457, 462 called the sort of things which are done for the benefit of the family without altering the title to property. The assertion that they do alter property rights seems to me to be, in substance, reverting to the idea of the 'family asset' which was rejected by the House of Lords in *Pettitt v Pettitt* [1970] AC 777. The decision in *Gissing v Gissing* [1971] AC 886 itself is really inconsistent with the contrary view since the parties lived together for ten years after the house was bought. ...

The result, in my opinion, is that the plaintiff fails to demonstrate the existence of any trust in her favour.

May LJ agreeing with Waller LJ and Fox LJ referred to the unfortunate position that the plaintiff found herself:

When one compares this ultimate result with what it would have been had she been married to the defendant, and taken appropriate steps under the Matrimonial Causes Act 1973, I think that she can justifiably say that fate has not been kind to her. In my opinion, however, the remedy for any inequity she may have sustained is a matter for Parliament and not for this court.
Appeal dismissed.

The principles were considered by Scott J in the following case:

Layton v Martin
[1986] 2 FLR 227, [1986] Fam Law 212, High Court, Chancery Division

The plaintiff met the deceased in 1967 and they became cohabitants. She was 29 and unmarried. He was a married man of 50, whose wife was in poor health. In a letter dated 25 May the deceased, whose wife was by then having medical treatment abroad, asked the plaintiff to live with him, offering 'what emotional security I can give, plus financial security during my life and financial security after my death'. He implied that he would marry her after his wife died. Thereafter, the plaintiff lived with him as his wife in all but name. He paid her a salary of £100 per month, later raised to £120, plus £30 per week for housekeeping. The deceased wife's died in 1977 but he did not in the event marry the plaintiff. It seemed that the plaintiff brought no pressure upon him to do so. She gave him love and affection during their time together and was wholly unmercenary in her dealings with him. He made some provision for her in a number of wills.

However, the relationship between them ran into difficulties culminating in the deceased cutting the plaintiff out of his will and giving to her, in June 1980, a 'written notice of dismissal'. They parted without rancour and kept in touch from time to time up to the deceased's death in April 1982. In 1983 the plaintiff made a claim to financial provision out of the estate of the deceased, the defendants being the deceased's executors. Her claim was based on the contents of the letter of 25 May 1975 under three heads: (i) that the deceased had represented to her that if she came to live with him he would make financial provision for her in his will, that relying on that representation she had done so, and that in the circumstances the estate was subject to a constructive trust to give effect to their common intention; (ii) that under the doctrine of proprietary estoppel, equity would subject the estate to such beneficial interests in her favour as would give effect to the representation on which she relied; (iii) that the representation constituted an offer which she by her subsequent conduct had accepted and that she was entitled to enforce the contract thereby concluded.

The claim was dismissed under all three heads. We consider here the first head (see p. 177, below for head (ii)).

Scott J: I will assume, that the plaintiff when she went to live with the deceased did so in reliance on the deceased's representation that if she did he would make financial provision for her.

Counsel for the plaintiff contends that one partner in a quasi-matrimonial relationship can claim a beneficial interest in assets owned by the other partner provided that the claimant should have a beneficial interest therein, and provided that it can be regarded in all the circumstances of the case as unconscionable that the beneficial interest should be withheld from the claimant.

Counsel for the plaintiff supports this contention, first, by reliance on dicta from such well-known cases as *Pettitt v Pettitt* [1970] AC 777 at 818; *Gissing v Gissing* [1971] AC 886 and a more recent authority in the Court of Appeal, *Burns v Burns* [1984] FLR 216. These authorities and the dicta in them are, in my view, no use whatever to counsel for the plaintiff. They are all dealing with the circumstances in which a person can claim a beneficial interest in specific assets, standing in the name of another person, but which have been acquired or preserved, at least in part, by contributions made by the claimant. They establish a principle that if there is a common intention on the part of the parties that the contributing claimant should have a beneficial interest in the assets, then equity will impose on the assets and the legal owner thereof, a constructive trust to give effect to that beneficial interest. In *Pettitt v Pettitt* and *Gissing v Gissing*, as in most cases of this type, the critical question was whether the nature of the claimant's contribution to the acquisition or preservation of the assets justified attributing to the parties the common intention that on account of that contribution the claimant should have a beneficial interest in the assets. In both *Pettitt v Pettitt* and *Gissing v Gissing*, and also *Burns v Burns*, the conclusion was that it did not. In some cases there is evidence of an actual (as opposed to inferred) intention of the parties that the claimant should have a beneficial interest. In those cases the only question is the size of the beneficial interest justified by the actual contribution made by the claimant. *Eves v Eves* [1975] 1 WLR 1338 was a case of this type. It is to be noted, however, that it was made clear by the Court of Appeal in *Eves v Eves* that an express common intention that the claimant should have a beneficial interest, unsupported by any *quid pro quo* moving from the claimant, would not suffice to entitle the claimant to a beneficial interest in accordance with the common intention (see the judgment of Brightman J (as he then was)).

But all these cases, of whichever type, involve an inferred or actual common intention directed to specific property. They involve contributions to the acquisition or preservation of specific property. This feature is not just an incidental circumstance. It lies at the heart of the circumstances which create the claimant's equitable interest in the specific assets in question.

... An agreement by one party to pay the other, say £5,000 a year, or a lump sum of £15,000, is enforceable, if it complies with the requirements of contracts, as a contract. It does not create any equitable interest in any assets of the promissor. An agreement to pay an unspecified amount can obviously not be in any better state to create an equity in the promissor's assets. Nor can an agreement in such general terms as 'to make provision', or 'to provide financiai security' create any equity in the promissor's assets.

Judgment for the defendant.

Grant v Edwards

[1986] Ch 638, [1986] 2 All ER 426, [1986] 3 WLR 114, [1987] 1 FLR 87, [1986] Fam Law 300, Court of Appeal

The plaintiff, a married woman who was separated from her husband, set up a home with the defendant. In 1969, the defendant purchased a house and moved into it with the plaintiff, their child and the two children of the plaintiff's first marriage. The house was conveyed into joint names of the defendant and his brother. It was alleged that the defendant told the plaintiff that her name was not included in the title simply because of possible difficulties in relation to her divorce. He paid the deposit and the mortgage instalments, although the plaintiff made substantial contributions to general household expenses. The parties separated in 1980 and the plaintiff claimed a beneficial interest in the house. The judge dismissed the claim, and the plaintiff appealed.

Nourse LJ: In order to decide whether the plaintiff has a beneficial interest in 96, Hewitt Road we must climb again the familiar ground which slopes down from the twin peaks of *Pettitt v Pettitt* [1970] AC 777 and *Gissing v Gissing* [1971] AC 886. In a case such as the present, where there has been no written declaration or agreement, nor any direct provision by the plaintiff of part of the purchase price so as to give rise to a resulting trust in her favour, she must establish a common intention between her and the defendant, acted upon by her, that she should have a beneficial interest in the property. If she can do that, equity will not allow the defendant to deny that interest and will construct a trust to give effect to it.

In most of these cases the fundamental, and invariably the most difficult, question is to decide whether there was the necessary common intention, being something which can only be inferred from the conduct of the parties, almost always from the expenditure incurred by them respectively. In this regard the court has to look for expenditure which is referable to the acquisition of the house: see *per* Fox LJ in *Burns v Burns* [1984] Ch 317, 328H–329C. If it is found to have been incurred, such expenditure will perform the twofold function of establishing the common intention and showing that the claimant has acted upon it.

There is another and rarer class of case, of which the present may be one, where, although there has been no writing, the parties have orally declared themselves in such a way as to make their common intention plain. Here the court does not have to look for conduct from which the intention can be inferred, but only for conduct which amounts to an acting upon it by the claimant. And although that conduct can undoubtedly be the incurring of expenditure which is referable to the acquisition of the house, it need not necessarily be so.

The clearest example of this rarer class of case is *Eves v Eves* [1975] 1 WLR 1338. That was a case of an unmarried couple where the conveyance of the house was taken in the name of the man alone. At the time of the purchase he told the woman that if she had been 21 years of age, he would have put the house into their joint names, because it was to be their joint home. He admitted in evidence that that was an excuse for not putting the house into their joint names, and this court inferred that there was an understanding between them, or a common intention, that the woman was to have some sort of proprietary interest in it; otherwise no excuse would have been needed. After they had moved in, the woman did extensive decorative work to the downstairs rooms and generally cleaned the whole house. She painted the brickwork of the front of the house. She also broke up with a 14-lb. sledge hammer the concrete surface which covered the whole of the front garden and disposed of the rubble into a skip, worked in the back garden and, together with the man, demolished a shed there and put up a new shed. She also prepared the front garden for turfing. Pennycuick V-C at first instance, being unable to find any link between the common intention and the woman's activities after the purchase, held that she had not acquired a beneficial interest in the house. On an appeal to this court the decision was unanimously reversed, by Lord Denning MR on a ground which I respectfully think was at variance with the principles stated in *Gissing v Gissing* [1971] AC 886 and by Browne LJ and Brightman J [in a different way, see before, p. 165].

About that case the following observations may be made. First, as Brightman J himself observed, if the work had not been done the common intention would not have been enough. Secondly, if the common intention had not been orally made plain, the work would not have been conduct from which it could be inferred. That, I think, is the effect of the actual decision in *Pettitt v Pettitt* [1970] AC 777. Thirdly, and on the other hand, the work was conduct which amounted to an acting upon the common intention by the woman.

It seems therefore, on the authorities as they stand, that a distinction is to be made between conduct from which the common intention can be inferred on the one hand and conduct which amounts to an acting upon it on the other. There remains this difficult question: what is the quality of conduct required for the latter purpose? The difficulty is caused, I think because although the common intention has been made plain, everything else remains a matter of inference. Let me illustrate it in this way. It would be possible to take the view that the mere moving into the house by the woman amounted to an acting upon the common intention. But that was evidently not the view of the majority in *Eves v Eves* [1975] 1 WLR 1338. And the reason for that may be that, in the absence of evidence, the law is not so cynical as to infer that a woman will only go to live with a man to whom she is not married if she understands that she is to have an interest in their home. So what sort of conduct is required? In my judgment it must be conduct on which the woman could not reasonably have been expected to embark unless she was to have an interest in the house. If she was not to have such an interest, she could reasonably be expected to go and live with her lover, but not, for example, to wield a 14-lb. sledge hammer in the front garden. In adopting the latter kind of conduct she is seen to act to her detriment on the faith of the common intention.

. . . .

Was the conduct of the plaintiff in making substantial indirect contributions to the instalments payable under both mortgages conduct upon which she could not reasonably have been expected to embark unless she was to have an interest in the house? I answer that question in the affirmative. I cannot see upon what other basis she could reasonably have been expected to give the defendant such substantial assistance in paying off mortgages on his house. I therefore conclude that the plaintiff did act to her detriment on the faith of the common intention between her and the defendant that she was to have some sort of proprietary interest in the house. ...

For these reasons, I would allow this appeal.

Questions

(i) What if in *Burns v Burns,* the man had left and he had then tried to evict the woman?
(ii) Is *Burns v Burns* a different case, or do you think the decision simply reflects the consensus amongst the judiciary that Lord Denning had gone too far?

Windeler v Whitehall
[1990] FCR 268, [1990] 2 FLR 505, High Court, Chancery Division

The plaintiff went to live with the defendant and they became cohabitants. The defendant was very much in love with her and wanted to marry her, but she consistently refused and occasionally had affairs with other men. The defendant was a successful theatrical agent, first as an employee of an agency and then on his own with a partner. The plaintiff looked after his house and entertained for him, but the work of the agency was essentially done by the defendant in his office. In 1979 the defendant sold his house and bought a larger one. The plaintiff made no contribution to the purchase. She had no money of her own, never worked or earned money and was supported by the defendant. She supervised some minor building works carried out on the new house. In June of that year the defendant made a will leaving the plaintiff his residuary estate. By 1980 the relationship was deteriorating and in 1984 it ended. The plaintiff accepted some money from the defendant and removed her belongings from the house, together with some items belonging to the defendant. In January 1987 the plaintiff brought a claim for a proprietary interest in the house and the business.

Millett J: If this were California, this would be a claim for palimony, but it is England and it is not. English law recognises neither the term nor the obligation to which it gives effect. In this country a husband has a legal obligation to support his wife even if they are living apart. A man has no legal obligation to support his mistress even if they are living together. Accordingly, the plaintiff does not claim to be supported by the defendant but brings a claim to a proprietary interest in his business and his home. ...

The plaintiff, Victoria Windeler, claims a share in the house in which she formerly lived with the defendant, Michael Whitehall, and a share in his business as a successful West End theatrical agent. They never married. To succeed, therefore, it is not enough for Miss Windeler to persuade me that she deserves to have such a share. She must satisfy me that she already owns it. In each case legal ownership is vested in Mr Whitehall. Miss Windeler, therefore, must satisfy me that in equity she is a part owner. This depends on the intention of the parties and such intention must be proved directly or inferred from their conduct. But it is important to bear in mind, that it is to that narrow issue alone that the parties' conduct is relevant.

... Miss Windeler ... was essentially immature. She never shook off an adolescent desire to be free and to avoid being tied down. Her counsel submitted to me that she saw her life and future with Mr Whitehall. I do not think she did. I do not think she ever saw the relationship as a permanent arrangement. She saw it only lasting as long as she chose to make it last.

She told me in the witness box that she gave Mr Whitehall the stability necessary to pursue his career. I think that is the last thing she gave him. She had no stability herself. I think she gave him love and beauty and excitement. But, apart from her love, the greatest gift that a woman can bring to a man is security, tranquillity and peace of mind; something I think Miss Windeler was never able to give to Mr Whitehall.

Not only is there no direct evidence of any common intention but there is evidence which I accept that it was not Mr Whitehall's intention that Miss Windeler should have an interest in the house or, for that matter, in the business. That really is the end of the case.

But as to the business, Millett J went further:

This is not a case where a woman has worked full-time or for substantial periods in the business without wages and in a way which would lead anyone to believe that she must have been encouraged in the expectation that she had or would have an interest in the business. What Miss Windeler did was not work for which Mr Whitehall would have paid anyone to do in any circumstance whatever. In the present case Miss Windeler would not have been entitled even to a quantum meruit claim, and the idea that her conduct entitled her to a proprietary interest in the business is, in my judgment, ridiculous. I dismiss the action.

If it *were* California:

Marvin v Marvin
134 Cal Reptr 815, 557 P 2d 106 (1976), Supreme Court, State of California

Michelle Marvin contended that in 1964, she and the defendant, the film actor Lee Marvin, entered into an oral agreement that: 'while the parties lived together they would combine their efforts and earnings and would share equally any and all property accumulated as a result of their efforts whether individual or combined.' Furthermore, she said that they had agreed to hold themselves out to the general public as husband and wife, and that she would 'further render her services as a companion, housekeeper and cook.' She gave up what she said was a lucrative career as an entertainer and a singer to devote herself full time to Lee Marvin. She alleged that she lived with the defendant for six years and fulfilled her obligations under the agreement. When the relationship broke up, the plaintiff sought a declaration of constructive trust upon one-half of the property acquired during the course of the relationship.

Tobriner J: We base our opinion on the principle that adults who voluntarily live together and engage in sexual relations are nonetheless as competent as any other persons to contract respecting their earnings and property rights. Of course, they cannot lawfully contract to pay for the performance of sexual services, for such a contract is, in essence, an agreement for prostitution and unlawful for that reason. But they may agree to pool their earnings and to hold all property acquired during the relationship in accord with the law governing community property; conversely they may agree that each partner's earnings and the property acquired from those earnings remains the separate property of the earning partner. So long as the agreement does not rest upon illicit meretricious consideration, the parties may order their economic affairs as they choose, and no policy precludes the courts from enforcing such agreements.

In the present instance, plaintiff alleges that the parties agreed to pool their earnings, that they contracted to share equally in all property acquired, and that defendant agreed to support plaintiff. The terms of the contract as alleged do not rest upon any unlawful consideration. We therefore conclude that the complaint furnishes a suitable basis upon which the trial court can render declaratory relief.

The court went on to add that, in the absence of an express agreement, the court may look to a variety of other remedies in order to protect the parties' legitimate expectations:

The courts may inquire into the conduct of the parties to determine whether that conduct demonstrates an implied contract or implied agreement of partnership or joint venture ..., or some other tacit understanding between the parties. The courts may, when appropriate, employ principles of constructive trust ... or resulting trust. ... Finally, a nonmarital partner may recover in quantum meruit for the reasonable value of household services rendered. ...

We conclude that the judicial barriers that may stand in the way of a policy based upon the fulfillment of the reasonable expectations of the parties to a nonmarital relationship should be removed.

The mores of the society have indeed changed so radically in regard to cohabitation that we cannot impose a standard based on alleged moral considerations that have apparently been so widely abandoned by so many. Lest we be misunderstood, however, we take this occasion to point out that the structure of society itself largely depends upon the institution of marriage, and nothing we have said in this opinion should be taken to derogate from that institution. The joining of the man and woman in marriage is at once the most socially productive and individually fulfilling relationship that one can enjoy in the course of a lifetime.

There was further litigation in this case culminating in the California Court of Appeal (1981) (122 Cal App 3d 871) deleting the trial judge's rehabilitative award of $104,000 to the plaintiff. The Appellate Court held that there was no basis for a finding of damage or unjust enrichment, and there was no evidence of a wrongful act on the part of the defendant with respect to either the relationship or its termination.

Question

Perhaps the situation between England and California is not all that different?

As well as the constructive trust, other legal mechanisms have been employed by the courts to deal with this kind of situation.

Tanner v Tanner
[1975] 3 All ER 776, [1975] 1 WLR 1346, 119 Sol Jo 391, 5 Fam Law 193, Court of Appeal

The facts of this case are given in the judgment of Lord Denning MR:

In 1968 Mr Eric Tanner, the plaintiff, was a milkman during the day and a croupier at night. He had been married for many years. He had a daughter then aged 19 and a son aged 12. They lived together at 26 Achilles Road in West Hampstead. But, to use his own words, he got 'disgusted' with his marriage and went out and had 'a good time.' He went out with three women, he said, 'simultaneously,' meaning separately but during the same weeks or months. One of these women was an attractive Irish girl, Miss Josephine MacDermott, the defendant. She was a cook in a nursing home. She had a flat in 33 Steels Road, Hampstead, on the third floor. He visited her frequently. She became pregnant by him. She took his name and became known as Mrs Tanner. In November 1969 she gave birth to twin daughters. They decided it was best to get a house for her and the twin babies. They found one at 4 Theobalds Avenue, North Finchley. The plaintiff borrowed a sum on mortgage with a local authority. In applying for it, he filled in a form. He said that he was 45. His wife was 41. He had a son aged 14, a daughter age 20 and twin daughters of 6 months. That was a very misleading application, because he was not getting it for his wife and his older children. He wanted it for the defendant and the twin babies. By means of that misrepresentation the plaintiff got the house on mortgage. It was in his own name. The defendant and the baby twins moved in there. She brought a good deal of her furniture and spent £150 on furnishings for it. She moved into the ground floor. They let the first floor. She managed the lettings and collected the rent. Previously, whilst she was in her flat in Steels Road, Hampstead, the plaintiff had paid her £5 a week maintenance for the twins. But after she moved into Theobalds Avenue he paid her nothing for them or for her. She got a supplementary allowance under social security from the local authority.

This was an appeal by the defendant against the order of the county court for vacation of the premises.

Lord Denning MR: It is said that they were only licensees – bare licensees – under a licence revocable at will: and that the plaintiff was entitled in law to turn her and the twins out on a moment's notice. I cannot believe that this is the law. This man had a moral duty to provide for the babies of whom he was the father. I would go further. I think he had a legal duty towards them. Not only towards the babies. But also towards their mother. She was looking after them and bringing them up. In order to fulfil his duty towards the babies, he was under a duty to provide for the mother too. She had given up her flat where she was protected by the Rent Acts – at least in regard to rent and it may be in regard also to security of tenure. She had given it up at his instance so as to be able the better to bring up the children. It is impossible to suppose that in that situation she and the babies were bare licensees whom he could turn out at a moment's notice. ... In all the circumstances it is to be implied that she had a licence – a contractual licence – to have accommodation in the house for herself and the children so long as they were of school age and the accommodation was reasonably required for her and the children. There was, it is true, no express contract to that effect, but the circumstances are such that the court should imply a contract by the plaintiff – or, if need be, impose the equivalent of a contract by him – whereby they were entitled to have the use of the house as their home until the girls had finished school. It may be that if circumstances changed – so that the accommodation was not reasonably required – the licence might be determinable. But it was not determinable in the circumstances in which he sought to determine it, namely, to turn the defendant out with the children and to bring in his new wife with her family. It was a contractual licence of the kind which is specifically enforceable on her behalf: and which the plaintiff can be restrained from breaking; and he could not sell the house over her head so as to get her out in that way.

Browne LJ: ... I agree that there was here a licence by the plaintiff to the defendant for good consideration: it could not be revoked at will. What has troubled me is what the duration of this licence was to be. With some hesitation I agree with Lord Denning MR's view of what it was to be; that is, in substance it was a licence to the defendant to occupy accommodation in the house so long as the children were of school age and such accommodation was reasonably required for her and the twins, subject to any relevant change of circumstances, such as her remarriage.

There was no express contract in *Tanner v Tanner*. However, the court decided that it could infer the existence of a contractual licence because of the presence of consideration, namely the giving up of the flat and looking after their children.

Nevertheless, the contractual licence has only very rarely been used. A more fruitful device has been proprietary estoppel. This was described by Edward Nugee QC (sitting as a Deputy High Court Judge) in *Re Basham* [1987] 1 All ER 405 at 410 as follows:

Where one person, A, has acted to his detriment on the faith of a belief, which was known to and encouraged by another person, B, that he either has [been] or is going to be given a right in or over B's property, B cannot insist on his strict legal rights if to do so would be inconsistent with A's belief.

Thus we are looking at one person encouraging another, by words or actions, to act to his detriment, rather than at an agreement or common intention. Proprietary estoppel differs from the constructive trust, at least in theory, in that the interest awarded to the claimant is at the court's discretion. Patricia Ferguson (1985) explains:

Conceptually the constructive trust is closer to the resulting trust than to proprietary estoppel. Both constructive and resulting trusts are mechanisms whereby the conduct of the parties leads by operation of law to the creation of a proprietary interest. ... Estoppel is conceptually different ..., the remedy for estoppel is discretionary and may be merely personal.

Pascoe v Turner
[1979] 2 All ER 945, [1979] 1 WLR 431, 123 Sol Jo 164, 9 Fam Law 82, Court of Appeal

In 1961, the plaintiff met the defendant, a widow. In 1963, the defendant moved into the plaintiff's home, at first as his housekeeper. In 1964, the plaintiff and defendant began to 'live in every sense as man and wife'. In 1965, they moved to another house. The plaintiff paid the purchase price and he also paid for the contents. In 1973, the plaintiff moved out. The defendant stayed on in the house and, in reliance upon the plaintiff's declarations that he had given her the house and the contents, she spent money and herself did work on redecorations, improvements and repairs. In 1976, the plaintiff tried to evict the defendant from the house. It was the man's determination to get her out of the house which persuaded the Court of Appeal to conclude that a fee simple rather than a life licence was the right answer.

Cumming Bruce LJ: ... The principle to be applied is that the court should consider all the circumstances and, the (defendant) having no perfected gift or licence other than a licence revocable at will, the court must decide what is the minimum equity to do justice to her having regard to the way in which she changed her position for the worse by reason of the acquiescence and encouragement of the legal owner. The defendant submits that the only appropriate way in which equity can here be satisfied is by perfecting the imperfect gift as was done in *Dillwyn v Llewelyn* (1862) 4 De GF & J 517.

This court appreciates that the moneys laid out by the defendant were much less than in some of the cases in the books. But the court has to look at all the circumstances. When the plaintiff left her she was, we were told, a widow in her middle fifties. During the period that she lived with the plaintiff her capital was reduced from £4,500 to £1,000. Save for her invalidity pension that was all that she had in the world. In reliance upon the plaintiff's declaration of gift, encouragement and acquiescence she arranged her affairs on the basis that the house and contents belonged to her. So relying, she devoted a quarter of her remaining capital and her personal effort upon the house and its fixtures. In addition she bought carpets, curtains and furniture for it, with the result that by the date of the trial she had only £300 left. Compared to her, on the evidence the plaintiff is a rich man. He might not regard an expenditure of a few hundred pounds as a very grave loss. But the court has to regard her change of position over the years 1973 to 1976.

We take the view that the equity cannot here be satisfied without granting a remedy which assures to the defendant security of tenure, quiet enjoyment, and freedom of action in respect of repairs and improvements without interference from the plaintiff. The history of the conduct of the plaintiff since 9 April 1976, in relation to these proceedings leads to an irresistible inference that he is determined to pursue his purpose of evicting her from the house by any legal means at his disposal with a ruthless disregard of the obligations binding upon conscience. The court must grant a remedy effective to protect her against the future manifestations of his ruthlessness. It was conceded that if she is granted a licence, such a licence cannot be registered as a land charge, so that she may find herself ousted by a purchaser for value without notice.

If she has in the future to do further and more expensive repairs she may only be able to finance them by a loan, but as a licensee she cannot charge the house. The plaintiff as legal owner may well find excuses for entry in order to do what he may plausibly represent as necessary works and so contrive to derogate from her enjoyment of the licence in ways that make it difficult or impossible for the court to give her effective protection.

Weighing such considerations this court concludes that the equity to which the facts in this case give rise can only be satisfied by compelling the plaintiff to give effect to his promise and her expectations. He has so acted that he must now perfect the gift.

Coombes v Smith
[1986] 1 WLR 808, [1987] 1 FLR 352, High Court, Chancery Division

The plaintiff, Mrs Coombes, sought relief against the defendant, Mr Smith in respect of property owned by the defendant but in which the plaintiff had been living since 1977. She sought an order that the defendant convey and transfer the property to her absolutely. As an alternative, she sought a declaration that the defendant was bound to allow her to occupy the property during her life and to discharge the mortgage. The plaintiff's action was based on proprietary estoppel and contractual licence. The trial judge distinguished *Pascoe v Turner* [1979] 2 All ER 945, [1979] 1 WLR 431, CA (see p. 175, above) on the ground that in this case the plaintiff had not held a belief that she would have a right to remain in the house indefinitely, and she had not acted to her detriment in any way on the facts of the case (this was despite becoming pregnant, leaving her husband, looking after the house and child, improving the house and not looking for a job!). On the contractual licence point, the judge, Jonathan Parker QC, said:

Nor in the instant case is there any evidence before me as to the plaintiff's circumstances when she was living with her husband, save that they were living in a council maisonette, and that the marriage was not a happy one. This is in contrast to *Tanner v Tanner* [1975] 1 WLR 1346, where the court found that the defendant was granted a licence in consideration for her giving up her rent-controlled flat and looking after the children in the new property. All I am left with in the instant case is the mere fact that the plaintiff decided to leave her husband and move to 67, Bulwark Road, with a view to the defendant joining her there subsequently. No doubt the plaintiff hoped that her relationship with the defendant would prove happier than her marriage had been, and that the defendant would look after her. But on the evidence before me I am wholly unable to infer an enforceable contract under which, as from the moment when the plaintiff moved to 67, Bulwark Road, the defendant became obliged to provide a roof over her head for the rest of her life. Nor was any lesser contractual right either pleaded or contended for. Accordingly, in my judgment, the plaintiff's claim based on contractual licence fails.

In the result, the action was dismissed on the defendant's undertaking to provide free accommodation at the house for the plaintiff and child until the child was 17.

Questions

(i) Given the undertaking by the defendant, is the result any different in this case to *Tanner v Tanner*?
(ii) Is it consideration to look after the child of the relationship?
(iii) In *Layton v Martin* [1986] 2 FLR 227 (see p. 169, above for the discussion on constructive trusts), the judge dismissed the claim based on proprietary estoppel. He said that the question whether an owner of property could by insisting on his strict legal rights defeat an expectation of an interest which he had raised by his conduct could not arise otherwise than in connection with some specific asset. A mere promise of 'financial security' did not suffice. Can you distinguish *Layton v Martin* from *Pascoe v Turner*, and if so, how?

Naturally, none of these property law concepts is restricted to the enforcement of claims by women against men, as the following two cases illustrate.

Walton v Walton
14 April 1994, CA (Lexis transcript)

This was a claim by Alfred Walton, who had worked on the farm that had belonged to his father and grandfather since he was 15 in 1960. His father died in 1962, and thereafter he worked for his mother; at some times of the year he worked a 70 hour week. When compared with the minimum agricultural wage for that period, his pay was very poor; he received considerably less than a farm worker who did no overtime. Hoffmann LJ explained:

From time to time he complained. His mother would tell him that he could not expect more because he was working for his future. 'You can't have more money and a farm one day,' was her stock phrase.

During that period he married and had two children. From 1977 his circumstances improved as his mother rearranged her business affairs so as to enable him to draw on the profits of the farm. In the years that followed

... he incurred expenditure ... by making improvements with his own labour and money which would otherwise have been profits which he could draw from the business. All these acts were to his detriment.

In 1988 Mrs Walton senior contracted to sell the farm to a neighbouring landowner; Alfred issued proceedings, and shortly afterwards his mother died. In her will she disposed of her property in such a way that the farm would have had to be sold to meet pecuniary legacies, leaving a small residue for the plaintiff's children and nothing for the plaintiff. He therefore pursued his claim on the basis of estoppel. Hoffmann LJ explained:

Mrs Walton's promise was not, of course, made under seal and ... I do not think that it was part of a contract. So if there was nothing more than the promise, she would have been free to change her mind. ... But the position is different if the person who has been promised some interest in the property has, in reliance upon it, incurred expense or made sacrifices which he would not otherwise have made. In such a case the law will provide a remedy. It can take various forms. It may order the maker of the promise to provide compensation for the expense which has been incurred. It may make payment of compensation a charge on the property. Or it may require the promise to be kept.

In this case, he concluded, there were various options:

The plaintiff says [the court should order] a transfer to him of the farm, subject to the existing mortgage. ... [Counsel for the defendant] puts forward various alternative proposals. One is that the transfer should be subject to a payment of £50,000, representing what Mrs Walton might have required to buy herself a house if she had moved off the farm during her lifetime. But Mrs Walton did not move off the farm and now has no need of a house. The only effect of the payment would be to provide money for the payment of the legacy to her niece. She seems to me to have no equitable claim superior to that of the plaintiff's right to take the farm in whatever state it was at the date of Mrs Walton's death. An alternative proposal is that the plaintiff should take a life interest (or, to avoid making him tenant for life under the Settled Land Act 1925, an agricultural tenancy for life) with remainder to his son Simon. ... There is no evidence that Mrs Walton ever told the plaintiff that he could expect only a life interest with remainder to Simon. ... In my judgment, therefore, the only way to satisfy the equity on the plaintiff's favour is to order a transfer to him of the farm subject to the mortgage.

In *Wayling v Jones* (1993) 69 P & CR 170, CA, the plaintiff, Paul Wayling, had lived with Daniel Jones as his homosexual partner from 1971 until Mr Jones' death in 1987. Throughout that time Mr Wayling worked for Mr Jones, helping him to run various hotel businesses; in return he received little more than pocket money. On more than one occasion Mr Jones promised Mr Wayling that he would leave him, in his will, the hotel they were running at the time. He did not do so. Mr Wayling's claim, based upon proprietary estoppel, foundered in the County Court on the issue of reliance. Balcombe LJ in the Court of Appeal set out the parts of Mr Wayling's evidence that were fatal to his claim at first instance:

In his affidavit evidence the plaintiff stated that he relied on the deceased's promises. In his oral evidence in chief he said:

Q: One question, Mr Wayling. Assuming you were in the Hotel Royal bar, before Dan's death and Dan was there, if Dan had told you that he was not going to give the Royal Hotel to you but to somebody else after his death, what would you have done?
A: I would have left.

... Later in cross-examination came the following questions and answers:

Q: If he had not made that promise to you, would you still have stayed with him?
A: Yes ... .
Q: Just to continue on from that. So far as you are concerned, from that reply you gave, you would have remained with the deceased whether or not he made the promises?
A: Whatever business venture he would have had, yes.
Q: The promises were not the reason why you remained with the deceased?
A: No, we got on very well together.

The Court of Appeal held that, nevertheless, Mr Wayling had relied upon the promises made to him. Balcombe LJ said that 'the only question that mattered' was the one asked in examination-in-chief, namely, 'What would you have done if the deceased had told you that he was no longer prepared to implement his promises?' The court was not concerned with the hypothetical question, 'What would you have done if the promises had not been made?' Accordingly, the plaintiff's claim succeeded. As the hotel had by the date of the hearing been sold, he was awarded the net proceeds of sale.

Question

What is meant by 'reliance upon a promise'? For some doubts on the views expressed by the Court of Appeal here, see Cooke (1995).

Look back again at *Eves v Eves* and at *Grant v Edwards* (pp. 164, 169). These cases were decided on the principles of the constructive trust and therefore on the basis of an agreement between the parties. Gardiner (1993) has this to say about that finding:

In *Eves v Eves* and *Grant v Edwards*, the court found an *express* agreement that a woman should have a share in a house owned by her partner. In both, the woman's only hope of success lay with the finding of an express agreement, because she had not made the direct financial contribution needed to allow discovery of an implied agreement. But in both, the partner had explicitly told the woman that she was not to have a share. So on the face of it, there was most decidedly no agreement that she should. The courts based their contrary finding on the fact that in each case the man had added a reason for this refusal to let the woman share the house, which was in truth a bad reason. In one case, it was that at 20 years of age the woman was legally too young to have an interest in land; in the other, it was that any share she had would cause some prejudice in the matrimonial proceedings she was currently undergoing with her estranged husband. In each case the court characterised this as an "excuse", and went on to say that the man's giving an excuse showed that he actually acknowledged the existence of an agreement that the woman should have a share.

But the fact that the men's statements were excuses (i.e. neither objectively valid nor even sincerely uttered) does not mean that the men were thereby acknowledging an agreement whereby the woman should have a share. If I give an excuse for rejecting an invitation to what I expect to be a dull party, it does not mean that I thereby agree to come: on the contrary, it means that I do not agree to come, but for one reason or another find it hard to say so outright. The fallacious quality of the reasoning in *Eves v Eves* and *Grant v Edwards* is thus clear. It is hard to think that the judges concerned really believed in it. One can only conclude that they too were engaged in the business of inventing agreements on women's behalf, but this time widening the catchment beyond merely those women who work outside the home.

The facts of *Hammond v Mitchell* [1991] 1 WLR 1127, [1992] 1 FLR 233, were that Mr H and Miss M began living together in 1977, and in 1979 Mr H bought a bungalow as a home for them both and their child. He explained to Miss M that the bungalow must be put in his name because of tax problems connected with his divorce, but assured her: 'Don't worry about the future because when we are married it will be half yours anyway and I'll always look after you and the boy.' Subsequently Miss M participated in Mr H's business activities, including two speculative ventures which involved considerable financial risk. In proceedings between them when the relationship broke down after 11 years, Mr H's statements were taken as evidence of an understanding between the parties that the Miss M was to have a beneficial interest in the property, as a result of which she acted to her detriment. Linda Clarke and Rod Edmunds, in *H v M: Equity and the Essex Cohabitant* (1992), comment:

With respect, this could be seen as an ex post facto rationalisation, necessary in order to give the worthy claimant an interest in the property. Strictly speaking, the conduct in the present case (especially the words spoken after the bungalow had been acquired) looks less like a bilateral understanding or agreement and more in the nature of a unilateral assurance by Mr H that once married (an event which never took place) Miss M would have an interest in the bungalow. Such an assurance, like that made to the mistress in *Pascoe v Turner*, might then be relied upon to assert a successful proprietary estoppel claim.

Question

Do you think that the law is in need of any rationalisation in this area? What solution can you suggest?

4 Legislative interventions

Charles Harpum, in *Adjusting Property Rights between Unmarried Cohabitees* (1982) states:

What is required is a broad statutory discretion (broader than that conferred by the Matrimonial Causes Act 1973 because the situations that exist are far more varied) to adjust the rights of cohabitees when they cease to live together. Already by statute, on the death of one cohabitee the other may have a claim against the estate of the deceased for reasonable financial provision, if the survivor was in some way economically dependent on the deceased: s. 1(1)(*e*) of the Inheritance (Provision for Family and Dependants) Act 1975. If on death, why not in life? The example of the 1975 Act could be followed and the trigger for the discretion could be a situation of total or partial economic dependence by one cohabitee on the other. The sooner such legislation is enacted the better.

(a) AUSTRALIA AND CANADA

One of the most significant legislative interventions comes from New South Wales where the De Facto Relationships Act 1984 was passed to put into effect the recommendations of the New South Wales Law Reform Commission (1983) relating both to property rights and to contractual claims.

14.—(1) Subject to this Part, a de facto partner may apply to a court for an order under this Part for the adjustment of interests with respect to the property of the de facto partners or either of them or for the granting of maintenance, or both.

(2) An application referred to in subsection (1) may be made whether or not any other application for any remedy or relief is or may be made under this Act or any other law.

...

17.—(1) Except as provided by subsection (2), a court shall not make an order under this Part unless it is satisfied that the parties to the application have lived together in a de facto relationship for a period of not less than 2 years.

(2) A court may make an order under this Part where it is satisfied –

(*a*) that there is a child of the parties to the application; or

(*b*) that the applicant –

(i) has made substantial contributions of the kind referred to in section 20(1)(*a*) or (*b*) for which the applicant would otherwise not be adequately compensated if the order were not made; or

(ii) has the care and control of a child of the respondent,

and that the failure to make the order would result in serious injustice to the applicant.

18.—(1) Except as provided by subsections (2) and (3), where de facto partners have ceased to live together as husband and wife on a bona fide domestic basis, an application to a court for an order under this Part shall be made before the expiration of the period of 2 years after the day on which they ceased, or last ceased, as the case may require, to so live together.

(2) A court may, at any time after the expiration of the period referred to in subsection (1), grant leave to a de facto partner to apply to the court for an order under this Part (other than an order under section 27(1) made where the court is satisfied as to the matters specified in section 27(1)(*b*)) where the court is satisfied, having regard to such matters as it considers relevant, that greater hardship would be caused to the applicant if that leave were not granted than would be caused to the respondent if that leave were granted.

(3) Where, under subsection (2), a court grants a de facto partner leave to apply to the court for an order under this Part, the de facto partner may apply accordingly.

19. In proceedings for an order under this Part, a court shall, so far as is practicable, make such orders as will finally determine the financial relationships between the de facto partners and avoid further proceedings between them.

20.—(1) On an application by a de facto partner for an order under this Part to adjust interests with respect to the property of the de facto partners or either of them, a court may make such order adjusting the interests of the partners in the property as to it seems just and equitable having regard to –

(*a*) the financial and non-financial contributions made directly or indirectly by or on behalf of the de facto partners to the acquisition, conservation or improvement of any of the property of the partners or either of them or to the financial resources of the partners or either of them; and

(*b*) the contributions, including any contribution made in the capacity of homemaker or parent, made by either of the de facto partners to the welfare of the other de facto partner or to the welfare of the family constituted by the partners and one or more of the following namely:

(i) a child of the partners;

(ii) a child accepted by the partners or either of them into the household of the partners, whether or not the child is a child of either of the partners.

(2) A court may make an order under subsection (1) in respect of property whether or not it has declared the title or rights of a de facto partner in respect of the property. ...

45.—(1) Notwithstanding any rule of public policy to the contrary, a man and a woman who are not married to each other may enter into a cohabitation agreement or separation agreement.

(2) Nothing in a cohabitation agreement or separation agreement affects the power of a court to make an order with respect to the right to custody of, maintenance of or access to or otherwise in relation to the children of the parties to the agreement.

46. Except as otherwise provided by this Part, a cohabitation agreement or separation agreement shall be subject to and enforceable in accordance with the law of contract, including, without limiting the generality of this section, the Contracts Review Act, 1980.

47.—(1) Where, on an application by a de facto partner for an order under Part III, a court is satisfied –

(*a*) that there is a cohabitation agreement or separation agreement between the de facto partners;

(*b*) that the agreement is in writing;

(*c*) that the agreement is signed by the partner against whom it is sought to be enforced;

(*d*) that each partner was, before the time at which the agreement was signed by him or her, as the case may be, furnished with a certificate in or to the effect of the prescribed form by a solicitor which states that, before that time, the solicitor advised that partner, independently of the other partner, as to the following matters:

(i) the effect of the agreement on the rights of the partners to apply for an order under Part III;

(ii) whether or not, at that time, it was to the advantage, financially or otherwise, of that partner to enter into the agreement;

(iii) whether or not, at that time, it was prudent for that partner to enter into the agreement;

(iv) whether or not, at that time and in the light of such circumstances as were, at that time, reasonably foreseeable, the provisions of the agreement were fair and reasonable; and

(*e*) that the certificates referred to in paragraph (*d*) are endorsed on or annexed to or otherwise accompany the agreement.

the court shall not, except as provided by sections 49 and 50, make an order under Part III in so far as the order would be inconsistent with the terms of the agreement.

(2) Where, on an application by a de facto partner for an order under Part III, a court is satisfied that there is a cohabitation agreement or separation agreement between the de facto partners, but the court is not satisfied as to any one or more of the matters referred to in subsection (1)(*b*), (*c*), (*d*) or (*e*), the court may make such order as it could have made if there were no cohabitation agreement or separation agreement between the partners, but in making its orders, the court, in addition to the matters to which it is required to have regard under Part III, may have regard to the terms of the cohabitation agreement or separation agreement.

(3) A court may make an order referred to in subsection (2) notwithstanding that the cohabitation agreement or separation agreement purports to exclude the jurisdiction of the court to make that order.

48. Where a cohabitation agreement or separation agreement does not satisfy any one or more of the matters referred to in section 47(1)(*b*), (*c*), (*d*) or (*e*), the provisions of the agreement may, in proceedings other than an application for an order under Part III, be enforced notwithstanding that the cohabitation agreement purports to exclude the jurisdiction of a court under Part III to make such an order.

49.—(1) On an application by a de facto partner for an order under Part III, a court may vary or set aside the provisions, or any one or more of the provisions, of a cohabitation agreement (but not a separation agreement) made between the de facto partners, being a cohabitation agreement which satisfies the matters referred to in section 47(1)(*b*), (*c*), (*d*) and (*e*), where, in the opinion of the court, the circumstances of the partners have so changed since the time at which the agreement was entered into that it would lead to serious injustice if the provisions of the agreement, or any one or more of them, were, whether on the application for the order under Part III or on any other application for any remedy or relief under any other Act or any other law, to be enforced.

(2) A court may, pursuant to subsection (1), vary or set aside the provisions, or any one or more of the provisions, of a cohabitation agreement notwithstanding any provision of the agreement to the contrary.

50. Without limiting or derogating from the provisions of section 46, on an application by a de facto partner for an order under Part III, a court is not required to give effect to the terms of any cohabitation agreement or separation agreement entered into by that partner where the court is of the opinion –

(*a*) that the de facto partners have, by their words or conduct, revoked or consented to the revocation of the agreement; or

(*b*) that the agreement has otherwise ceased to have effect.

For a discussion of these provisions see Parkinson, 'The Property Rights of Cohabitees – Is Statutory Reform the Answer?' in *Frontiers of Family Law*, ed. Bainham, Pearl and Pickford (1995).

Question

Is this what Harpum (see p. 180) is suggesting for England?

(b) SCOTLAND

The Scottish Law Commission's Discussion Paper on the *Effects of Cohabitation on Private Law* (1990) describes the New South Wales Act as well as other legislation from Australia and Canada.

5.2 Several Canadian provinces have enacted legislation which enables a cohabitant to apply to a court, during the cohabitation or within a specified period after its end, for an order for support against the other cohabitant. [Institute of Law Research and Reform, Alberta, *Towards Reform of the Law Relating to Cohabitation Outside Marriage* (Issues Paper No 2, 1987).] The details vary. In Ontario, for example, an application may be made by

'either a man or a woman who are not married to each other and have cohabited

(*a*) continuously for a period of not less than 3 years, or

(*b*) in a relationship of some permanence if they are the natural or adoptive parents of a child.' [Family Law Act 1986, s. 29. The New Brunswick Family Services Act 1980 s. 112(3) is broadly similar.]

In Manitoba the required period of cohabitation is 1 year if there is a child of the union and 5 years if there is not. [Family Maintenance Act 1978 (as amended) s. 2(3).] In British Columbia the required period of cohabitation is not less than 2 years, whether or not there is a child of the union. [Family Relations Act 1979, s. 1(*c*).] In Nova Scotia one year's cohabitation as husband and wife suffices [Family Maintenance Act 1980 (as amended) s. 2(*m*)], while in the Yukon Territory all that is required is cohabitation in a relationship of some permanence. [Matrimonial

Property and Family Support Ordinance 1979 (as amended) s. 30.6.] In a recent report the Alberta Law Reform Institute has, by a majority, recommended that an order for the maintenance of one cohabitant by the other should be possible where

'(i) the applicant for maintenance has the care and control of a child of the cohabitational relationship and is unable to support himself or herself adequately by reason of the child care responsibilities; or

(ii) the earning capacity of the applicant has been adversely affected by the cohabitational relationship and some transitional maintenance is required to help the applicant to re-adjust his or her life.' [*Towards Reform of the Law Relating to Cohabitation Outside Marriage* (Report No 53, 1989).]

5.3 There have also been interesting developments in Australia. One of them took place more than a hundred and fifty years ago. Tasmania has had since 1837 a provision [now in s. 16 of the Maintenance Act 1967] enabling a woman who has cohabited with a man for at least a year to obtain a maintenance order if the man, without just cause or excuse, leaves her without adequate means of support, or deserts her, or is guilty of such misconduct as to make it unreasonable to expect her to continue to live with him. More recently, New South Wales, following on a report by the New South Wales Law Reform Commission [1983] passed the De Facto Relationships Act of 1984. This allows a cohabitant, who must normally have cohabited with his or her partner for at least two years, to claim maintenance if he or she is unable to support himself or herself adequately and if the inability is due either to having the care of a child of the union or to having suffered a reduction in earning capacity as a result of the cohabitation. An order based on the applicant's reduced earning capacity resulting from the cohabitation ceases 3 years from the date of the order or 4 years from the end of the cohabitation, whichever is earlier. The Act also gives the court power to make such order adjusting the interests of the cohabitants in their property as seems just and equitable, having regard to their contributions (financial or otherwise) to the property and to their financial resources. In Victoria, the Property Law (Amendment) Act 1988 enables a court in settling property disputes between cohabitants to take into account contributions of various kinds to the property of the cohabitants and the welfare of the family. The Northern Territory Law Reform Committee in its Report on *De Facto Relationships* [1988] recommended rules on maintenance and property adjustment similar, in their essential features, to those enacted in New South Wales.

The Scottish Discussion Paper (1990) identified a number of options for reform; the Scottish Law Commission's subsequent *Report on Family Law* (1992) reviewed these options and reported on the responses to consultation. The approach taken was to consider whether or not various aspects of the law on financial provision on divorce in Scotland should be made applicable to cohabitants (see p. 305, below).

16.15 We do not favour a comprehensive system of financial provision on termination of cohabitation comparable to the system of financial provision on divorce in the Family Law (Scotland) Act 1985. That would be to impose a regime of property sharing, and in some cases continuing financial support, on couples who may well have opted for cohabitation in order to avoid such consequences. Almost all consultees agreed with our provisional view that there was no adequate justification for applying to cohabitants the principle of equal sharing of property in section 9(1)(*a*) of the Family Law (Scotland) Act 1985. There was also general support for our provisional view that one cohabitant should not be ordered, on termination of the cohabitation, to make financial provision for the other on principles analogous to those in section 9(1)(*d*) or 9(1)(*e*) of the Family Law (Scotland) Act 1985. Section 9(1)(*d*) relates to an award of short-term financial support to enable one party to adjust, over a period of not more than three years from the date of the divorce, to the loss of financial support from the other. Almost all consultees considered that this would be inappropriate on the termination of a cohabitation, given that there would be no obligation of support during the cohabitation and that cases involving child care or compensation for contributions or sacrifices in the interests of the family could be otherwise covered. Section 9(1)(*e*) is concerned with the relief of long-term financial hardship which is likely *as a result of the divorce*. Again, this is linked to the loss of the obligation of support which exists during marriage and almost all consultees agreed with our provisional view that it would be inappropriate to apply it on the termination of a cohabitation. In the public opinion survey, respondents were shown a card saying

> 'Suppose that a couple cohabited for 5 years and then separated. They have no child. Should the one who is better off financially be bound to pay aliment (or maintenance) to the other?'

Over three-quarters (76%) of all respondents thought that the one who was better off should not be bound to pay aliment to the other. ... This ... was the only question which resulted in a negative response in relation to improved rights for cohabitants. We therefore do not recommend the introduction of principles for property-sharing or financial provision, on or after the end of a cohabitation, corresponding to the principles on section 9(1)(*a*), (*d*) or (*e*) of the Family Law (Scotland) Act 1985.

16.16 In the discussion paper we favoured the introduction of a principle designed to share the economic burden of child-care after the end of a cohabitation. ... In the event, this ... has been overtaken by the provisions in the Child Support Act 1991. ...

16.17 We asked in the discussion paper whether, on the termination of a cohabitation, a cohabitant should be able to apply to a court for an order for financial provision based on the principle in section 9(1)(*b*) of the Family Law (Scotland) Act 1985. This provides that

> 'fair account should be taken of any economic advantage derived by either party from the contributions of the other, and of any economic disadvantage suffered by either party in the interests of the other party or of the family'.

If this principle were applied to cohabitants it would enable some provision to be made for cases where, for example, one party has worked unpaid for years helping to build up the other's business or one party has given up a good pensionable career in order to look after the children of the relationship. ...

16.18 The principle on section 9(1)(*b*) could be applied, quite readily and appropriately, to cohabitants. The argument for applying it is that it would be unfair to let economic gains and losses arising out of contributions or sacrifices made in the course of a relationship of cohabitation simply lie where they fall. To allow a remedy for the type of situation covered by section 9(1)(*b*) would not be to impose on cohabitants a solution based on a particular view of marriage. It would merely be to give them the benefit of a principle designed to correct imbalances arising out of the circumstances of a non-commercial relationship where the parties are quite likely to make contributions and sacrifices without counting the cost or bargaining for a return. ...

16.19 ... respondents to the public opinion survey ... were asked the following question.

> 'Suppose that a couple cohabited for some years. They do not have a child. They have now split up. During the cohabitation one of them worked unpaid to help build up the other's business. Should that person have any financial claim against the other because of this contribution to the other's wealth?'

Over four-fifths (85%) of respondents believed that a person should have such a financial claim. ...

16.23 We recommend that ...

(*a*) Where a cohabitation has terminated otherwise than by death, a former cohabitant should be able to apply to a court, within one year after the end of the cohabitation, for a financial provision on the basis of the principle in section 9(1)(*b*) of the Family Law (Scotland) Act 1985 – namely that fair account should be taken of any economic advantage derived by either party from contributions by the other, and of any economic disadvantage suffered by either party in the interests of the other party or of any child of the family.

...

(*d*) The court hearing an application should have power to award a capital sum (including a deferred capital sum and a capital sum payable by instalments) and to make an interim award.

Questions

(i) How would you have responded to the questions quoted here from the public opinion survey?
(ii) Do you agree with the Scottish Law Commission's recommendation and, if so, why?
(iii) In England, different considerations apply. Will it be necessary to introduce a law similar to the Family Law (Scotland) Act 1985 for divorcing couples prior to providing relief for former cohabitants, or would the extension of the principles in the Matrimonial Causes Act 1973 to former cohabitants suffice?

(iv) The Law Commission are investigating the property rights of unmarried cohabitants. Are there any suggestions that you would make on this topic?
(v) Charles Harpum, in *Cohabitation Consultation* (1995), wrote: 'Home-sharers are not denizens of some black hole of outlawry. Is it better for the law that regulates their affairs to be developed by legislation after an exhaustive consideration of the issues or should it continue to be left to the chances of litigation?' What is your view?

Although this recommendation from the Scottish Law Commission's Report on Family Law has not been enacted, Scots law has taken one inconspicuous step that has been under discussion recently in this jurisdiction. It will be recalled (see p. 149, above) that the Family Law Act 1996 enables a spouse to seek a transfer of certain types of tenancy on the granting of a decree of divorce, etc, or at any time thereafter. The Matrimonial Homes (Family Protection) (Scotland) Act 1981, ss. 18 and 13 gives this right to cohabitants.

The Family Law Act 1996 makes similar provisions for cohabitants (again, only in respect of tenancies with statutory security of tenure), so that, say, a girlfriend living in her boyfriend's council house could apply for an order that the tenancy be transferred to her. The court is required to bear a number of considerations in mind, including the housing needs and resources of each party, the health, safety and well-being of the parties and any child living with them, and the nature and length of the parties' relationship. The provisions are to be found in Part III of the Act which is concerned both with occupation rights and with mechanisms for protection from domestic violence; but there is no requirement that there need have been any violence or misconduct before such an order can be made.

Question

This provision for cohabitants has given rise to considerable controversy. It was originally contained in the Family Homes and Domestic Violence Bill 1995, and it was partly because of objections to this provision that the bill was withdrawn. Why do you think it was so controversial? Why do you suppose it was nevertheless retained when the provisions of the Family Homes and Domestic Violence Bill 1995 were reproduced, with modifications, in Part III of the Family Law Act 1996?

5 Property claims for children

When married parents divorce, the court can adjust the parents' property rights under the Matrimonial Causes Act 1973 (see Chapter 8, below), and will have as its 'first consideration ... the welfare while a minor of any child of the family who has not attained the age of eighteen' (s. 25(1)). The order made will provide a home for the children if possible. Unmarried couples cannot resort to this jurisdiction, and we have seen enough of the principles involved in property law to know that the party who is to look after the children may well be left homeless.

The Family Law Reform Act 1987 introduced a power for the court to make property adjustment orders in favour of children, following the recommendations made by the Law Commission in their Report on *Illegitimacy* (1982). Paragraph 1(2)(*d*) and (*e*) of Sch 1 of the Children Act 1989 enables the court to make:

> (*d*) an order requiring a settlement to be made for the benefit of the child, and to the satisfaction of the court, of property –
> (i) to which either parent is entitled (either in possession or in reversion); and
> (ii) which is specified in the order;
> (*e*) an order requiring either or both parents of a child –
> (i) to transfer to the applicant, for the benefit of the child; or
> (ii) to transfer to the child himself,
> such property to which the parent is, or the parents are, entitled (either in possession or in reversion) as may be specified in the order.'

This may enable the court to order the transfer of a council tenancy from one parent to the other, as in *K v K* [1992] 2 FLR 220, or to require one parent to settle a capital sum on a child, as in *H v P (Illegitimate Child: Capital Provision)* [1993] Fam Law 515. Such a settlement will be made so as to last for the child's minority or while he is in full-time education, rather than to make an outright transfer of a capital asset. In *A v A* [1994] 1 FLR 657 an application had been made for an order for the benefit of a child whose father was immensely wealthy; the settlement made for the child in *A v A* was described by Ward J as follows:

> The terms of the trust, the detail of which can be settled on further argument and if necessary with liberty to apply, should be that the property be conveyed to trustees, preferably … the nominees of the mother and father to hold the same for A for a term which shall terminate 6 months after A has attained the age of 18, or 6 months after she has completed her full-time education, which will include her tertiary education, whichever is latest. I give her that period of 6 months to find her feet and arrange her affairs. The trustees shall permit her to enjoy a reasonable gap between completing her school education and embarking upon her further education. I have regard to para 4(1)(*b*) which requires me to consider the financial needs, obligations and responsibilities of each parent and also subpara (*c*) which requires me to have regard to the financial needs of the child. The mother's obligation is to look after A, and A's financial need is to provide a roof over the head of her caretaker. It is, indeed, father's obligation to provide the accommodation for the live-in help which A needs. Consequently, it must be a term of the settlement that while A is under the control of her mother and thereafter for so long as A does not object, the mother shall have the right to occupy the property to the exclusion of the father without paying rent therefor for the purpose of providing a home and care and support for A.

Question

What would happen if the young lady decided, later in her teenage years, that she did object to her mother living in the house?

The facts of *A v A* are unrepresentative because of the father's great wealth. Nevertheless, similar provision could well be ordered in a family of more moderate means – see *T v S* [1994] 1 FCR 743, [1994] 2 FLR 883.

Obviously, the availability of these orders for children has an effect upon the housing position, and in some cases the property rights, of unmarried partners. Thus, while the mothers of the children concerned in *A v A* and

T v S obtained, as a side-effect of the order, the right to live in the child's home until it was eventually disposed of, the mother in *K v K* (above) had the council tenancy transferred to her on a permanent basis.

Question

How does a consideration of the orders available under Sch 1 of the Children Act 1989 affect your answer to question (iv) on p. 185?

6 Rights of inheritance

(a) FIXED SHARE FOR THE SURVIVING SPOUSE?

In their Working Paper (1971) the Law Commission discuss a system of inheritance under which a surviving spouse would be entitled as of right to a fixed proportion of the estate of the deceased spouse whether he died intestate or testate and regardless of the terms of the will:

0.37 Such a system is to be distinguished from community of property and from the right to apply for family provision. Although theoretically it could co-exist with 'community', it would be a needless complication in a law which recognised and enforced a genuine community of property; accordingly we discuss it as an alternative or substitute for 'community'. It differs from the law of family provision in that an order for family provision is discretionary [see p. 189, below], and the amount of the order is assessed having regard to the means, needs and conduct of the applicant. A legal right of inheritance would be a property right in no way dependent upon the means, needs and conduct of the surviving spouse, all of which factors would be irrelevant. The system put forward for consideration is comparable with systems in certain other countries, including Scotland.

0.39. Questions which arise are: –

(*a*) what minimum amount or proportion of the estate should go, *as of right*, to the survivor,
(*b*) whether a spouse should be able to waive a right of inheritance,
(*c*) whether, and if so, how benefits received from the deceased during his life should be taken into account,
(*d*) how to deal with dispositions made by the deceased with the intention of defeating rights of inheritance,
(*e*) the relationship between rights of inheritance and the intestacy rules,
(*f*) whether children should enjoy rights of inheritance.

0.40 We make a number of tentative suggestions as to the way in which these questions might be answered. For instance, we reach the provisional view that children should not have a legal right of inheritance; we suggest £2,000 or one-third of the estate (whichever is the greater) for the surviving spouse; and we indicate that it may be better not to complicate the law by seeking a solution within a system of rights of inheritance of the problems of benefits received or dispositions made during the lifetime of the deceased. The appropriate context in which to consider these problems may well be that of family provision, where the courts will continue to have a discretion to set aside dispositions and to make such financial orders as are considered necessary for the support of the survivor.

Question

Would this raise problems similar to those of common law dower?

The Working Paper itself drew attention to a major disadvantage of fixed rights of inheritance:

4.71 A system of legal rights would be an imprecise way of protecting the survivor's interest in the family assets. It would take no account of the fact that the bulk of the family assets might already be vested in the survivor: the survivor's assets would be irrelevant unless derived from the deceased. It would not be limited to that part of the deceased's estate which could properly be regarded as family assets, and since it would operate only on death it would create a distinction between property rights on divorce and those on death.

The First Report (1973) noted the lack of support for the principle of legal rights of inheritance for a surviving spouse:

38. In the light of all the comments and views received we have considered again the principle of fixed legal rights of inheritance for a surviving spouse and its relation to family provision law. If one were starting from the position as it was in England before the introduction of family provision law [in 1939], it would be necessary to consider the best means of protecting the interests of the family of a deceased person and to weigh up the relative advantages and disadvantages of an automatic system of legal rights and a discretionary system of family provision operating through an application to the court. However, as the Working Paper suggested, and as the results of our consultation confirm, the issue now is whether it is necessary to supplement or reinforce family provision law by a system of legal rights.
39. Under family provision law the court can, in the exercise of its discretion, take into account the means and needs of all the parties concerned.

The Law Commission recommend substantial improvements to the family provision legislation. They rejected the introduction of a principle under which the surviving spouse would have a *legal* right to inherit part of the estate of the deceased spouse.

(b) INTESTACY

Legal rights of inheritance are seldom of significance when a spouse dies intestate. Under the present law, the surviving spouse inherits personal chattels, a statutory legacy of £125,000 of the estate and a life interest in half of any residue where there are children; or the personal chattels, a statutory legacy of £200,000 plus half the balance where there are no children but other close relatives. In other cases, the surviving spouse inherits the whole estate.

In 1989 the Law Commission in their Report *Distribution on Intestacy* (1989) considered the position of the surviving spouse on intestacy.

17. There was virtually unanimous agreement among respondents to our working paper that the present law is in need of reform. Consultees also agreed that its principal defect is the failure to ensure adequate provision for a surviving spouse. There are several reasons for this.
18. First, the statuary legacy is often insufficient to ensure that the surviving spouse is able to remain in the matrimonial home, even though the estate is otherwise large enough to enable him or her to do so. House values vary considerably in different parts of the country and also rise (or fall) at different rates. A figure which is large enough to cover the price of an average home in central London would give a substantial surplus to widows living elsewhere. Secondly, even if the legacy is sufficient to retain the home, it will often leave the survivor with very little on which to live or maintain the home.
19. This basic defect is compounded by two other, more technical problems. First, even supposing that the purpose of the statutory legacy is to enable the survivor to keep the home, the present rules make no distinction according to how the home is owned or tenanted. If the home

was beneficially jointly owned by the couple, the survivor acquires the deceased's interest automatically and therefore receives the whole home and a full statutory legacy. If the couple were tenants in common, perhaps because they owned unequal shares or one had contributed to the purchase of the home in the other's name, the deceased's interest forms part of his or her estate and thus counts towards the statutory legacy. If the home was wholly owned by the deceased, of course, it will count. ... Such disparities in what survivors receive will often seem arbitrary and unfair.

20. Secondly, the statutory legacies must from time to time be uprated by statutory instrument. The legacy applicable is that in force at the date of death. This can lead to gross disparity in the treatment of deaths taking place on either side of the date on which the legacy changed. Further, if the survivor has the house appropriated, in or towards satisfaction of the legacy, the legacy is that at the date of death, whereas the house is valued at the date of appropriation which could be years later.

21. If these rules can produce results which seem arbitrary or unfair in relation to the surviving spouse, the same can be said in relation to issue or other relatives. The children's expectations will depend, not upon how well their surviving parent is provided for, but upon the nature and tenure of their deceased parent's assets.

22. A further defect of the present rules is that, in places, they are complex and expensive to administer. ...

They therefore recommended that on intestacy the surviving spouse should receive the whole estate.

When the Law Reform (Succession) Bill was introduced in the House of Lords in February 1995, Lord Mishcon pointed out that the Bill as drafted did not implement this recommendation, and it was agreed that the question be discussed further at the Committee stage. However, the Bill was not amended.

Question

Why do you suppose the recommendation has not been enacted?

(c) FAMILY PROVISION

Family provision legislation is a means of providing for family members for whom *either* the provisions of the deceased's will *or* the intestacy rules were not adequate.

Writing in 1974, Miller said that 'the aim of the present law of family provision is to ensure that reasonable provision is made for the *maintenance* of certain dependants of the deceased. It is not designed to enable members of the deceased's family to acquire a share in his estate without reference to their need for support, or in other words, dependency.'

The Law Commission at first advanced the belief that maintenance should remain as the governing factor. However, they subsequently had second thoughts and, so far as the wife is concerned, in their First Report (1973) recommended a change in objective:

41. At present, the aim, as expressed in the legislation, is to secure reasonable provision for the *maintenance* of the deceased's dependants, and this is clearly narrower in concept than the provision of a fair share (although in any particular case it may amount to much the same thing). 'Maintenance' is no longer the principal consideration in fixing the amount of financial provision for a spouse on divorce, and we have come to the conclusion that it would be anomalous to retain it as the main objective in determining family provision for a surviving spouse.

The recommendations of the Law Commission were enacted in the Inheritance (Provision for Family and Dependants) Act 1975 (as now slightly amended by the Family Law Act 1996):

1. Application for financial provision from deceased's estate

(1) Where after the commencement of this Act a person dies domiciled in England and Wales and is survived by any of the following persons: –

(*a*) the wife or husband of the deceased;

(*b*) a former wife or former husband of the deceased who has not remarried;

(*c*) a child of the deceased;

(*d*) any person (not being a child of the deceased) who, in the case of any marriage to which the deceased was at any time a party, was treated by the deceased as a child of the family in relation to that marriage;

(*e*) any person (not being a person included in the foregoing paragraphs of this subsection) who immediately before the death of the deceased was being maintained, either wholly or partly, by the deceased;

that person may apply to the court for an order under section 2 of this Act on the ground that the disposition of the deceased's estate effected by his will or the law relating to intestacy, or the combination of his will and that law, is not such as to make reasonable financial provision for the applicant.

(2) In this Act 'reasonable financial provision' –

(*a*) in the case of an application made by virtue of subsection (1)(*a*) above by the husband or wife of the deceased (except where at the date of death, a separation order under the Family Law Act 1996 was in force in relation to the marriage and the separation was continuing), means such financial provision as it would be reasonable in all the circumstances of the case for a husband or wife to receive, whether or not that provision is required for his or her maintenance;

(*b*) in the case of any other application made by virtue of subsection (1) above, means such financial provision as it would be reasonable in all the circumstances of the case for the applicant to receive for his maintenance.

(3) For the purposes of subsection (1)(*e*) above, a person shall be treated as being maintained by the deceased, either wholly or partly, as the case may be, if the deceased, otherwise than for full valuable consideration, was making a substantial contribution in money or money's worth towards the reasonable needs of that person.

2. Powers of court to make orders

(1) Subject to the provisions of this Act, where an application is made for an order under this section, the court may, if it is satisfied that the disposition of the deceased's estate effected by his will or the law relating to intestacy, or the combination of his will and that law, is not such as to make reasonable financial provision for the applicant, make any one or more of the following orders: –

(*a*) an order for the making to the applicant out of the net estate of the deceased of such periodical payments and for such term as may be specified in the order;

(*b*) an order for the payment to the applicant out of that estate of a lump sum of such amount as may be so specified;

(*c*) an order for the transfer to the applicant of such property comprised in that estate as may be so specified;

(*d*) an order for the settlement for the benefit of the applicant of such property comprised in that estate as may be so specified;

(*e*) an order for the acquisition out of property comprised in that estate of such property as may be so specified and for the transfer of the property so acquired to the applicant or for the settlement thereof for his benefit;

(*f*) an order varying any ante-nuptial or post-nuptial settlement (including such a settlement made by will) made on the parties to a marriage to which the deceased was one of the parties, the variation being for the benefit of the surviving party to that marriage, or any child of that marriage, or any person who was treated by the deceased as a child of the family in relation to that marriage.

(2) An order under subsection (1)(*a*) above providing for the making out of the net estate of the deceased of periodical payments may provide for –

(*a*) payments of such amount as may be specified in the order,

(*b*) payments equal to the whole of the income of the net estate or of such portion thereof as may be so specified, (*c*) payments equal to the whole of the income of such part of the net estate as the court may direct to be set aside or appropriated for the making out of the income thereof of payments under this section,

or may provide for the amount of the payments or any of them to be determined in any other way the court thinks fit.

(3) Where an order under subsection (1)(*a*) above provides for the making of payments of an amount specified in the order, the order may direct that such part of the net estate as may be so specified shall be set aside or appropriated for the making out of the income thereof those payments; but no larger part of the net estate shall be so set aside or appropriated than is sufficient, at the date of the order, to produce by the income thereof the amount required for the making of those payments.

(4) An order under this section may contain such consequential and supplemental provisions as the court thinks necessary or expedient for the purpose of giving effect to the order or for the purpose of securing that the order operates fairly as between one beneficiary of the estate of the deceased and another and may, in particular, but without prejudice to the generality of this subsection –

(*a*) order any person who holds any property which forms part of the net estate of the deceased to make such payment or transfer such property as may be specified in the order;

(*b*) vary the disposition of the deceased's estate effected by the will or the law relating to intestacy, or by both the will and the law relating to intestacy, in such manner as the court thinks fair and reasonable having regard to the provision of the order and all the circumstances of the case;

(*c*) confer on the trustees of any property which is the subject of an order under this section such powers as appear to the court to be necessary or expedient.

3. Matters to which court is to have regard in exercising powers under s. 2

(1) Where an application is made for an order under section 2 of this Act, the court shall, in determining whether the disposition of the deceased's estate effected by his will or the law relating to intestacy, or the combination of his will and that law, is such as to make reasonable financial provision for the applicant and, if the court considers that reasonable financial provision has not been made, in determining whether and in what manner it shall exercise its powers under that section, have regard to the following matters, that is to say –

(*a*) the financial resources and financial needs which the applicant has or is likely to have in the foreseeable future;

(*b*) the financial resources and financial needs which any other applicant for an order under section 2 of this Act has or is likely to have in the foreseeable future;

(*c*) the financial resources and financial needs which any beneficiary of the estate of the deceased has or is likely to have in the foreseeable future;

(*d*) any obligations and responsibilities which the deceased had towards any applicant for an order under the said section 2 or towards any beneficiary of the estate of the deceased;

(*e*) the size and nature of the net estate of the deceased;

(*f*) any physical or mental disability of any applicant for an order under the said section 2 or any beneficiary of the estate of the deceased;

(*g*) any other matter, including the conduct of the applicant or any other person, which in the circumstances of the case the court may consider relevant.

(2) Without prejudice to the generality of paragraph (*g*) of subsection (1) above, where an application for an order under section 2 of this Act is made by virtue of section 1(1)(*a*) or 1(1)(*b*) of this Act, the court shall, in addition to the matters specifically mentioned in paragraphs (*a*) to (*f*) of that subsection, have regard to –

(*a*) the age of the applicant and the duration of the marriage;

(*b*) the contribution made by the applicant to the welfare of the family of the deceased, including any contribution made by looking after the home or caring for the family;

and, in the case of an application by the wife or husband of the deceased, the court shall also, unless at the date of death a separation order under the Family Law Act 1996 was in force and the separation was continuing, have regard to the provision which the applicant might reasonably have expected to receive if on the day on which the deceased died the marriage, instead of being terminated by the death, had been terminated by a divorce order.

(3) Without prejudice to the generality of paragraph (*g*) of subsection (1) above, where an application for an order under section 2 of this Act is made by virtue of section 1(1)(*c*) or 1(1)(*d*) of this Act, the court shall, in addition to the matters specifically mentioned in paragraphs (*a*) to (*f*) of that subsection, have regard to the manner in which the applicant was being or in which

he might be expected to be educated or trained, and where the application is made by virtue of section 1(1)(*d*) the court shall also have regard –

(*a*) to whether the deceased had assumed any responsibility for the applicant's maintenance and, if so, to the extent to which and the basis upon which the deceased assumed that responsibility and to the length of time for which the deceased discharged that responsibility;

(*b*) to whether in assuming and discharging that responsibility the deceased did so knowing that the applicant was not his own child;

(*c*) to the liability of any other person to maintain the applicant.

(4) Without prejudice to the generality of paragraph (*g*) of subsection (1) above, where an application for an order under section 2 of this Act is made by virtue of section 1(1)(*e*) of this Act, the court shall, in addition to the matters specifically mentioned in paragraphs (*a*) to (*f*) of that subsection, have regard to the extent to which and the basis upon which the deceased assumed responsibility for the maintenance of the applicant and to the length of time for which the deceased discharged that responsibility.

(5) In considering the matters to which the court is required to have regard under this section, the court shall take into account the facts as known to the court at the date of the hearing.

(6) In considering the financial resources of any person for the purposes of this section the court shall take into account his earning capacity and in considering the financial needs of any person for the purposes of this section the court shall take into account his financial obligations and responsibilities.

4. Time-limit for application

An application for an order under section 2 of this Act shall not, except with the permission of the court, be made after the end of the period of six months from the date on which representation with respect to the estate of the deceased is first taken out.

Questions

(i) Do you think that orders for periodical payments should cease on the remarriage of a *surviving* spouse?

(ii) Do you think that such orders should cease on the remarriage of a *former* spouse?

An examination of the special criteria applicable to claims by the surviving spouse is found in the following case:

Moody v Stevenson
[1992] Ch 486, [1992] 2 All ER 524, Court of Appeal

The applicant had married his wife in 1971 when he was 61 and she 66. In 1984 the wife went to live in a nursing home; she died in 1985, leaving all her property to her stepdaughter. More of the facts appear in the course of Waite J's judgment, when he considered the requirements of s. 3(2):

... the Act of 1975, when stripped down to its barest terms, amounts to a direction to the judge to ask himself in surviving spouse cases: 'What would a family judge have ordered for this couple if divorce instead of death had divided them; what is the effect of any other section 3 factors ...; and what, in the light of those two inquiries, am I to make of the reasonableness, when viewed objectively, of the dispositions made by the will and/or intestacy of the deceased?' If the judge finds those dispositions unreasonable, he will go on to ask himself: 'What, in the light of those same inquiries, would be a reasonable provision for me to order for the applicant under section 2?'

The result of applying that approach to the present case would be likely, in our judgment, to produce the following result at stage one. Looking first at the notional entitlement of the applicant on a presumed divorce at the date of death, it is necessary to visualise the probable reaction of a family judge when faced with a husband of 81 claiming from a wife of 86 financial relief in a case when he was still living in the former matrimonial home and she was permanently housed in a nursing home; where the only assets they had between them were £6,000 (his) and the former matrimonial home and £1,000 (hers); where the marriage had endured for 17 years, although for the last four years the parties had been separated through the wife's illness without contact with each other; where there were no children of the marriage as such, although the wife had an adult stepdaughter now living on her own; and where, this being a late marriage, the husband's contribution to the material welfare of the family unit had been limited to his earnings during the four years between the wedding and his retirement.

Applying his mind to those circumstances under section 25(1), and having regard to the various specific factors to which the court is required to have regard under section 25(2) of the Matrimonial Causes Act 1973, which of course closely resemble those set out in section 3 of the Act of 1975, a family judge would in our view be most unlikely to regard the case as one for refusing financial relief to the husband altogether. Periodic maintenance would clearly be inappropriate to a case where both sides were dependent on state benefit or state pension, or both. A lump sum order would be equally inappropriate because there would be no free capital to fund it. The most probable outcome, in our expectation, is that the court would make cross-orders under section 24 of the Act of 1973 directing on the one hand a settlement of the property on terms which, without going to the lengths of constituting him a life tenant, would give the husband a right of occupation so long as he was able and willing to exercise it; and on the other hand a transfer of part of the husband's £6,000 to, or for the benefit of, the wife, so that she might enjoy some small additional comforts in the nursing home in her last years.

Regard must next be had to those section 3 factors not already subsumed in that inquiry. It would, in particular, be necessary to consider the position of the respondent under section 3(1)(*c*) and (*d*), taking note of the fact that she lives in council accommodation with very limited financial resources, but at the same time could not be described as a person towards whom the deceased could be said to have had any obligations or responsibilities.

When the matter is approached in that way, and the stage one question is then asked, namely, whether the disposition of the deceased's estate was such, when viewed objectively, as to make reasonable provision for the applicant, who was of course wholly excluded from it, the answer must in our judgment be 'No'.

A settlement of the house for the husband's benefit was accordingly directed; in the end no order was made about any corresponding payment to the respondent, since it became apparent legal fees had left the husband without cash resources.

The fact that the surviving spouse's claim is not restricted to what is required for maintenance does not necessarily mean that he is entitled to capital provision.

Davis v Davis
[1993] 1 FLR 54, [1993] Fam Law 59, Court of Appeal

The widow, who was the second wife of the deceased and had been married to him for seven years, was left a life interest in his estate, which amounted at the time of his death to £177,000 and would later be increased to some £267,000 when the capital of the deceased's father (at present subject to a life interest in favour of his mother) became available. The estate included a house which the widow would be able to live in, although of course she did not own it absolutely. The judge at first instance said:

The Act of Parliament makes it plain that the court's powers only arise if the court is satisfied that the disposition of the deceased's estate by his will fails to make reasonable financial provision for the plaintiff. It seems to me that the plaintiff has manifestly failed to cross the threshold. It is not for this court to rewrite the testamentary provisions of deceased persons lightly.

The Court of Appeal saw no reason to interfere with that finding, and no further provision was made.

Consider the difference in these provisions between the position of the surviving spouse and the cohabitant, who could only apply for provision in the event that he falls within s. 1(1)(*e*), as a person who was being maintained by the deceased. In its report on *Intestacy* in 1989 the Law Commission recommended that:

Cohabitants should be provided for, not under the intestacy rules, but where appropriate under the Inheritance (Provision for Family and Dependants) Act 1975:

(*a*) Cohabitants should be able to apply for reasonable financial provision ... without having to show dependence.

(*b*) The definition of a cohabitant should be the same as that used in s. 1(3)(*b*) of the Fatal Accidents Act 1976 ... .

(*c*) The definition of 'reasonable financial provision' should be what is reasonable for the applicant's maintenance but the relevant factors for the court to consider should be the same as those for spouses. ...

The Law Reform (Succession) Act 1995 inserts the following provisions in the 1975 Act:

2. – (2) In section 1 [of the 1975 Act] ... the following paragraph shall be inserted after paragraph (*b*) –

'(*ba*) any person (not being a person included in paragraph (*a*) or (*b*) above) to whom subsection (1A) below applies;'.

(3) In that section, the following subsection shall be inserted after subsection (1) –

'(1A) This subsection applies to a person if the deceased died on or after 1st January 1996 and, during the whole of the period of two years ending immediately before the date when the deceased died, the person was living –

(*a*) in the same household as the deceased, and

(*b*) as the husband or wife of the deceased.'

(4) In section 3 ... , the following subsection shall be inserted after subsection (2) –

'(2A) Without prejudice to the generality of paragraph (*g*) of subsection (1) above, where an application for an order under section 2 of this Act is made by virtue of section 1(1)(*ba*) of this Act, the court shall, in addition to the matters specifically mentioned in paragraphs (*a*) to (*f*) of that subsection, have regard to –

(*a*) the age of the applicant and the length of the period during which the applicant lived as the husband or wife of the deceased and in the same household as the deceased;

(*b*) the contribution made by the applicant to the welfare of the family of the deceased, including any contribution made by looking after the home or caring for the family.'

Questions

(i) The plaintiff in *Wayling v Jones* (see p. 178, above) also made an application under the 1975 Act; this failed at first instance, and the Court of Appeal did not have to consider it in view of the conclusion on estoppel. If Mr Wayling had not had the estoppel claim, would the newly inserted subsections have been of any assistance to him?

(ii) Would you extend the provisions of the new subsections to include (*a*) those who can benefit under the Ontario Family Law Reform Act (see p. 182, above); (*b*) those who would benefit under the reforms of the Alberta Law Reform Institute (1989) (see p. 183, above); (*c*) some other definition; or (*d*) leave well alone?

It is still the case that claims by any person other than a surviving spouse must be for 'such financial provision as it would be reasonable ... for the applicant to receive for his maintenance.' The effect of this is seen in the following case.

Re Jennings, deceased
[1994] Ch 286, [1994] 3 All ER 27, Court of Appeal

The plaintiff sought an order for family provision from the estate of his father. He was now fifty years old, and had been brought up by his mother and step-father since he was four. His father left his estate, worth about £300,000 mostly to charities. The plaintiff was married with two adult children; he and his wife owned a four-bedroomed house, subject to a mortgage, and ran two successful companies. The Court of Appeal held that he therefore had no need for maintenance, and his claim failed. The members of the court looked at the matters to be taken into consideration under s. 3(1)(*a*)–(*g*) and concluded that there was no reason why any provision should now be required, since the plaintiff appeared to have no financial needs beyond, perhaps, an unspecified need for better retirement provision. Under s. 3(1)(*d*) the question was whether or not the deceased's failure to provide for the plaintiff as a child gave rise to an obligation to make provision now. Nourse LJ said:

While it is true that [the subsection] requires regard to be had to obligations and responsibilities which the deceased 'had', that cannot mean 'had at any time in the past'. At all events as a general rule that provision can only refer to obligations and responsibilities which the deceased had immediately before his death. An Act intended to facilitate the making of reasonable financial provision cannot have been intended to revive defunct obligations and responsibilities as a basis for making it. Nor, if they do not fall within a specific provision such as section 3(1)(*d*), can they be prayed in aid under a general provision such as section 3(1)(*g*).

Question

As a matter of statutory interpretation, do you agree with Nourse LJ? Do you think that the plaintiff should have succeeded?

In this chapter we have looked at issues in property law on the basis that the rights of husband and wife can be ascertained without awaiting a divorce adjustment. Leaving divorce on one side has, however, to some extent been artificial, if only because many of the circumstances which create the difficulties only arise on marriage breakdown. It is therefore to divorce that we now turn.

Chapter 6

Divorce

'Divorce is an institution only a few weeks later in origin than marriage.' [Voltaire, quoted in A. Alvarez, (1981).]

An American psychologist, Gerald Alpern in *Rights of Passage* (1982) has tried to provide a guide to the emotional realities of divorce:

Some divorces are simple happenings, a graceful parting in which two people go off in different directions to new lives. Other divorces occur so gradually, over so many years, that the divorce process is not a deeply felt experience. For others, the marriage involved a connection so casual that a legal divorce is but a formality.

However, the majority of divorces are very powerful experiences which, for many, are devastating. For most people, divorce necessitates major revisions in life goals, expectations and personal identities. People involved in divorce find themselves acting in unfamiliar ways. They may behave irrationally, become vicious or promiscuous, or suddenly plan to desert loved children. These unfamiliar actions and feelings are very frightening and cause grave self-doubts which exacerbate the depression so common to divorcing men and women. The most disorienting experience is the wide mood swings which accompany the vacillating positive and negative feelings about the divorce. At one moment the person is high on thoughts of being independent, of being free of a spouse no longer loved. The next moment or day the same person may be crying, longing for the missing spouse and planning an attempt at reconciliation.

John Cleese and Robin Skynner in *Families and How to Survive Them* (1993) remind us that we are perhaps asking for trouble by entering into the types of marriage expected of us in this period of our history:

John Let's start with an easy one ... Why do people decide to marry each other?
Robin Because they're in love.
John Oh, come on.
Robin No, I'm being serious.
John Well, perhaps, but this falling in love routine is very bizarre. You find perfectly ordinary, rational people like computer programmers and chartered accountants, and there they are, happily computing and chartering away, and suddenly they see someone across a crowded room and think, 'Ah, that person is made for me, so I suppose I'd better spend the rest of my life with them.' It borders on the occult.
Robin Perhaps you'd have preferred it three hundred years ago when parents arranged all the marriages for sensible reasons like land and money and social climbing. They all regarded 'falling in love' as the worst possible basis for marriage – a recipe for disaster.
John Yes, Samuel Johnson said that all marriages should be arranged by the Lord Chancellor without reference to the wishes of the parties involved.
Robin So the point I'm making is that nowadays we are free to marry the person we love, the one who can really make us happy.
John And of course we have the highest divorce rate in history.
Robin Since you and I have both made a contribution to those statistics, we'd better not sound too critical.

John I'm sorry if I did. Actually, I think divorce is underrated. It gives you insights into some of the trickier aspects of marriage, the more delicate nuances as it were, that couples who've been happy together for thirty years wouldn't begin to grasp. But nevertheless, divorced or not, here we are, millions upon millions of us, all blithely pairing off, thinking, 'This is the one for me.' So what's going on, Doctor?
Robin What do you think falling in love is about?

We turn our attention first of all to the history of our divorce law up until the major changes of the Divorce Reform Act 1969.

1 The history of English divorce law

We should first ponder on the important words of Lawrence Stone in *Road to Divorce* (1990). It is his view that there does not exist any single model of change which can explain the history of marital breakdown and divorce in a single country for all periods of time and for all classes of society. He writes:

Any historian who claims that either the law has always shaped marital practices or that marital practices have always shaped the law, or that the causes of change were at bottom either legal, or economic and social, or cultural and moral, or intellectual, is offering a simplistic solution which is unsupported by the evidence. History is messier than that.

The Gospel according to St Mark, in Chapter 10, lays the foundation for the Christian view of marriage and divorce which has influenced our law for so long.

2. And the Pharisees came to him, and asked him, Is it lawful for a man to put away his wife? tempting him.
3. And he answered and said unto them, What did Moses command you?
4. And they said, Moses suffered to write a bill of divorcement, and to put her away.
5. And Jesus answered and said unto them, For the hardness of your heart he wrote you this precept.
6. But from the beginning of the creation God made them male and female.
7. For this cause shall a man leave his father and mother, and cleave to his wife.
8. And they twain shall be one flesh: so then they are no more twain, but one flesh.
9. What therefore God hath joined together, let not man put asunder.
10. And in the house his disciples asked him again of the same matter.
11. And he saith unto them, Whosoever shall put away his wife, and marry another, committeth adultery against her.
12. And if a woman shall put away her husband, and be married to another, she committeth adultery.

An almost identical account appears in St Matthew's Gospel (Chapter 19, verses 3 to 9), but with the significant addition of the words 'except it be for fornication' in his version of Mark's verse 11.

A helpful summary of developments up until the second Royal Commission on Divorce (1912) appears in *The History of the Obligation to Maintain*, by Sir Morris Finer and Professor O.R. McGregor, which is Appendix 5 to the *Report of the* (Finer) *Committee on One-Parent Families* (1974):

The canon law of marriage
1. In medieval times most men, whether of high or low degree, married with the primary object of advancing their interests. For women, marriage was a protective institution. Monogamy did not

require, or imply, that people should contract only one marriage in a lifetime, and remarriage was a frequent occurrence in all social groups thereby helping to fill the gaps among the married population which resulted from early deaths. Remarriage protected widows from the dangers of living alone in a violent society as well as feudal superiors from the risk that unmarried dependants would fail in the full performance of services due from them. Moreover, the medieval laity were motivated by a desire 'to place the satisfaction of the flesh under the shelter of the sacrament'.

2. From the middle of the twelfth century until the Reformation, the law regulating marriage in England was the canon law of the church of Rome administered in courts christian. The canon law was framed in the belief that marriage is a permanent union of the natural order established by God in the creation, and consequently it affirmed that marriage made man and woman one flesh and partook of the nature of a sacrament signifying the unity betwixt Christ and his Church. Medieval christendom regarded marriage as an eternal triangle within which spouses established unbreakable bonds not only with each other but also with God. For this reason, the church maintained that marriage was indissoluble and that no earthly power, not even the Pope himself, could break the bond of a christian marriage. ...

The canon law of nullity

4. In early English law, church and state recognised divorce *a vinculo matrimonii.* This was a divorce in the full sense. It dissolved the bond of marriage and left the parties free to marry again. The church of Rome, treating marriage as indissoluble, abolished divorce in this sense. Thereafter, the ecclesiastical courts granted in the case of a validly contracted marriage only a more limited form of relief. As against a spouse guilty of adultery, cruelty, heresy or apostasy, they might pass sentence of divorce *a mensa et thoro.* This had the effect of a modern judicial separation. It relieved the spouses of the obligation to live together – to share board and bed – but preserved intact the marriage tie.

5. Yet the practical realities of life in the middle ages demanded a method of legitimate avoidance of the rigours of the doctrine of indissolubility. The church provided such a method by developing an elaborate theory of nullity. It was argued that only a valid, consummated, christian marriage was indissoluble. If an impediment to the validity of a marriage had existed when it was contracted, then that marriage would be held by the ecclesiastical courts never to have taken place at all. Many impediments were soon established; the most important were the degrees of consanguinity and affinity within which marriage was prohibited. Before the Lateran Council of 1215, marriage was forbidden between persons to the seventh degree of blood relationship; afterwards, the prohibition was narrowed to the fourth degree, that is, to third cousins. To the impediments of blood were added those of affinity. Since sexual union made man and woman one flesh, it followed that all the blood kinswomen of a man's wife or even of his mistress, were themselves connected to him by affinity. To the impediments of sexual affinity the church then added yet another series created by the spiritual relationships of godchildren. ... [See further in Chapter 1, above.]

The effect of the Reformation

6. By the time of the Reformation, many reformers were rejecting the canon law of marriage developed by the medieval church. They no longer regarded virginity as superior to marriage; they abandoned sacerdotal celibacy; they urged that marriage should be treated as a civil contract regulated by the state; and they favoured the dissolubility of marriage, although differing as to the grounds on which a divorce *a vinculo* ought to be granted. Nevertheless, the protestant doctrines of divorce, though much discussed in the second half of the sixteenth century, did not become part of the law of the land. On the contrary, by the beginning of the seventeenth century, the new church of England had affirmed its belief in the indissolubility of marriage mitigated only by divorce *a mensa et thoro.* ... At the same time, it rejected the extravagances of the canon law of nullity. Thus, ironically enough, the principal effect of the Reformation on marriage in England was the sealing up of the loopholes and the rejection of the evasions and absurdities by which the medieval system had been made tolerable in practice. Yet whatever formal respect the rich and powerful accorded to christian theology, they were no more prepared than were their ancestors to tolerate the inconveniences inseparable from a system of rigidly indissoluble marriage. In seventeenth and eighteenth century England, these classes both sustained monogamous marriage and encouraged the accumulation of private property. It was natural, therefore, for them to be more sensitive to the immediate damage which hasty and easily contracted marriages could inflict upon the orderly disposition of family property than to the remoter danger that sexual immorality might imperil their immortal souls. For these reasons, the state broke the exclusive familial jurisdiction of the ecclesiastical courts in two ways. First, it stepped in to regulate and formalise

the procedure by which a valid marriage could be contracted. Secondly, it provided a machinery for the dissolution of valid marriages by Act of Parliament. ...

Parliamentary divorce[1]

13. As the ecclesiastical courts had no power to dissolve a valid marriage *a vinculo* and as the secular courts refused to invade the spiritual jurisdiction, only Parliament could break the indissoluble bond of marriage by intervening in particular cases through the procedure of sovereign legislation. The following Table shows the extent of its interference for this purpose by the passing of private Acts of divorce:

Period	Number	Percentage
Before 1714	10[2]	3
1715–1759	24	8
1760–1779	46	14
1780–1799	53	17
1800–1819	49	15
1820–1839	59	19
1840–1856	76	24
Total	317	100

Source: Adapted from PP 1857, Session 2 (106–I), Volume XLII, page 117.

[The table] shows how rare parliamentary divorces were before the accession of George I and how their use increased steadily thereafter, so that one quarter of all the private Acts were passed in the twenty years before the system was abolished in 1857. Before the eighteenth century the main reason for Parliament's willingness to grant the privilege of marrying again was to continue the succession to peerages in the male line. When the Duke of Norfolk successfully petitioned the House of Lords for his divorce bill of 1700, he stated that his wife had 'made full proof of her adultery' and that he 'hath no issue, nor can have any probable expectation of posterity to succeed him in his honours, dignities, and estate, unless the said marriage be declared void by authority of Parliament. ...'[3] This soon ceased to be the only circumstance in which Parliament would intervene. Later Acts were passed in favour of professional men (including seventeen clergymen) and people engaged in business; indeed, such folk accounted for half the Acts passed between the middle of the eighteenth century and 1857. Nevertheless all the promoters had one characteristic in common: they were very wealthy. They had to be, for the cost of a private Act and the related proceedings was formidable.

14. After the adoption of a series of Resolutions framed by Lord Chancellor Loughborough in 1798, the House of Lords imposed a standard procedure upon all applications. Before coming to Parliament a petitioner had first to obtain both a decree of divorce *a menso et thoro* from the spiritual court, and an award of damages for criminal conversation against the wife's seducer in the secular court. The Resolutions further required that the petitioner should attend the House so that he might if necessary be examined as a witness, with reference both to collusion or connivance and also to another point which was always deemed of primary importance in judging divorce bills: whether at the time of the adultery he was living apart from his wife and had thereby contributed to her offence. ...

17. This procedure, cumbersome, expensive and intricate as it was, could in practice be utilised only by aggrieved husbands. Only four wives were ever granted Acts and these were all passed in

---

1. See also Sybil Wolfram, 'Divorce in England 1700–1857', Oxford Journal of Legal Studies vol. 5 (1984) pp. 155–186, and S. Anderson, 'Legislative Divorce – Law for the Aristocracy' in G. Rubin and D. Sugarman (eds) *Law, Society and Economy. Essays in Legal History* (1984).

2. The case of Lord Roos in 1670 is discussed in detail by Stone (1990). The case, described by Charles II as 'better than a play', apparently gave birth to the famous nursery rhyme 'Mary Mary quite contrary, how does your garden grow ... pretty maids all in a row' after the alleged succession of extramarital liaisons of his wife Anne. Unlike 'Mary', 'Anne' does not rhyme with 'contrary'!

3. Stone (1990) informs us that Norfolk died in 1701 before he had had time to remarry so that the whole purpose of the Act was frustrated.

the nineteenth century. The first occurred in 1801. We quote Frederick Clifford's account of Mrs Addison's Act in full, both for its intrinsic interest and to show how, even at the close of the Age of Reason, the House of Lords could still be moved and bemused by arguments based upon the canonists' doctrine of the carnal affinities.

> 'Mr Addison had maintained a criminal intercourse with his wife's sister, a married woman. Her husband, Dr Campbell, obtained a verdict against him with £5,000 damages. Mrs Addison, after obtaining in the Ecclesiastical Court a divorce *a mensa et thoro*, applied to Parliament for a divorce *a vinculo*. Her husband did not appear. Lord Thurlow ... made a powerful speech for the Bill. Every principle of justice, he said, would be violated by its rejection. But Lord Thurlow did not assert a woman's general right to the same legislative relief as was given to an injured husband. He found his chief defence of the Bill upon the old doctrine of the canonists, that commerce between the sexes creates affinity. In this case, he argued, if Mr Addison had previously had illicit intercourse with her sister, he could not have married his present wife, because such marriage would have been tainted by incest, and might have been pronounced void by an Ecclesiastical Court. A like result occurred by reason of this incestuous adultery. It made reconciliation legally impossible, for, by the affinity it had created, renewed cohabitation between Mr and Mrs Addison would become incestuous.'

Lord Thurlow's subtleties prevailed upon the Lord Chancellor, Lord Eldon, to withdraw his intended opposition to the establishment of this precedent. There is no record of any opposition in the House of Commons, and Mrs Addison obtained her Act. But Parliament held thereafter to the principle that adultery without more by the husband was not a sufficient ground for a wife to obtain an Act. Of the three other instances, in Mrs Turton's case in 1830 the adultery was incestuous; in Mrs Battersby's case in 1840 there was adultery aggravated by cruelty and followed by bigamy for which her husband was transported; and in Mrs Hall's case in 1850 there was also bigamy.

18. Two of the characteristics of the procedure of divorce by private Act of Parliament are now plain. It was so expensive that only the wealthy could avail themselves of it, and within the exclusive social sphere for which the procedure catered, it made a further discrimination between men and women. The discrimination which Parliament maintained between husbands and wives, in respect of the grounds on which it was prepared to dissolve a marriage, was justified in terms of the different effect of their adultery. As Lord Chancellor Cranworth explained to the House of Lords:

> 'A wife might, without any loss of caste, and possibly with reference to the interests of her children, or even of her husband, condone an act of adultery on the part of the husband but a husband could not condone a similar act on the part of a wife. No one would venture to suggest that a husband could possibly do so, and for this, among other reasons ... that the adultery of the wife might be the means of palming spurious offspring upon the husband, while the adultery of the husband could have no such effect with regard to the wife.'

R v Hall (1845) 1 Cox CC 231 (cited by Stone (1990))

Maule J: Prisoner at the bar, you have been convicted before me of what the law regards as a very grave and serious offence: that of going through the marriage ceremony a second time while your wife was still alive. You plead in mitigation of your conduct that she was given to dissipation and drunkenness, that she proved herself a curse to your household while she remained mistress of it, and that she had latterly deserted you; but I am not permitted to recognise any such plea ... Another of your irrational excuses is that your wife had committed adultery, and so you thought you were relieved from treating her with any further consideration – but you were mistaken. The law in its wisdom points out a means by which you might rid yourself from further association with a woman who had dishonoured you, but you did not think proper to adopt it. I will tell you what that process is. You ought first to have brought an action against your wife's seducer, if you could have discovered him; that might have cost you money, and you say you are a poor working man, but that is not the fault of the law. You would then be obliged to prove by evidence your wife's criminality in a Court of Justice, and thus obtain a verdict with damages against the defendant, who was not unlikely to turn out pauper. But so jealous is the law (which you ought to be aware is the perfection of reason) of the sanctity of the marriage tie, that in accomplishing all this you would only have fulfilled the lighter portion of your duty. You must then have gone, with your verdict in your hand, and petitioned the House of Lords for a divorce. It would cost you perhaps five or six hundred pounds, and you do not seem to be worth as many pence. But it is the boast of the law that it is impartial, and makes no difference between the rich and the poor. The wealthiest man in the kingdom would have had to pay no less than that sum for the same luxury; so that you would have no reason to complain. You would, of course, have to prove your case over again, and at the end of a year, or possibly two, you might obtain a divorce which would enable you legally to do what you have thought proper to do without it. You have thus wilfully rejected the boon the legislature offered you, and it is my duty to pass upon you such a sentence as I think your offence deserves, and that sentence is, that you be imprisoned for one day; and in as much as the present assizes are three days old, the result is that you will be immediately discharged.

Question

As we can see from this sentence on the unfortunate Mr Hall, there was one law for the rich and another law for the poor. Could it be that only the rich needed to divorce? What social changes in the years leading up to 1857 might have made it necessary for others to seek this remedy?

The story is taken up by Sir Morris Finer and Professor O.R. McGregor:

The first Royal (Campbell) Commission on divorce

30. In 1850 a Royal Commission, under the chairmanship of Lord Campbell, was appointed 'to enquire into the present state of the law of divorce'. The commission was an explicit response to the dissatisfaction with the existing law we have been describing: 'the grave objection,' as Lord Chancellor Cranworth explained, 'that such complicated proceedings were too expensive for the pockets of any but the richest sufferers, and that relief was put beyond the reach of all but the wealthiest classes.' It followed, as Lord Campbell himself said, that the object of the commission was not in any way to alter the law, but only the procedure by which the law was carried into effect. The same points were made repeatedly in the debates on the Matrimonial Causes Act 1857, whereby the recommendations of the Campbell Report were given effect. Thus, the Act of 1857 did not, as is sometimes mistakenly thought, introduce divorce into England or discard a hitherto sacred principle of indissolubility of marriage. The Act (apart from some minor innovations) did no more than consolidate and transfer to a civil and more accessible court of law the jurisdictions that were already being respectively exercised by Parliament and the ecclesiastical courts. The only substantial change which it effected was to make more widely available matrimonial remedies which only the very few had until then enjoyed.

The Matrimonial Causes Act 1857

31. The principal provisions of the Act of 1857 were, accordingly, as follows. The matrimonial jurisdiction of the ecclesiastical courts was abolished, but re-created in a new court called 'the Court for Divorce and Matrimonial Causes'. In exercising the transferred jurisdiction, the divorce court was to proceed on the same principles as had guided the ecclesiastical courts. The remedy which those courts had formerly granted under the name of a decree of divorce *a mensa et thoro* was henceforth to be called a decree of judicial separation. The divorce court would also deal with petitions for the dissolution of marriage. A husband could present a petition for divorce on the ground of his wife's adultery; a wife, on the ground of adultery aggravated by some other conduct (such as incestuous adultery, adultery coupled with cruelty or with desertion for two years or upwards) or on the ground of sodomy or bestiality. It is notable that Gladstone, while vigorously opposing the passage of the Act, was equally strong in contending that if it were passed at all it should not discriminate between the sexes:

> 'It is impossible to do a greater mischief than to begin now, in the middle of the nineteenth century, to undo with regard to womankind that which has already been done on their behalf, by slow degrees, in the preceding eighteen centuries, and to say that the husband shall be authorised to dismiss his wife on grounds for which the wife shall not be authorised to dismiss her husband. If there is one broad and palpable result of Christianity which we ought to regard as precious, it is that it has placed the seal of God Almighty upon the equality of man and woman with respect to everything that relates to these rights.' [See the extract from St Mark's Gospel at the beginning of this chapter.]. ...

The number of divorces

34. The Act of 1857 opened the door to matrimonial relief for many whom the expense of the earlier procedures had excluded. In the four years following the passing of the Act 781 petitions for divorce and 248 petitions for judicial separation were filed in the new court. On the other hand, the Act, as these figures demonstrate, opened no floodgate. The highest number of decrees granted in any one year up to 1900 was 583 divorces (in the year 1897) and 57 decrees for judicial separation (in the year 1880). The new jurisdiction was wholly centralised in London, which acted as a deterrent to its employment by those who resided at a distance. Further, although the costs were not so wildly exorbitant as previously, they were still very considerable, and beyond the reach of people of ordinary means. It was not long before the criticisms which had preceded the Act regained currency. ...

The Second Royal (Gorell) Commission on Divorce

42. In 1909, a Royal Commission was appointed, under the chairmanship of Lord Gorell 'to enquire into the present state of the law of England and the administration thereof in divorce and matrimonial causes and applications for separation orders, especially with regard to the position of the poorer classes in relation thereto.' By this time, while the High Court was dealing every year with some 800 petitions for divorce and judicial separation, the magistrates were dealing with some 15,000 applications for matrimonial orders. [This jurisdiction is discussed in Chapter 3, above.] In the ten years 1897–1906 the magistrates made more than 87,000 separation orders. Almost all of the magistrates' clientele were the poor, whose problems the terms of reference expressly recognised. Indeed, the themes and anxieties which had dominated the discussion in the preceding century, and which the intervening reforms had not laid to rest, continued to be strongly reflected in the evidence given to the commission: discrimination between the sexes; discrimination against the poor. ... It continues ... to impress by a quality of vision and humanity which may be illustrated by a passage which refers to the obligation:

> 'to recognise human needs, that divorce is not a disease but a remedy for a disease, that homes are not broken up by a court but by causes to which we have already sufficiently referred, and that the law should be such as would give relief where serious causes intervene, which are generally and properly recognised as leading to the break-up of married life. If a reasonable law, based upon human needs, be adopted, we think that the standard of morality will be raised and regard for the sanctity of marriage increased.'

43. As regards the law of divorce and its administration, the Gorell Report proposed, first, 'that the law should be amended so as to place the two sexes on an equal footing as regards the grounds on which divorce may be obtained'. ... This recommendation was not followed until 1923. Next, the report proposed the broadening of the grounds on which either spouse might petition for divorce, by adding to adultery the offences of desertion for three years and upwards, cruelty, incurable insanity, habitual drunkenness and imprisonment under commuted death sentence. Extensions on these lines had to wait upon the Matrimonial Causes Act 1937. Thirdly, the Gorell Report recommended a decentralisation of procedure so that the High Court could sit and exercise divorce jurisdiction locally, for the benefit, in particular, of people of small means. It took another committee, in 1946, to produce any effective change in this respect.

The story since then is taken up in the main body of the Finer Report:

Lord Buckmaster's Act in 1923 had put husbands and wives on a footing of formal equality in respect of the grounds of divorce, by making it possible for each to petition against the other on the grounds of simple adultery. But it was not until the legal aid scheme of 1949 compensated wives for their lack of income or low earnings that they won practical equality of access to the court.[4]

The Third Royal (Morton) Commission on Marriage and Divorce

4.30 In 1951, Mrs Eirene White proposed, in a private member's bill, to permit divorce to spouses who had lived apart for seven years: that is to say, divorce which depended on the fact of separation over this period, and did not involve the proof, by one spouse against the other, of the commission of a matrimonial offence. Coming as it did, at the time when legal aid regarded as a social service was replacing help for the poor as a form of professional charity dispensed by

---

4. This observation is based upon the respective proportions of husbands and wives who were subsequently legally aided (Gibson and Beer, 1971), but it should be recalled that part of the husband's common law duty to maintain his wife was to give security for her costs in litigation.

lawyers, and the financial bar to the divorce courts was being lifted, Mrs White's bill was seen by its opponents as a measure to open the floodgates. Nevertheless, to the alarm of its opponents, and to the surprise of many of the supporters of the bill, it appeared as though the House might respond favourably. At this juncture, the government offered Mrs White a Greek gift in the shape of a Royal Commission. Mrs White accepted.

4.31 The Report of the Morton Commission in 1956, though divided, was decidedly against change. Reformers had urged that the doctrine of the matrimonial offence was out of step with people's actual behaviour and expectations in marriage, that the law was brought into contempt by the perjury thereby encouraged, and that the result was illicit unions and the birth of illegitimate children. The Church of England was the most influential opponent of change in the matrimonial law. It explained to the Royal Commission that the doctrine of the matrimonial offence was 'entirely in accord with the New Testament', asserted that divorce was 'a very dangerous threat to the family and to the conception of marriage as a lifelong obligation', and upheld its traditional view that, although much individual. suffering and hardship might be relieved by making divorce easier to obtain, the damage to the social order must outweigh such benefits. ...

The pressure for reform

4.32 In 1956, it must have seemed that the Morton Commission and the Church of England had between them put the quietus on divorce law reform for many years to come. But the appearances were deceptive. The report proved to be little more than a ripple on the surface of a tide that was moving strongly in the other direction.

Nevertheless, it was a group set up in the 1960s by the Archbishop of Canterbury (under the chairmanship of the Rt. Rev. R.C. Mortimer, Lord Bishop of Exeter) that cleared the way for major reform. Its report was published in 1966, under the title *Putting Asunder – A Divorce Law for Contemporary Society*. It drew three main conclusions.

First, as Jesus himself had accepted the Mosaic law for those whose 'hardness of heart' made them unable to understand the truth of Jesus' own teaching about life-long fidelity, and today's secular society was full of such people:

17. There is therefore nothing to forbid the Church's recognizing fully the validity of a secular divorce law within the secular sphere. It follows that it is right and proper for the Church to co-operate with the State, and for Christians to co-operate with secular humanists and others who are not Christians, in trying to make the divorce law as equitable and as little harmful to society as it can be made. Since ex hypothesi the State's matrimonial law is not meant to be a translation of the teaching of Jesus into legal terms, but [to] allow properly for that 'hardness of heart' of which Jesus himself took account, the standard by which it is to be judged is certainly not the Church's own canon law and pastoral discipline. ...

18. The only Christian interests that need to be declared are the protection of the weak and the preservation and strengthening of those elements in the law which favour lasting marriage and stable family life; and these are ends which Christians are by no means alone in thinking socially important. ...

Secondly, having considered the interpretation of the fault-based grounds; the stratagems to which these put couples who were determined on divorce; and the inconsistency of having some fault and some (like incurable insanity and cases of cruelty for which the respondent could not morally be blamed) no-fault grounds:

45(*f*) ... We are far from being convinced that the present provisions of the law witness to the sanctity of marriage, or uphold its public repute, in any observable way, or that they are irreplaceable as buttresses of morality, either in the narrower field of matrimonial and sexual relationships, or in the wider field which includes considerations of truth, the sacredness of oaths, and the integrity of professional practice. As a piece of social mechanism the present system has not only cut loose from its moral and juridical foundations: it is, quite simply, inept.

Thirdly, the courts should be empowered, after an enquiry into every case, to recognise in law the fact that a marriage had irretrievably broken down:

55. ... As we see it, the primary and fundamental question would be: Does the evidence before the court reveal such failure in the matrimonial relationship, or such circumstances adverse to that relationship, that no reasonable probability remains of the spouses again living together as husband and wife for mutual comfort and support? That is in line with Lord Walker's definition of a broken marriage as 'one where the facts and circumstances affecting the lives of the parties adversely to one another are such as to make it improbable that an ordinary husband and wife would ever resume cohabitation' (Morton Report, 1956). The evidence falling to be considered by the court would be all the relevant facts in the history of the marriage, including those acts and circumstances which the existing law treats as grounds for divorce in themselves. The court would then dissolve the marriage if, and only if, having regard to the interests of society as well as of those immediately affected by its decision, it judged it wrong to maintain the legal existence of a relationship that was beyond all probability of existing again in fact.

In the light of what eventually happened, however, one further conclusion reached by the group should be stressed:

69. We may enumerate three principal objections to reducing the principle of breakdown to a verbally formulated 'ground' and introducing it into the existing law cheek by jowl with the 'grounds' defining matrimonial offences.

(a) The mutual incompatibility of the two principles would be glaringly obvious
The existing law is almost entirely based on the assumption that divorce ought to be seen as just relief for an innocent spouse against whom an offence has been committed by the other spouse. If then there were inserted into this law an additional clause enabling a guilty spouse to petition successfully against the will of an innocent, the whole context would proclaim the addition unjust. Conversely, if the legislature came to the conclusion that it was right and proper to grant divorce, on the petition of either party and without proof of any specific offence, when – and only when – a marriage was shown to have broken down irreparably, how could it justify retaining grounds which depended on the commission of specific offences, on which only injured parties might petition, and which required no evidence of breakdown at all? ...

(b) The superficiality inseparable from verbally formulated 'grounds' would tend to render the principle of breakdown inoperative
One of our reasons for recommending the principle of breakdown is that it would enable the courts to get to grips with the realities of the matrimonial relationship instead of having to concentrate on superficialities. But if the principle were introduced into the law in the shape of yet another verbally formulated 'ground' ..., the advantage hoped for would be lost. ...

(c) The addition of a new 'ground' embodying the principle of breakdown would make divorce easier to get without really improving the law
As we have said, we have no reason to believe that the entire substitution of breakdown for the matrimonial offence would, in the long run, make divorce easier or increase the number of decrees granted to a significant extent; but quite obviously the mere addition of a 'ground of separation' would do both, since it would make divorce available where now it is not, while leaving undisturbed the opportunities now existing. ...

Immediately following the publication of *Putting Asunder*, the Lord Chancellor referred the matter to the Law Commission. Their report, entitled *Reform of the Grounds of Divorce – The Field of Choice*, was published only five months later. Their conclusions were summarised thus:

120. (1) The objectives of a good divorce law should include (*a*) the support of marriages which have a chance of survival, and (*b*) the decent burial with the minimum of embarrassment, humiliation and bitterness of those that are indubitably dead. ...

(2) The provision of the present law whereby a divorce cannot normally be obtained within three years of the celebration of the marriage may help to achieve the first objective. ... But the

principle of matrimonial offence on which the present law is based does not wholly achieve either objective. ...

(3) Four of the major problems requiring solution are:

(*a*) The need to encourage reconciliation. Something more might be achieved here; though little is to be expected from conciliation procedures after divorce proceedings have been instituted. ...

(*b*) The prevalence of stable illicit unions. As the law stands, many of these cannot be regularised nor the children legitimated. ...

(*c*) Injustice to the economically weaker partner – normally the wife. ...

(*d*) The need adequately to protect the children of failed marriages. ...

(4) The field of choice for reform is circumscribed by a number of practical considerations and public attitudes, which cannot be ignored if acceptable and practicable reforms are to be undertaken. ...

(5) The proposals of the Archbishop's Group on Divorce made in *Putting Asunder*, though they are to be welcomed for their rejection of exclusive reliance on matrimonial offence, are procedurally impracticable. They propose that there should be but one comprehensive ground for divorce – breakdown of the marriage – the court being required to satisfy itself by means of a thorough inquest into the marriage that it has failed irretrievably. It would not be feasible, even if it were desirable, to undertake such an inquest in every divorce case because of the time this would take and the costs involved. ...

(6) However, the following alternative proposals, if any of them were thought desirable, would be practicable in the sense that they could be implemented without insuperable legal difficulty and without necessarily conflicting with the critical factors referred to in (4):

(*a*) *Breakdown without Inquest* – a modification of the breakdown principal [sic] advocated in *Putting Asunder*, but dispensing in most cases with the elaborate inquest there suggested. The court would, on proof of a period of separation and in the absence of evidence to the contrary, assume that the marriage had broken down. If however this were to be the sole comprehensive ground of divorce, it would not be feasible to make the period of separation much more than six months. If, as seems likely, so short a period is not acceptable, breakdown cannot become the sole ground, but might still be introduced as an additional ground on the lines of proposal (*c*) below. ...

(*b*) *Divorce by Consent* – This would be practicable only as an additional, and not a sole comprehensive, ground. It would not be more than a palliative and would probably be unacceptable except in the case of marriages in which there are no dependent children. Even in the case of childless marriages, if consent were the sole criterion, it might lead to the dissolution of marriages that had not broken down irretrievably. ...

(*c*) *The Separation Ground* – This would involve introducing as a ground for divorce a period of separation irrespective of which party was at fault, thereby affording a place in the law for the application of the breakdown principle. But since the period would be substantially longer than six months, it would be practicable only as an addition to the existing grounds based on matrimonial offence. The most comprehensive form of this proposal would provide for two different periods of separation. After the expiration of the shorter period (two years is suggested) either party, subject to safeguards, could obtain a divorce if the other consented, or, perhaps, did not object. After the expiration of the longer period (five or seven years) either party, subject to further safeguards, could obtain a divorce even if the other party objected. ...

(7) If any of these proposals were adopted, the following safeguards would appear to be necessary: –

(*a*) The three year waiting period should be retained. ...

(*b*) The court should have power to adjourn for a limited period to enable the possibilities of reconciliation to be explored. ...

(*c*) The court should have a discretion to refuse a decree if attempts had been made by the petitioner wilfully to deceive it; but the present absolute and discretionary bars would be inapplicable to petitions on these new grounds. ...

(*d*) Additional safeguards would be needed to protect the respondent spouse and the children. These should include: –

(i) A procedure to ensure that the respondent's decision to consent to or not oppose a divorce, had been taken freely and with a full appreciation of the consequences. ...

(ii) Retention, and possible improvement, of the provisions of the present law designed to ensure that satisfactory arrangements are made for the future of the children. ...

(iii) Provisions protecting an innocent party from being divorced against his or her will unless equitable financial arrangements are made for him or her. …

(*e*) It is for consideration whether there should be a further discretionary bar based on protection of interests wider than those of the parties alone. If such a bar were introduced, it should be defined as precisely as possible so as to promote consistency in its exercise and to enable legal advisers to give firm advice to their clients. …

Question

In the light of this summary, do you think that to title the Report *The Field of Choice* was 'inaccurate'?

The 'practical considerations and public attitudes' referred to in paragraph 120(4) above are of particular interest:

52. …

(*a*) Public opinion would not accept any substantial increase in the difficulty of obtaining a divorce or of the time it takes, unless it could be shown that an appreciable number of marriages would be mended as a result.

(*b*) Experience shows that the chances of reconciliation between the parties have become almost negligible by the time that a petition for a divorce is filed.

(*c*) Whether a divorce is obtainable or not, husbands and wives in modern conditions will part if life becomes intolerable. The ease with which names can be changed under English law simplifies the establishment of a new and apparently regular 'marriage'; where the deception is not complete, the resulting children are the main sufferers because of the stigma that still attaches to the status of illegitimacy.

(*d*) Children are at least as vitally affected by their parents' divorce as are the parents themselves.

(*e*) Breakdown of a marriage usually precedes the matrimonial offence on which the divorce petition is based. Thus, an isolated act of adultery or isolated acts with different partners may be the grounds for divorce, but are likely to be the result of the breakdown of the marriage rather than its cause.

(*f*) Public opinion would be unlikely to support a proposal which had the effect of, say, doubling the amount spent on divorce proceedings; in so far as more Judges, more courts and more Legal Aid would impose a burden on public funds, it would be felt that the money could be better spent on other subjects, including, for example, marriage guidance and conciliation.

(*g*) Public opinion would be equally unlikely to support a great expansion of the Queen's Proctor's Office or the employment of additional public servants with the function of investigating the truth of the evidence given by parties to divorce proceedings. At the present time there is a shortage of trained welfare officers attached to the courts and no sudden addition to their numbers can be hoped for in the near future.

(*h*) Even where a marriage is childless, divorce granted automatically if the parties consent ('Post Office divorces') would not be acceptable; there must be an independent check if only to ensure that the economically weaker party really and freely consents to the divorce and to approve the financial arrangements worked out by the parties and their solicitors. The need for outside intervention is, of course, far greater where there are children.

Question

The Law Commission did not base these statements on any scientific opinion poll (although they were described as 'hard facts' in the Report) – how many of them would hold good today?

2 The present law: the Matrimonial Causes Act 1973

The Divorce Reform Act 1969, by and large, translated the Law Commission's clear preferences into law. It came into force on 1 January 1971 and has since been consolidated with other relevant legislation in the Matrimonial Causes Act 1973. Until the Family Law Act 1996 comes into force, the 1973 Act remains the present law on divorce.

1. **Divorce or breakdown of marriage** (1) Subject to section 3 below, a petition for divorce may be presented to the court by either party to a marriage on the ground that the marriage has broken down irretrievably.

(2) The court hearing a petition for divorce shall not hold the marriage to have broken down irretrievably unless the petitioner satisfies the court of one or more of the following facts, that is to say –

(*a*) that the respondent has committed adultery and the petitioner finds it intolerable to live with the respondent;

(*b*) that the respondent has behaved in such a way that the petitioner cannot reasonably be expected to live with the respondent;

(*c*) that the respondent has deserted the petitioner for a continuous period of at least two years immediately preceding the presentation of the petition;

(*d*) that the parties to the marriage have lived apart for a continuous period of at least two years immediately preceding the presentation of the petition (hereafter in this Act referred to as 'two years' separation') and the respondent consents to a decree being granted;

(*e*) that the parties to the marriage have lived apart for a continuous period of at least five years immediately preceding the presentation of the petition (hereafter in this Act referred to as 'five years' separation').

(3) On a petition for divorce it shall be the duty of the court to inquire, so far as it reasonably can, into the facts alleged by the petitioner and into any facts alleged by the respondent.

(4) If the court is satisfied on the evidence of any such fact as is mentioned in subsection (2) above, then, unless it is satisfied on all the evidence that the marriage has not broken down irretrievably, it shall, subject to sections 3(3) and 5 below, grant a decree of divorce.

(5) Every decree of divorce shall in the first instance be a decree nisi and shall not be made absolute before the expiration of six months from its grant unless the High Court by general order from time to time fixes a shorter period,[5] or unless in any particular case the court in which the proceedings are for the time being pending from time to time by special order fixes a shorter period than the period otherwise applicable for the time being by virtue of this subsection.

2. **Supplemental provision as to facts raising presumption of breakdown** (1) One party to a marriage shall not be entitled to rely for the purposes of section 1(2)(*a*) above on adultery committed by the other if, after it became known to him that the other had committed that adultery, the parties have lived with each other for a period exceeding, or periods together exceeding, six months.

(2) Where the parties to a marriage have lived with each other after it became known to one party that the other had committed adultery, but subsection (1) above does not apply, in any proceedings for divorce in which the petitioner relies on that adultery the fact that the parties have lived with each other after that time shall be disregarded in determining for the purposes of section 1(2)(*a*) above whether the petitioner finds it intolerable to live with the respondent.

(3) Where in any proceedings for divorce the petitioner alleges that the respondent has behaved in such a way that the petitioner cannot reasonably be expected to live with him, but the parties to the marriage have lived with each other for a period or periods after the date of the occurrence of the final incident relied on by the petitioner and held by the court to support his allegation, that fact shall be disregarded in determining for the purposes of section 1(2)(*b*) above whether the petitioner cannot reasonably be expected to live with the respondent if the length of that period or of those periods together was six months or less.

(4) For the purposes of section 1(2)(*c*) above the court may treat a period of desertion as having continued at a time when the deserting party was incapable of continuing the necessary intention if the evidence before the court is such that, had that party not been so incapable, the court would have inferred that his desertion continued at that time.

---

5. The period is now fixed at six weeks.

(5) In considering for the purposes of section 1(2) above whether the period for which the respondent has deserted the petitioner or the period for which the parties to a marriage have lived apart has been continuous, no account shall be taken of any one period (not exceeding six months) or of any two or more periods (not exceeding six months in all) during which the parties resumed living with each other, but no period during which the parties lived with each other shall count as part of the period of desertion or of the period for which the parties to the marriage lived apart, as the case may be.

(6) For the purposes of section 1(2)(*d*) and (*e*) above and this section a husband and wife shall be treated as living apart unless they are living with each other in the same household, and references in this section to the parties to a marriage living with each other shall be construed as references to their living with each other in the same household.

(7) Provision shall be made by rules of court for the purpose of ensuring that where in pursuance of section 1(2)(*d*) above the petitioner alleges that the respondent consents to a decree being granted the respondent has been given such information as will enable him to understand the consequences to him of his consenting to a decree being granted and the steps which he must take to indicate that he consents to the grant of a decree.

5. **Refusal of decree in five year separation cases on ground of grave hardship to respondent** (1) The respondent to a petition for divorce in which the petitioner alleges five years' separation may oppose the grant of a decree on the ground that the dissolution of the marriage will result in grave financial or other hardship to him and that it would in all the circumstances be wrong to dissolve the marriage.

(2) Where the grant of a decree is opposed by virtue of this section, then –

(*a*) if the court finds that the petitioner is entitled to rely in support of his petition on the fact of five years' separation and makes no such finding as to any other fact mentioned in section 1(2) above, and

(*b*) if apart from this section the court would grant a decree on the petition,

the court shall consider all the circumstances, including the conduct of the parties to the marriage and the interests of those parties and of any children or other persons concerned, and if of opinion that the dissolution of the marriage will result in grave financial or other hardship to the respondent and that it would in all the circumstances be wrong to dissolve the marriage it shall dismiss the petition.

So that we can see the English law in context, we reproduce Table 2 (opposite) from Mary Anne Glendon in *Abortion and Divorce in Western Law* (1987). As Mary Ann Glendon explains, England was not alone:

Between 1969 and 1985 divorce law in nearly every Western country was profoundly altered. Among the most dramatic changes was the introduction of civil divorce in the predominantly Catholic countries of Italy and Spain, and its extension to Catholic marriages in Portugal. Other countries replaced or amended old, strict divorce laws. Most of these laws had been virtually unchanged since the grounds for ecclesiastical separation from bed and board became the basis for the secular institution of divorce. The chief common characteristics of all these changes were the recognition or expansion of nonfault grounds for divorce, and the acceptance or simplification of divorce by mutual consent. When California in 1969 became the first Western jurisdiction completely to eliminate fault grounds for divorce, the move was thought by some to prefigure the direction of reforms in other places. But it soon became clear that the purist approach was not to find wide acceptance. That same year England, too, passed a new divorce law which purported to make divorce available only when a marriage had irretrievably broken down. But since the English statute permitted marriage breakdown to be proved by evidence of traditional marital offences as well as by mutual consent or long separation, it did not really repudiate the old fault system. As it turned out, compromise statutes of the English type (resembling those already in place in Australia, Canada, and New Zealand) became the prevailing new approach to the grounds of divorce.

Glendon writes:

The changes in divorce law were themselves part of a more general process in which the legal posture of the state with respect to the family was undergoing its most fundamental shift since family law had begun to be secularized at the time of the Protestant Reformation. Beginning in the 1960s, movement in Western family law had been characterized, broadly speaking, and in

Table 2: Grounds for divorce in nineteen countries[a]

Mixed Fault and Non-fault Grounds						Non-fault Grounds Only			
Required waiting period of more than 1 year for contested unilateral non-fault divorce		Required waiting period of 1 year or less for contested unilateral non-fault divorce		Mutual consent required for non-fault divorce		Judicial discretion to deny contested unilateral divorce		No judicial discretion to deny divorce	
Austria	(1978)	Canada	(1968–86)	U.S. (2 states)		Netherlands	(1971)	Sweden	(1973)
Belgium[b]	(1974–82)	Switzerland[b]	(1907)			West Germany	(1976)	U.S.	(18 states and D.C.)
Denmark	(1969)	U.S.	(22 states)						
England[b]	(1969)								
Finland[c]	(1929–48)								
France[b]	(1975)								
Greece	(1983)								
Iceland[b]	(1921)								
Italy	(1970–75)								
Luxembourg[b]	(1975–78)								
Norway	(1918)								
Portugal	(1975–77)								
Spain	(1981)								
U.S.	(8 states)								

[a] This table classifies countries according to two criteria: the extent to which their divorce statutes have (1) abandoned the fault principle and (2) accepted the possibility of divorce by one spouse of a partner who opposes the divorce and has committed no marital 'fault.' The dates of the most recent major changes relating to the grounds of divorce are in parentheses. Countries vary, of course, in the extent to which these ideas are put into practice by the courts, the cost of implementing statutory rights, the opportunities offered for tactical delay, and so on. Ireland, which allows no divorce, is not included in table.

[b] In these systems of mixed grounds, the court has discretion to deny a divorce sought by one spouse against a non-consenting partner who has committed no 'fault' in the technical sense of the divorce laws.

[c] In 1986, the Finnish government introduced a bill to make marriage dissolution available on non-fault grounds only, with no discretion to deny divorce.

varying degrees, by a withdrawal of much official regulation of marriage: its formation, its legal effects, and its termination. The removal of many legal obstacles to marriage; the effect of new attitudes of tolerance for diversity combined with older policies of nonintervention in the ongoing marriage; and the transformation of marriage itself from a legal relationship terminable only for serious cause to one increasingly terminable at will, amounted to a dejuridification of marriage. This process of deregulation of the formation and dissolution of marriage, and of the relations of the spouses during marriage, was typically accompanied, however – again in varying degrees – by a continued, and sometimes intensified, state interest in the economic and child-related consequences of marriage dissolution.

Questions

(i) Do you agree with Glendon's analysis of the fundamental shift, and if you do, do you welcome this process of 'deregulation' and 'dejuridification'?
(ii) Does it surprise you to learn that the Divorce Act 1985 in Canada provides for divorce after one year's separation, or for physical or mental cruelty, or for adultery?
(iii) Does it surprise you to learn that the Scottish Law Commission conclude that adultery and behaviour should be retained as alternatives to the two separation 'facts'; these should be reduced to one year in the case of consent and two years where there is no consent (Report on *Reform of the Ground for Divorce* (1989))?

(a) THE 'FAULT-BASED' FACTS

At first sight, these provisions combine fault and no-fault 'grounds' for divorce in just the way so deplored by the Archbishop's group in *Putting Asunder*. In fact, as the following cases illustrate, the apparently fault-based 'grounds' are not always what they seem.

Cleary v Cleary
[1974] 1 All ER 498, [1974] 1 WLR 73, 117 Sol Jo 834, Court of Appeal

The wife left her husband and committed adultery. She then returned to her husband and they lived together for five or six weeks. She left again but did not repeat the adultery. She took proceedings unsuccessfully in a magistrates' court complaining of her husband's persistent cruelty and wilful neglect to maintain her. A few months later she petitioned for divorce on the basis of her husband's behaviour. The husband denied this and cross-prayed for divorce on the basis of her adultery. She withdrew her petition and the case proceeded undefended upon the husband's cross-prayer. The county court judge dismissed the suit and the husband appealed.

Lord Denning MR: ... [On the words of section 1(2)(*a*)] a point of law arises on which there is a difference of opinion between the judges. The question is whether the two facts required by section [1(2)(*a*)] are severable and independent, or whether they are interconnected. In other words, is it sufficient for the husband to prove (*a*) that the wife has committed adultery and (*b*) that he finds it intolerable to live with her? Or has he to prove that (*a*) the wife has committed adultery and (*b*) that *in consequence thereof* he finds it intolerable to live with her? Are the words 'in consequence thereof' to be read into section [1(2)(*a*)]?

On the one hand, in *Goodrich v Goodrich* [1971] 2 All ER 1340, [1971] 1 WLR 1142, Lloyd-Jones J quoted from *Rayden on Divorce*, 11th ed. (1971), p. 175, where it was submitted that the two phrases are in the context independent of one another. The judge said: 'In my judgment that view is acceptable.' On the other hand, more recently in *Roper v Roper and Porter* [1972] 3 All ER 668, [1972] 1 WLR 1314, Faulks J took a different view. He said:

> 'I think that common sense tells you that where the finding that has got to be made is that the respondent has committed adultery, and the petitioner finds it intolerable to live with the respondent, it means, "*and in consequence* of the adultery the petitioner finds it intolerable to live with the respondent." '

So Faulks J would introduce the words 'in consequence thereof,' whereas Lloyd-Jones J would not. Which is the right view?

As a matter of interpretation, I think the two facts in section [1(2)(*a*)] are independent and should be so treated. Take this very case. The husband proves that the wife committed adultery and that he forgave her and took her back. That is one fact. He then proves that, after she comes back, she behaves in a way that makes it quite intolerable to live with her. She corresponds with the other man and goes out at night and finally leaves her husband, taking the children with her. That is another fact. It is in consequence of that second fact that he finds it intolerable – not in consequence of the previous adultery. On that evidence, it is quite plain that the marriage has broken down irretrievably. He complies with section [1(2)(*a*)] by proving (*a*) her adultery which was forgiven; and (*b*) her subsequent conduct (not adultery), which makes it intolerable to live with her.

I would say one word more. In *Rayden on Divorce*, 11th ed., p. 175, it is suggested (referring to an extra-judicial lecture by Sir Jocelyn Simon [Riddell Lecture 1970, see *Rayden*, pp. 3227, 3234]): 'It may even be his own adultery which leads him to find it intolerable to live with the respondent.' I cannot accept that suggestion. Suppose a wife committed adultery five years ago. The husband forgives her and takes her back. He then falls in love with another woman and commits adultery with her. He may say that he finds it intolerable to live with his wife, but that is palpably untrue. It was quite tolerable for five years: and it is not rendered intolerable by his love for another woman. That illustration shows that a judge in such cases as these should not accept the man's bare assertion that he finds it intolerable. He should inquire what conduct on the part of the wife has made it intolerable. It may be her previous adultery. It may be something else. But whatever it is, the judge must be satisfied that the husband finds it intolerable to live with her.

On the facts of this case I think the judge could and should have found on the evidence the two elements required, (1) the adultery of the wife and (2) the husband found it intolerable to live with her.

Appeal allowed.

Questions

(i) Husband and wife agree that they will live on the wife's earnings from prostitution; after some months of this the husband falls in love with a young virgin; he finds it intolerable to live with his wife; is he entitled to an immediate divorce?

(ii) The same husband leaves his wife to wait until he is free to marry his young virgin; is his wife entitled to an immediate divorce?

(iii) Do you find your answers to questions (i) and (ii) either (*a*) just, or (*b*) sensible?

(iv) If you are not happy with the answers to questions (i) and (ii), ought the result to be (*a*) that neither is entitled to an immediate divorce, or (*b*) that both are entitled to an immediate divorce?

(v) What difference, if any, would it have made to any of your answers if the husband's distaste for his wife had developed because she contracted the AIDS virus in the course of her prostitution?

(vi) Does not the answer to Lord Denning's last example lie in s. 2(1)?

(vii) But if 'adultery' and 'intolerability' need have nothing to do with one another, why is s. 2(2) expressed as it is?[6]

Livingstone-Stallard v Livingstone-Stallard
[1974] Fam 47, [1974] 2 All ER 766, [1974] 3 WLR 302, 118 Sol Jo 462, 4 Fam Law 150, High Court, Family Division

The husband and wife married in December 1969; they were then aged 56 and 24 respectively. Two months later, 'as the result of one of the few scenes of violence which took place during the marriage', the wife left. But in September 1970 they were reunited. The marriage ended for practical purposes in September 1972, when the wife left after the husband became enraged in the course of an argument. The wife petitioned on the basis of her husband's behaviour. Most of the incidents were 'trivial in themselves', and we quote only one of those described because of the significance attached to it by the judge. It took place shortly after the wedding and before the first parting.

Dunn J: ... The wife also complained about another incident which was, perhaps, the most illuminating incident so far as the husband's character was concerned. They had, naturally, had some photographs taken at their wedding, and not very long afterwards the photographer came round with the wedding album. The husband was out and the wife, exercising what one would imagine was normal courtesy and hospitality, offered the photographer a glass of sherry which he accepted and she had a glass of sherry too to keep him company. When the husband came home he went to his cocktail cabinet, took out the sherry bottle and said, 'You have drunk half a bottle of sherry. Don't you ever go to my cocktail cabinet again.' He asked her who she had been drinking with and she told him what had happened. He forbade her to 'give refreshment to trades people again.' He was naturally cross-examined about his attitude and it appeared to be that if his wife took a glass of sherry with a tradesman – and he apparently classed the photographer as a tradesman – then the glass of sherry might, as he put it, impair her faculties, so that the tradesman might make some kind of indecent approach to her; and that was the justification of his conduct on that occasion. To my mind, it is typical of the man. ...

I am quite satisfied that this marriage has broken down. The wife told me that in no circumstances would she continue to live with her husband, partly because he is so irresponsible with Jason [their son] and takes so little interest in him. I cannot, of course, dissolve this marriage unless I am satisfied that the husband has behaved in such a way that the wife cannot reasonably be expected to live with him. That question is, to my mind, a question of fact, and one approach to it is to suppose that the case is being tried by a judge and jury and to consider what the proper direction to the jury would be, and then to put oneself in the position of a properly directed jury in deciding the question of fact.

... I ask myself the question: Would any right-thinking person come to the conclusion that this husband has behaved in such a way that this wife cannot reasonably be expected to live with him, taking into account the whole of the circumstances and the characters and personalities of the parties? It is on that basis that I approach the evidence in this case.

The wife was young enough to be the husband's daughter and plainly considerable adjustment was required on both sides. Mr Reece submitted that she had known him a long time and that she knew exactly the kind of man that she was marrying; that the complaints which she made are trivial; and that she cannot bring herself within section 1(2)(*b*) simply because the character of her husband does not suit her. He further submitted that the reality of this case was that this young woman had simply got fed up and walked out, and walked out pretty soon too. I accept that the wife was a strong-minded young woman, but I am satisfied that she was anxious for the marriage to last and wished it to continue, that she wished to have children and bring them up and to have her own home, and that she did her best so far as she was able to adjust to her husband's character.

---

6. A differently constituted Court of Appeal was troubled by this point in *Carr v Carr* [1974] 1 All ER 1193, [1974] 1 WLR 1534, but reluctantly accepted the *Cleary* interpretation of s. 1(2)(*a*).

The husband was said, by Mr Reece, to be meticulous. I agree with Mr Beckman [for the wife] that more suitable adjectives would be self-opinionated, didactic and critical and I accept that the husband's approach was to educate the wife to conform entirely to his standards. He, in my judgment, patronised her continually and submitted her, as I have found, to continual petty criticisms and his general attitude is well exemplified by the incident of the sherry and the photographer whom he called 'the tradesman.' I accept that many of the incidents were, or might appear to be, trivial in themselves and that there is a paucity of specific incidents between September 1970 and November 1972. But taking the facts as I have found them in the round in relation to the husband's character, in my judgment, they amount to a situation in which this young wife was subjected to a constant atmosphere of criticism, disapproval and boorish behaviour on the part of her husband. Applying the test which I have formulated, I think that any right-thinking person would come to the conclusion that this husband had behaved in such a way that this wife could not reasonably be expected to live with him. There will accordingly be a decree nisi under section 1(2)(*b*) of the Matrimonial Causes Act 1973.

Buffery v Buffery
[1988] FCR 465, [1988] 2 FLR 365, Court of Appeal

The parties were married in 1964. In December 1985 the wife petitioned for divorce under s. 1(2)(*b*) of the Matrimonial Causes Act 1973. The recorder considered that the conduct alleged against the husband had to be 'grave and weighty' and such that the wife could not reasonably be expected to continue to live with him. He concluded from the evidence that the cause of the breakdown of the marriage could not be blamed on the husband in the sense that he had been guilty of misbehaviour of a grave and weighty nature and that the breakdown could not be directed at either party since they had merely drifted apart. Accordingly, he held that the wife had failed to prove her case under s. 1(2)(*b*) and dismissed the petition. The wife appealed.

May LJ considered the meaning of s. 1(2)(*b*) and concluded that:

... on a proper reading of the statute and an assessment of the facts of a given case, the gravity or otherwise of the conduct complained of is of itself immaterial. What has to be asked ... is whether the behaviour is such that the petitioner cannot reasonably be expected to live with the respondent.

One considers a right-thinking person looking at the particular husband and wife and asks whether the one could reasonably be expected to live with the other taking into account all the circumstances of the case and the respective characters and personalities of the two parties concerned. ...

Looking at the facts in this case, May LJ went on:

The matters of which complaint is made in the original and supplemental particulars went, first, to the questions of finances between husband and wife and the way in which the husband had dealt with them and, secondly, to whether the husband ever took his wife out on social occasions, she contending that he did not. That failure on his part was at least part of the behaviour of which she complained, which led to the reasonable conclusion that she could not be expected to live with him.

In so far as going out together socially was concerned, the recorder made a more precise finding:

> 'I think the situation was this – the wife was not keen to go out when the children were growing up and they simply got to a stage when they did not go out socially except on rare occasions. By the time the children had grown up and they could have gone out socially, they were quite unable to communicate. In that respect, I do not think the blame is attached to one more than the other. As the wife put it on more than one occasion – we just do not communicate. We have nothing in common.'

Then, towards the end of his judgment, the recorder said:

> 'Although the [wife] has established that the marriage has irretrievably broken down, the cause of the breakdown cannot really be levelled at the [husband] in the sense that he has been guilty of misbehaviour of a grave and weighty nature. The [wife] has been quite candid about this; when asked she said the marriage has broken down; we cannot communicate; we have nothing in common – and there lies, in my view, the crux of the matter. The situation is that neither is really at fault.'

Reading the judgment of the recorder in full, I conclude that in so far as any dissension over money matters was concerned, although the husband had been somewhat insensitive, nevertheless this did not constitute sufficient behaviour within the relevant statutory provision. In truth, what has happened in this marriage is the fault of neither party; they have just grown apart. They cannot communicate. They have nothing in common and there lies, as the recorder said, the crux of the matter.

It was submitted that if the matter went back to the recorder he could make various findings on the evidence about the sensitivity, for instance, of the wife in relation to these matters and various further findings of fact about the nature and extent of the husband's behaviour complained of. I, for my part, do not think he could. He heard all the evidence and the conclusion to which he came was that nobody was really at fault here, except they both had grown apart. In those circumstances, in my judgment, clearly the wife failed to make out her case under s. 1(2)(*b*), although she satisfied the recorder that the marriage had broken down irretrievably. I do not think any advantage would be gained by sending this matter back for a retrial. The matter was fully investigated and the recorder made the findings to which I have referred. In those circumstances, I would reach the same conclusion as did the recorder, namely that the petition should be dismissed.

Appeal dismissed.

Questions

(i) If Mr Livingstone-Stallard and Mr Buffery had petitioned for divorce based on s. 1(2)(*b*), what would have been the result?

(ii) The facts in *Pheasant v Pheasant* [1972] Fam 202, [1972] 1 All ER 587, to which Dunn J refers, were that a husband complained that the wife was unable to provide him with the 'spontaneous, demonstrative affection' which his character and personality demanded. This lack of affection made it impossible for him to live with his wife. The husband's petition was rejected by Ormrod J. If Mrs Pheasant had petitioned for divorce based on s. 1(2)(*b*) would she have obtained the same result as Mrs Livingstone-Stallard?

(iii) Desertion is leaving without consent or a good reason; the deserted party cannot petition for two years. Would a jury think it reasonable to expect her to live with a person who was no longer there to be lived with?

(iv) Should the test for 'unreasonable behaviour' be the same as the test for a good reason to leave?

Thurlow v Thurlow

[1976] Fam 32, [1975] 2 All ER 979, [1975] 3 WLR 161, 119 Sol Jo 406, 5 Fam Law 188, High Court, Family Division

The wife suffered from epilepsy and a severe physical neurological disorder. From June 1969, her mental and physical condition gradually deteriorated. Her husband made a 'genuine, sustained and considerable effort' to cope with her at home, but was forced to give up, and since July 1972 she had required full-time institutional care and would continue to do so for the rest of her life. In 1974, the husband petitioned on the basis of her behaviour.

Rees J: ... The husband's case therefore consists of allegations of both negative and of positive behaviour on the part of the wife. The negative behaviour alleged and proved is that between the middle of 1969 and 1 July 1972, she gradually became a bedridden invalid unable to perform the role of a wife in any respect whatsoever until she reached a state in which she became unfitted even to reside in an ordinary household at all and required to be removed to a hospital and there reside for the rest of her life. The positive behaviour alleged and proved is that during the same period she displayed bad temper and threw objects at her mother-in-law and caused damage by burning various household items such as towels, cushions and blankets. From time to time she escaped from the home and wandered about the streets causing alarm and stress to those trying to care for her.

I am satisfied that by July 1972 the marriage had irretrievably broken down and since the wife, tragically, is to spend the rest of her life as a patient in a hospital the husband cannot be expected to live with her. But the question remains as to whether the wife's behaviour has been such as to justify a finding by the court that it is unreasonable to expect him to do so. ...

Questions of interpretation of the words in section 1(2)(*b*) of the Act of 1973 which arise from the facts in the instant case include the following: Does behaviour which is wholly or mainly negative in character fall within the ambit of the statute? Is behaviour which stems from mental illness and which may be involuntary, capable of constituting relevant behaviour?

I consider these questions separately. As to the distinction which has been made between 'positive' and 'negative' behaviour I can find nothing in the statute to suggest that either form is excluded. The sole test prescribed as to the nature of the behaviour is that it must be such as to justify a finding that the petitioner cannot reasonably be expected to live with the respondent. It may well be that in practice such a finding will more readily be made in cases where the behaviour relied upon is positive than those wherein it is negative. Spouses may often, but not always, be expected to tolerate more in the way of prolonged silences and total inactivity than of violent language or violent activity. I find myself in respectful agreement with the views expressed by Davies LJ in the Court of Appeal in *Gollins v Gollins* [1964] P 32 at 58:

> '... I do not find the contrast between "positive" conduct and "negative" conduct either readily comprehensible or helpful, although these expressions are undoubtedly to be found in the decided cases. Almost any sort of conduct can at one and the same time be described both as positive and as negative. An omission in most cases is at the same time a commission.'...

I now turn to the question as to whether behaviour which stems from mental illness and which may be involuntary is capable of falling within the statute. ...

... I propose to follow the principle stated by Lord Reid in *Williams v Williams* [1964] AC 698 at 723 and cited by Sir George Baker P in *Katz v Katz* [1972] 3 All ER 219 at 224:

> 'In my judgment, decree should be pronounced against such an abnormal person ... simply because the facts are such that, after making all allowances for his disabilities and for the temperaments of both parties, it must be held that the character and gravity of his acts were such as to amount to cruelty.'

Sir George Baker P usefully suggested that this statement of principle may be adapted to meet the present law by substituting for the final words: '... the character and gravity of his behaviour was such that the petitioner cannot reasonably be expected to live with him.'

Accordingly the facts of each case must be considered and a decision made, having regard to all the circumstances, as to whether the particular petitioner can or cannot reasonably be expected to live with the particular respondent. If the behaviour stems from misfortune such as the onset of mental illness or from disease of the body, or from accidental physical injury, the court will take full account of all the obligations of the married state. These will include the normal duty to accept and to share the burdens imposed upon the family as a result of the mental or physical ill-health of one member. It will also consider the capacity of the petitioner to withstand the stresses imposed by the behaviour, the steps taken to cope with it, the length of time during which the petitioner has been called upon to bear it and the actual or potential effect upon his or her health. The court will then be required to make a judgment as to whether the petitioner can fairly be required to live with the respondent. The granting of the decree to the petitioner does not necessarily involve any blameworthiness on the part of the respondent, and, no doubt, in cases of misfortune the judge will make this clear in his judgment.

In the course of his most helpful submissions on behalf of the wife Mr Holroyd Pearce drew attention to some difficulties which he urged would arise if the law were such as to enable a decree to be granted in the instant case. It would mean, he said, that any spouse who was afflicted by a mental or physical illness or an accident so as to become a 'human vegetable' could be divorced under section 1(2)(*b*) of the Matrimonial Causes Act 1973. This was repugnant to the sense of justice of most people because it involved an implication of blameworthiness where none in truth existed and it was not what Parliament intended. The remedy was open to the petitioner in such cases to seek a decree of divorce on the ground of five years' separation under section 1(2)(*e*) of the Act of 1973 and if this were done no blame would be imputed to the respondent and also the special protection for the interests of the respondents provided by sections 5 and 10 of the Act of 1973 would be available whereas it would not if a decree were granted under section 1(2)(*b*). He cited two extreme examples to illustrate the point. One was the case of a spouse who was suddenly reduced to the state of a human vegetable as a result of a road traffic accident and was immediately removed to a hospital and there remained for life. The other was one in which supervening permanent impotency brought marital relations to an end.

There is no completely satisfactory answer to these submissions but what may properly be said is that the law as laid down in *Williams v Williams* [1964] AC 698, [1963] 2 All ER 994 does provide a remedy by divorce for a spouse who is the victim of the violence of an insane respondent spouse not responsible in law or fact for his or her actions and in no respect blameworthy. The basis for that decision is the need to afford protection to the petitioner against injury. So also in the insanity cases where the behaviour alleged is wholly negative and no violence in deed or word is involved but where continuing cohabitation has caused, or is likely to cause injury to health, it should be open to the court to provide a remedy by divorce. Before deciding to grant a divorce in such cases the court would require to be satisfied that the petitioner could not reasonably be expected to live with the respondent and would not be likely to do so in the case referred to by Mr Holroyd Pearce unless driven to it by grave considerations which would include actual or apprehended injury to the health of the petitioner or of the family as a whole. It is now common knowledge that health may be gravely affected by certain kinds of negative behaviour whether voluntary or not and if the granting of a decree under section 1(2)(*b*) is justified in order to protect the health of petitioners injured by violence so it should be in cases where the petitioner's health is adversely affected by negative behaviour. The safeguard provided for the interests of respondents is that it is the judge and not the petitioner who must decide whether the petitioner can reasonably be expected to live with the respondent; and that decision is subject to review upon appeal.

I do not propose to state any concluded view upon the case postulated in which a spouse is reduced to a human vegetable as the result of a road traffic accident and is removed at once to hospital to remain there for life ...

In reaching the decision the judge will have regard to all the circumstances including the disabilities and temperaments of both parties, the causes of the behaviour and whether the causes were or were not known to the petitioner, the presence or absence of intention, the impact of it upon the petitioner and the family unit, its duration, and the prospects of cure or improvement in the future. If the judge decided that it would be unreasonable to expect the petitioner to live with the respondent then he must grant a decree of divorce unless he is satisfied that the marriage has not irretrievably broken down.

Approaching the facts in the instant case upon the basis of these conclusions I feel bound to decide that a decree nisi of divorce should be granted. This husband has conscientiously and courageously suffered the behaviour of the wife for substantial periods of time between 1969 and July 1972 until his powers of endurance were exhausted and his health was endangered. This behaviour stemmed from mental illness and disease and no blame of any kind can be nor is attributed to the wife.

Questions

(i) Is it possible for anyone nowadays to define the 'obligations of the married state'? How can a judge guess what a jury of 'right-thinking' people would think they were?

(ii) The Family Law Sub-Committee of the Law Society, in *A Better Way Out* (1979), stated that, in undefended cases, 'the evidence presents little difficulty – after several years of marriage, virtually any spouse can assemble a list of events which, taken out of context, can be presented as unreasonable behaviour [sic] sufficient on which to found a divorce petition.' Does this surprise you?

(iii) If you were drafting a petition based upon the other's behaviour would you be inclined to make it look as bad as possible (lest the court be tempted

to probe more deeply) or as little as you think you can get away with (lest the respondent be goaded into defending either the petition itself or ancillary issues)?
(iv) How little do you think you can get away with?

A selection of newspaper cuttings on defended divorce petitions during the period 1984–1991 reveals successful petitions brought against the following:

(i) a handyman husband who started many jobs in the house and garden, but seldom finished them. He was moody, aggressive and difficult (2 November 1984);
(ii) a husband who deliberately annoyed his wife by hiding her underwear; if she did or said something he did not like he would become moody and not speak to her for days (17 April 1986);
(iii) a husband who sat in the matrimonial home all day in his pyjamas shouting his opinions at anyone prepared to listen and even those not prepared to (1 March 1985);
(iv) a wife who often forced her husband to sleep in the car and did not allow him to use the downstairs bathroom (14 February 1986);
(v) a husband who was something of 'a martinet' and put his children on parade before him from time to time (17 June 1985);
(vi) a wife who went to Athens where her husband was a diplomat, and attacked his mistress in a public cinema. Earlier, when they were stationed in Istanbul where she was unhappy with the sewerage system, she had threatened to pour a pail of sewage over the Consul General's dining-room table if something was not done (25 March 1987);

And unsuccessful petitions against the following:

(vii) an undemonstrative husband (16 April 1986);
(viii) a man of 'outstanding forbearance' who had shown 'patience and sympathy' for a wife who was 'cold, utterly self-centred and somewhat neurotic' (24 January 1985);
(ix) a man who was alleged to be 'of dominant mind and character', especially in financial matters (18 January 1990).

The following feature in *The Times*, 19 February 1996, gives some more recent examples of particulars of 'unreasonable behaviour':

So what's unreasonable behaviour?

1. Allegation made by the petitioner – the husband – that his full-time working wife would only ever cook him 'microwave suppers' and not the 'real meals' his mother used to cook.
2. The allegation made by the petitioner – the wife – that her husband was an incompetent do-it-yourself fanatic who spent all his spare time constructing things around the house that would later fall down or – on one occasion – had caused actual structural damage to their home.
3. The wife who petitioned the husband on the ground that he would not speak to her for a year because he had been advised by a medium that he should not do so.
4. The wife who petitioned that her husband would count all the plants in the garden in an obsessive manner each night, making notes about how many blooms there were on each rose bush.
5. The wife who petitioned that her husband was obese and physically repugnant to her. On receiving the petition he was so upset that he lost four stone and they eventually became reconciled.

6. The husband who petitioned that his partner, a housewife, would spend all her evenings talking on the telephone to her friends, recalling every dull detail of her day.
7. The husband who alleged that his wife had claimed that she could not make love to him because she believed he was a reincarnated god and she should remain chaste.
8. The woman who petitioned that her husband would not give up control of the television zapper and would compulsively switch channels when she wanted to watch something. She could cope with this until he installed cable TV. With 24 channels to zap through, she finally left him.
9. The woman who claimed that her husband's problem with flatulence made it necessary for her to move into the spare room and eventually out of the marriage.
10. The man who alleged that his wife was so concerned about being seen without makeup that she never took it off, even at night, and the sight of her clogged face was repugnant to him.

Questions

(i) Was there really any point defending the petitions in the first six cases on p. 217?
(ii) Would you have advised the respondents in cases (vii) to (ix) to defend? What would have happened if they had been undefended?
(iii) Look back now to *Buffery* (p. 213). Do you think that, if the facts of that case were to recur today, the petition would be defended? In any event, do you think the petitioner would obtain a divorce?
(iv) Is 'adultery' or 'unreasonable behaviour' the more acceptable basis for a marriage to be terminated against (*a*) a male respondent, and (*b*) a female respondent?

(b) THE 'NO-FAULT' FACTS

Santos v Santos
[1972] Fam 247, [1972] 2 All ER 246, [1972] 2 WLR 889, 116 Sol Jo 196, Court of Appeal

This was a wife's undefended petition on the basis of two years' separation and her husband's consent. The judge dismissed the petition because on three occasions since the separation the wife had stayed with her husband for a short while. These did not amount to more than six months and they had been apart for the requisite total of two years in all, but the judge's attention was not drawn to what is now s. 2(5) of the Matrimonial Causes Act 1973. The wife appealed and the Court of Appeal took the opportunity to consider a totally new point as to the meaning of 'living apart.' The judgment was that of the whole court.

Sachs LJ: ... The appeal first came before the court, differently constituted, on November 11, 1971. Then, after having heard the submissions of Mr Picard for the wife, it became apparent that it raised a very important issue as to the meaning of the words 'living apart' in section [1(2)(*d*)]. Does this relate simply and solely to physically not living under the same roof, or does it import an additional element which has been referred to in various terms – 'absence of consortium,' 'termination of consortium,' or an 'attitude of mind' – phrases intended to convey either the fact or realisation of the fact that there is absent something which is fundamental to the state of marriage.

In the course of the argument before us reference was frequently made to the position of diplomats en poste in insalubrious foreign capitals, to those serving sentences in prison, to those in mental and other hospitals, and to prisoners of war – in the main, involuntary separations. None the less there are larger and no less important categories of separations which start voluntarily, such as business postings, voyages of exploration or recuperation trips when one party has been ill – all of which must also be looked at when endeavouring to determine what the legislature intended by the words 'living apart.'

Their lordships then reviewed the Commonwealth authorities on comparable divorce legislation and the English authorities on similar expressions in English tax and criminal legislation.

The cogent volume of authority, to which we have been referred, makes it abundantly clear that the phrase 'living apart' when used in a statute concerned with matrimonial affairs normally imports something more than mere physical separation. This is something which obviously must be assumed to have been known to the legislature in 1969. It follows that its normal meaning must be attributed to it in the Act of 1969, unless one is led to a different conclusion either by the general scheme of the statute coupled with difficulties which would result from such an interpretation, or alternatively by some specific provision in that statute. ...

Obviously this element is not one which necessarily involves mutual consent, for otherwise the new Act would not afford relief under head (*e*) in that area where it was most plainly intended to be available – where the 'innocent' party adheres to the marriage, refusing to recognise that in truth it has ended, often despite the fact that the 'guilty' one has been living with someone else for very many years. So it must be an element capable of being unilateral: and it must, in our judgment, involve at least a recognition that the marriage is in truth at an end – and has become a shell, to adopt a much-used metaphor.

If the element can be unilateral in the sense of depending on the attitude of mind of one spouse, must it be communicated to the other spouse before it becomes in law operative? That is a question that gave particular concern in the course of the argument. There is something unattractive in the idea that in effect time under head (*e*) can begin to run against a spouse without his or her knowledge. Examples discussed included men in prison, in hospital, or away on service whose wives, so far as they knew, were standing by them: they might, perhaps, thus be led to fail to take some step which they would later feel could just have saved the marriage. On the other hand, communication might well be impossible in cases where the physical separation was due to a breakdown in mental health on the part of the other spouse, or a prolonged coma such as can occasionally occur. Moreover, need for communication would tend to equate heads (*d*) and (*e*) with desertion – which comes under head (*c*) – something unlikely to be intended by the legislature. Moreover, bowing to the inevitable is not the same thing as intending it to happen.

In the end we have firmly concluded that communication by word or conduct is not a necessary ingredient of the additional element.

On the basis that an uncommunicated unilateral ending of recognition that a marriage is subsisting can mark the moment when 'living apart' commences, 'the principal problem becomes one of proof of the time when the breakdown occurred'. ... Sometimes there will be evidence such as a letter, reduction or cessation of visits, or starting to live with another man. But cases may well arise where there is only the oral evidence of the wife on this point. One can only say that cases under heads (*d*) and (*e*) may often need careful examination by the first instance judge and that special caution may need to be taken. ...

... Therefore 'living apart' referred to in grounds (*d*) and (*e*) is a state of affairs to establish which it is in the vast generality of cases arising under those heads necessary to prove something more than that the husband and wife are physically separated. For the purposes of that vast generality, it is sufficient to say that the relevant state of affairs does not exist whilst both parties recognise the marriage as subsisting. ...

The case was therefore sent back for trial before a High Court judge.

Questions

(i) From the point of view of the innocent and loyal wife of the long-sentence prisoner, why is it 'absurd and unjust' if he makes up his mind to divorce her

just before he is released, but apparently not if he makes up his mind five years earlier and tells her nothing about it?
(ii) Is the real reason not that this is absurd and unjust to her, but that such a recent decision is not conclusive evidence that the breakdown is irretrievable?
(iii) Suppose a couple whose marriage is going through a bad patch have a trial separation but keep returning to one another for brief periods until they finally decide that it is all over: is that decision any less likely to be 'irretrievable' than that of a couple whose initial separation was 'for good' but who kept changing their minds? (The logic of *Santos* coupled with s. 2(5) would appear to be that the second couple get their divorce whereas the first couple do not.)

However, the notion that 'living with each other in the same household' is as much an abstraction as a physical reality can be very helpful to those couples who are still under the same roof:

Fuller (otherwise Penfold) v Fuller
[1973] 2 All ER 650, [1973] 1 WLR 730, 117 Sol Jo 224, Court of Appeal

Husband and wife separated in 1964, when the wife left the matrimonial home, taking their two daughters, and went to live with a Mr Penfold in the latter's home. She took the name of Mrs Penfold and they lived together as husband and wife. Four years later, Mr Fuller had a coronary thrombosis and was no longer able to live alone. He therefore 'went and became a lodger in the house' where his wife lived with Mr Penfold. The wife gave him food and he ate with others in the house. The wife also did the washing. He paid a weekly sum for board and lodging. After four years of this, the wife petitioned for divorce on the basis of five years' separation and the husband did not defend. The judge refused the decree and the wife appealed.

Lord Denning MR: ... At the hearing the judge held that he had no jurisdiction to grant a divorce because he thought that when the husband came back to the house, he and his wife were not living apart. The judge referred to the cases under the old law, such as *Hopes v Hopes* [1949] P 227, [1948] 2 All ER 920; and also the cases under the new Act: *Mouncer v Mouncer* [1972] 1 All ER 289, [1972] 1 WLR 321 and *Santos v Santos* [1972] 2 All ER 246.

In *Santos v Santos* this court stressed the need, under the new Act, to consider the state of mind of the parties and, in particular, whether they treated the marriage as subsisting or not. Clearly they treated it in this case as at an end.

... In this case the wife was living with Mr Penfold as his wife. The husband was living in the house as a lodger. It is impossible to say that husband and wife were or are living with each other in the same household. It is very different from *Mouncer v Mouncer* where the husband and wife were living with the children in the same household – as husband and wife normally do – but were not having sexual intercourse together. That is not sufficient to constitute 'living apart'. I do not doubt the correctness of that decision. But the present case is very different. I think the judge put too narrow and limited a construction on the Act. I would allow the appeal and pronounce the decree nisi of divorce.

Stamp LJ: I agree. I can only say that to my mind the words 'living with each other in the same household' in the context of the Act relating to matrimonial proceedings are not apt to describe the situation where the wife is indisputably living with another man in the same household and her husband is there as a paying guest in the circumstances Lord Denning MR has described. 'Living with each other' connotes to my mind something more than living in the same household: indeed the words 'with each other' would otherwise be redundant.
Appeal allowed.

Questions

(i) Until this case, we had all thought that the operative concept was that of a common 'household' – were they sharing such things as meals and television, and was the wife still doing some things for her husband, even if they were not sharing a bed? – but does it now seem that the operative words are 'with each other'? Does that make the words 'in the same household' redundant?
(ii) If that be so, why should not withdrawal to a separate bedroom, together with the state of mind envisaged in *Santos v Santos* [1972] Fam 247, [1972] 2 All ER 246, be sufficient?
(iii) Why do the judges apparently think that it is more important when a wife stops cooking and washing for her husband than when she refuses to share a bed with him?
(iv) Suppose a woman comes to you and explains that she and her husband have had little to do with one another for some time and would now like a divorce, although for convenience they are still living under the same roof: will you explain the law carefully to her before you seek further and better particulars of their circumstances?
(v) What questions would you then ask?
(vi) How do you think all this accords with the concern felt by the Archbishop of Canterbury's group for 'considerations of truth, the sacredness of oaths and the integrity of professional practice'?

We turn now to the s. 5 defence:

Le Marchant v Le Marchant
[1977] 3 All ER 610, [1977] 1 WLR 559, 121 Sol Jo 334, Court of Appeal

The husband was a post office employee and about to retire. He petitioned for divorce on the basis of five years' separation. The wife alleged that the possible loss of an index-linked widow's pension would cause her grave financial hardship. The judge granted a decree and the wife appealed.

Ormrod LJ: ... It would be quite wrong to approach this kind of case on the footing that the wife is entitled to be compensated pound for pound for what she will lose in consequence of the divorce. She has to show, not that she will lose something by being divorced, but that she will suffer grave financial hardship, which is quite another matter altogether. It is quite plain that, prima facie, the loss of the pension, which is an index-linked pension, in the order of £1,300 a year at the moment, is quite obviously grave financial hardship in the circumstances of a case like this unless it can be in some way mitigated. The learned judge, however, did not approach the case in this way. He said that s. 5 had to be read with s. 10 of the 1973 Act. Section 10 is the section which provides, in sub-s (3), that before a decree nisi is made absolute in cases such as the present, the court is required at the request of the wife to investigate the financial position and not to make the decree absolute until it is satisfied either that the petitioning husband should not be required to make any financial provision for the wife or that the financial provision made by him is reasonable and fair or (and these are the words which cause the trouble) is 'the best that can be made in the circumstances'. So, as counsel for the wife says, s. 10 offers an elusive or, perhaps better, an unreliable protection to a wife placed in the position in which this wife is placed. The marriage would have been dissolved by the decree nisi, there would have been therefore a finding of fact that she has not suffered grave financial hardship in consequence of the decree and she would then have to do the best she could under s. 10.

It is also right to point out that there are many cases, and this is one, in which the powers of the court, extensive as they are under ss. 23 and 24 as well as s. 10, are not wide enough to enable the court to carry out by order various things which a petitioner husband can do voluntarily, even if compelled to do it voluntarily, so s. 10 is not an adequate substitute. The learned judge, in a sentence, took the view that if he could see from the husband's financial position that he would be able one way or the other to alleviate sufficiently the financial hardship falling on the wife as a result of the loss of her pension, that was good enough. In the view of this court, that is not right. The right way to approach this problem is Cumming-Bruce J's approach in *Parker v Parker* [1972] Fam 116, [1972] 1 All ER 410, that is that the answer should set up a prima facie case of financial hardship, that the petition should be dismissed unless the petitioner can meet that answer in his reply by putting forward a proposal which is acceptable to the court as reasonable in all the circumstances and which is sufficient to remove the element of grave financial hardship which otherwise would lead to the dismissal of the petition. ...

Now, at the last minute, and this is really one minute to midnight, counsel for the husband has at least made an offer. The offer is this. His client offers to transfer the matrimonial home or his interest in the matrimonial home to the wife forthwith. Secondly, he offers to pay her £5,000 when he receives the capital sum under his pension scheme (his position has clearly improved since the figures in the document P1 were worked out) and in addition to that he proposes to take out a life insurance policy on his own life to provide on his death the sum of £5,000 which will be payable to the wife if she survives him and which she can then use as she thinks fit. That offer is without prejudice to any order for periodical payment which may be made hereafter by a registrar when the respective income positions have been investigated. ...

The view which I have formed is that the present offer is a reasonable one in the sense that it will, if implemented, remove the element of grave financial hardship so far as the wife is concerned, and remove therefore the defence which she has to the present petition. ...

I need only say that the decree absolute will not be made in this case until the matrimonial home has been transferred and the insurance policy has been taken out, and the lump sum paid over, to the satisfaction of the wife's advisers. In those circumstances, and in those circumstances only, would I be in favour of allowing a decree nisi to stand.

In *Reiterbund v Reiterbund* [1974] 2 All ER 455, [1974] 1 WLR 788, Finer J held that the possible loss of a state widow's pension to a woman of 52 who would have to rely, as she was then relying, on supplementary benefit was *not* a grave financial hardship.

The grave hardship does not, of course, have to be financial.

Rukat v Rukat
[1975] Fam 63, [1975] 1 All ER 343, [1975] 2 WLR 201, 119 Sol Jo 30, 4 Fam Law 81, Court of Appeal

The husband, a Pole, and the wife, a Sicilian, married in 1946. Both were Roman Catholics. They had not lived together since 1947, when the wife had visited Sicily with their daughter and the husband had written telling her not to return as he had fallen in love with another woman. Since then the wife had kept up the pretence that the marriage was still subsisting. In 1972, the husband petitioned for divorce on the basis of five years' separation. The wife alleged that this would cause her hardship on the grounds that: (i) the prospect of divorce was an anathema to her on religious and moral grounds because she was a Roman Catholic; (ii) because of the social structure of the area where she lived, divorce would cause serious repercussions for her and her child; and (iii) if a decree were pronounced she would not be accepted in her community in Sicily and would not be able to return to her home. The judge granted a decree and the wife appealed.

Lawton LJ: ... One has to start, I think, by looking at the context in which the phrase 'grave financial or other hardship' occurs. The word 'hardship' is not a word of art. It follows that it must be construed by the courts in a common sense way, and the meaning which is put on the word 'hardship' should be such as would meet with the approval of ordinary sensible people. In my judgment, the ordinary sensible man would take the view that there are two aspects of 'hardship' – that which the sufferer from the hardship thinks he is suffering and that which a reasonable bystander with knowledge of all the facts would think he was suffering. That can be illustrated by a homely example. The rich gourmet who because of financial stringency has to drink vin ordinaire with his grouse may well think that he is suffering a hardship; but sensible people would say he was not.

If that approach is applied to this case, one gets this situation. The wife undoubtedly feels that she has suffered a hardship; and the learned judge, in the passages to which Megaw LJ has referred, found that she was feeling at the time of the judgment that she could not go back to Sicily. That, if it was genuine and deeply felt, would undoubtedly be a 'hardship' in one sense of that word. But one has to ask oneself the question whether sensible people, knowing all the facts, would think it was a hardship. On the evidence, I have come to the conclusion that they would not, and for this reason. The wife has been separated from her husband now since 1947. She returned in that year to Sicily. She has been living in Palermo with her mother and father. Her relatives have been around her; they must have appreciated that something had gone wrong with the marriage. I make all allowances for the undoubted fact that many male Sicilians leave their country to work elsewhere, and wives may be left alone for months and years on end. Nevertheless, 26 years is a very long time; and such evidence as there was before the learned judge was to the effect that it was almost inevitable that her family and those who knew her would have appreciated that there was something wrong. There would be some social stigma attached to that; she might be thought to have failed as a wife. But she has lived that down; and the fact that there had been a divorce in some foreign country would add very little to the stigma. ...

Ormrod LJ: ... The court has first to decide whether there was evidence on which it could properly come to the conclusion that the wife was suffering from grave financial or other hardship; and 'other hardship' in this context, in my judgment, agreeing with Megaw and Lawton LJ, must mean other *grave* hardship. If hardship is found, the court then has to look at the second limb and decide whether, in all the circumstances, looking at everybody's interests, balancing the respondent's hardship against the petitioner's interests in getting his or her freedom, it would be wrong to dissolve the marriage. ...
Appeal dismissed.

In *Balraj v Balraj* (1980) 11 Fam Law 110, Court of Appeal, another case where the wife's defence was based upon hardship arising from cultural and religious factors, the judge dismissed the defence. The wife appealed, and counsel for the wife submitted that the judge should have applied a subjective rather than an objective test. The Court of Appeal rejected this submission:

Cumming-Bruce LJ: ... in my view the President was right in taking the view that, having made that appraisal of the respondent's own expectation about her suffering, he must stand back and then look at all the circumstances and form an objective view as to whether the prospective situation for the lady would constitute grave hardship or not.
Appeal dismissed.

Questions

(i) Can you describe a case, other than one such as *Le Marchant v Le Marchant* [1977] 3 All ER 610, [1977] 1 WLR 559, see p. 221, in which a divorce would cause grave hardship to the respondent *and* it would be wrong to dissolve the marriage? (See *Johnson v Johnson* (1981) 12 Fam Law 116.)
(ii) Is it necessary for the 'grave hardship' to be caused by the divorce rather than by the breakdown of the marital relationship?
(iii) If it is necessary, why should this be?

(iv) What advice would you give to Mrs Balraj and Mrs Rukat? [Read s. 10(2)(3), MCA 1973.]

(c) DOES FAULT MATTER?

Grenfell v Grenfell
[1978] Fam 128, [1978] 1 All ER 561, [1977] 3 WLR 738, 121 Sol Jo 814, 7 Fam Law 242, Court of Appeal

Husband and wife married in 1951 and separated in 1969. In 1974, shortly before they had been separated for five years, the wife petitioned for divorce on the basis of her husband's behaviour. The husband waited until the five years had elapsed and then filed an answer denying her allegations of behaviour and cross-praying on the basis of five years' separation. The wife filed a reply admitting separation but alleging that a divorce would cause her grave hardship, for the following reasons:

(1) She is of the Greek Orthodox faith. (2) As a practising Christian her conscience would be affronted if the marriage were to be dissolved otherwise than for grounds of substance whereby the true cause of the breakdown of the marriage will be determined by the court and a decree pronounced accordingly. (3) Further and alternatively the petitioner contends that the financial provisions set forth in the reply are inadequate in any event and that if implemented after a decree had been granted to the respondent the petitioner would suffer grave financial hardship.

The third reason was later abandoned. The registrar ordered, in effect, that the wife's reply should be struck out and that the case should proceed first on the prayer in the husband's answer. The wife appealed, first to the judge without success, and then to the Court of Appeal.

Ormrod LJ: ... It is quite clear that the purpose of section 5 is to permit a party to a marriage to object to a decree being granted on the ground of five years' separation where dissolution of the marriage would result in grave financial or other hardship to that party. The only thing to be looked at is the dissolution of the marriage. The question is simply and solely: Will the dissolution of this marriage cause grave financial or other hardship? It has got nothing to do, in my judgment, with which of the parties initiates the proceedings, nor with the ground for the proceedings. The wife in this case, having herself asked for a decree of dissolution, cannot be heard to say that if her marriage is dissolved she will suffer grave financial or other hardship. It would be a plain case of blowing hot and cold, which, of course, is not a form of pleading which can be tolerated. Consequently, in my judgment, the registrar and the judge were entirely right to strike out the reply.

I turn now to the second matter. The second point in this appeal is whether the wife should be permitted to go on with the allegations of behaviour in her petition in view of what has happened. It might be more accurate perhaps to put the question the other way round, in view of Mr Ewbank's submission [for the wife], and ask whether the court has power to grant a decree on the husband's answer on the ground of five years' separation, all the necessary facts being admitted, and to refuse to hear the allegations of behaviour set out in the petition. ...

Mr Ewbank has sought to rely on section 1(3) of the Act of 1973, which provides:

> 'On a petition for divorce it shall be the duty of the court to inquire, so far as it reasonably can, into the facts alleged by the petitioner and into any facts alleged by the respondent.'

He says that that requires the court, imposes a statutory duty on the court, to conduct an inquiry into the facts alleged by the petitioner and by the respondent. ... But, in the nature of things, on the facts in this case, there are no other relevant facts, other than the fact that the parties have been apart for five years and that the wife herself has asked for a decree and has herself admitted that the marriage has irretrievably broken down. There is nothing else to be inquired into.

There is no point, as I see it, in a case like this of conducting an inquiry into behaviour merely to satisfy feelings, however genuinely and sincerely held by one or other of the parties. To do so would be a waste of time of the court and, in any event, would be running, as I think, counter to the general policy or philosophy of the divorce legislation as it stands today. The purpose of Parliament was to ensure that where a marriage has irretrievably broken down, it should be dissolved as quickly and as painlessly as possible under the Act, and attempts to recriminate in the manner in which the wife in this case appears to wish to do should be, in my judgment, firmly discouraged. ...

In those circumstances, I am quite satisfied that it would be entirely wrong to permit the wife to go on with her petition in this case, for the simple reason that facts sufficient to enable the court to grant a decree of dissolution are plain on the face of the pleadings.

Appeal dismissed.

Questions

(i) Do you think, from what you can gather from all these cases, that 'the general policy or philosophy of the divorce legislation as it stands today' is the same as it was in 1971? You might consider this question again in the light of your reading on divorce procedure (below).

(ii) The 1973 Act being still in force,

(*a*) What advice would you give to a couple who came to you wanting an immediate divorce? and

(*b*) What advice would you give to a wife who wanted to divorce as soon as possible from a husband who did not? and

(*c*) What advice would you give to the husband in question (ii)(*b*)?

(iii) Do you think that the answers you have given to the questions: (*a*) reflect any credit upon the law; or (*b*) represent the reformers' original intentions?

(d) THE PROCEDURE UNDER THE 1973 ACT

One feature which has militated against attempts to restrict divorce is the impossibility of forcing respondents to defend. By 1966, 93% of divorces were undefended, and the position now is that less than 1,000 cases a year are likely to result in a defended divorce hearing. (In 1989, only 285 defended divorces proceeded to a hearing.) A so-called 'special procedure' was invented for the very simplest of cases and extended to all undefended divorces in 1977. The 'special procedure' is described in appendix C to the Law Commission's Report *The Ground for Divorce* (1990):

26. ... This requires the [district judge] to scrutinise the petition, supporting affidavit and any other evidence, in order to satisfy himself that the contents of the petition have been proved and that the petitioner is entitled to a decree. Thus the documents are checked both for their procedural regularity and for their sufficiency in substance to prove the petitioner's case. If they are found to be lacking in some way, the [district judge] may request further information or evidence. If the [district judge] is satisfied, he will issue a certificate that the petitioner is entitled to a decree and the judge will pronounce it formally in open court. If the [district judge] is not satisfied, he will remove the case from the special procedure list and require that it be heard before the judge.

Appendix C to the Report is a summary of a *Court Record Study* carried out by the Law Commission. One of the major aims of the study was to discover more about the circumstances in which district judges refused their certificates. This is what they report:

31. Procedural or administrative problems fell into the following broad categories: inaccuracies on the face of the documents, ... documents, for example the marriage certificate, not filed or the wrong document, for example an acknowledgement of service relating to the wrong fact, filed; disagreement or problems over costs; problems with service; and respondents under a disability for whom a guardian ad litem might have to be appointed ...
32. Substantive problems arose where the [district judge] had questioned the method or sufficiency of proof of the fact asserted in the petition and whether the petitioner was entitled to a decree. These fell into the following broad categories: insufficient evidence of adultery ...; failure to name the person with whom the adultery was alleged to have been committed[7] ... and parties still living at the same address. ...

And in behaviour cases:

44. It might have been thought that assessing behaviour cases would also cause some problems. [district judges] might have been unpersuaded, either that the behaviour complained of had in fact taken place or had the effect alleged, or that however accurately described it was such that it was unreasonable to expect the petitioner to live with the respondent. The files examined did not reveal evidence of this, apart from the problems arising where the couple were still living at the same address. The behaviour itself was generally proved by the assertions made in the petition and subsequently confirmed in the petitioner's affidavit.

The study concludes:

51. It is certainly difficult to conclude from the files which we studied that the intervention of the courts, considerable though this may be, has a noticeable impact upon the outcome of cases. Of the cases which failed to proceed, far more did so because of the decisions of the parties themselves than because of the problems of proving the ground. Of the cases where there had been such problems, the great majority eventually reached a decree.

John Haskey in *Divorce and Children: Fact Proven and Interval between Petition and Decree* (1996) presents the statistics for the duration of divorce proceedings in 1994, in the following table:

Table 2: Median interval of time, in months, between petition and decree absolute, 1994, England and Wales

Months

Type of divorcing couple	Fact proven					
	Adultery	Unreasonable behaviour	Desertion	2 years' separation (with consent)	5 years' separation	Total
Decrees granted to wives						
with children aged under 16	7.1	7.6	9.3	6.4	7.7	7.3
all couples	6.8	7.3	8.3	5.9	6.6	6.8
Decrees granted to husbands						
with children aged under 16	6.8	7.7	7.3	6.2	7.5	6.9
all couples	6.3	7.0	6.8	5.7	6.7	6.3

Note: Calculated for single fact divorces granted to a single party. Intervals calculated using full dates of petition and decree absolute.

7. It is no longer necessary to do this: Family Proceedings Rules 1991, r. 2.7(1).

At the same time as the so-called special procedure was introduced, legal aid was withdrawn from undefended divorce proceedings, although it remains available for 'ancillary relief'. The impact of this has been studied by Gwynn Davis, Alison Macleod and Mervyn Murch in *Special Procedure in Divorce and the Solicitor's Role* (1982):

Background to the procedural changes

The measures in question were introduced primarily to save money. The proportion of people qualifying for legal aid declined after 1950 as the eligibility limits did not keep pace with inflation, but civil legal aid expenditure escalated rapidly during the 1970s. By 1976, divorce accounted for the bulk of the civil legal aid budget. This was due to a number of factors, including the rising divorce rate, the increasing proportion of women petitioners who were more likely to be legally aided, and the growing practice of financially assisted petitioners not applying for costs against the respondent. Research had shown that judicial hearings of undefended divorce petitions served little practical purpose (Elston, Fuller and Murch, 1975). It was thought that their abolition, by removing the need for representation, would bring savings to the legal aid fund. It was also hoped that the changes would encourage more petitioners to prepare their own petitions, although this could still be done with a solicitor's help under the legal advice and assistance ('Green Form') scheme. This is limited to specified sums for petitioner and respondent, although solicitors can apply to the Area Legal Aid Committee for extensions. The services covered are also limited and do not normally include representation in court.

Although the primary legislation remained the same, when the changes were introduced they were thought to be significant for the following reasons:

(i) formal responsibility for the conduct of the divorce in Green Form cases passed from the solicitor to the petitioner;

(ii) it was thought that the changes might contribute to a greater use of alternative sources of legal help, such as citizens' advice bureaux and law centres; they might also bring more people into direct contact with county court staff and increase reliance on their informal advice;

(iii) there was no longer to be a judicial hearing of the petition in open court;

(iv) for the first time since the legal aid scheme was introduced it was being withdrawn from one area; and

(v) since almost all divorces are now undefended, the above changes were likely to affect the majority of the divorcing population.

The Lord Chancellor's withdrawal of legal aid was challenged by The Law Society. They argued that:

(i) the Green Form limits (then £45 for petitioners, £25 for respondents) would be inadequate to allow the necessary work to be done and would dilute the quality of service to clients;

(ii) people would need representation at the new judicial appointments;

(iii) the use of legal advice and assistance 'in tandem' with legal aid, with an unclear division of responsibility between solicitor and client, would be confusing and inefficient;

(iv) the restrictions would mean a two-tier system, with one level of service for those who could afford to pay and another for those who could not.

The authors then describe their research and its results, which they summarise as follows:

1. The great majority of petitioner and respondent [parties] still consult solicitors. While technically they may be 'petitioners in person', this phrase is misleading, as practically all are advised by solicitors at some stage.

2. Although a quarter of our sample had sought information from CABs or legal advice centres, most had done so as a preliminary to seeking solicitors' advice.

3. Solicitors continue to deal with most of the paperwork associated with special procedure divorce. The complexity of the documentation and procedure encourages dependence on solicitors.

4. Some solicitors find it necessary to do work not covered by the Green Form.

5. Some of those interviewed told us that, at least in retrospect, they thought that their solicitor had not adequately explored the possibility of reconciliation. [See Chapter 7, below.]

6. The research identified a number of problems concerning the legal aid and advice schemes. These include:

(*a*) people's uncertainty concerning whether or not they are eligible for help;
(*b*) the distinction between the role of adviser under the Green Form scheme and representation under legal aid is not understood;
(*c*) some people are deterred by worries about cost from seeking a lawyer's help as early as they might do otherwise;
(*d*) some disturbing cases were encountered where it appeared that solicitors had not adequately informed their clients about their entitlement to legal aid;
(*e*) some respondents are being advised not to defend the divorce because of cost and many feel aggrieved about this.

Conclusion
What impact has the extension of the special procedure and the withdrawal of legal aid had upon the provision of legal services for those who divorce? The changes relate primarily to people's entry into the legal system. They affect the mechanics of obtaining an undefended divorce but do not touch custody battles, disputes about finance or property, or contested divorces, all of which may be pursued under a full legal aid certificate as before.

Much of the policy debate between the Lord Chancellor's Legal Aid Advisory Committee and The Law Society about the withdrawal of legal aid from undefended divorce hinged on the question of what legal services were necessary in these cases. Many solicitors were unhappy with the limits. As we have seen, some provide their clients with extra services for which they do not get paid. This raises the question of whether the State should provide anything other than the minimum service necessary to meet the strictly legal requirements of the case.

We would argue that the divorce lawyer also has a responsibility to consider the social and emotional aspects, if only because these have a bearing on the legal issues. For example, clients may well use their lawyers as sounding-boards while working out problems such as access arrangements. ... Some solicitors refuse to see their role as consisting entirely in the performance of a series of straightforward administrative tasks, although the Green Form scheme is designed to support little more than this:

> 'The special procedure has simplified the process but divorce is an emotional experience and people want support. Currently there is no system designed to do this. I'd say that three-quarters of my time is spent counselling.'

We may at present have the worst of both worlds: a system of legal advice and representation which does not allow solicitors to give adequate time to their divorcing clients and yet, through comparatively generous support for representation in ancillary matters, encourages a litigious approach.

Meanwhile, the hope that divorce under the Green Form would substantially reduce the cost to the legal aid fund of ancillary matters has not been realized. The number of legal aid certificates in matrimonial cases rose by 18% in 1980/81. The Law Society comment that the number of certificates in matrimonial proceedings has increased 'at a rate far in excess of the increase in the number of divorce petitions'. There has been no fall in the use of solicitors because there has been no fundamental change in divorce law or procedure. Overall the measures have made little impact on a system which is still largely adversarial in character and which, therefore, does not encourage genuine litigants in person.

Gwynn Davis and Mervyn Murch bring together the research on the Special Procedure and the research on Conciliation (see, p. 237 below) in *Grounds for Divorce* (1988):

It is worth noting, incidentally, that one party's need to obtain a quick divorce can leave them open to pressure to grant what they consider to be unreasonable concessions in respect of 'ancillary' matters, usually finance or property. This, for example, was the experience of one man who petitioned for divorce on the basis of his wife's adultery: 'They held out the adultery confession as the prize for being a good boy and splitting up the house. If I'd refused, I probably wouldn't have got the divorce – or I *may* not; it would have been more difficult. I'd have had to get a private detective or whatever people do.' The fact of there being a judicial test of breakdown – which in practice is allowed to rest entirely on the respondent's acceptance of behaviour or adultery allegations – is bound to invite manipulation of this kind. Anyone anxious to obtain a quick divorce is vulnerable in this respect.

Many of the couples whom we interviewed had come to recognize the truth of Chester and Streather's dictum that 'whatever the client's reason for wanting divorce, the lawyer's function is to discover grounds' (Chester and Streather, 1972). In the words of one husband, 'As it stands now you choose a reason, whatever is the easiest, and you don't ever really involve the courts in the real reason for the breakdown of the marriage. It's just something that they recognize, so you choose one of them.' This element of contrivance (and of acceptance on the respondent's part) was most marked in respect of petitions based on adultery, a point also noted by Eekelaar (1984). Use of the 'behaviour' basis was, however, far more problematic. This emerged in the course of our Special Procedure survey when we asked the parties how 'amicable' their divorce had been. The 'behaviour' basis stood out, containing proportionately far fewer 'amicable' (or even remotely reasonable) partings than did the other four 'facts'. Divorces based on 'adultery', on the other hand, were said to have been 'amicable' (or 'fairly amicable') as often as those based on two years separation. 'Adultery', in other words, appears to be employed with a degree of emotional neutrality, whereas 'behaviour' seldom is.

Since divorce can no longer be refused because the suit is collusive, there is little doubt that 'adultery' is employed by many couples who simply find it inconvenient to wait two years to obtain a decree. ...

Questions

(i) Do you think the introduction and the extension of the 'special procedure' and the withdrawal of legal aid more radical departures than the introduction of irretrievable breakdown as the sole ground of divorce?
(ii) Is it necessary or desirable that the termination of the marriage be obtained in a formal or judicial manner?
(iii) In some circumstances, we recognise divorces obtained abroad by judicial or other proceedings and even, on occasions, in cases where the divorce is not accompanied by 'other proceedings' (Family Law Act 1986, s. 46(2)(*b*)). If we recognise such divorces obtained abroad, why not allow administrative divorces here?
(iv) Or do we already have that given that almost all divorces are granted each year under the 'special procedure'?
(v) Although we no longer have many defended divorces, the number of cases where the respondent at some stage indicates an intention to defend is by no means insignificant. (See the Law Commission's *Court Record Study* (1990).) Why is it that so few of these initially contested cases reach the point of a full hearing before a judge?

(e) TIME RESTRICTIONS ON PETITIONING

One stratagem, introduced in 1937, to stem the tide of divorce was the so-called 'three-year' rule. This rule prevented divorce petitions being presented to court before the expiration of the period of three years from the date of the marriage unless special leave was granted on the ground either of exceptional hardship suffered by the petitioner or of exceptional depravity on the part of the respondent. This restriction was recommended to be retained both by *Putting Asunder* (1966) and the *Field of Choice* (1966). However, the Law Commission reconsidered it in a Working Paper (1980) and Report, *Time Restrictions on Presentation of Divorce and Nullity Petitions* (1982) which recommended replacing the previous discretion with an absolute bar on petitioning within a year of the marriage.

2.14 ... It is perhaps a little simplistic to think of measuring the effectiveness of the restriction solely, for example, in terms of the number of marriages saved, as the underlying objective is more subtle: it is to shape an attitude of mind. ...

2.30 In the Working Paper we said that the arguments in favour of the proposal that there should be an absolute bar on the presentation of divorce petitions within a stipulated period from the date of the marriage could be put in this way:

> 'The justification for a time restriction is one of public policy; it would devalue the institution of marriage to make divorce readily obtainable within days of the marriage. The present law is on this view based on a sound principle, but is objectionable because of the unsatisfactory nature of the exceptions whereby the court may allow a petition to be presented on proof of exceptional hardship or depravity. Although it would be possible to construct other exceptions, none of them is entirely satisfactory. The law would on this view be simpler and more comprehensible if it asserted the general policy by means of an absolute bar on divorce early in marriage.'

2.31 There was widespread support in the response to the Working Paper for the view that such a bar would have the obvious advantage of certainty and consistency, and would provide an adequate expression of public concern that the institution of marriage should not be devalued by precipitate divorce. It is, of course, true that such a bar may involve hardship. However, the response to the Working Paper reinforces us in our view that such hardship may, in many cases, be more apparent than real (provided that the period during which petitions may not be presented is comparatively short) particularly in view of the fact that, even where a marriage breaks down in the very early stages, the parties are eligible to apply for a wide range of legal remedies, by way of financial provision, protection and arrangements for custody of and access to children. Indeed the only relief which will not be available is the liberty to re-marry. Thus the number of cases involving actual hardship is likely to be minimal. ...

2.33 We are, however, conscious that a considerable number of those who wrote to us favoured the total abolition of the restriction. We have sympathy with the logic of their arguments; yet we firmly believe in the public policy arguments recited above and the need to avoid the apparent scandal of divorce petitions being presented immediately after the marriage. We think that a one-year absolute bar is the least intrusive and most straightforward of restrictions which accords with many of the views which have been expressed to us and is, accordingly, likely to be the most generally acceptable.

The reform proposed by the Law Commission was implemented by s. 1 of the Matrimonial and Family Proceedings Act 1984.

Questions

(i) After the three year bar was reduced to one year in 1984, the number of petitions for judicial separation fell sharply. The number of petitions in 1989 was 2,741 and there were 1,678 decrees. The figures in 1983 were 7,430 petitions and 4,852 decrees; in 1994 there were 4,358 petitions and 1,350 decrees. Do you agree with the Law Commission (1990) that judicial separation should remain available as an alternative to divorce, and if so, why?

(ii) The effect of the Family Law Act 1996 (see, p. 260, below) is that no divorce can be granted until at least 21 months after the marriage, and in many cases two years and three months. Do you anticipate hardship in some cases as a result of these provisions?

3 The factual context

We now turn to the facts behind the law, in order to look briefly at a number of different areas of research.

(a) THE USE OF THE FIVE FACTS

First, given the availability of divorce on proof of a single ground, which can only be proved by the use of one of the five facts set out in s. 1(2) of the Matrimonial Causes Act 1973, it is interesting to consider the use made of these facts by different people. The following table, produced by the Office of Population Censuses and Surveys in November 1995, shows the distribution of divorces by fact proven, granted to husbands and wives in 1994:

Divorces by fact proven, 1994, England and Wales

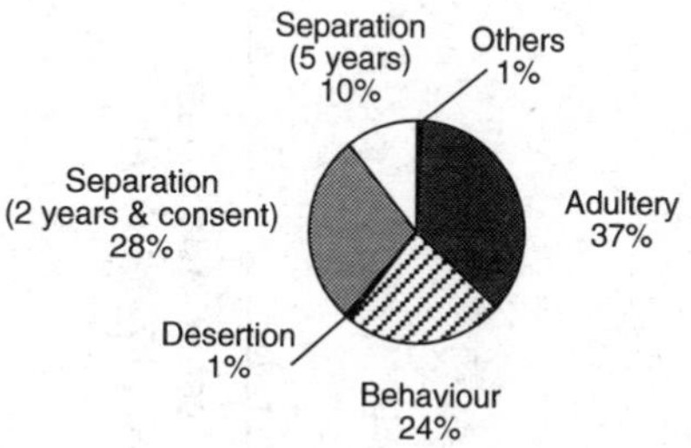

Divorces granted to husbands (44,914)

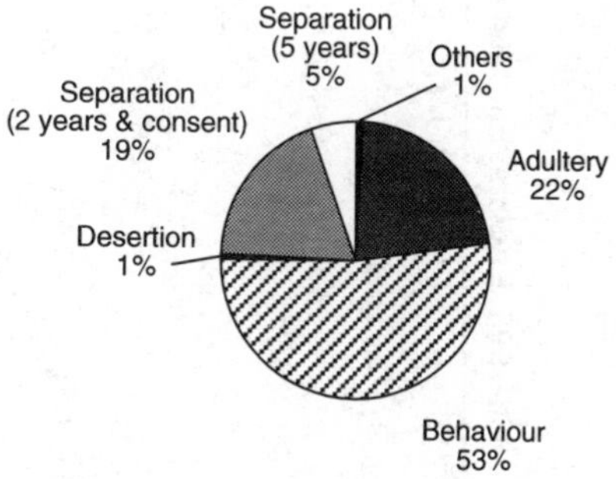

Divorces granted to wives (112,407)

The proportion of petitions brought by husbands and wives has changed over the years, as the graph from Haskey, *Trends in Marriage and Divorce 1837–1987* (1987) (p. 232) makes clear.

Question

In 1994, 71% of all divorce petitions were brought by wives. Do you think that (*a*) there is a greater desire among women for divorce or (*b*) there is a greater desire among women to be the petitioner? In either case, why might that be?

Some answers may be supplied by the relative use of the five 'facts' by husbands and by wives. These are set out in *Social Trends* 21 (1991), p. 233, below.

Before we leap to conclusions, we should take a slightly closer look. John Haskey, in *Grounds for Divorce in England and Wales – A Social and Demographic Analysis* (1986), analysed the decrees obtained in 1981, firstly by age groups, p. 234, below.

Then by social class of husband (1979) and of wife (1981) and by whether they had children (1981), p. 235, below.

Haskey returns to the question of children of divorcing couples in a further study *Children in Families Broken by Divorce* (1990) as shown in the chart on p. 236, below.

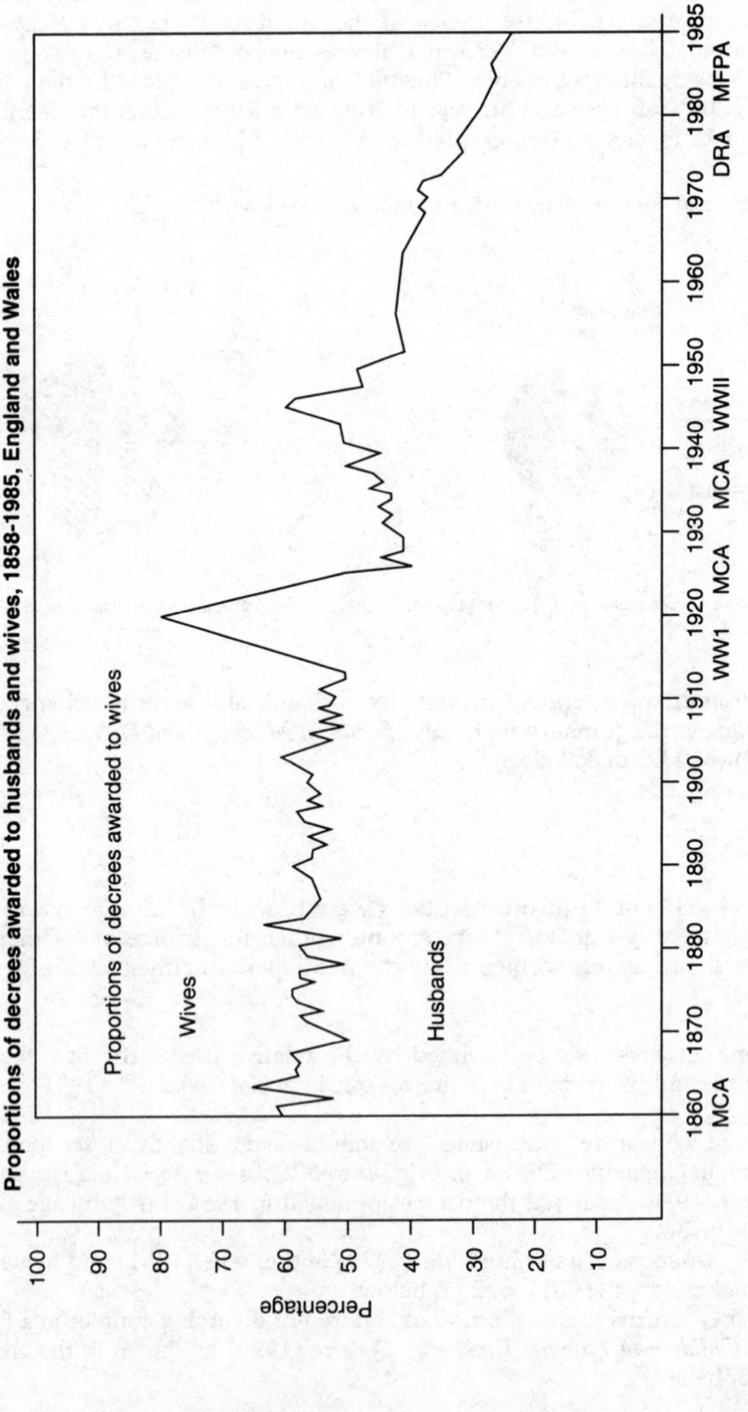

Proportions of decrees awarded to husbands and wives, 1858-1985, England and Wales

Divorce – party granted decree: by grounds[1]

England and Wales

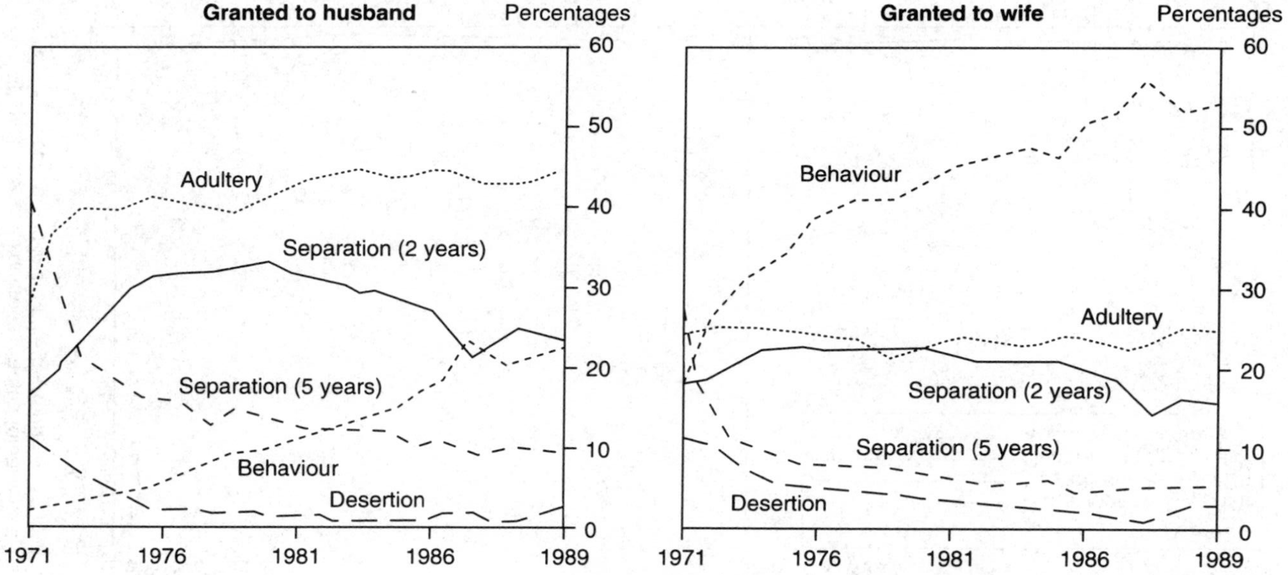

1 Decrees granted to one party on more than one ground are included in the 100 per cent base but have not been plotted.

Source: Lord Chancellor's Department

Divorces by class of decree; by age of and party granted decree, 1981, England and Wales

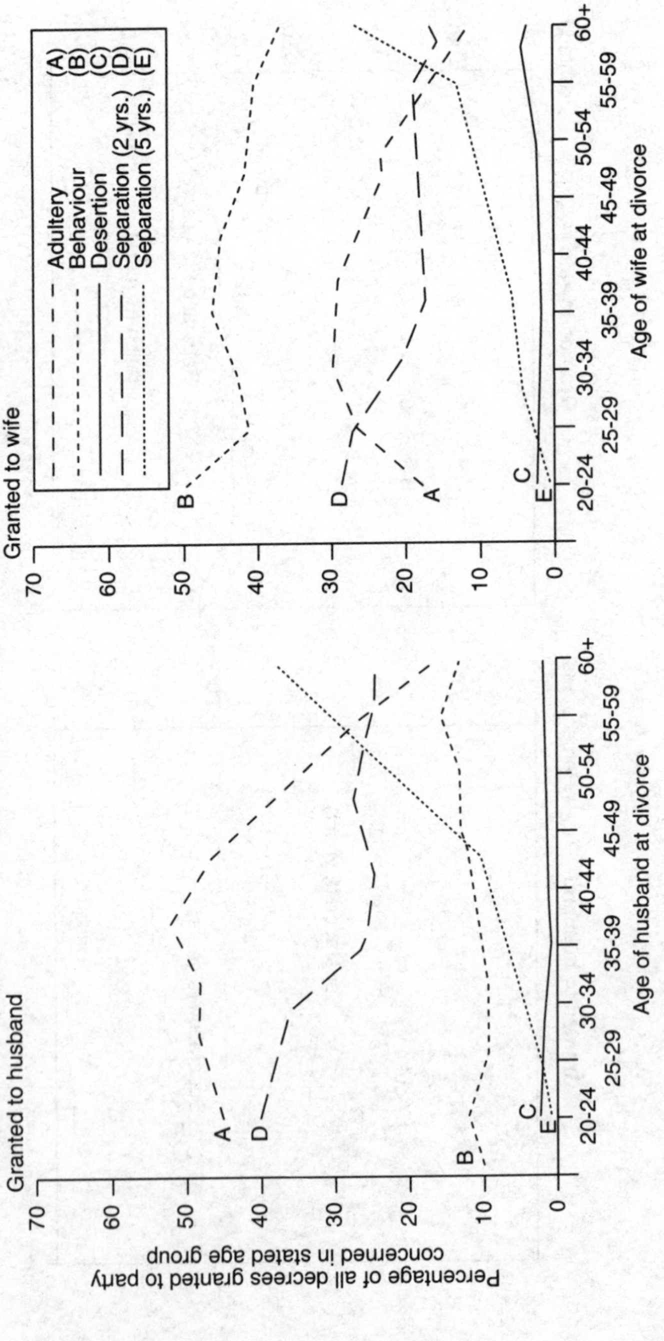

Table 3: Distribution of divorces by class of decree, party granted decree and social class of husband (1979) and of wife (1981), England and Wales

Social class		Granted to husband (%)					Granted to wife (%)					
				Separation					Separation		% of decrees	
		Adultery	Behaviour	2 years	5 years	All classes N*	Adultery	Behaviour	2 years	5 years	All classes N*	granted to wife
Social class of husband, 1979												
I	Professional	46	0	33	13	24	25	25	38	9	32	57
II	Intermediate	40	4	45	9	121	37	27	31	2	228	65
IIIN	Skilled non-manual	45	10	34	11	71	30	40	21	6	150	68
IIIM	Skilled manual	46	6	34	11	202	25	41	23	8	482	70
IV	Partly skilled	39	7	33	12	85	22	43	25	5	212	71
V	Unskilled	32	11	25	25	28	15	67	13	4	123	81
	Armed forces	64	0	36	0	11	24	55	17	3	29	73
	Economically inactive	37	10	23	21	52	12	46	25	10	223	81
	Unemployed	34	11	17	26	35	13	57	21	2	107	75
All social classes, 1979†												
	Sample	42	6	34	13	628	24	42	24	6	1,540	71
	England and Wales	40	9	33	14	42,407	24	41	24	7	96,661	70
Social class of wife‡												
II	Intermediate	37	8	44	10	93	27	39	26	6	203	69
IIIN	Skilled non-manual	44	7	39	9	198	31	35	27	4	382	66
IIIM	Skilled manual	33	17	37	10	30	30	38	22	7	73	71
IV	Partly skilled	47	6	37	9	79	19	51	21	6	193	71
V	Unskilled	18	32	14	32	22	27	56	8	3	62	74
	Housewives	47	15	22	14	219	28	49	15	5	591	73
All social classes, 1981												
	Sample	41	10	33	13	781	27	45	21	5	1,723	69
	England and Wales	43	11	31	12	43,088	25	44	23	6	103,643	71
Family characteristics of couple, 1981												
Pre-maritally conceived child		60	11	16	10	97	23	54	16	4	274	74
Dependent children		55	13	22	7	368	28	50	16	3	1,066	75
Children		48	12	22	15	491	27	49	16	5	1,275	72
No dependent children		29	8	43	8	413	25	35	28	8	652	61
No children		30	8	50	8	290	25	31	35	5	448	61

* Forms base of 100%; includes decrees of nullity and of divorce for desertion. Multiple facts counted under each fact and joint decrees counted in figures for both husbands and wives.

† Includes those whose occupation was inadequately described and those not normally assigned a social class.

‡ By own occupation.

Divorcing couples and children* in their families, 1970-89, England and Wales

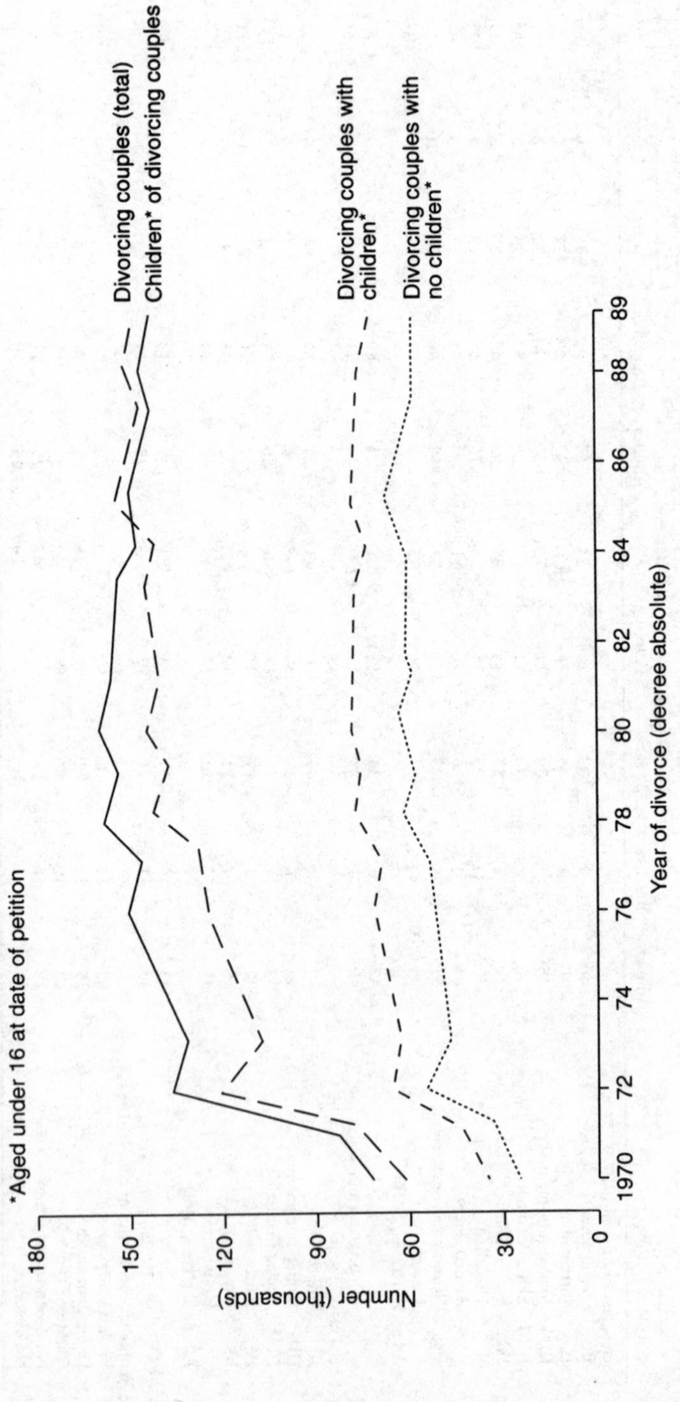

The point about social class is emphasised in an earlier article on *Social Class and Socio-economic Differentials in Divorce in England and Wales* (1984), in which Haskey calculated the 'expected' number of divorces in each social class and compared it with the actual number, giving a standardised rate showing the extent of deviation from the expected 100:

Social class of husband		*Standardised divorce rate*
I	Professional	47
II	Intermediate	83
IIIN	Skilled, non-manual	108
IIIM	Skilled, manual	97
IV	Partly skilled	111
V	Unskilled	220
	Armed Forces	270
	Unemployed	225

Some observations from these and other statistics, as well as more general arguments relating to questions of 'fault' are provided for us by the work of Davis and Murch (see p. 228, above) and Martin Richards. Davis and Murch in *Grounds for Divorce* (1988) write:

It is clear that choice of 'fact' is class-based. Social Classes I and II opt for 'adultery' in about 45 per cent of cases and have as many petitions based on two years separation as they have on 'behaviour'. The lower the social class, the more popular 'behaviour' petitions become until, in Social Class V, they comprise 57 per cent. Correspondingly, the proportion of 'adultery' petitions declines to the point where in Social Class V it is less than half that in Social Class I.

These patterns are confirmed by the larger (and more assuredly representative) study conducted by Haskey (1986). He also points out the parallels with the social class distribution under the old law, particularly in relation to the ground of 'cruelty' as analysed by Chester and Streather (1972). Those researchers found that amongst petitions based on the ground of cruelty, there was an over-representation of couples where the husband worked in a partly skilled or unskilled occupation, and a corresponding under-representation of Social Classes I and II.

Whilst it is possible to derive a degree of harmless amusement from speculating as to why adultery should be so popular amongst the upper classes, it is certain that we need to look for more broadly social (or extra-marital) explanations for these patterns, rather than regard them as reflecting (albeit with many distortions) the actual marital circumstances of couples within these social groups. They may reflect, for example, different social groups' tolerance of the stigma of fault, or commitment to an interactionist view of marital breakdown.

The class breakdown may also reflect legal practitioners' views as to what is an appropriate (or acceptable) basis for divorce for couples from a given social background. These days, 'adultery' provides an almost totally non-stigmatic route to divorce. This is especially true of those cases in which the third party is not even cited, it being alleged simply that the respondent has committed adultery with a person unknown to the petitioner. 'Behaviour' ... has not been sanitized in this way. Middle class people, perhaps more aware of the various options, or more anxious to preserve their dignity, tend to avoid it; or else their solicitors, alive to the social cost which a 'behaviour' petition entails, avoid it on their behalf.

As with the evidence relating to the parties' age or to the sex of the petitioner, one possible conclusion to be drawn from this breakdown of 'fact' by social class is that it undermines any case for the continued existence of the present legal categories. This is on the assumption, difficult to establish empirically, that social class variation in the choice of 'fact' does not reflect an objective reality in terms of marital circumstances.

The variation in use of the five 'facts' across the social classes probably accounts for the different patterns which we observed *within each court*. In Table 13 we give this breakdown for each of the courts in which we conducted the Special Procedure survey, focusing on the three most commonly used 'facts' of adultery, behaviour, and two years separation. It can be seen that choice of 'fact' does vary quite significantly by court. ... The underlying influence of social class is suggested by the fact that Newport and Cardiff, which had the highest incidence of 'behaviour' petitions, also had considerably more men who were unemployed or working in unskilled occupations. It is doubtful, therefore, whether Yeovil is the hotbed of adultery that the figures might suggest, or whether one should regard intolerable behaviour within marriage as another manifestation of Welsh culture, along with fine singing voices and a genius for rugby football.

Table 13: 'Fact' cited by court (Special Procedure survey)

Court	*No.*	*Adultery* %	*Behaviour* %	*2 years sep.* %
Bristol	615	32	42	20
Cardiff	255	24	55	15
Gloucester	447	34	45	14
Newport	273	30	51	13
Swindon	268	37	37	20
Taunton	222	37	32	23
Yeovil	163	44	34	19

…

Despite the elements of collusion and contrivance which are readily apparent in present-day decree proceedings, we would not wish to suggest that the parties' marital history plays *no* part in the choice of 'fact', even if the relationship between the two is not clear-cut. For example, when in the course of the Special Procedure project we asked petitioners what had led them to start divorce proceedings, 31 per cent of those petitioning on adultery cited their former spouse's relationship with someone else; only 4 per cent of 'behaviour' petitioners give this as the main reason. We also asked petitioners whether there had been any incidents of physical violence in their marriage. Of those petitioning on 'behaviour', 55 per cent said that there had been violence, as compared with 35 per cent of those petitioning on 'adultery' and 32 per cent of those petitioning on two years separation. It is also possible that the more severe or repeated violence may have been experienced by 'behaviour' petitioners, although this cannot be determined on the basis of our quantifiable information.

But rather than trying to ascertain whether there is any objective relationship between behaviour in marriage and 'fact' cited in the divorce petition, it might be more fruitful to ask whether the parties regard it as appropriate that the law should allow scope for public recrimination in divorce: if the answer to that question is 'yes', it might be argued that the 'fault' element should be retained. In the Special Procedure survey we asked everyone whether the idea of 'the guilty party' had any relevance as far as they were concerned. Thirty-one per cent said that it did, with a further 16 per cent giving equivocal responses. Since the Special Procedure research focused on uncontested cases, amongst which questions of 'fault' might be thought to have less relevance, it is evident that questions of guilt or innocence are still important for many people. But it was also apparent that the listing of one spouse's marital failings, whilst giving expression to the resentment felt by the petitioner, often provoked a sense of profound injustice on the part of the respondent. This, indeed, was the reason given by some men for wanting divorce to remain a public matter: they wished to see these false allegations openly challenged.

Not surprisingly, petitioners and respondents who had experienced the fault-based 'facts' were more likely to regard the question of which party was responsible for the marriage breakdown as being an appropriate element in divorce law, although the variation across the five 'facts' was not very dramatic. In general, respondents were more likely than petitioners to say that the issue of guilt or blame mattered to them. This was particularly true of those who had experienced the 'behaviour' fact, with 60 per cent of respondents saying that they were concerned about questions of 'fault', as against only 33 per cent of petitioners. This might suggest that the experience of being on the receiving end of a 'behaviour' petition actually promotes this way of thinking, so that the respondent is prompted to defend the allegations, or perhaps to recriminate in turn. The 'adultery' group was the only one in which petitioners were more likely than respondents to say that questions of guilt or innocence still mattered to them (52 per cent as against 37 per cent).

Our informants advanced a number of arguments in favour of retaining the 'fault' element. The first was that the drift away from fault has undermined the significance of marriage, making it more akin to other types of relationship. As one male respondent put it, 'It [the question of responsibility for the breakdown] matters a hell of a lot to me. By getting away from that, they've taken a lot of the importance out of marriage.'

Secondly, there was the argument that the 'innocent' spouse should be protected against divorce; in other words, if you lead a blameless marital life, you should be able to feel secure in your marital status. As it was put by another man whom we interviewed, 'To my mind, if you've done something wrong – OK, let someone divorce you. But if you've done nothing at all wrong, how can the other person divorce you?' Whilst some 'innocent' petitioners regarded it as appropriate that their spouse should be identified as the person whose conduct ended the marriage, they might nevertheless feel very aggrieved that all the trauma and responsibility of obtaining the divorce fell to them, so that in that sense the 'guilty' party escaped scot-free.

Maybe where you live has something to do with it as the researchers show. Haskey provides the following table in *Regional Patterns of Divorce* (1988):

Table 6: Estimated divorce rates by standard region of England and Wales, 1981 and 1985

Standard region or area	1981		1985	
	Divorce rate (per 1,000)	– as a percentage of that for England and Wales	Divorce rate (per 1,000)	– as a percentage of that for England and Wales
South West	12.8	106	13.6	101
Yorkshire and Humberside	12.7	106	14.3	107
East Anglia	12.6	105	13.0	97
South East	12.5	104	13.0	97
North West	12.4	103	13.5	101
England and Wales	*12.0*	*100*	*13.4*	*100*
North	11.9	99	13.0	97
West Midlands	11.2	93	11.8	88
Wales	10.2	85	12.2	91
East Midlands	9.6	80	10.3	77
(Greater London)	(14.8)	(124)	(14.9)	(111)

Questions

(i) The percentage of decrees granted to wives is higher (*a*) in the lower socio-economic classes, and (*b*) when there are dependent children: why is that?
(ii) What conclusions do you draw from the fact that the most numerous single category is behaviour petitions by wives?
(iii) Why are so few petitions based on desertion?
(iv) Do the figures on the five year fact confirm or dispel fears that it would become a 'Casanova's Charter'?
(v) How would you account for Haskey's finding that 'husbands who divorce their wives who are housewives tend to establish irretrievable marriage breakdown on their wives' adultery relatively more often than the average husband'?
(vi) Couples without children are more than twice as likely to divorce by consent after two years' separation as couples with children. Why do you think that is so?
(vii) Can you hazard a guess at which groups of petitioners would be most affected by moves to make divorce (*a*) easier, or (*b*) more difficult?

The figures for the use of the five facts 1994 are given by the Office of Population Censuses and Surveys in its February 1996 *Update*:

Table 1: Divorces by party to whom granted and presence of children in family

Thousands

Type of divorcing couple	Party to whom granted: Wife	Husband	Both parties	Total
with children aged under 16	68	21	0.3	88
with no children aged under 16	45	24	0.1	69
all divorcing couples	112	45	0.4	158

Note: Table excludes annulments. Components may not sum to totals because of rounding.

Table 2: Divorces* by fact proven, party to whom granted, and presence of children in family

Percentages

Type of divorcing couple	Fact proven: Adultery	Unreasonable behaviour	Desertion	2 yrs' separation (with consent)	5 years' separation	Total
Decrees granted to wives						
with children aged under 16	22	60	0.4	15	3	100
all couples	22	54	0.6	19	5	100
Decrees granted to husbands						
with children aged under 16	46	26	0.5	22	6	100
all couples	37	24	0.9	28	10	100

*Single fact divorces granted to a single party.

The overall figures for proceedings over the years are summarised in the Judicial Statistics for 1994–95:

Table 5.5: Matrimonial suits: summary of proceedings in selected years since 1938

	1938	1958	1968	1978	1988	1990	1991	1992	1993	1994
Dissolution of marriage:										
Petitions filed	9,970	25,584	54,036	162,450	182,804	191,615	179,103	189,329	184,471	175,510
Decrees nisi	7,621	23,456	47,959	151,533	154,788	157,344	153,258	149,126	160,625	154,241
Decrees absolute	6,092	22,195	45,036	142,726	152,139	155,239	155,927	156,679	162,579	154,873

Question

Why is there such a gap (which is never retrieved in later years) between (*a*) the number of petitions and decrees nisi, and (*b*) the number of decrees nisi and decrees absolute?

(b) WHY DIVORCE?

The more fundamental question why people divorce is a remarkably difficult one. Martin Richards in *Divorce Research Today* (1991) makes some suggestions:

The incidence of divorce

After a lull in the 1950s, divorce rates in Britain and, indeed, through most of the industrialised world, began to rise steeply in the early 1960s. This increase persisted until the late 1970s when the curve flattened out and it has remained more or less stable ever since. The fact that this pattern of change is so widespread, geographically, means that we should not look for its causes in local factors. Clearly, attitudes to marriage have undergone a very widespread change in the post-war years.

While it is widely believed that increasing rates of divorce are the consequence of reducing the legal hurdles involved in ending a marriage, the evidence suggests the opposite process is the more important: that as divorce has become more common, jurisdictions have found it necessary to reform their divorce law and to simplify the process in order to accommodate the growing numbers.

There have been many suggestions about how we might account for the rising rates. Rising expectations for marriage and a growing feeling that, if you do not succeed at first, you should try again, seem part of the pattern. Rising divorce rates, at least until very recently, have been associated with parallel increases in rates of remarriage, so the increasing divorce rates seem more to reflect a disenchantment with a particular partner, rather than any more general flight from marriage. But in recent years there may have been a change in this pattern and in many countries there has been an increase in cohabitation, especially for those who have been previously married. As the great majority of divorces are initiated by women, it is reasonable to assume that they most often make the decision to leave the marriage, so it is not surprising to find evidence that divorce rates are associated with the ease, or difficulty, with which women with children can support themselves financially on their own. Housing is probably of great importance and it has been suggested that the housing shortage and, especially the lack of council housing, may currently be acting to depress divorce rates especially in South-East England.

Regional differences in rates remain significant, so that, within the UK, we have very low rates in Northern Ireland, among the lowest in Europe, while those in England are towards the upper end of the European distribution.

It is often suggested that divorce is contagious. There may well have been an effect of this kind while rates were rising rapidly. As people saw those around them divorce and were increasingly likely to have friends or relatives who had been through the process, they may have been encouraged to use this means of trying to alleviate their own domestic problems. In the 1960s the literature on divorce tended to emphasise its potential positive results for adults and had little to say about the difficulties. But in recent years there have been indications of an opposite kind of influence. As the negative effects of divorce, in both personal and economic terms, become much more widely appreciated, people may be much more reluctant to leave a marriage and instead may try to make greater efforts to keep it going.

In *Private Worlds and Public Intentions – the Role of the State at Divorce* (1995) Richards makes some further points:

There is a belief, especially among some of those associated with the law, that if divorce was made harder to obtain, the numbers would be reduced and some of the attendant consequences for children would therefore be avoided. ...

All these kinds of arguments seem to miss two basic points. The first is that marriage rates are now dropping and cohabitation is increasing. It is probable that cohabitation is being transformed from a prelude to marriage to its alternative. Perhaps we are moving towards the Scandinavian model which is approaching a situation where only a minority of the population marries. In Britain approaching a third of all children are born outside marriage and in two thirds of these cases the birth registration is made jointly. It seems reasonable to assume that many of these are cohabiting couples. As yet we lack any information about the consequences of the ending of a cohabitation for children but there seem to be few reasons to believe that they will be any more benign than the ending of a marriage. Given the relative lack of institutionalised processes for dispute resolution at the ending of cohabitation, outcomes could be worse. Attempts to regulate marriage – either at entry or exit – seem likely to increase cohabitation. If we provide legal processes for regulating the exit from marriage partly on the grounds that they may serve to protect the welfare of children, should we not do the same for the ending of cohabitation?

The second point concerns the reason for the increased rates of divorce. The rise in divorce is associated with the development of companionate marriage. ... Expectations for marriage have risen as have the range of functions it is expected to fulfil. Spouses are now seen as friends, lovers, helpmates and companions for leisure time as well as lifelong marital partners. These extended functions, the high ideals of what marriage should provide, have made marriage relationships both more exclusive and more vulnerable. This vulnerability is further increased by the growing extent to which close relationships among the unmarried are now sexual and most spouses enter marriage with the experience of several earlier sexual relationships. This changing nature of marriage has meant that increasing numbers of spouses, especially women, find that their satisfaction with their marriages may fall quite steeply after the early years. This is particularly true after the arrival of children. I suggest that reasons for divorce in many cases are different for men and women. I believe that if men initiate a divorce it is more often because they have another partner to go to, while women are more likely to be motivated by a desire to leave an unsatisfactory marriage. The great majority of divorces are now initiated by women, a point to which I will return. ...

The influences that have led to the present day style of marriage have a long history and may be traced back to developing ideals of domestic life early in the nineteenth century ... They have been shaped by complex social and economic forces and seem most unlikely to be directly controllable by the action of any government. Leaving aside the effects of world wars which produced marked peaks in the marriage and divorce rates, there are a number of other factors which in the short-term do seem to influence divorce rates and probably lie behind some of the fluctuations in recent years. The following all seem likely to depress divorce rates: high house prices and a shortage of state housing, low rates of welfare support for poor single parent households, lack of child care facilities and high cost of child care in relation to the earning abilities of women. It seems undesirable to try and manipulate any of these factors in order to try to influence the divorce rate, not least because all of them are damaging to the welfare of children.

Another aspect of the relationship between cohabitation and the divorce rate is reflected in the following table produced by John Haskey in *Pre-marital Cohabitation and the Probability of Subsequent Divorce* (Population Trends, Summer 1992) (see opposite).

Haskey comments:

Of course, these results do not establish a *causal* link between pre-marital cohabitation and divorce; there may be other factors common to both. For example, couples who marry with a civil ceremony are more likely than those who marry with a religious ceremony to have cohabited pre-maritally; and marital breakdown rates are higher amongst the former group of couples than the latter. The type of marriage ceremony probably reflects not so much the presence or absence of religious belief or church affiliation, but more the commitment to – and the likely extent of external support for – the union; it is generally easier and quicker and involves far fewer family members and friends to marry with a civil, rather than a religious, ceremony.

Possibly couples who cohabit pre-maritally view marriage in a different light to those who do not; certainly the evidence we do possess – from the British Social Attitudes Survey, albeit based on a small sample size – suggests that, compared with those who are married, cohabitees have the most liberal views towards marriage and divorce and 'are emphatically against making divorce more difficulty to obtain and markedly less sympathetic to the notion that society ought to do more to protect marriage'. In view of these differences, it would be understandable if those who pre-maritally cohabit were less likely – compared with those who do not pre-maritally cohabit – to think of marriage as a life-long commitment.

A number of other considerations could have a bearing on the observed results. For the most part, the pre-marital cohabitation of the couples included in the 1989 GHS sample took place in earlier decades when pre-marital cohabitation carried much greater social stigma than today. As a result, these marriages may have been under greater strain, and the couple not so completely accepted in their local community, compared with the 'traditional' married couple. In addition, given that, historically, pre-marital cohabitation was a socially unconventional pattern of behaviour, partners who so cohabited before marriage may have been unconventional in their expectations of – and behaviour within – marriage. Possibly individuals who were divorce-prone might be 'selected into' marriages which were preceded by pre-marital cohabitation.

It should also be borne in mind that results from the GHS depend upon the respondents' statements about pre-marital cohabitation; there could be an association between the willingness to mention pre-marital cohabitation and of having subsequently divorced or separated. Another possible mechanism could operate as follows. Couples who were unsure about the stability of

Fig. 3: Cumulative percentages of first marriages, from a hypothetical standard population, ending in (*a*) divorce, (*b*) divorce or separation, by duration of marriage, and by whether or not there was pre-marital cohabitation, based on data for 1970–89, Great Britain

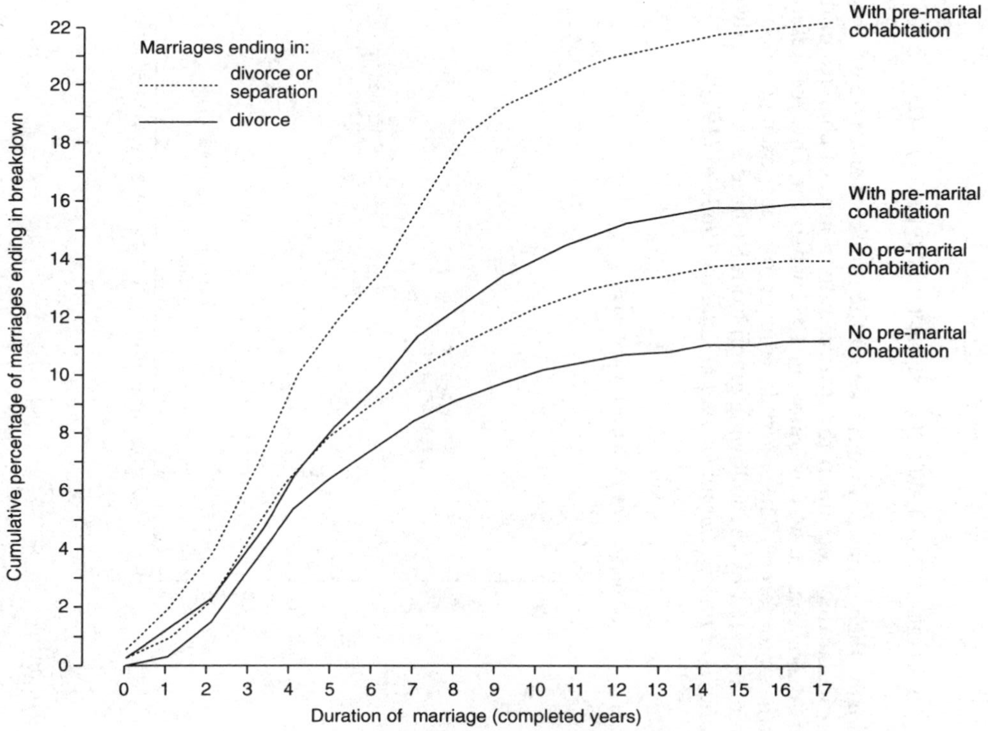

their union may have decided to cohabit for a short period before marriage to test their relationship. The greater probability of subsequent marital breakdown could be associated more with the initial doubts about the durability of the union than with the pre-marital cohabitation itself.

Overall, most authors tend to think that there are two main explanations for the observed phenomenon. One is that pre-marital cohabitation reflects a weaker commitment to the institution of marriage and that the higher rates of marital breakdown result from that weaker commitment. The other is that cohabitation attracts those who are more unconventional in their beliefs and lifestyles – characteristics which, by their very nature, tend to be held by those who are more likely to consider and seek divorce.

(c) THE EFFECT OF LAW REFORM ON THE DIVORCE RATE

Finally, then, what can we say about the numbers and rate of divorces, and in particular the effect upon the divorce rate, if any, of changes in the law? The last major change was of course in 1971 when the Divorce Reform Act 1969 came into force. The possible impact of that change upon numbers is demonstrated by the following graph from Richard Leete's study of *Changing Patterns of Family Formation and Dissolution 1964–76* (1979):

Divorces, 1966-76 England and Wales

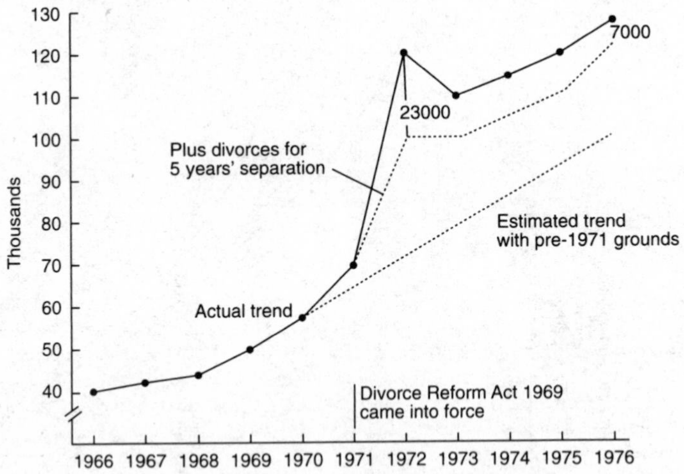

Questions

(i) If in 1976 there were 7,000 more divorces than might have been expected from an extrapolation of the pre-1971 trend together with the five year cases, how would you account for the increase? Is it (*a*) that the law was allowing more already broken marriages to be dissolved; or (*b*) that more marriages were breaking down than even the pre-1971 trend would have suggested; or (*c*) a bit of both?

(ii) If you are inclined to favour explanation (*b*), does the increase of 7,000 (in a total of 126,000 in 1976) strike you as being large or small?

(iii) If you think that the law contributes to an attitude of mind (see the views of the Law Commission on p. 206, above), do you think that this is most potent when the law is changed? Does the trend in the 1980s and 1990s support this?
(iv) How many *other* reasons can you think of for the rise in the divorce rate?

In 'Formation and Dissolution of Unions in the Different Countries of Europe' (1993) John Haskey produces tables showing the divorce rate in various countries (see pp. 246–7, below). In 'Patterns of Marriage, Divorce and Cohabitation in the Different Countries of Europe' (1992) he comments:

The trend in divorce in many countries in the early 1950s still showed some evidence of the aftermath of the War. Immediately after the War there had been a large surge in divorce, followed by a decline to a level which nevertheless still exceeded that which had existed before the War. Levels were fairly steady during the 1950s, although somewhat erratic for some of the Eastern European countries. There was a large variation in the level of divorce between different countries – even between countries in the same part of Europe. Thus, throughout the 1950s, Denmark's TDR was more than double that of England and Wales, Austria's was twice Belgium's, and Poland's was more than double Hungary's.

Between the mid-1950s and the mid-1960s, the level of divorce was remarkably level in most Northern and Western European countries, but was already increasing slowly in many of the Eastern European countries. In general, divorce was very low or virtually non-existent in the countries of Southern Europe; indeed, there were no provisions for divorce in Italy, Spain, or Portugal. In the mid-1960s, the pace of increase in divorce rates quickened in the Northern and Western European countries, and also in some of the countries of Eastern Europe.

In the period 1965 to 1975, the increase in divorce in all the Northern European countries was substantial; the TDR doubled in Norway and Denmark and trebled both in Sweden and in England and Wales. The increase was generally smaller in the Western European countries; although the TDR doubled in Luxembourg and West Germany, it increased by only about 50 per cent in France, Austria, and Switzerland. Divorce tended to be resorted to at younger ages in countries where divorce rates were high, and at older ages in countries where divorce rates were comparatively low.

The decade 1965–75 was an extremely busy one as far as new divorce legislation was concerned – very few countries in Europe did not amend their law on divorce, and Italy, Spain, and Portugal introduced divorce legislation for the first time. Festy has examined the timing of the revision in divorce law and pointed out that countries which introduced legislation early in the 1970s – Denmark, England and Wales, and Sweden – saw a much greater increase in divorce than in those countries which introduced it later, such as France and West Germany. In addition, divorce had started to increase *before* the enactment of the new legislation, in those countries which had changed the law in the early 1970s.

After 1975, the rate of growth in divorce slowed down considerably in the Northern European countries. The level of divorce actually fell in Sweden after 1974, but this decline followed a massive rise of 70 per cent between 1973 and 1974 after the implementation of a radical reform of the law on divorce. In contrast, the rate of growth in the TDR for the countries of Western Europe continued at much the same pace as had occurred in the previous decade, 1965–75. The large fall in the rate for West Germany resulted from a complete overhaul of the law in 1976, which gave rise to uncertainty regarding the validity of a large number of cases which were temporarily suspended. Between 1975 and 1988, the level of divorce rose by about 50 per cent in Austria, Switzerland, and West Germany, and by about 90 per cent in France and The Netherlands. The picture for the Eastern European countries was somewhat mixed: for one group of countries, including Albania and Poland, the TDR scarcely changed, or else increased only slightly; whereas for another group of countries, such as East Germany and Czechoslovakia, it increased by a larger amount.

Figure 2a: Total period divorce rate for selected countries of Eastern Europe, 1950–1988

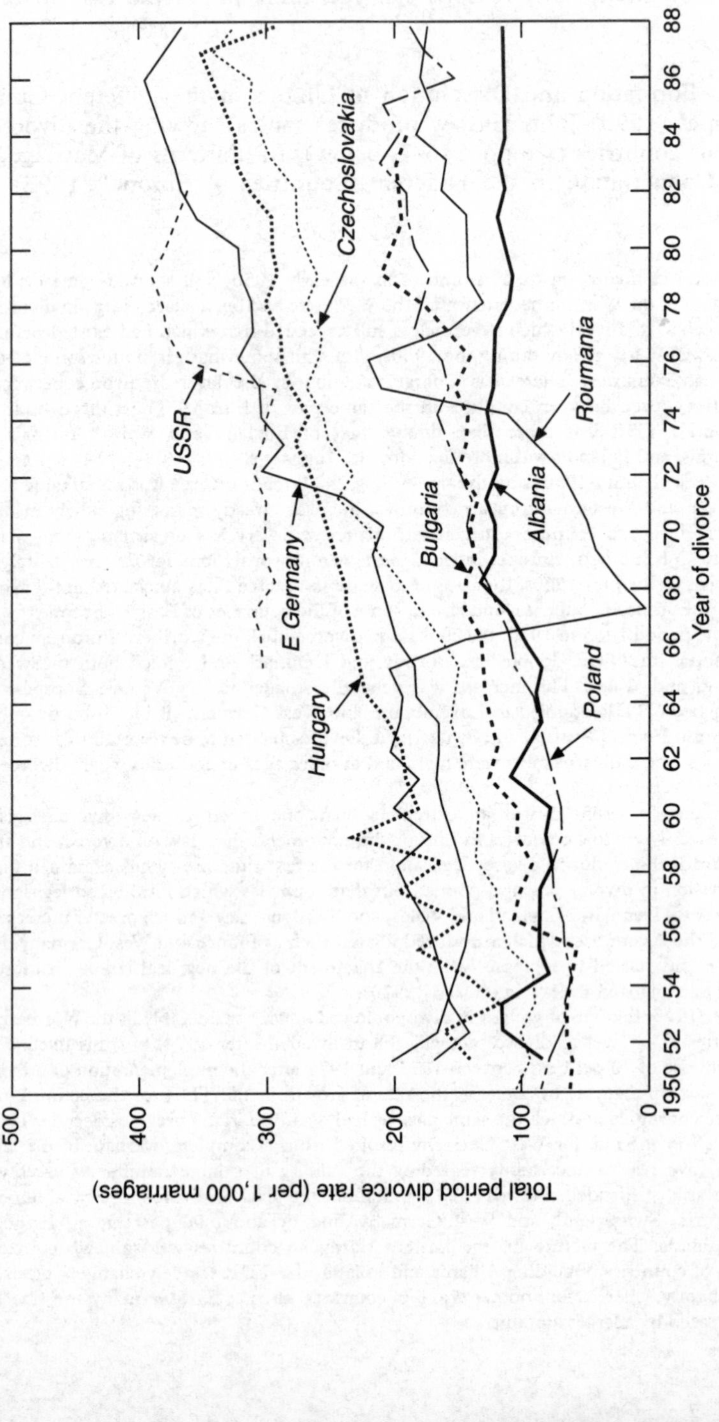

Figure 2b: Total period divorce rate for selected countries of Northern and Western Europe, 1950–1988

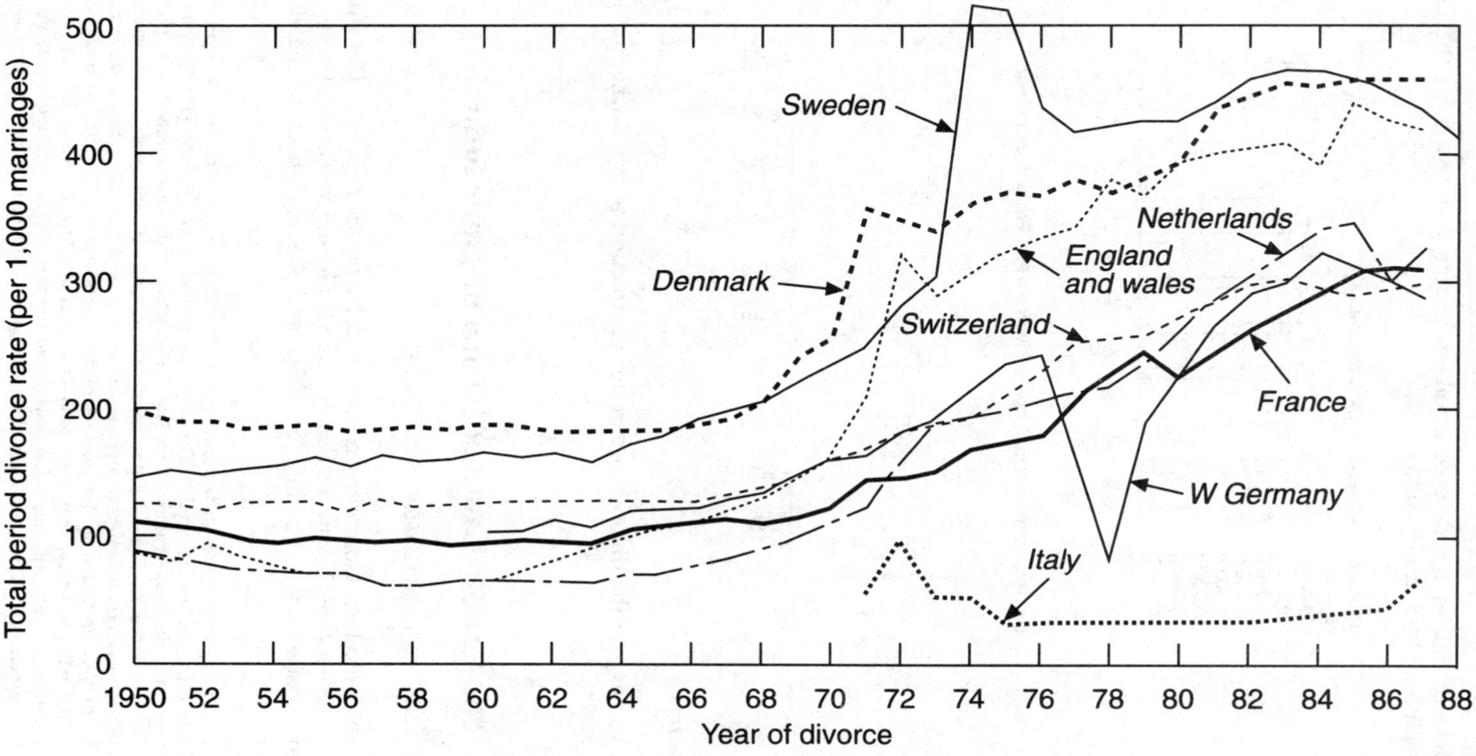

Recent figures for divorce numbers in this country, from the OPCS in November 1995, are as follows:

Divorces, 1984-1994, England and Wales

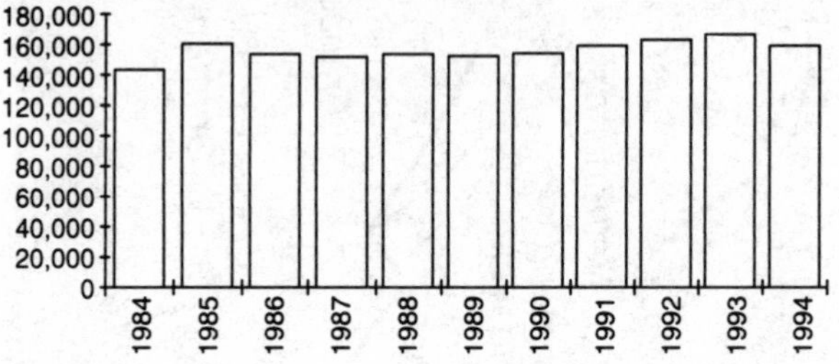

Median duration of marriage at divorce, 1994, England and Wales

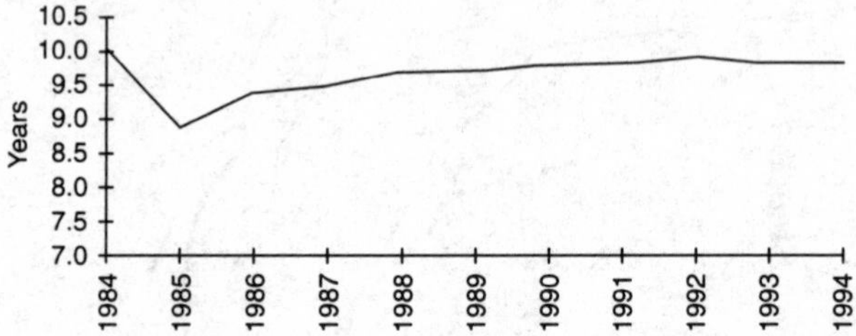

Question

Do you expect the divorce rate in this jurisdiction to rise during the 1990s? If so, why?

4 The Family Law Act 1996: a brighter future?

(a) THE LAW COMMISSION'S PROPOSAL

In 1988, the Law Commission published *Facing the Future: A Discussion Paper on the Ground for Divorce*. In *Family Law: A Ground for Divorce* (1990) the Law Commission report on their inquiries and the responses to the discussion paper:

1.5 Our inquiries have made three things absolutely plain. First, of the existence of the problem there can be no doubt. The response to Facing the Future [1988] overwhelmingly endorsed the criticisms of the current law and practice which it contained. The present law is confusing and unjust. It now fulfils neither of its original objectives. These were, first, the support of marriages which have a chance of survival, and secondly, the decent burial with the minimum of embarrassment, humiliation and bitterness of those that are indubitably dead.

1.6 Secondly, it is clear that those basic objectives of a 'good' divorce law, as set out by our predecessors in 1966, still command widespread support, difficult though it may be to achieve them in practice. In 1990, however, any summary would include two further objectives: to encourage so far as possible the amicable resolution of practical issues relating to the couple's home, finances and children and the proper discharge of their responsibilities to one another and their children; and, for many people the paramount objective, to minimise the harm that the children may suffer, both at the time and in the future, and to promote so far as possible the continued sharing of parental responsibility for them.

1.7 Thirdly, there was overwhelming support for the view expressed in Facing the Future that irretrievable breakdown of the marriage should remain the fundamental basis of the ground for divorce. This means, first, that divorce should continue to be restricted to those marriages which have clearly broken down and should not be available for those which are capable of being saved; and secondly, that any marriage which has broken down irretrievably should be capable of being dissolved. The criticism is not of the principle itself, but of the legal rules and processes by which the irretrievable breakdown of a marriage is at present established in the courts.

1.8 Our consultations have led us to the firm conclusion that there is one particular model for reform which is to be preferred. It has not only received the support of the great majority of those who responded to Facing the Future, but has also been shown by our public opinion survey to be acceptable to a considerable majority of the general population. This was the model described in Facing the Future as divorce as a 'process over time' but here described as divorce after a period of consideration and reflection, colloquially a 'cooling-off' period or breathing space. [Our recommendations] constitute in many ways a radical departure from the present law: one designed to retain what are seen as the strengths of the present system while meeting the most serious criticisms.

They identify six criticisms of the present law and practice:

(i) *It is confusing and misleading*

2.8 There is a considerable gap between theory and practice, which can only lead to confusion and lack of respect for the law. Indeed, some would call it *downright dishonest*. There are several aspects to this. First, the law tells couples that the only ground for divorce is irretrievable breakdown, which apparently does not involve fault. But next it provides that this can only be shown by one of five 'facts', three of which apparently do involve fault. There are several recent examples of divorces being refused despite the fact that it was clear to all concerned that the marriage had indeed irretrievably broken down.[8] The hardship and pain involved for both parties can be very great.

2.9 Secondly, the fact which is alleged in order to prove the breakdown need not have any connection with the *real reason* why the marriage broke down.[9] The parties may, for example, have separated because they have both formed different associations, but agree to present a petition based on the behaviour of one of them, because neither wishes their new partner to be publicly named. The sex, class and other differences in the use of the facts make it quite clear that these are chosen for a variety of reasons which need have nothing to do with the reality of the case. This is a major source of confusion, especially for respondents who do not agree with the fact alleged. As has long been said, 'whatever the client's reason for wanting divorce, the lawyer's function is to discover grounds'. [See p. 228, above.]

2.10 The behaviour fact is particularly confusing. It is often referred to as 'unreasonable behaviour', which suggests blameworthiness or outright cruelty on the part of the respondent; but this has been called a 'linguistic trap',[10] because the behaviour itself need be neither unreasonable nor blameworthy: rather, its *effect* on the petitioner must be such that it is unreasonable to expect him or her to go on living with the respondent, a significantly different and more flexible concept which is obviously capable of varying from case to case and court to court. Although the test is to be applied by an objective reasonable outsider, the character and personality of the petitioner are particularly relevant in deciding what conduct he or she should be expected to bear.[11]

2.11 Finally, and above all, the present law pretends that the court is conducting an inquiry into the facts of the matter, when in the vast majority of cases it can do no such thing. This is not the fault of the court, nor is it probably any more of a problem under the present law and procedure than it was under the old. It may be more difficult to evaluate the effect of the

---

8. *Buffery v Buffery* [1988] FCR 465, [1988] 2 FLR 365 (see p. 213, above).
9. *Stevens v Stevens* [1979] 1 WLR 885.
10. *Bannister v Bannister* (1980) 10 Fam Law 240 per Ormrod LJ.
11. *Astwood v Astwood* (1981) 131 NLJ 990.

respondent's behaviour from the papers than from the petitioner's account in the witness box, but it has always been difficult to get at the truth in an undefended case. Moreover the system still allows, even encourages, the parties to lie, or at least to exaggerate, in order to get what they want. The bogus adultery cases of the past may have all but disappeared, but their modern equivalents are the 'flimsy' behaviour petition or the pretence that the parties have been living apart for a full two years. In that 'wider field which includes considerations of truth, the sacredness of oaths, and the integrity of professional practice',[12] the present law is just as objectionable as the old.

(ii) *It is discriminatory and unjust*

2.12 83% of respondents to our public opinion survey thought it a good feature of the present law that couples who do not want to put the blame on either of them do not have to do so, but these couples have to have lived apart for at least two years. This can be extremely difficult to achieve without either substantial resources of one's own, or the co-operation of the other spouse at the outset, or an ouster order from the court. A secure council house tenancy, for example, cannot be re-allocated between them without a court order which is only obtainable on divorce or judicial separation.[13] The law does recognise that it is possible to live apart by conducting two separate households under the same roof. In practice, this is impossible in most ordinary houses or flats, especially where there are children: it inevitably requires the couple to co-operate in a most unnatural and artificial lifestyle. It is unjust and discriminatory of the law to provide for a civilised 'no-fault' ground for divorce which, in practice, is denied to a large section of the population. A young mother with children living in a council house is obliged to rely upon fault whether or not she wants to do so and irrespective of the damage it may do.

2.13 The fault-based facts can also be intrinsically unjust. 'Justice' in this context has traditionally been taken to mean the accurate allocation of blameworthiness for the breakdown of the marriage. Desertion is the only fact which still attempts to do this: it requires that one party has brought about their separation without just cause or consent. Desertion, however, is hardly ever used, because its place has been taken by the two year separation fact. A finding of adultery or behaviour certainly need not mean that the respondent is any more to blame than the petitioner for the breakdown of the marriage. If one has committed adultery or behaved intolerably there is usually nothing to stop the other obtaining a divorce based upon it, even though that other may have committed far more adulteries or behaved much more intolerably himself or herself. Nor does the behaviour fact always involve blame: it may well be unreasonable to expect a petitioner to live with a spouse who is mentally ill or disabled[14] or has totally incompatible values or lifestyle.[15] Even when the catalogue of complaints contained in the petition includes violence or other obviously blameworthy behaviour, this might look different if weighed against the behaviour of the other. In a defended case, the petitioner's own character and conduct may be relevant in determining the effect of the respondent's conduct upon her, but if his conduct is sufficient, it is irrelevant that she may have behaved equally badly in some other way. In an undefended case, of course, the matter will appear even more one-sided.

2.14 This inherent potential for injustice is compounded by the practical problems of defending or bringing a cross-petition of one's own. It is extremely difficult to resist or counter allegations of behaviour. Defending them requires time, money and emotional energy far beyond the resources of most respondents. Even if the parties are prepared to go through this, what would be the point? If the marriage is capable of being saved, a long-fought defended divorce, in which every incident or characteristic that might amount to behaviour is dragged up and examined in detail, is not going to do this. It can only serve to make matters worse and to consume resources which are often desperately needed elsewhere, particularly if there are children. Legal aid will only be granted if the case cannot be disposed of as an undefended suit without detriment to the interests of either party. As the basis on which the divorce is granted is usually irrelevant to ancillary issues, the parties' *legal* positions are unlikely to be affected whatever their personal views. Small wonder, then, that lawyers advise their client not to defend and that their clients feel unjustly treated.[16]

---

12. *Putting Asunder* (1966) (see p. 203, above).
13. Unless it is a joint tenancy and one of them voluntarily surrenders it, but this brings the whole tenancy to an end. See *Greenwich London Borough Council v McGrady* (1982) 81 LGR 288 (see p. 150, above).
14. *Thurlow v Thurlow* [1976] Fam 32 (see p. 214, above).
15. *Livingstone-Stallard v Livingston-Stallard* [1974] Fam 47 (see p. 212, above).
16. See particularly the work of Davis and Murch (see p. 228, above).

(iii) *It distorts the parties' bargaining positions*

2.15 Not only can the law be unjust in itself, it can also lead to unfair distortions in the relative bargaining positions of the parties. When a marriage breaks down there are a great many practical questions to be decided: with whom are the children to live, how much are they going to see of the other parent, who is to have the house, and what are they all going to live on? Respondents to Facing the Future told us that the battles which used to be fought through the ground for divorce are now more likely to be fought through the so-called ancillary issues which in practice matter so much more to many people. The policy of the law is to encourage the parties to try and resolve these by agreement if they can, whether through negotiation between solicitors or with the help of a mediation or conciliation service. Questions of the future care of children, distribution of family assets, and financial provision are all governed by their own legal criteria. It is not unjust for negotiations to be affected by the relative merits of the parties' cases on these matters. Yet negotiations may also be distorted by whichever of the parties is in a stronger position in relation to the divorce itself. The strength of that position will depend upon a combination of how anxious or reluctant that party is to be divorced and how easy or difficult he or she will find it to prove or disprove one of the five facts. That might not matter if these represented a coherent set of principles, reflecting the real reasons why the marriage broke down; but as we have already seen, they do not. The potentially arbitrary results can put one party at an unfair disadvantage.

(iv) *It provokes unnecessary hostility and bitterness*

2.16 A law which is arbitrary or unjust can exacerbate the feelings of bitterness, distress and humiliation so often experienced at the time of separation and divorce. Even if the couple have agreed that their marriage cannot be saved, it must make matters between them worse if the system encourages one to make allegations against the other. The incidents relied on have to be set out in the petition. Sometimes they are exaggerated, one-sided or even untrue. Allegations of behaviour or adultery can provoke resentment and hostility in a respondent who is unable to put his own side of the story on the record. We are not so naive as to believe that bitterness and hostility could ever be banished from the divorce process. It is not concerned with cold commercial bargains but with the most intimate of human relations. The more we expect of marriage the greater the anger and grief when marriage ends. But there is every reason to believe that the present law adds needlessly to the human misery involved. Our respondents confirmed this.

(v) *It does nothing to save the marriage*

2.17 None of this is any help with the law's other objective, of supporting those marriages which have a chance of survival. The law cannot prevent people from separating or forming new relationships, although it may make it difficult for people to get a divorce. The law can also make it difficult for estranged couples to become reconciled. The present law does make it difficult for some couples – in practice a very small proportion – to be divorced, but does so in an arbitrary way depending upon which facts may be proved. It also makes it extremely difficult for couples to become reconciled. A spouse who wishes to be divorced is obliged either to make allegations against the other or to live apart for a lengthy period. If the petitioner brings proceedings based on behaviour, possibly without prior warning, and sometimes while they are still living together, the antagonism caused may destroy any lingering chance of saving the marriage. The alternative of two or five years' separation may encourage them to part in order to be able to obtain a divorce, when their difficulties might have been resolved if they had stayed together. From the very beginning, attention has to be focused on how to prove the ground for divorce. The reality of what it will be like to live apart, to break up the common home, to finance two households where before there was only one, and to have or to lose that day-to-day responsibility for the children which was previously shared, at least to some extent: none of this has to be contemplated in any detail until the decree nisi is obtained. If it had, there might be some petitioners who would think again.

2.18 It is a mistake to think that, because so few divorces are defended, the rest are largely consensual. There are many, especially behaviour cases, in which the respondent indicates an intention to defend, but does not file a formal answer, or files an answer which is later withdrawn. Some of these are a reaction to the unfairness of the allegations made against them, but some reveal a genuine desire to preserve the marriage. A defended suit is not going to do this, and if a case is, or becomes, undefended, there is little opportunity to explore the possibility of saving the marriage. An undefended decree can be obtained in a matter of weeks. If both parties are contemplating divorce, the system gives them every incentive to obtain a 'quickie' decree based on behaviour or separation, and to think out the practical consequences later.

(vi) *It can make things worse for the children*

2.19 The present system can also make things worse for the children. The children themselves would usually prefer their parents to stay together. But the law cannot force parents to live amicably or prevent them from separating. It is not known whether children suffer more from their parents' separation or from living in a household in conflict where they may be blamed for the couple's inability to part.[17] It is probably impossible to generalise, as there are so many variables which may affect the outcome, including the age and personality of the particular child. But it is known that the children who suffer least from their parents' break-up are usually those who are able to retain a good relationship with them both. Children who suffer most are those whose parents remain in conflict.[18]

2.20 These issues have to be faced by the parents themselves, as they agonise over what to do for the best. However regrettably, there is nothing the law can do to ensure that they stay together, even supposing that this would indeed be better for their children. On the other hand, the present law can, for all the reasons given earlier, make the conflict worse. It encourages couples to find fault with one another and disputes about children seem to be more common in divorces based on intolerable behaviour than in others. The alternative is a long period of separation during which children can suffer from the uncertainty before things can be finally sorted out or from the artificiality of their parents living in separate households under the same roof. This is scarcely an effective way of encouraging the parents to work out different ways of continuing to discharge their shared parental responsibilities. It is often said that couples undergoing marital breakdown are too wrapped up in their own problems to understand their children's needs. There are also couples who, while recognising that their own relationship is at an end, are anxious to do their best for their children. The present system does little to help them to do so.

Conclusion

2.21 These defects alone would amount to a formidable case for reform. The response to Facing the Future very largely endorsed its conclusion that 'Above all, the present law fails to recognise that divorce is not a final product but part of a massive transition for the parties and their children'. It is all too easy to think of divorcing couples in simple stereotypes. In fact they come in many different shapes and sizes. But for most, if not all, the breakdown of their relationship is a painful process, and for some it can be devastating. It affects each party in different ways: one may be far ahead of the other in withdrawing from the relationship before the other even realises that there is a problem. The anger, guilt, bitterness and regret so often felt have little to do with the law, which can seem an irrelevant game to be played by the lawyers. But the law does nothing to give the parties an opportunity to come to terms with what is happening in their lives, to reflect in as calm and sensible a way as possible upon the future, and to re-negotiate their relationship. Both emotionally and financially it is better for them and their children if they can do this by agreement rather than by fighting in the courts. There are always going to be some fights and the courts are there to resolve them. But the courts should be kept to their proper sphere of adjudicating upon practical disputes, ensuring that appropriate steps are properly taken, and enforcing the orders made. They should not be pretending to adjudicate upon matters they cannot decide or in disputes which need never arise.

Questions

(i) Do you accept these criticisms?

(ii) Can you think of other criticisms which can be levelled at the present law and practice of divorce?

---

17. That there are adverse effects upon some children from some divorces cannot be doubted; see, eg J.S. Wallerstein and J.B. Kelly, *Surviving the Breakup* (1980); however the claims of J.S. Wallerstein and S. Blakeslee in *Second Chances* (1989) as to the high risks of such effects, have to be treated with some caution. One difficulty is distinguishing the effects of divorce itself from the poverty and consequent disadvantages which so often result; see M. Maclean and R.E.J. Wadsworth 'The Interests of Children after Parental Divorce: A Long-Term Perspective' (1988) 2 Int J of Law and the Family 155.

18. M.P.M. Richards and M. Dyson, *Separation, Divorce ond the Development of Children: a Review* (1982).

(iii) Those are the criticisms. What are the strengths of the present law?

The Law Commission rejected the retention of 'fault'; the introduction of a full judicial inquest into the marriage and the possibility of saving it; immediate divorce either unilaterally or by mutual consent; and a divorce after a fixed minimum period of separation. They recommended a divorce after a fixed minimum period for reflection and consideration of the arrangements: the process over time.

3.29 Several features particularly commended themselves to respondents. One was the recognition that divorce is not a single event but a social, psychological and only incidentally a legal process, which takes place over a period of time. Relate Marriage Guidance considered that acknowledging the time people need to adapt emotionally, socially and psychologically to their new circumstances could have far reaching – and beneficial – effects, not only for the parties and their children, but also for any new families formed through re-marriage. It is thought that one reason why so many re-marriages fail is the unresolved legal and emotional legacy of the first.

3.30 Another advantage emphasised was the encouragement given to focus upon the practical consequences of separation and divorce and to work these out *before* rather than after the divorce itself. Several respondents, including Relate, the Law Society, and the Association of Chief Officers of Probation, believed that the encouragement to look to the future instead of attacking the past would foster constructive rather than destructive attitudes towards the practical issues. The removal of the need to allege fault should reduce the temptation to adopt hostile and adversarial positions in the parties' discussions. This was seen as an incentive for the parties to recognise and meet their responsibilities towards the family, and therefore as a protection for the children and the financially weaker party. The financial position of the weaker spouse would also be improved by the power to make orders during this period. The period itself would assist in negotiations by providing a clear beginning and end to the process.

3.31 The potential for the increased use of conciliation and mediation, in order to resolve practical issues in a more constructive atmosphere, was also favoured, not only by professionals who are currently engaged in conciliation or mediation, including the Association of Chief Officers of Probation, the National Family Conciliation Council, and the Family Mediators' Association, but also by the legal profession and many others. One advantage seen was that the parties could set their own pace for the proceedings, giving time for a person who was less ready to cope emotionally, rather than progress at a pace dictated by one of them. The more constructive environment which this proposal would bring to the provision of counselling services was also welcomed by many respondents, including Relate Marriage Guidance.

3.32 Several features were thought likely to increase rather than decrease the chances of reconciliation. First was the removal of the need to separate or allege fault, with all the accompanying stigma and bitterness. Second was the encouragement to work out the practical consequences of a divorce before committing themselves to it. Third was the period of time itself, which would prevent hasty divorces and discourage people from rushing into remarriage. One respondent thought that it might even be sufficiently onerous to act as a deterrent to divorce itself.

3.33 Finally, it was thought that all these features would foster more constructive and co-operative attitudes towards the children's future and reduce the damage which they can suffer from prolonged uncertainty and hostility.

3.34 This model therefore received very substantial support from a wide variety of quarters. There is also good reason to believe from our public opinion survey that it would be acceptable to the general public. 87% of respondents to our public opinion survey thought a model along these lines might be 'acceptable', but that was alongside other models. More importantly, it was approved as the sole ground for divorce by 67% and disapproved by 15%, an 'acceptability' rate well above that for separation as the sole ground for divorce. If the law is to be reformed, as respondents to Facing the Future clearly thought that it should, then this is evidently the model to be preferred.

3.35 However, there was understandable concern among some of our respondents about the details of how it would work in practice. We ... should point out here the central features which were implicit, or in some cases explicit, in the support which it received. First, a substantial period of time should be required to elapse, in order to demonstrate quite clearly that the marriage has irretrievably broken down. There can be no better proof of this than that one or both parties to the marriage have stated their belief that their marital relationship has broken down and that either or both of them persist in that belief after the lapse of a considerable period. This must be longer than the present interval between petition and decree, which is six months or less in a substantial proportion of cases. It must also give the parties a realistic timescale within which, in the great majority of cases, the practical questions about the children, the home and the finances can be properly resolved. It must avoid rushing them towards a resolution of those issues, so that they can go at their own pace and draw back if they wish. It must discourage hasty and ill-thought-out applications. In our views, an overall period of one year would be required to achieve all these objectives. ...

3.36 Secondly, there should be an orderly but unhurried procedural timetable during the period, for the exchange of information and proposals, the negotiation of those matters which can be resolved by agreement, and the adjudication of those which cannot, together with the possibility of making orders to have effect during the period, and of extending it where matters have not been properly resolved.

3.37 Many respondents also attached particular importance to the provision of adequate counselling and conciliation services during this time. The National Campaign for the Family, for example, argued that there should be professionally monitored counselling and conciliation services available in all localities, with trained staff and a firm funding base. ... counselling and conciliation are two very different things: counselling may either help a couple who wish to try to save their marriage or give support to one or both of them, or to a child, who is suffering particular trauma or distress from the breakdown of a marriage which cannot be saved. Conciliation or mediation provide a neutral figure who helps both parties to negotiate an agreed solution to the issues concerning their children, and sometimes their property and finances, which will have to be resolved if the divorce proceeds. It was considered important that both such services should be available for all couples (and their children) who want them and that opportunities to make use of them should be built into the procedure itself.

3.38 We share our respondents' views of the importance of both counselling and conciliation services. Indeed, we think this just as great whether or not the law of divorce is to be changed. Similarly, we would consider our proposals a great improvement upon the present law, whether or not more resources were to be made available for these services; but there is no doubt that, just as our proposals would provide a much more constructive and less damaging context for both counselling and conciliation to be successful, so would our proposals greatly benefit from increased provision for them. We say this because we believe that it is by the provision of these services, to the people who want and need them, that the most harmful emotional, social and psychological effects of marital breakdown and divorce can best be avoided or mitigated. The law and legal processes cannot do this, although they can, and at present do, make matters worse. The law's processes are principally designed to adjudicate disputes and to oblige people to meet their financial and legal liabilities. This is an important element in the model which we propose.

3.39 There were of course some respondents who specifically rejected this model. It is necessary, therefore, both to explain their objections and if possible to attempt to meet them.

3.40 Some objections centred round the removal of fault from the ground for divorce. Two different types of advantage are claimed for retaining fault. The first is that it provides a moral base for conduct within marriage. The main difficulty with this is that, logically, it can only be done by returning to a system based wholly on fault. The present mixed system of fault and no-fault 'grounds' is, as the authors of *Putting Asunder* recognised in 1966, incapable of supplying a coherent and consistent moral base. ... Furthermore, granting or withholding the divorce itself is an inappropriate and ineffective sanction against marital misbehaviour; the real and effective sanction is the unwanted breakdown of the marriage. Conduct still has a part to play in determining the practical consequences of that breakdown.

3.41 Secondly, it is argued that the retention of fault provides a public affirmation of 'guilt' and 'innocence' within the marriage which enables the innocent party to feel vindicated in his or her decision to end it. This is an important psychological point. However, one of the difficulties with the whole concept of divorce for fault is that it assumes that fault is the only possible justification for divorce. People who hold this belief, whether for religious or other reasons, may well need to feel that they are morally justified in what they have done. Unfortunately for them, experience has shown the law cannot accurately allocate moral blameworthiness, for there are always two sides to every marital history and different people assess these in different ways; nor do the great majority of divorcing couples want it to do so. They may wish that something could have been done to stop the other spouse behaving as he or she did, or even for the other to be publicly branded in some way, but they shrink from the detailed examination of their marital lives which would necessarily be involved in making a proper assessment in every case. The human as well as the financial costs in making the attempt would be enormous. If that is so, then the sometimes (although obviously not invariably) inaccurate allocation which takes place at present is itself morally wrong, quite apart from the other problems it can cause.

3.42 Another objection was that this model amounts to divorce by unilateral demand, albeit not immediately. This is the inevitable consequence of any system based on irretrievable breakdown of the marriage, including the present one. The present law expressly provides for unilateral divorce after five years' separation, and 71% of respondents to our public opinion survey thought this period too long. In practice, it also provides for divorce by unilateral demand a great deal more quickly, because of the practical and legal problems of defending a petition based on behaviour or, sometimes, adultery.

3.43 It is also the case that this model does not supply an opportunity for one spouse to contest the other's allegation that the marriage has broken down. There are many divorces where one party believes that the marriage can be saved. Sometimes both may do so. Contests in court, however, cannot be the way to do this. As the Booth Committee observed, 'The court itself discourages defended divorce not only because of the futility of trying a contention by one party that the marriage has not broken down despite the other party's conviction that it has, but also because of the emotional and financial demands that it makes upon the parties themselves and the possible harmful consequences for the children of the family'. A reasonably long period of delay, where each party has every opportunity to reflect upon the position and explore the alternatives, coupled with the availability of counselling services if need be, and the removal of the necessity to make damaging allegations against one another, stand a better chance of helping those marriages which can and should be preserved.

3.44 However, it is one thing to accept that the marriage has irretrievably broken down once one party has become convinced, after a considerable period of delay, that it has done so. It is another thing to conclude that that person should 'be able to switch resources to a new family' irrespective of the hardship caused to the first. Under the present law, it is possible to resist a divorce, although only if based on five years' separation, on the ground that the divorce will cause the respondent grave financial or other hardship. In the vast majority of marriages, of course, it is the break-up and separation which cause the hardship, rather than the divorce as such. However, it would be both possible and logical to combine this model with such a hardship bar, if this were considered appropriate. [See p. 258, below.] ...

3.45 On the other hand, there were some respondents who objected that this model would in fact make divorce more difficult, particularly for couples who are agreed upon divorce and for petitioners who need a speedy decree for other reasons. Both groups would, however, be catered for by the availability of ancillary remedies at the outset, so that all they have to wait for is the decree itself, with its consequent permission to remarry. While we appreciate that there are young and childless couples who realise early in their marriage that they have made a mistake, it does not seem unduly intrusive to require a period of delay before granting what is, in effect, a licence to remarry.

Easier or harder?

3.46 This debate indicates quite clearly how impossible it is to characterise any particular divorce system as 'too easy' or 'too difficult'. 'Easy' may mean short or painless, whereas 'hard' may mean long or painful. For some, the model we are recommending might provide 'easier' divorce, in that they would not have to separate for years before proceeding; for others, for example most of those who now rely on adultery or behaviour, it would be 'harder' because they would have to wait for longer than they do at present. For some, it might be 'easier', because they would no longer, justly or unjustly, be branded the wrongdoer; for others, it might be 'harder', because they would have to disclose their financial circumstances and confront their responsibilities towards their families before they could obtain a decree.

3.47 The emotional pain which many people feel at the breakdown of their marriages is not necessarily linked in any way to the ease or difficulty of the legal process. Divorce is almost always painful for their children, but if there is to be a divorce at all, the system should certainly try to make it as easy for them as it can. This was the unanimous view of all those organisations whose principal concern is the welfare of children.

Conclusion

3.48 For all these reasons, we therefore *recommend*:

(i) that irretrievable breakdown of the marriage should remain the sole ground for divorce; and

(ii) that such breakdown should be established by the expiry of a minimum period of one year for consideration of the practical consequences which would result from a divorce and reflection upon whether the breakdown in the marital relationship is irreparable.

Ruth Deech is no supporter of the Law Commission's work in this area. She puts her point in the following article in The Independent (1990):

Marriage as a short-term option

The last time divorce law was reformed, we all still believed that human behaviour was rational and could be shaped by legal rules.

The Law Commission said its 1969 Act, which introduced simpler divorce by separation, would promote marriage stability and reconciliation. It would encourage spouses to omit recriminations from their petitions.

Twenty-one years later, the inaccuracy of the reformers' predictions about the new law's effect on people's lives is striking.

Cohabiting couples would regularise their unions, they said, the illegitimacy rate would drop as a result of the freedom to remarry, and the divorce rate would not rise. Instead, we find a marked increase in cohabitation and a divorce rate that has trebled to some 190,000 petitions each year.

So why are we about to embark on another reform, and why is the Law Commission ... implicitly repeating naïve claims that a new law will improve the lot of children?

Liberalised divorce law has not, so far, resulted in a greater sum of human happiness. It has given us over one million unremarried divorcees, many of whom are largely dependent on social security.

Feminists have remained largely silent on the question of easier divorce, presumably because women have diametrically opposed personal interests: one woman's bitter divorce and abandonment is another woman's freedom to claim the man or liberty she wants. Yet it could be argued that, if women as a sex ought to be protesting about anything, it is about this issue.

The public at large does not seem to want any change in the law, including the latest proposal to rid it of fault-based grounds and allow a couple to divorce after working out arrangements over children and finances. Neither is there any pressing need to liberalise the law, because all those whose marriages have broken down can readily obtain their divorces under the existing arrangements.

The reason for reform is one given several times before: that the law should reflect social reality and the fact that many divorces are undefended and uninvestigated.

On each occasion the law has been brought into line with practice, however, it has simply made divorce easier. Once the rate rises it never drops back to its previous level. The resulting increased faith in divorce as a solution to marital problems leads to increased willingness to use it, which in turn leads to a relaxation of divorce procedure and then a fresh call for further changes to bring the law into line with reality.

That happened in 1937, 1949 and 1969 and is about to happen again. It is a spiralling process that Parliament should not encourage, for the sake of children, if no one else.

Common sense, as well as academic research, has shown us that the children of divorce (unlike widows' children) suffer from the divorce itself. It results in lower educational achievement and worse employment and emotional prospects for the children.

From the research, it seems that the most hurtful episode for children in the divorce process is the time of separation. The proposals for a more effective maintenance system and for civilised agreements between parents about access can have no remedial effect: most children want their parents to stay together. Any change in divorce law is irrelevant to children's post-divorce suffering and we should not delude ourselves otherwise.

Rational lawyers, such as the Lord Chancellor, are reported to believe that something can be built into a new divorce process to encourage parents to concentrate on their children's welfare, and maybe to change their minds for the sake of their offspring.

That is much wishful thinking because, by the time a couple has initiated the divorce process, it is too late. In the great majority of cases, the children will remain with their mother and there are no real alternatives on offer. Many fathers soon stop visiting, and recent research by Newcastle University shows that conciliation services have little lasting impact.

The law reformers' argument is that divorce law should bury a dead relationship; it is never conceded that the law itself might have played a part in infecting the couple with a fatal virus.

Everything except the law, has been blamed for the breakdown of marriage – housing shortages, shotgun marriages, youthful marriages, unions, unemployment, living longer and legal aid.

My own hypothesis is that the most important element in divorce law is the *message* it conveys to the public. We all absorb the prevailing divorce ethos long before we ourselves ever seriously consider ending a marriage, and it is that earlier influence which counts in determining our response. ...

Everything points to the desirability of leaving the law of divorce unchanged. It would be better for the reformers to focus their efforts on informing teenagers and married couples of the harm done by divorce. It is far too late in a relationship to rely on the divorce law to do so.

Deech makes a further point, about the economic aspects of divorce, in *Divorce Dissent: Dangers in Divorce Reform* (1994):

We cannot afford serial marriage in our society: poverty is as inevitable as the damage to children from the emotional state of their parents. Yet it seems to be an unspoken political decision that attempts to make divorce more difficult are totally unacceptable. Even while public debate focuses on the plight of single parents and their children, the fact that over half of them are created by divorce and separation is overlooked. It is astonishing that any government should seriously contemplate easing divorce law while simultaneously expressing anxiety about single parents, their children and society's health.

She concludes:

1. The Government should abandon plans to reform the ground of divorce.
2. No decree absolute should be granted until at least twelve months have elapsed from service of the petition.
3. An education for marriage programme should be drawn up for school use.
4. The statutory provisions giving legal status to cohabitation and unmarried fathers should be reviewed.

The final recommendation refers to provisions such as the opportunities under the Children Act 1989 for unmarried fathers to obtain parental responsibility for their children (see p. 499), inheritance rights for unmarried partners (p. 194) and the protection of unmarried non-owning partners under Part IV of the Family Law Act 1996 (p. 388).

In *Divorce and the Lord Chancellor* (1994) Andrew Bainham comments:

I must take issue with Ruth Deech who suggests that there is a correlation between divorce reform and the rate of marriage breakdown. Deech confuses the rate of marriage breakdown with the rate of *divorce*. For while it is indisputable that the rate of dissolution is connected to the ease with which the law allows that dissolution to be obtained, it is quite another matter to suggest that divorce law has any significant influence on the *quality* of relationships within marriage – surely the factor most likely to determine whether those relationships end or survive.

Questions

(i) Ruth Deech is concerned about the message the new law conveys to the public. Can you write a short paragraph describing that message? Now write another short paragraph describing the message the Matrimonial Causes Act 1973 conveys to the public.

(ii) Do you think it is possible to establish any connection between the divorce rate, the provisions of divorce law, and the rate of relationship breakdown within the community?

(iii) Do you agree with Ruth Deech that to take away those elements of legal recognition given to unmarried fathers would support the institution of marriage? Would that have any effect upon the rate of relationship breakdown?

The Law Commission wished to retain, and indeed extend, the s. 5 bar (see p. 255, above):

5.75 ... those respondents to Facing the Future who discussed this issue were all in favour of retaining the bar. It provides an important protection for a small group of people who may still face serious hardship which the law is unable at present to redress in other ways. If it retains substantially the same form as the present bar, it is unlikely to be invoked, and even less likely to succeed, in any but a tiny minority of cases. On balance, therefore, we *recommend* that it should be possible to resist the grant of a divorce, on the ground that the dissolution of the marriage would result in grave financial or other grave hardship to the person concerned, and that it would be wrong, in all the circumstances, for the marriage to be dissolved.

5.76 Given that the hardship bar can only apply to divorce rather than separation, it follows that an application to invoke such a bar can only be made once an application for a divorce order has been made. The court will then normally have only the one month period of transition to consider the merits of such an application before the divorce order is issued. However, this should not usually cause insuperable difficulties, as it is almost inconceivable that the financial position of the parties as it is likely to be after divorce would not already have become clear to the court. The person wishing to invoke the bar should have made his or her position apparent in all the exchanges taking place during the period of consideration and reflection. ... [I]n appropriate cases, the court should give consideration at the preliminary assessment to whether or not the bar is likely to be raised. It should at that stage be possible to require a spouse to state whether he or she intends to invoke it should an application for divorce be made, and if so on what grounds. Occasionally, however, it may be impossible to resolve matters within the month between application and divorce. The court must therefore have power to delay the divorce for this purpose. It is vital, however, that this be strictly limited, so that it cannot be used as a tactical weapon in every case. Accordingly, we *recommend* that the court should have power to postpone the divorce but only where it is probable that the hardship part of the grounds can be established, there are exceptional circumstances making it impracticable to decide the application within the month, and postponement is desirable in order to enable it to be properly determined. Any delay in notifying the other party of an intention to invoke the bar, or any matters relevant to it, should be taken into account in deciding this. Thus, for example, it may only just have become apparent that the applicant will suffer hardship, because the other spouse has only just disclosed details of his pension scheme. On the other hand, the applicant may now be seeking to rely on matters which she could easily have raised much earlier. In the one case delay might well be desirable, in the other not. Only if it is probable that the applicant will succeed in establishing hardship should it be possible to delay in order for the full circumstances to be properly explored.

5.77 It would also be unjust were a bar imposed by the court on the ground of hardship to remain in force indefinitely, despite any change in the financial position of the parties. We therefore *recommend* that the court have power to revoke an order imposing a bar, upon application by either or both parties, where it is satisfied that the grounds for continuing the bar no longer exist. Revocation might be appropriate, for example, where the party who applied for the bar wished to re-marry or where the other party found the financial resources to compensate for any loss of pension rights. We further *recommend* that, provided all the other conditions have been met, the court should then have power to make an order for divorce either after the usual one month period of transition or earlier if appropriate. It would not at that stage make sense to require a further period of consideration.

Questions

(i) Given that the Law Commission has rejected the philosophy of the fault-based divorce, why retain the bar?
(ii) Do you think the retention of the bar will be (*a*) the last recourse of the bloody-minded or (*b*) provide much needed protection for dependants and spouses who would otherwise be discarded at will?
(iii) Is pension splitting an answer? (See pp. 350ff, below.)

(b) DIVORCE UNDER THE FAMILY LAW ACT 1996

In 1993 the Green Paper, *Looking to the Future: Mediation and the Ground for Divorce* sought views and reactions to proposals for the reform of divorce law, including the Law Commission's recommendations but also a number of other possibilities ranging from a return to a system based on matrimonial offences to divorce by consent or immediate divorce on unilateral demand. The White Paper of the same title in 1995 set out the Government's proposals for reform, largely following the Law Commission's proposals, and these have been enacted in the Family Law Act 1996. The Act is not yet in force, and will initially be put into effect in a limited geographical area as a pilot project.

The conditions for the making of a divorce order are set out s. 3 of the Act:

3. – (1) If an application for a divorce order or for a separation order is made to the court under this section by one or both of the parties to a marriage, the court shall make the order applied for if (but only if) –

(*a*) the marriage has broken down irretrievably;
(*b*) the requirements of section 8 about information meetings are satisfied;
(*c*) the requirements of section 9 about the parties' arrangements for the future are satisfied; and
(*d*) the application has not been withdrawn.

(2) A divorce order may not be made if an order preventing divorce is in force under section 10.

These conditions are further defined as follows:

5. – (1) A marriage is to be taken to have broken down irretrievably if (but only if) –

(*a*) a statement has been made by one (or both) of the parties that the maker of the statement (or each of them) believes that the marriage has broken down;
(*b*) the statement complies with the requirements of section 6;
(*c*) the period for reflection and consideration fixed by section 7 has ended; and
(*d*) the application under section 3 is accompanied by a declaration by the party making the application that –
(i) having reflected on the breakdown, and
(ii) having considered the requirements of this Part as to the parties' arrangements for the future,

the applicant believes that the marriage cannot be saved.

(2) The statement and the application under section 3 do not have to be made by the same party.

...

6. – (1) A statement under section 5(1)(*a*) is to be known as a statement of marital breakdown; but in this Part it is generally referred to as 'a statement'.

(2) If a statement is made by one party it must also state that that party –

(*a*) is aware of the purpose of the period for reflection and consideration as described in section 7; and
(*b*) wishes to make arrangements for the future.

(3) If a statement is made by both parties it must also state that each of them –

(*a*) is aware of the purpose of the period for reflection and consideration as described in section 7; and
(*b*) wishes to make arrangements for the future.

...

7. – (1) Where a statement has been made, a period for the parties –

(*a*) to reflect on whether the marriage can be saved and to have an opportunity to effect a reconciliation, and
(*b*) to consider what arrangements should be made for the future,

must pass before an application for a divorce order or for a separation order may be made by reference to that statement.

(2) That period is to be known as the period for reflection and consideration.

(3) The period for reflection and consideration is nine months beginning with the fourteenth day after the day on which the statement is received by the court.

...

(6) A statement which is made before the first anniversary of any marriage to which it relates is ineffective for the purposes of any application for a divorce order.

(10) Where an application for a divorce order is made by one party, subsection (13) applies if –

(*a*) the other party applies to the court, within the prescribed period, for time for further reflection; and

(*b*) the requirements of section 9 (except any imposed under section 9(3), are satisfied.

(11) Where any application for a divorce order is made, subsection (13) also applies if there is any child of the family under the age of sixteen when the statement is received by the court.

(12) Subsection (13) does not apply if –

(*a*) at the time when the application for a divorce order is made, there is an occupation order or a non-molestation order in force in favour of the applicant, or of a child of the family, made against the other party; or

(*b*) the court is satisfied that delaying the making of a divorce order would be significantly detrimental to the welfare of any child of the family.

(13) If this subsection applies, the period for reflection and consideration is extended by a period of six months, but without invalidating the application for a divorce order.

8. – (1) The requirements about information meetings are as follows.

(2) A party making a statement must (except in prescribed circumstances) have attended an information meeting not less than three months before making the statement.

...

(5) Where one party has made a statement, the other party must (except in prescribed circumstances) attend an information meeting before –

(*a*) making any application to the court –

(i) with respect to a child of the family; or

(ii) of a prescribed description relating to property or financial matters; or

(*b*) contesting any such application.

(6) In this section 'information meeting' means a meeting organised, in accordance with prescribed provisions for the purpose –

(*a*) of providing, in accordance with prescribed provisions, relevant information to the party or parties attending about matters which may arise in ccnnection with the provisions of, or made under, this Part of Part III; and

(*b*) of giving the party or parties attending the information meeting the opportunity of having a meeting with a marriage counsellor and of encouraging that party or those parties to attend that meting.

...

9. – (1) The requirements as to the parties' arrangements for the future are as follows.

(2) One of the following must be produced to the court –

(*a*) a court order (made by consent or otherwise) dealing with their financial arrangements;

(*b*) a negotiated agreement as to their financial arrangements;

(*c*) a declaration by both parties that they have made their financial arrangements;

(*d*) a declaration by one of the parties (to which no objection has been notified to the court by the other party) that –

(i) he has no significant assets and does not intend to make an application for financial provision;

(ii) he believes that the other party has no significant assets and does not intend to make an application for financial provision; and

(iii) there are therefore no financial arrangements to be made.

(3) If the parties –

(*a*) were married to each other in accordance with usages of a kind mentioned in section 26(1) of the Marriage Act 1949 (marriages which may be solemnized on authority of superintendent registrar's certificate), and

(*b*) are required to co-operate if the marriage is to be dissolved in accordance with those usages,

the court may, on the application of either party, direct that there must also be produced to the court a declaration by both parties that they have taken such steps as are required to dissolve the marriage in accordance with those usages.

(4) A direction under subsection (3) –

(*a*) may be given only if the court is satisfied that in all the circumstances of the case it is just and reasonable to give it; and

(*b*) may be revoked by the court at any time.

(5) The requirements of section 11 must have been satisfied.

(6) Schedule I supplements the provisions of this section.

(7) If the court is satisfied, on an application made by one of the parties after the end of the period for reflection and consideration, that the circumstances of the case are –

(*a*) those set out in paragraph 1 of Schedule 1,

(*b*) those set out in paragraph 2 of that Schedule, or

(*c*) those set out in paragraph 3 of that Schedule, or

(*d*) those set out in paragraph 4 of that Schedule,

it may make a divorce order or a separation order even though the requirements of subsection (2) have not been satisfied.

10. – (1) If an application for a divorce order has been made by one of the parties to a marriage, the court may, on the application of the other party, order that the marriage is not to be dissolved.

(2) Such an order (an 'order preventing divorce') may be made only if the court is satisfied –

(*a*) that dissolution of the marriage would result in substantial financial or other hardship to the other party or to a child of the family; and

(*b*) that it would be wrong, in all the circumstances (including the conduct of the parties and the interests of any child of the family), for the marriage to be dissolved.

[Section 11 sets out the duty of the court to consider whether or not its powers under the Children Act 1989 should be exercised with respect to any child of the family.]

Questions

(i) Using these provisions, explain to a client the steps to be taken in order to obtain a divorce order. (For a useful summary, see John Eekelaar's article: 'The Family Law Bill: The Politics of Family Law' in [1996] Family Law 46.)

(ii) Why is it necessary for the new provisions to be brought into force initially only in a pilot project?

Section 9(3) and (4) addresses a problem discussed by Helen Conway in *Divorce and Religion* (1995):

The failure of the legal system to allow a religious law influence in the dissolution of marriages has the potential to cause injustice to members of religious minorities.

A prime example of this is where a civil divorce is obtained but the Jewish Get is not forthcoming. In Jewish law a divorce can be obtained by consent without the commission of a matrimonial offence. A wife is divorced when a husband executes and delivers a Get to her, Get being the Aramaic word for a formal deed of severance. It is only the husband who may formally initiate the divorce. There are set grounds on which parties may compel the other to either execute or accept a Get. ...

... Problems occur when a civil divorce exists but one party refuses a Get. If the wife refuses to accept a Get, the husband has certain religious solutions. ... However, a wife is left in a position where she would be forbidden by religious law to contract a second Jewish marriage. Such women are known within their community as the *agunot* or 'the chained'.

... there is an argument to say that the English civil law ought to address this issue and offer some assistance to potential *agunot*.

Section 9(3) and (4) of the 1996 Act makes provision for this by enabling the wife (whether petitioner or respondent) to prove that the marriage was of a Jewish nature and to say that she requires her husband to consent to a Get. The court can then give a direction requiring him to do so.

Questions

(i) Why has the law of divorce been adapted in this way to meet the needs of religious communities, when (as we have seen) it is the policy of the law not to accommodate those whose conscience is offended by the grant of a divorce (pp. 222ff, above)?
(ii) Can you foresee problems with this provision where either party has changed their religious views since the marriage?

(c) CONSIDERING AND REFLECTING

Section 7(3) states that the period for consideration and reflection which must elapse between the making of a statement of marital breakdown and the making of the divorce order is nine months. However, the effect of sub-ss (10)–(13) is that the period is extended by a further six months if either party so requests or if there are children of the marriage under 16. In these circumstances, it may nevertheless be reduced to one year if there is in force a domestic violence injunction (see Chapter 9, below), or if the court considers that the longer period would be significantly detrimental to the children. (It remains the law that divorce proceedings cannot be initiated during the first year of marriage.)

In *Family Law: A Ground for Divorce* (1990) the Law Commission explained that the period:

5.25 ... is primarily designed to provide convincing proof that the breakdown in the marital relationship is indeed irreparable. It should also give the parties a realistic time within which to resolve the practical questions and to decide whether or not they wish to be reconciled.

They then considered the length of the period:

Length

5.27 There was overwhelming agreement amongst respondents to Facing the Future that these objectives could not be achieved in less than nine months. The great majority favoured a period of nine or twelve months, with only a few suggesting longer. It was pointed out that a twelve month period would make divorce a significantly more lengthy process for a substantial number of people. Respondents to our public opinion survey chose periods ranging from six months to over two years, with the highest number (35%) choosing one year. We *recommend* an overall period of twelve months. This should give sufficient time to enable all but the most difficult and complex matters to be decided and to establish that the breakdown is indeed irreparable. It should also allow sufficient time for the benefits of conciliation or mediation to be explored. We also *recommend* that the actual application for a separation or divorce order should not be made until at least eleven months of the period have elapsed. However, there would be no compulsion to apply for an order upon expiration of this time. Parties could take longer if they wished, as an order should not be made unless it is actually applied for. Once applied for, it would not be granted for a further month, making a minimum total of one year overall.

5.28 A few respondents to Facing the Future suggested that the period should be longer if there were children. Most, however, did not support this. A child's sense of time is quite different from an adult's and considerable harm can be done by prolonged uncertainty. Harm may also be done by the additional bitterness which can be caused by having to wait longer on their account. The general view, both on this and on previous occasions, has been that to make divorce inevitably more difficult for those who have children will not benefit the children themselves and could make matters worse. Thus, 'it would amount to a denial that childless marriage is real marriage. ... Unhappy motives would be introduced for having, or not having, children; and a child once there could become a focus of bitterness for the parent who wanted to be free.' We *recommend*, therefore, that the period should not automatically be longer where there are children. The parties and the court will, however, have to consider what arrangements should be made for them and, if it is desirable to prolong the period in their interests, this should be done.

Although the Family Law Bill as originally drafted imposed a one year period in all circumstances, it was amended in the House of Commons and s. 7(10)–(13) added. The aim of the amendment was, in the words of Edward Leigh, MP, in the House of Commons Debate, to:

... send the important message that, if there are children in a marriage, that should also make a difference to the divorce process. In such circumstances, the parties should think not just of themselves but of the interests of the children.

He also expressed concern that:

... if the period is as short as 12 months, it is simply impossible to have a meaningful period of reconciliation – there is not enough time because there is so much to sort out. If children are involved and if there is not consent to the divorce, reconciliation will not be effective.

Questions

(i) Do you agree that there should be a longer period for reflection and consideration where there are children of the marriage?
(ii) Do you think that the extension of the period to 15 months increases the chance of reconciliation?
(iii) Bearing in mind the provisions of s. 7(10)(*a*), how could a couple with children ensure that they only had to wait nine rather than 15 months?

Another departure from the Law Commission's recommendations is contained in s. 3(1)(*c*), the requirement that financial arrangements be settled before a divorce order can be made. Paragraphs 1, 2, 3 and 4 of Sch. 1 set out the circumstances when a divorce order may be made before the parties' financial arrangements are resolved:

The first exemption

1. The circumstances referred to in section 9(7)(*a*) are that –
   (*a*) the requirements of section 11 have been satisfied;
   (*b*) the applicant has, during the period for reflection and consideration, taken such steps as are reasonably practicable to try to reach agreement about the parties' financial arrangements; and
   (*c*) the applicant has made an application to the court for financial relief and has complied with all requirements of the court in relation to proceedings for financial relief but –
      (i) the other party has delayed in complying with requirements of the court or has otherwise been obstructive; or
      (ii) for reasons which are beyond the control of the applicant, or of the other party, the court has been prevented from obtaining the information which it requires to determine the financial position of the parties.

The second exemption

2. The circumstances referred to in section 9(7)(*b*) are that –
   (*a*) the requirements of section 11 have been satisfied;
   (*b*) the applicant has, during the period for reflection and consideration, taken such steps as are reasonably practicable to try to reach agreement about the parties' financial arrangements;

(*c*) because of –
 (i) the ill health or disability of the applicant, the other party or a child of the family or (whether physical or mental), or
 (ii) an injury suffered by the applicant, the other party or a child of the family,
the applicant has not been able to reach agreement with the other party about those arrangements and is unlikely to be able to do so in the foreseeable future; and
(*d*) a delay in making the order applied for under section 3 –
 (i) would be significantly detrimental to the welfare of any child of the family; or
 (ii) would be seriously prejudicial to the applicant.

The third exemption

3. The circumstances referred to in section 9(7)(*c*) are that –
(*a*) the requirements of section 11 have been satisfied;
(*b*) the applicant has found it impossible to contact the other party; and
(*c*) as a result, it has been impossible for the applicant to reach agreement with the other party about their financial arrangements.

The fourth exemption

4. The circumstances referred to in section 9(7)(*d*) are that –
(*a*) the requirements of section 11 have been satisfied;
(*b*) an occupation order or a non-molestation order is in force in favour of the applicant or a child of the family, made against the other party;
(*c*) the applicant has, during the period for reflection and consideration, taken such steps as are reasonably practicable to try to reach agreement about the parties' financial arrangements;
(*d*) the applicant has not been able to reach agreement with the other party about those arrangements and is unlikely to be able to do so in the foreseeable future; and
(*e*) a delay in making the order applied for under section 3 –
 (i) would be significantly detrimental to the welfare of any child of the family; or
 (ii) would be seriously prejudicial to the applicant.

Question

What effect do you think this requirement will have upon (*a*) the use made of the period for reflection and consideration, or upon (*b*) the chances of the parties' concluding, upon reflection, that the marriage has not irretrievably broken down?

Stephen Cretney in 'The Divorce White Paper – Some Reflections' (*Family Law*, 1995) comments:

The Government commissioned a MORI poll which, apparently, showed that divorce on demand by one partner without having to give a reason was widely thought to be unacceptable. The requirement to deal with financial and child upbringing issues before the divorce order is made may be thought significantly to reduce the force of the criticism ... that divorce by repudiation was, in substance, on offer. But the White Paper seems curiously naive about what is likely to happen during the 'period of reflection'. Far from spending the evenings, as the White Paper, para 4.16 suggests, 'reflecting on whether their marriage can be saved and, if not to face up to the consequences of their actions and make arrangements to meet their responsibilities' some, at least, of those concerned seem likely to spend the time in the far more pleasurable activity of conceiving – necessarily illegitimate – babies. Some will spend the time exploiting their emotional or financial advantage; others will brood on their grievances.

(d) MEDIATION

The title to the Green and the White Papers, *Looking to the Future: Mediation and the Ground for Divorce* draws one's attention to the fact that the ground for divorce is not the only concern of the reforms. We have seen that the Law Commission recommended that the use of mediation be encouraged (see p. 253, above). One of the questions raised in the Green Paper was whether or not mediation should be compulsory; responses to the consultation process indicated that it should not, and this was accepted in the White Paper. At the same time, the Government was encouraged by the positive conclusions of the *Rowntree Report* (discussed further in Chapter 7). Accordingly, the Act contains provision for the court to adjourn proceedings in order for the parties to resolve matters, and to direct that they attend a meeting to have the available mediation facilities explained to them (sections 13 and 14); Part III of the Act amends the Legal Aid Act 1988 so as to make Legal Aid available for mediation in family matters.

The Green Paper *Legal Aid – Targeting Need* (May 1995) adds some further detail to the mediation proposals. It discusses the relationship between the provision of funding for legal representation and its availability for mediation:

The assessment of whether to grant publicly funded legal representation will need to take into account the availability of family mediation. The Government does not believe that family mediation should be compulsory. Family mediation is a process that is unlikely to work effectively unless couples enter it voluntarily. The Government accepts that family mediation may not be suitable in certain types of case. The Government does consider, however, that family mediation is both more effective and more suited to resolving the kinds of problems that arise in most family cases than representation in negotiations by solicitors, or litigation. As a result, the Government believes that the manner in which funding for the two services is organised should provide a definite encouragement to couples to choose family mediation. In particular, the Government believes that those who seek publicly funded legal representation should have to demonstrate their need for such representation rather than mediation.

Point blank refusal to mediate would not be considered a good reason, and the solicitor would not be able to represent a client who could offer no reason for their decision not to choose to mediate.

The Green Paper gives examples of acceptable reasons – some would be set out in regulations, including for example cases where there had been violence; others might emerge from an initial meeting with an intake officer at a mediation service, for example where the mediator felt that the matter involved legal technicalities beyond the scope of mediation.

Why mediation? The White Paper states that:

Family mediation encourages couples to:
- seek marital counselling if it is appropriate to attempt to save the marriage;
- accept responsibility for the ending of the marriage;
- acknowledge that there may be conflict and hostility, and a strong desire to allege fault and attribute blame;
- deal with their feelings of hurt and anger;
- address issues which may impede their ability to negotiate settlements amicably, particularly the conduct of one spouse;
- focus on the needs of their children rather than on their own personal needs.

The Green Paper also spelt out a further motivation:

9.28 Evidence of the current costs of mediation services is limited. National Family Mediation – whose services deal more frequently with child-related mediation – estimates the average cost of a comprehensive mediation at £550 per mediation and of a child-related mediation at £180 to £200. The FMA, which offers comprehensive mediation and is largely self-financing, charges £180 per 90 minute session per couple for an average of 3 sessions (i.e. £540 per mediation).

9.29 Given the likely increase in the number of couples seeking mediation, which will reduce unit costs, and the pressure to offer professional mediators competitive rates of remuneration, which will tend to increase unit costs, the likely average cost of a mediation could be assumed to be of the order of £550 per case.

9.30 The average cost of a matrimonial bill paid out of the Legal Aid Fund in 1992/93 was £1,565. Many privately paying spouses will have paid more.

National Family Mediation (NFM; see p. 283, below) produced a flow chart depicting the mediation process, while the 1996 Act was being debated in Parliament (p. 267, below). It shows the routes to mediation, and something of the interaction between mediation and legal services. This leads us to consider the whole question of the court system and the alternatives to it, and in particular the nature, scope and purpose of mediation. These issues are the subject of the next chapter.

(e) DIVORCE AND MARRIAGE

We began this chapter with a comment on the emotional realities of divorce. During the debate about the new law before it was enacted there were frequent expressions of concern about the emotional and practical effects of divorce on the parties and their children, and about the stability of marriage.

Cardinal Basil Hume in *The Times*, 20 January 1996, suggested that:

... any necessary reform of the divorce law can only be part of a larger project of strengthening the institution of marriage and family life.

One urgent need is for better marriage preparation to be available to all. I am often struck by the thought that a monk has to wait five years before being allowed to take solemn vows. Monastic vows are no more solemn than the vows of marriage. And monks do not have the grave responsibility of bringing new life into the world and nurturing young children. We are spending too much money and energy focusing on the ending of marriages, when what is needed is more investment on preparing for marriage and sustaining couples, especially in the early years. Maybe we should make entry into marriage more difficult. ...

Questions

(i) Is it (*a*) practicable or (*b*) desirable for the law to make entry into marriage more difficult?

(ii) If more people cohabit instead of marrying, who loses – the man, the woman, their children, or all of us?

(iii) In a secular context, what form might 'better marriage preparation' take?

Thelma Fisher, in *Impressions of the Family Law Bill in the House of Lords* (1996) commented that the debate in the House of Lords gave the impression

... of a grandparent generation's deep anxiety about marriage breakdown. There have been speeches about the effects of divorce at a personal level (several peers have given accounts of their own and others' experiences), about the effects of divorce upon children ... and about a 'throwaway' culture of relationships. The elders of the tribe have been grieving and casting about for explanations. However, the retention of the fault clauses has seemed a misguided way of tackling these issues. ... Lord Habgood made one of the most telling speeches, positively arguing the principle of the period of a year:

The mediation process

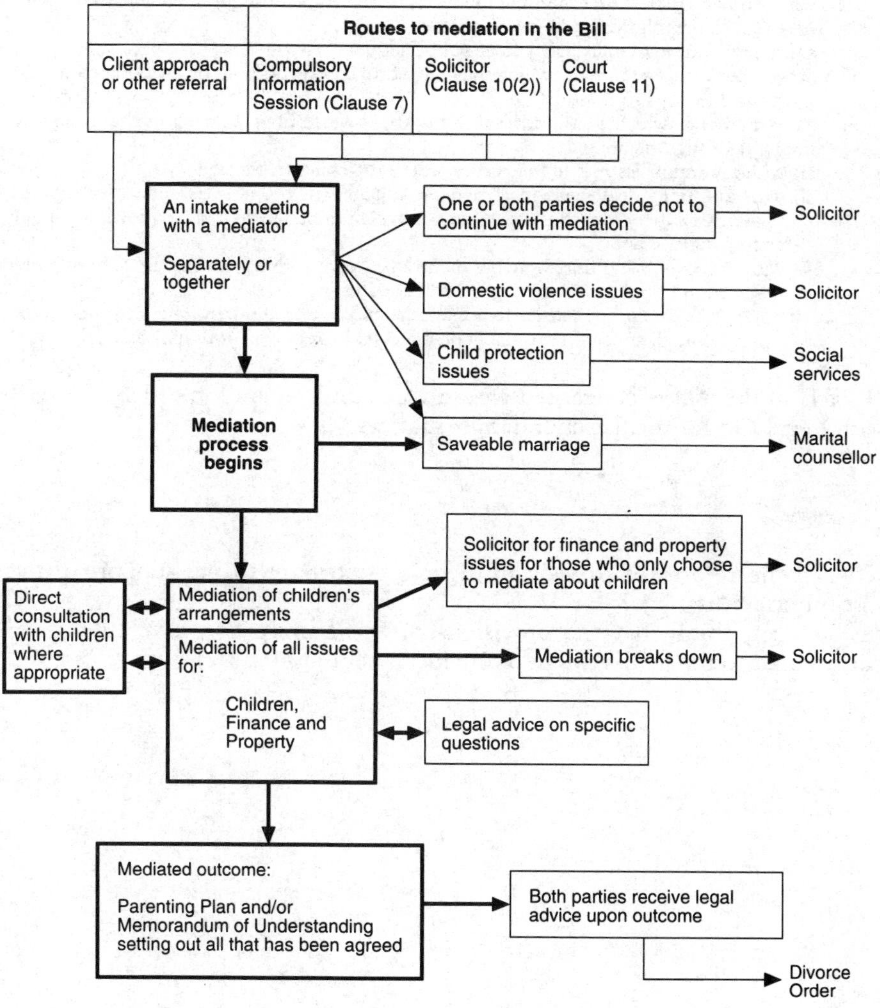
Routes to mediation in the Bill
Client approach or other referral
Compulsory Information Session (Clause 7)
Solicitor (Clause 10(2))
Court (Clause 11)
An intake meeting with a mediator
Separately or together
One or both parties decide not to continue with mediation
Solicitor
Domestic violence issues
Solicitor
Child protection issues
Social services
Mediation process begins
Saveable marriage
Marital counsellor
Solicitor for finance and property issues for those who only choose to mediate about children
Solicitor
Direct consultation with children where appropriate
Mediation of children's arrangements
Mediation of all issues for:
Children, Finance and Property
Mediation breaks down
Solicitor
Legal advice on specific questions
Mediated outcome:
Parenting Plan and/or Memorandum of Understanding setting out all that has been agreed
Both parties receive legal advice upon outcome
Divorce Order

'Surely this Bill strikes at the right point by giving legal significance to the passage of time. It says "Slow down. What is wrong is precisely that you do want everything immediately." Time is itself important. Time is important not just for what can be done in it – reflection, negotiation, mediation, although they are important. *Time is important as a public assertion that marriages are not easily undone.*'

These concerns and aspirations are reflected in s. 1 of the Family Law Act 1996, added to the Family Law Bill as a House of Lords amendment:

1. The court and any person, in exercising functions under or in consequence of Parts II and III, shall have regard to the following general principles –
   (*a*) that the institution of marriage is to be supported;
   (*b*) that the parties to a marriage which may have broken down are to be encouraged to take all practicable steps to save it;
   (*c*) that a marriage which has irretrievably broken down and is being brought to an end should be brought to an end –
      (i) with minimum distress to the parties and to the children affected;
      (ii) with questions dealt with in a manner designed to promote as good a continuing relationship between the parties and any children affected as is possible in the circumstances; and
      (iii) without costs being unreasonably incurred in connection with the procedures to be followed in bringing the marriage to an end; and
   (*d*) that any risk to one of the parties to a marriage and to any children, of violence from the other party should, so far as reasonably practicable, be removed or diminished.

(Part II of the Act is concerned with divorce and separation orders, Part III with Legal Aid for mediation in family matters.)

Questions

(i) Can the reform of the law of divorce contribute to the support of the institution of marriage?
(ii) Do you think that the provisions of the Family Law Act 1996 have contributed to the achievement of the ideals set out in s. 1(*c*)?

Chapter 7

Adjudication and mediation

Americans preach that the procedure of the family court must be therapeutic. This means no more (but no less) than that, just as the juvenile court seeks to do what is best for the child, so the family court should approach its wider jurisdiction inspired by a similar philosophy. In every case it would seek to diagnose and cure the underlying cause of the family disorder. Thus, in divorce it would think first of marriage-mending before marriage-ending. For this remedial function it would need to be buttressed with adequate expert assistance, whether within the court or in the local community. Where, however, cure proved impossible, the family court would perform its legal operation (such as divorce) with the least traumatic effect on the personalities involved.

This extract from Neville Brown's discussion of *The Legal Background to the Family Court* (1966) would be highly controversial today. Elizabeth Szwed, in 'The Family Court', her contribution to Michael Freeman's collection on *The State, the Law and the Family: Critical Perspectives* (1984), says:

I believe that there is a real possibility that enthusiasm for the therapeutic and conciliatory, or the reassuring and accessible, atmosphere could produce unfair and adverse consequences. Unbridled abrogation of the customary rules of court proceedings is probably more likely to result in sloppiness and disrespect rather than reassurance.

The object of this chapter is to look at the role of the courts and other agencies in the resolution of conflict in the family. This is particularly important at a time when that role is being challenged, and may be on the brink of radical change. We have placed this discussion immediately after our examination of divorce. This is partly because, for many people, divorce marks their first encounter with the legal system, and may prompt them to question its operation; and principally because it is in the context of divorce that the latest challenge to the court system has arisen (see Chapter 6, above).

1 The family courts debate

The first comprehensive official discussion of family courts came in the *Report of the Committee on One-Parent Families* (the Finer Report) in 1974. The Report deals first with general principles:

CRITERIA

4.282 Our approach owes little to American experience or writings, or to any preconceived attachment to the notions of a 'family court'. We have been guided pragmatically by specific considerations emerging from our study of the matrimonial law and courts in this country, which has established for us the need for and the character of the institution we have in mind. We have, in the first place, traced the personal and social mischiefs to which the dual system of matrimonial jurisdiction gives rise. We have also shown how this system offers financial provision to wives, mothers and their children by means of orders which in many cases are not honoured by those whose obligation to maintain their dependants has been affirmed by the courts. To ensure that these women and children survive, the social security authorities provide the subsistence which the law promises. The contribution of the private obligation to maintain is interstitial; that of social security is fundamental. We therefore conclude that only an institution which is shaped by the recognition of these facts can adequately serve the needs of broken families. The second major point is that members of families which have collapsed come to court at a stage when critical decisions will have to be taken about issues, other than those directly affecting matrimonial relief or finance, around which conflicts are likely to develop. There may be disputes over the custody of the children, or the ownership or occupation of the matrimonial home. Such practical matters have to be settled or determined at some time, and the presence of the parties in court provides the best opportunity that may ever occur for discussion and decision. Thus, we have come to think of the family court as an institution which will improve on our inherited system by eliminating the overlap, the contradictions and the other weaknesses and defects of the legal jurisdictions we have exposed earlier in this Part of the Report, and which at the same time will also improve the machinery and services which are available to deal realistically with the practical problems resulting from marriage breakdown.

4.283 In the light of the foregoing considerations, we set out the six major criteria which a family court must in principle satisfy:

(1) the family court must be an impartial judicial institution, regulating the rights of citizens and settling their disputes according to law;

(2) the family court will be a unified institution in a system of family law which applies a uniform set of legal rules, derived from a single moral standard and applicable to all citizens;

(3) the family court will organise its work in such a way as to provide the best possible facilities for conciliation between parties in matrimonial disputes;

(4) the family court will have professionally trained staff to assist both the court and the parties appearing before it in all matters requiring social work services and advice;

(5) the family court will work in close relationship with the social security authorities in the assessment both of need and of liability in cases involving financial provision;

(6) the family court will organise its procedure, sittings and administrative services and arrangements with a view to gaining the confidence and maximising the convenience of the citizens who appear before it.

Criterion (1) is elaborated thus:

THE FAMILY COURT AS A JUDICIAL INSTITUTION

4.285 The fundamental principle which must govern the family court is that it shall be a judicial institution which, in dealing with family matters, does justice according to law. This may seem to be so obvious a point as hardly to be worth mentioning; but the need to emphasise it arises from the nature of a jurisdiction which aims to do good as well as to do right. To promote welfare is an unusual function for a court of law. To some extent, the courts which deal with matrimonial disputes and with children are already familiar with that function through references in the statutes to reconciliation in husband and wife disputes, and through the statutory obligation in many forms of proceedings which involve children to have first and paramount regard, in any decision the court may reach, to their welfare. But the deliberate attempt to expand and systematise the welfare function, which is an essential part of the family court concept, carries risks, as well as potential advantages, which can be eliminated only by clear thinking and firm practice regarding boundaries and priorities. The court must remain, and must be seen to remain, impartial. This is of particular importance now that local authorities and governmental agencies of various kinds have powers and duties imposed on them which bring them into the proceedings, either as interested parties or as advisers to the court. The object of achieving welfare must not be permitted to weaken or short cut the normal safeguards of the judicial process – the dispassionate examination of evidence properly adduced to the court, regular procedures which promote an orderly and fair hearing, and the allowance of legal representation. The court must not see the men, women and children with whom it is concerned as 'clients', and still less as 'patients' for whom the court process is one form of, or a preliminary to, 'treatment'. Professional staff serving the court, including any who are responsible for assisting the court to reach sound conclusions on welfare issues, must be answerable to the court for what they do and how they do it. The aim must be to make adjudication and welfare march hand in hand, but there should be no blurring of the edges, either in principle or in administration. Through the family court it should be possible to make a new and highly beneficial synthesis between law and social welfare, and the respective skills, experience and efforts of lawyers and social workers; but the individual in the family court must in the last resort remain the subject of rights, not the object of assistance.

Question

To what extent have criteria (2) and (5) been overtaken by later developments?

The Finer Committee were heavily influenced by the differences between the higher courts, the magistrates' courts, and the social security authorities in their approach to financial relief (see Chapters 3 and 4, above). The plethora of jurisdictions relating to children was, however, even more confusing.

Reform of the substantive law can, however, lead to changes in the courts. Thus the Department of Health in *An Introduction to the Children Act 1989* (1989) explain the main features of the new code of remedies:

3.4 The Children Act creates a single code for court orders about the welfare of children. The main features of this code are that for the first time:

(*a*) each court which is considering a matter affecting a child's future will be able to make orders in the interests of the child's welfare;
(*b*) any person will be able to apply to court for an order concerning a child's upbringing (either with or without the court's leave);
(*c*) the range of orders available in each court and the criteria applied by the courts will be the same;
(*d*) the effect of court orders is clarified, including the effect of one order on another;
(*e*) where aspects of a case affecting the same child come before more than one court, the proceedings can be brought together in one venue.

Their guidance on *Court Orders* (1991) explains the new concurrent jurisdiction thus:

1.13. The Children Act creates a concurrent system of jurisdiction for a wide range of family proceedings in new magistrates' family proceedings courts, county courts and the High Court. Rules governing the allocation and transfer of cases either vertically between the various tiers, or horizontally within tiers, will ensure that cases are directed to the most appropriate court.

1.14. In practice the majority of public law cases will be heard entirely in the magistrates' family proceedings court as usually this will be the most appropriate court. Different considerations apply to private law cases where for the time being it will continue to be possible to exercise free choice about which court is used.

1.15. Most public law applications will start in the magistrates' family proceedings court but in certain circumstances can be transferred to a higher court. Subject to the overriding principle that delay is likely to prejudice the welfare of the child the criteria for transfer are:

(*a*) exceptional complexity, importance or gravity;
(*b*) the need to consolidate with other proceedings;
(*c*) urgency.

Questions

(i) Do you think that magistrates' family proceedings courts will usually be the 'most appropriate court' to handle care proceedings?

(ii) Why should the applicant local authority not be allowed to choose where to bring the case?
(iii) Could we not achieve a family court by the simple expedient of abolishing the family jurisdiction of magistrates' courts?
(iv) What are the objections to doing that?
(v) Do you think that a single family court will ever be achieved?

It was the inefficiency of overlapping jurisdictions and inconsistent remedies which most concerned the Interdepartmental Review of Family and Domestic Jurisdictions (Consultation Paper, 1986) and which has now been addressed to some extent in the Children Act 1989. Others have been more concerned that the nature of family disputes, and hence the functions of the courts in relation to them, demand a rather different sort of court. For example, the report of a working party set up by British Agencies for Adoption and Fostering and the Association of Directors of Social Services on Family Justice (1986) identified a number of characteristics shared by family matters, including these:

30 c) Decisions in family matters have far-reaching consequences for the adults and children concerned. Those who have to dispense justice require not only a thorough knowledge of complex areas of law and a consistent response to difficult aspects of interpretation but also an understanding of the social and emotional factors which influence the well-being of individuals.
d) Those adults and children who come into contact with the courts through civil proceedings are likely to be experiencing considerable stress and to be angry with or alienated from each other. At the same time they may have to cope with readjustments in personal, social, economic and other practical areas of their lives. Personal satisfaction and the ability to deal constructively with the legal resolution of disputes will be affected by the degree of privacy, respect, sensitivity and efficiency which is reflected in all aspects of the court's operation. ...

Questions

(i) Do you think that some or all family cases should be heard in private? If so, which? What are the advantages and disadvantages of privacy for (*a*) adult parties, (*b*) children, or (*c*) courts?
(ii) Cases heard in private cannot be reported in the media unless the court allows this. What, if any, restrictions should there be on the reporting of family cases?
(iii) Do you think that specialist skills are needed by the judiciary in family cases? If so, what are they, and how can such skills be acquired?

A recurring theme of discussions about family courts has been the need for greater informality and for inquisitorial rather than adversarial procedures. The Finer Report (1974) had this to say:

4.404 We are impressed by the unanimity of the commentators in favour of greater informality in family matters. But we are impressed, too, by the lack of studies of the effect of legal ritual upon citizens who use the courts. We do not know how representative a figure is the trade union leader who observed of the Industrial Relations Court that, if his members are to be sent to prison for contempt of court, he desires it to be done by a judge properly robed in scarlet and ermine. On these aspects of court procedure, we think that decisions should be delayed until they can be based on knowledge of what will best satisfy the citizen user's desire for fairness and dignity in the determination of matrimonial cases.

4.405 Another much canvassed procedural question is how far the hearings in the family court should be inquisitorial rather than adversary in nature. In the accusatorial or adversary form of procedure, as it characterises our civil litigation, the parties not only choose the issues which form the subject matter of the dispute, but also determine what evidence shall be brought before the court. The court has no right and no means to act as its own fact-gatherer. In the inquisitorial form of procedure, the court is not confined to acting as a referee, but may, so far as it has the means, take steps of its own to inform itself of the facts and circumstances it considers it ought to know in order to make a just determination. But the two forms of procedure are not, in truth, mutually exclusive. In the divorce jurisdiction, the court has always been charged with the duty of being 'satisfied' that it can grant relief, which must involve, in appropriate cases, a duty to enquire into matters as to which the parties themselves may not be in dispute. So again, in matters affecting custody of and access to children the court has to have regard to the child's paramount interests, which is a matter which the views of the parties, even to the extent that they coincide, do not determine. The proper balance of the two forms of procedure in the family court should, in our view, be determined by the following considerations. It is desirable that the court itself should not come into the arena. To the extent that the court requires assistance by way of investigation or expert assessment of circumstances which it considers material, this function should be discharged by ancillary services which are attached to or can be called upon by the court, but whose personnel are not themselves members of the court. The bench of the family court is to consist only of judges, professional or lay, and experts or assessors should not be constituents. On the other hand, the bench as so constituted should, in every aspect of its jurisdiction, be able to call upon the aid of a competent person to make social and welfare enquiries and reports.

Question

Should a judge dress up in purple dressing gown and curly wig (*a*) to grant an adoption order to which the birth parents have agreed, or (*b*) to try a hotly contested parental dispute about where the children are to live, or (*c*) to decide whether or not a ten-year-old girl has been sexually abused, or (*d*) to grant or enforce an ouster injunction against a violent man, or (*e*) to decide whether a child should be called by a new surname, or (*f*) in any family law case?

Consider again a dispute about whether or not a ten-year-old girl has been sexually abused, in the context of care proceedings. As the above extract from the Finer Report points out, the parties can determine what evidence shall be brought before the court. The judge may therefore be asked to give leave to the local authority to instruct a child psychiatrist as an expert witness; he may grant leave for the guardian ad litem to instruct another expert, and perhaps for the girl's mother to instruct another.

Question

Is this acceptable? Would you prefer to see one expert consulted by the court? (The procedural mechanism exists, in RSC Ord 40.)

The Children Act Advisory Committee considered this problem briefly in its annual report for 1993/94. It had the assistance of a report made to it by a working group, the Expert Witness Group, chaired by Dr. Eileen Vizard, Consultant Child Psychiatrist from the Tavistock Clinic, which recommended:

That one expert should, wherever possible, be appointed with the agreement of all parties. The Group was divided on the issue of court appointed experts with all the experts favouring a move in this direction and most lawyers opposing this or expressing reservations.

Questions

(i) What would be your reservations, if any?
(ii) Reverting to our last example, suppose that the girl's mother, who maintains she has not been abused, instructs a psychiatrist who, to her consternation, reports that she has. What is mother going to do with that report? Why should she not simply decide not to use that evidence at the trial?

The Children Act Advisory Committee, in its 1993/94 report, recommended that in giving leave for papers to be shown to an expert (who should always be named, never merely 'an expert') the court should:

- Provide for the disclosure of any written expert report both to all parties and to the other experts in the case. When a report is disclosed it should include a copy of the letter of instruction.
- Provide for discussions between experts following mutual disclosure of reports and for the filing of further evidence by the experts stating the areas of agreement and disagreement between the experts. Parties should only instruct experts who are willing to meet in advance of the hearing. When granting leave, the court must make this a condition of the appointment.

Question

Why is it desirable for the letter of instruction to an expert to be disclosed?

In *Re L (minors) (police investigation: privilege)* [1996] 2 All ER 78, [1996] 2 WLR 395 the House of Lords by a majority held that in care proceedings (unlike other litigation) experts' reports are not privileged. Accordingly, where leave is given to a party to instruct an expert, this is usually done on condition that his report be disclosed to the court and to the other parties, and the court may, if it is in the child's interests to do so, order the disclosure of the report to a non-party such as the police.

Behind all these questions lies the essential role of the court in family cases: is it there to regulate and supervise family life, to help solve family problems, to resolve disputes by adjudication or by other means, or all of these things? We shall look at each of them in turn.

2 Public regulation or private ordering?

Robert Mnookin's celebrated article *Bargaining in the Shadow of the Law – The Case of Divorce* (1979) begins:

I wish to suggest a new way of thinking about the role of law at the time of divorce. It is concerned primarily with the impact of the legal system on negotiations and bargaining that occurs *outside* of court. Rather than regard order as imposed from above, I see the primary function of contemporary divorce law as providing a framework for divorcing couples themselves to determine their respective rights and responsibilities after dissolution. This process, by which parties to a marriage are empowered to create their own legally enforceable commitments, I shall call *'private ordering'*.

In *Divorce Bargaining: The Limits on Private Ordering* (1984), he explains both the advantages and the disadvantages which have to be countered:

The advantages of private ordering

Let me begin with the arguments supporting the presumption in favour of private ordering. The core reason is rooted in notions of human liberty. Private ordering is supported by the liberal ideal that individuals have rights, and should largely be left free to make of their lives what they wish. In Charles Fried's words, a regime of law that 'respects the dispositions individuals make of their rights, carries to its logical conclusion the liberal premise that individuals have rights'.

Private ordering can also be justified on grounds of *efficiency*. Ordinarily, the parties themselves are in the best position to evaluate the comparative advantages of alternative arrangements. Each spouse, in the words of John Stuart Mill, 'is the person most interested in his own well-being: ... with respect to his own feelings and circumstances, the most ordinary man or woman has means of knowledge immeasurably surpassing those that can be possessed by anyone else.' Through negotiations, there are opportunities for making *both* parents better off than either would be if a court or some third party simply imposed a result. A consensual solution is, by definition, more likely to be consistent with the preferences of each spouse than would a result imposed by a court. Parental preferences often vary with regard to money and child-rearing responsibilities. Through negotiations, it is possible that the divorcing spouses can divide money and child-rearing responsibilities to reflect their own individual preferences.

Finally, there are obvious and substantial *savings* when a couple can resolve the distributional consequences of divorce without resort to formal adjudication. The financial cost of litigation, both private and public, is minimised. The pain of the formal adversarial proceedings is avoided. A negotiated settlement allows the parties to avoid the risks and uncertainties of litigation, which may involve all-or-nothing consequences. Given the substantial delays that often characterize contested judicial proceedings, agreement can often save time and allow each spouse to proceed with his or her life. In short, against a backdrop of fair standards in the shadow of which a couple bargains, divorcing couples should have very broad powers to make their own arrangements. Significant limitations are inconsistent with the premises of no-fault divorce. Parties should be encouraged to settle the distributional consequences of divorce for themselves, and the state should provide an efficient and fair mechanism for enforcing such agreements and for settling disputes when the parties are unable to agree.

Capacity

On an abstract level, I find the general defence of private ordering both appealing and persuasive. But it is premised on the notion that divorce bargaining involves rational, self-interested individuals – that the average adult has the intelligence and experience to make a well-informed judgment concerning the desirability of entering into a particular divorce settlement. Given the tasks facing an individual at the time of divorce, and the characteristics of the relationship between divorcing spouses, there are reasons to fear that this may not always be the case.

...

Some might think that the stresses and emotional turmoil of separation and divorce undermine the essential premise of private ordering – the idea that individuals are capable of deliberate judgments. I disagree. After all, for most persons the emotional upheaval is transitory, and the stresses are an inevitable consequence of having to make a new life. Temporary incapacity does not justify state paternalism for an extended period of time. Nonetheless, safeguards are necessary, and the wooden application of the traditional contract defence of 'incompetence' may not provide sufficient protection. ...

Professor Eisenberg recently suggested a concept of 'transactional incapacity' to capture the notion that 'an individual may be of average intelligence and yet may lack the aptitude, experience, or judgmental ability to make a deliberative and well-informed judgment concerning the desirability of entering into a given complex transaction.'...

An analogous concept could be applied to divorce bargaining within a system that encourages private ordering at the time of divorce. When one spouse knows or has reason to know of the diminished capacity, and exploits this incapacity, a court should reopen the agreement. Proof of exploitation is essential, however. For this I would require a showing that the terms of the agreement considered as a whole fall outside the range of what would have been acceptable to a competent person at the time of the settlement. By providing a remedy only if a party exploited the other side's incapacity by securing an unusually one sided bargain, this test will not create uncertainty in most cases.

A second prophylactic to guard against transitory diminished capacity would involve a 'cooling-off' period, during which either party would be free to rescind a settlement agreement. In a commercial context, this period is often very short – typically three days. In the divorce context, I would make it considerably longer – perhaps sixty or ninety days. Like any safeguard, this one has costs. Some agreements may come apart even though they involve no exploitation whatsoever, simply because of ambivalence or a change of heart. Moreover, this cooling-off period might be used strategically by a party – a tentative agreement may be reached, only to be later rescinded, in order to wear an opponent down.

...

Unequal bargaining power

Let me now turn to a second possible justification for imposing limits on private ordering – the basic idea is simple; in negotiations between two competent adults, if there are great disparities in bargaining power, some bargains may be reached that are unconscionably one-sided.

The notion of bargaining power has intuitive appeal, but turns out to be very difficult to define. Without a complete theory of negotiations, it is hard to give precise substantive content to the notion of bargaining power, much less define precisely the idea of 'relative bargaining power'. Nonetheless, by briefly analyzing the five elements of the bargaining model I described in an earlier article, it is possible to suggest why some divorcing spouses may be seen as having unequal bargaining power.

First, there are *the legal endowments*. The legal rules governing marital property, alimony, child support, and custody give each spouse certain claims based on what each would get if the case goes to trial. In other words, the outcome the law will impose if no agreement is reached gives each parent certain bargaining chips – an endowment of sorts.

...

Second, a party's bargaining power is very much influenced by his or her *preferences* – i.e., how that party subjectively evaluates alternative outcomes. These preferences are not simply matters of taste – they can depend upon a party's economic resources and life circumstances. ...

A third element that effects bargaining power has to do with uncertainty, and the parties' attitudes towards risk. Often the outcome in court is far from certain, and the parties are negotiating against a back-drop clouded by substantial uncertainty. Because the parties may have different risk preferences, this uncertainty can differentially affect the bargaining power of the two spouses. ...

A fourth element that can create differences in bargaining power relates to the differential ability to withstand the transaction costs – both emotional and economic – involved in negotiations. ...

A fifth element concerns the bargaining process itself, and strategic behaviour. In divorce bargaining, the spouses may not know each other's true preferences. Negotiations often involve the attempts by each side to discern the other side's true preferences, while making credible claims about their own, and what they intend to do if a particular proposal is not accepted. Some people are more skilled negotiators than others. They are better at manipulating information and managing impressions. They have a more refined sense of tactical action. These differences can create inequalities in negotiations.

Externalities – third party effects

Third party effects provide the last set of reasons that justify limiting private ordering. ...

A divorce settlement may affect any number of interests not taken into account in the spouses' negotiations. The state's fiscal interests can be affected, for example. The economic terms of the bargain between the two spouses may substantially affect the odds that a custodial parent will later require public transfer payments. The most important third party effects concern the children, although there can be externalities with respect to other family members as well. At a conceptual level, it is easy to see how a negotiated settlement may reflect parental preferences but not the child's desires or needs. ...

Concerns about the effects of the divorce on the children underlie many of the formal limitations on private ordering – e.g., the requirement of court review of private agreements relating to custody and child support; the legal rules prohibiting parents from making nonmodifiable and binding agreements concerning these elements. ...

I believe divorcing parents should be given considerable freedom to decide custody matters – subject only to the same minimum standards for protecting the child from neglect and abuse that the state imposes on *all* families. The actual determination of what is in fact in a child's best interests is ordinarily quite indeterminate. It requires predictions beyond the capacity of the behavioural sciences and involves imposition of values about which there is little consensus in our society. It is for this reason that I conclude that the basic question is who gets to decide on behalf of the child.

Because primary responsibility for child-rearing after divorce does and *should* remain with parents there should be a strong presumption in favor of the parental agreement and limits on the use of coercive state power by judges or other professionals to force parents to do what the professional thinks is best. On the other hand, I think the state has an important interest in encouraging parents to understand that the responsibility for their children extends beyond the divorce, that children are in many ways at risk during the divorcing process, and that in deciding about the child-rearing arrangements, the parents have an important obligation to meet their children's needs. Moreover, there is reason to think that by facilitating parental agreement, and helping the parents transform their old relationship into one in which they can now do business together with respect to the children's future needs, the interests of the children are being served.

Questions

(i) Why are significant limitations on private ordering 'inconsistent with the premises of no-fault divorce'?
(ii) How far does English law in the Family Law Act 1996 reflect Mnookin's model?
(iii) Do the arguments in favour of allowing people to make their own arrangements when they separate or divorce apply equally to allowing them to make pre-marital or pre-cohabitation contracts (see p. 43, above)?
(iv) What if the parties find it difficult to make their own arrangements? What help should they be given?
(v) How far, if at all, does the concept of private ordering help us to decide what sort of court would be best suited to adjudicating upon those issues which the parties cannot decide for themselves?

One suggestion is put forward by Mervyn Murch in *Justice and Welfare in Divorce* (1980):

(i) Primary task
The participant model defines the primary task of legal and welfare processes in a new way. It starts from the assumption that there is a common objective about which all parties could reach agreement, even though they may differ as to the means of reaching that objective. This common objective is that of arriving at a fair and reasonable basis upon which the family can reconstitute itself following divorce, paying due regard to the interests of the children. In other words, the primary task of divorce machinery is to find a way of providing for the interests and welfare of family members after divorce. I doubt very much whether more than a small minority of divorcing parents would not subscribe to this objective, likewise few lawyers or welfare officers would dissent fundamentally.

(ii) Membership of the conflict-resolving system
Once it is accepted that there is a common objective, all the actors within the machinery of justice – judges, members of the Bar, solicitors, welfare officers and the family members themselves, who have temporarily become part of the system – can be perceived as being bound together in a common pursuit of an agreed objective. This becomes the task, and each actor within the system has a responsibility to work towards the common goal. To a large extent therefore the task of working towards the common goal becomes itself an authority from which the actors derive their responsibility and by which their roles are defined and differentiated.

Murch (1995), in his contribution to *Frontiers of Family Law*, anticipates criticisms of his theory in the following extract:

... there are those who argue that there is something about the lawyers' world view and approach to family and child welfare issues which is fundamentally at odds with those of other occupational groups. ... Thus Michael King and Christine Piper in their challenging book *How the Law Thinks about Children*, argue that a multi-disciplinary approach to family justice is not really possible. Using propositions developed by the German legal sociologist Gunther Teubner, that law is essentially a powerful, closed, self-referring and self-sustaining (autopoietic) system of thought, they suggest that legal process will inevitably 'enslave' all other disciplines ... and distort other views to fit its own particular intellectual discourse. This leads King and Piper to the view that the legal approach to child welfare matters is bound to suffer from the following basic shortcomings:

First, it over-simplifies the child's social world, excluding from consideration, for example, environmental factors such as poverty, bad housing, social security provision and taxation – matters which the judicial process generally cannot address in any meaningful way. ... Of course one could respond that much the same thing applies to other intellectual discourses; that, for example, behaviourist or psycho-dynamic theories have their own autopoietic character which tends to alter accounts of people and their relationships in order to accord to the basic tenets of the discourse.

Second, King and Piper argue that the legal approach traditionally individualises parent/child relationships and tends to 'root them' in notions of individual morality and responsibility. Thus a functional systemic view of family interaction upon which various models of family therapy and mediation have been developed cannot be properly encompassed by the legal process. ... While as a generalisation this view may have a certain validity, particularly as it applied to court practice before the Children Act 1989, I think King and Piper have failed to appreciate where it now clearly has to be modified. Take for example those instances when courts refer cases to child welfare experts for assessment and then simply accept the experts' recommendation. ... Similarly where mediation is arranged through the agency of the court it generally accepts the resulting settlements, sometimes as a basis for a subsequent order if that is what the parties and the children wish. ...

Third, King and Piper suggest that the legal approach concentrates decision-making on dyadic relationships – child/mother, mother/father etc – and thus excludes factors seen as irrelevant to these relationships, ruling out other versions of reality which it is unable or unwilling to handle. Again it seems to me that law is not alone in this tendency. In the child welfare field, different schools of thoughts will tend to shape and focus practitioners' thoughts in ways which include favoured or familiar perceptions while excluding others. For example those using family systems theory will focus on the interaction of the whole family, whereas those adopting a child development perspective may view the child's early attachments as the crucial factor.

Fourth, King and Piper argue that the very nature of the litigation process, particularly if based on the adversarial model of justice, encourages distortion and exaggeration. Parties are obliged to defend their corner and press their case to the limit, notwithstanding that children's proceedings under the Children Act 1989 are 'officially deemed to be an enquiry into the future welfare of the child'. Again, one readily sees a certain validity in the observation, yet on reflection one might argue that any form of dispute or interpersonal conflict tends to generate a defensive dynamic which encourages exaggeration and polarisation. ...

Fifth, King and Piper argue that law is reductionist in its approach to child welfare matters – reducing the findings of child welfare science to simple rules of thumb, such as 'continuing contact between child and non-custodial parent is a good thing'. Even here one could argue that law is not alone in this tendency. Indeed there is much evidence to suggest that social work is being strongly developed and managed along similar lines. Thus we find a developing corpus of professional guidelines and rules of 'best practice' limiting the individual social worker's professional discretion. ...

All this means that while not totally dismissing the validity of the so-called autopoietic nature of law and the problems it may pose for collaborative work between the disciplines, I find King and Pipers' arguments somewhat overstated.

Question

To what extent to you think that lawyers and other professionals share a common objective in family law cases? (Consider this question again when you have read the Solicitors' Family Law Association Code of Practice, p. 292, below).

This brings us to the question whether the court's role is to help solve family problems or simply to resolve disputes.

3 Marriage mending or marriage ending?

Explicit in Neville Brown's conception of a family court was a commitment to 'marriage mending' – a court-based attempt to solve the family's problems and reunite the parties. The Finer Report (1974) recounts the English experience:

4.298 It may, indeed, be said to be the virtually unanimous opinion of those who have the relevant experience that there is little room for optimism when the court to which the parties have presented themselves to formalise or regulate the breakdown of the marriage seeks to use that occasion for mending it. The Denning Report [1947] concluded on the evidence it received:

> 'The prospects of reconciliation are much more favourable in the early stages of marital disharmony than in the later stages. At that stage both parties are likely to be willing to co-operate in an effort to save the marriage; but if the conflict has become so chronic that one or both of the parties has lost the power or desire to co-operate further, the prospects sharply diminish. By the time the conflict reaches a hearing in the divorce court, the prospects are as a rule very small. It is important therefore that the general public should be brought to realise the importance of seeking competent advice, without delay, when tensions occur in marriage.'

4.299 The Morton Royal Commission on Marriage and Divorce [1956] which took a good deal of evidence on this subject, recorded:

> 'If matters are allowed to develop into a condition of chronic disharmony one or perhaps both of the spouses will probably have lost the ability or desire to make any attempt to restore the marriage, and by the time steps have been taken to institute divorce proceedings the prospects of bringing husband and wife together again are greatly reduced. This view won a wide measure of support from our witnesses.'

4.300 The Law Commission [1966] considered that reconciliation procedures started after the filing of the petition achieve little success and 'have tended to become pointless and troublesome formalities'.

The Law Society took a similar view in *A Better Way Out* (1979):

178. ... It is generally accepted that, by the time either spouse reaches the stage of consulting a solicitor about divorce proceedings, the breakdown of the marriage has reached the point of no return and it is too late for there to be any real prospect of reconciliation. If the spouses wanted help in saving the marriage, they will have sought it before then from family, friends or marriage guidance counsellors.

Gwynn Davis and Mervyn Murch, however, in *Grounds for Divorce* (1988) report that:

The results of our 'consumer' interviews indicate beyond doubt that this assessment is seriously wide of the mark. In particular, it fails to take account of the fact that the whole divorce process has speeded up, with many petitions being filed whilst the parties are still living together.

Earlier, they point to the evidence suggesting that, nowadays, the possibility of reconciliation may exist in a great many cases:

Our own research also suggests that there is a potential for reconciliation in a significant number of divorce cases. Even in the course of the Special Procedure survey (from which initially defended cases were excluded) 39 per cent of respondents and 23 per cent of petitioners claimed that they would have preferred to remain married to their former partner. In at least 50 per cent of these cases it appeared that the marriage breakdown reflected the will of only one party. Given that our interviews usually took place some months after the award of the decree nisi – and in some cases, several years after the initial separation – it is likely that the number wishing to continue with their marriage had, at the outset of proceedings, been even greater.

... we also asked respondents whether they believed that their own marriage had 'irretrievably broken down'. Fifteen per cent denied that it had done so, with a further 10 per cent saying that they were 'uncertain'. Few, if any, of those interviewed in the course of this research had attempted to defend the divorce petition.

This evidence of *doubt* or *regret* should not be taken as an indication that a great many of these marriages could have been 'saved'. ...

The findings of the Law Commission's *Court Record Study* (1990) also lend support to the view that there is more scope for reconciliation during divorce proceedings than had previously been acknowledged:

13. The original 477 files resulted in one nullity decree, five judicial separation decrees, 433 decrees nisi of divorce and 418 decrees absolute. One decree nisi was later rescinded. Thus 53 cases (11.1% of the total) fell by the wayside at some stage, 28 without any decrees at all, and 15 between decree nisi and decree absolute. These included one case (mentioned earlier) where the fact was not recorded. Otherwise, Table 6 shows the facts relied on in the unsuccessful petitions:

Table 6 Facts relied on in unsuccessful petitions

	No.	*(%)*	*% of petitions on that fact*
Adultery	13	(24.5%)	9.3%
Behaviour	30	(56.6%)	16.2%
Desertion	0	(0%)	0%
Two years	6	(11.3%)	5.4%
Five years	4	(7.5%)	11.1%
Total:	53	(99.9%)	

14. The behaviour cases did tend to run into more difficulty than the others, but it is significant that more than a quarter of these couples were still living at the same address at the date of the petition. This in itself was associated with a higher rate of failure to proceed.
15. It was not always possible to deduce the reason why a case had failed to reach decree or decree absolute. It was rarely associated with, let alone attributable to, the intervention of the court. The most common reason appeared to be reconciliation; there were also some who had obtained non-molestation or ouster injunctions but apparently gone no further, some where the proceedings on the file had been superseded by a new petition in that or another court, and some which proceeded no further than notification of an intention to defend.

Questions

Davis and Murch nonetheless conclude 'It would be absurdly facile to assume, just because some couples decide, in the end, to remain together, that *courts* have much (if any) role in the marriage mending business. Perhaps the most we can ask of courts and legal procedure is that they do not make life *even more difficult* for couples facing these decisions.' (*a*) Do you agree? (*b*) In what respects might the present law make life even more difficult?

The law gives some encouragement to reconciliation: s. 6(2) of the Matrimonial Causes Act 1973 allows the court to adjourn divorce proceedings for an attempt to reconcile the parties if at any stage it appears that there is a reasonable possibility of success; and the 'period for reflection and consideration' required by the Family Law Act 1996 to elapse before a divorce order is made is stated by s. 7(1) to be a period for the parties '(*a*) to reflect on whether the marriage can be saved and to have an opportunity to effect a reconciliation, and (*b*) to consider what arrangements should be made for the future'. Another provision is explained in the Law Commission's *Court Record Study* (1990):

Reconciliation certificates

21. A solicitor acting for a petitioner is obliged, under section 6(1) of the 1973[1] Act, to file with the petition a certificate stating whether or not he has discussed reconciliation with the client or given the client the names and addresses of persons qualified to assist. There were at least five cases in which certificates were filed apparently unnecessarily because the solicitor was not acting for the purposes of the petition; and four cases where there was no certificate but there should have been. Hence there were certificates in 121 of the 125 cases in which solicitors were acting.

22. Generally, therefore, solicitors were fulfilling their duty to file certificates. More interestingly, perhaps, they gave positive responses in what might be thought a surprisingly high proportion of cases. Thus 85 out of the 125 certificates reported that the solicitor *had* discussed reconciliation with his client, and 29 reported that they had referred the client to other agencies.

Solicitors now rarely act for the purposes of the petition itself, because of the special procedure (see p. 225, above). The perhaps surprisingly high proportion (also found by Davis and Murch) who had nevertheless discussed 'reconciliation' or made referrals may have done so because of a practice direction (see p. 284, below) that 'reconciliation' can also include 'conciliation'. The Finer Report drew the following distinction:

4.288 In the discussion which follows we shall be using the terms 'reconciliation' and 'conciliation' to denote two different concepts. By 'reconciliation' we mean the reuniting of the spouses. By 'conciliation' we mean assisting the parties to deal with the consequences of the established breakdown of their marriage, whether resulting in a divorce or a separation, by reaching agreements or giving consents or reducing the area of conflict upon custody, support, access to and education of the children, financial provision, the disposition of the matrimonial home, lawyers' fees, and every other matter arising from the breakdown which calls for a decision on future arrangements.

4.289 The distinction between reconciliation and conciliation, and the influence which the family court may bring to bear in promoting either of them, is of cardinal importance in the consideration of any proposal for a family court.

In their Report on *The Ground for Divorce* (1990), the Law Commission try to sum up the different kinds of processes and objectives:

Counselling, conciliation and mediation

5.29 ... The umbrella term 'counselling' is used in Australia and New Zealand to encompass a variety of different types of help. All share the characteristic of keeping an open mind about the eventual outcome, while helping the couple or individuals involved to gain a greater understanding of their situation and to reach their own decisions about the future. The focus and method, however, can differ sharply, as can the organisational context in which the service is offered.

5.30 Broadly speaking, there are three different types of activity which may be involved:

(i) Marital counselling is offered, either to a couple or to an individual spouse, with a view to helping the couple to strengthen or maintain their marital relationship. If they are estranged or separated, the aim is to reconcile or reunite them. Historically, attempts at reconciliation were part of the role of 'police court missionaries' who became the probation and divorce court welfare service of today. Generally speaking, however, such services are offered by voluntary organisations, principally Relate Marriage Guidance. Relate counsellors are carefully selected and trained, but do not hold any particular professional qualification and offer their services voluntarily;

(ii) Divorce counselling and other forms of therapy aim to assist individuals, couples, and their children, to come to terms with the fact that their relationship is breaking down, to reduce the sense of personal failure, anger and grief, to disengage from and negotiate a new relationship with the former spouse and with the children, and eventually to move on to new relationships with confidence, avoiding the mistakes of the past. In other words, it seeks to minimise the harm done to either partner and to their children by the breakdown

---

1. Compare s. 12(2) of the Family Law Act 1996.

of their marriage. Once again, this is generally offered by voluntary organisations such as Relate, although some probation services offer divorce experience courses, and specialist therapy may be available privately or in some parts of the health service;

(iii) Conciliation or mediation is a way of resolving disputes without resort to traditional adjudication. The aim is to help the couple to reach their own agreements about the future, to improve communication between them, and to help them to co-operate in bringing up their children. Conciliation in this country developed first in the context of resolving disputes about children, often through the efforts of registrars and divorce court welfare officers at the court where a custody or access dispute was to be tried, but also through independent conciliation services, most of which are now affiliated to the National Family Conciliation Council. Conciliators generally hold professional qualifications in social work, undergo specialist training in family conciliation, and are paid for their services. The costs and benefits of various conciliation services have recently been the subject of a major research study conducted by the University of Newcastle. This has revealed that conciliation is indeed effective, both in reducing the areas of conflict and in increasing the parents' well-being and satisfaction with the arrangements made. In general, these benefits are greater when the service is provided away from the courts. The problems with conciliation conducted by or at the court, valuable and effective though it can often be, include the inevitable pressure to reach a settlement quickly, the inevitable authority of the registrar or court welfare officer conducting it, which may unconsciously or consciously dictate the outcome, and the risks of confusing the welfare officer's different roles of reporting to the court and assisting the couple to reach agreement. However, this is a fast-moving field in which developments are taking place all the time. For example, the independent sector is beginning to develop methods of comprehensive mediation, covering property and finance as well as child-related issues.

As had the Finer Report, but for rather different reasons, they concluded that reconciliation attempts should *not* be a mandatory part of the divorce process:

5.33 Some of our respondents argued that counselling aimed at saving the marriage should be a compulsory part of the divorce process, but most were opposed to this. The matter has been considered on many previous occasions, most notably by the Denning Committee on Procedure in Matrimonial Causes in 1947, by the Royal Commission on Marriage and Divorce in 1956, by the Law Commission in The Field of Choice in 1966, and by the Finer Committee on One-Parent Families in 1974. They all concluded that mandatory reconciliation attempts within the court process were unlikely to succeed. We do not take the view that no reconciliation is possible once a person has taken the momentous step of consulting a solicitor and making a statement of marital breakdown: the evidence suggests that, even under the present law, couples become reconciled between petition and decree, and even between decree nisi and decree absolute. Removing the need to separate or to make hostile allegations against one another should increase the prospect of reconciling those who can be reconciled; but we do not believe that the courts should require them, on pain of punitive sanctions, to make the attempt. There are several reasons for this. First, there are the views of the organisations at present involved in providing these services. They would of course like there to be a properly funded network of services readily available to all who wish to use them. But such counselling is a two-way process which can only be offered to volunteers, not conscripts. The hostility and bitterness induced by conscription is unlikely to lead to a real and lasting resolution. Secondly, and perhaps more importantly, there are some marriages which it would be wrong in principle to attempt to save. A wife who is regularly subjected to violence or abuse from her husband needs rescuing from her marriage, not pressure to return to it. A system of mandatory reconciliation could not be justified without some attempt to distinguish between marriages, which would only reintroduce the very inquiry into past misbehaviour which it is the object of these proposals to avoid. Thirdly, it would be impossible to justify the enormous public expenditure which would be involved in requiring such attempts in every case, without a better prospect of success than can be demonstrated at present. Finally, it was felt by some respondents that *conciliation* might, paradoxically, be more likely to result in reconciling some couples, by encouraging them to find a way through their difficulties relating to future arrangements while they were still amenable to discussion.

Questions

(i) Do you agree that 'there are some marriages which it would be wrong in principle to attempt to save'?
(ii) Can you think of other ways in which encouragement to seek whatever help might be needed by either party could be built into the divorce process?
(iii) Do you think that it is the role of the state to provide such help?
(iv) If you do, how might it be funded? Would a levy on banns, licences, and certificates to marry be appropriate? If not, why not?

4 Mediation: development, and the way ahead

The term 'mediation' is now used instead of 'conciliation', following recommendations made in the *Newcastle Report* urging greater clarity and common terminology. In 1993 the National Council for Family Conciliation was renamed National Family Mediation (NFM); NFM and the Family Mediation Association (FMA) are now the two national organisations offering mediation.

We now consider in more detail the nature of mediation in the light of the prominence now given to it in the Family Law Act 1996 (see Chapter 6, above). In *Mediation: the Making and Remaking of Co-operative Relationships* (1994) by Janet Walker, Peter McCarthy and Noel Timms (the Rowntree Report) mediation is defined as follows:

Family mediation is a process in which an impartial third person, the mediator, assists couples considering separation or divorce to make arrangements, to communicate better, to reduce conflict between them, and to reach their own agreed joint decisions. The issues to be decided may concern separation, the divorce, the children, finance and property.

The mediator has no stake in any disputes, is not identified with any of the competing interests, and has no power to impose a settlement on the participants, who retain authority to make their own decisions.

Couples enter mediation voluntarily, to work together on the practical consequences of family breakdown, and to reach proposals for settlements which may then be endorsed by their legal representatives and the court, wherever appropriate. Mediation offers an alternative to negotiation by solicitors and to adjudication through the court, but is not a substitute for legal advice and representation.

Looking first at the development of mediation, an outline of its history in this country is given in the University of Newcastle's Conciliation Project Unit's Report to the Lord Chancellor on the *Costs and Effectiveness of Conciliation in England and Wales* (1989):

Early Forms of Family Conciliation

2.21 Conciliation in the area of family disputes has been a relatively recent development in England and Wales. It is difficult to trace its precise source simply because the further one delves into the past the greater the confusion between 'conciliation' and 'reconciliation' (Eekelaar and Dingwall (1988)). 'Conciliation' is reported to have been widely practised in the magistrates' courts before the Second World War – and not only by the probation service – but the context makes it clear that the primary aim was to preserve the marriage relationship and, in particular, to persuade wives not to pursue legal claims against their husbands (Manchester and Whetton (1974)).

2.23 The notion that divorce procedures should enable parties to resolve their differences with the minimum of bitterness and conflict, once the breakdown of the marriage was irretrievable, can be discerned in the change of attitude to collusion which, in 1969, became a discretionary, rather than an absolute bar to divorce (see the remarks of Lord Scarman in *Minton v Minton* [1979] AC 593, 608). The first official, explicit recognition of the distinction between 'conciliation' and 'reconciliation' would appear to be the Practice Direction of the President of the Family Division, issued on 27 January 1971 (*Practice Note (Divorce: Conciliation)* [1971] 1 WLR 223), and which coincided with the coming into force of the Divorce Reform Act 1969:

> 'Where the Court considers that there is a reasonable possibility of reconciliation *or that there are ancillary proceedings in which conciliation might serve a useful purpose*, the Court may refer the case, or any particular matter or matters in dispute therein, to the Court Welfare Officer.'

The Court Welfare Officer would then, if he decided that conciliation 'might assist the parties to resolve their dispute', refer the case on to a probation officer, a marriage guidance counsellor or 'some other appropriate person or body indicated by the special circumstances ... of the case'.

The Finer Report and its Aftermath

2.24 The impact of the 1971 Practice Direction on the divorce courts is unclear, but when the Finer Committee investigated the question it found that the court welfare services had concentrated almost exclusively on reconciliation rather than conciliation (Finer (1974)). ...

2.25 Having reviewed conciliation and reconciliation practices both in Britain and in some foreign jurisdictions, the committee concluded that, whereas reconciliation procedures undertaken at the time when parties seek to formalise their marriage breakdown have small success, 'conciliation procedures conducted through the court at this same stage have substantial success in civilising the consequences of the breakdown'. In its view, the policy of the law should be that:

> 'dead marriages should be decently buried. Decency in this connection involves diagnosing the practical needs of the family at the time when the court assumes control over the relationship between its members and their affairs, invoking the help of other appropriate agencies to minister to those needs, and encouraging the victims of the family breakdown to wind up their failure with the least possible recrimination, and to make the most rational and efficient arrangements possible for their own and their children's future'.

The Committee envisaged that the 'agencies' referred to would comprise not only the court welfare service but also other bodies, including the social services and specialised organisations offering marriage guidance.

2.26 These suggestions for conciliation were made in the context of the Finer proposals for a family court and this may help to explain why they elicited no centralised response. Instead, initiatives were taken at a local level by different groups with different aims. Indeed, the very breadth of the Finer definition of conciliation encouraged a multitude of approaches. ... Parkinson [1986] lists six concerns which, in her view, fuelled the rapid growth of conciliation in Britain from 1975:

(i) to provide an alternative to the adversarial system in the divorce courts;
(ii) to protect children involved in their parents' divorce;
(iii) to give people more control over their own affairs and reduce their reliance on formal institutions;
(iv) to achieve greater administrative efficiency by processing contested cases more quickly;
(v) to reduce public expenditure, particularly on legal aid;
(vi) to stem the rising tide of divorce. (Parkinson (1986)).

The Development of In-Court Conciliation

2.27 The first attempt to institute a formal conciliation service within the court process took place at the Bristol County Court. The Avon Probation Service, as a response to the Finer proposals, had organised a specialist civil work team and, following discussions with the judiciary, a system of preliminary appointments in defended divorced cases was set up in 1976. In 1978, the service was extended to cases of disputes over custody or access, the term 'mediation' being used to describe appointments in cases of this kind (Parmiter (1981)).

... [It] is clear ... is that growth has been very rapid, particularly in areas where the enthusiasm of the probation service was matched by that of local judges or registrars. ...

2.29 Legally, it is clear that parties cannot be compelled to attend conciliation appointments (*Clarkson v Winkley* [1987] FCR 33) but there is evidence that they perceive the process to be compulsory (Davis and Bader (1985)). As will be revealed elsewhere in this Report, both the style of the conciliation appointment and the procedure of referral vary considerably. In some courts, once the existence of a dispute has been located, the parties are invited to an appointment with a court welfare officer. In others, the process is initiated by a registrar who seeks to identify the area of disagreement and then encourages the parties to meet with the conciliator in a separate room, with the possibility of a further appointment should this be necessary.

2.30 It was this approach to conciliation which the Booth Committee, reporting in July 1985, found to be so appealing, for it squared with its own view that much of the difficulty and cost associated with matrimonial litigation could be reduced by earlier institutional interventions, primarily through an 'initial hearing' which would take place as soon as practicable after the fiiing of the petition (Booth (1985)). ...

The Development of Independent Conciliation Services

2.34 It has been argued by some that conciliation is most effective when undertaken independently of the judicial process (Davis and Bader (1985)). As recognised by the Booth Committee (para 3.12), this is, in part, based on a belief that the earlier the intervention the better, and court services can, of course, only be used when proceedings have begun. But other advantages are also regarded as important (Parkinson (1986): p 76), such as quick accessibility in crisis situations and availability to unmarried as well as married couples and to those who wish to avoid court proceedings. It has also been argued (Roberts (1983) and (1987)) that the essence of conciliation being to enable the parties themselves to make joint decisions on disputed matters, the process may be seriously inhibited by its location within the institutional framework of the courthouse or any connection with it.

2.35 Arguments such as these were deployed by those, including lawyers, who helped to launch the independent conciliation services. As with court schemes, Bristol took the lead with the establishment of the Bristol Courts Family Conciliation Service in 1979 (the word 'Courts' was abandoned in 1987 to avoid confusion with the court-based service). Perhaps the other most important pioneering service was the South-East London Family Conciliation Bureau, established also in 1979 at Bromley. ...

The debate about whether mediation should be provided as part of the court's own processes, or by an independent agency, has swung in favour of the latter option. An Inter-departmental Committee in 1983 had favoured 'in court' conciliation, whereas the *Report of the Matrimonial Causes Procedure Committee* (the Booth Report) was in favour of conciliation both in and out of court:

3.11 ... There are three main factors which lead us to the conclusion that conciliation should be available to parties to matrimonial litigation. The first is that conciliation places responsibility squarely on the parties to seek agreement. This is consistent with our fundamental approach to matrimonial litigation, that contested proceedings are generally only appropriate where parties have been unable to reach agreement after being given every assistance and encouragement to do so. Secondly, conciliation, by its very nature, emphasises that parties are jointly responsible for dealing with the consequences of marriage breakdown and that it is not a matter just to be left to lawyers. This is particularly important in relation to children, for if both parents are to remain involved in the children's care and upbringing it is necessary that they should co-operate in making the necessary arrangements. Thirdly, we believe that if conciliation were generally available early in the proceedings it would encourage parties to face up to difficulties which might otherwise be suppressed, only to emerge at a later date as contested issues. *However, we do not think that conciliation should be concerned with the deep-seated and complex and emotional problems which stem from marriage breakdown: counselling for those problems should be available elsewhere.* The object of conciliation is to marshal such reasonableness and objectivity as exist and to direct the parties towards solving the essentially practical problems which arise.

3.12 Under our proposals the obvious place for conciliation is at the initial hearing. However, we have been greatly impressed by the view that in many cases conciliation is likely to be most effective before court proceedings have been started. *We also see much force in the argument that the distinction between out-of-court and in-court conciliation is somewhat arbitrary and is not necessarily relevant to the central question as to what form of conciliation service is likely to be most effective. We remain convinced that early intervention can be a major factor in developing a positive and conciliatory approach. Equally, we think that conciliation has a crucial role to play in helping parties to resolve issues which arise, or emerge, only when proceedings have started.*

The Newcastle unit were asked to investigate the comparative costs and effectiveness of various types of conciliation service. The Newcastle Report draws the following broad policy conclusions:

20.19 Our identification of the factors which, as regards existing services, seem to hinder the effectiveness of conciliation leads us to the view that conciliation:

(*a*) should not be mandatory for all couples;
(*b*) should not focus exclusively on child issues;
(*c*) should not be surrounded by ambiguous terminology; and
(*d*) should not overlap with other legal and welfare processes.

More positively, for effectiveness to be maximised, we believe that:

(*e*) conciliation should be recognised as an alternative mechanism to legal, adjudicatory procedures for the resolution of disputes and be identifiable as a discrete, unambiguous process;
(*f*) its distinguishing feature should be to enable couples to retain control of the decision-making process consequent on separation and divorce, encouraging them to reach their own agreements; and
(*g*) the arena in which it takes place should be conducive to civilised discussion with an appropriate degree of informality.

The Law Commission in their Report on *The Ground for Divorce* (1990) were heavily influenced by these conclusions in making their recommendations on conciliation and the legal process:

5.34 A more difficult question, therefore, is whether conciliation or mediation should be mandatory, if not in all cases at least in those which the court identifies as suitable for it. Once again, however, the majority of our respondents thought it should not. The professionals practising in the field said that mandatory conciliation or mediation was unlikely to be successful and indeed might be counter-productive. The Newcastle research indicated that the greatest benefits came from independent conciliation which was clearly distinguished from the coercive setting of the court. It is also clear that, whatever its benefits in some cases, there are many issues or relationships in which it is quite unsuitable. If so, the aim must be to ensure that adequate services are available to those who wish to use them, and to secure efficient information and referral machinery, rather than coercive sanctions to achieve this. There are also dangers in relying too heavily upon conciliation or mediation instead of more traditional methods of negotiation and adjudication. These include exploitation of the weaker partner by the stronger, which requires considerable skill and professionalism for the conciliator to counteract while remaining true to the neutral role required; considerable potential for delay, which is damaging both to the children and often to the interests of one of the adults involved; and the temptation for the court to postpone deciding some very difficult and painful cases which ought to be decided quickly. It is important that, whatever encouragement is given by the system to alternative methods of dispute resolution, the courts are not deterred from performing their function of determining issues which require to be determined. Where time permits, alternative methods can be explored so as to enable the parties to try and reach their own agreements away from the pressures of the court door. Where, however, an immediate decision is needed in the interests of either party or of their children, the courts should be prepared to give it.
5.35 We therefore *recommend* that undertaking either relationship counselling whether reconciliation or divorce motivated, or conciliation or mediation should be purely voluntary.
5.36 We further *recommend* that opportunities and encouragement to resolve matters amicably should be built into the system where appropriate. The first opportunity will be when the statement of marital breakdown is made; the second will be at the preliminary and subsequent assessments by the court; and the third will be whenever any contested issue arises for decision. Throughout, it can be encouraged by placing obligations upon the parties' legal advisers as to the provision of information and discussing the possibilities of both reconciliation and conciliation.
5.37 Furthermore, although participation in conciliation or mediation should be voluntary, we *recommend* that the court should have two additional powers to encourage it. Neither of these powers should be seen as placing any pressure on the parties to participate. They are designed to ensure that the parties are better-informed and to facilitate participation if they wish. They are also designed to some extent to regulate what happens informally at present. ...

Referral for an explanation of conciliation or mediation

5.38 It is likely that in a number of cases one spouse, or perhaps both spouses, will not appreciate the nature and effectiveness of conciliation or mediation, or even if aware have a totally closed mind on the subject. Many people are confused about the distinctions between counselling, reconciliation and conciliation and are instinctively resistant to reconciliation. We therefore *recommend* that the court should have power, whether on application or of its own motion, to give a direction that the spouses meet a specified conciliator or mediator, in order to discuss the nature and potential benefits of conciliation or mediation in their case. ...

Adjournment for participation
5.39 We further *recommend* that, where the parties are in dispute about any issue arising in the context of divorce or separation, the court should have power, whether on application or of its own motion, to adjourn the hearing of that issue, for the purpose of enabling them to participate in conciliation or mediation, or generally with a view to the amicable resolution of the dispute. In deciding to do this, the court should take the interests of any children into account (whether, for example, they will be more helped by the amicable resolution or harmed by the delay). It should, of course, be open to the parties not to participate and if either of them feels unable to do so this should not affect the handling of the case thereafter.

This was all very encouraging to the mediation movement, which has continued to develop and to gather momentum. The focus recently has been on the development of comprehensive mediation out of a system that began by concentrating on child-related issues. The authors of the Rowntree Report explain:

In [the Newcastle Report] we recommended more co-ordinated, comprehensive services for families facing separation through marital breakdown, including marital and divorce counselling, advice, and mediation on all issues. Our research had shown that it was unusual for couples to be in dispute about a single issue: those who could not agree about arrangements for children were likely to be in dispute about other matters. As one dispute was apparently 'settled' others might emerge. The lastingness of settlements in services focusing on one dispute in isolation from others was problematic. At the end of our study as many as 25 per cent of couples who had mediated child-related issues were still in dispute about child maintenance, and some 27 per cent about property issues. While mediation generated many social benefits, it had serious limitations also. We recommended not only that mediation should be all-embracing, but also that it could not be a true alternative dispute resolution mechanism while parties are obliged to seek separate legal representation. Such a stratagem adds to the costs of divorce rather than reducing them. Extending the mediation remit in turn extends the possibility of offering mediation to couples without dependent children, who may nevertheless face disputes about finance and property distribution, notably young dual-career couples, or older couples for whom accumulated property and pension benefits can be the source of considerable conflict. We contended that if, for all couples in dispute, mediation were effective in keeping dispute resolution out of the courts, there would be a noticeable and important change in the amount and costs of business for the courts and for lawyers, as well as a promotion of valued social and personal benefits. But such a shift has far-reaching implications for mediation services supported by child-based charitable organisations.

It was as a result of this recommendation that in 1990 the Joseph Rowntree Foundation funded five pilot projects, whereby comprehensive mediation was offered by mediation services affiliated to NFM (at Bristol, Cambridge, Coventry, Northumberland and Tyneside, and Sussex). The Relate Centre for Family Studies, in the University of Newcastle upon Tyne, was invited to evaluate and compare the five projects, and the Rowntree Report records their findings. The FMA has also begun to offer comprehensive mediation; the FMA, and NFM in its pilot projects, have regarded the involvement of lawyers as crucial to this new development, because of the range of issues now to be addressed, and the pilot projects were able to experiment with different ways of involving them. In some cases a lawyer joined the mediator for some sessions, in others a lawyer met the couple separately, or was available in the background as a consultant.

The picture that emerges from the Rowntree Report is a complex one, and no simple conclusions are drawn. The following extract gives something of the flavour of clients' reactions to the process:

> 'I think it has moved us into this frame of mind to try to be co-operative which might not have happened if we had gone through this hostility that people often get going through solicitors. ... The children have been put first an awful lot of the time and conciliation has helped with that.' (F)

The benefits would seem to relate to mediation as preventing tension –

> 'I feel it has helped to keep me from getting tense and wound up and I have been able to keep things happier for the children.' (M)

– or managing it more effectively and over a shorter time period:

> 'Because of the way we have done it we are still quite friendly.' (F)
>
> 'At the worst time of the post-separation period my wife and I were able to meet and not scream at one another and I thought that was quite impressive and it didn't come from us I am sure.' (M)
>
> 'I think it has reduced the amount of bitterness over a shorter period than perhaps would have been the case. ... A plus, but not one that I had considered beforehand.' (M)

Even when feelings were largely negative between partners, the majority did not see themselves in a state of high conflict with each other. Several questioned whether they would have been suitable candidates for mediation if this had been the case:

> 'Overall I felt it was a very valuable exercise. It did help to reduce the tension because of having to talk about something in not a formal atmosphere, but with third parties present. It does tend to concentrate the mind far better than two of you sitting over a table. Although there were a few areas of disagreement it was more of establishing what had to be done and how we could best do it, both in a practical manner and also in an emotional manner. Providing a couple are not coming to blows at the service I would thoroughly recommend it to anyone else. ... I find it very difficult to envisage that situation being handled by the mediators.' (M)
>
> 'Had we been spitting blood I don't know how they would have coped. Certainly the one who was not quite so confident – I think she would have run out of the room screaming.' (M)
>
> 'I can see that the downfalls in that [mediation] would be that if you got two people sitting there and they really are at loggerheads then that must be one of the biggest problems because it then starts to get personal.' (M)
>
> 'Everything was amicable anyway and whether or not it would be different if you had a couple who were at loggerheads and trying to sort things out I can't say. In many ways we were giving the mediators a fairly easy ride.' (M)

Indeed, one client commented:

> 'Had there been a dispute no doubt we would have had to go elsewhere.' (M)

This view does seem rather odd to a process of which the main objective is dispute resolution, but it introduces what might become a major debate in divorce reform, namely the extent to which mediation can helpfully be considered as 'assisted decision-making' in which couples manage their own divorce with a mediator rather than through advising solicitors. Or does the concept of *dispute* resolution dominate, thus restricting the service to couples with identifiable disputes about which they need to reach agreement before the divorce can be finalised? The broader objectives associated with mediation could be viewed as equally important as resolving actual disputes, but this would raise a theoretical conceptual argument about the nature and meaning of mediation.

> 'It's a very good way of sorting out troubles in a friendly way without involving judges and courts and it didn't cost as much. It seemed more friendly and logical.' (F)

'Sorting out troubles' is somewhat removed from dispute resolution, yet would be said to be very valuable, particularly in relation to wider concerns to protect children from the experience and consequences of parental conflict:

> 'It gave me peace of mind where I'd been afraid and it freed me to concentrate on the children and on looking after myself. I don't think I'd have been able to deal with it as well as I did if I hadn't gone there. ... It's left me free to focus on the children, learn to do finances, look after the house, adjust my identity to being a single person and things like that.' (F)

The theme of 'assisted decision-making' is one to which we return since it seems to fit well with the ideal of encouraging a 'civilised' approach to marriage breakdown.

The most common response from mediation clients to the question of what they did not like about the outcome related quite clearly to the failure to meet *any* of the expected objectives. The majority of clients were satisfied with the service provided, and this was not dependent on either the reaching of agreements or the time spent in mediation.

> 'I haven't got a bad word to say about them. I thought it was brilliant.' (F)
>
> 'I think there would have been a big void if there hadn't been comprehensive mediation.' (F)
>
> 'The conciliation process was excellent. I cannot praise it highly enough. I know that if it hadn't been for the service, I would be still now feeling and manifesting considerable anger all the time over the separation. The availability of this service providing a non-confrontational, non-adversarial mechanism for dealing with issues at a time when both parties are suffering extreme emotional anguish was opportune, soothing, comforting and helpful. I am not certain whether, without it, my wife and I would have been able to come to any agreement at all.' (M)

One user was especially keen to ensure we had recorded his satisfaction:

> 'Just to make sure, in case you haven't got it down, that if the funding for this place doesn't carry on it would be a big mistake because I can't see how we would have got by without it. It made it very clean. I cannot think of any criticism of the way it was run.' (M)

Marian Roberts, Assistant Director of Professional Practice and Training at NFM, in a letter to Family Law (1995), wrote:

... mediation is about helping people to make their own decision about their own arrangements. It is not the aim to resolve conflict.

Lord Hapgood (the former Archbishop of York) sums it up neatly in a letter to *The Times* (6 April 1996):

It is a basic principle of mediation that couples must reach their own decisions, which are then given legal force by being referred to a lawyer. The task of the mediator is to provide a controlled, supportive and yet searching context in which a couple can face the practical implications of divorce together.

Not all couples are suitable for this, especially when there has been violence, and mediators are alert to the dangers of coercion. When the conditions for mediation are inappropriate they advise couples to seek independent legal advice. Alternatively if the couple show signs of changing their minds about divorce they are advised to use the reconciliation services.

In their concluding chapter, the writers of the Rowntree Report have this to say about the different influences working upon mediation, and the different perceptions of what it can achieve:

'Mediation', as a process to the 'sanctity' of which mediators come increasingly to attest, seems in fact to be a permeable form of intervention, subject to the 'pushes and pulls' of interests: those of users, of providers and the state. Moreover, these interests interact in a dynamic manner. Thus, when in the course of our investigations we observed protracted discussions between the Law Society and the comprehensive mediation schemes on the emerging distinction between legal information and legal advice we could not help connecting this with the expressed disappointment of clients of mediation at the absence of 'guidance' and at a lack of information concerning legal norms. Similarly, when the Green Paper refers to the several distinct purposes the state wishes to realise in the 'initial' mediation interview we juxtapose the confused, changing and hesitant purposes clients themselves from time to time propose. Confusion, ambivalence and conflict cannot be adequately addressed by providing a catholic but confused service: distinct objectives require specification in an overall description and the ability to move between the procedures necessary for their particular achievement.

Anne Bottomley, in 'Resolving Family Disputes: a Critical View', her contribution to Michael Freeman's collection on *The State, the Law and the Family: Critical Perspectives* (1984) had this to say about the nature of mediation:

The idea ... has an older pedigree than is often assumed. ... Other forms of dispute resolution share the objective of agreement rather than judgment; however in conciliation it is the parties who are deemed to be in control. The presence of a third party is simply to further face-to-face negotiations by 'assisting in' helping communication (the language here slips often into a quasi-therapeutic discourse) and, when necessary, to give technical assistance with the symbols of social recognition of an agreement having been reached, whether by eating and drinking or by the drafting of a document. The anthropological literature has long alerted us to the need to look behind the presentation of such a form of dispute resolution and ask two questions. First, is there equality of power in the relationship between the parties, and between the parties and the mediator? Such an 'open' process is open to manipulation. To be persuaded may be an invidious form of judgment and control. Second, despite the presentation of the mediator in terms of neutrality and objectivity the mediator may be the purveyor of a particular pattern of beliefs that would tend to favour a particular 'resolution' to which the parties give their formal agreement.

[T]he conciliator is clearly not neutral but the purveyor of certain ideologies and practices. Psychology, therapy, or social policy are not neutral bodies of knowledge. ... Social workers and probation officers tend to share a common belief in the functionalism of the family, and a particular familial ideology in which roles are cast and those who do not fit are deemed not to be fit. They also share a concern with the increase in divorce and the need somehow to 'normalize' divorce so that it becomes less challenging to the images of stability and continuity that remain at the core of the family image. Much emphasis is placed on the fact that parents never divorce, only spouses: 'The court is asked in a divorce petition to dissolve the legal bonds of marriage, not the bonds of parenthood' (Parkinson 1983a: 24).

What we are experiencing at the moment is a pincer movement. On the one hand family law is being squeezed out of the formal legal system on arguments of cost and on the other hand it is being enticed out with promises of more fruitful pastures elsewhere. This shift towards de-legalization (Glendon 1977) must not be simply accepted but must be more closely examined. We need to recognize that the process of de-legalization is not one of de-regularization but is a shift from one form of social discipline to another. While the articulate middle classes will continue to buy the services of professional groups, others will become more and more the subjects of control by 'welfarism' (Donzelot 1980). Those who are most vulnerable will be caught between the unequal power relations of private ordering and a familial ideology rendered benign by welfarism in informal dispute resolution.

Questions

(i) Is mediation simply a form of alternative dispute resolution in family cases or is it yet another cloak for yet another type of professional to take over?
(ii) How far might these concerns be dismissed as lawyers' special pleading?
(iii) Do you now have a clear perception of what mediation is and what it can achieve? How would you describe it to a client?
(iv) If mediation fails or is inappropriate, should the court procedure seek to promote a non-adversarial approach in more conventional dispute resolution?
(v) What is a non-adversarial approach? Is it the same thing as an informal approach? Or an inquisitorial approach?
(vi) We are, of course, civilised people: when you have read Chapter 9, look back to this chapter and ask yourself what sort of family court is required to meet the needs of victims of domestic violence?
(vii) Can the same system be made to work *both* for divorce and for child care cases?

One of the aims of the writers of the Rowntree Report was:

... to address some of the key questions raised in the Government Consultation Paper on family mediation and the ground for divorce (December 1993), and to make recommendations that can be considered by the mediation services and Government at what is undoubtedly a critical point in the development of family mediation.

We have seen (in Chapter 6, above) something of the Government's response to the report in the White Paper and the Family Law Act 1996. Dr Stephen Cretney, in *The Divorce White Paper – Some Reflections* (1995) comments upon the perceptions of mediation seen there:

The Government's conversion to the merits of mediation ... is remarkable; but it has to be said that the White Paper reveals a view of the functions of the mediation process which is, in many respects, idiosyncratic. For example, how many mediators believe that their function is to enable spouses 'to take responsibility for the breakdown in their marriage' or to acknowledge responsibility for the ending of their marriage (White Paper, para. 5.22), or that where conduct is in issue mediation enables the parties 'to address face to face the questions of fault and blame' (White Paper, para. 7.5), and that 'mediation offers an opportunity to address what went wrong with the marriage'. It may be that these functions – although, perhaps, regarded by some as more appropriate for the confessional or the re-education programmes associated with totalitarian regimes – could form a part of the mediation process; but those involved in conciliation seem to have a rather different view. Indeed, Walker, McCarthy and Timms [the Newcastle Report], at p. 62, state that 'not addressing the past is much appreciated by clients who are feeling guilt. For them it came as a relief to discover that the mediators were not judgmental and that fault was not an issue'.

In the Joseph Jackson Memorial Lecture in January 1996 Cretney returns to this theme, commenting on what was then the Family Law Bill and the provisions one might expect to see for the provision and regulation of mediation services. He recalls the recognition in the White Paper of the need for a national professional body for mediators to lay down standards for its members, and compares the requirements in statutes such as the Chiropractors Act 1994 and the Osteopaths Act 1993 for accreditation, indemnity insurance and so on:

So you have expectations of the kind of provision you would expect to find in a statute concerned with the provision of mediation and other related services. I am afraid the Family Law Bill is unlikely to meet these expectations. You look for the duty to provide mediation services or at least a duty to ensure that mediation services are provided. There is none. You look for the duty – or even the power – to ensure that proper professional standards are maintained amongst all mediators; so that – for example – a mediator who abuses his or her position of trust can be prevented from offering such services in the future. There is no such provision.

In January 1996 the UK College of Family Mediators came into being, and it is intended by its founders (National Family Mediation, the Family Mediators Association and Family Mediation Scotland) to become the single regulatory body for mediators. Cretney's point is, of course, that there is no statutory basis for its operations. Meanwhile the Family Law Act 1996 is to be brought into force, although not yet on a nationwide basis; the White Paper explains that the Government intends to set up 'a major comprehensive pilot project which will monitor and test the new arrangements' (para. 7.39).

Questions

(i) The pilot project is to be independently evaluated. By what criteria would you evaluate its effectiveness?
(ii) One of the aspects to be examined in the pilot project is the use of lawyers (para. 7.40). As we have seen (p. 287, above), the developing comprehensive mediation services have regarded the involvement of lawyers as crucial. The White Paper states (at para. 6.21) that 'The Government believes that with

suitable quality assurance mechanisms in place, it will not be necessary for lawyers to "shadow" mediation.' How would you design quality assurance mechanisms to ensure that mediators do not need the assistance of lawyers? What are the advantages of doing so?
(iii) How important do you think it is for an agreement reached by mediation to be checked by a lawyer?

In *Involvement of Lawyers in the Mediation Process* (1996) Peter McCarthy and Janet Walker report on a survey of mediators and their views on the involvement of lawyers in mediation. They conclude:

The practice of all-issues mediation in England and Wales has involved considerable participation from lawyers, either as mediators or as legal advisers to couples who use mediation. In some services operating under the auspices of National Family Mediation, lawyers also act as consultants to mediators. Although mediation which is attended by the parties' legal advisers is practised in other jurisdictions, it is not an approach which would be welcomed by most FMA mediators. On the other hand, there is considerable support for suggestions that parties using mediation should have access to independent legal advice at all stages of the process and especially at the conclusion of mediation. ... Most respondents accept that the lawyer's legal knowledge and experience regarding financial issues make an important contribution to the mediation process, although lawyer mediators also seem to appreciate the contributions of family mediators. It is the balance that the sharing of skills brings to mediation which is valued, allowing mediation to deal with all issues and help mediators to cope with stress. Most survey respondents ... regard legal expertise as an essential component to the mediation process. Indeed, 83% of lawyer mediators, and 61% of family mediators, suggest that lawyers ought to be able to offer mediation as part of their legal practice. Moreover, 40% of ... mediators ... suggest that mediation training should be compulsory for all lawyers practising family law.

The Solicitors' Family Law Association introduces its Code of Practice as follows:

An SFLA solicitor believes that in resolving the problems arising at the end of family relationships or in family crises, it is preferable to promote a conciliatory atmosphere and to deal with matters in a sensitive, constructive and cost-effective way. To help put this into practice, SFLA members subscribe to a Code of Practice.

The Association was created in 1982 when there was widespread concern that too often solicitors and the court process were adding to the distress and anger that can arise on the breakdown of a family relationship. Our members believe that solicitors could and should deal with matters in a way designed to ensure that people's dignity is preserved, with every encouragement to reach agreement and avoid unnecessary litigation. The result will be to achieve the same or more satisfactory solutions but at less cost – in terms of emotion and money.

Most importantly, they will be solutions that do not destroy the possibility of former family members dealing with each other in a civilised way, for example in parents agreeing arrangements for the benefit of their children notwithstanding their own differences. Experience shows that agreed solutions are more likely to be adhered to than those imposed by a Court. Even when proceedings are inevitable so that a court has to decide matters, it is to the advantage of the whole family that proceedings are conducted in a constructive and realistic manner rather than as if in the midst of a war zone.

Questions

(i) In view of efforts such as these on the part of lawyers, why are lawyers and the courts still perceived by many as adding to the difficulties of family breakdown?
(ii) Can we be sure that mediation will escape the same reputation?

(iii) If you were involved in divorce proceedings, would you rather have a lawyer who was 'on your side', or a mediator dealing impartially with you and your spouse? What do you think would be the advantages and disadvantages of both?

Chapter 8

Maintenance and capital provision on divorce

1 The historical background

At common law the wife acquired the right to be supported by her husband throughout the marriage, albeit how and when the husband chose. (See Chapter 3, above.) When divorce was introduced into English law in 1857, it was thought to be only correct that the wife would have the right to apply to a court to obtain an order for support to substitute the voluntary payments to which she would have been entitled had the marriage continued.

Until recently, English law was dominated by a system of divorce based on the doctrine of the matrimonial offence (see Chapter 6, above). It necessarily followed that the court would attempt to make awards which kept an 'innocent' wife in the position in which she would have been had her husband properly discharged his marital obligations towards her. The Law Commission discussion paper entitled *The Financial Consequences of Divorce: the Basic Policy* (1980) reminds us of the following never to be forgotten words of Sir James Wilde (later Lord Penzance) in the Victorian case *Sidney v Sidney* (1865) 4 Sw & Tr 178, 34 LJPM & A 122:

> ... If, it was said, a man can part with his wife at the door of the Divorce Court without any obligation to support her, and with full liberty to form a new connection, his triumph over the sacred permanence of marriage will have been complete. To him marriage will have been a mere temporary arrangement, conterminous with his inclinations, and void of all lasting tie or burden. To such a man the Court may truly say with propriety, 'According to your ability you must still support the woman you have first chosen and then discarded. If you are relieved from your matrimonial vows it is for the protection of the woman you have injured, and not for your own sake. And so much of the duty of a husband as consists in the maintenance of his wife may be justly kept alive and enforced upon you in favour of her whom you have driven to relinquish your name and home.'

Further,

> It is the foremost duty of this Court in dispensing the remedy of divorce to uphold the institution of marriage. The possibility of freedom begets the desire to be set free, and the great evil of a marriage dissolved is, that it loosens the bonds of so many others. The powers of this Court will be turned to good account if, while meting out justice to the parties, such order should be taken in the matter as to stay and quench this desire and repress this evil. Those for whom shame has no dread, honourable vows no tie, and violence to the weak no sense of degradation, may still be held in check by an appeal to their love of money; and I wish it to be understood that, so far as the powers conferred by the section go, no man should, in my judgment, be permitted to rid himself of his wife by ill-treatment, and at the same time escape the obligation of supporting her.

Question

Do you think that the knowledge that there is no escape from the financial ties and obligations of a marriage would operate today as a deterrent against divorce and a buttress to the institution of marriage?

What of a 'guilty' wife? Historically, a wife who had deserted her husband or committed adultery lost her common law right of maintenance. Although the position was ameliorated to a certain extent, the function of divorce was seen to be that of giving relief where a wrong had been done. This inevitably deprived many women of support after a divorce.

Finer and McGregor describe the position in the following way in their *History of the Obligation to Maintain* (Appendix 5 to the Finer Report (1974)):

Alimony in the ecclesiastical courts

26. A right to maintenance in the strict sense – meaning a claim for the payment of money directly enforceable against the husband – was available to the wife only in the ecclesiastical courts, and even there was only ancillary to the power of these courts to pronounce a decree of divorce *a mensa et thoro*. Such a decree, if granted on its own, might have left the wife without the means of survival. The court would therefore at the same time pronounce a decree of alimony, under which the husband would be required to pay his wife an annual sum, calculated as a proportion of his income, or, if the wife had separate estate, a proportion of their joint incomes. It was common to award one third, sometimes less, sometimes – especially where the husband's property had come substantially from the wife – more. A decree of alimony could not be made separately from a decree of divorce *a mensa et thoro*, for which it followed that a wife who could not establish one of the offences on which such a decree could be granted could not be granted alimony either. Moreover, the means of enforcing an award of alimony were of more theoretical than practical utility. Alimony could not be sued for as a debt in the civil courts. Just as the common law courts refused to award maintenance on the grounds that this would have interfered with the ecclesiastical jurisdiction, so on the same grounds they refused to enforce the awards made in that jurisdiction. Before 1813, the only sanction for non-payment of alimony was excommunication or other ecclesiastical censure. Thereafter, a machinery for the imprisonment of the defaulting husband on a writ of *de contumace capiendo* became available, but there is little evidence to suggest that the threat of punishment here and now proved to be any more effective than the threat of punishment in the hereafter.

Maintenance after parliamentary divorce

27. A second species of maintenance attached to divorce by private Act of Parliament. The women who benefited from these awards of maintenance were very few in number. But the parliamentary practice is of cardinal historical importance because it established the principles that were adopted by the legislature as governing the right to maintenance when it established for the first time, in 1857, a system of divorce in the civil courts. The earliest Divorce Acts contained express provisions to ensure that the divorced wife should not be left in a state of destitution. Subsequently, a different practice prevailed:

> 'In the House of Commons there was a functionary called "The Ladies' Friend", an office generally filled by some member interested in the private business of Parliament, who undertook to see that any husband petitioning for divorce made a suitable provision for his wife. No clause to this effect was inserted in the Bill, lest it should be rejected in the other House, but, as a condition of obtaining relief, a husband was made to understand that, before the Bill passed through Committee, he must enter into a bond securing some moderate income to his wife.'

Two features of this practice call for special note. First, unlike the practice in the ecclesiastical court, which granted alimony only to an innocent wife, Parliament deliberately saw to it that a man could not use its process to rid himself of his wife, whatever her matrimonial misconduct might have been, without making some financial provision for her. Secondly, also in contrast with alimony, the provision which had to be made was not for the periodic payment of a sum of money. A husband seeking divorce by Act of Parliament had to make secured provision: that is to say, he had to make property available which, under the terms of an appropriate deed, was permanently set aside to secure whatever gross or annual amount he was to pay.

Finer and McGregor describe the beginning of the divorce court (as to which see Chapter 6, above) and then continue:

Maintenance for wives under the new procedure

32. ... The new divorce court could grant alimony ancillary to a decree of judicial separation on the same principles as alimony could previously attach to a decree of divorce *a mensa et thoro*. It could also in granting a decree of divorce dissolving the marriage, insist on the husband making financial provision for the wife of the kind which the Ladies' Friend, under the parliamentary divorce procedure, had previously secured for her benefit. In this connection, the Act provided that on any decree of dissolution of marriage the court might order the husband to secure to the wife such gross sum of money, or such annual sum of money for any term not exceeding her own life, as having regard to her fortune (if any), to the ability of the husband, and to the conduct of the parties, the court should deem reasonable.

33. The use which the divorce court made of its powers of securing maintenance to the wife when dissolving her marriage took rather a curious course. Despite the fact that the distinctive feature of the parliamentary procedure which the court was supposed to have inherited was precisely that it guaranteed provision for the guilty (respondent) wife, the divorce court at first ruled that it would do this only in the rarest of cases. More than that, by 1861 (*Fisher v Fisher* (1861) 2 Sw & Tr 410, 31 LJPM & A 1) Sir Cresswell Cresswell, the first Judge Ordinary of the court, was saying that a wife petitioner should be awarded less by way of maintenance on being granted a decree of divorce than she would have been granted by way of alimony had she sought a judicial separation, for this would tend towards the preservation of the sanctity of marriage. Four years later, this view of the law was rejected by the court (*Sidney v Sidney* (1865) 4 Sw & Tr 178, 34 LJPM & A 122), which indicated in the same case that it would welcome a power, in dissolving a marriage, to make financial provision for the wife by way of an order for periodical payments, as well as by way of a secured sum. This power was granted by the Matrimonial Causes Act 1866, which provided that if a decree for dissolution of marriage were obtained against a husband who had no property on which the payment of a gross or annual sum could be secured, he might be ordered to pay such monthly or weekly amounts to his former wife, during their joint lives, as the court should think reasonable. By about the 1880s, the maintenance jurisdiction in divorce had come to be exercised to the following broad effect: the guilty wife, as under the old parliamentary practice, would have some modicum awarded to her; the innocent wife, as under the old ecclesiastical practice, would be granted a proportion, almost always one third, of the joint income, and, in addition, an amount in respect of any children committed to her custody.

37. In 1873, as part of the general re-organisation of the superior courts which then took place, the jurisdiction of the Court for Divorce and Matrimonial Causes, set up in 1857, was transferred to the High Court of Justice to be exercised in the Probate, Divorce and Admiralty Division of the High Court.

38. ... the court began to state that the rule, borrowed from the ecclesiastical jurisdiction, of awarding one third of the joint income to the innocent wife was not a rule of thumb, and that in awarding maintenance it had to take into account all the circumstances of the particular case. Secondly, signs emerged of a recognition that the moral blame, if there was any, for the breakdown of a marriage might not be coincident with the finding of guilt in the divorce suit. It followed that an adulterous wife might in justice be entitled to a larger award than the sustenance which, following the former Parliamentary practice, the divorce court had conceded to her. As ultimately established, the rule was stated to be:

> 'Nowhere ... is there to be found any warrant for the view that a wife who had committed adultery thereby automatically loses her right to maintenance regardless of the other circumstances of the case. ... In practice a wife's adultery may or may not disqualify her from succeeding in her application for maintenance and may or may not reduce the amount allotted. At one end of the scale her adultery may indeed disqualify her altogether. It may do so, for example, where it broke up the marriage, where it is continuing and where she is being supported by her paramour. At the other end of the scale, her adultery will not disqualify her and have little, if any, influence on the amount' (*Iverson v Iverson* [1967] P 134, [1966] 1 All ER 258).

Nevertheless, the discretionary nature of the jurisdiction gave ample opportunity to judges so inclined to take an idiosyncratic view on these matters.

The Divorce Reform Act 1969 altered completely the conceptual basis of divorce (see Chapter 6, above). Necessarily, the preconceptions inherent in the legal status of the husband and the wife, especially in relation to the doctrine of unity and the concept of lifelong support obligation unless the wife committed a matrimonial offence – all this could no longer form the underlying philosophy of a marriage. At the same time, there was awareness that in reality, certainly in conventional marriages and perhaps also in dual career marriages (see p. 88, above) a wife's performing the 'domestic chores' *was* a significant contribution in its own right towards the resultant value of the family assets. There was also a view, although perhaps it did not play a major role in the reform, that marriage itself was a substantial impediment to a woman's self-sufficiency in many cases. All this resulted in the enactment of the Matrimonial Proceedings and Property Act 1970. That Act permitted all financial orders to be made in favour of either husband and wife, enabling the court to rearrange all the couple's assets through periodical payments (secured and unsecured), lump sum payments and property adjustment orders.

The Act also set out detailed guidelines designed to assist the court in the exercise of its powers. These guidelines were simply that; for the basic philosophy inherent in the Act was to permit a broad discretion within the framework of the legislative target. It is to that target that we must turn.

2 The law from 1970–1984; the principles and the criticisms

The 1970 Act was consolidated in the Matrimonial Causes Act 1973. Section 25, relevant to both maintenance and capital provision, provided that it was the duty of the court to:

> ... exercise those powers as to place the parties, so far as it is practicable and, having regard to their conduct, just to do so, in the financial position in which they would have been if the marriage had not broken down and each had properly discharged his or her financial obligations and responsibilities towards the other.

The Law Commission, in their discussion paper *The Financial Consequences of Divorce: the Basic Policy* (1980), identified four specific complaints:

(a) Inconsistency with the modern law of divorce

24. A fundamental complaint is, we think, that the underlying principle of the law governing the financial consequences of divorce is inconsistent with the modern divorce law. The law (it is said) now permits either party to a marriage to insist on a divorce, possibly against the will of the other party, regardless of the fact that the other party may have honoured every conceivable marital commitment. Why (it is asked), if the status of marriage can be dissolved in this way, should the financial obligations of marriage nevertheless survive – particularly in cases where divorce has been forced on an unwilling partner, or where a wholly innocent partner is required to support one whose conduct has caused the breakdown? Instead (it is argued), divorce ought to provide a 'clean break' with the past in economic terms as well as in terms of status, and, so far as possible, encourage the parties to look to the future rather than to dwell in the past.

(b) Hardship for divorced husbands

25. We have been told that the continuing financial obligations imposed by divorce often cause severe economic hardship for those who are ordered to pay, normally of course the husband. It is not uncommon for a man to be ordered to pay as much as one-third of his gross income to his ex-wife until she either remarries or dies, and to be deprived of the matrimonial home (which may well represent his only capital asset) at least during the minority of the children. Unless she

remarries this obligation to maintain an ex-wife can put divorced husbands under financial strain not only over a very long period of years but even into retirement. The obligation to maintain an ex-wife is particularly resented if the husband feels that it is his wife who is really responsible for the breakdown of the marriage; and such feelings are further exacerbated where he believes that his ex-wife has either chosen not to contribute toward her maintenance by working, or has elected to cohabit with another man, who might be in a position to support her but whom she has decided not to marry so as not to be deprived of her right to maintenance from her first husband.

(c) Hardship for second families

26. ... Particular resentment seems to be felt by men who have remarried after a divorce, and by their second wives. The burden of continuing to provide for a first wife can involve financial deprivation for a man who does not remarry, but the burden may well be acute if he remarries and has a second family. In such cases the impoverishment caused by the first wife's continuing claim upon her husband may well fall on all the members of his new family. ... In particular the effect on a man's second wife is a frequent source of comment. It is claimed that she is invariably forced to accept a reduced standard of living by reason of the fact that part of her husband's income is being diverted to support his first wife; it is also claimed that a second wife may be forced, notwithstanding family commitments, to work, even although her husband's first wife, who possibly has no family commitments, chooses not to do so. Indeed some second wives have told us that they feel that they are being required personally to support their husband's first wife because the courts take a second wife's resources into account when assessing a husband's financial circumstances and his capacity to make periodical payments to a former spouse.

(d) Hardship suffered by divorced wives

27. ... There is no doubt that many divorced wives feel that the law still fails to make adequate provision for them. Not only is the starting point for assessing the provision to be made for a divorced wife only one-third [see *Wachtel v Wachtel* [1973] Fam 72, [1973] 1 All ER 829, CA, p. 311, below] (as opposed to one-half) of the parties' joint resources, but in practice divorced wives often face great difficulty in enforcing any order which the court has made. The law, it is true, requires that so far as practicable, the wife should be kept in the position she would have been in had the marriage not broken down, but, as the Finer Committee remarked in 1974, private law is not capable of providing the 'method of extracting more than a pint from a pint pot'. We have seen that economic realities often make it difficult for a husband to provide for his second family. The same economic factors also make it difficult for him to provide for his former wife. ...

One particular aspect of the debate still relevant today is the question of whether married women are justified in looking primarily to their husbands for support if their marriages break down. After all, so the argument goes, emphasis is now placed on equality of opportunity for men and women, and it is indeed a fact that most women are employed outside the home for at least some period during their married lives. The argument has been forcefully presented by Ruth Deech. We quote here from *The Principles of Maintenance* (1977):

For some time now there have been available to married women reliable contraception, education and full legal status. Legislation provides for equal opportunities and equal pay: 40% of the working force of employees are female, of whom two-thirds are married and 85% of married women have been in employment at some time during their marriage. But the concept of female dependency on the male continues to permeate the maintenance laws and in addition the comparatively recent state pensions and tax provisions are based on sexual stereotypes of the husband as provider and the wife as full-time housekeeper and child-rearer. This legal supposition of female dependency tends to deny freedom of choice to married and formerly married persons; it is widely considered degrading to women and it perpetuates the common law proprietary relationship of the husband and wife even after divorce. While they express the superiority of the male the maintenance laws are at the same time an irritant to the increasing number of divorced men who have always to be able to provide and who suffer the perpetual drain on their income represented by a former wife. Maintenance awards are emotionally charged with the desire on the part of the wife for retribution and by their nature are unlikely to be readily enforceable because of the hostility surrounding their creation and the fact that the ex-husband is paying money without getting anything in return.

Deech concludes by stating that maintenance should be rehabilitative and a temporary measure confined to spouses who are incapable of work because of infirmity or child care.

A different view, however, is presented by Katherine O'Donovan in *The Principles of Maintenance: An Alternative View* (1978):

Whilst it cannot be denied that laws based on sexual stereotypes are undesirable and ought to be eliminated what both Deech and Gray (1977) fail to see is that the current organisation of family life is premissed on the assumption that one partner will sacrifice a cash income in order to rear children and manage the home. The dependence of the non-earning spouse on the wage-earner is inevitable under present family arrangements. This leads in turn to inequality of earning power of spouses. Without a major change in social and family structures the Deech or Gray proposals merely serve to perpetuate an already unfair situation and will not ensure equality.

...

... The idea of a family wage adequate to support a wife and children with the addition of child benefit has been built into wage structure since the nineteenth century. So the expectation of society is that a wife's work is covered by her husband's wages. On divorce, without maintenance, the housewife will have little or no income from wage-earning and no National Insurance benefits to fall back on. If she does get a job, as already pointed out, her earning ability will be low.

For the majority of couples there will be a period in their marriage when their major asset, other than possible ownership of the matrimonial home, is the earning ability of the husband. This is why the law gives dependants a right of support after [divorce], and not the fact that they are parasites – as suggested by Deech. ...

Ruth Deech's argument is ultimately against marriage itself. If the spouse who undertakes housekeeping and child care should not consider marriage as (in part) an alternative career to one which is economically productive, then the answer is either not to marry, or to engage in paid work during marriage. But society does not seem ready for marriages in which both spouses work full-time. The present provision for nursery and pre-school facilities is inadequate. Children are prone to illness and are naturally dependent. Schools are not open for a full working day. And at present there is high unemployment. Participation in the workforce is not necessarily the answer, where there are young children; at least not without major changes in society, with the provision of communal laundries, cheap family restaurants, full-time nurseries etc. And male work attitudes would have to change to enable fathers to share equally in child care functions. It seems unlikely that this will happen. Deech argues that mothers with children should receive maintenance on divorce, and that it is only those who could earn who should be deprived. But withdrawal from the labour market at any time, current or past, affects earning ability, and it is fair that this diminution in earning ability be shared by both spouses.

Carol Smart in *The Ties That Bind* (1984) points to the difficulty of both positions in the context of a feminist viewpoint:

The question that proponents on either side of this debate have posed is, 'Should individual husbands support their ex-wives after divorce?' This question does not allow for a 'feminist answer' as such because whichever side of the debate a woman supports she does a disservice to feminist arguments. Basically feminists have argued for the financial independence of women, hence dependency on men either during or after marriage is recognised as a major problem. But equally feminists have argued for a recognition of the value of domestic labour which benefits not only the state but also individual men. Hence it can be argued that if domestic labour has a value to both the state and individual men, *both* should recompense the woman who has lost material benefits whilst individual men and the state have been reaping them. If we consider these conflicting principles within the existing framework of family law there is no satisfactory solution. Abolishing maintenance for ex-wives does not give women their financial independence, it just means that even more women have to rely on inadequate supplementary benefit (assuming they cannot work outside the home or cannot earn a living wage). On the other hand arguing that individual men should pay for their privileges ignores the fact that many simply cannot afford to pay. But in addition this argument has the deleterious effect of containing the 'problem' within the private sphere, with the consequence that women's dependency remains a private issue and a personal conflict, and does not become a matter of public policy. It is an untenable situation for feminists *precisely* because the original question was framed outside feminist priorities.

Questions

(i) Notice that O'Donovan argues that Deech's argument is ultimately against marriage itself. We know Deech's views about the divorce law reforms (see p. 256, above). Can her argument on maintenance in her 1977 article be reconciled with her views on divorce law reform, and if so, how?
(ii) Why is the idea that men should be able to avoid all financial responsibility for their own children through realistic child benefits attractive to an 'emergent feminist policy'?
(iii) Should an able-bodied house-husband be expected to support himself after divorce?
(iv) What do you suppose Carol Smart means by the phrase 'feminist priorities'?
(v) Do you think that the main question is really about how women can advance in the labour market?

Deech thinks that matters will only improve when the ideological basis of a support-dominated maintenance law is abolished; O'Donovan believes that a support-dominated maintenance law can only be abolished after the infrastructure of employment laws, support services for child care, pension and social security laws, and taxation provisions have all been reorganised to permit a woman to survive without the need for support from her former provider.

Questions

(i) Which of these two views do you believe to be *politically* realistic?
(ii) Are they asking the right questions?

In Part IV of their discussion paper, *The Financial Consequences of Divorce: the Basic Policy* (1980), the Law Commission describe seven models which might form the basis of a law to govern the financial consequences of divorce. These are discussed as separate options, and more briefly in combination. It should be recalled that the Commission were dealing mainly with the parties' finances and only incidentally with reallocation of their property. We summarise below the major characteristics of each model:

Model 1: Retention of section 25 of the Matrimonial Causes Act 1973

59 ... Whilst it is true that the failure of the Act to give any indication of the weight to be attached to any particular circumstance, or indeed to 'the circumstances' as a whole, can make it difficult for practitioners to advise clients on how a case is likely to be decided, it is claimed that any such disadvantage is more than outweighed by the advantage to be gained from the court having a discretion which cannot only be adapted to the infinitely varied facts of each case (which can be foreseen neither by a judge nor by the legislature) but also to changing social circumstances. Moreover, in this view it is not only inevitable, but indeed desirable, that it should be left to case law to provide the coherent but evolving guidance on how to deal with such specific problems ...

Model 2: Repeal of the direction to the court in section 25 to seek to put the parties in the financial position in which they would have been had the marriage not broken down

66 ... We consider the most fundamental issue raised by the present controversy over section 25 to be whether or not it is desirable to retain the principle of life-long support which that section seems to embody. It might therefore be argued that the simplest solution to the criticisms of the

present law would be for Parliament to repeal the specific direction at the end of section 25(1), but otherwise to leave the section intact; the court would simply be directed to make whatever order it considered appropriate in the light of all the circumstances, including the circumstances listed in sub-sections (*a*) to (*g*) of section 25(1). This would enable the courts to adopt a flexible approach, taking into account not only all the relevant individual circumstances of the parties, but also changing economic factors such as the availability of housing and changing attitudes to the proper purpose of financial provision. ...

Model 3: The relief of need

70 Under this model, the economically weaker party would be eligible to receive financial assistance from the economically stronger party if, and so long as, he or she could show that, taking into account his or her particular social and economic conditions, there is actual need of such assistance. The principle adopted would thus be one of individual self-reliance: after a marriage had broken down neither of the parties would have any automatic right to support, but rather only a qualified right insofar as it could be justified by special circumstances. ...

Model 4: Rehabilitation

73 ... The concept of rehabilitative financial provision has been explained in a recent American case as:

> 'sums necessary to assist a divorced person in regaining a useful and constructive role in society through vocational or therapeutic training or retraining, and for the further purpose of preventing financial hardship on society or the individual during the rehabilitative process' *Mertz v Mertz* (1973, 287 So 2d 691 at 692).

The onus is therefore firmly placed on the spouse in receipt of a rehabilitative award to take steps to become self-sufficient, and in this respect we think that such an approach might often result in the wife having to accept a significantly lower standard of living after divorce than that which she enjoyed before. She would be given an opportunity to develop such skills as she possessed, but ultimately she would be expected to fend for herself. ...

75 ... The rehabilitative period might be limited by statute, to a maximum of two or three years or to the duration of some course of training, or it might lie in the discretion of the court. ...

Model 5: The division of property – the 'clean break'

77 The essence of this model is the analogy of partnership. Where a partnership is dissolved, the partnership property is divided amongst the partners and that is the end of the matter. This, it is said, should also be the case where a marriage is dissolved (Grey, 1977). The principle might be adopted in one of a number of forms. At the one extreme it would involve no continuing financial relationship between ex-spouses: their rights and duties inter se would be resolved at the time of the divorce by dividing the matrimonial property between them. Such division might involve using a fractional approach (e.g. both parties would be entitled to half of the property available for distribution) or it might reflect some other principle such as the 'rehabilitative' or 'needs' models suggested above. Alternatively, the division might be effected solely on the basis of the court's discretion in each individual case. However, other variations on the basic theme that the financial consequences of divorce ought to be resolved by means of a division of the matrimonial property might also be possible. Thus a law based on this model might provide, for instance, for a delay in the division where the matrimonial home is needed to accommodate a growing family, or for additional payments of maintenance on a rehabilitative or needs basis. ...

Model 6: A mathematical approach

80 ... On this approach the spouses' financial rights and duties inter se on divorce would be resolved by reference to fixed mathematical formulae which might then be adjusted to take into account particular factors such as the care of children or the length of the marriage. The result, it is said, would be two-fold. First, the parties and their legal advisers would in most cases be able to save time and money by negotiating a settlement in the knowledge that it accurately reflected current practice. Secondly, adjudicators would be able to decide cases in an entirely consistent fashion. ...

Model 7: Restoration of the parties to the position in which they would have been had their marriage never taken place

84 On this view (e.g. Gray) the court should seek to achieve 'not the position which would have resulted if the marriage had continued, but the position which would have occurred if the marriage had never taken place at all'. The model is therefore a guiding principle, and might be

carried into effect either by imposing an obligation to make periodical payments or by a once and for all division of the parties' capital (or a combination of both) which would be designed to compensate the financially weaker spouse for any loss incurred through marriage. ...

A combination of models

86 ... It might be argued however that many of the problems which could result if a particular model were to be adopted as the sole governing principle might be avoided if the law were to be based on a combination of these models. For instance, elements of the needs or rehabilitative approaches could be used to temper some of the difficulties that might arise if the division of property model were to be adopted by itself. Alternatively it would no doubt be possible, whilst maintaining the main structure of the existing law, to amend the guidelines at present contained in section 25, so as to direct the court's attention more specifically to certain matters, for example the possibility that a wife should be expected to rehabilitate herself after divorce.

In *The Financial Consequences of Divorce* (1981), the Law Commission make the following recommendation:

17. We have come to the conclusion that the duty now imposed by statute to seek to place the parties in the financial position in which they would have been if the marriage had not broken down is not a suitable criterion; and in our view it should be removed from the law.

The Report goes on to recommend that the guidelines in s. 25(1) should be revised to give greater emphasis: (*a*) to the provision of adequate financial support for children which should be an overriding priority, and (*b*) to the importance of each party doing everything possible to become self-sufficient. The latter should be formulated in terms of positive principle and weight should be given to the view that, in appropriate cases, periodical financial provision should be primarily concerned to secure a smooth transition from the status of marriage to the status of independence. Thus, of the models advanced in the discussion paper, the English report argues for the retention of a discretion-based framework.

The proposals were introduced into law by the Matrimonial and Family Proceedings Act 1984 replacing the old s. 25 and adding a new s. 25A of the Matrimonial Causes Act 1973, and further amendments have been made by the Family Law Act 1996:

25. – (1) It shall be the duty of the court in deciding whether to exercise its powers under any of sections 22A to 24A above and, if so, in what manner, to have regard to all the circumstances of the case, first consideration being given to the welfare while a minor of any child of the family who has not attained the age of eighteen.

(2) As regards the exercise of the powers of the court under section 22A or 23 above to make a financial provision order in favour of a party to a marriage or the exercise of its powers under section 23A, 24 or 24A above in relation to a party to the marriage, the court shall in particular have regard to the following matters –

(*a*) the income, earning capacity, property and other financial resources which each of the parties to the marriage has or is likely to have in the foreseeable future, including in the case of earning capacity any increase in that capacity which it would in the opinion of the court be reasonable to expect a party to the marriage to take steps to acquire;
(*b*) the financial needs, obligations and responsibilities which each of the parties to the marriage has or is likely to have in the foreseeable future;
(*c*) the standard of living enjoyed by the family before the breakdown of the marriage;
(*d*) the age of each party to the marriage and the duration of the marriage;
(*e*) any physical or mental disability of either of the parties to the marriage;
(*f*) the contributions which each of the parties has made or is likely in the foreseeable future to make to the welfare of the family, including any contribution by looking after the home or caring for the family;

(*g*) the conduct of each of the parties, whatever the nature of the conduct and whether it occurred during the marriage or after the separation of the parties or (as the case may be) dissolution or annulment of the marriage, if that conduct is such that it would in the opinion of the court be inequitable to disregard it;

(*h*) the value to each of the parties to the marriage of any benefit (for example, a pension) which, by reason of the dissolution or annulment of the marriage, that party will lose the chance of acquiring.

(3) As regards the exercise of the powers of the court under section 22A or 23 above to make a financial provision order in favour of a child of the family or the exercise of its powers under section 23A, 24 or 24A above in relation to a child of the family, the court shall in particular have regard to the following matters –

(*a*) the financial needs of the child;

(*b*) the income, earning capacity (if any), property and other financial resources of the child;

(*c*) any physical or mental disability of the child;

(*d*) the manner in which he was being and in which the parties to the marriage expected him to be educated or trained;

(*e*) the considerations mentioned in relation to the parties to the marriage in paragraphs (*a*), (*b*), (*c*) and (*e*) of subsection (2) above.

(4) As regards the exercise of the powers of the court under any of sections 22A to 24A above against a party to a marriage in favour of a child of the family who is not the child of that party, the court shall also have regard –

(*a*) to whether that party assumed any responsibility for the child's maintenance, and, if so, to the extent to which, and the basis upon which, that party assumed such responsibility and to the length of time for which that party discharged such responsibility;

(*b*) to whether in assuming and discharging such responsibility that party did so knowing that the child was not his or her own;

(*c*) to the ability of any other person to maintain the child.

...

25A. – (1) If the court decides to exercise any of its powers under any of sections 22A to 24A above in favour of a party to a marriage (other than its power to make an interim periodical payments order or an interim order for the payment of a lump sum), it shall be the duty of the court to consider whether it would be appropriate so to exercise those powers that the financial obligations of each party towards the other will be terminated as soon after the grant of a divorce order or decree of nullity as the court considers just and reasonable.

(2) Where the court decides in such a case to make a periodical payments or secured periodical payments order in favour of a party to the marriage, the court shall in particular consider whether it would be appropriate to require those payments to be made or secured only for such term as would in the opinion of the court be sufficient to enable the party in whose favour the order is made to adjust without undue hardship to the termination of his or her financial dependence on the other party.

(3) If the court –

(*a*) would have power under section 22A or 23 above to make a financial provision order in favour of a party to a marriage ('the first party'), but

(*b*) considers that no continuing obligation should be imposed on the other party to the marriage ('the second party') to make or secure periodical payments in favour of the first party,

it may direct that the first party may not at any time after the direction takes effect, apply to the court for the making against the second party of any periodical payments order or secured periodical payments order and, if the first party has already applied to the court for the making of such an order, it may dismiss the application.

...

The court's powers to make financial provision and property adjustment orders are now, following the Family Law Act 1996, set out in sections 21 to 24A of the 1973 Act:

21. Financial provision and property adjustment orders

(1) For the purposes of this Act, a financial provision order is –

(*a*) an order that a party must make in favour of another person such periodical payments, for such term, as may be specified (a 'periodical payments order');
(*b*) an order that a party must, to the satisfaction of the court, secure in favour of another person such periodical payments, for such term, as may be specified (a 'secured periodical payments order');
(*c*) an order that a party must make a payment in favour of another person of such lump sum or sums as may be specified (an 'order for the payment of a lump sum').
(2) For the purposes of this Act, a property adjustment order is –
(*a*) an order that a party must transfer such of his or her property as may be specified in favour of the other party or a child of the family;
(*b*) an order that a settlement of such property of a party as may be specified must be made, to the satisfaction of the court, for the benefit of the other party and of the children of the family, or either or any of them;
(*c*) an order varying, for the benefit of the parties and of the children of the family, or either or any of them, any marriage settlement;
(*d*) an order extinguishing or reducing the interest of either of the parties under any marriage settlement.

...

(6) In this section –
'marriage settlement' means an ante-nuptial or post-nuptial settlement made on the parties (including one made by will or codicil);
'party' means a party to a marriage; and
'specified' means specified in the order in question.

22A. Financial provision orders: divorce and separation

(1) On an application made under this section, the court may at the appropriate time make one or more financial provision orders in favour of –
(*a*) a party to the marriage to which the application relates; or
(*b*) any of the children of the family.
(2) The 'appropriate time' is any time –
(*a*) after a statement of marital breakdown has been received by the court and before any application for a divorce order or for a separation order is made to the court by reference to that statement;
(*b*) when an application for a divorce order or separation order has been made under section 3 of the 1996 Act and has not been withdrawn;
(*c*) when an application for a divorce order has been made under section 4 of the 1996 Act and has not been withdrawn;
(*d*) after a divorce order has been made;
(*e*) when a separation order is in force.
(3) The court may make –
(*a*) a combined order against the parties on one occasion,
(*b*) separate orders on different occasions,
(*c*) different orders in favour of different children,
(*d*) different orders from time to time in favour of the same child,
but may not make, in favour of the same party, more than one periodical payments order, or more than one order for payment of a lump sum, in relation to any marital proceedings, whether in the course of the proceedings or by reference to a divorce order or separation order made in the proceedings.

[Subsections (3) and (4) relate to interim orders, and to the payment of lump sums by instalments.]

22B. Restrictions affecting section 22A

(1) No financial provision order, other than an interim order, may be made under section 22A above so as to take effect before the making of a divorce order or separation order in relation to the marriage, unless the court is satisfied –
(*a*) that the circumstances of the case are exceptional; and
(*b*) that it would be just and reasonable for the order to be so made.

...

(4) No financial provision order may be made under section 22A after a divorce order has been made, or while a separation order is in force, except –

(*a*) in response to an application made before the divorce order or separation order was made; or

(*b*) on a subsequent applicaition made with the leave of the court.

...

23A. Property adjustment orders: divorce and separation

(1) On an application made under this section, the court may, at any time mentioned in section 22A(2) above, make one or more property adjustment orders.

(2) If the court makes, in favour of the same party to the marriage, more than one property adjustment order in relation to any marital proceedings, whether in the course of the proceedings or by reference to a divorce order or separation order made in the proceedings, each order must fall within a different paragraph of section 21(2) above.

(3) The court shall exercise its powers under this section, so far as is practicable, by making on one occasion all such provision as can be made by way of one or more property adjustment orders in relation to the marriage as it thinks fit.

(4) Subsection (3) above does not affect section 31 or 31A below.

(5) This section is to be read subject to any restrictions imposed by this Act and to section 19 of the 1996 Act.

23B. Restrictions affecting section 23A

(1) No property adjustment order may be made under section 23A above so as to take effect before the making of a divorce order or separation order in relation to the marriage unless the court is satisfied –

(*a*) that the circumstances of the case are exceptional; and

(*b*) that it would be just and reasonable for the order to be so made.

...

(4) No property adjustment order may be made under section 23A above after a divorce order has been made, or while a separation order is in force, except –

(*a*) in response to an application made before the divorce order or separation order was made; or

(*b*) on a subsequent application made with the leave of the court.

...

[Sections 23 and 24 relate to proceedings for nullity of marriage.]

24A. Orders for sale of property

(1) Where the court makes under any of sections 22A to 24A above a secured periodical payments order, an order for the payment of a lump sum or a property adjustment order, then, on making that order or at any time thereafter, the court may make a further order for the sale of such property as may be specified in the order, being property in which or in the proceeds of sale of which either or both of the parties to the marriage has or have a beneficial interest, either in possession or reversion.

(2) Any order made under subsection (1) above may contain such consequential or supplementary provisions as the court thinks fit and, without prejudice to the generality of the foregoing provision, may include –

(*a*) provision requiring the making of a payment out of the proceeds of sale of the property to which the order relates, and

(*b*) provision requiring any such property to be offered for sale to a person, or class of persons, specified in the order. ...

(4) Where an order is made under subsection (1) above, the court may direct that the order, or such provision thereof as the court may specify, shall not take effect until the occurrence of an event specified by the court or the expiration of a period so specified.

(5) Where an order under subsection (1) above contains a provision requiring the proceeds of sale of the property to which the order relates to be used to secure periodical payments to a party to the marriage, the order shall cease to have effect on the death or re-marriage of that person.

(6) Where a party to a marriage has a beneficial interest in any property, or in the proceeds of sale thereof, and some other person who is not a party to the marriage also has a beneficial interest in that property or in the proceeds of sale thereof, then, before deciding whether to make an order under this section in relation to that property, it shall be the duty of the court to give that other person an opportunity to make representations with respect to the order; and any representations made by that other person shall be included among the circumstances to which the court is required to have regard under section 25(1) below.

3 A Scottish alternative

Proposals from the Scottish Law Commission in *Aliment and Financial Provision* (1981) and the resultant legislation in Scotland provides an interesting contrast:

Need for balance between principle and discretion
3.62 One of the main criticisms made of the present law on financial provision is that it leaves too much to the unfettered discretion of the court. We think that this criticism is justified. On the other hand we have no doubt that the courts must be left with considerable discretion to take account of the great variety of circumstances in cases which come before them. One of our main concerns in this Report has been to try to strike the right balance between principle and discretion. We take as our starting point the proposition that an order for financial provision should be made if, and only if, it is justified by an applicable principle. ...

FAIR SHARING OF MATRIMONIAL PROPERTY

A principle of quantification
3.65 When we refer to the principle of fair sharing of matrimonial property we are not talking about the division of specific items of property. How the value of a spouse's share would be satisfied would depend on the resources available at the time of the divorce. The court's powers would not be limited to matrimonial property (as defined) but would extend to all of the spouses' resources at the time of the divorce. ... The basic idea is that it covers property acquired by the spouses, otherwise than by gift or inheritance, in the period between the marriage and their final separation.

The norm of equal sharing
3.66 It would be too vague to empower the courts to award simply a 'fair share' of matrimonial property. One of the major criticisms of the present law is that it provides no guidance on the amount of a capital sum which can be expected on divorce. It would, on the other hand, be too rigid to lay down a fixed rule of apportionment for all cases. We think that the best solution is to provide that matrimonial property should normally be divided equally between the parties but that the court should be able to depart from this norm of equal sharing in special circumstances. ... [We] can see no good reason for giving either spouse, whether legal owner or not, whether wife or husband, less than half of the matrimonial property. The underlying idea is that of partnership in marriage and the only fair solution seems to us to be an equal division of the 'partnership' assets as the norm. ...
3.68 Where there are special circumstances justifying a departure from equal sharing ... we think that the court should be directed to share the matrimonial property in such proportions as may be fair in those circumstances. It would be impossible to provide with precision for the infinite variety of special circumstances which may arise. We therefore recommend:

32. (*a*) The principle of fair sharing of matrimonial property is that the net value of the matrimonial property should be shared equally or, if there are special circumstances justifying a departure from equal sharing, in such other proportions as may be fair in those circumstances. ...

Having defined matrimonial property essentially in terms of property acquired during marriage and discussed the special circumstances justifying the departure from equal sharing, they turn to a discussion of the recognition of contributions:

3.92 The first is where the contributions of one spouse have contributed to an improvement in the other's economic position. A husband, for example, may have paid off a loan over a house owned by his wife before the marriage, or he may have worked for years extending and improving her house. Similarly a wife may have worked for years, unpaid, in a small business owned by her husband before the marriage and may have helped to build up its value. In all these cases one spouse has contributed to an increase in the capital of the other and we think it reasonable that the court should be able to award some financial provision on divorce in recognition of the contributions. The position is essentially the same where one of the spouses has contributed to an increase in the other's earning potential. ... A husband may have worked overtime to pay his wife's fees for some special course of further education or training. A wife may have helped her husband with his work on an unpaid basis ... but because of the nature of his work (e.g. author, doctor, advocate, professional sportsman, entertainer) the result of her contributions may be an increase in his earning potential rather than in the capital value of a business. Again, there may be cases where one spouse's unpaid services as a housekeeper, hostess, domestic manager and child-minder could be shown to have contributed directly or indirectly to an improvement in the other spouse's economic position. ... In all these cases, ... it seems to us that there is a strong case for enabling the contribution to be recognised where this is not already done by means of a share in matrimonial property.

3.93 The position becomes more difficult, however, if there is no link between the contributions and any improvement in the other spouse's economic position. Suppose, for example, that three men all started work in the same employment at the age of 20. The first married a wife who assumed the traditional housewife's role and did all the domestic work. The second married an idle woman and did most of the domestic work himself. The third remained unmarried and did all his own domestic work. All three lived in rented accommodation. None accumulated any savings. All advanced remorselessly up their salary scale. If the first man was divorced at the age of 40 it would certainly not be obvious that his wife's contributions over the years had contributed to any improvement in his economic position, although they may well have contributed to an increase in the time available to him for leisure activities. Should an industrious wife receive more than an idle wife in this case? Should the principle of fair recognition of contributions extend to contributions to the welfare of the family even if they have not improved the other spouse's economic position? One submission made to us was that such contributions were made voluntarily and should therefore be ignored. The same point could, however, be made about many contributions which have directly improved the other spouse's economic position. Another view put to us was that the law should take a hard line on the question of a housewife's contributions in order to encourage women to preserve their economic independence during marriage. In our view, however, it is not the function of financial provision on divorce to encourage people to adopt any particular life style during marriage. ... We therefore reject these two arguments. We think, however, that there are other grounds for not recognising a claim based on contributions which have not resulted in any improvement in the other spouse's economic position. First, such contributions will often be evenly balanced. If, in the traditional type of marriage, a housewife could make a claim on the basis of contributions in work towards the welfare of the family, her husband could often do the same. ... Moreover, if a wife could make a claim on the basis of her contributions in work, her husband could often make a claim on the basis of his contributions in money to the welfare of the family. In some cases (for example the lazy wife, the wife with domestic help) the husband would be able to make a claim on this basis for a payment out of the wife's separate property. We doubt whether this would be acceptable. Secondly, an attempt to work out which spouse had contributed more to the welfare of the family during the marriage would often involve an unproductive examination and investigation of conduct over many years. Thirdly, and more fundamentally, the purpose of financial provision on divorce is not, in our view, the punishment of bad conduct or the reward of good conduct. In our view its concern should be with the economic effects of marriage and divorce ...

3.94 There is a further problem. One spouse may have sustained an economic disadvantage in the interests of the other party or of the family. The standard illustration is the well-qualified woman who married, say, 20 or 30 years ago and who gave up her own career prospects, perhaps with the encouragement or passive approval of her husband, in order to look after and bring up the family. There are other illustrations. A husband may have given up career prospects (for example the chance of a lucrative post abroad) in his wife's interests. An older woman may have given up a good position on marriage in order to look after her husband and may be unable to obtain employment again after divorce. One of the parties may have given up a tenancy in order to live with the other party on marriage. In all such cases there should in our view be the possibility of financial provision on divorce in recognition of the economic disadvantages sustained. ...

FAIR PROVISION FOR ADJUSTMENT TO INDEPENDENCE

The principle

3.107 In many cases divorcing spouses will already be economically independent by the time of the divorce. In many cases an award of financial provision under one of the principles discussed above would be sufficient to provide for any necessary adjustment to post-divorce independence. In other cases, however, we think that a reasonable objective of an award of financial provision on divorce is to enable a spouse to adjust, over a relatively short period, to the cessation on divorce of any financial dependence on the other spouse. Depending on the circumstances, the purpose of the award might be to enable the payee to undertake a course of training or retraining, or to give the payee time to find suitable employment, or to enable the payee to adjust gradually to a lower standard of living. It would be essential to specify a maximum time over which the adjustment would have to be made because otherwise there would, in many cases, be no way of ensuring that a transitional provision did not become permanent life-long support. We think that a period of three years from the date of divorce would be an adequate maximum period, given that in most cases the final separation between the parties would be some considerable time before that. We considered whether an adjustment provision ought to be available for, say, three years after the termination of a period of childcare after divorce. We have concluded, however, that this would not be justified. The main purpose of a provision under this principle is to provide time to adjust. ...

Factors to be taken into account

3.108 In addition to the usual factors such as the needs and resources of the parties, we think that it would be desirable to refer specifically, in relation to this principle, to the earning capacity of the payee, to the duration and extent of the payee's past dependency on the payer and to any intentions of the payee to undertake a course of education or training. ...

3.109 We therefore recommend as follows:

35. (*a*) The principle of fair provision for adjustment to independence is that where one party to the marriage has been financially dependent on the other and the dependence has come to an end on divorce, the dependent party should receive such financial provision as is fair and reasonable to enable him to adjust, over a period of not more than three years from the date of divorce, to the cessation of that dependence.

(*b*) In deciding what financial provision is fair and reasonable under this recommendation the court should have regard to the age, health and earning capacity of the applicant, to the duration and extent of the applicant's past dependency on the payer, to any intention of the applicant to undertake a course of education or training, to the needs and resources, actual or foreseeable, of the parties, and to the other circumstances of the case. ...

RELIEF OF GRAVE FINANCIAL HARDSHIP

Purpose and scope

3.110 It could be argued that the ... principles which we have discussed so far are adequate to cover all cases where financial provision on divorce is justified. This would mean that if there was no matrimonial property, if there was no claim based on contributions or disadvantages, and if there were no dependent children, then a divorced spouse could be awarded at most a provision designed to ease his or her adjustment to independence over a period of not more than three years. Thereafter he or she would have no claim against the former spouse. While there is much to be said for this approach, we have rejected it. The ... principles discussed already would not always ensure that a spouse who suffered severe financial hardship as a result of the marriage and the divorce could recover some financial provision in appropriate cases. A wife might, for example, have gone with her husband to some tropical country and might have contracted a disabling disease. Or she might have been permanently disabled as a result of injury in childbirth. We think that in such cases financial provision on divorce would be justified if it were reasonable having regard to the parties' resources. We have more doubt about whether a former spouse should ever be expected to relieve the hardship of the other if the hardship does not arise in any way from the marriage. If we were approaching the matter as one of pure principle we would be inclined to reject such a proposition as contrary to the idea that divorce ends the marriage. Financial provision on divorce is not, however, simply a matter of abstract principle. It is essential that any system should be acceptable to public opinion and it is clear from the comments we have received that many people would find it hard to accept a system which cut off, say, an elderly or disabled spouse with no more than a three-year allowance after divorce, no matter how wealthy the other party might be. We have concluded therefore that the law ought to provide, as a 'long-stop', for the case where one spouse would suffer grave financial hardship as a result of the divorce. In such a case the court should be able to award such financial provision as is fair and reasonable in the circumstances to relieve the hardship over such period as the court may determine. We do not intend this principle to be a gateway to support after divorce in all cases just as if the marriage had not been dissolved. We do not think, for example, that a man who suffers hardship on being made

redundant at the age of 52 should have a claim for financial provision against a former wife whom he divorced thirty years before. We think that the general principle should be that after the divorce each party bears the risk of *supervening* hardship without recourse against the other. It should therefore be made clear in the legislation that it is only where the likelihood of grave financial hardship is established at the time of the divorce that a claim will arise under this principle.

Questions

(i) Does the approach of the Scottish Law Commission differ substantially from that of the English Law Commission?
(ii) If so, whose approach do you prefer?

The Family Law (Scotland) Act 1985 states:

Principles to be applied
9. – (1) The principles which the court shall apply in deciding what order for financial provision, if any, to make are that –
- (*a*) the net value of the matrimonial property should be shared fairly between the parties to the marriage;
- (*b*) fair account should be taken of any economic advantage derived by either party from contributions by the other, and of any economic disadvantages suffered by either party in the interests of the other party or of the family;
- (*c*) any economic burden of caring, after divorce, for a child of the marriage under the age of 16 years should be shared fairly between the parties;
- (*d*) a party who has been dependent to a substantial degree on the financial support of the other party should be awarded such financial provision as is reasonable to enable him to adjust, over a period of not more than three years from the date of the decree of divorce, to the loss of that support on divorce;
- (*e*) a party who at the time of the divorce seems likely to suffer serious financial hardship as a result of the divorce should be awarded such financial provision as is reasonable to relieve him of hardship over a reasonable period.

(2) In subsection (1)(*b*) above and section 11(2) of this Act –
'economic advantage' means advantage gained whether before or during the marriage and includes gains in capital, in income and in earning capacity, and 'economic disadvantage' shall be construed accordingly;
'contributions' means contributions made whether before or during the marriage; and includes indirect and non-financial contributions and, in particular, any such contribution made by looking after the family home or caring for the family.

Sharing of value of matrimonial property
10. – (1) In applying the principle set out in section 9(1)(*a*) of this Act, the net value of the matrimonial property shall be taken to be shared fairly between the parties to the marriage when it is shared equally or in such other proportions as are justified by special circumstances.

(2) The net value of the matrimonial property shall be the value of the property at the relevant date after deduction of any debts incurred by the parties or either of them –
- (*a*) before the marriage so far as they relate to the matrimonial property, and
- (*b*) during the marriage,

which are outstanding at that date.

(3) In this section 'the relevant date' means whichever is the earlier of –
- (*a*) subject to subsection (7) below, the date on which the parties ceased to cohabit;
- (*b*) the date of service of the summons in the action for divorce.

Question

Note that 'grave' financial hardship recommended by the Scottish Law Commission has been replaced by 'serious' financial hardship. Is there a difference?

Criticisms of the Scottish legislation are summarised by the Family Law Committee of the Law Society in their memorandum on *Maintenance and Capital Provision on Divorce* (1991):

2.17 The principles in the Scottish legislation were subject to criticism at the time of the legislation's enactment and this criticism has been borne out in research into the effect the Act has had on advice given by solicitors to their clients (see Wasoff, Dobash and Harcus *'The Impact of the Family Law Scotland Act 1985 on Solicitors' Divorce Practice'* 1990).
2.18 At the time the Act was passed [Stephen] Cretney argued in *'Money After Divorce – The Mistakes We Have Made'* (1986) that although the Scottish system does seem to reduce judicial discretion nevertheless three criticisms can be made of it. First, that although certainty has been achieved through the implementation of a framework of principles, scope for uncertainty still exists. If you take the judge's discretion under the existing English law as being as long as a piece of string, and replace it by five pieces of string each of indeterminate length, as under the Scottish legislation, it is far from clear that the position has been improved. Secondly, he argues that the Scottish legislation is unfavourable to women as the court cannot make an order for periodical payments unless it is satisfied that an order for the payment of a capital sum or transfer of property would not by itself be appropriate or sufficient to give effect to the five principles embodied in the legislation. Thirdly, if the court does order periodical payments they must not be for a longer period than three years from the date of divorce unless these payments are required in order to satisfy the two principles of fair sharing of the burden of child care or relief from serious financial hardship. In addition, another limitation on any settlement is the fact that spouses are entitled to receive 'fair recognition of contributions and disadvantages'. There is also a proviso that claims are only to be accepted under this heading if they have resulted in an improvement in the spouse's economic position.
2.19 Under the Scottish Code there is no reference to the welfare of the child(ren) because claims in respect of the child(ren) are dealt with independently of claims of parents in divorce proceedings. Thus, when considering the allocation of income and property, attention is not specifically directed to the interests of the children although the court must have regard to the economic burden of child care. It is the Family Law Committee's view that any set of principles dealing with maintenance and capital provision on divorce should include within it recognition that the interests of any children should be the first consideration.
2.20 The Committee believes that the principles in the Scottish legislation have the potential to produce arbitrary results. This concern is backed up ... by A R Dewar *'The Family Law (Scotland) Act 1985 in Practice'* (1989) in which he stated that the courts were relying on the fifth principle of relief from serious financial hardship to an unexpected degree in order to avoid this. The results of the research carried out by Wasoff, Dobash and Harcus [1990] also lend support to this argument as well as revealing a number of other problems experienced by solicitors in their interpretation of the legislation.
2.25 Difficulties encountered by English solicitors can be attributed to a lack of principles. However, it is clear from the analysis set out above that while a set of principles is a useful tool it does not represent the complete answer. Indeed, the use of principles seems to introduce a new problem of when and how to apply them. The Committee was particularly concerned about the problems experienced when a conflict between different principles arose and the possible adverse effect on the former wife's financial position. The Committee's view, therefore, is that their introduction would not greatly increase certainty – particularly if the effect is merely to shift an argument from the issue of which principles should be applied to when and how to apply them.

Emily Jackson, Fran Wasoff, Mavis Maclean and Rebecca Dobash, in their article 'Financial Support on Divorce: the Right Mixture of Rules and Discretion?' (1993) report on their research project, examining the practice of solicitors dealing with financial matters after divorce in England and Scotland. The aim was to study solicitors' views and behaviour in the context of the tension between rules and discretion, and not principally to compare the workings of the two systems; the researchers acknowledge that the two legal frameworks are different, but found, 'sufficiently similar themes to justify tying the two projects together'. This is their description of a legal practitioner's approach in Scotland:

Their collective approach can best be summarised as primarily needs-based within the wide constraints set by a framework of rules and rights codified in the main by the Family Law (Scotland) Act 1985. There was no evidence that they sought to use a formula or even a particularly systematic approach to quantifying awards. To a great extent, they sought to secure individualized justice, using discretion not simply for its own sake but in order to re-allocate (usually) scarce resources by giving first priority to meeting the needs of the custodial parent and dependent children, and, secondly, providing for the basic needs of the non-custodial parent/husband, only after that redistributing the remaining matrimonial resources.

Question

Do you see anything in such an approach that reflects the Scottish rather than the English legal principles?

This research was carried out before the implementation of the Child Support Act 1991 took the issue of maintenance for children out of the discretionary system; it is now, of course, a fixed amount, in the light of which all other issues, such as housing and spousal maintenance, have to be calculated. Jackson and her colleagues comment that its introduction is a sign of 'an international trend towards the use of rules within family law', and that 'although the divergence between English and Scottish legislation will remain when a nationwide Child Support Agency is in place, it will be of less significance'.

Question

What impact do you think the introduction of the Child Support Act 1991 has had upon the balance between principles and discretion in the Matrimonial Causes Act 1973?

4 Court decisions

(a) THE STARTING POINT

We start with the leading case on the pre-1984 law:

Wachtel v Wachtel
[1973] Fam 72, [1973] 1 All ER 829, [1973] 2 WLR 366, 117 Sol Jo 124, Court of Appeal

The parties were granted cross-decrees of divorce, and the dispute between the parties over the financial consequences of the divorce was dealt with in subsequent ancillary proceedings. The facts of the case are stated in the first few paragraphs.

Lord Denning MR: Mr and Mrs Wachtel were married on January 9, 1954. They were both then 28 years of age. They have two children, a son aged now 14, and a girl of 11. The husband is a dentist in good practice. On 31 March 1972, the wife left the home. On 21 July 1972, there was a divorce. ... In consequence many things have to be settled. The parties have made arrangements for the children. The son is with the father. He is a boarder ... where his fees are paid by his grandfather. The daughter is with the mother. She goes to day-school. There remain the financial consequences. ...

On 3 October 1972, Ormrod J ordered the husband to pay to his wife (i) a lump sum of £10,000, or half the value of the former matrimonial home in Norbury, South London, whichever be the less: (ii) periodical payments of £1,500 per annum, less tax: and (iii) further payments of £500 per annum (£9.50 weekly), less tax, in respect of the eleven-year-old daughter.

The husband appeals to this court. The appeal raises issues of wide importance. This court is asked to determine, for the first time, after full argument, the principles which should be applied in the Family Division when granting ancillary relief pursuant to the powers conferred by the Matrimonial Proceedings and Property Act 1970 (in this judgment called the Act of 1970). ...

The crucial finding of fact is that the responsibility for the breakdown of the marriage rested equally on both parties:. ... The judge, having made that finding, determined that the only capital asset, namely, the matrimonial home, should be divided more or less equally between the parties. Since the evidence before the judge showed that the equity of the house in Norbury, (after discharging the outstanding mortgage amounting to some £2,000) was about £20,000, he ordered the husband to pay to his wife a lump sum of £10,000 or half the net value of the house if and when sold, whichever was the less. So far as the periodical payment of £1,500 per annum is concerned, the judge appears to have worked on an earning capacity on the part of the husband of £4,000 to £5,000 gross taxable income. He appears not to have allowed anything for the wife's earning capacity, at least in terms of monetary value. On this basis the £1,500 represents about one-third of the judge's assessment of the husband's earning capacity. But if one adds to that figure of £1,500 the further sum of £500 gross which the judge ordered to be paid by the husband to the wife in respect of the eleven-year-old daughter, the total is £2,000 gross, considerably more than one-third of the figure which the judge took as the husband's earning capacity.

The husband's appeal was founded on the ground that in effect he had been ordered to pay his wife one-half of his capital, and about one-half of his income. Particular criticism was levelled in this respect at an important passage in the judge's judgment ..., stating that Parliament had intended in the Act of 1970 'to bring about a shift of emphasis from the concept of "maintenance" ... to one of re-distribution of assets and ... "purchasing power." ' Mr Ewbank, for the husband, contended that the judge had but lightly concealed his view that the Act of 1970 had brought about a new concept of community of property so that it was just to give every wife – or at least almost every wife – half the value of the matrimonial home on the break-up of the marriage, and about half her husband's income. If that were right in the case of a wife held equally to blame with her husband for the breakdown of the marriage, what, he asked rhetorically, was the position of a wife who was wholly innocent of responsibility for such a breakdown? He further asked this: If as in the past, one-third of the combined available income of the parties had been regarded as proper maintenance for a blameless wife, with a reduction (we avoid the use of the word 'discount') in the case of a wife who was not free from blame, how could periodical payments totalling nearly one-half of the husband's earning capacity be justified in a case where the wife was found equally to blame with the husband for the breakdown?

Mr Ewbank also complained that the judge had really started from a presumption that equal division was right and had worked back from the starting point and, allowing nothing – or almost nothing – for 'conduct' had arrived at the determination we have stated. He contested the judge's view that it was right to disregard conduct where blame had been found to exist, especially as Parliament in section 5(1) of the Act of 1970 [the unamended s. 25(1) of the Matrimonial Causes Act 1973] had enjoined the courts to have regard to the conduct of the parties. He also said that no, or no sufficient, account had been taken of the wife's earning capacity and that the £500 ordered to be paid for the child was in any event too high. He offered a lump sum of £4,000, together with a guarantee of any mortgage instalments which the wife might have to pay in connection with the acquisition of a new home for herself and the child. He urged this court in any event to reduce the £1,500 to £1,000; and the £500 to £300, or less.

Mr Gray, for the wife, supported the judgment on the broad ground that the long line of cases decided over the last century and more, which dealt with the issue of conduct, especially in relation to a guilty or blameworthy wife, were all decided when the foundation of the right to relief in matrimonial causes was the concept of a matrimonial offence. Now that concept had been swept away by the Act of 1969, the whole question of conduct in relation to ancillary relief required to be reconsidered, even though section 5(1) of the Act of 1970 preserved the obligation on the courts to have regard to 'conduct' in language not easily distinguishable from that of the earlier statutes from 1857 onwards. ... Mr Gray particularly criticised the continued application of the so-called 'one third rule' under present day conditions. ...

The conduct of the parties

It has been suggested that there should be a 'discount' or 'reduction' in what the wife is to receive because of her supposed misconduct, guilt or blame (whatever word is used). We cannot accept this argument. In the vast majority of cases it is repugnant to the principles underlying the new legislation, and in particular the Act of 1969. There will be many cases in which a wife (though once considered guilty or blameworthy) will have cared for the home and looked after the family for very many years. ... There will no doubt be a residue of cases where the conduct of one of the parties is in the judge's words[1] 'both obvious and gross,' so much so that to order one party to support another whose conduct falls into this category is repugnant to anyone's sense of justice. In such a case the court remains free to decline to afford financial support or to reduce the support which it would otherwise have ordered. But, short of cases falling into this category, the court should not reduce its order for financial provision merely because of what was formerly regarded as guilt or blame. ... Mr Ewbank disputed this and claimed that it was but justice that a wife should suffer for her supposed misbehaviour. We do not agree. Criminal justice often requires the imposition of financial and indeed custodial penalties. But in the financial adjustments consequent upon the dissolution of a marriage which has irretrievably broken down, the imposition of financial penalties ought seldom to find a place.

The family assets

The phrase 'family assets' is a convenient short way of expressing an important concept. It refers to those things which are acquired by one or other or both of the parties, with the intention that there should be continuing provision for them and their children during their joint lives, and used for the benefit of the family as a whole. ...

Until recently the courts had limited powers in regard to the capital assets. They could determine the property rights of the parties. They could vary any ante-nuptial or post-nuptial settlements. But they could not order a transfer of property from one to the other. ...

Now under the Act of 1970 the court has power, after a divorce, to effect a transfer of the assets of the one to the other. It set out in section 5 various criteria [now s. 25 of Matrimonial Causes Act 1973]. The Act of 1970 is not in any sense a codifying statute. It is a reforming statute designed to facilitate the granting of ancillary relief in cases where marriages have been dissolved under the Act of 1969, an even greater measure of reform. ...

The matrimonial home

... Before the Act of 1970 there might have been much debate as to whether the wife had made financial contributions of sufficient substance to entitle her to a share in the house. The judge said ..., that it 'might have been an important issue.' We agree. But he went on to say that since the Act of 1970 it was 'of little importance' because the powers of transfer under section 4 enabled the court to do what was just having regard to all the circumstances. We agree.

How is the court to exercise its discretion under the Act of 1970 in regard to the matrimonial home? We will lead up to the answer by tracing the way in which the law has developed. Twenty-five years ago, if the matrimonial home stood in the husband's name, it was taken to belong to him entirely, both in law and in equity. The wife did not get a proprietary interest in it simply because she helped him buy it or to pay the mortgage instalments. Any money that she gave him for these purposes would be regarded as gifts, or, at any rate, not recoverable by her: see *Balfour v Balfour* [1919] 2 KB 571, 88 LJKB 1054. But by a long line of cases, starting with *Re Rogers' Question* [1948] 1 All ER 328 and ending with *Hazell v Hazell* [1972] 1 All ER 923, [1972] 1 WLR 301, it has been held by this court that, if a wife contributes directly or indirectly, in money or money's worth, to the initial deposit or to the mortgage instalments, she gets an interest proportionate to her contribution. In some cases it is a half-share. In others less.

The court never succeeded, however, in getting a wife a share in the house by reason of her other contributions: other, that is, than her financial contributions. The injustice to her has often been pointed out.

---

1. Lord Denning MR here adopts the terminology of Ormrod J at first instance.

In 1965 Sir Jocelyn Simon, when he was President, used a telling metaphor [see p. 135, above]: 'The cock can feather the nest because he does not have to spend most of his time sitting on it.'...

But the courts have never been able to do justice to her. In April 1969 in *Pettitt v Pettitt* [1970] AC 777 at 811 [see p. 137, above] Lord Hodson said: 'I do not myself see how one can correct the imbalance which may be found to exist in property rights as between husband and wife without legislation.'

Section 5(1)(*f*) [see now s. 25(2)(*f*) of the Matrimonial Causes Act 1973]

Now we have legislation. In order to remedy the injustice Parliament has intervened. The Act of 1970 expressly says that, in considering whether to make a transfer of property, the court is to have regard, among other things, to:

> '(*f*) the contributions made by each of the parties to the welfare of the family, including any contributions made by looking after the home or caring for the family.'

Mr Ewbank suggested that there was nothing new in these criteria in section 5(1)(*f*). [See now s. 25(2)(*f*) of the Matrimonial Causes Act 1973.]

Lord Denning MR considered the Law Commission's Report on *Financial Provision in Matrimonial Proceedings* (1968) and continued:

... we may take it that Parliament recognised that the wife who looks after the home and family contributes as much to the family assets as the wife who goes out to work. The one contributes in kind. The other in money or money's worth. If the court comes to the conclusion that the home has been acquired and maintained by the joint efforts of both, then, when the marriage breaks down, it should be regarded as the joint property of both of them, no matter in whose name it stands. Just as the wife who makes substantial money contributions usually gets a share, so should the wife who looks after the home and cares for the family for 20 years or more.

The one-third rule

In awarding maintenance the divorce courts followed the practice of the ecclesiastical courts. They awarded an innocent wife a sum equal to one-third of their joint incomes. Out of it she had to provide for her own accommodation, her food and clothes, and other expenses. If she had any rights in the matrimonial home, or was allowed to be in occupation of it, that went in reduction of maintenance.

There was, we think, much good sense in taking one third as a starting point. When a marriage breaks up, there will thenceforward be two households instead of one. The husband will have to go out to work all day and must get some woman to look after the house – either a wife, if he remarries, or a housekeeper, if he does not. He will also have to provide maintenance for the children. The wife will not usually have so much expense. She may go out to work herself, but she will not usually employ a housekeeper. She will do most of the housework herself, perhaps with some help. Or she may remarry, in which case her new husband will provide for her. In any case, when there are two households, the greater expense will, in most cases, fall on the husband than the wife. As a start has to be made somewhere, it seems to us that in the past it was quite fair to start with one third. Mr Gray criticised the application of the so-called 'one-third rule' on the ground that it no longer is applicable to present-day conditions, notwithstanding what was said in *Ackerman v Ackerman* [1972] Fam 225, [1972] 2 All ER 420. But this so-called rule is not a rule and must never be so regarded. In any calculation the court has to have a starting point. If it is not to be one third, should it be one half or one quarter? A starting point at one third of the combined resources of the parties is as good and rational a starting point as any other, remembering that the essence of the legislation is to secure flexibility to meet the justice of particular cases, and not rigidity, forcing particular cases to be fitted into some so-called principle within which they do not easily lie. There may be cases where more than one third is right. There are likely to be many others where less than one third is the only practicable solution. But one third as a flexible starting point is in general more likely to lead to the correct final result than a starting point of equality, or a quarter.

There is this, however, to be noted. Under the old dispensation, the wife, out of her one third, had to provide her own accommodation. If she was given the right to occupy the matrimonial home, that went to reduce the one third.

Under the new dispensation, she will get a share of the capital assets: and, with that share, she will be able to provide accommodation for herself, or, at any rate, the money to go some way towards it.

If we were only concerned with the capital assets of the family, and particularly with the matrimonial home, it would be tempting to divide them half and half, as the judge did. That would be fair enough if the wife afterwards went her own way, making no further demands on the husband. It would be simply a division of the assets of the partnership. That may come in the future. But at present few wives are content with a share of the capital assets. Most wives want their former husbands to make periodical payments as well to support them; because, after the divorce, he will be earning far more than she; and she can only keep up her standard of living with his help. He also has to make payments for the children out of his earnings, even if they are with her. In view of those calls on his future earnings, we do not think she can have both – half the capital assets, and half the earnings.

Under the new dispensation, she will usually get a share of each. In these days of rising house prices, she should certainly have a share in the capital assets which she has helped to create. The windfall should not all go to the husband. But we do not think it should be as much as one half, if she is also to get periodical payments for her maintenance and support. Giving it the best consideration we can, we think that the fairest way is to start with one third of each. If she has one third of the family assets as her own – and one third of the joint earnings – her past contributions are adequately recognised, and her future living standards assured so far as may be. She will certainly in this way be as well off as if the capital assets were divided equally – which is all that a partner is entitled to.

We would emphasise that this proposal is not a rule. It is only a starting point. It will serve in cases where the marriage has lasted for many years and the wife has been in the home bringing up the children. It may not be applicable when the marriage has lasted only a short time, or where there are no children and she can go out to work.

Remarriage

In making financial provision, ought the prospects of remarriage to be taken into account? The statute says in terms that periodical payments shall cease on remarriage: see section 7(2)(*a*), (*b*). [See now s. 28(1) of the Matrimonial Causes Act 1973.] But it says nothing about the prospects of remarriage. The question then arises: ought the provision for the wife to be reduced if she is likely to remarry?

So far as the capital assets are concerned, we see no reason for reducing her share. After all, she has earned it by her contribution in looking after the home and caring for the family. It should not be taken away from her by the prospect of remarriage.

So far as periodical payments are concerned, they are, of course, to be assessed without regard to the prospects of remarriage. If the wife does in fact remarry, they cease. If she goes to live with another man – without marrying him – they may be reviewed.

The present case

Coming now to the facts of the present case. The matrimonial home belongs in law to the husband. On the figures before the judge, its gross value was about £22,000; and, as already stated, the equity is worth about £20,000. ...

So far as the husband's earning capacity is concerned, ... We propose to proceed on the basis of the husband's earning capacity (i.e. his gross taxable income) being not less than £6,000 per annum. ... We put the wife's potential earning capacity on part-time work as a dental nurse at £15 per week gross – say £750 per annum. The combined total earning capacity is thus £6,750 per annum gross, of which one third (if that be the right starting point) is £2,250. If one deducts the £750 from that latter figure of £2,250, the result is £l,500 – the same figure as the judge arrived at though he reached that figure by a different route.

The husband is presently living at the former matrimonial home. ...

Any lump sum ordered to be paid will, we were told, be raised by the husband by increasing the sum for which the house is mortgaged. To require him to pay a lump sum of £10,000 raised in this way might cost him around £900 per annum in interest; and, of course, he will have to repay the principal as well. If £900 is added to the total of £1,500, plus the £500 (i.e., £2,000), the result is the equivalent of an order for a periodical payment of almost half of what we have taken to be the husband's gross taxable income. We think an order for a periodical payment on this scale (omitting any consideration of a lump sum payment) would be too high, having regard to the wife's needs and to the husband's needs. But, even if the matter be approached by a different route, we still think the £10,000 figure is too high. The wife should be able to make a substantial deposit in order to purchase suitable accommodation (assuming she wishes to buy, and not to rent) with the aid of a considerably smaller sum; and, if the order for £1,500 as a periodical payment is upheld, there seems to us to be a margin within that figure beyond the requirements of ordinary living expenses out of which repayments of mortgage, principal and interest could be made. On the other hand, we think the husband's offer of £4,000 is too low …

On the basis that the order for a periodical payment of £1,500 per annum is left untouched, we think the proper lump sum, taking everything into account that the Act of 1970 requires, is £6,000, and we would vary the judge's order for £10,000 accordingly. We think the wife should have that sum, £6,000, free of any trust, or other terms.

We, therefore, see no reason to interfere with the order for £1,500 in favour of the wife on the basis of the figures we have just mentioned. …

Looking at it broadly

In all these cases it is necessary at the end to view the situation broadly and see if the proposals meet the justice of the case. On our proposals here the wife gets £6,000 (nearly one third of the value of the matrimonial home). She gets it without any conditions at all. This seems to represent a fair assessment of her past contributions, when regard is had to the fact that she will get periodical payments as well. She also gets £1,500 a year by way of periodical payments, which is about one third of their joint incomes. She will also have the management of £300 a year for the daughter who is at a good school, and aged 11. These provisions are as much as the husband can reasonably be expected to make. It will mean that each will have to cut down their standard of living: but it is as much as can be done in the circumstances.

Appeal allowed by varying lump sum payment of £10,000 to £6,000 and reducing payments in respect of daughter from £500 per annum to £300 per annum (£6 a week gross of tax).

Questions

(i) Lord Denning MR gives two reasons for substituting one-third for the one-half approach used by the trial judge: does either of them convince you?
(ii) Would either reason have been valid if the wife had been working full time and: (*a*) earning as much as her husband, or (*b*) earning less than he did?
(iii) Do you think that a court would reach a similar result to Lord Denning MR, applying the principles in s. 25 of Matrimonial Causes Act 1973 as amended?

The status of the 'one-third rule' in more recent years has been eroded considerably. The position is summarised in Rayden and Jackson's *Law and Practice in Family Matters* as follows:

Prior to the introduction of the new rules for maintenance contained in the Finance Act 1988 there was a considerable body of authority for the proposition that the 'one-third' rule (or ratio) was an appropriate basis upon which to calculate an applicant's entitlement to periodical payments, even if only as 'a useful rule of thumb'. Such calculations were, however, made on the basis of the parties' respective gross incomes, and took into account both the tax relief available to the payer and the individual reliefs available to different payees.

With the effective abolition of substantial tax relief on orders for periodical payments, and given in particular the fact that maintenance is not taxable in the hands of the payee, the current approach to periodical payments is to ascertain the net incomes of both husband and wife and to look at the net effect of the order on both parties. In this exercise it would seem (although there is as yet no authority on the point) that the 'one-third' rule has no part to play save as a check on the result to see that it is not unduly disproportionate.

An example of the 'net-effect' approach is seen in *Allen v Allen* [1986] 2 FLR 265, CA. It is described by Jill Black, Jane Bridge and Tina Bond in *A Practical Approach to Family Law* (1994) in the following way:

It is very helpful to the court to work out how a proposed order (be it a one-third order or an order arrived at on a different basis) would work in practice.

To do this it is necessary to calculate each party's tax liability on the basis of the proposed order. From the payer's gross income is then deducted the tax he would have to pay, and his expenses of earning it. What is left is his spendable income – is it enough to enable him to meet his reasonable expenses? If not, the proposed order may well be too high. If he would have a significant sum over after meeting his expenses, the order may be too low. The position of the payee must also be considered. From her gross income, including the proposed maintenance, child benefit and one-parent benefit, must be deducted tax and her earning expenses. Is her spendable income sufficient for her reasonable expenses?

The net effect approach can be a very valuable way of showing up inequalities between the parties that might not otherwise be apparent; for instance, if the proposed order leaves the husband with £200 a month to spend and the wife with minus £10, the proposed order will obviously have to be adjusted so that the husband pays more. It may well be, however, that *both* parties are left with too little to cover their expenses – an all too common situation following the breakdown of a marriage. In such a case there is no possibility of carrying out a fine balancing exercise to distribute surplus income – the court must do the best it can and may have to work on the basis that one or the other party (or both) will require state benefits.

An illustration of the modern approach to financial provision is provided by the unreported first instance decision in *B v B* (Fam Div, 17 March 1995):

Hale J: These are cross applications for all forms of ancillary relief. I shall call the parties husband and wife although they are now divorced. The wife is 51, a doctor, a partner in an eleven partner general medical practice. The husband is 50, a solicitor, a senior partner of a three partner firm. They were married in May 1969. They have three children: Helen, aged 24, who is a final year medical student; Lynne, aged 22, who is a fifth and penultimate year medical student; and Michael, aged 18, who is in his first of four years as a student of law and criminology. All three were educated at top flight independent schools. Sadly, since the breakdown of the marriage, all three children have become estranged from their father and look to their mother for financial and moral support.

It has been a typical dual career family. The husband worked full-time throughout the marriage. The wife continued to work during the early years of the marriage but only part-time while the children were young. She joined her present practice in 1980, at first part-time and then full-time a year later. For three and a half or four years when she first became full-time the family had a housekeeper. They have had a series of matrimonial homes in their joint names; the most recent is an attractive four bedroom house with an extension forming a separate flatlet. It was bought in 1976 and extended when the wife returned to full-time work.

The marriage went seriously wrong in 1992. No issue is now raised as to matrimonial conduct by either party; nor am I asked to take the conduct of this litigation into account in the assessment of ancillary relief.

I now turn to the consideration of the factors in section 25(2) of the Matrimonial Causes Act 1973. Paragraph (*a*) requires me to consider the resources which each of the parties has or is likely to have in the foreseeable future.

Firstly, the husband: the husband's share of the profits of his firm has fluctuated quite dramatically from £47,000 in 1987, up to £53,000 and £54,000 in 1988 and 1989, down to £47,000 in 1990 and then down to an all time low of £22,000 in 1991; up to £35,000 in 1992, back down to £26,000 in 1993, and last year it was £36,000.

He has a profession which will give him a reasonable income, more than adequate for the needs of a single man, for the rest of his working life. He works hard and the firm's turnover is still considerable. His evidence was that he would not expect to retire until 65 and possibly not even then. He thought that solicitors never retired.

The problem with the husband's position is that he has built up a deficit on his capital account with the firm of £73,000 and he has promised the bank to pay £60,000 out of the proceeds of these proceedings into the firm in order to reduce the firm's borrowings and thus enable the firm to continue in business. The reason for the deficit is that since 1990 his drawings have exceeded his share of the profits. ...

His initial explanation for the difficulties was that the wife was spending too much. He initially also contended that as a result the overdraft on their joint account was increasing, but this was not so. He then contended that he was drawing more out of the firm in order to meet their expenditure. Again this is not obviously demonstrated because his drawings have been comparable over the whole of the period under discussion. Also the allegation of excessive expenditure by the wife, although it has featured extremely heavily in the evidence in the case, is not maintained before me and on the evidence before me it could not possibly be. …

The truth of course is that the family's expenditure was inevitably heavy. They were maintaining three children at expensive schools and university; they were amassing, although most of it was before this period, a collection of paintings, porcelain and antiques, and of course the general expenditure of a household of this nature is in itself heavy. …

The capital position of the firm, according to the most recent accounts before me, is that the liabilities exceed the assets by £106,000 and the husband values the firm at nil. He is very pessimistic about the future of high street solicitors' firms. However he is a hard worker and he has a marketable skill which has brought him a good living in the past. I cannot speculate one way or another how his business will go over the next ten to fifteen years or whether by the time the husband comes to retire there will be any goodwill for him to sell. He may, of course, as he has been thinking of doing, go into another business in any event.

The husband has other assets of more limited value: guns, shares, premium bonds and cash totalling approximately £12,000 in value. He has recently acquired, presumably through the firm, an L registration Volvo estate worth approximately £18,000, presumably thinking it appropriate to continue to run the same sort of family car that he ran while the family were united. The husband also has a personal pension which at the moment has a value, depending on the method chosen of £97,500 or £106,000. The husband's parents are very elderly; their estate is worth about £80,000. In due course it will be shared between the husband and his sister. It cannot at the moment be foreseen whether his parents will soon both die leaving the estate intact or whether one or both will require expensive residential care. Very properly, the husband says he has no hopes of an inheritance from them.

As to his liabilities, I have already mentioned the loan account with his firm, in effect of £73,000, and his promise to repay £60,000 of it. However, it is now agreed that there are many items belonging to his firm which are currently housed in the matrimonial home. … They must have made a sizeable contribution to the firm's loan account. Their sale could obviously go some way towards reducing it. … The husband has also incurred actual costs of £28,200 up to the date of the trial of which £21,100 has been paid, leaving him with a debt of £7,100. …

Turning now to the wife, the wife's drawings from her practice range from £39,000 in 1991 to £71,000 last year. They have never exceeded her share of the profits. She also has a capital account, put at £101,000 in the recent partnership accounts, which she will be able to take out when she leaves. …

The precise value of a partner's capital account is worked out by reference to the partnership's assets at the time of leaving. The practice owns a surgery, an annex, which is let to various other practitioners and a chemist's shop, and four semi-detached properties; they get rent for these from the health authority and from tenants. They are currently building an extension to the surgery to improve the facilities for patients and nurses. There is a dispute about the valuation of these properties. The valuer used by the partnership gave two different valuations last year: one for the bank and one for the purpose of buying out a doctor leaving the practice. There is some discrepancy between them, but it has been agreed to take the higher figure which is £1,250,000. Of course the rental for the doctor's premises is to some extent notional because they could not be let for any other purpose which would attract such a rent and in any event they are not going to be sold. This is the only GP practice in the town and these are purpose built premises. The valuer instructed by the husband on the basis of the same information about rentals assumes the rental to represent about 10 per cent of the capital value and so values the whole at £1,745,000. When additional borrowings for the extension are taken into account the discrepancy is only put at some £80,500, which is not a great deal when divided amongst ten and a half partners, but in any event the rental figures have not yet been agreed and it is not clear what the effect will be of the new extension on the one hand and the lettings to the other practitioners on the other. …

She no longer hopes to retire before she is 60. However when she does retire, she can expect a capital sum which, at the moment, is in the region of £100,000. On retirement she will also have an NHS pension. The amount accrued in her 14 years' service to date would yield, when she is 60, a pension of approximately £8,500 and a lump sum of approximately £25,500 but this will increase with each year of service. The present transfer value is £109,000. …

The wife does have a residuary interest in her father's estate which is a share in a house worth on recent values around £29,400 plus securities of £29,100. Unlike her husband's expectations, this is an absolute and indefeasible interest but it will only come to her on the death of her father's widow who is now a fit 66-year-old with a life expectancy, I am told, of some 18 years.

The wife has other current assets: jewellery, stocks and shares, which again came from her father's estate; a building society account; insurance policy and premium bonds totalling in all approximately £39,600. She also has debts amounting in all to around £26,500. These include a legal expenses loan of £20,000; a debt to a family friend for Michael's school fees of over £2,000, and a debt of a similar sum to repay grant paid in error to Lynne, as well as normal fluctuating credit card purchases. ...

Thirdly their joint assets: this is a family in which until the marriage broke down the assets were pooled. The matrimonial home is worth something between £275–300,000. It has been agreed to take its value at £285,000. There is a mortgage of some £63,000 which with the cost of sale will bring this down to around £215,000.

Its contents are more than usually valuable because the couple enjoyed collecting water colours, porcelain and antiques. ... Together these valuables total approximately £61,000. The antiques and silver have been valued by antique dealers at just over £14,000, making a total of just over £75,000 worth of chattels. Those then are the assets and the debts of the parties.

I turn to paragraph (*b*), their respective financial needs obligations and responsibilities. Both have the needs of a single middle aged professional person. They will each need a home. The only special factor here is that the children are estranged from their father and he is not providing for them at all. The wife pays Helen's rent of £235 per month to the hospital and other sums when they are needed which she puts in all at about £500 per month. The wife also pays Lynne's hall fees of £250 per month and more if she is finding things difficult. Of the four terms of Michael's school fees left after the proceedings began she paid two full terms and two half term fees. The husband paid one half term and a friend lent the other. That is the debt that I referred to earlier. On a strict reading of the school fees account, therefore, this leaves the husband one and a half terms in deficit which would be some £6,600. She now pays Michael's hall fees of between £500 and £700 at the beginning of each term and some extra when she can. Whereas the girls of course can expect to become self-supporting within the relatively near future, Michael will be dependent for some years yet. It is of course to be hoped that the children will in due course be reconciled with their father but they will undoubtedly look to her for a home base. She needs at least a three bedroomed house and she also needs it ... either within the practice boundaries or within a reasonable distance of the surgery. Even if this were not a legal requirement, it is obviously necessary for the reasonable operation of a general practitioner who has to spend periods of time on-call.

The husband's housing needs as a single man are not quite so great, nor is he so restricted as to area, although of course he has to balance proximity to his practice against the problems of living too close to his clients.

Paragraph (*c*) refers to the standard of living enjoyed by the family while it was together and that of course was a good standard of living of the sort to be expected in these circumstances. Paragraph (*d*) refers to their ages and the duration of the marriage. The parties are in their early fifties, they are now well established in life, and it was a long marriage.

Paragraph (*e*) refers to the contributions that each has made and is likely to make in the foreseeable future to the welfare of the family. This was, as I have said, a typical dual career family in which both worked hard and contributed financially what they could at the time. They regarded themselves as a partnership. The husband worked throughout and of course contributed more financially when he was working full-time and the wife was not. He also put in extras from time to time, cashing in insurance policies and extra drawings from his firm to finance the extension and he also put in a sum of money received from his parents which was a result of the profit that they made on moving house. The wife bore and cared for the children but she also worked and everything she acquired went into the joint account; not only her earnings, but also the cash which she received immediately from her father's estate, amounting to some £41,000. They both did their best for the welfare of the family. Their contributions in the past are obviously equal. The wife's contributions since the breakdown and into the foreseeable future are undoubtedly greater, both financially and as to the welfare of the family, and this will continue for some time.

I have already pointed out that paragraph (*g*), conduct, is not an issue in this case, nor has any issue been made of paragraph (*h*), the loss of potential benefits which in the case of parties who each have their own profession and provision for retirement is no doubt appropriate.

Having considered all those factors, what conclusion should be drawn? No-one suggests that there should be periodical payments for either party or the children. The wife argues that their current joint assets, the house and the valuables, should be shared equally between them. Assuming that all the valuables were sold this would give them each roughly £145,000. The wife can get a suitable house for £175,000 with the help of a manageable mortgage. She has a little in hand after the payment of her debts, including legal fees, but not a great deal and she will still have to furnish and equip the house.

The husband also has a little in hand, but he has to reduce the firm's borrowing from the bank and this may take up to £60,000 from the proceeds. Some, of course, could be taken by the firm's valuables which will no longer be in the matrimonial home. If they are not sold to reduce the firm's debts, presumably they will remain on loan to him and will be of help to him in decorating his new home. He does not need quite such a large house and so he could manage with a similar sized mortgage.

In the future they will have their own incomes and pensions. The husband is free of commitments to the children. Their pension schemes are roughly equivalent in value at the moment and each will no doubt go on contributing between now and then. The husband's retirement plans are very far in the distance. Neither party has any plan to remarry or cohabit, although the husband does have a relationship with one of the other witnesses.

The husband argues that the wife should only have £30,000 and he should have the balance, on my figures, of £260,000. The way that he justifies this, on the face of it, entirely inequitable result is: firstly, his debt to the firm, which would bring it down to £200,000; secondly, that the wife has current extra resources that he does not; thirdly, that they both need the same sort of house, and fourthly, above all, that the wife can afford a huge mortgage now because of her expectations from the firm which will pay it off when she retires.

It seems to me in a case like this where there has been a long partnership marriage, and both have careers of their own, the Court should in principle seek to divide their current assets equally and let each go their separate ways into the future. Of course where one spouse has an income and pension and the other does not, or only has a very limited one, one has to take into account pension entitlements falling due in the foreseeable future as a resource and a lump sum order or other adjustment, or even an adjournment for the application of a lump sum, may be appropriate to take account of it. (See cases such as *Milne v Milne* (1981) 2 FLR 286; *Priest v Priest* (1980) 1 FLR 1989 and *Davies v Davies* [1986] 1 FLR 497.) However these cases do not come anywhere near saying that the Court should be seeking to achieve equality of results, not only now but also in the future. The statutory injunction to seek to put the parties in the position that they would have been had the marriage not broken down was repealed in 1984. ...

The strongest argument in favour of the husband is that the wife was enabled to build up her capital account because she did not increase her drawings at the time when the husband was beginning to become overdrawn. I accepted the wife's evidence that she would have done so if asked, but I do not accept that all the husband's deficit is due to his family responsibilities. ... The wife also contributed to the assets which are now to be shared a very substantial extra cash sum, which she might have kept separately, to be weighed in the balance now. In reality, the main reason for their different prospects, if that is how they turn out to be, is that the wife is a doctor and the husband is a solicitor.

I have been very properly urged by Miss Ball to consider what the position would be in reverse. This is indeed an important discipline, but in this case it merely serves to re-enforce my conclusions. I find it difficult to accept that on a clean break settlement, if the husband were in a profession where he earned more and had better pension prospects than his wife, he would be expected to take less than his half share of the accumulated joint assets just because the wife was also in good employment, but somewhat less well paid with less good prospects on retirement. This is all the more the case where the future in relation to the husband's practice is so difficult to predict. Above all, however, the wife has the extra burden of the children to support and this is more than enough to compensate for the eventual differences there may be in the parties' positions if life for solicitors continues to be as gloomy as the husband fears.

I therefore propose to order that the house be sold and the net proceeds be divided equally and that the valuables listed be divided by agreement in equal shares by value and in default of such agreement within a short period – as to which of course I will hear further argument but I will put it at one month – they should be sold and the proceeds of sale equally divided. ...

The husband appealed. In the Court of Appeal (*B v B*, CA, 7 February 1996) counsel for the husband argued that Hale J's approach had been incorrect because she appeared to have applied a rule of equal division of assets for dual career families, expressed in the sentence in her judgment beginning 'It seems to me that in a case like this ...'. Dismissing the appeal, Waite LJ (with whom Morritt LJ agreed) said:

... I would accept that, as a matter of grammatical interpretation, the judge's remarks – read in isolation – would be capable of being construed as applying a precept that the interests of working spouses in joint assets acquired through their combined efforts are to be treated equally. If that is the correct interpretation, then the judge would certainly be in error. ... But in my view, when her words are read in the context of a judgment which demonstrably seeks to apply s. 25 of the Act to the letter, and which produced nothing in its result which betrays the least sign of error or misplaced emphasis, it becomes clear that the judge was really intending to say no more than this. When the Court is dealing with the joint assets of working spouses, common sense and equity require that equality of interest should be adopted as a starting point. It is, however, only a starting point, and will yield to the requirements of all the circumstances of the case including the specific factors to which s. 25(2) requires regard. That is an unexceptionable approach.

Question

Is there now any discernible overall objective in the courts' approach to financial provision cases?

(b) THE MODERN APPROACH TO INCOME AND CAPITAL PROVISION

Examination of the case law illustrates the modern approach in a number of contexts; we have sought to highlight some of the issues by the following.

(i) Substantial assets

Gojkovic v Gojkovic
[1992] Fam 40, [1990] 2 All ER 84, [1990] FCR 119, [1990] 1 FLR 140, Court of Appeal

The husband and wife, both Yugoslavs, arrived in England in 1966 with very little money. In 1969 they started to live together and they were married in 1978. Their life together consisted of hard work and sacrifice. Whilst in other employment, they turned a property into a hotel. The wife worked hard from dawn to midnight, did night-portering and made the hotel successful. The husband and his brothers were involved in other enterprises and expanded their business into other hotels and properties. During the later years of the marriage, the wife ran the hotel side of the business and the husband and his brothers concentrated on successful property speculation. The marriage broke down in 1986 and they were divorced in 1987. In ancillary proceedings, the husband's share of the family assets was approximately £4m. The wife's legal share amounted to very little. It was agreed between the parties that there should be a 'clean break' order and that the wife should have a maisonette worth £295,000. The husband's solicitor offered the wife a lump sum of £532,000 calculated to reflect the reasonable needs and requirements of a former wife of a wealthy husband. The wife wanted to continue with the hotel business and asked for a lump sum to enable her to acquire and run her own hotel.

The judge awarded the wife a lump sum of £1m to enable her to buy and run a hotel. The husband appealed.

Butler-Sloss LJ: Prior to the hearing before the judge, the husband, through his legal advisers, made an open offer based upon calculations provided by the accountants Cooper and Lybrand. That open offer was that the wife should receive a maisonette worth £295,000, about which there is no dispute, and that she should receive a lump sum of £532,000. That figure was carefully calculated in accordance with what has been called the '*Duxbury* principles' or '*Duxbury* calculations',[2] ... The difference between the award of the judge and the offer of the husband is therefore approximately half a million pounds. It was agreed between the parties that this was a suitable case for a 'clean break' order.

This court has been urged to provide guidelines as to the correct approach to big money cases. Our attention has been drawn to the two cases of *Preston v Preston* (1981) 2 FLR 331 and *Duxbury v Duxbury* [1987] 1 FLR 7. In *Preston* the judge accepted that £500,000 was required to provide the wife with a net income after tax of £20,000 a year. In *Duxbury* the figure of £20,000 net income for the wife of a rich man in 1980 was accepted in principle by the legal advisers as an appropriate sum and was adjusted to the 1985 figure of £28,000. On that basis, and with the assistance of detailed figures, the judge in *Duxbury* arrived at the lump sum award of £540,000 to meet in full the wife's entitlement and reasonable requirements. The lack in *Preston* of detailed information as to the financial implications of a lump sum awarded to provide income, criticised by Ormrod LJ, was remedied in *Duxbury,* and the computerised formulation accepted by the judge in that case has provided, we are told, a very useful guide to the settlement of cases in this bracket in the last 2 years. ... It can only, however, be a guide and should not be elevated to a rigid mathematical calculation. Each case must be decided on its own facts and in accordance with the principles set out in s. 25 of the Matrimonial Causes Act 1973 as amended by the Matrimonial and Family Proceedings Act 1984. The wide discretion of the court under s. 25 must not be fettered.

Mr Wall, on behalf of the husband, in his attractive argument urges us to treat the present appeal as a *Duxbury* type of case. He makes two main points:

(i) that the judge was wrong in principle to make an award to enable the wife to buy and run a hotel; and

(ii) if not wrong in principle, the amount was excessive, and he erred in the exercise of his discretion in making so large an award.

In considering (i) he argued that the effect of the repeal and reenactment of s. 25 of the 1973 Act as amended by s. 3 of the Matrimonial and Family Proceedings Act 1984, had the effect of limiting the discretion of the court under the new s. 25 to providing for the wife to become self-sufficient. Considerations of the future standard of living of the former spouse were irrelevant, although he accepted that the contribution of the applicant spouse during the marriage would affect or enhance her subsequent standard of living after divorce.

For my part, I do not see the repeal and replacement of s. 25 as having that effect. ... The new s. 25A lays a responsibility upon the court to consider whether financial obligations should be terminated and to make orders designed to enable the spouse to adjust without undue hardship to the termination of financial dependence on the other spouse. By s. 25(1)(*a*) an applicant's future earning capacity is relevant. So also, however, is the standard of living enjoyed by the family before the breakdown of the marriage. The proposed standards of living of both spouses must be a relevant consideration and where finances permit, they should not be wholly out of proportion to each other.

... The judge found that the wife had made an exceptional contribution to the wealth generated during their relationship and marriage, a contribution greater than that often made by wives after long marriages. He found that in 1969, at the inception of their relationship, she 'was in at the beginning, committed – as he was – to contributing financially, physically and emotionally', and that she took with him the first steps towards the current financial empire of the wider family. As was said in *Page v Page* (1981) 2 FLR 198, 'this wife has earned her share'. That share is not to be calculated exclusively in relation to her needs. It is clear that her needs in one sense would be met by the offer of suitable accommodation and a lump sum producing an income of £30,000 a year net. Equally important as financial need is, however, the contribution made by each of the parties to the welfare of the family, a contribution found by the judge to be exceptional. ...

---

2. This principle is referred to by Ward J in *B v B (financial provision)* [1990] FCR 105, [1990] 1 FLR 20 in this way:

'... accountants or investment consultants calculate from a computer program the lump sum, which, if invested on assumptions as to life expectancy, inflation, return on investments, growth of capital and incidence of income tax, would produce enough to meet the recipient's needs for life ...'

The assumption is that both capital and income would be used so that at the end of the recipient's life the lump sum would be exhausted.

Mr Wall criticised the findings of the judge that they were engaged in a joint enterprise and a quasi-partnership. He argued that the wife was not considered by the husband to be a partner and was never so described. It was, indeed, a matter of dissent between the spouses, particularly when at a later stage other members of the family were made partners. This position may have owed much to the husband's view of the wife as his wife, rather than a recognition of her own contribution to the making of the business. Further, he saw himself as creating the wealth for the wider family of some sixteen people and being in a sense a trustee of it. It was available for use by all of them, according to him, but not individually. His view of the wealth of the family cannot displace an objective assessment of the wife's entitlement.

During the marriage, both spouses worked so hard that they did not have the time or opportunity to enjoy a comfortable standard of living. The wife does not now wish to sit back and be comfortable. The effect of the breakdown of the marriage was to deprive her of her way of life, the running of the hotel. She now desires to buy and run a small hotel. The judge found, and there was evidence upon which he could come to that finding, that she required £1.5m to buy such a hotel. She would be able to raise £500,000 and service the interest and therefore required £1m for her project. Mr Wall submitted that all her reasonable requirements were met by £532,000 and the property in which she was living, and the requirements of s. 25 did not include her needs at a higher level. She was self-sufficient at the figure of the husband's offer.

If his wife's contribution was adequately taken into account by the figure offered by the husband, her desire, however strong, to have a greatly increased lump sum to enable her to run a hotel would not be reasonable, but weight must be given to the fact that this is a working wife with a recognised expertise in the management of hotels. It is a viable proposition that she puts forward although one which will require her to continue a life of hard work. A wife who is entitled to a lump sum on the *Minton* 'clean break' principle is not obliged to deal with that money in any particular fashion. She is perfectly entitled to use it as working capital if this is the sum of money to which, taking into account her contribution and all other aspects of s. 25, she is entitled. In principle I cannot see how the judge can be criticised for making an order which enabled her to buy a hotel so long as all the relevant criteria were satisfied. This is not, in my view, an issue of principle.

Mr Wall's second question in my view is the only issue in this case: did the judge in exercising his discretion make an order which was so out of proportion that it was plainly wrong? However great the contribution of the wife to the family, the order to her must not be out of proportion to the total assets and must do justice between the parties. The judge considered this aspect very carefully. There was no suggestion that this order would be impossible for the husband to comply with or that it would cripple his business interests. On joint assets of £4m, subject to costs, he will retain £2.7m or so. The judge not only considered it from the point of view of the wife's desire to buy a hotel; he tested it in other ways: half the value of the hotel she had been running and approximately a third of the joint assets, though he was at pains to say he was not making his decision in reliance upon either of those bases.

This is an award which is not excessively generous and I cannot say it is outside the 'generous ambit of disagreement' that would entitle an appellate court to interfere with the discretion of the judge. I would dismiss this appeal.

Appeal dismissed.

With this case should be borne in mind the warning given by Thorpe J in another 'big money case', *H v H (Financial Provision: Capital Allowance)* [1993] 2 FLR 335, [1993] Fam Law 520. Here, the district judge had ordered the husband to pay a lump sum to the wife, simply in order to give her a capital resource or 'cushion'. Thorpe J reversed this, and commented:

The wife ... has got capital with a present value of approximately £227,000. The husband has present capital with a value of approximately £277,000. Why, in those circumstances, is it necessary for the court to make any capital adjustment between the spouses? The district judge, by his judgment, made a very substantial readjustment to capital without any express rationale. I believe that the discretionary powers of the court to adjust capital shares between the spouses should not be exercised unless there is a manifest need for intervention upon the application of the s. 25 criteria. In this case I can see no manifest need for intervention. ... It must be borne in mind that the allocation of money between spouses in substantial cases is nowadays principally directed to the estimable objective of obtaining a clean break and furthermore, in pursuit of that end, the *Duxbury* approach (*Duxbury v Duxbury* [1987] 1 FLR 7) has become common place. ...

It does not seem to me, in the age of *Duxbury*, that there is much principle for increasing a wife's capital award by reference to some specific cushion.

Whatever the scale of the family's finances, in all cases the level of child support must, of course, be determined not by the court but by the Child Support Agency; s. 8(3) of the Child Support Act 1991 provides that in any case where the child support officer has jurisdiction under the Act, 'no court shall exercise any power which it would otherwise have to make, vary or revive any maintenance order in relation to the child and absent parent concerned.' However, in very wealthy cases s. 8(6) may come into effect, which provides that if the absent parent's income is above a certain level (determined by the formula), the court may nevertheless order the absent parent to make periodical payments for the child in addition to the maintenance assessment carried out by the Agency, if 'the court is satisfied that the circumstances of the case make it appropriate' for him to do so.

(ii) Average resources

In many typical cases the family's only or main asset is the matrimonial home. Jackson and her colleagues (1993) describe the reasoning process of English solicitors when dealing with financial provision on divorce as follows:

The solicitors' first question was always directed at the needs of the two households. And since the interviewer was explicitly asking about the advice that would be given to a divorcing mother who would be seeking to retain custody, the highest priority was the needs of the first family. Indeed, it was their access to housing which was the primary concern; as one solicitor said 'I want to know how much the custodial parent needs to keep a home going'. Here, questions relating to the home will be separated from those concerning division of income. The home will be dealt with first, since it became clear, as in Scotland, that this is the order in which solicitors approach financial issues on divorce. Once a decision has been taken on the home, other resources and needs are assessed, but this secondary decision-making process is necessarily shaped by the prior resolution of the housing issue.

The following example illustrates this preoccupation:

Scallon v Scallon
[1990] FCR 911, [1990] 1 FLR 194, Court of Appeal

The parties were married in 1943 and divorced in 1987. In ancillary proceedings, the district judge ordered that on the husband's transfer of his interest in the matrimonial home to the wife together with its contents and certain insurance policies, all her other financial claims should be dismissed. The former matrimonial home had an equity value of £68,400. The husband had debts of £11,000. He appealed contending that the order had left him with no capital assets. At the time of the appeal, both parties were employed, the husband was earning £12,000 p.a. and the wife £8,500 p.a. The recorder discharged the district judge's order. She concluded that each party should be in a position to have alternative homes and that having regard to the long marriage and the wife's contributions towards the family, she should have the protection of a nominal periodical payments order in case she should need maintenance in the future. She ordered that the house be sold and the net proceeds of sale be divided three fifths to the wife and two fifths to the husband. Both parties were legally aided with costs estimated at £3,500 each. The wife appealed contending, inter alia, that the recorder should have taken into account the impact of the legal aid charge when considering the order and should have deducted that sum from the wife's share and that as things stood she would have insufficient funds to purchase an alternative home.

Parker LJ: ... The recorder proceeded on the basis that it would be just and equitable so to deal with the capital assets, if possible, as to provide that each party should be able to provide themselves with an alternative home. That approach is not challenged and, in my view, was clearly right. It is contended, however, that under the recorder's order neither party but principally the wife would be able to purchase an alternative property, and that that is wrong in principle. I accept that if the order made was an order which would result in the wife being unable to house herself, the husband's position being of less importance in this connection since it is the wife who is appealing, it would be proper for this court to interfere. The question, therefore, which is central to this appeal is whether the order ... did achieve the objective of enabling the wife to purchase a suitable alternative property.

The net proceeds, as I have said, were £68,400. The distribution ordered by the recorder results in a figure of £41,040 for the wife and £27,360 for the husband. The proceeds of the policies, as I have said, were £4,560. The debts of the wife were substantially the same, £4,645, so that the £41,000 was available to be spent upon a new property. As to the legal aid costs, it was submitted by Mr Pointer that those costs would have to be deducted, leaving in the wife's hands available for a new property the sum not of £41,040 but, broadly speaking, £37,500. That was based upon an observation which was made in the case of *Simmons v Simmons* (1983) 4 FLR 803, in which this court considered, somewhat incidentally, the matter of the position of the legal aid charges. The judgment of the court in essence was given by Purchas LJ, who in the last paragraph of his judgment said as follows:

> 'I revert to the comment made by the President [Sir John Arnold] in *Jones v Law Society*; amendments to s. 9(6) of the 1974 Act and the regs 88 and 91 to exclude the proceeds of the sale of the matrimonial home or funds allocated for the purchase of a primary home for either of the parties to the marriage or a child of the marriage to whom s. 41 of the 1973 Act applies would avoid the hardship caused in this case. A person's home and the tools of his trade are already excluded from assessment under the 1974 Act. However, a mere discretion granted to the Law Society would not, in my judgment, be sufficient to permit the court to assume that the monies would not be collected, nor a charge enforced unless the position was secured by direct enactment.'

Since then the regulations have been amended and the regulations presently in force are the Civil Legal Aid (General) Regulations 1989 (SI 1989 No. 339) which came into force on 1 April 1989. Regulation 96 reads as follows:

> **96 Postponement of enforcement of charges over money**
>
> (1) This regulation applies where in proceedings under – ...
>
> (*b*) The Matrimonial Causes Act 1973, ...
>
> there is recovered or preserved for the assisted person a sum of money which by order of the court, or under the terms of any agreement reached, is to be used for purchasing a home for himself or his dependants.
>
> (2) Where the assisted person –
>
> (*a*) wishes to purchase a home in accordance with the order or agreement; and
>
> (*b*) agrees in writing on a form approved by the Board to comply with the conditions set out in sub-paragraph (3) the Board may, if the Area Director is satisfied that the property to be purchased will provide adequate security for the sum referred to in paragraph 3(*b*), agree to defer enforcing any charge over that sum.

It is thus apparent that there is still a discretion in the Law Society, even where the order of the court is in the terms envisaged by para. (1). In the present case the wording of the order which was made appears to me to satisfy the condition, for it is in these terms:

> 'That the former matrimonial home ... be sold and that the net proceeds of sale be divided into three-fifths to the petitioner and two-fifths to the respondent to be used by each party for the purpose of purchasing a home.'

That condition is thus satisfied. But, it is true that a discretion still remains in the Legal Aid Board and it is not for this court to direct how the Legal Aid Board should exercise its discretion. However, in my view, the court is entitled to proceed on the basis that the Legal Aid Board would so exercise its discretion as to further and not to defeat an order of this court. In a case where the entire order of the court could be frustrated if the charge were enforced and the result was that neither party could obtain a home, it appears to me to be unlikely in the extreme that the Board would exercise the charge and thus frustrate the order of the court. Accordingly, it does not appear to me to be justified, when considering the figures in this case, to deduct from the wife's share of the proceeds of £41,040 any figure for legal aid costs. The amount available to her initially is, therefore, £41,040.

It is submitted that that figure is not sufficient to enable her to house herself. The evidence before the judge given by the wife was that she could support a mortgage of £25,000, albeit she was then contemplating that that mortgage would be on the matrimonial home, which was a three-bedroom house in which she could have taken lodgers and still provide for her son to have a room of his own on occasion when he visited her.

It is abundantly apparent from the evidence which was given and from a further document, which is not in the main court bundle but which was filed as a supplemental bundle which was before the court, that £25,000 is a sum which she could raise from the building society. Those two figures, taken together, amount to £66,000. The recorder concluded that the wife could purchase a suitable property for a figure in the region of £65,000. On that basis there would appear to be a margin of some £1,000 available to meet removal expenses. It is submitted by Mr Pointer that the recorder's figure of £65,000 was too low and that the figure should be considerably higher, probably as high as £69,000. But the recorder had before her a large number of particulars showing various house prices in and outside Oxford, some for one-bedroom accommodation, which should be disregarded because it was common ground that the wife should have a two-bedroom house, and some of which were, albeit it a short distance, outside Oxford. The recorder was left, because no evidence was given as to the suitability or outgoings or anything else relating to any of those houses, to do the best she could on the material before her. For my part I am quite unable to see how it could possibly be said that she erred in any way in reaching the figure of £65,000. The particulars, as one might expect, give the asking prices that the agents suggest the sellers require. It would be flouting common sense if one were to assume that those prices would be achieved in every case. Doing the best she could on the material which she had, it appears to me the recorder's conclusion that the wife could purchase a house for a sum in the region of £65,000 is unassailable. It indeed appears to me to be a figure which is towards the top figure rather than the lower figure, and it may well be that the wife can acquire a suitable property at less than £65,000. If that be right, then, on the face of it, the wife would only be short of a very small amount, if anything; and, bearing in mind that there is in existence a maintenance order, albeit a nominal one, should it turn out in the future that she is unable to meet her outgoings, it would be possible for her to apply to the court.

Next, it is said that the wife cannot really support a mortgage of £25,000. Although the matter was not developed in his opening, Mr Pointer in his reply put before us a number of figures to suggest that the wife was not able to support a mortgage of that amount. In my judgment, the position must be dealt with as it stood on the evidence, which was that the wife could afford a mortgage of £25,000. As against this, the only matter that is raised is that it appears on the evidence that she was then assuming that she would have an income from lodgers. But it must be borne in mind that the figures for outgoings, which were laid before the court in the form of the wife's affidavit, have to be reduced considerably because they include payments on the mortgage which would not be rightly included if one is doing the sort of calculation which Mr Pointer invited us to do. For my part I am not satisfied that she is unable to raise or should not prudently raise £25,000 on mortgage. Nor am I satisfied that the division of the proceeds in accordance with the recorder's order would not enable her to buy a suitable house elsewhere. It is, therefore, clear that although the recorder was dealing with figures which necessarily meant that she would be near the borderline in each case, I do not consider that it would be proper for this court to interfere on the ground that the figures demonstrate that the wife could not purchase a property. As to the husband, it is unnecessary to consider the matter. It is not suggested on his behalf that he would be unable to purchase another property and, indeed, it could not be so suggested because his percentage of the proceeds is £27,360 and his capacity in regard to raising a mortgage would be in the amount of some £36,000. It is thus abundantly apparent that, being a single man with no need for a two-bedroom residence, he could have purchased a property quite simply.

Appeal dismissed.

Question

Why has he no need for a two-bedroom residence?

The question of the 'statutory charge' for legally aided litigants has long exercised the courts. Even in cases where the Legal Aid Board *may* postpone its enforcement, it is not obliged to do so, and the consequences of immediate enforcement would be ruinous in most cases. There is no discretion to postpone enforcement against a lump sum payment that is not to be used to buy a home (although the first £2,500 is exempt); and even where it is, the charge must be paid off, with interest eventually (Civil Legal Aid (General) Regulations 1989, SI 1989/339, regs 94, 97, 99). In *Hanlon v Law Society*[3] [1981] AC 124, [1980] 2 All ER 199, [1980] 2 WLR 756, 124 Sol Jo 360, House of Lords, Lord Lowry commented:

I am attracted by the Royal Commission's recommendation that the matrimonial home should once again be freed from any charge (Royal Commission on Legal Services, Final Report (1979) (Cmnd. 7648), vol. I, para. 13.64, p. 149). If this is done, I suggest that reform should be radical. For example, the registrar could be treated as an arbitrator whose decision on a section 23 and 24 application would be final subject to a case stated on a point of law. To give the method a chance of working the registrar would have to discuss his proposals with the parties before making up his order.

Questions

(i) Do you think the matrimonial home should be freed from the statutory charge?
(ii) Do you think that the present system of the statutory charge places a fetter on the discretion of the judges in legally aided cases?
(iii) Do you think there is any possibility of Lord Lowry's suggestion of binding arbitration being implemented?

In the Green Paper *Looking to the Future: Mediation and the Ground for Divorce* (1993) the Government suggested that where a couple reached agreement through mediation, the statutory charge would not apply. The White Paper (1995) stated (at para. 6.28) that the Government is to review the future of publicly funded legal services in the family justice system, and that a Green Paper will be published on all aspects of this, including 'the applicability and operation of the statutory charge in all cases, including mediated cases'.

(iii) Limited resources

Cann v Cann [1977] 3 All ER 957, [1977] 1 WLR 938, 121 Sol Jo 528, 7 Fam Law 141, High Court, Family Division concerned an application by the husband to vary an order made in the magistrates' courts in 1960, when the parties were still married. They were divorced in 1961. The couple

3. The Legal Aid fund was formerly administered by the Law Society.

were pensioners, the husband's total weekly income was £23.46p and the wife's total weekly income was £13.30p. The husband also had small savings amounting to £830 and he owned a motor car valued at £250. The current amount of the order was £7.00 per week. The husband's application to vary was unsuccessful and he appealed. He was again unsuccessful.

Hollings J summarised the court's approach in such cases:

For myself I am satisfied that the one-third approach is quite inappropriate, in circumstances of this kind where neither party is earning; then one has to look at each party's needs and see what can best be done in all the circumstances. I have in mind particularly the words of the statute under which the justices have jurisdiction. What was a reasonable sum in all the circumstances of the case? Bearing that aspect in mind, I would hold that the justices were wrong in not effecting some reduction, but by no means a reduction of the size contended for on behalf of the husband. If one reduces the order made by the justices of £7 to the sum of £5, that is reducing it by £2, the wife will have £18 and the husband will be left with £18.46 to cover expenses of £19.61. That leaves him with £1.15 deficit. That deficit, I think, should properly be financed out of interest from his savings, such as are left, or if necessary the interest plus capital. In that way, the parties would, so far as it is possible in the circumstances of this case, be left with a fair division of the respective pensions to which they are entitled. ...

(iv) Short marriages

Foley v Foley
[1981] Fam 160, [1981] 2 All ER 857, [1981] 3 WLR 284, 125 Sol Jo 442, Court of Appeal

The parties began to cohabit in 1962 when each was married to someone else. They had three children. They married in 1969, separated in 1974, and were divorced in 1977. The wife applied for financial provision for herself and the one child who was living with her. She had good employment; she also had realisable capital assets. The husband was not working and his future prospects were not very good; he owned a property (not the matrimonial home). The wife agreed to her claim for periodical payments (for herself) being dismissed but she claimed a lump sum payment.

In assessing the amount of the lump sum payment the judge distinguished the period of the marriage and the period of cohabitation, indicating that in so far as s. 25(1)(*d*) of the Matrimonial Causes Act 1973 [now s. 25(2)(*d*)] referred to the duration of the marriage he was not prepared to treat this as a marriage which had subsisted prior to 1969 but that as part of 'all the circumstances of the case' he took into account the wife's contribution to the family during the whole of the period they were living together. The judge was of opinion that the one-third calculation was not an appropriate starting point for computing the lump sum in this case. The one-third calculation would have given the wife £14,000. The judge awarded her £10,000. The wife appealed. The appeal was dismissed.

Eveleigh LJ considered the question of the length of the marriage:

The learned judge [Balcombe J] came to the conclusion that the proper sum to award the wife was £10,000.

The wife now appeals and the first ground of her appeal is to the effect that the learned judge failed to take into account the period of cohabitation, that is to say, the period when the parties were living together before the marriage.

[However,] ... in my view, the two periods, namely, cohabitation and marriage, are not the same. What weight will be given to matters that occurred during those periods will be for the learned judge to decide in the exercise of his discretion, but one cannot say that those two periods are the same. Ten years of cohabitation will not necessarily have the same effect as 10 years of marriage. During the period of cohabitation the parties were free to come and go as they pleased. This is not so where there is a marriage. In the great majority of cases public opinion would readily recognise a stronger claim founded upon years of marriage than upon years of cohabitation. On the other hand, in deciding these difficult financial problems there may be cases where the inability of the parties to sanctify and legitimize their relationship calls for a measure of sympathy which will enable the court to take what has happened during the period of cohabitation into account as a very weighty factor. *Kokosinski v Kokosinski* [1980] Fam 72, [1980] 1 All ER 1106 is one such case. *Campbell v Campbell* [1976] Fam 347, [1977] 1 All ER 1 is certainly not.

I do not regard Balcombe J as saying that the years of cohabitation are irrelevant. He simply says that they are not years of marriage within section 25(1)(*d*). That section requires the court to have regard to all the circumstances. Circumstances may be relevant for consideration in one case which would not be relevant in another, and the two cases, *Campbell v Campbell* and *Kokosinski v Kokosinski*, provide examples of this. But the matters specifically listed in s. 25 will always be relevant, because Parliament has said so. ...

I therefore see no error in the approach of the learned judge to the problem and I cannot say that he wrongly exercised his discretion in this case, in so far, for the moment, as he considered what weight should be given to the years of cohabitation.

On the relevance of the one-third formula to the case, on which the Court of Appeal again supported the trial judge, Eveleigh LJ said:

... the second ground of appeal is that the learned judge should have started on the basis that one-third was the proper proportion for the wife. Mr Jackson [for the wife] argued that, starting from one-third, the wife, on the facts of this case, should actually have received more than the £14,000 which a 'one-third' calculation would have produced, and he referred the court to the authorities relating to the 'one-third' proportion. As I see it, one-third in many cases is a very useful starting point for the court in deciding what should be the final figure. It is a useful proportion to take and then adjust one way or another as the case demands. But it is in no way a rule of law, as I see it. It is an aid to the mental process when arriving at the appropriate figure and there are many cases where the 'one-third' figure would not enter the mind of the court, because it would be obvious from the start that the proportion would be nothing like that. For example, the young marriage that lasts but a day or two. It is an extreme case but it is not unknown in this court. So that I do not find it possible to criticize the learned judge because he in fact said that he did not regard the one-third as the starting point in this case.

Appeal dismissed.

Questions

(i) Judgments such as these are based, to some extent at least, on an ideological commitment to marriage. Do you think that they actually help to enhance the status of marriage? For further examples of the courts' approach to short marriages, see *H v H (Financial Provision; Short Marriage)* (1981) 2 FLR 392, *Attar v Attar (No 2)* [1985] FLR 653 and *Robertson v Robertson* (1982) 4 FLR 387.

(ii) On the facts of *Foley v Foley,* do you think that the one-third formula was rejected because, in the view of both the trial judge and the appellate court, a five-year marriage is a 'short' marriage?

(iii) The court's response to a short marriage may be to order periodical payments for a limited period to enable the financially weaker party to adjust and to get back on her feet. What should happen if she fails to get back on her feet during that period? (See *Richardson v Richardson* [1994] 1 FLR 286.)

(iv) Would legislating for automatic equal distribution of property deprive us: (*a*) of the net effect approach to income distribution, or (*b*) the rationale for *any* income distribution?
(v) Do you think that the one-third formula is appropriate in cases where the husband is applying for provision from his wife? If not, why not?
(vi) The cases we have looked at so far have enabled us to contrast rich families with poor (*Gojkovic*; *Cann*); and long marriages with short (*Scallon*; *Foley*). Consider some other contrasts: how, if at all, would the outcome in *B v B* (p. 317, above) have been different if the couple had had no children? What might have been the outcome in *B v B* if the wife had not had her own career? What if the husband had not?

(c) CONDUCT

You will recall that s. 25(2)(*g*) of the Matrimonial Causes Act 1973 states that the court shall have regard to the conduct of each of the parties if that conduct is such that it would in the opinion of the court be inequitable to disregard it. Lord Denning MR, in *Wachtel v Wachtel* [1973] Fam 72, [1973] 1 All ER 829, p. 313, above, used the phrase 'obvious and gross' when describing that conduct which would justify the court in departing from the then statutory objective. Sir George Baker P, in *W v W* [1976] Fam 107, [1975] 3 All ER 970, said that he would be entitled to take account of conduct in a case which would cause an ordinary mortal to throw up his hands and say 'surely that woman is not going to be given any money!' The problem with a definition such as that is that 'ordinary mortals' *are* ordinary mortals, and might be tempted to throw up their hands in cases where the judges would consider that some financial provision was appropriate. Consider some of the 'folk myths' identified by the authors of *Simple Quarrels* (p. 371, below).

It is of course not possible to conclude that it would be inequitable to disregard conduct without investigating the conduct of both parties in some depth. If conduct is raised, argument is likely to last for some considerable period of time. This is indeed what happened in the following case:

Leadbeater v Leadbeater
[1985] FLR 789, [1985] Fam Law 280, High Court, Family Division

The judge heard evidence lasting some two weeks. Both parties had been married before and both had children from earlier relationships. Balcombe J summarised the problems of the new marriage in this way:

Balcombe J: There was, first, the husband's obsessive feelings about the custody of his children. There were some 16 hearings in the divorce suit between the husband and the former wife about custody of their children, which eventually the husband largely lost, although in the event the eldest child, a girl who is some 18 years of age, has now come to live with him in Tenerife; the middle child tragically died; the youngest child, a boy, is with his mother and the husband does not see him. But that sort of litigation imposes an immense strain on the parties to it and that must have been, and clearly was, a great strain on the parties' marriage, and indeed everybody else concerned.

Another problem allied to the first was the wife's inability to establish any satisfactory relationship with the husband's children. She accepts that on one or two occasions when she was drunk she did make the remark that she wished they were dead, a remark which she regretted bitterly when later the middle child died. But that failure to establish a relationship with her husband's children by his first marriage was clearly another major problem.

Then a great problem throughout was the relationship of the wife's son, both with his sister and with the adults. He had had some psychiatric outpatient treatment during the first year or so of this marriage, but at the time, at any rate, that did not appear to be effective and, the suggestion of in-patient treatment was not followed up. The son's problems manifested themselves in outbreaks of violence.

Then there was the wife's alcoholism. That was only really under control during the first 9 months of the marriage. Again I quote but two passages from the evidence which I noted. In her own evidence under cross-examination she said: 'It was under control for the first 6 to 9 months of the marriage'; the husband, in his evidence, said: 'From early 1980 onwards she was regularly drunk'. Although I accept, as I indicated during the course of the hearing, that alcoholism is a disease, nevertheless one cannot ignore the effects that that disease may have on the other persons concerned, and that was a major problem.

Then there was the wife's adultery in Cyprus. The husband, naturally, was upset by it, but he treated it, as he himself said, in a civilized manner. He attributed it to her drink, and by itself it could probably have been overcome. But it was not.

Finally, at the end of the marriage, there was this introduction of the 16-year-old girl, Miss D, into the household. Even had there been no form of sexual attraction between the husband and Miss D, in my judgment the husband was wholly unreasonable in insisting that this 16-year-old girl should be a part of the family, against his wife's wishes. Even if there had been no other relationship, it seems to me quite unreasonable for a husband to insist that a complete stranger be adopted as part of a family against his wife's objections. But, in any event, I find that from an early stage there was some form of sexual attraction between the husband and Miss D. I do not say that there were actual sexual relations until much later. It is now accepted that there were sexual relations in November 1983 and Miss D had the husband's child born in July 1984. I do not accept that the husband's relationship with Miss D was wholly innocent from the beginning. It very soon must have become a question of sexual attraction and I accept the wife's evidence that the husband (as she put it) was besotted by Miss D. But the introduction of Miss D into the household was certainly not the sole, nor even the main cause, of the breakdown of this marriage. It was the last in a whole series of failures of relationships. …

In my judgment it would not be inequitable to disregard conduct in this case. To put it another way, if I have to take the husband's conduct into account in bringing Miss D into the house, then equally I have to take the wife's conduct into account in her attitude over her son, her alcoholism, and indeed also the question of the adultery in Cyprus. In my judgment it is proper in this case not to give any effect to conduct, even in the way that Mr Feder (for the wife) invited me to do, namely, by saying that if it had not been for the husband's conduct in bringing Miss D into the house this would not have been merely a 4-year marriage. I leave conduct out of account and there is here a 4-year marriage.

Question

Would you have left conduct out of account?

Conduct was deemed more relevant in the following case:

Kyte v Kyte
[1988] Fam 145, [1987] 3 All ER 1041, [1987] 3 WLR 1114, [1988] FCR 325, Court of Appeal.

Purchas LJ: … This is an appeal by … the husband against an order made by Ewbank J on 16 January 1987 at Manchester when the judge allowed an appeal from an order made by the [district judge] on 7 October 1986 to the extent that, in addition to the orders made by the [district judge], the husband was ordered to pay to … the wife a lump sum of £14,000. …

The short background to the application was as follows. The parties were married on 25 July 1975. There are four children of the family, two of whom were the wife's children by a former marriage, namely Paul, born on 21 September 1965, and Andrea, born on 29 January 1969; and two who were the issue of the parties to the marriage, Victoria, born on 7 October 1977, and Rachel, born on 17 January 1980. The marriage appears to have come under stress at or soon after the birth of Rachel. The husband suffered from depression and spent numerous periods in hospital under treatment for this condition. In the particulars of behaviour upon which the wife relied in support of her petition for dissolution of marriage based upon section 1(2)(*b*) of the Matrimonial Causes Act 1973, which generally were accepted by the husband, it appears that, as a result of his depression, he was unpredictable and suicidal. Particularly severe incidents are recorded in April 1981. In the summer of 1982 he attempted suicide at his office and was rescued only by the wife and his office driver who, missing him, had called the wife for assistance. Other suicidal incidents occurred in the summer of 1983.

On the findings of fact reached by the [district judge], which were generally accepted by the judge on appeal, the wife started associating with a Mr. Gregory as early as June 1983, although she did not start living with him permanently until 1984. The husband's case, which was accepted by the [district judge], was that, although one of the serious suicidal attempts in the summer of 1983 was caused by the wife withdrawing her support from him, he was not at that time aware of the wife's association with Mr. Gregory. Subsequently, he realised that she was only using his conduct as a means to dissolve the marriage and set up home with Mr. Gregory.

Having initiated the suit, the wife obtained an injunction ousting the husband from the matrimonial home in February 1984. It is his assertion that this application was contrived to enable her to set up home with Mr. Gregory in the matrimonial home. The [district judge] found that, in presenting her version of these events to him, the wife had lied on oath. ...

The district judge found that the wife had connived at his suicide attempts with a view to gaining as much of his assets as possible.

I accept the submission made by Mr. Burns [for the husband] that it is abundantly clear from the long and careful judgment of the [district judge] that he took into account the conduct of the wife in the context of the conduct of the husband and all the circumstances arising during the marriage and that the judge, with great respect to him, was not entitled to criticise his judgment in this respect in the way in which he did. ...

I have, reluctantly, come to the conclusion that the judge was wrong to have reversed the [district judge] on the findings of conduct. The test as to conduct which the [district judge] set for himself is as apt an interpretation of the phrase 'inequitable to ignore it' that I can readily envisage. The conduct of the wife not only in actively assisting or, alternatively, taking no steps to prevent the husband's attempts at suicide in the presence of the motive of gain which the [district judge] found on ample evidence to be established, together with her wholly deceitful conduct in relation to her association with Mr. Gregory, would amount to conduct of a gross and obvious kind which would have fallen within the concept under the old law and, in my judgment, could certainly render it inequitable to ignore it even against the conduct of the husband which contributed to the unhappy conditions which existed during the marriage and afterwards as a result of the husband's manic depression.

The approach which I propose to adopt is to vary the judge's apportionment of the £40,000 additional capital to take into account the question of conduct which he wrongly ignored. Bearing in mind that the interests of the minors have already been catered for and that the wife enjoys the support of Mr. Gregory, and her conduct, which I considered was extremely grave, even taking into account the difficulties of the marriage, I would reduce the lump sum to £5,000.

Appeal allowed with costs.

Questions

(i) Suppose that a divorced wife who is in receipt of periodical payments from her ex-husband has an affair with another man: is this conduct which the court should refuse to regard as relevant?

(ii) If the answer to question (i) is 'yes,' suppose further that she becomes pregnant as a result of the affair and is obliged to give up her part-time job: how would you put her ex-husband's case in reply to her application for an increase in her periodical payments?

(iii) Suppose that the behaviour of the ex-wife in *Kyte v Kyte* had been entirely due to her own psychiatric disorder: would this have made the situation any different?

A v A (Financial Provision: Conduct) [1995] 2 FCR 137, [1995] 1 FLR 345

The parties in this case were married in 1968 and divorced in 1992; they had three children, daughters aged over 21 and 18, and a son of 14. At the time of the financial provision application the matrimonial home was worth about £52,000, and was not subject to a mortgage, so that it would be worth about £50,000 after deducting the cost of sale. At the time of the marriage the husband was a carpenter and the wife a civil servant, but when their son was about 10 she decided to retrain as a teacher. Thorpe J described the husband's reaction:

Prior to that development the husband had no relevant medical history and his reaction to the wife's ambition was therefore peculiarly extreme. He became depressed and suicidal, a state which continues unalleviated by continuing medical supervision. During the course of the last 3 years he has made approximately 12 suicide attempts. More seriously on 4 September 1991, after an absence from the home of some months, he appeared at the door of a neighbour's house which the wife and the son were visiting. Although offered no provocation, he advanced on the wife and struck her a forceful blow on the chest with a kitchen knife. Fortunately he was overpowered by the neighbour, who disarmed him. He ran off and attempted suicide on a nearby railway line. The physical damage sustained to both the husband and the wife on that day proved to be relatively trivial. The knife inflicted a surface wound at the top of the wife's left breast which was only a quarter of an inch deep and which required no treatment other than cleansing. She was left with a minimal scar. The husband suffered severe bruising after being struck by a train. Criminal proceedings followed. The husband was charged with unlawful wounding and, after conviction at the Crown Court, received a sentence of 18 months' imprisonment suspended for 2 years and subject to probation. It seems that for a time he moved to the Midlands and then returned to the West Country. He now lives in the West Country and receives supplementary benefit. ... Since this extremely frightening episode on 4 September 1991 neither the wife nor the son has received any further molestation, although there was an incident in the district judge's chambers when the husband exploded and left the room leaving a piece of paper on which he had written, 'I will fight on. I will kill'.

At first instance, the district judge made an order settling the husband's half share in the property upon the children; the wife now appealed. Thorpe J explained why this order was incorrect, and substituted a different arrangement:

I reject his discretionary conclusion for three reasons:

(1) There is no doubt that he over-estimated the significance and effect of the disgraceful episode of 4 September 1991. I agree that it constitutes conduct which it would be inequitable to disregard not only as an incident of aggravated violence but also in its long-standing effects on both the wife and the children, particularly the son. But it is only one of the factors to be reflected in the s. 25 exercise and it is not one which in my judgment should drive the court to conclude that the husband must be deprived of his entire capital. ...
(2) He seems not to have considered the wife's claim or potential claim to the Criminal Injuries Compensation Board. ...
(3) The application of capital from a spouse to children is not a permissible objective of the statutory powers. It may have been intended as a sop to the husband but as a matter of principle, it cannot be supported.

What discretion should I then exercise? For my part the starting-point is the joint entitlement to the property at the net value of £50,000. But that starting-point needs to be adjusted to reflect the combination of conduct, responsibility, needs and contribution. The wife has the overall responsibility for the care and upbringing of the children until they reach independence. ... The extent of that responsibility and contribution is exacerbated by the husband's conduct. However, his responsibility for that conduct may be attributed in part to his uncontrollable psychological state. Applying all these considerations, I would reduce his proprietary entitlement from a half to a third and would unhesitatingly say that its realisation must be deferred until the wife has completed the responsibility for the children, particularly the responsibility to provide them with a secure home. ... But ... it would be unwise to perpetuate a financial relationship between the husband and the wife over the course of years to come. If ever there was a case in which it was desirable for both the husband and the wife that the order be clear and final, it is this. ... I come to the conclusion that, in substitution for the district judge's provision that the wife enter into a settlement of one-third of the property on the children, the order to transfer by the husband to the wife of all his share in the former matrimonial home be balanced by a lump sum payment of £15,000. A date for the payment of that lump sum need not be specified. There will be liberty to both parties to apply as to the date of payment. There are a number of possible sources from which the lump sum might be discharged, namely proceeds of sale, the wife's borrowing capacity and the wife's prospective award from the Criminal Injuries Compensation Board. ... It is in the interests of both that it should be paid sooner rather than later. But in view of the wife's responsibilities and the uncertainty of her resources, it would be wrong to impose any time for payment today.

Questions

(i) Do you suppose that a different order would have been made if the husband's psychiatric disorder had been more serious and consequently his conduct more violent?
(ii) Why is it regarded as incorrect to settle property on children in these circumstances? (Compare the approach to property adjustment orders under the Children Act 1989, p. 185, above.)

The term 'financial misconduct' may relate to the dissipation or mismanagement of assets during or after the marriage, or to failure to disclose assets or other improper behaviour during the ancillary relief proceedings. The following cases show two contrasting approaches:

Beach v Beach
[1995] 2 FLR 160, [1995] 2 FCR 526

The background is given by Thorpe J:

This ... is an unusual and a sad case, and its conclusion depends very much on findings of fact and upon the assessment of the evidence of the parties.

The husband is 53 and the wife is 51. Throughout, the husband was a dairy farmer, his principal unit being the farm at Selborne in Hampshire. He acquired the farm in 1969 and at that date his first wife acquired a proprietary interest in some proportion. When that marriage was dissolved in 1979, it was agreed that she should receive the sum of £100,000 in settlement of that share. There were two children of that marriage. The wife also had a previous marriage by which she had one son.

The marriage between these parties was celebrated on 21 October 1980 and an arrangement was worked out whereby the wife should step into the proprietary shoes of the former wife, providing the consideration of £100,000 from the proceeds of sale of her home.

The entitlement of the former wife was not the only burden on the farm and the business. It had been incurring losses and there were secured creditors for liabilities in the region of £300,000. The arrangement between the parties at marriage was that if the wife were to invest her capital in the venture she should be entitled to repayment by sale if the trade had not been turned into profit within a period of 3 years.

Unfortunately, the farm business went from bad to worse. This was largely due to the husband's irrational optimism and tendency to spending sprees. In addition, in 1983 the dairy herd was struck by a plague of leptospirosis. Mr Beach blamed this on the veterinary profession, and embarked upon a course of disastrous litigation, from which he emerged in 1989 without recovering damages, and liable for his own and his opponent's costs of £180,000. In February 1990 the husband and wife entered into an agreement, after legal advice on both sides, that the farm would be sold and that she would receive, on sale on or before 29 September 1990, £450,000 in respect of her interest in it. But the farm was not sold within that period, due to the husband's continued refusal to co-operate in a sale and his insistence that he would be able to continue running the farm. He was declared bankrupt in December 1990. The farm was sold by the trustee in bankruptcy. The wife, as a secured creditor, received about £412,000 on account of her interest and was still owed about £44,000 at the time of the husband's application for a lump sum. Thorpe J summarised the arguments on both sides:

The present position of the parties is that the husband resides with his parents. He is on income support. ... The wife's position contrasts strongly. With the money received from the sale of the commercial property, together with the money received from the trustee, she has assets of about £820,000. ...

The case for the husband is opened by Mr. Moor, who says that all the history is irrelevant to the decision that I have to take. The agreement of 20 February 1990 is an agreement that I am not bound to uphold. The principles contained in the judgment of Ormrod LJ in the root case of *Edgar v Edgar* (1980) 2 FLR 19 allow me to make proper provision for the husband. In particular, he says that the February 1990 agreement should be disregarded because of:

(1) pressure on the husband;
(2) change of circumstances; and
(3) gross disparity.

He says that I should simply do the s. 25 exercise upon the parties' positions as they now are, and that a fair, discretionary decision would give his client a lump sum of £270,000, being a third of the wife's capital.

Inevitably Miss Ralphs for the wife places the greatest stress on the history. She emphasises the agreement of 20 February 1990, freely entered into on independent advice. It is not asserted that that advice was bad or unsatisfactory, and the agreement protects the wife from any claim since she has not yet received her entitlement under its terms.

Alternatively, if this is a case to be assessed on the s. 25 criteria, it is a case of manifest financial misconduct and in the exercise of discretion the application for lump sum should be dismissed: the husband has nobody but himself to blame for his present circumstances.

Thorpe J had this to say about the 1990 agreement:

Against those findings, what is the fair conclusion? I do not regard this as being an *Edgar* case in simple classification. The classic *Edgar* case contains a litigant who seeks to depart unreasonably or capriciously from a fairly negotiated formal settlement. Here, in February 1990 both the husband and the wife concede that the net proceeds of sale left to the husband after paying the wife £450,000 would be some greater sum. Here I am not concerned with a contracting party who wilfully or capriciously seeks to depart from a formal agreement, freely negotiated. Here I contemplate circumstances which are totally different from the circumstances contemplated by the contracting parties. ... My conclusion, therefore, is that although the agreement of 20 February 1990 is of importance, it is only of importance as part of the developing history. My essential duty is to determine this application upon the criteria contained in s. 25, as amended.

After considering the s. 25 factors, Thorpe J concluded:

... the crux of the case is really the responsibility for the present near-destitution of the husband. How has this come about? Who is responsible for this state of affairs? Is it the product of the husband's misconduct?

I have already recorded the developments and find the history as the wife presents it. I utterly reject Mr. Moor's submission that this history is irrelevant to the outcome of this case. I think Miss Ralphs is fully entitled to suggest that the husband's conduct amounted to conduct which it would be inequitable to disregard.

He obstinately, unrealistically and selfishly trailed on to eventual disaster, dissipating in the process not only his money but his family's money, his friends' money, the money of commercial creditors unsecured and eventually his wife's money, insofar as the disaster that eventually developed did not even pay for her specified agreed sum. It would have been in her interest, it would have been in his interest, had she forced him into accepting a properly marketed sale in the 1980s. She cannot be blamed for having failed to achieve that result. She secured formal agreement, she obtained orders in Chancery. But I can understand how difficult it must have been for her, living under the same roof with somebody so deluded. The responsibility is, in my judgment, not shared, not hers, but his.

So, on one view, why should he have anything when she has not even had what should have been her due under the freely negotiated contract? My first impression was to dismiss this claim as Miss Ralphs invited me to do. However, on further reflection I have concluded that the disparity between the present position of the husband and the wife is so great that that would not be a fair application of the s. 25 criteria. ...

I have reached the conclusion that the sum that would enable him to obtain some basic accommodation without at the same time removing from the wife the return of her basic financial contribution is £60,000, and I order the wife to pay the husband a lump sum in that amount within 28 days.

T v T (Interception of Documents)
[1994] 2 FLR 1083, [1995] Fam Law 15, [1995] 2 FCR 745

In this case the wife anticipated – correctly, as it turned out – that the husband would not give full disclosure of his assets during the financial provision proceedings. She therefore engaged in some detective work of her own, and the husband retaliated in kind, intercepting her mail and at one point breaking into her premises and removing a large number of documents. He now claimed that her conduct was such that it would be inequitable to disregard it. Wilson J's decision was as follows:

[Counsel for the wife] implied that, since each party had behaved similarly in relation to the other's documents, the issue was of little moment. I cannot accept his submission: although I cannot condone the husband's actions ... they were the result of acute provocation and I do not propose further to consider them.

The first question, which is not straightforward, is to what extent the wife's activities in relation to documents were reprehensible. The fact is that the husband had not made a full and frank presentation to the court of his financial resources and that a few of the documents taken by the wife (or, like the diaries, scrutinised by her and then called for) have enabled this to be made clear. The wife anticipated – and I find that she reasonably anticipated – at the outset of the litigation that the husband would seek to reduce the level of her award by understating his resources in breach of his duty to the court. On balance, I consider that in those circumstances it was reasonable for the wife to take photocopies of such of the husband's documents as she could locate without the use of force and, for that matter, to scour the dustbin. But the wife went far beyond that. She:

(*a*) used force to obtain documents;
(*b*) intercepted the husband's mail; and
(*c*) kept original documents.

The timing of the wife's production of some of the documents through the solicitors is also unacceptable. The original and copy documents which she had taken were discoverable documents and all those that she had in her possession at the discovery stage of the litigation should have been disclosed at that time, i.e. at the time of the delivery of her questionnaire, or earlier upon request. Those coming into her possession at a later stage should have been disclosed forthwith. Instead the wife suppressed her possession of some of the documents for many months, producing one or two of them piecemeal and then a substantial number, like a rabbit from a hat, just prior to the hearing.

The next question is whether the reprehensible activities of the wife in relation to documents amount to relevant 'conduct' or to a relevant 'circumstance' within the subsections. I appreciate that it has been held that a spouse's behaviour in the ancillary litigation, specifically a dishonest failure to make full disclosure, amounts to such conduct: *Desai v Desai* (1982) 13 Fam Law 46 and *B v B (Real Property: Assessment of Interests)* [1988] 2 FLR 490. But I agree with Thorpe J in *P v P (Financial Relief: Non-Disclosure)* [1994] 2 FLR 381 at p. 392F–H that a dishonest disclosure will more appropriately be reflected in the inference that the resources are larger than have been disclosed (in which case it will fall within s. 25(2)(*a*)) and/or in the order for costs; indeed that is how I intend to approach the husband's disclosure in this case. I am also firmly of the view that the wife's activities in relation to documents should not be brought into my reckoning of the substantive award, whether as conduct or as a circumstance, but should prima facie have some relevance in respect of costs. The extent of their relevance will depend on the potency of other factors. Although the wife's activities may not have caused significant increase in the costs, the court's discretion is wide enough to permit their inclusion in its survey of the litigation.

Question

Do you now have a clear idea of what constitutes conduct which it would be 'inequitable to disregard', and of the effects of not disregarding it?

(d) HOUSING

It will have been apparent from the cases already discussed that one of the most significant problems concerns what is to be done with the matrimonial home. In this section we consider the different legal forms that the solution to that problem may take. There are a number of options available to the court. First, the court may decide to allow the husband to retain an interest in the matrimonial home even though the former wife remains in the home with the children. It may be considered appropriate for the sale of the home to be postponed until the youngest child has completed his or her education:

Mesher v Mesher and Hall
(1973) [1980] 1 All ER 126n, Court of Appeal

The marriage took place in 1956 and the one child of the marriage (aged 9) lived with the mother. The house was in joint names. The judge ordered that the house be transferred to the wife, and the husband appealed.

Davies LJ: ... Counsel for the husband submits that it would be quite wrong to deprive the husband of the substantial asset which his half-interest in the house represents ..., one has to take a broad approach to the whole case. What is wanted here is to see that the wife and daughter, together no doubt in the near future with Mr Jones [whom the wife intended to marry], should have a home in which to live rather than that she should have a large sum of available capital. With that end in view, I have come to the conclusion that counsel's submission for the husband is right. It would, in my judgment, be wrong to strip the husband entirely of any interest in the house. I would set aside the judge's order so far as concerns the house and substitute instead an order that the house is held by the parties in equal shares on trust for sale but that it is not to be sold until the child of the marriage reaches a specified age or with the leave of the court.

Harvey v Harvey
[1982] Fam 83, [1982] 1 All ER 693, [1982] 2 WLR 283, 126 Sol Jo 15, Court of Appeal

The parties were married in 1960. They had six children. The marriage broke down in 1979 and it was dissolved in May 1981. The judge made an order in the form used in *Mesher v Mesher,* namely that the home should be held in joint names of husband and wife on trust for sale in equal shares and that the sale of the property should be postponed until the youngest child attained 16 or completed her full-time education, whichever was later, when the wife should be at liberty to purchase the husband's share in the property at a valuation then made. The wife appealed.

Purchas J: ... I am of the opinion that the wife is entitled to live in this house as long as she chooses so to do, ... I do that on the basis that was adopted in *Martin v Martin* [1978] Fam 12, [1977] 3 All ER 762, that, had the marriage not broken down, that is precisely what she would have been entitled to do.

I would vary the judge's order, first of all to say that the asset (the matrimonial home) be transferred into the joint names of the wife and the husband on trust for sale in the shares two-thirds to the wife and one-third to the husband; and further that such sale shall be postponed during the lifetime of the wife, or her remarriage, or voluntary removal from the premises, or her becoming dependent on another man. I have in mind that if she begins to cohabit with another man in the premises, then obviously that man ought to take over the responsibility of providing accommodation for her. Until one or other of those events occur, she should be entitled to continue to reside at these premises, but after the mortgage has been paid off, or the youngest child has reached the aged of 18, whichever is the later, she should pay an occupation rent to be assessed by the [district judge].

Ormrod LJ: I agree. This is another case which illustrates very aptly the proposition which has been stated many times in this court, that the effect of making a *Mesher v Mesher* order is simply to postpone the evil day to avoid facing the facts now.

Questions

(i) Are you attracted by this solution? In *Carson v Carson* [1983] 1 All ER 478, [1983] 1 WLR 285, Ormrod LJ said that the facts of that case, where the judge had made the type of order in *Mesher v Mesher,* were 'a very good example of the chickens coming home to roost.' What exactly does he mean?
(ii) Why should a new man take over responsibility of providing accommodation for an ex-wife remaining in the former matrimonial home?
(iii) Assume the ex-wife is disabled and unable to contemplate moving out of a purpose built bungalow which is the former matrimonial home There are no children. Is her disability a sufficient reason by itself to transfer the matrimonial home into her name alone? (Read *Chadwick v Chadwick* [1985] FLR 606, [1985] Fam Law 96, CA.) What if the former spouse is terminally ill? (Consider *M v M (Property Adjustment: Impaired Life Expectancy)* [1993] Fam Law 521.)

In contrast, the court may decide not to postpone sale but rather to transfer title to the wife absolutely (*Hanlon v Law Society* [1981] AC 124, see p. 326, above). The husband may be ordered to continue to pay the mortgage. Or the wife may be ordered to pay a lump sum to the husband; in effect to buy him out. The deciding factor in determining whether to postpone sale or to transfer ownership is often whether the court considers that the husband cannot or will not pay periodical payments. However, the court is bound to think hard before it deprives the husband of the only real capital asset he has; and it will think even harder now that the Child Support Act 1991 may in the future deprive him of more of his income than can be envisaged at present (see *Crozier*, p. 122, above).

Comparative merits of *Mesher* orders, *Harvey* orders (or *Martin* orders as they are generally known) and orders transferring the home absolutely are discussed in the following case:

Clutton v Clutton
[1991] 1 All ER 340, [1991] 1 WLR 359, Court of Appeal

The parties, who were married in 1964, had two children, now aged 23 and 16. In 1970 the husband bought the matrimonial home in his sole name for about £4,500, subject to a small mortgage. The parties separated in 1984 and a decree absolute dissolving the marriage was granted in 1985. The husband remarried in that year. In 1984 the wife had applied for ancillary relief, seeking transfer of the matrimonial home into her sole name or at least an order that she be allowed to remain there with the children and be not required to sell the house until death or remarriage 'or such order as the court shall think fit.' The district judge made an order transferring the house to the wife, subject to a charge in the husband's favour for £7,000, not to be enforced until 1 January 1991. In addition he awarded the wife maintenance of £10 per week, arrears of maintenance and maintenance of £25 per week for the younger child. On appeal by the husband the judge was told that the matrimonial home was the sole capital asset of the parties, the equity being worth £50,000; that the husband, whose debts amounted to £17,000, had a net disposable income, taking account of debt repayments, of £127 per week, while his second wife ran a small business which brought in £2,000 per annum; and that the wife, who had a stable sexual relationship with another man but had declared her intention of not remarrying or cohabiting, earned £66 per week from part-time work. The judge held that it was a clear case for a 'clean break' and ordered that the charge over the matrimonial home in the husband's favour should be set aside and that the husband should pay maintenance of £25 per week for the younger child until the end of the July following her sixteenth birthday so long as she remained in full-time education. He made no order for payments of maintenance to the wife. The judge refused the husband's application for leave to appeal against the order transferring the matrimonial home to the wife absolutely.

Lloyd LJ: An order whereby the sale of the matrimonial home is postponed until the youngest child of the family is 18, or some other age, is usually known as a *Mesher* order: see *Mesher v Mesher and Hall* [1980] 1 All ER 126n. An order whereby the sale is postponed until the wife dies, remarries or cohabits with another man, is usually known as a *Martin* order: see *Martin (BH) v Martin (D)* [1978] Fam 12. It will be seen that while, in 1984, the wife was asking for an out-and-out transfer of the matrimonial home, she would have been content, in the alternative, with a *Martin* order.

The principle of the clean break was, of course, well established long before the Matrimonial and Family Proceedings Act 1984: see for example *Minton v Minton* [1979] AC 593, *per* Viscount Dilhorne, at p. 601, and *per* Lord Scarman, at p. 608. It is now enshrined in section 25A(1) of the Matrimonial Causes Act 1973 by virtue of section 3 of the Act of 1984. But there is perhaps a danger in referring to it as a 'principle', since it might lead courts to strive for a clean break, regardless of all other considerations. This is not what section 25A requires. It requires the court to consider the appropriateness of a clean break, neither more nor less. It is salutary to remind oneself from time to time of the language of section 25A(1):

> 'it shall be the duty of the court to consider whether it would be appropriate so to exercise those powers that the financial obligations of each party towards the other will be terminated as soon after the grant of the decree as the court considers just and reasonable.'

Another danger is that 'clean break' may mean different things to different people. In origin it referred to an agreement whereby the wife abandoned her right to claim maintenance in return for a transfer by the husband of a capital asset, usually, though not always, the matrimonial home, thus encouraging the parties to put the past behind them, and, in the words of Lord Scarman in *Minton v Minton,* at p. 608, 'to begin a new life which is not overshadowed by the relationship which was broken down.'

...

Where the judge went wrong, and plainly wrong in my opinion, was in refusing to make a *Martin* order. As I have pointed out, this is what the wife was originally content to accept. It is also what the husband was asking for. Why then did the judge not make a *Martin* order? We cannot tell, because we do not know his reasons. It cannot surely have been because a *Martin* order would offend against the principle of the clean break. A charge which does not take effect until death or remarriage could only be said to offend against the principle of the clean break in the most extended sense of that term. The only clue we have is the argument on behalf of the wife that she did not want to be spied on.

I see some force in that argument, although it was scarcely pressed before us. Indeed it was not mentioned at all until it was raised by the court. Whatever the force of the argument, it is far outweighed by the resentment which the husband will naturally feel if the wife remarries within a year or two and continues thereafter to occupy the matrimonial home. She says she has no intention of marrying Mr. Davidson. But it remains a distinct possibility. In *Leate v Leate* (1982) 12 Fam Law 121 Ormrod LJ recognised that it is 'very galling' for a husband if the family assets are handed over to the wife, who then remarries. He said:

> 'Some provision as to the wife's remarriage was reasonable and there ought to be a charge enforceable by the husband in the event of her death or remarriage.'

In *Simpson v Simpson* (16 March 1984, unreported), Court of Appeal (Civil Division) Transcript No. 119 of 1984, Lincoln J, giving the first judgment of the Court of Appeal, said:

> 'Such then was her intention. On that evidence the judge was entitled to conclude that on the balance of probability she did not then intend to and might never marry Mr. Cook, and that he was no more than a man friend employing her at £25 a week as his secretary and helping with petrol for the car and its insurance. But the matter does not stop there. Such a finding, if it had been expressly made, would not be inconsistent with a further finding that there was still a real possibility that she might marry him. She accepts that her feelings for him have deepened recently, she had been considering marriage with him and his relationship with her was clearly a close one. In the circumstances her intention, though truly and genuinely described today as negative, could change with the passage of time. If it did and if the present order for an out-and-out transfer remained, then the wife would be joined in her occupation at the matrimonial home by her second husband or cohabitee, the latter having contributed nothing to its original acquisition, and meanwhile the husband would have lost his half interest. I agree with the husband's contention that this would scarcely appear to be a just and fair solution. A trust for sale in which the power of sale becomes exerciseable on remarriage or permanent cohabitation would remedy that unfairness. An out-and-out order by definition cannot do so.'

In *Hendrix v Hendrix* (27 January 1981, unreported), Court of Appeal (Civil Division) Transcript No. 57 of 1981, where the facts were very similar to the present, a court consisting of Ormrod LJ and Purchas J ordered that the matrimonial home be transferred into the name of the wife, on her paying the husband a capital sum of £3,000, and further ordered that the house stand charged in favour of the husband as to 25 per cent of the proceeds of sale, payable on the wife's death or remarriage, or on her cohabiting. In other words, the court made a *Martin* order.

It is true that, in the present case, the husband's earning capacity is very much greater than that of the wife. In due course, when he has paid off his debts, he will be able to get back on to the property ladder without insuperable difficulty. But the same was also true in *Hendrix v Hendrix.* The question is whether the difference in earning capacity, and the severance of the maintenance tie, justified an out-and-out transfer of the sole capital asset to the wife. In my judgment it did not. The very least which the judge should have done was to order a charge in favour of the husband in the event of the wife's death or remarriage.

Cohabitation raises a separate problem. But if, as Lord Scarman said in *Minton v Minton* [1979] AC 593, the reason underlying the principle of the clean break is the avoidance of bitterness, then the bitterness felt by the husband when he sees the former matrimonial home occupied by the wife's cohabitee must surely be greater than the bitterness felt by the wife being subject, as she fears, to perpetual supervision.

Not to have made a *Martin* order in this case was therefore in my opinion manifestly unfair to the husband. It deprived him forever of any share in the sole capital asset of the marriage, without any sufficient corresponding benefit to the wife.

...

I would be happy to leave the matter there. But Mr. Mostyn is not now content with a *Martin* order, as was his instructing solicitor, who appeared in this case in the court below. He asks us to consider making a *Mesher* order so that the charge would become effective on Amanda attaining the age of 18 or some other age.

The rise and fall of the *Mesher* order has been charted in many previous decisions of this court. Though decided in 1973, the case was not reported until 1980: *Mesher v Mesher and Hall* [1980] 1 All ER 126n. It caught on very quickly, so much so that by the time of *Martin (BH) v Martin (D)* [1978] Fam 12 Ormrod LJ felt it necessary to say that the *Mesher* order was never intended to be a general practice.

> 'There is no magic in the fact that there are children to be considered. All it means is that the interests of the children take priority in these cases, so that often there can be no question of sale while the children are young. But the situation that will arise when the children reach the age of 18 requires to be carefully considered. Otherwise a great deal of hardship may be stored up in these cases by treating it as a rule of thumb that the matrimonial home should then be sold. It is not a rule of thumb.'

Omrod LJ went on to say, however, that in some cases a *Mesher* order might be the only way of dealing with the situation.

The dangers of the *Mesher* order were emphasised in a number of cases in the early 1980s. In *Mortimer v Mortimer-Griffin* [1986] 2 FLR 315 Sir John Donaldson MR said, at pp. 318–319:

> 'It does seem to me that both orders suffer from the defects to which Ormrod LJ drew attention, that "chickens come home to roost" at an unpredictable time and in unpredictable circumstances; and that while an adjustment based on percentages seems attractive at the time, experience shows that it is subject to all kinds of difficulties and objections when it is worked out in the event.'

Parker LJ said at p. 319:

> 'I would also add that I wholly endorse what my Lord, the Master of the Rolls, has said with regard to what is known as a *Mesher* order. It has been criticised since its birth; it is an order which is likely to produce harsh and unsatisfactory results. For my part, I hope that that criticism, if it has not got rid of it, will at least ensure that it is no longer regarded as the "bible".'

It seems to me, with respect to Parker LJ, that there are still cases where, if only by way of exception, the *Mesher* order provides the best solution. Such a case might be where the family assets are amply sufficient to provide both parties with a roof over their heads if the matrimonial home were sold, but nevertheless the interests of the children require that they remain in the matrimonial home. In such a case it may be just and sensible to postpone the sale until the children have left home, since, ex hypothesi, the proceeds of sale will then be sufficient to enable the wife to rehouse herself. In such a case the wife is 'relatively secure': see the judgment of Ormrod LJ in *McDonnell v McDonnell* (1976) 6 Fam Law 220, CA.

But where there is doubt as to the wife's ability to rehouse herself on the charge taking effect, then a *Mesher* order should not be made. That is, as I see it, the position here. The split suggested by the husband would give the wife two thirds of £50,000. It must be very uncertain whether this would be sufficient to enable the wife to rehouse herself in a few years' time when Amanda leaves home. That is no doubt the reason why the [district judge] declined to make a *Mesher* order. I would agree with him. But the *Martin* order does not suffer from the same disadvantages.

In conclusion I would reject Mr. Mostyn's submission that we should make a *Mesher* order, but accept his submission that we should make a *Martin* order. The split which he suggests seems about right. Accordingly, I would grant leave and allow the appeal to that extent.

Ewbank J: I agree. It is of course important to retain flexibility to meet the circumstances of individual cases and changes in social conditions. On the other hand, justice and the provisions of the statute usually indicate that an asset which has been acquired by the joint efforts of the spouses should eventually be shared. Where the only asset is a jointly acquired home of modest value it is often necessary to give its occupation to the parent with custody of children or to the spouse with the greater need. The clean break principle does not, however, mean that the other spouse is to be deprived for all time of any share. Experience has shown that postponing such an interest until the children are grown up often merely postpones and exacerbates the problems in re-housing that the occupying spouse will have. This is why the *Mesher* type of order is regarded as unsuitable unless there is going to be sufficient capital available to provide a suitable alternative home. But postponement until death, remarriage or cohabitation does not produce the same problem and is not generally disadvantageous to the occupying spouse. It does ensure that the other spouse receives eventually an appropriate share in the jointly acquired asset.

This is such a case. The judge was wrong, in my view, in depriving the husband of all interest in the house. The proper order would be for proceeds of sale of the house to be divided in the proportions of one third [to the husband] to two thirds [to the wife] on the death, remarriage or cohabitation of the wife.

Questions

(i) As a woman living in the former matrimonial home with your children which would you prefer: (*a*) the knowledge that the house has to be sold when the youngest of your children goes to university and you receive one half of the equity; (*b*) the knowledge that the house has to be sold when you commence a 'permanent cohabitation' with your boy friend so as to provide your husband with one third of the equity. Would your answer differ in either case according to whether you were in receipt of maintenance payments?
(ii) What would amount to evidence of 'permanent cohabitation' if that fact were in dispute?
(iii) Should property adjustment orders be capable of variation? (Read section 31 of the Matrimonial Causes Act 1973 and *Thompson v Thompson* [1986] Fam 38, [1985] 2 All ER 243.)
(iv) What happens when a property adjustment order is made, and circumstances subsequently change so as to make that order inappropriate (for example, the matrimonial home is transferred to the wife, to be a home for her and the children, and she dies soon after the order is made)? See *Barder v Caluori* [1988] AC 20, [1987] 2 FLR 480.

We now consider the question of tenancies. Whereas orders of the court regulating the occupation of the home can be made under the Family Law Act only during the marriage, there is jurisdiction to order the transfer of a private or council tenancy if there is security of tenure from one spouse to the other in a case where the marriage is terminated by divorce or a decree of nullity (Family Law Act 1996, Sch. 7). The court has the power to order the transfer, on granting a decree of divorce, nullity or judicial separation, or, with leave of the court, at any time thereafter. The landlord's consent is not required, but he does have a right to be heard before an order is made.

Questions

(i) Do you think (*a*) that this provision is an unnecessary interference in the powers and responsibilities of local authorities to determine housing priorities in their area; or (*b*) that to allow a housing authority to reallocate the home before the judicial decision was made would prejudge the matter and hamper the ousted party's chances of having the children?

(ii) But what is a local authority to do if (as is now usual) there is a joint tenancy and neither party will risk surrendering it (see *Hammersmith London Borough Council v Monk*, p. 150, above)?

(iii) There has been evidence that women are sometimes unable to obtain the children without housing and unable to obtain housing without the children. (Watson and Austerberry, 1986.) If this is correct, who should break this vicious circle, the court or the housing authority?

What of women who leave home because they find the relationship intolerable although there is no question of violence? Indeed one reason why courts are asked to make orders may be because housing authorities often treat childless women or women who have left their children behind as intentionally homeless under the Housing Act 1985 and therefore not under a duty to rehouse. Rosy Thornton (1987) discovered that 54% of housing authorities in her survey (more than 100) would find such women intentionally homeless.

(e) THE CLEAN BREAK

The doctrine of the clean break has emerged from the haze of the judicial involvement as a major target.

Minton v Minton
[1979] AC 593, [1979] 1 All ER 79, [1979] 2 WLR 31, 122 Sol Jo 843, House of Lords

In this case, the House of Lords collectively, and Lord Scarman in particular, stressed the requirement that the parties put the past behind them and begin a new life which is in no way overshadowed by a former relationship:

> ... There are two principles which inform the modern legislation. One is the public interest that spouses, to the extent that their means permit, should provide for themselves and their children. But the other – of equal importance – is the principle of 'the clean break.' The law now encourages spouses to avoid bitterness after family break-down and to settle their money and property problems. An object of the modern law is to encourage each to put the past behind them and to begin a new life which is not overshadowed by the relationship which has broken down. It would be inconsistent with this principle if the court could not make, as between the spouses, a genuinely final order unless it was prepared to dismiss the application. The present case is a good illustration. The court having made an order giving effect to a comprehensive settlement of all financial and property issues as between spouses, it would be a strange application of the principle of the clean break if, notwithstanding the order, the court could make a future order on a subsequent application made by the wife after the husband had complied with all his obligations.

Questions

(i) Is Lord Scarman being cruel to be kind?
(ii) Is the clean break approach consistent with the interests of the children?

Suter v Suter and Jones
[1987] Fam 111, [1987] 2 All ER 336, [1987] 3 WLR 9, 131 Sol Jo 471, Court of Appeal

The husband and wife, who had married in 1971, were divorced in 1985, on the husband's petition, on the ground of the wife's adultery with the co-respondent. Care and control of the two children of the marriage, born in 1972 and 1978, was awarded to the wife who continued to live with them in the former matrimonial home. The co-respondent, who earned £7,000 per annum, paid rent to his mother for a room in her house and had his meals there, but spent most nights with the wife, who neither sought nor received any contribution from him towards the expenses of running the home. The husband remarried. On the wife's application for financial provision, the district judge in the county court ordered, inter alia, the husband to transfer to the wife all his interest in the former matrimonial home, subject to the mortgage, together with the surrender value of two insurance policies, and to make periodical payments of £100 per month to her until she remarry or both children attain the age of 18 and periodical payments of £110 and £90 per month respectively to the children during their respective minorities. Without the periodical payments to her, the wife's outgoings would have exceeded her income by £570 per annum. The circuit judge dismissed the husband's appeal against the periodical payments order in favour of the wife, on the basis that a 'clean break' could not be ordered, under section 25A(2), where there were children under 18, that section 25(1) of the Act of 1973 made the welfare of the children the paramount consideration in deciding whether to make a periodical payments order and its amount, and that the children's welfare required the order to be made so as to ensure that they continued to have a roof over their heads.

On the husband's appeal:

Sir Roualeyn Cumming-Bruce: This appeal raises questions about the meaning and application of section 25(1) of the Matrimonial Causes Act 1973, as amended by section 3 of the Matrimonial and Family Proceedings Act 1984, and the correct exercise of the powers and duties conferred on the court by section 25A of the Act of 1973.

...

Counsel for the appellant husband's first submission was that the judge misdirected himself in that he never carried out the exercise prescribed as a mandatory duty upon the court by section 25A. By section 25A(1) it is the duty of the court to consider whether it would be appropriate to exercise the powers so that financial obligations of each party towards the other will be terminated as soon after the grant of the decree as the court thinks just and reasonable. By subsection (2), where the court decides to make a periodical payments order in favour of a party to a marriage, the court shall in particular consider whether it would be appropriate to require those payments to be made for such term as would in the opinion of the court be sufficient to enable the party in whose favour the order is made to adjust without undue hardship to the termination of his or her financial dependence on the other party.

Those provisions, introduced by the Act of 1984, enshrine in statute law the principle that after dissolution of marriage a time may have come, or can be foreseen in the future, when the party in whose favour financial provision has been made can so adjust his or her life as to attain sufficient financial independence to enable that party to live without undue hardship without any further dependence on the other party. This has been described as the principle of a 'clean break,' the phrase used by Lord Scarman in his speech in *Minton v Minton* [1979] AC 593, 608. In a number of cases which were decided before the new legislation came into force the court observed that where there were children for whom the parties shared a continuing obligation there is likely to be little or no room for the father and mother to have a clean break from each other: see, for example, *Pearce v Pearce* (1979) 1 FLR 261 and *Moore v Moore* (1980) 11 Fam Law 109, in which Ormrod LJ observed at p. 109:

> 'It is one thing to talk about a 'clean break' when there are sufficient financial resources to make a comprehensive settlement. Where there are no capital resources, as here, it is unrealistic to talk about a 'clean break' if there are children. It is not possible for the father and mother of dependent children to have a clean break from one another. ... So, in my judgment, the so-called principle of the 'clean break' has no application where there are young children.'

I agree with the submission of counsel that the new section 25A imposes a mandatory duty in every case to apply itself to questions set out in section 25A(2) whenever a court decides to make a periodical payments order in favour of a party to the marriage. The judgments in the cases before 1984 have to be read with that in mind. Though the parties may have to co-operate with each other over children still dependent upon them, it may be possible on the facts to recognise a date when the party in whose favour the order is made will have been able to adjust without undue hardship to the termination of financial dependence on the other party. I also agree that the judge appears to have been influenced by the earlier cases to approach the question of termination of financial dependence without specifically addressing himself to the question whether this wife could and should find a way of adjusting her way of life so as to attain financial independence of her husband. So this court is entitled to consider the facts for itself and to carry out the statutory duty prescribed by section 25A. Having said that, I am clear that on the facts it is not possible at this date to predict with any more confidence than the [district judge] when the wife will have been able to make the adjustment which leads to the inference that it will then be just and reasonable to terminate her right to claim periodical payments from her husband. The children are growing up. It is likely that it will become progressively easier for the wife to organise and increase her earning capacity. But there are too many uncertainties to predict the development of events over the next 10 years. Likewise in connection with the financial advantages which on the judge's finding she can expect to derive, if she wishes, from her association with the co-respondent. It is their declared intention at present not to marry. There has already been one interruption in the continuity of their cohabitation, if that is the right description of their present arrangements, as I think it is. She may become increasingly and permanently financially dependent on the co-respondent. She may not. Consideration of the facts in evidence before the [district judge] does not at this date enable the court to predict with any confidence whether she will in the next 10 years have had the opportunity so to adjust herself that her claim for periodical payments can be terminated without undue hardship. The [district judge] warned her that such would be the position once the younger child reached the age of 18. It may be that that situation will be attained earlier. It is not impossible that even after the younger child is 18, consideration of the wife's needs and earning capacity will still make it just and reasonable for her to claim some support from her husband, though I would expect it to be unlikely. For those reasons I reject the submission that the judge was wrong in refusing to make an order terminating the husband's financial obligations towards his wife.

I do not however found that conclusion upon the judge's reasoning and approach. I am satisfied for the reasons that I have stated, that he misdirected himself by failing to apply the test prescribed in section 25A(2). This court is therefore entitled to consider the facts in the way that section 25A(2) has enjoined, and then to exercise the discretionary power itself. So directing myself I come to the conclusion that it would be premature to make an order terminating the wife's claim for periodical payments for her support from her husband.

The second submission made on behalf of the husband is that the judge, following the approach of the [district judge], misdirected himself upon the proper construction and effect of section 25 of the Act of 1973, as amended by section 3 of the Act of 1984.

By section 25(1):

> 'It shall be the duty of the court in deciding whether to exercise its powers under section 23, 24 or 24A above and, if so, in what manner, to have regard to all the circumstances of the case, first consideration being given to the welfare while a minor of any child of the family who has not attained the age of 18.'

This subsection is new, and in effect replaces the words formerly enacted in section 25 at the end of the list of matters in paragraphs (*a*) to (*g*) of section 25(1) and paragraphs (*a*) to (*e*) of section 25(2) to which the court had to have regard amongst all the circumstances of the case.

The husband submits that both the judge and the [district judge] treated the welfare of the children as first and paramount, in the sense in which that phrase was interpreted by Lord MacDermott in the context of section 1 of the Guardianship of Infants Act 1925: see *J v C* [1970] AC 668, 711. There Lord MacDermott considered the two adjectives in the phrase, and said:

> 'That is the first consideration because it is of first importance and the paramount consideration because it rules upon or determines the course to be followed.'

I agree with the submission that counsel culled from a commentary by a distinguished commentator [F.A.R. Bennion (1976)] that the phrase 'first and paramount' means simply 'overriding,' and that if the draftsman had omitted the adjective 'first' the meaning and effect of the single adjective 'paramount' would have been the same. We are faced with the problem of discovering the intention of Parliament when it used the phrase 'the first consideration' without the conjunction of the adjective 'and paramount' which gave the phrase in section 1 of the Guardianship of Infants Act 1925 its dominant force and effect.

The duty of the court under section 25(1), as amended, is to have regard to all the circumstances, first consideration being given to the welfare while a minor of any child of the family under the age of 18. As regards the exercise of the powers in relation to a party to the marriage, the court shall in particular have regard to the matters set out in section 25(2) in the subparagraphs lettered *(a)* to *(h)*. Sub-paragraph *(g)* introduces a matter not previously included: 'the conduct of each of the parties, if that conduct is such that it would in the opinion of the court be inequitable to disregard it; ...'

Having regard to the prominence which the consideration of the welfare of children is given in section 25(1), being selected as the first consideration among all the circumstances of the case, I collect an intention that this consideration is to be regarded as of first importance, to be borne in mind throughout consideration of all the circumstances including the particular circumstances specified in section 25(2). But if it had been intended to be paramount, overriding all other considerations pointing to a just result, Parliament would have said so. It has not. So I construe the section as requiring the court to consider all the circumstances, including those set out in subsection (2), always bearing in mind the important consideration of the welfare of the children, and then try to attain a financial result which is just as between husband and wife.

Consideration of the judge's judgment, taken in conjunction with paragraphs 15 and 16 of the judgment of the [district judge] which he clearly approved, shows that the judge treated the consideration of the children's welfare as paramount; and controlling the effect of the interplay of all other matters. Though the [district judge] and the judge gave some effect by way of reduction of the periodical payments to the financial contribution of the co-respondent to the wife's finances, which the judge held would be substantial, the order was calculated in such a way as to provide the wife with a periodical payments order which would enable her to make all the mortgage payments. And the reasoning thus proceeded because it was considered that the children's welfare required that solution, although the [district judge] for the reasons that he gave thought that ordinary people would regard the result as unjust. In my view the judge fell into error in treating section 25(1) as requiring him to give effect to a consideration of the children's welfare as the overriding or paramount consideration. This was a misdirection, and this court is entitled to review the facts, apply the statute on its proper construction, and decide how to determine the wife's financial claim for periodical payments.

The judge then considered the position of the co-respondent.

... the wife has invited her lover to live for the foreseeable future in the former matrimonial home with herself and the children, without seeking or receiving any contribution to the expenses of maintaining that house. He is a bachelor aged 21 with a gross income of not less than £7,000, subject to tax. The figures demonstrate that the payment of the mortgage amounts to £2,148 per annum, and that after payment thereof she has a deficit of £570 per annum. It is reasonable to infer that the co-respondent is in a position to contribute at least £12 per week for the privileges which he enjoys in the furnished residence which, as a consequence of the husband's transfer of property, now belongs wholly to the wife, subject to the mortgage. It is material to bear in mind that since he moved to reside in the wife's house the co-respondent has continued to pay £16 per week to his mother for the room in which he no longer sleeps. As the wife is now for practical purposes living with the co-respondent in the former matrimonial home, it is just and reasonable to make an order on the basis that she require him to contribute not less than £600 per annum for the expenses of the house which she has invited him to enjoy. On that basis I would not think it just that the husband should do more than he has done by making the capital transfers already completed and by continuing to make payments to the children amounting to £200 per month. In that situation the wife's and children's needs are met, she can afford to run the home and pay the mortgage, and the husband and wife can expect to enjoy a comparable standard of living in the accommodation in which they respectively live.

I would move that the appeal be allowed and that the husband's obligation to contribute to her support be reduced to a nominal order of £1 per year.
Appeal allowed.

Questions

(i) Purchas LJ described a 'clean break' in *Scallon v Scallon* [1990] FCR 911, [1990] 1 FLR 194, CA (see p. 324, above) as follows:

Finally, I wish to say a word about 'clean break' which is a phrase which arises since the amendments to the 1973 Act were introduced to ensure that, where there were short-term marriages, one party should not get what is described as 'a meal ticket for life' upon the dissolution of such a marriage. Furthermore, it was to encourage spouses who hitherto had not earned their living to face up to the fact that after the dissolution they should earn their living.

But if the husband insisted that the wife remained at home during the marriage, is it really fair on her that she should now be encouraged to 'face up to the fact ... that she should earn her living?' Perhaps it is too late?
(ii) When making a 'clean break' should the emphasis be on 'need' or 'earned share'? (See *B v B (financial provision)* [1990] FCR 105, [1990] 1 FLR 20.)

The ideology of the clean break is discussed in *Indissolubility and the Clean Break* (1985) by Pamela Symes:

The Logic of the Clean Break Principle

The limitations of the old section 25 directive were soon apparent and therefore a realistic and workable alternative needed to be found. The clean break principle is arguably a logical step forward in the long march towards liberal divorce and sexual equality but it is possible that in principle, it carries almost as much potential conflict and inconsistency as the old directive – equally capable of producing unjust and inequitable results, but for different reasons. The former section 25 directive embodied an *inherent* contradiction ('to place the parties ... in the financial position in which they would have been if the marriage had not broken down'). By contrast, the clean break principle has an inherent logic about it based, as it is, on the assumption that the marital relationship is ending rather than being continued. The potential contradictions are not inherent – rather they are *internal* to the legislation (for example, trying to reconcile the clean break with the other policy objective of giving priority to children's needs) and *external*, such as when the clean break is not recognised by the D.H.S.S., for instance, who may still require contributions from an ex-husband after a clean break settlement. (*Hulley v Thompson* [1981] 1 All ER 1128.) [See now the Child Support Act (p. 116, above).]

After looking at the English and the Scottish proposals, Symes raises the basic issue of 'who pays'?

One very fundamental question was never satisfactorily answered before the Divorce Reform Act 1969 was enacted – namely, how is it going to be paid for? Divorce and remarriage it was realised would involve the creation of many new households; where were the extra resources to come from to finance this exercise? The wider fiscal implications of such a change in the divorce law seem to have been largely ignored ...

The husband's obligation to maintain his wife, is the very nub of the problem. It is debatable whether such an obligation should arise during marriage, but if it does not end on divorce then what does divorce mean? This leads to the second basic question which has still not been satisfactorily answered: does divorce constitute the termination of the marital relationship, or merely a readjustment of it? These two questions have chased one another in a kind of conundrum for the last 15 years. Unable to accept the full logic of the position that divorce should constitute a complete and final termination of the parties' legal and financial relationship with the parties reverting to being 'legal strangers,' we have been forced to accept that it must therefore be a readjustment of their former marital relationship. Our present law is still ambiguous; while apparently signalling the end of the marital relationship, the financial provisions point to its readjustive function. But in one respect the law is quite clear and unambiguous: it incorporates a licence to remarry.

She argues that marriage 'as it has been traditionally practised, is not intended to be ended by divorce':

Indeed, traditional housewife marriage has a most potent feature of indissolubility built right into it – dependency. When that dependency is reinforced in the social infrastructure (both explicitly through social security and taxation laws and implicitly in the underlying assumptions about marriage) then the marriage bond becomes practically indissoluble. The accumulation of responsibilities and obligations, the consequences of an unequal partnership based on dependency – all mean that an absolute severance of the bond without massive adjustment would be manifestly unjust, more likely impossible.

She ends her article in this way:

Conclusion

Present divorce is so often merely a readjustment of the former marital relationship. It results in the parties being released from the obligation to share bed and board but they are still saddled with the ongoing financial obligations of the marriage, not unlike judicial separation. Thus the licence to remarry is something of an illusion. In so many ways the parties are *not* free to remarry, as the evidence from numerous pressure groups will testify. Thus divorce, as granted in most cases, is only *a mensa et thoro* simply because most marriages are still indissoluble. True divorce *a vinculo matrimonii* can only be granted when, because the marriage is short, childless or the parties are sufficiently rich, the bond can be truly severed and a clean break imposed – the marriage is, by practical definition, dissoluble. This is because, at the time the reformed divorce law came into operation, we failed to introduce simultaneously the effective means whereby the *vinculum*, the marriage bond could be broken (*i.e.* the necessary changes in the infrastructure). The ongoing marriage tie is reflected in the continuing support obligation which is imposed – admittedly imposed but often not met ... If the support obligation is met, there is financial strain where remarriage follows as limited resources are spread between two families; if it is ignored or only partly met, then usually the resort is to subsistence on state benefit for the first family.

This was the inevitable result of attempting the impossible, of trying to introduce divorce for indissoluble marriage. With the passing of the Matrimonial and Family Proceedings Act 1984 the clean break principle now has embryonic statutory form. While it remains unsupported by a reformed social policy it will at best be a non-event, at worst, it will simply open the way to more injustice and suffering. For only when a radical change in the marital relationship takes place, when it becomes a partnership of two economically independent individuals through the abolition of marital dependency and when the corresponding changes in the social infrastructure are brought about, will there be any chance of formulating a coherent, clean break divorce law.

Questions

(i) After reading this, are you inclined to give up searching for a coherent policy?
(ii) Do you think that the policy of the 'clean break' is consistent with the principles behind the Child Support Act 1991? (See Chapter 4, above.)
(iii) Will a 'clean break' be harder to achieve following implementation of the Child Support Act 1991?

That brings us to some decisions taken in the light of the Child Support Act 1991, where the courts have had to grapple with this problem. The facts of *Mawson* are set out by Thorpe J:

Mawson v Mawson
[1994] 2 FLR 985, [1995] Fam Law 9

The marriage between the parties was preceded by a period of cohabitation. At the date of the marriage, on 21 June 1986, the husband was 28 and the wife 24. He was a flying officer in the Royal Air Force and the wife worked for Thomas Cook. Shortly after the marriage they changed homes. Their first was provided by the wife and on sale she received approximately £7500. The second home was purchased in the husband's sole name with an endowment mortgage but the wife provided the deposit of £1500. The balance of £6000 of her capital was subsequently spent on a motor car which was subsequently replaced more than once until it emerged as a Renault in the husband's possession at the date of the hearing.

There was one child of the marriage who was born on 5 June 1988. The separation took place in February 1990 and the husband's petition was filed in May 1991. So it can be seen that this is a young couple, they came together when each had a career, they separated after approximately 3 years of marriage, although the period of their partnership extended to about 5 years by virtue of the prior-to-marriage cohabitation.

The financial proceedings were undoubtedly protracted and in part by a manoeuvre on the part of the wife's advisers. In July 1993 she aborted what the husband had anticipated would be a final hearing by withdrawing her claim to financial provision for the child on the basis that she would submit that to the adjudication of the Child Support Agency (CSA). That adjudication resulted in an assessment on 4 December 1993 that the husband should pay to the CSA £596.70 per month, or £7,160.40 pa. That was a substantial sum and manifestly more than the court would have ordered by way of periodical payments to the child, applying the ordinary approach that district judges have for long adopted in cases in this range.

The order made at first instance by the district judge was for the transfer to the wife of the former matrimonial home and the endowment policy supporting the mortgage, a lump sum of £2,000, and periodical payments limited to a three-month term. The wife now appealed against that order, arguing for a greater lump sum and for an increased order for periodical payments, to continue during the parties' joint lives or until her remarriage or further order.

That raises the question of how a 'deferred clean break', whereby periodical payments are made for a time and then cease, can be achieved. If an order is made that payments continue for, say, three months, finality is not guaranteed because the recipient can apply before the end of that period for an extension of it (see *Richardson v Richardson* [1993] 4 All ER 673, [1994] 1 WLR 186, [1994] 1 FLR 286). However, s. 28(1A) of the Matrimonial Causes Act 1973 provides that when such an order has been made:

... the court may direct that the party shall not be entitled to apply under section 31 for the extension of the term specified in the order.

The question in *Mawson* was whether or not any such direction had been intended by the district judge, whose order was unclear in this respect, and, if so, whether or not such a direction was appropriate. Thorpe J concluded that if the order was intended to include such a direction, it could not stand, bearing in mind dicta in *Waterman v Waterman* [1989] 1 FLR 380 and in *N v N (Consent Order: Variation)* [1993] 2 FLR 868, CA, to the effect that such a direction should only be made in exceptional cases where there were, as in this case, very young children. Thorpe J concluded:

Clearly it would be quite inappropriate to fix upon any date at which the wife's claims for periodical payments could be absolutely and irrevocably terminated without some risk to the financial security of the only child to whose welfare particular regard must be paid.

On the other hand, a balance must be struck between the desirability of securing his financial future and the need to uphold the message from the amendments to the 1973 Act, namely the obligation on the wife to stand on her own feet and to bring an end to her financial dependency upon her former husband as soon as possible. I think in this case the right balance is struck by a periodical payments order for a finite term, but one which does not carry a s. 28(1A) direction prohibiting application under s. 31 for an extension of the term.

His order was therefore for periodical payments to continue for a further nine months, but without a s. 28(1A) direction.

Question

Does the court's order in this case strike a fair balance between the parties?

Finally, consider the following case:

Smith v McInerney
[1994] 2 FLR 1077, [1995] Fam Law 10

In this case the parties made a separation agreement in 1990, to the effect that the husband's share in the matrimonial home and collateral endowment policies be released to the wife, and that he would have no future liability to maintain her and the three children – although in fact he paid maintenance for the children voluntarily for some 15 months. The situation now was that the husband had been made redundant, and that he was applying for a property adjustment and lump sum order. The wife was now in a position when she would shortly become dependent upon income support, so that there would inevitably be a Child Support Agency assessment in respect of the one child, D, still living with his mother. The district judge made an order giving the husband 35 per cent of the net proceeds of the house (in which there was equity, at that date, of about £47,000), the order not to be enforced for five years without leave. On the wife's appeal, Thorpe J concluded:

It seems to me manifestly fair that if the husband parted with capital in February 1990, in part in commutation of his future obligations to maintain D, then he should have the right to look to the wife for indemnity in respect of any sums which are extracted from him in respect of D's maintenance. In reality, he would be paying twice to discharge the same obligation; once by capital, and secondly by periodical payments. Whilst the wife would not herself have laid claim to that second payment, she would indirectly have triggered it by her application for income support for herself.

The conclusion that I reach then is different to that reached by the district judge. I would set aside his order, charging the wife's home (the former matrimonial home). I would order the payment of a lump sum to recompense the husband for the cash that he advanced to the wife in 1990 and 1991. It is agreed that the sums paid total £3,000. I would also adjourn his application for a property adjustment order in respect of the former matrimonial home generally for the single purpose of providing a means of pursuing a claim for indemnity if, and only if, the Child Support Agency extracts from him substantive periodical payments in respect of D between this date and the date of D attaining financial separation from his mother by attaining the age of 17 or ceasing full-time education.

Obviously, that adjourned claim must await the termination of the potential liability. The quantification of the claim could not sensibly be attempted until D was off cost. When that stage is reached, possibly in 3 years' time possibly in more years, then with hindsight the court, in the absence of agreement between the parties, could quantify the sums paid by the husband and do justice to him by fixing some percentage interest, or charge, in relation to the capital from which he parted in February 1990 to settle his obligations in respect of D in part.

Question

(i) Do you see any possibility of the courts making this type of order on new applications (i.e. where separation has occurred since the implementation of the Child Support Act 1991)?
(ii) If not, do you think that the *Mesher* order will enjoy renewed popularity?

(f) PENSIONS

Section 25(2)(*h*) requires the court to have regard to 'the value to each of the parties to the marriage of any benefit (for example, a pension) which, by reason of the dissolution or annulment of the marriage, that party will lose the chance of acquiring.' Maggie Rae, in her article 'Pensions and Divorce: Time for Change' (1995) explains why pensions have posed such a problem on divorce.

Almost a third of all marriages in the United Kingdom end in divorce. About half of all those in work are members of occupational pension schemes and many others now invest in personal pensions. It follows that many of those who divorce are members of pension schemes or married to those who are. They constitute a major family asset but commonly, one spouse will have a much larger pension than the other one. The link between pension provision and divorce ought to be obvious. Equally obvious to divorce lawyers is the need to reform the law so that pensions can be dealt with on divorce in the same way as other family assets.

The core of the problem is that the courts usually have no power to divide pensions on divorce. This is because the Inland Revenue will not approve pension schemes which permit the assignment, charging or allocation of acquired pension rights to third parties including spouses. In addition, almost all occupational schemes and an increasing number of personal pensions contain 'Protective' or 'Spendthrift' trusts which mean that were a court to make an order against a member in relation to his/her pension rights, those pension rights would be forfeited.

This produces unfair results in a significant number of cases. Take for instance the couple who divorce in their early fifties when the children have grown up. The wife may not have worked for a decade or more while the children were young and after that only worked part-time. If she has a pension at all it will only be a small one, and much smaller than her husband's. In happier times both of them looked forward to a secure old age. Divorce changes all of that. Suddenly the wife finds herself unsure of what the future will bring. In the ensuing division of the assets, the family's largest potential asset cannot be the subject of division by the court. Widows' pensions and entitlements to death in service benefits are also affected and also outside the court's jurisdiction.

In this family, as in many others the decision that the wife should stay at home and then only work part-time, was one taken jointly – a family decision. The only fair way to look at this couple's pension provision is as a joint family asset. In some marriages that treatment would not necessarily be right. Nonetheless it ought to be available.

The Law Society Memorandum (1991) identifies six benefits which require consideration:

3.3 (*a*) the payment of a lump sum on retirement;
(*b*) the pension the husband will become entitled to on retirement;
(*c*) a widow's pension which may be payable following the husband's death after retirement;
(*d*) a lump sum which could be payable to the husband's estate should he die in service;
(*e*) a widow's pension payable should the husband die in service; and
(*f*) the possibility of substantial life cover which would be payable to the husband's estate in the event of his death.

However, there have been difficulties:

(*a*) Under Section 25(1)(*a*) of the Matrimonial Causes Act 1973 the court must look at what will occur in the foreseeable future. The courts seem to limit the foreseeable future to about four or five years following the divorce, or at most ten – thus, if a couple divorce more than ten years before a pension is due, the wife is unlikely to benefit.
(*b*) The court does not have the power to order a husband to take out life or term insurance, assign pension benefits, or continue pension or insurance premiums. It is also not possible to order that a service gratuity be split (see section 203 of the Army Act 1955). As a result most arrangements for pensions for divorcees are made by consent.
(*c*) It is very difficult to value a pension accurately before it has accrued as the value will either depend on the final salary of the contributor or the amount of contributions made to a personal scheme and the performance of the investment. Traditional reliance has been placed on transfer values, however, it appears that these tend to underestimate the benefits accrued.
(*d*) It has been suggested in relation to family trusts (see J.G. Miller *'Trusts and Financial Provision on Divorce'* (1990)) ... that orders contingent on an event occurring i.e. a pension accruing should be made. Although this approach has been used in the past (see *Milne v Milne* (1981) 2 FLR 286) it leaves a former wife dependent on a series of events occurring over which she has no control. It may be that her former husband becomes unemployed or dis-entitled to his pension or that he manages to avoid liability to his former wife by some other means.
(*e*) Often the terms of the pension schemes do not allow the assignment or commutation of benefits.
(*f*) Under the present system the only solution is often for a former husband to consent to taking out a policy for his former wife's benefit. This will often not be possible because of a lack of resources.
(*g*) Again, a sheer lack of resources often means that it is virtually impossible for a husband to compensate his wife adequately in some other way for the loss of pension rights, particularly when this is combined with the fact that women, whether married or divorced, tend to earn less (and therefore have lower pension entitlements) than their male counterparts.

The Memorandum then summarises the proposals of the Institute of Fiscal Studies (1988), the proposals of the Labour Party, as well as Scottish[4] and German law: the Memorandum concludes by recommending:

3.22 The Committee, therefore, *recommends* that
(i) the courts should be given power to make pension adjustment orders in proceedings for ancillary relief brought under the Matrimonial Causes Act 1973;
(ii) the courts should be provided with powers similar to those available under the Scottish legislation. In addition there should be a power to allow payments by a former husband into a personal pension scheme for a wife.
(iii) Guidance should be issued on how and when a pension should be valued and in what shares it should be split.

In 1992 the Pensions Management Institute (PMI) set up a working group, in conjunction with the Law Society; its report, *Pensions and Divorce*, was published in May 1993. The report summarised the possible ways of dealing with pensions on divorce as follows:

We have looked at four ways of reallocating the value of pension rights when divorce takes place before the pension comes into payment:

---

4. 3.17 The Family Law (Scotland) Act 1985 also makes some provision for pension splitting on divorce. Under the terms of section 10 of the Act [see p. 309, above], pensions and life assurance benefits are included in the definition of matrimonial property which should be split on divorce.

(*a*) pension rights continue undisturbed but their value is taken into account – any reallocation of resources between the couple is made by adjustment of non-pension assets;
(*b*) earmarking – pension rights continue undisturbed, but a specified amount of whatever benefit eventually becomes payable to or in respect of the scheme member is earmarked for payment direct to the former spouse when the time comes;
(*c*) pension splitting within a scheme – a scheme member's pension rights are reduced by the specified amount mentioned in (*b*), and the resources so released are used to provide, within the scheme, a package of benefit rights for the former spouse as an entirely separate member of the scheme;
(*d*) transfer – a scheme member's pension rights are reduced as in (*c*), and the resources so released are made available to the former spouse in the form of a transfer payment to another pension arrangement.

Method (*a*) is in use at present, particularly in Scotland, but it is effective only if there are adequate non-pension assets, and there are difficulties in comparing the value of pension assets, which enjoy favourable tax treatment, with the value of other assets. Methods (*b*), (*c*) and (*d*) would need changes in the law. We favour method (*d*). ...

In addition, the working group favoured the earmarking approach (*b*), coupled with life assurance, in cases where the marriage broke down after retirement.

Question

Can you see why these two different methods are appropriate in the two different situations?

Although the PMI report was widely welcomed, it did meet with some criticism. Jennifer Bispham's comments, in her article 'Pension Reform – Tilting at Windmills' (1994), may remind you of the debate about the maintenance after divorce and the position of women (see pp. 298ff, above):

We have, at present, a society in which both parties to a marriage will commonly work, and in which, whether from choice or necessity, the wife will continue to work after childbirth. She is encouraged to seek her own independence in life from the start of her schooling, and will normally have as her role models a working mother and other working female relatives. She will be brought up to believe that 'relationships', children and a career are her right, and that she can and must enjoy all to the full. The downside of this is that she must attempt to balance competing responsibilities without robbing Peter to pay Paul.

If, therefore, the female spouse is now a working woman for all or the greater portion of her working life, she will have or can be capable of having pension arrangements of her own, whether private or occupational. Since divorce statistically affects one in three marriages, if the wife elects not to make such provision for herself she is both short-sighted and culpably negligent, and the necessity for such fiscal prudence in such wives should, if necessary, be emphasised by the refusal of courts to make such pension provision as they could otherwise order, in the event that the court was satisfied that the wife had wilfully refused or unreasonably neglected so to do.

Question

To what extent is this view realistic?

While the PMI group was at work, the issue of pensions was being raised in a new way in the courts. Section 24(1)(*c*) of the Matrimonial Causes Act 1973 gave the court power to make 'an order varying for the benefit of the parties to the marriage ... any ante-nuptial or post-nuptial settlement ... made on the parties to the marriage' (see now section 21(2)(*c*), following the amendments made by the Family Law Act 1996). This provision has been put to perhaps unexpected use in the context of pensions.

Brooks v Brooks
[1996] 1 AC 375, [1995] 3 All ER 257, House of Lords

Mr and Mrs Brooks were married in 1977. Mr Brooks ran a building business, through his company, D.E. Brooks Ltd; the couple had a house in Sunningdale, Berkshire. When the marriage broke down in 1989, Mr Brooks was 63 and Mrs Brooks was 54; the assets available to the couple were the house, and several pension schemes of Mr Brooks. On Mrs Brooks' application for ancillary relief, District Judge Plumstead awarded her a substantial lump sum from the sale proceeds of the house, and periodical payments to be secured by an attachment of earnings order against the husband's pensions entitlement under the pension schemes. She also ruled that one of the schemes was a post-nuptial settlement, and made an order varying it to provide the wife with a pension of her own.

There were a number of unusual features in the case. First, the company was a 'one man band' where the husband was in effect the sole shareholder and the only member of the pension scheme. Second, the wife had for some time been company secretary, and therefore as an employee could herself have been a member of the scheme. Finally, there were surplus funds of about £166,000 in the pension scheme beyond what was needed to provide the husband with a pension of the maximum amount permissible under Inland Revenue rules; the rules of the scheme provided that this surplus was to be repaid to the company. The company had in fact ceased trading in 1989 and had been struck of the register. The District Judge's order envisaged that the surplus would be used to provide the wife's pension.

On the husband's appeal from the District Judge's decision, Ewbank J ([1993] Fam 322, [1993] 4 All ER 917, [1993] 3 WLR 548, [1993] 2 FLR 491) upheld the order varying the terms of the pension scheme. The Court of Appeal ([1995] Fam 70, [1994] 4 All ER 1065, [1994] 3 WLR 1292) by a majority did the same.

The decision of the House of Lords on the husband's final appeal ([1995] 3 All ER 257) was eagerly awaited, on the two questions raised by the case: was the scheme a post-nuptial settlement, and, if so, to what extent was that finding dependent upon the unusual facts of the case?

On the first question, Lord Nicholls of Birkenhead, giving the single judgment, upheld the earlier order, but to a limited extent. He held that the court had power to vary the settlement '*so far as it constituted a settlement made by the husband*', and therefore to the extent only of the funds available to him. He had power under the scheme to give directions about the use of his own pension benefit, and could have arranged for part of it to be used for separate provision for her. But the surplus in the scheme belonged to the company, and 'was never brought into the settlement by the husband.'

Accordingly the order was varied to provide that the separate pension for the wife be paid in priority to, and if necessary in diminution of, the husband's pension, rather than out of the surplus.

Lord Nicholls concluded his judgment as follows:

A variation of the scheme along these lines is expected to meet with the approval of the Commissioners of Inland Revenue in this case. In respect of the immediate pension the wife had earnings of her own from the company, paid for her nominal services as the company secretary. These earnings will support a pension for her of the amount in question. So to achieve this purpose, the scheme can be converted to a multi-member scheme. ... If the Inland Revenue approves, it is difficult to see any reason why the Equitable Life should wish to withhold its approval. Likewise with the trustees of the scheme, who are now the husband's accountant and sister. ...

This decision should not be seen as a solution to the overall pensions problem. Not every pension scheme constitutes a marriage settlement. And even when a scheme does fall within the court's jurisdiction to vary a marriage settlement, it would not be right for the court to vary one scheme member's rights to the prejudice of other scheme members. Directing a variation which does not meet with Inland Revenue approval would normally be prejudicial to the rights of the other scheme members. A feature of the instant case is that there is only one scheme member and, moreover, the wife has earnings of her own from the same employer which will sustain provision of an immediate pension for her. If the court is to be able to split pension rights on divorce in the more usual case of a multi-member scheme where the wife has no earnings of her own from the same employer, or to direct the taking out of life insurance, legislation will still be needed.

Thus the House of Lords' decision in *Brooks* will not resolve the problem of pensions in the majority of cases.

Reverting, then, to the moves towards legislative intervention: in September 1993 the Pension Law Review Committee, chaired by Professor Roy Goode QC, reported its findings on occupational pension schemes in *Pensions and Law Reform* (Cm 2342) and endorsed the recommendations of the PMI group. Nevertheless, in its White Paper *Security, Equality, Choice: The Future for Pensions* (June 1994) the Government's response to the question of pension rights on divorce was (para. 1.45):

As the PLRC recognised, the issue of pension rights on divorce is extremely complex. Any change to the current position could have significant implications for pension schemes. ... In any event, there is at present no clear evidence of the extent of the problem. A detailed research programme will be undertaken to ascertain the extent of the problem before the issue is considered further.

The Pensions Bill contained nothing about the problem when it was introduced in the House of Lords in January 1995. However, the issue figured prominently in debates. Baroness Hollis of Heigham argued:

The PMI report outlines three basic ways in which the courts might take [pension] assets into account. The first is offsetting; the second is earmarking; and the third is splitting. ... The first way ... is by offsetting. The courts can do that now; that is, they can offset against the pension, which must remain with the scheme member (who is usually the husband) other assets such as savings or the matrimonial home. The courts can do that now; and very often, all too often, it does not work ... [because] there are insufficient offsetting assets.

Alternatively, even where both the material and the pension assets balance each other out, immediate assets are being set against long-term assets. Therefore in order to keep a pension which he may never live to enjoy, the husband is stripped of his short-term assets such as the matrimonial home and savings. ...

The second route is to earmark so that the pension is divided at the point of retirement. That is uncertain unless one is receiving a pension at the time at which the divorce occurs. What happens when the scheme member changes jobs? Does he carry the earmarking with him to four, five, six different jobs, with the employer having to make a record of that? What happens if the scheme member dies before he is 65 and the scheme deeds allow a widow but not somebody who is divorced to be a beneficiary? What happens if there are two or three spouses each with a charge on a pension but not knowing what they will receive or when, so that they have to wait until the age of 65 to know what are their future prospects. ...

We have offsetting now and it does not work. Earmarking is messy and chancy and leaves all parties insecure. Therefore, what is the right way forward? … It is to divide pension rights at the point of divorce. …

On divorce, the cash value of the pension so far accrued would be calculated precisely as it is now, often several times during a working life, when a scheme member changes jobs and wants his pension rights transferred with him. In other words, in relation to divorce we should be using the well-established procedure which is easily and continually used by scheme professionals and members every time a scheme member changes jobs. …

If that were done, much of the bitterness over financial arrangements on divorce would be avoided. Both parties could get on with the rest of their lives. … It would apply to men and women alike. It would be clean, decent, fair and straightforward, and we could do that now.

As a result of pressure in the House of Lords debate amendments were made to the Pensions Bill, making additions and amendments to the Matrimonial Causes Act 1973 so as to allow the earmarking of pensions. Richard Malone, president of the Pensions Management Institute, commented in *The Times*, 26 August 1995 that the effect of earmarking a pension is:

The husband has all the usual rights of moving the pension around. The divorced partner has no say in that. She may not ever know. She also has to wait until her ex-husband retires to receive an income. He may retire early and get a reduced level of pension. Worse still, he might die, in which case the ex-wife's pension is cut off altogether.

Question

How can concern about pension rights on divorce be consistent with the wish to achieve a clean break wherever possible? Which is more consistent with the clean break, earmarking or splitting?

Finally, as a result of an amendment made to the Family Law Bill during its passage through the House of Lords, the Family Law Act 1996 has made a further amendment to the Matrimonial Causes Act 1973 so as to allow pension splitting. Sections 25B and 25C of that Act now provide as follows:

Pensions

25B. – (1) The matters to which the court is to have regard under section 25(2) above include –

(*a*) in the case of paragraph (*a*), any benefits under a pension scheme which a party to the marriage has or is likely to have, and

(*b*) in the case of paragraph (*h*), any benefits under a pension scheme which, by reason of the dissolution or annulment of the marriage, a party to the marriage will lose the chance of acquiring,

and, accordingly, in relation to benefits under a pension scheme, section 25(2)(*a*) above shall have effect as if 'in the foreseeable future' were omitted.

(2) In any proceedings for a financial provision order under section 22A or 23 above in a case where a party to the marriage has, or is likely to have, any benefit under a pension scheme, the court shall, in addition to considering any other matter which it is required to consider apart from this subsection, consider –

(*a*) whether, having regard to any matter to which it is required to have regard in the proceedings by virtue of subsection (1) above, such an order (whether deferred or not) should be made, and

(*b*) where the court determines to make such an order, how the terms of the order should be affected, having regard to any such matter,

(*c*) in particular, where the court determines to make such an order, whether the order should provide for the accrued rights of the party with pension rights ('the pension rights') to be divided between that party and the other party in such a way as to reduce the pension rights of the party with those rights and to create pension rights for the other party.

(3) The following provisions apply where, having regard to any benefits under a pension scheme, the court determines to make an order under section 23 above.

(4) To the extent to which the order is made having regard to any benefits under a pension scheme, the order may require the trustees or managers of the pension scheme in question, if at any time any payment in respect of any benefits under the scheme become due to the party with pension rights, to make a payment for the benefit of the other party.

(5) The amount of any payment which, by virtue of subsection (4) above, the trustees or managers are required to make under the order at any time shall not exceed the amount of the payment which is due at that time to the party with pension rights.

(6) Any such payment by the trustees or managers –

(*a*) shall discharge so much of the trustees or managers liability to the party with pension rights as corresponds to the amount of the payment, and

(*b*) shall be treated for all purposes as a payment made by the party with pension rights in or towards the discharge of his liability under the order.

(7) Where the party with pension rights may require any benefits which he has or is likely to have under the scheme to be commuted, the order may require him to commute the whole or part of those benefits; and this section applies to the payment of any amount commuted in pursuance of the order as it applies to other payments in respect of benefits under the scheme.

(8) If a pensions adjustment order under subsection (2)(*c*) above is made, the pension rights shall be reduced and pension rights of the other party shall be created in the prescribed manner with benefits payable on prescribed conditions, except that the court shall not have the power –

(*a*) to require the trustees or managers of the scheme to provide benefits under their own scheme if they are able and willing to create the rights for the other party by making a transfer payment to another scheme and the trustees and managers of that other scheme are able and willing to accept such a payment and to create those rights; or

(*b*) to require the trustees or managers of the scheme to make a transfer to another scheme –

(i) if the scheme is an unfunded scheme (unless the trustees or managers are able and willing to make such a transfer payment); or

(ii) in prescribed circumstances.

...

Pensions: lump sums

25C. – (1) The power of the court under section 22A or 23 above to order a party to a marriage to pay a lump sum to the other party includes, where the benefits which the party with pension rights has or is likely to have under a pension scheme include any lump sum payable in respect of his death, power to make any of the following provision by the order.

(2) The court may –

(*a*) if the trustees or managers of the pension scheme in question have power to determine the pension to whom the sum, or any part of it, is to be paid, require them to pay the whole or part of that sum, when it becomes due, to the other party,

(*b*) if the party with pension rights has power to nominate the person to whom the sum, or any part of it, is to be paid, require the party with pension rights to nominate the other party in respect of the whole of part of that sum,

(*c*) in any other case, require the trustees or managers of the pension scheme in question to pay the whole or part of that sum, when it becomes due, for the benefit of the other party instead of to the person to whom, apart from the order, it would be paid.

(3) Any payment by the trustees or managers under an order made under section 22A or 23 above by virtue of this section shall discharge so much of the trustees, or managers, liability in respect of the party with pension rights as corresponds to the amount of the payment.

Question

Upon what principles do you think the courts should make orders splitting pensions under s. 25B(2)(*c*) of the Matrimonial Causes Act 1973?

5 Empirical evidence

In most cases, the financial aspects of divorce are settled between the parties, usually with but sometimes without the help of lawyers; as we have seen

(Chapter 7, above), in a small but growing number of cases financial arrangements are the subject of mediation. Of the very few cases that are decided in court hearings, only a tiny proportion are reported. Research in recent years has examined, not only what actually happens to individuals after divorce, but also how that outcome is arrived at. The behaviour of divorce lawyers has been a particular focus of interest. The conclusion of Jackson and her colleagues (1993) in their study of English and Scottish solicitors was:

> It is clear that the role of solicitors in post-divorce financial arrangements is characterized by a high level of negotiation and compromise. ... [W]e found universal concern for the position of the other side and a strong desire for compromise. Whether this amounts to legal practitioners assuming the role of mediators is a question too broad for the ambit of this paper. Nonetheless, it would seem that family law represents a highly distinctive branch of legal practice, and the significance of the practitioners' role should not be underestimated.

In *Simple Quarrels* (1994), Gwynn Davis, Stephen Cretney and Jean Collins undertook an extensive study of the conduct of litigation on financial questions in divorce, and of the expectations and attitudes of solicitors and of their clients. The picture that emerges reinforces the impression that here is a 'distinctive branch' of the legal profession; it also reveals the diversity within it, and perhaps some unexpected features.

Compare these two views of the relevance of the law in this area (the authors have changed the names of clients studied in the book):

> This was how Mr Daniels's solicitor assessed the situation when we first spoke to him:
>
> > 'Let's just say the equity is £42,000 – it's probably a bit more – as a starting point, two thirds/one-third – automatic starting point. So if we divide that, that comes to about £14,000 for him, taking one third. We know that she can raise £16,000, so I will immediately go to the chap on the other side, and perhaps ask for ... I'll ask for £16,000, hoping I'll end up with £14,000, and then I can sell it to Mr Daniels and say : "Look, that's what the court will give you." I may be wrong here, because I think if I were him [the other solicitor] I'd come back and say: "Look, in normal circumstances I can see the approach you're adopting, but here we have [handicapped son] who is different, and this is a complication. We can't say, but [son] could put off somebody wanting to marry my client, [son] could really stop her getting full-time work, [son] may be a liability until he's 25–30, he may need a home for the rest of his life." I've said to Mr Daniels already : "Don't be too sure that you're going to get something." '
>
> Whilst this solicitor could not predict the final outcome (Mr Daniels's barrister agreed a lump sum of £7,500, in fact) and whilst he recognized and to some extent relished the bargaining element in the negotiation, he none the less regarded it as bargaining within narrow limits. The fact that there was an element of uncertainty did not dissuade him from making proposals. ...
>
> Many solicitors with whom we discussed this point likewise implied, or revealed in their case management, that as far as they were concerned the outcome of ancillary relief proceedings was wholly unpredictable. It was almost as if legal doctrine had no impact upon the actual administration of family law. This was the view of one solicitor, based in Newport:
>
> > 'I suppose it's a terrible reflection of how many things are done on the basis of nothing more than rough horse-trading, with only a very passing shadow of reference to case law. When one reads the models, the ways in which you should really deal with financial relief, they are so technical and so precise. In 9,999 cases out of a thousand it's all down to a wing and a prayer and what you can deal with off the back of a truck.'

Question

From what you have read so far, which of these two was right? Can we say that either was right or wrong?

Turning to the mediator's role in this context, John Haynes in *The Fundamentals of Family Mediation* describes this as 'being a mediator and not a judge', and as 'helping clients define a solvable problem':

When people have an intractable dispute that appears unresolvable, the mediator enters to assist them to settle the dispute by negotiating a mutually acceptable agreement. However, a significant part of the problem is the inability of parties to agree on the content of the dispute. Indeed, they often have quite different versions of its nature and history.

When the mediator first meets with the disputants each person has a story to tell. These stories consist of three parts – a version of the events, a complaint about the other, and a problem definition.

In specific versions of the events and of the past, the basic data may be similar, or even the same, but the interpretation each places on the facts colours their view of the situation. Each version is designed to show the mediator how good he or she is; how each is the innocent victim of the situation.

The second part, the complaint, is designed to show the mediator how bad the other is.

The hallmark of the definition of the problem is that each person defines it in such a way that it can be solved only by a change in the behaviour or position of the other. A's problem can only be solved by a change in B, and B's problem can only be solved by a change in A.

These three elements represent each party's definition of the problem. Their inability to agree on the content of the dispute means that the mediator's role in the early stages is to obtain agreement on the problem to be resolved. She helps the clients to arrive at a mutual and neutral definition of a problem which, when solved, benefits all participants.

Neither A nor B will change unilaterally, nor will either change to conform with the other's definition of the problem. The mediator's task is to help them discard their individual problem definitions and adopt a mutual and common definition. Only then can problem solving begin. ...

While mediators cannot avoid all legal questions or emotive behaviour, they can limit the non-useful dialogue. Their primary method is to focus on what they believe is relevant to the clients. Mediators test and clarify the difference between relevant and non-useful information. They clarify for the clients what is important, directing them away from emotive behaviour towards self-interests contained in the information about the problem and solutions to it. ...

Figure 1.2: Sorting information in mediation

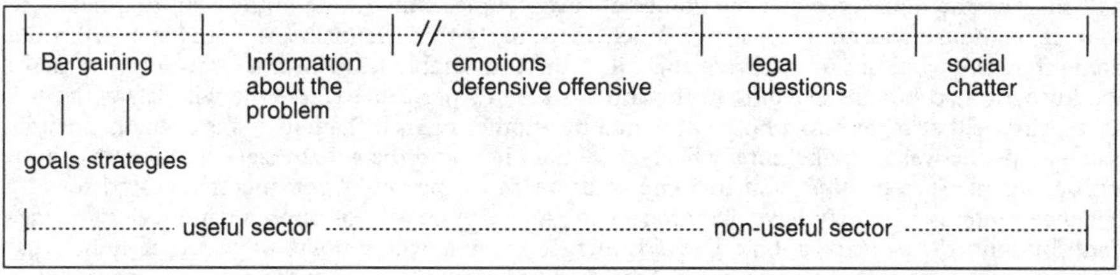

The client behaviour is divided into sectors. The right-hand sector is non-useful client information and the left-hand sector is useful client information. The mediator looks for useful data – information about the problem, the clients' bargaining goals and strategies. These data are collected and noted and form the basis of the next line of questioning. Client information that falls into the right-hand sector is ignored unless the client is persistent. Faced with client persistence, the mediator attempts to deal with the behaviour by acknowledging it and using other strategies to limit it.

Questions

(i) Why is legal material regarded as irrelevant in this process? Should it be?
(ii) Imagine yourself involved in a dispute about maintenance and capital provision on divorce. By what procedures would you like it to be resolved?

We now consider the outcomes of these procedures, what is needed is hard evidence of what actually happens. Evidence began to emerge in the 1980s, and is still relevant in the absence of more up-to-date information.

Eekelaar and MacLean in *Maintenance after Divorce* (1986) undertook to describe the present financial circumstances of a nationally representative sample of those who have divorced in England and Wales since the introduction of no-fault divorce in 1971. They chose an 'omnibus survey' which approached a quota sample of 8,000 individuals in England and Wales in May 1981; from this they were given permission to approach 92 of the men and 184 of the women. As the researchers admit, 'our final sample of 276 individuals is, of course, relatively small. It was, however, central to our strategy that it should be as closely representative of the divorcing population at large as we could make it. We therefore chose not to distort our original sample by interviewing additional cases with particular characteristics'.

They comment in detail on the housing position:

A distinction needs to be drawn between occupants of local authority housing at the time of separation and those enjoying other types of housing provision. In the former case, the childless invariably left the accommodation. But where there were children, 79 per cent of the women interview respondents (n = 52) and 30 per cent of the men (n = 21) stayed; all but one of the men having custody of the children. ... Of the few women who left, three returned (with their children) to their own families, four moved into a house with their new partners; and in one case both parents left and were re-housed by the local authority. For these people, then, housing circumstances in themselves played no significant role in altering their living standards on divorce. The effects of divorce would primarily be felt in respect to income. A similar pattern was found among the long-term mothers interviewed in 1984. Eight out of the ten in local authority housing at separation stayed there, the other two moving into owner-occupation (one with married children and one buying her council house).

But when we look at the housing outcome with respect to the owner-occupiers, a more complex picture emerges. ... childless and children divorces share one feature regarding the home. In almost half of each category, the owner-occupied home was sold on divorce. In the case of the childless, the reason for the sale seems to have been to allow the wife to realize her half-share in the house, for half the homes of such couples which were in their joint names were sold. If the house was not sold, it was much more likely that the husband would stay on in the home than the wife, but in the event the wife would invariably leave with a lump sum payment; the husband had bought her out. In the three cases (13 per cent) where the wife left without a share, she went straight into a home provided by another man. If the house was in the husband's name alone, he was overwhelmingly likely to remain in it and the wife to leave without any lump sum payment. It is possible that in some of those cases the wife went uncompensated for any beneficial interest she may have acquired in the home by reason of direct or indirect monetary contributions to its acquisition. The advantage, from a wife's point of view, of joint legal ownership is clear, and the message of these findings seems to be that for childless marriages, a lump sum payment made to the wife is likely to be in the form of strict compensation for the transfer to the husband of a property interest.

It is striking that owner-occupied homes are just as likely to be sold in the case of divorces involving dependent children as where the marriage was childless, despite the well-established policy of the courts that one of the primary goals of divorce settlement is to secure accommodation for the children, usually by keeping them in the matrimonial home. [See *H v H (family provision remarriage)* [1975] Fam 9, [1975] 1 All ER 367.] Are the children of divorcees who live in the owner-occupier sector subject to greater disruption than those of divorcees who live in public-sector housing?

In a number of cases it might be unnecessary to keep the home for the children because they and the wife will be moving into accommodation provided by another man. In four (28 per cent) of the cases where the house was sold the woman moved in with a new partner. So in over a quarter of the cases where the home was sold, no accommodation problem for the children arose. What of the other cases? It seems that the sales in these cases might either have been desired by the caregiving parent wanting to move from the area, or forced on her by the financial situation. This can be deduced from the fact that the wife stayed on in the house only once (3 per cent) in the childless cases, but did so in *one-quarter* of the children cases, irrespective of whether the house was in joint names or in the husband's name alone. Put another way, the wife stayed in half of the cases where the home was not sold. The reason for this is undoubtedly to provide accommodation for the children, and there is no reason to believe that this would not have happened in those cases where the house was sold were it not for the fact that the wife desired the sale or had it forced on her. Indeed, a small number of the sales (10 per cent) were in fact the result of foreclosure by the mortgagee. Others may well have taken place to prevent this eventuality.

It is at this point, of course, that the difficulties which the families with children experience over income have direct impact on their housing conditions. Yet, about three-quarters of the divorced mothers, still single and with dependent children, who had been in owner-occupation at the time of their separation were still living in *the private sector* at the time of interview. The lump sum acquired by the sale, or support from the former husband, or payments of mortgage interest by the supplementary benefit authorities, cushioned the *extent* of the deterioration in their housing circumstances; or, at least, the degree to which they needed to go to the public housing authorities for assistance. It is plausible to suppose that a move from the private sector will frequently cause greater social disruption, especially as regards the children's school environment, than moves within a sector. Our data showed that, of the women who moved, half (seven) were able to buy in the private sector (three of them later remarried). Only three (21 per cent) moved into public housing.

Our findings regarding the housing circumstances of divorcing men fail to show any disturbing degrees of hardship. In the childless cases, the man either kept the house or sold it, taking his share. Even where there were children, he stayed on in the house in one-quarter of the cases. Where the wife stayed, we found no evidence that she was joined by a cohabitee or new husband. The pattern seems clearly to be that, where a new partner enters the scene, he will provide a home for the wife and children. Where, in the divorces involving dependent children, the home was sold, the husband invariably took his share. There were, however, a few cases (thirteen (22 per cent) of those where either the house was sold or the wife remained in it) where the husband left without any apparent immediate compensation for his capital loss. However, four involved a 'Mesher' arrangement whereby the house is settled on trust for sale for both parents but sale is postponed until the youngest child reaches a certain age (usually eighteen or on completion of full-time education), or until a court order is made. Thus the husband is not deprived of his capital; his enjoyment of it is simply postponed. Of the seven cases where the husband left without taking any share of the asset, three forewent their share in discharge of their support obligation, one went to a new partner with a house and we had no information on the others. It should be remembered, of course, that when it is the man who leaves, it will usually be very difficult for the wife to raise sufficient capital to pay him a lump sum. Her inferior earning power and commitments to the children effectively preclude such a course.

The long-term mothers in owner-occupation at the time of separation were perhaps more firmly established in this sector. Even so, in half of the cases the home was sold and the proceeds shared enabled the women to buy a smaller property. Of the cases where the house was not sold, in half the house was occupied in lieu of maintenance (in one case with a 'Mesher' agreement), and in the two remaining cases the wife purchased her husband's interest, one with her own resources and the other with parental help.

We should conclude this review of the economic conditions of families after divorce by remarking on the significance of housing provision. Were it not for the relative security provided by public-sector housing, the position of many divorced single mothers would be far worse than it is. As we have seen, there is no potential in income transfers to substitute for its absence. We might make the same observation with respect to health care. It is fortunately not essential for these mothers to rely on income provision, from the state or from the absent parent, to meet the medical expenses of their children. These fall on the community through the national health service. But even outside the ambit of community-financed services, we note that, as far as accommodation is concerned, the position of mothers living in the private sector is not totally bleak. Most managed to stay in that sector, even if precariously. The attention given to the accommodation of children by judicial policy seems, according to our data, to have borne some fruit and, in so far as it has done so, has reduced the extent to which the receipt of income maintenance is critical to the most fundamental needs of these families [see Chapter 4, above]. The Social Security Review of 1985 revealed that the government was concerned about the burden which housing-related benefit (whether by way of rate rebates, payment of rent and mortgage interest, and of water and heating charges) was placing on the social security budget (*Reform of Social Security* (1985)). The implications of any erosion of these benefits for families broken by divorce do not seem to have been considered. The result might be to throw them into greater dependence on maintenance from the absent parent to undermine the already precarious degree to which stability in housing those in owner-occupation has been achieved and to put new pressure on the public sector.

Questions

(i) What conclusions do you draw from Eekelaar and Maclean's work?
(ii) Is dependence on maintenance from the absent parent a good thing or a bad thing? (See Chapter 4, above).
(iii) Ruth Deech in *Divorce Studies and Empirical Studies* (1990) has hard words to say:

Likewise, Eekelaar and Maclean's figures in *Maintenance After Divorce* do not assess, and overlook the value of lump sums and property transferred after divorce. In emphasising weekly payments, they are, by definition, but without sufficient clarification of the bias, concentrating on and counting the awards to the wives of poorer husbands. Of those that responded to the Eekelaar and Maclean request for a sample, more than half were in local authority housing. Where childless owner-occupiers were surveyed, conclusions were drawn from a total of only 27 houses, a number too small, it is suggested, for broad conclusions to be drawn. There are widely accepted scientific criteria for the taking of samples and their sizes, and many small exercises in family law would not be accepted as valid for national purposes by professional statisticians.

The preconceptions relating to policy held by researchers are in general spelled out by them but, it is submitted, detract from the wider significance of the figures gathered in support. A clear example of this is provided by Eekelaar and Maclean's study. There is a presumption throughout that a family unit, impliedly the first family, remains bonded despite divorce and therefore perpetually liable to each other after divorce. Moreover, the authors apparently disapprove of working mothers. It used to be argued that divorced mothers could not be expected to seek self-support because of the unemployment rates. Now that that argument is less tenable, child welfare is cited instead.

Has she a point?

The debate continues. In their reply to Deech, *Divorce Law and Empirical Studies – A Reply* (1991) Eekelaar and Maclean say:

Where small-scale studies do produce statistical data, it is well understood that the scope for statistical analysis is restricted. ... Nevertheless, if a number of small studies, using different methods, produce similar results, generalised conclusions may sometimes reasonably be drawn. ... Deech ... rightly points out that the data on the housing circumstances of childless owner-occupiers was too restrictive to allow 'broad conclusions to be drawn'. We had expressly recognised this ... yet confidence even in such small numbers can grow from learning that a much larger survey by the Australian Institute of Family Studies showed that a very similar percentage of women had left the home after the divorce. There were many other similarities between the Australian findings and our own, and between both these studies and another small-scale study, using different methods, by Davis, Macleod and Murch. Is this mere coincidence? ...

Deech says that we make 'a presumption throughout that a family unit, impliedly the first family, remains bonded despite divorce and therefore perpetually liable to each other after divorce.' But two chapters which set out *arguments* for principles upon which child support and spousal maintenance might be grounded demonstrate, not only that our position bears no relation to the presumption attributed to us, but that any *preconceptions* we might have held when we began the research have now, as a result of the experience of the research and principled argument, fructified into *conceptions*.

In 1987 the Australian Law Reform Commission's Report No 39, *Matrimonial Property* summarised the results of two major research projects:

84. The research projects. Two major projects were undertaken. With the co-operation of the Family Court, the Commission conducted a survey of property proceedings in all Registries of the

Family Court of Australia and the Family Court of Western Australia. The Report on that survey under the title 'A Survery of Family Court Property Cases in Australia' was published in July 1985. It is summarised in this chapter. The other project goes beyond a study of court proceedings, to examine property and income arrangements between spouses during marriage, the respective economic circumstances of husbands, wives and children after separation and divorce, and the experience and attitudes of divorced people relating to the law. This project, 'The Economic Consequences of Marriage Breakdown in Australia', was conducted by the Australian Institute of Family Studies in co-operation with the Family Court of Australia and the Commission. It is based on a detailed survey of a large sample of divorced people. The Institute's report on the project was published in 1986.[5]

Introducing the findings of the second project, the Report states:

143. Other studies. Recent research projects in the United States and England concluded that divorced women and the children in their custody suffer economic adversity which is only likely to be relieved significantly by a new marriage. Lenore Weitzman undertook a study of a sample of divorced people in California where, since 1970, a strict rule of equal property division has applied, together with attenuated maintenance rights. Her research suggested that one year after divorce, the living standard of former husbands had risen, while that of former wives and their children had fallen sharply. In England, Mavis MacLean and John Eekelaar found that female-headed single-parent families suffered a decline in living standards that was not shared by divorced people without the care of children, or by those who had remarried. These projects reinforced the Commission's view that it was essential to examine the situation of divorcing people in Australia, before concluding that as a general rule, equal sharing of property is fair sharing. The project which was undertaken for this purpose is the first systematic study in Australia of the economic consequences of divorce and, so far as the Commission is aware, it is the most comprehensive study of its type ever undertaken in any country. …

146. … The study concentrated on four components of standard of living: property, income, housing, and employment. A central hypothesis of the study was that these four components were closely inter-related and that a focus on property alone would yield a misleading picture. Particular attention was given to the changes in these measures of standard of living from the year preceding separation through to the time of the interview up to six years later, and to the extent to which these changes were modified by repartnering and responsibilities for children.

Table 12 on p. 364 shows the research findings on changes in household income.

The researchers conclude:

165. Disparities. While there is considerable individual variation, there are clear underlying trends. Former husbands and former wives who had established a new household with a partner and children had returned, on average, to roughly the pre-separation level. Men living alone, or as sole parents, or with a new partner with no children, had considerably improved their living standards. However, the most arresting finding of the survey is that women living alone or as sole parents sustained a drastic fall in living standards. Substantial numbers were below the poverty line – 41% of women living alone and 35% of sole parents. These women were rarely 'asset-rich but income-poor' as, despite the upward economic bias in the sample, 92% received property below the limit which entitles a person to the full social security benefit.

166. Major reason. The major explanation for the disparity of living standards after separation is that a husband's income earning capacity is generally not adversely affected either by marriage or separation. Wives generally emerge from a marriage with a lack of sustained workforce experience, resulting from child rearing. Of 456 women in the survey, all but 13 had worked at some time during the marriage, but only nine reported uninterrupted workforce participation. Women left the workforce predominantly to bear and rear children; many had repeated breaks for this reason (54% of responses). Other breaks were often for marriage-related reasons. Men

---

5. [P. McDonald, *Settling Up: Property and Income Distribution on Divorce in Australia*, 1986, Prentice-Hall of Australia (AIFS 1986).]

Table 12: Comparisons of household incomes* for the pre-separation period and the time of interview, by family type at interview and sex of respondent

Family type in 1984	Men				Women			
	alone	couple, no children	couple with children	sole parent	alone	couple, no children	couple with children	sole parent
Indicator								
Median excess/deficit over pre-separation level in dollars per week	+$72	$153	−$6	+$69	−$84	+$36	−$6	−$86
Per cent better off in 1984	75	75	47	69	29	**	48	22
Per cent worse off in 1984	25	25	53	31	71	**	52	78
Per cent below poverty line	6	2	12	12	41	**	8	35
Per cent 0–20% above poverty line	7	3	13	3	15	**	16	19
Per cent in various family types in 1984	33	20	30	10	8***	5	28	55
		+7 per cent 'with others'				+4 per cent 'with others'		

- Both pre-selection and 1984 incomes are adjusted using equivalence scales from the Commission of Inquiry into Poverty (1975). Pre-separation income is adjusted to 1984 values. Incomes are net after the payment of tax and the payment or receipt of maintenance by survey respondents.

** Not reliable due to small numbers.

*** These are all older women.

tended to increase their earning capacity during the marriage whereas discontinuity of work tended to diminish women's occupational progression. Upon separation husbands retained their income earning capacity, while wives generally had the major responsibility for the care of children. Maintenance and social security do not compensate for the disparity.

167. **Effect of wife's pre-separation income.** The women most likely to avoid poverty after separation were those who had a new partner and those who, immediately before separation, had personal incomes that permitted at least marginal independence for themselves and their children (estimated as $135 a week, being the supporting parent's benefit and family allowance for a single parent with two children in May 1984). Two thirds of the women who were single in 1984 and who had been dependent on their husbands immediately before separation (earning less than $30 a week in 1984 dollars), or had supplemented their husbands' earnings (earning $30–$134) had fallen beneath the level of 20% above the poverty line. Three quarters were receiving social security benefits. Many of the women who were earning supplementary incomes prior to separation were no longer working in 1984, presumably because of the costs of child care and the povery traps associated with the supporting parent's benefit.

The researchers also looked at the distribution of property:

182. **Strong determinants.** Three factors emerged as strong and consistent determinants of the wife's share even after the effects of other characteristics were taken into account. These were

- *Custody of the children.* The custodial parent received a greater share, but the additional share that the wife received if she was the custodial parent was much less than the share she lost if the husband was the custodial parent. The difference in shares between female custodial parents and female non-custodial parents after controlling for other determinants was 19.4% of the total property based on women's reports, and 24.6% based on men's reports.
- *The percentage that basic assets represented of total wealth.* The wife's share declined as the level of non-basic assets as a proportion of total wealth increased. As the percentage of non-basic assets was closely related to the overall level of wealth, this also meant that the higher the level of wealth, the lower was the wife's share.
- *Occupation of the matrimonial home in the initial period following separation.* The person who remained in the matrimonial home tended to receive a greater share than the one who left. On average, continued occupation of the matrimonial home led to an increase of between 15 and 20 percentage points in the share that a person received.

The effect of continued occupation of the matrimonial home is the more remarkable when it is considered for the younger couples in conjunction with custody. If the wife stayed in the house and had custody of the children, her share was about 8 percentage points above the average share for women. If she left the house and had custody her share was about 6 percentage points below the average for women. If she left and her husband had custody, her share was 18 percentage points below the average.

The researchers comment:

186. Significance of these findings. Several interpretations can be made:

- *Basic contributions.* Despite the emphasis in the present law upon individualised assessment of the parties' relative contributions, variations in contributions to household tasks and to the value of the house and contributions through workforce participation make little or no difference to the shares of property. Pervasive differences in spouses' perceptions of relative contributions suggest that the process of assessment of these basic contributions is impractical and aggravates conflict between the parties, as well as being ineffectual in determining the outcome.
- *Contributions to non-basic assets.* Contributions which do affect the shares of property are those related to non-basic assets such as businesses and farms, superannuation and investments. As these contributions mainly relate to the activities of husbands, variations in the contributions of wives play almost no part in property division.
- *Post-separation factors.* The only factor reflecting the future needs of the parties which has a significant bearing on the outcome is the need of the custodial parent. The effect of the marriage on the post-separation income earning capacity of husbands and wives is not a significant factor, even though the sample was drawn from groups where this factor was most likely to be strong.
- *Occupation of home immediately after separation.* This is a highly significant factor, carrying even more weight than custody. Yet it cannot be aligned with any of the factors prescribed by the Family Law Act. One explanation may be that the occupant of the house cannot raise the money to totally compensate the one who has left. An alternative, more subtle possibility is that departure from the matrimonial home is usually associated with having made the decision to end the marriage. Persons leaving may concede more in order to buy out of their marriages, while those who remain may press for more because they see themselves as not being responsible for the ending of the marriage. If the person who decides to separate manages to stay in the home, this is an indication of that person's power in the relationship, which may extend to the ultimate property division. This latter interpretation is supported to some extent by the fact that even when the house is ultimately sold at distribution, the one who remained in the house initially after separation benefits by about 8 percentage points of the overall property. This, however, could also merely indicate that at distribution, this party has a need for new housing because the matrimonial home is to be sold. It seems likely that to some extent, this factor is an indicator of the state of the relationship between spouses, as reflected in the decision to separate and their negotiations over property and financial arrangements. The question is whether the prominence of this factor shows that the flexibility of the present law helps couples in their negotiations or whether it shows that this degree of flexibility leads to injustice for those with less power or greater willingness to make concessions in order to reach a settlement.

In conclusion:

238. The strong influence upon the outcome of the occupation of the home immediately after separation has no policy basis. It suggests that there may be a tendency in the present law to permit results which are unfair to spouses with less negotiating power or a greater willingness to make concessions. This could be alleviated by a clearer prescription of the process of reasoning by which the spouses' shares in the value of their property are to be determined and the factors to be taken into account. This can be done without unduly restricting the scope for parties to reach mutually acceptable arrangements by negotiation.

239. ... The findings on the influence upon the outcome of the parties' respective contributions to property and to the welfare of the family reinforce the doubts raised in chapter 5 about the merit of individualised assessment of contributions, at least in marriages of the kind included in this survey. The only contributions which strongly influence property division are those relating to non-basic assets such as businesses and farms, superannuation and investments. If marriage is to be regarded as a co-operative relationship between parties of equal status, it must be asked why contributions to non-basic assets should have greater significance than other forms of contributions to property or to the welfare of the family.

A major study by Jonathan Bradshaw and Jane Millar, *Lone Parent Families in the UK* (1991) provides further detailed information relating both to maintenance and housing enjoyed by the parties after divorce. They summarise their findings as follows:

Maintenance

This is the first survey that has provided evidence on the proportion of all lone parents who received payments from the absent parents and the level of payments they receive. It has shown that 29 per cent of all lone parents at any one time receive regular payments from the absent parent and that the proportion varies with the marital status of the lone parent and whether or not they receive income support or are employed. Only 13 per cent of single lone parents on income support receive maintenance. One in five lone parents not receiving maintenance say they do not want it and a further 29 per cent think that the absent parent is unemployed or cannot afford to pay. Two thirds of lone parents receiving maintenance were receiving it in respect of their children only. The level of maintenance is variable but is low. The modal payment is £10 per week and the mean payment per child about £16 per week. (This was at a time when DSS expected the absent parents to pay the family premium, the lone parent premium and the children rates: this totals £22.15 per child per week for children under 11 in a one child family.) Multivariate analysis was not particularly successful in producing a reliable model which predicted whether lone parents received maintenance. Only about a third of lone parents receiving no maintenance thought that the absent parent could pay anything. Among those lone parents who knew the circumstances of the absent parent it was estimated that 41 per cent of those paying nothing could pay something. Sixty five per cent of the lone parents who had received income support had been asked for the name and address of the absent parent. Forty six per cent had given DSS the details and a further 21 per cent said they would now give details if asked. Eleven per cent who had been asked had refused and a further 13 per cent said they would refuse if asked. The main reasons for not giving the details was that they did not know where the absent parents were or did not want to have anything more to do with them. Only 17 per cent of those receiving less than £10 per week gave our interviewer the name and address of the absent parent. ...

Housing

The housing consequences of lone parenthood are profound. Fifty-eight per cent had to move following the breakdown of their relationship. Over half of those who moved thought that their accommodation was better than it had been before and only 25 per cent thought it was worse. Only 17 per cent of the sample were dissatisfied with their present housing.

Lone parents are very dependent on public sector housing. More lone parents come from local authority accommodation and the majority of those who move either pass through or eventually are housed by local authorities. It is a credit to public sector housing that satisfaction is as high as it is. The survey confirms previous research evidence that there is a shift downmarket following relationship breakdown. However it appears that absent parents experience this as much as lone parents. Absent parents are less likely to remain in owner occupied or local authority accommodation and they are also more likely to drift into households shared with others. In particular they are likely to go back to their parents.

Lone parents who moved tended to have had to move more than once in order to find a satisfactory housing solution and many of them had passed through episodes of living with relatives, or in temporary local authority or voluntary accommodation. Some lone parents had moved a number of times in a short while and 41 per cent of tenants had experienced rent arrears at some time since separation.

Question

Are you surprised by their conclusion?

The *General Household Survey 1993* (published 1995) considers first the general pattern of housing tenure over the previous two decades (Figure 3A, below), and then the relationship between divorce, re-marriage and housing tenure. It is claimed that:

'Almost two-thirds of divorced people who were owner-occupiers prior to separation were also owner-occupiers one year after divorce and almost three-quarters of those whose matrimonial home was rented were still living in rented accommodation one year after divorce. ... Twenty per cent of former owner-occupiers and 22% of former tenants had ceased to be householders in their own right one year after divorce. ... Men were more likely than women to have changed their tenure. ... Those whose tenure was unchanged a year after divorce, were unlikely to have changed their tenure later.'

These conclusions are represented in the following two tables (pp. 368–9, below). Of the second, the authors of the survey comment that the data should be viewed with caution because the time lapse between the point one year after divorce and the date of interview could vary from months to several years.

Figure 3A Tenure: Great Britain, 1971–93

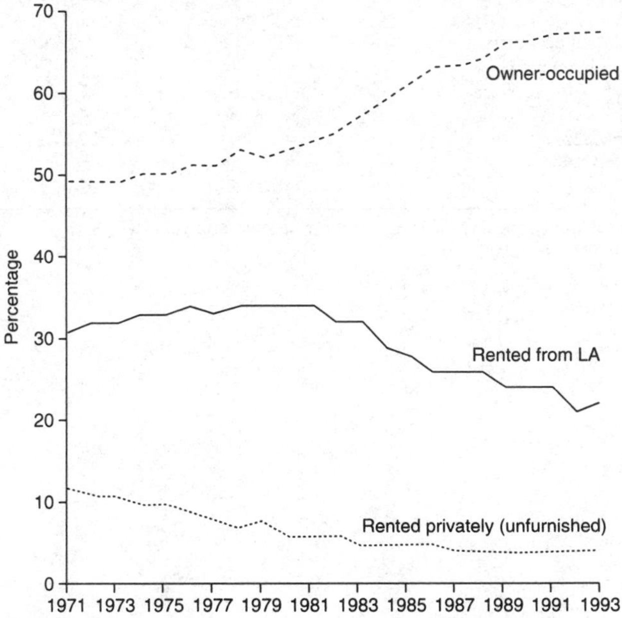

Table 3.23 Tenure one year after divorce by tenure of the former matrimonial home by sex

Divorced persons aged 20–59* *Great Britain: 1991–93 combined*

Tenure one year after divorce	Tenure of the former matrimonial home		
	Owner-occupied	Rented	Total
	%	%	%
Men			
Owner-occupied, owned outright	6	0	4
Owner-occupied, with mortgage	55	8	37
Rented from local authority, New Town or housing association†	3	40	17
Other rented	11	20	15
Not a householder	25	32	27
Base = 100%	*405*	*254*	*659*
	%	%	%
Women			
Owner-occupied, owned outright	10	1	6
Owner-occupied, with mortgage	57	6	37
Rented from local authority, New Town or housing association†	11	67	33
Other rented	5	11	7
Not a householder	18	16	17
Base = 100%	*672*	*438*	*1110*
	%	%	%
Total			
Owner-occupied, owned outright	8	0	5
Owner-occupied, with mortgage	56	7	37
Rented from local authority, New Town or housing association†	8	57	27
Other rented	8	14	10
Not a householder	20	22	21
Base = 100%	*1077*	*692*	*1769*

* Divorced since the beginning of 1980, and for at least one year.

† Includes Scottish Homes.

Table 3.26 Current tenure by tenure one year after divorce by sex

Divorced persons aged 20–59* *Great Britain: 1991–93 combined*

Current tenure	Tenure one year after divorce			
	Owner-occupied	Rented	Not a householder	Total
	%	%	%	%
Men				
Owner-occupied, owned outright	8	1	0	4
Owner-occupied, with mortgage	79	20	25	46
Rented from local authority, New Town or housing association†	1	45	19	20
Other rented	3	20	7	10
Not a householder	8	13	49	21
Base = 100%	*262*	*211*	*177*	*650*
	%	%	%	
Women				
Owner-occupied, owned outright	13	1	6	7
Owner-occupied, with mortgage	75	13	33	43
Rented from local authority, New Town or housing association†	4	71	28	35
Other rented	2	8	6	5
Not a householder	5	6	26	9
Base = 100%	*470*	*444*	*187*	*1101*
	%	%	%	
Total				
Owner-occupied, owned outright	12	1	3	6
Owner-occupied, with mortgage	77	16	29	44
Rented from local authority, New Town or housing association†	3	63	24	30
Other rented	3	12	7	7
Not a householder	6	9	37	14
Base = 100%	*732*	*655*	*364*	*1751*

* Divorced since the beginning of 1980, and for at least one year.

† Includes Scottish Homes.

Question

Do these data shed any more light upon the questions considered by Eekelaar and Maclean, and by the Australian researchers?

What is needed now is a more large scale survey of the financial effects of divorce after the implementation of the Child Support Act 1991 – which has an effect, of course, upon both housing and income for both partners.

Finally, research also reveals the gap between the perceptions and expectations of many members of the public and the reality of what happens after divorce.

Research on the reasons acceptable as justification for alimony payments (periodical payments) was carried out in 1978 in Los Angeles County, California by Lenore Weitzman and Ruth Dixon, *The Alimony Myth: Does no Fault Divorce Make a Difference* (1980). Weitzman summarises the findings in the following manner in *The Divorce Revolution* (1985):

Table 1: Attitudes toward alimony
From interviews with divorced men and women, Los Angeles County, California. 1978

	Percentage who agree (Weighted Sample)*	
	Women (n = 111)†	Men (n = 112)
	(Percentage)	
A. A woman deserves alimony if she has helped her husband get ahead because they are really *partners* in his work	68	54
B. A woman does not deserve alimony if she had an *affair* and was unfaithful to her husband	23	40
C. A woman deserves alimony for at least a year or two so she can *adjust* to the divorce	31	21
D. A woman deserves alimony if she wants to go back to school or to be *retrained* so that she can get a good job to support herself	73	52
E. A woman deserves alimony if she's been married a long time and is *too old* to get a good job	87	66
F. A woman deserves alimony if she has young *children* and wants to stay home to care for them	67	63
G. A woman does not deserve alimony if she can go to work and support herself	65	85
H. A woman deserves alimony if her husband left her for another woman	29	39
I. A woman deserves alimony if she is *disabled* and can't support herself	94	87
J. A woman deserves alimony because when she got married her *husband promised to* support her for the rest of her life	9	3
K. A woman deserves alimony because her husband should *pay her* back for her years of work as a homemaker and/or mother	25	19
L. A woman deserves alimony because she can never recapture the years she has given to her marriage and the *opportunities* she *missed* to have a career of her own	20	4

* The interview sample was weighted to reflect the characteristics of the total divorcing population in Los Angeles County.

† n refers to the number of cases (i.e., interviews) on which the percentages are based.

Questions

(i) How many of these 12 statements do you agree with, and how many do you disagree with?
(ii) Carry out a similar exercise amongst your colleagues.
(iii) The results may well be different. If they are, do you think that the differences result from the fact that the California research was confined to *divorced* men and women?
(iv) How many of these 12 statements do you think most English judges would agree with?
(v) Do you think any of these responses are contradictory?
(vi) Having read through this chapter: (*a*) what underlying principle would you adhere to in income and property redistribution on divorce? (*b*) what guidelines would you provide for the courts to reach solutions based on these principles? (*c*) would everyone be happy?
(vii) Do you think that a convincing case has been made for the moment of marriage as the date to merge 'human capital' between the husband and wife which should be equally split on the event of a subsequent divorce? But what about cohabitants – is there a similar moment in their relationship?

The authors of *Simple Quarrels* comment:

It is a mark of the relative powerlessness of the divorcing couple that they find themselves embroiled in procedures which they do not understand, while their quarrels are settled (or occasionally adjudicated) by reference to legal norms which they themselves do not accept. ... There is little prospect of evolving alternative structures to those provided by lawyers and courts.

Question

Which of the legal norms discussed in this chapter would some divorcing couples find particularly difficult to accept?

Interviews with one couple revealed the following disagreement:

For example, Mrs Merton did not consider that she should be expected to work to support the children post-divorce given that Mr Merton had not wanted her to work whist they were married. ... Mr Merton on the other hand made a very clear distinction between his wife's working when they were married and her doing so once they had separated. According to Mr Merton: 'There's no reason, other than her own choice, why she cannot get work and help to support herself. The marriage is over. The children are looked after. I don't see why she should, for the rest of her days, sit down on her bum. I've provided and supported her all these years. She's going to have to support herself now – we're no longer married. And as far as I'm concerned I'm not, morally, legally, or in any other way, obliged to keep her at the level I did when I was responsible for her because I was married to her.'

The authors identify a number of 'folk myths' which make for a gulf between the parties' thinking and the lawyer's assumptions:

- The man's belief that it is his money because he has earned it.
- The presumption of a 50:50 split (the authors comment that this is hardly a myth in Scotland where it is the principle upon which Scots law is based).

- The man's reluctance to pay maintenance on the basis that his former wife and children are provided for by the state.
- The belief that 'conduct', especially in opting to terminate the marriage, should have a bearing upon the financial resolution.

Questions

(i) Why are these 'folk myths' so prevalent?
(ii) Do you think it desirable that people's perceptions and expectations be changed? If so, how can this be accomplished? Do you think it a likely outcome of the way the law is developing at present?

Chapter 9

Dangerous families

Home is generally regarded as a place of safety but in this chapter we examine some of the dangers which can face family members. We shall look first at the different kinds of abuse and ill-treatment which can be suffered, and then at some of the research into explanations, before turning to the remedies in criminal and civil law. In this chapter, we shall deal only with the 'private law' remedies available to victims (usually women). Although these remedies are available to protect children (see p. 406, below), the abuse of children will usually require the involvement of local authority social services departments, or the NSPCC, exercising 'public law' powers. These will be considered in Chapter 13 after we have looked generally at the legal relationship between parents, children and the state.

1 What are the dangers?

I have had ten stitches, three stitches, five stitches, seven stitches, where he has cut me. ... I have had a knife stuck through my stomach; I have had a poker put through my face; I have no teeth where he knocked them all out; I have been burnt with red hot pokers; I have had red hot coals slung all over me; I have been sprayed with petrol and stood there while he has flicked lighted matches at me. ...

When I was carrying he used to start hitting me a bit more, you know. He wanted me to have an abortion, but I would not – I kept on refusing. He kept punching me in the stomach.

So said two of the women who gave evidence to the House of Commons Select Committee on Violence in Marriage (1975). Susan Edwards (1996) describes some of the brutality which has reached the criminal courts:

In *R v Davies* (1986) 8 Cr App Rep (S) 97, a husband struck a wife on the back of the head with a hammer and rendered two further blows to the face fracturing the bridge of her nose and the upper part of the bony cavity of the eye. He also fractured the jaw bone and the eyeball had to be removed. The court conceded, 'Indeed she was lucky to have survived', sentencing him to seven years' imprisonment. ... In *R v Bedford* (1992) 14 Cr App Rep (S) 336–337, the wife was doused with petrol and ignited when she refused to sleep with the appellant. She said she would sleep on the settee. The appellant left the room and returned with a container of petrol he kept in the car. He set her alight and when she tried to leave the burning room he held the door shut against her. She sustained 40 per cent burns. When arrested he said to police, 'You know what it's like, you know what women are like. I just snapped.' . ... In *R v Dearn* (1990) 12 Cr App Rep (S) 527, the husband admitted tying a piece of electric flex around his wife's neck. Medical evidence estimated that the flex must have been held for at least five minutes causing irreparable brain damage. The husband explained that she had been, '... nagging him all that day' and he had tried to shut her up by using the flexible cord of the vacuum cleaner cable. A sentence of fifteen years was reduced to twelve years.

Civil courts also encounter many cases of domestic violence. In 1995 there were 24,010 applications to county courts for orders under the Domestic Violence and Matrimonial Proceedings Act 1976 (Judicial Statistics, 1996). Research carried out in Leicester County Court over a six month period looked at the behaviour upon which such applications are based (Jones et al., 1995). This included: punching, kicking, choking/strangling, slaps, throwing across room, pushing/shoving, hitting, using a weapon, hair pulling, dragging across room, hitting with object, throwing objects at applicant, headbutting, pushing against wall, throwing downstairs, biting, burning, hitting head on ground, jumping on, pushing head through glass, stabbing, pinching, sexual abuse, and 'other violence'. In most cases there was a history of violence over several years before the first application was made.

However, many cases of domestic violence may not reach the criminal or civil courts. The House of Commons Home Affairs Committee recognised the difficulties in its report on *Domestic Violence* (1993):

9. Domestic violence is common, and its direct and indirect costs are high. There is clearly need for proper statistical information on which policy priorities can be set. Neither the Criminal nor the Judicial Statistics will ever provide a full picture of the incidence of domestic violence since many victims will neither report the violence to the police nor take action in the civil courts. Nor will the British Crime Survey (which involves asking a sample of the population about their experience of crime, whether they reported it or not) necessarily be entirely accurate, because of the shame which some victims may feel and which may discourage them from being frank. This may be particularly true of men – and one reason why statistics of male abuse by females appear insignificant.

Question

Can you think of any reasons, besides male shame, why the Leicester County Court study found that 98% of domestic violence applications were made by women (Jones et al., 1995)?

2 The search for explanations

In *Domestic Violence: Action for Change* (1993), Gill Hague and Ellen Malos review some of the different types of explanation which have been developed:

Individual pathological models of explanation
This kind of explanation is based on the idea that the individual using violence suffers from a pathological condition which leads to deviance from a non-violent norm. In practice it might only be quite extreme forms of violence or repeated violence that would be included in this kind of diagnosis. A certain kind of 'low-level' aggression might be seen as 'normal' at least in some families. Pathological deviance, however, might be thought to be based on either psychiatric illness or faults of temperament of one or both partners. Often it has been regarded as a sign of inadequacy, of an inarticulate person who had not learned to assert himself in non-violent ways.

When violence within families began to be perceived as a major problem in the early 1970s, it was in the context of medical evidence of the physical abuse of children in the United States.

Initial explanations of violence within families at that time arose from concern about child abuse and focused on 'abusive families'. Women, as mothers, were viewed as colluding in the abuse of their children and also colluding in, or provoking, violence against themselves. The early research into 'family violence' in the United States in particular, where most of the large-scale studies have been carried out, was often based on this kind of assumption.

Such ideas are still current in psychiatry and psychology. They also persist in certain kinds of therapeutic social work, most notably in family therapy, where individualistic explanations shade over into theories of group pathology in which those who experience the violence are themselves often seen as helping to cause it. Certain kinds of psychotherapy too involve the idea that violence arises from 'issues' which the individuals concerned have not 'worked through' in their relationship. In recent years, some researchers with such views have been moving towards other types of explanation as they have asked more sophisticated questions.

Cycles of violence

The 'cycle of violence' theory suggests that there is a direct transmission of violence down the generations by learned behaviour, creating a cycle in which the violence continuously reproduces itself. This theory has a variant in which it is argued that the behaviour is learned by children who either witness or experience violence within an individual family. There is also a 'sub-cultural model' in which the use of violence is learned as part of a wider way of life, either in neighbourhoods in criminal sub-cultures or gangs, or in certain professions such as the police and the army.

There is certainly some evidence that violence can be learned, but these theories cannot explain why some individuals who observe such behaviour or live in such environments are not violent, or why some people are violent who do not live in this kind of family or social setting. Nor can they explain why, according to a rather indiscriminate lumping together of different kinds of learned behaviour, it ends up that boys both observing and experiencing violence should, according to the theory, become perpetrators of violence whereas girls apparently learn to choose violent partners and 'enjoy', or passively put up with, violent assault.

The theory rests ultimately on assumptions about the natural aggressiveness of boys and men, and the passivity of girls and women. This kind of explanation also loses force if violence, and violence against women in particular, is both very common and often accepted in the whole society, as suggested by Elisabeth Wilson in *What's to be Done about Violence Against Women?* (1983):

> 'If you are one of only 500 [abused] women in a population of 50 million then you have certainly been more than unlucky and there may perhaps be something very peculiar about your husband, or unusual about your circumstances, or about you; on the other hand, if you are one of 500,000 women then that suggests something very different – that there is something wrong not with a few individual men, or women, or marriages, but with the *situation* in which *many* women and children regularly get assaulted – that situation being home and the family.'

Yet, as we will see in later chapters, the cycle of violence is still a very popular kind of explanation. One possible reason for its popularity is that it seems to suggest that those men who attack their wives or partners, and those women who experience violence, are not 'people like us' – but rather belong to a special deviant group of 'violent families', who are completely different from the rest of us. Even if the violence happens more often than we would like to think and is much worse than we ever imagined, it has been explained. And, using the theory, it can be dealt with, perhaps by removing children from the violent family or violent sub-culture – and thus 'breaking the cycle'.

As to the adults, it might be too late to change the ingrained pattern. Perhaps all you can do is to recognize that, or perhaps you can help the women and children to get away. Perhaps you prosecute the man, or break the cycle by re-educating the parents or the perpetrator (in more optimistic variants of the theory which think it is actually possible to change what happens). Ultimately, though, if you believe that this is why domestic violence takes place, all you can probably hope to do is to minimize the transmission of violence, because it is all a result of some unexplainable situation in the violent past. It is not about the present situation of many families, as Elisabeth Wilson suggests. Some people are 'just like that', even if there are a large number of them.

…

Social-structural explanations

This is another kind of explanation of 'family violence'. It bases itself on the stress caused by lack of access to money, housing and education common to both men and women in the family. This view was expressed very succinctly in a discussion document drawn up by the British Association of Social Workers in 1975:

> 'Economic conditions, low wages, bad housing, and isolation; unfavourable and frustrating work conditions for the man; lack of job opportunities for adolescent school leavers, and lack of facilities such as day care (e.g. nurseries), adequate transport, pleasant environment and play space and recreational facilities, for mother and children were considered to cause personal desperation that might cause violence in the home.'

This kind of explanation usually assumes that violence occurs mainly in working-class and poor families. There is a 'middle-class' version in terms of financial pressures and stressful careers, but more commonly in this view the greater resources of middle-class families or, in some cases, the ability of middle-class men to maintain dominance without resorting to violence are thought to explain what is believed to be the relative lack of violence in these families.

However, as Michael Freeman (1987) and others point out, it is likely that violence in middle-class families can more easily remain hidden from neighbours and public agencies like the police and social services. Borkowski, Murch and Walker found in their study *Marital Violence* (1983) that the more significant class differential was not in whether violence occurred but in the kind of agencies consulted, the middle class being more likely to use lawyers and the divorce courts than the police, social services or women's refuges. Although it seems very likely that the pressures of poverty might increase the occurrence of violence or make it worse, this type of analysis fails adequately to account for the predominant direction of serious violence from men towards women or the fact that it occurs in all social classes.

...

Feminist explanations

... In the feminist view, domestic violence arises out of men's power over women in the family. This male power has been built into family life historically, through laws which assume that men have the right to authority over both women and children within families, where this does not conflict with public policy and the interests of the state. Rebecca and Russell Dobash in *Violence Against Wives* (1980), for example, describe the inferior historical position of women in British and North American society and in marriage, which arose from laws and customs which excluded women from public life and placed them under the authority of their husband or their father within the private sphere of the family.

As Susan Schechter has pointed out in *Women and Male Violence* (1982), this does not necessarily mean that feminists are 'dismissing psychology or ignoring violent individuals'. Rather:

> 'They are stressing the need for a psychology that analyses wife beating in its proper contexts, accounts for power differentials, and asks why women have been brutalized. Rather than label battering as pathology or a family systems failure, it is more conceptually accurate to assume that violence against women, like that directed towards children, is behaviour approved of and sanctioned in many parts of the culture. Extreme cases in which women are mutilated by psychotic men are only one end of a continuum of violent behaviour the more moderate forms of which are viewed as normal. Many in this culture approve of hitting women.'

Many feminists would use the kind of explanation which stresses the need to examine the historical position of women in particular societies and the way in which it was, and still is, embodied in law and custom. However, some forms of feminist explanation, basing themselves on the male-dominated nature of most known forms of society, come close to arguing that inherent biological differences between men and women are at the core of male violence and female non-violence. Others argue that there can be no such definite, undifferentiated categories as 'men' and 'women', but that we live among conflicting or intersecting sets of inequalities and differences in power.

Most feminist accounts draw attention to the economic position of women. They point to the way in which the responsibility that society assigns to women for looking after children often places them in a position of enforced financial dependency on their partners or ex-partners, a situation which will be reinforced in Britain by the new Child Support Act. It is also used as an excuse for paying women low wages or minimal state income support. Some feminists would also want to argue that class and racial oppression, and social stresses such as unemployment, bad housing and poverty, are likely to increase violence and make it harder to escape. Yet they would point out that this does not explain why it is that it is predominantly men who become violent in these circumstances, or why so much of the violence is directed towards women whom the men would profess to love.

The view that domestic violence is a relatively common feature of women's lives is supported by the results of Jayne Mooney's research conducted in North London, *The Hidden Figure* (1993).

The prevalence of domestic violence in a woman's lifetime, by type of violence

Violent behaviours	%
Mental cruelty	
– including verbal abuse (e.g. name-calling, being ridiculed in front of other people), being deprived of money, clothes, sleep, prevented from going out etc.	37
Threats of violence or force	27
Actual physical violence	
– Grabbed or pushed or shaken	32
– Punched or slapped	25
– Kicked	14
– Head butted	6
– Attempted strangulation	9
– Hit with weapon/object	8
Injuries	
– Injured	27
– Bruising or black eye	26
– Scratches	12
– Cuts	11
– Bones broken	6
Rape (defined as made to have sex without consent)	23
– Rape with threats of violence	13
– Rape with physical violence	9
Composite violence	30

Lorna Smith expands upon the nature of feminist explanations in *Domestic Violence: an Overview of the Literature* (1989):

Feminist explanations

At the core of feminist explanations is the view that all violence is a reflection of unequal power relationships: domestic violence reflects the unequal power of men and women in society and also, therefore, within their personal relationships. It is a view propounded by sociologists (for example, Dobash and Dobash, 1980; Edwards, 1985), psychologists (for example, Walker, 1984), lawyers (for example, Freeman, 1979; 1984) and practitioners in the criminal justice system (for example, Pence, 1985) alike.

Dobash and Dobash (1980, 1984) employ the notion of patriarchy to explain women's subordinate status. Patriarchy comprises two elements: the structural – that is those societal institutions which define and maintain women's subordinate position and thus prevent them from influencing or changing the social order – and the ideological – that is the socialisation process which ensures acceptance of that order. Both the Dobashes' (1981) historical analysis of legal sources and their empirical 'context specific' study (1980, 1984) demonstrate how husbands have sought and still seek to control their wives by violence.

Pahl (1985) has explicitly pointed out that the 'taken-for-granted assumptions' about marriage and the role of the family shape the ways in which the roles of women are defined, the ways in which domestic violence is perceived and thus also agencies' response to domestic violence. The ideology of the family and the privacy accorded the family in our society mean that women are, and are seen to be, subordinate to the men they live with. Men are expected to assume their 'natural' role as the dominant adult within the family. Indeed, Wilson (1983) has argued that domestic violence can be better understood if it is seen as an extreme form of normality – an exaggeration of how society expects men to behave as the authority figure in the family – and both Freeman (1980) and Edwards (1985) argue that the legal system both reflects and sustains this male supremacy. The pathology is, therefore, moved from that of the individual or even of the individual family to the family structure itself and its unequal power structure. Moreover, the family is seen as a microcosm of an unequal society. Domestic violence thus becomes a symptom of the more general demonstration of male violence, a demonstration of the male ethos and the male domination of women.

A number of writers have drawn attention to the economic dependency of women (see, for example, Chapman and Gates, 1978; Homer et al., 1985; Kalmuss and Straus, 1981; Kaufman Kantor and Straus, 1987; Martin, 1976; 1978). Pahl's empirical study (1985) attests to the importance of the allocation of the control of money within the household. Although Pahl, herself, did not see this as important when she began her study, the women in her sample drew such consistent attention to it that she systematically investigated it: more than three quarters of the women named money a problem area. Husbands seemed to use the control of money as part of a more general attempt to control and subordinate wives. It appeared to be the key element in a marital relationship in which the husband assumed he would be the dominant partner. This finding is consistent with other studies. The Dobashes (1980) found that the majority of arguments preceding violence focused on husband's jealousy, differing expectations regarding the wife's domestic duties and the allocation of money. Roy (1977), in her American study, found that the four factors most often leading to violence were, in order of importance, arguments over money, jealousy, sexual problems and alcohol. Evason (1982), too, paid particular attention to financial arrangements within marriage. Her sample compared groups of women who had been victims of domestic violence with those who had not: those who had experienced violence were more likely to have had husbands who kept control over finances and who gave their wives money as and when they thought fit. Non-violent husbands were more likely to have opted for joint management of money. Assumptions and expectations about wives' appropriate behaviour were also identified as important by Evason (1982) and Klein (1982). Evason, for example, found that although there were no differences between her violent and non-violent groups in terms of education, social class, age at marriage or length of courtship prior to marriage, wives who had been abused were particularly likely to have had husbands who favoured a traditional model of marriage in which the husband was 'master in his own home'. Any attempt by wives to assert themselves or question that authority was interpreted as wives 'getting above themselves' and, therefore, they had to be 'put back in their place'.

Morash (1986) has pointed out that socio-structural cultural explanations and feminist explanations are not necessarily antithetical despite their use of different paradigms for theory building. ... Straus (1977), for example, agrees with feminists that:

> 'The most fundamental set of factors bringing about wife beating are those connected with the sexist structure of the family and society. ... The cultural norms and values permitting and sometimes encouraging husband-to-wife violence reflect the hierarchical and male dominant type of society which characterises the Western world.'

Moreover, some feminists (for example, Dobash and Dobash, 1980) would not reject the relevance of family history, social stresses, use of alcohol, sexual problems and so on, but argue rather that their explanatory power is not sufficient. Emphasising such factors leaves the question unanswered: why are women most frequently the victim?

Questions

(i) Why, then, do most men not beat their wives?

(ii) Do you think, as the magistrates (but not the Family Division) did in *Bergin v Bergin* [1983] 1 All ER 905, [1983] 1 WLR 279, that a wife who accepted three black eyes 'as part of married life' can reasonably be expected to go on living with her husband when he next turns violent?

3 But is it not a crime?

According to Erin Pizzey, in the book which first alerted the public to the modern realities of wife-beating, *Scream Quietly or the Neighbours will Hear* (1974):

The police attitude to wife-battering reveals an understandable but unacceptable schizophrenia in their approach to violence. Imagine that Constable Upright is on his beat one night and finds Mr Batter mugging a woman in the street. Mr Batter has already inflicted heavy bruises to the woman's face and is just putting the boot in when Constable Upright comes on the scene. The constable knows his duty and does it. He arrests Mr Batter, who is charged with causing grievous bodily harm and goes to prison for ten years.

Ten years later Constable Upright is on his beat when he is sent to investigate screaming which neighbours have reported coming from the home of the newly released Mr Batter. Mr Batter is mugging his wife. He's thrown boiling water at her, broken her nose, and now he's trying for her toes with a claw hammer. When Constable Upright arrives what does he do? Does he make an arrest? Of course not.

He knocks on the door and Mr Batter tells him to 'sod off'. He tells Mr Batter that the neighbours are complaining and he wishes to see his wife. Mr Batter says they have been having a minor row and he gets his wife who is looking bruised round the face and crying. The policeman will not arrest. In one case the husband even assaulted his wife in front of a policeman but still there was no arrest. All that he did was to advise her to go to the local magistrates' court the next morning and take out a summons against her husband, but he knew that she was unlikely to do this because she would have to live in the same house as her husband while she was taking him to court.

Confirmation for what she said came from the evidence of various police bodies to the House of Commons Select Committee on Violence in Marriage (1975). Thus the Association of Chief Police Officers (ACPO):

... Whilst such problems take up considerable Police time ... in the majority of cases the role of the Police is a negative one. We are, after all dealing with persons 'bound in marriage', and it is important, for a host of reasons, to maintain the unity of the spouses. Precipitate action by the Police could aggravate the position to such an extent as to create a worse situation than the one they were summoned to deal with. ...

Questions

(i) This was borne out by Jan Pahl's research (1982), which indicated that the police were far more likely to take action themselves if (*a*) the woman had already left for a refuge, or (*b*) although still under the same roof, the woman was not married to the man: can you list the 'host of reasons' why this might be?

(ii) How many of the reasons which might disincline a policeman to intervene appear to you to be valid?

(iii) What powers does Constable Upright have, if told to 'sod off' by a man who is apparently beating his wife inside the matrimonial home? (Consult *R v Thornley* (1980) 72 Cr App Rep 302, and also the Police and Criminal Evidence Act 1984, s. 17(1)(*e*) and (6), considered by the Court of Appeal in *McLeod v Metropolitan Police Comr* [1994] 4 All ER 553.)

Mildred Dow put her finger on one difficulty in 'Police Involvement', her contribution to *Violence in the Family* (edited by Marie Borland in 1976):

It has, however, been recognised in law for many centuries that the sanctity of marriage is something special. Until recent times a wife was seen as a chattel of her husband and had no real rights. In recent years it has become obvious to the writer, through years of police experience as a practical officer, that however often one says to a wife, 'Your rights are ... ' she will invariably be re-influenced by her husband and refuse to give the necessary evidence. Whether this is basically due to personal fear or to an essentially sexual attraction and influence or to fear for the children of the union, it is difficult to determine. I only know how frustrating it is for a police officer who has taken much care and trouble in the preparation of the presentation of the case at court to be let down because his principal witness has had 'second thoughts'. If positive action is desirable when injury has been caused, quite often severe injury, we must overcome the problem of the wife who is unwilling to give evidence. Often her decision not to do so is made at the last minute, either as a result of reconciliation or perhaps through fear of retribution. From a practical viewpoint it would appear better to charge the husband and keep him in custody, rather than to follow the practice in some few police areas where the husband is reported for summons, thus giving him time to influence his wife. If some aggressive husbands are, by these means, kept away from the matrimonial home, more wives may be prepared to give the relevant evidence.

Dobash and Dobash argue in *Women, Violence and Social Change* (1992) that it is the police themselves who are responsible for the problem:

Police officers continue to see victims as fundamentally 'unreliable and capricious', 'inadequate people', who are only worthy of police response. In light of such perceptions it is not surprising that arrest, even in areas of pro-arrest policies, is an unlikely outcome of police contact. ... Observations of police reactions and interviews with officers reveal that they discourage women from filing formal complaints, often give strong advice against arrest, present victims with all the potential 'negative effects of and barriers to pursuing a prosecution' and pressure women not to press charges [e.g. Sanders (1988)]. In this way the justice system helps create the reality of dropped charges and reluctant witnesses about which it complains.

In any event, both Dobash and Dobash (1980) and Wasoff (1982) in Scotland found that claims about wives dropping charges were 'greatly exaggerated', as did Tony Faragher, discussing *The Police Response to Violence against Women in the Home* (1985):

The degree of police concern over possible withdrawal of the complaint is not matched, however, by the frequency with which this occurs in practice. Only one in ten women in a local study were found to have withdrawn their complaint (Dawson and Faragher, 1977, 142). The only way in which this low level of withdrawal can be accounted for is that the police are extremely selective about who they sponsor to take legal action. This is borne out by observation at the scene of 'domestics' – women are time and again asked whether they really want to take legal action. Alternatively women are given time to 'think it over' in the belief that an 'unemotional' decision made the next day will be more realistic. In this sense the police abrogate their protective role, for their judgment is heavily influenced by prognoses of the woman's reliability as a witness in court proceedings.

But things may have begun to change in the late 1980s (see Cretney and Davis, 1996, p. 383, below). Morley and Mullender, in *Hype or Hope?* (1992), argued that, after the 1975 Select Committee Report:

... the issue of domestic violence largely disappeared from the public agenda until the second half of the 1980s. When it re-emerged, it did so in the context of an increasing tendency to view the police, and criminal justice system generally, as being in the forefront of solutions to the problem. And within policing, the new emphasis was firmly on domestic violence as a *criminal* act, and on *arrest* as the primary response to assailants.

In contrast to its view in 1975, the Association of Chief Police Officer's evidence to the Home Affairs Committee (1993) said that, during the late 1980s, 'the Police Service changed its focus from one of conciliation to intervention'. This development is demonstrated by the Home Office Circular (60/1990) on *Domestic Violence*:

Nature and extent of problem

2. Chief officers will be aware of the wide range of abuse which is covered by the term 'domestic violence'. It encompasses all aspects of physical, sexual and emotional abuse, ranging from

threatening behaviour and minor assaults which lead to cuts and bruises to serious injury, and sometimes even death. (In about 44% of homicide cases where the victim is a female the suspect is or was married to or lived with her.) Research has shown that, although the severity of the abuse varies, incidents of domestic violence have several common characteristics. They are rarely isolated occurrences. They tend to be repeated over a period of time, often increasing in their severity, and are particularly common during the woman's pregnancy. They often extend beyond the woman to children living within the home. The offender is likely to come from a family in which violence was used against women, but he may be in any stratum of society; domestic violence occurs across the whole social spectrum.

...

4. Domestic violence is not simply a challenge for the criminal justice system. Victims will often need assistance which is beyond the capacity of the police to provide, requiring close co-operation with medical, social work and housing authorities and with victim support groups. Domestic violence is, however, a crime and it is important that the police should play an active and positive role in protecting the victim and that their response to calls for help is speedy and effective.

...

Force policy statements

11. The Home Secretary recommends that chief officers should consider issuing a force policy statement about their response to domestic violence. ... Central features of the force policy statement should be:

- the overriding duty to protect victims, and children, from further attack;
- the need to treat domestic violence as seriously as other forms of violence;
- the use and value of powers of arrest;
- the dangers of seeking conciliation between assailant and victim;
- the importance of comprehensive record-keeping to allow the chief officer to monitor the effectiveness of the policy in practice.

Initial police response to incidents

(a) *Distinguish violent/non-violent incidents*

12. The first contact between a victim and the police is likely to be by telephone when a victim seeks police intervention or protection. The first priority for police officers answering such calls is to find out whether immediate police help is required, or whether there is no imminent danger of an assault. Even if immediate help is not sought, the call must be recorded and there should always be some sort of positive action to investigate the case – for instance, an interview with the victim to establish in more detail what prompted her call and whether it was part of a history of violence.

(b) *Check previous history of relationship*

13. All complaints of domestic violence by victims or witnesses should be properly recorded in the same way as similar incidents involving strangers. The seriousness of an incident should not be downgraded because it takes place in a domestic context and no incident should be 'no-crimed' unless the police conclude, after investigation, that the report was inaccurate or false.

...

(c) *Action at the scene of the incident: the victim*

14. In the past, police officers arriving at the scene of domestic violence have often tried to smooth over the dispute and reconcile the partners. Research suggests that this is not necessarily the best course of action and that what victims want is the enforcement of the law. Police officers should rarely attempt conciliation if the victim has been, or claims to have been, violently assaulted (bruises may not develop for some time after the incident so the absence of obvious injury may not be significant). Wherever possible, it is desirable for a woman police officer to be available to attend the incident so that the victim may be given a choice about the sex of the officer who assists her. If the victim is interviewed on the spot, the interview should not take place in the presence of her alleged assailant so that she does not feel pressurised into relating the incident in front of him. However, if she *chooses* to repeat the allegation in his presence and hearing, it may be given in evidence by the police at any subsequent court hearing. The victim should never be asked in the alleged assailant's presence whether she will be prepared to give evidence against him. In some cases, however, the immediate priority will simply be to remove her (and any children) to a place of safety.

...

(d) *Action at the scene of the incident: the assailant*
16. Police officers should be aware of their powers in respect to domestic violence. ... Experience in other countries suggests that the arrest of an alleged assailant may act as a powerful deterrent against his re-offending – at least for some time – and it is an important means of showing the victim that she is entitled to, and will receive, society's protection and support. The arrest and detention of an alleged assailant should therefore always be considered, even though the final judgement may be that this is inappropriate in the particular case.

(e) *Action at the scene: witnesses*
17. In view of the difficulties in bringing a prosecution in cases of domestic violence, there is a particular need to establish whether there are witnesses such as other members of the family or neighbours who can give evidence.

Action after the incident

(a) *Charging the suspect*
18. In considering whether or not to initiate criminal proceedings, police officers will wish to take into account the same factors as those which are relevant in the case of attacks by strangers. The fact that some women, having made a complaint, subsequently decide that they are not prepared to give evidence at court should not affect a police officer's decision to charge in a case in which the evidence justifies that course of action. Many women will be in a state of shock when the police first arrive, and unable to contemplate the prospect of a court case. With proper support, however, they may gain in confidence and, following discussion of all the aspects of their case, they may well come to recognise that prosecution is in their own interest. When there is sufficient evidence to justify a prosecution the police should charge the suspect and refer the case to the Crown Prosecution Service.

...

(c) *Reports to the Crown Prosecution Service*
21. Just as police officers will find it essential to have background information about the nature and history of the relationship readily to hand in order to deal with an incident, so Crown Prosecutors need the same information in order to prosecute the case effectively and ensure the protection of the victim and any children by the imposition of bail conditions or a remand in custody. In particular, Crown Prosecutors need to be kept informed if circumstances change. The information which is required by the Crown Prosecutor includes

(i) the composition of the family;
(ii) the nature of the relationship – marital status of the parties, history of the relationship including previous attacks if known, likelihood of recurrence if not self-evident;
(iii) domestic arrangements (relevant to bail);
(iv) the future of the relationship – whether complainant has ended/intends to end relationship, whether a reconciliation is in progress or seems likely, whether or not she seeks/intends to seek non-molestation order in civil courts. (This information may best be obtained in the presence of a third person eg relative or social worker or, at this early stage, the victim may not be able to discuss rationally the future of the relationship.)

...

Withdrawal of victim's complaint

24. In the past, the likelihood of the victim's withdrawing her complaint has often been used to justify not taking criminal proceedings against the alleged assailant. Recent research has established, however, that withdrawal of complaint is less common than has been supposed. The victim's refusal to testify against her partner may considerably lessen the prospect of a conviction, however. The CPS has power, under section 97 of the Magistrates' Courts Act 1980 or Section 80 of the Police and Criminal Evidence Act 1984 to seek to compel a spouse or partner to attend court for the purpose of giving evidence. The power is used infrequently and a decision to use it can only be taken in the light of the circumstances of the case, including the reasons why the complainant does not wish to give evidence and the views of the officer in the case. This underlines the need to give close support to the victim during the pre-trial period, so that she will feel sufficiently self-confident to give evidence.

Although the Circular is merely advisory, and its implementation may vary from area to area, it does indicate a change of attitude among senior police officers and Government officials. But are these new attitudes shared by the officers who actually respond to incidents of violence? A Home Office Research Study, *Policing Domestic Violence in the 1990s* (1995) by Sharon Grace, addresses this issue:

The general police response

Virtually all forces have developed policies on domestic violence which closely adhere to the recommendations in Home Office Circular 60/1990. However, the findings in this report suggest that the translation of this policy into practice has been limited. Just over half of the forces had a specialist unit with *some* responsibility for domestic violence but only five forces had domestic violence units dedicated solely to this offence. While there was a general awareness among officers about how domestic violence *should* be policed, this awareness was not always reflected in the way they dealt with such cases. It appeared that managers were overly optimistic about how effective they had been in getting the message across to their operational colleagues and were somewhat out of touch about what was happening at ground level.

Most officers felt that the policing of domestic violence had improved and that such incidents were now being taken more seriously with more positive intervention and more support and advice available for victims. There was evidence that officers had increased their awareness of domestic violence issues and showed a greater understanding and sympathy for victims. However, a third of operational officers had not heard of Circular 60/1990 at all and over half said that they had not received any new guidelines on domestic violence – despite their managers' confidence that the guidance had been successfully disseminated.

...

Although most officers were aware that arrest should be a priority in domestic violence cases, almost half of them put it below all other considerations (e.g. the safety of the victim and any children) when asked to prioritise their actions at a domestic violence scene. Their decision to arrest appeared to be heavily influenced by whether a complainant would support any police action. However, the use of informal responses to domestic violence incidents appeared from interviews to be unsatisfactory both for officers – who will usually have to return to that address at a later date – and for victims – who feel the police have not taken their plight seriously enough. If they are to follow the guidance in Circular 60/1990, officers need to consider arrest more often in domestic violence cases. In addition, it may be worth placing less emphasis on Breach of the Peace as a solution and making more use of assault charges. This will reassure the victim that her situation is being taken seriously, and may also have more of a long term impact on her assailant. CPS lawyers did say that, while Breach of the Peace was a speedy way of dealing with domestic violence cases, it probably did not help the victim in the long term nor was it likely to act as a deterrent.

Questions

(i) Are you surprised that operational police officers are more concerned about the safety of women and children than about making arrests?
(ii) Are these objectives incompatible?

Research by Antonia Cretney and Gwyn Davis (1996) suggests that domestic assaults are now much more likely to be prosecuted than in the past. A study of 448 assaults prosecuted in the Bristol courts between January 1993 and October 1993 found that 46% were 'domestics'. On this basis, the authors concluded that 'this is a hidden crime no longer'. However, they found that more than half of these prosecutions were discontinued (52%), whereas only 29% of the non-domestic cases were discontinued. They also found that the victim withdrew support for the prosecution in 30% of domestic cases, compared with 7% of non-domestic cases.

In its evidence to the Home Affairs Committee (1993), the ACPO highlighted some of the special problems attached to the investigation of domestic violence:

- Witnesses are likely to be related to one or more of the parties and are, therefore, likely to take sides.
- In many cases, there are no witnesses. Therefore abuse involving anything less than serious physical assault is unlikely to be referred to the court.
- Close relationships inhibit reporting until repeated extreme behaviour has occurred, by which time positions have become firmly entrenched.
- For a victim to report, takes courage. It may well result in the 'loss' of a partner, home and way of life, which could be replaced by near poverty line existence in hostel accommodation.
- Assuming there is sufficient evidence to arrest a suspect at the time a complaint is made, in most cases the Bail Act will ensure freedom within a short space of time.
- Conditions attached to bail/injunctions are regularly broken, resulting in considerable stress to the victim and increased work for the police. When the offender is returned to court, it is common practice to admonish the offender, then release him on the same conditions. This practice does little for the confidence of the victim.
- Regardless of the outcome of criminal proceedings, a very high percentage of those involved in domestic violence continue their relationship.
- A longer term consideration is the accommodation and welfare of the victim and her children. This tends to inhibit the reporting of any incidents.

Questions

(i) Why is it significant that a 'very high percentage' continue their relationship?
(ii) The Bristol study found that prosecutions were much more likely to be discontinued where the parties continued cohabiting (Cretney and Davis, 1996). How many reasons can you think of why a woman might withdraw support for prosecution in these circumstances?
(iii) Under what circumstances should prosecutions be continued against the wishes of the woman concerned (see *R v Renshaw* [1989] Crim LR 811; Edwards, 1989; Brownlee, 1990)?

The Police and Criminal Evidence Act 1984 made wives competent and compellable witnesses against their husbands (see p. 64, above). Before that, the House of Lords had held in *Hoskyn v Metropolitan Police Comr* [1979] AC 474, [1978] 2 All ER 136, HL, that a wife could not be compelled to give evidence against her husband in these cases. Lord Edmund Davies, who dissented, summed up the opposing viewpoints thus:

The noble and learned Lord, Viscount Dilhorne, has spoken of the repugnance created by a wife being compelled ' ... to testify against her husband on a charge involving violence, no matter how trivial and no matter the consequences to her and to her family'. For my part I regard as extremely unlikely any prosecution based on trivial violence being persisted in where the injured spouse was known to be a reluctant witness. Much more to the point, as I think, are cases such as the present ... , arising from serious physical maltreatment by one spouse of the other.

Such cases are too grave to depend simply on whether the injured spouse is, or is not, willing to testify against the attacker. Reluctance may spring from a variety of reasons and does not by any means necessarily denote that domestic harmony has been restored. A wife who has once been subjected to a 'carve up' may well have more reasons than one for being an unwilling witness against her husband. In such circumstances, it may well prove a positive boon for her to be directed by the court that she has no alternative but to testify. But, be that as it may, such incidents ought not to be regarded as having no importance extending beyond the domestic hearth. Their investigation and, where sufficiently weighty, their prosecution is a duty which the agencies of law enforcement cannot dutifully neglect.

Prosecutors must still decide whether to exercise their powers to compel a reluctant witness. The position of the Crown Prosecution Service is described in their evidence to the Home Affairs Committee (1993):

6.1.2 For a variety of reasons, it frequently occurs that the victim decides, during the course of criminal proceedings, not to support the prosecution and to withdraw the complaint. This is often accompanied by the victim taking the defendant back into the shared home (sometimes in breach of the defendant's bail conditions).

6.1.3 In such circumstances, the CPS obtains a statement from the victim setting out the reasons for the withdrawal of support together with a police report. The purpose of this is to attempt to ascertain whether the original complaint was true or false, and whether the victim is withdrawing support for the prosecution voluntarily or under duress.

6.1.4 Once in receipt of this information, the prosecutor has to decide what action to take. Assuming that the complaint is true, but that the victim voluntarily wishes to withdraw support, the dilemma facing the prosecutor is whether to accede to the victim's wishes, or to continue with the prosecution against the victim's wishes on the basis of the wider public interest.

...

6.3.1 The prosecution can only compel a spouse to give evidence in relation to offences of violence against her or her children [section 80, PACE]. Unmarried partners have always been competent and compellable witnesses for the prosecution.

...

6.3.3 Witnesses brought to the court in this manner will inevitably have been caused distress. Additionally the prosecutor is unlikely to know how the witness will react; some may give evidence apparently willingly and with a degree of relief that the decision to do so is out of their control; others will become 'hostile' to the prosecution and give evidence which only assists the defence; yet others may refuse to give evidence at all and thus find themselves at risk of being punished for contempt whilst the perpetrator of the original offence is discharged. This situation has, in the past, given rise to adverse publicity.

On the basis of their research in Bristol, Cretney and Davis (1996) conclude:

It now appears that offenders are being arrested and charged where once they would only have been 'advised', and that in general women who seek police help are receiving a better service, both in terms of the immediate response and in the support which they receive during the prosecution process.

We would suggest that further thought now be given to the management of those cases in which the woman indicates that she no longer wishes to proceed. It does not seem to us that the issue of intimidation and pressure has been effectively addressed. Much that police, prosecutors and courts currently do to ensure that a retraction is properly made appears designed to protect the prosecuting authorities rather than to uncover coercion. The fact that coercion is seldom if ever revealed by these means forces this conclusion. We would suggest therefore that the courts and the CPS abandon the practice of requiring withdrawal from the witness-box. Instead, the emphasis should be on facilitating private consultation between victim and prosecutor, a policy which we recognise does present certain difficulties for the CPS although it is managed well enough by some prosecutors. A second issue which we would identify is the tendency to *blame* the woman. It has been part of police culture to regard victims of domestic violence as vacillating women who in the end deserve what they get because they are unable to make a break with their abuser. With an apparent increase in the number of domestic violence cases coming before the courts there is a tendency to regard the woman who withdraws at this stage as failing all those (police, CPS and court) who have put themselves out on her behalf. ... We consider there to be very good reasons why some women withdraw, whether this withdrawal be early or late. Furthermore, withdrawal does not necessarily denote failure on anyone's part.

Questions

(i) Do you agree that the withdrawal of a prosecution should not necessarily be regarded as a failure?

(ii) What are the 'very good reasons' why some women withdraw support for prosecutions?

The arguments for and against 'diverting' cases out of the criminal justice system are put by Susan Maidment in *The Relevance of the Criminal Law to Domestic Violence* (1980):

Strong arguments can be put forward why the criminal law should be used in all cases of domestic violence. It would be a clear affirmation of social values, of condemnation by society, and a clear statement of the personal responsibility and accountability of the offender. We know that the criminal law can provide an effective and prompt protection for the victim. The criminal law can at least attempt to prevent an escalation of violence either through incarceration, or by making at the outset the strongest statement that society can make denouncing the act. The police are in any case often involved in emergency calls, and they may be the only agency with the authority and ability to cope with such volatile situations.

On the other side there are arguments against the use of the criminal law. It is a blunt tool. It misplaces emphasis on the offender, not the victim. There is no facility for treatment within the system, for example, for understanding and attempting to control aggression, except probation, but then the husband is still at large. No attempt is made to improve the marital relationship, to develop mutual respect between husband and wife. On a more technical level, there are problems of proof in criminal law, as compared with the easier standard of proof for an injunction. This may lead to some acquittals purely on technical grounds. For the wife however this means a lack of protection.

In more general terms a criminal conviction and sentence for the husband may be counterproductive for the wife in many ways. There may be financial disadvantage to the wife, emotional loss to the children. It may only escalate the problem because of the husband's anger and grudge against her; imprisonment is only a temporary respite (though this argument could equally apply to injunctions). It may not be what the wife really wants – she would like to have him treated. She may feel guilty and responsible for him being punished or locked away. Indeed her initial call to the police may not be a cry for criminal action at all; it is simply the only place she knows to turn to in an emergency.

Indeed the present operation of the criminal law, when it is invoked in these cases, makes a mockery of the criminal process, because of the derisory sentences that are passed, even for example where the charge is actual bodily harm (House of Commons, 1975; Pizzey, 1974). The basic problem to which the use of the criminal law gives rise has been well expressed in the following statement:

> 'Of all the areas in which an alternative to criminal treatment seems justified, the area of marital disputes is the most obvious. This is not to say that violence, theft or neglect between spouses should be ignored, but it does appear that these cases deserve different treatment than they are now given. Whether prosecution is decided upon or not, it would seem that beyond the point of immediate police response to danger, the criminal process is largely irrelevant in these cases. If anything, its very invocation may exacerbate poverty related and/or psychological problems. The summary, rather shallow treatment given these complainants does not answer the need that they have expressed for help.' (Subin, 1966)

Nevertheless there are some cases where the criminal law has to be used. These cases should be restricted to those occasions when there is a need present for coercive prevention of violence in view of serious physical or emotional danger to the wife. It is all the other cases, where there is a choice between the civil and criminal remedy, which give rise to problems of decision-making. At present the choice of remedy is, as already described, haphazard. It depends partly on the wife's choice as to whether she goes to a solicitor or to the police, and on the police as to whether they are willing to prosecute. In practice the choice will effectively be made by the police since they will usually be involved in the very initial stages. But the fact is that the choice of remedy can and ought to be a professional principled decision. There are some clear issues to be considered, and serious arguments for and against the use of the criminal law as already described. A professional decision needs to be arrived at after full consideration of the alternative remedies available.

Questions

(i) Which professionals might those be? Why should they be better qualified to decide than the police or the woman herself?

(ii) Do we need to distinguish between what Constable Upright does when called to the house in the middle of the night and what Inspector Morse or the Crown Prosecution Service do the next day?

Sharon Grace's study (1995) considered the views of victims of domestic violence:

What do victims want?
The clearest message to emerge from interviews with victims was that they wanted the police to treat their situations seriously and to take into account their needs and wishes when deciding what action to take. An understanding, sympathetic attitude from the police seems to help ensure that victims feel satisfied with the response they receive. The police should be able to offer long-term support to victims regardless of whether victims decide to pursue a criminal solution to their problems. To offer this support, officers need to know about the various non-criminal options available to victims and support them in whatever decision they decide to take.

Question

Are the police the most appropriate agency to give this type of long-term support?

4 Developing civil law remedies

In its evidence to the Home Affairs Committee (1993), the Women's Aid Federation England points out some of the reasons why victims of domestic violence might prefer to use civil remedies, rather than the criminal law:

From the point of view of the woman experiencing the abuse, it may seem preferable to apply for protection in the civil courts rather than to give evidence in a criminal prosecution of her partner. Firstly, the process seems to be more under her control: she instructs the solicitor, who will represent her in court, or will instruct a barrister on her behalf. Secondly, in most cases the hearing will be in a closed court or in the Judge's chambers, and there will be no publicity. Thirdly, her partner will not acquire a criminal record, which could hamper his employment prospects and hence indirectly affect the economic situation of the woman and her children. For all these reasons it is important that the process of obtaining injunctions or personal protection orders should be as straightforward as possible, and that the orders, once obtained should be effective and if breached, should be strictly enforced.

The victim's control over the process is a strength of the civil law, but it may also be a limitation. Jenny Clifton points to some of the difficulties which women face in taking action in her account of *Factors Predisposing Family Members to Violence*, in the Scottish Social Work Services Group's collection of papers on *Violence in the Family* (1982):

It is important to view the battered wife in the context of a family network which may tacitly or explicitly support the husband's position. The problems of the wife who does not think she will be believed if she tells how her apparently normal husband is a batterer ... represent a crucial component of the explanation for women remaining in a violent relationship. Women's own hopes and expectations of marriage and family life, added to the pressures from others to keep the family together, the very real hardships of life alone and the social disadvantages of divorced status offer plenty of scope for the explanation of women's apparent tolerance of a violent relationship without recourse to suppositions that women must need the violence in a pathological way (for example,

Marsden 1978). This is not to say that conflict which may occasionally spill into violence does not sometimes become an integral part of a marital relationship (Cade 1978) but the consistent picture from research studies is that women who are beaten do not come to need or enjoy their victimisation (Dobash and Dobash 1980). Neither are conflict-ridden marriages and relationships which occasionally involve physical combat quite the same as marriages in which the wife is frequently and brutally subjected to physical force.

Dobash and Dobash (1992) also explain some of the reasons why women may return to violent men:

Women return for a myriad of reasons: because men promise to reform; they are concerned about the welfare of their husband and children; they accept the powerful ideals associated with an intact family; they do not wish to discard their emotional and material investment in the relationship; they have no accommodation and few prospects for meaningful employment; and they fear the violent reprisals of men who are often at their most dangerous when women leave.

As John Stuart Mill pointed out in 1869, 'it is contrary to reason and experience to suppose that there can be any real check to brutality, consistent with leaving the victim still in the power of the executioner'. The first step had therefore to be to improve and extend the procedures for releasing wives from their lifelong promise and legal duty to live with their husbands. But it is one thing to be told that you need no longer live with your husband, and another thing to pluck up the courage to live through the interim before the divorce and to find somewhere to live both then and thereafter.

The law in this area has been comprehensively reformed by the Family Law Act 1996. However, before we consider the details of this legislation, we must consider the remedies which have been developed in this area of family law (and which will apply until this part of the 1996 Act is implemented). The Law Commission reviewed the law in their Report on *Domestic Violence and Occupation of the Family Home* (1992):

2.21 There are three different statutes giving the courts express powers to grant nonmolestation orders or injunctions and to regulate the occupation of the family home by way of ouster, exclusion or other orders. The Domestic Violence and Matrimonial Proceedings Act 1976 empowers county courts to grant injunctions against molestation or exclude one party from the home, not only between spouses but also between men and women living together as husband and wife, and also to attach powers of arrest to certain injunctions however granted [ss. 1 and 2]. The Domestic Proceedings and Magistrates' Courts Act 1978 gives magistrates' courts power to make orders protecting one spouse from violence by the other, and in some cases to exclude one spouse from the home and to attach powers of arrest [s. 16(2) and (3)]. The Matrimonial Homes Act 1983 gives one spouse the right to occupy a matrimonial home to which the other is entitled, makes those rights a charge upon the estate or interest of the entitled spouse, and enables the High Court or a county court to enforce or restrict the respective rights of spouses to occupy the home [ss. 1(2) and 9(1)].

2.22 These statutory powers were superimposed on the existing general powers of the High Court and county courts to grant injunctions [Supreme Court Act 1981, s. 37; County Courts Act 1984, s. 38]. Such powers are ancillary to some other remedy within the court's jurisdiction, or in support of a right recognised by the general law. Thus, for many years divorce courts have granted injunctions against molestation or even excluded a spouse from the matrimonial home in response to applications made ancillary to divorce, separation or nullity proceedings in order to enable the petitioner to pursue her action free from intimidation [e.g. *Silverstone v Silverstone* [1953] P 174; *Hall v Hall* [1971] 1 WLR 404. ...]. The High Court and county courts can also grant injunctions to protect victims from the torts of assault, battery, nuisance or trespass, or in support of any other unrecognised property right [e.g. *Egan v Egan* [1975] Ch 218; *Tabone v Seguna* [1986] 1 FLR 591, *Smith v Smith* [1988] 1 FLR 179; *Patel v Patel* [1988] 2 FLR 179].

2.23 There are many inconsistencies and anomalies in the present law. These have arisen largely as a result of piecemeal statutory development and the adoption or adaptation of a remedy developed for a particular purpose in one context for different purposes in another. [In an international review of remedies for violence against women in the family, the United Nations has commented that 'The scheme in England and Wales provided by three different pieces of legislation which apply to different relationships and in different circumstances and give different relief presents even experienced lawyers with difficulties': United Nations, 1989.] The existing remedies have been developed in response to a variety of needs. Those under the Matrimonial Homes Act 1983 were first introduced in 1967 [by the Matrimonial Homes Act 1967 at a time when it was more usual for matrimonial homes to be in the husband's sole name] in order to ensure that deserted wives were not left without a roof over their heads, by giving them rights of occupation in the matrimonial home which could be registered and enforced against third parties, and by giving the court power to regulate occupation of the matrimonial home in the long or short term. To this was later added a power to prohibit the exercise by the property-owning spouse of his right to occupy the home [Domestic Violence and Matrimonial Proceedings Act 1976, ss. 3 and 4, reversing the effect of *Tarr v Tarr* [1973] AC 254]. The remedies provided in sections 16–18 of the Domestic Proceedings and Magistrates' Courts Act 1978 and the Domestic Violence and Matrimonial Proceedings Act 1976 have protection against violence and molestation as their primary objective and were designed to provide an urgent legal response to this, which could include an exclusion order where the circumstances justified it. The principles applicable to regulating occupation of the home in the short or long term and to providing protection from violence and molestation are not necessarily the same. But it is impossible to treat them separately because, very often, the removal of one party from the house is the only effective protection which can be provided in cases of violence.

2.24 ... The fact that different remedies are available to different applicants on different criteria in different courts with different enforcement procedures has resulted in a vastly complicated system, made even more confusing by the complex inter-relationship between the statutory remedies and the general principles of property and tort law. In the first place, the scope of orders available under the different Acts differ. For instance, orders under the Domestic Violence and Matrimonial Proceedings Act 1976 can be wider than those under the Matrimonial Homes Act 1983 in that they can be tailored to allow the respondent to return to the property for the purpose of, for example, visiting children or carrying on a business [see also Domestic Proceedings and Magistrates' Courts Act 1978, s. 16(9)]; but at the same time they are narrower in that there is no power to make ancillary orders about the discharge of outgoings or payment for occupation [Matrimonial Homes Act 1983, s. 1(3)(*b*) and (*c*)]. Again, the Domestic Violence and Matrimonial Proceedings Act 1976 allows the exclusion of the respondent from an area around the family home [Domestic Violence and Matrimonial Proceedings Act 1976, s. 1(1)(*c*)] whereas this is not possible under the Domestic Proceedings and Magistrates' Courts Act 1978 or the Matrimonial Homes Act 1983. Yet we understand that exclusion zone orders are frequently made by the courts in the context of matrimonial proceedings in which the principles in the 1983 Act are applied.

2.25 The criteria applicable under the different Acts are also diverse and, in many ways, unsatisfactory in themselves. Neither the general powers under which the Courts grant injunctions in pending proceedings or the 1976 Act lay down any criteria for the exercise of the court's discretion. [Supreme Court Act 1981, s. 37 and County Courts Act 1984, s. 38 refer simply to what is 'just and convenient']. But, despite the fact that the courts had developed their own principles to govern the exercise of this jurisdiction [based mainly upon relative hardship to the parties and the interests of the children, see *Bassett v Bassett* [1975] Fam 76; *Walker v Walker* [1978] 1 WLR 533], in *Richards v Richards* [1984] AC 174 (p. 397, below) the House of Lords decided that the criteria set out in section 1(3) of the 1983 Act should be applied in any case where an ouster order is sought between spouses, whether under that Act, the 1976 Act or in pending matrimonial proceedings. [Section 1(3) provides that 'the court may make such order as it thinks just and reasonable having regard to the conduct of the spouses in relation to each other and otherwise, to their respective needs and financial resources to the needs of any children and to all the circumstances of the case'. The same criteria have also been extended to applications between cohabitants, despite the fact that the Matrimonial Homes Act 1983 does not apply to them; *Lee v Lee* [1984] FLR 243.] These criteria are not, however, applied in applications for exclusion orders under the Domestic Proceedings and Magistrates' Courts Act 1978. This Act has its own criteria based mainly on the use or threat of violence and danger of injury.

Before the Family Law Act 1996, the grounds for personal protection and exclusion orders in magistrates' courts were set out in s. 16(3) of the Domestic Proceedings and Magistrates' Courts Act 1978: the respondent must have (i) used violence against the applicant or a child of the family, or (ii) threatened to use violence against the applicant or child and actually used it against someone else, or (iii) threatened to use violence against the applicant or a child in breach of a personal protection order; and the applicant or child must be in danger of being physically injured by the respondent.

Questions

(i) Why, before the Family Law Act 1996, were the magistrates' powers limited (*a*) to cases involving the use or threat of violence, and (*b*) to husband and wife?
(ii) The number of applications to magistrates' courts has decreased dramatically from 8,720 in 1984 to 1,642 in 1993 (Edwards, 1996), while applications to county courts have increased from 7,110 in 1981 to 24,010 in 1995 (Judicial Statistics 1996). Can you think of reasons why a wife who has suffered violence might prefer to apply to a county court, despite being able to apply under the Domestic Proceedings and Magistrates' Court Act 1978?

The complexity of the different enactments, with different criteria, was one reason why reform was necessary. The lack of protection for former spouses and former cohabitants, as well as other family members, was another reason. Many of these problems have been addressed by the Family Law Act 1996 (see below). However, as the Law Commission's Report (1992) points out, it is not just the law's substantive defects which reduce its effectiveness:

2.8 Domestic violence is not simply a legal problem which can be eradicated by the appropriate legal remedies. It is also a social and psychological problem which can be eliminated only by fundamental changes in society and in attitudes to women and children. While legal remedies are an attempt to alleviate the symptoms of domestic violence, they can do little to tackle the causes. Also, their effectiveness can be hampered by various factors [see Women's National Commission, *Violence Against Women: report of an ad hoc Working group*, 1985]. First, they have to operate in an area where there is a constant tension between the need for instant protection to be given to the victim and the need to observe due process in the conduct of proceedings against the alleged perpetrator. A balance has to be struck between the victim's need and the rights of other people, although there is, of course, room for argument about what the correct balance should be. Also, legal remedies can be undermined by the gap which exists between the letter and spirit of the law and the law in practice. It has been said that those who work in this area, including solicitors, barristers, police, court staff and judiciary, can, perhaps unconsciously, deter applicants from pursuing their proceedings or prevent the law operating as effectively as it might, if their reactions are affected by particular perceptions of male and female roles or an ambivalence about the propriety of legal or police intervention within the family [for example, Edwards and Halpern, 1991; Maidment, 1977]. As a recent study has concluded, 'whatever legal reforms may be made, and whatever changes may be made to court procedures, without effective enforcement by police officers and by courts, injunctions and protection orders will continue to be "not worth the paper they are written on" ' [Barron, 1990].

Some of the reasons why women found that non-molestation orders were 'not worth the paper they were written on' are illustrated by Erin Pizzey (1974):

Joan took her husband before the High Court eleven times before she finally got him put in prison with a one-year sentence. The first time he broke in the police refused to come as they said there was nothing they could do on a High Court injunction. He beat her up and she came to Women's

Aid. After that the poor woman yo-yoed back and forth with her three children using us as a refuge when her husband was around. Eventually she went back and tried to live in the home that the court said was hers when the divorce had been granted. He broke in, beat her up, punctured her ear-drum and raped her at the point of a knife. When she got him back into the High Court, the judge did not appear to have read the previous judges' notes and accepted the husband's story that he dropped in for some urgent papers at 3 a.m. and his wife had refused to let him have them. The judge gave him seven days and told him in effect that he was a naughty boy.

Part of Joan's problem was that whenever she took her husband to court they appeared in front of a different judge, and none of the judges bothered to read the file of her husband's atrocities, which was steadily getting thicker and thicker.

She gave up trying to live in 'her' home and moved in with us. Her husband broke our windows, screamed and raged outside the house, pestered the school and tried to snatch the children. We took him back to court and this time saw the same judge twice. He did read the case and was appalled enough to put him inside for a year. It was too late for Joan to claim her council house, though – the rent arrears had mounted up and the council had taken it back.

Other problems are demonstrated by a woman whose experience was described in the evidence of Welsh Womens' Aid to the Home Affairs Committee (1993):

In May 1989, I was hospitalised for eight weeks by my partner's violence. Whilst I was in hospital, my ex-partner was allowed out of prison on bail. The bail conditions were that he stayed away from the hospital and the village where the 'matrimonial home' was. However, no one bothered to tell me this and I only found out by 'pestering' the police.

About four to five weeks after I returned home from hospital, my ex-partner simply walked in on me – he literally didn't even bother to knock on the door. He said that he had been back to court and the bail conditions no longer applied. He had been given two years probation. Again, no one had bothered to let me know when the hearing was or what the decision was. I was very shocked and frightened and managed to escape with great difficulty, using a zimmer frame, to my neighbour's.

I phoned the Probation Officer and was told that I would have to take out an injunction myself despite the fact that my partner was supposedly under the direction and control of this Probation Officer.

I applied for an injunction and it took nearly three weeks to come to court. I asked for an injunction with a power of arrest attached. This I did not get, in fact I only got an undertaking which was negotiated in the corridor whilst I was sitting in the courtroom waiting for my application to be heard. After the hearing, I had to come into contact with my ex-partner because there was only one way out. He asked me if I wanted a lift 'home' from court – the 'home' that he had just undertaken to stay away from! The charge for this ended up on my Legal Aid bill.

When the undertaking ran out, I sought another injunction. I was told that as I had suffered no further assaults, it would be very unlikely that I would be granted one. During this time, he had called up to my house every weekend to see the children and to work on me. He wanted to move back into the house permanently. I felt harrassed and under threat.

By June 1990, I gave way and agreed for him to move into the house for one week because he had to leave his accommodation and his new accommodation was not ready. However, once he moved back in he would not leave. In order to get an 'ouster', I would have had to wait until I was assaulted again. With my last experience of hospitalisation in my mind and knowing that if I did get an 'ouster', it would only last three months anyway, I decided to leave. I felt that I had no real choice, I didn't want to leave my home.

At the end of September 1990, I moved to Aberystwyth. In November, my ex-partner found me and threatened me with a knife. I had to run to the Women's Aid office and from there, moved into a Refuge. I was granted an emergency *ex-parte* non-molestation order which lasted until 20 December. Again, this ended up on my Legal Aid bill.

On 20 December, I got another non-molestation order but I had to move from the Refuge into hiding because my ex-partner had found the Refuge and was calling there. He was also going to the children's school and into lecture theatres in the University looking for me. For three weeks, the non-molestation order was void as it had not been served. Therefore, I could not even use the limited power of the order to take my ex-partner back to court for contempt. I had extensions to the injunction and so on and similar things happened.

It seems to me that I was a victim of someone else's violent and irresponsible behaviour and yet it has always been me that has had to pay. Somewhere along the line, I had a property put into my joint name. My name should have been on the property in the first place if it were not for my ex-partner's irresponsible behaviour. I have had to respond to my ex-partner's actions in order to seek protection, but the costs go on to my Legal Aid bill as a charge on my house which I must pay when the house is sold.

I feel that I should have been told when the hearings would be and of the sentence. My feelings should have been considered when the bail conditions (my only protection) were lifted. And I feel extremely let down by the Probation Service to whom I was an irrelevance. Every time I attended court no one met my eye. I was ignored. The judge would usually have a little joke with my ex-partner. I think I made them all feel uncomfortable. I am now a law student and, when they know this, they treat me very differently. I am no longer a victim but 'one of us'.

When I really needed protection I did not get it. If I knew then what I know now, I would not have bothered with all the distress of hours spent in solicitors' offices and court waiting rooms.

Although reform of the law cannot be a complete solution to the problem of domestic violence, it is important that the law should be as clear and comprehensible as possible. The Law Commission recommended in 1992 that there should be a consistent system of remedies available at all levels of the court system, replacing the confusing statutory framework already described. However, an attempt to introduce such a system in the Family Homes and Domestic Violence Bill 1995 proved unexpectedly controversial, and the Bill was withdrawn. An amended version of the Bill's provisions was eventually incorporated into the Family Law Act 1996. The Act provides for 'non-molestation orders' and 'occupation orders' to be available at all levels of the court system, replacing the various orders and injunctions which were available under the previous law.

Section 42 of the Family Law Act 1996 deals with non-molestation orders:

42. – (1) In this Part a 'non-molestation order' means an order containing either or both of the following provisions –

(*a*) provision prohibiting a person ('the respondent') from molesting another person who is associated with the respondent;

(*b*) provision prohibiting the respondent from molesting a relevant child.

(2) The court may make a non-molestation order –

(*a*) if an application for the order has been made (whether in other family proceedings or without any other family proceedings being instituted) by a person who is associated with the respondent; or

(*b*) if in any family proceedings to which the respondent is a party the court considers that the order should be made for the benefit of any other party to the proceedings or any relevant child even though no such application has been made.

...

(5) In deciding whether to exercise its powers under this section and, if so, in what manner, the court shall have regard to all the circumstances including the need to secure the heath, safety and well-being –

(*a*) of the applicant or, in a case falling within subsection (2)(*b*), the person for whose benefit the order would be made; and

(*b*) of any relevant child.

'Relevant child' is defined by s. 62(2) as:

(*a*) any child who is living with or might reasonably be expected to live with either party to the proceedings;

(*b*) any child in relation to whom an order under the Adoption Act 1976 or the Children Act 1989 is in question in the proceedings; and

(*c*) any other child whose interests the court considers relevant.

The category of 'associated persons' is defined in s. 62(3):

62. – ... (3) For the purposes of this Part, a person is associated with another person if –
(*a*) they are or have been married to each other;
(*b*) they are cohabitants or former cohabitants;
(*c*) they live or have lived in the same household, otherwise than merely by reason of one of them being the other's employee, tenant, lodger or boarder;
(*d*) they are relatives;
(*e*) they have agreed to marry one another (whether or not that agreement has been terminated);
(*f*) in relation to any child, they are both persons falling within subsection (4); or
(*g*) they are parties to the same family proceedings (other than proceedings under this Part).
(4) A person falls within this subsection in relation to a child if –
(*a*) he is a parent of the child; or
(*b*) he has or has had parental responsibility for the child.
(5) If a child has been adopted or has been freed for adoption by virtue of any of the enactments mentioned in section 16(1) of the Adoption Act 1976, two persons are also associated with each other for the purposes of this Part if –
(*a*) one is a natural parent of the child or a parent of such a natural parent; and
(*b*) the other is the child or any person-
(i) who has become a parent of the child by virtue of an adoption order or has applied for an adoption order, or
(ii) with whom the child has at any time been placed for adoption.
(6) A body corporate and another person are not, by virtue of subsection (3)(*f*) or (*g*), to be regarded for the purposes of this Part as associated with each other.

'Cohabitants' is defined by s. 62(1):

(*a*) 'cohabitants' are a man and a woman who, although not married to each other, are living together as husband and wife; and
(*b*) 'former cohabitants' is to be read accordingly, but does not include cohabitants who have subsequently married each other.

and 'relative' is defined by s. 63(1) as:

(*a*) the father, mother, stepfather, stepmother, son, daughter, stepson, stepdaughter, grandmother, grandfather, grandson or granddaughter of that person or of that person's spouse or former spouse, or
(*b*) the brother, sister, uncle, aunt, niece or nephew (whether of the full blood or of the half blood or by affinity) of that person or of that person's spouse or former spouse,

and includes in relation to a person who is living or has lived with another person as husband and wife, any person who would fall within paragraph (*a*) or (*b*) if the parties were married to each other.

Questions

(i) Do these provisions allow for non-molestation orders between: (*a*) a gay or lesbian couple living together; (*b*) a heterosexual couple who have separate homes, but frequently spend nights together; (*c*) a group of students sharing a house, which one of them sub-lets to the others; (*d*) cousins? Should they?
(ii) What makes households or families more deserving of such a remedy than other victims of harassment or molestation?

In its Report (1992), the Law Commission considered the possibility of allowing anyone to seek a non-molestation order, but decided against:

3.19 ... We do not think it is appropriate that this jurisdiction should be available to resolve issues such as disputes between neighbours, harassment of tenants by landlords or cases of sexual harassment in the workplace. Here there is no domestic or family relationship to justify special remedies or procedures and resort should properly be had to the remedies provided under property or employment law. Family relationships can, however, be appropriately distinguished from other forms of association. In practice, many of the same considerations apply to them as to married or cohabiting couples. Thus the proximity of the parties often gives unique opportunities for molestation and abuse to continue; the heightened emotions of all concerned give rise to a particular need for sensitivity and flexibility in the law; there is frequently a possibility that their relationship will carry on for the foreseeable future; and there is in most cases the likelihood that they will share a common budget, making financial remedies inappropriate.

However, in addition to the categories eventually included in the Family Law Act 1996, the Law Commission (1992) had recommended that non-molestation orders should be available between people who 'have or have had a sexual relationship with each other (whether or not including sexual intercourse)'. The inclusion of this category was supported by the Home Affairs Committee (1993):

109 ... People must be protected against harassment, violence and abuse from those with whom they have or have had close emotional and sexual relationships. Not all intense relationships between partners result in marriage or cohabitation – there are, for example, 'visiting' or adulterous relationships where the parties still live with their spouses or simply lovers who choose not to live together. Nor do we believe that sexual intercourse should be a determining factor because not all cohabitees, let alone non-cohabitees, have sexual intercourse with each other. We therefore think it inappropriate to attach any special significance here to the sexual act.

On the other hand, His Honour Judge Fricker QC (1995) supported the exclusion of this group:

... when a 'family' breaks down, it is likely that further contact between the members will be needed in relation to practical and continuing arrangements for their children, or adjustments to their finances or housing needs. Therefore a right to be protected from molestation is related to a likely continuing practical nexus in many situations. The problems arising in disentangling previous shared commitments based on family membership involving a mixture of personal and legal relationships.

If the [Act] were extended to cover persons who have had an intimate sexual relationship without having created a child, ... would there be a continuing practical nexus? The continuing nexus in most cases would, I suggest, be substantially an inability to 'let go' the relationship. Usually there will not be a practical need to adjust to a change in existing financial or housing arrangements.

...

One form of harassment which has recently been publicised is 'stalking', e.g. an obsessional admirer harasses someone in the entertainment world. People who are unfairly harassed do need protection.

I suggest that extending the [Family Law Act] beyond a sensible family nexus would create an anomalous legal right not founded on legal principle other than convenience. It would create what would be in effect a right not to be harassed under a stretched umbrella of family law, with an arbitrary boundary. The nettle should be grasped and the right not to be harassed should be founded in the law of tort, where it belongs.

The Court of Appeal has already gone some way to developing the law of tort in order to provide remedies for people who face violence or harassment from people with whom they have had a sexual relationship, as well as less intimate acquaintances, or complete strangers.

Burris v Azadani
[1995] 4 All ER 802, [1995] 1 WLR 1372, [1996] 1 FLR 266, Court of Appeal

A divorced woman with two children was being harassed by an acquaintance. He was seeking to establish an intimate relationship with her, which she did not want. She obtained an injunction restraining him from assaulting, molesting, harassing, threatening, pestering or interfering with her. He was also ordered not to come with 250 yards of her address. He was committed to prison for breach of these orders, and appealed.

Sir Thomas Bingham MR: ... In *Khorasandjian v Bush* [1993] QB 727, [1993] 2 FLR 66 the plaintiff and the defendant had previously been friends, although they had never cohabited. Their relationship had broken down, but the defendant had been quite unable to accept that it was over. The plaintiff made a number of complaints against the defendant: that he had assaulted her; that he had threatened violence; that he had abused her; that he had persecuted her with telephone calls, and not only her but her mother, her boyfriend, and her boyfriend's mother; that he had converted her property; and that he had damaged her property. For the defendant it was accepted on appeal that the court could properly restrain him from assaulting, or attempting to assault, or using violence against, or interfering with the property of, the plaintiff. But it was argued that the plaintiff could not complain of persistent unwanted telephone calls since she had no real property interest in her parents' house, and it was accordingly submitted that the judge had no jurisdiction to restrain the defendant from 'harassing, pestering or communicating with' the plaintiff, because those words did not reflect any tort known to the law and an interlocutory injunction could only be granted to protect a legal right of the plaintiff. In a judgment with which Rose LJ agreed, but from which Peter Gibson J dissented, Dillon LJ rejected these suggested restrictions on the jurisdiction of the court. He regarded it as 'ridiculous' if the law was that the making of deliberately harassing and pestering telephone calls to a person was only actionable in the civil courts if the recipient of the calls happened to have the freehold or a leasehold interest in the premises in which he or she had received the calls. If the wife of an owner of premises was, as a Canadian court had held, entitled to sue in respect of harassing telephone calls, he could not see why that should not also apply to a child living at home with her parents. He accepted that damage was a necessary ingredient of the tort of private nuisance but observed:

> 'So far as the harassing telephone calls are concerned, however, the inconvenience and annoyance to the occupier caused by such calls, and the interference thereby with the ordinary and reasonable use of the property are sufficient damage. The harassment is the persistent making of the unwanted telephone calls, even apart from their content; if the content is itself as here threatening and objectionable, the harassment is the greater.'

Having referred to earlier authority, Dillon LJ held that it did not preclude the court from taking a wider view of the telephone harassment under the heading of private nuisance in the light of the interference with the ordinary and reasonable enjoyment of property, and also that verbal threats made orally to a person could be actionable if they caused illness. He found on the facts an obvious risk that the cumulative effect of continued and unrestrained harassment such as the plaintiff had undergone could subject the plaintiff to such stress as would be likely to cause illness.

Furthermore, it was also lawful to order the defendant not to come within a defined area around the plaintiff's house. The Master of the Rolls continued:

Neither statute nor authority in my view precludes the making of an 'exclusion zone' order. But that does not mean that such orders should be made at all readily, or without very good reason. There are two interests to be reconciled. One is that of the defendant. His liberty must be respected up to the point at which his conduct infringes, or threatens to infringe, the rights of the plaintiff. No restraint should be placed on him which is not judged to be necessary to protect the rights of the plaintiff. But the plaintiff has an interest which the court must be astute to protect. The rule of law requires that those whose rights are infringed should seek the aid of the court, and respect for the legal process can only suffer if those who need protection fail to get it. That, in part at least, is why disobedience to orders of the court has always earned severe punishment. Respect for the freedom of the aggressor should never lead the court to deny necessary protection to the victim.

Ordinarily, the victim will be adequately protected by an injunction which restrains the tort which has been or is likely to be committed, whether trespass to the person or to land, interference with goods, harassment, intimidation or as the case may be. But it may be clear on the facts that if the defendant approaches the vicinity of the plaintiff's home he will succumb to the temptation to enter it, or to abuse or harass the plaintiff; or that he may loiter outside the house, watching and besetting it, in a manner which might be highly stressful and disturbing to a plaintiff. In such a situation the court may properly judge that in the plaintiff' s interest – and also, but indirectly, the defendant's – a wider measure of restraint is called for.

This case indicates the protective potential of the law of tort for people who cannot apply for non-molestation orders under the Family Law Act 1996. However, Mary Hayes is very critical of this position in *Non-molestation Protection: Only Associated Persons Need Apply* (1996):

The [Family Law Act 1996] will give rights to apply for non-molestation orders to spouses, cohabitants and a curious list of associated persons. The law of tort will make provision for those who fall outside this group. Instead what is needed is a clear and unambiguous civil law relating to non-molestation injunctions with a particular emphasis, in my view, on the courts being given effective powers to combat violence and threats of violence. Enabling anyone to benefit from such a proposal would, of course, increase the numbers of potential litigants and give extensive discretionary powers to the judges. Of course injunctions have the potential to interfere with civil liberties, and a balance must be struck between the rights and interests of the opposing parties. But the history of domestic violence legislation, and the exercise of judicial discretion generally in family and tort cases, reveals that there is no need to fear that courts will take an extreme, or radical, or over-protective stances, should all persons be drawn into the net of the courts' protective powers.

... [Parliament] should decide whether it wishes all its citizens to be protected effectively against violence and other forms of molestation, rather than a privileged group, and if it does it should provide the courts with a flexible and permissive framework within which to respond, coupled with strong enforcement powers. It should then draw back from legislating in a detailed manner and simply trust the courts to exercise their injunction powers wisely. They usually do.

Questions

(i) Do you agree, or do you share Judge Fricker's view that the remedies developed in family law should not be stretched to cover people who have never been part of the same family?

(ii) The Government announced in May 1996 that it intended to introduce legislation to combat the problem of 'stalking' (Home Office and LCD, 1996). Would such legislation be unnecessary if the 'associated person' requirement were removed from the Family Law Act 1996?

Under the Family Law Act 1996, a non-molestation order may be made for a specified period or until further order (s. 42(7)) and may be 'expressed so as to refer to molestation in general, to particular acts of molestation, or to both' (s. 42(6)). As the Law Commission point out in their Report (1992):

2.3 Domestic violence can take many forms. The term 'violence' itself is often used in two senses. In its narrower meaning it describes the use of threat of physical force against a victim in the form of an assault or battery. But in the context of the family, there is also a wider meaning which extends to abuse beyond the more typical instances of physical assaults to include any form of physical, sexual or psychological molestation or harassment which has a serious detrimental effect upon the health and well-being of the victim, albeit that there is no 'violence' involved in the sense of physical force. Examples of such 'non-violent' harassment or molestation cover a very wide range of behaviour [*Vaughan v Vaughan* [1973] 1 WLR 1159]. Common instances include persistent pestering and intimidation through shouting, denigration, threats or argument, nuisance telephone calls, damaging property, following the applicant about and repeatedly calling at her home or place of work. Installing a mistress into the matrimonial home with a wife and three children [*Adams v Adams* (1965) 109 Sol Jo 899], filling car locks with superglue, writing anonymous letters and pressing one's face against a window whilst brandishing papers [*Smith v Smith* [1988] 1 FLR 179] have all been held to amount to molestation. The degree of severity of such behaviour depends less upon its intrinsic nature than upon it being part of a pattern and upon its effect on the victim. Acts of molestation often follow upon previous behaviour which has been violent or otherwise offensive. Calling at the applicant's house on one occasion may not be objectionable. Calling frequently and unexpectedly at unsocial hours when the victim is known to be afraid certainly is. Such forms of abuse may in some circumstances be just as harmful, vicious and distressing as physical injuries.

In addition to non-molestation orders, the Family Law Act 1996 also provides for a variety of 'occupation orders'. The Law Commission (1992) recognised the importance of such orders in cases of domestic violence:

4.6 ... where the parties live together, an occupation order ousting the respondent from the home will often be the only way of supporting a non-molestation order and giving the applicant effective protection.

However, the Law Commission's Report (1992) also drew attention to the effect of such orders on the other party:

2.48 In principle, there must be a distinction between an order not to be violent towards or molest another family member, which can be obeyed without prejudice to the interests of the person concerned, and an order to leave or stay away from the home (or part of it), which obviously does prejudice those interests, however temporarily or justifiably.

Before the Family Law Act 1996, the criteria for 'ouster orders' were settled by the House of Lords:

Richards v Richards
[1984] AC 174, [1983] 2 All ER 807, [1983] 3 WLR 173, [1984] FLR 11, 13 Fam Law 256, House of Lords

The wife petitioned for divorce, relying upon allegations of behaviour, but remained in the matrimonial home for nearly three months performing 'wifely duties' but not sleeping with her husband. She then left taking the children, a girl of six and a boy of four, to a friend's cottage. She sought and obtained an order, inter alia, for the husband to leave the home. She then returned with the children; the parties had since arranged that she lived with them there during the week and the father lived with them there at weekends. The husband's appeal to the Court of Appeal was dismissed and he appealed to the House of Lords. The House of Lords decided that the judge had been wrong to give priority to the interests of the children. Instead, he should have applied the criteria in the Matrimonial Homes Act 1967 (later consolidated as the Matrimonial Homes Act 1983).

Lord Brandon of Oakbrook: ... That subsection requires the court to make such order as it thinks just and reasonable having regard to a number of specified matters. The matters so specified are these: (1) the conduct of the spouses to each other and otherwise; (2) the respective needs and financial resources of the spouses; (3) the needs of any children; and (4) all the circumstances of the case. With regard to these matters it is, in my opinion, of the utmost importance to appreciate that none of them is made, by the wording of s. 1(3), necessarily of more weight than any of the others, let alone made paramount over them. All the four matters specified are to be regarded, and the weight to be given to any particular one of them must depend on the facts of each case.

My Lords, I do not go so far as to say that the conduct of an applicant wife in the particular respect under discussion is necessarily and in all cases decisive, in a manner adverse to her of the question whether the order for which she has applied should be made or not. It is however, an important factor to be weighed in the scales, along with the other matters specified in s. 1(3) of the 1967 Act; and in a substantial number of cases at any rate it will be a factor of such weight as to lead a court to think that it would not be just or reasonable to allow her application. ...

When the Law Commission reviewed the law in 1992, they outlined the criticism of these criteria:

4.23 ... They do not give priority to the applicant's personal protection, but require this to be balanced against all other factors, including hardship to the respondent. Thus the level of protection provided for an applicant suffering from violence may not be adequate. Also a requirement to decide upon occupation of the family home on the basis (at least in part) of fault, thus encouraging parties to make allegations about behaviour, sits uneasily with the general trend in matrimonial law towards reducing the need for recrimination and fault-finding, and enabling the courts to deal with problems of family breakdown without allocating blame, with a view to enhancing the possibility of agreement or even reconciliation between the parties. The test is also thought to give insufficient weight to the interests of children as the balancing exercise throws the children into the scales along with all the other factors and gives no priority to their welfare.

However, the Law Commission stopped short of recommending that the welfare of children should be the paramount consideration. Instead they recommended a 'balance of harm' test should apply, so that a court should have a duty to make an order if it appears likely that the applicant or any relevant child will suffer significant harm if an order is not made and that such harm will be greater than the harm which the respondent or any relevant child will suffer if the order is made. They said:

4.34 ... It is likely that a respondent threatened with ouster on account of his violence would be able to establish a degree of hardship (perhaps in terms of difficulty in finding or unsuitability of alternative accommodation or problems in getting to work). But he is unlikely to suffer significant harm, whereas his wife and children who are being subjected to his violence or abuse may very easily suffer harm if he remains in the house. In this way the court will be treating violence or other forms of abuse as deserving immediate relief, and will be directed to make an order where a risk of significant harm exists. However, by placing an emphasis on the need for a remedy rather than on the conduct which gave rise to that need, the criteria will not actually put a premium on allegations of violence and thus may avoid the problems which would be generated by a scheme which focuses on it.

Question

Why was the Law Commission concerned not to put a premium on allegations of violence?

An amended version of the 'balance of harm' test appears in s. 33 of the Family Law Act 1996:

33. – ... (3) An order under this section may –

(*a*) enforce the applicant's entitlement to remain in occupation as against the other person ('the respondent');

(*b*) require the respondent to permit the applicant to enter and remain in the dwelling-house or part of the dwelling-house;

(*c*) regulate the occupation of the dwelling-house by either or both parties;

(*d*) if the respondent is entitled [to occupy the dwelling-house by virtue of a beneficial estate or interest or contract or by virtue of any enactment giving him the right to remain in occupation], prohibit, suspend or restrict the exercise by him of his right to occupy the dwelling-house;

(*e*) if the respondent has matrimonial home rights in relation to the dwelling-house and the applicant is the other spouse, restrict or terminate those rights;

(*f*) require the respondent to leave the dwelling-house or part of the dwelling-house; or

(*g*) exclude the respondent from a defined area in which the dwelling house is included.

...

(6) In deciding whether to exercise its powers under subsection (3) and (if so) in what manner, the court shall have regard to all the circumstances including –

(*a*) the housing needs and housing resources of each of the parties and of any relevant child;

(*b*) the financial resources of each of the parties;

(*c*) the likely effect of any order, or of any decision by the court not to exercise its powers under subsection (3), on the health, safety or well-being of the parties and of any relevant child; and

(*d*) the conduct of the parties in relation to each other and otherwise.

(7) If it appears to the court that the applicant or any relevant child is likely to suffer significant harm attributable to conduct of the respondent if an order under this section containing one or more of the provisions mentioned in subsection (3) is not made, the court shall make the order unless it appears to it that –

(*a*) the respondent or any relevant child is likely to suffer significant harm if the order is made; and

(*b*) the harm likely to be suffered by the respondent or child in that event is as great as, or greater than, the harm attributable to conduct of the respondent which is likely to be suffered by the applicant or child if the order is not made.

...

'Harm' is defined in s. 63 of the Act to mean ill-treatment or the impairment of physical or mental health, and (in the case of children) impairment of development.

Question

Why does sub-s. (7) require that the harm likely to be suffered is 'attributable to the conduct of the respondent'?

An application under s. 33 of the Family Law Act 1996 is only possible where the applicant is entitled to occupy the home by virtue of a legal or beneficial estate or interest or a contractual or statutory right. Section 33 will, therefore, always be available between spouses since, in the absence of any other right, they will have a statutory right of occupation under s. 30 of the Family Law Act 1996 (see p. 147, above). Occupation orders will be available between unmarried people, provided that they are 'associated' in the same way as for non-molestation orders, but only if the applicant can establish that he or she has some entitlement to occupy the property in question (s. 33(1)).

Of course, a person with no right to occupy the home may be just as much in need of protection, but under the Family Law Act 1996 such a person may only apply for an occupation order against a former spouse, cohabitant or former cohabitant, and there are different criteria for such applications. Sections 37 and 38 of the 1996 Act provide for occupation orders where neither of the parties has a right of occupation. A more common situation will be where a non-entitled applicant is seeking an occupation order against a former spouse, cohabitant or former cohabitant who is entitled to occupy the property. These applications are governed by s. 35 (for former spouses) and s. 36 (for cohabitants and former cohabitants).

It was established under the previous legislation that ouster orders could be made in favour of a cohabitant who had no right to occupy the home (*Davis v Johnson* [1979] AC 264). The Law Commission (1992) explained why it was, nevertheless, thought necessary to distinguish between 'entitled' and 'non-entitled' applicants:

4.7 ... the grant of an occupation order can severely restrict the enjoyment of property rights, and its potential consequences to a respondent are therefore more serious than those of a non-molestation order which generally only prohibits conduct which is already illegal or at least, anti-social. Such consequences may be acceptable when both parties are entitled to occupy, but they are more difficult to justify when the applicant has no such right. ... In the case of non-entitled applicants, particularly when the respondent is also entitled, an occupation has a purpose beyond short term protection, namely to regulate the occupation of the home until its medium or short term destiny has been decided, or in some cases, indefinitely. ... In the case of non-entitled applicants, an occupation order is essentially a short term measure of protection intended to give them time to find alternative accommodation, or, at most, to await the outcome of an application for a property law remedy.

Under ss. 35 and 36, there is a two-stage approach to non-entitled applicants. Under both sections, an applicant must first obtain an order under sub-s. (3) or (4) which gives the applicant the right to enter the home (if not already in occupation), and to remain there without being evicted or excluded by the respondent.

Before making such an order, the court is required to have regard to:

(6) ... all the circumstances including –
- (*a*) the housing needs and housing resources of each of the parties and of any relevant child;
- (*b*) the financial resources of each of the parties;
- (*c*) the likely effect of any order, or of any decision by the court not to exercise its powers under subsection (3) or (4) on the health, safety or well-being of the parties and of any relevant child; and
- (*d*) the conduct of the parties in relation to each other and otherwise.

This checklist occurs in identical form in ss. 35(6) and 36(6). However, the remainder of each subsection is different. In cases involving former spouses the court must also consider:

35. – ... (6) ...
- (*e*) the length of time that has elapsed since the parties ceased to live together;
- (*f*) the length of time that has elapsed since the marriage was dissolved or annulled; and
- (*g*) the existence of any pending proceedings between the parties –
  - (i) for an order under section 23A or 24 of the Matrimonial Causes Act 1973 (property adjustment orders in connection with divorce proceedings etc.);
  - (ii) for an order under paragraph 1(2)(*d*) or (*e*) of Schedule 1 to the Children Act 1989 (orders for financial relief against parents); or
  - (iii) relating to the legal or beneficial ownership of the dwelling-house.

In cases involving cohabitants or former cohabitants the court must consider:

36. – ... (6) ...

(*e*) the nature of the parties' relationship;
(*f*) the length of time during which they have lived together as husband and wife;
(*g*) whether there are or have been any children who are children of both parties or for whom both parties have or have had parental responsibility;
(*h*) the length of time that has elapsed since the parties ceased to live together; and
(*j*) the existence of any pending proceedings between the parties –
 (ii) for an order under paragraph 1(2)(*d*) or (*e*) of Schedule 1 to the Children Act 1989 (orders for financial relief against parents); or
 (iii) relating to the legal or beneficial ownership of the dwelling-house.

Furthermore, where the court is considering the 'nature of the relationship' of cohabitants or former cohabitants, the court is required by s. 41 to 'have regard to the fact that the parties have not given each other the commitment involved in marriage'.

Question

How helpful are these provisions, given that the court is obliged to consider 'all the circumstances'?

If a non-entitled applicant obtains an order under sub-ss. (3) or (4), the court may then consider whether to include a provision under sub-s. (5) to:

(*a*) regulate the occupation of the dwelling-house by either or both of the parties;
(*b*) prohibit, suspend or restrict the exercise by the respondent of his right to occupy the dwelling-house;
(*c*) require the respondent to leave the dwelling-house or part of the dwelling-house; or
(*d*) exclude the respondent from a defined area in which the dwelling-house is included.

In deciding whether to include such a provision, the court is once more required to consider the basic criteria in sub-s. (6)(*a*)–(*d*) (see p. 400, above). However there are further additional criteria at this stage, which differ according to whether the non-entitled applicant is a former spouse (applying under s. 35) or a cohabitant or former cohabitant (applying under s. 36).

In the case of former spouses, s. 35(7) requires the court to consider the length of time that has elapsed since the parties ceased to live together. In addition, the 'balance of harm' test (see p. 399, above) applies at this stage.

In the cases of a non-entitled cohabitant or former cohabitant, the court is required by section 36(7) and (8) to consider:

(*a*) whether the applicant or any relevant child is likely to suffer significant harm attributable to conduct of the respondent if the subsection (5) provision is not included in the order; and
(*b*) whether the harm likely to be suffered by the respondent or child if the provision is included is as great or greater than the harm attributable to conduct of the respondent which is likely to be suffered by the applicant or child if the provision is not included.

Finally, s. 36(10) provides that an occupation order in favour of a non-entitled cohabitant or former cohabitant must be limited to a period not exceeding six months, and may be extended on only one occasion for a further period not exceeding six months. Under the previous legislation ouster orders were rarely made for longer than three months (see *Practice*

Note [1978] 2 All ER 1056, [1978] 1 WLR 1123). The Law Commission (1992) recommended that occupation orders in favour of entitled applicants could be made for any specified period or until further order, but that orders in favour of non-entitled applicants could only be made for up to six months, but renewable any number of times for up to six months at a time. They were persuaded that there was a widespread problem of applicants being unable to find alternative accommodation in less than six months. Where an order is made at a full hearing after an initial ex parte order, the maximum period of the two orders taken together is six months (s. 45(4)(*b*)). However, in determining the number of renewals, the two orders are treated as a single order (s. 45(4)(*a*)) which may, therefore, be renewed once more.

Questions

(i) Why, contrary to the recommendations of the Law Commission (1992), does the balance of harm test not apply to applications by non-entitled cohabitants or former cohabitants?
(ii) Many of the complexities in the criteria for occupation orders for different types of non-entitled applicants were introduced after the failure of the Family Homes and Domestic Violence Bill in 1995 (see Horton, 1996). Is the complexity of the provisions justifiable?

As well as needing to satisfy the criteria in the legislation, a victim of domestic violence who is seeking a remedy will face many practical difficulties. One problem is graphically illustrated by Erin Pizzey (1974):

Going to court is quite an ordeal. The High Court in the Strand is as awe-inspiring as it sounds. It is a massive crenellated building with white towers and spires outside and a huge arched hall inside. The place is honeycombed with narrow corridors that run off the central hall to the small courtrooms. Everywhere ant-like uniformed figures bustle around. Barristers stride along in their black flapping gowns and wrinkled white wigs, best-suited solicitors scurry in their wake, blue-suited ushers look officious. The people waiting in little knots look shabby and out of place in this impersonal palace of justice.

If the case is to be heard in the morning we have to be there by 10. Waiting to meet the solicitor is always an anxious time because if the husband has been told to attend the court too, it will be the first time that his wife has had to face him since she ran away.

If you manage to avoid meeting him before, you usually find him crouched on the hard little benches that line the ill-lit, crowded corridor outside the courtroom. There, knee to knee and face to face, the couple must wait, sometimes for hours, before they are called into court.

My first time was with Lesley. Pat had come along to hold her other hand and together we had to hold Lesley upright because she was in such a state of fear at the prospect of seeing her husband. He had a terrible reputation, and on the night she had left him, he'd gone to see her friends with a gang and broken into the house. The gang beat up the old couple upstairs and their two sons. It took ten policemen to get them out, and though he was charged he was released on bail. Now we were in court to ask for an injunction to give her custody of the three children, maintenance while her divorce petition went through and a non-molestation order to keep him from carrying out his threat to kill her.

Waiting to go into the courtroom, we were all frightened. The solicitor and the barrister were quite unperturbed, and the barrister gave the impression that Lesley was making an unnecessary fuss. We were due in court mid-morning, so we settled down on the little benches to wait, morosely contemplating the other silent people waiting, and gazing at the stained walls.

The tedium and the peace were disturbed by the arrival of Lesley's husband and his henchmen. Then began a cat-and-mouse shuffle as we moved round the narrow corridors trying to prevent him upsetting Lesley even more. By the time it was our turn Lesley was speechless with fright and we half carried her between us into the court.

Fairness to the respondent requires that he be given a chance to hear the applicant's case, and respond to it. However, in some cases, the risk to the victim will be such that she should be able to seek an immediate remedy, either without informing the respondent at all, or without giving him as much notice of the application as would usually be required. A Practice Note issued in 1978 ([1978] 1 WLR 925) stated that 'an *ex parte* application should not be made, or granted, unless there is real immediate danger of serious injury or irreparable damage'. The Family Law Act 1996 provides new criteria for *ex parte* orders:

45. – (1) The court may, in any case where it considers that it is just and convenient to do so, make an occupation order or a non-molestation order even though the respondent has not been given such notice of the proceedings as would otherwise be required by rules of court.

(2) In determining whether to exercise its powers under subsection (1), the court shall have regard to all the circumstances including –

(*a*) any risk of significant harm to the applicant or a relevant child, attributable to conduct of the respondent, if the order is not made immediately;

(*b*) whether it is likely that the applicant will be deterred or prevented from pursuing the application if an order is not made immediately; and

(*c*) whether there is reason to believe that the respondent is aware of the proceedings but is deliberately evading service and that the applicant or a relevant child will be seriously prejudiced by the delay involved –

(i) where the court is a magistrates' court, in effecting service of proceedings; or

(ii) in any other case, in effecting substituted service.

(3) If the court makes an order by virtue of subsection (1) it must afford the respondent an opportunity to make representations relating to the order as soon as just and convenient at a full hearing.

...

Question

Which is the more unjust: making an alleged batterer leave the home for a short while before he has an opportunity of defending himself against the allegations, or making the alleged victim leave for a short while before she has an opportunity of putting her case before a court?

It is one thing to obtain an order, but it must also be enforced effectively if it is to ensure the applicant's safety. Because of difficulties with purely civil enforcement methods, s. 2 of the Domestic Violence and Matrimonial Proceedings Act 1976 contained a provision allowing a 'power of arrest' to be attached to an order in certain circumstances. This allowed a police officer to arrest someone whom he had reasonable cause to suspect was breaching the court's order. However, such orders were rarely granted for more than three months (see *Practice Note* [1981] 1 All ER 224, [1981] 1 WLR 27). In *Violence Against Women* (1985), a Working Group of the Women's National Commission commented:

108. The Working Group received evidence that these apparently helpful legislative measures have, in practice, achieved much less than was anticipated. ... Many battered women are wholly ignorant of the law and are deterred from consulting solicitors because too afraid or believing it would be too costly. The Courts have proved suspicious of the wide powers which can be taken against the allegedly violent partner including removing him from his own property, and if they agree to grant injunctions they may limit the period these remain in force. Practical difficulties

for complainants and their solicitors have proved to be great: the procedures are cumbersome and time consuming; it is virtually impossible for the police to assist in enforcing an injunction with no powers of arrest attached, and, probably through lack of specific training and lack of serious concern with domestic matters, police have often proved ill-informed about what to do, and sluggish to act, even where powers of arrest exist. ...

111. Parker (1985) refers to the fact that in 1980, out of 6,400 injunctions granted under Section 1 of the DVA, only 24% had powers of arrest attached to them (in the North East only 10%). Other authorities discuss in greater detail the practical difficulties solicitors for battered women and the women themselves may encounter in obtaining injunctions. Violent husbands can be clever and elusive. They may return during the night to the home from which they are excluded by injunction to attack their wife. Wives may have difficulty in establishing that a breach of the injunction has occurred. Injuries may need to be grave and obvious to convince sceptical authorities. If a power of arrest is attached, police may nevertheless be very reluctant to act and have to be convinced that a breach has occurred. Where there is no power of arrest, the battered wife has to apply to the Court for her husband to *be charged with contempt of court*, first ensuring notice is served on him. ... The period of any legal delays can be most dangerous for wives as violent men are often inflamed by wives taking legal steps. ...

113. The Working Group accepts that there are intrinsic difficulties for the Courts in establishing when violent partners should be subject to injunctions, especially when this makes a man homeless. If injunctions were granted to women without enquiry, judges would be criticised with some justification for failing to give a fair hearing to husbands to whom the asset of their home and the stability this represents for them will normally be very important. However, the Working Group urge judges to consider the frequently desperate situation of battered wives, who are obliged to seek safety and redress for acts of what may be extreme violence through an inadequate mechanism. They would like to see powers of arrest attached to all injunctions made under the DVA, unless the judge is satisfied that there is no danger of physical attack. It would be desirable if legislation could be amended to incorporate this principle.

Responding to concerns of this kind, the Family Law Act 1996 creates a presumption in favour of powers of arrest in cases of actual or threatened violence:

47. – ... (2) If –

(*a*) the court makes [an occupation order or a non-molestation order], and

(*b*) it appears to the court that the respondent has used or threatened violence against the applicant or a relevant child,

it shall attach a power of arrest to one or more provisions of the order unless satisfied that in all the circumstances of the case the applicant or child will be adequately protected without such a power of arrest.

This presumption does not apply to *ex parte* orders, but a court may attach a power of arrest to such an order if it appears:

47. – ... (3) ...

(*a*) that the respondent has used or threatened violence against the applicant or a relevant child; and

(*b*) that there is a risk of significant harm to the applicant or child, attributable to conduct of the respondent, if the power of arrest is not attached to those provisions immediately.

The court may accept an undertaking from any of the parties to the proceedings instead of making an occupation order or a non-molestation order (s. 46(1)). An undertaking may be enforced in the same way as an order (s. 46(4)). However a power of arrest cannot be attached (s. 46(2)). Therefore, the court cannot accept undertakings in cases where a power of arrest would have been added (s. 46(3)).

In cases where a power of arrest has not been granted, there is a new procedure under s. 47(8), allowing the court to grant a warrant of arrest if the court has reasonable grounds for believing that the respondent has failed to comply with the order.

The provisions relating to powers of arrest should help to provide additional security for victims of domestic violence, but civil remedies will rarely provide a complete or permanent solution. Gill Hague and Ellen Malos discuss the difficulties in *Children, Domestic Violence and Housing*, in the collection *Children Living with Domestic Violence*, edited by Morley and Mullender in 1994:

For very large numbers of women and children escaping domestic violence, the only way to achieve a safe and secure life is to leave the violent perpetrator completely and begin again somewhere else.

In our study [Malos and Hague (1993)], however, we collected evidence that women and children attempting to escape violence and seeking rehousing in various local authorities were refused any assistance from the council once they had obtained a legal order against the violent perpetrator. ... But, for women and children to be safe and secure in this situation, there will need to be an as yet unachieved level of effective legal protection and enforcement, accompanied by multi-layered support within the community and community intolerance of domestic violence. At the moment, this is not the situation in this country, and many women and children escaping violence in the home do not wish, under any circumstances, to return to their former home.

The availability of alternative housing will be crucial in these circumstances. The Working Group of the Women's National Commission (1985) discuss the possibilities:

115. ... An alternative to restraining the man is to remove the woman to a place of safety where she can begin a new separate existence if she wishes. ... Women's Aid refuges serve a number of purposes admirably, and are an exceedingly welcome development which needs supporting. But women often return to violent husbands because of concern about the quality of their own and their children's lives in refuges, which are often overcrowded. This underlines the importance of the Housing (Homeless Persons) Act 1977, which defines women victims of domestic violence as in 'priority need' and obliges a local authority to find permanent accommodation for them. Women's Aid groups normally find that the existence of the Act now enables them to negotiate some permanent local authority accommodation for women living in their refuges. But local authorities tend to strictly ration what is available. The assumption sometimes made that a very high proportion of women in refuges return permanently to their violent partners is not true. One research study undertaken by Jan Pahl (1985) found that:

> 'Out of the 42 women, 20 (48%) never lived with their husbands again after leaving the refuge, while only two lived with their husbands continuously from the time they left the refuge until the time of the second interview (about two years later). The remaining 20 of the women (48%) made between one and nine attempts at reconciliation. ... Of these only nine couples were still together at the second interview. ... '

Lack of a housing offer amongst other factors has forced large numbers of women to try again with their husbands and to suffer further violence. The Working Group therefore urge Housing Authorities to accept their responsibilities in relation to battered wives. It has been suggested that if Housing Authorities had a policy of seeking to find some accommodation (temporary or permanent) for violent husbands they would enable battered wives and children to remain in the family home in family sized accommodation which would be under-utilised by the man himself. To effect this kind of sensible solution probably requires multi-agency working groups to be set up on which police, personal social services, housing authority, and women's organisations representatives could serve.

Questions

(i) Knowing that a woman with children who is not intentionally homeless has a priority need under (now) Part III of the Housing Act 1985, would you be more or less inclined to grant an order ousting her husband from the matrimonial council house?

(ii) Will the court be able to transfer the tenancy into her name (see p. 185, above)? What if the couple are not married?
(iii) As the House of Commons Select Committee on Violence in Marriage (1975) asked during its proceedings, why do we not create hostels to receive the battering men?

5 What about the children?

Researchers have begun to explore the links between domestic violence and child abuse (see Morley and Mullender, 1994; Kelly, 1994; Department of Health, 1996), and there are indications that the abuse of mothers and children frequently occur in the same family. We have already seen that an adult may seek a non-molestation order or occupation order to protect a 'relevant child' (pp. 392, 398–401, above). It is also possible for a child to make an application under the Family Law Act 1996 him or herself. Section 43 of the Family Law Act 1996 provides for this:

43. – (1) A child under the age of sixteen may not apply for an occupation order or a non-molestation order except with the leave of the court.
(2) The court may grant leave for the purposes of subsection (1) only if it is satisfied that the child has sufficient understanding to make the proposed application for the occupation order or non-molestation order.

This section is based upon similar provisions of the Children Act 1989, which we will consider in the next chapter, but what if no member of the family is able or willing to make an application? Even if the children are not directly attacked, there will often be a risk that they will be physically injured during an attack on their mother. Besides the physical dangers, the impact on a child's emotional and psychological development may amount to 'significant harm' under s. 31 of the Children Act 1989. This raises the possibility of an application by the local authority for a care order which would allow for the children to be removed from the home. We will consider care proceedings in Chapter 13, below.

Questions

(i) If a woman is aware that her children might be removed from her care if she continues to live with their violent father, is she (*a*) more likely to leave him, or (*b*) less likely to seek any form of assistance? Is this another example of 'blaming the victim'?
(ii) Would it not be better to allow someone to apply for orders to protect both adults and children from domestic violence?

Section 60 was added to the Family Law Act 1996 at a late stage.

60. – (1) Rules of court may provide for a prescribed person, or any person in a prescribed category ('a representative'), to act on behalf of another in relation to proceedings to which this Part applies.

(2) Rules under this section may, in particular, authorise a representative to apply for an occupation order or for a non-molestation order for which the person on whose behalf the representative is acting could have applied.

(3) Rules made under this section may prescribe –

(*a*) conditions to be satisfied before a representative may make an application to the court on behalf of another; and

(*b*) considerations to be taken into account by the court in determining whether, and if so how, to exercise any of its powers under this Part when a representative is acting on behalf of another.

The Government spokesman explained the background to this provision (HC Official Reports (5th Series), Vol 279, cols 598–599, 17 June 1996):

The proposal to grant police powers to seek civil remedies on behalf of those suffering domestic violence has its origin in the Law Commission report of 1992. However the Homes Affairs Select Committee's inquiry into domestic violence in 1993 rejected the proposal, as did the House of Lords Special Public Bill Committee on the Family Homes and Domestic Violence Bill.

There was, and remains, concern that the police have neither the resources nor the expertise to take on this role. Interest groups were also divided on this issue, some fearing the further disempowerment of women already trapped in situations over which they have little control. In light of these considerations, it was decided not to include such a provision in the Bill. Whatever the pros and cons of the third party approach to attacking domestic violence, it is clear we are not yet in a position where it is wise to embark immediately on this course. ...

The Government remain of the view that there may need to be a good deal more thought, discussion and research before any rules are made under the new clause. ...

The Government also accept that ... the amendment does not prescribe that the police shall act as the representatives, and that others may more appropriately be able to do it in consultation with the police.

Questions

(i) Should rules be made under s. 60 to allow third parties to apply for non-molestation orders and occupation orders?

(ii) Should the representatives be police officers, or some other agency?

(iii) How much weight should the representative and the court be required to give to the wishes of the person on whose behalf the representative is acting?

Chapter 10

Parents and children

Relying on parents to bring up their children is seen as an essential feature of Western democratic society. But is this for the parents', the children's or society's sake? When should a child's interests or wishes prevail over his parents'? How much help should the parents be given to perform their task? These are large issues which can only be touched on here, but they serve as an introduction to the philosophy of the Children Act 1989, with its transition from rights to responsibility for parents.

1 Parental rights and children's welfare

The concept of parental 'rights' achieved its greatest legal prominence in the nineteenth century. An example of eighteenth century thinking is provided by Sir William Blackstone in the first volume of his *Commentaries on the Laws of England* (1765):

1. And, first, the duties of parents to legitimate children: which principally consist in three particulars; their maintenance, their protection, and their education.

The duty of parents to provide for the *maintenance* of their children is a principle of natural law; an obligation, says Puffendorf, laid on them not only by nature herself, but by their own proper act, in bringing them into the world: for they would be in the highest manner injurious to their issue, if they only gave the children life, that they might afterwards see them perish. By begetting them therefore they have entered into a voluntary obligation, to endeavour, as far as in them lies, that the life which they have bestowed shall be supported and preserved. And thus the children will have a perfect *right* of receiving maintenance from their parents. ...

After discussing the relevant provisions of English law, including its deficiencies in the matter of education, he continues:

2. The *power* of parents over their children is derived from the former consideration, their duty; this authority being given them, partly to enable the parent more effectually to perform his duty, and partly as a recompence for his care and trouble in the faithful discharge of it. And upon this score the municipal laws of some nations have given a much larger authority to the parents, than others. The ancient Roman laws gave the father a power of life and death over his children; upon this principle, that he who gave had also the power of taking away. ...

The power of a parent by our English laws is much more moderate; but still sufficient to keep the child in order and obedience. He may lawfully correct his child, being under age, in a reasonable manner; for this is for the benefit of his education. The consent or concurrence of the parent to the marriage of his child under age, was also *directed* by our ancient law to be obtained: but now it is absolutely *necessary;* for without it the contract is void. And this also is another means, which the law has put into the parent's hands, in order the better to discharge his duty; first, of protecting his children from the snares of artful and designing persons; and, next of settling them properly in life, by preventing the ill consequences of too early and precipitate marriages. A father has no other power over his son's *estate,* than as his trustee or guardian; for, though he may receive the profits during the child's minority, yet he must account for them when he comes of age. He may indeed have the benefit of his children's labour while they live with him, and are maintained by him: but this is no more than he is entitled to from his apprentices or servants. The legal power of a father (for a mother, as such, is entitled to no power, but only to reverence and respect) the power of a father, I say, over the persons of his children ceases at the age of twenty one: for they are then enfranchised by arriving at years of discretion, or that point which the law has established (as some must necessarily be established) when the empire of the father, or other guardian, gives place to the empire of reason. Yet, till that age arrives, this empire of the father continues even after his death; for he may by his will appoint a guardian to his children. ...

3. The *duties* of children to their parents arise from a principle of natural justice and retribution. For to those, who gave us existence, we naturally owe subjection and obedience during our minority, and honour and reverence ever after; they, who protected the weakness of our infancy, are entitled to our protection in the infirmity of their age; they who by sustenance and education have enabled their offspring to prosper, ought in return to be supported by that offspring, in case they stand in need of assistance. Upon this principle proceed all the duties of children to their parents, which are enjoined by positive laws.

Questions

(i) How much of this represents the modern law?
(ii) Do you think that Blackstone's account of the rationale underlying parental power is equally applicable today?

If parents have rights, there might be two ways of enforcing them: either by an action in tort against anyone who interfered or by an action to recover the child and impose the parental will upon him. There was a common law action in tort, but only if the third party, either by enticement, seduction or harbouring, or by a wrongful act against the child, caused a loss of services actually being rendered by the child to the father. These actions were abolished in 1970 and 1982 respectively. Hence in *F v Wirral Metropolitan Borough Council* [1991] Fam 69, [1991] 2 All ER 648, Stuart-Smith LJ announced that 'In my judgment [counsel's] submission that this court could now declare that a parent had an action for damages for interference with his or her right as a parent was wholly misconceived.' However, various remedies were available to recover a child and enforce the father's wishes as to his upbringing (see Pettitt, 1957). These reached their peak in a case which Lord Upjohn in *J v C* [1970] AC 668, [1969] 1 All ER 788, p. 411, below, could 'only describe as dreadful'.

Re Agar-Ellis, Agar-Ellis v Lascelles
(1883) 24 Ch D 317, 53 LJ Ch 10, 50 LT 161, 32 WR 1, Court of Appeal

A Protestant father agreed at his marriage that any children would be brought up Roman Catholics, but at the birth of the first child he changed his mind. The mother, however, taught the children Roman Catholicism and eventually they refused to go to a Protestant church. The father made them wards of court and the court (see (1878) 10 Ch D 49, 48 LJ Ch 1) restrained the mother from taking them to confession or to a Roman Catholic church and left the father to do what he thought fit for their spiritual welfare. He therefore took the children from their mother and placed them with other people, allowing her to visit only once a month and censoring her letters. In 1883, the second daughter, then aged 16, wrote to the judge begging to be allowed the free exercise of her religion and to live with her mother. The father agreed to the former but not the latter. Accordingly, she and her mother petitioned the court to allow them a two-month holiday together and freedom of correspondence and access. The father opposed this because he feared that the mother would alienate his child's affections. Pearson J dismissed the petition. The petitioners appealed.

Brett MR: ... The rights of a father are sacred rights because his duties are sacred duties. ...

Bowen LJ: ... This is a case in which, if we were not in a Court of Law, but in a court of critics capable of being moved by feelings of favour or disfavour, we might be tempted to comment, with more or less severity, upon the way in which, so far as we have heard the story, the father has exercised his parental right. But it seems to me the Court must not allow itself to drift out of the proper course; the Court must not be tempted to interfere with the natural order and course of family life, the very basis of which is the authority of the father, except it be in those special cases in which the state is called upon, for reasons of urgency, to set aside the parental authority and to intervene for itself. ...

... Judicial machinery is quite inadequate to the task of educating children in this country. It can correct abuses and it can interfere to redress the parental caprice, and it does interfere when the natural guardian of the child ceases to be the natural guardian, and shews by his conduct that he has become an unnatural guardian, but to interfere further would be to ignore the one principle which is the most fundamental of all in the history of mankind, and owing to the full play of which man has become what he is. ... If that were not so we might be interfering all day and with every family. I have no doubt that there are very few families in the country in which fathers do not, at some time or other, make mistakes, and there are very few families in which a wiser person than the father might not do something better for that child than is being done by the father, who however has an authority which never ought to be slighted.

Appeal dismissed.

Questions

(i) Take out the sex discrimination and apply these arguments to a couple's decision: (*a*) that their child shall not go on the school trip to France; (*b*) that their child shall go to Sunday school every week; (*c*) that their child shall not be vaccinated against whooping cough; or (*d*) that their child should not receive sex education or attend 'peace studies' in school. Should the law interfere?

(ii) How relevant to your view of the *Agar-Ellis* decision was it (*a*) that mother and father disagreed with one another, and (*b*) that the child was, by the hearing, aged 17?

The position between mother and father was radically changed by or before the Guardianship of Infants Act 1925, later consolidated in the Guardianship of Minors Act 1971. Section 1 of each required any court considering a question of the custody or upbringing of a child, or the use of his income or property, to regard his welfare as the 'first and paramount consideration' and not to take into consideration whether 'from any other point of view the claim of the father, or any right at common law possessed by the father ... is superior to that of the mother' or vice versa. The same principle was later applied to disputes between parents and non-parents:

J v C
[1970] AC 668, [1969] 1 All ER 788, [1969] 2 WLR 540, 113 Sol Jo 164, House of Lords

It is almost impossible to summarise the facts dispassionately, but Lord Guest perhaps comes closest to doing so:

The story began in the autumn of 1957 when the infant's parents came to Britain from Madrid for the purpose of bettering their financial position by entering domestic service. The father was at that time a very lowly-paid worker living in poor housing conditions in Madrid. They are both of the Roman Catholic faith. They left behind a daughter then aged 4 who lived with the maternal grandmother. The mother became pregnant shortly after their arrival in Britain and the infant was born in hospital on 8 May 1958. As the mother was found to be suffering from tuberculosis and had to remain in hospital for some considerable time a home was found for the infant through the kind offices of a married couple who have been called the 'foster parents'. The infant was taken care of, from the age of four days, by them in their house in Northamptonshire while the mother remained in hospital. The foster parents had been both previously married and between them have four children by their previous marriages and now have two by their own marriage. The infant continued to remain with the foster parents until the mother was discharged from hospital in April 1959. The infant's father remained in employment near the foster parents' house and visited the infant from time to time. The infant thereafter rejoined his parents who had obtained employment in Surrey. The foster parents had also moved to Surrey. The infant remained with his parents at C for about ten months: the foster mother assisted the mother in looking after the infant and the parents kept in touch with the foster parents' family. In February 1960, the mother again became pregnant. As she was afraid of having another baby in this country she and her husband went back to Madrid taking the infant with them.

During the infant's stay in Madrid in the summer of 1960 his parents lived in what has been described as little better than a 'hovel'. The father was still a lowly-paid worker and the family lived in what were virtually slum conditions. In the summer heat of Madrid the infant's health rapidly deteriorated due to malnutrition and the local conditions which did not suit him. He only remained in Madrid with his parents for 17 months. In July 1961, he returned to Britain to stay with the foster parents. This move was made at the specific request of the parents who, through the intermediary of a Spanish maid of the foster parents, M, conveyed their request to the foster parents. This request was made on the ground of the infant's health. On his return to this country the infant's health rapidly improved and he has continued thereafter to enjoy good health. He has not lived with his parents since July 1961, and has continued to live with the foster parents ever since. ...

Up to [February 1963] the parents had evinced no wish to the foster parents to have the infant back with them in Madrid apart from a suggestion for a holiday. But in July 1963, the foster mother wrote to the mother what has been described as a tactless and most unfortunate letter. In this letter she described how the infant had become integrated with their family; he had gone to an English school and he had grown up an English boy with English habits, and that it would be most disturbing for him to have to return to live with his parents in Madrid. She also made critical remarks about the infant's father. This letter produced the not unexpected reaction from the mother who, after some previous correspondence, wrote on 25 September 1963, to the Surrey County Council, in whose official care the infant was, asking for the infant's return. The local authority did not act with conspicuous consistency or good sense. After appearing to agree to the mother's request they subsequently, after receipt of a letter from the foster parents expressing their point of view, resolved, on the advice of counsel, to apply to the Chancery Division to have the infant made a ward of court, which was done on 16 December 1963.

The proceedings took some considerable time to reach the judge and the parents were unfortunately led to believe by a letter from the Surrey County Council that they would be represented by counsel at the hearing who would state their case for them. For this reason the parents only lodged written representations which had been prepared for them by a Spanish lawyer. These, however, did express their wish for the infant's return. Affidavits were lodged by various other parties. After a hearing on 22 July 1965, Ungoed-Thomas J ordered that the infant remain a ward of court, that the care and control be committed to the foster parents, that the infant be brought up in the Roman Catholic faith and in the knowledge and recognition of his parents and in knowledge of the Spanish language.

Two years were to elapse before the final stage of the proceedings took place before the same judge. This stage had been initiated by the parents' summons – asking that they should have the care and control of the infant. This was made on 10 May 1967. An application was also made by the foster parents in January 1967, that the infant be brought up in the Protestant faith. This request for a change in the boy's religious upbringing was prompted by a desire on the foster parents' part that he should enter a choir school so as to avoid expense. The most convenient school was a Protestant school. The official solicitor also entered the proceedings, having been appointed next friend. On this occasion the judge heard evidence from all the parties and his judgment was given on 31 July 1967. No order was made on either application. ...

... It may be that if more expedition had been exercised by the parties in bringing the case to trial and the full facts had been known at the time, the judge's decision might well have been different in 1963. In 1963 when the parents first asked for the infant's return he was only 5 years old and he had only been parted from his parents for a matter of two years. Even in 1965 he was only 7 years old, but at the time of the second hearing he was 9½ and he is now 10½ years old. He has been at school in England since January 1963. He has not seen his parents since 1961 when he was 3, and apart from a matter of 27 months he has been living continually in the home of the foster parents with their family. There is no doubt, as the learned judge found, that the infant lives in happy surroundings in a united and well-integrated family. The mixed families have made it particularly easy for him to become integrated. He speaks English and only pidgin Spanish. He is especially friendly with P the child of the marriage of the foster parents who is only a little younger than him.

It is right at this stage to say that the house in which the parents now live in Madrid is entirely suitable for the reception of the infant. It contains three bedrooms and is in a modern block of flats in quite different surroundings from the previous home. The father is in good steady employment at a weekly wage of about £18 and the mother's health has been completely restored.

The reason which has impelled the judge to take the unusual step of taking the care and control from the parents and giving it to strangers is that, in his view, the risk of plunging this boy of 10½ years into a Spanish family, where he has not seen his parents since he was aged 3 and into a foreign country, would be too great to take and that the adjustment necessary might well permanently injure the infant's health at the impressionable age at which he has arrived. The judge has regarded the infant's welfare as the paramount consideration and he has decided that this demands that he should remain with his foster parents.

The account of the law which has been most frequently quoted in subsequent decisions is that of Lord MacDermott:

All parties were agreed that the courts had jurisdiction and a duty to interfere with the natural right of parents to have the care, control and custody of their child if the welfare of the child required and the law permitted that course to be taken. But there agreement ended. For the parents it was submitted that the courts were in law bound to presume that the welfare of the child was best served by allowing him to live with his parents unless it was shown that it was not for his welfare to do so because of their conduct, character or station in life. Counsel for the infant and counsel for the foster parents submitted, on the other hand, that there was no such presumption of law, that the paramount and governing consideration was the welfare of the child and that the claim of natural parents, although often of great weight and cogency and often conclusive, had to be regarded in conjunction with all other relevant factors, and had to yield if, in the end, the welfare of the child so required.

... I have already mentioned counsel for the parents' concession as to the position if his argument does not prevail. I may add here that if it does prevail the appeal, in my opinion, is bound to succeed since: (*a*) the evidence shows no defects of character or conduct on the part of the parents sufficient to disentitle them to custody; and (*b*) their position in life has so improved as to be no longer capable in itself of constituting an answer to their claim.

His lordship then reviews the developments in case law and statute before 1925 and continues:

I have referred to these Acts because, as in the case of the authorities, they record an increasing qualification of common law rights and the growing acceptance of the welfare of the infant as a criterion. In this way, and like the trend of the cases, they serve to introduce the enactment which has been so closely canvassed on the issue of law under discussion. It is s. 1 of the Guardianship of Infants Act 1925 [see above, p. 410].

The part of this section referring to 'the first and paramount consideration' has been spoken of as declaratory of the existing law. See *Re Thain, Thain v Taylor* [1926] Ch 676, 95 LJ Ch 292 per Lord Hanworth MR (p. 689) and Sargant LJ (p. 691); and *McKee v McKee* [1951] AC 352 at 366 per Lord Simonds. There have been different views about this, but whether the proposition is wholly accurate or not, the true construction of the section itself has to be considered as a matter of prime importance.

Two questions arise here. First, is the section to be read as referring only to disputes between the parents of the child? In *Re Carroll* [1931] 1 KB 317, 100 LJKB 113, Slesser LJ appears to have approved such an interpretation for he said (p. 355):

> 'This statute, however, in my view, has confined itself to questions between the rights of father and mother which I have already outlined – factors which cannot arise in the case of an illegitimate child ... '

Now, the latter part of the section is directed to equalising the legal rights or claims of the parents, and the preamble speaks only of achieving an equality between the sexes in relation to the guardianship of infants. But these considerations, do not, in my opinion, suffice to constrict the natural meaning of the first part of the section. The latter part beginning with the words 'shall not take into consideration ... ' does not call for or imply any such constriction for it does not necessarily apply to all the possible disputes which the earlier part is capable of embracing; and as for the preamble, it could only be used to restrict the applicability of the earlier part of the section if that part were ambiguous. See *A-G v HRH Prince Ernest Augustus of Hanover* [1957] AC 436 at 463 per Viscount Simonds. Having read the whole Act, I cannot find this important earlier part to be other than clear and unambiguous. On the contrary, its wording seems to be deliberately wide and general. It relates to *any* proceedings before *any* court, and as Eve J said in *Clarke-Jervoise v Scutt* [1920] 1 Ch 382 at 388: ' "Any" is a word with a very wide meaning, and prima facie the use of it excludes limitation.'...

The second question of construction is as to the scope and meaning of the words '... shall regard the welfare of the infant as the first and paramount consideration.' Reading these words in their ordinary significance, and relating them to the various classes of proceedings which the section has already mentioned, it seems to me that they must mean more than that the child's welfare is to be treated as the top item in a list of items relevant to the matter in question. I think they connote a process whereby, when all the relevant facts, relationships, claims and wishes of parents, risks, choices and other circumstances are taken into account and weighed, the course to be followed will be that which is most in the interests of the child's welfare as that term has now to be understood. That is the first consideration because it is of first importance and the paramount consideration because it rules on or determines the course to be followed. It remains to see how this 'first view', as I may call it, stands in the light of authority.

After a review of the authorities, he concludes:

... I conclude that my first view construction of s. 1 should stand, and that the parents' proposition of law is ill-founded and must fail. The consequences of this present little difficulty, but before coming to them I would add in summary form certain views and comments on the ground surveyed in the hope that they may serve to restrict misunderstanding in this difficult field. These may be enumerated as follows:

1. Section 1 of the Act of 1925 applies to disputes not only between parents, but between parents and strangers and strangers and strangers.
2. In applying s. 1, the rights and wishes of parents, whether unimpeachable or otherwise, must be assessed and weighed in their bearing on the welfare of the child in conjunction with all other factors relevant to that issue.
3. While there is now no rule of law that the rights and wishes of unimpeachable parents must prevail over other considerations, such rights and wishes, recognised as they are by nature and society, can be capable of ministering to the total welfare of the child in a special way, and must therefore preponderate in many cases. The parental rights, however, remain qualified and not absolute for the purposes of the investigation, the broad nature of which is still as described in the fourth of the principles enunciated by FitzGibbon LJ in *Re O'Hara* [1900] 2 IR 232 at 240. [I.e. the court should act cautiously, and in opposition to the parent only when judicially satisfied that the welfare of the child requires it.]
4. Some of the authorities convey the impression that the upset caused to a child by a change of custody is transient and a matter of small importance. For all I know that may have been true in the cases containing dicta to that effect. But I think a growing experience has shown that it is not

always so and that serious harm even to young children may, on occasion, be caused by such a change. I do not suggest that the difficulties of this subject can be resolved by purely theoretical considerations, or that they need to be left entirely to expert opinion. But a child's future happiness and sense of security are always important factors and the effects of a change of custody will often be worthy of the close and anxious attention which they undoubtedly received in this case.

... The learned judge applied the appropriate principles of law and I can find no ground for interfering with the manner in which he exercised his discretion. On these grounds I am of opinion that the appeal fails and should be dismissed.

Their lordships all concurred in dismissing the appeal. Lord Upjohn, however, had this to say:

My Lords, Eve J [in *Re Thain* [1926] Ch 676] said that among other considerations the wishes of an unimpeachable parent undoubtedly stand first, and I believe, as I have said, that represents the law. ... The natural parents have a strong claim to have their wishes considered first and principally, no doubt, because normally it is part of the paramount consideration of the welfare of the infant that he should be with them but also because as the natural parents they have themselves a strong claim to have their wishes considered as normally the proper persons to have the upbringing of the child they have brought into the world. It is not, however, a question of the onus being on anyone to displace the wishes of the parents; it is a matter for the judge ...

Lord Donovan's short, sharp speech contains the following:

I think the section means just what it says – no more and no less; and although the claim of natural parents to the custody and upbringing of their own children is obviously a most weighty factor to be taken into consideration in deciding what is in the best interests of the infant, yet the legislature recognised that this might not always be the determining factor, whether the parents were unimpeachable or not.

The Law Commission discuss the point of principle in their Working Paper on *Custody* (1986):

6.20 There may still be doubts whether the child's 'best interests' should determine the issue between parents and non-parents. Respect for family life is guaranteed under the European Convention on Human Rights [see p. 714, below] and parents may require protection from unwarranted interference. Local authorities are not permitted compulsorily to intervene in the care of children simply because they could provide something better, but only where specific shortcomings in the home or the parents can be proved. In adoption, parental agreement is required, unless it can be dispensed with on defined grounds, and the child's welfare is only the 'first' rather than the 'paramount' consideration. In relation to custody and upbringing, however, the House of Lords decided in *J v C* that there is no presumption in favour of even the 'unimpeachable' natural parents of the child, although their relationship with the child will often carry great weight as they 'can be capable of ministering to the total welfare of the child in a special way'.

6.21 Although we recognise that this is a difficult question, several arguments persuade us that the present position in English law should be maintained. First, the child may have a much closer relationship with someone other than his 'natural' parent. The emotional and psychological bonds which develop between a child (especially a very young child) and those who are bringing him up are just as 'natural' as are his genetic ties. To give preference over such a 'psychological' parent to one whose interest may be based solely on a blood tie could on occasion be highly detrimental to the child. Secondly, the analogy with intervention by local authorities is not exact. By definition, the authority cannot be or become such a 'psychological' parent. Whereas a non-parent applicant will usually be seeking to secure the child's existing home and an established relationship, the local authority will usually be seeking to remove him from such a home in favour of an unspecified alternative. Unlike a case between private individuals, the court is not faced with a choice between two (or more) identifiable homes. There are also strong objections in principle to the authority of the state being used to impose standards upon families unless it can be shown that the children are suffering, or are likely to suffer, unacceptable harm.

6.22 We conclude, therefore, that the welfare of each child in the family should continue to be the paramount consideration whenever their custody or upbringing is in question between private individuals.

The Children Act 1989 has replaced s. 1 of the Guardianship of Minors Act 1971 as follows:

1. – (1) When a court determines any question with respect to –
(*a*) the upbringing of a child; or
(*b*) the administration of a child's property or the application of any income arising from it,
the child's welfare shall be the court's paramount consideration.

Questions

(i) Do you agree with the principle?
(ii) The facts of *J v C* were very similar to those of Sifiso Mahlangu, a 10-year-old Zulu boy looked after by his mother's employer and brought to this country with her consent; but on 4 May 1996 Sifiso was sent back to his parents in South Africa even though he wanted to stay here; can you think why the courts reached a different conclusion in his case?
(iii) It is one thing to decide between competing sets of parents, one 'natural' and the other 'social': but what about interfering in a particular upbringing decision made by otherwise 'unimpeachable' parents?

Of course, some decisions are more important than others:

Re D (a minor) (wardship: sterilisation)
[1976] Fam 185, [1976] 1 All ER 326, [1976] 2 WLR 279, 119 Sol Jo 696, High Court, Family Division

D, now aged 11, was born with 'Sotos syndrome', the symptoms of which included epilepsy, clumsiness, an unusual facial appearance, behavioural problems, and some impairment of intelligence. Her mother was convinced that she was seriously mentally handicapped and would be unable to care either for herself or a child of her own. The paediatrician who had taken an interest in her case from an early stage took a similar view. When she reached puberty, therefore, mother and paediatrician arranged with a gynaecologist that she should be sterilised immediately, because they were afraid that she might be seduced and bear an abnormal child. The people responsible for her education, however, thought that it would be wrong to perform an irreversible and permanent operation upon her; her behaviour and social skills were improving steadily; she was of dull normal intelligence and it was common ground that she had sufficient intellectual capacity to marry in due course. The educational psychologist therefore made her a ward of court and applied for an order continuing the wardship in order to delay or prevent the proposed operation. It was not proposed that D should be removed from the care and control of her widowed mother, who had looked after her 'splendidly'.

Heilbron J: ...

Is wardship appropriate?
I have first of all to decide whether this is an appropriate case in which to exercise the court's wardship jurisdiction. Wardship is a very special and ancient jurisdiction. Its origin was the sovereign's feudal obligation as parens patriae to protect the person and property of his subjects,

and particularly those unable to look after themselves, including infants. This obligation, delegated to the chancellor, passed to the Chancery Court, and in 1970 to this division of the High Court.

The jurisdiction in wardship is very wide, but there are limitations. It is not in every case that it is appropriate to make a child a ward, and counsel for Mrs B has argued with his usual skill and powers of persuasion that, as this case raises a matter of principle of wide public importance, and is a matter which affects many people, continuation of wardship would be inappropriate.

In his powerful argument, counsel for the Official Solicitor, on the other hand, submitted that the court in wardship had a wide jurisdiction which should be extended to encompass this novel situation, because it is just the type of problem which this court is best suited to determine when exercising its protective functions in regard to minors. As Lord Eldon LC said many years ago in *Wellesley v Duke of Beaufort* (1827) 2 Russ 1, 5 LJOS 85:

> 'This jurisdiction is founded on the obvious necessity that the law should place somewhere the care of individuals who cannot take care of themselves, particularly in cases where it is clear that some care should be thrown around them.'

It is apparent from the recent decision of the Court of Appeal in *Re X (A Minor)* [1975] Fam 47, [1975J 1 All ER 697 that the jurisdiction to do what is considered necessary for the protection of an infant is to be exercised carefully and within limits, but the court has, from time to time over the years, extended the sphere in the exercise of this jurisdiction.

The type of operation proposed is one which involves the deprivation of a basic human right, namely the right of a woman to reproduce, and therefore it would, if performed on a woman for non-therapeutic reasons and without her consent, be a violation of such right. ... As the evidence showed, and I accept it, D could not possibly have given an informed consent. What the evidence did, however, make clear was that she would almost certainly understand the implications of such an operation by the time she reached 18.

This operation could, if necessary, be delayed or prevented if the child were to remain a ward of court, and as Lord Eldon LC, so vividly expressed it in *Wellesley's* case: 'It has always been the principle of this Court, not to risk the incurring of damage to children which it cannot repair, but rather to prevent the damage being done.'

I think that is the very type of case where this court should 'throw some care around this child', and I propose to continue her wardship which, in my judgment, is appropriate in this case.

The operation – should it be performed?

In considering this vital matter, I want to make it quite clear that I have well in mind the natural feelings of a parent's heart, and though in wardship proceedings parents' rights can be superseded, the court will not do so lightly, and only in pursuance of well-known principles laid down over the years. The exercise of the court's jurisdiction is paternal, and it must be exercised judicially, and the judge must act, as far as humanly possible, on the evidence, as a wise parent would act. As Lord Upjohn pointed out in *J v C* [1970] AC 668, [1969] 1 All ER 788 the law and practice in relation to infants –

> 'have developed, are developing and must, and no doubt will, continue to develop by reflecting and adopting the changing views, as the years go by, of reasonable men and women, the parents of children, on the proper treatment and methods of bringing up children; for after all that is the model which the judge must emulate for ... he must act as the judicial reasonable parent.'

It is of course beyond dispute that the welfare of this child is the paramount consideration, and the court must act in her best interests.

The judge then reviews some of the evidence and arguments, including the facts that D had as yet shown no interest in the opposite sex, and had virtually no opportunities for promiscuity; that other methods of contraception or even abortion would be available should the need arise; and that there was no therapeutic reason for performing the operation now. She continues:

Dr Gordon, however, maintained that, provided the parent or parents consented, the decision was one made pursuant to the exercise of his clinical judgment, and that no interference could be tolerated in his clinical freedom.

The other consultants did not agree. Their opinion was that a decision to sterilise a child was not entirely within a doctor's clinical judgment, save only when sterilisation was the treatment of choice for some disease, as, for instance, when in order to treat a child and to ensure her direct physical well-being, it might be necessary to perform a hysterectomy to remove a malignant uterus. Whilst the side effect of such an operation would be to sterilise, the operation would be performed solely for therapeutic purposes. I entirely accept their opinions. I cannot believe, and the evidence does not warrant the view, that a decision to carry out an operation of this nature performed for non-therapeutic purposes on a minor, can be held to be within the doctor's sole clinical judgment.

It is quite clear that once a child is a ward of court, no important step in the life of that child can be taken without the consent of the court, and I cannot conceive of a more important step than that which was proposed in this case.

A review of the whole of the evidence leads me to the conclusion that in a case of a child of 11 years of age, where the evidence shows that her mental and physical condition and attainments have already improved, and where her future prospects are as yet unpredictable, where the evidence also shows that she is unable as yet to understand and appreciate the implications of this operation and could not give a valid or informed consent, but the likelihood is that in later years she will be able to make her own choice, where, I believe, the frustration and resentment of realising (as she would one day) what had happened could be devastating, an operation of this nature is, in my view, contra-indicated.

For these, and for the other reasons to which I have adverted, I have come to the conclusion that this operation is neither medically indicated nor necessary, and that it would not be in D's best interests for it to be performed.

Questions

(i) In what circumstances do you think that the court should allow the sterilisation of (*a*) a female child, or (*b*) a male child?

(ii) In *Re B (a minor) (wardship: sterilisation)* [1988] AC 199, at 205–206, [1987] 2 All ER 206, at 214, Lord Templeman observed:

In my opinion sterilisation of a girl under 18 should only be carried out with the leave of a High Court judge. A doctor performing a sterilisation operation with the consent of the parents might still be liable in criminal, civil or professional proceedings. A court exercising the wardship jurisdiction emanating from the Crown is the only authority which is empowered to authorise such a drastic step as sterilisation after a full and informed investigation.

Why would it otherwise be a crime or a tort?

(iii) What difference would it have made if an operation had been necessary to save D's life?

Some life-saving problems are easier than others:

Re R (a minor) (blood transfusion)
[1993] 2 FLR 757, [1993] Fam Law 577, High Court, Family Division

The facts are set out in the judgment.

Booth J: This is a sad case and one which, tragically, is not uncommon. The application, which is made by the local authority, is for an order which will enable a child to receive blood transfusions. Her parents, who are baptised members of the faith of Jehovah's Witnesses, are not able to compromise their beliefs to give their consent to this treatment. ...

The little girl with whom I am concerned is 10 months old, the only child of her parents, Mr and Mrs R. She suffers from B-cell lymphoblastic leukaemia and is presently in hospital receiving treatment. She has already been given blood products as a life-saving measure at the time of her admission, but she is likely to need more in the future. The evidence is that blood products could be necessary at any time over the next 2 years, which is the length of time during which she will need treatment. The medical consultants responsible for her believe that this is the only treatment likely to maximise the little girl's chances of being successfully treated.

The parents are extremely anxious that their daughter should receive the best possible medical care. Their primary objection to the proposed medical procedure is one of scriptural conscience. But the parents are also aware of the known hazards of blood transfusions and are anxious on this account. They further make the telling point that advances in medical science are so rapid that alternative blood management becomes possible in many procedures and as parents they want to be able to argue for their use whenever possible. If the court authorises the use of blood the parents are concerned to ensure that it is not a blanket authority to the doctors to do whatever they wish without consultation with them. ...

I therefore turn to consider the application and the matters to which the court must have regard under s. 1 of the Act. The welfare of the little girl is the court's paramount consideration. At 10 months of age she is too young to express her wishes and feelings. The evidence is clear, however, that because of her medical condition the opinion of those who are responsible for her treatment supports the use of blood products. Without that treatment, the consensus is that the treatment will be unsuccessful and she will suffer harm. Only because they cannot give their consent to this treatment are her caring parents unable to meet her needs. But so overwhelming is her need for blood and so much is it in her best interests to have it in the light of current medical knowledge that, for her welfare, I am bound to override the parents' wishes and authorise the use of blood products, thus enabling the doctors to give her transfusions.

[Counsel], however, makes the powerful submission that such an order should not provide the medical consultants with a blanket authority to carry out such treatments without any further reference to the parents. They wish not only to be involved as far as possible in the care of their daughter but also to be able to draw attention to treatments alternative to the use of blood products and this is a field in which medical science is advancing rapidly and more such treatments are quickly becoming available. I consider this to be a perfectly proper approach. In a life-threatening emergency situation, the doctors clearly could not consult with the parents; but in the normal course of events it is reasonable that they should do so. [Counsel], on behalf of the local authority, has been able to agree this. ...

The order was as follows:

It is ordered that there be a specific issue order in respect of the child, namely that:

(1) In any imminently life-threatening situation, when it is the professional opinion of those medically responsible for the said child, that she is in need of the administration of blood products, she shall be given such blood products without the consent of her parents.

(2) In any situation which is less than imminently life-threatening, those medically responsible for the child shall consult with the parents and will consider at every opportunity all alternative forms of management suggested by the parents. In the event that those medically responsible for the child conclude, after such consultation, that there is no reasonable alternative to the administration of blood products, they shall be at liberty to administer such blood products without the consent of the parents.

(3) No order for costs save legal aid taxation of the respondents' costs.

Questions

(i) Parents and guardians are deemed (by virtue of s. 1(2)(*a*) of the Children and Young Persons Act 1933) to have neglected a child 'in a manner likely to cause injury to his health' (for the purpose of the offence of wilfully assaulting, ill-treating, neglecting, abandoning or exposing him in such a manner under s. 1(1)) if they fail to provide 'adequate food, clothing, medical aid or lodging' for him. Religious belief is no defence (*R v Senior* [1899] 1 QB 283, CCR). Should these parents have been prosecuted (*a*) as well as, or (*b*) instead of applying for an order? If not, why not?

(ii) How much harm should a child be at risk of suffering before the courts intervene in this way?

Re R was about when a child should be treated to save his life; it is even more difficult to decide when he should not.

Re J (a minor) (wardship: medical treatment) [1991] Fam 33, [1990] 3 All ER 930, [1991] 2 WLR 140, Court of Appeal

J had been born very prematurely. He suffered very severe and permanent brain damage at the time of his birth. He was epileptic and the medical evidence was that he was likely to develop serious spastic quadriplegia, would be blind and deaf and was unlikely ever to be able to speak or to develop even limited intellectual abilities, but it was likely that he would feel pain to the same extent as a normal baby. His life expectancy was uncertain but he was expected to die before late adolescence, although he could survive for a few years. He had been ventilated twice for long periods when his breathing stopped, that treatment being both painful and hazardous. The medical prognosis was that any further collapse which required ventilation would be fatal. However he was neither on the point of death nor dying. The judge made an order that J should be treated with antibiotics if he developed a chest infection but should not be reventilated if his breathing stopped unless the doctors caring for him deemed it appropriate given the prevailing clinical situation. The Official Solicitor appealed …

Lord Donaldson MR: … No one can *dictate* the treatment to be given to the child, neither court, parents nor doctors. There are checks and balances. The doctors can recommend treatment A in preference to treatment B. They can also refuse to adopt treatment C on the grounds that it is medically contra-indicated or for some other reason is a treatment which they could not conscientiously administer. The court or parents for their part can refuse to consent to treatment A or B or both, but cannot insist on treatment C. The inevitable and desirable result is that choice of treatment is in some measure a joint decision of the doctors and the court or parents. …

Taylor LJ: The plight of baby J is appalling and the problem facing the court in the exercise of its wardship jurisdiction is of the greatest difficulty. When should the court rule against the giving of treatment aimed at prolonging life?

Three preliminary principles are not in dispute. First, it is settled law that the court's prime and paramount consideration must be the best interests of the child. That is easily said but not easily applied. What it does involve is that the views of the parents, although they should be heeded and weighed, cannot prevail over the court's view of the ward's best interests. In the present case the parents, finding themselves in a hideous dilemma, have not taken a strong view so that no conflict arises.

Second, the court's high respect for the sanctity of human life imposes a strong presumption in favour of taking all steps capable of preserving it, save in exceptional circumstances. The problem is to define those circumstances.

Third, and as a corollary to the second principle, it cannot be too strongly emphasised that the court never sanctions steps to terminate life. That would be unlawful. There is no question of approving, even in a case of the most horrendous disability, a course aimed at terminating life or accelerating death. The court is concerned only with the circumstances in which steps should not be taken to prolong life.

Two decisions of this court have dealt with cases at the extremes of the spectrum of affliction. *Re C (a minor) (wardship: medical treatment)* [1990] Fam 26, [1989] 2 All ER 782 was a case in which a child had severe irreversible brain damage such that she was hopelessly and terminally ill. This court held that the best interests of the child required approval of recommendations designed to ease her suffering and permit her life to come to an end peacefully with dignity rather than seek to prolong her life.

By contrast, in the earlier case of *Re B (a minor) (wardship: medical treatment)* (1981) [1990] 3 All ER 927, [1981] 1 WLR 1421, the court was concerned with a child suffering from Down's syndrome, who quite separately was born with an intestinal obstruction. Without an operation this intestinal condition would quickly have been fatal. On the other hand, the operation had a good chance of successfully removing the obstruction, once and for all, thereby affording the child a life expectation of some 20 to 30 years as a mongol. The parents genuinely believed it was in the child's interests to refrain from operating and allow her to die. The court took a different view. …

Those two cases thus decide that where the child is terminally ill the court will not require treatment to prolong life; but where, at the other extreme, the child is severely handicapped although not intolerably so and treatment for a discrete condition can enable life to continue for an appreciable period, albeit subject to that severe handicap, the treatment should be given. ...

This leads to the arguments presented by counsel for the Official Solicitor. His first submission propounded an absolute test, that, except where the ward is terminally ill, the court's approach should always be to prolong life by treatment if this is possible, regardless of the quality of life being preserved and regardless of any added suffering caused by the treatment itself. I cannot accept this test which in my view is so hard as to be inconsistent at its extreme with the best interests of the child. Counsel for the Official Solicitor submits that the court cannot play God and decide whether the quality of life which the treatment would give the child is better or worse than death. He referred to dicta in *McKay v Essex Area Health Authority* [1982] QB 1166, [1982] 2 All ER 771. ...

Despite the court's inability to compare a life afflicted by the most severe disability with death, the unknown, I am of the view that there must be extreme cases in which the court is entitled to say: 'The life which this treatment would prolong would be so cruel as to be intolerable.' If, for example, a child was so damaged as to have negligible use of its faculties and the only way of preserving its life was by the continuous administration of extremely painful treatment such that the child either would be in continuous agony or would have to be so sedated continuously as to have no conscious life at all, I cannot think counsel's absolute test should apply to require the treatment to be given. In those circumstances, without there being any question of deliberately ending the life or shortening it, I consider the court is entitled in the best interests of the child to say that deliberate steps should not be taken artificially to prolong its miserable life span.

Once the absolute test is rejected, the proper criteria must be a matter of degree. At what point in the scale of disability and suffering ought the court to hold that the best interests of the child do not require further endurance to be imposed by positive treatment to prolong its life? Clearly, to justify withholding treatment, the circumstances would have to be extreme. Counsel for the Official Solicitor submitted that if the court rejected his absolute test, then at least it would have 'to be certain that the life of the child, were the treatment to be given, would be intolerably awful'.

I consider that the correct approach is for the court to judge the quality of life the child would have to endure if given the treatment and decide whether in all the circumstances such a life would be so afflicted as to be intolerable to that child. I say 'to that child' because the test should not be whether the life would be tolerable to the decider. The test must be whether the child in question, if capable of exercising sound judgment, would consider the life tolerable. This is the approach adopted by McKenzie J in *Re Superintendent of Family and Child Service and Dawson* (1983) 145 DLR (3d) 610 at 620–621. ... It takes account of the strong instinct to preserve one's life even in circumstances which an outsider, not himself at risk of death, might consider unacceptable. The circumstances to be considered would, in appropriate cases, include the degree of existing disability and any additional suffering or aggravation of the disability which the treatment itself would superimpose. In an accident case, as opposed to one involving disablement from birth, the child's pre-accident quality of life and its perception of what has been lost may also be factors relevant to whether the residual life would be intolerable to that child.

Counsel for the Official Solicitor argued that, before deciding against treatment, the court would have to be *certain* that the circumstances of the child's future would comply with the extreme requirements to justify that decision. Certainty as to the future is beyond human judgment. The courts have not, even in the trial of capital offences, required certainty of proof. But, clearly, the court must be satisfied to a high degree of probability.

In the present case, the doctors were unanimous that in his present condition, J should not be put back on to a mechanical ventilator. That condition is very grave indeed. ... In reaching his conclusion, the judge no doubt had three factors in mind. First, the severe lack of capacity of the child in all his faculties which even without any further complication would make his existence barely sentient. Second, that, if further mechanical ventilation were to be required, that very fact would involve the risk of a deterioration in B's condition, because of further brain damage flowing from the interruption of breathing. Third, all the doctors drew attention to the invasive nature of mechanical ventilation and the intensive care required to accompany it. They stressed the unpleasant and distressing nature of that treatment. To add such distress and the risk of further deterioration to an already appalling catalogue of disabilities was clearly capable in my judgment of producing a quality of life which justified the stance of the doctors and the judge's conclusion. I therefore agree that, subject to the minor variations to the judge's order proposed by Lord Donaldson MR, this appeal should be dismissed.

Appeal dismissed.

Questions

(i) *Re J* concerned artificial breathing. In *Airedale National Health Service Trust v Bland* [1993] AC 789, at 884, [1993] 1 All ER 821, at 883, Lord Browne-Wilkinson said that

> ... the critical decision to be made is whether it is in the best interests of Anthony Bland to continue the invasive medical care involved in artificial feeding. That question is not the same as, 'Is it in Anthony Bland's best interests that he should die?'

Do you find this distinction helpful?

(ii) In a second *Re J (a minor) (child in care: medical treatment)* [1993] Fam 15, [1992] 4 All ER 614, Waite J had ordered the health authority to provide artificial ventilation if this became necessary to prolong the child's life; allowing the appeal, Lord Donaldson MR (with whom Balcombe and Leggatt LJJ expressly agreed) repeated his views:

> The fundamental issue in this appeal is whether the court in the exercise of its inherent power to protect the interests of minors should ever require a medical practitioner or health authority acting by a medical practitioner to adopt a course of treatment which in the bona fide clinical judgment of the practitioner concerned is contra-indicated as not being in the best interests of the patient. I have to say that I cannot at present conceive of any circumstances in which this would be other than an abuse of power as directly or indirectly requiring the practitioner to act contrary to the fundamental duty which he owes to his patient. This, subject to obtaining any necessary consent, is to treat the patient in accordance with his own best clinical judgment, notwithstanding that other practitioners who are not called upon to treat the patient may have formed quite a different judgment or that the court, acting on expert evidence, may disagree with him.

But if a court can take a child away from parents who are not acting in his best interests, should it not take a child away from a doctor who is not doing so and give him to one who will?

(iii) Money may be the reason. In *R v Cambridge Health Authority, ex p B* [1995] 2 All ER 129, Laws J in judicial review proceedings had quashed the authority's decision not to fund further chemotherapy and a second bone marrow transplant for a child with leukaemia. Allowing the appeal, Sir Thomas Bingham MR said:

> I have no doubt that in a perfect world any treatment which a patient, or a patient's family, sought would be provided if the doctors were willing to give it, no matter how much it cost, particularly when a life was potentially at stake. It would however, in my view, be shutting one's eyes to the real world if the court were to proceed on the basis that we do live in such a world. ... Difficult and agonising judgments have to be made as to how a limited budget is best allocated to the maximum advantage of the maximum number of patients. That is not a judgment that the court can make.

Now do you understand why Bowen LJ said (p. 410, above) that 'judicial machinery is quite inadequate to the task of educating children in this country'?

(iv) Are parents also entitled to make such judgments, for example, when considering (*a*) where the family should go on holiday, or (*b*) where each of their children should go to school, or (*c*) whether to provide 'cosmetic' surgery?

(v) Ian Kennedy, in *The Karen Quinlan Case: Problems and Proposals* (1976) supports the view of a *doctor's* obligations to his patient put forward in 1957 by Pope Pius XII:

Doctors, he said, were obliged to continue with 'ordinary' measures but were not obliged to carry out 'extraordinary' measures. The latter he defined not in terms of what a doctor would regard as extraordinary or non-standard procedures, a definition which would change as developments occurred, but rather as whatever 'cannot be obtained or secured without excessive expense, pain or other inconvenience for the patient or for others, or which, if used, would not offer a reasonable hope of benefit to the patient'.

Does this also strike you as a reasonable definition of the limits of a parent's duty under s. 1(2)(*a*) of the Children and Young Persons Act 1933 to secure adequate medical aid for his child?

(vi) Do you agree that the test of 'best interests' in matters of life and death should be what the child himself would have wanted? Or should the court adopt the 'same attitude as a responsible parent ... in the case of his or her own child' (per Balcombe LJ in the earlier *Re J*)? What difference would it make?

Re R, *Re D* and *Re J* concerned a single, albeit vital, question about the child's upbringing. There was no dispute about where the child should live or who should bring him up. But when the state wishes to challenge the parents' claim to bring the child up at all, should it be enough to prove that the state will probably be able to provide the child with a better life than they can? The *Review of Child Care Law* (1985) thought not:

2.12 ... We have had to consider whether a simple welfare or 'best interests' test should now be adopted where the state, in the shape of local authority, is in conflict with the parents.

2.13 We are firmly of the opinion that it should not and that in cases where compulsory committal to local authority care is in issue the present balance between the welfare of the child and the claims of his parents should be maintained. Taken to its logical conclusion, a simple 'best interests' test would permit the state to intervene whenever it could show that the alternative arrangements proposed would serve the children's welfare better than those proposed by their parents. But 'the child is not the child of the state' and it is important in a free society to maintain the rich diversity of lifestyles which is secured by permitting families a large measure of autonomy in the way in which they bring up their children. This is so even, or perhaps particularly, in those families who through force of circumstances are in need of help from social services or other agencies. Only where their children are put at unacceptable risk should it be possible compulsorily to intervene. Once such a risk of harm to the child has been shown, however, his interests must clearly predominate. [Later on:]

15.11 We have considered whether it would be sufficient to qualify a broad welfare test by a requirement that, as in family cases, the responsible body should first be satisfied that there are exceptional circumstances making it impracticable or undesirable that the child should be entrusted to his parents or to some other person. In our view that criterion would add very little to the broad welfare ground, given that only in exceptional circumstances would a court or local authority even consider compulsory intervention and given the readiness of the courts in applying section 1 of the 1971 Act to assume that generally a child's welfare is best served by his being brought up by his parents [see *J v C* [1970] AC 668]. The judges of the Family Division in proposing the criterion agreed that it might leave too much to subjective interpretation by the courts. We did consider whether adding guidelines to the criterion might overcome its apparent drawbacks, as has been suggested to us. However we doubt that these would be sufficient to direct the court's mind to the principles underlying restrictions on state intervention.

Questions

(i) We shall come to the 'threshold conditions' for state intervention in Chapter 13, but how would you define the cases where a child is 'put at unacceptable risk'?

(ii) The threshold conditions apply before a child can be placed in care or under supervision, but not where a social worker, educational psychologist,

doctor or other representative of the caring agencies of the state seeks a 'specific issue order' dealing with a particular aspect of how the child should be brought up, as happened in *Re R*: can this distinction be justified?
(iii) Do you think that this will make much difference to what courts actually do?

2 Arguments for parental autonomy

In *Before the Best Interests of the Child* (1980), Goldstein, Freud and Solnit employ psychological concepts of a child's development to support their argument for severe limitations upon the state's power to intervene between parent and child:

... Constantly ongoing interactions between parents and children become for each child the starting point for an all-important line of development that leads toward adult functioning. What begins as the experience of physical contentment or pleasure that accompanies bodily care develops into a primary attachment to the person who provides it. This again changes into the wish for a parent's constant presence irrespective of physical wants. Helplessness requires total care and over time is transformed into the need or wish for approval and love. It fosters the desire to please by compliance with a parent's wishes. It provides a developmental base upon which the child's responsiveness to educational efforts rest. Love for the parents leads to identification with them, a fact without which impulse control and socialization would be deficient. Finally, after the years of childhood comes the prolonged and in many ways painful adolescent struggle to attain a separate identity with physical, emotional, and moral self-reliance.

These complex and vital developments require the privacy of family life under guardianship by parents who are autonomous. The younger the child, the greater is his need for them. When family integrity is broken or weakened by state intrusion, his needs are thwarted and his belief that his parents are omniscient and all-powerful is shaken prematurely. The effect on the child's developmental progress is invariably detrimental. The child's need for safety within the confines of the family must be met by law through its recognition of family privacy as the barrier to state intrusion upon parental autonomy in child rearing. These rights – parental autonomy, a child's entitlement to autonomous parents, and privacy – are essential ingredients of 'family integrity.' 'And the integrity of that life is something so fundamental that it has been found to draw to its protection the principles of more than one explicitly granted Constitutional right.'...

Beyond these biological and psychological justifications for protecting parent-child relationships and promoting each child's entitlement to a permanent place in a family of his own, there is a further justification for a policy of minimum state intervention. It is that the law does not have the capacity to supervise the fragile, complex interpersonal bonds between child and parent. As *parens patriae* the state is too crude an instrument to become an adequate substitute for flesh and blood parents. The legal system has neither the resources nor the sensitivity to respond to a growing child's ever-changing needs and demands. It does not have the capacity to deal on an individual basis with the consequences of its decisions, or to act with the deliberate speed that is required by a child's sense of time. Similarly, the child lacks the capacity to respond to the rulings of an impersonal court or social service agencies as he responds to the demands of personal parental figures. Parental expectations, implicit and explicit, become the child's own. However, the process by which a child converts external expectations, guidance, commands, and prohibitions into the capacity for self-regulation and self-direction does not function adequately in the absence of emotional ties to his caretakers.

A policy of minimum coercive intervention by the state thus accords not only with our firm belief as citizens in individual freedom and human dignity, but also with our professional understanding of the intricate developmental processes of childhood.

Question

Would it trouble you if a child's belief that his parents are omniscient and all powerful is broken prematurely?

There is also the question of the role of the state where parent and child are at odds with one another. This issue has arisen in the United States in connection with the right of parents to 'volunteer' their children for treatment in a psychiatric hospital. The following anonymous discussion of the *Mental Hospitalisation of Children and the Limits of Parental Authority* (1978) provides a summary of the arguments:

Five justifications are most often advanced to support parental authority. They may for convenience be termed *social pluralism*, *social order*, *parental privilege*, *family autonomy* and *child's welfare*. Once each of these proffered justifications have been considered, the constitutional limits on a parent's power to admit his child to a mental hospital will emerge.

A. Social pluralism
It is a 'fixed star in our constitutional constellation,' especially with respect to the education of children, that the state shall not impose an orthodoxy 'in politics, nationalism, religion, or other matters of opinion.' And, especially in matters that relate to families and childrearing, the Constitution also disfavors state practices that threaten to impose on all a single conception of a worthwhile way of life. The institution of parental authority, by fragmenting decisions about the goals and methods of childrearing, serves to militate against such an orthodoxy. This, historically, has been part of its rationale and is today one reason for treating parental authority, when asserted against the state, as a constitutional right. It is therefore not surprising that the Supreme Court has acted more readily to protect parental authority against state intrusion when the threat to social pluralism has been acute.[1]

... Yet where, as here, the conflict under consideration is between parents and their children, the social pluralism rationale offers little direct guidance. Although a rule favoring parents over the state will always be a bulwark against a state-imposed orthodoxy of social values, a rule favoring parents over their children may or may not have that effect. The goal of social pluralism might just as well be advanced by allowing children to decide for themselves. ...

B. Social order
Historically, the law recognized society's interest in having children reared so that as adults they would be economically self-sufficient and would conform their conduct to society's norms. Parents, according to one court, were ordinarily entrusted with this task 'because it [could] seldom be put into better hands,' but they were subject to state supersession if they failed. Parents are still, to some extent, viewed as child-socialization agents of the state. ...

To the extent that parents actually do admit their children to mental hospitals as a method of social control, they are acting in their role of child-socialization agents of the state and are, therefore, subject to the same constitutional constraints as would apply if the state had acted directly. ...

C. Parental privilege
It is not uncommon for parents to seek to express their own personalities through their children. This interest of parents may serve as the basis for the claim they advance to have 'the power to dictate their [children's] training, prescribe their education and form their religious opinions.' To

---

1. The author's footnote reads: Compare *Wisconsin v Yoder* 406 US 205 (1972) (invalidating state compulsory education law as applied to Amish children) and *Pierce v Society of Sisters* 268 US 510 (1925) (invalidating state law requiring parents to send their children only to public schools) with *Prince v Massachusetts* 321 US 158 (1944) (upholding statute prohibiting street solicitation by children as applied to Jehovah's Witnesses distributing religious literature). The Court in *Yoder* noted especially that the statute as applied 'substantially interfer[ed] with the religious development of the Amish child and his integration into the way of life of the Amish faith community' and 'carrie[d] with it a very real threat of undermining the Amish community and religious practice.' 406 US at 218. Enforcement of the statute in *Prince*, however, posed no such threat to the Jehovah's Witnesses' way of life; the Court in *Prince* took pains to note that its holding left parents free to accomplish the religious training and indoctrination of their children by all means 'except the public proclaiming of religion [by their children] in the streets.' 321 US at 171. More importantly, in *Yoder* and *Pierce* but not in *Prince* the effect of a holding in favour of the state would have been to compel children to confront daily a set of religious and social values antagonistic to those that their parents sought to foster.

the extent that the law protects this claim of parents, it creates a *parental privilege* – that is, a prerogative of a parent to rear his child to be a person whose conduct, character, and belief conform to standards of the parent's choosing. There can be no doubt that this interest of parents, when asserted against the state, is within the scope of liberty protected by the Constitution. ...

It is regarded by many as unjust for one adult to impose his conception of the good life on another and as demeaning to another's dignity not to respect his choice of his own life plan. Psychological studies show that at adolescence, children of normal intellect are in this respect substantially like adults: they have the basic cognitive capacities to choose intelligently among competing values and to formulate their own life plans. So, as applied to adolescents, parental privilege – the prerogative of parents to impose on their children values and styles of life that best express the *parents'* personalities – is especially hard to justify on moral grounds. ...

D. Family autonomy

The state's interest in preserving the family unit is often cited to justify state sanction of parental authority. But protecting the family from outside interference is quite distinct from fortifying the family's power over one of its members. ...

When a parent, in his role of family governor, exercises authority over the child, his action has a moral basis that the exercise of bare parental privilege lacks. But there are other criteria for the moral assessment of social institutions – whether an institution that makes claims against some provides some reciprocal benefit for each of those whose liberty it restricts, or whether it makes an equal relative contribution to the good life of each of its participants. Although family life may often require that some good of one individual be foregone for the well-being of the family as a whole, a family that excessively derogates the interests of one for the sake of the others undermines its own moral basis.

These moral considerations suggest a legal norm. The state need not intervene in every family dispute, but if it does, it must treat each family member affected as having a distinguishable interest, which is equally entitled to the protection of the state. ...

E. Child's welfare

The last of the proffered justifications of parental authority is that it serves the child's welfare. It has been suggested that allowing parents to be the supreme arbiters of their child's fate is justified because it is conducive to the child's long term psychological health. More commonly, parental authority is defended on the ground that someone must choose for children since they lack the capacity to choose for themselves; parents are assigned this role because they are presumed to be better able to perform the task than anyone else.

The legitimacy of parental authority based on the child's welfare rationale depends primarily on the child's capacity to choose for himself. This capacity will vary with age. Parental authority over preadolescents is justified because the assumption that children are not competent to make their own choices is, as applied to them, generally correct. Since, however, parents under this rationale are presumed to act as guardians of the child's interests, parental authority would lose its underlying legitimacy if exercised for purposes unrelated to the child's welfare or in ways that create for the child a substantial risk of harm. ...

For the adolescent, the situation is more complex. Psychologists agree that about the time of adolescence a major transformation occurs in the quality of a child's thought. As a consequence of a shift to what is called formal operational thought, the youngster is capable of abstract, logical, and scientific thinking, which enables him to see the practical possibilities of real-life situations and to anticipate and evaluate the consequences of his own conduct. Simultaneously, or perhaps as a consequence of the same underlying process, the individual acquires an appreciation for the social ramifications of individual conduct, and a capacity to formulate his own personal and social ideals.

When a person makes choices after having identified the likely consequences for himself and others and having evaluated those alternatives in light of an overall life plan, he has chosen intelligently, even if unwisely from someone else's point of view. By this criterion, the psychological evidence shows that the typical adolescent will have acquired a basic capacity for intelligent choice by about fourteen years old.

Questions

(i) In *R v Kirklees Metropolitan District Council, ex p C (a minor)* [1993] 2 FLR 187, CA, it was held that a local authority having the responsibilities of a parent

could arrange for the admission of a 12-year-old child to a psychiatric unit against her will without any of the safeguards in the Mental Health Act 1983. Do you consider this (*a*) a proper way to meet their parental responsibility, or (*b*) an unjustified invasion of the rights of the child?
(ii) Would it make any difference to your answer if the child had been 15 years old and able to choose 'intelligently, even if unwisely from someone else's point of view'?

3 Children's rights

That last point makes it clear that we are here considering a tri-partite relationship: between parents and the state (or other third parties) and between parents and children, but also between children and parents and children and the state.

Gillick v West Norfolk and Wisbech Area Health Authority
[1986] AC 112, [1985] 3 All ER 402, [1985] 3 WLR 830, [1986] 1 FLR 224, House of Lords

The plaintiff, mother of five daughters under the age of 16, sought a declaration that the guidance issued by the Department of Health and Social Security, to the effect that in exceptional circumstances a doctor might give contraceptive advice and treatment to a girl under 16 without her parents' consent, was unlawful. She failed at first instance, but succeeded in the Court of Appeal. On appeal to the House of Lords:

Lord Fraser of Tullybelton: ... Three strands of argument are raised by the appeal. These are: (1) whether a girl under the age of 16 has the legal capacity to give valid consent to contraceptive advice and treatment including medical examination; (2) whether giving such advice and treatment to a girl under 16 without her parents' consent infringes the parents' rights; and (3) whether a doctor who gives such advice or treatment to a girl under 16 without her parents' consent incurs criminal liability. I shall consider these strands in order.

1. *The legal capacity of a girl under 16 to consent to contraceptive advice, examination and treatment*
There are some indications in statutory provisions to which we were referred that a girl under 16 years of age in England and Wales does not have the capacity to give valid consent to contraceptive advice and treatment. If she does not have the capacity, then any physical examination or touching of her body without her parents' consent would be an assault by the examiner. One of those provisions is s. 8 of the Family Law Reform Act 1969, which is in the following terms:

> '(1) The consent of a minor who has attained the age of sixteen years to any surgical, medical or dental treatment which, in the absence of consent, would constitute a trespass to his person, shall be as effective as it would be if he were of full age; and where a minor has by virtue of this section given an effective consent to any treatment it shall not be necessary to obtain any consent for it from his parent or guardian. ...
> (3) Nothing in this section shall be construed as making ineffective any consent which would have been effective if this section had not been enacted.'

The contention on behalf of Mrs Gillick was that sub-s (1) of s. 8 shows that, apart from the subsection, the consent of a minor to such treatment would not be effective. But I do not accept that contention because sub-s (3) leaves open the question whether consent by a minor under the age of 16 would have been effective if the section had not been enacted. That question is not answered by the section, and sub-s (1) is, in my opinion, merely for the avoidance of doubt. ...

... It seems to me verging on the absurd to suggest that a girl or a boy aged 15 could not effectively consent, for example, to have a medical examination of some trivial injury to his body or even to have a broken arm set. Of course the consent of the parents should normally be asked, but they may not be immediately available. Provided the patient, whether a boy or a girl, is capable of understanding what is proposed, and of expressing his or her own wishes, I see no good reason for holding that he or she lacks the capacity to express them validly and effectively and to authorise the medical man to make the examination or give the treatment which he advises. After all, a minor under the age of 16 can, within certain limits, enter into a contract. He or she can also sue and be sued, and can give evidence on oath. Moreover, a girl under 16 can give sufficiently effective consent to sexual intercourse to lead to the legal result that the man involved does not commit the crime of rape: see *R v Howard* [1965] 3 All ER 684 at 685, [1966] 1 WLR 13 at 15, ...

Accordingly, I am not disposed to hold now, for the first time, that a girl aged less than 16 lacks the power to give valid consent to contraceptive advice or treatment, merely on account of her age.

2. *The parents' rights and duties in respect of medical treatment of their child*

... It was, I think, accepted both by Mrs Gillick and by the DHSS, and in any event I hold, that parental rights to control a child do not exist for the benefit of the parent. They exist for the benefit of the child and they are justified only in so far as they enable the parent to perform his duties towards the child, and towards other children in the family. If necessary, this proposition can be supported by reference to *Blackstone's Commentaries* (1 Bl Com (17th edn, 1830) 452), ...

From the parents' right and duty of custody flows their right and duty of control of the child, but the fact that custody is its origin throws but little light on the question of the legal extent of control at any particular age. ...

It is my view, contrary to the ordinary experience of mankind, at least in Western Europe in the present century, to say that a child or a young person remains in fact under the complete control of his parents until he attains the definite age of majority, now 18 in the United Kingdom, and that on attaining that age he suddenly acquires independence. In practice most wise parents relax their control gradually as the child develops and encourage him or her to become increasingly independent. Moreover, the degree of parental control actually exercised over a particular child does in practice vary considerably according to his understanding and intelligence and it would, in my opinion, be unrealistic for the courts not to recognise these facts. Social customs change, and the law ought to, and does in fact, have regard to such changes when they are of major importance. ...

Once the rule of the parents' absolute authority over minor children is abandoned, the solution to the problem in this appeal can no longer be found by referring to rigid parental rights at any particular age. The solution depends on a judgment of what is best for the welfare of the particular child. Nobody doubts, certainly I do not doubt, that in the overwhelming majority of cases the best judges of a child's welfare are his or her parents. Nor do I doubt that any important medical treatment of a child under 16 would normally only be carried out with the parents' approval. That is why it would and should be 'most unusual' for a doctor to advise a child without the knowledge and consent of the parents on contraceptive matters. But, as I have already pointed out, Mrs Gillick has to go further if she is to obtain the first declaration that she seeks. She has to justify the absolute right of veto in a parent. But there may be circumstances in which a doctor is a better judge of the medical advice and treatment which will conduce to a girl's welfare than her parents. ...

The only practicable course is, in my opinion, to entrust the doctor with a discretion to act in accordance with his view of what is best in the interests of the girl who is his patient. He should, of course, always seek to persuade her to tell her parents that she is seeking contraceptive advice, and the nature of the advice that she receives. At least he should seek to persuade her to agree to the doctor's informing the parents. But there may well be cases, and I think there will be some cases, where the girl refuses either to tell the parents herself or to permit the doctor to do so and in such cases the doctor will, in my opinion, be justified in proceeding without the parents' consent or even knowledge provided he is satisfied on the following matters: (1) that the girl (although under 16 years of age) will understand his advice; (2) that he cannot persuade her to inform her parents or to allow him to inform the parents that she is seeking contraceptive advice; (3) that she is very likely to begin or to continue having sexual intercourse with or without contraceptive treatment; (4) that unless she receives contraceptive advice or treatment her physical or mental health or both are likely to suffer; (5) that her best interests require him to give her contraceptive advice, treatment or both without the parental consent. ...

Lord Scarman: ... Parental rights clearly do exist, and they do not wholly disappear until the age of majority. Parental rights relate to both the person and the property of the child: custody, care and control of the person and guardianship of the property of the child. But the common law has never treated such rights as sovereign or beyond review and control. Nor has our law ever treated the child as other than a person with capacities and rights recognised by law. The principle of the law, as I shall endeavour to show, is that parental rights are derived from parental duty and exist only so long as they are needed for the protection of the person and property of the child. The principle has been subjected to certain age limits set by statute for certain purposes; and in some cases the courts have declared an age of discretion at which a child acquires before the age of majority the right to make his (or her) own decision. But these limitations in no way undermine the principle of the law, and should not be allowed to obscure it. ...

... The underlying principle of the law was exposed by Blackstone and can be seen to have been acknowledged in the case law. It is that parental right yields to the child's right to make his own decisions when he reaches a sufficient understanding and intelligence to be capable of making up his own mind on the matter requiring decision. Lord Denning MR captured the spirit and principle of the law when he said in *Hewer v Bryant* [1970] 1 QB 357 at 369, [1969] 3 All ER 578 at 582:

> 'I would get rid of the rule in *Re Agar-Ellis* (1883) 24 Ch D 317 and of the suggested exceptions to it. That case was decided in the year 1883. It reflects the attitude of a Victorian parent towards his children. He expected unquestioning obedience to his commands. If a son disobeyed, his father would cut him off with 1s. If a daughter had an illegitimate child, he would turn her out of the house. His power only ceased when the child became 21. I decline to accept a view so much out of date. The common law can, and should, keep pace with the times. It should declare, in conformity with the recent report on the Age of Majority that the legal right of a parent to the custody of a child ends at the eighteenth birthday; and even up till then, it is a dwindling right which the courts will hesitate to enforce against the wishes of the child, the older he is. It starts with a right of control and ends with little more than advice.'

But his is by no means a solitary voice. It is consistent with the opinion expressed by the House in *J v C* [1970] AC 668, [1969] 1 All ER 788, where their Lordships clearly recognised as out of place the assertion in the *Agar-Ellis* cases (1878) 10 Ch D 49; (1883) 24 Ch D 317 of a father's power bordering on 'patria potestas'. It is consistent with the view of Lord Parker CJ in *R v Howard* [1965] 3 All ER 684 at 685, [1966] 1 WLR 13 at 15, where he ruled that in the case of a prosecution charging rape of a girl under 16 the Crown must *prove* either lack of her consent or that she was not in a position to decide whether to consent or resist and added the comment that 'there are many girls who know full well what it is all about and can properly consent'. And it is consistent with the views of the House in the recent criminal case where a father was accused of kidnapping his own child, *R v D* [1984] AC 778, [1984] 2 All ER 449. ...

In the light of the foregoing I would hold that as a matter of law the parental right to determine whether or not their minor child below the age of 16 will have medical treatment terminates if and when the child achieves a sufficient understanding and intelligence to enable him or her to understand fully what is proposed. It will be a question of fact whether a child seeking advice has sufficient understanding of what is involved to give a consent valid in law. Until the child achieves the capacity to consent, the parental right to make the decision continues save only in exceptional circumstances. Emergency, parental neglect, abandonment of the child or inability to find the parent are examples of exceptional situations justifying the doctor proceeding to treat the child without parental knowledge and consent; but there will arise, no doubt, other exceptional situations in which it will be reasonable for the doctor to proceed without the parent's consent.

Lord Bridge agreed with them both. For him, however, the main ground for decision was that the DHSS guidance could only be challenged through judicial review, whereas Lord Scarman held that private rights were involved. Lord Brandon of Oakbridge did not discuss the rights of parents or children because he concluded from the provisions of the Sexual Offences Act 1956 relating to unlawful sexual intercourse that the provision of contraceptive facilities was unlawful in any event.

Lord Templeman: ... I accept also that a doctor may lawfully carry out some forms of treatment with the consent of an infant patient and against the opposition of a parent based on religious or any other grounds. The effect of the consent of the infant depends on the nature of the treatment and the age and understanding of the infant. For example, a doctor with the consent of an intelligent boy or girl of 15 could in my opinion safely remove tonsils or a troublesome appendix. But any decision on the part of a girl to practise sex and contraception requires not only knowledge of the facts of life and of the dangers of pregnancy and disease but also an understanding of the emotional and other consequences to her family, her male partner and to herself. I doubt whether a girl under the age of 16 is capable of a balanced judgment to embark on frequent, regular or casual sexual intercourse fortified by the illusion that medical science can protect her in mind and body and ignoring the danger of leaping from childhood to adulthood without the difficult formative transitional experiences of adolescence. There are many things which a girl under 16 needs to practise but sex is not one of them. ...

... In my opinion a doctor may not lawfully provide a girl under 16 with contraceptive facilities without the approval of the parent responsible for the girl save pursuant to a court order, or in the case of emergency or in exceptional cases where the parent has abandoned or forfeited by abuse the right to be consulted. Parental rights cannot be insisted on by a parent who is not responsible for the custody and upbringing of an infant or where the parent has abandoned or abused parental rights. And a doctor is not obliged to give effect to parental rights in an emergency.
Appeal allowed.

Question

Are all three of their Lordships saying the same thing? Does parental right yield to the child's autonomy? Or does the child's autonomy allow a third party to take over the decision of what will be best?

But what if a 'Gillick-competent' child does not want treatment? In *Re R (a minor) (wardship: medical treatment)* [1992] Fam 11, [1991] 4 All ER 177, it was held that the court could authorise the administration of anti-psychotic drugs to a 15-year-old girl despite her refusal; Lord Donaldson MR went further: adopting a keyholder analogy, he stated that the consent of either the parents or a competent child could unlock the door to treatment. He went further still in the next case.

Re W (a minor) (medical treatment: court's jurisdiction) [1993] Fam 64, [1992] 4 All ER 627, Court of Appeal

W. was a 16-year-old girl in local authority care who suffered from anorexia nervosa. She was admitted to an adolescent psychiatric unit but her physical condition had deteriorated so much that it was proposed to move her to a hospital specialising in eating disorders. She did not wish to go. The local authority asked the court, in the exercise of its inherent jurisdiction, to authorise this. Thorpe J held that she was competent to make the decision but that the court could make the order sought. She appealed, arguing that the Family Law Reform Act, s. 8 (see p. 426, above) gave her the exclusive right to consent and therefore an absolute right to refuse treatment.

Lord Donaldson of Lymington MR: ... *Gillick's case*
In *Gillick v West Norfolk and Wisbech Area Health Authority* [1986] AC 112 the central issue was *not* whether a child patient under the age of 16 could refuse medical treatment if the parents or the court consented, but whether the parents could effectively impose a veto on treatment by failing or refusing to consent to treatment to which the child might consent. Mrs. Gillick accepted that the court had such a power of veto and contended that the parents had a similar power. ...

The House of Lords decisively rejected Mrs. Gillick's contentions and held that at common law a child of sufficient intelligence and understanding (the '*Gillick* competent' child) could consent to treatment, notwithstanding the absence of the parents' consent and even an express prohibition by the parents. Only Lord Scarman's speech is couched in terms which might suggest that the refusal of a child below the age of 16 to accept medical treatment was determinative. …

In the light of the quite different issue which was before the House in *Gillick's* case I venture to doubt whether Lord Scarman meant more than that the *exclusive* right of the parents to consent to treatment terminated, but I may well be wrong. Thorpe J having held that 'there is no doubt at all that J. is a child of sufficient understanding to make an informed decision,' I shall assume that, so far as the common law is concerned, Lord Scarman would have decided that neither the local authority nor W.'s aunt, both of whom had parental responsibilities, could give consent to treatment which would be effective in the face of W.'s refusal of consent. This is of considerable persuasive authority, but even that is not the issue before this court. That is whether *the court* has such a power. That never arose in *Gillick's* case, the nearest approach to it being the proposition, accepted by all parties, that the court had power to override any minor's consent (*not* refusal) to accept treatment. …

The Latey Committee Report

It is common ground that the Family Law Reform Act 1969 was Parliament's response to the Report of the Committee on the Age of Majority (1967) (Cmnd 3342). The relevant part is contained in paragraphs 474–484. These show that the mischief aimed at was twofold. First, cases were occurring in which young people between 16 and 21 (the then age of majority) were living away from home and wished and needed urgent medical treatment which had not yet reached the emergency stage. Doctors were unable to treat them unless and until their parents had been traced and this could cause unnecessary suffering. Second, difficulties were arising concerning

> 'operations whose implications bring up the question of a girl's right to privacy about her sexual life. A particularly difficult situation arises in the case of a girl who is sent to hospital in need of a therapeutic abortion and refuses point blank to enter the hospital unless a guarantee is given that her parents shall not be told about it.'

The committee had recommended that the age of majority be reduced to 18 generally. The report, in paragraph 480, records that all the professional bodies which gave evidence recommended that patients aged between 16 and 18 shoulod be able to give an effective consent to treatment and all but the Medical Protection Society recommended that they should also be able to give an effective refusal. The point with which we are concerned was therefore well in the mind of the committee. It did not so recommend. It recommended that:

> '*without prejudice to any consent that may otherwise be lawful*, the consent of young persons aged 16 and over to medical or dental treatment shall be as valid as the consent of a person of full age.' (My emphasis.)

Conclusion on section 8

I am quite unable to accept that Parliament in adopting somewhat more prolix language was intending to achieve a result which differed from that recommended by the committee.

On reflection I regret my use in *In re R (A Minor) (Wardship: Consent to Treatment)* [1992] Fam 11, 22, of the keyholder analogy because keys can lock as well as unlock. I now prefer the analogy of the legal 'flak jacket' which protects the doctor from claims by the litigious whether he acquires it from his patient who may be a minor over the age of 16, or a '*Gillick* competent' child under that age or from another person having parental responsibilities which include a right to consent to treatment of the minor. Anyone who gives him a flak jacket (that is, consent) may take it back, but the doctor only needs one and so long as he continues to have one he has the legal right to proceed. …

Hair-raising possibilities were canvassed of abortions being carried out by doctors in reliance upon the consent of parents and despite the refusal of consent by 16- and 17-year-olds. Whilst this may be possible as a matter of law, I do not see any likelihood taking account of medical ethics, unless the abortion was truly in the best interests of the child. This is not to say that it could not happen. This is clear from the facts of *In re D (A Minor) (Wardship: Sterilisation)* [1976] Fam 185. …

Thus far I have, in the main, been looking at the problem in the context of a conflict between parents and the minor, either the minor consenting and the parents refusing consent or the minor refusing consent and the parents giving it. Although that is not this case, I have done so both because we were told that it would be helpful to all those concerned with the treatment of minors and also perhaps the minors themselves and because it seems to be a logical base from which to proceed to consider the powers of the court and how they should be exercised.

W.'s case

... I have no doubt that the wishes of a 16- or 17-year-old child or indeed of a younger child who is '*Gillick* competent' are of the greatest importance both legally and clinically, but I do doubt whether Thorpe J was right to conclude that W. was of sufficient understanding to make an informed decision. I do not say this on the basis that I consider her approach irrational. I personally consider that religious or other beliefs which bar any medical treatment or treatment of particular kinds are irrational, but that does not make minors who hold those beliefs any the less '*Gillick* competent'. They may well have sufficient intelligence and understanding fully to appreciate the treatment proposed and the consequences of their refusal to accept that treatment. What distinguishes W. from them, and what with all respect I do not think that Thorpe J took sufficiently into account (perhaps because the point did not emerge as clearly before him as it did before us), is that it is a feature of anorexia nervosa that it is capable of destroying the ability to make an informed choice. It creates a compulsion to refuse treatment or only to accept treatment which is likely to be ineffective. This attitude is part and parcel of the disease and the more advanced the illness, the more compelling it may become. ...

There is ample authority for the proposition that the inherent powers of the court under its parens patriae jurisdiction are theoretically limitless and that they certainly extend beyond the powers of a natural parent: see for example *In re R (A Minor) (Wardship: Consent to Treatment)* [1992] Fam 11, 25B, 28G. There can therefore be no doubt that it has power to override the refusal of a minor, whether over the age of 16 or under that age but '*Gillick* competent'. It does not do so by ordering the doctors to treat which, even if within the court's powers, would be an abuse of them or by ordering the minor to accept treatment, but by authorising the doctors to treat the minor in accordance with their clinical judgment, subject to any restrictions which the court may impose.

... This is not, however, to say that the wishes of 16- and 17-year-olds are to be treated as no different from those of 14- and 15-year-olds. Far from it. Adolescence is a period of progressive transition from childhood to adulthood and as experience of life is acquired and intelligence and understanding grow, so will the scope of the decision-making which should be left to the minor, for it is only by making decisions and experiencing the consequences that decision-making skills will be acquired. As I put it in the course of the argument, and as I sincerely believe, 'good parenting involves giving minors as much rope as they can handle without an unacceptable risk that they will hang themselves'. ...

Balcombe LJ delivered a judgment agreeing with Lord Donaldson. The third judge, however, was more cautious.

Nolan LJ: ... The general approach adopted by the House of Lords to the weight which should be attached to the views of a child who has sufficient understanding to make an informed decision is clearly of great importance, but it is essential to bear in mind that their Lordships were concerned with the extent of parental rights over the welfare of the child. They were not concerned with the jurisdiction of the court. It is of the essence of that jurisdiction that the court has the power and the responsibility in appropriate cases to override the views of both the child and the parent in determining what is in the child's best interests. Authoritative and instructive as they are, the speeches in *Gillick's* case do not deal with the principles which should govern the exercise of this court's jurisdiction in the present case. In my judgment, those principles are to be found in section 1 of the Children Act 1989. ...

In ... the circumstances of the present case the wishes and feelings of W., considered in the light of her age and understanding, are the first of the factors to which the court must have regard, but the court must have regard also to such of the other factors as may be relevant when discharging its overall responsibility for W.'s welfare.

... I am very far from asserting any general rule that the court should prefer its own view as to what is in the best interests of the child to those of the child itself. In considering the welfare of the child, the court must not only recognise but if necessary defend the right of the child, having sufficient understanding to take an informed decision, to make his or her own choice. In most areas of life it would be not only wrong in principle but also futile and counter-productive for the court to adopt any different approach. In the area of medical treatment, however, the court can and sometimes must intervene.

... One must, I think, start from the general premise that the protection of the child's welfare implies at least the protection of the child's life. I state this only as a general and not as an invariable premise because of the possibility of cases in which the court would not authorise treatment of a distressing nature which offered only a small hope of preserving life. In general terms, however, the present state of the law is that an individual who has reached the age of 18 is free to do with his life what he wishes, but it is the duty of the court to ensure so far as it can that children survive to attain that age.

To take it a stage further, if the child's welfare is threatened by a serious and imminent risk that the child will suffer grave and irreversible mental or physical harm, then once again the court when called upon has a duty to intervene. It makes no difference whether the risk arises from the action or inaction of others, or from the action or inaction of the child. Due weight must be given to the child's wishes, but the court is not bound by them. …

We are not directly concerned with cases in which the jurisdiction of the court has not been invoked, and in which accordingly the decision on treatment may depend upon the consent of the child or of the parent. I for my part would think it axiomatic, however, in order to avoid the risk of grave breaches of the law that in any case where time permitted, where major surgical or other procedures (such as an abortion) were proposed, and where the parents or those in loco parentis were prepared to give consent but the child (having sufficient understanding to make an informed decision) was not, the jurisdiction of the court should always be invoked. …

Appeal dismissed with costs against Legal Aid Board. Order below varied. Leave to appeal refused.

Questions

(i) Given what Lord Donaldson says about the girl's competence, how much of the rest of what he says is *ratio decidendi*?

(ii) Lord Donaldson points out that consent provides the 'flak jacket' against liability for administering the treatment; does it also follow that the consent of a parent or local authority with parental responsibility would provide a 'flak jacket' against liability for holding the patient down while treatment is forcibly administered? Do you consider such a possibility fanciful? Do you consider it hair-raising?

(iii) What would you advise a doctor to do if a mother insists that her pregnant daughter (*a*) of 17 or (*b*) of 13 should have an abortion which she does not want?

(iv) What would you advise a doctor to do if a mother wanted her pregnant daughter (*a*) of 17 or (*b*) of 13 to have a caesarian section without which there was a risk that (*a*) the daughter or (*b*) the baby would die?

The Children Act 1989 allows the child to make applications about his own care and upbringing. Usually he must first have leave (see p. 657, below).

Re SC (a minor) (leave to seek residence order)
[1994] 1 FLR 96, [1993] Fam Law 618, High Court, Family Division

S was a 14-year-old girl who had been in the care of a local authority under a care order for eight years. She was living in a children's home and wanted to apply for an order that she should live with a friend's family who were willing to provide her with a home. The local authority did not know whether they would oppose the eventual application but did not oppose letting her apply; her mother opposed the application for leave.

Booth J: … Mr Petrou, the solicitor instructed by S and who has presented the application on her behalf, submitted that the first test which must be satisfied is that contained in s. 10(8) of the Act. Section 10(8) provides:

> 'Where the person applying for leave to make an application for a section 8 order is the child concerned, the court may only grant leave if it is satisfied that he has sufficient understanding to make the proposed application for the section 8 order.'

S approached Mr Petrou of her own initiative in February 1993. She has given him clear instructions and he assesses her to have a good understanding of the situation. She does not suffer from any psychiatric or mental disability. The issues to which the substantive application would give rise are not complex, and the mother does not contend that S could not properly deal with them.

In the circumstances I am satisfied that the child does have sufficient understanding to enable the court to grant her leave to make the application. It does not, however, follow that the court is bound to grant leave once the test of s. 10(8) is satisfied. The court still has a discretion whether or not to do so. Where the application is made by a child, no guidance is to be found in the Act or in the rules as to the matters which should be taken into account in the exercise of this discretion. Where the person applying for leave is not the child, s. 10(9) lists the matters to which the court must have particular regard. No equivalent check-list exists in the case of an application by the child.

Mr Petrou makes two submissions. First, he submits that the court must be satisfied that the application for a s. 8 order might reasonably succeed. Such a test is analogous to that applied by the court in deciding whether to grant leave for an adoption application to be made in respect of a ward of court: see *F v S (Adoption: Ward)* [1973] Fam 203, CA. ...

I accept that submission. In my judgment it is right for the court to have regard to the likelihood of success of the proposed application and to be satisfied that the child is not embarking upon proceedings which are doomed to failure.

Secondly, Mr Petrou submits that the application for leave made by a child gives rise to a question with respect to the upbringing of the child and accordingly s. 1 of the Act applies. It would then follow that not only must the court have regard to the child's welfare as its paramount consideration, but that it must also have regard to the matters set out in the check-list in s. 1(3).

That submission I am unable to accept. In *Re A (Minors) (Residence Order: Leave to Apply)* [1992] Fam 182, [1992] 2 FLR 154. ... Balcombe LJ said (at pp. 191G and 160D respectively):

> 'In granting or refusing an application for leave to apply for a s. 8 order, the court is not determining a question with respect to the upbringing of the child concerned. That question only arises when the court hears the substantive application. The reasoning of this court in *F v S (Adoption: Ward)* [above] supports this conclusion.'

... Mr Brasse, on behalf of the mother, opposes the application on a number of grounds. He submits, first, that a child should not be permitted to apply for a residence order but that, as a matter of principle, the person in whom parental responsibility would vest under the order should make the application. If that person was not entitled to apply, he would have to seek leave to do so. On that application the court would then be bound to apply what Mr Brasse submits is the more stringent test of s. 10(9) of the Act and to have regard, among the other matters set out in that subsection, both to the local authority's plans for the child's future as well as to the wishes and feelings of the child's parents.

Mr Brasse submits that the court should not permit that more stringent test to be by-passed by allowing the child concerned, to whom it does not apply, to make the application instead.

... In my judgment the court should not fetter the statutory ability of the child to seek any s. 8 order, including a residence order, if it is appropriate for such an application to be made. Although the court will undoubtedly consider why it is that the person in whose favour a proposed residence order would be made is not applying, it would in my opinion be wrong to import into the Act any requirement that only he or she should make the application.

The second ground on which Mr Brasse relies is founded upon the fact that since Mrs B is a friend of S, the local authority is bound to consider her as a carer in accordance with the duty imposed upon them by s. 23(6)(*b*) of the Act. Despite the fact that she has already been considered and rejected as a carer the local authority are in the process of carrying out a further assessment and are thereby fulfilling their statutory duty. The local authority are under a duty to safeguard and promote S's welfare. In those circumstances, Mr Brasse submits, it is unnecessary and inappropriate for an application to be made for a residence order in favour of Mrs B. The decision whether or not it is in S's interests to live with Mrs B should be left to the local authority.

Although, again, those clearly are factors to be taken into account by the court on the issue of granting leave to S, I do not consider that they are determinative of it. They must be balanced against other circumstances which include the length of time S has been in care, the fact that in care she has not had settled accommodation and her wish now to live with and be cared for by Mrs B, a wish to which the court is statutorily bound to have regard whereas the local authority is not. I think that it may safely be assumed by the court that a child of S's age will, understandably, prefer to have parental responsibility for her vested in a trusted friend, if not a parent, rather than to be subject to a care order with parental responsibility vested in a local authority. It is also a matter for consideration that the local authority do not take the point themselves and remain neutral on the application. I do not, therefore, think that this argument should stand in the way of leave being granted to S.

These are not the only circumstances in which a child may become a party to proceedings; she may be allowed to make an application about another child, for example, for contact with a sibling who is living with another family; or she may be joined as a party in proceedings between her parents about her own future; or she may be a respondent to proceedings brought by others about her own child; mainly because of the last situation, the Family Proceedings Rules 1991, r. 9.2A, make an exception to the usual rules about child parties to litigation.

Re T (a minor) (child: representation)
[1994] Fam 49, [1993] 4 All ER 518, sub nom Re CT (a minor) [1993] 2 FLR 278, Court of Appeal

T. was a 13-year-old girl who had been adopted at the age of seven but now wanted to resume her links with her birth family and live with her birth mother's sister. She was given leave to apply for a residence order and a solicitor agreed to represent her without a 'next friend'. Her adoptive parents were strongly opposed to her application and instituted wardship proceedings. The judge made her a ward of court and appointed the Official Solicitor as her guardian ad litem in those proceedings. T. appealed against the imposition of a guardian to conduct the case for her.

Waite LJ: ...

2. *The child as a party generally*
Family proceedings are in general subject to the ordinary rules of disability, applying to all civil proceedings, which prevent a minor from bringing or defending any proceedings except by a next friend or guardian ad litem (as the case may be): see RSC Ord 80, r 2 and the Family Proceedings Rules 1991, SI 1991/1247, r 9.2. A next friend or guardian does not in those circumstances act merely as the child's representative. He has an independent function to perform, and must act in what he believes to be the minor's best interests, even if that should involve acting in contravention of the wishes of a minor who is old enough to articulate views of his own: see the authorities cited in the notes to RSC Ord 80, r 2 in *The Supreme Court Practice 1993* vol 1, paras 80/2/1–80/2/16. Those functions can be performed by anyone who has no interest in the proceedings ...: there is no need for a next friend or guardian ad litem in private law proceedings to be professionally qualified, or even a member of the panel of guardians recruited to discharge the public law functions established by s. 41 of the Children Act 1989. In practice, however, problems of representation and legal aid make it difficult for a lay person to act, and in the majority of private law cases the child's next friend or guardian ad litem will be the Official Solicitor, whose department has unrivalled experience in dealing with the problems to which such proceedings are apt to give rise. In function, however, he does not differ at all from any other next friend or guardian ad litem. He owes a loyalty which has by its very nature to be divided: to the child whose views he must fully and fairly represent; and to the court, which it is his duty to assist in achieving the overriding or paramount objective of promoting the child's best interests.

An exception to that long-established principle has been introduced, uniquely, into family law by r 9.2A of the 1991 rules (as amended by SI 1992/456) in certain specified instances. Those are: (1) where the court has given leave at the outset for a minor to begin or defend proceedings without a next friend or guardian ad litem. Such leave is only to be granted if the court considers that 'the minor concerned has sufficient understanding to participate as a party in the proceedings ... without a next friend or guardian ad litem' (r 9.2A(1)(*a*) and (6)). (2) Where a minor has a next friend or guardian ad litem in proceedings that are already on foot and applies successfully for leave to prosecute or defend the remaining stages of the proceedings without a next friend or guardian ad litem. Leave for that purpose is only to be granted if the court reaches the same conclusion as in case (1) (r 9.2A(4) and (6)). (3) Where a solicitor has accepted instructions from the minor to act in the proceedings, and where that solicitor 'considers that the minor is able, having regard to his understanding, to give instructions in relation to the proceedings' (r 9.2A(1)(*b*)(i) and (ii)).

3. *The child's 'understanding'*
This is a factor expressly to be considered by the court when considering whether to grant leave to apply under s. 10(8) of the 1989 Act, and also when considering whether to grant leave to initiate or continue proceedings without a next friend or guardian ad litem under cases (1) and (2) above. It is also a factor expressly to be considered by the solicitor in considering whether to accept instructions in case (3). No definition of 'understanding' is attempted by the 1989 Act or the 1991 rules, but guidance was offered by this court in *Re S (a minor) (independent representation)* [1993] Fam 263 at 276, [1993] 3 All ER 36 at 43–44, where Sir Thomas Bingham MR said:

> 'Different children have differing levels of understanding at the same age. And understanding is not absolute. It has to be assessed relatively to the issues in the proceedings. Where any sound judgment on these issues calls for insight and imagination which only maturity and experience can bring, both the court and the solicitor will be slow to conclude that the child's understanding is sufficient.'

...

(1) *Was the judge justified in directing or authorising the use of wardship proceedings – whether as a means of introducing the Official Solicitor or for any other reason?*
No one aware of the facts of this case could fail to sympathise with T., who must feel herself prey to torn loyalties and is clearly in need of all the help that can be given to her, or with the adoptive parents, who have shown her love and kindness and are still ready to offer her a permanent and loving home. It is throughly understandable, in such circumstances, that the judge should have wished to provide T. with the most objective representation and the most appropriate medical assessment that could be devised for her, and should have favoured the involvement of the Official Solicitor as her guardian ad litem as being an appropriate means to that end. It may even be fairly said that in placing this vulnerable child under the protection of a prerogative jurisdiction of great antiquity, which until the coming into force of the 1989 Act had become refined by the courts into an effective instrument for achieving continuity and flexibility in judicial supervision of child care procedures, the court was giving her, in juridical terms, the most favourable treatment possible.

The arguments [of counsel] have persuaded me, however, that the judge was wrong to have invoked the wardship jurisdiction. Rule 9.2A(1) gives T. exactly the same rights in wardship as she enjoys in proceedings under Pt II of the 1989 Act. Provided the conditions of that paragraph are satisfied, she can bring or defend wardship proceedings without a next friend or guardian ad litem, and the court would have no power to impose one upon her against her will. If, therefore, the judge believed that wardship provided a means of requiring T. to accept a guardian ad litem, he was mistaken. If he thought that wardship would secure for her, or for the adoptive parents, any advantage not available in ordinary family proceedings under Pt II of the 1989 Act, he was mistaken in that respect also. ...

Appeal allowed. Leave to appeal to the House of Lords refused.

Questions

(i) Is the understanding required to make an application about yourself the same as the understanding required to conduct the proceedings by yourself?
(ii) What would you do about (*a*) an 11-year-old boy who wanted to instruct his own lawyer in a bitterly contested dispute between his parents (as in *Re S (a minor) (independent representation)* [1993] Fam 263, [1993] 3 All ER 36, CA); (*b*) a twelve-year-old girl who had run away from home after an argument with her mother and wanted to live with her boy-friend's parents?

(iii) If a child is conducting the proceedings himself, should he be in court like any other party?
(iv) In public law proceedings (see Children Act 1989, s. 41) a child of sufficient understanding will have a professional social worker as a 'guardian ad litem' who must represent his best interests and a solicitor who must represent his views if these are different (see Family Proceedings Rules 1991, rr. 4.11, 4.12): why is this system not adopted in private law proceedings?
(v) How would you go about deciding whether what a child wanted was in his best interests?

In *The Emergence of Children's Rights* (1986) John Eekelaar discusses the concept of children's rights, and distinguishes three different kinds of interest they may have:

We may accept that the *social perception* that an individual or class of individuals has certain interests is a precondition to the conceptualization of rights. But these interests must be capable of isolation from the interests of others. I might believe that it is in my infant daughter's interests that I (and not she) take decisions concerning her medical welfare. This may even be supportable by objective evidence. But my interest, or right, to take such decisions is not identical with her interests. I might make stupid or even malicious decisions. Her interest is that I should make the best decisions for her. I am no more than the agent for fulfilling her interests. Hence we should be careful to understand that when we talk about rights as protecting interests, we conceive as interests only those benefits which the subject himself or herself might plausibly claim in themselves. This point is of great importance in the context of modern assertions of the right to parental autonomy. This has been advanced as a fuller enhancement of children's rights. Goldstein, Freud and Solnit [see p. 423, above] construct the concept of 'family integrity' which is a combination of 'the three liberty interests of direct concern to children, parental autonomy, the right to autonomous parents and privacy'. But can we say the children might plausibly claim any of these things in themselves? If they are claimed (which they may be) it will be because they are believed to advance other desirable ends (perhaps material and emotional stability) which are the true objects of the claims. Observe that the formulation refers to claims children might plausibly make. Not, be it noted, what they actually claim. We here meet the problem that children often lack the information or ability to appreciate what will serve them best. It is necessary therefore to make some kind of imaginative leap and guess what a child might retrospectively have wanted once it reaches a position of maturity. In doing this, values of the adult world and of individual adults will inevitably enter. This is not to be deplored, but openly accepted. It encourages debate about these values. There are, however, some broad propositions which might reasonably be advanced as forming the foundation of any child's (retrospective) claims. General physical, emotional and intellectual care within the social capabilities of his or her immediate caregivers would seem a minimal expectation. We may call this the 'basic' interest. What a child should expect from the wider community must be stated more tentatively. I have elsewhere [Eekelaar, 1984] suggested the formulation that, within certain overriding constraints, created by the economic and social structure of society (whose extent must be open to debate), all children should have an equal opportunity to maximize the resources available to them during their childhood (including their own inherent abilities) so as to minimize the degree to which they enter adult life affected by avoidable prejudices incurred during childhood. In short, their capacities are to be developed to their best advantage. We may call this the 'developmental' interest. The concept requires some elaboration.

It seems plausible that a child may expect society at large, no less than his parents, to ensure that he is no worse off than most other children in his opportunities to realize his life-chances. Could a child also plausibly claim that he should be given a *better* chance than other children, for example, by exploitation of his superior talents or a favoured social position? As an expectation addressed to the child's parents, such a claim might have some weight. A child of rich parents might retrospectively feel aggrieved if those resources were not used to provide him with a better chance in life than other children. On the other hand, such an expectation is less plausibly addressed to society at large, except perhaps with respect to the cultivation of singular talents. But from the point of view of a theory of rights, it does not much matter whether we decide that a privileged child has an interest in inequality favourable to himself. For, if the interest is to become a right, it must be acknowledged in the public domain as demanding protection for its own sake. As far as the 'developmental' interest is concerned, therefore, societies may choose to actualize it in harmony with their overall social goals, which may (but not necessarily) involve creating equality of opportunity and reducing socially determined inequalities, but encouraging diversity of achievement related to individual talent.

There is a third type of interest which children may, retrospectively, claim. A child may argue for the freedom to choose his own lifestyle and to enter social relations according to his own inclinations uncontrolled by the authority of the adult world, whether parents or institutions. Claims of this kind have been put forward on behalf of children by Holt (1975) and by Farson (1978). We may call them the 'autonomy' interest. Freeman (1983) has argued that such interests might be abridged insofar as children also have a right to be protected against their own inclinations if their satisfaction would rob them of the opportunity 'to mature to a rationally autonomous adulthood ... capable of deciding on [their] own system of ends as free and rational beings'. This may be no more than a version of the developmental interest defined earlier. The problem is that a child's autonomy interest may conflict with the developmental interest and even the basic interest. While it is possible that some adults retrospectively approve that they were, when children, allowed the exercise of their autonomy at the price of putting them at a disadvantage as against other children in realizing their life-chances in adulthood, it seems improbable that this would be a common view. We may therefore rank the autonomy interests subordinate to the basic and the developmental interests. However, where they may be exercised without threatening these two interests, the claim for their satisfaction must be high.

'Basic' interests are served by care proceedings, now under s. 31 of the Children Act 1989, p. 617, below:

... the statute does not confer rights to be free of deprivations suffered by parents which are reflected on the children. But it does, as applied in practice, seem to give children rights to be removed from the adverse consequences of care by parents who suffer social or personal inadequacy. The imposition of these duties is primarily perceived by the enforcement agencies as directed at advancing the interests of the rightholders, and represents a total reversal of earlier characterizations of the child-parent relationship. This reflects not only the social recognition of the basic interests of the rightholders as ends in themselves, but also a societal decision of the priority to be applied where those interests conflict with the interests of others, in this case, the parents.

'Developmental' interests present more problems:

When we turn to the developmental interests, there is more difficulty. The requirement to allocate resources so that an individual child does not suffer such deprivations during childhood that he is disadvantaged disproportionately, when compared to children generally, in the outset of his or her adult life, can for a large part be met only by the community at large. The cost appears in such areas as children's medical services and education. The duties lie primarily in the political domain and therefore become enmeshed in still broader considerations of public policy. Their legal articulation is at a very broad level of generality. ...

While children are resident with their parents, the law imposes no duty on the parents to fulfil the developmental interests, apart from ensuring their education. However we may justify it, the developmental interest for the vast majority of children is not protected as a right, but owes its satisfaction to the natural workings of the economies of families which are themselves dependent on the wider social and economic mechanisms of the community. Where, however, the family is split apart, the regulation of the distribution of resources between the families is thrown into the public domain. Failure to ensure some such distribution carries the risk of visible impoverishment of the mother and child, with attendant threats to social stability and community welfare funds. The developmental interests of children are also threatened in these circumstances, so it is of interest to discover how far the legal regulation of income distribution after family separation can be characterized as the protection of that interest. ...

Finally, he discusses the autonomy interest in the light of *Gillick*:

... Of the nine judges who gave a decision in this litigation, five were in favour of the plaintiff. This perhaps illustrates the ambiguity in current perceptions of the proper scope of children's autonomy interests. But the majority decision of the House of Lords has implications which extend beyond the parent-child relationship and into the scope of state power over the lives of children themselves. …

The significance of Lord Scarman's opinion with respect to children's autonomy interests cannot be over-rated. It follows from his reasoning that, where a child has reached capacity, there is no room for a parent to impose a contrary view, *even if this is more in accord with the child's best interests*. For its legal superiority to the child's decision can rest only on its status as a parental right. But this is extinguished when the child reaches full capacity. …

This recognition of the autonomy interests of children can be reconciled with their basic and developmental interests only through the empirical application of the concept of the acquisition of full capacity. This, as Lord Scarman made clear, may be no simple matter. The child must not only understand the nature of the transaction, but be able to evaluate its implications. Intellectual understanding must be supplemented by emotional maturity. It is easy to see how adults can conclude that a child's decision which seems, to the adult, to be contrary to his interests, is lacking in sufficient maturity. In this respect, the provision of the simple test of age to provide an upper limit to the scope of a supervisory, paternalistic power has advantages. We cannot know for certain whether, retrospectively, a person may not regret that some control was not exercised over his immature judgment by persons with greater experience. But could we not say that it is on balance better to subject all persons to this potential inhibition up to a defined age, in case the failure to exercise the restraint unduly prejudices a person's basic or developmental interests? It avoids judgments in which questions of fact and value will be impenetrably mixed. But the decision, it seems, has been taken. Children will now have, in wider measure than ever before, that most dangerous but most precious of rights: the right to make their own mistakes.

Questions

(i) Where does the child's 'autonomy interest' now stand in the light of *Re W (a minor) (medical treatment: court's jurisdiction)* [1993] Fam 64, [1992] 4 All ER 627, CA, p. 429, above?
(ii) Might not recognising the child's 'autonomy interest' itself be a means of recognising his 'basic' and 'developmental' interests (see, for example, Adler and Dearling, 1986)?
(iii) To what extent would you give priority to any of these interests, if they conflicted with those of adults?
(iv) Eekelaar acknowledges the political implications of society recognising the developmental interests of children: how far is it possible to go in a democracy?
(v) 'Is it not almost a self-evident axiom that the state should require and compel the education, up to a certain standard, of every human being who is born its citizen?' (Mill, 1859)
(vi) The European Convention on Human Rights, Protocol 1, Article 2 (see further p. 714, below) requires:

No person shall be denied the right to education. In the exercise of any functions which it assumes in relation to education and to teaching, the state shall respect the right of parents to ensure such education and teaching in conformity with their own religious and philosophical convictions.

Would you consider it a breach of this article (*a*) to impose a national curriculum including evolution within its compulsory science teaching upon children of a family who believed in the literal truth of the book of Genesis (probably not: *Kejeldson, Busk Madsen and Pederson* (1976), Series A, No 23; 1 EHRR 711); (*b*) to use corporal punishment to enforce school rules, contrary to the philosophical convictions of the parents (definitely: see *Campbell and Cosans v United Kingdom* (1982) 4 EHRR 293, Series A, No 48); (*c*) to

enforce a compulsory school leaving age of 16 against children whose parents believed that education over 14 would prejudice their upbringing in the Amish way of life (probably not: but see *Wisonsin v Yoder* 406 US 205 (1972))?
(vii) Is this article protecting the rights of the child or the rights of the parents?
(viii) What happens if a child with special educational needs wants to go to a special school but his parents want him to go to an ordinary school or vice versa?

4 Parental responsibility

The Children Act 1989 uses the basic concept of 'parental responsibility', defined as follows:

3. – (1) In this Act 'parental responsibility' means all the rights, duties, powers, responsibilities and authority which by law a parent of a child has in relation to the child and his property.
(2) It also includes the rights, powers and duties which a guardian of the child's estate (appointed, before the commencement of section 5, to act generally) would have had in relation to the child and his property.
(3) The rights referred to in subsection (2) include, in particular, the right of the guardian to receive or recover in his own name, for the benefit of the child, property of whatever description and wherever situated which the child is entitled to receive or recover.
(4) The fact that a person has, or does not have, parental responsibility for a child shall not affect –
(*a*) any obligation which he may have in relation to the child (such as a statutory duty to maintain the child); or
(*b*) any rights which, in the event of the child's death, he (or any other person) may have in relation to the child's property.
...

The reasons for what might be thought a purely cosmetic change appear in the Law Commission's Report on *Guardianship and Custody* (1988):

Parental responsibility
2.4 Scattered through the statute book at present are such terms as 'parental rights and duties' or the 'powers and duties', or the 'rights and authority' of a parent. However, in our first Report on Illegitimacy we expressed the view that 'to talk of parental "rights" is not only inaccurate as a matter of juristic analysis but also a misleading use of ordinary language.' The House of Lords, in *Gillick v West Norfolk and Wisbech Area Health Authority* [[1986] AC 112, [1985] 3 All ER 402, HL (p. 426, above)] has held that the powers which parents have to control or make decisions for their children are simply the necessary concomitant of their parental duties. To refer to the concept of 'right' in the relationship between parent and child is therefore likely to produce confusion, as that case itself demonstrated. As against third parties, parents clearly have a prior claim to look after or have contact with their child but, as the House of Lords has recently pointed out in *Re KD (A Minor) (Ward: Termination of Access)* [1988] AC 806, [1988] 1 All ER 577, HL, that claim will always be displaced if the interests of the child indicate to the contrary. The parental claim can be recognised in the rules governing the allocation of parental responsibilities, but the content of their status would be more accurately reflected if a new concept of 'parental responsibility' were to replace the ambiguous and confusing terms used at present. Such a change would make little difference in substance but it would reflect the everyday reality of being a parent and emphasise the responsibilites of all who are in that position. ...
2.5 One further advantage is that the same concept could then be employed to define the status of local authorities when children have been compulsorily committed to their care. The reports of the inquiries into the deaths of Jasmine Beckford and Tyra Henry indicate how helpful this would be in emphasising the continuing parental responsibility of the local authority even if the child has been allowed to live at home.

(a) The scope of parental responsibility

2.6 The concept of 'parental responsibility' can be defined by reference to all the incidents, whether rights, claims, duties, powers, responsibilities or authority, which statute and common law for the time being confer upon parents. It would be superficially attractive to provide a list of these but those who responded to our Working Paper on Guardianship recognised the practical impossibility of doing so. The list must change from time to time to meet differing needs and circumstances. As the *Gillick* case itself demonstrated, it must also vary with the age and maturity of the child and the circumstances of each individual case.

2.7 Three points should, however, be made clear. First, the incidents of parenthood with which we are concerned are those which relate to the care and upbringing of a child until he grows up. This does include some power to administer the child's property on his behalf but it does not include the right to succeed to the child's property on his death (which will almost always be without leaving a will because children under 18 can only make wills in very exceptional circumstances). The right to succeed is a feature of being related to the deceased in a particular way and operates irrespective of who has responsibility for bringing him up. ...

2.8 Secondly, it might also be helpful to clarify the nature and extent of a parent's powers to administer or deal with a child's property, for the law on this is most obscure ... a particular uncertainty is whether the parents have the same powers as do guardians, for example to receive a legacy on the child's behalf. Our provisional proposal that parents should be in no worse position than guardians in this respect was approved on consultation and we so recommend.

2.9 Thirdly, the fact that a person does, or does not, have parental responsibility for the care and upbringing of a child does not affect the rights of the child, in particular to be maintained or to succeed to a person's estate. The principle that children should have the same rights whatever the marital status of their parents was an essential feature of our recommendations on illegitimacy [see p. 492 et seq, below] which have recently been implemented by the Family Law Reform Act 1987. ...

Question

What do you think the Commission meant when they argued that the concept of parental 'responsibility' would 'reflect the everyday reality of being a parent'?

John Eekelaar, in *Parental Responsibility: State of Nature or Nature of the State?* (1991), has pointed out that the concept of parental responsibility can be used in two rather different senses:

It was ... in the context of appreciation that parental 'rights' needed to be exercised for the benefit of the child that the Law Commission (1982) first suggested that it might be more appropriate to talk about parental responsibilities than parental rights. Similarly, the Commission's confirmation in paragraph 1.11 of its 1985 Working Paper on Guardianship of its preference for speaking of 'powers and responsibilities' rather than 'rights and duties' follows the observation that a parent 'will not ... be permitted to insist upon action which is contrary to (the welfare of the child) or to resist action which will promote it' (Law Commission, 1985). The shift in terminology reflects a similar change made in West Germany as long ago as 1970, when 'parental power' (*elterliche Gewalt*) was replaced by 'parental care' (*elterliche Sorge*) (Frank, 1990) and the conception of 'parental responsibilities' recommended by the Committee of Ministers of the Council of Europe in 1984 (Recommendation No. R(84)4, February 28, 1984), which states that 'parental responsibilities are a collection of duties and powers which aim at ensuring the moral and material welfare of the child, in particular by taking care of the person of the child, by maintaining personal relationships with him and by providing for his education, maintenance, his legal representation and the administration of his property.' I shall refer to this sense of 'responsibility' as *responsibility (1)*.

However, also in paragraph 1.11 of its 1985 Working Paper, the Commission introduced a different concept of responsibility. 'Further,' they wrote, 'to the extent that the law enables parents to decide how to bring up their children without interference from others or from the state, it does so principally because this is a necessary part of the parents' responsibility for that upbringing and in order thus to promote the welfare of their children'. 'Responsibility' does not here refer to the way in which a parent behaves *towards* his child (as is reflected in the references to duties and supervision over parental conduct made earlier) but rather to a role which is to be exercised by the parent rather than some other entity. Of course, the assumption of responsibility for a child in this sense is not necessarily inconsistent with the presence of duties towards the child (as we shall see, it is sometimes thought that it encourages their performance). But the focus is not upon those duties but rather upon the distance between the parent and others in making provision for the child; indeed, on the degree of *freedom* given to parents in bringing up their children. And the more scope that is given to parental autonomy, the less room there is for external supervision over the way duties (under *responsibility (1)*) towards children are discharged. This will be referred to as *responsibility (2)*.

Question

As various provisions of the Children Act 1989 appear, try to identify whether they owe more to responsibility (1) or responsibility (2).

The Children Act 1989 also deals with some important features of parental responsibility:

2. – ... (5) More than one person may have parental responsibility for the same child at the same time.

(6) A person who has parental responsibility for a child at any time shall not cease to have that responsibility solely because some other person subsequently acquires parental responsibility for the child.

(7) Where more than one person has parental responsibility for a child, each of them may act alone and without the other (or others) in meeting that responsibility; but nothing in this Part shall be taken to affect the operation of any enactment which requires the consent of more than one person in a matter affecting the child.

(8) The fact that a person has parental responsibility for a child shall not entitle him to act in any way which would be incompatible with any order made with respect to the child under this Act.

(9) A person who has parental responsibility for a child may not surrender or transfer any part of that responsibility to another but may arrange for some or all of it to be met by one or more persons acting on his behalf.

(10) The person with whom any such arrangement is made may himself be a person who already has parental responsibility for the child concerned.

(11) The making of any such arrangement shall not affect any liability of the person making it which may arise from any failure to meet any part of his parental responsibility for the child concerned.

3. – ... (5) A person who –

(*a*) does not have parental responsibility for a particular child; but

(*b*) has care of the child,

may (subject to the provisions of this Act) do what is reasonable in all the circumstances of the case for the purpose of safeguarding or promoting the child's welfare.

Once again, these are explained in the Law Commission's Report (1988):

(b) *The power to act independently*

2.10 ... We believe it important to preserve the equal status of parents and their power to act independently of one another unless and until a court orders otherwise. This should be seen as part of the general aim of encouraging both parents to feel concerned and responsible for the welfare of their children. A few respondents suggested that they should have a legal duty to consult one another on major matters in their children's lives, arguing that this would increase parental co-operation and involvement after separation or divorce. This is an objective which we all share. However, whether or not the parents are living together, a legal duty of consultation seems both unworkable and undesirable. The person looking after the child has to be able to take decisions in the child's best interests as and when they arise. Some may have to be taken very quickly. In reality ... it is that person who will have to put those decisions into effect and that person who has the degree of practical control over the child to be able to do so. The child may well suffer if that parent is prevented by the other's disapproval and thus has to go to court to resolve the matter, still more if the parent is inhibited by the fear that the other may disapprove or by the difficulties of contacting him or of deciding whether what is proposed is or is not a major matter requiring consultation. In practice, where the parents disagree about a matter of upbringing the burden should be on the one seeking to prevent a step which the other is proposing, or to impose a course of action which only the other can put into effect, to take the matter to court. Otherwise the courts might be inundated with cases, disputes might escalate well beyond their true importance, and in the meantime the children would suffer. We recommend, therefore, that the equal and independent status of parents be preserved and, indeed, applied to others (principally guardians) who may share parental responsibility in future. This will not, of course, affect any statutory provision which requires the consent of each parent, for example to the adoption of the child.

(c) *The effect of court orders*

2.11 Allied to this is the principle that parents should not lose their parental responsibility even though its exercise may have to be modified or curtailed in certain respects, for example if it is necessary to determine where a child will live after his parents separate. Obviously, a court order to that effect will put many matters outside the control of the parent who does not have the child with him. However, parents should not be regarded as losing their position, and their ability to take decisions about their children, simply because they are separated or in dispute with one another about a particular matter. Hence they should only be prevented from acting in ways which would be incompatible with an order made about the child's upbringing. If, for example, the child has to live with one parent and go to a school near home, it would be incompatible with that order for the other parent to arrange for him to have his hair done in a way which will exclude him from the school. It would not, however, be incompatible for that parent to take him to a particular sporting occasion over the weekend, no matter how much the parent with whom the child lived might disapprove. These principles form part of our general aim of 'lowering the stakes' in cases of parental separation and divorce, and emphasising the continued responsibility of both parents, to which we shall return [see p. 529, below]. However, they are equally important where children are committed to local authority care. The crucial effect of a care order is to confer parental responsibilities upon the authority and there will be detailed regulations about how these are to be exercised. But the parents remain the parents and 'it will continue to be important in many cases to involve the parents in the child's care'. Clearly, the order will leave little scope for them to carry out their responsibilities, save to a limited extent while the child is with them, because the local authority will be in control of so much of the child's life [see p. 626, below]. But the parents should not be deprived of their very parenthood unless and until the child is adopted or freed for adoption.

(d) *Arrangements and agreements with parents and others*

2.12 ...

2.13 It is clearly important to maintain the principle that parental rights or responsibility cannot be legally surrendered or transferred without a court order and we so recommend. Equally, it is always possible, and a common practice, for parents to delegate the exercise of some or all of their parental responsibilities either between themselves or to other people or agencies, such as schools, holiday camps, foster parents or local authorities. It would be helpful for the law to recognise this expressly, for two reasons. First, parents are now encouraged to agree between themselves the arrangements which they believe best for their children, whether or not they are separated. It is important, therefore, that they should feel free to do so. Secondly ... it is helpful if, for example, a school can feel confident in accepting the decision of a person nominated by the parents as a temporary 'guardian' for the child while they are away. ...

2.14 We do not recommend, however, that such arrangements should be legally binding so that the parents cannot revoke or change them. ... It would scarcely be in the best interests of children for parents to be bound by such arrangements should they wish to change them. No court would uphold them if they were contrary to the child's interests but the burden of taking the case to court should not lie with the parents. This is particularly important in the context of arrangements made with or through local authorities. Both the Review of Child Care Law and the Government's response to it have emphasised that these should always be voluntary and that court proceedings should be required before any compulsory interference with the parents' responsibilities.

2.15 ... As between those who share parental responsibility, ... a provision for legally binding agreements might inhibit them from making whatever arrangements seem best at the time for fear that it might later be difficult to change them. Any disagreement will eventually have to be resolved by a court and in practice the burden will still lie on the one wishing to change the agreed arrangements. The court, in deciding what is best for the child, will no doubt take account of the arrangements agreed, the reasons for them, and the risks of changing them. But if they have already been changed in fact it would be wrong for there still to be a bias in favour of the previous agreement. ...

(e) *The position of those without parental responsibility*

2.16 However, it would be helpful to clarify the position of those who have actual care of a child without having parental responsibility for him in law. ... There is criminal liability for, *inter alia*, ill-treatment, neglect and failure to educate, whether or not a person has legal custody. ... But there may be confusion about the power of such people to take certain decisions about the child. We therefore recommend that it be made quite clear that anyone with actual care of a child may do what is reasonable in all the circumstances of the case for the purpose of safeguarding or promoting the child's welfare. The obvious example is medical treatment. If the child is left with friends while the parents go on holiday, it would obviously not be reasonable to arrange major elective surgery, but it would be reasonable to arrange whatever was advised in the event of an accident to the child. ...

The Department of Health's *Introduction to the Children Act 1989* (1989) sums it all up like this:

1.4 The Act uses the phrase *'parental responsibility'* to sum up the collection of duties, rights and authority which a parent has in respect of his child. That choice of words emphasises that the duty to care for the child and to raise him to moral, physical and emotional health is the fundamental task of parenthood and the only justification for the authority it confers.

1.5 The importance of parental responsibility is emphasised in the Act by the fact that not only is it unaffected by the separation of parents but even when courts make orders in private proceedings such as divorce, that responsibility continues and is limited only to the extent that any order settles certain concrete issues between the parties. That arrangement aims to emphasise that interventions by the courts where there is family breakdown should not be regarded as lessening the duty on both parents to continue to play a full part in the child's upbringing.

Questions

(i) Do you really believe that parents are for children rather than children for parents?

(ii) If you do, would you introduce any controls over who is allowed to have children (see also p. 482, below)?

However, as we shall see in the next chapter, not all parents have parental responsibility, but even those without it have a closer and better legal relationship with their children than does anyone else.

Chapter 11

Becoming a parent

Once upon a time there was only one way to become a mother and to become a father you had to be married to a mother. Nowadays you can become a father without being married to the mother. You can also become a parent of someone else's child by adoption, by assisted reproduction, and by surrogacy, which is a mixture of the two. We shall look briefly at each of these in turn, before examining what difference it makes whether or not the parents are married to one another.

1 Births in and out of marriage

Women are having fewer children these days. The first graph, from *Social Trends 26* (1996) shows that the total period fertility rate in the United Kingdom is now well below the rate of 2.1 which is associated with long-term population replacement.

Total period fertility rate[1]

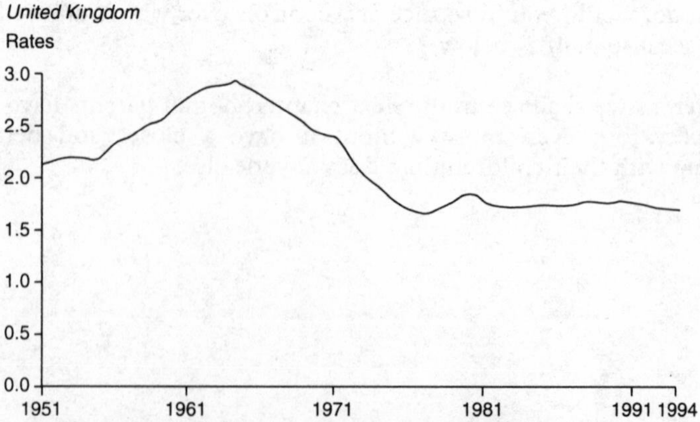

1 The average number of children which would be born per woman experienced the age specific fertility rates of the period in question throughout their child-bearing lifespan.

Source: Office of Population Censuses and Surveys; General Register Office (Scotland); General Register Office (Northern Ireland)

The second graph, from *Social Trends 25* (1995) shows how a rapidly increasing proportion of children are being born outside marriage.

Live births outside marriage as a percentage of all births

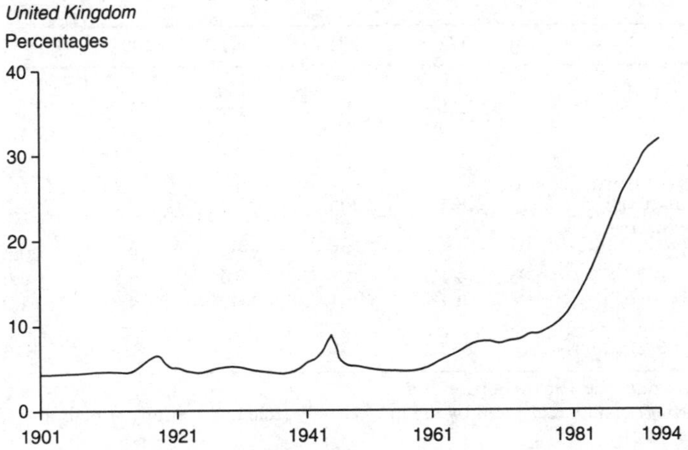

Source: Office of Population Censuses and Surveys

But the third graph, from *Social Trends 24* (1994) shows that many of their fathers are not only known but are living at the same address as their mothers.

Live births outside marriage as a percentage of all births: by registration

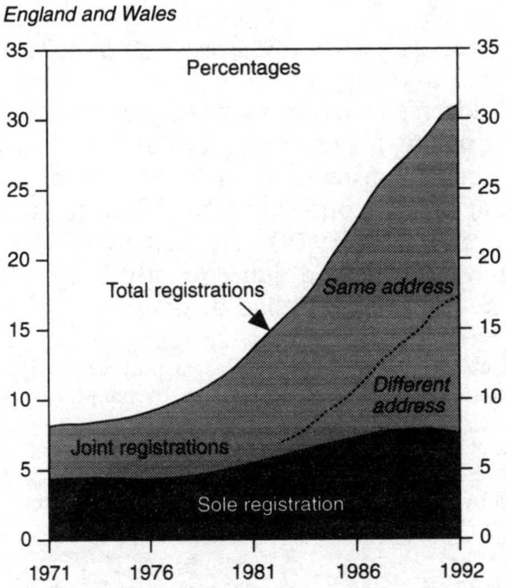

Source: Office of Population Censuses and Surveys

The final table, from *Social Trends 26* (1996) shows how responses to becoming pregnant have changed over the same period.

Conceptions: by marital status and outcome

England and Wales *Percentages*

	1971	1981	1991	1992	1993
Inside marriage					
Maternities	72.6	65.9	51.9	51.2	51.2
Legal abortions[1]	5.2	5.6	4.4	4.4	4.3
Outside marriage					
Maternities inside marriage	8.1	5.5	3.7	3.6	3.5
Maternities outside marriage[2]					
Joint registration	3.5	6.8	18.9	19.9	20.2
Sole registration	4.1	4.8	6.0	5.9	6.0
Legal abortions[1]	6.7	11.4	15.0	14.9	14.9
All conceptions (= 100%) (thousands)	835	752	854	829	819

1 Legal terminations under the 1967 Abortion Act.
2 Births outside marriage can be registered by the mother only (sole registration) or by both parents (joint registration).

Source: Office of Population Censuses and Surveys

Questions

(i) How would you account for the fall in shot-gun marriages?
(ii) As these marriages have in the past been twice as likely to break down, does this strike you as a good thing or a bad thing?
(iii) But has it got anything to do with the rise in 'same address' registrations?
(iv) Does this strike you as a good thing or a bad thing?

Of course, the children's situation may well change after their birth. If their natural parents later marry, for example, they are legitimated (Legitimacy Act 1976, s. 2) and can be re-registered as such. A study of the fate of those born outside marriage was carried out by Richard Leete, in *Adoption Trends and Illegitimate Births 1951–1977* (1979). He calculated the numbers of these children in a given year who had subsequently been adopted by a parent, adopted by strangers, legitimated or had died:

The figures show that between 7 and 8% of the generations born in the 1950s and 1960s were, or can be expected to be adopted by age 16 by couples of whom one at least is a parent. ...

The level of adoption of illegitimate children by non-parents is very much higher than that by parents. ... some 20% of children born illegitimate between 1951 and 1968 were, or can be expected to be, adopted by non-parents by the time they become adults; ... Since 1968 the rate of adoption in the first years of life has fallen greatly. Thus, just 9 per cent of children born illegitimate in 1974 had been adopted by age two, just half the proportion found for generations born during the early and mid 1960s. ...

Among generations born in the mid and late 1960s it is likely that some 20% of illegitimate children will have been legitimated by age 16. For generations born during the 1970s there has been a sharp fall in the level of legitimation ...

Percentage of selected generations of illegitimate children alive and still illegitimate by given age, England and Wales

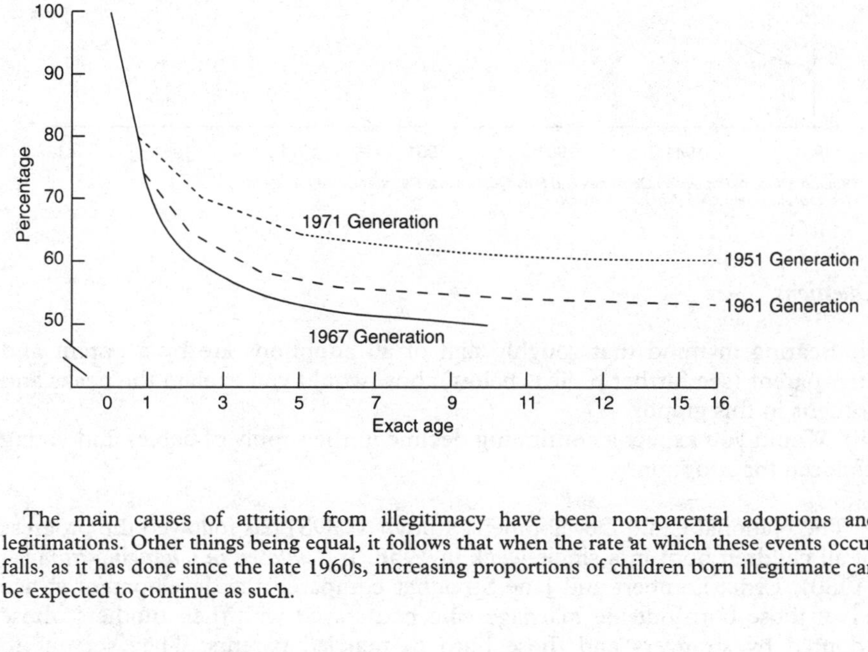

The main causes of attrition from illegitimacy have been non-parental adoptions and legitimations. Other things being equal, it follows that when the rate at which these events occur falls, as it has done since the late 1960s, increasing proportions of children born illegitimate can be expected to continue as such.

Questions

(i) Why do *you* think there has been a fall in *both* adoptions by strangers *and* legitimation?
(ii) Might it not have been expected that legitimation would increase following the Divorce Reform Act 1969?

The fluctuating fortunes of adoption over the years are shown in the following graph from *Social Trends 25* (1995):

Adoption orders

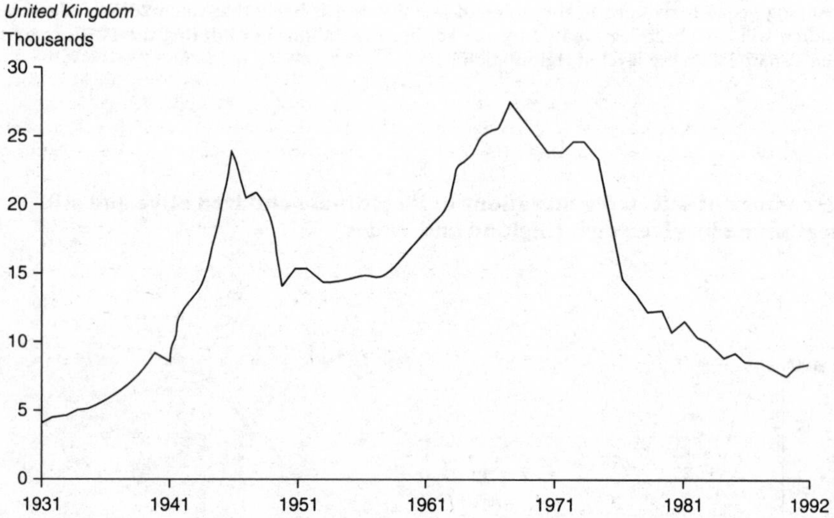

Source: Office of Population Censuses and Surveys; General Register Office (Scotland); General Register Office (Northern Ireland)

Questions

(i) Bearing in mind that roughly half of all adoptions are by a parent and step-parent (see further p. 561, below): how would you explain the peaks and troughs in this graph?
(ii) Would you expect a continuing decline in the supply of babies and young children for adoption?

The National Child Development Study (NCDS) has followed the progress of all children born in a single week in 1958. In *Children in Changing Families* (1980), Lydia Lambert and Jane Streather compared the development at age 11 of those born outside marriage who had stayed with their mothers, those adopted by strangers and those born to married parents. They set out to answer the question 'does birth status matter?' The raw data showed that the children who remained with their mothers were generally less likely to be living in favourable circumstances: 16% had been in local authority care at some time in their lives, compared with 3% of the marital children; only 12% were in non-manual ('middle class') homes, compared with 34% of the marital and 60% of the adopted; many more of their mothers had 'come down in the world' from their social class of origin; 35% were receiving supplementary benefit or free school meals, compared with 13% of the legitimate and 4% of the adopted; they were also more likely to be over-crowded, less likely to have sole use of basic amenities, and less likely to be owner-occupiers, even when both parents were together. But when the authors studied the children's physical development and school attainment after making allowances for their family situation and environmental circumstances, a different picture emerged:

When no allowance was made for background circumstances, adopted children were, for example, reading better at 11, on average, than either legitimate children or illegitimate children. This achievement deserves to be commended, but when we looked at the reading scores of children who came from homes with similar environmental characteristics, illegitimate as well as legitimate children were reading just as well as the adopted. Conversely, where the home circumstances were less favourable, illegitimate children were not reading any worse than other children in such circumstances. The fact that illegitimate children were more likely than other children to be living in disadvantaged situations, rather than their birth status, was associated with their lower reading scores at 11. For most of the children the same was also true when maths ability was considered. The findings also showed that at the age of 11 children's physical growth was unlikely to be related to birth status.

When the children's social adjustment at 11 was considered within the context of their background circumstances, there continued to be a difference between illegitimate and legitimate children, and the apparently equivocal position of the adopted children tilted in the direction of the illegitimate. Although the adjustment of these two groups appeared similar, varying stress factors may have been at work in each group, even if, ultimately, they were all linked with birth status.

At the age of 7 the adopted children had already been showing signs of having more behaviour problems than legitimate children (Seglow et al, 1972). Between the ages of 7 and 11 all children are likely to have had periods of doubt and uncertainty about their origins and identity, and all but a handful of the adopted children knew for a fact that they were born to a different parents [sic] but probably did not know a great deal about them. By 1969, when these children were 11, the policy of greater openness in talking to adopted children about their origins was increasingly encouraged by professionals and the media. But, with the best will in the world, it is not an easy matter to put into practice, and may have added to, rather than diminished, the children's difficulties in adjustment. The finding, in other studies of adopted children, that there was an increase in problems around this age, followed by a later settling down, suggests that it may be a healthy sign that the adopted children in the NCDS were more troublesome in mid-childhood. It will be extremely interesting to study their adjustment at 16 to see what was happening during adolescence. Obviously teachers and parents would be right to show concern for difficulties in social adjustment at any age, but it may be the case that these are only an indication of possible maladjustment if they persist.

Illegitimate children who were not adopted were also more likely than legitimate children to have experienced difficulties in resolving uncertainties about their origins. Their mothers may have been more reluctant than adoptive parents to discuss the subject, and while some of the children were living with their own fathers, others may have been told even less about them than adopted children. However, the illegitimate children had been less well adjusted than legitimate children at the age of 7, which suggests that unless uncertainty about their origins was the contributory reason at both ages, other factors, such as the greater amount of change in their environmental circumstances, were also associated with their relatively poorer social adjustment at 11.

In conclusion

The general lack of association between children's physical development or their school attainment at the age of 11 and their birth status is a salutory reminder of the powerful influence of the environment for good or ill. Some children were fortunate and lived in an exceptionally favourable environment, and many of the adopted children were among this group. For other children, living in families with poor housing and low income, and experiencing the difficulties mainly associated with low social status were far more pressing and ever-present problems than whether their parents had been married when they were born.

Even if they were legitimately born, diversity in family life was becoming the experience of an increasing proportion of children, as their parents' marriages were broken or remade. The importance of birth status fades before a recognition of the practical needs of families for such things as adequate incomes and adequate housing if children are to grow up without disadvantage.

Questions

(i) Could the greater tendency of these children to show signs of stress, both at seven and at eleven, have anything to do with their birth *status*?

(ii) Do you think that the findings of a similar study of children born during 1996 would be the same?

(iii) If not, why not?

2 How to become a father

The bastard, like the prostitute, thief, and beggar, belongs to that motley crowd of disreputable social types which society has generally resented, always endured. He is a living symbol of social irregularity, and undeniable evidence of contramoral forces; in short, a problem – a problem as old and unsolved as human existence itself.

These are the opening words of Davis' seminal article, *Illegitimacy and the Social Structure* (1939). But why should the child be the problem? Why not his parents? Why not marriage itself? Davis explains a sociological theory of illegitimacy thus:

... The gist of the theory is that the function of reproduction can be carried out in a socially useful manner only if it is performed in conformity with institutional patterns, because only by means of an institutional system can individuals be organized and taught to co-operate in the performance of this long-range function, and the function be integrated with other social functions. The reproductive or familial institutions constitute the social machinery in terms of which the creation of new members of society is supposed to take place. The birth of children in ways that do not fit into this machinery must necessarily receive the disapproval of society, else the institutional system itself, which depends upon favorable attitudes in individuals, would not be approved or sustained. ...

People are not supposed to have illegitimate children, but when they do an emergency machinery is set into operation to give the child a status (though an inferior one) and to define the positions of the parents. In this way society continues. No one ever completely transcends the institutional boundaries. If he did, he would not be human. On the other hand, no one ever remains completely within the narrowest institutional boundaries. If he did, he would not be human. The fundamental explanation of nonconformity to the marital institutions is the same as the explanation of institutional nonconformity in general. ...

The question as to why the child is punished for the sins of its parents is wrongly put. It assumes an explanation of what has yet to be explained. It should read: What is the status of the illegitimate child, and why is he given this status? Perhaps his status is partly explicable in terms of punishment, but not primarily. ... punishment for parental sin is not the sole motive for the treatment of illegitimate children and does not deserve the primacy generally given it. The inquiry must be pushed to a deeper level which will explain both the legal disabilities (concerning descent, inheritance, support, and domicile) and the social disabilities (concerning public opinion, folkways, and mores).

In other words, in order to understand the treatment meted out by society and the law towards those born outside marriage, we have to understand what marriage itself was designed to achieve. Lucy Mair, an anthropologist, discusses this in the first chapter of her book, *Marriage* (1971), intriguingly entitled, 'What is a husband for?' She first outlines Robin Fox's theory that in primitive societies, marriage is a mechanism for persuading father to stay at home in order to protect and support his children and their mother. She then examines some cultures in which, even though 'it is an ideal in all known societies that the begetting of children should be formally licensed in some way', illegitimacy is common. She concludes:

If it were essential for the protection – in modern times rather for the economic support – of a woman with young children that the father of her children should be legally tied to her, these populations would not be able to survive. But they do. So we come back to the question, what is a husband for?

Husbands, considered as recognized fathers, are most important where they are the source of their children's social status and claims to inheritance. ...

In the greater part of the world children take their status from the father; and even where the line of descent is traced through the mother it is usually no disadvantage to have a father of high status. There are societies. ... that are divided into *patrilineal* or *agnatic lineages*, groups recruited by descent through males and recognizing common descent as far back as the members can trace their ancestry. A lineage has its patrimony, in land, cattle or capital, and as long as commercial activity is not much developed men depend on inheritance more than on acquisition; where there is commercial activity there is still nothing like inheritance to give you a good start in life. Men are always informally ranked by wealth, and where there is a formal ranking system it is legitimate descent that assigns places in it. Public office is often hereditary; so is the ability to approach nonhuman beings in ritual to secure their benevolence towards the society or some section of it. Because of the rules that define whom one may or may not marry, status by descent is significant when one is seeking a spouse.

The implications of this aspect of husbandhood and fatherhood are much wider than practical matters of economic support. ...

A man is anxious to be the head of a numerous household when this provides him with a large working team; to be a member of a numerous lineage when this may be necessary for defence. He looks to his sons for support when he is old or sick. In societies organized in agnatic lineages religion is commonly focused on the cult of ancestors, and every man wishes to have descendants to make offerings to his spirit so that he will be commemorated in whatever is considered the appropriate way. In China up to the Communist revolution it was the first duty of a son to marry and produce a son to carry on the ancestor cult. The ancient Romans had very similar ideas. In lineage-based societies, and indeed in many others, marriage is an important way of forming alliances; this is one reason why men wish to become husbands as distinct from fathers.

In societies so organized, then, men wish to marry and women have no choice. Women do not have difficulty in inducing their consorts to marry them; but they are often penalized for entering into unlegalized unions, at any rate if these produce offspring.

Question

Engels (1884) described the development of such societies as the

... world historical defeat of the female sex ... In order to make certain of the wife's fidelity and therefore of the paternity of her children, she is delivered over unconditionally into the power of her husband ... [This type of marriage] is based on the supremacy of the man, the express purpose being to produce children of undisputed paternity; such paternity is demanded because these children are later to come into their father's property as his natural heirs.

In modern times, the reason given for the strength of the common law presumption that a child born to a married woman is her husband's child was that both woman and child would otherwise suffer the disabilities attached to adultery and illegitimacy. Is it at least possible that those disabilities were the *result*, not the cause, of that presumption?

Proving paternity has always been thought to be a problem. Somehow it is easier to remember the first part of Lancelot's speech to Old Gobbo – 'It's a wise father, that knows his own child' – than the second – 'Truth will come to light; murder cannot be hid long, a man's son may; but in the end, truth will out'. Hence there is a presumption that any child born to a married woman is her husband's child. This used to be extremely difficult to rebut. There was also a procedure for conclusively determining a person's legitimacy. Both are illustrated by the following case:

Ampthill Peerage Case
[1977] AC 547, [1976] 2 All ER 411, [1976] 2 WLR 777, 120 Sol Jo 367, House of Lords' Committee of Privileges

In 1921, Christobel, wife of the man who was later to become third baron Ampthill, gave birth to Geoffrey, who had been conceived by external fertilisation while his mother was still a virgin. Her husband petitioned for divorce, alleging that this was the result of Christobel's adultery. At the trial, the husband gave evidence that he had had no sexual intimacy of any kind with his wife at the probable date of conception and was granted a decree. On appeal, the House of Lords decided that evidence of non-access by a husband or a wife was inadmissible both in legitimacy proceedings and in divorce proceedings (*Russell v Russell* [1924] AC 687, 93 LJP 97: the rule was subsequently reversed in the Law Reform (Miscellaneous Provisions) Act 1949, s. 7(1)). The divorce decree was rescinded. In 1925, the High Court made a declaration that Geoffrey was the legitimate child of Christobel and her husband. Under the Legitimacy Declaration Act 1858, such declarations were binding on all the world, but could not prejudice anyone who had not been given notice or made a party (or did not claim through such a person) or if obtained by fraud or collusion. The marriage was eventually dissolved in 1937. In 1950, a son John was born of the third baron's third marriage. The third baron died in 1973 and both Geoffrey and John claimed to succeed him. Geoffrey relied upon the declaration, but John alleged that this was not binding, inter alia, because it had been procured by fraud. Blood samples were available from Christobel and the third baron, but not from Geoffrey.

Lord Simon of Glaisdale: ... There is one status for which Parliament, in the wisdom of experience, has made special provision. This is the status of legitimacy. Status means the condition of belonging to a class in society to which the law ascribes peculiar rights and duties, capacities and incapacities. Such, for example, is the status of a married person or minor. Legitimacy is a status: it is the condition of belonging to a class in society the members of which are regarded as having been begotten in lawful matrimony by the men whom the law regards as their fathers. Motherhood, although also a legal relationship, is based on a fact, being proved demonstrably by parturition. Fatherhood, by contrast, is a presumption. A woman can have sexual intercourse with a number of men any of whom may be the father of her child; though it is true that modern serology can sometimes enable the presumption to be rebutted as regards some of these men. The status of legitimacy gives the child certain rights both against the man whom the law regards as his father and generally in society. Among the peculiar rights which a child is entitled to enjoy by virtue of the status of legitimacy is the right to succeed to a hereditary title of honour. If the hereditary title of honour is a peerage of the United Kingdom, the oldest legitimate son when of full age is entitled to be called to your Lordships' House on the death of the man whom the law regards as his father.

It was probably for two reasons that Parliament made special provision for judgment as to the status of legitimacy. First, no doubt, because, since fatherhood is not factually demonstrable by parturition, it is questionable; and it is generally in the interest of society that open questions should be finally closed. Second, no doubt, because since the legitimate child, by virtue of his legal relationship with the man whom the law regards as his father, is entitled to certain rights both as against the father and generally in society, it is desirable that the legal relationship between father and child should be decisively concluded.

His lordship then reviews the law and the evidence and concludes that the decree was not obtained by fraud or collusion, not least because, as the law stood in 1925, Geoffrey was entitled to the benefit of the presumption *even if* his mother had confessed to committing adultery at the relevant time.

Questions

(i) This case demonstrates the strength of the courts' traditional reluctance to bastardise a child, but we repeat our earlier question: were the disabilities

attached to adultery and bastardy the *result*, rather than the cause, of the need to presume that the husband was father to his wife's children?
(ii) Now that most of the legal distinctions between birth in and outside marriage have been removed, is there any longer a need for this presumption?
(iii) Is it so obvious these days who is a child's mother (see p. 478, below)?

However, the position has since changed. First, the Family Law Reform Act 1969 now provides:

26. – Any presumption of law as to the legitimacy or illegitimacy of any person may in any civil proceedings be rebutted by evidence which shows that it is more probable than not that that person is illegitimate or legitimate, as the case may be, and it shall not be necessary to prove that fact beyond reasonable doubt in order to rebut the presumption.

The leading case on the meaning of this was decided shortly afterwards:

S v S; W v Official Solicitor
[1972] AC 24, [1970] 3 All ER 107, [1970] 3 WLR 366, 114 Sol Jo 635, House of Lords

Both were divorce cases in which the husband denied paternity of a child to whom the presumption of legitimacy applied. They are the leading authorities on whether or not the court should direct the use of blood tests to determine a child's paternity (as to which see the extracts quoted in *Re H (a minor) (blood tests: parental rights)*, p. 457, below). On the presumption of legitimacy:

Lord Reid: ... The law as to the onus of proof is now set out in s 26 of the Family Law Reform Act 1969, ...

That means that the presumption of legitimacy now merely determines the onus of proof. Once evidence has been led it must be weighed without using the presumption as a make-weight in the scale for legitimacy. So even weak evidence against legitimacy must prevail if there is not other evidence to counterbalance it. The presumption will only come in at that stage in the very rare case of the evidence being so evenly balanced that the court is unable to reach a decision on it. I cannot recollect ever having seen or heard of a case of any kind where the court could not reach a decision on the evidence before it. ...

Compare Lord Reid's remarks with those of Ormrod LJ in *Re JS* [1981] Fam 22, [1980] 1 All ER 1061, CA as to the standard of proof required to establish that a particular man *is* the father:

... The burden might be formulated on analogous lines, 'the plaintiff (or the party on whom the burden rests) must satisfy the court that it is reasonably safe in all the circumstances of the case to act on the evidence before the court, bearing in mind the consequences which will follow'.

The learned judge, rightly in our opinion, adopted this test. In the course of her judgment she said: 'The degree of probability in an issue of paternity should, in my opinion, be commensurate with the transcending importance of that decision to the child.'

Questions

(i) *Re JS* was applied in *W v K (proof of paternity)* [1988] 1 FLR 86. Mr and Mrs B and Mr and Mrs W agreed to swap partners. Mrs B became pregnant and only Mr B or Mr W could be father. Earlier sperm tests indicated that Mr B was likely to be infertile. Blood tests on Mr W indicated as follows:

(1) A combination of tests used in this investigation would be expected to exclude at least 95% of wrongly accused men.
(2) It is not the primary purpose of blood tests to attempt to prove paternity. Nevertheless, by comparing the chances that those genes, for which blood tests have been carried out, which the child must have inherited from its true father, have come from a putative father rather than a random man, a paternity index can be calculated. In this case the paternity index for Mr W and the baby is 97.4%.

(*a*) Would you have found (as the court did) that the presumption of legitimacy had been rebutted? (*b*) Would you also have found (as the court did) that Mr W was the father?
(ii) If your answer to (*a*) is 'yes', should the law allow you to answer 'no' to (*b*)?
(iii) Do you think that the standard of proof of paternity should be the same (*a*) if the mother is applying for financial provision or a property settlement for her child, or (*b*) if the father is applying for a contact, residence or parental responsibility order, or (*c*) if the child is applying for a declaration of parentage?

Provisions in the draft Bill attached to the Law Commission's original Report on *Illegitimacy* (1982) requiring paternity to be proved 'to the satisfaction of the court' were dropped from the revised version attached to the Commission's Second Report (1986), for these reasons:

3.18 ... It cannot be right that, as a matter of law, the standard of proof required to show that a particular man is not the father is necessarily less than the standard of proof required to show that he is. As a matter of evidence, it may be easier to show the one than the other, although with the advent of modern blood testing it is often possible to prove a likelihood of paternity to a degree of probability far higher than is possible for many other facts which may be in issue in litigation. The courts will also bear in mind, in appropriate cases, the general principle that the degree of proof should be commensurate with the gravity of the subject matter in dispute.
3.19 We therefore think that it would be unsatisfactory if some special standard of proof were automatically to prevent a child being granted access to or financial support from a man who, after fully fought proceedings, was shown on a balance of probabilities to be the father. Such a special provision might be seen as unnecessarily marking out the issue of paternity amongst the many issues faced by the courts in civil proceedings and as such contrary to the general principle of eliminating unnecessary discrimination in the law. ...

Question

Do you think that either dropping the requirement, or the approach of the House of Lords to the standard of proof in care proceedings (see *Re H (minors) (sexual abuse: standard of proof)* [1996] 1 All ER 1, [1996] 2 WLR 8, HL, p. 620, below), is likely to lead to a judicial change of heart?

The whole debate has now been overtaken by the scientific development known as 'DNA profiling' or 'fingerprinting', explained by Cellmark Diagnostics, who have patented the process, in their *DNA Fingerprinting Information and Procedures Guide*:

The DNA fingerprinting process

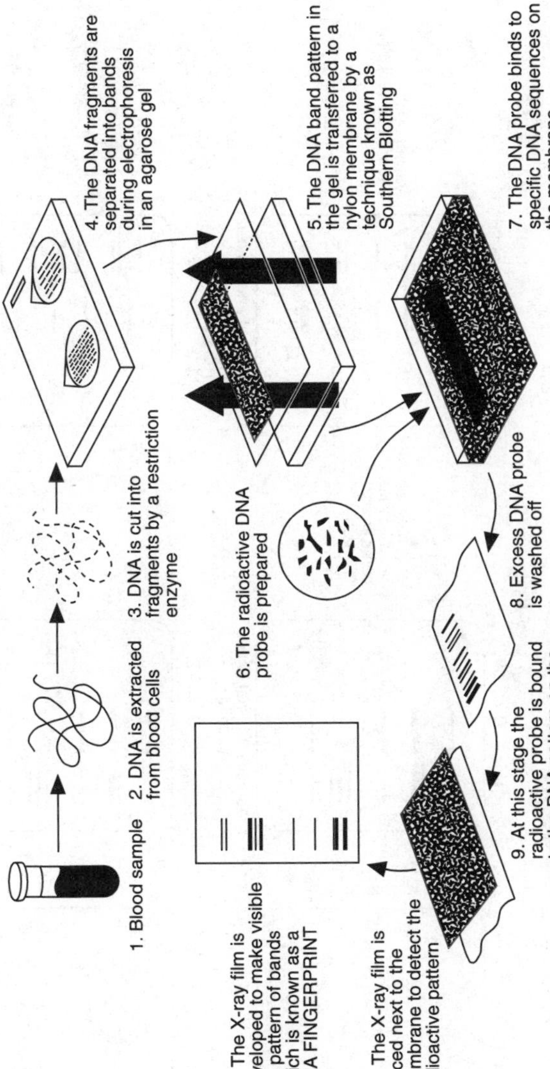
1. Blood sample
2. DNA is extracted from blood cells
3. DNA is cut into fragments by a restriction enzyme
4. The DNA fragments are separated into bands during electrophoresis in an agarose gel
5. The DNA band pattern in the gel is transferred to a nylon membrane by a technique known as Southern Blotting
6. The radioactive DNA probe is prepared
7. The DNA probe binds to specific DNA sequences on the membrane
8. Excess DNA probe is washed off
9. At this stage the radioactive probe is bound to the DNA pattern on the membrane
10. The X-ray film is placed next to the membrane to detect the radioactive pattern
11. The X-ray film is developed to make visible the pattern of bands which is known as a DNA FINGERPRINT

Analysis of DNA fingerprints in paternity testing

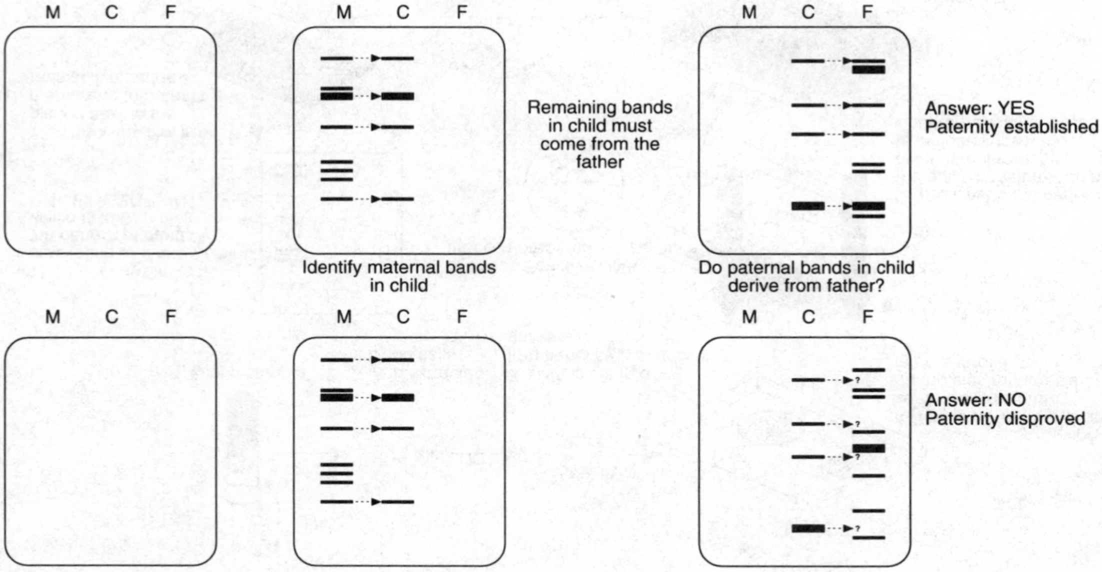

WHAT IS DNA FINGERPRINTING?

The technique known as DNA fingerprinting, or genetic fingerprinting, was developed by Professor Alec Jeffreys FRS, who is a Lister Institute Research Fellow at Leicester University. It has the ability to positively demonstrate relationships between individuals and is the subject of various patent applications by the Lister Institute of Preventive Medicine [UK Patent No. 2166445]. DNA is the genetic material contained in all living cells which makes every individual different (except for genetically identical twins) and can be extracted from blood, semen, hair roots or other body tissues that contain DNA. A blood sample taken under medical supervision is usually the simplest form of material that is used for testing. A pattern of chemical signals has been discovered within the DNA molecule which is as unique and individual to each person as their actual fingerprint, hence the colloquial term 'DNA fingerprinting'. This pattern is visualised by the laboratory process shown below as a series of bands on an X-ray film, rather like the bar codes now found on a wide variety of retail goods.

WHAT WILL IT RESOLVE?

Conventional methods previously used to resolve paternity/maternity may be lengthy and involve up to 17 different blood tests. They may only show whether an individual *is not* the father or mother of a child. DNA fingerprinting, in one single test, can show with certainty that an individual either *is* or *is not* the father or mother of a child, or whether a child is related to a particular individual.

HOW DOES THE TEST WORK?

As previously described, a genetic fingerprint is producted as a series of bands on an X-ray film. Just as all of us inherit out basic physical characteristics from our parents, then so do we inherit the DNA bands in our DNA fingerprint. Approximately half a person's DNA bands are inherited from the father and half from the mother. Positive proof of paternity is established by firstly identifying a child's maternally-inherited DNA bands by comparison of the DNA fingerprints from the mother and child. Any bands in the child's DNA fingerprint which do not match with the mother can only have been inherited from the true biological father. Analysis of the alleged father's DNA fingerprint will show that he has bands present in his DNA fingerprint which match the paternal bands in the child if he is indeed the true father. The statistical chance that a randomly-selected unrelated individual could possess all the same bands as the true father has been calculated to be as small as 30000 million to 1. In other words, if the father's bands and the child's paternal bands match, paternity is confirmed. [This is illustrated by the diagrams on the following pages.]

In order to provide *positive* proof of a relationship, a blood sample is required from the alleged father, the child and the mother. Testing *can* be carried out in cases where one of the parents may be deceased or simply unavailable for testing, but the method of analysis used is then based upon looking for the statistically expected band-sharing that is normally seen between related individuals. With just two individuals, the test will clearly indicate whether or not they are related but the nature of that relationship, i.e. mother to child, or aunt to nephew, can only be assessed upon the relative degree of band-sharing found. Therefore in this instance, the Test Report will indicate whether or not the DNA fingerprint analysis is *consistent* with that claimed relationship, rather than providing positive proof of it.

There may be some concerns over quality control in the forensic context, but there is no doubt as to the reliability of the technique in the family law context, where good quality samples are readily available, either by court order under Part III of the Family Law Reform Act 1969, or more commonly by agreement.

The leading case on blood test directions, apart from *S v S, W v Official Solicitor* [1972] AC 24, p. 453, above, used to be *Re F (a minor) (blood tests: parental rights)* [1993] Fam 314, CA; but recently, and on similar facts, the Court of Appeal has given what must have been intended as the definitive account:

Re H (a minor) (blood tests: parental rights)
[1996] 2 FLR 65, [1996] Fam Law 254, Court of Appeal

The mother's husband, Mr H, had a vasectomy in 1990. The mother became pregnant in March 1994. At the time she was having a sexual relationship with both her husband and the applicant, Mr B. The understanding then was that the husband would leave and the applicant move into the matrimonial home. The husband left in May 1994 but the mother changed her mind and ended the affair in July. A year later the mother and her husband were reconciled. The applicant applied for a blood test direction but the mother adamantly refused to agree that either herself or the child, Haydon, should be tested. The judge granted the application and the mother appealed.

Ward LJ: ... The mother is adamantly opposed to the use of blood testing to establish paternity. She is totally convinced that blood testing is likely to be detrimental to Haydon's welfare which she believes depends, for the foreseeable future, on his settled relationship in a happy family unit, the stability of which may be disturbed by a blood test and the pursuit of litigation by Mr B. which is doomed to fail. She saw no advantage in establishing the truth by science because, as she said:

> 'Haydon has a father, it is Mr H. ...'
>
> 'Even if a blood test or a DNA test were to show that B. is the father, I will never allow contact. ...'
>
> 'Even if H. died I would not let B. have any contact with Haydon. ...'
>
> 'Haydon will never know the truth. My husband's name is on the birth certificate as the father. He is Haydon's father. ...'

The following issues arise in this appeal:

1. Is refusal to undergo blood testing determinative of the application for a direction under section 20(1) of the Family Law Reform Act 1969?
2. Can an inference adverse to the refusing party be drawn only if the refusal is made after the court has directed the use of blood testing?
3. How does the child's welfare influence the decision?
4. How do the prospects of success in the proceedings influence the decision?
5. What are this child's best interests?

1. *Is the refusal determinative?*

In *Re F (a minor) (blood tests: parental rights)* [1993] Fam 314 the Court of Appeal posed the question but may not have given a clear answer. In *Re G (a minor) (blood tests)* [1994] 1 FLR 495 Mr Michael Horowitz QC sitting as a Deputy Judge of the High Court answered the question, 'No'; but in *Re CB (a minor) (blood testing)* [1994] 2 FLR 762 Wall J said, 'Yes'. His Honour Judge Coningsby QC declined to follow Wall J. Did he misdirect himself? The answer necessitates a somewhat semantic review of the authorities.

The Family Law Reform Act 1969 was passed after the Law Commission's Report No. 16 on Blood Tests and the Proof of Paternity in Civil Proceedings. This report had been prompted by the Judges of the old Probate, Divorce and Admiralty Division, possibly as a result of *W v W (No 4)* [1964] P 67 where the Court of Appeal refused to allow blood tests to determine paternity. ...

Danckwerts LJ said at p. 78:

> 'To compel persons to submit to a blood test without their consent seems to me a very serious interference with personal liberty and rights. Very convincing reasons would have to be shown before I could conclude that such power was within the inherent jurisdiction of the court.'

...

In *S v McC, W v W* [1972] AC 24 Lord Hodson summed it up in the observation:

> 'No one doubts that so far as adults are concerned the law does not permit such an operation to be performed against the wishes of the patient.'

That was and remains established law.

In their report the Law Commission said:

> '39. A more important question is how the court is to treat the refusal of one of the individuals concerned to submit to blood tests. We do not think that it would be acceptable to public opinion in general or to the medical profession in particular to exert physical compulsion in order to obtain blood samples. We recommend, therefore, that no blood samples should be taken from a person under a direction of the court without that person's consent or, if he is incapable of consenting, without the consent of someone entitled to act on his behalf. ... We would recommend that refusal be considered by the court as evidence from which it can draw whatever inferences it thinks warranted in the particular case. For

this reason we recommend that the court should be given the power to make a direction for the use of blood tests rather than an order requiring them to be made.

40. In our working paper we suggested that a person refusing to be tested ought to be able to show good cause, on religious or health grounds, why his or her refusal is justified. We still think that it should be open to a person refusing to be tested to satisfy the court that his or her refusal is justified but we do not think that it would be appropriate to provide specific grounds on which refusal can be justified.'

I venture to think that the distinction made in the last sentence of paragraph 39, which is reflected in the Family Law Reform Act 1969, has not always been fully understood and the misunderstanding has created confusion.

The scheme of the Act is as follows:

'**20. Power of court to require a blood test.** – (1) In any civil proceedings in which the paternity of any person falls to be determined by the court hearing the proceedings, the court may on an application by any party to the proceedings, give a direction for the use of blood tests to ascertain whether such tests show that a party to the proceedings is or is not thereby excluded from being the father of that person. …

21. Consents, etc, required for taking of blood samples. – (1) Subject to the provisions of subsections (3) and (4) of this section, a blood sample which is required to be taken from any person for the purpose of giving effect to a direction under section 20 of this Act shall not be taken from that person except with his consent.

(3) A blood sample may be taken from a person under the age of 16 years … if the person who has the care and control of him consents.

23. Failure to comply with direction for taking blood tests. – (1) Where a court gives direction under section 20 of this Act and any person fails to take any step required of him for the purpose of giving effect to the direction, the court may draw such inferences, if any, from that fact as appears proper in the circumstances.'

The Act carried the Law Commission's advice into effect; s. 20 does not empower the court to order blood tests, still less to take blood from an unwilling party: all it does is permit a direction for the use of blood tests to ascertain paternity. …

… If refusal simpliciter were a determinative reason for not giving the direction, then the Act would surely have said so. On the contrary the express provisions make it clear that Parliament was content to envisage a direction being made notwithstanding that it might never be carried into effect. The legislature would not have made express provision that a refusal to comply with the direction has specified consequence if a refusal to submit to tests would have compelled the court not to make any direction at all.

I conclude, therefore, that whereas refusal is a factor to take into account (and, for example, in the case of an haemophiliac, it may be a very powerful factor), it cannot be determinative of the application and I disagree with Wall J's conclusion in *Re CB* at 773H. In my judgment His Honour Judge Coningsby QC did not misdirect himself.

2. Can an inference be drawn only if the refusal to give blood samples is made after the court's direction? Mr Blair QC supports the judge's conclusion that, 'because of the existence of the statutory provision it must be only in the circumstances in which an adverse inference may be drawn as laid down in the Act that any such inference can be drawn and this cannot happen outside the Act'. …

The question seems to me to be not so much whether the court is entitled to draw an adverse inference but what, if any, inference can be drawn from a refusal. That is the way the Law Commission approached the question. They said:

'43. So far as adultery is concerned the wife knows, as a fact, whether or not she has committed adultery. It is, therefore, proper that the court should be able to infer from her refusal to be tested that she is trying to prevent it from discovering a fact of which she herself has knowledge. On the question of the child's paternity however the position is different. Here she does not know which of the two men is the child's father; she is refusing to be tested, not in order to hide facts of which she has knowledge, but because she does not want to run the risk of her child being shown to be illegitimate. Her refusal has no bearing on whether or not the child is illegitimate and the court may well decide that it cannot draw any inference on the issue of paternity.

44. The problem is not confined to cases where the child's mother refuses to be tested. A husband can also take advantage of the presumption of legitimacy and refuse to be tested if

he is anxious to have the child's legitimacy established. Let us take as an example the case where a husband is divorcing his wife on the ground of her adultery. The wife admits her adultery and it is clear that both the husband and the co-respondent had intercourse during the period of conception of the child concerned. The husband and wife are each applying for custody of the child. There is no way, apart from using blood test evidence, by which it can be established which of the men is the child's father. The wife, wanting custody and wanting to prove that the co-respondent, whom she is to marry, is the child's father, asks for blood tests. The husband also wanting custody, refuses to be blood tested because he wishes the child to be declared his. The court cannot properly draw from his refusal the inference that the child is illegitimate; neither the husband nor anyone else knows who is the child's father. The presumption of legitimacy is therefore applied and the husband is held to be the child's father.

45. How can parties be prevented from refusing to comply with a court order for blood tests, purely as a matter of tactics, so as to prevent the presumption of legitimacy being rebutted? We have already said that we do not think that it would be acceptable to force a person by physical compulsion to submit to an order for blood tests to be taken. We think it would be equally unacceptable to treat a refusal as contempt of court. ...

47. In our view the most effective way of dealing with this problem is to provide that where a direction for blood tests is made and a party to the proceedings is entitled to rely on the presumption of legitimacy in claiming relief, then if that party refuses to be tested the court may either draw inferences against him (if appropriate) or dismiss his application for relief.'

It should be remembered that at that time blood testing served only to exclude paternity: It did not establish it. It seems to me that a refusal to comply after the solemnity of the court's decision is more eloquent testimony of an attempt at hiding a truth than intransigent objection made as a forensic tactic. Science has now advanced. The whole truth can now be known. As Waite LJ said in *Re A (a minor) (paternity)* [1994] 2 FLR 463 at 473:

'Against the background of law and scientific advance, it seems to me to follow, both in justice and in common sense, that if a mother makes a claim against one of the possible fathers, and he chooses to exercise his right not to submit to be tested, the inference that he is the father of the child should be virtually inescapable. He would certainly have to advance very clear and cogent reasons for this refusal to be tested – reasons which it would be just and fair and reasonable for him to be allowed to maintain.'

Although that was a case of a refusal being made after a direction had been given, I, like Wall J, 'see no intellectual difference between the two situations'. Common sense seems to me to dictate that if the truth can be established with certainty, a refusal to produce the certainty justifies some inference that the refusal is made to hide the truth, even if the inference is not as strong as when the Court's direction is flouted.

3. *How do considerations of the child's welfare influence the decision?*

The judge correctly directed himself that he should 'refuse the test if satisfied it would be against the child's interests to order it'. This is wholly in accordance with *S v McC*. There Lord Reid said at p. 45D:

'I would, therefore, hold that the court ought to permit a blood test of a young child to be taken unless satisfied that would be against the child's interests.'

Lord Hodson said at p. 58G:

'The court in ordering a blood test in the case of an infant has, of course, a discretion and may make or refuse an order for a test in the exercise of its discretion, but the interests of the other persons than the infant are involved in ordinary litigation. The infant needs protection but that is no justification for making his rights superior to those of others.'

It is clear, therefore, that whereas welfare is the paramount consideration in deciding the applications for parental responsibility and contact orders, welfare does not dominate this decision.

4. *How do the prospects of success in the proceedings influence the decision?*

In *Re F* it was held at p. 32A that:

'If the probable outcome of those proceedings will be the same whoever may be the natural father of E., then there can be no point in exposing E. to the possible disadvantages of a blood test.'

The speeches in the House of Lords seem to take a somewhat different view. Lord MacDermott, at p. 48E says:

'If the court had reason to believe that the application for a blood test was of a fishing nature, designed for some ulterior motive to call in question the legitimacy, otherwise unimpeached, of a child who had enjoyed a legitimate status, it may well be that the court, acting under its protective rather than its ancillary jurisdiction, would be justified in refusing the application. ...

... It would be a backward step to start to whittle down the effect of section 1, but it would be just as bad to have to apply its final criterion on a finding of fact which was not reached on the best available evidence, and even worse if that had to happen because the court, having spied a paternity issue, considered that it should not be fully explored.'

Reading those authorities together, it seems to me that the correct approach must be:

1. The paternity issue must be judged as a free standing application entitled to consideration on its own.
2. The outcome of the proceedings in which the paternity issue has been raised, insofar as it bears on the welfare of child, must be taken into account.
3. Any gain to the child from preventing any disturbance to his security must be balanced against the loss to him of the certainty of knowing who he is.
4. The terms of section 10(4) of the Children Act 1989 are explicit in giving parent a right to apply for contact because they provide:

   'The following persons *are entitled to apply* to the court for *any section 8 order with respect to a child* –

   (*a*) any parent ... of the child; ... .'

   There is no statutory justification for transforming the paternity issue into a disguised application for leave to apply and judging the paternity issue by the criteria set out in section 10(9).
5. Accordingly, whilst the outcome of the section 8 proceedings and the risk of disruption to the child's life both by the continuance of the paternity issue as well as the pursuit of the section 8 order are obviously factors which impinge on the child's welfare, they are not, in my judgment, determinative of the blood testing question.

In this case the judge's conclusion was that 'it would be rather unlikely that the court would make an order for contact'. That is a conclusion he was plainly entitled to reach, and one which I would support. He did not, however, expressly deal with the parental responsibility order. ...

5. *What are the child's best interests?*

The mother submits that 'pursuing contact would be to destabilise her own marriage which has only recently been put together again to the disadvantage of the child'. Miss Scotland QC submits accordingly that the case is indistinguishable from *Re F*.

I do not agree. ... The material facts of the case under appeal before us include these features which may or may not have applied in *Re F*:

1. As the judge found, Mr B. has a substantial case for his claim to be this child's father. That can be seen from:
   a. The mother's clear belief, at least until she set eyes on her baby, that the child was born of her adulterous relationship. She now closes her mind even to the possibility that might be so.
   b. The fact that Mr H. has had a vasectomy. He admitted thinking that it was 'unlikely that I would be the father'.
2. If Mr and Mrs H. were reconciled in that state of mind, having their worst fears realised is unlikely of itself to be the cause for the breakdown of a fragile reconciliation. ...
3. It may well be correct, as Miss Scotland submits, that denial of the truth is essential to this mother for the restoration of her self-esteem and for the expiation of her guilt. That creates a danger in putting her welfare to the forefront, not the child's. ...
4. This secret cannot be hidden forever. Mr H. knows the substantial difficulty of his position. Moreover, and most importantly, 14 year old Christopher knows, because his mother told him, that his father may not be Haydon's father. It is unrealistic to pretend that the time will not come when Haydon has to face these doubts about his paternity. If his peace of mind is likely to be threatened, and if he has a right to know, the question then becomes one of when it is best he should learn the truth.
5. In my judgment every child has a right to know the truth unless his welfare clearly justifies the cover up. The right to know is acknowledged in the United Nations Convention on the Rights of the Child (Treaty Series No 44 of 1992) (Cm. 1976) which has been ratified by the United Kingdom and in particular Article 7 which provides 'that a child has, as far as possible, the right to know and be cared for by his or her parents'. In *Re F* the putative

father submitted that the child's welfare included her right to know under this Article. Balcome LJ said at p. 321A:

> 'Whether or not B is included in this definition of parent within the meaning of this Article, it is not in fact possible for E to be cared for by both her parents (if B is such). No family unit exists, nor has it ever existed, between B and Mrs F, and if B were able to assert his claims to have share in E's upbringing it would inevitable risk damaging her right to be cared for by her mother, Mrs F.'

That passage concentrates on the child's right to be cared for by his or her parents. I do not read it as refuting what to me seems the clear intent of the Article that there are two separate rights, the one to know, and the other to be cared for by, one's parents. …

6. This is the whole tenor of the speeches in the House of Lords. Lord Reid (and Lord Guest) said at p. 45D:

> 'The court must protect the child, but it is not really protecting the child to ban a blood test on some vague and shadowy conjecture that it may turn out to be to its disadvantage: it may equally turn out to be for its advantage or at least do it no harm.'

…

Lord Hodson at p. 59B asked:

> 'Who is to say what is in the interest of the child and whether knowledge of true paternity would or would not favour his or her future prospects in life? How are these interests to be assessed? I find these questions especially difficult to answer in view of the fact that it must surely be in the best interests of the child in most cases that paternity doubts should be resolved on the best evidence, and, as in adoption, the child be told the truth as soon as possible.'

7. Lord Hodson's reference to adoption produces interesting parallels. The Houghton Committee reporting in 1972 called for greater openness in adoption. That call was heeded. Section 51 of the Adoption Act 1976 now enables adopted persons to obtain access to their birth records. The Inter-departmental Review of Adoption Law in 1992 expressed the opinion that 'it is fundamental to the welfare of the child that he or she is told (when of sufficient age and understanding) about his or her adoptive status'. It is a recognition that the child's shock at discovering the truth about his origins at a later stage in childhood will be increased by the realisation that his adopted parents have, to date, allowed him to believe in a falsehood that he was their child.
8. Section 56 of the Family Law Act 1986 gives Haydon the right to apply for a declaration –
'(*a*) that a person named in the application is or was his parent: or
(*b*) that he is the legitimate child of his parents.'
9. Given the real risk bordering on inevitability that Haydon will at some time question his paternity, then I do not see how this case is not concluded by the unassailable wisdom expressed Lord Hodson at p. 57H:

> 'The interests of justice in the abstract are best served by the ascertainment of the truth and there must be few cases where the interests of children can be shown to be best served by the suppression of truth.'

If, as she should, this mother is to bring up her children to believe in and to act by the maxim, which is her duty to teach them at her knee, that honesty is the best policy, then she should not sabotage that lesson by living a lie.

10. If the child has the right to know, then the sooner it is told the better. The issue of biological parentage should be divorced from psychological parentage. Acknowledging Mr B.'s parental responsibility should not dent Mr H.'s social responsibility for a child whom he is so admirably prepared to care for and love irrespective of whether or not he is the father. If the cracks in the H. marriage are so wide that they will be rent asunder by the truth then the piece of paper which dismisses the application hardly seems adhesive enough to bind them together.
11. If Haydon grows up knowing the truth, that will not undermine his attachment to his father figure and he will cope with knowing he has two fathers. Better that than a time-bomb ticking away.

Conclusions

The judge concluded that it was not within his power to prevent this father pursuing his application. I agree. …

Appeal dismissed. Order below varied to direct rather than to order taking of blood samples from applicant, mother and child.

Questions

(i) What would your answer have been if (*a*) it had been the applicant who had had the vasectomy, and/or (*b*) there was a strong physical resemblance between the child and the mother's husband?
(ii) If everyone has the right to know who their biological parents are, does this apply (*a*) to all adopted people, (*b*) to all people born of donated sperm, or (*c*) to all people born of donated eggs?

Thus far we have been looking at proof for the purpose of legal proceedings, but of course there are other people (such as social workers or personal representatives) who may have to decide the facts. What other sources of information are available? One is birth registration. The Law Commission's *Working Paper* (1979) had this to say:

9.18 For birth registration purposes the registrar should be entitled to accept a paternity statement from either parent without the explicit consent of the other parent –
(i) where the registration reflects the application of the presumption of paternity based on marriage; or
(ii) where paternity has been established by a court order.
This would constitute a change in the law only to the extent that it would allow a father to insist on his fatherhood appearing on the register (if necessary, by re-registration), where he has either obtained a declaration of parentage under the procedure dealt with below, or where an order giving him custody or access, or ordering him to pay maintenance, has been made. …

Formal methods of acknowledging paternity other than by court order
9.23 A considerable number of other jurisdictions, including New Zealand, most of the Australian states, Ontario, parts of the United States, and many civil law countries, have provided for acknowledgement of paternity otherwise than through the register of births. In New Zealand, for instance, an instrument of acknowledgment executed by the father and mother either as a deed or in the presence of a solicitor constitutes prima facie evidence of paternity. Such an instrument may be filed with the Registrar General.
9.24 We entirely agree that voluntary acceptance of paternal responsibilities is to be encouraged, but we suggest that the formal adoption of any such procedures here, by legislation, would be superfluous. The best solution, we think, would be to ensure that our registration system is sufficiently flexible to enable the evidence of paternity to be derived from the register. It would clearly not be helpful if the register and other instruments recognised by statute told different stories. An instrument recording an agreement between parties as to a child's paternity would still have evidential value; but in our view it should not be given any special status.

Court orders
9.27 … Our suggestion is that whenever a maintenance, custody, access or other similar order is made in proceedings in which the paternity of the child has been found or admitted, such finding or admission should, if either of the parties so wishes, appear on the face of the order. …
9.28 It should be repeated here that an incidental finding of paternity would only be recorded in the manner indicated above where the court goes on to make an order for maintenance, custody, access or the like. For example, if a man applies to the court for access to a child, and an order is refused on the merits despite the court being satisfied that he is the child's father, his application should simply be dismissed. It is only the existence of immediate rights or obligations in relation to a child which would justify the proposition that an application to the registrar of births may be made unilaterally. Furthermore, any reference to a finding of paternity in a case where no substantive order is made would be tantamount to the making of a declaration of paternity, and (as we argue later) we do not think that persons other than the child in question should have unrestricted access to the courts for such a purpose. …

Declaration of parentage

...

9.33 We think that there is a strong case for introducing a procedure for obtaining a declaration of parentage. There may be cases where it is important to establish parentage, but inappropriate to apply for any other relief, such as maintenance, custody or access under the Guardianship of Minors Acts or otherwise. We have two particular instances in mind. First, future entitlement to property may turn on the issue. It is, we think, insufficient to say that the question could always be determined at the date of distribution, since by then the best evidence may no longer be available. It has to be remembered that blood test evidence is most satisfactory only when the child, his mother, and all likely fathers can be tested. Hence the sooner a test is carried out the better, in order to minimise the risk of the evidence becoming unobtainable by reason of the death or disappearance of relevant persons. In any event, questions of parentage cannot in all cases be determined solely by blood testing, and it may be important to have those concerned available to give evidence. Secondly the child, or indeed those claiming to be his parents, may think it emotionally important to have the issue judicially determined. The right to know the facts about one's origins is increasingly recognised, and it would be unsatisfactory if the law provided only artificial means (such as an application for a nominal award of maintenance) for doing so. ...

9.40 It is clear that a child should be able to obtain a declaration that a named person is his father (or mother). Should the alleged parent, or any other person, be able to obtain a declaration of parentage? We think that there are cases in which it would be right to allow such applications. First, those claiming to be parents may have a proprietary or emotional claim to have the matter resolved just as much as the child himself. Secondly, a grandparent or other person may think it important in the child's interest that the matter be cleared up, even though the child's mother, for example, is unwilling to permit it. However, we have to accept that applications by parents and others might not be in the child's interests – for instance, where there is real doubt about parentage which the court is unlikely to be able to resolve, and the trial of the issue could only disturb a settled relationship. Hence we suggest that, in addition to the child, any other person should be able to seek a declaration that the child is the child of a named person or persons if, but only if, he can satisfy the court that it is appropriate, having regard to the welfare of the child, that the issue be tried.

Earlier in the Working Paper, the Commission considered but rejected one further possibility:

9.12 In some Commonwealth jurisdictions – for example Tasmania, New South Wales and Ontario, but not New Zealand or Queensland – cohabitation is treated in the same way as marriage, as prima facie evidence of paternity. Needless to say, only cohabitation as defined by statute counts for this purpose, the definitions ranging from the arbitrary (for example twelve months, as in Tasmania) to the vague ('a relationship of some permanence', as in Ontario). We incline to the view that this complication should not be introduced into the law. The value of a 'prima facie evidence rule' lies in its general applicability without further evidence. ... But cohabitation (or rather, cohabitation 'as husband and wife', for only such cohabitation can be relevant) is by no means self-proving, especially if there are further statutory definitions going to the durability of the relationship.

Questions

(i) Was your stereotype of the unmarried father a man who was anxious to avoid his responsibilities or a man who was anxious to assert his relationship in the face of the mother's determination to have nothing more to do with him? Should the law on establishing paternity be the same in each case?

(ii) How easy is it to judge what will be in the child's best interests? Suppose for example, that Miss B is brutally raped by Mr X, who is a very rich man, and a child Y results; 20 years later X is killed in a road accident having left no will. Should he have been registered as Y's father when his application for contact with the baby was refused?

(iii) Do you think that the mother should be obliged to name the father (*a*) for the purpose of claiming benefits (so that steps can be taken to recover a contribution from him), or (*b*) in all cases?

Given the current enthusiasm, in the Child Support Act 1991 (see *Children Come First* (1990), para. 5.33 and p. 121, above), for obliging mothers to name their children's fathers, the Law Commission's doubts about extending the formal machinery for recognising paternity seem somewhat out of date. Their Working Paper's proposals about birth registration were enacted in s. 10 of the Family Law Reform Act 1987. Their proposals for declarations of paternity had a more chequered history. Eventually, they were enacted in what is now s. 56 of the Family Law Act 1986. Section 56(1) allows only the child to apply for a declaration (*a*) that a person named in the application is or was his parent; or (*b*) that he is the legitimate child of his parents. Section 56(2) allows him to apply for a declaration that he has or has not become a legitimated person.

Questions

(i) Why should only the child himself be able to apply? Why not a grandchild? Why not a father? Why not a mother?
(ii) If you know who your parents are, in what circumstances might you also have to know whether you were legitimate or legitimated?

3 How to adopt a child

Adoption means a great many different things. For a summary of the extraordinary diversity of the institution, we may turn to *Adoption: A Second Chance* (1977), Barbara Tizard's account of her study comparing the adoption or rehabilitation of children in care:

The essence of adoption is that a child not born to you is incorporated into your family as though he were your own. This practice can be found in some form in most cultures – one of the best-known early adoptions was that of Moses. But just as the family, although a constant feature of all societies, has assumed many different forms and functions, so the characteristics of adoption have varied enormously during history. Today most people think of adoption as a process in which a young child, usually an infant, is permanently incorporated into a family into which he was not born. Typically, the adoptive parents and the biological parents are strangers, and the adoption is arranged through an agency or other third party. Great stress is laid on keeping the two sets of parents from meeting or even knowing each others' identity. All links between the adopted child and his natural parents are severed, and the adopted child has all the rights, and is treated in the same way, as a natural child of his new family. The primary purpose of the adoption is seen to be the satisfaction of the desire of a married couple to rear a child; at the same time, a home is provided for a child whose natural parents are unable to rear it. ...

Perhaps the greatest contrast is with the custom of child exchange, or kinship fostering, formerly prevalent in Polynesia and parts of Africa. In these societies children were often not reared by their biological parents but sent to be raised by relatives, sometimes after weaning, sometimes from the age of 6 or 7. The exchange of children was arranged by the parents, who continued to maintain some contact with their biological child. It was believed that aunts, uncles and grandparents would bring children up and train them more effectively than their parents. This custom of child exchange seems to have been part of a system of mutual kinship obligations.

Adoption played a very different role in such ancient civilisations as the Babylonian, Chinese and Roman. There, its function was primarily to ensure the continuity of wealthy families by providing for the inheritance of property and the performance of ancestral worship. Roman law, for example, permitted adoption only in order to provide an heir to the childless, and laid down that the adopters must be past child-bearing age and the adoptee must be an adult. Until recently, the adoption laws of many European countries were influenced by Roman law; often adoptive parents had to be childless and over the age of 50.

Hindu law also recognised adoption as a method of securing an heir, both for religious purposes and for the inheritance of property. It specified, however, that the adopted child should be if possible a blood relative, and that the transaction must take place directly between the two sets of parents. For this reason, orphans could not be adopted. In most ancient civilisations adoption was only one among several possible ways of providing an heir, and often not the preferred one. In Islam, for example, divorce and remarriage, polygamy, and the legitimisation of children by maidservants were common practices, while adoption was not permitted.

In all these societies adoption was essentially concerned with preserving the property and the religious observances of the families of the ruling class. It was very much a service for the rich, and for men; it was men who wanted heirs, and for this purpose they wanted boys. The emotional needs of childless wives were not recognised; indeed if they did not produce an heir they were likely to be divorced or otherwise replaced. Nor was it a service for homeless children; the adoptees were often adult, or, if children, they were given to the adoptive parents by their biological parents in order to better their social status.

Question

It may be easy to see why the modern idea of providing a home for an illegitimate and often pauper child found little favour in medieval England, but how do you account for the fact that the great English families did not wish to do as the Romans had done – so that, even now, an adopted child cannot succeed to a peerage or other hereditary title?

Tizard resumes her account thus:

It is only relatively recently that adoption has become a recognised practice in Western society. Before this time bastards were sometimes legitimised by the rich, but the orphans and illegitimate children of the poor were sent to the workhouse and contracted out as soon as possible to private employers for domestic service, or work in factories, mills or mines. Often, of course, the orphans of both rich and poor were cared for by relatives, but they were rarely accorded the same status as the biological children of the family. The position of illegitimate children was worse, because of the social and moral stigma attached to illegitimacy, coupled with a strong belief in the inheritance of moral qualities. Not only the unmarried mother but also her child were regarded as morally inferior. There was also a general belief that to care for the illegitimate child would condone or even encourage the immorality of his mother. People were reluctant even to admit illegitimate children into a household; it was thought that 'bad blood will out', and the sins of the mother would be visited on the child.

It was in the United States, where more egalitarian ideas prevailed, heredity was at a discount, and human labour was in short supply, that the modern practice of adoption began to evolve. The first modern adoption law was enacted in Massachusetts in 1851. But long before that time American homesteaders took homeless children and reared them, benefiting in exchange from their help on the farm. Often, these children were treated very much as second-class citizens. Indeed, for half a century after adoption was legitimised in the USA it continued to be seen as a charitable act, and the adopted child was expected to work harder than a natural child and repay his debt of gratitude. …

Adoption at this stage, then, was a way of giving a homeless child a more humane upbringing than he would have received in an institution, with the expectation of receiving services from the child in return. It was only gradually that adoption began to be seen as a way of giving infertile couples all the emotional satisfaction that they would have had from a biological child.

The English were still deeply suspicious. In 1921, the Hopkinson Committee reported in favour of providing for legal adoption, but its recommendations proved so controversial that a second Committee was appointed, under the chairmanship of Mr Justice Tomlin. The *Report of the Child Adoption Committee* in 1925 is far from enthusiastic:

4. ... There have no doubt always been some people who desire to bring up as their own the children of others but we have been unable to satisfy ourselves as to the extent of the effective demand for a legal system of adoption by persons who themselves have adopted children or who desire to do so. It may be doubted whether any such persons have been or would be deterred from adopting children by the absence of any recognition by the law of the status of adoption. The war led to an increase in the number of de facto adoptions but that increase has not been wholly maintained. The people wishing to get rid of children are far more numerous than those wishing to receive them and partly on this account the activities in recent years of societies arranging systematically for the adoption of children would appear to have given to adoption a prominence which is somewhat artificial and may not be in all respects wholesome. The problem of the unwanted child is a serious one; it may well be a question whether a legal system of adoption will do much to assist the solution of it.

...

9. [Nevertheless] ... we think that there is a measure of genuine apprehension on the part of those who have in fact adopted other people's children, based on the possibility of interference at some future time by the natural parent. It may be that this apprehension has but a slight basis in fact notwithstanding the incapacity of the legal parent to divest himself of his parental rights and duties. The Courts have long recognised that any application by the natural parent to recover the custody of his child will be determined by reference to the child's welfare and by that consideration alone. The apprehension, therefore, in most cases has a theoretical rather than a practical basis. There is also a sentiment which deserves sympathy and respect, that the relation between adopter and adopted should be given some recognition by the community. We think, therefore, that a case is made out for an alteration in the law. ...

Having reluctantly reached that conclusion, the Committee went on to consider how adoption should take place, and to what effect. Some of their arguments cast an interesting light upon more recent debates:

11. ... some form of judicial sanction should be required. ... The transaction is one which may affect the status of the child and have far-reaching consequences and from its nature is not one which, without judicial investigation, there is likely to be any competent independent consideration of the matter from the point of view of the welfare of the child.

Inasmuch as many cases of adoption in fact have their origin in the social or economic pressure exercised by circumstances upon the mother of an illegitimate child, it is desirable that there should be some safeguard against the use of a legal system of adoption as an instrument by which advantage may be taken of the mother's situation to compel her to make a surrender of her child final in character though she may herself, if a free agent, desire nothing more than a temporary provision for it. Further, there are many who hold that a system of adoption so far as it tends to encourage or increase the separation of mother and child may of itself be an evil and should be therefore, if introduced, operated with caution. ...

...

15. ... Whichever be the tribunal selected it is important that the judicial sanction, which will necessarily carry great weight, should be a real adjudication and should not become a mere method of registering the will of the parties respectively seeking to part with and take over the child. To avoid this result we think that in every case there should be appointed ... some body or person to act as guardian ad litem of the child with the duty of protecting the interests of the child before the tribunal.

...

18. ... No system of adoption, seeking as it does to reproduce artificially a natural relation, can hope to produce precisely the same result or to be otherwise than in many respects illogical, and this is made apparent in the diversity of provisions in relation to succession and marriage which appear in the adoption laws of other countries.

19. We think that in introducing into English law a new system it would be well to proceed with a measure of caution and at any rate in the first instance not to interfere with the law of succession ... it does not require any profound knowledge of the law of succession to bring home to an enquirer (1) the impracticality of putting an adopted child in precisely the same position as

a natural child in regard to succession, and (2) the grave difficulties which would arise if any alteration were to be made in the law of succession for the purpose of giving an adopted child more limited rights ... but ... the tribunal which sanctions the adoption should have power if it thinks fit, to require that some provision be made by the adopting parent for the child.

Question

What, if anything, was so different about the system of succession in classical Roman law that the complete absorption of the adopted child into his new family presented none of the difficulties apparently so obvious to English lawyers in 1925?

If these passages in the report betray (although they do not confess to) deep-seated attitudes about 'natural' and 'artificial' relationships, there is one point upon which the Committee's views have a decidedly modern ring:

28. ... Certain of the Adoption Societies make this feature an essential part of their policy. They deliberately seek to fix a gulf between the child's past and future. This notion of secrecy has its origin partly in a fear (which a legalised system of adoption should go far to dispel) that the natural parents will seek to interfere with the adopter and partly in the belief that if the eyes can be closed to facts the facts themselves will cease to exist so that it will be an advantage to an illegitimate child who has been adopted if in fact his origin cannot be traced. Apart from the question whether it is desirable or even admissible deliberately to eliminate or obscure the traces of a child's origin ... we think that this system of secrecy would be wholly unnecessary and objectionable in connection with a legalised system of adoption.

The first cautious steps were taken in the Adoption of Children Act 1926. Since then three quite different kinds of adoption have emerged: the voluntary, if deeply painful, surrender of a baby or young child to complete strangers; the adoption of a child by a step-parent or other member of his existing family network; and the compulsory removal from one family to another of a child who usually already has a family history of his own. We shall here concentrate on the first, dealing with the others in Chapters 12 and 14.

The principal Act is now the Adoption Act 1976. It preserves one principle which has been taken for granted from the start:

57. – (1) Subject to the provisions of this section, it shall not be lawful to make or to give to any person any payment or reward for or in consideration of –
(*a*) the adoption by that person of any child;
(*b*) the grant by that person of any agreement or consent required in connection with the adoption of a child;
(*c*) the handing over of a child by that person with a view to the adoption of the child;
(*d*) the making by that person of any arrangements for the adoption of a child.

Questions

(i) What is so wrong about paying an unmarried mother to let you have her baby?
(ii) Can it be distinguished from paying a doctor to inseminate you with the semen of an unknown donor?
(iii) Or paying a woman to bear your child? (See p. 485, below.)
(iv) Wait a moment – is not that what husbands do?

At first, however, while payment was prohibited, adoptions could be arranged either by adoption societies, or by individual third parties (such as doctors or lawyers) or by the mother herself. Regulation of adoption societies was introduced in 1939 and improved in 1950. The increasing professionalism of adoption societies led to an increasing concern about the private placement of children for adoption, discussed in the *Report of the Departmental Committee on the Adoption of Children* (the Houghton Report) in 1972:

83. The Hurst Committee estimated that in 1954 more than one-third of non-relative adoptions resulted from placements by third parties or by the natural parents. The 1966 survey figures [Grey, 1971] ... show that the proportion was then very much less. Nevertheless there were some 1,500 children a year placed in this way. There are a number of reasons why people make independent arrangements without using agency services. One is the inaccessibility of agencies in some areas, which our recommendations are designed to remedy. Others are people's dislike of the idea of enquiries by an agency, a desire to keep control of the situation themselves, or their trust in a person known to them, such as their family doctor. Some would-be adopters have been turned down by agencies, and others may seek independent placements because they realise that no adoption agency would consider them suitable.

84. Much concern has been expressed about these placements. The decision to place a child with a particular couple is the most important stage in the adoption process. Adoption law must give assurance of adequate safeguards for the welfare of the child at this stage, otherwise it is ineffective. This assurance rests mainly upon the skilled work of the adoption services, which includes preparation for adoptive parenthood. An independent adoption is one in which this assurance is lacking. We therefore suggested in our working paper that independent placements with non-relatives should no longer be allowed.

85. The evidence we received was divided. The main arguments against our proposal were that it was an interference with individual liberty, particularly in the case of direct placements by the mother; that there was no research evidence to prove that independent placements were any worse than agency placements, and that they should not be banned until agency work had improved; and that the investigation by the guardian ad litem and a court hearing were sufficient safeguards against adoption orders being made in respect of unsuitable placements.

86. Virtually no recent research has been done to compare the outcome of independent placements with that of agency placements, but there is no lack of evidence of unsatisfactory independent placements. Information received from the Church of England Board for Social Responsibility, which has contact with agencies working with unmarried mothers, revealed that in the course of a year a considerable number of highly unsatisfactory independent placements came to the notice of the social workers. Local authorities with experience of acting as guardians ad litem or carrying out welfare supervision of children placed for adoption have come across unsatisfactory independent placements which would not have been made by a reputable adoption agency. This is confirmed by the written and oral evidence we have received and by the personal experience of some of our members.

87. ... The greater imbalance between the numbers of couples wishing to adopt and the number of babies needing adoption could lead to an increase in third party activity in future. We have received no direct evidence of financial transactions in third party placements, but it is within the knowledge of some of our members that couples have alleged that they have paid an inflated fee for the investigation of infertility on the understanding that a child would be found for them to adopt, and that mothers have alleged that services, such as nursing home facilities, have been provided on the understanding that the child would be available for adoption.

88. Adoption is a matter of such vital importance to a child (who is usually too young to have any say in the matter) that society has a duty to ensure that the most satisfactory placements are made. Society manifestly does not do so while it is open to anybody to place a child for adoption. While the court hearing is intended as a final safeguard, safeguards are needed much earlier. Moreover courts are in difficulty about refusing to make an adoption order because there is no agency to which the child can be returned. Adoption agencies are increasingly staffed by social workers whose professional skills and knowledge are increasing. Agency practice has built-in safeguards through the Adoption Agencies Regulations and through general accountability to the public. We therefore adhere to the view expressed in our working paper that independent placements should not be allowed once the new registration system for adoption agencies is in force, when these safeguards will be even greater. We include in this proposal direct placements

by the parents, although, if they wished a particular placement to be made, the agency arranging the adoption should give this sympathetic consideration.

In *Growing Up Adopted* (1972), Jean Seglow, Mia Kellmer Pringle and Peter Wedge report upon a follow-up study of all the NCDS children (born in a single week in 1958) who were adopted by non-parents: they were studied at birth, then again at seven, and further enquiries were made of their adoptive parents in 1967 and 1971. As Jane Rowe says in her foreword:

The outstanding fact to emerge from this careful study is the power of the environment to affect children's development for good or ill. The adopted children are shown to have enjoyed a more favourable environment than the much larger group of illegitimate children who remained with their natural mothers. The illegitimate children were found to be vulnerable at birth. By the age of 7 years, the care, affection and material advantages provided by their new parents had enabled the adopted children to overcome their earlier handicaps and to compare very favourably with their peers in the general population. …

[Nevertheless] no-one reading this book carefully could spring to the conclusion that adoption is an easy solution to the problems of illegitimacy or childlessness. Not all the placements were happy and successful. Some of the agencies' work was evidently poor. Adoption is shown to have its own built in stresses. Many of the cherished theories of agency policy are once more challenged by the findings that factors such as age, health, social class and family composition are rather unimportant, while the authors demonstrate over and over again the importance of such intangible factors as attitudes, feelings and expectations.

One of the greatest advantages of agency placement might be thought by lay people to be the enhanced opportunities it provides for suiting the child to the particular adopters, but Mia Kellmer Pringle has this to say:

'Matching' for similarities in physical appearance, temperament, intelligence, etc., is yet another myth which needs to be abandoned for a number of reasons. Being led to expect similarities between their adopted children and themselves, adoptive parents will feel cheated and justifiably resentful if their expectations are subsequently not fulfilled. Also, the younger the baby the more impractical it is to ensure any measure of success. Moreover, it increases the risk of playing into the hands of those adoptive parents who want to deny the reality of adoption.

But perhaps most important of all 'none of the evidence showed matching to be a favourable factor. The only associations, in fact, were in the opposite direction. Families in the "very high" match group on physical resemblance and ethnic background had more children in the problem groups at follow-up, and those in the "very low" match group had fewer children showing problems' (Ripple, 1968). In matching for intelligence it has been shown that children with a very unpromising background who are placed into adoptive homes of a much superior level tend to develop intellectual abilities more closely in keeping with those of their adoptive parents.

Perhaps, therefore, it is not surprising that in discussing the overall results of the study, Peter Wedge reports:

Privately placed children accounted for some 21% of our sample. The remainder were placed by recognized adoption agencies. The former group of children did not differ significantly from children placed by an agency when their overall assessment of success in adoption was considered. The importance of this is not only that private placements seemed to be no less successful than agency placements, but that agency placements were no more successful than private placements. One would have expected that, where children were placed by agencies (presumably using specialist staff), then those children would have a more successful outcome than children placed privately, and so relatively haphazardly. If the practice of private placements justifies the criticism that has been frequently levelled at it, then now how necessary is it that the whole standard of adoption work among agencies should be raised above the level implied by this finding? Rather than banning independent arrangements, the first step must surely be to improve the alternative. …

Nevertheless the Adoption Act 1976 provides:

11. – (1) A person other than an adoption agency shall not make arrangements for the adoption of a child, or place a child for adoption, unless –
(*a*) the proposed adopter is a relative of the child; or
(*b*) he is acting in pursuance of an order of the High Court.

By s. 11(3), contravening this, or receiving a child placed in contravention of this, or taking part in the management of a body which exists to arrange adoptions but is not an approved adoption agency, is an offence.

Questions

(i) Now that so few babies are offered for adoption here, many more couples are going abroad, often to South America or China, to adopt: what can we do to insist that ss. 11 and 57 are obeyed?
(ii) If they succeed in finding one and bring him back here, should we allow them to adopt?
(iii) What can we do (*a*) to stop them or (*b*) to protect the children?

We look at these issues in Chapter 15. The professionals' main concerns are that such adopters may abandon the child if things do not turn out as they had hoped, or find it difficult to cope with a child from another culture, and would not have been thought eligible to adopt a child from this country. Eligibility to adopt here is discussed in the *Review of Adoption Law* (1992):

26.4 We recommend that agencies should not be allowed to operate absolute rules governing people's eligibility for consideration as adopters. In other words, a person who meets the statutory criteria for an adoptive parent should not automatically be excluded from consideration on account, say, of his or her age. An agency may, however, decide that, having regard to the needs of the children for whom adoptive families are required and to agency guidelines on suitability, it would not be appropriate to accept that person for consideration.
...

Upper age limits

26.7 Agencies may not impose strict age limits on adopters, as there is no provision for this in legislation, but they do operate their own age guidelines in relation to people who want to adopt healthy infants. These vary from the early to late thirties, and few agencies will accept applicants over 40 for consideration as adopters for healthy infants. The guidelines reflect the view that it is better for very young children to be placed with adopters who are not older by too wide a margin than most couples starting a family.
26.8 We do not consider it appropriate to set down requirements or guidelines in relation to an upper age for adopters, or a maximum interval between the ages of adopter and child. Some children may benefit from having adoptive parents who do not differ greatly in terms of age from their birth parents or from the parents of their peers. But there may be circumstances where older applicants, by virtue of their maturity, experience, or other special qualities, are particularly well-qualified to provide a home for a child. Agencies should always be satisfied, however, that adopters have a reasonable expectation of retaining health and vigour to care for a child until he or she is grown up; age is one of a number of factors which should be taken into account in determining whether an applicant meets this criterion.

Marital status

26.9 At present, an adoption order may be made on the application of a married couple. A single person may also apply for an adoption order. However, a married person may only adopt alone if the court is satisfied that the spouse cannot be found or is incapable of applying by reason of physical or mental ill-health; or that the couple have separated and are living apart, and the separation is likely to be permanent.

26.10 In practice, some agencies assess and prepare unmarried couples together, although only one partner may apply for the order and become the child's legal parent. It has been asked whether an unmarried couple should be allowed to adopt jointly. Family structures are changing and more children are born to parents who are not married but are living in stable unions. Under section 4 of the Children Act 1989, an unmarried father may acquire the same parental status as one who is married. On the other hand, unmarried parents do not have the same legal obligations to one another as a married couple have. Should the relationship break down, the caring parent may therefore be less financially secure than if they were married. Furthermore, one of the special features of adoption is that it transfers a child from one family to another and gives the child a legal relationship with all members of the new family, including grandparents, aunts and uncles. However great the commitment of unmarried adoptive parents to a child might be, it is open to question how far their wider families would be willing to accept that child as part of their family.

26.11 It is also important to bear in mind Article 6(1) of the European Adoption Convention which prohibits adoption by unmarried couples. Although some unmarried couples might be suitable adoptive parents for a child, we feel that the security and stability which adopted children need are still more likely to be provided by parents who have made a publicly recognized commitment to their relationship and who have legal responsibilities towards each other. Taking into account also the United Kingdom's international obligations, we consider that it would not be appropriate to allow two unmarried people to adopt jointly.

26.12 The fact that two people are married to each other is not of course in itself a sufficient guide to the likely stability of their relationship. Agencies generally expect applicants to have been married for at least three years, although some are prepared to take into account periods of co-habitation preceding marriage, where there is evidence of it available. We consider that agencies should have flexibility to operate their own criteria in forming views on the likely stability of a marriage, and that this should be the subject of guidance.

26.13 We do not propose any changes to the law relating to single applicants, including lesbians and gay men. There are examples of extremely successful adoptions, particularly of older children and children with disabilities, by single adopters. Some children are only able to settle in single-parent households, as a result of experiences in their early lives.

26.14 Some agencies may place a child with a single applicant who is living with a partner. As a matter of practice, to safeguard the child, they also assess the suitability of the partner. We have suggested above that an unmarried couple should not be allowed to adopt jointly, ie that it should not be possible for them to have the same legal relationship towards a child which they would have if they were a married couple adopting together. We do not feel that this is necessarily incompatible with allowing a single person who has a partner to adopt. We recommend that, where assessing a single applicant, agencies should have a duty to assess any other person who is likely to act in a parental capacity towards the adopted child.

Health

26.15 There are no statutory requirements in respect of the health of adopters. Adoption agencies are required to obtain a report on the prospective adopters' health, covering matters such as personal and family health history and current state of health, and consumption of tobacco, alcohol and other habit-forming drugs.

26.16 Professionals, agencies and courts can face difficult decisions in relation to the extent to which health factors may influence a prospective adopter's suitability. Agencies appear to employ a variety of approaches, particularly in relation to smoking. Central guidelines on general principles might help to achieve a greater sense of fairness among prospective adopters and assist agencies in making difficult decisions.

Questions

(i) Who do *you* think would be more suitable to bring up a little girl of two, recently released for adoption by her mother, who had found it impossible to cater for either her physical or her psychological needs: (*a*) a childless couple in their 30s, who have turned to adoption in desperation after unsuccessful attempts to cure the wife's infertility, or (*b*) a couple in their 40s whose own three children are now aged 18, 15 and 10 and who have been acting as short-term foster parents but would prefer a permanent placement?

(ii) Would you say the same if the child were of mixed race and couple (*a*) were white and couple (*b*) were black?
(iii) Do you agree that unmarried couples should not be able to adopt?

But what should adoption mean? Is it simply a way of providing a home for a child who needs one, or is it a total transfer from one family to another? And can that transfer ever be quite complete? The next step after the first cautious moves in 1926 is described by Heywood in *Children in Care* (1978) thus:

The policy reflected in legislation for adoption ... has moved on from providing legal *status*, for those who lacked this, to providing a legal *relationship* between adopted child and adopters as similar as possible to that which exists between a child and his natural parents. This principle was expressed in the Adoption of Children Act 1949, introduced as a private members' bill by Sir Basil Nield. The Act took great care to see, particularly by the safeguarding of consents, that the divestment of the natural family, and particularly the mother, should not be lightly undertaken, but that, where it was, the integration of the child with his new family should be complete and natural.

The process was still not complete, as the Houghton Report (1972) explains:

Interpretation of wills and other instruments

326. The present law provides that for the purposes of inheritance (in Scotland, succession) and of the interpretation of dispositions made after an adoption order, an adopted person shall be treated as if he is a child born to the adopter in lawful wedlock and not the child of any other person. This means that an adopted child has the same rights on an intestacy occurring after the adoption order as a child born to the adopter in wedlock. In England and Wales an adopted person does not, however, benefit under a general gift to, say, grandchildren of the testator, where the disposition was made before the date of the adoption order unless it can be construed to include adopted children as such. ...

327. If adoption means the complete severance of the legal relationship between the child and his natural parents and the establishment of a new and irrevocable relationship, designed to make the child a full member of another family, it follows that that child should have exactly the same rights under wills and other instruments as a natural child of the adoptive family. We proposed that this should be the case and none of the evidence dissented from our proposition. It was pointed out to us that the passing of the Family Law Reform Act 1969 had placed illegitimate children in England and Wales in a better position than adopted children by providing, in section 15, that an illegitimate child may take under any disposition made after the Act came into force whether he was born before or after the disposition.

These recommendations were implemented in 1975, so that there are now only three important exceptions to the principle that an adopted child is the same as a child born to married parents: he cannot succeed to peerages and similar dignities; the rules prohibiting marriages with certain relatives in his birth family remain and he is only debarred from marriage with his adoptive parent in the new family; and if he is adopted abroad he will not gain the same rights under nationality and immigration laws as would a child born abroad to United Kingdom parents or adopted here.

Nevertheless, a total legal transplant does not mean a total physical or psychological transplant, as shown by these quotations from adopted adults who had sought their original birth certificates, as then permitted by Scottish but not English law, in John Triseliotis' study *In Search of Origins* (1973):

'You look at yourself in the mirror and you can't compare it with anybody. You're a stranger because you don't know what your real mother looks like or what your father looks like. ...'

'All through my life I had the feeling of unreality about myself; a feeling of not being real, something like an imitation antique ... I have been told that I was born in the Poor House and that my birth mother was a bad lot. This has been haunting me. I tried desperately to avoid being like her but then who am I like? I feel I have nothing to pass on to my children. ... '

'My parents were kind people but very isolated. We had few relatives calling and we had no habit of calling on others. My parents' relatives meant nothing to me and I must have meant nothing to them. ... When I was 15 or 16 I was very curious to know "who I was" and especially to know about my natural parents and their families. With your adoptive family you can only go as far back as they are and not beyond. But with your natural ones you feel you want to go further back. ... '

The adopted person's needs are discussed by Christine Walby and Barbara Symons in *Who am I?* (1990):

The need to know

A major task faced by adopted people is the development of a sense of separate identity out of what Sants in 1967 called 'genealogical bewilderment'. Triseliotis in 1974 posed the question of 'how far adopted people face similar or different developmental tasks from those who have not been adopted'. These 'growing-up' tasks may be seen as achieving a mature independence and a clear sense of identity, and being able to give and receive love. They are inextricably linked with knowledge and feelings about heritage and about how other people see us and behave towards us.

Thus while the growing-up tasks may be common to all, the adopted person's development may be hampered by lack of knowledge. Margaret Kornitzer described the situation graphically in 1971 when writing of the effect upon the adopted person's natural development of a sense of identity when there has been a failure to provide information about 'blood and bones':

'Background knowledge of one's family is like baby food – it is literally fed to a person as part of the normal nourishment that builds up his [or her] mental and emotional structure and helps the person to become acquainted with what he [or she] is so that he can seize his inheritance of himself.'

She goes on to discuss the importance of knowing what our (biological) parents were like in understanding much about ourselves, and of the reality being 'healthier' than the fantasy. The point is made that simply being honest with adopted children is not enough: 'Even those adopted children whose adopters have been quite honest with them do feel left out on a limb at a certain point in their development because they can have no visual or mental picture of the couple who gave them their physical continuity in the chain of life': a fact denied by many practitioners and adopters.

At a more mundane level, as McWhinnie [1970] reports, the simplest tasks of adult life, such as completing medical data on forms, can become an ordeal because of the adopted person's lack of very basic information about biological background which others possess as a matter of course.

An adopted person has, in Triseliotis' view, to base his or her identity on 'the concept of two sets of parents'. Rowe [1970], Kirk [1964], Triseliotis [1974] and Rosner [1961] agree that adopters need to feel and experience the child as their own, and have confidence in the validity of their family. Jan de Hartog, a novelist and adopter, goes as far as to say that the adoptive mother should totally exclude the birth mother for a time in order to make the child her own.

The crucial issue, says Rowe, is that adopters should not pretend that being an adoptive parent is the same as being a biological parent, but should have a 'sturdy belief that their form of parenthood really is parenthood'. They also need to be able to feel 'some sense of kinship with the people who gave their child birth', and truly absorb the child's background into their family traditions.

Attitudes in the outside world

Unfortunately, as Triseliotis illustrated, the problems encountered by adopted persons in the maturation process are not limited to the resolution of attitudes, roles and relationships within the family. The community too has a subtle but profound effect: 'However successful adoptive parents are in their parental task, they cannot protect the child from the nuances of the outside world'. He also refers to 'covert negative messages', which are best illustrated by some of his examples from discussion with adopted people:

'When I told my fiance I was adopted his reply was "I do not know what my father and mother will feel ..."

When my boy was born and my mother-in-law visited me in hospital she exclaimed: "Thank God that he has taken from our side of the family." I know what she was getting at and it hurt.

Somehow I felt that my parents were ashamed to talk about it and they gave me the feeling that adoption was unnatural ... '

Thus the concept of access to birth records must be considered against a shifting foundation of confusion about the real nature of adoption. On the one hand we have absolute legal precision about the status of adoption and on the other, highly complex cultural and emotional uncertainty. It is in this context, and that of the complicated development of maturity and independence, that adopted people seek information on, and sometimes direct contact with, their origins.

The arguments for and against access to birth records were summarised in the Houghton Report (1972):

301. ... It seems that where an adopted person has been told of his adoption at an early age and his relationship with his adopters is good he is less likely to seek access to his original birth record. Two-thirds of those in [Triseliotis'] sample who sought this information came to know about their adoption when they were 11 or more years old, half of them being 16 or over and one as old as 40. Only two-fifths of those who applied had been told of their adoption by their adoptive parents, the others finding out by discovering documents or letters or from chance remarks by people outside the family, mainly other children. For many of them the late disclosure of their adoption came as a shock, and they had difficulty in coming to terms with it. It was also noticeable that two out of every five who sought this information had lost one or both adoptive parents by death, separation or divorce before they reached the age of 16, and in one-third of all the applications it was the death of an adoptive parent that triggered off the search for information about the natural parents. Two-thirds of those who sought this information had the immediate reaction that it was helpful or of some help to them, while one-third felt very upset by the information they had obtained. Some were unhappy to discover that they were illegitimate, while the few who were legitimate were equally sad to think that their parents, although married, had 'given them away'. When seen four months later, however, nine out of ten had no regrets about having taken steps to find out this information.

302. The other evidence we received was divided. ... Some witnesses urged that the right of an adult adopted person to know the names of his natural parents was a basic human right. Others were concerned about the distress which might be caused as a result of widespread attempts by adopted children to seek out their original parents. The Scottish research showed that although 42 adopted persons, or 60% of the sample, sought to trace their natural parents, only four succeeded in doing so, although seven others were able to contact blood relations. The Deputy Registrar General for Scotland said that he could not recall any complaint made by natural relatives who had been traced through the Registrar General's records. The fear of being traced may therefore have been unduly magnified, particularly as all the indications are that the climate of opinion is changing and mothers are becoming less concerned to conceal the fact that they have had an illegitimate child. Research into the views of a sample of adoptive parents revealed that 63% considered that their adoptive children should be allowed free access to their original records.

303. The weight of the evidence as a whole was in favour of freer access to background information, and this accords with our wish to encourage greater openness about adoption. ... We therefore recommend that all adopted adults in England and Wales, whenever adopted, should in future be permitted to obtain a copy of their original birth entry.

This probably provoked more public debate and controversy than all the other recommendations in the report. For example, on 10 October 1976, the *News of the World* declared:

Thousands of women are facing the fear that a secret shadow from the past may soon knock at their door and wreck their marriages. They are the mothers who have never told their husbands and their families that they had an illegitimate baby whom they gave for adoption.

As a compromise, all those adopted before 12 November 1975, when the Children Act 1975 was passed, were obliged to accept counselling before gaining access to their original birth certificate. John Triseliotis looked at the debate and at the various studies of how the provisions had operated, in *Obtaining Birth Certificates* (1984) and concluded:

Only a minority of adopted people seek access to their birth records ... The calamities anticipated by sections of the media, politicians, and some organizations have not materialized. The various studies carried out so far suggest that the vast majority of adoptees act thoughtfully and with great consideration for the feelings of both their birth and adoptive parents. The value of access facility is not now in dispute. ... The vast majority of adoptees had no intention of setting out on a quest. Their main explanation was that they had parents, their adoptive ones, they were leading a 'happy' life and they were not interested in quests or in meetings with an original parent. ...

It is difficult to escape my earlier conclusions that though there is a curiosity and deep psychological need in every adoptee to know about his background and personal history, the need for access to records, for meetings or reunions with birth parents is frequently a characteristic of those who were not given reasonable explanations and information about their origins, of those who have recently gone through some major event or crisis in their lives, or of those who may have experienced unsatisfactory growing-up experiences. Contrary to some assumptions identity confusion does not necessarily go with adoption. Studies have shown that the vast majority of adopted people have a firm and secure sense of self.

Walby and Symons, however, were able to explore the feelings of their small sample in some depth:

One of the most interesting facts to emerge from this data is that those respondents who were voluntarily told of their adoption by their parents did not necessarily feel better about their situation than those who were not told. The crucial elements appear to be the amount and the accuracy of the information available, the ability of the adoptive parents to recognise and share in the feelings of the adopted child about the adoption, and particularly their appreciation of the child's need to explore the question 'Who am I?'. The experiences and feelings of respondents in both groups were markedly similar.

No respondents had received any meaningful information about their origins; many spoke of extreme tensions and even taboo preventing any discussion of adoption; all had feelings ranging from discomfort in their difference from others, and anger about not having information to which they felt entitled, to guilt about causing distress to their adoptive parents. The majority felt stigmatised by their adoptive state. In terms of Goffman's [1963] description of the three main types of stigma, this feeling would derive from 'abominations of the body' and 'blemishes of individual character', the first a subtle product of common attitudes towards childlessness (traditionally the main motivation to adoption), the second a more obvious, and for the respondents more potent, reaction to illegitimacy.

Question

Is this a question of psychological welfare or human rights (see p. 461, above)? In *R v Registrar General, ex p Smith* [1990] 2 QB 253, the Divisional Court held that, on public policy grounds, the Registrar General could refuse to disclose the original birth certificate to an adopted man who had committed a brutal and sadistic murder and while in prison had killed another prisoner whom he thought was his adoptive mother: was this right?

4 Assisted reproduction and the 'social parent'

Nowadays, one can become a parent, not by adopting the child, but by adopting the sperm or the egg which go to make up the child. The Law Commission considered the parentage of children born as a result of artificial insemination with sperm from a donor other than the mother's husband (now known as donor insemination or DI) in their Working Paper on *Illegitimacy* (1979):

10.9 The policy of the legislation, we are at present inclined to think, should therefore be that where a married woman has received A.I.D. treatment with her husband's consent, the husband rather than the donor should, for all legal purposes, be regarded as the father of a child conceived as the result. ...

10.11 The simplest way of implementing the policy which we have suggested would be a statutory provision deeming the husband to be the father of an A.I.D. child born to his wife; the only ground on which the husband could challenge the operation of this deeming provision would be that he had not consented to his wife receiving A.I.D. treatment. This approach seems to us to have the merit not only of simplicity, but also of giving effect to the likely feelings and wishes of the wife and husband. We note that statutory provision of the type we envisage has been made in several States of the USA. ...

10.17 Although there are many advantages to such a statutory deeming provision, there are two main objections to it. The first involves a major point of policy: it could be said that the proposal involves a deliberate falsification of the birth register. The second objection is more theoretical: that the proposal would involve a transfer of legal rights from the donor to the husband, and that the law should accurately mirror that transfer.

A comment upon the first objection may be taken from a Ciba Foundation Symposium on the *Law and Ethics of A.I.D. and Embryo Transfer* (1973):

McLaren [*geneticist*]: Even though the genetic register which Canon Dunstan proposed might not be very useful, through being erroneous (owing to the possibility that occasionally the supposedly infertile husband fertilizes the egg), our present registry system is itself erroneous in all those cases where the husband is not actually the father of the child. Are there any statistics on how common this is? This is probably more frequent than the cases where a supposedly infertile husband was really the father of an A.I.D. child.

Philipp [*consultant obstetrician and gynaecologist*]: We blood-tested some patients in a town in south-east England, and found that 30% of the husbands could not have been the fathers of their children ...

JH Edwards [*geneticist*]: ... Analysis of some blood group data, making allowance for the fact that one could not detect all the illegitimacies, showed that in the 1950s in the West Isleworth area about 50% of premarital conceptions were not fathered by the apparent father. As the apparent fathers were questioned while visiting their wives immediately after the birth, most of them obviously thought they were the father. I think the group Mr Philipp referred to is also highly biased. In spite of much talk about artificial insemination by donor and all the difficulties with genetics and so on, natural insemination by donor is practised on quite a substantial scale on an amateur basis.

Meanwhile, the Government had set up the Warnock Committee of Inquiry into Human Fertilisation and Embryology. This dealt with other techniques for counteracting infertility, which are usefully summarised in the DHSS Consultation Paper on *Legislation on Human Infertility Services and Embryo Research* (1986):

In vitro fertilisation

8. This technique is used mainly where a woman has no fallopian tubes or they are blocked. Currently about 1,000 births in the UK are thought to have involved IVF. It has also been used in dealing with some types of male infertility and where the cause of infertility is unknown. A ripe egg is taken from the woman's ovary shortly before it would have been released naturally. It is then mixed with sperm in a dish (in vitro) so that fertilisation can occur. Once the fertilised egg has started to develop it is transferred back to the woman's womb. If a pregnancy is to be established the embryo must then implant in the womb.

9. IVF although simple in concept is not an easy technique in practice. To increase the chances of success (currently the success rate is thought to be of the order of 15 per cent) it is usual to create and transfer to a woman more than one embryo. Several eggs are thus required. To obtain these eggs the woman is given superovulatory drugs which ensure that a number of eggs is produced in one menstrual cycle and these are available for fertilisation.

10. Fertilisation of these eggs may result in more embryos than it is appropriate to transfer to the woman's womb. These embryos can then be preserved by freezing for later transfer to the

womb or scientific use or they may be left to perish. At present it is not possible for embryos to grow outside a woman's body for longer than 9–10 days.

Egg donation

11. The IVF technique allows a pregnancy to be achieved where the woman cannot produce an egg. An egg by another woman is fertilised with the husband's sperm in vitro and the resulting embryo is then transferred to the infertile woman. One case involving sisters was reported in this country in 1985.

Embryo donation

12. In this case donated eggs and sperm would be used to create an embryo for transfer to the infertile woman. The technique could apply where both partners are infertile. Embryo donation is thought not yet to have been used in the UK.

Surrogacy

13. This practice involves one woman carrying a child for another with the intention that the child be handed over after birth. Surrogacy can make it possible for a woman to obtain a child in cases where she cannot carry the pregnancy at all, or for long enough for the fetus to be capable of being born alive. Artificial insemination of the surrogate mother by sperm of the commissioning mother's husband makes it possible for that child to be conceived without the need for sexual intercourse. However, by means of IVF it may be possible in some instances for the commissioning mother's eggs to be used.

As the Warnock Committee pointed out in their Report (1984):

6.8. Egg donation produces for the first time circumstances in which the genetic mother (the woman who donates the egg), is a different person from the woman who gives birth to the child, the carrying mother. The law has never, till now, had to face this problem. There are inevitably going to be instances where the stark issue arises of who is the mother. In order to achieve some certainty in this situation it is our view that where a woman donates an egg for transfer to another the donation should be treated as absolute and that, like a male donor she should have no rights or duties with regard to any resulting child.

These proposals are all now implemented by the Human Fertilisation and Embryology Act 1990:

27. – (1) The woman who is carrying or has carried a child as a result of the placing in her of an embryo or of sperm and eggs, and no other woman, is to be treated as the mother of the child.

...

28. – (1) This section applies in the case of a child who is being or has been carried by a woman as a result of the placing in her of an embryo or of sperm and eggs or her artificial insemination.

(2) If –

(*a*) at the time of the placing in her of the embryo or the sperm and eggs or of her insemination, the woman was a party to a marriage, and

(*b*) the creation of the embryo carried by her was not brought about with the sperm of the other party to the marriage,

then, subject to subsection (5) below, the other party to the marriage shall be treated as the father of the child unless it is shown that he did not consent to the placing in her of the embryo or the sperm and eggs or to her insemination (as the case may be).

(3) If no man is treated, by virtue of subsection (2) above, as the father of the child but –

(*a*) the embryo or the sperm and eggs were placed in the woman, or she was artificially inseminated, in the course of treatment services provided for her and a man together by a person to whom a licence applies, and

(*b*) the creation of the embryo carried by her was not brought about with the sperm of that man,

then, subject to subsection (5) below, that man shall be treated as the father of the child.

(4) Where a person is treated as the father of the child by virtue of subsection (2) or (3) above, no other person is to be treated as the father of the child.

(5) Subsections (2) and (3) above do not apply –

(*a*) in relation to England and Wales and Northern Ireland, to any child who, by virtue of the rules of common law, is treated as the legitimate child of the parties to a marriage,

...

(6) Where –

(*a*) the sperm of a man who had given such consent as is required by paragraph 5 of Schedule 3 of this Act was used for a purpose for which such consent was required, or

(*b*) the sperm of a man, or any embryo the creation of which was brought about with his sperm, was used after his death,

he is not to be treated as the father of the child.

(7) The references in subsection (2) above to the parties to a marriage at the time there referred to –

(*a*) are to the parties to a marriage subsisting at that time, unless a judicial separation was then in force, but

(*b*) include the parties to a void marriage if either or both of them reasonably believed at that time that the marriage was valid; and for the purposes of this subsection it shall be presumed, unless the contrary is shown, that one of them reasonably believed at that time that the marriage was valid.

...

29. – (1) Where by virtue of section 27 or 28 of this Act a person is to be treated as the mother or father of a child, that person is to be treated in law as the mother or, as the case may be, father of the child for all purposes.

(2) Where by virtue of section 27 or 28 of this Act a person is not to be treated as the mother or father of the child, that person is to be treated in law as not being the mother or, as the case may be, father of the child for any purpose.

(3) Where subsection (1) or (2) above has effect, references to any relationship between two people in any enactment, deed or other instrument or document (whenever passed or made) are to be read accordingly.

(4) In relation to England and Wales and Northern Ireland, nothing in the provisions of section 27(1) or 28(2) to (4), read with this section, affects –

(*a*) the succession to any dignity or title of honour or renders any person capable of succeeding to or transmitting a right to succeed to any such dignity or title, or

(*b*) the devolution of any property limited (expressly or not) to devolve (as nearly as the law permits) along with any dignity or title of honour.

Questions

(i) How many arguments can you think of for making (*a*) the carrying mother, or (*b*) the genetic mother the mother in law?

(ii) Are the arguments for recognising 'social' rather than 'genetic' fatherhood stronger or weaker?

(iii) Does the widespread availability of donor insemination, whether by artificial or more conventional methods, on a 'do-it-yourself' basis, affect matters?

(iv) Why should not the same provisions apply when a husband accepts his wife's naturally born child by another man?

(v) If it is not right to allow unmarried couples to adopt (see p. 471, above), why is it right to extend 'social' fatherhood to unmarried relationships?

(vi) What if the husband or partner consented to *in vitro* fertilisation of the woman's egg by a donor's sperm and the resulting embryo was frozen for some years before implantation? Should he be able to change his mind?

(vii) As donors can never be fathers, what do you think of the re-introduction of a class of children who are inevitably 'fatherless by law'?

(viii) Do you think that all this is, or is not, in the best interests of the children?

The Law Commission (1979) also considered a further problem raised by their basic approach:

10.25 A problem which would arise whichever method were used for dealing with A.I.D. is whether or not legal provision should be made so that the child would be entitled to ascertain the facts about his parentage. Under the present law and practice the truth about the child's genetic identity may well be concealed from him if he has been registered as the legitimate child of the mother and her husband; in any event it is up to his mother and her husband to decide whether or not to disclose the fact that he is an A.I.D. child. Even if they do decide to tell him what they know, they will not usually be able to tell him who the donor was.
10.26 The argument in favour of a procedure giving the child the right to know the facts about his conception is essentially that a person has the right to know the truth about his origins. This principle is now accepted in adoption law, and an adopted child is entitled to discover the recorded facts about his natural parentage on attaining his majority. It therefore seems logical that an A.I.D. child should have the same right. On the other hand, if the only fact which the child is able to discover is that he is not genetically the offspring of his mother's husband, but of a donor wholly unknown not only to him but to his mother and her husband, it is difficult to see that this would be of any real advantage to him. To go further, by giving the child the right to know the identity of the donor would involve a major, and probably unacceptable, change of policy and practice.

The Warnock Committee's Report (1984) took much the same view:

4.19 It is the practice of some clinics in the USA to provide detailed descriptions of donors, and to permit couples to exercise choice as to the donor they would prefer. In the evidence there was some support for the use of such descriptions. It is argued that they would provide information and reassurance for the parents and, at a later date, for the child. They might also be of benefit to the donor, as an indication that he is valued for his own sake. A detailed description also offers some choice to the woman who is to have the child, and lack of such choice can be said to diminish the importance of the woman's right to choose the father of her child.
4.20 The contrary view, also expressed in the evidence, is that detailed donor profiles would introduce the donor as a person in his own right. It is also argued that the use of profiles devalues the child who may seem to be wanted only if certain specifications are met, and this may become a source of disappointment to the parents if their expectations are unfulfilled.
4.21 As a matter of principle we do not wish to encourage the possibility of prospective parents seeking donors with specific characteristics by the use of whose semen they hope to give birth to a particular type of child. We do not therefore want detailed descriptions of donors to be used as a basis for choice, but we believe that the couple should be given sufficient relevant information for their reassurance. This should include some basic facts about the donor, such as his ethnic group and his genetic birth. A small minority of the Inquiry, while supporting the principle set out above, and without compromising the principle of anonymity, consider that a gradual move towards making more detailed descriptions of the donor available to prospective parents, if requested, could be beneficial to the practice of AID, provided this was accompanied by appropriate counselling. **We recommend that on reaching the age of eighteen the child should have access to the basic information about the donor's ethnic origin and genetic health and that legislation be enacted to provide the right of access to this.** This legislation should not be retrospective.
4.22 We were agreed that there is a need to maintain the absolute anonymity of the donor, though we recognise that in privately arranged donation, for example between brothers, a different situation would of course apply; such domestic arrangements, however, fall outside any general regulation. Anonymity would give legal protection to the donor but it would also have the effect of minimising the invasion of the third party into the family. Without anonymity, men would, it is argued, be less likely to become donors ... We recognise that one consequence of this provision would be that AID children, even if informed about the circumstances of their conception would never be entitled to know the identity of their genetic fathers.

Questions

(i) What is the 'principle' which would prevent would-be parents from designing their own baby?
(ii) Should a white woman be able to ask for sperm from a black man?

(iii) Has this principle got anything to do with whether or not the child should later on know something about his genetic parents?

On the last point, the contrary view is succinctly put by Eric Blyth in his article, *Assisted reproduction: what's in it for the children?* (1990):

However, available evidence serves to undermine justification of both donor anonymity and secrecy. Research conducted in Sweden (Sverne, 1986), Australia (Daniels, 1989) and New Zealand (Daniels, 1987) indicates that sperm donors would be prepared to continue to donate in the absence of anonymity. A report prepared for the European Commission (Grover, 1989) recommends the removal, for an evaluated trial period, of donor anonymity.

Empirical evidence concerning AR families is restricted to those brought about following DI, but this clearly reveals both the disadvantages of maintaining secrecy and the benefits of openness. Secrecy, it appears, can only be sustained at high psychological cost to the parent(s). It deprives them of social support, whilst inadvertent disclosure remains a potentially lifelong fear. Children who found out about their genetic origins by less than direct means often expressed bitterness about their experiences (Snowden and Snowden, 1984).

Conversely, children whose parents had been open with them valued their parents' honesty, experienced few emotional consequences of being told, and fears about the specific effect of openness on the father-child relationship were not substantiated. Parents who were open felt that they no longer had to carry the burden and guilt of secrecy and were able to obtain support from others (Snowden and Snowden, 1984). The task of telling children at an early age about the nature of their conception could be considerably lightened by the development of story books similar to those currently available for adopted children.

The positive experiences of 'open' AR families are supported by the experience of both traditional adoption (McWhinnie, 1984) and more recent practices of 'open adoption' where contact between the child and birth-parent(s) is maintained (Fratter, 1989).

Nigel Bruce takes the argument a stage further in a later article, on *The importance of genetic knowledge* (1990):

Adopted young people now have the legal right in Britain, on reaching maturity, to see their original birth certificates. Those conceived by means of DI do not as yet enjoy this legal right. The main purpose of this article is to argue that, at least in the contemporary culture of Western Europe, such young people have strong moral claims to know their genetic identities; and that these moral claims should now be converted to legal rights.

In any civilised moral code, the truth is preferable to deception; without respect for truth, social institutions could not operate. Truth-telling is a basic legal, as well as moral, principle; the courts oblige us to swear or affirm to tell the truth, and they can punish us if we resort to deception.

In any civilised moral code, trustworthiness is more meritorious than unreliability. Sociologists say that society depends upon honesty and trustworthiness if it is to function properly. Psychologists say that trust is a basic component in the social development of the child.

In any civilised moral code, individual members of society have a *prima facie* right to personal autonomy. They must not be enslaved or imprisoned without trial; they must not be bought or sold; and they have legal rights not to be discriminated against or unjustly treated. In contemporary Western law, this personal autonomy also includes the right to personal information about themselves which may be held on official commercial or welfare files. John Harris (1985, p. 209) discussed personal autonomy in relation to medical ethics in *The Value of Life* and reached the conclusion that 'if one clear principle emerges from this discussion of autonomy, it is that there is an obligation to tell all to those who wish to be told'.

Linked with this claim to autonomy is the need which we all have to possess and develop a personal identity. There are two aspects of the term 'identity': the objective identity perceived by authority, which we possess; and the subjective identity which we develop within our 'selves' and which is the way we perceive and come to terms with our 'selves'.

The United Nations Declaration of the Rights of the Child (1959) referred only to the objective aspect of identity when it declared in Principle 3: 'The child shall be entitled from his birth to a name and a nationality'. The new United Nations Convention on the Rights of the Child (1989) contains a broader concept of identity in Articles 7 and 8. Article 7 requires that:

> '... the child shall be registered immediately after birth and shall have the right to a name, the right to acquire a nationality, and as far as possible the right to know and be cared for by his or her parents.'

Article 8 requires the States Parties:

> '... to respect the right of the child to preserve his or her identity, including nationality, name and family relations as recognised by law, without unlawful interference.'

The Convention also contains an Article 13 on freedom of expression and of information, which must surely include the right to obtain medical information about one's conception and birth. Even if the release of such information may be seen as an infringement of the privacy of the adults involved, it is now well established in the law of most developed countries that when there is a conflict between the interests of children and adults, the interests of the children should be paramount. Principle 2 of the UN Declaration of the Rights of the Child states that 'in the enactment of laws for this purpose, the best interests of the child shall be the paramount consideration'. Article 3 of the UN Convention contains the less definitive statement that:

> '... in all actions concerning children, whether undertaken by public or private social welfare institutions, courts of law, administrative authorities or legislative bodies, the best interests of the child shall be the primary consideration.'

Thus the claim that children should be legally as well as morally entitled to know the facts of their conception and birth rests equally on the argument that it is in their best interests to be treated with honesty and respect and on the relevance of the legal provisions prohibiting traffic in children, protecting their mental health and guaranteeing free access to information.

Questions

(i) Section 31 of the Human Fertilisation and Embryology Act 1990 leaves it to regulations to specify what information about the donor should be given to people born as a result of licensed treatment services (i.e. egg or sperm donation or *in vitro* fertilisation) when they grow up, but insists that information identifying the donor cannot be released unless regulations provided for this at the time of the donation: should such regulations be made now or should they wait until public opinion has developed further?
(ii) If they should be made now, should they provide (*a*) for identifying information to be released if the donor consents, or (*b*) for such information to be released even if he or she does not consent, and (*c*) what other information about the donor should be provided to his or her offspring?

The concern here is with the long-term welfare and interests of a person who has been born as a result of licensed treatment. But what about the welfare of children who *may be* born if treatment is given? Section 13(1) of the 1990 Act provides that it shall be a condition of every licence to provide treatment service under the Act that:

> **13.** – (5) A woman shall not be provided with treatment services unless account has been taken of the welfare of any child who may be born as a result of the treatment (including the need of that child for a father), and of any other child who may be affected by the birth.

The Lord Chancellor explained what this meant to the House of Lords (*Hansard* (H.L.), vol. 516, c.1097) thus:

> I think everyone would agree that it is important that children are born into a stable and loving environment and that the family is a concept whose health is fundamental to the health of society in general. A fundamental principle to our law about children, including the legislation which this House considered in such detail last Session and which became the Children Act 1989, is that the welfare of children is of paramount consideration. I think that it is, for these general reasons,

entirely right that the Bill should be amended to add that concept. It could be argued that the concept of the welfare of the child is very broad and indeed all-embracing. That I think is inevitable given the very wide range of factors which need to be taken into account when considering the future lives of children who may be born as a result of techniques to be licensed under the Bill. ...

... The amendment will place on clinicians in statutory form a responsibility which I believe most, if not all, of them already perform. I accept that that is an important responsibility and it may in particular cases be far from easy to discharge.

Among the factors which clinicians should take into account will be the material circumstances in which the child is likely to be brought up and also the stability and love which he or she is likely to enjoy. Such stability is clearly linked to the marital position of the woman and in particular whether a husband or long-term partner can play a full part in providing the child with a permanent family setting in the fullest sense of that term, including financial provision.

The House does not need to be reminded of the plight of childless people and the very strong and deeply felt emotions which those in that position experience. We may on the one hand pay the tribute which is due to the importance of ensuring that children are born into the family environment by specifically excluding from treatment women who are not married or have no stable partner to be involved in the decision about treatment and in counselling beforehand, but I wonder what will happen if we do that. Surely there is a risk that such women, driven by the very strong desire for a child, may turn elsewhere for treatment. I am advised that it is a relatively easy matter for AID to be carried out in clinically unsupervised conditions. It may be that the result of the amendment would be to encourage those few single woman who are infertile to seek unsuitable donors if we were to introduce such a restriction. Any children who may be born as a result of uncontrolled treatment are at risk of serious disease, including HIV infection.

On the other hand, if the law recognises that in a very small number of cases single women will come forward for treatment, it may be better to encourage them to seek clinical advice. With the child and welfare amendments we have just discussed there is a likelihood that through counselling and discussion with those responsible for licensed treatment they may be dissuaded from having children once they have fully considered the implications of the environment into which their child would be born for its future welfare.

Guidance on the welfare of the child is given by the Human Fertilisation and Embryology Authority in its *Code of Practice* (Second Revision, December 1995):

3.13 The condition applies only to centres with a treatment licence, but it covers any of the services they offer to assist conception or pregnancy, whether or not these require a licence. However, the degree of consideration necessary will be greater if the treatment is required to be licensed under the Act and particularly if it involves the use of donated gametes.
3.14 Centres should have clear written procedures to follow for assessing the welfare of the potential child and of any other child who may be affected. The HFE Act does not exclude any category of woman from being considered for treatment. Centres should take note in their procedures of the importance of a stable and supportive environment for any child produced as a result of treatment.

Factors to be considered

...

3.16 People seeking treatment are entitled to a fair and unprejudiced assessment of their situation and needs, which should be conducted with the skill and sensitivity appropriate to the delicacy of the case and the wishes and feelings of those involved.
3.17 Where people seek licensed treatment, centres should bear in mind the following factors:

a. their commitment to having and bringing up a child or children;
b. their ability to provide a stable and supportive environment for any child produced as a result of treatment;
c. their medical histories and the medical histories of their families;
d. their ages and likely future ability to look after or provide for a child's needs;
e. their ability to meet the needs of any child or children who may be born as a result of treatment, including the implications of any possible multiple births;
f. any risk of harm to the child or children who may be born, including the risk of inherited disorders, problems during pregnancy and of neglect or abuse; and
g. the effect of a new baby or babies upon any existing child of the family.

3.18 Where people seek treatment using donated gametes, centres should also take the following factors into account:

a. a child's potential need to know about their origins and whether or not the prospective parents are prepared for the questions which may arise while the child is growing up;
b. the possible attitudes of other members of the family towards the child, and towards their status in the family;
c. the implications for the welfare of the child if the donor is personally known within the child's family and social circle; and
d. any possibility known to the centre of a dispute about the legal fatherhood of the child ...

3.19 Further factors will require consideration in the following cases:

a. where the child will have no legal father. Centres are required to have regard to the child's need for a father and should pay particular attention to the prospective mother's ability to meet the child's needs throughout their childhood. Where appropriate, centres should consider particularly whether there is anyone else within the prospective mother's family and social circle willing and able to share the responsibility for meeting those needs, and for bringing up, maintaining and caring for the child.
b. where it is the intention that the child will not be brought up by the carrying mother. In this case, centres should bear in mind that *either* the carrying mother and in certain circumstances her husband or partner, *or* the commissioning parents may become the child's legal parents. Centres should therefore consider the factors listed in paragraphs 3.17 and 3.18 as applicable in relation to all those involved, and any risk of disruption to the child's early care and upbringing should there be a dispute between them. Centres should also take into account the effect of the proposed arrangement on any child of the carrying mother's family as well as its effect on any child of the commissioning parents' family.

Questions

(i) Can you improve upon this? Would it also be useful in adoption placements?
(ii) What is the case for imposing these requirements upon couples who need IVF or other assistance but can use their own eggs and sperm?
(iii) Not all candidates for assisted reproduction are infertile: do you think that it should be available to a single, virgin or lesbian woman or to a woman who would like another child so that her first is not brought up alone?
(iv) Should it be available to a woman who is HIV positive?
(v) What difference, if any, does it make that treatment is more readily available for people who can pay for it? How rigorously do you think that the Code will be applied (*a*) in an NHS hospital and (*b*) in a private clinic?
(vi) Blyth (1990) points out that 'the extent to which welfare principles might apply to children in the field of AR is questionable ... Firstly, it is hardly valid to claim that anyone would have been better off not having been born in the first place. Secondly, the implication that alternatives exist from which a choice may be made does not hold'. Do you agree?

Blyth (1990) also has some interesting observations about controlling access to assisted reproduction which might be applied in a wider context:

... the Warnock Committee itself recognised the problems of restricting access to AR services on social grounds and that it would not be possible to 'draw up comprehensive (social) criteria that would be sensitive to the circumstances of every case' (1984). Such reservations are justified given the discriminatory criteria currently employed by some AR practitioners (Snowden and Mitchell, 1981). That intentions to be more open about receipt of AR should be perceived as a potential contra-indication for treatment is an extreme but iniquitous example (Braidwood, 1989; Saunders, 1980).

Although the use of a screening process has been justified by reference to the potential psychopathology of infertile people, recent studies indicate a lack of support for the existence of a psychogenic basis to infertility. Similarly, the extent to which infertility inevitably represents a 'psychic trauma' can be challenged (e.g. Edelmann and Connolly, 1986).

Conventional assumptions about the 'ideal' environment for child-rearing, based on theological doctrine and the stereotype of the contemporary, white, westernised middle class nuclear family, result in the denial of parental aspirations to those who do not conform to the norm. Specifically, the claims to AR services by single women and lesbians are rejected as a 'threat to normal family life' by failing to provide children with a 'nurturing father-figure' (Council for Science and Society, 1984). Similarly the Warnock Committee believed that it would be 'morally wrong' for the state to deliberately seek to create single parent families.

Golombok *et al.* (1983), who have provided empirical evidence about both single parent and lesbian families, complain that the debate has been characterised by 'dogma rather than argument'. Their own research failed to substantiate generally held stereotypes about lesbian families, at the same time concluding that the deprivations children in both single parent and lesbian households did experience were essentially the result of societal prejudice.

In a recent literature review evaluating the impact of a variety of family forms on children's psychological development, Schaffer (1988, p. 95) concluded there was:

> '... no indication that departures from the conventional norm of family structures are necessarily harmful to children; psychologically healthy personalities can develop in the context of a great variety of social groupings.'

Evidence to support the validity of selection criteria is scarce. There has been little follow-up of children born following AR or their families or of those who have been rejected for treatment (Snowden and Snowden, 1984). Outcomes of adoption might be seen to offer some guidance, although these are not without their difficulties. ...

Criteria for successful child care placements are also somewhat elusive, although some studies have identified certain factors contributing to successful adoption placements: parental attitudes and the adopted child's perception of being fully accepted and integrated into family life, although the mechanics of telling and talking about adoption appear not to be significantly associated with outcome (Smith, 1984). Triseliotis' recent review of studies of foster placements (1989) identifies certain factors associated with *unsuccessful* outcomes which appear to be of relevance to AR:

(i) the child's ignorance about her or his origins;
(ii) the carer's ambivalence/hostility towards genetic parents.

There is considerable evidence of the limitations on the ability to successfully predict 'good parents' and indeed define with any degree of confidence what characteristics one should even be looking for, let alone try and find. Smith (1984) catalogues the specific problems associated with the implementation of selection criteria in adoption practice:

(i) restrictions on the time available for this process limit the depth of investigation;
(ii) applicants have a lot at stake and are out to impress;
(iii) social workers' skills in assessment are not particularly sophisticated;
(iv) there are few generally accepted assessment techniques for determining who will make a good or bad parent, or clear cut predictors of potential for successful parenthood.

Some adoption workers have explicitly abandoned conventional practices of 'matching' and 'assessment' on the grounds that:

> '... there is no evidence to indicate that social workers have any proven expertise in the prediction of which adoptive parents are likely to provide a continuing, stable relationship and a secure family environment for an adopted child (Howell and Ryburn, 1987, p. 38)'

In their place they have developed practice which focuses on *preparation and education* designed to help applicants decide if adoption is for them and provide the necessary information and support. Similar practices could well be developed in AR.

Paragraph 3.19b of the HFEA Code refers to surrogacy, which may involve either sperm donation alone, or egg and sperm donation. The Warnock Committee's Report (1984) summarised the arguments like this:

Arguments against surrogacy

8.10 There are strongly held objections to the concept of surrogacy, and it seems from the evidence submitted to us that the weight of public opinion is against the practice. The objections turn essentially on the view that to introduce a third party into the process of procreation which should be confined to the loving partnership between two people, is an attack on the value of the marital relationship. Further, the intrusion is worse than in the case of AID, since the contribution of the carrying mother is greater, more intimate and personal, than the contribution of a semen donor. It is also argued that it is inconsistent with human dignity that a woman should use her uterus for financial profit and treat it as an incubator for someone else's child. The objection is not diminished, indeed it is strengthened, where the woman entered an agreement to conceive a child, with the sole purpose of handing the child over to the commissioning couple after birth.

8.11 Again, it is argued that the relationship between mother and child is itself distorted by surrogacy. For in such an arrangement a woman deliberately allows herself to become pregnant with the intention of giving up the child to which she will give birth, and this is the wrong way to approach pregnancy. It is also potentially damaging to the child, whose bonds with the carrying mother, regardless of genetic connections, are held to be strong, and whose welfare must be considered to be of paramount importance. Further it is felt that a surrogacy agreement is degrading to the child who is to be the outcome of it, since, for all practical purposes, the child will have been bought for money.

8.12 It is also argued that since there are some risks attached to pregnancy, no woman ought to be asked to undertake pregnancy for another, in order to earn money. Nor, it is argued should a woman be forced by legal sanctions to part with a child, to which she has recently given birth, against her will.

Arguments for surrogacy

8.13 If infertility is a condition which should, where possible, be remedied it is argued that surrogacy must not be ruled out, since it offers to some couples their only chance of having a child genetically related to one or both of them. In particular, it may well be the only way that the husband of an infertile woman can have a child. Moreover, the bearing of a child for another can be seen, not as an undertaking that trivialises or commercialises pregnancy, but, on the contrary, as a deliberate and thoughtful act of generosity on the part of one woman to another. If there are risks attached to pregnancy, then the generosity is all the greater.

8.14 There is no reason, it is argued, to suppose that carrying mothers will enter into agreements lightly, and they have a perfect right to enter into such agreements if they so wish, just as they have a right to use their own bodies in other ways, according to their own decision. Where arguments are genuinely voluntary, there can be no question of exploitation, nor does the fact that surrogates will be paid for their pregnancy of itself entail exploitation of either party to the agreement.

8.15 As for intrusion into the marriage relationship, it is argued that those who feel strongly about this need not seek such treatment, but they should not seek to prevent others from having access to it.

8.16 On the question of bonding, it is argued that as very little is actually known about the extent to which bonding occurs when the child is *in utero*, no great claims should be made in this respect. In any case the breaking of such bonds, even if less than ideal, is not held to be an overriding argument against placing a child for adoption, where the mother wants this.

The Committee were divided between those who wanted an almost complete ban on the practice and those who wanted only profit-making agencies banned. The Surrogacy Arrangements Act 1985 banned commercial agencies and advertising of and for surrogacy services. The Human Fertilisation and Embryology Act 1990 inserted a further provision making all surrogacy arrangements unenforceable (and see *A v C* (1978) [1985] FLR 445). The HFEA *Code of Practice* (1995) advises (as does the British Medical Association, 1996) that:

3.20 The application of assisted conception techniques to initiate a surrogate pregnancy should only be considered where it is physically impossible or highly undesirable for medical reasons for the commissioning mother to carry the child.

However, the 1990 Act provides a convenient method of avoiding its own rules about parentage and allowing the commissioning parents to take over:

30. – (1) The court may make an order providing for a child to be treated in law as the child of the parties to a marriage (referred to in this section as 'the husband' and 'the wife') if –

(*a*) the child has been carried by a woman other than the wife as the result of the placing in her of an embryo or sperm and eggs or her artificial insemination,
(*b*) the gametes of the husband or the wife, or both, were used to bring about the creation of the embryo, and
(*c*) the conditions in subsections (2) to (7) below are satisfied.

(2) The husband and the wife must apply for the order within six months of the birth of the child or, in the case of a child born before the coming into force of this Act, within six months of such coming into force.

(3) At the time of the application and of the making of the order –
(*a*) the child's home must be with the husband and wife, and
(*b*) the husband or the wife, of both of them, must be domiciled in a part of the United Kingdom or in the Channel Islands or the Isle of Man.

(4) At the time of the making of the order both the husband and the wife must have attained the age of eighteen.

(5) The court must be satisfied that both the father of the child (including a person who is the father by virtue of section 28 of this Act), where he is not the husband, and the woman who carried the child have freely, and with full understanding of what is involved, agreed unconditionally to the making of the order.

(6) Subsection (5) above does not require the agreement of a person who cannot be found or is incapable of giving agreement and the agreement of the woman who carried the child is ineffective for the purposes of that subsection if given by her less than six weeks after the child's birth.

(7) The court must be satisfied that no money or other benefit (other than for expenses reasonably incurred) has been given or received by the husband or the wife for or in consideration of –
(*a*) the making of the order,
(*b*) any agreement required by subsection (5) above,
(*c*) the handing over of the child to the husband or the wife, or
(*d*) the making of any arrangements with a view to the making of the order,
unless authorised by the court.

...

(9) Regulations may provide –
(*a*) for any provision of the enactments about adoption to have effect, with such modifications (if any) as may be specified in the regulations, in relation to orders under this section, and applications for such orders, as it has effect in relation to adoption, and applications for adoption orders, and
(*b*) for references in any enactment to adoption, an adopted child or an adoptive relationship to be read (respectively) as references to the effect of an order under this section, a child to whom such an order applies and a relationship arising by virtue of the enactments about adoption, as applied by the regulations, and for similar expressions in connection with adoption to be read accordingly.
and the regulations may include such incidental or supplemental provision as appears to the Secretary of State necessary or desirable in consequence of any provision made by virtue of paragraph (*a*) or (*b*) above.

Questions

(i) In *A v C* (1978) [1985] FLR 445, Ormrod LJ referred to a surrogacy arrangement (from which the mother had repented) as a 'quite bizarre and unnatural arrangement' and Cumming-Bruce J called it a 'kind of baby-farming operation of a wholly distasteful and lamentable kind': do you agree?
(ii) How much of the law relating to adoption would you apply to the procedure under s. 30?
(iii) (*a*) In 1987, Mrs Pat Anthony gave birth to triplets. Doctors in South Africa had implanted into her eggs from her daughter Karen which had been fertilised by Karen's husband's sperm. Mrs Anthony therefore became the world's first surrogate grandmother (see Reid, 1988). Should treatment be provided in such a case? (*b*) In 1989, an English husband, infertile as a result

of mumps, was told that it was 'ethically impossible' for his wife to be artificially inseminated with his brother's sperm. Can you think what the ethical objection might be? (*c*) How relevant are the Houghton Committee's doubts (p. 656, below) about adoption by relatives?
(iv) Why do we not feel able to allow the carrying mother to decide what she finds 'inconsistent with [her] human dignity'?

5 Illegitimate children or illegitimate parents?

For centuries the law tried, with varying success, to deter parents from having children outside marriage. Deterrence began in the medieval ecclesiastical courts, but the secular authorities took a hand once it appeared that failures in spiritual control were likely to cost the community money. The following examples are offered by Peter Laslett in *The World We Have Lost* (1971):

Anyone who committed or tried to commit a sexual act with anyone not his spouse, whether or not conception took place, ran the risk of a summons to the archdeacon's court – the lowest in the hierarchy of spiritual courts – a fine, and then penance in church at service time, or in the market place. If a person about whom a *fame of incontinency* had got abroad (that is a suspicion of a sexual escapade) ignored the summons or refused the punishment, then excommunication followed. This meant exile from the most important of all social activities, isolation within the community.

The lay courts and lay authority could be invoked for the more serious offences, and this often happened for the begetting of bastards. ...

If the records of the church courts are filled with notices of sexual incontinence, those of the magistrates courts are studded with measures taken in punishment of unmarried mothers, and sometimes of unmarried fathers too, with provision for the upkeep of the child:

> 'Jane Sotworth of Wrightington, spinster, swears that Richard Garstange of Fazarkerley, husbandman, is the father of Alice, her bastard daughter. She is to have charge of the child for two years, provided she does not beg, and Richard is then to take charge until it is twelve years old. He shall give Jane a cow and 6s. in money. Both he and she shall this day be whipped in Ormeskirke.'

So ordered the Lancashire justices at the Ormskirk Sessions on Monday, 27 April 1601, though the language they used was Latin and lengthier. At Manchester, in 1604, they went so far as to require that Thomas Byrom, gentleman, should maintain a bastard he had begotten on a widow, and be whipped too. On 10 October 1604, he was whipped in Manchester market place. ...

The legal warrant for Thomas Byrom's punishment is explained by Elisofon in *A Historical and Comparative Study of Bastardy* (1973):

The year 1576 was especially important in relation to rights of the bastard child; for this was the first time in English history that a duty of support was imposed upon the parents of an illegitimate child. The statute passed by Parliament read, in part:

> 'Concerning bastards begotten and born out of lawful matrimony (an offence against God's law and man's law), the said bastard being now left to be at the charge of the parish where they be born, to the great burden of the same parish, and in defrauding of the relief of the impotent and aged true poor of the same parish, and to the evil example and encouragement of lewd life; it is ordained and enacted that two justices of the peace, upon examination of the cause and circumstances, shall and may by their discretion take order as well for the *punishment of the mother and reputed father* of such bastard child, as also for the better relief of every such parish in part or in all, and shall make likewise by like discretion, take order for the keeping of every such bastard child, *by charging such mother or reputed father with payment of money weekly or other substentation for the relief of such child* and such ways as they think covenant. And if ... the reputed mother and father shall not observe and perform the order, then the party making the default in not performing the order, be committed to the common gayle.' (emphasis added) ...

Question

Which do you suppose was the more serious – the offence against God's law or burden of the parish?

The deterrent approach was thus carried on through the poor law. Its more recent history is taken up by Sir Morris Finer and Professor O.R. McGregor, in *A History of the Obligation to Maintain*, printed as an appendix to the Report of the Committee on One-Parent Families (1974). They begin with the Report of the Royal Commissioners on the Poor Laws which led to the 'new' poor law of 1834:

56. In the case of such a mother, the report did not recommend any change in the methods of relief, but it urged the repeal of all legislation which punished or charged the putative father of a bastard who should become, the Commissioners said:

> 'what Providence appears to have ordained that it should be, a burden on its mother, and, where she cannot maintain it, on her parents. The shame of the offence will not be destroyed by its being the means of income and marriage, and we trust that as soon as it has become both burthensome and disgraceful, it will become as rare as it is among those classes in this country who are above parish relief. ... If we are right in believing the penalties inflicted by nature to be sufficient, it is needless to urge further objections to any legal punishment. ... In affirming the inefficiency of human legislation to enforce the restraints placed on licentiousness by Providence, we have implied our belief that all punishment of the supposed father is useless.'

Behind this extreme statement of the providential foundations of the double standard of sexual morality lay the experience of abuses under the old bastardy laws. Under these, if a single woman declared herself pregnant and charged a man with being responsible, the overseers of the poor or any substantial householder could apply to any justice of the peace for a committal warrant. This would issue unless the accused man could give security to indemnify the parish or to enter into a recognisance to appear at Quarter Sessions and to perform any order which might there be made. The Commissioners thought that poor men were at the mercy of blackmail and perjury by unscrupulous women, and that the bastardy laws promoted social demoralisation.

57. The bastardy clauses of the Act of 1834 were in line with the opinions of the Poor Law Commissioners. ...

However, not all sections of society took the same view of the problem:

59. With the dislike of Tories for the centralising tendency of Benthamite administrative reforms, went also a different view of sexual morality and obligation. The urban Victorians inherited a strict moral code. They got it from evangelical religious teachers who imposed it on the new middle class, the executive agents of the expanding industrial economy; and they planted it, as far as they could, on their lower orders. Their bookshelves carried the weight of such typical products of the evangelical outlook as Thomas Bowdler's *The Family Shakespeare, In which nothing is added to the Text; but those Words and Expressions are omitted which cannot with Propriety be read aloud in a Family.* These ten volumes reached a sixth edition in 1831, six years before the adolescent Victoria came under the influence of her first prime minister, a cultivated Whig who had been heard to respond to an evangelical sermon with the observation that 'things are coming to a pretty pass when religion is allowed to interfere with private life'. 'That d – d morality' which disturbed Lord Melbourne did not result from religious enthusiasm only. Differing provisions for the inheritance of family property were an important factor, too. The sexual waywardness of the territorial aristocracy did not endanger the integrity or succession of estates which were regulated by primogeniture and entail. Countless children of the mist played happily in Whig and Tory nurseries where they presented no threat to the property or interest of heirs. But middle class families handled their accumulating industrial wealth within a system of partible inheritance which demanded a more severe morality imposing higher standards upon women than upon men. An adulterous wife might be the means of planting a fraudulent claimant upon its property in the heart of her family; to avoid this ultimate catastrophe, middle class women were required to observe an inviolable rule of chastity. Just as the new poor law of 1834 represented a political triumph for philosophic radicalism by establishing an effective means of policing poverty, so it imposed middle class morality upon pauper women by seeking to police their sexual virtue.

60. Despite protests, the Poor Law Commissioners remained stout, for a time, in their insistence that to afford the mother of an illegitimate child a direct claim against the putative father for its maintenance would, by extending the rewards of matrimony to the unqualified and undeserving, tend to the destruction of the institution. In their sixth annual report in 1840, they printed with approval a report on the law of bastardy submitted to them by Sir Edmund Head, an Assistant Commissioner. ...

> '... We were told by many eminent members of the legislature that, to afford a woman who had once broken the marriage tie an opportunity of even seeing her children for a few minutes was an encroachment on the privileges of wives who had remained faithful, and in this way a direct encouragement to immorality. If this be so, what shall we say to the infringement of the exclusive privileges of the married state implied by conferring on the mother of a bastard that claim for its support from a definite father, which it is one great object of matrimony to secure? Does not the principle that anything short of marriage is sufficient to fix the paternity of the child involve in itself a direct attack on that institution?'

Against such arguments were set the findings of the Commissioners of Inquiry for South Wales who were appointed to investigate the Rebecca Riots. They reported in 1844 that the bastardy laws had:

> 'altogether failed of the effect which sanguine persons calculated they might produce on the caution or moral feelings of the weaker sex. (There was little prostitution in South Wales but) subsequent marriage – and that not a forced one – ... almost invariably wiped out the light reproach which public opinion attached to a previous breach of chastity. (Now subsequent marriage was becoming rarer and women were exposed to) all the temptations of a life of vice (while) the man evades or defies the law, with a confidence and effrontery which has outraged the moral feeling of the people to a degree that can hardly be described.'

61. In the end, the Poor Law Commissioners gave ground and recommended in their tenth annual report that a mother should be given a civil action for maintenance against the putative father of her child. The Poor Law Amendment Act 1844 made a complete change by taking bastardy proceedings out of the hands of the poor law authorities and turning them into a civil matter between the parents. ...

62. The Poor Law Amendment Act 1868 restored to the parish the power to recover from the putative father the cost of maintenance of a bastard child by providing that, where a woman who had obtained an order against the father of her child herself became a charge of the parish, the justices might order the payments to be made to the relieving officer. ...

64. If the history of the legal rules which determine responsibility for the maintenance of bastards and their mothers is complicated, their treatment under the poor law was entirely straightforward. The mother was regarded as an able-bodied woman of demonstrated immorality, and relief was accordingly provided on a strictly deterrent basis in the workhouse. Mothers and babies were separated after the confinement and initial period of nursing. Most unmarried mothers could only use the workhouse as an immediate refuge during childbirth, after which they abandoned their children within it. Such unfortunates shared the fate of orphans and other deserted children who suffered deprivation as pauper children. But girls suffered worse than boys, because the workhouse served as a manufactory of prostitutes. Frances Power Cobbe's observation in 1865 remained true throughout the nineteenth century:

> 'The case of the girls is far worse than of the boys, as all the conditions of workhouse management fall with peculiar evil on their natures. ... Among all the endless paradoxes of female treatment, one of the worst and most absurd is that which, while eternally proclaiming "home" to be the only sphere of a woman, systematically educates all female children of the State, without attempting to give them even an idea of what a home might be. ... '

Workhouse children gained in the later decades of the nineteenth century from such advances in institutional care as cottage homes, sheltered homes and boarding out. But the need for change was only just beginning to be recognised in the early years of this century. ...

Question

Does the difference in patterns of inheritance between the landed aristocracy and the commercial bourgeoisie strike you as a plausible explanation for the difference in their attitudes to illegitimacy?

The primacy of succession is reflected in the view of Sir William Blackstone, in his *Commentaries on the Laws of England* (1765):

The incapacity of a bastard consists principally in this, that he cannot be heir to any one, neither can he have heirs, but of his own body; for, being *nullius filius*, he is therefore of kin to nobody, and has no ancestor from whom any inheritable blood can be derived. A bastard was also, in strictness, incapable of holy orders; and, though that were dispensed with, yet he was utterly disqualified from holding any dignity in the church: but this doctrine seems now obsolete; and in all other respects, there is no distinction between a bastard and another man. And really any other distinction, but that of not inheriting, which civil policy renders necessary, would, with regard to the innocent offspring of his parents' crimes, be odious, unjust, and cruel to the last degree.

Thus, if inheritance has been the principal explanation for our laws of both marriage and legitimacy, it has little importance in the modern world. The expectations which a child may have of his parents were spelt out by the Court of Appeal when allowing the appeal of a millionaire father against an order that, on divorce, he should settle £25,000 on each of his children:

Lord Lilford v Glynn
[1979] 1 All ER 441, [1979] 1 WLR 78, Court of Appeal

Orr LJ: ... a father, even the richest father, ought not to be regarded as under 'financial obligations or responsibilities' to provide funds for the purposes of such settlement as are envisaged in this case on children who are under no disability and whose maintenance and education are secure. ...

There is not in this context, one rule for millionaires and another for less wealthy fathers, and in our judgment there was no means of judging whether the father, if the marriage had continued, would or would not have made a settlement in favour of the daughters. He might or he might not, and there was no reason to suppose that the first course was more likely than the other in view of the fact that he had already made a substantial settlement for the daughters in the form of the trust deed.

Similarly, under the Inheritance (Provision for Family and Dependants) Act 1975 (p. 190, above) children of the deceased can only upset the provisions of his will or the rules of intestacy if these fail to make 'such financial provision as it would be reasonable in all the circumstances of the case for the applicant to receive for his maintenance' (s. 1(2)(*b*)). The leading case is *Re Coventry* [1980] Ch 461 (doubting *Re Christie* [1979] Ch 168 and applied in *Re Dennis* [1981] 2 All ER 140). The Court of Appeal upheld the decision of Oliver J that a 46 year old son was not entitled to a share in his father's estate, even though they had shared a house for 19 years, which the son would now have to leave, while the deceased and his widow (who was entitled to the whole estate under the rules of intestacy) had lived apart. Buckley LJ said this:

His approach was that where an applicant is an adult male in employment, and so capable of earning his own living, some special circumstance is required to make a failure on the part of the deceased to make some financial provision for the applicant unreasonable. ...

...

Later on he said:

> 'It seems to me, however, that in regarding the circumstances and in applying the guidelines set out in s. 3, it always has to be borne in mind that the 1975 Act, so far as it relates to applicants other than spouses, is an Act whose purpose is limited to the provision of reasonable maintenance. It is not the purpose of the Act to provide legacies or rewards for meritorious conduct. Subject to the court's powers under the 1975 Act and to fiscal demands, an Englishman still remains at liberty at his death to dispose of his own property in whatever way he pleases or, if he chooses to do so, to leave that disposition to be regulated by the laws of intestate succession. In order to enable the court to interfere with and reform those dispositions it must, in my judgment, be shown, not that the deceased acted unreasonably, but that, looked at objectively, his disposition or lack of disposition produces an unreasonable result in that it does not make any or any greater provision for the applicant and that means, in the case of an applicant other than a spouse, for that applicant's maintenance.'

In my judgment the judge there correctly states the problem, and I think he states the appropriate test to be applied.

The view that children are entitled to be maintained but not necessarily to inherit may help to explain why the *Report of the Committee on the Law of Succession in Relation to Illegitimate Persons* (the Russell Report, 1966) took a simple line on intestate succession to both mother and father:

19. At the root of any suggestion for the improvement of the lot of bastards in relation to the laws of succession to property is, of course, the fact that in one sense they start level with legitimate children, in that no child is created of its own volition. Whatever may be said of the parents, the bastard is innocent of any wrongdoing. To allot to him an inferior, or indeed unrecognised, status in succession is to punish him for a wrong of which he was not guilty.

All children do not start level, however, if they have not had what the modern world thinks is due to every child – proper attention to their physical, emotional and intellectual needs throughout childhood. The differences at that time between children born in and out of wedlock were summarised thus in the Law Commission's Working Paper on *Illegitimacy* (1979):

Discrimination directly affecting the illegitimate child

2.10 It may be that the biggest discrimination suffered by a person born out of wedlock is the legal characterisation of him as 'illegitimate': we deal with the perpetuation of this label in Part III of this paper. The main practical areas in which there is legal discrimination are:

(i) the maintenance of an illegitimate child is subject to the restrictions affecting the jurisdiction of the magistrates' courts: no lump sum exceeding £500 can be awarded and financial provision cannot be secured;

(ii) although an illegitimate child can now inherit on the intestacy of either of his parents, he cannot take on the death intestate of any remoter ascendant or any collateral relation. In effect, therefore, he is treated as having no grandparents, brothers or sisters;

(iii) despite recent reforms, an illegitimate child cannot succeed as heir to an entailed interest or succeed to a title of honour; and

(iv) an illegitimate child if born outside the United Kingdom is not entitled as of right to United Kingdom citizenship even if both his parents are United Kingdom citizens.[1]

Discrimination affecting the father of an illegitimate child

2.11 From a strictly legal point of view, the father of an illegitimate child is today probably at a greater disadvantage than the child himself; and while many fathers may take little or no interest in their children born out of wedlock, other fathers who have lived with the mothers for perhaps many years are clearly affected by the discrimination. This discrimination takes a number of different forms:

---

1. Under the British Nationality Act 1981, s. 50(9), an illegitimate child may claim citizenship through his mother but not through his father.

(i) the father has no automatic rights of guardianship, custody or access, even where an affiliation order has been made against him. Any such rights are obtainable by him only by court order or, if the mother has died, under the mother's will. The basic principle is set out in section 85(7) of the Children Act 1975: 'Except as otherwise provided by or under any enactment, while the mother of an illegitimate child is living she has the parental rights and duties exclusively'.

(ii) Even if the father is awarded custody, he (unlike the father of a legitimate child) cannot obtain maintenance for the child from the mother, whatever her means.

(iii) The father's agreement to the child's adoption is not required unless he has already been granted custody or has become the child's guardian by court order or by appointment under the mother's will. His position is therefore different from that of the mother, and of both parents of a legitimate child, whose agreement is required.

(iv) The father's consent to a change of the child's name is not required unless he has become the legal guardian of the child by court order or under the mother's will.

(v) The father's consent to the marriage of the child during the child's minority is not required unless he has been granted custody of the child or has become the child's guardian under the mother's will.

(vi) There is no legal procedure by which the father can establish his paternity without the consent of the child's mother.

Procedural discrimination

2.12 There are, in addition, a number of procedural matters which point to the illegitimate child as 'different':

(i) Maintenance for an illegitimate child involves the institution by the mother of a special form of proceedings (affiliation proceedings) which many people regard as involving a stigma.

(ii) The mother cannot obtain maintenance for the child unless she is a 'single woman' at the date of the application for maintenance, or was so at the date of the child's birth. The phrase 'single woman' includes not only an unmarried woman (spinster, widow or divorcee) but also a married woman who is living apart from her husband and who has lost the right at common law to be maintained by him.

(iii) Only the magistrates' court has jurisdiction in affiliation proceedings, whereas the High Court, the county court and the magistrates' court all have jurisdiction in cases where maintenance is sought for legitimate children.

(iv) Subject to certain exceptions, an application for maintenance by way of affiliation proceedings must be made within three years of the child's birth. There is no such time limit as respects legitimate children.

(v) There is a special rule of evidence applicable to affiliation proceedings: if the mother gives evidence, her evidence must be corroborated.

(vi) There is a special form of appeal from a magistrates' court in affiliation proceedings.

Questions

(i) Why, do you suppose, did the Law Commission choose the word 'discrimination' instead of, for example, 'distinction'?

(ii) Should the lack of an automatic relationship with the father be classified as 'discrimination affecting the father' or 'discrimination affecting the child' or both?

(iii) Why are the matters described in paragraph 2.12 not labelled discrimination against the mother?

The Law Commission went on to survey the basic question of discrimination in this way:

3.2 ... It is not now easy to put convincing arguments in favour of discrimination, because such arguments would logically justify a return to the strict common law position, and it is difficult to believe that there would be any substantial support for turning the clock back in this way. Nevertheless, arguments in favour of preserving the principle of discrimination may still be used by those who are prepared reluctantly to accept, as an accomplished fact, the changes which have already been made towards improving the legal status of the illegitimate child, but think that no further reform should be made. …

3.3 First, it is said that the legal distinction between 'legitimacy' and 'illegitimacy' reflects social realities. This was certainly true at one time. The birth of an illegitimate child was regarded as bringing disgrace not only on the mother but also on her immediate family. The child could no more expect to be recognised as a member of the family and be received into the family home than he could expect to inherit family property. He was not a real member of the family group. However, although there may still be cases where the illegitimate child is in this position, the evidence suggests that a significant and increasing proportion of all illegitimate children born each year are recognised by both their parents, at least if the parents have a relationship of some stability. …

3.4 Secondly, it is said that the distinction serves to uphold moral standards and also to support the institution of marriage. In relation to the preservation of moral standards, it is difficult to say how far the fear of producing illegitimate children influenced sexual behaviour in the past; since the risk of an unwanted pregnancy can now usually be avoided by contraceptive measures it seems improbable that such fears still influence sexual behaviour to any substantial extent. Support for the institution of marriage is of course of great importance, especially in the present context, because a married relationship between parents should in principle be more stable than an unmarried one, so creating a better environment for the child's upbringing. However, many marriages are not stable, and statistically it seems that marriages entered into primarily for the purpose of ensuring that an expected child is not born illegitimate are especially at risk. …

3.5 The third argument in favour of preserving discriminatory treatment asserts that the legal relationship between the child's parents should be relevant in determining the child's legal status: that as the legal relationship of marriage results in legitimate status for the child, so a relationship which does not accord with the norm should not result in normal status for the child. On this view it is regarded as significant not only that a legitimate child is the issue of a legally recognised union, the incidents of which are fixed by law and which can only be dissolved by formal proceedings but also that marriage, at least in its inception, is intended to be permanent. The relationship of an illegitimate child's parents, on the other hand, is not in general legally recognised and may never have been intended to be more than transient. However this argument is based on the premise that a child's status ought to be affected by that of his parents. This is the proposition which we do not accept; it is, after all, the child's status, and the nature of the relationship between his parents need not and should not affect this.

Two further reasons for reform were put forward in the Scottish Law Commission's Consultative Memorandum on *Illegitimacy* (1982):

1.15 Reform would be in line with this country's treaty obligations. The United Kingdom has ratified the European Convention on the Legal Status of Children born out of Wedlock. The preamble to this Convention notes that in a great number of member States of the Council of Europe efforts have been, or are being, made to improve the legal status of children born out of wedlock by reducing the differences between their legal status and that of children born in wedlock which are to their legal or social disadvantage. It records that the signatory States believe that the situation of children born out of wedlock should be improved and that the formulation of certain common rules concerning their legal status would assist this objective. The Convention then binds each Contracting Party to ensure the conformity of its law with the provisions of the Convention. A State is, however, allowed to make not more than three reservations. The present law of Scotland [and England] does not conform to two provisions of the Convention and the United Kingdom accordingly reserved the right not to apply, or not to apply fully, those provisions in relation to Scotland.[2] The policy of the Convention is to allow 'progressive stages for those States which consider themselves unable to adopt immediately' all of its rules and reservations are valid for only five years at a time. It is clear that the general policy of the Convention is the reduction of legal discrimination against illegitimate children and that the United Kingdom's position would be more in accord with that policy if the reservations were unnecessary.

---

2. The provisions in question are: – Art. 6(2) 'Where a legal obligation to maintain a child born in wedlock falls on certain members of the family of the father or mother, this obligation shall also apply for the benefit of a child born out of wedlock.'
Art. 9 'A child born out of wedlock shall have the same right of succession in the estate of its father and its mother and of a member of its father's or mother's family, as if it had been born in wedlock.'

1.16 The United Kingdom is also a party to the European Convention on Human Rights. It has been held in the case of *Marckx v Kingdom of Belgium* that the provisions of Belgian law prohibiting an illegitimate child from inheriting from his close maternal relatives on their intestacy contravened Article 8 [see p. 714, below] and that these different inheritance rights of legitimate and illegitimate children lacked objective and reasonable justification. In Scots law, as in Belgian 1aw, an illegitimate child has no such inheritance rights, so that changes are necessary to prevent the continuing breach of Article 8 by the United Kingdom.

Having concluded that there was no justification for retaining the status quo, the English Law Commission (1979) went on to discuss two possible models for reform:

(b) First model for reform: abolition of adverse legal consequences of illegitimacy

3.8 In this model the concepts of legitimacy and illegitimacy are preserved, but further steps are taken to remove by statute certain of the practical and procedural consequences of illegitimacy: in particular, all consequences which are adverse to the child. ...

3.9 The particular reforms for inclusion within such a scheme could be selective; and the model has what some may regard as the advantage of not necessarily involving the automatic removal of all discrimination against the father of an illegitimate child. ...

(c) Second model for reform: abolition of the status of illegitimacy

3.14 This model involves the total disappearance of the concept of 'legitimacy' as well as of 'illegitimacy', for the one cannot exist without the other. It goes beyond the mere assimilation of the legal positions of children born in and out of wedlock, since that solution, which has been considered above, would still preserve the caste labels which help artificially to preserve the social stigma now attached to illegitimacy.

3.15 The case for abolishing illegitimacy as a status is in our view supported by the fact that such a change in the law would help to improve the position of children born out of wedlock in a way in which the mere removal of the remaining legal disabilities attaching to illegitimacy would not. No change in the law relating to legitimacy would help to improve the economic position of a child born out of wedlock in so far as he suffers from being the child of a 'one-parent family'; but an illegitimate child suffers a special disadvantage which does not affect the child of a widow or divorcee. He has a different *status*, even if the incidents of that status do not differ greatly from those attached to the status of a legitimate child; attention is thus focused on the irrelevant fact of the parents' marital status. We believe that the law can help to lessen social prejudices by setting an example clearly based upon the principle that the parents' marital relationship is irrelevant to the child's legal position. Changes in the law cannot give the illegitimate child the benefits of a secure, caring, family background. They cannot even ensure the he does not suffer financially, since his father may not be in a position to support him. But they can at least remove the *additional* hardship of attaching on opprobrious description to him. ...

3.16. If the law were changed so that there was no longer a legal distinction between the illegitimate child, it would also follow that in principle there would be no distinction between parents: both parents would have equal rights and duties unless and until a court otherwise ordered. ... We have tentatively concluded that the advantages of removing the status of illegitimacy altogether from the law outweigh the disadvantages of giving all fathers parental rights.

The response of the National Council for One-Parent Families, *An Accident Birth* (1980), supported the end but not the means:

In discussing the abolition of illegitimacy, we believe that it is necessary to draw a clear distinction between the rights of the child and the rights of the parents. We do not believe that the two models – that of abolishing the status of illegitimacy and that of preserving some distinction between the parental rights and duties of married and unmarried parents – are necessarily mutually exclusive. We believe that by giving all children equal rights, irrespective of the marital status of their parents, the status of illegitimacy is abolished. Any remaining difference in the custodial relationship of parents is a consequence of the status of marriage, of which we are not proposing the abolition. We recognise the need for reform in the area of parental rights, and would certainly support an increase in father's rights to encourage unmarried fathers to play a greater role in the upbringing of their children. However, we feel that there are strong arguments against giving all fathers *automatic* equal parental rights. ...

(*a*) In our experience, the majority of illegitimate children during early childhood are living with and being cared for by their mothers alone, and either have no contact, or very erratic contact, with their natural fathers. We believe that giving fathers automatic rights will remove the existing protection and security an unmarried mother has in bringing up her child alone, and will lead to increased pressure and distress, caused not only in the event of intervention by an estranged father, but also by the uncertainty of never knowing whether or not the father will exercise his rights, unless the issue is decided by the court.

(*b*) If an unmarried father is to be given automatic parental rights, the question of establishing paternity takes on increased significance. We believe that many mothers will be deterred from entering the father's details on the birth certificate or will deny the identity of the father if automatic parental rights flow from paternity being established. This will act against the child's right to know the facts about his or her origins and will undermine the Law Commission's recommendation on this subject.

[However:] ... There is a need to provide a procedure available to all unmarried parents, whether cohabiting or not, to make a *mutual declaration* of parentage and joint custody, and to register it with the court. Simple forms could be available at the Municipal Offices where births are registered, where such a declaration could be formalised. This would give full custody rights to unmarried fathers where the mother consents. Although we believe that such a consensual arrangement is the only one having a reasonable chance of success, it could be viewed as giving an unjustifiable veto to the mother. We therefore recommend that a further amendment should be made to the Guardianship of Minors Act 1971, to allow unmarried fathers to apply to the court for joint custody if the mother should not agree to a mutual declaration. In reaching its decision, the court would have to apply the cardinal principle of family law in regarding the welfare of the child as paramount.

[Finally:] We deplore the Law Commission's statement that 'One-parent families remain a major social problem'. The one-parent family is not problematic per se and it is not a deviation from the two-parent family. Despite the fact that one-parent families suffer both economic and social discrimination we believe that a one-parent family is a normal and viable family form in its own right and is able to carry out required family functions such as parenting. Given such negative attitudes it is not surprising that laws developed to suit a two-parent family fit so awkwardly on a one-parent family.

Residual social stigma affects the confidence of single women in their undoubted ability to provide a satisfactory upbringing for their children. Attitudes towards illegitimacy are part of wider social and moral codes affecting sexual behaviour and particularly attitudes towards women. The sense of shame, of feeling different and inferior, which has been the experience of so many illegitimate children in the past, is the result of society's punishing attitude towards the mother for contravening the moral code. In our concern to give equality to all children, we should not overlook that in the early childhood years, the fate of many children will be in the hands of one custodian only, usually the mother. The law must strike a balance which protects and respects her as custodian whilst at the same time keeping open the channels of access to the father.

Somewhat similar criticisms were voiced by Mary Hayes in her comment on the Working Paper (1980):

One weakness of their paper is that only superficial attention is given to the practical implications of giving rights to fathers, while the emotional dimensions of implementing such a change are virtually ignored. Furthermore the effect of giving rights to fathers is not tested against the welfare principle; this means that the Law Commission fail to ask themselves some fundamental questions before they conclude, at an early stage, that abolishing illegitimacy promotes the welfare of the child.

The Commission's Report on *Illegitimacy* (1982) therefore paid much greater heed to the arguments against according automatic rights to fathers:

4.26 ...

(*a*) It was said that automatically to confer 'parental rights' on fathers could well result in a significant growth in the number of mothers who would refuse to identify the father of their child. Mothers would be tempted to conceal the father's identity in order to ensure that in practice he could not exercise any parental rights. If this were to happen, it would detract from the desirable objective of establishing, recognising and fostering genuine familial links.

(*b*) It was said that to confer rights on the father might well be productive of particular distress and disturbance where the mother had subsequently married a third party, who had put himself *in loco parentis* to the child. The possibility – however unlikely in reality – of interference by the child's father could well engender a damaging sense of insecurity in the family; matters would be all the worse if the father did intervene. Some commentators argued that the result in such a case might be that the mother and her new partner would seek, for instance by an application for custody or adoption, to forestall any possible intervention by the natural father with the result that the child would be prematurely denied the possibility of establishing a genuine link with him.

(*c*) It was said that automatically to confer 'rights' on the father of a child born outside marriage could put him in a position where he might be tempted to harass or possibly even to blackmail the mother at a time when she might well be exceptionally vulnerable to pressure. In this context a number of commentators made what seems to us to be the valid point that what is in issue is not so much how the law is perceived by the professional lawyer or the experienced social worker, but how it might be perceived by a fearful and perhaps ill-informed mother. Sometimes what the law is thought to be may be almost as important as what it in fact is. Thus the partners of a child might well attach more significance to the fact that the law had given the father 'rights' than would a lawyer who is accustomed to the forensic process and able dispassionately to consider the likelihood of a court in fact permitting a father to exercise those rights, given its overriding concern to promote the child's welfare.

(*d*) It was also suggested that the experience of countries which have sought to abolish the discrimination affecting those born outside marriage is generally against automatically conferring 'parental rights' on the father of an illegitimate child. In most of those countries the father does not have the full range of parental rights unless he has obtained a court order or he falls within a delimited category of fathers in whom the law automatically recognises parental rights.

(*e*) Finally it was suggested that if all fathers automatically possessed parental authority over their illegitimate children, practical difficulties would be encountered where the child was in the care of a local authority. ... These would arise because a local authority is not entitled to keep a child in its care if a person having parental rights expresses a desire to take over the child's care. The result might therefore be either that the father would, contrary to its best interests, take the child out of care, or alternatively that long-term planning for the child's future would be delayed until the father's rights had been terminated. In such cases the child might well suffer.

Questions

(i) Which of the following do you think would be the best for most children: (*a*) abolishing the status and giving *all* fathers automatic parental responsibility: (*b*) abolishing the child's exclusion from his father's lineage, giving him the same claims to financial provision and property adjustment as any other child, but not giving the father automatic parental responsibility; or (*c*) abolishing the status and giving *no* fathers automatic parental responsibility?

In their First Report on *Illegitimacy* (1982), the Law Commission opted for a package of reforms corresponding to model (*b*):

4.44 ... Some commentators expressed the view ... that it would be perfectly possible to abolish the status of illegitimacy whilst preserving the existing rules whereby parental rights vest automatically only in married parents. We do not accept this view. The argument for 'abolishing illegitimacy' (rather than merely removing such legal consequences of that status as are adverse to the child) is essentially that the abolition of any legal distinction based on the parents' marital status would itself have an influence on opinion. The marital status of the child's parents would cease to be *legally* relevant, and thus the need to refer to the child's distinctive legal status would (in this view) disappear. This consequence could not follow if a distinction – albeit relating only to entitlement to parental rights – were to be preserved between children which would be based solely on their parent's status. There would remain two classes of children: first, those whose parents were married and thereby enjoyed parental rights; secondly, those whose parents were unmarried and whose fathers did not enjoy such rights. ...

4.49 In the result, we have come to the conclusion that the advantages of abolishing the status of illegitimacy are not sufficient to compensate for the possible dangers involved in an automatic extension of parental rights to fathers of non-marital children. ...

4.51 For almost all purposes the effect of the changes which we recommend will be that all children – irrespective of their parents' marital status – will be treated alike by the law. However, in a few areas (the most important of which is obviously the question of entitlement to parental rights) there will continue to be a difference between those children whose parents have married and those whose parents have not. To this extent it will be necessary to preserve the concepts of 'legitimacy', 'illegitimacy' and 'legitimation'. On the question of terminology, however, we would at this stage make one small, but we think important, recommendation: namely, that whenever possible the terms 'legitimate' and 'illegitimate' should cease to be used as legal terms of art. The expressions that we favour in their stead, and that we use generally in this Report and in the draft legislation attached hereto, are 'marital' and 'non-marital', which avoid the connotations of unlawfulness and illegality which are implicit in the term 'illegitimate'.

The Scottish Law Commission, in their Report on *Illegitimacy* (1984), reached the same conclusions about what the law should be, but approached the questions of terminology and status in this way:

9.2 ... We would endorse the view of the Law Commission for England and Wales that the terms 'legitimate' and 'illegitimate' should, wherever possible, cease to be used as legal terms of art. We do not agree with the Law Commission, however, that it would be desirable to replace these terms with 'marital' and 'non-marital'. This is just another way of labelling children, and experience in other areas, such as mental illness, suggests that new labels can rapidly take on old connotations. In our view it should so rarely be necessary to discriminate between children on the basis of whether their father was married to their mother that no special legal label is required for this purpose. There are already children, for example, whose fathers, although married or formerly married to the mother, have been deprived of custody and other parental rights. It has not been found necessary to invent a special legal label for them. In short, we would not wish to see a discriminatory concept of 'non-maritality' gradually replace a discriminatory concept of 'illegitimacy'. We would rather see future legislation distinguish, where distinctions based on marriage are necessary, between fathers rather than between children. Where it is thought necessary to distinguish between people on the basis of whether or not their parents were married to each other at any relevant time – and we hope this will be a very rare exception – we would suggest that this should be done expressly in those terms. ...

9.3 *The legal status of illegitimacy.* Implementation of our recommendations would remove most remaining legal differences between children which depend on whether or not their parents are, or have been, married to each other. It would not, however, remove all and, as we have seen, the words 'legitimate' and 'illegitimate' would not be entirely removed from the statute law. In these circumstances, it would be a matter for argument whether it was any longer justifiable to refer to a legal status or illegitimacy in Scots law. This, in our view, is not a matter on which it would be appropriate to legislate. Legislation is concerned with rules. Whether minor differences in the rules applying to different classes of persons justify the ascription of a distinct status is a matter for commentators rather than legislators.

Questions

(i) On terminology, the Law Commission in their Second Report (1986) agreed with the Scots: do you?

(ii) On status, could they have gone further and purged the statute book of the concepts of legitimacy and legitimation altogether?

The Family Law Reform Act 1987 provides:

GENERAL PRINCIPLE

1. – (1) In this Act and enactments passed and instruments made after the coming into force of this section, references (however expressed) to any relationship between two persons shall, unless the contrary intention appears, be construed without regard to whether or not the father and mother of either of them, or the father and mother of any person through whom the relationship is deduced, have or had been married to each other at any time.

(2) In this Act and enactments passed after the coming into force of this section, unless the contrary intention appears –

(*a*) references to a person whose father and mother were married to each other at the time of his birth include; and

(*b*) references to a person whose father and mother were not married to each other at the time of his birth do not include,

references to any person to whom subsection (3) below applies, and cognate references shall be construed accordingly.

(3) This subsection applies to any person who –

(*a*) is treated as legitimate by virtue of section 1 of the Legitimacy Act 1976;

(*b*) is a legitimated person within the meaning of section 10 of that Act;

(*c*) is an adopted child within the meaning of Part IV of the Adoption Act 1976; or

(*d*) is otherwise treated in law as legitimate.

(4) For the purpose of construing references falling within subsection (2) above, the time of a person's birth shall be taken to include any time during the period beginning with –

(*a*) the insemination resulting in his birth; or

(*b*) where there was no such insemination, his conception.

and (in either case) ending with his birth.

The Children Act 1989, however, provides:

2. – (1) Where a child's father and mother were married to each other at the time of his birth, they shall each have parental responsibility for the child.

(2) Where a child's father and mother were not married to each other at the time of his birth –

(*a*) the mother shall have parental responsibility for the child;

(*b*) the father shall not have parental responsibility for the child, unless he acquires it in accordance with the provisions of this Act.

(3) References in this Act to a child whose father and mother were, or (as the case may be) were not, married to each other at the time of his birth must be read with section 1 of the Family Law Reform Act 1987 (which extends their meaning).

(4) The rule of law that a father is the natural guardian of his legitimate child is abolished.

The 1989 Act also provides for several ways in which the father may come to share parental responsibility with the mother:

4. – (1) Where a child's father and mother were not married to each other at the time of his birth –

(*a*) the court may, on the application of the father, order that he shall have parental responsibility for the child; or

(*b*) the father and mother may by agreement ('a parental responsibility agreement') provide for the father to have parental responsibility for the child.

(2) No parental responsibility agreement shall have effect for the purposes of this Act unless –

(*a*) it is made in the form prescribed by regulations made by the Lord Chancellor; and

(*b*) where regulations are made by the Lord Chancellor prescribing the manner in which such agreements must be recorded, it is recorded in the prescribed manner.

(3) Subject to section 12(4), an order under subsection (1)(*a*), or a parental responsibility agreement, may only be brought to an end by an order of the court made on the application –

(*a*) of any person who has parental responsibility for the child; or

(*b*) with leave of the court, of the child himself.

(4) The court may only grant leave under subsection (3)(*b*) if it is satisfied that the child has sufficient understanding to make the proposed application.

...

12. – (1) Where the court makes a residence order in favour of the father of a child it shall, if the father would not otherwise have parental responsibility for the child, also make an order under section 4 giving him that responsibility.

...

(4) Where subsection (1) requires the court to make an order under section 4 in respect of the father of a child, the court shall not bring that order to an end at any time while the residence order concerned remains in force.

Section 4(1)(*a*) replaced s. 4 of the Family Law Reform Act 1987. The purpose and effect of this were explained by the Law Commission in their Second Report (1986) like this:

3.1 At present, an unmarried father may be granted legal custody of his child, but he cannot share that custody with the mother. The Report Bill provided that a court could grant him the full legal status of parenthood, that is all the parental rights and duties, usually sharing these with the mother in the same way that married parents do. It was thought that such an order would normally be sought where the mother and father were living together and both wanted it, or where the mother had died without appointing the father testamentary guardian (although in that case he may at present apply to be made guardian), or where the parents had separated and he wanted full parental status rather than simply legal custody. However, in providing that the father should share that status with the mother 'unless otherwise directed,' the Report Bill incidentally gave the court the unprecedented power to remove all the mother's parental authority. We think that this result was unintentional and could be undesirable. ...
3.2 The new clause 4 [permits] the court to order that the father shall have all parental authority, sharing it with the mother. Such an order will place him in essentially the same position as a married father. ...
3.3 There is one respect in which the position of a father who has been granted all the parental rights and duties by means of an order under clause 4 of the draft Bill will differ from that of a married father, in that the court will have power to revoke the order. This was provided for in our earlier Report and, in the present state of the law relating to family responsibilities, we consider that it should be retained. We recognise that, owing to the widely varying extent to which unmarried fathers in fact assume responsibility towards their children (and indeed towards the mothers who bring those children up), it would not be in the best interests of the children if fathers were automatically to enjoy full parental status. Where the parents are in fact living together and co-operating in bringing up their children, we hope that such orders will frequently be applied for and granted. However, unless the courts are able to remove parental powers where it subsequently proves not to be in the child's best interests for the father to have them, the courts may be reluctant to make such orders at all. A court will necessarily have to have regard to the extent to which it will be able to protect the child's interests should the need arise in the future and under the present law the powers of the divorce courts in relation to married couples are somewhat more extensive than those under the Guardianship of Minors Acts. The time may come when the general framework of the law relating to the responsibilities of parents, not only towards their children but also towards one another, is such that this can be reconsidered. ...

Question

Do you think that it should be reconsidered straightaway?

The many reported cases on parental responsibility orders, including the often cited *Re H (minors) (local authority: parental rights) (No 3)* [1991] Fam 151, [1991] 2 All ER 185, CA, are conveniently summarised in:

Re S (Parental Responsibility)
[1995] 2 FLR 648, [1995] Fam Law 596, Court of Appeal

The parents lived together from 1985 and the child was born in January 1988. The parents separated when she was 18 months old. The father regularly paid the mother £500 per month. In 1990 he was convicted of possessing obscene literature. The mother stopped contact for a while but resumed it because of the child's distress. It developed into staying contact. The father applied for a parental responsibility order but was refused. He appealed.

Ward LJ: ... At the risk of being tedious, it may be necessary for me to recite some of the principles on which these applications ought to be judged. The case of *D v Hereford and Worcester County Council* [1991] Fam 14, [1991] 1 FLR 205 was, I believe, the first of this kind of application and it happened to come before me. I endeavoured to explain my understanding of the precursor to s. 4 of the Children Act, namely s. 4 of the Family Law Reform Act 1987 which gave the power to grant parental rights, as it was phrased, in the language of the day. I endeavoured to explain how the Law Commission had wrestled over a number of years and in a number of reports, with the dilemmas that the question posed seen against the background that it was right and proper in this day and age to sweep aside those distinctions between legitimacy and illegitimacy which bore unfavourably upon the children.

The logic would have suggested that one should also sweep away any disability that remained vested in the father of the illegitimate child. Since science could conclusively determine the fact of fatherhood the concept of filius nullius was no longer one which could command respect. But there are obvious difficulties, which the Law Commission recognised, in giving a total equality of status to the father who has married the mother, and to the putative father who had not. At its most emotive, but none the less pertinent point of distinction, it would cause offence to right-thinking people that the rapist should claim parental rights or parental responsibilities over the child which that criminal act produced. That led to the Commission entertaining the debate as to whether or not they should do what I believe may have been done in Scotland, that is to say, to confer parental responsibility on the father but with a right upon the mother to apply to disenfranchise him. They grappled with the concept of defining an irresponsible father who should not be afforded this status and eventually they left it to the court to decide. ...

No guidance is given as to how the court should approach the exercise of that broad discretion given to it. My puny efforts to provide that guidance in the case of *D v Hereford and Worcester* were distilled and approved by the Court of Appeal in the first important case on this subject. It is *Re H (Minors) (Local Authority: Parental Rights) (No 3)* [1991] Fam 151, sub nom *Re H (Illegitimate Children: Father: Parental Rights) (No 2)* [1991] 1 FLR 214. Balcombe LJ. ... suggested, and most helpfully, this test at pp. 158B and 218F respectively:

> 'In considering whether to make an order under s. 4 of the 1987 Act, the court will have to take into account a number of factors of which the following will undoubtedly be material (although there may well be others, as the list is not intended to be exhaustive):
> (1) the degree of commitment which the father has shown towards the child;
> (2) the degree of attachment which exists between the father and the child; and
> (3) the reasons of the father for applying for the order.'

There followed the case of *Re C (Minors) (Parental Rights)* [1992] 1 FLR 1. This is another judgment often cited for the eloquent words of Waite J, as he then was. He was there dealing with the problem of how parental rights were to be enforced and what would happen if it was not possible fully to enforce them. He said at p. 3F:

> 'Given, therefore, that the prospective enforceability of parental rights is a relevant consideration for a judge deciding whether or not to grant them, there is, in our judgment, nothing in the Act to suggest that it should be an overriding consideration. It would be quite wrong, in our view, to assume that just because few or none of the parental rights happen to be enforceable under conditions prevailing at the date of the application, it would necessarily follow as a matter of course that a PRO [parental rights order] would be refused. That can be illustrated by looking – as the legislation clearly requires one to look – at the position of a lawful father in analogous circumstances. Conditions may arise (for example in cases of mental illness) where a married father has, regretfully, to be ordered, in effect, to step out of his children's lives altogether. In such a case, his legal status as a parent remains wholly unaffected, and he retains all his rights in law, although none of them may be exercisable in practice. This does not mean that his parental status becomes a dead letter or a mere paper title. It will have real and tangible value, not only as something he can cherish for the sake of his own peace of mind, but also as a status carrying with it rights in waiting, which it may be possible to call into play when circumstances change with the passage of time. It is not difficult to imagine situations in which similar considerations would apply in the case of a natural father. Though existing circumstances may demand that his children see or hear nothing of him, and that he should have no influence upon the course of their lives for the time being, their welfare may require that if circumstances change he should be reintroduced as a presence, or at least as an influence, in their lives. In such a case a PRO, notwithstanding that only a few or even none of the rights under it may currently be exercisable, may be of value to him and also of potential value to the children.'

He set out, later at p. 8G, his test in similar terms to that of Balcombe LJ in these words:

> '... was the association between the parties sufficiently enduring, and has the father by his conduct during and since the application shown sufficient commitment to the children, to justify giving the father a legal status equivalent to that which he would have enjoyed if the parties had been married, due attention being paid to the fact that a number of his parental rights would, if conferred on him by a PRO, be unenforceable under current conditions?'

It is, therefore, important to observe the interrelation between the rights and the status and the exercise of those rights and, of course, the restrictions upon the exercise of those rights. *Re H (A Minor) (Parental Responsibility)* [1993] 1 FLR 484 was another case where, although contact had been denied yet the question posed by Waite J, in the passage I have just read, was answered affirmatively by the court and parental responsibility was granted. Waite J gave more guidance in *Re CB (A Minor) (Parental Responsibility Order)* [1993] 1 FLR 920. ...

Re T (A Minor) (Parental Responsibility: Contact) [1993] 2 FLR 450 was one of the few cases where a refusal of the parental responsibility order was upheld. ... There the mother and father separated during the mother's pregnancy. The cause of the separation was a totally violent assault by the father on the mother, so severe that he had to take her to hospital. He was utterly feckless in his payment of maintenance. He was a man of unbridled hostility, who head-butted the mother on another occasion when one of the few attempts to arrange contact dissolved into this violence. He abducted the little girl from the mother for a period of days, which was an act rightly described by my Lady, Butler-Sloss LJ, as cruel and callous behaviour in respect of a young child, with no thought for her welfare.

It is not surprising, in those circumstances, that the judge below, Ewbank J, found that he had no worthwhile part whatever to play in the life of this child and declined to afford him parental rights. Later Eastham J denied him all his contact and debarred him under s. 91(4) from making any further application. That gives a clue to the nature of the beast in that particular case.

Another case where parental responsibility was refused was *W v Ealing London Borough Council* [1993] 2 FLR 788. ... In that case the father's conduct was so outrageous that his attempt to apply for a residence order, in respect of the child in care, was dismissed without being heard on its merits. ...

In *Re G (A Minor) (Parental Responsibility Order)* [1994] 1 FLR 504, again a decision of the Court of Appeal, Balcombe LJ at p. 508A said this ...:

> '... I am quite prepared to accept that the making of a parental responsibility order requires the judge to adopt the welfare principle as the paramount consideration. But having said that, I should add that, of course, it is well established by authority that, other things being equal, it is always to a child's welfare to know and, wherever possible, to have contact with both its parents, including the parent with whom it is not normally resident, if the parents have separated.
>
> Therefore, prima facie, it must necessarily also be for the child's benefit or welfare that it has an absent parent sufficiently concerned and interested to want to have a parental responsibility order. In other words, I approach this question on the basis that where you have a concerned although absent father, who fulfils the other test about which I spoke in *Re H*, namely having shown a degree of commitment towards the child, it being established that there is a degree of attachment between the father and the child, and that his reasons for applying for the order are not demonstrably improper or wrong, then prima facie it would be for the welfare of the child that such an order should be made.'

The next in this long litany is a judgment of first instance, a judgment of Wilson J in *Re P (A Minor) (Parental Responsibility Order)* [1994] 1 FLR 578. There the justices had decided that a parental responsibility order might be used by the father to question aspects of the child's upbringing which would normally remain in the domain solely of the person with day-to-day care. As to that Wilson J said this at pp. 584G–585D:

> 'It is important to be quite clear that an order for parental responsibility to the father does not give him a right to interfere in matters within the day-to-day management of the child's life. ...'

...

The final case is that of *Re E (Parental Responsibility: Blood Tests)* [1995] 1 FLR 392. ...

I have engaged in this laborious review of the authorities because it is my increasing concern, both from the very fact that there are so many reported cases on this topic and from my experience when dealing with the innumerable appeals from justices to the Family Division, that applications under s. 4 have become one of these little growth industries born of misunderstanding. Misunderstanding arises from a failure to appreciate that, in essence, the granting of a parental responsibility order is the granting of status. It is unfortunate that the notion of 'parental responsibility' has still to be defined by s. 3 of the Children Act to mean '... all the rights, duties, powers, responsibilities and authority which by law a parent ... has in relation to the child and his property', which gives outmoded pre-eminence to the 'rights' which are conferred. That it is unfortunate is demonstrated by the very fact that, when pressed in this case to define the nature and effect of the order which was so vigorously opposed, counsel for the mother was driven to say that her rooted objection was to the rights to which it would entitle the father and the power that it would give him. That is a most unfortunate failure to appreciate the significant change that the Act has brought about where the emphasis is to move away from rights and to concentrate on responsibilities. She did not doubt that if by unhappy chance this child fell ill whilst she was abroad, her father, if then enjoying contact, would not deal responsibly with her welfare.

It would, therefore, be helpful if the mother could think calmly about the limited circumstances when the exercise of true parental responsibility is likely to be of practical significance. It is wrong to place undue and therefore false emphasis on the rights and duties and the powers comprised in 'parental responsibility' and not to concentrate on the fact that what is at issue in conferring upon a committed father the status of parenthood for which nature has already ordained that he must bear responsibility. There seems to me to be all too frequently a failure to appreciate that the wide exercise of s. 8 orders can control the abuse, if any, of the exercise of parental responsibility which is adverse to the welfare of the child. Those interferences with the day-to-day management of the child's life have nothing to do with whether or not this order should be allowed.

There is another important emphasis I would wish to make. I have heard, up and down the land, psychiatrists tell me how important it is that children grow up with good self-esteem and how much they need to have a favourable positive image of the absent parent. It seems to me important, therefore, wherever possible, to ensure that the law confers upon a committed father that stamp of approval, lest the child grow up with some belief that he is in some way disqualified from fulfilling his role and that the reason for the disqualification is something inherent which will be inherited by the child, making her struggle to find her own identity all the more fraught.

Trying, therefore, to apply those principles to this case, at the heart of it lies the finding by the judge that in terms of commitment, attachment and bone fides this father passed the test. She rightly stated that that was not the conclusive list of requirements, and she rightly had regard to the fact of his conviction. But it seems to me that however disreputable the conviction, it was not one which demonstrably and directly affected the child in her day-to-day life. ...

I would therefore allow the appeal.

Simon Brown LJ: I agree.

Butler-Sloss LJ: I also agree. ...

It is important for parents and it is important, indeed, for these parents to remember the emphasis placed by Parliament on the order which is applied for. It is that of duties and responsibilities as well as rights and powers. Indeed, the order itself is entitled 'parental responsibility'. A father who has shown real commitment to the child concerned and to whom there is a positive attachment, as well as a genuine bona fide reason for the application, ought, in a case such as the present, to assume the weight of those duties and cement that commitment and attachment by sharing the responsibilities for the child with the mother. This father is asking to assume that burden as well as that pleasure of looking after his child, a burden not lightly to be undertaken.

Appeal allowed.

Questions

(i) If a father is granted a residence order, s. 12(1) insists that a parental responsibility order must also be made; there is no corresponding requirement whenever a contact order is made; did Parliament intend that all fathers who have contact should also have parental responsibility?

(ii) In *Re H (minors) (local authority: parental rights) (No 3)* [1991] Fam 151, the Court of Appeal held that a father should be granted parental responsibility, so that his agreement to the child's adoption was required, but then that this could be dispensed with on the ground that it was unreasonably withheld: what good did this do either the father or the child?

(iii) Do you think that the Law Commission had such cases in mind?
(iv) Ward LJ was mistaken about the position in Scotland. The Scottish Law Commission, in their Report on *Family Law* (1992), had concluded that:

2.48 The question is not whether there should be an unalterable recognition or denial of parental responsibility and rights. Whatever the initial position may be, a court order could alter it in the interests of the child. The question is whether the starting position should be that the father has, or has not, the normal parental responsibilities and rights. Given that about 25% of all children born in Scotland in recent years have been born out of wedlock, and that the number of couples cohabiting outside marriage is now substantial, it seems no use that the balance has now swung in favour of the view that parents are parents, whether married to each other or not. If in any particular case it is in the best interests of a child that a parent should be deprived of some or all of his parental responsibilities and rights, that can be achieved by means of a court order.

But the Children (Scotland) Act 1995, ss. 4 and 11, make provision equivalent to that in England and Wales. (*a*) Do you agree with the Scottish Law Commission? (*b*) Is opinion amongst you on this matter divided according to gender?
(v) In their second Report on *Illegitimacy* (1986), the Law Commission argued that the agreement of a father with contact should not automatically be required to an adoption:

3.4 ... Our earlier Report recognised that the arguments for and against including a mere right of access were finely balanced. On the one hand, 'such an order clearly suggests that the court believed that a link between father and child should be recognised and fostered'. On the other hand, a father with access can be heard on the merits of the adoption order in any event. A court which considers that it is in the best interests of the child for the father to continue to have the right of access can always refuse the order, whereas if his agreement is required that agreement may only be dispensed with in defined and limited circumstances in which the interests of the child are not the first and paramount consideration. We now consider that a right to access, which may be very limited and may or may not be being exercised, is too flimsy a basis on which to give the father rights which may not be in the best interests of the child. ...

Do you agree? Bear in mind that the better the relationship between father, mother and child, the less likely it is that there will be any contact order at all.

Section 4(1)(*b*) provides for parental responsibility agreements. We have already mentioned One-Parent Families' proposal for a voluntary sharing procedure (p. 496, above). The Law Commission's response in their first Report on *Illegitimacy* (1982) was this:

4.39 It may, however, be argued that the father should be entitled to parental rights in cases where *both* parents of the child agree that he should. After all (it might be argued) the law already accords parental rights to all married parents without any prior scrutiny of what is in the child's best interests. Why should it not equally accord such rights to unmarried parents who are in agreement? We see force in this argument, but have nevertheless rejected it. The most powerful factor influencing our decision was the strong body of evidence from those best acquainted with the problems of the single parent family about the vulnerable position of the unmarried mother in many cases. Such mothers may well be exposed to pressure, and even harassment, on the part of the natural father; and it would, in our view, give unscrupulous natural fathers undesirable bargaining power if they were to be placed in a position where they might more easily extort from the mother a joint 'voluntary' acknowledgement, having the effect of vesting parental rights in the father, perhaps as the price of an agreement to provide for the mother or her child, or even as the price of continuing a relationship with the mother. For this reason, we think it appropriate for the court to investigate and sanction even a joint request that parental rights vest in the father. In reaching this conclusion we have, as we have said, been particularly impressed by the need to protect single mothers from the risk of pressure. But we should make it plain that we do not, in any event, accept the argument that since a couple can acquire parental rights over their child by marriage they should be able to do so by some other formal act. Apart from the consideration (to which some will attach considerable importance) that to do so would debase the institution of marriage, it must be borne in mind that marriage is still, in principle, a permanent relationship. In contrast, there is no such unifying factor in the case of unmarried relationships, which are infinitely variable in their nature and in the intentions of the partners to them. This diversity suggests to us that scrutiny by a court is a not unreasonable protection for the interests of the child of unmarried parents.

Questions

(i) Is not the threat of legal proceedings just as much harassment for the mother, at least if her consent is not required for an order?
(ii) Does not the new order debase the institution of marriage just as much as a voluntary agreement might do?
(iii) Why should a parent be able to appoint a guardian to share parental status with the other parent after her death, but not to share her own status while she is alive?

The Commission were able to return to this question in the course of their review of the whole of the private law relating to the upbringing of children. In their Report on *Guardianship and Custody* (1988) they concluded:

2.18 … In our Working Paper on Guardianship, we pointed out that such judicial proceedings may be unduly elaborate, expensive and unnecessary unless the child's mother objects to the order. We suggested, therefore, that the mother might be permitted to appoint the father guardian to share responsibility while she was alive. A large majority of those who responded, including the leading organisations representing single parents and children's interests, supported this suggestion. It was pointed out, however, that it would be more consistent with the primary concept of parenthood if the father were to acquire the same status by such an appointment as he would by a court order. We therefore recommend that mother and father should be able to make an agreement that the father shall share parental responsibility with the mother. This will have the same effect as a court order. Both, for example, will confer upon him the power to give or withhold agreement to the child's adoption or to appoint a guardian. More importantly perhaps, both an agreement and an order may only be brought to an end by a court order made on the application of either parent (or a guardian). The child should also be able to make such applications, but only if the court is satisfied that he has sufficient understanding to do so.
2.19 For this reason, we also recommend that the agreement be made in a prescribed form. … The object is to ensure that, as far as possible, both parents understand the importance and effects of their agreement. Overall, this should provide a simple and straightforward means for unmarried parents to acknowledge their shared responsibility, not only for the support, but also for the upbringing of their child.
2.20 … Given the serious concern about the pressures to which mothers may be subject, which was expressed at the time of our first Report on Illegitimacy, it is appropriate for the machinery for such sharing appointments to be different from, and more formal and deliberate than, the machinery for appointment of a guardian. However, although it is hoped that more and more unmarried parents will agree to share parental responsibility, there may still be cases in which they would prefer the mother to have sole responsibility during her life-time but for the father to assume it in the event of her death. It should therefore remain possible for the mother to appoint him guardian. …

The following table is taken from the Children Act Advisory Committee's Annual Report 1994/1995:

Table 4: Parental responsibility orders made and agreements registered in the PRFD

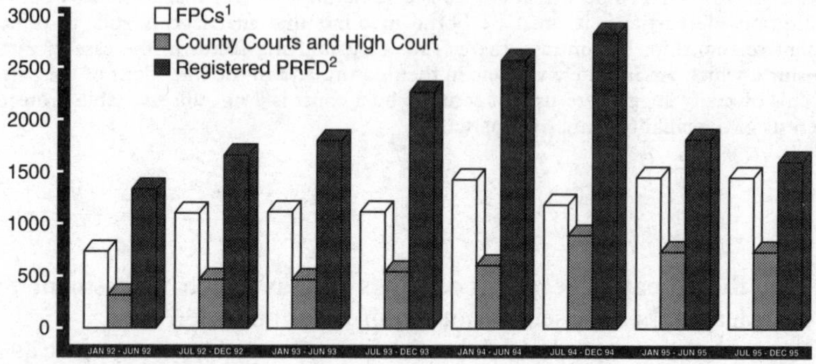

1 Family Proceedings Courts.
2 Principal Registry of the Family Division.

Questions

(i) Given the courts' attitude to making parental responsibility orders when the mother does not agree, how strict should the formalities be when she does agree?
(ii) What now are the advantages and disadvantages, from the father's point of view, of being married to the mother?
(iii) What now are the advantages and disadvantages, from the mother's point of view, of being married to the father?
(iv) What now are the advantages, from the child's point of view, of his mother being married to his father?

Chapter 12

When parents part

Doreen: I feel very angry sometimes, that a man can literally decide that he wants to be free, free of responsibilities that *somebody* must take. Somebody needs to when children are involved. But men can just walk off. I think because they know that the woman is going to be the strong one, that *she* will not ... walk away.

Michael: The effects on my career have hurt. ... The company begins to assess you a bit lower perhaps because your mind has family welfare as a higher priority than it should be. ... I took Anne down to junior church as I always have done ... but I'd never brushed her hair before or tied ribbons, and this was actually impossible to me.

These two lone parents, and others, talked about their lives to Catherine Itzin for her book on *Splitting Up* (1980). This chapter is concerned with how it is decided what should happen to the children when their parents part. We shall look first at the circumstances in which these children find themselves and the effects of this upon them and their parents; then at the present law and the reasons for it, together with a few illustrative cases; and then at what happens if the lone parent family is reconstituted into a step-family.

1 Lone-parent families

Everyone knows that the proportion of families with children where there is only one parent in the household has grown dramatically over the past 25 years. This is illustrated by the graph overleaf, taken from *Social Trends 26* (1996). But there are many different kinds of lone-parent household, and the ways in which these have changed over the years are shown in the figure overleaf, taken from David Utting, *Family and Parenthood – Supporting Families, Preventing Breakdown* (1995).

If we look at it from the point of view of the children, we can see the proportions who are living with one or both natural parents from the table on p. 509, taken from *Social Trends 25* (1995), with the following commentary:

... This shows that in 1991 three quarters of children lived in married couple families with both their natural parents, although some will have step-brothers and sisters living with them. Of the remainder, another 3 per cent lived with both natural but unmarried parents and a further 6 per cent were step-children in a couple family. The remaining 17 per cent lived in lone-parent families.

Children who live with only one of their natural parents are more likely to live with their mother: in 1991, 19 per cent of all dependent children lived with their natural mother but not with their natural father while only three per cent lived with their natural father but not with

Families headed by lone parents as a percentage[1] of all families with dependent children

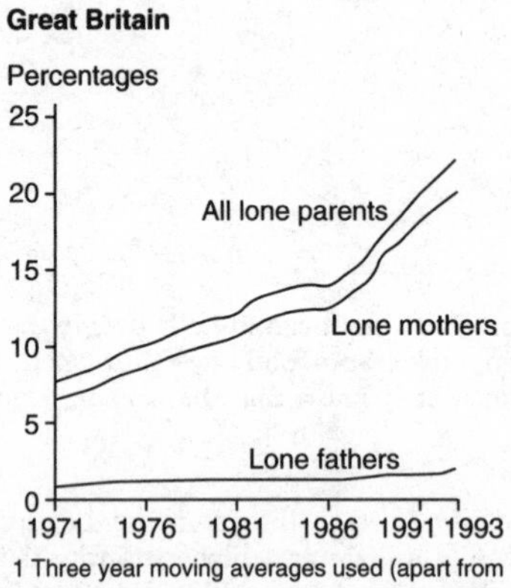

1 Three year moving averages used (apart from 1993).

Source: General Household Survey, Office of Population Censuses and Surveys

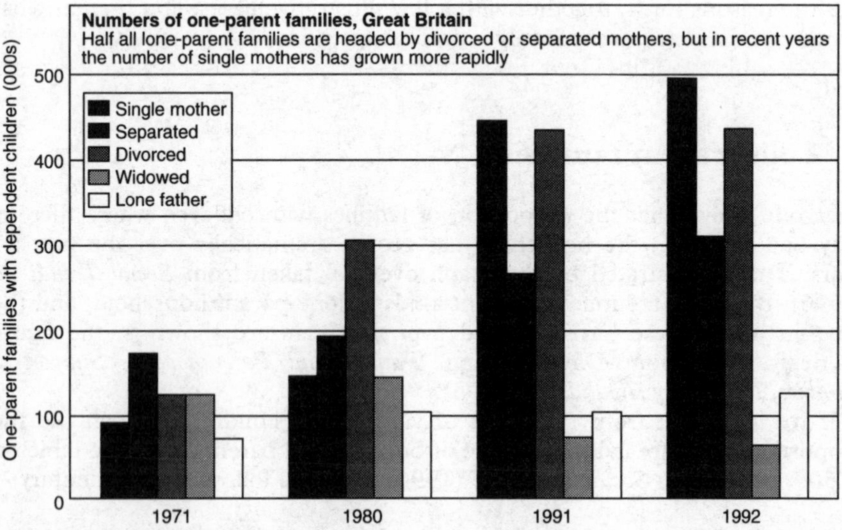

Source; Burghes, L (1994) / Haskey, J (1994b)

Note: 1992 figures are provisional estimates

their natural mother. These children were very likely to be in a lone-parent family if they lived with their mother, but those who lived with their natural father were almost as likely to live as step-children in a couple family.

Dependent children: by family type, 1991

Great Britain *Percentages*

	Couple families			Lone-parent families	All families
	Married	Cohabiting	All		
Children living in families with their natural mother and natural father with:					
No step-brothers/sisters	72.8	2.7	75.5	–	75.5
Step-brothers/sisters[1]	1.8	0.3	2.1	–	2.1
Children living with one natural parent					
Mother	2.9	1.5	4.4	14.8	19.2
Father	1.0	0.4	1.4	1.8	3.2
All dependent children	78.5	4.9	83.4	16.6	100.0

1 Of either or both parents.

Source: Office of Population Censuses and Surveys

Questions

(i) Why, do you think, has the proportion of lone-parent families headed by fathers gone up?
(ii) But why, do you think, are children who are living with their fathers more likely to have a step-mother than children who are living with their mothers are to have a step-father?
(iii) Why do we talk about 'lone-parent' rather than 'one-parent' families these days?

We do not know quite how much impact the decisions of courts have on what happens to children whose parents part. The major published studies of orders made relate to divorce proceedings before the Children Act 1989 abolished the old concepts of legal and actual custody, joint custody, and access. These are summarised by Jacqueline Priest and Jonathan Whybrow in *Custody Orders in Practice in Divorce and Domestic Courts* (1986):

Table 6: Custody orders in divorce proceedings (Percentages)

Study	Year of Data	Custody of Wife	Custody of Husband	Joint Custody	Others	Total Number[7]
Maidment[1]	1973	77.6	19.0	3.4	0	58
Wolfson[2]	1974	81.4	13.2	5.2	.2	428
Bristol[3]	1979–80	81.4	11.6	7.0	0	1,290
National[4]	1985	77.4	9.2	12.9	.7	82,059
Bristol(2)[5]	1985	73.0	9.6	16.9	.5	4,676
Wolfson(2)[6]	1985	72.2	9.2	18.1	.5	12,771

Notes to Table 6
1. A random sample of 95 undefended divorce petitions involving children, which had been filed in a North Midlands county court in 1973: Maidment, 'A Study in Child Custody' (1976) 6 Fam Law 195 and 236, p. 198.

Notes (continued)
2. A study of 625 divorces involving children in 1974, from a sample of 10 courts selected to reflect a cross-section of the divorcing population: Eekelaar and Clive with Clarke and Raikes, *Custody After Divorce*, Family Law Studies No. 1, Centre for Socio-Legal Studies, Wolfson College, Oxford, Table 33.
3. Research into 1,550 children's appointments between May 1979 and June 1980 in five courts in the Western Circuit and two courts on the Wales and Chester Circuit: Davis, MacLeod and Murch, 'Undefended Divorce: Should Section 41 of the Matrimonial Causes Act 1973 be Repealed?'(1983) 46 M.L.R. 121, 132.
4. The figures collected from the returns of 174 divorce registries in 1985.
5. The courts used by the Bristol study, updated using the figures noted in 4.
6. The courts used by the Wolfson study, updated using the figures noted in 4. These are the county courts at Birmingham, Bournemouth, Carmarthen, Guildford, Lincoln, Newcastle-upon-Tyne, Nottingham, Sheffield and Shrewsbury, and the Principal Registry of the Family Division. The latter's returns have been extrapolated from our own survey's results.
7. The total number of custody orders made by the divorce court, that is excluding care committals and previous courts' orders. In rows 1, 2 and 3 orders splitting the children between husband and wife have been counted as orders in favour of *each* of them.

But their own study of returns from ten courts showed that, even though the proportion of orders giving the parents joint *legal* custody varied widely, the proportion of children who were in the *actual* custody or care and control of their mothers varied only from 85% to 92.6%. This research did not examine the court records in detail, as the Wolfson study, *Custody after Divorce* (1977) by John Eekelaar and Eric Clive, with Karen Clarke and Susan Raikes, had done. The earlier study revealed more about the parties' behaviour:

13.7 Proposals of the parties
The vast majority of petitioners/pursuers simply sought the court's approval for the continuation of the existing state of affairs. In England and Wales only 4.8% of petitioners and in Scotland only 2.5% of pursuers proposed any substantial change in the child's residence, and those cases generally contained some abnormal feature (e.g. the children were in care or with third parties). ... Since children generally lived with their mother, this meant that petitioners/pursuers generally wished this to continue. Indeed, it was relatively rare for a husband to challenge the continued care for his children by the mother. In England and Wales husbands expressed an initial intention to apply for custody of children currently in their wife's care only in 10.3% of such cases, whereas in 34.3% of cases where the children were living with the husband, the wife expressed an initial intention to seek custody herself. However, in only a few of these cases was the challenge pressed to a contest in the court. ... In Scotland ... as well as England and Wales ... the evidence showed a very strong tendency on the part of mothers to claim custody of children in contrast to the fathers.

Earlier, the authors comment:

3.6 ... Wives are more tenacious than husbands in their attempts to obtain possession of the children. In most cases the husbands are content to leave to the wife the task of bringing up the children. If they seek to do so themselves, they are far more likely to be challenged by the wife than is a wife who keeps the children. That the wife is seen as prima facie the proper person to have care of the children therefore appears as a factor of community opinion which is shared by the parties themselves. However, the very low success rate of wives where they did challenge their husbands' possession of the children shows that the courts do not necessarily share that assumption, or, if they do, they have regard to other factors in making their decisions.

The authors conclude:

13.29 Another striking finding emerged in the examination of the contested cases. This is that the courts did not favour either sex as the more suitable custodian (although they displayed more caution when the husband was the custodian), nor did they appear to operate in accordance with presumptions relating to the age or sex of the children. Instead, they followed the principle advocated by Goldstein, Freud and Solnit [see p. 517, below] ... of minimum disruption to the child's existing emotional ties.

Fathers who want their children and are prepared to fight, therefore, would appear, statistically at least, to have a reasonable chance of success. The reasons why fathers do not fight, however, are likely to vary. Some are suggested by Martin Richards in his discussion of *Post-Divorce Arrangements for Children: A Psychological Perspective* (1982):

Mother or father?

Though the law itself does not favour mothers or fathers as potential custodial parents, if all else is equal and, especially if the children are young ('of tender years'), the mother is more likely to be granted custody in a dispute. Not all would concur with this point, but I think the weight of the evidence from reported cases and the surveys support a principle of a presumption that custody should be vested in the mother. Of course, I am not suggesting that the courts are entirely responsible for the fact that only in a small percentage of cases does a father have custody of his children after a divorce. In most cases the father has not sought custody and does not challenge his wife's claim. The main reason for this situation is that the general assumptions that are held about the sexual division of labour within marriage are extended to the post-divorce situation. Within most marriages, the prime responsibility for childcare falls on women and so it is after the marriage ends. A small and probably increasing proportion of men would like to have the custody and care and control of their children. In many of these cases it seems that they are so certain that this will not be granted to them that they do not bother to raise the issue with their solicitors. One man I interviewed recently thought that it was 'against the law' for men to have custody 'especially if they had daughters.' (He, incidentally, was looking after his children on his own and had consulted a solicitor. Later, after he received some counselling, he asked for and got the custody and care and control of his children.) In turn, solicitors are unlikely to suggest to their male clients that they might seek custody (or joint custody). If the client does bring it up the common advice seems to be that it is not worthwhile to proceed unless their partners will agree to the proposal. So [in] almost all cases where a man does get custody, it is because the spouses have agreed to this, or because the wife has left the matrimonial home and has not maintained contact with the children.

Question

But might there be another reason not to fight? As the *New English Bible* relates:

So they went on arguing in the king's presence. ... Then he said, 'Fetch me a sword.' They brought in a sword and the king gave the order: 'Cut the living child in two and give half to one and half to the other.' At this the woman who was the mother of the living child, moved with love for her child, said to the king, 'Oh! sir, let her have the baby; whatever you do, do not kill it.' The other said, 'Let neither of us have it; cut it in two.' Thereupon the king gave judgement: 'Give the living baby to the first woman; do not kill it. She is its mother.'

Can you think of less drastic ways in which a legal system might try to achieve the same?

For most children, therefore, the vital question is not where, or with whom, they will live but how their parents will resolve what Murch (1980) has called the 'fundamental dilemma facing divorcing parents. This is how to disengage from the broken marriage while preserving a sense of being a parent with a part to play in the children's future.' Many 'absent' parents lose touch with their children. The Wolfson study of *Custody After Divorce* (Eekelaar and Clive, 1977) found a marked falling off in contact over time:

England and Wales **Access by time from separation**

Whether access exercised	Time from separation in years						
	0–½	½–1	1–2	2–3	3–5	5–10	over 10
Access exercised %	66.6	59.0	50.6	49.6	48.6	33.3	18.1
Access not exercised %	28.3	33.7	37.7	37.6	38.9	56.1	54.5
Access infrequent[1] %	5.1	7.4	11.7	12.8	12.5	10.5	27.3
Total number of cases[2]	99	95	77	125	72	57	11

1 Once or twice in previous year or since separation
2 Excluding cases where exercise of access unknown

When Jonathan Bradshaw and Jane Millar studied a representative sample of *Lone Parent Families in the UK* (1991), however, they found some interesting differences (but see also Simpson, McCarthy and Walker, 1995):

Table 2.8: Proportion of absent parents having contact with their children

	%
Divorced	65
Separated	71
Single	38
Length of lone parenthood	
< 6 months	79
6 months–<1 year	65
1–<2 years	61
2–<3 years	60
3–<4 years	55
4–<5 years	67
5–<6 years	54
6–<10 years	52
10+ years	43
Female absent parent	72
Male absent parent	56
Total	57
Base	(1373)

Table 2.10: Absent parent's contact with the lone parent by contact with their children

	Contact between lone parent and absent parent			
	once a week %	once a month %	less than once a month %	no contact %
Contact between children and absent parent				
Once a week	90	11	14	6
Once a month	4	77	21	6
Less than once a month	1	3	51	10
No contact	6	9	15	78
Total	100	100	100	100
Base	(309)	(116)	(219)	(721)

Martin Richards (1982) also addresses the question 'why do non-custodial parents disappear?'

Almost all the evidence we have is about absent fathers so I will discuss this. However, there is no reason to think that male non-custodial parents disappear any more or less often than female ones, although the reasons may differ somewhat in the two cases. I will list some of the reasons that have been uncovered in the research studies.

(*a*) Some men believe that it is in their children's interests for them to disappear. They may feel that their visits will upset the children or that their continued presence makes it less likely that their ex-spouses will settle down with a new partner. Often, and especially in the early days after separation, a child's upset at what has happened is most likely to be apparent before and after a visit from the father. This may lead either parent to try to reduce or stop the visiting. It is hardly surprising that the child's feelings are most likely to be expressed at these times as they will be the most vivid reminders of what has happened. Indeed, it would be odd if any child accepted such a radical change in their lives without upset and in the long term it is probably much better that these feelings are expressed at the time. The real issue here is the capacity of the parents to accept the expression of such feelings at a time when they are likely to be feeling very vulnerable and upset themselves.

(*b*) It is often said, not least by mothers with custody that some fathers are uninterested in their children. Doubtless this is sometimes true but I suspect that this reason is often used to cover others.

(*c*) Some men believe, incorrectly of course, that if they do not see their children they will not be required to pay maintenance. More realistically, others assume that if they have no contact with their old families it will be hard for them to be traced and forced to pay maintenance. Others connect maintenance and access in another way so that they see the money they pay as an entitlement to visit. If they can only afford a little, they see themselves as having little entitlement to visit.

(*d*) Some men are prevented from seeing their children by their ex-spouse. Preventing contact with children is the most obvious weapon available to a custodial parent and some use it. After a long journey the father arrives to find the house empty. Or perhaps a child may always turn out to be 'ill' on access days. More bluntly, a father may simply be told at the doorstep that he cannot see his children. As I have mentioned above, the sanctions are few in such cases and without persistence and the ability to find the right kind of help the situation may seem hopeless.

(*e*) Some men feel that after a separation they want to move away and start again. Particularly if their spouse has a new partner, they may not want to live nearby. Distance may then create too many problems for the visiting arrangements to survive.

(*f*) A new partner may be very resentful of the contact with the children of the first marriage and bring pressure to try to end it. Not infrequently the custodial parent will attempt to argue for access orders which try to prevent the children having contact with a new partner. Although it is not hard to understand the feelings that give rise to such attempts, these are unrealistic and unreasonable from the point of view of both the adults and children and, in general, courts have not sanctioned them. But pressures from both the new and old spouse may effectively reduce access.

(*g*) Access visits may be so painful and upsetting that a father cannot bear to continue with them. This may be because the visits involve meeting the ex-spouse or because the father finds it very difficult to readjust to a new kind of relationship with his children. The latter is particularly likely if access visits are brief. Sometimes the conditions in an access order are such that it seems impossible that any parent could conform, e.g. two hours a month in the old matrimonial home in the presence of the ex-spouse (and often her new partner). If access is brief and the father's home is far away there is the problem of where to take the children. There is also the 'father Christmas syndrome' – where the father seems only able to relate to his children by giving gifts and treats. Anything more realistic and normal may seem threatening to his relationship with the children. As one might expect the problems of access are most acute at the beginning and they usually resolve over time provided, of course, that access continues.

(*h*) Last among the reasons I shall mention, but certainly not least, is the point made to me by many men I have interviewed – that all too often continued contact is not supported or encouraged by anyone. Indeed, I have been told of men being advised by a whole variety of professional people that access was a kind of selfish private indulgence they should give up as soon as possible. Very few had received any sensible advice or help – if they had it was usually from a court welfare officer, one of the few solicitors who specialise in family law or from another parent who had experienced a divorce. ...

There is much debate about the effects of family disruption upon the children. There is also a large research literature. Something of the flavour of this may emerge from the summary in David Utting, *Family and Parenthood – Supporting Families, Preventing Breakdown* (1995):

Separation and divorce – the effects on children

'There is no indication that divorce is entered into lightly. Quite the reverse.'

If children were, miraculously, able to live through their parents' separation or divorce without experiencing any ill (or positive) effects, the personal and social consequences of relationship breakdown might be of limited interest. As it is, there is accumulated evidence that children whose birth parents separate run increased risks of adverse educational, health and behavioural outcomes when compared with those from similar social backgrounds whose parents stay together. Modest, but statistically significant, differences have been observed in terms of reading and arithmetic skills, general health, psychological adjustment, delinquency and personal relationships [Burghes, 1994]. Furthermore, where studies at one time suggested that ill-effects were mostly confined to the years immediately following relationship breakdown, it is now apparent that *some* consequences for *some* children continue into adult life. The chances have been shown to be greater, for example, of leaving school at the minimum age, failing to obtain educational qualifications, leaving home due to friction, cohabitation, marriage and childbearing at an early age, and of poor mental health.

Attempts to unravel the processes responsible for these effects are hampered by methodological difficulties [Amato and Keith, 1991], but few would nowadays deny their existence. There is, however, considerable disagreement over their scale and interpretation – a matter of no small importance if available research is to contribute to practical policy-making. Louie Burghes [1994], in a review of the literature, has, rightly, issued a warning that there is no single or straightforward relationship between family disruption and the consequences for children. Poorer outcomes can occur separately or in association with other factors such as low income, unemployment, reduced parental supervision, mental and physical illness and inadequate schooling. She has also emphasised the equally valid point that there is no *inevitable* path down which children who experience their parent's separation can be expected to travel.

Conflicting perspectives

'It makes good copy for the media to claim that divorce is either a disaster for children or that it does no harm at all. Neither case is true.'

Outcomes observed by comparison with children living in intact families may be less good on average, but that does not mean that every child whose parents divorce – or more than a small minority of children in many cases – is likely to experience a particular difficulty. If, for example, one-third of divorced parents report behaviour difficulties among their children compared with only a fifth of parents in intact families (as was the case in one American study [Peterson and Zill, 1986]), a seemingly impressive statistic emerges that problems were more than 50 per cent more prevalent among the children of divorce. Yet it is equally true that a large majority of children whose parents had divorced did *not* display behaviour problems. Is the policy-maker to conclude that the glass was, in this instance, an encouraging two-thirds empty or a worrying one-third full [Furstenberg and Cherlin, 1991]?

Louie Burghes has concluded that a wide range of psychological, economic and social factors are at work in families affected by parental separation whose subtle connections are only beginning to be understood. Others have warned their academic colleagues and the media against exaggeration and over-simplification when trying to unravel the processes involved [eg Richards, 1994]. This has not deterred less prudent analysts from asserting the primacy of one set of influences over another. The rival theoretical perspectives can be considered under three broad headings [Amato and Keith, 1991]:

- *Father absence*: these focus on the loss of one birth parent – in most cases the father – as the key to understanding the deficits associated with separation and divorce. In Britain, this approach has been given polemical force by Norman Dennis and George Erdos [1992] who argue its relevance to one-parent families whether they result from parental separation or births to single mothers. In their view: 'The longer the same father has been part of the child's life and the more effectively the father has taken part in the life of the family, the better the results for the child.'

- *Child poverty*: interpretations emphasising the economic disadvantage that commonly results from the breakdown of a parental relationship. Children growing up in families that are relatively poor are more likely to encounter health, educational and housing problems. It is also self-evident that families which divide into two households are going to be poorer than they were before. Yet poverty is more obviously one of the consequences of breakdown – six out of ten separated or divorced lone mothers are, at any one time, receiving Income Support [Bradshaw and Millar, 1991] – than a cause.
- *Parental conflict*: a view that what children find most upsetting is high levels of conflict between their parents and that this can prove damaging regardless of whether it leads to separation. Hence the results obtained by the Cambridge Study in Delinquent Development which found similar rates of juvenile criminal involvement among children from 'broken homes' and from high conflict families that were intact [West, 1982; also Utting, 1993]; likewise, analyses of longitudinal studies in Britain and the United States showing that educational and behaviour deficits found among children aged 16 whose parents had divorced could also be observed *before* the divorce took place [Elliott and Richards, 1991; Cherlin, 1991].

One attempt to measure the relative strengths of these perspectives, using the statistical technique of meta-analysis, has looked at results from 92 American and British studies concerned with the well-being of children affected by divorce. It concludes that there is evidence to support all three hypotheses, but that the strongest – or more accurately the 'least weak' – effects are associated with parental conflict [Amato and Keith, 1991].

New dimensions

'You cannot predict anything sensible about an adult's life from just knowing that his or her parents were divorced.'

Almost inevitably, further research will not only reinforce parts of the existing picture, but add new and sometimes unexpected dimensions. To take just one example, the researchers who traced behaviour problems among 16-year-old children whose parents had divorced back to a time before the break-up (see above) have since examined social handicaps and mental health problems among the same sample of children when they were interviewed at age 23 [Cherlin, 1994]. Their study shows that emotional disorders, leaving home due to friction and having a child outside marriage were found significantly more often among the children of divorce than those from intact families (although those affected were only a small minority in both cases). Intriguingly, however, these particular effects did *not* relate to what was observed about the children's emotional state and behaviour at age 7 before their parents' divorce. In other words, studying a different set of outcomes at a later age pinpointed a *different* group of children from divorce backgrounds whose particular problems had emerged during a *different* period of their lives. Those determined to characterise the available research in black and white, rather than multiple shades of grey should, once again, beware.

Re-ordered families

'It is critical that we address the way that an increasing number of children are moving through different family households.'

Understanding the events in children's lives before, during and after their parents' separation can be assisted by examining them as a sequence of events or 'process'. Research, as already seen, suggests that the behaviour and educational achievement of some children is affected by conflict between their parents long before it leads to divorce. Where children have been the unhappy witnesses of domestic violence between their parents, the consequences can be especially traumatic [NCH – Action for Children, 1994; see also p. 409, above]. It is also well-established that children whose parents divorce commonly go through a crisis period of at the time of separation from which they recover with varying degrees of resilience and speed [e.g. Hetherington and Clingempeel, 1992]. For some (see above), there may be long-term consequences.

But that is only part of the story. While some children may remain living with one parent for many years, others will find themselves part of a step-family living with a new parent figure and, perhaps, his or her children from a previous relationship. Half-brothers and sisters may also be born. There is the possibility, too, that this second partnership will break down (if current trends are maintained, 50 per cent of re-marriages will end in divorce) to be followed by further transitions. The question which research has, in recent years, begun to consider is what influence this 're-ordering' of families exerts over children's lives, health and happiness.

According to one study, young people who have lived in a lone-parent family [headed by their mother] before the age of 16 as a result of divorce are more likely to leave school at the minimum age and to leave home by 18 compared with those in intact families. However, the chances of those events occurring among children who become part of a step-family following divorce are *also* significantly greater [Kiernan, 1992]. In addition, there are increased risks (compared with intact families) of girls and boys in step-families leaving home due to friction, marrying before the age of 20 and becoming a parent by an equally young age.

Such findings could not be expected if children's outcomes after divorce were determined entirely by economic poverty, since a lone parent's re-partnering would normally increase rather than diminish family income. They would not, likewise, be expected if the outcomes depended on whether families were headed literally by one parent or two. The fact that children living in step-families following the death of one parent were generally not found to have been affected in the same way is further evidence that the particular reason for family disruption is relevant to the outcomes for children rather than disruption *per se*.

There is even more contention about what can be done to minimise any short- or long-term ill effects for children. For a long time, ideas about what was best for children were influenced by the work of John Bowlby, whose book *Child Care and the Growth of Love* was first published in 1953. The gist of his theory is stated at the outset:

... What is believed to be essential for mental health is that an infant and young child should experience a warm, intimate, and continuous relationship with his mother (or permanent mother-substitute – one person who steadily 'mothers' him) in which both find satisfaction and enjoyment. It is this complex, rich and rewarding relationship with the mother in the early years, varied in countless ways by relations with the father and with the brothers and sisters, that child psychiatrists and many others now believe to underlie the development of character and of mental health.

A state of affairs in which a child does not have this relationship is termed 'maternal deprivation'. This is a general term covering a number of different situations. Thus, a child is deprived even though living at home if his mother (or permanent mother-substitute) is unable to give him the loving care small children need. Again a child is deprived if for any reason he is removed from his mother's care. ...

The ill-effects of deprivation vary with its degree. Partial deprivation brings in its train anxiety, excessive need for love, powerful feelings of revenge, and, arising from these last, guilt and depression. A young child, still immature in mind and body, cannot cope with all these emotions and drives. The ways in which he responds to those disturbances of his inner life may in the end bring about nervous disorders and instability of character. ...

Bowlby goes on to explain why the discussion in the book concentrates upon the mother and does not deal in detail with the father:

The reason for this is that almost all the evidence concerns the child's relation to his mother, which is without doubt in ordinary circumstances by far his most important relationship during these years. It is she who feeds and cleans him, keeps him warm and comforts him. It is to his mother that he turns when in distress. In the young child's eyes father plays second fiddle and his value increases only as the child becomes more able to stand alone. Nevertheless, as the illegitimate child knows, fathers have their uses even in infancy. Not only do they provide for their wives to enable them to devote themselves unrestrictedly to the care of the infant and toddler, but, by providing love and companionship, they support the mother emotionally and help her maintain that harmonious contented mood in the atmosphere of which her infant thrives.

Question

It is noticeable that this paragraph is phrased, not in terms of how things necessarily *should* be, but of how they in fact are: do you think that his estimate of the respective roles of mother and father in caring for very young children generally holds good today?

In *Maternal Deprivation Reassessed* (1981), Michael Rutter examined the components of the theory and concluded that various modifications are required. In particular:

A further point of departure from Bowlby's views concerns the supposedly special importance of the mother. He has argued that the child is innately monotropic and that the bond with the mother (or mother-surrogate) is different in kind from the bonds developed with others. The evidence on that point is unsatisfactory but what there is seems not to support that view. Two issues are involved. The first is whether or not the main bond differs from all others. It is suggested here that it does not. The chief bond is especially important because of its greater strength, but most children develop bonds with several people and it appears likely that these bonds are basically similar. The second concerns the assumption that the 'mother' or 'mother-surrogate' is the person to whom the child is necessarily most attached. Of course in most families the mother has most to do with the young child and as a consequence she is usually the person with whom the strongest bond is formed. But it should be appreciated that the chief bond need not be with the chief caretaker and it need not be with a female.

Furthermore, it seems to be incorrect to regard the person with whom there is the main bond as necessarily and generally the most important person in the child's life. That person will be most important for some things but not for others. For some aspects of development the same-sexed parent seems to have a special role, for some the person who plays and talks most with the child and for others the person who feeds the child. The father, the mother, brothers and sisters, friends, school-teachers and others all have an impact on development, but their influence and importance differs for different aspects of development. A less exclusive focus on the mother is required. Children also have fathers!

In *Beyond the Best Interests of the Child* (1973), Joseph Goldstein, Anna Freud and Albert J. Solnit, respectively a lawyer, a psychoanalyst and a psychiatrist collaborate in an attempt to use 'psychoanalytic theory to develop generally applicable guidelines to child placement.' That theory 'establishes, for example, as do developmental studies by students of other orientations, the need of every child for unbroken continuity of affectionate and stimulating experiences with an adult.' The authors develop three basic concepts. The first is that of the relationship between a 'psychological parent' and a 'wanted child' whom they later define as follows:

A wanted child is one who receives affection and nourishment on a continuing basis from at least one adult and who feels that he or she is and continues to be valued by those who take care of him or her.

A psychological parent is one who, on a continuing, day-to-day basis, through interaction, companionship, interplay, and mutuality, fulfills the child's psychological needs for a parent, as well as the child's physical needs. The psychological parent may be a biological ..., adoptive, foster, or common law ... parent, or any other person. There is no presumption in favor of any of these after the initial assignment at birth. ...

Secondly, they stress the need for continuity in this relationship:

Continuity of relationships, surroundings, and environmental influence are essential for a child's normal development. Since they do not play the same role in later life, their importance is often underrated by the adult world.

Physical, emotional, intellectual, social, and moral growth does not happen without causing the child inevitable internal difficulties. The instability of all mental processes during the period of development needs to be offset by stability and uninterrupted support from external sources. Smooth growth is arrested or disrupted when upheavals and changes in the external world are added to the internal ones.

Disruptions of continuity have different consequences for different ages:

In *infancy*, from birth to approximately 18 months, any change in routine leads to food refusals, digestive upsets, sleeping difficulties, and crying. Such reactions occur even if the infant's care is divided merely between mother and baby-sitter. They are all the more massive where the infant's day is divided between home and day care center; or where infants are displaced from the mother to an institution; from institutional to foster care; or from fostering to adoption. Every step of this kind inevitably brings with it changes in the ways the infant is handled, fed, put to bed, and comforted. Such moves from the familiar to the unfamiliar cause discomfort, distress, and delays in the infant's orientation and adaptation within his surroundings.

Change of the caretaking person for *infants and toddlers* further affects the course of their emotional development. Their attachments, at these ages, are as thoroughly upset by separations as they are effectively promoted by the constant, uninterrupted presence and attention of a familiar adult. When infants and young children find themselves abandoned by the parent, they not only suffer separation distress and anxiety but also setbacks in the quality of their next attachments, which will be less trustful. Where continuity of such relationships is interrupted more than once, as happens due to multiple placements in the early years, the children's emotional attachments become increasingly shallow and indiscriminate. They tend to grow up as persons who lack warmth in their contacts with fellow beings.

For *young children* under the age of 5 years, every disruption of continuity also affects those achievements which are rooted and develop in the intimate interchange with a stable parent figure, who is in the process of becoming the psychological parent. The more recently the achievement has been acquired, the easier it is for the child to lose it. Examples of this are cleanliness and speech. After separation from the familiar mother, young children are known to have breakdowns in toilet training and to lose or lessen their ability to communicate verbally.

For *school-age children*, the breaks in their relationships with their psychological parents affect above all those achievements which are based on identification with the parents' demands, prohibitions, and social ideals. Such identifications develop only where attachments are stable and tend to be abandoned by the child if he feels abandoned by the adults in question. Thus, where children are made to wander from one environment to another, they may cease to identify with any set of substitute parents. Resentment toward the adults who have disappointed them in the past makes them adopt the attitude of not caring for anybody; or of making the new parent the scapegoat for the shortcomings of the former one. In any case, multiple placement at these ages puts many children beyond the reach of educational influence, and becomes the direct cause of behavior which the schools experience as disrupting and the courts label as dissocial, delinquent, or even criminal.

With *adolescents*, the superficial observation of their behavior may convey the idea that what they desire is discontinuation of parental relationships rather than their preservation and stability. Nevertheless, this impression is misleading in this simple form. It is true that their revolt against any parental authority is normal developmentally since it is the adolescent's way toward establishing his own independent adult identity. But for a successful outcome it is important that the breaks and disruptions of attachment should come exclusively from his side and not be imposed on him by any form of abandonment or rejection on the psychological parents' part.

Adults who as children suffered from disruptions of continuity may themselves, in 'identifying' with their many 'parents,' treat their children as they themselves were treated – continuing a cycle costly for both a new generation of children as well as for society itself.

Thus, continuity is a guideline because emotional attachments are tenuous and vulnerable in early life and need stability of external arrangements for their development.

Thirdly, they discuss the child's sense of time:

A child's sense of time, as an integral part of the continuity concept, requires independent consideration. That interval of separation between parent and child which would constitute a break in continuity for an infant, for example, would be of no or little significance to a school-age youngster. The time it takes to break an old or to form a new attachment will depend upon the different meanings time has for children at each stage of their development.

Unlike adults, who have learned to anticipate the future and thus to manage delay, children have a built-in time sense based on the urgency of their instinctual and emotional needs. As an infant's memory begins to incorporate the way in which parents satisfy wishes and needs, as well as the experience of the reappearance of parents after their disappearance, a child gradually develops the capacity to delay gratification and to anticipate and plan for the future.

Emotionally and intellectually an infant and toddler cannot stretch his waiting more than a few days without feeling overwhelmed by the absence of parents. He cannot take care of himself physically, and his emotional and intellectual memory is not sufficiently matured to enable him to use thinking to hold on to the parent he has lost. During such an absence for the child under two years of age, the new adult who cares for the child's physical needs is latched onto 'quickly' as the potential psychological parent. The replacement, however ideal, may not be able to heal completely, without emotional scarring, the injury sustained by the loss.

For most children under the age of five years, an absence of parents for more than two months is equally beyond comprehension. For the younger school-age child, an absence of six months or more may be similarly experienced. More than one year of being without parents and without evidence that there are parental concerns and expectations is not likely to be understood by the older school-aged child and will carry with it the detrimental implications of the breaches in continuity we have already described. After adolescence is fully launched an individual's sense of time closely approaches that of most adults.

Finally, they point to the limits of the law's ability to supervise personal relationships and of knowledge to predict long-range outcomes:

While the law may claim to establish relationships, it can in fact do little more than give them recognition and provide an opportunity for them to develop. The law, so far as specific individual relationships are concerned, is a relatively crude instrument. It may be able to destroy human relationships; but it does not have the power to compel them to develop. It neither has the sensitivity nor the resources to maintain or supervise the ongoing day-to-day happenings between parent and child – and these are essential to meeting ever-changing demands and needs. Nor does it have the capacity to predict future events and needs, ... [However] placement decisions can be based on certain generally applicable and useful predictions. We can, for example, identify who, among *presently available adults*, is or has the capacity to become a psychological parent and thus will enable a child to feel wanted. We can predict that the adult most likely suited for this role is the one, if there be one, with whom the child has already had and continues to have an affectionate bond rather than one of otherwise equal potential who is not yet in a primary relationship with the child. Further, we can predict that the younger the child and the more extended the period of uncertainty or separation, the more detrimental it will be to the child's well-being and the more urgent it becomes even without perfect knowledge to place the child permanently.

Beyond these, our capacity to predict is limited.

These concepts lead the authors to propose the following guidelines for all child placement decisions:

As an overall guideline for child placement we propose, instead of the 'in-the-best-interests-of-the-child' standard, 'the least detrimental available alternative for safeguarding the child's growth and development.' The new standard has as its major components the three guidelines which we have already described. The least detrimental alternative, then, is that specific placement and procedure for placement which maximizes, in accord with the child's sense of time and on the basis of short-term predictions given the limitations of knowledge, his or her opportunity for being wanted and for maintaining on a continuous basis a relationship with at least one adult who is or will become his psychological parent.

However, the reasoning behind this proposal also reveals how unhelpful it is in the normal dispute between parents:

To use 'detrimental' rather than 'best interest' should enable legislatures, courts, and child care agencies to acknowledge and respond to the inherent detriments in any procedure for child placement as well as in each child placement decision itself. It should serve to remind decision-makers that their task is to salvage as much as possible out of an unsatisfactory situation. It should reduce the likelihood of their becoming enmeshed in the hope and magic associated with 'best,' which often mistakenly leads them into believing that they have greater power for doing 'good' than 'bad'.

The concept of 'available alternatives' should press into focus how limited is the capacity of decisionmakers to make valid predictions and how limited are the choices generally open to them for helping a child in trouble. If the choice, as it may often be in separation and divorce proceedings, is between two psychological parents and if each parent is equally suitable in terms of the child's most immediate predictable developmental needs, the least detrimental standard would dictate a quick, final, and unconditional disposition to either of the competing parents.

It is difficult not to sympathise with the comment of Mnookin, in *Child Custody Adjudication: Judicial Functions in the Face of Indeterminacy* (1975):

I believe that psychologists and psychiatrists can rather consistently differentiate between a situation where an adult and a child have a substantial relationship of the sort we characterize as parent-child and that where there is no such relationship at all. But I do not think that existing psychological theories provide the basis to choose generally between two adults where the child has some relationship and psychological attachment to each. …

Often each parent will have a different sort of relationship with the child, with the child attached to each. One may be warm, easy-going, but incapable of discipline. The other may be fair, able to set limits, but unable to express affection. By what criteria is an expert to decide which is less detrimental? Moreover, even the proponents of psychological standards have acknowledged how problematic it is to evaluate relationships from a psychological perspective unless a highly trained person spends a considerable amount of time observing the parent and child interact or talking to the child. Superficial examinations by those without substantial training may be worse than nothing. And yet, that is surely a high risk. …

While the psychologists and psychiatrists have made substantial therapeutic contributions, they are not soothsayers capable of predicting with any degree of confidence how a child is likely to benefit from alternative placements. When the expert does express a preference, it too often is based on an unexpected value preference. What is psychologically least detrimental will usually be no more determinate for expert and nonexpert alike than what is in a child's best interests; and to reframe the question in a way that invites predictions based on the use of labels and terminology developed for treatment is both demeaning to the expert and corrupting for the judicial process.

Questions

(i) Dingwall and Eekelaar (1986) would go further: 'Psychology is used selectively to legitimate an ideal of social organisation so that moral or political choices are made to appear matters of natural law.' How would you describe the moral and political choices of Goldstein, Freud and Solnit?

(ii) Goldstein, Freud and Solnit's footnote to the last passage quoted from their book suggests that 'a judicially supervised drawing of lots between two equally acceptable psychological parents might be the most rational and least offensive process for resolving the hard choice.' Do you agree?

Goldstein, Freud and Solnit's arguments, however, did lead to some firm and controversial conclusions on post-separation contact:

Children have difficulty in relating positively to, profiting from, and maintaining the contact with two psychological parents who are not in positive contact with each other. Loyalty conflicts are common and normal under such conditions and may have devastating consequences by destroying the child's positive relationships to both parents. A 'visiting' or 'visited' parent has little chance to serve as a true object for love, trust, and identification, since this role is based on his being available on an uninterrupted day-to-day basis.

Once it is determined who will be the custodial parent, it is that parent, not the court, who must decide under what conditions he or she wishes to raise the child. Thus, the noncustodial parent should have no legally enforceable right to visit the child, and the custodial parent should have the right to decide whether it is desirable for the child to have such visits. What we have said is designed to protect the security of an ongoing relationship – that between the child and the custodial parent. At the same time the state neither makes nor breaks the psychological relationship between the child and the noncustodial parent, which the adults involved may have jeopardized. It leaves to them what only they can ultimately resolve.

Martin Richards (1982), however, argues that continued contact is so much in the interests of the child that the system should try harder to encourage it. In discussing the needs of children, he first points to the lack of good direct evidence either way, and continues:

There are a couple of findings in the psychological studies which have turned up several times and are at least consistent with my hypothesis. The first is that some of the long-term disruptive effects on children whose parents divorce are most marked if the separation comes earlier (say before the age of five) rather than later (eg Douglas, 1970). Several explanations are possible but one of these is that the likelihood of losing contact with the non-custodial parent will increase over time and so is most likely to be lost after an earlier separation. A similar explanation can be given of the evidence that divorce is more upsetting for children who remain with their mothers if those mothers remarry (Douglas, 1970), as the presence of a step-father almost always reduces contact with the father (Furstenberg, 1981).

The nearest we get to a direct study of the question of continuing contact is an American one where groups of children spending varying amounts of time with each of their divorced or separated parents were compared (Keshet and Rosenthal, 1978). Here the children (and parents) who spent at least 25% of their time with each of their parents seem to adjust best. However, in this study we cannot be certain that factors other than the post-separation arrangements determined the outcome. For instance, it could be that parents who decide to share their time with their children after separation are also parents who prepare their children for the separation and support them before it occurs. However, this evidence is in the same direction as the hints which can be found in all the recent studies of children of divorced parents that continuing relations with both parents are desirable from the point of view of the children's adjustment (Weiss 1975, 1979; Wallerstein and Kelly, 1980). ...

A continued relationship with the non-custodial parent would appear to offer many psychological advantages for children. One of the most obvious is that it offers a wider variety of experience; the experience of a relationship with a second parent. A child is not denied a close and continuing relationship with a parent of each gender. This may be of special value in the development of his or her own gender identity (which has been shown to be disturbed in some studies of children of divorce) (Hetherington, 1972). With two parents a child is given the opportunity of learning how to move from one relationship to another. Often this is seen in a rather negative sense as something a child must learn to cope with. But I think we should see it much more positively as a very necessary skill for adult life that allows us to live within a whole network of relationships of differing kinds and qualities. It might be argued that these aspects of development should be satisfied equally by any two (or more) adults, not just a child's parents. To some extent this may be true, but there are many indications that parental relations are usually very special and cannot be replaced by other adults in any easy way. To say this is not to evoke any concept of a blood tie but one of a psychological parent. The potency of a psychological parent lies in the continuity of the relationship with their child and their symbolic position as a parent. A separation that does not involve the loss of one parent is likely to be much less disturbing of a child's social connections outside the immediate family. Friends and relatives of the non-custodial parent are not lost to the child. The child has a much better chance of maintaining links with both sets of grandparents.

At a separation, it is usual that among the many feelings a child is likely to experience is anger (Wallerstein and Kelly 1980). This anger is associated with the wish or fantasy that the parents will come back together again and it is generally expressed towards the parent who spends most time looking after the child regardless of their role in the separation. If a child is able to maintain a relationship with both parents this anger gradually dissipates as the child begins to feel confident in the new kind of relationship that develops with both parents. The separation of the parents gradually ceases to be the total threat to the child's life it once had seemed. In a case where the child does not have contact with the non-custodial parent the resolution of the anger at the parents' separation may be much more complex and prolonged. The absent parent, just because he or she is absent, may be built up into a totally idealised figure while the custodial parent's role is seen as that of the person who has driven out the 'ideal' parent. Everything that goes wrong or frustrates the child may be laid at the door of the custodial parent. Under this emotional pressure even the strongest of parents begins to react so that the child may feel signs of rejection or anger in return. This in turn increases the child's anger and insecurity. Of course, not all children of divorce react in this way, but those who do are probably those who have lost contact with one parent.

It has been suggested that a continued relationship with both parents makes the acceptance of a step-parent much more difficult for a child. There is no evidence to support this idea, which is improbable in view of our understanding of a child's parental relations. The unlikely assumption here is that a child has the capacity for two parental relations and if both spaces are filled there will be no space for anybody else. In fact there is great variation in number and kind of relations that a child can maintain (Shaffer and Emerson, 1964). It seems much more likely that if children feel confident that they are going to lose neither of their parents despite the marital separation, that they will accept a new adult more easily. Certainly, we need to move beyond the simplistic notion of very fixed parental roles which can be occupied by anybody that a parent or a court chooses to place in that position.

At the social level there are several very powerful arguments that can be given for the maintenance of ties with both parents.

For many, if not most children, a marital separation is followed by a permanent or temporary period in a single-parent family. We have abundant evidence that these families suffer from many disadvantages (Ferri, 1976). Among these are the effects of a single person providing for all the children's needs day in and day out and the low incomes typical of such families. Both of these are likely to be reduced by continuing [contact] with the non-custodial parent. Such a parent not only provides the child with an alternative home but is also a relief for the custodial parent. These breaks allow the custodial parent to recharge emotional batteries and indulge in some adult life uninterrupted by the demands of childcare.

In principle, there is no connection between access and the payment of maintenance by non-custodial parents. However, this is not the way it is always seen by those involved. Parents who have regular contact with their children and maintain a close relationship are much more likely to want to pay maintenance and feel that it is fair and reasonable to do so. If the contact is maintained the needs of the children including financial ones will be more obvious and are likely to be more freely met.

One can also see the non-custodial parent as a kind of insurance policy for children. Lives of custodial parents cannot be predicted with certainty; changes may occur which make it very difficult or impossible for them to cope with children. If there is a disaster a second parent who is in close touch can often take the children and so avoid another major upheaval.

But what of the negative side – what arguments are there against the continuing involvement of both parents? There is a general belief, which is borne out by the research studies, that many difficulties are associated with access visits. However, the extent of these should not be exaggerated. Murch's study (1980), for instance, found a majority who are satisfied with their access arrangements and he also noted that initial difficulties often resolved in time. That difficulties occur around access visits is hardly surprising as this will often be the one point of contact between spouses (Eekelaar, 1982). The remedy of cutting off the contact may be superficially attractive, but in the long term is unlikely to help the adults to resolve their difficulties, apart from its likely effects on the children.

Part of our ambivalence about access is expressed in the common attitude that, though access is desirable, it can easily be overdone and so it is necessary to limit visits in terms of both their duration and frequency. Over-long or frequent visits are held to lead to confusions of loyalty for the children and to undermine their security in their main home. Clearly, if two parents are determined to continue their battles via their children, heavy pressures can be brought to bear which, if long-lasting, could make life a misery for children. However, such battles are usually relatively short-lived. As the separated parents begin to rebuild their lives and acquire new concerns and interests the old battles begin to lose their fire. Also children are surprisingly resourceful in avoiding situations which cause them pain.

One of the feelings that most concerns children at a parental separation is the fear of loss of both parents. If one parent has chosen to leave home and live elsewhere, why should not the other one make the same decision at a future date? The only way in which these fears can be countered is by a demonstration that there is continuity in the new arrangements. But it is not always understood that a child's fears are best countered if continuity is demonstrated in *both* parental relationships. Part of the mistaken fear that access visits are disturbing rests on the assumption that they may unsettle the relationship with the custodial parent. However, unless the child has a reasonable amount of time with the non-custodial parent there is no chance to regain confidence in that relationship.

Perhaps the most common cause of difficulties in access is that visits are too brief. We are well-used to descriptions of the Sunday afternoon access visit spent in the park and cafe. Only a moment's reflection is required to see how difficult or impossible it would be to recreate a normal parental relationship on that kind of basis. What children and adults need is the chance to share some of the very ordinary and routine aspects of life. Access visits must be long enough to remove the sense that they are a special occasion. Excessive gifts and the provision of 'treats' are sure signs that an ordinary relationship has not been recreated. The matter was summed up very clearly by a man I interviewed who told me that it was only after he had first got angry with his children during a visit that he began to feel that they were getting back to a reasonable relationship.

Given the many factors that will influence a particular situation and the practical constraints in making visiting arrangements I feel it would be unwise to try to lay down norms for the length of visits. However, I think it is fairly obvious that difficulties will be more common if overnight stays are not possible.

Sometimes it is felt important that things like rules about bedtimes should be as similar as possible in the two homes. Children often make comparisons and talk about any differences they have noted. In general, I would take the ability to talk openly about such differences as evidence that they were coming to terms with the separateness of their parents. Children will, of course, also try to exploit differences between the homes, supposed and real, to get what they want from a parent. But it is simple enough to make it clear to them that rules between the homes may differ and the fact that they are allowed to do X in the other house is no reason why they should do it here. Far from seeing differences in rules and routines in the two homes as confusing for children, I think there are good reasons for viewing them as advantages. They are ways of seeing something of variety in life and learning that there is not always a single answer to a problem. If different activities are possible in the two homes, just as the two relationships with the two parents will each have its own characteristics, so much the better for the children.

Richards makes several suggestions about how we might encourage continued contact but primarily he says this:

The awarding of custody to a single parent at divorce is a public acknowledgment and notice that the role of the non-custodial parent is expected to be reduced. My first suggestion is that we cease to give such notice in the majority of cases. Much more appropriate would be a public reaffirmation that, in spite of the adults' separation, parental duties persist. The most obvious way in which this could be done is by making joint custody the norm – courts could either automatically make such an order unless strong and specific arguments against it were brought forward or they could make no order as to custody in this situation so that the position existing before divorce could persist.

The evidence to support this hypothesis is, however, questioned by sociologists Frank Furstenberg and Andrew Cherlin, in *Divided Families – What Happens to Children When Parents Part* (1991):

WHAT MAKES A DIFFERENCE?

A critical factor in both short-term and long-term adjustment is how effectively the custodial parent, who usually is the mother, functions as a parent. We have noted how difficult it can be for a recently separated mother to function well. The first year or two after the separation is a difficult time for many mothers, who may feel angry, depressed, irritable, or sad. Their own distress may make it more difficult to cope with their children's distress, leading in some cases to a disorganized household, lax supervision, inconsistent discipline, and the coercive cycles between mothers and preschool-aged sons that have been identified by Hetherington and others [Chase-Langdale and Hetherington, 1990; Hetherington, 1987, 1989]. Mothers who can cope better with the disruption can be more effective parents. They can keep their work and home lives going from day to day and can better provide love, nurturing, consistent discipline, and a predictable routine.

Quite often their distress is rooted in, or at least identified by, financial problems. Loss of the father's income can cause a disruptive, downward spiral in which children must adjust to a declining standard of living, a mother who is less psychologically available and is home less often, an apartment in an unfamiliar neighborhood, a different school, and new friends. This sequence of events occurs at a time when children are greatly upset about the separation and need love, support, and a familiar daily routine.

A second key factor in children's well-being is a low level of conflict between their mother and father. This principle applies, in fact, to intact as well as disrupted families. Recall the finding from the NSC [National Study of Children] that children who live with two parents who persistently quarrel over important areas of family life show higher levels of distress and behavior problems than do children from disrupted marriages. Some observers take this finding to imply that children are better off if their parents divorce than if they remain in an unhappy marriage. We think this is true in some cases but not in others. It is probably true that most children who live in a household filled with continual conflict between angry, embittered spouses would be better off if their parents split up – assuming that the level of conflict is lowered by the separation. And there is no doubt that the rise in divorce has liberated some children (and their custodial parents) from families marked by physical abuse, alcoholism, drugs, and violence. But we doubt that such clearly pathological descriptions apply to most families that disrupt. Rather, we think there are many more cases in which there is little open conflict, but one or both partners finds the marriage personally unsatisfying. The unhappy partner may feel unfulfilled, distant from his or her spouse, bored, or constrained. ... Under these circumstances, divorce may well make one or both spouses happier; but we strongly doubt that it improves the psychological well-being of the children.

A possible third key factor in children's successful adjustment is the maintenance of a continuing relationship with the noncustodial parent, who is usually the father. But direct evidence that lack of contact with the father inhibits the adjustment of children to divorce is less than satisfactory. A number of experts have stressed the importance of a continuing relationship, yet research findings are inconsistent. The main evidence comes from both the Hetherington and Wallerstein [Wallerstein and Kelly, 1980] studies, each of which found that children were better adjusted when they saw their fathers regularly. More recently, however, other observational studies have not found this relationship [see Emery, 1988].

And in the NSC, the amount of contact that children had with their fathers seemed to make little difference for their well-being. Teenagers who saw their fathers regularly were just as likely as were those with infrequent contact to have problems in school or engage in delinquent acts and precocious sexual behavior. Furthermore, the children's behavioral adjustment was also unrelated to the level of intimacy and identification with the nonresidential father. No differences were observed even among the children who had both regular contact and close relations with their father outside the home. Moreover, when the children in the NSC were reinterviewed in 1987 at ages 18 to 23, those who had retained stable, close ties to their fathers were neither more nor less successful than those who had had low or inconsistent levels of contact and intimacy with their fathers [Furstenberg et al., 1987].

Another common argument is that fathers who maintain regular contact with their children also may keep paying child support to their children's mothers. Studies do show that fathers who visit more regularly pay more in child support [Furstenberg et al., 1983]. But it's not clear that they pay more *because* they visit more. Rather, it may be that fathers who have a greater commitment to their children both visit and pay more. If so, then the problem is to increase the level of commitment most fathers feel, not simply to increase the amount of visiting.

These puzzling findings make us cautious about drawing any firm conclusions about the psychological benefits of contact with non-custodial parents for children's adjustment in later life. Yet despite the mixed evidence, the idea that continuing contact with fathers makes a difference to a child's psychological well-being is so plausible and so seemingly grounded in theories of child development that one is reluctant to discount it. It may be that evidence is difficult to obtain because so few fathers living outside the home are intimately involved in childrearing. It is also likely that, even when fathers remain involved, most formerly married parents have difficulty establishing a collaborative style of childrearing. We remain convinced that when parents are able to cooperate in childrearing after a divorce and when fathers are able to maintain an active and supportive role, children will be better off in the long run. But we are certain that such families are rare at present and unlikely to become common in the near future.

DOES CUSTODY MAKE A DIFFERENCE FOR CHILDREN?

The belief that the father's involvement is beneficial to children was an important reason why many states recently adopted joint-custody statutes. ...

Joint *legal* custody seems to be hardly distinguishable in practice from maternal sole custody [Albiston et al., 1990]. ... It appears that joint legal custody does not substantially increase the father's decision-making authority, his involvement in childrearing, or the amount of child support he pays. Why is it so hard to increase fathers' involvement after divorce? For one thing, ... many men don't seem to know how to relate to their children except through their wives. Typically, when married, they were present but passive – not much involved in childrearing. When they separate, they carry this pattern of limited involvement with them; and it is reinforced by the modest contact most have with their children. Uncomfortable and unskilled at being an active parent, marginalized by infrequent contact, focused on building a new family life, many fathers fade from their children's lives.

Less is known about joint physical custody. But a few recent studies suggest that it isn't necessarily better for children's adjustment than the alternatives. Among all families in the Stanford Study in which children still were seeing both parents about two years after the separation, parents in dual-residence families talked and coordinated rules more; but they quarreled about the children just as much as did parents in single-residence families [Maccoby et al., 1990]. Several colleagues of Wallerstein followed 58 mother-physical-custody families and 35 joint-physical-custody families for two years after the families had been referred to counseling centers in the San Francisco area. Many of the parents were disputing custody and visitation arrangements. Children from the joint-physical-custody families were no better adjusted than children from the mother-physical-custody families: their levels of behavior problems, their self-esteem, their ease at making friends were very similar. What did make a difference for the children was the depression and anxiety levels of their parents and the amount of continuing verbal and physical aggression between them, regardless of the custody arrangements. The authors suggest that children whose parents are having serious disputes may have more behavior problems, lower self-esteem, and less acceptance by friends if they shuttle between homes. They are exposed to more conflict, and their movement back and forth may even generate it [Kline et al., 1989].

The admittedly limited evidence so far suggests to us that custody arrangements may matter less for the well-being of children than had been thought. It is, of course, possible that when more evidence is available, joint custody will be shown to have important benefits for some families. As with father involvement, the rationale for joint custody is so plausible and attractive that one is tempted to disregard the disappointing evidence and support it anyway. But based on what is known now, we think custody and visitation matter less for children than the two factors we noted earlier: how much conflict there is between the parents and how effectively the parent (or parents) the child lives with functions. It is likely that a child who alternates between the homes of a distraught mother and an angry father will be more troubled than a child who lives with a mother who is coping well and who once a fortnight sees a father who has disengaged from his family. Even the frequency of visits with a father seems to matter less than the climate in which they take place.

For now, we would draw two conclusions. First, joint physical custody should be enouraged only in cases where both parents voluntarily agree to it. Among families in which both parents shared the childrearing while they were married, a voluntary agreement to maintain joint physical custody probably will work and benefit the children. Even among families in which one parent did most of the childrearing prior to the divorce, a voluntary agreement won't do any harm – although we think the agreement likely will break down to sole physical custody over time. But only very rarely should joint physical custody be imposed if one or both parents do not want it. There may be a few cases in which the father and mother truly shared the childrearing before the divorce but one of them won't agree to share physical custody afterward. These difficult cases call for mediation or counseling, and they may require special consideration. But among the vastly larger number of families in which little sharing occurred beforehand and one or both parents doesn't want to share physical custody afterward, imposing joint physical custody would invite continuing conflict without any clear benefits. Even joint legal custody may matter more as a symbol of fathers' ties to their children than in any concrete sense. But symbols can be important, and joint legal custody seems, at worst, to do no harm. A legal preference for it may send a message to fathers that society respects their rights to and responsibilities for their children.

Our second conclusion is that in weighing alternative public policies concerning divorce, the thin empirical evidence of the benefits of joint custody and frequent visits with fathers must be acknowledged.

On the other hand, Martin Richards, in *Private Worlds and Public Intentions* (1993), suggests that the need for contact should dictate where the children are to live:

The principle of the primacy of the welfare of the children should still obtain in such situations but I suggest it should be given a single simple definition, that the children should reside with whichever parent is able to convince the court that they are the parent most likely to foster and maintain the children's links with the other parent. Such a criterion has a long history (Solomon, 1 Kings 3.16–28) and should ensure that attention is focused on the welfare of the children rather than the supposed moral worth of each parent. Here my argument directly contradicts that of those feminists who have argued for a system based exclusively on who was the primary caretaker within marriage (Smart and Sevenhuijsen, 1989). While such a system is attractive in its simplicity, it fails to take account of the changes in living arrangements and employment that divorce may bring and seems likely to reinforce further the expectation that child care should remain a mother's duty.

This is how sociologist Carol Smart explains the argument about caring in *The Legal and Moral Ordering of Child Custody* (1990):

We are now in a position to recognise the complexity of the concept of 'care' and to appreciate that it is not simply a natural outpouring of instinctual love but a *moral practice*. As Tronto (1989) has summarised, there is a distinction to be made between 'caring about' and 'caring for'. Typically we have taken 'caring about' to be a moral position. Hence caring about what happens to people is regarded as taking a moral stance. But 'caring for' has not been regarded as a moral stance, merely a maternal activity which arises from instinct which is, if anything, amoral.

Herein lies an important distinction between the moral claims that women and men make in relation to children. In relation to fathers it is common to hear the sort of statement that takes the form, 'He is their father after all'. What is meant by this and how does it compare with how both men and women typically talk about mothers' relationships to children?

'He is their father after all'

This statement carries two quite contradictory meanings. The first is an assertion of a right arising from biological fatherhood. This is a statement which implies a legal or moral right arising out of a procreative act. But why isn't it sufficient to say 'He is their father' or 'I am their father'? Why is the 'after all' added? What does this add or take away? This 'after all', which men add as often as women, is a form of apology. It means 'I may not have done much but I am still their father'. It means 'I may not occupy the same moral terrain in terms of what I should claim, but I shall claim it anyway because of my biological status'.

Consider the following statement.

Maureen: He said he hadn't been a bad father and he didn't see why any judge would say to him that he couldn't have joint custody. I thought he had quite a good point really because he hadn't been a bad father. He *had* left them, but before that he wasn't cruel or vindictive and we didn't go short of anything so really I couldn't say that he had abused the children in any way.

In this construction it is enough for this mother that her husband has not done any harm for her to acknowledge his legal rights. But consider her reaction when asked how she might have felt if her husband had tried to gain care and control of their sons.

Maureen: I would have fought tooth and nail that he couldn't have them. There is no way he would have taken the children off me because I am a good mother and I love my children. ... Yes, I think mothers and fathers feel differently about their children and a mother's love is a strong deep love and even though they are boys, and boys are supposed to be closer to their father, I think in a stable background I would give them the best stability and love in their lives until they are old enough to go on their own.

Now, we can dismiss this as special pleading based on an outdated ideology of motherhood and mother love. It might even be that she is mistaken and that she can't give her sons what they most need and so on. But this is not the point. She was making a moral claim which had its foundations in the years of care she had given to her sons. If we say this is nothing, or that it counts for little, we are adopting a position which affirms that the act of 'caring for' has no (moral) value in our culture. We continue to place 'caring about' above 'caring for' and turn the moral content of acts of caring into self-interest.

In her statement Maureen is obviously associating the moral claim that arises out of caring with gender identity. That is to say she does use the language of the ideology of motherhood which is held as suspect in many quarters. Indeed one of the main claims of fathers' rights groups is that there is nothing intrinsic to being a woman/mother which means you can love deeply and care well. But this is not the end of the story as it is so often presumed. We can accept that there is nothing intrinsically caring about being a woman, but that does not mean we should reject the meanings that arise from providing care and nurture. Indeed, this research has indicated quite clearly that as soon as men begin to 'care for' children dramatic changes can occur. They become, metaphorically, 'born again'.

She also has something to say (echoing findings of earlier researchers discussed by Maidment, 1975) about the practical problems of sharing parenthood after separation:

... Maureen had been devastated when her husband left her and she remained extraordinarily sad at the turn of events she had endured. Notwithstanding her pain she was able to see how hard it was for her husband to (re)form and sustain his relationship to their sons and she was working hard to make this possible even though she was not prepared to include the 'other' woman in her efforts. Finally Tina was faced with a husband who was doubly dependent on drugs and alcohol. Her reaction was one of sympathy rather than mutual understanding, nonetheless she regarded her husband in a caring way and was prepared to work to sustain his role as father even though it had been entirely minimal until that time.

What comes as a shock to many parents who have had little involvement in 'caring for' children during a marriage is the emotional work that is required to sustain relationships after divorce. The parents who were successfully sharing parenting shared this work. That is to say they took on an extra dimension of planning and negotiating in order to make it work. This was arduous but regarded as essential. The parents who had 'cared about' but had done little 'caring for' often seemed angry at the emotional work that was required. One father remarked that he could not see why things could not be just like they were during their marriage. He did not want to do the emotional work that was necessary to keep things going. In other cases the mothers merely took on the work of keeping access going. They prepared the children emotionally for their fathers, they consoled the children when their fathers left, they kept up the flow of information and so on. The work of 'caring for' merely extended beyond the boundaries of divorce and dealing with access and sustaining their former husbands as adequate fathers became an additional task in the repertoire of care giving.

It is interesting that when mothers refuse to take on this extra work they become identified as bad or vindictive mothers. The work of sustaining access is like housework, it is only visible when it is not done. When it is done it is expected to be its own reward, but when it is not done the mother becomes blameworthy.

If we accept that sustaining parenting after divorce is hard work, that it adds a dimension to caring that is not an element of an ongoing marriage, we need to consider that there may be circumstances in which parents are reluctant to do the extra work without regarding this as a moral failure or as emotional immaturity.

Questions

(i) How would you define (*a*) a 'good father', and (*b*) a 'good mother'? And in each case (*a*) while they were living together, and (*b*) after they had separated?

(ii) Smart (1990) also points out that:

there has grown up over time the argument that merely because a father does not pay child support a mother cannot deprive the child of the opportunity of seeing her father because the child's psychological needs are paramount – or at least can be separated from her substantive needs. Mothers who deny access because of maintenance arrears are therefore bad mothers.

Do you agree?

(iii) Do you believe that children mainly live with their mothers because it is better for them or because their mothers have earned the right to go on looking after them by doing so in the past?

(iv) Do you believe that children should go on seeing their fathers because it is better for them or because their fathers have a right to go on seeing them?

2 The law

(a) THE ORDERS AVAILABLE

The Children Act 1989 replaces the old orders for custody, joint custody, care and control, access, and the resolution of disputes about the exercise of parental rights, as follows:

8. – (1) In this Act –
'a contact order' means an order requiring the person with whom a child lives, or is to live, to allow the child to visit or stay with the person named in the order, or for that person and the child otherwise to have contact with each other;
'a prohibited steps order' means an order that no step which could be taken by a parent in meeting his parental responsibility for a child, and which is of a kind specified in the order shall be taken by any person without the consent of the court;
'a residence order' means an order settling the arrangements to be made as to the person with whom a child is to live; and
'a specific issue order' means an order giving directions for the purpose of determining a specific question which has arisen, or which may arise, in connection with any aspect of parental responsibility for a child.

(2) In this Act 'a section 8 order' means any of the orders mentioned in subsection (1) and any order varying or discharging such an order.

As between parents (married or unmarried) these may be made in the following circumstances:

10. – (1) In any family proceedings in which a question arises with respect to the welfare of any child, the court may make a section 8 order with respect to the child if –
(*a*) an application for the order has been made by a person who –
(i) is entitled to apply for a section 8 order with respect to the child; or
(ii) has obtained the leave of the court to make the application; or
(*b*) the court considers that the order should be made even though no such application has been made.

(2) The court may also make a section 8 order with respect to any child on the application of a person who –
(*a*) is entitled to apply for a section 8 with respect to the child; or
(*b*) has obtained the leave of the court to make the application.

...

(4) The following persons are entitled to apply to the court for any section 8 order with respect to a child –
(*a*) any parent or guardian of the child;
(b) any person in whose favour a residence order is in force with respect to the child.

There are also various supplementary provisions:

11. – (3) Where a court has power to make a section 8 order, it may do so at any time during the course of the proceedings in question even though it is not in a position to dispose finally of those proceedings.

(4) Where a residence order is made in favour of two or more persons who do not themselves all live together, the order may specify the periods during which the child is to live in the different households concerned.

(5) Where –
(*a*) a residence order has been made with respect to a child; and
(*b*) as a result of the order the child lives, or is to live, with one of two parents who each have parental responsibility for him,

the residence order shall cease to have effect if the parents live together for a continuous period of more than six months.

(6) A contact order which requires the parent with whom a child lives to allow the child to visit, or otherwise have contact with, the other parent shall cease to have effect if the parents live together for a continuous period of more than six months.

(7) A section 8 order may –

(*a*) contain directions about how it is to be carried into effect:

(*b*) impose conditions which must be complied with by any person –

(i) in whose favour the order is made;

(ii) who is a parent of the child concerned;

(iii) who is not a parent of his but who has parental responsibility for him; or

(iv) with whom the child is living,

and to whom the conditions are expressed to apply;

(*c*) be made to have effect for a specified period, or contain provisions which are to have effect for a specified period;

(*d*) make such incidental, supplemental or consequential provision as the court thinks fit.

...

13. – (1) Where a residence order is in force with respect to a child, no person may –

(*a*) cause the child to be known by a new surname; or

(*b*) remove him from the United Kingdom;

without either the written consent of every person who has parental responsibility for the child or the leave of the court.

(2) Subsection (1)(*b*) does not prevent the removal of a child, for a period of less than one month, by the person in whose favour the residence order is made.

(3) In making a residence order with respect to a child the court may grant the leave required by subsection (1)(*b*), either generally or for specified purposes.

These provisions are explained in the Law Commission's Report on *Guardianship and Custody* (1988):

Orders between parents

4.2 There are three main difficulties with the present law. First, ... the orders available differ according to the proceedings brought. ...

4.3 The second difficulty is that the effect of these orders is no longer clear or well-understood. Parents not unnaturally think that a sole custody order puts the custodial parent in sole control, but the Court of Appeal appeared to say otherwise in *Dipper v Dipper* [1981] Fam 31, [1980] 2 All ER 722. Parents who are reluctant to concede sole custody are advised that joint custody is 'an important ratification of their continued parental role' [Priest and Whybrow, 1986, para. 8.4]. Parents with care and control who see joint custody as a threatening interference are told that it is simply 'a matter of words'. In most cases, this is obviously right, because the strategic matters over which a power of veto might be exercised very rarely arise. The fact that a joint custody order technically gives a power of veto may not be generally appreciated. ...

4.4 The third difficulty is that the views and practices of courts differ very considerably, largely because of differences of opinion amongst judges, legal practitioners and clients about the merits of joint custody orders. ...

4.5 In framing a scheme of orders to replace the present law, we have had in mind throughout the clear evidence that the children who fare best after their parents separate or divorce are those who are able to maintain a good relationship with them both [e.g. Wallerstein and Kelly, 1980; Lund, 1987; Richards and Dyson, 1982; Maidment. 1984]. The law may not be able to achieve this – indeed we are only too well aware of the limits of the law in altering human relationships – but at least it should not stand in their way. Our respondents were generally agreed on three points. Where the parents are already able to co-operate in bringing up their children, the law should interfere as little as possible. Where they may be having difficulty, it should try to 'lower the stakes' so that the issue is not one in which 'winner takes all' or more importantly 'loser loses all'. In either case, the orders made should reduce rather than increase the opportunities for conflict and litigation in the future.

4.6 The scheme which we provisionally proposed in the Working Paper had three basic elements. The first, as we have already explained, [see p. 441, above] is that the parents should retain their equal parental responsibility and with it their power to act independently unless this is incompatible with the court's order. A parent who does not have the child with him should still be regarded in law as a parent. He should be treated as such by schools and others, so that he can be given information and an opportunity to take part in the child's education. He should not be able to exercise a power of veto over the other, but should be able to refer any dispute to the court if necessary. A parent who does have the child with him should be able to exercise his responsibilities to the full during that time.

...

4.8 The second element in our proposals was designed to reflect the practical reality that parental status is largely a matter of everyday responsibility rather than rights. It is 'a mistake to see custody, care and control and access as differently-sized bundles of powers and responsibilities in a descending hierarchy of importance'. Most parental responsibilities can only be exercised while the parent has the child, for only then can the parent put into effect the decisions taken. Equally, however, it is then that the parent must be in a position to meet his responsibilities as the circumstances and needs of the child dictate. Parental responsibilities, therefore, largely 'run with the child'. Clearly, in most cases, one parent carries a much heavier burden of that responsibility than does the other. The present system of orders, by concentrating on the allocation of 'rights', appears more concerned with whether one parent can control what the other parent does while the child is with the other, than with ensuring that each parent properly meets his responsibilities while the child is with him. The practical question in most cases is where the child is to live and how much he is to see of the other parent. Hence we provisionally proposed that custody and access orders should be replaced by a single order, possibly termed 'care and control', allocating the child's time between the parents.

...

4.10 However, several respondents who approved of the general thrust of our provisional proposals suggested different terminology from 'care and control' which still carries some of the proprietorial connotations of 'custody'. There is also a practical disadvantage in having only a single order which divides the child's time between his parents. Most children will live with one parent for most of the time and spend variable amounts of time with the other. The usual order at present is for 'reasonable' access. Our respondents did not think it desirable for orders to spell this out in any more detail unless and until disputes arose. Parents are usually able to agree upon their own arrangements, which have to be flexible enough to meet changing needs and circumstances. Rather than being required to specify the periods of time intended, therefore, the court should normally deal with where (or, more accurately, with whom) the child is to live, whom he should see, and any other specific matters which have to be resolved.

...

(a) *Residence orders*

4.12 Apart from the effect upon the other parent, ... the main difference between a residence order and a custody order is that the new order should be flexible enough to accommodate a much wider range of situations. In some cases, the child may live with both parents even though they do not share the same household. It was never our intention to suggest that children should share their time more or less equally between their parents. Such arrangements will rarely be practicable, let alone for the children's benefit. However, the evidence from the United States is that where they are practicable they can work well and we see no reason why they should be actively discouraged. None of our respondents shared the view expressed in a recent case [*Riley v Riley* [1986] 2 FLR 429] that such an arrangement, which had been working well for some years, should never have been made. More commonly, however, the child will live with both parents but spend more time with one than the other. Examples might be where he spends term time with one and holidays with the other, or two out of three holidays from boarding school with one and the third with the other. It is a far more realistic description of the responsibilities involved in that sort of arrangement to make a residence order covering both parents rather than a residence order for one and a contact order for the other. ...

4.14 The effect of a residence order is simply to settle where the child is to live. If any other conditions are needed they must usually be specified. However, the Matrimonial Causes Rules 1977 at present specify two conditions which must be included in divorce court custody orders unless the court otherwise directs. First, the parent with custody must not change the child's surname without the written consent of the other parent or the leave of a judge. The child's surname is an important symbol of his identity and his relationship with his parents. While it may well be in his interests for it to be changed, it is clearly not a matter on which the parent with whom he lives should be able to take unilateral action. ...

4.15 Secondly, a divorce court order for custody or care and control must provide for the child not to be removed from England and Wales without leave of the court except on such terms as the court may specify in the order. This means that, unless the court makes an exception at the outset, the child cannot be taken on holiday abroad (or even to Scotland), even if the other parent agrees, without the trouble and expense of an application for leave. This is clearly quite unrealistic these days and we suspect that the requirement is often ignored. Otherwise, an order for legal custody does not permit a person to arrange the child's emigration unless he is a parent or guardian but the order contains no more stringent requirement unless the court specifically prohibits removals and we understand that it rarely does so. The matter could be dealt with entirely by the criminal law [s. 1, Child Abduction Act 1984]. However, taking the child abroad indefinitely can obviously have a serious effect upon his relationship with the other parent and it may be important to remind the residential parent of this, and of the steps to be taken if she wishes to do so. A simple, clear general rule seems most likely to be remembered and observed.

...

(b) *Contact orders*

4.17 Where the child is to spend much more time with one parent than the other, the more realistic order will probably be for him to live with one parent and to visit the other. There are important differences between this and the present form of access order. It will not provide for the 'non-custodial' parent to have access to the child. It will provide for the child to visit and in many cases stay with the parent. While the child is with that parent, the parent may exercise all his parental responsibilities. He must not do something which is incompatible with the order about where the child is to live. The court may also attach other conditions if there are particular anxieties or bones of contention but these should rarely be required. If visiting is not practicable, the court may nevertheless order some other form of contact with the child, including letters or telephone calls or visits to the child. We would expect, however, that the normal order would be for reasonable contact, which would encompass all types. ...

(c) *Specific issue orders*

4.18 Specific issue orders may be made in conjunction with residence or contact orders or on their own. ... As with conditions attached to other orders, the object is not to give one parent or the other the 'right' to determine a particular point. Rather, it is to enable either parent to submit a particular dispute to the court for resolution in accordance with what is best for the child. A court can determine in the light of the evidence what decision will be best for the child at the time. It may equally be content for decisions to be taken by each parent as they arise in the course of everyday life in the future. It may even attach a condition to a residence or contact order that certain decisions may not be taken without informing the other or giving the other an opportunity to object. But to give one parent in advance the right to take a decision which the other parent will have to put into effect is contrary to the whole tenor of the modern law [e.g. the disapproval of the old form of 'split' orders, giving custody to one and care and control to the other, *Williamson v Williamson* [1986] 2 FLR 146]. A court can scarcely be expected to know in advance that the first parent's decision will be the best for the child.

4.19 However, a specific issue order is not intended as a substitute for a residence or contact order. There is obviously a slight risk that they might be used, particularly in uncontested cases, to achieve much the same practical results but without the same legal effects. We recommend, therefore, that it should be made clear that a specific issue order cannot be made with a view to achieving a result which could be achieved by a residence or contact order.

(d) *Prohibited steps orders*

4.20 Prohibited steps orders are also modelled on the wardship jurisdiction. The automatic effect of making a child a ward of court is that no important step may be taken without the court's leave. An important aim of our recommendations is to incorporate the most valuable features of wardship into the statutory jurisdictions. It is on occasions necessary for the court to play a continuing parental role in relation to the child, although we would not expect those occasions to be common. If this is in the best interests of the child, it should be made clear exactly what the limitations on the exercise of parental responsibility are. Hence, instead of the vague requirement in wardship, that no 'important step' may be taken, the court should spell out these matters which will have to be referred back to the court. We would expect such orders to be few and far between, as in practice the wardship jurisdiction is more often invoked to achieve a particular result at the time than to produce the continuing over-sight of the court. One example, however, might be to ensure that the child is not removed from the United Kingdom, especially in a case where there is no residence order and so the automatic prohibition cannot apply. As with specific issue orders, however, we recommend that these orders should not be capable of being made with a view to achieving a result which could be achieved by a residence or contact order.

(e) *Supplemental provisions*
4.21 The courts have interpreted their powers under section 42 of the Matrimonial Causes Act 1973 so flexibly as to enable them to make interim orders, delay implementation or attach other special conditions. The other legislation contains specific provisions for similar purposes. The object of our recommendation is to preserve the present flexibility of the divorce courts' powers within the new scheme of orders. We would not expect these supplemental powers to be used at all frequently, as most cases will not require them and all are subject to the general rule that orders should only be made where they are the most effective means of safeguarding or promoting the child's welfare.

Question

The new scheme of orders has to be read in conjunction with the provisions on parental responsibility, and in particular the rule that each person with parental responsibility may act alone in meeting it, unless this is inconsistent with a court order (see pp. 441–443, above). Do you think that the new scheme would appeal more to Martin Richards (see p. 523, above) or to Carol Smart (see p. 526, above) or would they both like or dislike it equally?

(b) THE WELFARE PRINCIPLE

The Children Act 1989 restates the welfare principle (first enacted in s. 1 of the Guardianship of Infants Act 1925, p. 410, above) with additions:

1. – (1) When a court determines any question with respect to –
(*a*) the upbringing of a child; or
(*b*) the administration of a child's property or the application of any income arising from it,
the child's welfare shall be the court's paramount consideration.
...
(3) In the circumstances mentioned in subsection (4), a court shall have regard in particular to –
(*a*) the ascertainable wishes and feelings of the child concerned (considered in the light of his age and understanding);
(*b*) his physical, emotional and educational needs;
(*c*) the likely effect on him of any change in his circumstances;
(*d*) his age, sex, background and any characteristics of his which the court considers relevant;
(*e*) any harm which he has suffered or is at risk of suffering;
(*f*) how capable each of his parents, and any other person in relation to whom the court considers the question to be relevant, is of meeting his needs;
(*g*) the range of powers available to the court under this Act in the proceedings in question.
(4) The circumstances are that –
(*a*) the court is considering whether to make, vary or discharge a section 8 order, and the making, variation or discharge of the order is opposed by any party to the proceedings; or
(*b*) the court is considering whether to make, vary or discharge an order under Part IV [see p. 617, below].

Section 1(1), however, differs in two respects from the recommendations of the Law Commission:

3.13 We suggested, however, two modifications in the present formulation of the paramountcy rule. First, the interests of the child whose future happens to be in issue in the proceedings before the court should not in principle prevail over those of other children likely to be affected by the decision. Hence their welfare should also be taken into consideration. Secondly, the world 'first' had caused confusion in that it had in the past led some courts to balance other considerations *against* the child's welfare rather than to consider what light they shed upon it [e.g. *Re L (infants)* [1962] 3 All ER 1, [1962] 1 WLR 886]. Since *J v C* [1970] AC 668 [p. 411, above], that view has been decisively rejected in the courts [*Re K (a minor) (children: care and control)* [1977] Fam 179, [1977] 1 All ER 647, below] and a modern formulation should reflect this. These proposals were approved by all those who commented upon them.

3.14 It could be said that, given its recent interpretation in the courts, retaining the present formula does no harm. However, merely to drop 'first', as a piece of 'draftsman's duplicity (now obsolete)' [Bennion, 1976], does nothing to resolve the earlier confusion. Litigants might still be tempted to introduce evidence and arguments which had no relevance to the child's welfare, in the hope of persuading the court to balance one against the other. The whole aim of these proposals is to state the modern law simply and clearly. We recommend, therefore, that in reaching any decision about the child's care, upbringing or maintenance, the welfare of any child likely to be affected by the decision should be the court's only concern. ...

Questions

(i) Is there a difference between a 'paramount' and a 'sole' consideration?
(ii) If other considerations can be taken into account, should they include, for example, (*a*) the 'justice' of the matrimonial dispute, (*b*) the need to minimise public expenditure, or (*c*) the wishes and feelings of any of the adults involved?
(iii) What would an economist or utilitarian think of a law which, in theory, required that a small gain to the child's welfare, in living with the marginally more suitable parent, should outweigh a much greater detriment to the welfare of a parent who would be devastated by the loss of his or her child?

The position which the courts had already reached before the 1989 Act is well illustrated by the following case:

Re K (Minors) (Children: Care and Control)
[1977] Fam 179, [1979] 1 All ER 647, [1977] 2 WLR 33, 121 Sol Jo 84, Court of Appeal

The parents married in 1969. They had a son in 1971, who was now aged 5, and a daughter in 1974, who was now two and a half. The father was a Church of England clergyman. Through church activities, the mother met a young man named Martin in 1973. By March 1975, their friendship had become adulterous. The father wished the mother to give up her relationship with Martin and be reconciled. The mother wished to leave the father and set up home in a house to be bought jointly with Martin, but she was unwilling to go without the children. Accordingly, in May 1976 she applied to the local magistrates' court for their custody. The father halted those proceedings by applying to make the children wards of court. Reeve J granted care and control to the mother and the father appealed.

StampLJ: Before turning to the facts of the case, I would make some introductory observations. In the first place the law which is to be applied is not in doubt. It is that the welfare of the children is, in the words of the statute, the first and paramount consideration. It was stated with clarity and precision by Lord MacDermott in *J v C* [1970] AC 668, [1969] 1 All ER 788 [p. 411, above] in a passage in his speech which should be in the mind of every judge who tries an infant case, ...

> 'The second question of construction is as to the scope and meaning of the words "... shall regard the welfare of the infant as the first and paramount consideration". Reading these words in their ordinary significance, and relating them to the various classes which the

section has already mentioned, it seems to me that they must mean more than that the child's welfare is to be treated as the top item in a list of items relevant to the matter in question. I think they connote a process whereby, when all the relevant facts, relationships, claims and wishes of parents, risks, choices and other circumstances are taken into account and weighed, the course to be followed will be that which is most in the interests of the child's welfare as that term has now to be understood. That is the first consideration because it is of first importance and the paramount consideration because it rules on or determines the course to be followed.'

Applying the law so stated, this court in *S (BD) v S (DJ) (infants: care and consent)* [1977] Fam 109, [1977] 1 All ER 656 held that the earlier case of *Re L (infants)* [1962] 3 All ER 1, [1962] 1 WLR 886, where this court appears to have balanced the welfare of the child against the wishes of an unimpeachable parent or the justice of the case as between the parties, was no longer to be regarded as good law. ...

The second thing I would say at the outset is, ... that although one may of course be assisted by the wisdom of remarks made in earlier cases, the circumstances in infant cases and the personalities of the parties concerned being infinitely variable, the conclusions of the court as to the course which should be followed in one case are of little assistance in guiding one to the course which ought to be followed in another case.

Thirdly I would emphasise that where a judge has seen the parties concerned, has had the assistance of a good welfare officer's report and has correctly applied the law, an appellate court ought not to disturb his decision unless it appears that he has failed to take into account something which he ought to have taken into account or has taken into account something which he ought not to have taken into account, or the appellate court is satisfied that his decision was wrong; it is not enough that a judge of the appellate court should think, on reading the papers, that he himself would on the whole have come to a different conclusion. ...

It is clear that, from the point of view of the children, nothing could be much worse than a continuation of the situation which the judge described, to which must be added the fact that the mother is, as I have indicated, continuing her intimate association with M and that one of them at least knows that something is wrong, and that both the children are, so it appears, fond of M, with whom they have become very well acquainted. As I have indicated, the father, because of his beliefs, will not divorce his wife, or consent to a divorce, so that the couple face for a period of five years during which they cannot marry, a situation which cannot I think continue from the point of view of any of the three adults concerned, or which could be tolerable for any lengthy period. To the extent that it does endure, the strains will become intolerable and the damage to the children incalculable.

The mother appears to have been somewhat ambivalent on the question whether if care and control were denied to her, she would stay in the home to look after the children, maintaining her liaison with M, or whether she would go and live with him. The judge thought that she could not contemplate the possibility of giving up either her children or M, but he considered that if care and control were given to the father, the greatest possibility was that she would go and live with M alone, but of course what she wants to do is to set up home with M and the children.

The arrangements which the father would make if he were to have care and control and the mother in fact went to live with M were summarised by the judge thus:

'Moreover, I bear this matter in mind. That the arrangements which the father can make – I refer to the roster which is exhibited to one of his affidavits – is on the face of it satisfactory in that these children will be cared for by worthy persons at all hours of the day, nevertheless it is not a satisfactory way, through no fault of the father's, in having children cared for. As has been pointed out, during the course of one week there may be five different persons who may be responsible for looking after these children. There will be some continuity in the care that the father can lavish on them. Nevertheless there would be a succession of other persons who would be assisting in that regard. That, as I say, is not the fault of the father, he is making the best arrangements that he can.'

...

I agree with the learned judge that the arrangements are far from satisfactory and that if the matter rested there it could hardly be doubted that it would be for the benefit of these children that effect should be given to the dictates of nature which make the mother the natural guardian, protector and comforter of the very young. But, as the judge pointed out in a judgment which shows the greatest possible sympathy with the father – a sympathy which I would emphasise that I share – in considering the welfare of the children one has to look also to their moral and spiritual welfare.

The father, who naturally holds his beliefs very strongly, not only wants to live according to his faith, but wants his children to be brought up in that faith, to hold the same beliefs as he does and to live their lives as he intends to live his life. I cannot do better than quote the words in which the learned judge put it; he said this:

> 'And he takes the view that if the care and control is committed to the mother this may do considerable harm, and he would put it a little higher perhaps, very considerable harm, to the children in that it would be hurtful to them spiritually. He does not attach so much importance to the difficulty which might exist in explaining to these children what it entails if their mother is living in sin, if one can use that old fashioned Victorian expression, with M. He does not attach any great importance to the difficulty that there no doubt will be in due course if the children are committed to the care and control of their mother of explaining to them how professed Christians can ignore one of the commandments, or any of them. But what he feels will do very considerable harm to these children is that they should be brought up in a home where their mother and another man are living together in blatant defiance of church doctrine and all that the father believes in. And as appears very clearly from their demeanour in the witness box where those two persons with whom the children would be living in those circumstances show no repentance.'

The judge remarked that there was considerable force in that argument.

But unfortunately, as the judge pointed out, if one yielded to that submission and committed the care of these children to the father, it would not in great measure protect them from the moral and spiritual harm which the father fears. The plain fact is that the children's mother intends to live with a young man who is not her husband. No one suggests that she should be denied access to the children and the judge thought, and I share that view, that it would have to be liberal access, including staying access. How could the children then fail to be aware, and constantly aware, that their mother was living with M in, to quote the judge's words 'blatant defiance of church doctrine and all that [the father] believes in'? And, if, as appears to be the case, the children are children who love their mother and are fond of M, to deprive them of her would, in my judgment, be as likely as not to cause a revolt against the very teaching that the father would have them imbibe and a revolt, so I would have thought, which in due course would be a revolt against the father himself. ...

One cannot be sure that the relationship between the mother and M will remain a stable one; the judge said that that was possibly one of the most difficult aspects of the case on which to express a view with any degree of certainty. He said of it:

> 'That is possibly one of the most difficult aspects of this case on which to express a view with any degree of certainty. I know that they met in January 1975 [that was a slip for 1973], that their adulterous association has continued for about a year now and that at the moment there can be no question that they feel they are going to stay with each other and that the union between them, whether they are married or not, is going to be a permanent one. Moreover M has purchased a house which would be the "matrimonial home". I appreciate that there must be some question that this association between them may be no more than a temporary infatuation which will burn itself out when the glamour of what I suppose one could call their courtship over the last few months has gone. I face that danger. It is also submitted that if I took the children away from the home which the boy has known for over three years, and that is really the whole of his life which he can remember (and this is the only home that the girl has known) that that would cause a great upheaval in their lives. I attach no importance to that. These children would settle down perfectly well in any other environment if they are with their mother.'

...

I turn now to how the learned judge described the mother; at one point in his judgment he said this:

> 'But again I can appreciate the situation in which she now is. She is a desperately unhappy person. She cannot control her own emotions. She has the laudible and natural maternal instincts for her children. For that she can only be praised. But unfortunately – and the fact I criticise her for this is neither here nor there – she has equally strong emotions for M and those two emotions are so strong that she can write the notes to which I have referred but not in detail and are so strong that she cannot really see the wickedness of the step that she is taking in disrupting this family. And also she cannot see the very real goodness that there is in her husband both as a husband and as a father.'

The judge also says this of her earlier in his judgment:

> 'So far as their material welfare is concerned no sort of criticism has been made against the mother. As a mother she has been quite excellent. And there is no reason to suppose that in that regard she will change. These children will need for nothing if they are being fed, clothed and brought up in all those material particulars by their mother; they could not expect to have a better mother.'

And it was at that point that the judge went on to point out that he also had to consider the children's spiritual and moral welfare. I would add this, that it is not suggested that the mother is in any degree lacking in the warmth which such very young children so much need.

The judge made it abundantly clear that if he were deciding the case by trying to do justice between the father and the mother, there could be only one way in which he could possibly decide it, and that was in favour of the father; but he correctly applied what was laid down in *J v C* and refused to set that consideration against the welfare of the children. ...

I can only say that I am quite unable to conclude that the judge came to a wrong conclusion; I agree with it and would dismiss this appeal.

Ormrod LJ: ... For my part, I do not think that justice between parents in these cases is ever simple. On the contrary, it is a highly complex question which can very rarely be answered satisfactorily, and then only after exhaustive investigation. In the present case this aspect of it was, quite rightly, not pursued in any detail, because I do not think the welfare of the children required any such enquiry. So I prefer to keep an open mind as to where the justice of the case, as between the father and the mother, lies. It seems to me that all experience shows that, particularly serious-minded people such as the mother in this case, do not break up their marriages unless their relationship with their spouses has deteriorated very severely indeed. So I hesitate to make moral judgments in this class of case; I do not find it particularly helpful. ...
Appeal dismissed.

Questions

(i) Do you consider that this decision was 'unfair' to the father?
(ii) If you do think it unfair, is that because: (*a*) the law requires the court to determine the case on the basis of the children's welfare and not upon the rights and wrongs of the marital dispute, or (*b*) the court gave effect to the 'dictates of nature which make the mother the natural guardian, protector and comforter of the very young'?
(iii) What do you think was best for these two children?

On the third point made by Lord Justice Stamp, the House of Lords affirmed a slightly wider view of the role of appellate courts in children cases:

G v G (Minors) (Custody: Appeal)
[1985] 2 All ER 225, [1985] 1 WLR 647, [1985] FLR 894, [1985] Fam Law 321, House of Lords

Lord Fraser of Tullybelton: ... We were told by counsel that practitioners are finding difficulty in ascertaining the correct principles to apply because of the various ways in which judges have expressed themselves in these cases. I do not think it would be useful for me to go through the cases and to analyse the various expressions used by different judges and attempt to reconcile them exactly. Certainly it would not be useful to inquire whether different shades of meaning are intended to be conveyed by words such as 'blatant error' used by the President in the present case, and words such as 'clearly wrong', 'plainly wrong', or simply 'wrong' used by other judges in other cases. All these various expressions were used in order to emphasize the point that the appellate court should only interfere when they consider that the judge of first instance has not merely preferred an imperfect solution which is different from an alternative imperfect solution which the Court of Appeal might or would have adopted, but has exceeded the generous ambit within which a reasonable disagreement is possible. The principle was stated in this House by my noble and learned friend Lord Scarman in *B v W (wardship: appeal)* [1979] 3 All ER 83, [1979] 1 WLR 1041: ...

> 'But at the end of the day the court may not intervene unless it is satisfied either that the judge exercised his discretion upon a wrong principle or that, the judge's decision being so plainly wrong, he must have exercised his discretion wrongly.'

The same principle was expressed in other words, and at slightly greater length, in the Court of Appeal (Stamp, Browne and Bridge LJJ) in *Re F (a minor) (wardship: appeal)* [1976] Fam 238, [1976] 1 All ER 417, CA ... Browne LJ said:

> 'Apart from the effect of seeing and hearing witnesses, I cannot see why the general principle applicable to the exercise of the discretion in respect of infants should be any different from the general principle applicable to any other form of discretion.'

... The decision in *Re F* is also important because the majority rejected, rightly in my view, the dissenting opinion of Stamp LJ, who would have limited the right of the Court of Appeal to interfere with the judge's decision in custody cases to cases 'where it concludes that the course followed by the judge is one that no reasonable judge having taken into account all the relevant circumstances could have adopted'. That is the test which the court applies in deciding whether it is entitled to exercise judicial control over the decision of an administrative body, see the well-known case of *Associated Provincial Picture Houses Ltd v Wednesbury Corpn* [1948] 1 KB 223. It is not the appropriate test for deciding whether the Court of Appeal is entitled to interfere with the decision made by a judge in the exercise of his discretion.

Questions

(i) 'But to say that the judge below is deemed to have "exceeded the generous ambit within which a reasonable disagreement is possible" is surely to say no more, nor less, than that his decision was one which no reasonable judge could make' (Eekelaar, 1985)?
(ii) How much importance should be attached to 'the effect of seeing and hearing witnesses' in children cases?
(iii) Do you think appeals should be encouraged or discouraged? Why?

The Law Commission went on to explain the 'checklist' in s. 1(3) like this:

3.18 The 'checklist' received a large majority of support from those who considered the matter. It was perceived as a means of providing a greater consistency and clarity in the law and was welcomed as a major step towards a more systematic approach to decisions concerning children. Respondents pointed out that it would help to ensure that the same basic factors were being used to implement the welfare criterion by the wide range of professionals involved, including judges, magistrates, registrars, welfare officers, and legal advisers. One respondent, for example, who is a magistrates' clerk, thought that the list would be particularly useful when advising magistrates in making decisions in contested custody cases and in formulating reasons in the event of an appeal. It would also provide a practical tool for those lacking experience and confidence in this area. Perhaps most important of all, we were told that such a list could assist both parents and children in endeavouring to understand how judicial decisions are made. At present, there is a tendency for advisers and their clients (and possibly even courts) to rely on 'rules of thumb' as to what the court is likely to think best in any given circumstances. A checklist would make it clear to all what, as a minimum, would be considered by the court. At the very least, it would enable the parties to prepare and give relevant evidence at the outset, thereby avoiding the delay and expense of prolonged hearings or adjournments for further information. Moreover, we were informed that solicitors find the checklist applicable to financial matters most useful in focusing their clients' minds on the real issues and therefore in promoting settlements. Anything which is likely to promote the settlement of disputes about children is even more to be welcomed. We recommend, therefore, that a statutory checklist similar to that provided for financial matters be provided for decisions relating to children.

3.19 We recognise, however, that a statutory checklist contains certain dangers against which the legislation must be careful to guard. It should not appear to increase the burden upon courts in uncontested cases and thus encourage them to intervene unnecessarily in the course of considering the arrangements proposed for the children. There is no evidence at all that the checklist for financial matters has had this effect. The courts would only apply it where an issue had arisen. Secondly, while the checklist may provide a clear statement of what society considers the most important factors in the welfare of children, it must not be applied too rigidly or be so formulated as to prevent the court from taking into account everything which is relevant in the particular case. Thirdly, a statutory checklist is only practicable if it is confined to the major points, leaving others to be formulated elsewhere. If a detailed checklist is provided, it cannot be appropriate to all types of decision and thus separate lists would be needed to deal with each issue. This would lead to unnecessary complexity, not only in the statute, but also in legal proceedings, where issues of custody and access (or residence and contact) often go side-by-side. The more detailed the list, the greater the risk of an appeal if the court were to fail to cover every single point in the course of explaining its decision. Finally, if a detailed list is prescribed by statute, it can only be changed by statute, yet knowledge and understanding of children and their needs is developing all the time and the courts must be able to keep pace with this.

Questions

(i) The list deliberately steers clear of statements like 'young children need their mothers', or 'boys need a masculine influence', or 'brothers and sisters need to stay together': is this a good thing (and see p. 548, below)?
(ii) Factor (*g*) was added later: why?

Eekelaar (1973) was inclined to describe access as one of the few remaining 'rights' of parenthood. Since then, the courts have turned the terminology, but not the practice, on its head:

M v M (child: access)
[1973] 2 All ER 81, High Court, Family Division

The parents married in 1956 and adopted the child, a boy now aged seven, in 1966. The mother was not able to give him 'full maternal care' and in 1969 a supervision order was made. In 1970, the mother left both father and boy. Her matrimonial complaint to the local magistrates' court was unsuccessful and custody was awarded to the father, with reasonable access to the mother. Access did not run smoothly, because of the parties' extreme hostility to one another. Each began to commit adultery, but once the mother became pregnant, the father refused to allow her to see the boy. She applied for access to be defined; the father applied for it to be revoked. By the time of the hearing she had not seen the boy for a year. There was evidence that access had an extremely disturbing effect upon the boy and the justices revoked it. The mother appealed.

Wrangham J: ... it seems to me ... that the companionship of a parent is in any ordinary circumstances of such immense value to the child that there is a basic right in him to such companionship. I for my part would prefer to call it a basic right in the child rather than a basic right in the parent. That only means this, that no court should deprive a child of access to either parent unless it is wholly satisfied that it is in the interests of that child that access should cease, and that is a conclusion at which a court should be extremely slow to arrive. It is not without significance that Edmund Davies LJ in *B v B* [1971] 3 All ER 682, [1971] 1 WLR 1486,CA said:

> 'For a court to deprive a good parent completely of access to his child is to make a dreadful order. That is what has been done here, and the impact on both parent and child must have lifelong consequences. Very seldom can the court bring itself to make so Draconian an order, and rarely is it necessary.'

I should add that in that case the boy was in his teens, so that there was little prospect of making a change in the access arrangements later. The order cutting off access could only in the circumstances of that case be regarded as effectively final, whereas of course in many cases, and this is one, there would be no reason for supposing that the cessation of access need be final.

I think before parting with *B v B* one should also note that the members of the Court of Appeal criticised very strongly the mother who had had the care and control of this boy during the years in which he grew up and had used it to alienate him from his father. I cite the words of Edmund Davies LJ, who quoted the report of the Official Solicitor, who said he did not suggest that the mother had wilfully attempted to turn the boy against his father, but, because she honestly believed it was not in the interests of the boy for there to be access, she had done nothing towards creating an atmosphere in which the boy would willingly go to the father for access. Edmund Davies LJ's comment was this:

> 'In general, one parent who takes that attitude in relation to the other parent is undertaking a tremendous responsibility and discharging it thoroughly badly. Again speaking generally, it is the duty of parents, whatever their personal differences may be, to seek to inculcate in the child a proper attitude of respect for the other parent.'

For these reasons I do not think it can be said that the justices, in reaching the conclusion which they did, were acting contrary to the law as laid down by the Court of Appeal. Quite clearly they placed before themselves the rule that the welfare of the child is the paramount consideration; they say so in terms; and they came to their conclusion on the ground that the welfare of the child would not be promoted by the continuance of access and would be promoted by the cessation of access. ...

Latey J: ... where the parents have separated and one has the care of the child, access by the other often results in some upset in the child. Those upsets are usually minor and superficial. They are heavily outweighed by the long term advantages to the child of keeping in touch with the parent concerned so that they do not become strangers, so that the child later in life does not resent the deprivation and turn against the parent who the child thinks, rightly or wrongly, has deprived him, and so that the deprived parent loses interest in the child and therefore does not make the material and emotional contribution to the child's development which that parent by its companionship and otherwise would make.
Appeal dismissed.

Questions

(i) How does one distinguish between upset to a child which is 'minor and superficial' and upset which is seriously damaging to the child?
(ii) Was this child being deprived of his right of access to his mother because she was not a 'good mother' (see p. 526, above)? Do you think that the result would have been the same if the positions of mother and father had been reversed?

The principles in *M v M* have frequently been repeated with approval but usually to the opposite effect. An oft-cited case is:

Re H (minors) (access)
[1992] 1 FLR 148, [1992] Fam Law 152, Court of Appeal

The parents married in 1980 and had two daughters, born in 1984 and 1986. They separated in June 1987. The children had regular contact with their father until November 1987 when the mother stopped it because one of them had been upset by the father's remark that they might come to live with him. The father took no immediate action, but in March 1989 he applied for access and his parents joined in the application. It was refused in May 1990. The father applied again early in 1991. This was again refused and the father appealed.

Balcombe LJ: ... in most cases, by the time the matter comes to be decided by the court, it is more than likely that access has ceased because (as in this case) the custodial parent has taken the unilateral decision (whether rightly or wrongly matters not for this purpose) to terminate access to the non-custodial parent who then applies for access. ... Judge Heald said:

> '... I am not asked to try that issue whether access should cease, access has ceased for a period now of over 3 years. What I am being asked to do is to reintroduce access'.

With respect to Judge Heald, there was no difference between this case and *M v M* [p. 538, above]. He then continued:

> 'Now, quite clearly, the actual reintroduction on the first occasion may be somewhat upsetting for a child, but one has to consider it from the child's point of view. Is there anything positive to be gained by reintroducing access to the father at the present time?'

...

The judge says, in effect, that they can have contact with their father by writing and continues:

> '... but the actual meeting of them is, of course, an upsetting experience. And I am by no means satisfied that contact access is of benefit in the circumstances in this case where there has been no access for such a long period. ...'

It seems to me that [counsel] is correct in her submission that Judge Heald applied the wrong test in this case and he should have asked himself the question: are there here any cogent reasons why this father should be denied access to his children?; or, putting it another way: are there any cogent reasons why these two children should be denied the opportunity of access to their natural father?

Accordingly, in my judgment, the decision to which Judge Heald came was wrong, and this court should set aside his order. The question then arises, what order should be made in its place? ... There must be an introductory period and, in the meantime, the court below should have the benefit of a welfare officer's report to indicate how access has gone – whether it has been successful or not.

I would propose three periods of visiting access between now and Christmas, in circumstances which will enable the welfare officer to observe the reaction of the children to access. A report should then be prepared, directed to the question of how access has taken place – whether it has been successful or not – and its future development. The matter should then be referred back to the Nottingham County Court as early in the new year as is possible.

Appeal allowed.

Sometimes face to face, or 'direct', contact is not possible:

Re O (contact: imposition of conditions)
[1995] 2 FLR 124, [1995] Fam Law 541, Court of Appeal

The parents did not marry but lived together for three and a half years, separating in July 1992. Their son was born in November 1992. The father undertook not to pester or molest the mother, and was punished for breaking that undertaking. Early on, the father made clear his wish to have contact with his son and the mother made clear her intention to resist this. There were orders for contact at a contact centre but the child became upset. The court welfare officer's view was that contact would only work if the mother was prepared to take part until the boy became acquainted with his father. An order was made for indirect contact with conditions that the mother send photographs every three months, inform the father if the child began at nursery or playgroup and send copies of all reports on his progress, inform the father of any significant illness and send copies of all medical reports, accept delivery of cards and presents from the father, read and show them to the child and give him any present. The mother objected to these conditions because she was not prepared to have any contact with the father.

Sir Thomas Bingham MR: ... It may perhaps be worth stating in a reasonably compendious way some very familiar but none the less fundamental principles. First of all, and overriding all else as provided in s. 1(1) of the 1989 Act, the welfare of the child is the paramount consideration of any court concerned to make an order relating to the upbringing of a child. It cannot be emphasised too strongly that the court is concerned with the interests of the mother and the father only insofar as they bear on the welfare of the child.

Secondly, where parents of a child are separated and the child is in the day-to-day care of one of them, it is almost always in the interests of the child that he or she should have contact with the other parent. The reason for this scarcely needs spelling out. It is, of course, that the separation of parents involves a loss to the child, and it is desirable that that loss should so far as possible be made good by contact with the non-custodial parent, that is the parent in whose day-to-day care the child is not. This has been said on a very great number of occasions and I cite only two of them. In *Re H (Minors) (Access)* [1992] 1 FLR 148 [p. 539, above], Balcombe LJ quoted, endorsing as fully as he could, an earlier passage in a judgment of Latey J [*M v M (child: access)* [1973] 2 All ER 81, p. 538, above].

My second citation is from *Re J (A Minor) (Contact)* [1994] 1 FLR 729 at p. 736B–C, where Balcombe LJ said:

> 'But before concluding this judgment I would like to make three general points. The first is that judges should be very reluctant to allow the implacable hostility of one parent (usually the parent who has a residence order in his or her favour), to deter them from making a contact order where they believe the child's welfare requires it. The danger of allowing the implacable hostility of the residential parent (usually the mother) to frustrate the court's decision is too obvious to require repetition on my part.'

Thirdly, the court has power to enforce orders for contact, which it should not hesitate to exercise where it judges that it will overall promote the welfare of the child to do so. I refer in this context to the judgment of the President of the Family Division in *Re W (A Minor) (Contact)* [1994] 2 FLR 441 at p. 447H, where the President said:

> 'However, I am quite clear that a court cannot allow a mother, in such circumstances, simply to defy the order of the court which was, and is, in force, that is to say that there should be reasonable contact with the father. That was indeed made by consent as I have already observed. Some constructive step must be taken to permit and encourage the boy to resume contact with his father.'

...

Fourthly, cases do, unbappily and infrequently but occasionally, arise in which a court is compelled to conclude that in existing circumstances an order for immediate direct contact should not be ordered, because so to order would injure the welfare of the child. In *Re D (A Minor) (Contact: Mother's Hostility)* [1993] 2 FLR 1 at p. 7G, Waite LJ said:

> 'It is now well settled that the implacable hostility of a mother towards access or contact is a factor which is capable, according to the circumstances of each particular case, of supplying a cogent reason for departing from the general principle that a child should grow up in the knowledge of both his parents. I see no reason to think that the judge fell into any error of principle in deciding, as he clearly did on the plain interpretation of his judgment, that the mother's present attitude towards contact puts D at serious risk of major emotional harm if she were to be compelled to accept a degree of contact to the natural father against her will.'

I simply draw attention to the judge's reference to a serious risk of major emotional harm. The courts should not at all readily accept that the child's welfare will be injured by direct contact. Judging that question the court should take a medium-term and long-term view of the child's development and not accord excessive weight to what appear likely to be short-term or transient problems. Neither parent should be encouraged or permitted to think that the more intransigent, the more unreasonable, the more obdurate and the more unco-operative they are, the more likely they are to get their own way. Courts should remember that in these cases they are dealing with parents who are adults, who must be treated as rational adults, who must be assumed to have the welfare of the child at heart, and who have once been close enough to each other to have produced the child. It would be as well if parents also were to bear these points in mind.

Fifthly, in cases in which, for whatever reason, direct contact cannot for the time being be ordered, it is ordinarily highly desirable that there should be indirect contact so that the child grows up knowing of the love and interest of the absent parent with whom, in due course, direct contact should be established. This calls for a measure of restraint, common sense and unselfishness on the part of both parents. If the absent parent deluges the child with presents or writes long and obsessive screeds to the child, or if he or she uses his or her right to correspond to criticise or insult the other parent, then inevitably those rights will be curtailed. The object of indirect contact is to build up a relationship between the absent parent and the child, not to enable the absent parent to pursue a feud with the caring parent in a manner not conducive to the welfare of the child.

The caring parent also has reciprocal obligations. If the caring parent puts difficulties in the way of indirect contact by withholding presents or letters or failing to read letters to a child who cannot read, then such parent must understand that the court can compel compliance with its orders; it has sanctions available and no residence order is to be regarded as irrevocable. It is entirely reasonable that the parent with the care of the child should be obliged to report on the progress of the child to the absent parent, for the obvious reason that an absent parent cannot correspond in a meaningful way if unaware of the child's concerns, or of where the child goes to school, or what it does when it gets there, or what games it plays, and so on. Of course judges must not impose duties which parents cannot realistically be expected to perform, and it would accordingly be absurd to expect, in a case where this was the case, a semi-literate parent to write monthly reports. But some means of communication, directly or indirectly, is essential if indirect contact is to be meaningful, and if the welfare of the child is not to suffer.

...

The sixth submission in the skeleton reads:

> 'The court had no power to compel the mother to send photographs, medical reports and school reports to the father when she was unwilling to do so.'

Sections 8 and 11(7) of the Children Act 1989 are given as authority for that proposition. In my view they provide no such authority. The court has ample power to compel the mother to send photographs, medical reports and school reports in order to promote meaningful contact between the father and the child, which would almost certainly wither and die if the father received no information about the child's progress. It is in my view plain that the court does have power under these sections as a necessary means of facilitating contact. ...

Appeal dismissed.

Questions

(i) There is no hint in this, or any recent case, that it was relevant that the parents had not married one another: should there have been?

(ii) No mention is made of a parental responsibility order: look back at pp. 499–504: should there have been?

(iii) In what circumstances would you consider that a parent's 'implacable hostility' to contact was justified?

Psychologist Kevin Hewitt makes a few suggestions in *Divorce and Parental Disagreement* (1996):

In my own exposure (both as expert witness and as therapist) to the problems of children of divorced or separated parents, I have come across several cases where it seems that it is contact with the absent parent which appears to have become the paramount consideration, rather than what is in the best interests of the child. Although, generally speaking, contact with the absent parent is usually of value to the child, there are also cases which really do challenge and question whether or not any contact at all is in the child's best interests (for example non-resident parents who repeatedly break promises about when contact will occur; parents who use contact to expose the child to further hostility about the resident parent; parents who use contact as a means of winning a battle, rather than having the child's needs at heart once contact is finally obtained; parents who are frankly abusive to the child or expose the child to abuse of the mother as a result of contact). There are also situations where it seems that applications for contact are being used to perpetuate contact between the non-resident and the resident parent, perhaps, in the context of a perpetuation of some pre-existing power struggle in their relationship.

Question

The law reports are full of the problems of dealing with parents who are opposed to contact but there is another side: if continued contact is the right of the child, how can the law enforce the corresponding duty of a parent to keep in touch?

In *Divorce and the Reluctant Father* (1980), Anne Heath-Jones gives a vivid account of the problem and her solution to it:

When my husband and I separated 12 years ago, we had two children who were then one and three years of age with long years of childhood ahead of them. …

James was never a doting father, which had been one of the problems of the marriage. In effect I had always been a single parent. The boys were very young and their awareness of, and attachment to, their remote father was slight. James was all set to vanish from our lives completely.

But somehow in all the mess, in all my own grief and loneliness, and in spite of all the bitterness I harboured against him, I knew that if I had strength to fight for anything it should be to maintain contact between the children and their father. …

In those early years the fact that he saw them at all was due to every imaginable ploy. Persuasion, appeal, anger and tears. I met him more than half-way on any arrangement that he was prepared to concede. I would deliver them to his flat and collect them. If he refused to have them to stay overnight then I settled for one day – or half a day. I felt anything was better than that they should lose touch and become strangers.

Meanwhile, I kept James informed of progress at nursery and later primary school. I made sure the boys remembered his birthday; I showed him school reports. I begged him (swallowing large hunks of indigestible pride) to attend school open days, birthday parties and Guy Fawkes parties. Most important of all I kept his image intact for his children. They never heard from me any criticism of his character, or knew of my deep hurt and resentment that their father needed so much coercion to see them or be involved in their lives.

For many years all the initiative for contact came from us. He never 'phoned or wrote or asked to see them. Then slowly, very slowly, the years of effort began to pay off. The boys and I moved from London into the country. James came down occasionally for the weekend and I would clear off and leave the cottage to them. After he re-married a more or less regular arrangement was worked out for the school holidays.

We were lucky in his choice of a new wife. She was friendly and accepted her two step-sons, and in time they formed an easy relationship with her. Christmases were now peopled with a whole new branch of extended family. Instead of moping alone with me (and some Christmases were very mopey) they had a welcome at their father's and his relations and even at the big family gatherings of his new wife. …

Now, 1967 seems a long time ago and their childhood is nearly over. The relationship with their father now is mutually warm, positive and spontaneous. At times the price to pay for nurturing that relationship has been high. If you idealise the absent parent you must be prepared for the consequences.

When life got tough for us, when the boys were unhappy with school or friends, or when they sobbed for the father whose contact I had so carefully preserved, the cry was 'I want to live with Dad.' It hurt of course because I had provided the years of love and security, it hurt because I knew their father wouldn't want them and it hurt because that was the last thing in the world that I could explain to the crying child.

In spite of the upheavals of those early years we have all survived. They now have a father they can respect and admire, a man they can talk to and learn from, and a model to emulate when they become husbands and fathers themselves.

But while it can be hard for the parent with whom the children are living, it can also be hard for the other one, as an anonymous mother explained in *'Saturday Parent'* (1980):

One morning nine years ago, when she was seven years old, I watched my youngest daughter walk across the school yard, knowing that it would not be me who collected her at the end of school that day. I do not care to describe the pain of that moment, nor the many pains that followed in the years to come. The decision had been made in court the day before – henceforward she was to live with her father, my ex-husband, and his new wife and her two adopted children. From that day on I have been a 'Saturday Parent' – the one who has access – that part-time travesty of parenting that is shared by an increasing number of separated parents in our present society. For years I could not see the problems with any kind of objectivity – I merely experienced them. ...

It is this vexed question of management which I wish to highlight – by-passing all the aggravation of actually settling on mutually convenient times and places – a most flourishing battle ground for embittered ex-spouses. I would like to enumerate some of the areas of difficulty personally experienced.

Firstly, there is the passage of time. Access is usually fixed at one hearing at a given point in time when the child is of a certain age. Obviously times and frequency of contact negotiated then frequently become obsolete, a child passes rapidly from toddler, to schoolchild, to independent teenager, and unless there is good-will – a scarce commodity in the devastation of a broken marriage – the poor youngster is stuck with every second Saturday from 9 a.m. to 7 p.m. whether it will or no. *Access is for the benefit of children.* The law acknowledges this; many parents do not.

Then there is the vexed question of discipline and training – something which was an everyday part of living, suddenly becomes a major issue. There is no time to confront, disagree, sulk and make-up when all you have is a truncated week-end. One vacillates between turning a 'blind eye' to everything and jumping on the poor kid at every turn. Related to this is one's attitude to the 'other' set of parents – the real (?) parents – does one share their values, opinions, standards? It is all too easy to fall into the role of permissive Aunty who lets the kid go to parties and stay out late, only to find that a 10 p.m. ban is standard at home. (No one bothered to tell you, though – unless something goes wrong!)

Matters of loyalty to ex-spouses, towards whom one's feelings are, to say the least, ambivalent, arise continually. 'So-and-so (in my case, step-mother) would not let me do so-and-so, isn't she unfair?' 'Well no, actually. If you were with me all the time, I too would' ... etc.

One had to fight an overwhelming desire to put all one's frustrated love into the small parcel of time allowed – a present on the bed, a cake specially baked – one yearns to be perceived as loving and lavishing, for after all one has also to cope with one's own feeling of guilt about letting the child go. However it happened, and whatever your reasons, you did it. Recounting the story of Solomon's wise judgment to a colleague, he remarked sadly: 'Trouble is, there's no one around with Solomon's wisdom or his knowledge.' Too true. Judges have to make life decisions for people they hardly know and who are not likely to be presenting themselves in the best light anyway.

We have already seen (pp. 441–443, 529–532, above) how the Children Act's provisions on parental responsibility and the new range of orders were trying to redress the balance between the two parents in situations such as this. The courts have given a more cautious welcome to the possibility of even more equal sharing:

A v A (minors) (shared residence order)
[1994] 1 FLR 669, [1994] Fam Law 431, Court of Appeal

The parents married in 1985 and separated in 1991. By mid 1992, it had been ordered that the children were to live with their mother, but spend alternate weekends and half of every school holiday with their father. The effect was to share equally between mother and father the time when they were not at school. The father applied for this arrangement to be reflected in a shared residence order. This was granted and the mother appealed.

Connell J: ... The mother, through counsel, says that shared orders for residence should rarely be made and then in exceptional circumstances. In support of that submission she relies upon the case of *Re H (A Minor) (Shared Residence)* [1994] 1 FLR 717. She relies in particular upon the judgment of Purchas LJ at p. 728:

> 'It is for those reasons that, in any event, I would not support the making of a joint residence order. That such an order is open to the court, ... is clear from the provisions of s. 11(4) of the Children Act 1989, as was indicated during the debate on the Bill by the Lord Chancellor. But, at the same time, it must be an order which would rarely be made and would depend upon exceptional circumstances. A child, as was emphasised in the case of *Riley v Riley* [1986] 2 FLR 429, should have one home, and the other place of spending time, including overnight, is not the home but a place where visits may regularly and frequently be made. The establishment, as it were, of two competing homes only leads to confusion and stress and would be contrary to the paramount concept of the welfare of the child himself.'

... I do not believe that it is constructive in this instance for this court to attempt to do more than support general principles, including the principle that shared orders are not appropriate in normal, conventional circumstances where parents are separated. They should only be made where there is something unusual about the case which justifies making such an order in the best interests of the child or children concerned.

... It is to be doubted whether the case of *Riley v Riley* remains a binding authority, so far as this aspect of the law is concerned, now that the Children Act is in place. In making that observation, I have in mind the guidance and regulations provided under *The Children Act 1989 Guidance and Regulations* (HMSO, 1991), *vol. 1: Court Orders*, para 2.28 at p. 10, which reads thus:

> 'A residence order may be made in favour of more than one person at the same time even though they do not live together, in which case the order may specify the periods during which the child is to live in the different households concerned. A shared residence order could therefore be made where the child is to spend, for example, weekdays with one parent and weekends with the other or term time with one parent and school holidays with the other, or where the child is to spend large amounts of time with each parent. This latter arrangement was disapproved of by the Court of Appeal in *Riley v Riley*, which must now be taken to have been overruled by s. 11(4). But it is not expected that it would become a common form of order, partly because most children will still need the stability of a single home, and partly because in the cases where shared care is appropriate there is less likely to be a need for the court to make any order at all. However, a shared care order has the advantage of being more realistic in those cases where the child is to spend considerable amounts of time with those parents, brings with it certain other benefits (including the right to remove the child from accommodation provided by a local authority under s. 20), and removes any impression that one parent is good and responsible whereas the other parent is not.'

... In the particular case with which we are dealing, the following features are of particular relevance. First of all, the movements of the children are agreed. There is no issue about the quantum of time which they are to spend, on the one hand, with their mother and, on the other hand, with their father. The only issue is: what is the appropriate order to recognise those movements, and what order will, in the circumstances prevailing, best serve the interests of the children? The father specifically accepts in his application, and in his evidence, that the children's main home is with their mother. ...

[The judge] gave a number of specific reasons for making the order. First of all, he said that the orders made by the court must reflect the day-to-day reality of the care of these children. I would only differ from the way in which the matter was put by the judge in using the word 'must', by observing that it is usually helpful if an order or orders made by the court do reflect the reality of the situation. The judge went on to say:

> 'This court finds exceptional circumstances as follows ...'

He then set out his reasons for so finding which included first that there would be no confusion or stress to the children caused by the making of such an order. Secondly, the father has an exceptional relationship with the children. Thirdly, and in the light of the submissions made this is of particular importance, the court accepted that the communication between the mother and the father, although very poor, was improving. The court looked to the possibility that the making of such an order might assist such improvement.

...

Fourthly, the judge ... pointed to the fact that the welfare officer, who had experience of this case over a significant period of time, recommended such an order. ...

In those circumstances, I would dismiss this appeal.

Butler-Sloss LJ: ... In the light of the statutory framework of s. 8 and s. 11(4) the disapproval of a joint custody order stated in the decision of this court in *Riley v Riley* [1986] 2 FLR 429 can no longer be good law and has, as the guidance suggested, been overruled by the statute.

... We are, at this moment, still feeling our way through the implications of the Children Act. But we must none the less do so in the light of the wisdom of the past distilled in many cases, and the fact that children's problems have not changed and the emotions of parents equally have not changed. ...

... The usual order that would be made in any case where it is necessary to make an order is that there will be residence to one parent and a contact order to the other parent. Consequently, it will be unusual to make a shared residence order. ... a shared residence order would, in my view, be unlikely to be made if there were concrete issues still arising between the parties which had not been resolved, such as the amount of contact, whether it should be staying or visiting contact or another issue such as education, which were muddying the waters and which were creating difficulties between the parties which reflected the way in which the children were moving from one parent to the other in the contact period.

If a child, on the other hand, has a settled home with one parent and substantial staying contact with the other parent, which has been settled, long-standing and working well, or if there are future plans for sharing the time of the children between two parents where all the parties agree and where there is no possibility of confusion in the mind of the child as to where the child will be and the circumstances of the child at any time, this may be, bearing in mind all the other circumstances, a possible basis for a shared residence order, if it can be demonstrated that there is a positive benefit to the child. It does not mean it will be; it may be. In this case, the children stay with the father for approximately one-third of the year and a very substantial portion of their free time. He plays a particularly important part in their life. ...

The judge followed the decision of this court in *Re H* ... and imposed upon himself the test of exceptional circumstances which was referred to by Purchas LJ at p. 728B. ...

In [that] case it was plain as a pikestaff that a shared residence order ought not to have been made. But insofar as the Lord Justice imported a general test of exceptional circumstances into the interpretation of s. 11(4) of the Children Act, his observations appear to me to have been obiter. I respectfully disagree with him. The section does not import such a constraint. Having said that, I would like to reiterate ... that the usual order would be a sole residence order, and that there has to be positive benefit to the children in making an order which is not the conventional order. Consequently, a shared residence order is an unusual order which should only be made in unusual circumstances.

For those reasons, as well as the reasons given in the judgment of Connell J, I agree that this appeal should be dismissed.

Appeal dismissed.

Questions

(i) What is the difference between 'unusual' and 'exceptional' circumstances?
(ii) In the light of the recent research evidence (p. 525, above), do you think that there was 'wisdom' in the earlier decisions?
(iii) Compare this case with *Re H (shared residence: parental responsibility)* [1995] 2 FLR 883, [1996] Fam Law 140, CA, p. 567, below: do you think that judicial 'wisdom' may be changing?
(iv) Is the main difference between now and then the so-called 'non-intervention' principle (see below)?

(c) THE NON-INTERVENTION PRINCIPLE

Section 1 of the Children Act 1989 contains another, important, but novel principle:

1. – (5) Where a court is considering whether or not to make one or more orders under this Act with respect to a child, it shall not make the order or any of the orders unless it considers that doing so would be better for the child than making no order at all.

The Law Commission's explanation (1988) was this:

3.2 A tendency seems to have developed to assume that some order about the children should always be made whenever divorce or separation cases come to court. This may have been necessary in the days when mothers required a court order if they were to acquire any parental powers at all, but that is no longer the case. Studies of both divorce and magistrates' courts have shown that the proportion of contested cases is very small so that orders are not usually necessary in order to settle disputes. Rather, they may be seen by solicitors as 'part of the package' for their matrimonial clients and by courts as part of their task of approving the arrangements made in divorce cases [Priest and Whybrow, 1986, para. 8.2]. No doubt in many, possibly most, uncontested cases an order is needed in the children's own interest, so as to confirm and give stability to the existing arrangements, to clarify the respective roles of the parents, to reassure the parent with whom the children will be living, and even to reassure the public authorities responsible for housing and income support that such arrangements have in fact been made. However, it is always open to parents to separate without going to court at all, in which case there will be no order. If they go to court for some other remedy, they may not always want an order about the children. The proportion of relatively amicable divorces is likely to have increased in recent years and parents may well be able to make responsible arrangements for themselves without a court order. Where a child has a good relationship with both parents the law should seek to disturb this as little as possible. There is always a risk that orders allocating custody and access (or even deciding upon residence and contact) will have the effect of polarising the parents' roles and perhaps alienating the child from one or other of them.

3.3 For these reasons, the Working Paper proposed a more flexible approach, in which it was not always assumed that an order should be made, but the court would be prepared to make one even in uncontested cases if this would promote the children's interests. Most of those who responded agreed with this approach. Such a change would be consistent with the view that anything which can be done to help parents to keep separate the issues of being a spouse and being a parent will ultimately give the children the best chance of retaining them both. [Clulow and Vincent, 1987]. On the other hand, the impression should not be given that an application or an order is a hostile step between them. We therefore recommend that the court should only make an order where this is the most effective way of safeguarding or promoting the child's welfare.

Carol Smart (1990) exposes these arguments to a feminist critique:

The Law Commission report espoused a policy of non-intervention by the courts into matters of child care arrangements on the basis that parents are the best people to decide what is right for their children. This exalted principle was wisely underscored by the recognition that even if parents were not, there is not a great deal of evidence to suggest that judges or local authority social workers are much better equipped for the job (except in cases of actual harm or abuse). The legislation therefore seeks to allow parents to make their own decisions. In practice this is what happens in the vast majority of cases anyway and the courts merely legitimate arrangements which have occurred elsewhere (even though these agreements take place in the shadow of the law (Mnookin, 1979)). On the face of it the Act simply acknowledges this, but at the same time it goes further and promotes a 'hands off' approach as the ideal. …

The criticism which has been made of non-interventionist family law in general (Olsen, 1984; Smart, 1984), and this provision in particular (Brophy, 1989), is that non-intervention is really intervention by another name. In other words to stand outside the 'fray' and do nothing is to be just as influential as doing something. The classic examples are, of course, domestic violence and child abuse where critics of non-intervention have shown that 'inaction' is not a position which is somehow morally superior to intervention. Non-intervention is therefore not automatically good but, by the same token, research in both of these fields has also shown that some caution must be applied to rushing to embrace intervention as if it must be better. Olsen suggests that we really should abandon such terms as indications of political orientation rather than as objective statements of how the law operates in relation to the family and there is some merit in this.

There is, however, another side to this argument (and it is one which was reflected in the interviews for this research). Murch, as long ago as 1980, pointed to the resentment caused to parents by the experience of state intervention into their lives at the point of marriage breakdown. It is also often remarked upon that if we allow parents to raise children according to their own values whilst a relationship is ongoing, there is no reason to assume that they become especially incapacitated in this respect just because the relationship ends. … [We] do not require a judge to be satisfied with arrangements made for a child when a spouse dies or simply leaves. In other words there is no reason to drawn the line between intervention and non-intervention at the point of divorce although we may still wish to draw it where violence occurs for example.

The non-intervention principle is closely linked to the role of the court in divorce cases where there are relevant children, even if the parties have agreed. As the Law Commission (1988) explain:

3.5 ... one possible reason why orders are almost always made at present is the divorce court's present duty under section 41 of the Matrimonial Causes Act 1973 to declare itself satisfied as to the arrangements made for the children of the family before making absolute a decree of nullity or divorce or making a decree of judicial separation. ...

3.6 The original main aims [Royal Commission on Marriage and Divorce 1951–1955, 1956, paras. 366 at seq.] of section 41 procedure were to ensure that divorcing parents made the best possible arrangements for their children and to identify cases of particular concern where protective measures might be needed. In our Working Paper on Custody we concluded that the procedure had not been successful in achieving either of these aims. The information currently available to the court is too limited, being based on a brief statement from the petitioner alone; the arrangements are usually discussed in a short interview with the judge, which cannot be other than perfunctory in many cases; and, most importantly, the practical power of the court to produce different outcomes is very limited, nor can it ensure that the approved arrangements are subsequently observed. Although there are undoubtedly exceptional cases in which protective measures of supervision or even care may be needed, the present process is not principally designed to discover these.

3.7 Hence the Working Paper provisionally proposed replacing the divorce court's present duty to declare that the arrangements are 'satisfactory' or 'the best that can be devised in the circumstances' with the domestic court's more modest duty to consider what order, if any, to make. ...

3.8 There was a large measure of support for these proposals ... But it was thought by some of our respondents that a duty invariably to have decided what order to make before granting the decree absolute went too far. We accept that this requirement would be too strong if it meant that no divorce could be granted while a custody dispute existed. This would create a serious risk of children becoming pawns in their parents' own battles. ...

3.9 We recommend, therefore, that once divorce, nullity or judicial separation proceedings have been initiated, the court should have a duty to consider the arrangements proposed for the children in order to decide whether to exercise any of its powers under this legislation. Where this is so, but only in exceptional circumstances, the court should also have power to direct that the decree absolute (or a decree of judicial separation) cannot be made until the court allows it.

The Children Act 1989 substituted a new s. 41 accordingly. The Family Law Act 1996, however, contains something stronger:

Welfare of children

11. – (1) In any proceedings for a divorce order or a separation order, the court shall consider –

(*a*) whether there are any children of the family to whom this section applies; and

(*b*) where there are any such children, whether (in the light of the arrangements which have been, or are proposed to be, made for their upbringing and welfare) it should exercise any of its powers under the Children Act 1989 with respect to any of them.

(2) Where, in any case to which this section applies, it appears to the court that –

(*a*) the circumstances of the case require it, or are likely to require it, to exercise any of its powers under the Children Act 1989 with respect to any such child;

(*b*) it is not in a position to exercise the power, or (as the case may be) those powers, without giving further consideration to the case; and

(*c*) there are exceptional circumstances which make it desirable in the interests of the child that the court should give a direction under this section,

it may direct that the divorce order or separation order is not to be made until the court orders otherwise.

(3) In deciding whether the circumstances are as mentioned in subsection (2)(*a*), the court shall treat the welfare of the child as paramount.

(4) In making that decision, the court shall also have particular regard, on the evidence before it, to –

(*a*) the wishes and feelings of the child considered in the light of his age and understanding and the circumstances in which those wishes were expressed;

(*b*) the conduct of the parties in relation to the upbringing of the child;

(*c*) the general principle that, in the absence of evidence to the contrary, the welfare of the child will be best served by –

(i) his having regular contact with those who have parental responsibility for him and with other members of his family; and

(ii) the maintenance of as good a continuing relationship with his parents as is possible; and

(*d*) any risk to the child attributable to –

(i) where the person with whom the child will reside is living or proposes to live;

(ii) any person with whom that person is living or with whom he proposes to live; or

(iii) any other arrangements for his care and upbringing.

(5) This section applies to –

(*a*) any child of the family who has not reached the age of sixteen at the date when the court considers the case in accordance with the requirements of this section; and

(*b*) any child of the family who has reached that age at that date and in relation to whom the court directs that this section shall apply.

Questions

(i) Can you see why there are different checklists in s. 12(4) and in s. 1 of the Children Act 1989 (p. 532, above)?
(ii) What effect, if any, would s. 12(4)(*b*) have in a case like *Re K (minors) (children: care and control)* [1977] Fam 179, p. 533, above?
(iii) Do you agree with the value judgments in s. 12(4)(*c*)?
(iv) How can the court find out about the child's wishes and feelings if the parents have agreed what should happen?
(v) What can it do if the child disagrees with his parents?

(d) THE CHILD'S SENSE OF TIME

There is one value judgment in the Children Act 1989 about what is good for children:

1. – (2) In any proceedings in which any question with respect to the upbringing of a child arises, the court shall have regard to the general principle that any delay in determining the question is likely to prejudice the welfare of the child.

The Law Commission (1988) are to blame:

4.55 ... Prolonged litigation about their future is deeply damaging to children, not only because of the uncertainty it brings for them, but also because of the harm it does to the relationship between the parents and their capacity to co-operate with one another in the future. Moreover, a frequent consequence is that the case of the parent who is not living with the child is severely prejudiced by the time of the hearing. Regrettably, it is almost always to the advantage of one of the parties to delay the proceedings as long as possible and, what may be worse, to make difficulties over contact in the meantime. At present, particularly in divorce courts, the responsibility for the progress of the proceedings lies principally with the adult parties, although a considerable source of delay is the time taken to prepare welfare officers' reports and sometimes to attempt conciliation between the parties.

4.56 ... there is serious concern, particularly among the judiciary, about the present delays and ... action is required to remedy the situation. There may be problems in preparing welfare reports, given the other constraints within which welfare officers have to work, and in some cases time may be beneficial in enabling an agreed solution to emerge, perhaps with the help of conciliation. Nevertheless, the 'child's sense of time' is quite different from the adults' and it is the child's interests which should prevail.

4.57 The most effective practical action which can be taken to remedy matters is to place a clear obligation upon the court to oversee the progress of the case and to ensure that the court regards all delay as prejudicial to the child's interests unless the contrary is shown. (An example might be where the benefit to the child from a thorough report outweighed the detriment of having to wait for it, but the Court of Appeal has said that if one has to wait as long as nine months it is better to do without one [*Re C (a minor) (custody of child)* (1980) 2 FLR 163].) This approach is something of a novelty within our legal system, which is generally content to leave such matters to the parties themselves.

(e) THE VIEWS OF THE CHILD

The Law Commission (1988) dealt with the 'wishes and feelings' of the child himself (item (*a*) in the Children Act checklist, p. 532, above) in this way:

3.22 The Working Paper on Custody provisionally proposed that, at least in contested cases, the court should have to ascertain the 'wishes and feelings' of the child and give due consideration to them in the light of his age and understanding. Such a requirement already exists in adoption cases [s. 6 of the Adoption Act 1976]. Views were invited upon whether the requirement should be expressed independently or as part of a 'checklist' and on whether it should extend to uncontested cases. ...

3.23 The opinion of our respondents was almost unanimously in favour of the proposal to give statutory recognition to the child's views. Obviously there are dangers in giving them too much recognition. Children's views have to be discovered in such a way as to avoid embroiling them in their parents' disputes, forcing them to 'choose' between their parents, or making them feel responsible for the eventual decision. This is usually best done through the medium of a welfare officer's report, although most agreed that courts should retain their present powers to see children in private. Similarly, for a variety of reasons the child's views may not be reliable, so that the court should only have to take due account of them in the light of his age and understanding. Nevertheless, experience has shown that it is pointless to ignore the clearly expressed wishes of older children [*M v M (transfer of custody: appeal)* [1987] 1 WLR 404, [1987] 2 FLR 146]. Finally, however, if the parents have agreed on where the child will live and made their arrangements accordingly, it is no more practicable to try to alter these to accord with the child's views than it is to impose the views of the court. After all, united parents will no doubt take account of the views of their children in deciding upon moves of house or employment but the children cannot expect their wishes to prevail [King, 1987, p. 190].

3.24 These considerations all point towards including the child's views as part of a statutory checklist, which in practice will be limited to contested cases, rather than as a separate consideration in their own right. This solution was generally favoured by our respondents and we so recommend. Were there not to be a statutory checklist, however, the increasing recognition given both in practice and in law to the child's status as a human being in his own right [*Gillick v West Norfolk and Wisbech Area Health Authority* [1986] AC 112], rather than the object of the rights of others, would clearly require an independent duty in the court to take account of his views to the same extent as that in adoption cases.

3.25 ... The courts' present powers to make custody and access orders endure until the child reaches 18, although the court will rarely, if ever, make a custody order which is contrary to the wishes of a child who has reached 16 [*Hall v Hall* (1945) 175 LT 355]. Any other approach is scarcely practicable, given that this is the age at which children may leave school and seek full-time employment and become entitled to certain benefits or allowances in their own right. However, the matter goes beyond the question of what is practicable. There are powers of direct enforcement of custody orders which operate upon the child rather than the adults involved [e.g. s. 34 of the Family Law Act 1986]. The older the child becomes, the less just it is even to attempt to enforce against him an order to which he has never been party. As we explain below, it is usually thought unnecessary to accord party status to children in family disputes and in general we would not disagree. We recommend, therefore, that orders relating to the child's residence, contact or other specific matters of upbringing should not be made in respect of a child who has reached 16 unless there are exceptional circumstances and that orders made before that age should expire then unless in exceptional circumstances the court orders otherwise.

Questions

(i) Does this cause you to reconsider your views on s. 11 of the Family Law Act 1996 (p. 548, above) at all?
(ii) The Family Law Act 1996 also provides for the Lord Chancellor to make regulations about the separate representation of children in divorce and other proceedings between the adults. Look back at pp. 432–436, above. When should children be separately represented in proceedings about their own futures? Should it depend upon whether or not there is a dispute between their parents? Should they be represented by a lawyer, a social worker, or both?
(iii) A consortium of children's charities was unsuccessful in getting a provision into the Family Law Act 1996 for a children's officer whose role would be very like that of the Children's Ombudsman recommended in a Justice Report on *Parental Rights and Duties and Custody Suits* as long ago as 1975. Are you attracted by the following idea?

89. ...
(*h*) The family court would include among its staff a new officer, having training in both law and applied social sciences. Among other things, his duty would be to act as overseer of children's interests in custody suits. We have referred to him already in our report as the 'Children's Ombudsman.'...

91. The role we envisage for the Children's Ombudsman includes that of a clearing agency, one branch at each family court. Everyone would know of his existence and would be expected to report to him. All relevant information would end up under one hand. He would have the power to request a welfare report whenever he thought it necessary. On behalf of a child the subject of a custody suit, he would act as the child's spokesman and would have the duty of instructing solicitors and counsel to represent the child's interests so that the interests of the child might be separately represented to the court independently of the adults and local or other authorities concerned. (He would have the power to do so in other legal proceedings as well.) As the child's spokesman, it would be his particular duty to ensure that the views of any child able to express them, verbally or otherwise, were ascertained in the absence of the parents or other adult 'custodian' and then made known to the tribunal. He would be responsible to the Lord Chancellor (the traditional delegate of the Crown as *parens patriae*).

3 Court welfare officers

The usual way of ascertaining the child's views and protecting his interests in private law proceedings is to obtain a welfare officer's report. At present the family court welfare service is part of the probation service. In addition to writing reports for the court, they may also help couples to reach agreement, or provide short term family assistance (under s. 16 of the Children Act 1989) to help with difficulties, for example over contact arrangements. The mediation and reporting functions should be kept separate (*Re H (conciliation: welfare reports)* [1986] 1 FLR 476). Great weight is attached to a report and the court should not depart from a clear recommendation without explaining why (*Re T (A Minor) (welfare report recommendation)* (1977) 1 FLR 59). The courts' expectations of reports are spelled out by Johnson J in *Re P (a minor) (inadequate welfare report)* [1996] 2 FCR 285:

The whole point of the court welfare officer system is that, because in the nature of things the court cannot itself observe the relationships between the children and the parents, the welfare officer acts as the eyes and ears of the court and provides the court with an independent and

objective assessment of the relationships involved. Here the report was inadequate. The welfare officer's inquiry was conducted in such a way as to make it impossible for her to form any view about the relationships involved.

Decisions such as this require a very delicate balance of a number of considerations, principal among which must surely be the relationships between the children and the parents. Such assessments cannot be made in an office, they have to be made in a natural environment. All that was done here was that the children went along to the welfare officer's office and were interviewed.

A better example is set by the following specimen, used by welfare officers for training purposes:

SPECIMEN WELFARE REPORT

BLANKSHIRE PROBATION & AFTER-CARE SERVICE

WOOD & WOOD

Applicant:	Mrs Jean WOOD	– 22 years
Respondent:	Mr John WOOD	– 35 years
Child concerned:	Richard WOOD	– 3 years
Child:	Amanda FORBES	– 6 years
Respondent's cohabitant:	Janet SMITH	– 32 years
Children:	Mary SMITH	– 6 years
	Brian SMITH	– 5 years

1. ENQUIRIES

I have read the Court file concerning this matter
I have had discussions with:
– the Applicant with Richard
– the Respondent and Cohabitant with Richard
– Richard by himself
I have had a telephone conversation with the Housing Department
I have had a telephone conversation with Dr Jones, the Respondent's Physician

2. BACKGROUND RELATING TO THE CHILD

I understand from both parties that initially their relationship was good though the Applicant claims the Respondent spent too much time with his mother. In March 1995 Mr Wood's father died and he invited his mother to live with him and his wife. The Applicant and her mother-in-law had never enjoyed a good relationship and there were immediate problems. Mrs Wood senior it is claimed assumed control of the family, gradually taking over responsibility for the housework and the care of both the Respondent and the child – Richard. There were constant quarrels and in November 1994 following a violent disagreement, the Applicant left the matrimonial home on an impulse and stayed for a short period with a relative. Being without accommodation she did not feel it fair to Richard to take him with her at that time. Within three weeks she had found accommodation in a very small bedsitting room sharing a kitchen and bathroom with a family of five people; again a situation she felt unsuitable for Richard.

3. APPLICANT MOTHER

Mrs Jean WOOD – Mrs Wood, a full time housewife, impressed as a bright, outgoing young woman who is obviously deeply attached to her son. She told me she had found the situation in the former matrimonial home quite intolerable from the time her mother-in-law moved in. She claimed Mrs Wood senior had undermined her discipline of Richard and had tried to cause difficulties between her and the Respondent. She said that her reason for staying had been the fear that she might lose Richard and that she left only when she felt she could no longer cope with the situation. I understand that Richard's behaviour was untypically bad from the time she left home causing the Respondent to contact the family doctor. I am told the child's behaviour returned to normal once contact with his mother was re-established in December 1994. Mrs Wood visits Richard twice weekly at the former matrimonial home. The Respondent has been quite adamant that he will not allow her to take the child away from the home. Until very recently, there were no difficulties with contact. The Applicant feels, however, that the atmosphere has become tense since the Respondent's cohabitant moved into the home in January 1995 whereupon the grandmother left.

4. Of her own relationship with her cohabitant, Mr Forbes, the Applicant tells me she had known him some years ago and met him again soon after leaving her husband. She has lived with Mr Forbes since the beginning of January 1995 and has already formed an excellent relationship with his daughter, Amanda, who lives with them. The Applicant and Mr Forbes plan to marry as soon as both are free to do so.

5. The Applicant Mother feels very strongly that she is the appropriate person to have the day to day care of Richard. She feels he has already been subjected to too many changes and that she can now offer him the stability he needs. She has made tentative enquiries concerning a playschool for Richard, but if he comes to live with her would delay any decision until he was completely settled in his new home. Mrs Wood appears to fully appreciate the importance of the child having regular contact with the Father and would have no objection to reasonable contact which she suggests could be staying on alternate weekends.

6. APPLICANT'S COHABITANT

Mr Michael FORBES – Mr Forbes presented as a pleasant, mature personality. He told me he had married very young, that his wife had had difficulty in managing on a low income and the resulting debts had caused difficulties between them. He told me that his wife left him 2 years ago and he has not heard from her since. He has made enquiries concerning her whereabouts as he is anxious now to petition for divorce. Mr Forbes has had the care of his daughter since his wife left and has coped admirably with the help of a neighbour. He is employed as a clerk. He tells me that because of the demands made on him in caring for his daughter, he has not been able to take advantage of promotion. However, now that the Applicant is caring for his daughter Amanda, he feels his employment prospects are excellent. Because the Respondent has refused to allow Richard to leave the home with his mother, Mr Forbes has not met the child. He is realistic about the possible difficulties should Richard come to live with them but feels his experience with his own child will help.

7. APPLICANT'S HOME

The home is a 2-bedroomed flat which is adequately furnished and well kept. Mr Forbes expects to move to a 3-bedroomed maisonette in the near future having negotiated an exchange with another family. I have contacted the Housing Department who confirm that there are no objections to this transfer.

8. RESPONDENT

Mr John WOOD – Mr Wood is a quiet, introspective man. He tells me he was the youngest son in a large family. He has always enjoyed a very close relationship with his mother who did not approve of his relationship with the Applicant. Mr Wood tells me that his wife coped well with the home and the child until his mother moved in with them. He claims that the Applicant then became lazy and lost interest in the home, leaving everything to the grandmother. The Respondent is employed as a Sales Manager. In the course of his work he travels extensively, often away overnight and sometimes travels abroad. His cohabitant – Mrs Smith – has lived with him since mid January 1995 and although he has not known her for very long, the relationship appears to be sound and based on mutual interests. The Respondent told me that Richard has caused him some anxiety since Mrs Smith arrived and the grandmother left the home. He has again consulted the family doctor but feels that if a firm line is taken with Richard, he will quickly adapt to the new situation. The Respondent tells me that he is asking Richard to stay with him as he does not wish to have another man involved in bringing up his son. He also feels he is in a better position to care for Richard's material needs than is the Applicant. He would have no objection to the present arrangement for contact being continued but would oppose staying visits.

9. RESPONDENT'S COHABITANT

Mrs Janet SMITH – Mrs Smith is a quiet, intelligent woman who is studying for a degree with the Open University and would like a teaching career. She talked frankly about her own children saying that she was not very maternal and although she very much enjoys her children's monthly visits, she does not wish to see them more often. She expressed some reservations about bringing up Richard, especially with the Respondent being often away from home. She told me however, that she is fond of Richard and is anxious to do whatever Mr Wood wishes.

10. RESPONDENT'S HOME

The home is a spacious, 4-bedroomed house where material standards are high. The property is owned by Mr Wood subject to a mortgage.

11. CHILD CONCERNED

Richard WOOD – Richard is a bright and lively child, obviously well cared for. I have seen him with the Applicant and also separately with the Respondent. When I saw Richard with the Respondent and Mrs Smith, he appeared to be anxious to do and say the right thing and was quieter and more subdued than when I interviewed him with the Applicant. With the Applicant, Richard was talkative and lively and very upset when the time came for her to leave. Although Richard is hardly 4, it appears that given the choice, he would wish to spend most of his time with his mother.

12. CONCLUSION

From my enquiries, it would appear that both parents care about Richard's welfare and either could offer him a good home. The Respondent is in a position to offer material advantages and wishes Richard to be privately educated. The Applicant Mother's means are more modest but the bond between mother and child is particularly close and the separation was of such short duration that it appears to have done no damage to the relationship. It has not been possible to see the Applicant's cohabitant with the child. On the other hand the child's relationship with the Respondent's cohabitant is not yet a close one. In fact, the child appears to be having some difficulty in relating to a third mother figure.

13. In view of the very close relationship between mother and child, it would appear to be in Richard's long-term best interests if he were to live with his Mother. The court will want, however, to ensure that he sees as much as possible of his father.

14. It is clear that whatever the decision Richard will experience problems in adjusting to the new step-parent. The Court may consider, therefore, that a short period of assistance would be of benefit to Richard in making this adjustment.

February 1996 *Court Welfare Officer*

Questions

(i) If you were counsel for the mother in this case, what features of the report would you emphasise to the court?
(ii) If you were counsel for the father, would you advise him to settle the dispute along the lines suggested by the welfare officer? How does the new law differ from the old?
(iii) If the father wished to fight the case, which features would you as counsel emphasise to the court?
(iv) As counsel for the father, how would you go about challenging the suggestion in para. 11 of the report that 'although Richard is hardly four, it appears that given the choice, he would wish to spend most of his time with his mother'?

The issue raised by the questions above is whether the conventional investigative report may be usurping the decision-making role of the court. When welfare officers adopt a rather different role, the issues become even more complex, as is shown in a large scale study of their work conducted by James and Hay (1992). Adrian James discusses some of the issues in *Social Work in Divorce: Welfare, Mediation and Justice* (1995):

What emerged strongly, however, was the enormous variation, both between and within areas, in numerous aspects of practice: the length of time taken to complete reports; the range and frequency of checks undertaken (with probation records, child abuse registers, police records); the extent of enquiries, both of other agencies (schools, social services departments, doctors, health visitors, etc) and of parents; different patterns of contact with mothers and fathers; different use of home visits and office-based contacts; different levels of contact with and involvement of children; and different levels of reference to children's needs and wishes in reports.

Such differences reflect the results of a decade of innovation, in the absence of a common framework provided by either policy (national or local) or training, with the emergence of sometimes widely different philosophies and theoretical frameworks. These were reflected, for example, in the fact that a minority of welfare officers do not regard assisting the court as part of their role at all, instead defining this solely in terms of their professional competence, their theoretical perspectives, and their skills in assisting parents either to reach an agreement or to identify the emotional obstacles which are preventing them from reaching agreement. Others, however, derive their orientation as welfare officers almost exclusively from their statutorily defined tasks and their duty to assist the court.

In spite of these extremes of orientation and the richness and diversity of practice, however, the research also revealed a broad area of consensus. ... A key element of this consensus lies in the almost universal belief that children should retain contact with both parents, that this is central to both the social and legal construction of 'the best interests of the child', and therefore that a significant part of the welfare remit of the Family Court Welfare Officer is to work with families to ensure that this happens. Thus, although the role of the FCWO is defined above in terms of investigation, assessment and reporting – as an adjunct to the legal process and essentially to assist the court in discharging its legal function – as a consequence of this belief and the impact of conciliation and mediation on the conceptualization of family court welfare work, many welfare officers now regard their role as providing a service to courts *and* to families. ...

...

Many FCWOs are thus concerned in practice not only to assist in court with the legal process but also in various ways to assist the parties through the social process of divorce – try to bridge the gap between the legal and the social processes and perspectives. For some, this involves working with families using various therapeutic techniques and approaches. ...

...

For others, their concern to incorporate the social perspective into their report writing function and to assist with the social process of divorce is reflected in their attempts to help families to understand and resolve their disputes.

> 'A starting point for every report is sitting down with the parents and saying to them "if we can find a solution (...) that will be reported to the court. If we can't do that, then (...) I will have to do an investigative report" (...) I will contact the school, doctor, and determine how and when I'm going to see the children. (Area B)'

...

Such approaches are intended to increase parents' awareness of their children's needs and to reduce conflict which, it is argued, is the best way of ensuring that the best interests of the child are met and that the child's welfare remains paramount, thereby assisting the court to respond to the principal imperative of the Children Act 1989. ...

...

It also provides strong support for the argument that a key role for welfare has become that of trying to bridge the gap between the legal and the social processes and perspectives. In providing a welfare service to the courts, FCWOs increasingly present mediation as the primary and preferred means of securing children's welfare in divorce, thereby helping the courts to ensure the paramountcy of the child's welfare, whilst also offering parents some assistance with the social process of divorce. From this perspective, therefore, mediation becomes synonymous with welfare, it becomes the *leitmotif* for the welfare perspective – mediation as welfare.

4 Step-families

As every child knows, there have always been step-parents, but their stereotype is the wicked step-mother who invades the family after their real mother is dead. Nowadays, the more appropriate stereotype would be the divorced father who has gradually faded out of his own children's lives, and has now married a woman with children from a previous marriage or relationship. What little is known about the increasing incidence of step-families is summarised by David Utting (1995):

Data gathered by the Office of Population Censuses and Surveys in 1991 suggests there are nearly 500,000 stepfamilies in Great Britain including some 800,000 stepchildren and another 300,000 children born to both parents (Table 3).

Table 3: Stepfamilies with dependent children, Great Britain

The number of stepfamilies with resident children is estimated at almost 500,000	
Married-couple stepfamilies	
– with resident children	330,000
– with non-resident children	140,000
Cohabiting-couple stepfamilies	
– with resident children	150,000
– with non-resident children	50,000

Source: Haskey, J. (1994)

This means that just under 7 per cent of families with dependent children are stepfamilies and that 8 per cent of all dependent children are living in them. Stepfamilies based on marriage currently outnumber those based on cohabitation by more than two to one, but the growing extent of cohabitation suggests that this margin will diminish in future years.

The children in three out of four stepfamilies, whether the parents are married or cohabiting, have come from the woman's previous relationship. Only one in five is headed by a stepmother living with the children's birth father and fewer than one in twenty include children from *both* partners' previous relationships.

Table 4: Children living in stepfamilies

Over 1 million children are estimated to be living in stepfamilies	
Married-couple stepfamilies	
– stepchildren	520,000
– natural children	240,000
Cohabiting-couple stepfamilies	
– stepchildren	250,000
– natural children	40,000
Total	1,050,000

Source: Haskey, J. (1994)

Data from the General Household Survey has been used to estimate that – if current trends continue – one in 18 children are likely to become part of a married-couple stepfamily before their sixteenth birthday and one in fifteen to live in a stepfamily based on cohabitation. Some children will, of course, experience both.

We have already seen (p. 516, above) that the finances of a lone parent family may improve if the mother has a new partner but the well-being of the children does not necessarily improve as well. The research is summarised by Louie Burghes in *Lone Parenthood and Family Disruption – The Outcomes for Children* (1994):

Repartnership

Step families may be formed after separation and divorce or following single motherhood. Some single mothers may form partnerships with their children's natural father. (Although strictly speaking this is a first partnership rather than a repartnership.)

Crellin et al [1971] showed that it is not always the case that children born 'illegitimately' who move from a single mother family to living with both natural parents fare better than those who remain with their lone mother (in some cases as part of a larger household).

Elliott and Richards [1991] found significantly more disruptive behaviour among children in step families than among those who remained with a lone mother (although all their caveats about the difficulties of these measures must be borne in mind). But there was no such difference on the 'unhappy and worried' score. Nor were there significant differences in achievement in maths and reading or in the chances of getting a university qualification by age 23 between those living with a lone mother or with their mother and a step father.

Maclean and Wadsworth [1988] and Kuh and Maclean [1990] found that repartnership following bereavement increased the chances of achieving educational qualifications. But this was not the case where it followed separation or divorce. Indeed, Maclean and Wadsworth found that likehood of higher educational qualifications increased where remarriage followed bereavement.

Kiernan [1992] found that just as there was little difference in the ages at which young people from intact and bereaved families made adult transitions, there was not a great deal of difference where the lone parent repartnered or remarried (following the bereavement).

By contrast, there were differences between transitions made by young people in intact families and for those whose lone parent had repartnered or remarried following separation or divorce.

The only exception was for young people in step families. They were more likely than those in intact families to leave home by 18 years whether the family disruption was due to separation, divorce or bereavement.

In her study of step children in the NCDS, Ferri [1984] found that overall:

> '… the deveopment of children with stepmothers did not differ very markedly from that of their peers in unbroken families or of those living with lone fathers.'

On the other hand,

> 'The results relating to children with stepfathers, however, were rather less reassuring. These children, and particularly the boys, frequently compared unfavourably with those in unbroken families, and differed little from children living with lone mothers.'

The outcomes from step-family life were generally less favourable when following the divorce of natural parents than the death of one of them.

But despite these observations, Ferri concludes that:

> 'For the majority of children we studied, there was no discernible adverse effect and little to distinguish them from their peers living with two natural parents.'

It was also true that

> '… there was sufficient indication of unhappiness and development difficulties among a minority of stepchildren to suggest that remarriage should not be seen as an instant, all-purpose "cure" for the many problems faced by the one-parent family, especially if those problems are viewed from the child's perspective.'

Research in Australia [Funder et al., 1992] of a cross-section of step-families looked at the relationships that 66 children had with their absent fathers and resident step-fathers. Children seemed to be happy at home where their step-father was involved with the family, but even more so where the step-father was well liked but slightly less involved. Moreover, good relations with their natural father seemed to be associated with better relations with their step-father. The researchers concluded that:

> 'Whatever the explanation, children tend to be involved with two fathers, or have little involvement with either.'

The complexities of the step-relationship are explored from the point of view of a step-mother by Brenda Maddox in *Step-parenting* (1980):

If families in which there is a step-parent differ from adoptive families, they differ far more from ordinary families. The reason is that the basic rules that govern family life are disturbed in families where the children are not the biological offspring of both the husband and wife in the household. These rules concern sex and money: who may have sexual relations with whom, who must support whom and who may inherit from whom. Father sleeps with a woman who is not his son's mother, and is therefore not explicitly forbidden to the son by the recognised incest taboo. The child sits at the table of the breadwinner of the household, but the child is actually supported by a father living somewhere else. Often children who ordinarily would expect to inherit from their father and mother find their parent's new spouse will take away some or all of what might have been their portion. Or, if there are children of the new marriage as well as of a former marriage, there often exists an uncomfortable situation in which there are two sets of children who live under the same roof, or who spend vacations together, but who have quite different financial expectations. One might be, say, the daughter of the late Aly Khan and the other of Orson Welles. …

Still, there is no model for how a step-parent should behave. The parent's obligations, by contrast, are clear. The anthropologist Bronislaw Malinowski has pointed out that 'the mother, besides feeling inclined to do all she does for her child, is none the less obliged to do it'. Step-parents often do not feel inclined to do anything for their step-children, yet they feel strong pressure from the community, and from their spouse, to do something. But what? For natural parents, not only the obligations but the ideals are clear. …

The social questions posed by the remarriage of parents have hardly been faced by a society that ostensibly accepts divorce as the right solution to an unhappy marriage. We have been told that the marriage bond is the structural keystone in our kinship system and that our identity depends entirely on the marriage unit (unless we come from old-established lineage like the Devonshires or the Rothschilds). Who we are depends entirely on two families – our family of origin and our family of procreation; we are the children of our parents and the parents of our children. But we are not told how to preserve our sense of identity if we have a mother in one family, a father in another, a son in a third, and a daughter in a fourth.

Jacqueline Burgoyne and David Clark, in *Reconstituted Families* (1982) draw upon their research with step-families in Sheffield to reach the following conclusions:

We have tried to suggest that it is still often the case that step-families are reconstituted according to a normative blueprint which is based on the unbroken nuclear family. Those who marry again are, therefore, heavily reliant on criteria of success, failure and adequacy which are drawn from 'normal' family life. Consequently evaluations of stepfamily life are typically made according to criteria of 'ordinariness'. However it is clear that stepfamilies differ in the extent to which they consciously attempt to 'pass' as an unbroken nuclear family by, for example, taking a new job and moving to a new area. Naturally this may seem to be the most obvious strategy; it brings about the normalisation of family life and, in the case of young adults with small children where divorce and custody are uncontested, this may well prove to be both practical and expedient. However, this may be impossible for other families. Where legal aspects of custody, access and maintenance arrangements are disputed and where older children and non-custodial parents are in regular contact, then the stepfamily is less likely to succeed in attempts at normalisation. For these families two possible strategies are available. Some may, out of a sense of guilt, propriety or confusion, choose to fly in the face of the structural factors which make their existence as a stepfamily both visible and incontrovertible. The pursuit of the goal of normal family life is inevitably frustrated, as subjective ideals clash continually with external and material constraints. Others, to the extent that they recognise the nature of these problems, may reject, either explicitly or implicitly, such a course. Members of these families, sensitised by media coverage of trends in divorce and remarriage, see themselves as pioneers of an alternative life. Having accepted their situation, they formulate an ideology and practice to match it. In marked contrast to some of the literature which emphasised the negative aspects of step-relationships, they are clear that their way of life may also represent a source of potential rewards and satisfactions of a type absent from more conventional nuclear families. Typically, these step-families emphasise the material and social benefits which stepsiblings derive from one another's presence in the family, the value and importance of additional parental figures, and the fulfillment which results from reconstituting a single family from its disparate elements.

In *Making a Go of It* (1984), Burgoyne and Clark construct the following typology to reflect these variations:

Table 6.1: A typology of stepfamilies

1 *'Not really a stepfamily'*
The stepchildren of the family were young at the time of divorce and remarriage; within a short time they were able to think of themselves as an 'ordinary' family.
Children of new marriage confirm this.

2 *'Looking forward to the departure of the children'*
Older couples with teenage children await departure of dependent children so that they can enjoy their new partnership more fully.
Too old for children in new marriage.

3 *The 'progressive' stepfamily*
Prototype 'new' stepfamily in which conflicts with ex-partners have been resolved. They stress the advantages of their circumstances.
Few barriers to additional children of new marriage.

4 *The successful conscious pursuit of an 'ordinary' family life together*
Stepparent becomes full 'social' parent transferring allegiance to stepchildren. Their initial problems are solved or successfully ignored.
Children of new marriage symbolise 'normality' of their family life.

5 *The conscious pursuit of 'ordinary' family life frustrated*
The legacy of their past marriage(s) frustrates their attempts to build an ordinary family life together.
Children of new marriage are unlikely because of continuing problems.

Step-families began increasingly to resort to adoption as a solution to these difficulties. In 1970, however, a Departmental Committee on the Adoption of Children published a *Working Paper* in which they voiced the doubts of many professionals about this practice and made a radical suggestion:

93. Just as openness about adoption and illegitimacy is desirable, so is it desirable to recognise openly the fact and the consequences of divorce and of death. One of the consequences of divorce is that many children are living with a parent and a step-parent and retain contact with, or even live for part of the time with, their other parent, who may also have remarried. Such a situation may well be disturbing to the child, but it is not appropriate to use adoption in an attempt to ease the pain or to cover up these consequences of divorce. The legal extinguishment of a legitimate child's links with one half of his own family, which adoption entails in such circumstances, is inappropriate and may well be damaging. We consider therefore that adoption of a legitimate child by a natural parent and step-parent should no longer be possible.
94. We recognise that we are drawing a distinction between legitimate and illegitimate children in that a step-parent will be able to adopt his step-child only if the child is illegitimate. This distinction might be regarded as invidious, and it may be thought that adoption by a step-parent should be available in both cases or in neither. On the other hand the two situations are not truly analogous. An illegitimate child, by adoption, obtains a legal status and a family which he did not have before. ...

The final Report of the Committee (1972) stated that:

108. The evidence we received was overwhelmingly opposed to our suggestion. Some witnesses pointed to the positive advantages of adoption to a legitimate child whose other parent is dead or where contact with that parent and his family is negligible or non-existent. Others were strongly opposed to the distinction between legitimate and illegitimate children, pointing out that a parent may have a legitimate and an illegitimate child and on the remarriage of the parent the illegitimate child could be adopted by the step-parent but not the legitimate child.

The Children Act 1975 accordingly introduced statutory discouragement of all types of step-parent adoption. The courts have always been reluctant to dispense with the agreement of an estranged father who does not want his children adopted, but they had difficulty in working out when they ought to refuse an adoption which everyone wanted.

Re D (minors) (adoption by step-parent)
(1980) 2 FLR 102, 10 Fam Law 246, Court of Appeal

The parents of two girls, now aged 13 and 10½, were divorced in 1973. In 1976 the mother married her present husband, who was also divorced and had the two children of his first marriage living with him. The girls' name was changed to his by deed poll with the consent of their father. There was contact between the father and the eldest child until the end of 1977 and between him and the younger child until September 1978. In 1980 the mother and step-father applied to adopt the girls and the father consented. Both girls indicated to the guardian ad litem that they wished to be adopted. The family planned to emigrate to Australia. The guardian ad litem, after a thorough examination of the advantages and disadvantages, concluded that on balance the adoption order should not be made. The judge reached the same conclusion and the applicants appealed.

Ormrod LJ: ... the natural father of these children has dropped out of their lives both physically and psychologically to an extent which is much greater than one usually meets in this type of post-divorce situation. It is reasonable to infer that the children see themselves as members of the D family to a much, much greater extent than children of divorced parents normally do. There is no question of regarding Mr D as 'Uncle Tom' or whatever his name is. They clearly regard him as 'Dad'.

So it is a case in which, to my mind, all the indications are in favour of making an adoption order, more particularly as the family is about to emigrate to Australia. I can well understand the adults feeling that it would put their position in their new country much more clearly and explicitly if they go there with these two children as the adopted children of the family.

The points which troubled [the guardian ad litem] mainly seem to me to be, first, the fact that the children in this case had a full recollection of their natural father, and so it was not one of those cases where the children themselves have no recollection of their natural father and where the making of an adoption order gives legal effect to a situation which already exists in fact. But, to my mind, this is not a crucial distinction. The fact that they remember their natural father cannot be, in itself, a reason for not making an adoption order if the other indications suggest that it would be desirable. Of course these children remember their father.

Then it is said that the effect of an adoption order is to cut them off entirely from their father's family – to which, to my mind, the answer is that it may or may not do so. There is no magic in an adoption order. The fact that the child becomes a child of the new family does not, in itself, automatically cut off the children from the natural family. Of course it may do. An adoption order has that effect when the child is very young. I am always impressed by the differences in the considerations to be taken into account where one is concerned with the adoption of a small child, say up to two years, and an older child. The effect of adoption of a child up to two is to effect a complete severance with the natural family and, hopefully, a complete integration into the new family; but, once the child is older than that and has experience of a natural parent, adoption can never have that effect in fact. It may have in law that effect, but there is no reason why, if everyone is agreeable, children like these should not see their [paternal] grandparents should it be desirable. In fact, in this case we are told they are completely out of touch with the whole of the father's family, not only with the father himself. So that, with respect to [the guardian] and recognizing his extreme care in this case, I personally do not attach great significance to the fact that the children are fully aware of the existence of their natural father.

He was also troubled by what he thought would be the disturbing effect of the adoption order on the existing family unit. That I find hard to understand, because there seems to be no indication that an adoption order will materially alter anything in this new family except, if anything, to increase its cohesion and not diminish it. The judge was worried that, possibly, after an adoption order had been made, one of the children might turn on the adoptive father and challenge him as not being their own father. But, with respect, that point must apply with even more force to a situation where Mr D's position is simply that of a joint custodian ...

He also took the point – and one sees the force of it again – that there was a distinction here between the two children that we are dealing with and the two children of the husband because there was no suggestion of an application by the step-mother, Mrs D, for an adoption order in respect of them. We are told that the reason for that is that their mother, that is the first Mrs D, has so completely disappeared out of the children's lives that the proposed adopters in this case regarded proceedings for an adoption order in respect of those children as being quite superfluous and unnecessary. If that is right – and it seems to me, on the face of it, reasonable to suppose that it is – then there does not seem to be any serious objection from that point of view. ...

Appeal allowed.

Questions

(i) Do you think there is 'no magic' in an adoption order?

(ii) Why was it right for the step-father to adopt his wife's children (whose father had completely dropped out of their lives) but not for the wife to adopt her husband's children (whose mother had completely dropped out of their lives)? Does it bear out what Furstenberg and Cherlin (p. 524, above) have to say about how fathers relate to their children?

The numbers of step-parents have increased dramatically, but the numbers of step-parent adoptions have not. They remain, however, a sizeable proportion of the diminishing number of adoption orders, as the *Judicial Statistics 1995* show:

During 1995, 5,317 orders for adoption were made (16% less than in 1994). Of these, 54% (2,877) were made to step-parents which, proportionally, was almost 5% more than in 1994.

Table 5.4 Adoption of children: summary of proceedings, 1995

Nature of proceedings	High Court	County courts	Family proceedings courts	Total
Applications:				
by step-parents	38	2,465	725	3,228
by others	219	2,001	161	2,381
Total	**257**	**4,466**	**886**	**5,609**
Orders made:				
to step-parents	37	2,270	570	2,877
to others	212	2,115	113	2,440
Total	**249**	**4,385**	**683**	**5,317**

Under the Children Act 1989, the court may make any s. 8 order instead of an adoption order whenever it wishes, although it has no duty to consider doing so. Step-parent adoptions are no longer expressly discouraged. If the child is treated as a 'child of the family' (see p. 7, above) of the new marriage, the step-parent is always entitled to apply for a residence or contact order (s. 10(5)(*a*)). He may be ordered to make financial provision for the child, although he will not be automatically liable under the new child support scheme (see Chapter 4). The child may also apply for family provision from his estate (see p. 190, above). So what does an adoption order do that a residence order in favour of parent and step-parent does not? Most of the cases concern emigration and change of surname, which are prohibited unless the other parent consents or the court gives leave (see p. 529, above).

Barnes v Tyrrell
(1981) 3 FLR 240, Court of Appeal

The mother had custody of the two children of her former marriage, a boy now 12 and a girl now 11. Since the divorce in 1977, the father had had liberal access. The mother was now married to an Australian and wished to return with him to Australia. Her first application to take the children was refused, because of the welfare officer's evidence that the boy might be upset at losing regular contact with his father. After a successful holiday in Australia, however, the boy changed his mind and both children now wished to go, although also to keep contact with their father. The judge granted leave to take the children permanently, with an annual holiday in this country. The father appealed.

Dunn LJ: ... In these cases one always has a great deal of sympathy for the parent who is, in effect, left behind. What is said in this appeal on behalf of the father is that the judge gave insufficient weight to the fact that these children had had very regular contact with the father, notwithstanding the breakdown of the marriage. It was not a case such as *P (LM) (otherwise E) v P (GE)* [1970] 3 All ER 659, where there was a very young child who hardly knew his father, but in this case the children obviously have a good relationship with their father and have been cared for by him for a period after the mother left.

Then it was said that these children of 11 and 12 would be uprooted from their schools, they would be sent to an entirely new system of education in Australia, and they would be taken away from what is nowadays called their 'extended' family, namely their grandparents, uncles and aunts and cousins, and would go to a strange country where they would only have their mother as a blood relation.

Speaking for myself it seems to me that all these matters were taken into account by the judge before he made the order. The principle which is followed by the court in these cases was stated by Sachs LJ in *P (LM) (otherwise E) v P (GE)* [1970] 3 All ER 659 at 662, where he said:

> 'When a marriage breaks up, a situation normally arises when the child of that marriage, instead of being in the joint custody of both parents, must of necessity become one who is in the custody of a single parent. Once that position has arisen and the custody is working well, this court should not lightly interfere with such reasonable way of life as is selected by that parent to whom custody has been rightly given. Any such interference may ... produce considerable strains which would not only be unfair to the parent whose way of life is interfered with but also to any new marriage of that parent. In that way it might well in due course reflect on the welfare of the child. The way in which the parent who properly has custody of a child may choose in a reasonable manner to order his or her way of life is one of those things which the parent who has not been given custody may well have to bear, even though one has every sympathy with the latter on some of the results.'

The judge plainly had that passage in mind because he dealt at length with the arrangements for these children in Australia. He had the evidence not only of the mother and Mr B, but also of Mr B's father as to what the circumstances were in Australia. It appears from the evidence, which the judge accepted, that Mr B's financial prospects are better in Australia than they are in this country. He would be likely to command a better salary there than he does here. There is apparently a suitable house in a suburb of Sydney, where his parents live, and the judge had evidence from Mr B's father as to the schools available in Australia. The judge summed it up in this way:

> 'The prospect of the family, accordingly, is one of prosperity in Australia, or a very much more uncertain prospect in England. Mr B is very anxious to go back to his home. The baby is an Australian, and he would wish to bring her up in Australia.'

The judge came to the conclusion, accordingly, that the mother's wish to take the children to Australia was an entirely reasonable one and upon that basis he made the order.

Appeal dismissed.

Questions

(i) What difference might it have made if the mother had not remarried but was herself an Australian and wished to return with the children (see *Tyler v Tyler* [1989] 2 FLR 158)?

(ii) Or are the courts likely to see things differently after the Children Act in any event?

Fathers who are anxious to maintain links with their children may be just as anxious to avoid a change of surname as they are to oppose an adoption. The Court of Appeal has expressed differing views:

R (BM) v R (DN)
[1978] 2 All ER 33, [1977] 1 WLR 1256, 121 Sol Jo 758, Court of Appeal

The case was a custody dispute about whether the youngest of four children, a boy now aged 6 and a half, should continue to live with his father and new partner or should join the other children, who lived with their mother and her new partner, in army quarters at the rural camp where he was stationed. The trial judge gave custody to the mother and Stamp LJ described the father's appeal as 'hopeless'. One element in the father's objections to the transfer was the fact that the three older children were using the surname of their mother's new partner, Sergeant W:

Ormrod LJ: ... I remember that [the original rule] was directed to preventing parents with custody or care and control orders changing children's names by deed poll or by some other formal means, but, unfortunately, it now seems to be causing a great deal of trouble and difficulty to school authorities and to children and the very last thing that any rule of this court is intended to do is to embarrass children. It should not be beyond our capacity as adults to cope with the problem of dealing with children who naturally do not want to be picked out and distinguished by their friends and known by a surname other than their mother's, if they are thinking about it at all. It is very embarrassing for school authorities and indeed to the court if efforts have to be made to stop a little girl signing her name 'W' when it really is 'R'. We are in danger of losing our sense of proportion. All one can say in this particular case is that one can understand the situation, which is not at all unusual, and I just hope that no one is going to make a point about this name business, in other words, to treat it as a symbol of something which it is not. There is nothing in this case that suggests that the mother or Sergeant W want to make a takeover bid for this family from the father and turn these children into their own children, nothing at all. Therefore, I hope that it can be treated as counsel in his exchanges with the learned judge below observed, 'This is a peripheral matter.' I would endorse that strongly.

W v A (child: surname)
[1981] Fam 14, [1981] 1 All ER 100, [1981] 2 WLR 124, 124 Sol Jo 726, 11 Fam Law 22, Court of Appeal

The parents separated in 1971 when their children were aged 3 and 1½. They were granted joint custody, with care and control to the mother and reasonable access, which was exercised, to the father. After divorce, both remarried; the mother married an Australian who wished to return with her and the children to his home country. The father agreed, provided that the mother undertook not to change the children's surname. The mother and both children, now aged 12 and 10, wished to use the step-father's name. The trial judge refused leave to change and the mother appealed.

Dunn LJ: ... When the question of the change of name came before the judge, he was faced with the dilemma that there are two apparently conflicting lines of authority in this court on the question of changing children's surnames. The first is that the change of a child's surname is an important matter, not to be undertaken lightly. The second is that the change of a child's surname is a comparatively unimportant matter. The judge, faced with the choice between those two lines of authority, opted for the first.

... As in all cases concerning the future of children whether they be custody, access, education or, as in this case, the change of a child's name, s. 1 of the Guardianship of Minors Act 1971 requires that the court shall regard 'the welfare of the [child] as the first and paramount consideration'. It is a matter for the discretion of the individual judge hearing the case, seeing the witnesses, seeing the parents, possibly seeing the children, to decide whether or not it is in the interests of the child in the particular circumstances of the case that his surname should or should not be changed; and the judge will take into account all the circumstances of the case, including no doubt where appropriate any embarrassment which may be caused to the child by not changing his name and, on the other hand, the long-term interests of the child, the importance of maintaining the child's links with his paternal family, and the stability or otherwise of the mother's remarriage. I only mention those as typical examples of the kinds of considerations which arise in these cases, but the judge will take into account all the relevant circumstances in the particular case before him. ...

Speaking for myself, I think the judge was entirely right not to attach decisive importance to the views of two young children of 12 and 10 who were about to embark on the excitement of going to Australia with their mother and their new stepfather.

Other criticisms were made of the judge. It was said that there were positive advantages to these children in changing their surname. They were about to make a fresh start in a new country and it would be an advantage to them to go out as a united family. A change of name, it was said, would not make much difference to the father because the children would be at the other end of the world and he has two sons by his second marriage, so the name of A will survive in Gloucestershire. It is also said that, when they get older, if the children wished to change their name back to A they could always do so.

I have no doubt that the judge had all these matters in mind and there is nothing in his reasons, in his short judgment, which leads me to suppose that he did not. On the contrary, it seems to me that the judge approached this matter entirely rightly.

Appeal dismissed.

Questions

(i) Do you think that children of this age are any less entitled to a view on this point than they are on adoption?

(ii) Do you think that *either* of the opposing camps in the Court of Appeal was indeed putting the children's interests before those of the adults?

(iii) There are many cases in which a child's surname might be changed without resort to litigation – for example, if any of these fathers had consented,

or if they were dead, or if the children had used their names although the parents were unmarried – are the arguments against allowing this any less strong in such cases?
(iv) *W v A* has undoubtedly won the day; what do you think the answer would be if a divorced mother reverted to her maiden name and wanted her children to use it too (see *Re F (child: surname)* [1993] 2 FLR 837n)?

Judith Masson, Daphne Norbury and Sandra Chatterton, in *Mine, Yours or Ours? A Study of Step-parent Adoption* (1983), found, as others have done, that step-parents are not very interested in an alternative to adoption. They discuss a new way of giving them some status:

Applicants we interviewed had little or no idea of the legal implications of adoption. They wanted to make the family like a 'proper family' but did not intend that the child be considered as 'adopted' rather than as 'their own'. Mothers did not want to become adoptive mothers and some were disturbed that the birth certificate had to be replaced with an adoption certificate. What they appeared to want was recognition for the step-parent, permission to change the child's name and something to reassure them that their family was secure. Adoption went far beyond this and legally made fundamental changes in the family structure. The belief that adoption is essential if members of the step-family are to be treated as belonging to a complete family unit or the step-parent is to enjoy legal rights arises largely from ignorance. ...

There is need for recognition of the step-parent during the life of his spouse: a need currently met, albeit inadequately for a minority, by adoption. The criticisms of the present and former laws suggest that whether or not there is a thorough investigation of the family, it has simply not been possible to assess families for a different status because there are no accepted criteria. If this is true, it follows that any new status should be available to all step-parents on demand. If there were no assessment and no selection then there would be no place for either a guardian *ad litem* or a judge. An administrative process could be used, just as adoption applicants themselves had expected in the past.

If a status is to be available without investigation to all who seek it, it should involve neither the exclusion of the other natural parent nor the creation of extra rights in the step-family. This could be achieved by a change in legislation enabling the step-parent to *share those parental rights which his spouse has*. There would be no need for the law to allocate these rights between the parent and the step-parent; this would be a matter for the parties, as it is in families of first marriage. Both parent and step-parent, and the other natural parent, would be able to challenge a decision or refer a dispute to the court, as can parents and guardians at present. Disputes would be settled applying the welfare principle. ... It would avoid the necessity of the natural parent naming the step-parent as guardian by will or deed if she wished him to act in the event of her death. The status which a step-parent can be given on the death of his spouse would exist *during* the marriage, thus problems would not arise as they do now merely because the natural parent dies intestate. ... This new status would not automatically provide for inheritance between the child and step-parent on intestacy; this would, perhaps, be too fundamental a change in English law. Nor would it permit the *post-divorce* parent and step-parent to change the child's name without the permission of either the other natural parent or the court. In fact, the status provided would be similar to the guardianship which the step-parent (or any other person) may obtain on the parent's death.

The *Review of Adoption Law – Report to Ministers of an Interdepartmental Working Group* (1992) took up the argument once more:

19.2 Adoption by a step-parent and parent severs the legal links between a child and the other side of his or her birth family. There may be circumstances in which this is appropriate, for instance where the other parent has never acted in a parental capacity and the child has never really known any member of that side of the birth family. But where the child has some relationship with the parent, or with his or her relatives, it is unlikely to be in the child's interests for their legal relationship to be extinguished. A parent may agree to adoption simply because he has no interest in the child, or even where he has such an interest and is keen to retain it but wishes to end the payment of maintenance. Where the other parent has died or is no longer in the picture, the possible benefits to the child of retaining a legal relationship with grandparents or other relatives may be overlooked. Of course, the adoption order need not mean severance of practical links. But where the prime motivation behind an adoption application is the wish to cement the family unit and put away the past, this may be confusing and lead to identity problems for the child, especially if (as is statistically not unlikely) the new marriage breaks down. It is also possible that the step-parent's family has little or no involvement or interest in the adopted child, so that the child loses one family without really gaining another. As divorce has become more common, it is less necessary for families to pursue step-parent adoption in order to avoid embarrassment and difficult explanations. We do not consider it appropriate to prevent step-parent adoptions; but there may be ways in which the law can help to discourage inappropriate applications.

Step-parent adoption orders

19.3 Where adoption by a step-parent *is* in a child's interests, we consider it anomalous that the parent who is caring for the child should also become an adoptive parent. It can be disturbing for a birth parent and child to have the birth certificate replaced by an adoption certificate on which the birth parent is shown as an adoptive parent. We therefore recommend that there should be a new type of adoption order, available only to step-parents, which does not make the birth parent (ie the step-parent's spouse) an adoptive parent but in almost all other respects resembles a normal adoption order. Application for the order would be by the step-parent with the agreement of his or her spouse. The order could not be made unless the child's other parent (if he or she had parental responsibility) – and the child (if 12 or over) – agreed to the adoption, or the court dispensed with agreement on one of the specified grounds [see p. 673, below]. The child's legal links with the other birth parent and family would be severed. Consideration would have to be given to an appropriate way of amending the adoption certificate and of recording the adoption on the Adopted Children Register. The order should only be open to a step-parent, not to an unmarried partner.

19.4 We are concerned by the relative incidence of breakdown of second and subsequent marriages. Where a step-parent who has adopted a child subsequently becomes divorced from the child's birth parent, it is possible that the parent and child may wish to have restored their legal relationship with the other side of the child's birth family. We therefore recommend that there should be provision for a step-parent adoption order to be undone where the marriage ends by divorce or death and the child is under the age of 18. Application would be by the birth parent whose parental responsibility had been extinguished by the adoption order. Agreement to the revocation of the order would be required from the step-parent, the parent who retained parental responsibility and the child if aged 12 or over. If any of these people did not agree to the revocation of the order, it would stand unless their agreement could be dispensed with. ... Consideration should also be given to whether, and if so in what circumstances, a child who has reached the age of 18 should be able to apply for the revocation of an order.

Alternative orders

19.5 We have already made clear our concern that some applications by step-parents appear to be made without full consideration of the needs of the child. It is likely that in many circumstances a residence order would be a better way of confirming a step-parent's responsibility for a child, because it does not alter a child's legal relationship with his or her parents and family. ...

19.6 ... we do not feel it would be advisable to have a ... legislative presumption in favour of residence orders for step-parents. We have already recommended (see above, paragraph 6.3) that the court should have a duty to consider alternative orders, including residence orders. It is even more imporant that any step-parent who is considering applying for an adoption order should be encouraged to explore alternative orders before the application comes to court. ...

Acquisition of parental responsibility by step-parents

19.8 Inappropriate applications might also less frequently be made if step-parents were able to acquire parental responsibility without a court order by making an agreement with the birth parent, in the same way that unmarried fathers may now acquire parental responsibility under section 4 of the Children Act 1989. A person with parental responsibility has all the rights, duties, powers, responsibilities and authority which by law a parent of a child has in relation to the child and the child's property. A person with a residence order has parental responsibility but only while the residence order remains in force. ... It would therefore be a significant step to allow step-parents to acquire parental responsibility, but one which we feel is justified in view of the public relationship which the step-parent has with the child's parent and their entitlement to

apply for an adoption order, which is likely to be far less appropriate. We therefore propose that a step-parent should acquire parental responsibility for a child if at any time he and both parents make an agreement to share parental responsibility (in a form prescribed under regulations made by the Lord Chancellor). We propose also that a court should have the power to make a parental responsibility order in favour of a step-parent. Where the other parent does not agree to the step-parent's acquisition of parental responsibility, the step-parent could apply for such an order. It would also be one of the alternatives available to a court (and which the court would have a duty to consider) when considering an application for a step-parent adoption order.
19.9 It should not be possible, under this system, for an unmarried co-habitant to acquire parental responsibility in respect of his or her partner's child, or for the court to grant it.

Questions

(i) Suppose that your parents divorced, your mother remarried and your step-father adopted you; but some time after that your mother died and your step-father was no longer able to look after you; meanwhile your father had remarried and wanted you to live with him; and so did you: should it be possible for the adoption order to be revoked (see *Re M (minors) (adoption)* [1991] 1 FLR 458, CA, and *Re B (adoption: jurisdiction to set aside)* [1995] Fam 239, [1995] 2 FLR 1, CA)?
(ii) Why do you suppose that the Government, in its White Paper, *Adoption: The Future* (1993) and draft Bill, *Adoption – A Service for Children* (1996), while accepting the recommendation in paragraph 19.3 has rejected the one in paragraph 19.4?
(iii) The recommendations in paragraph 19.8 have been accepted: how do they differ from the proposals made by Judith Masson and her colleagues?
(iv) Would you have banned step-parent adoptions altogether?

Consider what effect any of those recommendations would have had upon the following case:

Re H (shared residence: parental responsibility)
[1995] 2 FLR 883, [1996] Fam Law 140, Court of Appeal

The mother had married when she was pregnant by another man. Her husband had treated the child (now aged 14) as his. They also had a child of their own (now aged 11). The marriage broke down in 1992 and in 1993 a shared residence order was made by consent. In fact the boys did not spend alternate weeks with each parent, as had been contemplated, but did stay with the father at least one whole weekend a fortnight. Each parent applied for a sole residence order. During the proceedings, the mother told the older boy about his paternity; he was upset but gratified that the father had been prepared to treat him as his own son. The judge maintained the current arrangements and made a shared residence order so that the father would have parental responsibility for the older child. The mother appealed.

Ward LJ: Orders for shared residence are still unusual orders. They may gradually win more grudging approval from the courts as the judges begin to acknowledge that such orders can reflect practical arrangements made by parents and their children which work well in putting into satisfactory practice that purpose promoted by the Act which emphasises that parenting is a continuing and shared responsibility even after a separation.

... Having set out the history and the wishes of the boys, [the judge] referred himself to some of the authorities and directed himself that the orders of shared residence were at least unusual, if not exceptional. He put himself on guard not easily to make such an order. He approached the question in a wholly proper and conventional way by asking himself where the welfare of these boys lay. He followed the checklist of factors which s. 1(3) of the Children Act 1989 requires him to bear in mind. He took account of the wishes of the boys. I see no force in the submission urged on behalf of the mother that P's expressed desire to live with the mother was an indication that he could not easily accept a shared residence order: the implications of that and a grant of parental responsibility that accompanies it would have been beyond his comprehension. He was dealing with a wholly different possibility, namely that he should live entirely in the respondent's home, something, as I have indicated, he found unacceptable. The judge moved from due regard to the boys' wishes to the next checklist factor of their respective needs, and those he analysed in a way to which exception cannot be taken. Both of these parties had discharged their duty to meet the needs of the children, especially of their educational needs. He looked then to the likely effect on the children of any change. He said this:

> 'The factual situation, which I have to say has clearly existed now for well over a year, has been this on-going contact arrangement, where the boys in their different ways go to their father's home. That has been an on-going situation. The impact of the various proposals by the parents on that situation does have to be examined.
>
> If the mother's application is accepted, so that there is a residence order in her favour only, there would be a loss of parental responsibility by the father for P. He has parental responsibility at the moment by virtue of the current order. I have to say that this is a very important matter. Its significance cannot be under-estimated.'

He found that the loss of that benefit would bring about a very significant change to the children's current situation. It is difficult, he said, to see that there was any pressing need to make such a significant change. He felt that it would be a recipe for continuing confusion, quite apart from the fact that it would be impossible to implement for P if these arrangements were changed.

The capabilities of the parents were eventually matched and he concluded in the exercise of his discretion that this shared residence order should be made. He gave these reasons for it:

> '... first of all, [it] reflects the actual situation that pertains to the parents and the children. Secondly, this order ensures that during P's childhood the father retains parental responsibility, which I consider should not be lost, because this is a case where both parents are acknowledging that the relationship between P and his father is one of father and son, even though there is no biological link.
>
> In every other respect, it is a straightforward father-and-son relationship. I consider it of vital importance that that relationship should not be disturbed in any way. There would be a disturbance if I made an order which took away the parental responsibility from the father.
>
> Thirdly, I consider that this order, in the terms I have made, is appropriate because if I went to an order for sole residence, discontinuing the father's position, the children might well be confused, perceiving the father as having done something as a result of which the court has taken something from him. They might, indeed, think that in some way their father was being punished. I think there is a potential for great confusion in that regard, because the father has made himself continuously available for the children for the period since the order of 4 November 1993 and before. That must be recognised. I do not see why I should make an order which suggests in some way that the father might be perceived by a court, viewed from the children's point of view, as having done something wrong and something being taken away from him.
>
> A fourth reason for making an order in the terms I have indicated is that it preserves the equality, which I consider must be maintained, as between P and L.
>
> A fifth reason, which is one I address to the parents, [is that] I make this order to reinforce for both parents the need for the exercise of parental responsibility for these children in a responsible manner.'

He went on to deal with that aspect.

He fully appreciated that he was making an order contrary to the recommendation of the court welfare officer but he properly gave reasons why he disagreed with that conclusion, those reasons being that it safeguarded P in one important aspect of his identity and it ensured and met the needs for dealing with P and L alike. It is said that the boys are treated alike, feel on the same footing and have the same opportunities with time with their father and their mother.

It is submitted that it was quite inappropriate to use a shared residence order for the purpose of conferring parental responsibility on a stepfather in circumstances like this. I see nothing in the authorities which compel that conclusion. In one of the early cases in which shared residence orders had to be considered, Connell J in *A v A (Minors) (Shared Residence Order)* [1994] 1 FLR 669 at p. 672G [p. 544, above] wisely declined the invitation proffered to him then to deliver a declaratory judgment of the type sought in the skeleton argument advanced by counsel as to what does or does not amount to an appropriate circumstance for the making of a shared residence order. ...

It is important not to forget that each case will depend upon its own facts. On the facts of the decision in *Re WB (Residence Orders)* [1995] 2 FLR 1023 Thorpe J was absolutely right. That case was similar to this in the sense that it was an unmarried father seeking a residence order, but the circumstances there were very different. The circumstances in that case were found by justices, from whom the appeal went to Thorpe J, to be such that a shared residence order would be likely to ferment disputes which would ill-serve the welfare interests of the children.

This case is at once different. The essential element of the judge's decision was to alleviate the confusion that would arise in the children's minds if they did not have the comfort and security of knowing not only that the father wished to treat the boy as if he was his father, but that the law would give some stamp of approval to that de facto position.

Given the boy's shock at the discovery of his paternity, everything must be done for this child to lead him to believe that life has not changed. It is important, in my judgment, that the benefits of the parental responsibility order, which by virtue of s. 12(2) of the Children Act flows from the making of a shared residence order, be impressed upon the boy to give him the confidence that he has not suffered some life-shattering blow to his self-esteem.

... Residence orders are, as their words indicate, practical orders which settle the arrangements to be made as to the person with whom the child is to live. Here it was important that the boys retain the perception that they lived with their father when they did not live with their mother. Shared residence has a different psychological impact from residence with one, contact to another because, as contact is defined, it requires that the parent with whom the child lives, must allow the child to visit or stay with the other parent. Here it was necessary for the boys to know they lived with the respondent and that they did not just visit him. I would therefore dismiss the appeal.

Order accordingly.

Questions

(i) Do you think that this couple should (*a*) have adopted or (*b*) (if they could have done) made a parental responsibility agreement when the older boy was born?

(ii) Who do you think should be treated as his father for the purpose of any calculations under the Child Support Act 1991?

(iii) Compare *A v A (minors) (shared residence order)* [1994] 1 FLR 669, p. 544, above; do you think that (*a*) the Court of Appeal, or (*b*) the Law Commission would have considered a shared residence order appropriate in this case even if the father had been the natural father of both boys?

Chapter 13

Social services for children and families

In this chapter we shall consider the legal mechanisms available to local authority social services departments to meet the needs of children and families. We will briefly consider the range of needs which must be met, and the influences which have shaped the law in this area, before considering the comprehensive code in the Children Act 1989. A recurring theme has been the risk of confusion, both in law and practice, between *providing a service* for children in need and *compulsory intervention* to protect either the child from his family or society from the child. The 1989 Act aimed to draw a clear distinction.

1 Children in need

Social workers are frequently confronted by some of the most horrifying aspects of family life:

I burned him later with the iron; I did it deliberately. I'd look at him, and think, oh you little bastard, you know? I just got hold of him and burned him on the back of the hand. I was so fed up! He'd been grizzling; he was tired out in the daytime because he didn't sleep at night. And of course *I* was tired too, and he wouldn't stop grizzling. I was ironing on the floor in the lounge because it was just something quick I wanted – I was kneeling down and he was sitting over by the window. I just got hold of his hand and I said, *that'll* make you sleep! It was all done in such a quick second, you know, that I didn't ... it wasn't sort of premeditated; I just looked at him, had the iron in my hand, and did it.

Jasmine Beckford died at the age of 4 and a half, in Kensal Rise, North-West London, at the home of Mr Morris Beckford (her step-father) and Miss Beverley Lorrington (her mother) of cerebral contusions and subdural haemorrhage as a direct result of severe manual blows inflicted on the child's head shortly before death. At the time of her death, and for some months (if not years) before, Jasmine was a very thin little girl, emaciated as a result of chronic undernourishment. When she was discharged from hospital after being taken into care she weighed 18 lbs, 14 ozs. Seven months later, when she was reunited with her parents after being fostered, she weighed 25 lbs, 5 oz. She died, 27 months later, weighing 23 lbs. Apart from her stunted development, she had been subjected to parental battering over a protracted period, multiple old scars appearing both to the pathologist who conducted the post-mortem and to the consultant orthopaedic surgeon who gave evidence to us, as being consistent with repeated episodes of physical abuse, to say nothing of the psychological battering she must have undergone.

Samantha's mother died when she was very young and her father brought up her younger brother and herself singlehanded. He began to abuse her when she was 4. When she was little he covered her head and top half with a blanket and interfered with her vagina. By the age of 10 it was regular sexual intercourse and thereafter it included buggery and oral intercourse. 'He made me say that I enjoyed it, that I wanted it. He wouldn't like any disagreement.' As she got older she began to realise that this did not happen to other girls. She said that: 'it got to the stage that if I wanted a favour, to go out with a friend, or buy a new pair of shoes, I had to let him do it first.'

She had no-one to confide in, no-one to turn to: 'I thought any adult would not believe me – they would think I was making up a story. ... I didn't know what might happen. For my brother's sake I didn't want my family split up. ... I loved my father so much. I respected him as a father. But I was confused, didn't understand. I wanted it to stop. I hated that part of it so much.'

So said, respectively, the mother who told her story to Jean Renvoize for her investigation into *Children in Danger* (1974), the report of the panel of inquiry into the circumstances surrounding the death of Jasmine Beckford, *A Child in Trust* (1985), and 'Samantha' whose history is told in the Report of the *Inquiry into Child Abuse in Cleveland 1987* (1988). Understandably, tragic cases like these receive a great deal of professional and public attention. However, local authority social services departments are concerned with a much wider range of problems. Three broad types of children (the 'victims', the 'villains', and the 'volunteered') were identified by Jean Packman, John Randall and Nicola Jacques, in *Who Needs Care?* (1986):

... Admission to care is not a unitary concept: it clearly has several purposes, and is a response to a wide range of different problems and situations, as this study has underlined. At its simplest, there are at least three distinct sorts of public child care on offer. One is for families who are beset by difficulties or handicaps which interrupt or interfere with their capacity to look after their children. Their problems may be acute or chronic, one-dimensional or, more usually, multifaceted and interconnected, and they are likely to be short on supportive networks of relatives or friends to help out, and without the means to pay for child-care services outside these networks. For such families the local authority can provide – and, indeed, is legally obliged to provide (under the old 1948 Act and its [successors]) – a child-care service. Provided that it is judged to be in the interests of the child's welfare, no limits are set on the circumstances in which an admission can take place, nor (apart from an upper age limit) to the time the child may spend in care. Parents can and do request such admissions (more properly, 'receptions' into care), though they can also be effected in their absence. In the words of one commentator, it 'does not imply any criticism of parents who may seek care for their child as a solution to a crisis. It can be a very constructive move by the parents.' [Holden, 1980] It is therefore a type of admission that responds to parents as unfortunate rather than blameworthy, and casts the local authority in the role of the child's caretaker, acting on the parents' behalf. As such, it can be seen to be at one end of a continuum of services which includes domiciliary help and day care for children. It therefore forms, in our view, part of a range of child-care services for *families* and not, as the narrower interpretations of 'care' and 'prevention' would imply, a stark alternative to such services. Given the severity of poverty and disruption in most of the families with whom social services departments come into contact, and the undoubted increase in their number through rising rates of unemployment and divorce, it is disturbing that the provision of such a service seems to be shrinking, relative to other forms of public child care.

A second type of admission provides a protection and rescue service for children who are thought to be in danger, whether it be physical, sexual, moral, emotional or developmental. Here the emphasis is on parental faults and failings and on the child as a victim of inadequate or inappropriate parenting. The local authority intervenes on the child's behalf, and, more often than not, if an admission is arranged (and even if it is requested by the parents) the local authority itself takes over parental rights as well as duties. In essence, the child-care service offered is protection for very vulnerable *children*.

The third type of admission relates to the child whose own behaviour is causing problems. Children whose behaviour troubles no one but their own families, or who behave in ways which adults too easily overlook – depressed and withdrawn children, for example – are unlikely candidates for care. But children whose disruptive and antisocial behaviour spreads beyond the family, and is visible to schools, police, neighbours and strangers, may well be so. For them, admission to care has a more ambiguous meaning. The intentions of the 1969 Children and Young Persons Act were to cast admitted 'villains' in the role of 'victims' of another sort –

vulnerable youngsters from difficult backgrounds who had succumbed to family, neighbourhood and societal pressures, and were in need of care or control not otherwise available to them. In practice, familiar elements of punishment, containment and deterrence are also in the minds of decision-makers and, it must be said, the parents themselves. In the event, the child-care service offered to this group is as much a retributive and protective service for the *public* as it is a 'care' service for the young people themselves.

More than 30,000 children started to be looked after by local authorities during the year ending 31 March 1994. The Department of Health's statistics on *Children Looked After by Local Authorities* (1996) show the reasons:

Table J: Children who started to be looked after during the year ending 31 March 1994 by reason for being looked after and age on admission

England — Numbers

Reason for being looked after	All children	Under 1	1–4	5–9	10–15	16 & 17	18 & over
All children[1]	30,400	3,100	6,300	5,700	12,500	2,700	10
Parents' health	4,500	390	1,700	1,500	950	50	–
No parents	270	10	20	30	160	50	*
Abandoned or lost	780	60	180	150	350	40	–
Family homeless	230	30	70	50	60	30	–
Parent(s) in prison	330	30	100	120	80	*	–
Parents need relief							
– disabled child	600	30	110	130	280	60	*
– other	7,900	490	1,700	1,700	3,800	310	–
Request of child	1,100	*	10	10	380	670	*
Child homeless	280	–	–	–	10	270	*
Concern for child's welfare	3,000	360	520	440	1,600	130	*
Preliminary to adoption	530	470	40	10	10	*	–
Freed for adoption	60	10	*	*	30	10	–
Abuse or neglect	5,200	970	1,500	1,100	1,400	110	–
Own behaviour	1,400	10	30	60	1,100	130	–
Guilty of an offence	130	–	–	–	80	50	–
Accused of an offence	1,300	–	–	–	720	600	–
Other	2,800	250	380	410	1,500	230	–

1 Figures for children looked after in this table exclude series of short-term placements.

More than 24,000 of these children (80%) were looked after as the result of a voluntary agreement under s. 20 of the Children Act 1989 (see p. 584, below). The Department of Health statistics (1996) also show that the majority of children looked after under voluntary agreements remain in local authority accommodation for less than eight weeks. Children subject to compulsory measures are likely to remain in local authority accommodation for much longer.

2 Out of the Poor Law

Jean Heywood explains the beginnings of the public service for the deprived child in her classic history of *Children in Care* (now 1978):

In pre-Reformation England the orphaned or illegitimate child had a place in a feudal and employed community, though opportunities were open and found for human nature to exploit him. His safeguard, if it existed, lay in the communal nature of the society and its ethical canons, expressed – though not always observed – in the teaching against usury, on the duty of almsgiving, on the efficacy of the corporal works of mercy. In the fact that life was centred round the community rather than the family there lay the possibility of opportunity and protection for the unwanted child. In the community obligations of medieval society a way could be found to provide for him and the family setting was less vital to him than it is to us today. The medieval Church had exalted not the private family but rather the greater one, Christian society, endowing chastity, asceticism and celibacy with greater virtue than the sacrament of marriage. It was at the Reformation period when economic as well as religious changes were taking place, that men turned from the Church's teaching on celibacy, and as they found the social order crumbling away they discovered that in family life there could also be an opportunity to witness to the glory of God.

The ideal of the small home and personal family life could hardly be achieved until a middle class came into existence. The sixteenth century Tudor households of yeomen farmers, of small merchants and tradesmen provided the setting in which real family life became possible, and in a growing urban society, which was neither stable economically, nor ruled any longer by a philosophy of the good of a united community, the family became of major significance. Without it the individual was unsupported in society and became without identity.

The spread of destitution which followed the social and economic changes of the sixteenth century was the cause of the increasing legislation dealing with poor relief in the Tudor era. Vagrancy increased with unemployment, and everywhere the old order was breaking down and a new and as yet unstable society being formed.

The discharging of servants and apprentices increased the numbers of deprived children while the growth of poverty, vagrancy and unemployment made it more difficult for them to find a home or to be fitted in to the pattern of village life. Collections made for the poor in the parish churches were unable to meet the demand for alms. The dissolved houses of the monks and nuns were no longer able to provide out-relief, and the hospitals were falling into decay. In consequence laws were passed to make each parish responsible for providing a place where the sick, the old and the 'succourless poor child' could receive shelter and care. At this time, too, the right of destitute children to beg was recognised and they were given a licence.

... In 1530, authority was first given for the compulsory apprenticing of vagrant children between the ages of five and fourteen, though sixteen years afterwards further legislation had to reduce the severity of apprenticeship regulations and give justices power to liberate children badly treated by master and mistress.

The crowds of vagrants and unemployed at this time (which included the child 'unapt to learning') were seen not only as a chronic nuisance but a serious danger to society, as social failures for whom the community was now legally and financially responsible. ...

So many of the composite hospitals which were established at this time, at first by persuasive and finally by compulsory taxation, for the relief of the poor became also houses of correction and punishment for the idle, as well as technical schools for the young. The deprived child, in need of training, and old and sick people in need of care were accommodated together with vagrants sent for punishment. The degradation of the pauper had begun.

It was the Elizabethan statute, the Poor Relief Act of 1601, which set the pattern for our system of relief to the poor until 1948. Those responsible for the care of deprived children, the churchwardens and the parish overseers, were to take such measures as were necessary for setting them to work or binding them as apprentices. These bald embodiments of a constructive principle of care remained unaltered in our legislation for three hundred and forty-seven years, until the shadow of a grim farm-house fell across them, and darkened them for ever.

However, Heywood also notes that the Report of the Committee on Parish Apprentices (1815) stated that in London poor relief was 'seldom bestowed without the parish claiming the exclusive right of disposing, at their pleasure, of all the children of the person claiming relief'. The parental right of custody emerged as a powerful factor in upper class litigation during the nineteenth century (p. 409, above) and began to pose a challenge both for the poor law authorities and for the philanthropists seeking to rescue children from their supposedly corrupting environment:

In all the planning of the various systems of care for the deprived child, the natural family, where it existed, remained a problem which, if it was not being treated, was certainly to be reckoned with. Separating the child and the unfit parent or relative of bad influence was a definite attempt to prevent pauperism reproducing itself in the next generation, but the policy was often difficult to effect even if it was considered ethically sound. The constructive work which the poor law attempted by providing a better environment for the child was frequently brought to nothing by what was described as the 'pernicious influence of the child's relations' particularly when the children passed out of the guardians' care at 16. Two solutions were found for coping with this problem: ...

Boards of Guardians were empowered under the Poor Law Amendment Act of 1850 to emigrate orphan or deserted children under the age of 16 years, provided the child gave his consent. There were real opportunities, particularly in Canada where there was a shortage of labour and where food was cheap, and the guardians made use of these opportunities, though not to any great extent. In general voluntary organisations, such as Dr Barnardo's Homes or the Roman Catholic Emigration Agency, were used as agents, the fittest and most promising of the eligible pauper children being chosen for this new life.

The more difficult problem of the child and the unfit parent was grappled with by Acts of 1889 and 1899. These gave the boards of guardians in England and Wales authority to assume complete rights and responsibilities of a parent over a child in care until he reached the age of 18. Such rights could be assumed only in respect of deserted children at first, but in 1899 their application was widened to include orphans and children of parents who were disabled or in prison, or unfit to have the care of them. This power to assume parental rights by the state was an expression of the public interest in the welfare of children and was intended to lay down a definite standard of parental care. ...

However, the standard of care provided by the local authorities which became responsible for administering the poor law left a great deal to be desired. The 'grim farmhouse' to which Heywood refers was where Dennis O'Neill died in 1945, as recounted by Sir Walter Monckton in his Report (1945):

2. ... Dennis and Terence O'Neill were born respectively on the 2 March 1932, and the 13 December 1934, and were the children of Thomas John O'Neill, a labourer, of Newport, Monmouthshire, and Mabel Blonwyn O'Neill, his wife. On the 30 May 1940, Dennis and Terence were committed by the Newport Juvenile Court to the care or protection of the Newport County Borough Council, as a 'fit person' within the meaning of Sections 76 and 96 of the Children and Young Persons Act 1933, hereinafter referred to as the 1933 Act. Dennis was boarded out at Bank Farm, Minsterley, Shropshire, on the 28 June 1944. The foster-parents were Reginald Gough and Esther Gough, his wife, Terence joined Dennis at Bank Farm on the 5 July 1944. Dennis died there on the 9 January 1945. Terence was removed from Bank Farm to a place of safety on the 10 January 1945.

3. An inquest was held on the boy Dennis. The coroner's jury returned a verdict that his death was due to acute cardiac failure following violence applied to the front of the chest and back while in a state of under-nourishment due to neglect and added a rider that there had been a serious lack of supervision by the local authority. Reginald and Esther Gough were charged with manslaughter. At Stafford Assizes on the 19 March 1945, Reginald Gough was found guilty of manslaughter and was sentenced to six years' penal servitude. Esther Gough was found not guilty of manslaughter but guilty of neglect and was sentenced to six months' imprisonment.

The children had been boarded out with the Goughs in an emergency, but thereafter there had been no adequate inquiry into their suitability, no medical examination, and no proper supervision. Sir Walter concluded, however, that little change in the law was needed:

54. ... What is required is rather that the administrative machinery should be improved and informed by a more anxious and responsible spirit. ... The personal relation in which the local authority, which has undertaken care and protection stands to the child should be more clearly recognized. ... It may well be that, in order to ensure that those who supervise are competent for

the purpose, some training or instruction should be required; but this is a question which would need fuller consideration. The duty to be sure in the care of children must not be put aside, however great may be the pressure of other burdens.

By that time, however, plans were already afoot to abolish the Poor Law and a different approach was being urged to the care of children:

WHOSE CHILDREN?
WARDS OF STATE OR CHARITY

To the Editor of *The Times*

Sir,
Thoughtful consideration is being given to many fundamental problems, but in reconstruction plans one section of the community has, so far, been entirely forgotten.

I write of those children who, because of their family misfortune, find themselves under the guardianship of a Government Department or one of the many charitable organisations. The public are, for the most part, unaware that many thousands of these children are being brought up under repressive conditions that are generations out of date and are unworthy of our traditional care for children. Many who are orphaned, destitute, or neglected, still live under the chilly stigma of 'charity'; too often they form groups isolated from the main stream of life and education, and few of them know the comfort and security of individual affection. A letter does not allow space for detailed evidence.

In many 'Homes', both charitable and public, the willing staff are, for the most part, overworked, underpaid, and untrained; indeed, there is no recognised system of training. Inspection, for which the Ministry of Health, the Home Office, or the Board of Education may be nominally responsible, is totally inadequate, and few standards are established or expected. Because no one Government Department is fully responsible, the problem is the more difficult to tackle.

A public inquiry, with full Government support, is urgently needed to explore this largely uncivilised territory. Its mandate should be to ascertain whether the public and charitable organisations are, in fact, enabling these children to lead full and happy lives, and to make recommendations how the community can compensate them for the family life they have lost. In particular, the inquiry should investigate what arrangements can be made (by regional reception centres or in other ways) for the careful consideration of the individual children before they are finally placed with foster-parents or otherwise provided for; how the use of large residential homes can be avoided; how staff can be appropriately trained and ensured adequate salaries and suitable conditions of work, and how central administrative responsibility can best be secured so that standards can be set and can be maintained by adequate inspection.

The social upheaval caused by the war has not only increased this army of unhappy children, but presents the opportunity for transforming their conditions. The Education Bill and the White paper on the Health Services have alike ignored the problem and the opportunity.

Yours sincerely,

Marjory Allen of Hurtwood.
15 July 1944. Hurtwood House, Albury, Guildford.

The public inquiry was conducted by the Care of Children Committee, chaired by Miss Myra Curtis, 'into the existing methods of providing for children who from loss of parents or from any cause whatever are deprived of a normal home life with their own parents or relatives'. This covered almost 125,000 children, some 57,000 of whom were cared for under the poor law. The Curtis Report (1946) paints a gloomy picture:

138. .... It was clear that in some areas the workhouse served as a dumping ground for children who could not readily be disposed of elsewhere, and that in some districts where children's Homes provided insufficient accommodation, or boarding out had not been well developed, older children, for whom there had never been any properly planned accommodation, were looked after in the workhouse for a considerable length of time.

...

140. An example of this kind of motley collection was found in one century-old Poor Law institution providing accommodation for 170 adults, including ordinary workhouse accommodation, an infirmary for senile old people and a few men and women certified as either mentally defective or mentally disordered. In this institution there were twenty-seven children, aged 6 months to 15 years. Twelve infants up to the age of 18 months were the children of women in the institution about half of them still being nursed by their mothers. In the same room in which these children were being cared for was a Mongol idiot, aged 4, of gross appearance, for whom there was apparently no accommodation elsewhere. A family of five normal children, aged about 6 to 15, who had been admitted on a relieving officer's order, had been in the institution for ten weeks. This family, including a boy of 10 and a girl of 15, were sleeping in the same room as a 3 year old hydrocephalic idiot, of very unsightly type, whose bed was screened off in the corner. The 15 year old girl had been employed in the day-time dusting the women's infirmary ward. These children had been admitted in the middle of the night when their mother had left them under a hedge after eviction from their house. No plan appeared to have been made for them.

...

144. One nursery which was structurally linked to the Public Assistance Institution had sunk to the lowest level of child care which has come under our notice. ... The healthy children were housed in the ground floor corrugated hutment which had been once the old union casual ward. The day room was large and bare and empty of all toys. The children fed, played and used their pots in this room. They ate from cracked enamel plates, using the same mug for milk and soup. They slept in another corrugated hutment in old broken black iron cots some of which had their sides tied up with cord. The mattresses were fouled and stained. On enquiry there did not appear to be any available stocks of clothes to draw on. ... The children wore ankle length calico or flanelette frocks and petticoats and had no knickers. Their clothes were not clean. Most of them had lost their shoes; ... Their faces were clean; their bodies in some cases were unwashed and stained.

This nursery was an exception, and some were very good, but even for the children who found their way into children's homes, conditions might not be much better:

171. ... In another Single Home with accommodation for 18 boys there were 24 present at the time of our visit. They had only one small sitting room for meals, reading and play. The dormitories were tightly packed and there was no room for any provision in the way of lockers or other receptacles for the boys' own possessions, though they were said to be on order. Outside was a small asphalt yard.

It was attitudes, as much as organisation and resources, which were to blame:

154. ... We do not mean to suggest that we found evidence of harshness for which the staff was responsible. Except in the one instance of the nursery unit described in paragraph 144 the ill-usage was of a negative rather than a positive kind and elsewhere sprang directly from unsuitability of buildings, lack of training and of appreciation of children's needs. Officials of local authorities suggested that the children suffered from the attitude of the public to children maintained under the poor law. This attitude had affected some members of the Public Assistance Committees, some of whom had survived as Committee members from the days of the old Boards of Guardians and still held old-fashioned views about what was suitable for a destitute child.

The Committee also visited some of the 27,800 children who were boarded out:

370. ... 'The contrast between the children in Homes and the boarded out children was most marked. The boarded out children suffered less from segregation, starvation for affection and lack of independence. They bore a different stamp of developing personality, and despite occasional misfits were manifestly more independent. For example, they were much more indifferent to visitors, were much better satisfied by their environment (by which we mean the special features of security and love). There was, we thought, much greater happiness for the child integrated by boarding out into a family of normal size in a normal home.'

Question

Why was the fact that the children 'were much more indifferent to visitors' regarded as a good sign?

When it came to recommending solutions, the Committee assumed that most of the children would remain in public care for a long time. It was clear about what their substitute home should provide:

427. ... If the substitute home is to give the child what he gets from a good normal home it must supply –

(i) Affection and personal interest; understanding of his defects; care for his future; respect for his personality and regard for his self esteem.
(ii) Stability; the feeling that he can expect to remain with those who will continue to care for him till he goes out into the world on his own feet.
(iii) Opportunity of making the best of his ability and aptitudes, whatever they may be, as such opportunity is made available to the child in the normal home.
(iv) A share in the common life of a small group of people in a homely environment.

Some at least of these needs are supplied by the child's own home even if it is not in all respects a good one; it is a very serious responsibility to make provision for him to be brought up elsewhere without assurance that they can be supplied by the environment to which he is removed.

Hence:

447. ... Every effort should be made to keep the child in its home, or with its mother if it is illegitimate, provided that the home is or can be made reasonably satisfactory. The aim of the authority must be to find something better – indeed much better – if it takes the responsibility of providing a substitute home. The methods which should be available may be treated under three main heads of adoption, boarding out and residence in communities. We have placed these in the order in which, subject to the safeguards we propose and to consideration of the needs of the individual, they seem to us to secure the welfare and happiness of the child.

Question

Do you agree with this order to priorities?

The Committee's main solution was for new local authority Children's Departments to take responsibility for all kinds of children's homes, including approved (reform) schools, boarding out, and adoption, and for children found in need of care and protection by a court. At its head would be a universal mother:

441. ... We desire ... to see the responsibility for the welfare of the deprived children definitely laid on a Children's Officer. This may indeed be said to be our solution of the problem referred to us. Throughout our investigation we have been increasingly impressed by the need for the personal element in the care of children, which Sir Walter Monckton emphasised in his report on the O'Neill case. No office staff dealing with them as case papers can do the work we want done – work which is in part administrative, but also in large part field work, involving many personal contacts and the solution of problems by direct methods. ...

443. ... She (we use the feminine pronoun not with any aim of excluding men from these posts but because we think it may be found that the majority of persons suitable for the work are women) will of course work under the orders of her committee or board but she will be a specialist in child care as the Medical Officer of Health is a specialist in his own province and the Director of Education is in his; and she will have no other duties to distract her interests. She would represent the council in its parental functions. The committal of the child to the care of a

council which takes over parental rights and duties is not without incongruity. To be properly exercised the responsibility must be delegated to an individual, and that individual one whose training has fitted her for child care and whose whole attention is given to it. ...

Hence the Children Act 1948 set up the new departments and gave them, among other things, the duty to care for orphaned, abandoned or deprived children, the power to assume parental rights over children in their care who had no parents or parents who were in some way incapable or unfit to look after them, and the duty to act as a fit parent for children compulsorily removed from home by a court. The compulsorily removed children fell into three different categories, which were eventually brought together in s. 1 of the Children and Young Persons Act 1969. John Eekelaar, Robert Dingwall and Topsy Murray in *Victims or Threats? Children in Care Proceedings* (1982) explain how this came about:

... A significant report published in 1816 by an unofficial Committee of the Society for Investigating the Causes of the Alarming Increase of Juvenile Delinquency in the Metropolis, attempted a radical assessment of the problem. Although it is sometimes thought that the significance of the home and community environment among the causative factors of delinquency is a modern realisation, this is not so. The 1816 Report numbered 'the improper conduct of parents, the want of education and the want of suitable employment' as the first of the five most significant causes of delinquency. Here is a recognition of human nature as being a product of environment, of behaviour being socially caused. The work of the reformatory movement was inspired by the same idea and it received statutory recognition in the Youthful Offenders Act 1854. But the scope of reform schools in combating juvenile delinquency was restricted by the major limitation that children were committed there only after having been convicted of an offence. ...

[Nineteenth century reformers] maintained a distinction in classification between children who had committed offences and those who had not. They were to be kept in separate establishments. The industrial schools, which catered for the latter category, were a development of the 'ragged schools' of the eighteenth century which, as the Departmental Committee on Young Offenders of 1927 noted 'were an attempt to deal more radically with the problem of child welfare by providing education and industrial training for the class of children from whom delinquents were mainly drawn.' ...

Yet it is clear that the children in industrial schools were there at least as much because they were thought of as being a *risk* to society as being *at risk* themselves and already by 1870 the Inspector of Industrial Schools reported that those schools had been assimilated to reformatories 'in their necessary arrangements and regulations and the main features of their management.' The children were sent there by warrant of a magistrate. The schools had become 'houses of detention for the young vagabond and petty misdemeanant.' ...

The third source which makes up the composition of section 1(2) of the 1969 Act had its origin in the Prevention of Cruelty to, and Protection of, Children Act 1889. The most significant provision of this Act created an offence if anyone over 16 who had custody, control or charge of a boy under 14 or a girl under 16 wilfully ill-treated, neglected or abandoned the child in a manner likely to cause unnecessary suffering or injury to health. On conviction of a parent for this offence, the court could commit the child to the charge of a relative or anyone else willing to have the care of the child who would have 'like control over the child as if he were its parent and shall be responsible for its maintenance, and the child shall continue under the control of such person, notwithstanding that it is claimed by its parents'.

The necessity of conviction of the parent is significant, for it reflects the basis of the justification for state intervention on which this provision rests. This is that the parent's conduct offends against the moral conception of society held by the Act's proponents. The purpose for the intervention was, indeed, to protect children, but the method by which this was sought was morally to reform the parents. ...

But in 1933 this category of children was included in the category of children formerly covered by the industrial schools legislation as being 'in need of care and protection.' This was a highly significant move for, as we have seen, children found to be in need of care and protection could be committed to approved schools as young offenders could be. It seems odd to find children who, even more clearly than the 'neglected' category, were in need of protection *from* adults, being dealt with under the very same statutory provisions, and indeed, court procedure, as children from whom the community sought to protect itself. It is revealing therefore to discover how this happened. The 1927 Committee was required 'to inquire into the treatment of young offenders and young people who, owing to bad associations or surroundings require protection and training.' They considered that their inquiry was concerned not only with the 'young offender' but also with 'the neglected boy or girl who has not yet committed offences but who, owing to want of parental control, bad associations or other reasons needs protection and training.' ... However, the Committee went on to say: 'There are also young people who are the victims of cruelty or other offences committed by adults and whose natural guardianship having proved insufficient or unworthy of trust must be replaced.' We may note here what has been characteristic of all these investigations into the condition of children, that the concern has primarily been with the problem of troublesome children, and the question of child protection has been tagged on very much as a subsidiary and secondary question. ...

There is no doubt that the result was to strengthen the provisions for protecting such children because local education authorities were now placed under a duty to inquire into such cases and bring them before a court and the courts were empowered to commit them into the care of local authorities. But these children had now become irredeemably intertwined with a group of children with entirely different problems and who were regarded by society as virtually inseparable from delinquent children.

In the meantime another significant development had been occurring in attitudes towards neglected and abused children. The evangelical movement had declined, but the growth of community health services provided an alternative model for intervention in family life. ... The immediate impetus arose from the prosecution by the NSPCC of a blind couple for neglecting their children, and in 1952 the Children and Young Persons (Amendment) Act removed the requirement of prosecution of parents as a condition precedent for finding a child to be in need of care and protection within the 1933 Act. Hence forward it would be enough if the child had no parent or guardian or if his parent or guardian was 'unfit to exercise care or guardianship or (was) not exercising proper care and guardianship' and 'he was being ill-treated or neglected in a manner likely to cause him unnecessary suffering or injury to health.' Failure (for whatever cause) in the parenting function leading to a specified condition in the child became a ground for intervention. Although the approach is now overtly welfarist, the requirement that the child's condition should arise from parental failure still serves to maintain a distinction between this class of children and those from whom society sought to protect itself. The distinction was not to last for long.

The Ingleby Committee (1960) and the 1969 Act

... In dealing with the general issue of the circumstances in which the state may properly intervene in proceedings against parents for child neglect, the Committee states that 'difficulty has not arisen for several years over the reasonable requirements for nutrition, housing, clothing and schooling' although there had been some cases where parents had refused to give their children proper medical attention. No mention is made at all by the Committee of child abuse cases and the Committee proceeds, throughout the rest of the chapter, to consider the issue solely in terms of delinquency cases. By 1960, then, our society had become blind to potential conflicts between family autonomy and child protection. Apart from a few troublesome cases involving unconventional religious sects, the resolution of welfarist child protection and family autonomy was considered simple and unproblematic. In fact, it had been obscured by the overwhelming preoccupation with delinquency. ...

The two Government White Papers, *The Child, the Family and the Young Offender* and *Children in Trouble* (Home Office, 1965 and 1968) were, as their titles indicate, wholly concerned with the problem of juvenile delinquents. They set the basis for the policy of the 1969 Act. One cornerstone of that policy was that children should progressively cease to be prosecuted for offences and should, instead, be made subject to care proceedings under the Act. Accordingly, the grounds for bringing care proceedings were to be extended to include a ground that the child had committed an offence (excluding homicide). Child offenders were now to be treated under (almost) exactly the same process as troublesome children who were not offenders. And, as we have seen, child *victims* had by now been assimilated into this category. The logic of this assimilation compelled the abandonment, *for all categories of these children*, of any reference to parental inadequacy among the conditions precedent to bringing care proceedings. For, as the Home Office observed in its official guide to the Act, such a provision 'meant that proceedings inevitably appeared to cast blame for the child's situation or behaviour directly into his parents or those looking after him' a fact which was quite irrelevant for the delinquent child (though, as will be argued below, crucially relevant in the case of the child victim). The Act, therefore, took the line originally proposed by the Ingleby Report and simply required that it be shown that the child was in need of 'care of control' which he would not receive if an order was not made.

Implementation of the 1969 Act, which tried to cater for the villains and the victims by the same process, coincided with the Local Authority Social Services Act 1970, which amalgamated the children's services with those provided for the old, the mentally disordered or handicapped, and the disabled, into new all-purpose social services departments. As Jean Packman explains in *The Child's Generation* (1981):

Developments in prevention and work with delinquency not only strained, modified and redefined the original aims and methods of the child care service; they also contributed to its eventual demise. The pursuit of both policies increased the children's departments' involvement with and dependence upon other agencies and threw into relief their relationship with one another and the illogical and wasteful effects of the fragmented pattern of personal social services. As the two policies drew closer together, with prevention of neglect being seen more and more as a key means of forestalling delinquency, the pressure to change that pattern and to provide an integrated 'family service' in its place mounted.

However, not everyone was delighted:

Oxfordshire's Children's Committee, in preparing its own evidence to Seebohm, said 'it would in our opinion, for instance, be damaging to the highly personal type of work done by the child care service to place it in such a large and general group of functions that the old pattern of the former Public Assistance Service might recur, with the disadvantages that would entail'. The spectre of the Poor Law still haunted the local councillors.

But there was another spectre, which soon came to haunt those responsible for local authority social services departments. There were some 18 reports of child abuse inquiries between 1973 and 1980 (see DHSS, 1982), beginning with Maria Colwell (1973) and including Susan Auckland (1975) and Wayne Brewer (1977). Between 1980 and 1989 there were at least 19 more (see DH, 1991), including Jasmine Beckford (1985), Heidi Koseda (1986), Tyra Henry (1987) and Kimberley Carlile (1987). The Cleveland Report (1988) dealt with the issue of child sexual abuse:

1. Child abuse, the non-accidental injury of a child, received increasing attention in this country in the 1960s, and followed upon its recognition in the United States. ... A parallel can be drawn between the reluctance to recognise physical abuse in the United Kingdom in the 1960s and the reluctance by many to accept the reality of certain aspects of child sexual abuse in the 1980s.
2. Child abuse has many forms; the concerns may centre upon physical abuse, sexual and emotional abuse, or upon neglect. Dr Cameron in discussing the 3 categories of active child abuse: physical, emotional, and sexual abuse, pointed out that, while it was helpful to the diagnostician to have distinct forms of child abuse in mind, not infrequently, in practice, a child is subject to more than one form of abuse. It is obviously important to recognise that the categories of the abuse are not closed. Experts gave us figures indicating that as much as 30% of children referred because of other forms of abuse may also show medical evidence of sexual abuse.

Definitions of child sexual abuse

4. The definition of child sexual abuse by Schechter and Roberge is widely quoted:

   'Sexual abuse is defined as the involvement of dependent, developmentally immature children and adolescents in sexual activities that they do not fully comprehend and to which they are unable to give informed consent or that violate the social taboos of family roles.'

In other words it is the use of children by adults for sexual gratification. Dr Cameron described it as inappropriate behaviour which involved: 'the child being exploited by the adult either for direct physical gratification of sexual needs or for vicarious gratification'.

5. Child sexual abuse may take place within the family circle or outside, for example, by a neighbour or a complete stranger. According to Dr Paul (1986) abuse within the family is the most common form. The type of sexual abuse, its degree of seriousness, the age of the child and whether it is within the family all affect not only the presentation but also the response to it by the community and the action required of the professionals charged with the duty of protecting the abused child. It is essential in any consideration of child sexual abuse to be clear at all times as to the definition and description being used.

...

The children

12. The Inquiry was provided with evidence about Cleveland children primarily in respect of allegations of the most serious offences of incest, unlawful sexual intercourse and buggery of girls and buggery of boys and indecent assault almost all within the family, including digital penetration, fondling, mutual masturbation, anal and oral/genital contact. From the evidence presented to the Inquiry a majority of children sexually abused in the U.K. are girls but there are significant numbers of boys. ...

13. The abuse may be one incident, occasional, a gradual but escalating level of abuse; or it may be frequent and regular. For some children it may become a way of life and only in adolescence do they realise they have not enjoyed a 'normal' family life. At the time it may not necessarily be experienced as distasteful by the child and it is only later that the child realises it is what it is. On the other hand it may be coercive and frightening from the beginning.

14. Some children appear to be specially vulnerable, for example those with physical or mental handicaps, others treated as scapegoats, or those who are particularly immature. It may occur where the older child has a parenting role. Alcohol, drugs, absence of the other parent from home; a single parent with succession of male partners, violence, marital or sexual difficulties may be factors. Other factors suggested include chaotic or inadequate families, or the sub-normality of a parent.

15. The children caught up in the crisis in Cleveland ranged in age from under a year to adolescence. It would be impossible to say how many sexually abused children in Cleveland were boys. But there were some boys sexually abused during the period and significant proportions in respect of whom allegations were made.

16. There were some unusual complaints, for example: one little girl of 7 complained that her father and girl friend squirted tea in a syringe up 'her front'; one little boy of 4 spoke of an iron bar being pushed up his bottom; one boy said he had a toilet roll pushed up as a punishment. In several instances children who were later found to have been abused at home engaged in sexualised behaviour towards each other or with other children at school.

Pressure to keep the secret

17. Many children who have been subject to sexual abuse are put under pressure from the perpetrator not to tell; there may be threats of violence to the child or that the perpetrator will commit suicide, of being taken away from home and put into care, threats that someone they love will be angry with them, or that no-one would believe them. Children may elect not to talk because of a genuine affection for the perpetrator and an awareness of the consequences to the perpetrator, to the partner, to the family unit, or for an older child an understanding of the economic considerations in the break-up of the family and the loss of the wage earner. The secretive element persists. Professor Sir Martin Roth in evidence said: 'There is a powerful disincentive to disclosing the fact that one has been subject to sexual abuse. The person who discloses this has fears that he may be regarded as having permitted himself, as having collaborated in it, as having been lastingly damaged in a sexual way. He is likely to fear ridicule, humiliation, obloquy and so on'.

18. This pressure upon the child not to tell and the desire of all to keep the secret is also apparent in the pressure brought upon children to retract once they have made a complaint. The pressure comes from the family, mother, siblings and the extended family as well as the abuser. The withdrawal of the complaint is a common situation with child complainants and presents particular difficulties for the police.

19. In Cleveland we heard of examples of pressure on children. A girl of 12 told the Official Solicitor that her step-father said no-one would believe her. A girl of 8 expressed relief at the death of her father who committed suicide after she revealed the abuse. One little girl of 5 told the police that her father had sexually abused her. According to a letter from her mother she explained why

she had not told before: 'It was because my daddy told me I would lose my voice if I told anyone'. The mother wrote: 'These are the things she has told me: she was told, somebody will come and take her away, people would hit her for telling lies, Mammy will cry if you tell her'.

The children may become 'double victims'

20. Those who fear a child has been sexually abused naturally wish to protect the child from further assaults; to stop the abuser having the opportunity to abuse again. The ideal would be to protect the child within his or her home and neighbourhood, preferably after identifying and excluding the abuser. However, if, as is often the case, the perpetrator is unknown, or is suspected but denies the abuse, how can the child be protected? In practice, it is the child who is taken away from home, friends and school and it is the child who is placed in hospital, in a childrens' home or in a foster home, in strange surroundings and among strangers.

21. The plight of the 'double victim' is well illustrated by what happened to one of the children in Cleveland. The girl told the police that she had been sexually abused by her father. She said that the threat from the perpetrator was that she would be taken away from home and placed in care if she told anyone what was going on. As it happened the effect of the complaint was a place of safety order and she was removed from home, and suffered twice over. That child retracted her story.

…

Relationships within the family

28. The mother, we are told, is by no means certain to be the protector of the child. Some may have themselves been abused as children. Some may be afraid of the man, inadequate personalities ill-equipped to give the child protection, or even prefer him to pay attention to the child rather than to themselves. Some mothers can not or will not believe it to be possible. There is a very acute dilemma for a mother in the conflict between her man and her child, in which the relationship with the man, the economic and other support which she received from him may disincline her to accept the truth of the allegation. Some mothers choose sexual offenders as partners more than once.

Again quoting Professor Sir Martin Roth: 'In many cases mothers play a role in the genesis of the sexual abuse of their daughters. They may be too physically ill or inadequate in personality to provide proper care and protection for their children. In other cases mothers elect the eldest or one of the oldest daughters to the role of 'child mother'. The girl in her early teens or even earlier is expected to take the responsibility for the caring of younger children whose mothering role is allowed to slide into a sexual relationship with the father. This is tolerated with little or no protest. I refer to lack of protest on the part of the mother for a variety of reasons and the mother may in such cases deny what is happening. She conceals the truth from herself as well as others; the relationship continues and when the situation is brought to light it may be insisted by the mother that it had been unknown to her'.

29. In the evidence presented to the Inquiry several children who described abuse indicated that their mothers either were present or knew what was going on.

The lasting effects of sexual abuse in childhood

30. We have been provided with a considerable amount of written material on various aspects of the long term effects on the abused child. …

33. Professor Sir Martin Roth told us in evidence of the serious harm sexual abuse had done to some of his patients. He warned that 'Those who have been intimidated by threats into incestuous relationships in childhood proved to be at high risk of abusing their own children thus transmitting the effects of deprivation. The ill effects are not confined to feelings of guilt, self-reproach and humiliation aroused after incest has begun or when its character has come to be appreciated. Emotional development may be seriously deranged or arrested and ability to form normal personal and sexual relationships to be fulfilled and happy in marriage and to prove emotionally equal to the responsibility of rearing children suffer lasting impairment. Although it is the more intrusive and more aggressive forms of abuse that cause the most grave damage, forms of incestuous relationship that leave no sign may inflict a lasting wound.'

Question

Before Cleveland, all of the other public inquiries concerned the authorities' failure to protect children from physical abuse or neglect either at home or in care. In Cleveland the concern was that the authorities might have been too anxious to protect the children. Is it significant that Cleveland involved allegations of sexual abuse?

The Department of Health's summary of research, *Child Protection – Messages from Research* (1995), suggests the importance of seeing child protection issues within the wider context of social services functions:

Protection issues are best viewed in the context of children's wider needs. It is important to ensure that inappropriate cases do not get caught up in the child protection process, for this could have several undesirable consequences. Of particular concern is the unnecessary distress caused to family members who may then be unwilling to co-operate with subsequent plans. Professionals have to weigh up which stages in the protection process are relevant to each case. They may have to rebuild a sense of trust with family members to enable them to participate. Ultimately, it will be necessary to decide when and how to permit a case to leave the child protection arena. ... The Children Act 1989 requires local authorities to provide a range of services for children in need and intends that only extreme cases will require adjudication by courts. For all but the most serious cases there are many intermediate stages between a child first coming to the notice of welfare agencies, the removal of the child from home and/or a court hearing being necessary. The child protection process encompasses some of these stages. The idea of a 'threshold' which includes the criteria for moving a child from one stage in the process to another has been introduced. In the following pages several thresholds for action are described, as are the criteria on which they are based.

...

Psychological evidence suggests that while children suffer in an environment of low warmth and high criticism, the intervention of professionals in these situations is seldom necessary or helpful. If, however, family problems endure, some external support, perhaps using Section 17 services [see p. 584, below], will be required to ensure that the health and development of the child is not significantly impaired. If the child's fraught situation endures, then he or she is likely to suffer significant harm and may need to be looked after away from home. There are, in addition, a small proportion of cases in which the abuse is extreme and will not be reduced by family support alone. For children who have been grossly injured or sexually abused, swift child rescue, sometimes using emergency powers, will be necessary. However, the research evidence suggests that, for the majority of cases, the need of the child and family is more important than the abuse or, put another way, the general family context is more important than any abusive event within it. This message applies when defining maltreatment, designing interventions or assessing outcomes.

Thus, in addition to the considerable burden of child protection work, professionals also offer family support and provide child welfare for the small proportion who live away from home. For a child-care system to be effective, some overlap between these services is inevitable. But the research studies have questioned whether the balance between child protection and the range of supports and interventions available to professionals is correct. This is an issue Area Child Protection Committees and professionals associated with this group must constantly raise about services in their region.

The research studies suggest that too much of the work undertaken comes under the banner of child protection. ...

A more balanced service for vulnerable children would encourage professionals to take a wider view. There would be efforts to work alongside families rather than disempower them, to raise their self-esteem rather than reproach families, to promote family relationships where children have their needs met, rather than leave untreated families with an unsatisfactory parenting style. The focus would be on the overall needs of children rather than a narrow concentration on the alleged incident.

Question

Is it possible to support families in a non-threatening way, and also protect children effectively?

3 Services for children and families

Working Together (DH, 1991) emphasises the importance of working in 'partnership' with parents:

1.4 Local authorities have, under the Children Act 1989, a general duty to safeguard and promote the welfare of children within their area who are in need and so far as is consistent with that duty to promote the upbringing of such children by their families. As parental responsibility for children is retained notwithstanding any court orders short of adoption, local authorities must work in partnership with parents, seeking court orders when compulsory action is indicated in the interests of the child but only when this is better for the child than working with the parents under voluntary arrangements.

The key provisions of the Children Act 1989 are these:

17. – (1) It shall be the general duty of every local authority (in addition to the other duties imposed on them by this Part) –
(*a*) to safeguard and promote the welfare of children within their area who are in need; and
(*b*) so far as is consistent with that duty, to promote the upbringing of such children by their families

by providing a range and level of services appropriate to those children's needs.

(2) For the purpose principally of facilitating the discharge of their general duty under this section, every local authority shall have the specific duties and powers set out in Part I of Schedule 2.

(3) Any service provided by an authority in the exercise of functions conferred on them by this section may be provided for the family of a particular child in need or for any member of his family, if it is provided with a view to safeguarding or promoting the child's welfare

...

(10) For the purposes of this Part a child shall be taken to be in need if –
(*a*) he is unlikely to achieve or maintain, or to have the opportunity of achieving or maintaining, a reasonable standard of health or development without the provision for him of services by a local authority under this Part;
(*b*) his health or development is likely to be significantly impaired, or further impaired, without the provision for him of such services; or
(*c*) he is disabled, and 'family', in relation to such a child, includes any person who has parental responsibility for the child and any other person with whom he has been living.

(11) For the purposes of this Part, a child is disabled if he is blind, deaf or dumb or suffers from mental disorder of any kind or is substantially and permanently handicapped by illness, injury or congenital deformity or such other disability as may be prescribed; and in this Part – 'development' means physical, intellectual, emotional, social or behavioural development; and 'health' means physical or mental health.

Part I of Sch. 2 lists a great many specific services for children living at home or elsewhere. Day care is dealt with in ss. 18 and 19. Section 20 deals with the provision of accommodation:

20. – (1) Every local authority shall provide accommodation for any child in need within their area who appears to them to require accommodation as a result of –
(*a*) there being no person who has parental responsibility for him;
(*b*) his being lost or having been abandoned; or
(*c*) the person who has been caring for him being prevented (whether or not permanently, and for whatever reason) from providing him with suitable accommodation or care.

(2) Where a local authority provide accommodation under subsection (1) for a child who is ordinarily resident in the area of another local authority, that other local authority may take over the provision of accommodation for the child within –
(*a*) three months of being notified in writing that the child is being provided with accommodation; or
(*b*) such other longer period as may be prescribed.

(3) Every local authority shall provide accommodation for any child in need within their area who has reached the age of sixteen and whose welfare the authority consider is likely to be seriously prejudiced if they do not provide him with accommodation.

(4) A local authority may provide accommodation for any child within their area (even though a person who has parental responsibility for him is able to provide him with accommodation) if they consider that to do so would safeguard or promote the child's welfare.

(5) A local authority may provide accommodation for any person who has reached the age of sixteen but is under twenty-one in any community home which takes children who have reached the age of sixteen if they consider that to do so would safeguard or promote his welfare.

(6) Before providing accommodation under this section, a local authority shall, so far as is reasonably practicable and consistent with the child's welfare –

(*a*) ascertain the child's wishes regarding the provision of accommodation; and

(*b*) give due consideration (having regard to his age and understanding) to such wishes of the child as they have been able to ascertain.

(7) A local authority may not provide accommodation under this section for any child if any person who –

(*a*) has parental responsibility for him; and

(*b*) is willing and able to –

(i) provide accommodation for him; or

(ii) arrange for accommodation to be provided for him,

objects.

(8) Any person who has parental responsibility for a child may at any time remove the child from accommodation provided by or on behalf of the local authority under this section.

(9) Subsections (7) and (8) do not apply while any person –

(*a*) in whose favour a residence order is in force with respect to the child; or

(*b*) who has care of the child by virtue of an order made in the exercise of the High Court's inherent jurisdiction with respect to children,

agrees to the child being looked after in accommodation provided by or on behalf of the local authority.

(10) Where there is more than one such person as is mentioned in subsection (9), all of them must agree.

(11) Subsections (7) and (8) do not apply where a child who has reached the age of sixteen agrees to being provided with accommodation under this section.

The 'continuum' of services provided under the Act can be traced back to the ideas in the Curtis Report (p. 575, above). Jean Packman, in *The Child's Generation* (1981), explains the development, after the 1948 Act, of the concept of 'prevention':

Research studies of the period [principally Bowlby (1953), see p. 516, above] stressed the importance of the mother-child relationship and the damaging effects on a child's mental, emotional and even physical development, if the relationship were inadequate, disturbed or broken. Most studies examined the latter – deprivation by separation – the phenomenon in its most readily observable form. The emphasis therefore tended to rest on the temporary, or even irreversible damage caused to children by removing them from home. To these studies were added the observations of the child care workers themselves. Seeing, at first hand, the unhappiness and distress of many children in care, they were naturally spurred to seek ways of avoiding admissions. Depressingly, too, they saw that many deprived children themselves grew up to be inadequate parents whose children were, in turn, deprived. A 'cycle of deprivation' was acknowledged long before it became a political catchphrase.

To this central concern to avoid separating children from their parents, was added the complicating factor that some families were clearly incapable of providing even a minimum of physical or emotional care and stability for their children. Social workers were therefore faced with decisions about whether or not the deprivations suffered by a child within his family were worse and more hazardous than those he would suffer by removal from home. Such decisions were also affected by estimates of their own skills and the resources available to them, to intervene and improve the family situation, to the child's benefit; and by the standards of substitute care that might offset and compensate the child for the effects of separation.

Prevention thus came to be a two-pronged concept; prevention of admission to care; and prevention of neglect and cruelty in the family. A variety of methods of working towards each of these ends can be seen emerging, in response to the differing circumstances of the families concerned. With some families the work was clearly directed to their weaknesses, whether these were problems of poor home management and low standards of hygiene, or of disturbed and volatile relationships. ...

In other situations more stress was laid on family and community strengths. Child care workers were aware that many children came into care at a time of family crisis, for lack of any alternative. It was their task to explore and encourage links with kin or with neighbours who could offer care for the children in a familiar environment. ...

A third dimension to preventive work grew from the knowledge that some families collapsed through external pressures which were beyond their control, yet were within the power of children's departments to influence. A prime example lies in the field of housing. As early as 1951 concern was expressed at the effects on children, separated from their parents because of homelessness. ...

The Review of Child Care Law (1985) and the Government's White Paper on *The Law on Child Care and Family Services* (1987), which led to the 1989 Act, emphasised the importance of preventative services:

18. It is proposed to give local authorities a broad 'umbrella' *power* to provide services to promote the care and upbringing of children, and to help prevent the breakdown of family relationships which might eventually lead to a court order committing the child to the local authority's care. Within this power the local authority will be able to provide services to a child *at home*, for example a family aide to assist within the home; at a *day centre*, for example a day nursery for pre-school children, an after school scheme for school age children or placement with a childminder; or *residential facilities* allowing a child to stay for short or long periods away from home, say with a foster family or in a children's home. The local authority will also be able to offer financial assistance in exceptional circumstances. ...

20. Local authorities have a duty under current legislation to receive children into their care in special circumstances, generally where there is a need to care for the child away from home because of the absence or incapacity of parents. This duty will be maintained broadly as at present. So will the duty to return the child to his family where this is consistent with his welfare.

21. The Government wish to emphasise, however, that the provision of a service by the local authority to enable a child who is not under a care order to be cared for away from home should be seen in a wider context and as part of the range of services a local authority can offer to parents and families in need of help with the care of their children. Such a service should, in appropriate circumstances, be seen as a positive response to the needs of families and not as a mark of failure either on the part of the family or those professionals and others working to support them. An essential characteristic of this service should be its voluntary character, that is it should be based clearly on continuing parental agreement and operate as far as possible on a basis of partnership and co-operation between the local authority and parents.

Hence the abolition of the power to assume parental rights by administrative resolution and the insistence (in s. 20(8), (9) and (10)) that any person who is entitled to have the child living with him may remove the child from local authority accommodation at any time. One reason for this emphasis on the voluntary provision of services was the recommendation of the Review of Child Care Law (1985) that child care legislation should be combined with the health and welfare legislation, under which services are provided for mentally handicapped and disabled children, to embody the best features of both. The White Paper agreed:

16. The health and welfare legislation generally makes no provision for the supervision of the welfare of individual children provided with services. Thus, for example, under this legislation a child may remain away from home for long periods without any legal requirement for the caring agency to review his case, or to give first consideration to his welfare or to consult him where practicable in taking any decisions about him all of which are requirements under child care law. Nor are there any provisions about local authority responsibilities to children when they leave facilities provided under this legislation. This again contrasts with child care law. There are also inconsistencies between health and welfare legislation and child care law over such matters as charging for services.

17. The Government therefore propose the unification of these two sets of legislation as recommended by the Review. In reaching this decision the Government considered carefully the reservations expressed by some that this would cause concern to those parents of handicapped and disabled children who provide expert and devoted care but from time to time need respite care provided by the local authority. This concern it was said flowed from the perception that reception into care by local authorities under the present legislation was frequently associated with parental shortcomings. ... The intention of the Government is to ensure that in all cases the children concerned receive the standard of care and protection and professional review appropriate to their needs and that those ends are achieved where possible in a partnership with parents.

A clear distinction should therefore be drawn between children 'in care', who are the subject of care orders (see p. 617, below), and other children who are simply provided with accommodation by the authority. A sharp eye, however, is needed to recognise the differences in the sections of the 1989 Act dealing with all children being 'looked after':

22. – (1) In this Act, any reference to a child who is looked after by a local authority is a reference to a child who is –

(*a*) in their care, or
(*b*) provided with accommodation by the authority in the exercise of any functions (in particular those under this Act) which stand referred to their social services committee under the Local Authority Social Services Act 1970.

(2) In subsection (1) 'accommodation' means accommodation which is provided for a continuous period of more than 24 hours.

(3) It shall be the duty of a local authority looking after any child –

(*a*) to safeguard and promote his welfare; and
(*b*) to make such use of services available for children cared for by their own parents as appears to the authority reasonable in his case.

(4) Before making any decision with respect to a child whom they are looking after, or proposing to look after, a local authority shall, so far as is reasonably practicable, ascertain the wishes and feelings of –

(*a*) the child;
(*b*) his parents;
(*c*) any person who is not a parent of his but who has parental responsibility for him; and
(*d*) any other person whose wishes and feelings the authority consider to be relevant, regarding the matter to be decided.

(5) In making any such decisions a local authority shall give due consideration –

(*a*) having regarded to his age and understanding, to such wishes and feelings of the child as they have been able to ascertain;
(*b*) to such wishes and feelings of any person mentioned in subsection (4)(*b*) to (*d*) as they have been able to ascertain; and
(*c*) to the child's religious persuasion, racial origin and cultural and linguistic background.

(6) If it appears to a local authority that it is necessary, for the purpose of protecting members of the public from serious injury, to exercise their powers with respect to a child whom they are looking after in a manner which may not be consistent with their duties under this section, they may do so.

(7) If the Secretary of State considers it necessary, for the purpose of protecting members of the public from serious injury, to give directions to a local authority with respect to the exercise of their powers with respect to a child whom they are looking after, he may give such directions to the authority.

(8) Where any such directions are given to an authority they shall comply with them even though doing so is inconsistent with their duties under this section.

Questions

(i) Subsections (6) to (8) of s. 22 stem from the Children and Young Persons Act 1969, when local authorities were given responsibility for most juvenile

offenders: now that committal to local authority accommodation is no longer available as a disposal in criminal cases (except on remand or as a short residential condition in a supervision order) can they still be justified?
(ii) Why are they not limited to 'children in care'?

23. – (1) It shall be the duty of any local authority looking after a child –
(*a*) when he is in their care, to provide accommodation for him; and
(*b*) to maintain him in other respects apart from providing accommodation for him.
(2) A local authority shall provide accommodation and maintenance for any child whom they are looking after by –
(*a*) placing him (subject to subsection (5) and any regulations made by the Secretary of State) with –
(i) a family;
(ii) a relative of his; or
(iii) any other suitable person, on such terms as to payment by the authority and otherwise as the authority may determine;
(*b*) maintaining him in a community home;
(*c*) maintaining him in a voluntary home;
(*d*) maintaining him in a registered children's home;
(*e*) maintaining him in a home provided by the Secretary of State under section 82(5) on such terms as the Secretary of State may from time to time determine; or
(*f*) making such other arrangements as –
(i) seem appropriate to them; and
(ii) comply with any regulations made by the Secretary of State.
(3) Any person with whom a child has been placed under subsection (2)(*a*) is referred to in this Act as a local authority foster parent unless he falls within subsection (4).
(4) A person falls within this subsection if he is –
(*a*) a parent of the child
(*b*) a person who is not a parent of the child but who has parental responsibility for him; or
(*c*) where the child is in care and there was a residence order in force with respect to him immediately before the care order was made, a person in whose favour the residence order was made.
(5) Where a child is in the care of a local authority, the authority may only allow him to live with a person who falls within subsection (4) in accordance with regulations made by the Secretary of State.
(6) Subject to any regulations made by the Secretary of State for the purposes of this subsection, any local authority looking after a child shall make arrangements to enable him to live with –
(*a*) a person falling within subsection (4); or
(*b*) a relative, friend or other person connected with him, unless that would not be reasonably practicable or consistent with his welfare.
(7) Where a local authority provide accommodation for a child whom they are looking after, they shall, subject to the provisions of this Part and so far as is reasonably practicable and consistent with his welfare, secure that –
(*a*) the accommodation is near his home; and
(*b*) where the authority are also providing accommodation for a sibling of his, they are accommodated together.
(8) Where a local authority provide accommodation for a child whom they are looking after who is disabled, they shall, so far as is reasonably practicable, secure that the accommodation is not unsuitable to his particular needs.
(9) Part II of Schedule 2 shall have effect for the purposes of making further provision as to children looked after by local authorities and in particular as to the regulations that may be made under subsections (2)(*a*) and (*f*) and (5).

The Arrangements for Placement of Children (General) Regulations 1991 require:

3. – (4) In any other case [i.e. except when child is 16 and agrees to be accommodated under s. 20(11), above] in which a child is looked after or accommodated but is not in care the arrangements shall so far as is reasonably practicable be agreed by the responsible authority with –

(*a*) a person with parental responsibility for the child, or
(*b*) if there is no such person the person who is caring for the child before a placement is made and if that is not practicable as soon as reasonably practicable thereafter.

By reg. 4(2), these arrangements must if practicable include the matters listed in Sch. 4:

MATTERS TO BE INCLUDED IN ARRANGEMENTS TO ACCOMMODATE CHILDREN WHO ARE NOT IN CARE

1. The type of accommodation to be provided and its address together with the name of any person who will be responsible for the child at that accommodation on behalf of the responsible authority.
2. The details of any services to be provided for the child.
3. The respective responsibilities of the responsible authority and –
(*a*) the child;
(*b*) any parent of his; and
(*c*) any person who is not a parent of his but who has parental responsibility for him.
4. What delegation there has been by the persons referred to in paragraph 3(*b*) and (*c*) of this Schedule to the responsible authority of parental responsibility for the child's day to day care.
5. The arrangements for involving those persons and the child in decision making with respect to the child having regard –
(*a*) to the local authority's duty under sections 20(6) (involvement of children before provisions of accommodation) and 22(3) to (5) of the Act (general duties of the local authority in relation to children looked after by them);
(*b*) the duty of the voluntary organisation under section 61(1) and (2) of the Act (duties of voluntary organisations); and
(*c*) the duty of the person carrying on a registered children's home under section 64(1) and (2) of the Act (welfare of children in registered children's homes).
6. The arrangements for contact between the child and –
(*a*) his parents;
(*b*) any person who is not a parent of his but who has parental responsibility for him; and
(*c*) any relative, friend or other person connected with him, and if appropriate the reasons why contact with any such person would not be reasonably practicable or would be inconsistent with the child's welfare.
7. The arrangements for notifying changes in arrangements for contact to any of the persons referred to in paragraph 6.
8. In the case of a child aged 16 or over whether section 20(11) (accommodation of a child of 16 or over despite parental opposition) applies.
9. The expected duration of arrangements and the steps which should apply to bring the arrangements to an end, including arrangements for rehabilitation of the child with the person with whom he was living before the voluntary arrangements were made or some other suitable person, having regard in particular, in the case of a local authority looking after a child, to section 23(6) of the Act (duty to place children where practicable with parents etc.) and paragraph 15 of Schedule 2 to the Act (maintenance of contact between child and family).

Questions

(i) The Review of Child Care Law (1985, para. 7.16) recommended against 'allowing legal powers over a child to be settled by informal agreement in individual cases. Great care would need to be taken to ensure that the parent was fully aware of the consequences of such an agreement and was in no way overawed or pressurised (however unwittingly) by the person obtaining consent.' What is the legal effect of the agreed arrangements under these regulations?
(ii) What is the position of a parent who wishes herself to meet one of the parental responsibilities delegated in the agreement (see p. 442, above)?

(iii) What is a parent to do if (*a*) the agreed arrangements for contact are not kept, or (*b*) she wishes to make some different arrangements?
(iv) Do you think that the parent will see herself as being in partnership with the local authority (or voluntary organisation) to look after her child?
(v) What is meant by an 'other person connected with him' (in para. 6(*c*) above)? What if a 13 year old girl in local authority accommodation has a boyfriend (*a*) to whom the local authority objects but the parents do not, or (*b*) to whom the parents object but the local authority does not?

Before the Children Act 1989 abolished the concept of 'voluntary care', the research evidence painted a depressing picture (e.g. Rowe and Lambert, 1973; DHSS, 1985). Once admitted to care, children frequently lost contact with their families, and there was a lack of planning to meet their long-term needs. We deal with these questions in the next chapter, but some of the concerns are addressed in s. 26, which requires regular reviews of why and how children are being looked after and a formal complaints mechanism:

26. – (3) Every local authority shall establish a procedure for considering any representations (including any complaint) made to them by –
- (*a*) any child who is being looked after by them or who is not being looked after by them but is in need;
- (*b*) a parent of his;
- (*c*) any person who is not a parent of his but who has parental responsibility for him;
- (*d*) any local authority foster parent;
- (*e*) such other person as the authority consider has a sufficient interest in the child's welfare to warrant his representations being considered by them,

about the discharge by the authority of any of their functions under this Part in relation to the child.

(4) The procedure shall ensure that at least one person who is not a member or officer of the authority takes part in –
- (*a*) the considerations; and
- (*b*) any discussions which are held by the authority about the action (if any) to be taken in relation to the child in the light of the consideration.

...

(7) Where any representation has been considered under the procedure established by a local authority under this section, the authority shall –
- (*a*) have due regard to the findings of those considering the representation; and
- (*b*) take such steps as are reasonably practicable to notify (in writing) –
  - (i) the person making the representation;
  - (ii) the child (if the authority consider that he has sufficient understanding); and
  - (iii) such other persons (if any) as appear to the authority to be likely to be affected, of the authority's decision in the matter and their reasons for taking that decision and of any action which they have taken, or propose to take.

(8) Every local authority shall give such publicity to their procedure for considering representations under this section as they consider appropriate.

Questions

(i) You are a child aged 15 being looked after by Blankshire County Council in a small residential home. You like this because it is near to your school and friends. Visits to or from your family are easy. Blankshire then decides to privatise its provision of residential care and to close the home. You are likely to be sent to a similar home 50 miles away. What can you do?
(ii) Your mother is a disabled widow who found it impossible to look after you as well as your two sisters because your mild mental handicap has made

your adolescence difficult for both of you. The relationship between you is still very close. What can she do?
(iii) Your mother's sister would have you to live with her, provided that she can have some financial and social work support. You have mixed feelings about this, but would prefer it to moving away. What can she do (see also p. 657, below)?
(iv) Your 16-year-old sister thinks you have a lovely life in the home and would like to join you. What can she do?
(v) Your 21-year-old boy friend would like to visit you in the home, but the home's rules prohibit such visits. What can he do?

The operation of many of the provisions considered in this section are illustrated in the following case:

Re T (accommodation by local authority)
[1995] 1 FCR 517, [1995] 1 FLR 159, High Court, Queen's Bench Division

T, aged 17, had 'escaped' from an inadequate background, and found a home with Mr and Mrs B. It was agreed that she should remain living with them. Initially the local authority paid £25 per week to support this arrangement, and later this was replaced by £33 per week, paid by the Department of Social Security. If T was accommodated by the local authority and placed with Mr and Mrs B, they would receive a fostering allowance of £79 a week. The local authority refused to accommodate her, and T applied for judicial review.

Johnson J: ... T's wish to be accommodated would, if successful, no doubt lead to payment of the fostering allowance and (as I think, every bit as importantly) would lead to the provision of the local authority's support after she becomes 18 and until she is 21.

The local authority decided, in considering s. 20(3), that T's welfare would not be likely to be seriously prejudiced if they did not provide her with accommodation. That decision was made on 21 July 1992, and thereafter a complaints procedure was put in motion.

I think it needs to be said, in fairness to this local authority, that they were not seeking to escape their obligation to T for any blameworthy reason; simply that they had to allocate their resources as they thought best. The fact is that, throughout this episode of T's life, she has been supported by a social worker who has given her commitment to her to a degree that is deserving of the very highest praise.

As to the complaints procedure, that resulted in a meeting of the complaints review panel of the local authority which took place on 15 January 1993. It is described as having been a 'searching and vigorous inquiry'. It upheld T's complaint. The matter of her application under s. 20(3), therefore, came to be considered once again by the local authority's director of social services. It is usually the case that this director of social services follows the recommendations of such review panels but, on this occasion, he did not. It is plain to me that he considered the matter carefully and conscientiously. In the exercise of the discretion vested in the local authority, he concluded that T's welfare would not be likely to be seriously prejudiced if the local authority did not provide her with accommodation. That decision is attacked now on T's behalf.

I direct myself according to the dictum of Lord Brightman in *R v Hillingdon London Borough Council, ex p Puhlhofer* [1986] AC 484. In matters such as this, it is the local authority, not the court, which is to judge the facts. It is not for the court to monitor the actions of local authorities, save in exceptional cases where, by way of example, there has been a mistake as to the applicable law or there has been unreasonableness in the *Wednesbury* sense; in the words of Lord Brightman, 'unreasonableness verging on an absurdity'.

Under s. 20(6), before providing accommodation under s. 20, the local authority shall give due consideration to the wishes of the child in T's situation. Those wishes had been made known to the local authority, were clearly known to the director of social services and, in my judgment, he clearly took them into consideration. However, it is plain from the letters which were written on his behalf at the time that a factor that weighed with him very considerably was the existence of the local authority's duties under s. 17 of the Children Act 1989. That duty is expressed to be a general duty to safeguard and promote the welfare of children within the area of the local authority and to promote the upbringing of such children by their families. Unusually, for the purpose of this statute, 'family' has an exceptionally wide meaning and includes any person with whom a child has been living; here, Mr and Mrs B.

This local authority had been exercising its duty and its powers under s. 17. It had allocated social work support, and it had been making discretionary financial payments, albeit not of the amount desired by T, and certainly not with the regularity that they might have been. The powers under s. 17 can, I think, fairly be described as being the provision of support on an ad hoc emergency basis. They are none the less valuable for that. However, in reaching his decision, the director of social services was satisfied that the past provision of support under s. 17 made it unlikely that T's welfare would be seriously prejudiced if she was not provided with accommodation. In my judgment, the director was here in error.

As in other provisions of the Children Act 1989, the focus of attention is, or should be, upon the likelihood of significant harm (s. 31) or here, serious prejudice; but in the future. Under s. 31, the court, and under s. 20(3), the local authority, must put its mind to the future and seek to form a judgment about the future. ...

... As at present advised, it seems to me that, in exercising its discretion under s. 20(3), the local authority should look at all the circumstances of the case, and for my part I would not think it right that anything should be excluded: in particular, the powers and the duties under s. 17 should not be excluded. However, because those powers and duties are discretionary in nature, it does not seem to me that they can amount to factors to which much weight should be attributed for the purpose of s. 20(3).

... I do accept that, in a practical situation, it will usually be very difficult for a local authority to decline an application under s. 20(3) on the basis of the possibility (because it can be no more) of the provision of support under s. 17. Accordingly, I grant the relief asked.

It is to be noted, in passing, that if T had not had the advantage of living with Mr and Mrs B, then it might well have become necessary for the local authority to obtain a care order, so that under s. 22 she would have become a child being looked after by the local authority, and so would have become a qualifying person under s. 24 and entitled to the ongoing relief there provided.

Questions

(i) Do you agree that s. 17 is concerned only with 'ad hoc emergency' support?
(ii) Can T's parents demand that she is returned to them? What if she had been 15 years old?
(iii) Suppose that you are 12, and have been accommodated under s. 20 for several years. Blankshire Social Services thinks that returning you to your family at this crucial stage in your education and development will not be for the best. If your mother decides to take you away from them, what can Blankshire do? What can your foster parents do?

This last question involves the use of compulsion against parents, which is dealt with below (p. 616). Remember, however, that compulsion is also used against the children themselves. *The Pindown Experience and the Protection of Children: The Report of the Staffordshire Child Care Inquiry 1990* (1991) examined the harsh and restrictive regime ('Pindown') to which some children were subjected. This is Susan's story:

11.17 Susan, who was born in 1976, was put into Pindown when she was 9 years old.

11.18 At the beginning of 1986 Susan, her half-sister aged 13, and her mother were living with the maternal grandfather. Her half-sister is the child of her mother's former marriage. Susan's father was one of her mother's subsequent boyfriends

11.19 Over a period of about a month, in early 1986, the mother contacted Staffordshire social services on a number of occasions requesting help with coping with Susan's behaviour. Susan was said to be mixing with older girls and smoking, stealing and upsetting her grandfather who did not want her to remain in his home.
11.20 Susan was then received into care and placed at 245 Hartshill Road.
11.21 She went straight into Pindown. The first entry in the log book was as follows: '(Susan) admitted – *very basic programme be very nasty to her*' (emphasis added).
11.22 Susan was required to wear pyjamas and kept in a sparsely furnished room. She was not allowed contact with other children or non-Pindown staff and was not permitted to attend school. She was required to knock on the door before going to the toilet. She remained in Pindown for a week and then returned home. Subsequently five 'family reviews' were held at The Birches at about weekly intervals before social services contact with the family ceased and the case was closed.
11.23 Immediately after Susan's admission to Pindown an entry in the log book at 245 Hartshill Road recorded a residential worker's conversation with her headmaster: he was concerned that she was in care because she was no trouble at all in school being a good attender, well-behaved, and a hard worker. She was also in his view very bright.
11.24 Further entries in the log book during her week in Pindown included:

- 'wants to go to the toilet a lot, soon put a stop to that. Had harsh words twice. Once for calling through the bedroom wall (to another child in Pindown).'
- 'will try anything to get out of her room, after several telling offs (sic) she stopped trying.'
- 'she thinks I'm room service, hasn't anyone told her its not an hotel.'
- 'the little knocker has not knocked so much tonight, when I go in I usually look for a tip as I feel like a waiter.'

11.25 On the evening of Susan's third day in Pindown a 'review' was held. Neither the log book nor the social services file on Susan records who was present. 'Susan's problems' were 'highlighted'. It was noted that the grandfather would not allow her back and her mother was prepared to move out of his home. It was 'agreed that [Susan] remain in care'. It was recorded in the log book that 'mother saw her 2 mins. Cried a little. Then later cried wanting to go home. Was her mother still here. Explained review system. Spoke to her about contract and may well come back if she breaks the rules. Bath, bed. Toilet a lot still. First sign of hope for her, maybe! ! !'
11.26 Susan is twice recorded in the log book as 'working hard'. What she was doing in the Pindown room is not specified.
11.27 A further 'review' was held after Susan had been in Pindown for 7 days. It was agreed that she should 'return home' on various conditions, one of which was that she should write a letter of apology to her grandfather.
11.28 Susan returned to the home of her grandfather. Soon afterwards she and her mother and half-sister were re-housed.
11.29 Just over a year later, the mother again brought Susan, then aged 10, to the social services office. She said that she had been having problems with Susan's behaviour for some considerable time. She would not do what she was told, called her mother unpleasant names and embarrassed her in public. The mother said that she had eventually lost her temper and attempted 'to strangle' Susan. She could not look at Susan without wanting to attack her and Susan was unrepentant about her behaviour. There were also problems with the mother's boyfriend who was living in their home and about whom Susan complained.
11.30 Susan was again received into care and placed into Pindown. The entry in the log book at 245 Hartshill Road records that '[Susan] admitted to pindown after family meeting. ... she is an extremely naughty and manipulative little girl: so much so that she has driven her mother to the point of violence. *Basic Pindown – plenty of schoolwork.*' Later on the day of admission to Pindown it is recorded that 'if she knocked on the door once, she knocked ten thousand times. Other than that *no* problems, she did *not* eat much tea, had a bath at 6.30 tucked up in bed 7 p.m.'
11.31 Three days later the following entry was made in the log book: '[Susan] reviewed this afternoon. She fully expected to go home. When she realised that this wasn't going to happen she became very upset. Cried off and on until 8.30 – at times becoming hysterical. She will go to school on Monday; she understands that this is a privilege and is the only one she will be given for some time to come.'
11.32 After ten days of Pindown it was noted by the child's social worker in the social services file that 'there are no complaints about [Susan's] behaviour at Hartshill Road but she is in no position to misbehave as she is restricted'.
11.33 Subsequently the mother recognised that 'problems can only be resolved at home' and Susan spent some of her time at home and some in Pindown at 245 Hartshill Road. It would seem that she actually spend some 20 days in Pindown before being transferred to The Birches.

11.34 After spending about 3 months at The Birches during which time she spent regular weekends at home, Susan was moved to another children's home. She eventually went home at the beginning of 1988, some six months after being received into care for the second time. More recently further problems occurred and Susan was placed in a foster home.
11.35 Susan at 9 years of age was one of the youngest children placed in Pindown. During her two spells in care in 1986 and 1987 she spent at least 27 days in the unit.

Questions

(i) Why should it be regarded as a privilege to be allowed to go to school?
(ii) Under s. 36 of the Education Act 1944, 'It shall be the duty of the parent of every child of compulsory school age to cause him to receive efficient full-time education suitable to his age, ability and aptitude and to any special educational needs he may have, either by regular attendance at school or otherwise'; under s. 114(1) (as amended by the Children Act 1989), 'parent' includes 'any person (*a*) who is not a parent of his but has parental responsibility for him, or (*b*) who has care of him' but for this purpose only includes such a person if he is an individual: should local authorities be under the same legal obligation as others to educate the children they are looking after properly?

There are limits on the circumstances in which children may be placed in 'secure accommodation', now contained in the Children Act 1989:

25. – (1) Subject to the following provisions of this section, a child who is being looked after by a local authority may not be placed, and, if placed, may not be kept, in accommodation provided for the purpose of restricting liberty ('secure accommodation') unless it appears –

(*a*) that –
  (i) he has a history of absconding and is likely to abscond from any other description of accommodation; and
  (ii) if he absconds, he is likely to suffer significant harm; or
(*b*) that if he is kept in any other description of accommodation he is likely to injure himself or other persons.

(2) The Secretary of State may by regulations –
(*a*) specify a maximum period –
  (i) beyond which a child may not be kept in secure accommodation without the authority of the court; and
  (ii) for which the court may authorise a child to be kept in secure accommodation;
(*b*) empower the court from time to time to authorise a child to be kept in secure accommodation for such further period as the regulations may specify; and
(*c*) provide that applications to the court under this section shall be made only by local authorities.

Questions

(i) Why is this not restricted to 'children in care'?
(ii) Should the welfare of the child be the paramount consideration when a court is asked to authorise the use of secure accommodation (see *Re M (secure accommodation order)* [1995] Fam 108, [1995] 2 All ER 407, [1995] 2 WLR 302, [1995] 1 FLR 418, CA)?
(iii) What legal action (if any) might be available to Susan and others like her?

(iv) Section 51 of the Act allows the Secretary of State to exempt from criminal liability for harbouring or assisting runaways specified voluntary organisations and others who provide refuges for children 'at risk': is this a better solution?
(v) Why should we tolerate a public care system from which children want to run away?

4 Child protection enquiries

Section 47 of the Children Act 1989 imposes extensive obligations upon local authorities to investigate cases of suspected child abuse and take action where necessary and upon other agencies to assist them. The reasons appear in the White Paper, *The Law on Child Care and Family Services* (1987):

42. Under existing legislation the local authority have a duty to investigate cases where information is received which suggests that there are grounds for care proceedings. The Review proposed that this should be replaced by a more active duty to investigate in any case where it is suspected that the child is suffering harm or is likely to do so. The Government endorse that proposal and accept that the enquiries made should be such as are necessary to enable the local authority to decide what action, if any, to take.
43. The Jasmine Beckford Report declared that there were powerful reasons why the duty on local authorities or health authorities to co-operate under section 22 of the NHS Act 1977 should in the context of child abuse be made more specific, to include the duty to consult and the duty to assist by advice and the supply of information so as to help in the management of such cases. Such a duty would, it was argued, operate as a positive and practical step to promote multidisciplinary working in this area, which is important not only at the stage of identification of abuse but also in subsequent follow-up action. The Government accept this view, and therefore intend to make legal provision for co-operation between statutory and voluntary agencies in the investigation of harm and protection of children at risk.

One of the startling things about almost all of the cases on which there have been official inquiries (see DHSS, 1982; DH, 1991) is that the family was well known to the social services and other agencies. Co-operation between health, education and social services, and the police, is seen as the key to effective protection by the Department of Health in *Working Together – A Guide to Arrangements for Inter-agency Co-operation for the Protection of Children from Abuse* (1991). It defines child abuse thus:

6.40 The following categories should be used for the register and for statistical purposes. They are intended to provide definitions as a guide for those using the register. In some instances, more than one category of registration may be appropriate. This needs to be dealt with in the protection plan. The statistical returns will allow for this. Multiple abuse registration should not be used just to cover all eventualities.

Neglect: The persistent or severe neglect of a child, or the failure to protect a child from exposure to any kind of danger, including cold or starvation, or extreme failure to carry out important aspects of care, resulting in the significant impairment of the child's health or development, including non-organic failure to thrive.

Physical Injury: Actual or likely physical injury to a child, or failure to prevent physical injury (or suffering) to a child including deliberate poisoning, suffocation and Munchausen's syndrome by proxy.

Sexual Abuse: Actual or likely sexual exploitation of a child or adolescent. The child may be dependent and/or developmentally immature.

Emotional Abuse: Actual or likely severe adverse effect on the emotional and behavioural development of a child caused by persistent or severe emotional ill-treatment or rejection.

All abuse involves some emotional ill-treatment. This category should be used where it is the main or sole form of abuse.

Child Protection – Messages from Research (DH, 1995) outlines some of the difficulties involved in defining what is 'abusive':

A look at changes over the last century would suggest that the threshold beyond which child abuse is considered to occur is gradually being lowered. This is happening for a variety of reasons, including an emphasis on the rights of children as individuals, ease of disclosures, the influence of feminist social theories about victimisation and public expectation that the state should intervene in the privacy of family life. Society continually reconstructs definitions of maltreatment which sanction intervention; in 1871 the concern was abuse by adoptive parents; in 1885 it was teenage prostitution; in 1923 incest; then, later, neglect, physical abuse, sexual and emotional abuse. The state remains selective in its concerns and there is a difference between behaviour known to be harmful to children and behaviour which attracts the attention of child protection practitioners. For example, professionals' interest in school bullying is perhaps not as great as parents and children would wish it to be and domestic violence is only just beginning to achieve salience as a cause of concern. Jane Gibbons helpfully summarises the situation when she says that 'as a phenomenon, child maltreatment is more like pornography than whooping cough. It is a socially constructed phenomenon which reflects values and opinions of a particular culture at a particular time'.

Questions

(i) Can you think of any cultures in which it would not be considered abusive to deliberately inflict injury upon a child, or for an adult to have sexual intercourse with a child?
(ii) Is corporal punishment of a child abusive, or is 'moderate chastisement' an aspect of parental responsibility?
(iii) Would you expect there to be widespread agreement about what is emotional abuse or neglect?

Working Together (1991) describes the process of referral:

5.11.1 The starting point of the process is that any person who has knowledge of, or a suspicion that a child is suffering significant harm, or is at risk of significant harm, should refer their concern to one or more of the agencies with statutory duties and/ or powers to investigate and intervene – the social services department, the police or the NSPCC. Referrals may come from members of the public, those working with children and families who are not accustomed to dealing with child protection or from other professionals who are regularly engaged in child protection work. All referrals, whatever their origin, must be taken seriously and must be considered with an open mind which does not prejudge the situation. The statutory agencies must ensure that people know how to refer to them, and they must facilitate the making of referrals and the prompt and appropriate action in response to expressions of concern. It is important in all these cases that the public and professionals are free to refer to the child protection agencies without fear that this will lead to unco-ordinated and/or premature action. The [Area Child Protection Committee] should publish advice about whom to contact with details of addresses and telephone numbers.
5.11.2 It is essential that professionals who work with children and families should be alert to the signs of child abuse. Locally agreed procedures should make it clear that each agency should provide appropriate training and guidance to ensure that all professionals can recognise signs of abuse and respond appropriately.

For health professionals, this overrides the normal rules of confidentiality. The General Medical Council has revised its guidance for the medical profession several times. Its most recent advice appears in an addendum to *Working Together, Child Protection – Medical Responsibilities* (DH et al., 1994):

4.1 … The [General Medical] Council's current advice, issued in May 1993, is that 'where a doctor believes that a patient may be the victim of abuse or neglect the patient's interests are paramount and will usually require a doctor to disclose information to an appropriate, responsible person or officer of a statutory agency'. This advice will guide a doctor's decisions on whether to disclose confidential information relating to abuse and neglect, both to medical colleagues and staff of the statutory agencies. The statutory agencies are social services, NSPCC and the police.

…

4.5 Distinction needs to be made between disclosing information which relates directly to a child and disclosing information which relates to a third party but which is directly relevant to child protection issues.

4.6 A doctor may be in possession of information relating to a third party and which is of direct relevance to child protection issues e.g. violent behaviour, sexual arousal to children, or information about a known or alleged perpetrator who may pose a continuing risk to children. It is essential that doctors are aware of risk factors and weigh this information very carefully. Disclosure of such information will usually be justified in relation to child protection.

Question

Despite what the guidance says, health professionals are under no legally enforceable duty to report suspicions of child abuse: should they be? What about other people?

D v National Society for Prevention of Cruelty to Children [1978] AC 171, [1977] 1 All ER 589, [1977] 2 WLR 201, 121 Sol Jo 119, 76 LGR 5, House of Lords

Lord Diplock: … The uncontradicted evidence of the director of the NSPCC is that the work of the society is dependent upon its receiving prompt information of suspected child abuse and that, as might be expected, the principal sources of such information are neighbours of the child's family or doctors, school-teachers, health visitors and the like who will continue to be neighbours or to maintain the same relationship with the suspected person after the matter has been investigated and dealt with by the NSPCC. The evidence of the director is that without an effective promise of confidentiality neighbours and others would be very hesitant to pass on to the society information about suspected child abuse. There is an understandable reluctance to 'get involved' in something that is likely to arouse the resentment of the person whose suspected neglect or ill-treatment of a child has been reported. …

The fact that information has been communicated by one person to another in confidence, however, is not of itself a sufficient ground from protecting from disclosure in a court of law the nature of the information or the identity of the informant if either of these matters would assist the court to ascertain facts which are relevant to an issue on which it is adjudicating. … The private promise of confidentiality must yield to the general public interest that in the administration of justice truth will out, unless by reason of the character of the information or the relationship of the recipient … to the informant, a more important public interest is served by protecting the information or the identity of the informant from disclosure in a court of law. The public interest which the NSPCC relies on as obliging it to withhold from the respondent and from the court itself material that could disclose the identity of the society's informant is analagous to the public interest that is protected by the well-established rule of law that the identity of police informers may not be disclosed in a civil action, whether by the process of discovery or by oral evidence at the trial (*Marks v Beyfus* (1890) 25 QBD 494; 59 LJQB 479) … in *Rogers v Home Secretary* [1973] AC 388, [1972] 2 All ER 1057 this House did not hesitate to extend to persons from whom the Gaming Board received information for the purposes of the exercise of their statutory functions, under the Gaming Act 1968, immunity from disclosure of their identity analogous to that which the law had previously accorded to police informers. Your Lordships' sense of values might well be open to reproach if this House were to treat the confidentiality of information given to those who are authorised by statute to institute proceedings for the protection of neglected or ill-treated children as entitled to less favourable treatment in a court of law than information given to the Gaming Board so that gaming may be kept clean. …

Question

The identity of informants is still protected under the Access to Personal Files Act 1987 and Access to Personal Files (Social Services) Regulations 1989, reg. 9(3): should busy-bodies be encouraged or discouraged?

Messages from Research (DH, 1995) emphasises that a relatively small proportion of referrals will lead to more formal stages of the child protection process:

It is helpful to view the children and families caught up in the child protection process in the context of all vulnerable children. Although the evidence is not absolutely conclusive, it has been estimated by Smith and colleagues [1996] that, each year, 350,000 children will be in an environment of low warmth and high criticism. These children are 'in need' to the extent that their health and development will be significantly impaired if their families do not receive some help. Many of these children will be supported through the routine work of health visitors and other preventative strategies. We do not know how many, but a proportion of these children will receive help via Section 17 of the Children Act, 1989 including some who are accommodated under voluntary arrangements.

Many, however, will be subject to Section 47 enquiries to establish whether the local authority needs to take action to safeguard the child, what many currently think of as the start of the child protection process. We can interpret the work of Gibbons and colleagues [1995] to suggest that about 160,000 such enquiries take place in England each year, including 25,000 where suspicions of maltreatment or neglect are unsubstantiated.

Because the decision to investigate abuse is influenced by social and administrative factors, the family characteristics of the 160,000 children dealt with under child protection procedures are not typical of families and children generally; nor are they typical of all families in which children are maltreated. Gibbons and colleagues [1995] found that over a third (36%) were headed by a lone parent and in only 30% of cases were both natural parents resident. Nearly three fifths (57%) lacked a wage earner and over half (54%) were dependent on income support. Domestic violence (27%) and mental illness (13%) within the family also featured prominently and, in Thoburn and colleagues' study [1995], nearly a quarter (23%) had suffered an accident or serious ill health during the previous year. One in seven parents under suspicion were known to have been abused themselves as children. Most (65%) children had previously been known to social services and a previous investigation had been undertaken in almost half (45%) of the 1,888 cases Gibbons and colleagues [1995] scrutinised. So, it is the most vulnerable in our society who are most likely to become the object of a Section 47 enquiry. What should they expect from the child protection process?

...

The diagram on page [600] describes the child protection process, showing – as accurately as the research evidence will allow – what happens each year to the 11 million children in England; it focuses especially on those dealt with under child protection procedures. The diagram also brings to notice approximately 25,000 children who come to the attention of child protection agencies even though they are found not to have been maltreated. It can be seen, first of all, that the process has four clearly identifiable stages, pre-investigation, first enquiry, family visit, and conference and registration.

First enquiry

Having described the characteristics of families subject to an abuse enquiry, what is it that triggers the interest of professionals? Cleaver and Freeman [1995] found that abuse came to official attention in one of three ways. Most commonly, someone, usually the child or another member of the family, disclosed their concerns to a professional; just over half (51%) of enquiries began in this way. In about two-fifths (39%) of cases, professionals already working with the family identified child abuse. In the remaining 10% of all enquiries, abuse was suggested during an unrelated event, such as an arrest or home visit.

Family visit

Over a decade ago, Dingwall [Dingwall et al, 1983] stated that the most important step in a child abuse investigation occurs when an allegation becomes public property. This finding remains true. When the allegation becomes public, family members usually learn that they are under suspicion. Whatever else happens in the days, weeks, months and years following, the impact at this moment of realisation can be devastating. The Dartington [Cleaver and Freeman, 1995] and Oxford [Sharland et al, 1996] teams talked at length to parents in these early stages. The following quotation, from a mother who learned from a social worker that her son's teacher suspected sexual abuse, was typical:

> 'When I got the letter I was very shocked. I said 'Ah-ah ... what's happening with the social worker! What have I done? Are they coming to take my child away?' I was scared. I hoped what happened to the Orkneys isn't going to happen to me now. I was just – 'Oh, God, if anyone rings this bell, I hope – Oh God, it's not them!' Anyone who rings the bell, I look out of the window first – don't open the door and I say 'Who is this?' From what I've heard from the telly, you know, I was very, very scared. And I phoned the social worker up. She wasn't in there! And I left a message. But I didn't get a reply from her.'

As the diagram on [page 600] shows, a tiny minority of parents lose their children at the point of the first enquiry, but it is this wrench, more than anything else, that parents fear. Unease which lingers as the case conference approaches hinders parental participation.

Conference and registration
Only a quarter of referrals lead to a meeting of professionals. Several weeks can elapse between the first enquiry and the meeting: Gibbons and colleagues [1995] found the interval was 34 days on average, longer than the eight days recommended in guidance. The primary function of such conferences is to assess risk and decide how best to protect the child, but Farmer and Owen [1995] discovered several others: the conference acted as a gateway to resources; it ensured that vulnerable children were subject to regular monitoring and review; more important, it provided a context in which sensitive information could be shared.

The purpose of the child protection conference is explained in *Working Together* (1991):

6.1 The child protection conference is central to child protection procedures. It is not a forum for a formal decision that a person has abused a child. That is a matter for the courts. It brings together the family and the professionals concerned with child protection and provides them with the opportunity to exchange information and plan together. The conference symbolises the inter-agency nature of assessment, treatment and the management of child protection. Throughout the child protection process, the work is conducted on an inter-agency basis and the conference is the prime forum for sharing information and concerns, analysing risk and recommending responsibility for action. It draws together the staff from all the agencies with specific responsibilities in the child protection process (health, social services, police, schools and probation), and other staff who can offer relevant specialist advice, for example psychiatrists, psychologists, lawyers, and provides them with the forum for conducting and agreeing their joint approach to work with the child and family.

...

The responsibility to convene a child protection conference
6.3 A child protection conference will be convened by the agency with statutory powers (the [Social Services Department] or the NSPCC) following an investigation and indication that a decision has to be made about further action under the child protection procedures. At the time of the initial conference, it will be agreed if and when a child protection review will be needed. In addition, any concerned professional may ask the agency with statutory powers to convene a child protection review when he or she believes that the child is not adequately protected or when there is a need for a change to the child protection plan. If a child's name is placed on the child protection register, a review conference should be held at a time agreed at the initial conference and the intervening period should be no more than six months. For the first review it will be less, unless the initial conference had before it enough material to assess fully the risk to the child.

...

The organisation of the child protection conference
6.10 Child protection conferences are only fully effective and useful if they have a clearly defined purpose and are task centred, chaired by an experienced and trained person. For reasons of both efficiency and confidentiality, the number of people involved in a conference should be limited to those who need to know and to those who have a contribution to make. In addition

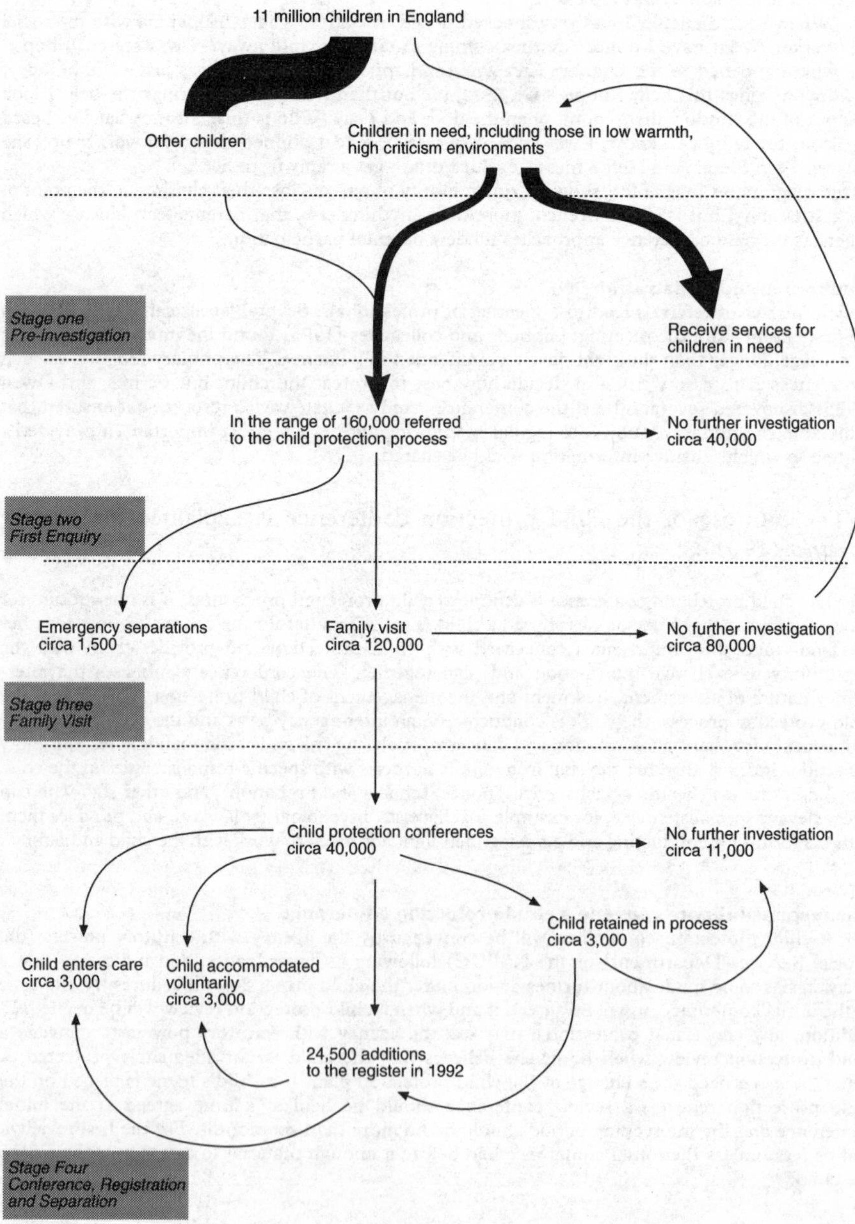
11 million children in England
Other children
Children in need, including those in low warmth, high criticism environments
Stage one
Pre-investigation
Receive services for children in need
In the range of 160,000 referred to the child protection process
No further investigation circa 40,000
Stage two
First Enquiry
Emergency separations circa 1,500
Family visit circa 120,000
No further investigation circa 80,000
Stage three
Family Visit
Child protection conferences circa 40,000
No further investigation circa 11,000
Child retained in process circa 3,000
Child enters care circa 3,000
Child accommodated voluntarily circa 3,000
24,500 additions to the register in 1992
Stage Four
Conference, Registration and Separation

there should be proper administrative arrangements for convening conferences and producing minutes. The involvement of parents and children in the child protection process requires that conferences are well organised and managed.

...

Involvement of children

6.13 A local authority has a specific duty to promote the welfare of the child looked after. In relation to any decisions taken, the authority has a duty to ascertain as far as is practicable his or her wishes and feelings and give due consideration to them, having regard to his or her age and understanding. Whenever children have sufficient understanding and are able to express their wishes and feelings and to participate in the process of investigation, assessment, planning and review, they should be encouraged to attend conferences. They may feel more able to do so if there is a friend or supporter present. ... If a child does not wish to attend, or his or her age and/or understanding makes this inappropriate, the conference should be provided with a clear and up-to-date account of the child's views by the professionals who are working with the child. The conference should, therefore, expect the key worker to be able to inform them about the views of a child who is not attending the meeting. Equally the professional who is working most closely with a child should keep the child informed about the decisions and recommendations reached at the conference and any changes in the inter-agency protection plan.

...

Exclusion from child protection conferences

6.15 While there may be exceptional occasions when it will not be right to invite one or other parent to attend a case conference in whole or in part, exclusion should be kept to a minimum and needs to be especially justified. The procedure should lay down criteria for this, including the evidence required. A strong risk of violence, with supporting evidence, by the parents towards the professionals or the child might be one example or evidence that the conference would be likely to be disrupted. The possibility that one of the parents may be prosecuted for an offence against the child does not in itself justify exclusion.

...

Involvement of others

6.18 It may be that the parent or relative will feel more confident to attend if they are encouraged to bring a friend or supporter. If they are accompanied by a friend or professional such as a lawyer, it will be incumbent on the chair to clarify the role of the additional person. The conference is not a tribunal to decide whether abuse has taken place and legal representation is therefore not appropriate.

...

Attendance at the child protection conference

6.24 Those who attend conferences should be there because they have a contribution to make. Meetings that are unnecessarily large inhibit discussion and do not use valuable resources to the best advantage. Large numbers of professionals, some of whom make no apparent contribution, are particularly inhibiting to parents and children who will in any event probably find the conference a difficult occasion.

6.25 All the agencies which have specific responsibilities in the child protection process should be invited to send representatives. These include:

- the social services,
- the NSPCC (when operational in the area),
- the police,
- education (when the child is of school age),
- the health authority,
- the general medical practitioner,
- the health visiting service,
- the probation service,
- appropriate voluntary organisations, and
- a representative of the armed services in each case where there is a Service connection.

6.26 All those who are invited should be informed that the child, the parents and other carers have been invited. A child protection conference may be a large gathering in the early stages of work, where a number of agencies may be contributing to an investigation or an assessment for planning. However, once a long-term plan has been formulated, and a group led by the key worker has been identified to work with the family, the number attending the child protection review will probably be reduced. It is the responsibility of the chair to ensure that the appropriate people are invited to the conference.

6.27 The chair must be able to call on advice from a lawyer from the local authority's legal section particularly when court action is under consideration and on other specialist advice when necessary, for example, the advice of a psychiatrist, psychologist or workers and interpreters with special knowledge either of working with people with a disability or of working with people from a particular race or culture.

6.28 On occasions it may be useful to invite others working with the family to join in the conference, for example, volunteer workers. It will be necessary for the key worker or the person most closely involved to brief him or her about the purpose of the conference, the duty of confidentiality and the primacy of the child's interest. Issues about attendance, written contributions and substitute representation are matters to be addressed in the local child protection procedures.

Apart from the services to be provided and the possibility of legal proceedings, case conferences discuss whether children should be placed on the child protection register:

6.36 In each area covered by a social services department, a central register must be maintained which lists all the children in the area who are considered to be suffering from or likely to suffer significant harm and for whom there is a child protection plan. This is not a register of children who have been abused but of children for whom there are currently unresolved child protection issues and for whom there is an interagency protection plan. The registers should include children who are recognised to be at risk and who are placed in the local authority's area by another local authority or agency. Registration does not of itself provide any protection and it must lead to an inter-agency protection plan. Registration should not be used to obtain resources which might otherwise not be available to the family.

The purpose of the register

6.37 The purpose of the register is to provide a record of all children in the area for whom there are unresolved child protection issues and who are currently the subject of an inter-agency protection plan and to ensure that the plans are formally reviewed every six months. The register will provide a central point of speedy inquiry for professional staff who are worried about a child and want to know whether the child is the subject of an inter-agency protection plan. The register will also provide useful information for the individual child protection agencies and for the ACPC in its policy development work and strategic planning.

Requirements for registration

6.39 Before a child is registered the conference must decide that there is, or is a likelihood of, significant harm leading to the need for a child protection plan. One of the following requirements needs to be satisfied:

(i) There must be one or more identifiable incidents which can be described as having adversely affected the child. They may be acts of commission or omission. They can be either physical, sexual, emotional or neglectful. It is important to identify a specific occasion or occasions when the incident has occurred. Professional judgement is that further incidents are likely; or

(ii) Significant harm is expected on the basis of professional judgement of findings of the investigation in this individual case or on research evidence.

The conference will need to establish so far as they can a cause of the harm or likelihood of harm. This cause could also be applied to siblings or other children living in the same household so as to justify registration of them. Such children should be categorised according to the area of concern.

Criteria for de-registration

...

6.44 For de-registration to occur all the members of the review conference must be satisfied that the abuse or risk of abuse (either the original type or any other) is no longer present or is no longer of a level to warrant registration. Their decision must be based on a careful and thorough analysis of current risk.

Some parents find all this rather unfair and heavy-handed. As 'Mrs Jones', the mother who burned her child (p. 570, above), says:

You know, once you get the authorities in you never get them out. They look at everything you do. Never a week goes past without there's somebody in our flat checking up. They think you'll think it's just a social visit-but it's not, you know what they're looking for. Once you're on their books! They keep having case conferences about our family, I think it's appalling: *it's wrong!* They call them without you knowing, they hold them behind your back and so many outsiders go to them. People you've never met before know you. You go in and there's a new doctor, and when you give your name they say, Oh, *hello* Mrs Jones! – just like that – and you know they know all about you. I mind it, I really do mind it. All sorts of people who've got no reason to know about me get told all the details – they sit in on conferences about me, that I know nothing about, and *I'm* not told about them. I don't think it's right. I feel I've no privacy left at all.

R v Harrow London Borough Council, ex p D
[1990] Fam 133, [1990] 3 All ER 12, [1989] 3 WLR 1239, [1989] FCR 729, [1990] 1 FLR 79, Court of Appeal

Following divorce proceedings, the mother was granted custody of three children, with fortnightly access to the father and a supervision order to the local authority. Access to the two elder children had been a cause of continuing litigation between the parents and there was a dispute over the paternity of the youngest child. In May 1986, following the father's allegations that the children were victims of physical abuse by the mother, the eldest child was examined by a paediatrician who found serious bruising and formed the view that the injuries were non-accidental. The child accused the mother of inflicting the injuries. A place of safety order was obtained and the two elder children were detained overnight in hospital and were examined by a consultant paediatrician the following day. The youngest child was never removed from home. The paediatrician found injuries to the eldest child which were incompatible with the mother's account. In June 1986 a case conference was convened, attended by the two paediatricians and the headmistress of the children's school. The mother's request to attend was refused but she was allowed to and did make written representations. As a result of the conference, the names of the children and the mother were placed on the 'at risk' register. The two children were then returned home. The mother applied for judicial review of the local authority's decision, on the basis that the conclusion of the case conference and the subsequent placing of the mother's and children's names on the register were unfair and unreasonable and contrary to natural justice. The judge dismissed the application and the mother appealed. The local authority contended, *inter alia,* that judicial review did not lie in respect of a decision to place a name on the register.

Butler-Sloss LJ: ... Before the judge it was argued that the mother should have been permitted to attend the case conference and to have been heard. That suggestion is not pursued before this court. Rather, it is urged upon us that the lowest degree of fairness to the mother, the opportunity to know about and to be allowed to meet the material allegations made against her, was not afforded to her. It is said that the decision was unfair, and the decision-making process was defective on *Wednesbury* principles.

[Counsel], for the appellant mother, made a number of points. The effect of entry on the register, even if the names of the children are subsequently removed, is to leave a stigma on the character of the mother. He asserts that the inclusion of the name of the mother in the register was the equivalent of a 'finding of guilt', that she had physically abused J. The record of J reads:

> '3. Nature of injury and by whom inflicted, whether child abuse has been substantiated: bruise on back and forehead, graze on side of nose, near eye (black eye), inflicted by mother. Child abuse substantiated.'

That finding had to be on the basis of suitable evidence which she was entitled to know about and to have an opportunity to answer. He accepts that not all the minutiae require to be disclosed, but asserts that relevant and important matters were taken into account without prior disclosure.

The case conference was given background information about the family, which included the information that the child J had previously been on the register shortly after birth in 1979 for about 2 years. The mother says that she was unaware of that fact, and the accuracy of that statement was not explored. There were other matters relating to why J did not attend swimming lessons, why the children did not drink milk at school, the failure of the mother to take the youngest for medical check-ups, the explanation for an earlier accident to D and the failure of the social workers to ask the mother for an explanation of the injuries to J.

In the context of these facts, the earlier registration was of peripheral relevance.

What was critical was whether the mother was responsible for J's injuries. What the mother required was an opportunity of giving her account as to how these injuries could have occurred, and this was given to her by the consultant paediatrician. She took advantage of the opportunity to give her account, both orally and in written representations.

The child J was clearly on the register as a result of the findings and conclusions of the consultant paediatrician, together with the allegations of the child J and the unsatisfactory explanations of the mother. The failure of a social worker to elicit an explanation from the mother was not only unders andable but, in my view, probably wise. In allegations of physical injury, the most appropriate person to be given the account of the parent is likely to be the paediatrician who is often specially qualified to assess its probability in the light of the type, place, severity and other aspects of the injuries which have occurred.

Although the mother's request to attend, be represented and speak at the case conference was refused, [counsel for the mother] does not submit that the case conference erred in that respect. She was permitted to make written representations, both from herself and a friend. The representations were placed before the case conference. The decision to place the name of J on the register cannot, in my view, be faulted. [Counsel for the mother] accepts that if J's name was properly there, the inclusion of the other children was reasonable since they would be at risk.

I am satisfied that the procedure and the result did not in any way offend the *Wednesbury* principles. The conclusion of the judge was that the appellant failed ' ... to show that the decision was in any way unfair, unreasonable, or contrary to natural justice' (see [1989] 2 FLR 51, at p. 55F).

I agree with him.

That would be sufficient to dispose of this matter, but it has been contended by the respondent council that judicial review does not lie in respect of a decision to place a name upon the child abuse register. [Counsel for the Local Authority] also submits that the decision of Waite J to grant judicial review of such a decision in *R v Norfolk County Council, ex p X* [1989] 2 FLR 120 was wrong. The facts in the *Norfolk* case were very different, of a plumber working in a house where a teenage girl made allegations of sexual abuse by him. She had twice previously been the victim of sexual abuse, and a few days later made similar allegations against another man. The plumber's name was entered in the child abuse register as an abuser, after a case conference. His employers were informed and suspended him, pending an internal inquiry. The first knowledge the plumber had of the allegations was the letter informing him of the decision to place his name on the register. He was not told that his employers had been informed. Although the contents of the register are confidential, a significant number of people inevitably have to aware of the information contained in it. As the *Norfolk* case demonstrates, the effect upon outsiders may be dramatic. If the decision to register can be shown to be utterly unreasonable, in principle I cannot see why an application to review the decision cannot lie. In coming to its decision, the local authority is exercising a most important public function which can have serious consequences for the child and the alleged abuser. I respectfully agree with the decision of Waite J.

It would also seem that recourse to judicial review is likely to be, and undoubtedly ought to be rare. Local authorities have laid on them by Parliament the specific duty of protection of children in their area. The case conference has a duty to make an assessment as to abuse and the abuser, if sufficient information is available. Of its nature, the mechanism of the case conference leading to the decision to place names on the register, and the decision-making process, is unstructured and informal.

It is accepted by [Counsel for the mother] that it is not a judicial process. It is part of a protection package for a child believed to have been the victim of abuse.

In balancing adequate protection to the child and fairness to an adult, the interest of an adult may have to be placed second to the needs of the child. All concerned in this difficult and

delicate area should be allowed to perform their task without looking over their shoulder all the time for the possible intervention of the court.
Appeal dismissed.

Questions

(i) Do you agree that it was 'probably wise' of the social worker not to 'elicit an explanation' from the mother?
(ii) What are the objections to parental attendance at case conferences? What are the advantages?
(iii) What are the objections to a more structured and formal procedure at case conferences? What are the advantages (*a*) to the child, (*b*) to the parents or carers, or (*c*) to third parties (e.g. plumbers)?

Working Together (1991) gives guidance on keeping information about abusers:

6.52 Some local authorities and other agencies have found it helpful for general social work and child protection purposes to maintain a list of all offenders in the area who have been convicted of offences listed in Schedule I of the Children and Young Persons Act 1933. Such a list has its limitations because it is difficult to keep it up to date. Although the prison service, through the probation service, notifies local authority social service departments of the discharges of Schedule I offenders, such people are often highly mobile.
6.53 Appendix 4 advises that child protection registers should include information on relevant offences committed by members of and regular visitors to the household. Who constitutes a 'regular visitor' will be a matter of judgement in relation to the circumstances of the case and would normally be identified in the course of the comprehensive assessment of the family. A 'relevant offence' will be an offence established by a criminal conviction which is relevant to the reasons for which the child is thought to be at risk and the child's name entered on the register. Information about such offences will normally emerge from the assessment of the family or at the initial conference but should also be considered during child protection reviews, particularly if the household composition has changed. It is not envisaged that the names of members of, or regular visitors to the household will be automatically checked against police records except where there are grounds to suspect the individual concerned.
6.54 Care should be taken with case records which contain information about adults suspected but not convicted of offences against children and a list of such people should not be held. The confidentiality of such records must be safeguarded and should not be shared except for child protection purposes. Any publicity given to such records could leave the agency subject to legal challenge. Where there is information about an abuser they must be informed and told of the possibility of questioning the details or making representations about the entry. See *R v Norfolk County Council, ex p M* [1989] QB 619 and *R v Harrow London Borough Council, ex p D* [1990] Fam 133 [see p. 603, above].

Questions

(i) Suppose that a local authority are convinced that a man has sexually abused children in the past, but there has never been a successful prosecution. If he moves into a household with a single mother and two small children, should the local authority warn her of their suspicions?
(ii) Should the local authority tell her that they will initiate care proceedings unless she takes steps to force him out of the household?
(iii) What can the man do to 'clear his name' (see *R v Devon County Council, ex p L* [1991] 2 FLR 541 and comment by Mary Hayes (1992))?

An important part of the investigation, particularly when sexual abuse is suspected, is to 'interview' the child. *Working Together* (1991) says this:

Focus on the child

5.14.7 Awareness of the needs of the child should focus the enquiry on the child. Every effort should be made to help him or her to relax and feel at ease. Consideration should be given to the child having a parent, relative, friend or supporter present during the investigative interviews, as the circumstances of the case determine. In spite of these efforts many children and young people will find it difficult to talk about very private matters. They may be reluctant to make statements and accusations the outcome of which they are unsure. The interviewer must listen carefully to what the child has to say and communication with him or her must be in a responsive and receptive manner. He or she must work at the child's pace and use language that the child can understand and thus enable the child to talk about and give as clear an account as possible of events that have taken place. The interviewer must always be open to the possibility that the events have not taken place. Sometimes consideration should be given to the need to provide a separate worker specifically for the parent.

Any interview which does not follow the guidance given in the Report of the *Inquiry into Child Abuse in Cleveland 1987* (1988) will certainly attract judicial criticism and will probably lose the case (see *Re E* [1990] FCR 793, [1991] 1 FLR 420):

Introduction

12.1 An essential part of the investigation of an allegation or a complaint of sexual abuse will be an interview with the child if he or she is old enough to say what did nor did not happen to them. The child telling of abuse was often referred to as 'in disclosure' and assisting the child to talk of it as 'disclosure work'. The use and potential abuse of 'disclosure work' was the subject of a considerable amount of evidence to the Inquiry. Dr David Jones defined 'disclosure' as: 'a clinically useful concept to describe the process by which a child who has been sexually abused within the family gradually comes to inform the outside world of his/her plight'. He defined 'disclosure work' as: the 'process by which professionals attempt to encourage or hasten the natural process of disclosure by a sexually abused child'.

When the child speaks of abuse

12.2 The young child may speak innocently of behaviour which an adult recognises as abuse; an older child may wish to unburden and tell of abuse to anyone they may trust and that may occur informally to, for instance, a parent, school teacher, paediatrician on a medical examination or foster mother. Dr Zeitlin told us that: 'There is evidence that material produced spontaneously without prompting is undoubtedly the most reliable form of statements that children make, and often these have been made before disclosure interviews to various people.' However as a step in the inter-disciplinary investigation of sexual abuse there needs to be the formal process of interviewing the child.

12.3 During the Inquiry the question as to whether any child involved was or was not telling the truth was not an issue. The problems related to the interpretation by professionals of the comments of children who were not making clear allegations against their parents. Nevertheless, the question of whether or not to believe the child where there is concern about sexual abuse is important and evidence was given to the Inquiry about it.

12.4 What should an adult do when a child speaks of abuse? According to Dr Bentovim, until a few years ago, it was the practice for professionals to disbelieve the child. He said: 'If a child described a sexual experience, you first of all disbelieved and it had to be proven to you, rather than you first of all taking it seriously and saying he is entitled to belief and then obviously investigating it properly and thoroughly.'

12.5 In the [draft] DHSS paper 'Child Abuse – Working Together' (April 1986) it is stated: 'A child's statement that he or she is being abused should be accepted as true until proved otherwise. Children seldom lie about sexual abuse.' …

Professor Kolvin said that the Royal College of Psychiatrists was not happy with the statement of the DHSS document: 'They felt that a statement by the child that sexual abuse has occurred should be taken seriously, but you are pre-judging the issue if you say that you believe it; in other words that you believe the child entirely.' He went on to say: 'Always listen to the child and always take what they say seriously.' …

The interview with the child

12.10 When the possibility of sexual abuse is raised the formal interview with a child of sufficient age and understanding is a necessary step in the investigation. Different types of interview must be distinguished and the purposes for which the interview is being held must be clear.

12.11 In Cleveland there was confusion as to whether some interviews were being conducted to ascertain the facts or for therapeutic purposes or a mixture of both. It must also be clear whether it is intended to 'facilitate' or assist the child to speak and if so in what way and using which aids.

...

Disclosure work

12.18 The problem arises when there is reason to believe there may be abuse and the child may need help to tell, or where the assessment to that date is inconclusive and then a somewhat different type of interview may take place. This is a second or so-called facilitative stage which needs further consideration. The interviewer at this time may be trying a more indirect approach, with the use of hypothetical or leading questions, or taking cue from the child's play or drawings. According to Dr Bentovim, it should be used sparingly by experts, who may include suitably trained social workers. ...

12.19 There is a danger, which should be recognised and avoided from the experience in Cleveland, that this facilitative second stage may be seen as a routine part of the general interview, instead of a useful tool to be used sparingly by experts in special cases. In the first stage the child tells the interviewer. The second stage is a process whereby the professional attempts to encourage the child who may be reluctant to tell the story.

...

Disagreement between the professionals

12.27 The main area of disagreement between the child psychiatrists from whom the Inquiry received contributions, is as to the desirability of and limits upon the facilitative second stage.

12.28 On the one hand, in Dr Bentovim's opinion the use of leading, alternative, hypothetical questions should be available 'but it is very important that whoever uses such techniques should be very aware of what the consequences are in terms of the fact that the interviewer immediately has problems in terms of its probability, in terms of evidential value and there is always a balance between those factors. ... My reading of the research is that a free statement, a spontaneous statement made by a child is going to be the most acute.'

12.29 The experience of his team was that children were usually highly relieved by the interview

On the other hand Professor Kolvin said: 'I am uneasy with the concept of disclosure, which really goes hell-bent for trying to get some idea of 'yes' or 'no' on the basis of almost a coercive interview with the child and also does not take into consideration the possibility that perhaps nothing has happened or that perhaps we will not know.'

...

Agreement of the professionals

12.34 All those who provided evidence to the Inquiry were agreed on the following points to be observed in conducting all interviews. We endorse their views:

1. The undesirability of calling them 'disclosure' interviews, which precluded the notion that sexual abuse might not have occurred.
2. All interviews should be undertaken only by those with some training, experience and aptitude for talking with children.
3. The need to approach each interview with an open mind.
4. The style of the interview should be open-ended questions to support and encourage the child in free recall.
5. There should be where possible only one and not more than two interviews for the purpose of evaluation, and the interview should not be too long.
6. The interview should go at the pace of the child and not of the adult.
7. The setting for the interview must be suitable and sympathetic.
8. It must be accepted that at the end of the interview the child may have given no information to support the suspicion of sexual abuse and position will remain unclear.
9. There must be careful recording of the interview and what the child says, whether or not there is a video recording.
10. It must be recognised that the use of facilitative techniques may create difficulties in subsequent court proceedings.

11. The great importance of adequate training for all those engaged in this work.
12. In certain circumstances it may be appropriate to use the special skills of a 'facilitated' interview. That type of interview should be treated as a second stage. The interviewer must be conscious of the limitations and strengths of the techniques employed. In such cases the interview should only be conducted by those with special skills and specific training.

Parents at interviews

12.35 The professionals who gave evidence to the Inquiry were unanimous about the unsuitability of having a parent present at an interview held because of the suspicion of sexual abuse. Dr Bentovim said the presence of parents made the interview very difficult, but the presence of a person familiar to the child, such as teacher or social worker, may be helpful to the child. However he/she must not take part in the interview.

...

Disclosure work in Cleveland

12.40 In Cleveland before 1987 sexual abuse had been identified by complaint from the child or from an adult. The need to interview children believed to be sexually abused but reluctant to disclose such abuse was not widely recognised and there was a lack of expertise in the Cleveland area (and almost certainly in many other areas) in this specialised field. A number of social workers had attended conferences and work shops on the subject, some of them at Great Ormond Street.

12.41 During 1987 there appears to have been an immediate response to a suspicion of child sexual abuse that somebody should do disclosure work with the child. It is not clear whether this was intended to listen to the child's account or to use specialised techniques learnt at workshops attended by some professionals.

12.42 There can however be no doubt that there were interviews carried out in Cleveland during 1987 which fall into the type of interviews criticised in the Family Law Reports. It was apparent that various feelings came together at the time of interviewing some at least of these children – anxiety, the need for a solution, beliefs about 'denial' and the therapeutic benefits for children of talking about abuse, the perceived need to believe the child and some learnt information about techniques of interviewing. These included matching the pressure on the child not to tell with pressure by the interviewer on the child at the interview. There was in many instances a presumption that abuse had occurred and the child was either not disclosing or denying that abuse. There was insufficient expertise, over-enthusiasm, and those conducting the interviews seemed unaware of the extent of pressure, even coercion, in their approach. There were dangers, which became apparent in some cases, of misinterpretation of the content of the interview. Some interviews we saw would not be likely to be acceptable in any court as evidence of sexual abuse. The Official Solicitor refers to an aspect of this – the dangers with such interviews of costly and protracted litigation. There is also a danger with a great deal of written material available on how to conduct an interview, of the inexperienced interviewer going through each of a number of stages with each child interviewed, rather than considering the best way to interview a particular child.

The Guidance in the Cleveland Report was developed in the *Memorandum of Good Practice on Video Recorded Interviews with Child Witnesses for Criminal Proceedings* (Home Office, 1992). This is primarily concerned with providing evidence which can be admitted in criminal proceedings, under s. 32A of the Criminal Justice Act 1988. However, the need to minimise the number of times when the child has to be interviewed will mean that there will frequently be a joint interview involving both police and social services for use in both civil and criminal proceedings if necessary. The *Memorandum* recommends that interviews should take place in phases, beginning with *Rapport* in which the child is helped to relax, followed by a *Free Narrative Account* stage, where the child gives an account in his or her own words. Then there is a *Questioning* phase, where the interviewer first asks open-ended questions, then specific yet non-leading questions, then closed questions, before moving to leading questions if necessary. Finally there is a *Closing* phase.

Questions

(i) Should interviews be conducted primarily to meet the evidential requirements for possible criminal proceedings, or should the needs of civil proceedings take priority?
(ii) If a psychiatrist views a video of the interview and comments on the credibility of the child's account, is this usurping the role of the judge (cf *Re S and B (minors)* [1991] FCR 175, [1990] 2 FLR 489 and *Re M and R (minors) (expert opinion: evidence)* [1996] 2 FCR 617, CA)?

The Children Act Advisory Committee describes the current situation in its Report 1994/5 (1996):

Children's evidence: the conflict of principle
A striking feature of the research and conferences ... was the widespread expression of views by the police, social workers and other child care professionals that the criminal justice system was at present not able to serve and promote the welfare of children involved in its processes. This stems in part from some of the issues already noted but in significant part it is connected with an irreconcilable conflict of principle. Thus it is the legal duty of child care professionals to promote the welfare of any child for whom they have a responsibility. It is the purpose of the criminal justice system to prosecute, bring to trial and, if convicted, to punish those guilty of proscribed conduct. It is the duty of those involved in the trial process to ensure that a defendant, whose liberty may be significantly at risk, is not convicted unless and until guilt is proved beyond reasonable doubt. In respect of abused children those duties will inevitably conflict with one another. Thus either society prefers one principle over another (eg by decriminalising child abuse) or balances those in conflict. Our society has chosen the latter course; consequently no one group will be entirely satisfied with the resultant outcome. That does not mean, of course, that there can be no improvement but it does preclude any one group's ideal.

Children's evidence: the family court
Whilst in criminal proceedings a child complainant will give evidence unless what is alleged is accepted by the defence, the position in family proceedings is quite different. Here only rarely will a child give direct evidence. What has exercised minds is how the child's voice should be heard and whether a child should be at court, particularly where he or she is a party to those proceedings.

A child can be spoken to informally by the court only on rare occasions. In its last report the Committee drew attention to the restrictions placed on that by the Court of Appeal in the case of *B v B (minors: residence and care disputes)* [1994] 2 FCR 667. Generally a child's evidence is received at second hand and his or her wishes and views conveyed to the court by the guardian ad litem in public law cases or court welfare officer in private law proceedings.

The child at court
The High Court and county courts have always inclined strongly against the presence of a child at court even where he or she is a party. Their views, it is said, can always be sufficiently ascertained by guardians or welfare officers or, exceptionally, their solicitor. Further their interests are unlikely to be served by hearing damaging allegations or evidence about those in whom they trust.

The view of the family proceedings court is traditionally different as under the former legislation the convention was that the child was usually physically produced before the court. Thorpe J has recently spelt out the problem in the case of *Re A (care: discharge application by child)* [1995] 1 FLR 599:

> 'The balance to be maintained between recognising and upholding the rights of children who are parties to Children Act litigation to participate and be heard and the need to protect children from exposure to material that might be damaging is a delicate one, and is essentially to be performed by the trial judge with a full perspective of the issues and the statements and reports, and at a relatively early stage in the proceedings.'

Clearly on these questions there is room for more than one view and it seems inevitable that such a balance will simply have to be struck on a case by case basis.

Questions

(i) What are the benefits for the child of being present in court, and what are the dangers?
(ii) Should the court exclude children unless they stand to benefit from being in court, or should children be allowed to be present unless there is evidence that they might be harmed by the experience?
(iii) Why is it appropriate for children to be encouraged to attend child protection conferences (p. 601, above), but not the resulting legal proceedings?

5 Assessment and protection orders

Before the Children Act 1989, research showed that a high proportion of compulsory admissions to care began with a 'place of safety' order, which could be obtained ex parte and last for up to 28 days with no right of appeal (Packman, 1986; Dartington, 1986). The Cleveland Report (1988) described something remarkably like abuse:

Place of safety orders
10.6 The initial route to the Juvenile Court was by way of place of safety orders. Between 1st January and 31st July 1987, 276 place of safety orders were applied for by social workers under the powers granted in s. 28 of the Children and Young Persons Act 1969. ... All but one application appears to have been made ex parte, that is to say without the parent present, and none appears to have been refused. ...
10.7 The Social Services Department operated a highly interventionist policy in the use of place of safety orders. The effect of their general approach to the use of these orders was accentuated by the memorandum of the 29th May issued by Mr Bishop, directing social workers to apply for them on receiving a diagnosis of child sexual abuse from a paediatrician. Further a trend away from applications for the maximum 28 days to periods not exceeding 7 days as advocated in their manual was not maintained in 1987 and was specifically reversed in early June. ...
10.8 Before the crisis period of May/June and before the 29th May memorandum a number of place of safety orders in cases of diagnosis of sexual abuse were applied for and granted for 28 days. The reason for the longer order was not so much the need to protect the child as the need perceived by social workers to have sufficient time to engage in 'disclosure work' with the child .
10.9 Of the 276 orders were applied for out of hours by the Emergency Duty Team. The majority of the orders were likely to have been granted during the day. We learnt however that of those 227, 174 were heard by a single magistrate at home, during the hours of court sittings, despite a clear understanding between the Clerk to the Justices and the Social Services Department that social workers would make these applications in the first instance to the full court. ...

Interim care orders
10.10 During early June the numbers of interim care orders applied for dramatically increased. On Monday 8th June there were 45 applications for interim care orders waiting to be heard. This increase in the workload led the Clerk to the Justices, Mr Cooke, to talk to one of the Court Liaison Officers, Mr Morris to discuss the implications for resources and to ask for a meeting with the Director of Social Services. In the evidence to the Inquiry there was some difference of recollection as to what was said between Mr Cooke and Mr Morris. Mr Morris went away with the impression that Mr Cooke was suggesting that Social Services should apply for 28 day orders to ease the strain on the courts, and he then advised the Emergency Duty Team to apply for 28 day orders.

Level of concern
10.13 Mr Davies said that there were three matters of special concern to magistrates receiving the applications.

1. The effect on the courts of applications which were increasing in volume and complexity. There was great concern about the backlog of cases and the delay to the regular work of the courts.
2. Prior to 1987 it was not the practice of the Social Services Department to refuse access to parents on the obtaining of a place of safety order and this approach was known to the Bench. Mr Morris told us that in the past access was almost invariably granted and denial was a marked change of policy. The requirement of separation of child from parents during 'disclosure work', which might take weeks or months was a new development. Mr Davies said that the denial of access on a place of safety order or on an interim care order was recognised by the magistrates as a most serious deprivation for parents and children and knowledge that it was now a common practice was a matter of deep concern. The reason for denying access in particular circumstances was known to the magistrates but there was unease that access might be denied too readily.
3. The conflict of medical evidence was also of great concern. Mr Davies told us that: 'It was the first time in my experience that Teesside magistrates had been invited to assess the quality of conflicting medical evidence provided by experts in child abuse.' Mr Cooke said that his magistrates were not used to dealing with that sort of thing. ...

Questions

(i) Look back at the account of child sexual abuse on p. 580: what level of concern do you think might justify removing a child and keeping him away from his parents for weeks in order to undertake disclosure work?
(ii) Look back to the discussion of ex parte orders in domestic violence cases on p. 403: why do you think that well-meaning social workers prefer to remove the child before telling the parents that they are bringing proceedings?

Working Together (1991) encourages a different approach to removing children from home:

3.8 The removal of children from their home gives rise to public and professional concern, causes great distress if not handled sensitively, and can be damaging both for the child and for the rest of the family. Therefore, except when a child is in acute physical danger it is essential that the timing of the removal of children from their homes should be agreed following consultation with all appropriate professionals. They should weigh up the likely immediate and long term effects of removing the child against the possibility of harm if they leave the child at home, and balance this with the need to secure evidence of criminal offences and, in some cases, to arrest the suspects. In many cases there will be no need to remove a child and simultaneously arrest a suspect living in the same home. In other cases, however, particularly those involving several children and adults in different households, it may be important to prevent suspects from communicating with each other or destroying evidence. In those cases it may be necessary for co-ordinated police action, distressing though this may be, at a time of day when the whole family is at home. In other cases, although early morning police action might secure better forensic evidence, such action may not be crucial to the overall welfare of the child(ren) and should not therefore be part of the plan for investigation. In all cases, the long term protection of and well-being of the child will be the overriding concern; the likelihood of securing the child's well-being through the courts will be an important consideration.

As for the law, the Cleveland Report supported the proposals, made in the Review of Child Care Law (1985) and the White Paper (1987), to replace place of safety orders with a new Emergency Protection Order. The changes are explained by the Department of Health in *Court Orders* (1991), volume 1 of their Guidance and Regulations on the Children Act 1989:

4.28 Emergency protection orders replace the much-criticised place of safety orders which could be obtained under a number of provisions in previous legislation. The purpose of the new order, as its name suggests, is to enable the child in a genuine emergency to be removed from where he is or be kept where he is, if and only if this is what is necessary to provide immediate short-term protection. Nearly every aspect of the new provisions, including the grounds for the order, its effect, opportunities for challenging it and duration are different.

4.29 The essential features of the new provisions are:

(*a*) the court has to be satisfied that the child is likely to suffer significant harm or cannot be seen in circumstances where the child might be suffering significant harm;
(*b*) duration is limited to eight days with a possible extension of seven days;
(*c*) certain persons may apply to discharge the order (to be heard after 72 hours);
(*d*) the person obtaining the order has limited parental responsibility;
(*e*) the court may make directions as to contact with the child and/or medical or psychiatric examination or assessment;
(*f*) there is provision for a single justice to make an emergency protection order;
(*g*) applications may be made in the absence of any other interested parties (ie ex parte), and may, with the leave of the clerk of the court, be made orally;
(*h*) the application must name the child, and where it does not, must describe him as clearly as possible.

4.30 These key provisions have been limited to what is necessary to protect the child, but it remains an extremely serious step. It must not be regarded – as sometimes was the case with place of safety orders – as a routine response to allegations of child abuse or as a routine first step to initiating care proceedings. The new grounds require some evidence that the situation is sufficiently serious to justify such severe powers of intervention being made available.

Nevertheless decisive action to protect the child is essential once it appears that the circumstances fall within one of the grounds in section 44(1). Under section 47(6) the authority must apply for an emergency protection order or another of the orders specified if they are refused access to the child or denied information about his whereabouts while carrying out enquiries, unless they are satisfied that the child's welfare can be satisfactorily safeguarded without their taking such action. …

The grounds for an order are these:

44. – (1) Where any person ('the applicant') applies to the court for an order to be made under this section with respect to a child, the court may make the order if, but only if it is satisfied that –

(*a*) there is reasonable cause to believe that the child is likely to suffer significant harm if –
  (i) he is not removed to accommodation provided by or on behalf of the applicant; or
  (ii) he does not remain in the place in which he is then being accommodated;
(*b*) in the case of an application made by a local authority –
  (i) the enquiries are being made with respect to the child under section 47(1)(*b*); and
  (ii) those enquiries are being frustrated by access to the child being unreasonably refused to a person authorised to seek access and that the applicant has a reasonable cause to believe that access to the child is required as a matter of urgency; or
(*c*) in the case of an application made by an authorised person –
  (i) the applicant has reasonable cause to suspect that a child is suffering, or is likely to suffer, significant harm;
  (ii) the applicant is making enquiries with respect to the child's welfare; and
  (iii) those enquiries are being frustrated by access to the child being unreasonably refused to a person authorised to seek access and the applicant has reasonable cause to believe that access to the child is required as a matter of urgency.

As the Department of Health Guidance observes:

4.44 As with all orders under the Act, even where the above conditions apply the court will not automatically make an emergency protection order. It must still consider the welfare principle and the presumption of no order [see pp. 532 and 546, above]. In most cases it is unlikely that the parents will be present at the hearing. With only one side of the case before it the court will want to examine very carefully the information it is given, especially where the basis of the application is likelihood of future harm or inability to see the child. It may be that the initial order will be made for a very short time such as the next available hearing date so that an extension to the order will be on notice to parents and others.

Section 44(1)(*b*) (local authorities) and (*c*) (authorised persons, see p. 618, below) seek to provide for children like Kimberley Carlile (see Greenwich,

1987), where the social worker was refused access but did not feel that he had sufficient cause to seek a place of safety order under s. 28 of the Children and Young Persons Act 1969 or a warrant under s. 40 of the Children and Young Persons Act 1933 (also repealed).

A local authority may begin legal proceedings because of some crisis, requiring immediate action to protect the child. Other cases, may be brought because of a refusal by the parents to 'work in partnership' with the local authority in meeting the child's needs. The Review of Child Care Law (1985), White Paper (1987), and Cleveland Report (1988) did not adopt the idea of a 'lesser' order requiring the parents to co-operate with a multi-disciplinary assessment of the child, but this found its way into the Children Act 1989 during its passage through Parliament. Its purpose is explained in the Departmental of Health Guidance as follows:

4.6 The child assessment order, established by section 43, had no parallel in previous legislation. It deals with the single issue of enabling an assessment of the child to be made where significant harm is suspected but the child is not thought to be at immediate risk (requiring his removal, or keeping him in hospital), the local authority or authorised person considers that an assessment is required, and the parents or other persons responsible for him have refused to co-operate. Its purpose is to allow the local authority or authorised person to ascertain enough about the state of the child's health or development or the way in which he has been treated to decide what further action, if any, is required. It is less interventionist than the emergency protection order, interim care order and interim supervision order and should not be used where the circumstances of the case suggest that one of these orders would be more appropriate.

4.9 A child assessment order will usually be most appropriate where the harm to the child is long-term and cumulative rather than sudden and severe. The circumstances may be nagging concern about a child who appears to be failing to thrive; or the parents are ignorant of or unwilling to face up to possible harm to their child because of the state of his health or development; or it appears that the child may be subject to wilful neglect or abuse but not to such an extent as to place him at serious immediate risk. Sexual abuse, which covers a wide range of behaviour, can fall in this category. The harm to the child can be long-term rather than immediate and it does not necessarily require emergency action. However, emergency action should not be avoided where disclosure of the abuse is itself likely to put the child at immediate risk of significant harm and/or where there is an urgent need to gather particular forensic evidence which would not otherwise be forthcoming in relation to the likelihood of significant harm.

4.12 The court can allow up to 7 days for the assessment. The order must specify the date which the assessment is to begin. The applicant should make the necessary arrangements in advance of the application, so that it would usually be possible to complete within such a period an initial multidisciplinary assessment of the child's medical, intellectual, emotional, social and behavioural needs.

4.15 Section 43(9) provides for keeping the child away from home for the purposes of the assessment. This is intended to be a reserve provision, and if used the number of overnight stays should be kept as low as possible. The assessment should be conducted with as little trauma for the child and parents as possible. It is important that the child assessment order is not regarded as a variant of the emergency protection order with its removal power: The purposes of the two orders are quite different. The child may only be kept away from home in the circumstances specified, namely:

(*a*) the court is satisfied that it is necessary for the purposes of the assessment;
(*b*) it is done in accordance with directions specified in the order; and it is limited to such period or periods (which need not be the full period of the order) specified in the order.

Questions

(i) Are you convinced by these arguments of the need for a child assessment order?

(ii) Why is it thought less drastic than an emergency protection order?
(iii) What sort of assessment could usefully be undertaken during the period of a child assessment order?
(iv) What should the local authority do if the parents refuse to cooperate with an assessment which will take longer?

Despite the provision of s. 1(2) of the Children Act 1989 (see p. 549, above), care proceedings can be a very lengthy process. The latest figures in the Children Act Advisory Committee Report 1994/5 (1996) show that the average time from application to final hearing was 56 weeks in the High Court, 43 weeks in county courts, and 30 weeks in magistrates' courts.

Questions

(i) Do you think that it is acceptable for child protection cases to take so long to be completed? Are there any advantages?
(ii) How can the child be protected during this period (see Children Act 1989, s. 38)?

It may be better for the child to stay at home while the proceedings are decided, provided that he can be adequately protected. The Department of Health Guidance talks about removing the alleged abuser rather than the child:

4.31 Where the need for emergency action centres on alleged abuse of the child the local authority will always want to explore the possibility of providing services to and/or accommodation for the alleged abuser as an alternative to the removal of the child. This could be on a voluntary basis backed up by the provisions of schedule 2 paragraph 5 which gives authorities the discretion to provide assistance with finding alternative housing or assistance to the person who leaves the family home. Such practical assistance may be crucial in persuading the alleged abuser to co-operate in this way. Existing legislation makes no public law provision empowering a court to order an alleged abuser out of the family home. However, in certain circumstances private law remedies may be used to achieve the same effect, and the local authority should explore these where it is in the child's best interest to do so. The non-abusing parent may agree to apply [for an occupation order], forcing the alleged abuser out of the home. This may be particularly appropriate in sexual abuse cases where the non-abusing parent has no wish to protect or shield the alleged abuser and where immediate removal of the child is not always in the child's best interests.

Occupation orders under the Family Law Act 1996 are considered in Chapter 9, above, but the 1996 Act also amends the Children Act 1989, so that an 'exclusion requirement' may be added to an emergency protection order:

44A. – (1) Where –
(*a*) on being satisfied as mentioned in section 44(1)(*a*), (*b*) or (*c*), the court makes an emergency protection order with respect to a child, and
(*b*) the conditions mentioned in subsection (2) are satisfied,

the court may include an exclusion requirement in the emergency protection order.

(2) The conditions are –
(*a*) that there is reasonable cause to believe that, if a person ('the relevant person') is excluded from a dwelling-house in which the child lives, then –
(i) in the case of an order made on the ground mentioned in section 44(1)(*a*), the child will not be likely to suffer significant harm, even though the child is not removed as mentioned in section 44(1)(*a*)(i) or does not remain as mentioned in section 44(1)(*a*)(ii), or

(ii) in the case of an order made on the ground mentioned in paragraph (*b*) or (*c*) of section 44(1), the enquiries referred to in that paragraph will cease to be frustrated, and

(*b*) that another person living in the dwelling-house (whether a parent of the child or some other person) –

(i) is able and willing to give to the child the care which it would be reasonable to expect a parent to give him, and

(ii) consents to the inclusion of the exclusion requirement.

(3) For the purposes of this section an exclusion requirement is any one or more of the following –

(*a*) a provision requiring the relevant person to leave a dwelling-house in which he is living with the child,

(*b*) a provision prohibiting the relevant person from entering a dwelling-house in which the child lives, and

(*c*) a provision excluding the relevant person from a defined area in which a dwelling-house in which the child lives is situated.

(4) The court may provide that the exclusion requirement is to have effect for a shorter period than the other provisions of the order.

(5) Where the court makes an emergency protection order containing an exclusion requirement, the court may attach a power of arrest to the exclusion requirement.

(6) Where the court attaches a power of arrest to an exclusion requirement of an emergency protection order, it may provide that the power of arrest is to have effect for a shorter period than the exclusion requirement.

(7) Any period specified for the purposes of subsection (4) or (6) may be extended by the court (on one or more occasions) on an application to vary or discharge the emergency protection order.

(8) Where a power of arrest is attached to an exclusion requirement of an emergency protection order by virtue of subsection (5), a constable may arrest without warrant any person whom he has reasonable cause to believe to be in breach of the requirement.

(9) Sections 47(7), (11) and (12) and 48 of, and Schedule 5 to, the Family Law Act 1996 shall have effect in relation to a person arrested under subsection (8) of this section as they have effect in relation to a person arrested under section 47(6) of that Act.

(10) If, while an emergency protection order containing an exclusion requirement is in force, the applicant has removed the child from the dwelling-house from which the relevant person is excluded to other accommodation for a continuous period of more than 24 hours, the order shall cease to have effect in so far as it imposes the exclusion requirement.

An exclusion requirement can also be attached to an interim care order under s. 38A, which may be renewed as many times as necessary up to the final hearing of the local authority's application.

Questions

(i) Can you think of any reasons why the person mentioned in sub-s. (2)(*b*) would not apply for an occupation order under the Family Law Act 1996?
(ii) Why is it necessary for the local authority to have an emergency protection order, or interim care order, *as well as* the exclusion requirement?
(iii) Should local authorities be able to apply for an order excluding someone from the child's home indefinitely (see p. 630, below)?

Under s. 46, where a police officer has reasonable cause to believe that a child would otherwise be likely to suffer significant harm, he may take the child into police protection for up to 72 hours.

Question

Why should such a power be thought necessary?

6 The 'threshold' test

Care proceedings no longer cover both the villains and victims: they are designed solely for cases where the parental shortcomings are such that the local authority should assume parental responsibility for the child. The Review of Child Care Law (1985) recommended that the criteria for care and supervision orders should focus upon the condition of the child, the shortcomings of the home and the comparative advantages of local authority intervention:

15.12 In our view the primary justification for the state to initiate proceedings seeking compulsory powers is actual or likely harm to the child. ...

...

15.14 We consider that newly drafted grounds should make it clear that 'harm' consists of a deficit in or detriment to the standard of health, development and well-being which can reasonably be expected for the particular child. By 'development' we mean not only his physical progress but also his intellectual, emotional and social or behavioural development, so that it is clear that a child who is failing to learn to control his anti-social behaviour as others do is included. We refer to the standard expected for the particular child because some children have characteristics or handicaps which mean that they cannot be expected to be as healthy or well-developed as others, but equally it must be clear that if the child needs special care or attention (perhaps, for example, because he is unusually difficult to control) then this is to be expected for him. However, the standard should only be that which is reasonable to expect, rather than the best that could possibly be achieved, for each particular child. To apply the 'best' standard would be to introduce by other means the risk that a child could be removed from home simply because some other arrangements could cater better for his needs than care by his parents.

15.15 We consider that, having set an acceptable standard of upbringing for the child, it should be necessary to show some *substantial* deficit in that standard. Minor short-comings in the health care provided or minor deficits in physical, psychological or social development should not give rise to compulsory intervention unless they are having, or are likely to have, serious and lasting effects upon the child. The courts are used to assessing degrees of harm, for example in the context of prosecution for assaults, and we consider that they could also do so here

15.16 The inclusion of 'well-being' in the standard to be expected is intended to cover those deficits which cannot necessarily be described in terms of health or development but which may equally amount to 'harm' to a child. Principal amongst these is ill-treatment. A child who has suffered non-accidental injury may not have suffered any lasting impairment in his health and the resulting emotional damage may be difficult to prove. The same may be said of older children who suffer sexual abuse. We consider that the concept of substantial detriment to their well-being will cover such cases and adequately distinguish between cases of real harm to the child and cases of acceptable variation in parenting standards.

...

15.18 In our view, a requirement that the harm be 'likely' will place a burden of proof upon local authorities which will be sufficiently difficult for them to discharge, especially in relation to mental or emotional harm, and this will prevent unwarranted intervention. A substantial or serious likelihood would be much more difficult to assess than substantial or serious harm and is not recommended. We have also considered whether anticipatory harm should be restricted by reference to specific circumstances from which risk could be inferred. ... However, a list would inevitably leave gaps unless the categories of risk were themselves very broadly expressed. Such broad expression would defeat the purpose of having express reasons for apprehended harm. In any event, it would perpetuate the arbitrariness and unfairness complained of by the Select Committee, would be complex and unwieldy, and would amount to a consolidation of the existing conditions rather than a genuine simplification in the law. ...

15.20 As regards more specific free-standing conditions, ... we do not consider them desirable. Their operation can be arbitrary or unfair and we doubt the traditional claim that specific preconditions of that sort operate to protect parents and children against unwarranted interference by the state. Rather we consider that such specific preconditions in practice may have the opposite effect and operate as magnets for drawing children within the sphere of compulsory care. ... Overall, there is a danger that very specific preconditions lead to a generalised view that once the conditions are satisfied an order follows unless there is some special reason for refusing one. What is more, the section 3 grounds, by focusing on parental unfitness, may have a stigmatising effect which may itself provoke unnecessary conflict and be detrimental to all concerned by unnecessarily prolonging proceedings and adding to their traumatic effects. We therefore, recommend that the sole primary ground should be actual or likely harm.

15.23 In our view the ground should also require that the source of the harm is the absence of a reasonable degree of parental care. Put another way, the court should be expressly required to find that the care available to the child is not merely wanting, but falls below an objectively acceptable level or that he is beyond parental control so that he cannot benefit from the care on offer. At present, the use of words such as 'prevented or neglected' or 'avoidably impaired', together with the care or control test in section 1(2), carry with them the flavour of lack of parental care. They fail, however, to express it clearly and more importantly give no indication of how great that failure must be. ...

15.24 We also consider that the grounds should in future make a clear reference to the likely effectiveness of an order. At present in section 1(2) there is the requirement that the child's need for care or control is unlikely to be met unless the court makes an order. Our impression is that the test is often satisfied by proof that his needs will not be met outside care, rather than by positive proof that a care order or supervision order will result in his needs being met or at least better catered for, and further that intervention will not do more overall harm than good. In our view the matter should be put beyond doubt. We consider that this might be achieved best by linking the idea of effectiveness with the child's best interests, that being the ultimate purpose of an order and in our view itself a matter which needs to be drawn expressly to the court's attention. Accordingly, we think there is a strong case in future for requiring the court to be satisfied before it makes an order that it is the most effective means available to it (including refusing an order) of safeguarding and promoting the child's welfare.

The Children Act 1989 provides as follows:

31. – (1) On the application of any local authority or authorised person, the court may make an order –

(*a*) placing the child with respect to whom the application is made in the care of a designated local authority; or

(*b*) putting him under the supervision of a designated local authority or of a probation officer.

(2) A court may only make a care order or supervision order if it is satisfied –

(*a*) that the child concerned is suffering, or is likely to suffer, significant harm; and

(*b*) that the harm, or likelihood of harm, is attributable to –

(i) the care given to the child, or likely to be given to him if the order were not made, not being what it would be reasonable to expect a parent to give to him; or

(ii) the child's being beyond parental control.

(3) No care order or supervision order may be made with respect to a child who has reached the age of seventeen (or sixteen, in the case of a child who is married).

(4) An application under this section may be made on its own or in any other family proceedings.

(5) The court may –

(*a*) on an application for a care order, make a supervision order;

(*b*) on an application for a supervision order, make a care order.

(6) Where an authorised person proposes to make an application under this section he shall –

(*a*) if it is reasonably practicable to do so; and

(*b*) before making the application, consult the local authority appearing to him to be the authority in whose area the child concerned is ordinarily resident.

(7) An application made by an authorised person shall not be entertained by the court if, at the time when it is made, the child concerned is –

(*a*) the subject of an earlier application for a care order, or supervision order, which has not been disposed of; or

(*b*) subject to –

(i) a care order or supervision order;

(ii) an order under section 7(7)(*b*) of the Children and Young Persons Act 1969; or

(iii) a supervision requirement within the meaning of the Social Work (Scotland) Act 1968.

(8) The local authority designated in a care order must be –

(*a*) the authority within whose area the child is ordinarily resident; or (*b*) where the child does not reside in the area of a local authority, the authority within whose area any circumstances arose in consequence of which the order is being made.

(9) In this section –

'authorised person' means –

(*a*) the National Society for the Prevention of Cruelty to Children and any of its officers; and

(*b*) any person authorised by order by the Secretary of State to bring proceedings under this section and any officer of a body which is so authorised;

'harm' means ill-treatment or the impairment of health or development;

'development' means physical, intellectual, emotional, social or behavioural development;

'health' means physical or mental health; and

'ill-treatment' includes sexual abuse and forms of ill-treatment which are not physical.

(10) Where the question of whether harm suffered by the child is significant turns on the child's health or development, his health or development shall be compared with that which could reasonably be expected of a similar child.

(11) In this Act –

'a care order' means (subject to section 105(1)) an order under subsection (1)(*a*) and (except where express provision to the contrary is made) includes an interim care order made under section 38; and

'a supervision order' means an order under subsection (1)(*b*) and (except where express provision to the contrary is made) includes an interim supervision order made under section 38.

Question

Does the idea of a 'similar' child in s. 31(10) mean a child (*a*) with similar physical or psychological characteristics, or (*b*) of a similar racial, ethnic or religious background?

The use of the present tense in the first limb of s. 31(2)(*a*) – 'is suffering' – has caused some difficulty:

Re M (a minor) (care order: threshold conditions)
[1994] 2 AC 424, [1994] 3 All ER 298, [1994] 3 WLR 558, [1994] 2 FLR 577, House of Lords

When the child, G, was 4 months old, his mother was murdered by his father. He went to live with foster parents, and his older siblings and half-siblings were looked after by the mother's cousin, Mrs W. The father was sentenced to life imprisonment, with a recommendation that he be deported on release. At first Mrs W did not feel able to care for G, and the local authority applied for a care order. Later Mrs W decided to seek a residence order for G, and the local authority supported this application. However, the child's guardian *ad litem*, and the child's father, argued that G should be adopted. Bracewell J decided that the s. 31 threshold test was satisfied because of the harm that the child had suffered when he was deprived of the love and care of his mother. A care order was made. The Court of Appeal allowing Mrs W's appeal, held that a court must decide whether the child is suffering or is likely to suffer significant harm at the time of the hearing. Since G was being adequately cared for by foster parents at the time of the final hearing, it was not possible to say that he was suffering harm. The father appealed to the House of Lords.

Lord Mackay LC: ... In my opinion the opening words of s. 31 link the making of an order by the court very closely with the application to the court by a local authority or authorised person. Section 31(2) then goes on to specify the conditions which are necessary to be satisfied before the court can make a care order or supervision order, but it is plain from this and the statute as a whole that even if these conditions are satisfied the court is not bound to make an order but must go through the full procedure particularly set out in s. 1 of the statute. It is also clear that Parliament expected these cases to proceed with reasonable expedition and in particular I refer to s. 32 in which the hearing by the court is not regarded only as taking place at the time when the applications are disposed of. Indeed, I think there is much to be said for the view that the hearing that Parliament contemplated was one which extended from the time the jurisdiction of the court is first invoked until the case is disposed of and that was required to be done in the light of the general principle that any delay in determining the question is likely to prejudice the welfare of the child. There is nothing in s. 31(2) which in my opinion requires that the conditions to be satisfied are disassociated from the time of the making of the application by the local authority. I would conclude that the natural construction of the conditions in s. 31(2) is that where, at the time the application is to be disposed of, there are in place arrangements for the protection of the child by the local authority on an interim basis which protection has been continuously in place for some time, the relevant date with respect to which the court must be satisfied is the date at which the local authority initiated the procedure for protection under the Act from which these arrangements followed. If after a local authority had initiated protective arrangements the need for these had terminated, because the child's welfare had been satisfactorily provided for otherwise, in any subsequent proceedings it would not be possible to found jurisdiction on the situation at the time of initiation of these arrangements. It is permissible only to look back from the date of disposal to the date of initiation of protection as a result of which local authority arrangements had been continuously in place thereafter to the date of disposal. It has to be borne in mind that this in no way precludes the court from taking account at the date of the hearing of all relevant circumstances. The conditions in sub-s. (2) are in the nature of conditions conferring jurisdiction upon the court to consider whether or not a care order or supervision order should be made. Conditions of that kind would in my view normally have to be satisfied at the date on which the order was first applied for. It would in my opinion be odd if the jurisdiction of the court to make an order depended on how long the court took before it finally disposed of the case. ...

... It is true that an important change has been made in the statutory provisions in respect that it is now permissible under the second branch of s. 31(2)(*a*) to look to the future even if no harm has already occurred in the past. This is an important difference from the previous legislation but in my opinion to read the present legislation as the Court of Appeal has done is substantially to deprive the first branch of s. 31(2)(*a*) of effect, as in the argument before your Lordships became very apparent. It is also clear that while Parliament added the new provisions looking to the future without any necessary connection with harm already suffered, it wished to retain the first branch in respect of harm which the child is suffering. In my opinion the provisions of s. 31(2) must be considered before the question of any competing order under the provisions of Pt II of the Act are decided upon. The scheme of s. 1(3) and (4) and in particular s. 1(3)(*g*) appears to me to require that the court decide whether or not it has power available to it to make a care order or a supervision order before it decides whether or not to make an order at all and in particular whether or not to consider a s. 8 order. ... It remains to consider what should now be done in the present case. As I said, the information available to your Lordships at the hearing before your Lordships suggests that G's stay with Mrs W has been very satisfactory to date. In the light of the options available, and the provisions of s. 1 of the Children Act 1989, I am of opinion that the choice is between a residence order in favour of Mrs W or a care order as asked for by the appellant father. I am clearly of the view that it would be quite wrong at present to disturb the arrangements presently existing for G's residence and that whether or not a care order is made, the local authority would be perfectly right to continue the present arrangements for G making his home with Mrs W. However, we cannot foresee the future and the learned judge who heard all the evidence did foresee the possibility in the longer term of difficulties. Although I hope that no difficulties will materialise I think it best in the difficult circumstances of this child that your Lordships should restore the care order which will enable the local authority to monitor the progress of the child and also has features such as that provided for by s. 33(3)(*b*) which might enable appropriate action to be readily taken if circumstances so required to determine the extent to which the father should meet his parental responsibility for G. ...

Questions

(i) If a local authority initially responds to a situation by providing services under s. 17, but later decides to seek a care order, can it argue that 'protective arrangements' have been continuously in place?
(ii) An 18 month old boy has been accommodated by the local authority since birth. His mother was homeless and immature, but she has a decent home to offer. Can the local authority apply for a care order on the grounds that the child 'is suffering' significant harm, based on the facts at the date when accommodation was first provided? Alternatively, could they argue that the child would be likely to suffer significant harm if he was removed from the only parents he knows?
(iii) Can a local authority apply for a care order in order to acquire parental responsibility for an orphan who is currently accommodated under s. 20 (cf *Birmingham City Council v D* [1994] 2 FLR 502, [1994] 2 FCR 245, which was decided before the decision of the House of Lords in *Re M* (above), and *Re SH (care order: orphan)* [1995] 1 FLR 746)?

The House of Lords has also considered the second limb of s. 31(2)(*a*) – 'likelihood' of significant harm:

Re H (minors) (sexual abuse: standard of proof)
[1996] AC 563, [1996] 1 All ER 1, [1996] 2 WLR 8, [1996] 1 FLR 80, [1996] 1 FCR 509, House of Lords

The case concerned four girls (referred to as D1, D2, D3 and D4). When she was 15, the eldest girl (D1) complained that she had been sexually abused by her step-father, who was the father of D3 and D4. He was charged with rape, but acquitted. D1 was no longer living in the household, but the local authority were concerned that the younger children were at risk of abuse. They sought care orders arguing that, although sexual abuse could not be proved to the standard required for a criminal conviction, there was sufficient evidence to satisfy the civil standard of proof in care proceedings. The judge dismissed the applications because he said that he could not be sure 'to the requisite high standard of proof' that D1's allegations were true. He said: 'This is far from saying that I am satisfied the child's complaints are untrue. ... I am, at the least, more than a little suspicious that [her step-father] has abused her as she says. If it were relevant, I would be prepared to hold that there is a real possibility that her statement and her evidence are true.' By a majority, the Court of Appeal dismissed the local authority's appeal, and an appeal to the House of Lords was also dismissed by a majority of 3 to 2. Lord Nicholls gave the leading speech, with which Lord Goff and Lord Mustill agreed.

Lord Nicholls: ...

'Likely' to suffer harm
I shall consider first the meaning of 'likely' in the expression 'likely to suffer significant harm' in s. 31. ... In everyday usage one meaning of the word likely, perhaps its primary meaning, is probable, in the sense of more likely than not. This is not its only meaning. If I am going walking on Kinder Scout and ask whether it is likely to rain, I am using likely in a different sense. I am inquiring whether there is a real risk of rain, a risk that ought not to be ignored. In which sense is

likely being used in this subsection? In s. 31(2) Parliament has stated the prerequisites which must exist before the court has power to make a care order. These prerequisites mark the boundary line drawn by Parliament between the differing interests. On one side are the interests of parents in caring for their own child, a course which prima facie is also in the interests of the child. On the other side there will be circumstances in which the interests of the child may dictate a need for his care to be entrusted to others. In s. 31(2) Parliament has stated the minimum conditions which must be present before the court can look more widely at all the circumstances and decide whether the child's welfare requires that a local authority shall receive the child into their care and have parental responsibility for him. The court must be satisfied that the child is already suffering significant harm. Or the court must be satisfied that, looking ahead, although the child may not yet be suffering such harm, he or she is likely to do so in the future. The court may make a care order if, but only if it is satisfied in one or other of these respects. In this context Parliament cannot have been using likely in the sense of more likely than not. If the word likely were given this meaning, it would have the effect of leaving outside the scope of care and supervision orders cases where the court is satisfied there is a real possibility of significant harm to the child in the future but that possibility falls short of being more likely than not. Strictly, if this were the correct reading of the Act, a care or supervision order would not be available even in a case where the risk of significant harm is as likely as not. Nothing would suffice short of proof that the child will probably suffer significant harm. The difficulty with this interpretation of s. 31(2)(*a*) is that it would draw the boundary line at an altogether inapposite point. What is in issue is the prospect, or risk, of the child suffering significant harm. When exposed to this risk a child may need protection just as much when the risk is considered to be less than fifty-fifty as when the risk is of a higher order. Conversely, so far as the parents are concerned, there is no particular magic in a threshold test based on a probability of significant harm as distinct from a real possibility. It is otherwise if there is no real possibility. It is eminently understandable that Parliament should provide that where there is no real possibility of significant harm, parental responsibility should remain solely with the parents. That makes sense as a threshold in the interests of the parents and the child in a way that a higher threshold, based on probability, would not. In my view, therefore, the context shows that in s. 31(2)(*a*) likely is being used in the sense of a real possibility, a possibility that cannot sensibly be ignored having regard to the nature and gravity of the feared harm in the particular case. By parity of reasoning, the expression likely to suffer significant harm bears the same meaning elsewhere in the Act; for instance, in ss. 43, 44 and 46. Likely also bears a similar meaning, for a similar reason, in the requirement in s. 31(2)(*b*) that the harm or likelihood of harm must be attributable to the care given to the child or 'likely' to be given to him if the order were not made.

The burden of proof

The power of the court to make a care or supervision order only arises if the court is 'satisfied' that the criteria stated in s. 31(2) exist. The expression 'if the court is satisfied', here and elsewhere in the Act, envisages that the court must be judicially satisfied on proper material. ... The legal burden of establishing the existence of these conditions rests on the applicant for a care order. ...

The standard of proof

Where the matters in issue are facts the standard of proof required in non-criminal proceedings is the preponderance of probability, usually referred to as the balance of probability. This is the established general principle. There are exceptions such as contempt of court applications, but I can see no reason for thinking that family proceedings are, or should be, an exception. By family proceedings I mean proceedings so described in the 1989 Act, ss. 105 and 8(3). Despite their special features, family proceedings remain essentially a form of civil proceedings. Family proceedings often raise very serious issues, but so do other forms of civil proceedings. The balance of probability standard means that a court is satisfied an event occurred if the court considers that, on the evidence, the occurrence of the event was more likely than not. When assessing the probabilities the court will have in mind as a factor, to whatever extent is appropriate in the particular case, that the more serious the allegation the less likely it is that the event occurred and, hence, the stronger should be the evidence before the court concludes that the allegation is established on the balance of probability. Fraud is usually less likely than negligence. Deliberate physical injury is usually less likely than accidental physical injury. A step-father is usually less likely to have repeatedly raped and had non-consensual oral sex with his under-age step-daughter than on some occasion to have lost his temper and slapped her. Built into the preponderance of probability standard is a serious degree of flexibility in respect of the seriousness of the allegation. Although the result is much the same, this does not mean that where a serious allegation is in issue the standard of proof required is higher. It means only that the inherent probability or improbability of an event is itself a matter to be taken into account when weighing the probabilities and deciding whether, on balance, the event occurred. The more improbable the event, the stronger must be the evidence that it did occur before, on the balance of probability, its occurrence will be established. Ungoed-Thomas J expressed this neatly in *Re Dellow's Will Trusts, Lloyd's Bank v Institute of Cancer Research* [1964] 1 WLR 451 at p. 455:

> 'The more serious the allegation the more cogent is the evidence required to overcome the unlikelihood of what is alleged and thus to prove it.'

...

The threshold conditions

There is no difficulty, in applying this standard to the threshold conditions. The first limb of s. 31(2)(*a*) predicates an existing state of affairs: that the child is suffering significant harm. The relevant time for this purpose is the date of the care order application or, if temporary protective arrangements have been continuously in place from an earlier date, the date when those arrangements were initiated. This was decided by your Lordships' House in *Re M (A Minor) (Care Order: Threshold Conditions)* [1994] 2 AC 424, [1994] 2 FLR 577. Whether at that time the child was suffering significant harm is an issue to be decided by the court on the basis of the facts admitted or proved before it. The balance of probability standard applies to proof of the facts. The same approach applies to the second limb of s. 31(2)(*a*). This is concerned with evaluating the risk of something happening in the future: aye or no, is there a real possibility that the child will suffer significant harm? Having heard and considered the evidence and decided any disputed questions of relevant fact upon the balance of probability, the court must reach a decision on how highly it evaluates the risk of significant harm befalling the child, always remembering upon whom the burden of proof rests.

...

A conclusion based on facts

The starting-point here is that courts act on evidence. They reach their decisions on the basis of the evidence before them. When considering whether an applicant for a care order has shown that the child is suffering harm or is likely to do so, a court will have regard to the undisputed evidence. The judge will attach to that evidence such weight, or importance, as he considers appropriate. Likewise with regard to disputed evidence which the judge accepts as reliable. None of that is controversial. But the rejection of a disputed allegation as not proved on the balance of probability leaves scope for the possibility that the non-proven allegation may be true after all. There remains room for the judge to have doubts and suspicions on this score. This is the area of controversy. In my view these unresolved judicial doubts and suspicions can no more form the basis of a conclusion that the second threshold condition in s. 31(2)(*a*) has been established than they can form the basis of a conclusion that the first has been established. ...

Thus far I have concentrated on explaining that a court's conclusion that the threshold conditions are satisfied must have a factual base, and that an alleged but unproved fact, serious or trivial, is not a fact for this purpose. Nor is judicial suspicion, because that is no more than a judicial state of uncertainty about whether or not an event happened.

I must now put this into perspective by noting, and emphasising, the width of the range of facts which may be relevant when the court is considering the threshold conditions. The range of facts which may properly be taken into account is infinite. Facts include the history of members of the family, the state of relationships within a family, proposed changes within the membership of a family, parental attitudes, and omissions which might not reasonably have been expected, just as much as actual physical assaults. They include threats, and abnormal behaviour by a child, and unsatisfactory parental responses to complaints or allegations. And facts, which are minor or even trivial if considered in isolation, when taken together may suffice to satisfy the court of the likelihood of future harm. The court will attach to all the relevant facts the appropriate weight when coming to an overall conclusion on the crucial issue. I must emphasise a further point. I have indicated that unproved allegations of maltreatment cannot form the basis for a finding by the court that either limb of s. 31(2)(*a*) is established. It is, of course, open to a court to conclude there is a real possibility that the child will suffer harm in the future although harm in the past has not been established. There will be cases where, although the alleged maltreatment itself is not proved, the evidence does establish a combination of profoundly worrying features affecting the care of the child within the family. In such cases it would be open to a court in appropriate circumstances to find that, although not satisfied the child is yet suffering significant harm, on the basis of such facts as are proved there is a likelihood that he will do so in the future. That is not the present case. The three younger girls are not at risk unless D1 was abused by Mr R in the past. If she was not abused, there is no reason for thinking the others may be. This is not a case where Mr R has a history of abuse. Thus the one and only relevant fact is whether D1 was abused by Mr R as she says. The other surrounding facts, such as the fact that D1 made a complaint and the fact that her mother responded unsatisfactorily, lead nowhere relevant in this case if they do not lead to the conclusion that D1 was abused. To decide that the others are at risk because there is a possibility that D1 was abused would be to base the decision, not on fact, but on suspicion: the suspicion that D1 may have been abused. That would be to lower the threshold prescribed by Parliament.

Conclusion

I am very conscious of the difficulties confronting social workers and others in obtaining hard evidence, which will stand up when challenged in court, of the maltreatment meted out to children behind closed doors. Cruelty and physical abuse are notoriously difficult to prove. The task of social workers is usually anxious and often thankless. They are criticised for not having taken action in response to warning signs which are obvious enough when seen in the clear light of hindsight. Or they are criticised for making applications based on serious allegations which, in the event, are not established in court. Sometimes, whatever they do, they cannot do right. I am also conscious of the difficulties facing judges when there is conflicting testimony on serious allegations. On some occasions judges are left deeply anxious at the end of a case. There may be an understandable inclination to 'play safe' in the interests of the child. Sometimes judges wish to safeguard a child whom they fear may be at risk without at the same time having to fasten a label of very serious misconduct onto one of the parents. These are among the difficulties and considerations Parliament addressed in the Children Act when deciding how, to use the fashionable terminology, the balance should be struck between the various interests. As I read the Act Parliament decided that the threshold for a care order should be that the child is suffering significant harm, or there is a real possibility that he will do so. In the latter regard the threshold is comparatively low. Therein lies the protection for children. But, as I read the Act, Parliament also decided that proof of the relevant facts is needed if this threshold is to be surmounted. Before the s. 1 welfare test and the welfare 'checklist' can be applied, the threshold has to be crossed. Therein lies the protection for parents. They are not to be at risk of having their child taken from them and removed into the care of the local authority on the basis only of suspicions, whether of the judge or of the local authority or anyone else. A conclusion that the child is suffering or is likely to suffer harm must be based on facts, not just suspicion.

Questions

(i) When the Child Care Law Review (p. 616, above) recommended that harm must be 'likely', do you think that they intended to exclude only cases where there was 'no real risk' of harm?

(ii) Horrendous sexual abuse is, hopefully, less common than relatively trivial failures of parental care, but is a child who claims to have been repeatedly raped more likely to be lying than a child who claims to have been slapped once?

(iii) Lord Nicholls pointed out that the case was unusual because everything turned on one allegation. He said that there would be some cases where alleged maltreatment could not be proved, but other proven facts would demonstrate a likelihood of future harm. What sort of facts would demonstrate that someone is likely to harm a child, without demonstrating that he or she has already done so?

The two dissenting speeches focused on whether the evidence, although not enough to prove past abuse, might be sufficient to establish a likelihood of harm:

Lord Browne-Wilkinson: ... To be satisfied of the existence of a risk does not require proof of the occurrence of past historical events but proof of facts which are relevant to the making of a prognosis. ... So in the present case, the major issue was whether D1 had been sexually abused (the macro fact). In the course of the hearing before the judge a number of other facts (the micro facts) were established to the judge's satisfaction by the evidence. The judge in his careful judgment summarised these micro facts: that D1 had been consistent in her story from the time of her first complaint; that her statement was full and detailed showing 'a classic unfolding revelation of progressively worse abuse'; that there were opportunities for such abuse by Mr R and that he had been lying in denying that he had ever been alone either with D1 or with any of the other children; that D2 had made statements which indicated that she had witnessed 'inappropriate' behaviour between Mr R and D1; that the mother (contrary to her evidence) also suspected that something had been going on between Mr R and D1 and had sought to dissuade D2 from saying anything to the social workers.

...

[The judge's] conclusion that there was a real possibility that the evidence of D1 was true was a finding based on evidence and the micro facts that he had found. It was not a mere suspicion as to the risk that Mr R was an abuser: it was a finding of risk based on facts. My Lords, I am anxious that the decision of the House in this case may establish the law in an unworkable form to the detriment of many children at risk. Child abuse, particularly sex abuse, is notoriously difficult to prove in a court of law. The relevant facts are extremely sensitive and emotive. They are often known only to the child and to the alleged abuser. If legal proof of actual abuse is a prerequisite to a finding that a child is at risk of abuse, the court will be powerless to intervene to protect children in relation to whom there are the gravest suspicions of actual abuse but the necessary evidence legally to prove such abuse is lacking. Take the present case. Say that the proceedings had related to D1, the complainant, herself. After a long hearing a judge has reached the conclusion on evidence that there is a 'real possibility' that her evidence is true, ie that she has in fact been gravely abused. Can Parliament really have intended that neither the court nor anyone else should have jurisdiction to intervene so as to protect D1 from any abuse which she may well have been enduring? I venture to think not. My Lords, for those reasons and those given by my noble and learned friend Lord Lloyd of Berwick I would allow the appeal.

Lord Lloyd: ... The case has been fought on the basis that the sole cause for concern is the allegations of sexual abuse made by [D1]. It may be that in that respect the case is unusual, and that in many, if not most cases, a local authority applying for a care order will rely on a number of contributing factors. It is only when the local authority relies, as here, on a single incident or series of incidents relating to the same child, that the problem arises in a stark form. If the court finds on the balance of probabilities that the incidents did not occur, how can it go on to hold that by reason of those incidents there is a real or substantial risk of significant harm in the future?

...

In the usual case, there will be a number of interlocking considerations, all of which will give rise to separate issues of fact, and on all of which, if the Court of Appeal be right, the court would have to make separate findings on the balance of probabilities before proceeding to the second stage. Suppose, for example, there are three or four matters for concern which have led the social services to the belief that a child is at risk, on each of which there is credible evidence, supported, it may be, by evidence from a child psychiatrist, but suppose the evidence is insufficient on any of them to justify a finding that the child has been abused. Is the court powerless to proceed to the second stage? This is not what Parliament has said, and I do not think it is what Parliament intended. Parliament has asked a simple question: Is the court satisfied that there is a serious risk of significant harm in the future? This question should be capable of being answered without too much over-analysis. In an unusual case such as the present, which has been fought on the basis of a single issue of past fact, it will no doubt make sense for the court to start by deciding whether that issue has been proved to its satisfaction, or not. But this is only the beginning. Even if the evidence falls short of proof of the fact in issue, the court must go on to evaluate the evidence on that issue, together with all the other evidence in the case, and ask itself the critical question as to future risk. ...

Questions

(i) Do you agree with Lord Browne-Wilkinson that the opinion of the majority has left the law in an unworkable state?

(ii) What would you advise a local authority to do, if they were very worried that a child was being sexual abused, but did not feel able to prove it?

In many cases, medical evidence will be required to establish whether the threshold test is met.

Re AB (child abuse: expert witness)
[1995] 1 FLR 181, [1995] 1 FCR 280, High Court, Family Division

A baby of 10 weeks was found to have multiple fractures and some brain damage. Several expert witnesses gave evidence that the injuries were non-accidental. However, the parents called an expert who gave evidence that the child's injuries were due to 'temporary brittle bone disease'. Wall J found that the injuries were non-accidental, and gave guidance on the role of expert witnesses in cases of alleged child abuse.

Wall J: ...

The duties of experts in children's cases

...

In my judgment it is of critical importance in discussing the role of the expert witness in children's cases to bear in mind throughout the respective functions of expert and judge. The expert forms an assessment and expresses his opinion within the particular area of his expertise. The judge decides particular issues in individual cases. It is therefore not for the judge to become involved in medical controversy except in the extremely rare case where such a controversy is itself an issue in the case and a judicial assessment of it becomes necessary for the proper resolution of the proceedings. ... The judge's task is difficult enough as it is in sensitive child cases. To have, in addition, to resolve a subtle and complex medical disagreement or to make assessments of the reliability of expert witnesses not only adds immeasurably to the judge's task but, given his fallibility and lack of medical training, may help to lead him to a false conclusion. It is partly for this reason that the current practice of the courts in children's cases is to require disclosure of all medical reports and to invite the experts to confer pre-trial. By these means the ambit of agreement and disagreement can be defined. ...

... there are sometimes cases in which there is a genuine disagreement on a scientific or medical issue, or where it is necessary for a party to advance a particular hypothesis to explain a given set of facts. Where that occurs, the judge will have to resolve the issue which is raised. Two points must be made. In my view, the expert who advances such a hypothesis owes a very heavy duty to explain to the court that what he is advancing is a hypothesis, that it is controversial (if it is) and to place before the court all the material which contradicts the hypothesis. Secondly, he must make all his material available to the other experts in the case. ...

There is also no doubt that unnecessary investigation of medical issues is very expensive and time-wasting. In the instant case, four specialists were called: they all came from different parts of the country. More than a day was spent hearing the medical evidence.

Question

Does justice require that parents should always be able to obtain expert evidence to challenge a local authority's case?

7 The choice of final order

If the s. 31 threshold criteria are established, the court must go on to apply the welfare test in the light of the 'checklist' (p. 532, above) and the 'non-intervention principle' (p. 546, above). Expert evidence may also be important at this stage, and the court will also consider the recommendations of the child's guardian ad litem (see s. 41). The principal options are: a care order, a supervision order, a s. 8 order, or no order at all.

In many cases, the choice will be between a care order or a supervision order. The effect of a care order is the same as the effect of a residence order in favour of a non-parent (p. 658, below), except for the following:

33. – (3) While a care order is in force with respect to a child, the local authority designated by the order shall –

(*a*) have parental responsibility for the child; and

(*b*) have the power (subject to the following provisions of this section) to determine the extent to which a parent or guardian of the child may meet his parental responsibility for him.

(4) The authority may not exercise the power in subsection (3)(*b*) unless they are satisfied that it is necessary to do so in order to safeguard or promote the child's welfare.

(5) Nothing in subsection (3)(*b*) shall prevent a parent or guardian of the child who has care of him from doing what is reasonable in all the circumstances of the case for the purpose of safeguarding or promoting his welfare.

...

(9) The power in subsection (3)(*b*) is subject (in addition to being subject to the provisions of this section) to any right, duty, power, responsibility or authority which a parent or guardian of the child has in relation to the child and his property by virtue of any other enactment.

Before the Children Act 1989, supervision orders were not widely used in child abuse cases. The Review of Child Care Law (1985):

18.5 The Select Committee were concerned about the small number of cases in which supervision orders were made (in 1983 there were about 1,400 supervision orders made in care proceedings as compared with about 3,000 care orders). They suggested that the reason was the perceived ineffectiveness of supervision orders and that these might be used more widely if the supervisor were given greater powers not only over the child but over the parents as well. In particular supervision might be used instead of a care order where the local authority intended to place the child at home on trial if a care order was obtained.

Imposing requirements on parents

18.6 One way forward would be to enable the court to impose conditions on the parent or whoever has the actual custody of the child provided that the actual custodian has had an opportunity to be heard. ...

18.7 Whether the requirements under a supervision order are met may depend on the parent rather than the child, especially where the child is young. At present orders may be frustrated, for example simply by the parent refusing the supervisor access to the child. Refusal to allow a supervised child to be visited or medically examined is now automatically reasonable cause for suspicion so that a warrant to search for and remove the child may be obtained. Nevertheless, where the object of the supervision is in fact to impose requirements on the parents for the protection of the child we consider that the court should have express power to do so. ...

18.9 As to what requirements precisely the court should be able to impose on adults the following list has occurred to us:

a. to keep the supervisor informed of his address and that of the child;

b. to allow the supervisor access to the child in the home and to assess the child's welfare, needs and condition;

c. to allow the child to be medically examined;

d. to comply with the supervisor's direction to attend with the child at a specified place (such as a clinic or day centre) for the purpose of medical examination, medical or psychiatric treatment, or participation in specified activities;

e. to permit the child to receive medical or psychiatric treatment; and

f. to comply with the supervisor's directions on matters relating to the child's education.

18.15 The power to require the child to live with a named individual will in our view be largely overtaken by our recommendation that the court in care proceedings should have power to grant legal custody to another person for example a relative or friend and should therefore be abolished. This will have the advantage of clarifying the legal status of the other person and enabling him to combine both the powers and responsibilities of a parent. The order could be coupled with a supervision order if required.

The Children Act 1989 implemented these recommendations in s. 15 and Sch. 2, Parts I and II. However, supervision orders are still made much less often than care orders. Judicial statistics show that during 1995 there were 4,238 care orders made, compared with 1,321 supervision orders (Lord Chancellor's Department, 1996). Some of the reasons why care orders are often preferred are shown by the next case:

Re D (a minor) (care or supervision order)
[1993] 2 FCR 88, [1993] 2 FLR 423, High Court, Family Division

While in the father's care, a child aged 4 had been injured, and a baby aged 2 months had died from a fractured skull and many other injuries. The father had been convicted of wilful cruelty, but acquitted of murder. The case concerned a baby, R, who was born after the father was released from prison. The local authority applied for a care or supervision order, and the judge found that the s. 31 threshold test was satisfied because there was a serious risk of violence from the father towards the child. The local authority argued that a care order would undermine the co-operation which they were receiving from the child's parents. The guardian ad litem argued that a care order was necessary to protect the child.

Ewbank J: ... At first sight it would appear that a supervision order should be made if the child is living with the parents, a care order if the child is not living with the parents. But the statute is more flexible than that. ... it is open under a care order for the child to live with the parents, as in this case.

A supervision order can only be made in the first instance for one year, as provided by Sch. 3, para. 6(1) to the Children Act. Paragraphs 6(3) and (4) allow an extension for a further 2 years. Schedule 3, paras 2, 3 and 4 provide for directions to be given on a supervision order. ... It is suggested that these paragraphs and the powers given to the supervising officer would enable the child's welfare to be monitored by regular medical examinations, by attendance at a children's centre, and directions as to where the child should live, and any other directions which seem appropriate.

If there is a breach of a supervision order the supervising officer, under s. 35(1)(*c*), has to consider whether to apply to the court for a variation of the supervision order or the discharge of the order. There is no direct way of enforcing the directions made under a supervision order.

...

If a care order were made then, under s. 33(3)(*a*), the local authority would have parental responsibility for R and they would have the power to limit the parental responsibility of the mother and father if they thought it was necessary under s. 33(3)(*b*). Under reg. 9 of the Placement of Children with Parents Etc Regulations 1991 the local authority have to satisfy themselves of the welfare of a child who has been placed by them and might visit the child in any event at intervals of not more than 6 weeks during the first year of the placement and thereafter at intervals of not more than 3 months. The advantage of a care order as opposed to a supervision order, in the submission of the guardian ad litem, is that a care order is unlimited in time and can only be revoked by an application to the court and even when revoked the court can substitute a supervision order. That is under s. 39 of the Children Act. The local authority feel that a care order is too strong an order to be made in the circumstances of this case. They feel that they are working well together with the parents and that a care order would undermine that. But in my judgment that approach misses the real point in the case. The point in the case is the protection of R. ...

... The life of this family is harmonious. The child is thriving and much loved by his mother and father. But the protection of the child, in my judgment, is the most important aspect of this case and the decisive point in coming to a decision whether there should be a supervision order or a care order is that, in my judgment, if there is to be a lifting of the safeguards surrounding this child that lifting ought to be done by the court on consideration of the evidence and the lifting of the safeguards ought not to be left to the responsibility of individuals. So, in my judgment, a care order should be made in this case, despite the views of the local authority. ...

Questions

(i) Are you surprised that the local authority placed so much weight on the need to maintain the co-operation of the parents?
(ii) Could the court have made a care order against the wishes of the local authority, if the local authority had not originally applied for a care or supervision order (see *Nottinghamshire County Council v P* [1994] Fam 18, [1993] 3 All ER 815, [1993] 3 WLR 637, [1993] 2 FLR 134, p. 630, below)?

However, supervision orders are sometimes appropriate, even when there are very serious concerns about children's safety:

Manchester City Council v B
[1996] 1 FLR 324, [1996] Fam Law 202, High Court, Family Division

A baby, Z, was admitted to hospital and was found to have brain haemorrhages. After neurosurgery, he eventually recovered. There was a conflict of expert evidence as to whether the injuries were non-accidental. The local authority applied for a care or supervision order. At the hearing the guardian ad litem and the local authority both proposed that the child should be rehabilitated with his parents under a supervision order.

Bracewell J: ... On the totality of all the evidence, I find to the appropriate standard of proof, and commensurate with the serious nature of these allegations, that these normally loving, caring parents, were driven beyond their endurance and tolerance by the difficulties presented by this child and by the frustration of lack of medical support and in their stress, behaved wholly out of character in one desperate incident of shaking, probably accompanied by projection of the child onto a cot or bed. It was a temporary phase. It is even understandable in the light of their youth and inexperience and the difficulty of this child and I am sure it was not done out of any malice or desire to hurt the child. I find it was some act of despair but, of course, it was life-threatening and, in consequence, represents significant harm and it was not the care which it would be reasonable to expect a parent to give within the meaning of s. 31.

In those circumstances, I am satisfied that the threshold criteria are established. Once that is established, the court has a menu of options governed by the welfare checklist and s. 1 which I apply.

It was a life-threatening injury, but it is agreed by all, and I accept, that the welfare of the child demands rehabilitation to these parents who, apart from this isolated lapse, have demonstrated a high standard of care and commitment.

The question arises whether protection of any order is needed and, if one is needed, which order is best for the welfare of the child. I am satisfied that some statutory protection is required to safeguard the child, so that the local authority can monitor the situation. I have considered very carefully if a supervision order would be adequate. The parents have expressed willingness to co-operate and have done so in the past. Of course, it has to be borne in mind that a supervision order does not have teeth, does not lay down statutory level of intervention, does not give the local authority parental responsibility, does not allow for rapid intervention to remove the child without further order of the court.

The potential consequences to the child of any further incident are very serious indeed. However, although a care order is in no way inconsistent with rehabilitation nor partnership with the family, I have been extremely impressed with the very careful and helpful analysis of the guardian ad litem. I would like to thank him for the way in which he has approached this task and I have concluded, in all the circumstances, that a supervision order for one year to the local authority is the order which will protect and provide for Z's welfare.

Question

Would the parents regard a supervision order as having 'no teeth'?

Another possibility, introduced by the Children Act 1989, is for the court to make s. 8 orders (see p. 528, above). Local authorities are prohibited from applying for residence or contact orders by s. 9(2) of the Children Act 1989. However, they can invite the court to make an order of its own motion under s. 10(1)(*b*), or support an application by another person. If the parents have separated, a residence order in favour of one parent may be appropriate where the risk to the child comes from the other parent, or there may be a member of the extended family who is able to care for the child adequately. However, as in *Re M* (p. 618, above), a care order may still be appropriate in such cases.

Re K (care order or residence order)
[1995] 1 FLR 675, [1996] 1 FCR 365, High Court, Family Division

The local authority applied for care orders in relation to two children, aged 5 and 6. One of them had suffered an injury while in the care of their mother, who was schizophrenic. The children went to live with their grandparents under interim care orders. They were diagnosed as suffering from an incurable muscle-wasting disease which would confine them to wheelchairs by the age of 10. The local authority asked the court to make a supervision order and a residence order in favour of the grandparents. The grandparents' position was that a care order would give them greater support, and they did not want the responsibility of a residence order. The mother supported the making of a care order because that would require the local authority to promote contact between her and the children (s. 34, see p. 649, below). The local authority eventually withdrew its opposition to a care order.

Stuart-White J: ... First, I find it rather difficult to conceive of circumstances in which it would not be wrong in principle to oblige an individual who has not applied for and does not desire a residence order, with its concomitant parental responsibility, to accept such an order and such responsibility. I accept that the power to make such an order does exist under s. 10(1)(*b*) of the Act, but it seems to me that the cases in which it would be right to exercise that power in the circumstances which I have mentioned, must be wholly exceptional, and this is not a wholly exceptional case of that kind.

The second principle which seems to me to emerge is this: that if I do not exercise the power to impose a residence order and parental responsibility on individuals who do not want it, then the only persons with parental responsibility will be the mother and the father. It is not suggested, as I understand it, that there exist any practicable means of preventing their exercising that parental responsibility with potentially harmful and possibly disastrous effects on the children, save by the making of a public law order: see *Nottinghamshire County Council v P* [1993] 1 FLR 514, and the Court of Appeal decision in the same case at [1994] Fam 18, [1993] 2 FLR 134. Thus, in the absence of a residence order, it seems to me that the argument that there are no child protection concerns could not be and cannot be maintained.

The third point of principle is this: I accept that in ordinary circumstances the court should be slow indeed to make a care order to a local authority which has applied for it but ultimately decides that it does not want it. The court will plainly, it seems to me, only make such an order under what may be unusual circumstances. The power to do so of course not only exists, it is in a sense emphasised by the Family Proceedings Rules 1991 (SI 1991/1247), r. 4.5, which provides that any application may only be withdrawn with leave. ... If the court concludes that the threshold criteria are satisfied and the welfare of the child demands it, a conclusion of course which would only be reached after considering the matters set out in s. 1(3) of the Act, then in my judgment the court should not shrink from making such a care order, even if the local authority which has applied for it should change its mind. Similarly, where the application is for a supervision order, the court should not in like circumstances shrink from exercising its powers under s. 31(5)(*b*) of the Act to make a care order.

Thirdly, whereas it will often be unnecessary and inappropriate to make a care order within the context of a family placement, I am not prepared to go so far as to say that it is only in exceptional circumstances that such an order should be made in that context. There may very well be circumstances where the making of a care order is the only way to protect children placed with members of their extended families from significant harm.

Fourthly, whilst it would be wholly inappropriate to make a care order solely for the purpose of conferring a financial benefit on the carers, the fact that such a financial benefit if it accrues will materially contribute to the welfare of the child, is in my judgment a factor which can properly be regarded as relevant in the balancing exercise which in any case like this is demanded. There is a complex interrelation between the general duties owed by all local authorities to children in need in their areas and the specific duties owed to children in care, as set out in ss. 31, 22, 23 and 24 of the Act, and in the relevant regulations, including the Review of Children's Cases Regulations 1991 (SI 1991/895) and the Foster Placement (Children) Regulations 1991 (SI 1991/910), to the details of which I have helpfully had my attention drawn.

...

Now bearing in mind these general principles as I have endeavoured no doubt inadequately to enunciate them, and on the overwhelming weight of the evidence in this unusual and in many ways tragic case, I have no hesitation in holding that the welfare of these children demands that a care order be made. That will provide them with security and protection during their minorities. I am quite sure that the applicant local authority has shown both good sense and, as one would expect, a true concern for these children in making the concession that it has made. I therefore make care orders in each case.

With leave of the court, local authorities can apply for specific issue orders and prohibited steps orders under s. 8. However, these are limited by s. 9(5) of the 1989 Act, and their use in child protection cases has been restricted following the decision of the Court of Appeal in the following case:

Nottinghamshire County Council v P
[1994] Fam 18, [1993] 3 All ER 815, [1993] 3 WLR 637, [1993] 2 FLR 134, [1994] 1 FCR 624, Court of Appeal

The eldest of three sisters claimed that she had been sexually abused by her father, and that he was also abusing her younger sisters aged 16 and 13. Leave was granted for the local authority to apply for a prohibited steps order requiring the father not to live in the same household as the girls, and not to have contact with them. The local authority decided not to seek care or supervision orders, which it considered would be ineffective. Ward J at first instance decided that s. 9(5) prevented him from making the order requested. The local authority appealed.

Sir Stephen Brown P: ... Section 9(5) of the Act of 1989 provides:

> 'No court shall exercise its power to make a specific issue order or prohibited steps order – (*a*) with a view to achieving a result which could be achieved by making a residence or contact order; or (*b*) in any way which is denied to the High Court [by section 100(2)] in the exercise of its inherent jurisdiction with respect to children.'

In the view of this court the application for a prohibited steps order by this local authority was in reality being made with a view to achieving a result which could be achieved by making a residence or contact order. Section 9(2) specifically provides:

> 'No application may be made by a local authority for a residence order or contact order and no court shall make such an order in favour of a local authority.'

The court is satisfied that the local authority was indeed seeking to enter by the 'back door' as it were. It agrees with Ward J that he had no power to make a prohibited steps order in this case. Submissions were made to the court to the effect that a contact order in any event necessarily implied a positive order and that an order which merely provided for 'no contact' could not be construed as a contact order. There are certain passages in editorial comment which seem to support that view. We do not share it. We agree with the judge that the sensible and appropriate construction of the term contact order includes a situation where a court is required to consider whether any contact should be provided for. An order that there shall be 'no contact' falls within the general concept of contact and common sense requires that it should be considered to fall within the definition of 'contact order' in section 8(1). We agree with the reasoning of Ward J and would therefore dismiss the appeal of the local authority against his refusal of its application for a prohibited steps order. A wider question arises as to policy. We consider that this court should make it clear that the route chosen by the local authority in this case was wholly inappropriate. In cases where children are found to be at risk of suffering significant harm within the meaning of section 31 of the Children Act 1989 a clear duty arises on the part of local authorities to take steps to protect them. In such circumstances a local authority is required to assume responsibility and to intervene in the family arrangements in order to protect the child. Part IV specifically provides them with wide powers and a wide discretion. As already pointed out the Act envisages that local authorities may place children with their parents even though they may have a care order under section 31. A supervision order may be viewed as being less draconian but it gives the local authority a wide discretion as to how to deal with children and with the family. A prohibited steps order would not afford the local authority any authority as to how it might deal with the children. There may be situations, for example where a child is accommodated by a local authority, where it would be appropriate to seek a prohibited steps order for some particular purpose. However, it could not in any circumstances be regarded as providing a substitute for an order under Part IV of the Act of 1989. Furthermore, it is very doubtful indeed whether a prohibited steps order could in any circumstances be used to 'oust' a father from a matrimonial home. Although counsel had prepared detailed submissions upon this aspect of the matter it has not been necessary to consider the point in order to resolve this appeal. It is a most regrettable feature of this case that the local authority having initially intervened under Part V of the Act of 1989 in order to obtain an emergency protection order did not then proceed to seek orders under section 31 in Part IV of the Act. This is even more regrettable after Judge Heald had directed the local authority to consider the position pursuant to a direction under section 37 of the Act. ...

... Since the fact of the risk of significant harm to the children has been established and not contradicted there remains upon the local authority the clear duty to take steps to safeguard the welfare of these children. It should not shrink from taking steps under Part IV of the Act. It appears from submissions made by all counsel in this court that the mother, the father and the children by their guardian ad litem would not resist the making of a supervision order in favour of the local authority pursuant to section 31 of the Act. That at least would afford a basis for the local authority to take some constructive steps in order to protect these children. This court is deeply concerned at the absence of any power to direct this authority to take steps to protect the children. In the former wardship jurisdiction it might well have been able to do so. The operation of the Children Act 1989 is entirely dependent upon the full co-operation of all those involved. This includes the courts, local authorities, social workers, and all who have to deal with children. Unfortunately, as appears from this case, if a local authority doggedly resists taking the steps which are appropriate to the case of children at risk of suffering significant harm it appears that the court is powerless. The authority may perhaps lay itself open to an application for judicial review but in a case such as this the question arises, at whose instance? The position is one which it is to be hoped will not recur and that lessons will be learnt from this unhappy catalogue of errors. For the reasons set out in this judgment, the court dismisses the appeal of the local authority and allows the appeals of the other appellants.

Questions

(i) Would a care or supervision order have adequately protected the children in this case?
(ii) Should a court be able to require a reluctant local authority to bring proceedings under s. 31?

The restrictions of the High Court's inherent (wardship) jurisdiction are contained in s. 100 of the Children Act 1989, which was one of the most controversial parts of the legislation:

Restrictions on use of wardship jurisdiction
100. – (1) Section 7 of the Family Law Reform Act 1969 (which gives the High Court power to place a ward of court in the care, or under the supervision, of a local authority) shall cease to have effect.
(2) No court shall exercise the High Court's inherent jurisdiction with respect to children –
(*a*) so as to require a child to be placed in the care, or put under the supervision, of a local authority;
(*b*) so as to require a child to be accommodated by or on behalf of a local authority;
(*c*) so as to make a child who is the subject of a care order a ward of court; or
(*d*) for the purpose of conferring on any local authority power to determine any question which has arisen, or which may arise, in connection with any aspect of parental responsibility for a child.
(3) No application for any exercise of the court's inherent jurisdiction with respect to children may be made by a local authority unless the authority have obtained the leave of the court.
(4) The court may only grant leave if it is satisfied that –
(*a*) the result which the authority wish to achieve could not be achieved through the making of any order of a kind to which subsection (5) applies; and
(*b*) there is reasonable cause to believe that if the court's inherent jurisdiction is not exercised with respect to the child he is likely to suffer significant harm.
(5) This subsection applies to any order –
(*a*) made otherwise than in the exercise of the court's inherent jurisdiction; and
(*b*) which the local authority is entitled to apply for (assuming, in the case of any application which may only be made with leave, that leave is granted).

These provisions mean that local authorities can only invoke the inherent jurisdiction in order to achieve a result which cannot be achieved under another provision of the Children Act 1989, and only then if there is reasonable cause to believe that the child is otherwise likely to suffer significant harm. These provision were considered in the following case:

Devon County Council v S
[1994] Fam 169, [1995] 1 All ER 243, [1994] 3 WLR 183, [1994] 1 FLR 355, High Court, Family Division

The local authority were concerned because the mother of several children was prepared to treat a man with three convictions for sexual offences as a member of the family. The children were successfully protected by prohibited steps orders, until *Nottinghamshire County Council v P* (p. 630, above). Following that decision, the local authority attempted to achieve a similar result by an application under the inherent jurisdiction. Leave was refused by the District Judge, and the local authority appealed.

Thorpe J: ... It is common ground between counsel that the terms of section 100(4)(*b*), namely, that there is reasonable cause to believe that if the court's inherent jurisdiction is not exercised with respect to the child he is likely to suffer significant harm, were satisfied. ... To my mind it is simple and not erroneous to conclude that the county council intends to invite the court to exercise its inherent jurisdiction to protect children rather than to have protective powers conferred on itself [contrary to section 100(2)(*d*)]. In relation to section 100(4)(*a*), [Mr. Meredith] submitted that the result at which the prospective application aimed was not one that could be achieved by any other route. Whilst the county council might apply for a care order under section 31, that would result in a far wider invasion of the mother's parental responsibility, with the risk of destabilisation of the children's parental care and with some risk of local stigma. In short, it might do more harm than good. He distinguished *Nottingham County Council v P* [1994] Fam 18, where the resident father constituted the risk to the children. That situation was classically managed by a care order, which would not necessarily be used to separate the children from their mother. But it would be quite inappropriate to protect the children from an external risk. Equally, Mr. Meredith submitted, a supervision order did not achieve the same result. All that would do would be to direct the functions of the mother, functions which she was already performing satisfactorily without direction. It did not control the only individual who required control, namely, Y. ... I cannot see how injunctions preventing an external adult from contacting or communicating with children at any time or in any place could be equated with either a care order or a supervision order. I did wonder why the possibility of the local authority protecting children from a potential abuser by invoking the inherent jurisdiction had not been considered in *Nottingham County Council v P*. Mrs. Gifford, who appeared for the father in that case throughout, said that it had been considered by the local authority to protect the eldest child who had left home. However, when mooted her client had offered an undertaking so that the point had not been argued. In respect of the younger children the local authority had relied exclusively on the prohibited steps application. I therefore conclude that the decision which I have reached is not at odds with the principles established by the judgment of Sir Stephen Brown P in *Nottingham County Council v P*. Any member of the family, or any other with a sufficient standing, might apply to the court to exercise its inherent power to protect these children. Where no one else invokes that protection, it seems to me quite wrong that the local authority should be excluded from doing so by a restrictive construction of section 100 of the Children Act 1989. I therefore allow the appeal and grant the leave sought.

Questions

(i) Why was the local authority in this case not criticised for failing to seek a care or supervision order, as the local authority in the *Nottinghamshire* case (p. 630, above) had been?
(ii) Could a local authority use the inherent jurisdiction to order a father to leave his home because he is a risk to his children (see *Re S (minors) (inherent jurisdiction: ouster)* [1994] 1 FLR 623, cf *Pearson v Franklin* [1994] 2 All ER 137, [1994] 1 WLR 370, [1994] 1 FLR 246, CA)?
(iii) The Family Law Act 1996 amends the Children Act 1989, so that an exclusion requirement may be attached to an emergency protection order or an interim care order under ss. 38A and 44A of the Children Act (see p. 614, above). Why do these provisions not allow the court to exclude an abuser from the child's home indefinitely?

Further difficulties arise following another decision of the Court of Appeal:

Re H (prohibited steps order)
[1995] 4 All ER 110, [1995] 1 WLR 667, [1995] 1 FLR 638, Court of Appeal

A man, Mr J, sexually abused one of the mother's children while living with the mother. The local authority was granted a care order on one child and supervision orders on the rest. The judge placed a condition on the supervision orders that there be no contact with Mr J, and also made a prohibited steps order against the mother to prevent contact between Mr J and the children. He refused to make a prohibited steps order against Mr J, who was not a party to the proceedings. The children's guardian ad litem appealed.

Butler-Sloss LJ: ... The prohibited steps order appears to me directly to contravene s. 9(5) since to make a prohibited steps order against the mother would achieve the same result as a contact order requiring the mother not to allow contact with Mr J and could be enforced in the same way. Equally, the condition made as part of the supervision order does not appear to come with the provisions of Sch. 3, Parts I and II. ... [A condition of no contact] cannot be imposed as part of a supervision order.

In my view a prohibited steps order which requires Mr J not to have nor to seek contact with the children does not contravene s. 9(5). If a 'no contact order' had been made in this case to the mother the order would be directed at the mother as the subject of the order and the obligation would be placed upon her to prevent any contact by the children with Mr J. There could not be a 'no contact order' which would direct Mr J not to have nor seek contact with the four children since he does not live with the children. A contact order directed at the mother would not achieve the required result. ... With the best will in the world this mother could not protect her children going to or from school or at school or at play, nor could the school or even the police in the absence of any injunctive order directed at Mr J.

... [In *Nottinghamshire County Council v P* (p. 630, above)] the local authority sought to rely upon a prohibited steps order by the local authority in preference to applying for an order under Part IV of the Act. The objections expressed in the judgment of the court, with which I respectfully agree, to the application in private proceedings for a prohibited steps order, do not arise on this appeal. ... In the present case the local authority has obtained s. 31 orders and the mother and the guardian ad litem of the children seek the prohibited steps order to meet a situation which cannot be achieved by a contact order.

Question

In the light of this decision, do you think that Thorpe J was right to find that s. 100(4)(*a*) was satisfied in *Devon County Council v S* (p. 632, above)?

As well as limits on the ability of local authorities to use the inherent jurisdiction to protect children, there are also limits on the ability of the courts to control local authorities. In *Nottinghamshire County Council v P* (p. 630, above) the court was concerned about its inability to force a local authority to make an application for a care and supervision order. In other cases, the concern relates to the inability to supervise the local authority after a care order has been made.

Whereas a supervision order can be combined with a s. 8 order, the Children Act 1989 made it clear that s. 8 orders and care orders are incompatible:

9. – (1) No court shall make any section 8 order, other than a residence order, with respect to a child who is in the care of a local authority.

91. – (1) The making of a residence order with respect to a child who is the subject of a care order discharges the care order.

(2) The making of a care order with respect to a child who is the subject of any section 8 order discharges that order.

(3) The making of a care order with respect to a child who is the subject of a supervision order discharges that other order.

(4) The making of a care order with respect to a child who is a ward of court brings that wardship to an end.

(5) The making of a care order with respect to a child who is the subject of a school attendance order made under section 37 of the Education Act 1944 discharges the school attendance order.

(6) Where an emergency protection order is made with respect to a child who is in care, the care order shall have effect subject to the emergency protection order.

Furthermore, the inherent jurisdiction cannot be used to dictate how a local authority exercises its responsibilities under a care order.

A v Liverpool City Council
[1982] AC 363, [1981] 2 All ER 385, [1981] 2 WLR 948, 145 JP 318, 125 Sol Jo 396, 79 LGR 621, House of Lords

This was a 'leap-frog' appeal direct from the High Court to the House of Lords against the decision of Balcombe J that he was bound by authority to dismiss a mother's application to have her child made a ward of court without investigating the merits of her case.

Lord Roskill: ... My Lords, I do not think it necessary to review the authorities on the inter-relationship between prerogative and statutory powers. The basic principles were authoritatively determined by your Lordships' House in *A-G v De Keyser's Royal Hotel Ltd* [1920] AC 508: see especially the speech of Lord Summer ([1920] AC 508 at 561). My Lords, I do not doubt that the wardship jurisdiction of the court is not extinguished by the existence of the legislation regarding the care and control of deprived children, a phrase I use to include children whose parents have for some reason failed to discharge their parental duties towards them. I am not aware of any decision which suggests otherwise. ...

[This was the view] which found favour with the Court of Appeal in *Re M.* Lord Evershed MR, with whom Upjohn and Pearson LJJ expressly concurred, stated his first two conclusions thus ([1961] Ch 328 at 345, [1961] 1 All ER 788 at 795):

> '(i) The prerogative right of the Queen as parens patriae in relation to infants within the realm is not for all purposes ousted or abrogated as the result of the exercise of the duties and powers by local authorities under the Children Act, 1948: in particular the power to make an infant a ward of court by invocation of s. 9 of the Act of 1949 is unaffected. (ii) But even where a child is made a ward of court by virtue of the Act of 1949, the judge in whom the prerogative power is vested will, acting on familiar principles, not exercise control in relation to duties or discretions clearly vested by statute in the local authority, and may, therefore, and in a case such as the present normally will, order that the child cease to be a ward of court.'

The statutory codes which existed in 1954 and in 1961 have been elaborated and extended and amended several times since these decisions as the social needs of our society have changed and, unhappily, the number of deprived children in the care of local authorities has tragically increased. ... This hardly suggests an intention by Parliament to restrict the scope of the statutory control by local authorities of child welfare in favour of the use by the courts of the prerogative wardship jurisdiction. On the contrary, the plain intention of this legislation is to secure the continued expansion of that statutory control.

I do not think that the language of s. 1 of the Guardianship of Infants Act 1925 and of its statutory successor in any way points in a contrary direction. The former statute, as its preamble shows, was largely designed to secure equality of rights as between father and mother in relation to their children and making the welfare of those children paramount in relation to those two henceforth equal interests. Nor do I think that the emphasis laid on that section in your Lordships' House in *J v C* [1970] AC 668, [1969] 1 All ER 788 [p. 411, above] casts any doubt on the correctness of the several earlier decisions to which I have already referred.

I am of the clear opinion that, while prerogative jurisdiction of the court in wardship cases remains, the exercise of that jurisdiction has been and must continue to be treated as circumscribed by the existence of the far-ranging statutory code which entrusts the care and control of deprived children to local authorities. It follows that the undoubted wardship jurisdiction must not be exercised so as to interfere with the day-to-day administration by local authorities of that statutory control.

My Lords, to say that is not to suggest that local authorities are immune from judicial control: in an appropriate case, as Lord Evershed MR himself said in *Re M,* the Wednesbury principle is available. The remedy of judicial review under RSC Ord. 53 is also available in an appropriate case.
Appeal dismissed.

Questions

(i) Is this reasoning on the inter-relationship of prerogative and statutory powers convincing?
(ii) Do you agree with the Law Commission (1987) that there must be 'concern that nothing can be done for the child's welfare even where a local authority have acted in breach or disregard of their statutory responsibilities'?

It follows that when the court makes a care order, it cannot dictate how the local authority should implement the order.

Re T (a minor) (care order: conditions)
[1994] 2 FLR 423, [1994] 2 FCR 721, Court of Appeal

Seven girls had been taken into care, following allegations that the two eldest had been sexually abused by their step-father. He was the father of the two youngest girls, and of a baby boy who was born after the care orders were made. The local authority obtained an emergency protection order, and applied for a care order. The judge made an interim care order, and ordered the local authority to carry out an assessment while the child was living at home. The child was returned home, and the parents' care of the child was found to be excellent. The local authority, supported by the guardian ad litem, asked for a care order with a view to adoption. The judge decided that the s. 31 threshold criteria were met because of 'a real, albeit low, risk of sexual abuse', but decided to make a supervision order. The local authority appealed, and made it clear that the child would be removed from home and placed for adoption if a care order was granted. By the time the appeal was heard, the guardian ad litem had changed her mind. She recommended that there should be a care order, but the child should remain at home. The Court of Appeal considered whether it was possible to achieve this result:

Nourse LJ: ... the proposition that the court's general inherent power is always available to fill gaps or to supplement the powers of the local authority cannot be applied to a situation in which Parliament by express enactment, has committed specific powers exclusively to the local authority.

It follows that the court does not have the power to make a care order containing either a direction or a condition that the child in question shall reside at home ... Our final observation on the law is that it is the duty of any court hearing an application for a care order carefully to scrutinise the local authority's care plan. If it does not agree with the care plan, it can refuse to make a care order: see *Re J (Minors) (Care: Care Plan)* [1994] 1 FLR 253 at p. 261C–D. The cases in which it is appropriate to take such a course will no doubt be rare.

... The threshold criteria for both care and supervision orders are the same. It follows that there will be cases (of which this is one) where the court finds the threshold critera to be met, and then has to decide whether the level of risk is such that a care order is necessary to protect the child, or whether the risk of harm can be catered for by a supervision order. The judge plainly took the view that this case fell into the latter category and, given his finding both that the parents were capable of bringing up the child and that it would be inimical to his welfare to be removed from their care (both findings that it was open to him to make), it was not then open to him to make a care order.

The local authority's appeal was dismissed. However, because of concerns that the father had been sleeping in the same bed as the child, the Court of Appeal made a residence order in favour of the parents and attached a condition under s. 11(7) of the Children Act 1989 that the father not share a bed with the child under any circumstances.

Questions

(i) Why is it appropriate for a court to attach conditions to a s. 8 order but not a care order?
(ii) How can the court decide whether a care order is in a child's interests, if it cannot be sure whether the child will be rehabilitated with the parents, or placed in a children's home, with a succession of short-term foster-parents, or with a long-term substitute family?
(iii) Is it possible to separate the decision about the child's placement, from the decision about the level of contact to be allowed between the child and the parents?

These questions require us to consider the legal framework which governs contact between children in care and their parents, and the provision of substitute families for these children. The next chapter will consider these issues.

Chapter 14

The 'permanency' principle: who are my family?

Former foster child A: It was only recently I was told that my natural parents could have removed me at any time if they wanted to. Even now when I think of it I shudder. ... For me they would have been total strangers. Why remove me when I was so happy? I have met my natural mother recently and I see her from time to time. There is no bond between us. My 'mum' is my foster mum and my 'dad' is my foster dad. If I call my natural mother 'mum' when I meet her it is just for saving face. ...
Former foster child D: I must have been 7 when I went to live with my foster parents. They were the second family I went to. The first family went abroad after promising to take me with them. They didn't and it broke my heart at the time. ... The [foster parents] had two of their own and another foster child. Somehow I never felt I belonged there. We foster children did not fit in very well. I cannot say that I developed much attachment to them. My foster mother often threatened to send me back to the Corporation. Sometimes she would ring them but they would make her change her mind. I suppose I was difficult too, and I would hark back or argue. She would then smack me and send me to bed ... I could be nasty and so could my foster mother ... I left at 17 when our quarrels became worse, and I went to live in a hostel.

These telling quotations come from John Triseliotis' study, *Growing Up in Foster Care and After* (1980). Whenever children have to be looked after away from home for any length of time, for whatever reasons, three questions arise. First, is the ultimate plan that they should go back home eventually, as most children do, or is it that they should stay away permanently? Secondly, if they are to stay away, what should be the legal basis on which they do so – fostering, adoption or something in between? Thirdly, what in any event should be their links with their family of origin? We shall look first at the development of social work thinking and research on these issues, then at how these have affected the law on family links, the position of relatives and foster carers, and finally the law and practice of adoption.

1 The 'permanency' principle

The evolution of the 'permanency' principle in child care began with the problems experienced with foster care, summed up by Jean Packman in *The Child's Generation* (1981):

Originally, fostering had frequently been seen as an *alternative* to parental care, when the latter had proved inadequate. Before children's departments existed many children who were fostered lost all contact with their natural families and the fostering became a 'de facto' adoption ... The Children Act [1948], moving away from this position, stipulated that children must be rehabilitated with their own families, when this was consistent with their welfare, and ... the concept was increasingly applied. Though fostering was the favoured method of care, promising as it did a 'natural' upbringing and the warmth and intimate relationships that children need, it was now more often a short-term or impermanent arrangement, incorporating a far greater degree of sharing. If children were to be rehabilitated, they must be kept in close touch with their natural parents. ... What was expected of foster parents became at once more subtle and more difficult. They must confer on the child all the benefits of loving family care, but should not seek to replace the parents in his affections. Their compassion and acceptance must be extended from the child himself, to his parents as well – even where the latter seemed 'to blame' for some of his past deprivations. They should act toward him as a good parent, yet give him up when the department judged the time to be ripe.

If it was difficult for the foster carers, it was even more difficult for the children, as Jane Rowe and her colleagues point out in *Long-Term Foster Care* (1984):

Being a foster child is not easy. The study children have revealed something of the stresses of having to answer questions, of feeling different and of anxieties and unanswered questions about the past and the future. ... Our findings confirm those of Triseliotis (1983) and of Fanshel and Shinn (1978). Summing up the differences between young adults who had been adopted as older children and young adults who had been fostered, Triseliotis concluded:

> 'Compared to those who grew up in long-term fostering, adoptees in general appeared more confident and secure with fewer doubts about themselves and about their capacity to cope with life ... In spite of the strong psychological bonds between those fostered and their foster parents, the ambiguous nature of the arrangement seemed to have a qualitative impact on the former's sense of identity.'

A very similar conclusion is drawn by Fanshel and Shinn (1978) though they, too, are tentative. At the end of their massive five-year longitudinal study of 624 children, these authors support the view that children should be afforded permanency in their living arrangements if at all possible, though they hasten to add that they do not take this position on the basis of their data but because:

> 'We are not completely sure that continued tenure in foster care over extended periods is not in itself harmful to children ... We fear that in the inner recesses of his heart, a child who is not living with his own family or who is not adopted may come to think of himself as being less than first-rate, as an unwanted human being.'

... The inescapable conclusion of our findings is that many long-term foster children would be better off if they were adopted by their foster parents, not because being fostered is so bad but because it is not quite good enough. However, one must hasten to add that it would be a serious mistake to assume that *all* long-term foster children could or should be adopted. ...

Distinguishing which children should be adopted is not easy and cannot be done by any general rule about length of stay or even on the basis of parental contact, though both may be useful guides. In our study we had examples of children who were in touch with parents but who nevertheless wanted very much to be adopted. There were a few children who had no parental contact who, nevertheless felt a strong sense of natural family identity. For them, adoption would have seemed like an intrusion. ... there are also foster parents who do not want to adopt even though they have a strong bond to the child and are committed to providing a permanent home. A crucial issue is whether or not the child *feels* secure.

The development of thinking about 'permanency' is described by Judith Stone in *Making Positive Moves – Developing Short-term Fostering Services* (1995):

Rethinking policy

A number of worrying themes had emerged in the early part of the 1970s. George's study [1970] confirmed that high levels of foster placement breakdown continued. Rowe and Lambert, in *Children Who Wait* [1973] had highlighted the problem of 'drift' in care and the deficiency in planning for children, and showed that policies of prevention and rehabilitation were not working as people had hoped. An estimated 7,000 children were adrift in residential care needing substitute families. At the same time the tragedy of the death of Maria Colwell [DHSS, 1974], abused and killed by her step-father on her return to the care of her birth mother after spending much of her early childhood in foster care, emphasised other personal costs that might be paid by some children as a consequence of policies that emphasised prevention or rehabilitation as the only goals in child care. The result was a rethink of policy which, occurring at the same time as the Houghton Committee, influenced the Children Act 1975, and paved the way for more assertive planning for children entering the care system.

In 1973 the first of two books by Goldstein, Freud and Solnit [*Beyond the Best Interests of the Child*, 1973; see p. 517, above] raised the issue of 'psychological parenting' and its relation to the whole concept of 'permanence'. By 'psychological parenting' was meant the permanent and exclusive relationship between a child and his or her 'parent' (irrespective of blood ties) which was seen as all important for the satisfactory emotional growth and development of a child.

...

Other studies stressed permanence as a developmental need and in consequence as a 'right'. Rowe and Lambert [1973] made apparent the harmful effects when separation resulted in limbo and drift:

> 'It is our conviction that no child can grow emotionally while in limbo, never really belonging to anyone except on a temporary and ill-defined or partial basis. He cannot invest except in a minimal way (just enough to survive) if tomorrow the relationship may be severed. ... To grow the child needs at least the promise of permanency in relationships and some continuity of environment.'

Later research produced equally worrying findings: children stayed in temporary foster care for long periods; children moved frequently between placements; the state of being a foster child was likely to destroy their relationships with their birth family; and children themselves found the temporary nature of their foster home a source of deep anxiety and concern [see Morris, 1984].

The 1970s–1980s: permanency planning – the least detrimental alternative

...

'Permanency planning' was a new approach to the provision of care for children, which had been developed in the USA (where over half of all foster children had typically been in temporary care for two years or more) in response to problems similar to those being experienced in the UK. This had shaped the philosophy, goals and services of child welfare agencies, re-forming them to accept the primacy of the needs of children over the 'blood tie'.

...

The concept of permanency planning is built on a number of basic beliefs. It stresses the value of rearing children in a family setting, based on a belief in the primacy of the family in the child's growth and development, and in the continuing need of each human being to belong to a family and the significance of the family in 'human connectedness'. The primacy of the parent–child attachment is part of the rationale behind permanency planning, which also emphasises the importance of stability in living arrangements, and of continuity, stability and mutuality in parent–child relationships [Maluccio, Fein and Olmstead, 1986].

...

Permanency planning also implies the right of every child to be provided with a stable home, quickly and with as few moves or temporary situations as possible. Adcock and White [1980] expressed this belief very firmly: 'No child should be deprived of an opportunity to grow up either in his own family or in a new family which he can legally call his own, unless there is a very strong reason to justify this.'

...

Permanency planning – the response in the UK

The most novel aspect of these policies was the placement for adoption of children who had previously been considered unadoptable, principally older children and those with physical and mental disabilities, or emotional and behaviour difficulties [Thoburn, 1990]. ...

... When permanency policies became part of child care practice in the UK it was, according to Thoburn, 'the adoption aspects of permanence which were to the fore, at the expense of preventive and rehabilitative aspects'. Such policies, it was hoped, would minimise 'drift' in unplanned care and cut down the numbers of young people leaving care at 18 who were attached to neither their birth families nor to substitute families. It aimed to give them, according to Triseliotis [1983], 'a family for life, with its network of support systems not only for them but also for their future children'.

The 1975 Children Act made adoption a more likely alternative for some children in long-term care, and both fostering and adoption were seen as options in a range of susbtitute family placements. In the UK there had always been the possibility that children in long-term foster care could be adopted by their foster carers, but the 1975 Children Act strengthened the position of foster families considering adoption. As adoption was to be considered an available option for a greater number of children in care, the adoption of children whose parents did not request it, and who might actively oppose it, became a possibility. Such an extension of the ranks of 'adoptable' children was, and still is, highly controversial.

…

The unacceptable face of permanence

Since the mid 1970s permanence had been seen predominantly to refer to substitute family care. In the mid 1980s it was, however, acknowledged that the emphasis upon adoption had perhaps gone too far. The Report of the House of Commons Social Services Committee [1984] regretted this trend towards equating 'permanence' with adoption:

> 'There is at the moment considerable confusion over the significance of the search for permanence in a placement. It should not have become a synonym for adoption. Adoption is only one eventual outcome among many. It is however, the most permanent possible outcome for a child unable to live with his natural family.'

Permanence within the child's birth family did not seem to be as energetically pursued. …

Rowe [1983] surveying foster care in the eighties, suggested that one of the benefits of planning for permanence was the urgency and emphasis it brought to providing services to birth parents which would enable them to resume care of their children before they had put down roots elsewhere and developed bonds with psychological parents. Agencies which worked hard to achieve permanence reported a significant increase in rehabilitation of children to their birth families.

However, there were serious doubts as to whether enough was being done in this regard. Rowe also reported that conspicuous by its absence in most discussion of foster care was any adequate consideration of work with natural parents. …

In 1986, Thoburn et al [1986] voiced the concern that the move towards greater compulsion in child care in order to facilitate planning for permanence may have had the unforeseen consequence of a less appropriate and sensitive service to those who should go home. …

In 1986 Millham et al [1986] demonstrated that the majority of children coming into care did in fact eventually return to their birth families or move into independent living situations. Of the 170 children under six years on admission to care in this Dartington study, only 24 were in long-term care two years later. This finding was an important reminder that agencies, in initiating policies for the small numbers who needed permanent family placement, must take care that these did not result in inappropriate and unhelpful services to the far greater numbers who would eventually return to their parents and needed to be helped to do so as quickly as possible. Millham and his colleagues confirmed in a later study [1993] that 90 per cent of children and adolescents who are taken away from their families into the care of a local authority eventually go home.

The simple dichotomy between the permanence of adoption and the permanence of a return home is called in question by the research which pointed to the importance of maintaining family links, described by the Department of Health in *Patterns and Outcomes in Child Care* (1991):

a) Contact and placement stability

By the mid 1980s there was cumulative research evidence from both the USA and Great Britain showing that the well-being of children being cared for by social agencies is enhanced if they maintain links with parents and other family members. Unfortunately, other research showed that all too often links were not being maintained. …

Berridge and Cleaver [1987] found that frequent access to parents was associated with fewer fostering breakdowns. Thoburn and Rowe's adoption survey [1988] showed that when other variables were held constant, few placements broke down when family links were maintained, while Wedge and Mantle [1991] discovered that even among a group of children who were being placed in permanent substitute families, those whose links with their birth families had been maintained were protected against the adverse effects of long periods in care. They noted that 50% of children referred for permanent placement had some link with their birth family at that time. They tended to be older children who presumably could maintain links themselves. These researchers conclude: 'The increasing trend towards access of family members to children in care needs to be further developed and extended if placements in substitute families are to be as successful as possible and if children are to acquire and retain the self-identity which is a crucial component in healthy emotional development.'

The findings, insights and conclusions from the Dartington Research Unit's study 'Lost in Care' (Millham *et al*, 1986) are admirably summarised in their follow-up research 'Access Disputes in Child Care' (1989). They are sufficiently important to require quoting at some length:

'... Managing a crisis, finding a suitable placement, coping with the anxiety, grief and frequent hostility of parents and children make it difficult for social workers to give the maintenance of links between parents and absent children high priority. Contacts are left to emerge, consequent upon other social worker decisions.

As a result, withering links with home affect many children in care; from the outset, nearly three-quarters of children experience great difficulty in maintaining contact with their parents. The barriers that they face are of two kinds. The first are specific restrictions, which are placed by social workers on the access of individuals, usually family or other household members. Such difficulties affect one-third of the children on entry. The second barrier is created by non-specific restrictions, difficulties inherent in placements, such as hostility, distance and inaccessibility. These hindrances affect two-thirds of the children in the early days of care.

As time passes, child isolation increases and restrictions on parental access to children actually increase, often to help maintain placements in difficulty, although the disruptive potential of visiting parents is over-estimated. Restrictions on contact do not receive continual scrutiny by social workers and constraints on unwelcome family members are frequently allowed to linger long after the original reasons for discouraging visits have evaporated. ...

Other factors increase the child's isolation. Social workers' visits to parents, children and care givers decline over time. ... Thus, the bridge between absent child and his or her family weakens and the social worker fails to stress the significance of parent/child reciprocal contact. Unfortunately, parents need encouragement to maintain relationships with their absent children, particularly when haunted by a sense of failure and bereft of a useful role.

... As a result, a third of those who remain in care will have lost contact with mother or father, siblings or the wider family at the end of two years and will be likely to stay in care for the foreseeable future. In the majority of cases, there are no cogent social work reasons for contacts with the family to wither. ...

...

Although Wedge and Mantle speak of 'the increasing trend' toward access, other researchers point out the low base from which this trend is starting. Thoburn's intensive and extensive studies of 'permanent' placements both show that family links which children wished to maintain were not always preserved, and in their studies of fostering breakdown Berridge and Cleaver noted an 'anti-family ideology' in some instances and more general lack of encouragement of contact, which meant that family links were too often allowed to wither and die.

The use of relations as a placement resource has received little attention until the last few years and has sometimes been frowned on as likely to exacerbate family tensions. However, if children's parents are unable or unwilling to care for them, an obvious way to preserve close links is to turn to the wider family, and the high level of stability and satisfaction found in foster placements with relatives which was first emphasised in 'Long-Term Foster Care' (Rowe et al, 1984) has been strongly reinforced in recent studies. ...

In 'Foster Home Breakdown' Berridge and Cleaver report a remarkable success rate for fostering by relatives and in 'Child Care Now' Rowe et al [1989] report that relatives tend to foster older children with more complex problems and still achieve better results than unrelated foster carers. Despite this, local authorities vary greatly in their use of fostering by relatives and their willingness to provide financial support for people looking after relatives' children.

b) Sibling relationships merit closer attention

Research underlines and supports the requirement in the Children Act 1989 (s. 23(7)(*b*)) that siblings should be accommodated together whenever 'reasonably practicable and consistent with the child's welfare'. Psychologists such as Judy Dunn [1988] point out that siblings provide our longest lasting relationships and can be a powerful influence on personality and development.

However, this explicit attention to the question of siblings is relatively recent and there are few references to siblings in local authority policy documents or practice guides.

...

There is also confirmation from research that children who are away from home, like being with siblings, but separation is a common experience. ...

Rowe et al (1984) found that long-term foster children placed with a sibling were usually glad about this and mentioned the benefit of having someone to talk to about their family of origin, while Fisher et al [1986] learned that children and young people who had been separated sometimes thought that this was a punishment.

...

The pros and cons of keeping siblings together if their needs seem very different is inevitably a matter for anxious debate among practitioners and decision makers. Until recently, research provided little assistance, but some useful pointers are emerging from recent studies. Although the evidence is sometimes conflicting, the overall conclusion seems to be that being with a sibling usually has a helpful effect on stability.

(1) *Placement at home.* In the Farmer and Parker study [1991], returning 'home on trial' with a sibling was associated with successful outcomes.

(2) *Long-term foster placements.* Berridge and Cleaver reported more breakdowns when the child had siblings in care but was separated from all of them (50% breakdown) than when placed with *all* siblings in care (33% breakdown) or with *some* siblings (26% breakdown). However, these findings were not entirely supported by the outcomes data in 'Child Care Now'.

(3) *Adoption and 'permanent' foster placements.*

(i) In a survey of the outcomes of over a thousand 'special needs' adoption placements Thoburn and Rowe found that sibling placements break down *less* often. Only 18% of placements with one or more siblings broke down compared with 24% of single child placements. (This difference is statistically significant and still found when other variables are held constant.)

(ii) After studying 'permanent' placements of siblings placed together or separately, Wedge and Mantle concluded that the impact can work both ways. Multiple placements may put too much stress on the new parents, but a child's adverse reaction to separation from siblings can also cause disruption. When siblings are placed together, the younger one may be more in jeopardy because of problems in the older one(s), but conversely, being placed with a younger sibling may reduce the chance of an older child feeling rejected by the new family.

(iii) Intensive study of a small number of adoption placements of 9–10 year old boys left Rushton et al [1989] equally uncertain about the wisdom of splitting or separating sibling groups. They noted more progress in children placed with one or more siblings but point out that those placed alone tended to have more serious problems to start with.

Amongst the conclusions drawn were:

(16) Agency policies and practice need to take seriously the now well established research finding that visiting is the key to discharge. Contact enhances the welfare of placed children and does not increase the risk of breakdown.

(17) Concepts of permanence should be broadened to include the possibility of continued family contact through open adoption or permanent fostering.

(18) Informal barriers to contact are widespread but may not be recognised. Agencies ought to examine not just their stated policies but the prevailing climate of opinion among their staff about birth parents and the maintenance of family contact. Staff may need more support and encouragement to do this work.

(19) Premature or routine termination of contact when permanent placements are planned can do children a serious disservice by precluding the possibility of continued contact of some sort.

(20) Relatives provide a placement resource which should always be considered. The stability of such placements – especially for long-term cases – makes it worth trying hard to seek out relatives and overcome obstacles.

(21) Relatives are also an important source of family contact. Visits by grandparents or aunts and uncles can often be encouraged even if visiting by parents cannot be permitted.

(22) More attention should be paid to the role of siblings and other children. The importance of child-to-child relationships has been insufficiently recognised. Changes in the child members of the family to which a child returns or the presence of 'own' children close in age to a foster child are both associated with negative outcome, whereas placement with siblings is generally beneficial and sibling ties are valued by children.

Combining permanence and openness is also difficult. Seven points are made by Michael Little in a paper on *Research on Open Adoption* (1995):

1. There is no research evidence which conclusively shows that contact with birth relatives is *good* for adopted children. On the other hand, there is no evidence that such contact is harmful for children. Lack of research on this question is a significant gap, and I think contrasts with our knowledge on children looked after by social services departments which, for the great majority of cases, attests to the benefits of contact between parents and their absent children.
2. There is now considerable research evidence which sheds doubt on the efficacy of adoption for certain groups of children; and it is in this context that questions about openness have come to the fore. The latest such research comes from Jane Gibbons and colleagues at the University of East Anglia [p. 645, below] who monitored the progress of children whose names were placed on the protection register because they had been physically maltreated. Most of these children stayed at home, but over the 10 year follow up some were placed in foster settings and some were adopted.

It was found that, in terms of their emotional and psychological health, it was the children who stayed at home who did best; those fostered with support from the local authority did less well but they prospered better than the adopted children.

It is not known why such results should occur. The outcomes cannot be explained by the differing degrees of difficulty posed by children from the three groups: the cases were carefully matched. The findings might reflect a lack of preparation or support for the adoptive parents; it is true that an extremely difficult child placed at home will receive more social work support than one who is adopted.

These are interpretations of the results. It is clear that questions about openness are taking place in the context of placements which are themselves difficult and which do not necessarily lend themselves to good outcomes.
3. Adoption is becoming increasingly rare, especially for children with special needs such as those in public care.

Of a cohort of children entering care in 1980, studied by the Dartington Unit, less than 5% were eventually adopted. A similar cohort of children looked after since the implementation of the Children Act 1989 suggests that the proportion of children in care who are adopted is much the same. Since fewer children are now separated, this means that the number of adoptions of children in care will be lower – much lower – than 10 years ago.

So adoption cases represent a tiny part of all public law work and, for the most part, represent the most difficult cases.
4. It takes a considerable amount of time to adopt a child. It can take as little as one year between separation and adoption if everything goes according to plan, but it is just as likely to take five years as 12 months. The average is three years and two months. This period of waiting causes the child much anxiety and is likely to involve placement breakdown and education disruption, all factors that will make the adoption more vulnerable when it occurs.

The principal reason for delay is an understandable reluctance on the part of birth parents to give up their children. They fight to stay in touch even when they recognise that they are inadequate parents and could never expect to look after their child. It is the severing of contacts that contributes the greatest amount of time to the three years between separation and adoption.
5. Professor June Thoburn at the University of East Anglia has undertaken research [p. 646, below] which sheds much light on the question of openness. She looked at over 1,000 special needs adoptions and long-term foster placements. She found that over a 10 year period 22% broke down. In simple terms, this finding tells us that a so-called permanent placement is not necessarily permanent.

More relevant to the question of openness are findings on adoption breakdown by age of placement. The graph [on p. 646, below] shows that a child placed for adoption in the first few years of life is highly unlikely to experience disruption. Over a fifth of those placed in their eighth year experience breakdown as do almost a half of those placed in the first years of secondary school.

Thoburn looked at risk factors – which contributed towards breakdown – and protective factors – which reduced the chances of breakdown. ... For the older children and others who were high risk of breakdown, the best protective factor was found to be some degree of openness in the placement. So there is no evidence pointing to the benefits of contact for children placed for adoption in infancy but there is clear evidence in favour of openness for those placed between their fifth and 12th birthday.

It is safe to suggest that where it is found that a nine, 10, or 11 year old is to be adopted (bearing in mind that the actual placement might be one or two years hence) some degree of openness should be a part of the thinking of all those involved with the child (not only because it will help the placement survive but also because if the family is on the scene, contingency plans can be fashioned if the placement does disrupt).

6. Naturally, there is a lot of research evidence on questions of openness from the United States. Much of it is of highly dubious quality but some is very useful. Principally, colleagues in North America can help us with the question of the willingness of adoptive parents to stand for some degree of openness.

To summarise several books and many hundreds of articles, I think the answer is that adoptive parents are initially reluctant to work with birth parents but it becomes easier with time and, with good preparation, there need not be any long-term sequelae caused by continued contact. There is sound scientific evidence to suggest that similarities in class, culture and ethnicity between birth parents and adoptive parents makes openness both easier to manage and more productive.

7. Finally, before closing, it might be helpful to dwell on the subject of adopting adolescents, particularly those of 15 or 16 years. This is very much a grey area. The evidence on outcome is shaky because there are so few orders and there is good research to suggest that adolescents find open adoptions extremely difficult to cope with. Adolescents in these cases have enough to deal with and they can find continued openness with birth parents an unnecessary distraction.

The results of the study of *Development after Physical Abuse in Early Childhood* (1995) by Jane Gibbons and her colleagues are indeed surprising:

Discussion

The results showed that children placed on registers following physical abuse were highly likely to lose one or both natural parents in the nine to ten year follow-up period. This came about through official protective intervention to remove a child from an abusive home, but also from action by parents themselves. Mothers in particular often acted to dissolve a violent relationship and eject an abusive partner from the household. They were then about as likely to end up as lone parents in conditions of some poverty as to share their households with another man. Children who remained with their natural parents were severely materially disadvantaged in comparison with the children who were placed in substitute families.

The children in substitute families in this sample did show some advantages in physical development and verbal ability, related to the professional and managerial backgrounds of the new parents. But measures of behaviour problems at home and school failed to find any advantages for the separated group of children.

Particular advantages have been claimed for adoption as opposed to foster care. In the present study the two forms of placement had been used rather differently, with children being adopted earlier while those in foster care tended to have been removed later, after further failures of home care. Thus the foster children might be expected to have less chance of overcoming the problems resulting from early poor rearing. In fact, there was no consistent association between age at placement and children's outcomes. There was a consistent trend for the children in foster care to have fewer behaviour problems, as rated by parents and teachers, fewer problems with peers and less depression, while the adopted group tended to have higher problem scores than children who remained with natural parents. It should be noted that this result is out of line with the weight of evidence from other studies, suggesting more favourable outcomes for children in adoptive homes (Sinclair, pers. comm.).

How might the negative findings be explained? First, the follow-up point, while nine to ten years on from placement on the child protection register, still marked a relatively early stage in children's lives – they were only 11 on average. There is time for further maturation and a very different picture might be revealed after another ten years. Second, there is some evidence that around the age of 11 there may be a 'dip' in adopted children's performance for reasons that are not clear (Maughan and Pickles, 1990). If this were so, then the adopted group might come out of the dip in a further few years. Thirdly, it is possible that the adopted children differed from the remainder in some characteristics that weighed heavily against good outcome and were not captured by the study's baseline measures. There could have been pre-existing differences between the groups that were not identified because of the limitations of records. Lastly, even though a high proportion of the original sample took part in the follow-up and no more children in substitute families were 'missed', it is possible that the missing cases in some way distorted the findings.

However, the most obvious difference between the adopted and fostered groups lay in their current experiences of family life. It seemed that adoptive parents were not always using particularly sensitive methods of child-rearing. They tended to be more punitive and to use more physical punishment and these parenting styles were associated with poor outcomes for children in the total sample. Adoptive parents also tended to have more personal problems and to be more depressed than foster carers. They were often faced with children showing difficult and disturbed behaviour but, unlike the foster carers, they rarely had professional support and advice and they felt more isolated. It is perhaps not surprising that some fell back on punitive methods.

The need for more consistent post-adoption services is being increasingly recognised (Howe, 1992; Rushton et al., 1993).

In considering these results, it is important to take into account the climate of opinion at the time most of the social work was carried out. Within social service departments there was a strong policy emphasis on planning for permanence, and this was usually interpreted to mean rapid replacement in adoptive homes if parents were assessed as inadequate carers. The majority of the adopted children in the study had been separated from natural parents who wanted to keep them by means of legal methods which are no longer available. Such a start may have influenced the subsequent course of the placement. Current adoption policy is also more aware of the need to take children's cultural backgrounds into account when planning placement, so that the very wide discrepancies in the present study would probably not be found in today's climate of professional opinion.

This chapter should not end without some recognition of the loving and patient approach of many substitute families to the damaged children in their care. ... The records of some children showed how improvements in behaviour and adaptation to school were slowly occurring, even though there were setbacks. However, it is important to recognise that the provision of a new family for a child who has suffered abuse is not of itself enough to improve that child's life chances. Placement creates some new problems – more changes of carer, need to adjust to changing parental demands and expectations, loss of important aspects of one's own identity. 'New' parents can rarely hope for quick returns for their love and care, and ultimate success may well depend on exceptional levels of altruism, child-rearing skills and confidence.

The risk of breakdown in permanent placements, and the relationship with continued contact, are shown in the graph and figure, together with a commentary on the choices available, from June Thoburn's (1991) account of the findings and conclusions of her survey of over 1,000 special needs placements made by voluntary agencies in Britain between 1980 and 1984:

Age at placement and percentage of placements disrupting

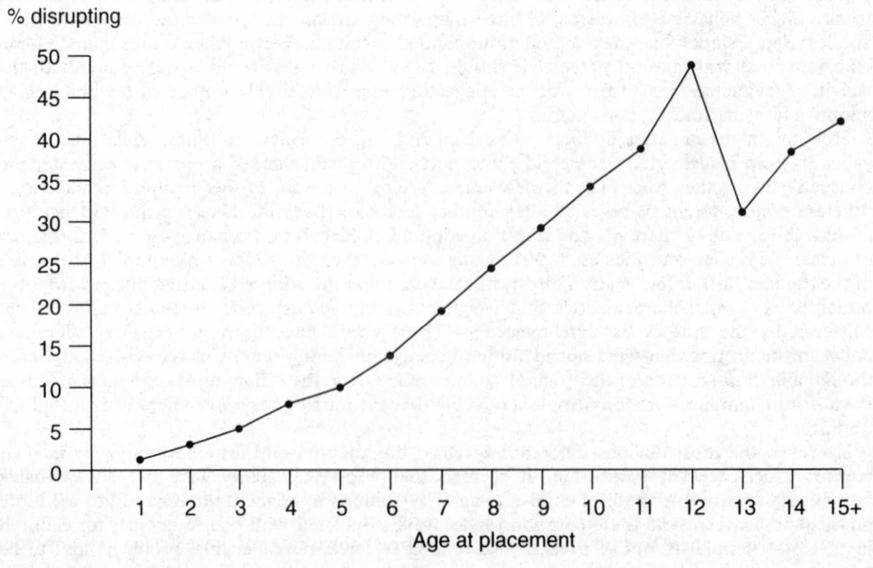

Outcome by continued contact and age at placement

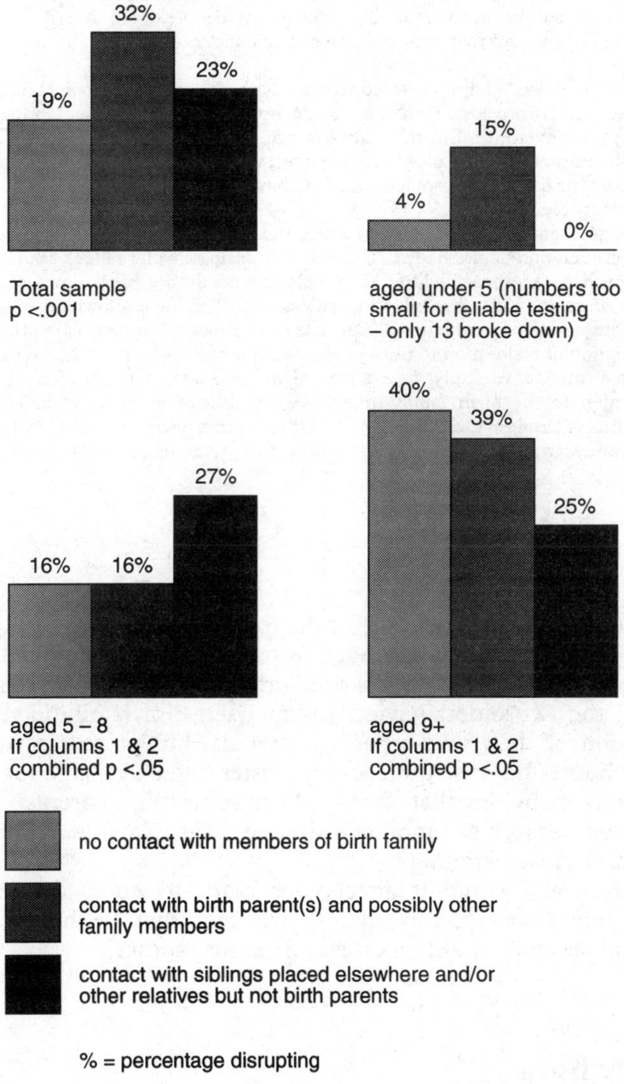

In view of the fact that the increased risk of breakdown is often given as a reason for placing for adoption rather than in foster care, and for terminating contact with birth parents, it is important to note that when age at placement was held constant, there was no significant difference in breakdown rates between adoption or permanent foster placement. Having continued contact with parents and other members of the birth family was a protective factor. However, it must be emphasised that all these placements were made with the intention that they would be permanent, and the social work service was based on maximising the sense of permanence of the new families.

This is a possible explanation for the lower breakdown rates for primary school-age children in this study compared with those in the study by Berridge and Cleaver [1987] of long-term foster placements (46 per cent broke down in the Berridge and Cleaver study, and 22 per cent in this study). However, there was no difference between breakdown rates of those placed at 11 or older in the two studies. It may be that, had it been possible to consider other outcome measures, the positive effects of foster placement intended to be permanent from the start, and the intensive work which goes with it both on the part of social workers and parents, would have been apparent even for the older group. There was some evidence from the qualitative study that even when placements broke down, the majority of the young people could describe positive benefits for themselves and were glad that their placement had happened.

...

How, then, should we advise those concerned with the placement of children in care to incorporate our results into their practice and decision-making? First, it is important to warn against a swing from overoptimism to overpessimism. Our finding that there is a greater risk of breakdown with children who are older at placement; who are described as institutionalised or as having behavioural or emotional problems; or who have a history of deprivation or abuse, should not lead to blanket rules. ...

New knowledge about groups of children where the risk of breakdown is high should lead to a more careful consideration of alternatives. Other studies, using a wider range of outcome measures, have also shown that even those children whose placements do not break down continue to need post-placement support, and often adoption allowances. This new knowledge should lead to a more careful consideration of whether a similar level of financial and social work support could make a viable option of restoration to birth parents or other relatives, or a 'shared care' placement. Trent, in a small qualitative study, found that when the same methods of work were used to support restoration to the birth family, those placements had as good a chance of lasting as placements with new families. Our finding that children with a history of abuse or deprivation are a particularly high risk group should act as an antidote to the 'rescue fantasies' which it is so easy to engage in.

Questions

(i) What would your care plan be for the following children:

(*a*) a family of four, ranging in age from 11 to three, removed from their parents because of father's drinking and mother's inability to cope alone, the two oldest having a strong sense of family identity and all still fond of their now-separated parents, but placed in two different foster homes because there was no foster home available for them all;

(*b*) the new baby in that family, born after the parents' separation, removed because the mother's situation was unstable, and placed with a different foster mother?

(ii) How, if at all, would it affect your plans to know that the father's drinking problem was mainly due to the fear that he had inherited an incurable and severely disabling disease from his mother?

2 Family links

Among other things, Sch. 2 to the Children Act 1989 contains this duty towards all children who are looked after by local authorities:

15. – (1) Where a child is being looked after by a local authority, the authority shall, unless it is not reasonably practicable or consistent with his welfare, endeavour to promote contact between the child and –

(*a*) his parents;

(*b*) any person who is not a parent of his but who has parental responsibility for him; and

(*c*) any relative, friend or other person connected with him.

(2) Where a child is being looked after by a local authority –

(*a*) the authority shall take such steps as are reasonably practicable to secure that –
(i) his parents; and
(ii) any person who is not a parent of his but who has parental responsibility for him,
are kept informed of where he is being accommodated; and
(*b*) every such person shall secure that the local authority are kept informed of his or her address.

If the child is in compulsory care, and so cannot simply go home, this duty is reinforced with the powers of the courts:

34. – (1) Where a child is in the care of a local authority, the authority shall (subject to the provisions of this section) allow the child reasonable contact with –
(*a*) his parents;
(*b*) any guardian of his;
(*c*) where there was a residence order in force with respect to the child immediately before the care order was made, the person in whose favour the order was made; and
(*d*) where, immediately before the care order was made, a person had care of the child by virtue of an order made in the exercise of the High Court's inherent jurisdiction with respect to children, that person.

(2) On an application made by the authority or the child, the court may make such order as it considers appropriate with respect to the contact which is to be allowed between the child and any named person.

(3) On an application made by –
(*a*) any person mentioned in paragraphs (*a*) to (*d*) of subsection (1); or
(*b*) any person who has obtained the leave of the court to make the application;
the court may make such order as it considers appropriate with respect to the contact which is to be allowed between the child and that person.

(4) On an application made by the authority or the child, the court may make an order authorising the authority to refuse to allow contact between the child and any person who is mentioned in paragraphs (*a*) to (*d*) of subsection (1) and named in the order.

(5) When making a care order with respect to a child, or in any family proceedings in connection with a child who is in the care of a local authority, the court may make an order under this section, even though no application for such an order has been made with respect to the child, if it considers that the order should be made.

(6) An authority may refuse to allow the contact that would otherwise be required by virtue of subsection (1) or an order under this section if –
(*a*) they are satisfied that it is necessary to do so in order to safeguard or promote the child's welfare; and
(*b*) the refusal –
(i) is decided upon as a matter of urgency; and
(ii) does not last for more than seven days.

(7) An order under this section may impose such conditions as the court considers appropriate.

(8) The Secretary of State may by regulations make provision as to –
(*a*) the steps to be taken by a local authority who have exercised their powers under subsection (6);
(*b*) the circumstances in which, and conditions subject to which, the terms of any order under this section may be departed from by agreement between the local authority and the person in relation to whom the order is made;
(*c*) notification by a local authority of any variation or suspension of arrangements made (otherwise than under an order under this section) with a view to affording any person contact with a child to whom this section applies.

(9) The court may vary or discharge any order made under this section on the application of the authority, the child concerned or the person named in the order.

(10) An order under this section may be made either at the same time as the care order itself or later.

(11) Before making a care order with respect to any child the court shall –
(*a*) consider the arrangements which the authority have made, or propose to make, for affording any person contact with a child to whom this section applies; and
(*b*) invite the parties to the proceedings to comment on those arrangements.

Section 34 cases tend to fall into two categories:

Re B (minors) (termination of contact: paramount consideration) [1993] Fam 301, [1993] 3 All ER 524, Court of Appeal

Two little girls, now aged four and two and a half, had been removed from their mother because she left them unattended and placed with a short-term foster mother for some two years. The mother then had a baby boy, S, and was looking after him successfully with social work support. Contact with the girls was re-established and they visited her home twice a week. The local authority applied for an order under s. 34(4) of the Children Act 1989, authorising them to refuse contact so that the girls could be placed for adoption. The judge considered that it was not open to him to use the powers in s. 34 to challenge the local authority's plan. He made the order and the girls' guardian ad litem appealed.

Butler-Sloss LJ: ... The underlying reason for the continuing contact was the hope of the mother that it might lead to rehabilitation and the return of the girls to her. The contact already taking place was incompatible with placing the children with prospective adopters. The local authority accepted that they had never attempted to assess the mother's ability to care for the three children. Their view was, and is, that the mother has made significant strides in her ability to care for S, but to expect her to care for three children is too much and will probably lead to the breakdown of all three placements, including the placement for S. They were concerned about the length of time the girls had lived with the short-term foster mother and the delay in placing them permanently. They considered that the children would not miss the contact with their mother, which the judge found to be true since their primary carer remains the foster mother. But they accepted that the contact visits had been successful and enjoyable for the children. The local authority had identified particularly suitable potential adopters who were, like the children, of mixed race and who would not be willing to accept continuing contact with the mother.

[Apart from the duty and powers in section 34] there is another important difference [between the old law and the new] of which the judge was well aware and which had a marked effect upon his approach to this case. Before the implementation of the Children Act 1989 the powers of the magistrates' court to make care orders did not extend beyond the making of the order. Thereafter the local authority took over the care of the child and was not subject to judicial control or monitoring other than by the limited remedy of judicial review: see *A v Liverpool City Council* [1982] AC 363 [p. 635, above] and *In re W (A Minor) (Wardship: Jurisdiction)* [1985] AC 791. By contrast, when a child was committed to care by a judge exercising the wardship jurisdiction in the High Court, or a Matrimonial Causes Act 1973 care order in the High Court or the county court, the judge was able to make directions and require the case to return for further consideration by the court. This monitoring by the court of a child in care has been specifically excluded by the Act of 1989. ...

... If the local authority's plan to place for adoption is not capable of reconsideration, the judge was clearly right in his decision that contact was not possible in this case. The question arises as to the interplay between the plans of the local authority and the jurisdiction of the court and the proper exercise of its discretion under the wider range of orders available under the Act of 1989.

[Counsel] for the local authority submitted that the principle in *A v Liverpool City Council* [1982] AC 363 still inhibits the court from any interference with the adoption plans made for the two girls and the judge's approach was entirely correct. *A v Liverpool City Council* is still, in my respectful opinion, of the greatest relevance beyond the confines of child care law and the principle set out by Lord Wilberforce is equally applicable today, that the court has no reviewing power over the exercise of the local authority's discretionary decisions in carrying out their statutory role. ... I do not, however, believe that the important principle set out in *A v Liverpool City Council* [1982] AC 363 and *In re W* [1985] AC 791 applies to the intervention of the court in response to an application which is properly made, or fetters the exercise of the judicial discretion in an application, under the Children Act 1989.

...

My understanding of the Act of 1989 is that it aims to incorporate the best of the wardship jurisdiction within the statutory framework without any of the perceived disadvantages of judicial monitoring of administrative plans. It provides for the court a wide range of options and the possibility of its own motion to set in train a line of investigation not contemplated or asked for by the parties. Like wardship, however, these wide powers are to be sparingly used.

The present position of a child whose welfare is being considered under Part IV of the Act appears to me to be that he will not be placed in care unless a court has been satisfied that the threshold conditions in section 31 have been met and that it is better to make a care order than not to do so. After the care order is made, the court has no continuing role in the future welfare of the child. The local authority has parental responsibility for the child by section 33(3). However, issues relating to the child may come before the court, for instance on applications for contact or leave to refuse contact, to discharge the care order or by an application for a section 8 residence order. The making of a residence order discharges the care order: section 91(1). At the moment that an application comes before the court, at whichever tier, the court has a duty to apply section 1, which states that when a court determines any question with respect to the upbringing of a child, the child's welfare shall be the court's paramount consideration. The court has to have regard to the prejudicial effect of delay, to the checklist including the range of orders available to the court and whether to make an order. On a section 34 application, therefore, the court has a duty to consider and apply the welfare section.

Contact applications generally fall into two main categories: those which ask for contact as such, and those which are attempts to set aside the care order itself. In the first category there is no suggestion that the applicant wishes to take over the care of the child and the issue of contact often depends on whether contact would frustrate long-term plans for the child in a substitute home, such as adoption, where continuing contact may not be for the long-term welfare of the child. The presumption of contact, which has to be for the benefit of the child, has always to be balanced against the long-term welfare of the child and, particularly, where he will live in the future. Contact must not be allowed to destabilise or endanger the arrangements for the child and in many cases the plans for the child will be decisive of the contact application. There may also be cases where the parent is having satisfactory contact with the child and there are no long-term plans or those plans do not appear to the court to preclude some future contact. The proposals of the local authority, based on their appreciation of the best interests of the child, must command the greatest respect and consideration from the court, but Parliament has given to the court, and not to the local authority, the duty to decide on contact between the child and those named in section 34(1). Consequently, the court may have the task of requiring the local authority to justify their long-term plans to the extent only that those plans exclude contact between parent and child. In the second category, contact applications may be made by parents by way of another attempt to obtain the return of the children. In such a case the court is obviously entitled to take into account the failure to apply to discharge the care order, and in the majority of cases the court will have little difficulty in coming to the conclusion that the applicant cannot demonstrate that contact with a view to rehabilitation with the parent is a viable proposition at that stage, particularly if it had already been rejected at the earlier hearing when the child was placed in care. The task for the parents will be too great and the court would be entitled to assume that the plans of the local authority to terminate contact are for the welfare of the child and are not to be frustrated by inappropriate contact with a view to the remote possibility, at some future date, of rehabilitation.

But in all cases the welfare section has to be considered, and the local authority have the task of justifying the cessation of contact. There may also be unusual cases where either the local authority have not made effective plans or there has been considerable delay in implementing them and a parent, who has previously been found by a court unable or unwilling to care for the child so that a care order has been made, comes back upon the scene as a possible future primary carer. …

I unhesitatingly reject the local authority argument. As I have already said, their plan has to be given the greatest possible consideration by the court and it is only in the unusual case that a parent will be able to convince the court, the onus being firmly on the parent, that there has been such a change of circumstances as to require further investigation and reconsideration of the local authority plan. If, however, a court were unable to intervene, it would make a nonsense of the paramountcy of the welfare of the child which is the bedrock of the Act, and would subordinate it to the administrative decision of the local authority in a situation where the court is seized of the contact issue. That cannot be right.

But I would emphasise that this is not an open door to courts reviewing the plans of local authorities. …

This court, therefore, has to decide whether the mother should be assessed as the potential carer of all three children. There is a large question mark over the wisdom of straining the placement for S. by the possibility of putting all three children together in the care of a relatively untried mother. But the guardian ad litem and the social worker saw a real possibility that she might become an adequate mother for all three children. The decision requires consideration of the competing factors that on the one side there is the prospect that the mother may come up trumps and, if so, the enormous advantage for these three children to be brought up together by their own mother in preference to a substitute family, however suitable. On the other side there is the real danger that the problems would be too great, that the assessment would be disappointing and, most worrying of all, the danger that this attempt might imperil the relationship between the mother and S., who would be devastated by losing his mother at this stage. We must add to those factors the need to settle these children and the fragility of their present placement from which they will have to move in any event, and the question of delay is very important. However, I have come to the clear conclusion that the mother's potential must be investigated and not to do so would be unfair to the children and, if the prospective adoption application were to be made, might create a serious obstacle on the special facts of this case.

Appeal allowed.

Re E (a minor) (care order: contact)
[1994] 1 FCR 584, [1994] 1 FLR 146, Court of Appeal

The parents of two little boys aged five and a half and nearly four at the date of the hearing had personality problems which made it difficult for them to look after the children. Over some 22 months before the hearing, the boys had been looked after first by family friends, then accommodated by the local authority, and then the subject of care proceedings. Everyone agreed that there should be a care order. But the local authority also applied for an order under s. 34(4) because the care plan was adoption. The judge adopted the approach that he could not order contact which was incompatible with the care plan unless this could be attacked as capricious or invalid in judicial review terms. He granted the application and the parents and guardian ad litem appealed.

Sir Stephen Brown P: ... Section 34 of the Children Act 1989 quite plainly begins with the provision that a local authority shall allow a child in care reasonable contact with, among others, his parents; there is therefore a presumption of contact: the onus is on the local authority to apply to the court for an order authorising it to refuse to allow contact; that is to say, to terminate contact. The emphasis is heavily placed on the presumption of continuing parental contact. ...

The submission made in this case therefore is that although the judge had before him evidence from the social worker in charge of the case, and evidence from the social worker in charge of adoption cases to the effect that in the relevant area, there was no real likelihood of the discovery or identification of proposed adopted parents who would countenance continuing contact after adoption; nevertheless, no specific investigation was made about the actual situation; ...

The case was strongly argued on behalf of the local authority that the care plan devised by the local authority was appropriate to these children; first of all because there was no prospect of actual rehabilitation with their parents; and secondly because the level and quality of contact between the children and the parents was of a relatively low quality. That matter took up a good deal of the hearing; ... The evidence of the guardian and Dr Williams ... was to the effect that although these children were in a particular category, if I may put it that way, they were not bonded in the full sense of the word with their parents; nevertheless, there was a benefit to the children of contact with their parents because the parents were in no way likely to undermine a permanent placement in another 'parent setting' whether it was an adoptive parent setting or a long-term foster setting and that in the light of a very strong likelihood in the view of the doctor, that an adoptive placement would either not be satisfactory or would break down, the constant presence of the parents in the lives of the children would have a stabilising effect. ... Dr Williams said that ideally, these children would prosper in a secure foster placement growing up knowing who their parents were and having regular access to them. ...

...

...I consider that in the light of very strong representation by the doctor and the guardian as to the particular value in this case of some continuing face-to-face contact, it was not sufficient for the local authority to dismiss the likelihood of obtaining suitable adopters prepared to entertain face-to-face contact upon the basis that there were none on the register at the time.

... The court has been very strongly pressed ... to give 'guidance' on s. 34 of the Children Act 1989. I do not consider it appropriate to say more than that this court endorses the approach indicated by Butler-Sloss LJ in the case of *Re B* [p. 650, above] emphasising that contact must not be allowed to destabilise or endanger the arrangements for the child. However, since the court has a duty to consider contact between the child and the parents, it may require the local authority to justify its long-term plan where their plan excludes contact between the parents and the child.

Simon Brown LJ: ... even when the s. 31 criteria are satisfied, contact may well be of singular importance to the long-term welfare of the child: first, in giving the child the security of knowing that his parents love him and are interested in his welfare; secondly, by avoiding any damaging sense of loss to the child in seeing himself abandoned by his parents; thirdly, by enabling the child to commit himself to the substitute family with the seal of approval of the natural parents; and, fourthly, by giving the child the necessary sense of family and personal identity. Contact, if maintained, is capable of reinforcing and increasing the chances of success of a permanent placement, whether on a long-term fostering basis or by adoption.

There is, I appreciate, an ongoing debate regarding the merits of open or closed adoption and it is not one that I propose to enter. But whatever be the arguments, there will undoubtedly be cases, and this I believe to be one, in which some continuing face-to-face contact is clearly desirable and which call, accordingly, at the very least for some positive efforts on the local authority's part to find, if at all possible, prospective open adopters; here, it seems to me, there have been none.

Even, therefore, were the appeal to be decided without reference to further evidence, I myself would have been inclined to allow it. For good measure, however, there is now before the court further evidence indicating at the very least this: that the admirable short-term foster-mother in whose care over the last 17 months these children have continued to thrive has indicated a wish to be considered, together with her husband, as a long-term foster-parent for these children, a placement which would allow continuing face-to-face contact.

For that reason too it seems to me highly desirable that this matter be considered afresh ... by a judge who will have the advantage of hearing from the local authority, both (a) what upon further investigation appears to be the up-to-date prospects of open adoption, and (b) their considered views upon the merits or otherwise of long-term fostering by the foster-parents.

Those advantages, in my judgment, clearly outweigh the disadvantages of delaying yet further a final decision upon the long-term placement of these children.

Order accordingly.

Question

Do you think that these appeals would have been allowed if the judges had not in each case applied the wrong approach in principle?

Families are not only parents and siblings, but grandparents, uncles, aunts, cousins and many more. Before turning to them, however, we must look at the law governing applications or claims by all non-parents, whether or not they are related to the child.

3 Families and foster homes

We have already seen how, in *J v C* [1970] AC 668, [1969] 1 All ER 788, p. 411, above, the House of Lords decided that there was no presumption of law in favour of parents in private law disputes with non-parents. We have also seen how the Children Act 1989 deliberately endorses the paramountcy of the child's welfare. Even so, the courts have sometimes been more conservative in their utterances:

Re K (a minor) (wardship: adoption)
[1991] FCR 142, [1991] 1 FLR 57, Court of Appeal

The parents had two older children and, despite some social services involvement with the family, there was no question of removing them. The marriage was a stormy one, the father was addicted to gambling and had a criminal record, and the mother was receiving treatment for heroin addiction. The mother became unexpectedly pregnant with this child, N, during a particularly difficult time. A private arrangement was made to hand the child over to foster parents, as they thought permanently. This was done when the child was six weeks old but less than three months later the mother wanted her back. The foster parents made the child a ward of court and obtained interim care and control. When the child was seven and a half months old, the judge gave them care and control with a view to adoption and terminated the mother's access. Mother, father and local authority all appealed.

Butler-Sloss LJ: ... This is a very sad case in which the little girl was handed over by the mother at a time of great stress and financial difficulty within 6 weeks of the birth of the child to a much older couple who are childless and have for some years hoped to care for a child on a long-term basis. The mother and the father have repented of their decision to hand over N and wish to reintroduce her into the family with her elder brother and sister. She has, however, settled into a warm and loving family who are currently caring for her admirably and wish to continue to do so. If she moves there will be inevitable upheaval and upset for the child. If she goes back to her natural family there are question marks as to their suitability. There are also question marks as to the long-term suitability of the family with whom she is at present.

The core of counsel's submissions on behalf of the mother was that the judge correctly stated the law but did not apply it. The judge referred to ... the decision in *Re K (A Minor) (Custody)* [1990] 2 FLR 64, 67F in which Fox LJ stated:

> 'I come now to the law. In *Re KD (A Minor) (Access Principles)*, Lord Templemen said:
>
> > "The best person to bring up a child is the natural parent. It matters not whether the parent is wise or foolish, rich or poor, educated or illiterate, provided the child's moral and physical health are not endangered."
>
> ... The question was not where would R get the better home? The question was: was it demonstrated that the welfare of the child positively demanded the displacement of the parental right? The word "right" is not really accurate insofar as it might connote something in the nature of a property right (which it is not) but it will serve for present purposes. The "right", if there is one, is perhaps more that of the child.'

...

The difficulty in this case is that if the child had not been placed in such an unorthodox fashion with the plaintiffs and had been put into short-term care to help the mother it is most unlikely that efforts would not have been made to reintroduce the child back to her mother and brother and sister, unless there were exceptional circumstances which do not, in my view, arise in this case.

The mother must be shown to be entirely unsuitable before another family can be considered, otherwise we are in grave danger of slipping into social engineering. The question is not: would the child be better off with the plaintiffs? but: is the natural family so unsuitable that, as Fox LJ said, 'the welfare of the child positively demanded the displacement of the parental right'? I agree with Fox LJ that it is the right of the child rather than the parent and, borrowing from the philosophy of the Children Act 1989, I would rephrase it as the displacement of the parental responsibility. Once the judge found that this mother genuinely wanted her child back and was a mother who cared properly for the other two children, not to give her at least an opportunity to try to rehabilitate the family was to deprive the child of any chance of her own family. I recognise that the placement of the child back with the natural family poses considerable risks and requires careful consideration from the local authority concerned. But, backed as it is by all the professionals who gave evidence, it cannot be said to be wholly unreasonable. One attempt at rehabilitation with a young baby and a mother capable of loving her children would have been likely to have been attempted if this private arrangement had not been entered into ...

There is a second matter raised in the arguments of the local authorities. ... the position of the plaintiffs as permanent caretakers presents its own problems and would have done so even if the natural family had been entirely unsuitable. ...
Appeal allowed.

However, parents and non-parents do not have equal rights of access to the courts. The Children Act 1975 allowed non-parents to apply for 'custodianship' once they had looked after the child for some time. Even this was not implemented until 1985 and was little used. Emma Bullard and Ellen Malos summarise the results of their study of *Custodianship* (1990) thus:

9.31 The largest group of applicants were the grandparents applying for young children who had been living with them for all or most of their lives. The mothers themselves were likely either to have been in their teens at the time of their child's birth or to be in their early twenties and to be described as 'immature' either by their parents and the social workers or, among those we interviewed, to have that perception of themselves.
9.32 In the majority of such cases the reason for the application was the desire of the grandparents to safeguard the children's place with them, to be given a clear legal right to make the normal day-to-day decisions about their upbringing and to symbolise the child's place in the family.
9.33 In the cases involving relatives it appeared that the need for such an order arose most often in situations where there had been a substantial degree of agreement by the parents to the placement but also an element of uncertainty about its stability or about the formal powers of the carers to make day-to-day decisions about the children's care. ...
9.34 In some cases there had been a background of concern about the children's well-being while they were living with their parents and in a smaller number of cases the children had come into the grandparents' care from that of a local authority social services department following physical or sexual abuse.
9.35 There were also other circumstances in which relatives applied for custodianship but these were more common in the wider family than among grandparents. These included bereavement and marital breakdown and the most unusual case was one where custodianship was granted in adoption proceedings to an aunt who had taken over the care of the daughter of her brother and sister-in-law who were living in the same multi-generation family household.
9.37 The circumstances in which the children came into the care of the unrelated foster carers had features in common with those where relatives were caring for children following bereavement or marital breakdown or where the children had suffered or had been at risk of neglect or abuse. There were a small number of cases where children who had been in care before the application were suffering from severe health problems or disabilities.

They also looked into the reasons for *not* applying for custodianship:

9.39 ... Most of the responses received were from unrelated foster carers. 14% of the respondents had not heard of custodianship until receiving our letter and questionnaire. The great majority (90%) of non-users described it as an advantage that, under a custodianship order, the child in their care could not be moved to another placement by a social worker. Nevertheless they had not wanted to apply for custodianship, and gave a variety of reasons for their decision.
9.40 Apart from the people who had not heard of custodianship, there was a group who had heard of it but had found the available information confusing and inadequate. Some carers had decided that adoption was preferable, while others said simply that they could see no advantages to be gained by applying for custodianship. Financial considerations were mentioned by some carers who were caring for a child with special needs or who were dependent on state benefits. A number of respondents felt that they needed continued social work support for a variety of reasons such as making access arrangements, the child's special needs, or behaviour problems in adolescence.

The researchers concluded that 'there was and will continue to be a need for some such provisions as custodianship'. Quite what these might be is discussed by the Law Commission in their Working Paper on *Custody* (1986):

Custodians

5.15 Custodianship was devised to meet two distinct needs. The Houghton Committee on the Adoption of Children was mainly concerned to provide an alternative to adoption by step-parents (which had by then become very common, especially after divorce) [see p. 559, above] or by relatives such as grandparents. Both will sever the child's legal relationship with one side of his family, which may be detrimental in emotional and financial terms. Both also carry the risk of confusion and distress to the child, through the distortion of his relationship, not only with the adopters but also with his parents. ...

5.17 Secondly, the Committee had in mind the need to provide security and status for some foster parents, in particular where 'the parents are out of the picture, and the foster parents and the child wish to legalise and secure their relationship and be independent of the local authority or child care agency, but the child is old enough to have a sense of identity and wishes to keep this and retain his own name'. There might also be cases where the parents were still in touch but recognised that they would never be able to provide a home for the child. Finally, some foster parents might not be able to afford to adopt, but could become guardians if financial assistance were available.

5.19 In the event, while the Committee's recommendations for adoption were implemented without significant change, further qualifications were imposed for 'custodianship.' It might have been argued that no special qualifications were needed, as the courts would be able to take all the relevant factors into account when deciding what would best promote the child's welfare. However, that would have increased the courts' powers to review the placement decisions made by local authorities. ...

Later, they make proposals for reform:

5.37 The simplest way of removing the arbitrariness, gaps and inconsistencies in the present law is to allow non-parents the same rights to apply for custody as have parents. They already have the right to apply for care and control in wardship proceedings, so that no new principle is involved in extending the statutory procedures to them. Given the large numbers of children who have experienced divorce, after which in theory any person can intervene to seek custody (or indeed access), it might not be such a radical step in practice as it at first sight appears.

...

5.39 It may therefore be that a requirement of leave, which currently applies to most interventions in divorce suits, would be a sufficient deterrent against unwarranted applications and would allow the court to judge whether the applicant stood a reasonable prospect of success in the light of all the circumstances of the case.

Special considerations apply, however, to children in care:

5.41 As already seen, children in care are treated differently from others in both the matrimonial and wardship jurisdictions and the restrictions in custodianship have been devised partly with their special circumstances in mind. Most children are received into care under section 2 of the Child Care Act 1980 without any compulsory measures against them or their parents. ... Under the Review's recommendations, local authorities would only compulsorily acquire parental rights if they could show, not only that they could do better than the parents, but also that the child was suffering or was likely to suffer harm as a result of shortcomings in his home. It would therefore be surprising if local authority foster parents could acquire the parental right of custody more readily than could the authority.

5.42 The unqualified right in foster parents to apply for custody could also be seen as an unprecedented interference in the child care responsibilities of the local authority. As has recently been emphasised, both by the Review of Child Care Law and by the report of the inquiry team in the Jasmine Beckford case, it is important to strengthen rather than to undermine the responsibility of local authorities to make the best possible provision for each child in their care. If foster parents were able to challenge their placement decisions in the courts, there would clearly be even greater pressure to allow parents to do so.

5.46 ... The security and stability which might be gained from a custodianship order must be set against the difficulties which premature applications might cause in the making and realisation of the local authority's plans, particularly for children who have been compulsorily removed from inadequate homes. Current child care practice places great emphasis upon planning a secure and permanent home for children who might otherwise have to grow up in care. This may be achieved either through making strenuous efforts to solve the family's problems and reach a position where parents and child may be reunited or through finding an alternative family which can provide the sort of care which is best suited to the child's needs. Such plans may obviously take some time to formulate and put into effect.

The end result, in the Children Act 1989, is a modified 'open door'. We have already seen (p. 528, above) how s. 10(1) and (2) provide for the court to make any s. 8 order, either in any family proceedings or on free-standing application, and that applications can be made either by people entitled to do so or by anyone with the court's leave. The section continues:

10. – (5) The following persons are entitled to apply for a residence or contact order with respect to a child –

(*a*) any party to a marriage (whether or not subsisting) in relation to whom the child is a child of the family;
(*b*) any person with whom the child has lived for a period of at least three years;
(*c*) any person who –
  (i) in any case where a residence order is in force with respect to the child, has the consent of each of the persons in whose favour the order was made;
  (ii) in any case where the child is in the care of a local authority, has the consent of that authority; or
  (iii) in any other case, has the consent of each of those (if any) who have parental responsibility for the child.

(6) A person who would not otherwise be entitled (under the previous provisions of this section) to apply for the variation or discharge of a section 8 order shall be entitled to do so if –

(*a*) the order was made on his application; or
(*b*) in the case of a contact order, he is named in the order.

(7) Any person who falls within a category of person prescribed by rules of court is entitled to apply for any such section 8 order as may be prescribed in relation to that category of person.

(8) Where the person applying for leave to make an application for a section 8 order is the child concerned, the court may only grant leave if it is satisfied that he has sufficient understanding to make the proposed application for the section 8 order.

(9) Where the person applying for leave to make an application for a section 8 order is not the child concerned, the court shall, in deciding whether or not to grant leave, have particular regard to –

(*a*) the nature of the proposed application for the section 8 order;
(*b*) the applicant's connection with the child;
(*c*) any risk there might be of that proposed application disrupting the child's life to such an extent that he would be harmed by it; and
(*d*) where the child is being looked after by a local authority –
  (i) the authority's plans for the child's future; and
  (ii) the wishes and feelings of the child's parents.

(10) The period of three years mentioned in subsection (5)(*b*) need not be continuous but must not have begun more than five years before, or ended more than three months before, the making of the application.

However, those local authority foster parents who require leave have an additional hurdle to surmount:

9. – (3) A person who is, or was at any time within the last six months, a local authority foster parent of a child may not apply for leave to apply for a section 8 order with respect to the child unless –

(*a*) he has the consent of the authority;
(*b*) he is a relative of the child; or
(*c*) the child has lived with him for at least three years preceding the application.

(4) The period of three years mentioned in subsection (3)(*c*) need not be continuous but must have begun not more than five years before the making of the application.

The consequences of obtaining a residence order are spelled out later (and see p. 442, above, for the consequences for the parents):

12. – (2) Where the court makes a residence order in favour of any person who is not the parent or guardian of the child concerned that person shall have parental responsibility for the child while the residence order remains in force.

(3) Where a person has parental responsibility for a child as a result of subsection (2), he shall not have the right –

(*a*) to consent, or refuse to consent, to the making of an application with respect to the child under section 18 of the Adoption Act 1976;

(*b*) to agree, or refuse to agree, to the making of an adoption order, or an order under section 55 of the Act of 1976, with respect to the child; or

(*c*) to appoint a guardian for the child.

Questions

(i) Do you approve of either (*a*) the open door or (*b*) the restrictions on local authority foster parents?
(ii) How many reasons can you think of why (*a*) the applicants, (*b*) the child, (*c*) the parents, or (*d*) the local authority might prefer (1) an adoption, (2) long-term fostering, or (3) a residence order?

The approach to leave applications is shown by the following two cases.

Re A (minors) (residence order: leave to apply) [1992] Fam 182, [1992] 3 All ER 872, Court of Appeal

Six children came into local authority care in 1989 and were placed with a 'supermum' foster carer who specialised in looking after children from very disturbed and difficult backgrounds. The two oldest ones ran away from her and in June 1991 the local authority decided to remove the other four for assessment. The foster mother was given leave to apply for judicial review; but before the case came on in December 1991 the Children Act 1989 had come into force and it was nearly six months since she had ceased to be the children's foster parent. The judge gave her leave to apply for a residence order and the local authority appealed.

Balcombe LJ: ... In my judgment the judge was wrong in holding that on an application for leave to apply for a section 8 order by a person other than the child concerned, the child's welfare is the paramount consideration. I reach that conclusion for the following reasons. (1) In granting or refusing an application for leave to apply for a section 8 order, the court is not determining a question with respect to the upbringing of the child concerned. That question only arises when the court hears the substantive application. ... (2) Some of the express provisions of section 10(9) – for example paragraphs (*c*) and (*d*)(i) – as to the matters to which the court is to have particular regard in deciding an application for leave to apply for a section 8 order would be otiose if the whole application were subject to the overriding provisions of section 1(1). (3) There would have been little point in Parliament providing that the court was to have particular regard to the wishes and feelings of the child's parents, if the whole decision were to be subject to the overriding (paramount) consideration of the child's welfare.

Thus in my judgment the judge applied the wrong test in approaching the exercise of his discretion. ... The application of this incorrect test may have materially affected the judge's decision, since he may well have considered that the children's welfare overrode the mother's wishes and feelings, a matter to which he should have had particular regard under section 10(9)(*d*)(ii). The judge's failure to apply the correct test in this respect was compounded by the fact that he was deprived of the material which was necessary for the proper exercise of his discretion because of his failure to require that the mother be notified of the foster mother's application for leave ...; had he done so he would have learned ... that if the matters to which she spoke were correct (viz. the foster mother's preventing her having access to and contact with the children, and allegations which she says the children made to her of their physical and emotional abuse by the foster mother and other members of her 'family'), then the mother's wishes and feelings were not lightly to be ignored. ...

... [S]ection 10(9)(*d*)(i) provides that the court is to have particular regard to the authority's plans for the child's future. And section 22(3) provides that it is the duty of a local authority to safeguard and promote the welfare of any child in its care. Accordingly, the court should approach the application for leave on the basis that the authority's plans for the child's future are designed to safeguard and promote the child's welfare and that any departure from those plans might well disrupt 'the child's life to such an extent that he would be harmed by it.'

...

It is now nearly a year since the children left the foster mother. If there is to be a full hearing of her application for a residence order it seems improbable that it could now be heard [for at least another three months]. Because of the nature of the allegations and counter-allegations it would be necessary for all the children to be subjected to psychiatric examination: the Official Solicitor recognises this but has postponed arranging any such examination pending the result of this appeal. Again, because of the nature of the allegations and counter-allegations, it seems probable that the hearing would be lengthy and bitter, and in view of their ages it seems to me impossible that the children would not know all about the hearing and the issues raised by it and be caught up in that bitterness. And, if they maintain their attitude expressed freely to the Official Solicitor's representative and to their mother, it would be all to no purpose, since no court would make a residence order in favour of the foster mother against the wishes of the children concerned who are of an age to know their own minds.

Appeal allowed.

Re M (care: contact: grandmother's application for leave)
[1995] 2 FLR 86, [1995] Fam Law 540, Court of Appeal

Two boys, now aged twelve and a half and nine, had been in care since 1987, some seven and a half years, because of their mother's psychiatric illness. They still had contact with both their mother and their grandmother, even after they had been made wards of court and the court had endorsed the plan that they be placed for adoption, but the contact caused difficulties and was suspended in 1991. Shortly after that the older boy ran away to his grandmother and she returned him to care. The boys were not placed with prospective adopters until 1993. In 1994, the grandmother sought leave to apply for contact. The judge had no information on the children's views or those of the prospective adopter. He refused leave and the grandmother appealed.

Ward LJ: ... It is clear to me that those concerns felt by the judge were overcome by the expectation he reasonably held on the information presented to him then that the prospective adopter was on the point of making her application for an adoption order. Unfortunately she has not done so as yet. ... It seems to me, therefore, that the whole basis upon which the judge dealt with the matter has been undermined. In a case redolent with delay, further delay and uncertainty is adverse to the interests of these children. Five years ago it was the opinion of Dr Wolkind and Dr James that contact should be stopped on the identification of the long-term foster-parents but reconsidered later and that view was accepted by Ewbank J. Contact in fact ended 4 years ago. It may be too late to reintroduce it but if during these years the children have retained a memory of their grandmother and would wish to have some even indirect contact to her, then a grave injustice will have been done to them if this matter is allowed to drift and the grandmother's application is not allowed to receive full consideration. Because I am satisfied that the whole basis of the judge's approach has been undermined, I would allow the appeal.

... Section 34(3) [p. 649, above] gives the court a wide and unfettered discretion in dealing with such applications. This can be contrasted with s. 10(9) which deals with leave to apply for s. 8 orders [p. 657, above].

... If the court were faced with an application by a grandparent for leave to apply for a residence order, alternatively a contact order, it would be anomalous, in my judgment, were the court not to take into account for the exercise of the s. 34(3) discretion the criteria specifically laid out for consideration in s. 10(9). Those particular factors seem to me to be also apposite for s. 34(3). The court must, of course, have regard to all the circumstances of the case, for each case is different, but in my judgment the court should always have particular regard at least to the following:

(*a*) *The nature of the contact which is being sought.* Contact to children in care varies infinitely from that which is frequent, to that which takes place two, three or four times a year to keep memory alive. It varies from contact which is face-to-face, to contact which is indirectly maintained through the exchange of letters, cards, photographs and gifts.

(*b*) *The connection of the applicant to the child.* The more meaningful and important the connection is to the child, the greater is the weight to be given to this factor. Grandparents ought to have a special place in any child's affection worthy of being maintained by contact but it is easy to envisage family circumstances, very much like those before us in this case where, however loving the grandparent may be, life's wheel of misfortune has diminished the importance to the child of that blood tie and may, for example, have strengthened the claims for contact by former foster-parents who have forged close attachment to the child. The fact is that Parliament has refused to place grandparents in a special category or to accord them special treatment. Nevertheless, by virtue of Sch. 2, para. 15 [p. 648, above], contact between a child and his or her family will be assumed to be beneficial and the local authority will need to file evidence to justify why they have considered that it is not reasonably practicable or consistent with the child's welfare to promote that contact.

(*c*) *Disruption.* This seems to me to be the factor of crucial significance, a fortiori when the child is in care. The child will only have come into care if life had already been so thoroughly disrupted that such intervention was judged to be necessary. The need then for stability and security is usually vital. The breakdown of the foster placement may be so harmful that it should not be placed at risk. All that is obvious. It is, none the less, significant and appropriate that the risk of disruption which is primarily contemplated in s. 10(9)(*c*) is the risk 'there might be of that *proposed application* [for a s. 8 order] disrupting the child's life to such an extent that he would be *harmed* by it'. I add the emphasis to make two points. The harm envisaged is harm which, through s. 105(1), is defined by s. 31(9) to mean impairment of health or development as those words are there defined. A child's upset, unhappiness, confusion or anxiety, needs to be sufficiently severe before it can amount to an impairment of emotional, social or behavioural development. Secondly, the risk must arise from the proposed application. The very knowledge that litigation is pending can be sufficiently unsettling to be harmful; if leave is given, the process of investigating the merits of the application can be sufficiently disruptive if it involves the children in more interviews, psychiatric investigations and so forth. The stressfulness of litigation may impair the ability of those who have care of the child properly to discharge their responsibility to the child's detriment. Questions of that sort are the narrow focus of the court's attention in weighing this factor. That is not to say that the court shuts its eyes to what prospects of eventual success the application has, and if the making of a contact order would be so manifestly disruptive as to be totally inimical to the child's welfare, then such an obviously unsustainable claim will not be permitted to get off the starting-blocks. Except in the most obvious case, it is incumbent on the respondent to the application to produce some evidence to establish disruption.

(*d*) *The wishes of the parents and the local authority.* They are very material, though not determinative. That the parents' wishes are relevant is consistent with the whole underlying philosophy of the Act, a cornerstone of which is the protection of the integrity and independence of the family. When a care order is made, the local authority acquires parental responsibility. Their exercise of that responsibility commands equal protection from unwarranted interference. ...

[Reference is then made to *Re B*, p. 650, above.]

I have attempted to identify the main factors which will be material for the court considering any application for leave. The list is not, however, intended to be exhaustive. I turn next to the question of what test the court must apply to decide whether or not to grant leave.

...

In my judgment the approach should be this:

(1) If the application is frivolous or vexatious or otherwise an abuse of the process of the court, of course it will fail.

(2) If the application for leave fails to disclose that there is any eventual real prospect of success, if those prospects of success are remote so that the application is obviously unsustainable, then it must also be dismissed: ...

(3) The applicant must satisfy the court that there is a serious issue to try and must present a good arguable case. 'A good arguable case' has acquired a distinct meaning: see the long line of authorities setting out this as the convenient approach for the grant of leave to commence proceedings and serve out of the jurisdiction under RSC Ord. 11. One should avoid unprofitable inquiry into what precisely these turns of phrase mean. Their sense is well enough known – is there a real issue which the applicant may reasonably ask the court to try and has he a case which is better than merely arguable yet not necessarily one which is shown to have a better-than-even chance, a fair chance, of success? One should avoid over-analysis of these 'tests' and one should approach the matter in the loosest way possible, looking at the matter in the round because only by such imprecision can one reinforce the importance of leaving the exercise of discretion unfettered. ...

It would be equally unwise to circumscribe rigidly the manner of the exercise of discretion. Each case is different and the weight to be given to the various factors will accordingly vary from case to case. The weight to be given to those factors is the very essence of the exercise of discretion.

Appeal allowed and case remitted to the High Court. Official Solicitor to act as guardian ad litem. Contact application to be heard on same day and immediately preceding adoption application.

Question

In 1992 the grandmother had applied for care and control, but because of the Children Act 1989, the boys were no longer wards of court and the court had no jurisdiction. It does not seem to have occurred to anyone that she could have sought leave to apply for a residence order. Who was most to blame for the drift and delay: (*a*) the social workers who had taken so long to find a placement, (*b*) the lawyers who had presumably given defective advice in 1992, or (*c*) the courts which had not taken the point then and later took over a year to determine her request for leave?

We have already seen (p. 656, above) that one reason for the invention of custodianship was disapproval of the distorting and confusing effects of adoption by grandparents and other relatives. The courts, however, were sometimes more sympathetic:

Re S (a minor) (adoption or custodianship)
[1987] Fam 98, [1987] 2 All ER 99, [1987] 2 WLR 977, Court of Appeal

The applicants were the mother's father and his second wife, who had taken full responsibility for the child (now 4) since he was 6 months old. The mother had consented to adoption, but the local authority favoured custodianship, because adoption would not enhance the quality of the relationship between the applicants and the child and could confuse existing relationships. The judge made a custodianship order and the applicants appealed.

Sir Roualeyn Cumming-Bruce: ... It seems to me that the paramount factor affecting his future welfare is to make an order that will secure him in his de facto relationships in such a way as to minimise the risk of the natural mother, or anyone else, seeking to disrupt them. This an adoption order can achieve with a greater prospect of success than a custodianship order. The legal relationships will then coincide with the actual relationships on which T is, by now, totally reliant. It seems to me that an adoption order will promote the welfare of T in another way. When he is tactfully introduced to the true facts about his parentage, the adoption order will have already conferred upon him the legal status of child of the applicants. This is likely to reduce, not increase, the risk of emotional confusion, or the onset of insecurity.

Glidewell LJ: ... In this case, however, whether T is adopted or not, he will be brought up by the applicants, and the decision when and how to tell him will be made by them. The female applicant said in her evidence in the county court: 'T will grow up understanding; we've spoken to him already about adoption.' She also then said, and counsel repeated before us, that she and her husband would seek the help and advice of the county council social workers. That being so, whatever the prospects are of T being in a state of some confusion when he not only knows but is old enough to appreciate and understand the true relationships in his family, I cannot see how that confusion will be greater, or its effect made worse, if he is adopted than if the applicants are his custodians.
Appeal allowed.

The Review of Adoption Law (1992), however, still favours residence orders over adoption and has looked for ways of making the former more attractive:

6.2 Where a child is living away from his parents and it is unlikely that he will be able to return home, he and his carers – be they relatives, foster-parents, or people with a residence order – may wish to enhance the security and stability of their relationship. Unless the child no longer feels part of his parents' family and would prefer to look on his present carers as his parents, his needs are more likely to be met by a residence order under the Children Act 1989 than by an adoption order. A residence order confers parental responsibility upon the child's carers without interfering with the child's identity and family relationships. Although it can be revoked, in practice a residence order will generally provide the necessary permanence for the family concerned, as once a child is settled the courts are reluctant to disturb the status quo and are most unlikely to discharge the order in favour of another party. Extra security may be gained by applying for a prohibited steps order restraining the parent from meeting aspects of parental responsibility without the permission of the court. The court may also prohibit any named person from applying for an order under the Act without the court's leave: this power could be used to prevent a parent disturbing the status quo by applying for a residence or contact order.
6.3 We are concerned that a number of adoption applications, particularly by relatives and step-parents, are made without giving proper consideration to the needs of the child and the effect of being cut off from his or her birth family. Adoption is too often regarded as the only way of securing permanence, in part no doubt because it is more familiar than other orders and because its long-term implications are not always fully understood. We therefore recommend that the court should have a duty when deciding whether or not to make a placement order or an adoption order to consider the alternative orders available under the 1989 Act or adoption legislation. ...
6.4 Responses to the review revealed a wide degree of concern that residence orders are not perceived as being likely to offer a sufficient sense of permanence for a child and his carers. It is hoped that in time residence orders will grow in familiarity and acceptance. One must nonetheless recognise the importance of the public perception of an order of this kind: some potential applicants may be deterred by the possible difficulty of explaining to other people what their relationship with the child is and by the relative attractiveness of an order which enables them to be regarded as the child's parents. It may therefore be beneficial to enhance the attractiveness of residence orders in certain circumstances.
6.5 We propose that, where a court makes a residence order in favour of a person other than a parent or step-parent and considers that that person will be responsible for the child's upbringing until he grows up, the court should have a further power to appoint, where appropriate, that person as the child's inter vivos guardian. Such a guardian would have parental responsibility until the child reached the age of 18, even though the residence order would normally come to an end at the age of 16. The guardian would have all the rights, duties and powers of a guardian under section 5 of the Children Act 1989 except for the right to agree or withhold agreement to the adoption of the child and the power to change the child's surname except with leave of the court. The appointment could of course be ended in the usual way by the court. An inter vivos guardian would be able to appoint a person to be the child's guardian after his or her death. Any guardian so appointed would have the right to agree or refuse to agree to the adoption of the child.

As for adoption applications by relatives or carers:

20.4 We do not wish to rule out the possibility of adoption by relatives. There may be circumstances, however few, where it is appropriate: for instance, where a child's parents are dead, or they are living in another country and are unlikely ever to be able to make parental decisions in respect of the child's upbringing, and the child would like to be able to look upon a relative as a parent. But, as with applications by step-parents, we feel that the legislative framework must provide adequate opportunity for applicants to explore other possibilities, particularly residence orders.

...

21.1 There does not appear to be any reason why a child's carers should not at some point be able to apply for adoption. It would not be in the interests of a child to deny him the opportunity of adoption where, with the passage of time and changes in circumstances, carers find themselves fulfilling the role of parent and a child has come to look upon the carers as parents, and their family as his.

21.2 We propose, in line by and large with the requirements under the Children Act relating to applications for residence orders, that a person with whom a child is living should be allowed to apply for an adoption order at any time with the agreement of those with parental responsibility including, where the child is in care, the care authority; and that, where the necessary agreement has not been given, a person should be allowed to apply if the child has lived with him for a cumulative period of three years (within the previous five years). The leave of the court may be obtained in other cases but a local authority foster parent needs the consent of the authority.

21.3 We suggest that these recommendations should apply equally to applications by non-relatives and relatives. We think it important that rules for applying for residence orders and adoption orders are similar to avoid the foster parents making one application where their real intention is to secure the other. ...

22.1 Once an application has been made, there is a need to investigate the relationship between the child and the applicants; to ascertain the wishes and feelings of the child, parents, relatives and any other relevant persons; and to give the applicants and child opportunities to discuss the application in the light of any other possible arrangements that could be made. It is proposed that, for these purposes, there should be a mandatory period of 12 months between the application and the making of an adoption order in all non-agency applications.

Questions

(i) Do you think that inter vivos guardianship will be any more popular than custodianship with grandparents who have looked after their grandchildren from infancy?

(ii) The draft Bill published for consultation in *Adoption – A Service for Children* (1996) does not implement the recommendation about appointing guardians. Do you see why the Review recommended that an inter vivos guardian could not give or withhold consent to an adoption but a guardian appointed by such a guardian could?

(iii) Do you agree with the Review team (para. 6.1) that 'it is also important that adoption is not seen as the only or best means of providing a child with a permanent home'?

4 Adoption now

We have already looked at the traditional type of adoption in Chapter 11, at adoption by step-parents in Chapter 12, and at adoption by relatives and foster carers above. Now we must draw the threads together by looking at adoption as a child care resource and the implications of this for the status of parents and the continuation of family links. Barbara Tizard explains the development in *Adoption: A Second Chance* (1977):

Since the twenties adoption had been seen primarily as a service for childless couples – a way of providing them with a substitute child to satisfy their emotional needs and cement their marriage. ...

The essence of the new view of adoption is that it is a form of child care, one among several possible ways of rearing children whose parents can't, or won't, look after them. At first sight this change in emphasis may seem to be only a verbal distinction, since adoption must necessarily provide a service to both adoptive parent and homeless child. The implications of the two viewpoints are, however, very different – different couples and different children are considered suitable for adoption, depending on whether adoption is seen primarily as a cure for infertility or as a form of care. According to the first viewpoint, which until recently prevailed, only infertile couples would be offered a child. Prolonged investigations into infertility were the rule, because it was assumed that if the couple subsequently had a child of their own they would reject the adopted child. The health, racial origins and family history of the infant were closely examined, because it would not be 'fair' to place with the couple a child dissimilar to the healthy infant who under optimal circumstances might have been born to them. Only healthy infants with a 'good' family history were offered. ...

If, however, adoption is seen primarily as a way of providing care for a child outside his natural family, then any child in need can be considered for adoption, whatever his colour, family history, state of health or age. Adoptive parents for these children are selected not for their infertility but because of evidence (often from the rearing of their own children, or from the kind of work they have done) that they are likely to provide a loving, stable home for a child in need.

This 'child-centred' view of adoption is enshrined in the following section of the Adoption Act 1976:

Duty to promote welfare of child

6. – In reaching any decision relating to the adoption of a child a court or adoption agency shall have regard to all the circumstances, first consideration being given to the need to safeguard and promote the welfare of the child throughout his childhood; and shall so far as practicable ascertain the wishes and feelings of the child regarding the decision and give due consideration to them, having regard to his age and understanding.

The Review of Adoption Law (1992) made this comment:

7.2 The present welfare test requires courts and agencies to have regard to the child's welfare throughout his childhood. One of the special features of adoption is that it has a significant effect on a person's identity and family relationships not just during childhood but after the age of 18. It is known that some adopted people who have had no great difficulties during childhood coming to terms with the fact that they are adopted and have enjoyed a close relationship with their adoptive parents subsequently experience difficulties in the area of personal identity. We recommend that the legislative framework should underline the long-term significance of an adoption order and that the welfare test should refer not only to the welfare of the child throughout childhood but his welfare in adult life as well. We also recommend that one of the factors which the court must take into account in deciding whether to grant an order should be the likely effect on the child's adult life of any change in his legal status.

This is reflected in the draft Bill published for consultation in *Adoption – A Service for Children* (1996):

Considerations applicable to the exercise of powers

1. – (1) This section applies whenever a court or adoption agency is coming to a decision relating to the adoption of a child.

(2) The paramount consideration of the court or adoption agency must be the child's welfare, in childhood and later.

(3) The court or adoption agency must at all times bear in mind that any delay in coming to the decision is likely to prejudice the child's welfare.

(4) The court or adoption agency must have regard to the following matters (among others) –

(*a*) the child's ascertainable wishes and feelings regarding the decision (considered in the light of the child's age and understanding),

(*b*) the child's particular needs,

(*c*) the likely effect on the child (during childhood or later) of having ceased to be a member of the original family and become an adopted person,

(*d*) the child's age, sex, background and any of the child's characteristics which the court or agency considers relevant,

(*e*) any harm which the child has suffered or is at risk of suffering, and

(*f*) the relationship which the child has with relatives, and with any other person in relation to whom the court or agency considers the question to be relevant, including –

(i) the value to the child of any such relationship continuing,

(ii) the ability and willingness of any of the child's relatives, or of any such person, to provide the child with a secure environment in which the child can develop, and otherwise to meet the child's needs,

(iii) the wishes and feelings of any of the child's relatives, or of any such person, about the child.

(5) The court or adoption agency must always consider the whole range of powers available to them in the child's case (whether under this Act or the Children Act 1989) and, if it exercises any power, must only exercise the most appropriate one; and the court must not make any order under this Act unless it considers that making the order would be better for the child than not doing so.

(6) In this section –

'coming to a decision relating to the adoption of a child', in relation to a court, includes (among other things) –

(*a*) coming to a decision in any proceedings where the orders that might be made by the court include an adoption order or the making or revocation of a placement order, or

(*b*) coming to a decision about granting leave in respect of any action (other than the initiation of proceedings in any court) which may be taken by an adoption agency or individual under this Part,

but does not include coming to a decision about granting leave in any other circumstances, and

'relative', in relation to a child, includes any adoptive relative and the mother and father (including an adoptive mother or father);

and references to making an order include dispensing with parental consent.

The last sentence, however, is directly contradictory to another recommendation of the Review of Adoption Law (1992):

7.1 ... We recommend that the welfare principle in adoption legislation should be brought into line with that in the Children Act in making the child's welfare the paramount consideration, but with the important exception that the child's welfare should *not* be the paramount consideration in determining whether to make an adoption order without the agreement of the child's parent. If the principle of the paramountcy of the child's welfare were to apply in this respect, the court would be able to override completely a parent's wishes, which we would consider unacceptable in relation to an order which irrevocably terminates a parent's legal relationship with a child.

This leads us to the vital subject of parental consent. The Tomlin Committee (p. 467, above) treated adoption as a 'transaction' between natural and adoptive parents, in which the court's task was to ensure that their agreement did not prejudice the welfare of the child. Later developments have increased the role of agencies and professionals and decreased the influence of parents. But the agreement of each parent with parental responsibility is still required unless it can be dispensed with on defined grounds. Over the years, the circumstances in which the court has been empowered to dispense with the parent's consent have increased. The present list is in s. 16 of the Adoption Act 1976:

16. – (2) ... that the parent or guardian –
(*a*) cannot be found or is incapable of giving agreement;
(*b*) is withholding his agreement unreasonably;
(*c*) has persistently failed without reasonable cause to discharge the parental duties in relation to the child;
(*d*) has abandoned or neglected the child;
(*e*) has persistently ill-treated the child;
(*f*) has seriously ill-treated the child (subject to subsection (5)).
...
(5) Subsection (2)(*f*) does not apply unless (because of the ill-treatment or for other reasons) the rehabilitation of the child within the household of the parent or guardian is unlikely.

Question

Compare these grounds with those for making a care order under s. 31 of the Children Act 1989 (see p. 617, above). Do these grounds appear to you to be wider or narrower? Do the differences seem, at least at first sight, to be justified by the different circumstances in which the procedures are used?

In practice, dispensing with parental agreement to an adoption order arises in two quite different contexts: first, the parent who places her child for adoption and later changes her mind, and second, the parent who has never agreed to adoption.

Re W (an infant)
[1971] AC 682, [1971] 2 All ER 49, [1971] 2 WLR 1011, 115 Sol Jo 286, House of Lords

The mother was unmarried, in her early 20s. She was living in one room with her two little girls by an earlier relationship, now broken, when she found herself unintentionally pregnant again. She was a good mother to the girls but was doubtful of her ability to cope with a third child in that accommodation. Accordingly she made arrangements before the birth for the child to be adopted. She was offered better accommodation just before the birth, but still had doubts and so did not alter the arrangement. The child went to the applicants as temporary foster parents when he was 8 days old and had been there ever since. They began adoption proceedings when he was 10 months old, and the mother signed the consent form a few days later. She withdrew that consent the day before the hearing was first due to take place. She was now well settled with her two daughters and a cousin in her new flat, but she had had no contact at all with the child, who was 16 months old when the county court judge came to decide the case. He decided that she was withholding her consent unreasonably and made the order. Her appeal to the Court of Appeal was upheld, on the ground that her conduct had not been 'culpable' or 'blameworthy' ([1970] 2 QB 589, [1970] 3 All ER 990, CA) but a differently constituted Court of Appeal refused to follow this test in *Re B (CHO) (an infant)* [1971] 1 QB 437, [1970] 3 All ER 1008, CA and the applicants in this case appealed to the House of Lords.

Lord Hailsham of St Marylebone LC: ... [Section 16(2)(*b*)] lays down a test of reasonableness. It does not lay down a test of culpability or self-indulgent indifference or of failure or probable failure of parental duty. ... It is not for the courts to embellish, alter, subtract from, or add to words which, for once at least, Parliament has employed without any ambiguity at all. I must add that if the test had involved me in a criticism of the respondent involving culpability or callous or self-indulgent indifference, I might well have come to the same conclusion on the facts as did Sachs and Cross LJJ. But since the test imposed on me by the Act is reasonableness and not culpability I have come to the opposite conclusion.

The question then remains as to how to apply the correct test. The test is whether at the time of the hearing the consent is being withheld unreasonably. As Lord Denning MR said in *Re L (an infant)* (1962) 106 Sol Jo 611:

> 'In considering the matter I quite agree that: (1) the question whether she is unreasonably withholding her consent is to be judged at the date of the hearing; and (2) the welfare of the child is not the sole consideration; and (3) the one question is whether she is unreasonably withholding her consent. But I must say that in considering whether she is reasonable or unreasonable we must take into account the welfare of the child. A reasonable mother surely gives great weight to what is better for the child. Her anguish of mind is quite understandable; but still it may be unreasonable for her to withhold consent. We must look and see whether it is reasonable or unreasonable according to what a reasonable woman in her place would do in all the circumstances of the case.'

This passage was quoted with approval by Davies LJ in *Re B (CHO) (an infant)*, by Lord Sorn in *A B and C B v X's Curator*, by Pearson LJ in *Re C* [1971] 1 QB 437, [1970] 3 All ER 1008, *Re C (L)* [1965] 2 QB 449, [1964] 3 All ER 483 and by Winn LJ in *Re B (CHO)*. In my view, it may now be considered authoritative. ...

From this it is clear that the test is reasonableness and not anything else. It is not culpability. It is not indifference. It is not failure to discharge parental duties. It is reasonableness, and reasonableness in the context of the totality of the circumstances. But, although welfare per se is not the test, the fact that a reasonable parent does pay regard to the welfare of his child must enter into the question of reasonableness as a relevant factor. It is relevant in all cases if and to the extent that a reasonable parent would take it into account. It is decisive in those cases where a reasonable parent must so regard it. ...

I only feel it necessary to add on this part of the case that I entirely agree with Russell LJ when he said in effect ([1970] 2 QB 589, [1970] 3 All ER 990) that it does not follow from the fact that the test is reasonableness that any court is entitled simply to substitute its own view for that of the parent. In my opinion, it should be extremely careful to guard against this error. Two reasonable parents can perfectly reasonably come to opposite conclusions on the same set of facts without forfeiting their title to be regarded as reasonable. The question in any given case is whether a parental veto comes within the band of possible reasonable decisions and not whether it is right or mistaken. Not every reasonable exercise of judgment is right, and not every mistaken exercise of judgment is unreasonable. There is a band of decisions within which no court should seek to replace the individual's judgment with his own.

Appeal allowed.

Question

How many points of difference can you find between this case and *Re K (a minor) (wardship: adoption)* [1991] FCR 142, [1991] 1 FLR 57 (p. 654, above)? Are they enough to account for the difference in result?

Re H (infants) (adoption: parental consent)
[1977] 2 All ER 339n, [1977] 1 WLR 471n, 121 Sol Jo 303, Court of Appeal

An unmarried mother of about 20 gave birth to twins in January. They were fostered until April when she signed a provisional form of consent to adoption and the children were placed with the applicants. In May she signed the formal consent forms but still had doubts. In July she indicated that she opposed the adoption. The hearing took place in December. The trial judge found that the children had formed a special attachment to the adoptive mother which it might be harmful to break and that the mother was immature and vacillating. He dispensed with her agreement and the mother appealed.

Ormrod LJ, delivering the first judgment at the invitation of Stamp LJ, stated the facts and said that it was impossible for the court to come to any other conclusion than that the judge's judgment must be upheld. His Lordship continued: The attitude of the court to the question of dispensing with consent, or holding that the consent is unreasonably withheld, has changed over the years, since adoption became possible in 1926. It has changed markedly since Lord Denning MR's judgment in *Re L (an infant)* and perhaps even more markedly since the House of Lords' decision in *Re W (an infant)* and probably it will change even more in consequence of the Children Act 1975, although, at the moment, this court has said that s. 6 of the Adoption Act 1976 does not apply to this particular issue (*Re P (an infant) (adoption: parental consent)* [1977] Fam 25, [1977] 1 All ER 182). However, it is safe to say this: the relative importance of the welfare of the children is increasing rather than diminishing in relation to dispensing with consent. That being so, it ought to be recognised by all concerned with adoption cases that once the formal consent has been given or perhaps once the child has been placed with the adopters, time begins to run against the mother and, as time goes on, it gets progressively more and more difficult for her to show that the withdrawal of her consent is reasonable.
Appeal dismissed.

Question

Do you think that, on its proper construction, s. 6 of the Adoption Act 1976 (p. 664, above), should apply to the court's decision about whether the parent's decision to withhold agreement is unreasonable?

Cases where the parent has never consented usually arise after a child has been taken into care and the local authority plans a permanent substitute home rather than rehabilitation. The court's approach is first to decide 'where does the child's future lie?'; if it lies in a substitute home, the court must then decide whether a hypothetical reasonable parent would object. The law is the same whether it is an application to adopt or to free the child for adoption.

Re D (a minor) (adoption: freeing order)
[1990] FCR 615, [1991] 1 FLR 48, Court of Appeal

The child was 4 and a half years old. The father played no part in her life, the mother's relationship with him having ended before the child's birth. Following unexplained injuries and evidence of emotional deprivation, a care order was made. The child was placed with short-term foster parents and visits with the mother were arranged. At about the same time the mother gave birth to a second child by another man. The relationship between the mother and that other man was unstable. The child returned home to the mother on trial with intense social work involvement. However, the child had a continuing loss of weight and suffered unexplained injuries. There was hostility by the mother towards the child. The child was again placed with foster parents. The local authority decided not to try further rehabilitation but to consider adoption. The mother was at first in favour of adoption but later changed her mind. By this time she was living with a different man. Contact between mother and the child continued, albeit infrequently, after the child was placed with prospective adopters. The local authority applied to free the child for adoption. The judge dismissed that application and the local authority appealed.

Butler-Sloss LJ: ... [Counsel] for the local authority has criticised the judge's approach to both tests of welfare and consent. The first ground is that the judge confused the two tests and did not apply them in two stages. The judge said:

> 'I have been referred to a large number of authorities and there are two questions:
> (1) Is adoption in the best interests of the child?
> (2) Is the natural mother unreasonable in withholding her consent?
> Whether these two matters should be dealt with separately or together is arguable, there being conflicting authorities, but the end result in this case in my opinion is the same.'

In our judgment, the judge, having correctly identified the questions to be asked, fell into a fundamental error in considering it made no difference whether they were dealt with separately or together. Our understanding is that there are not now any conflicting authorities on the matter and none was cited to us. Moreover, ... the test under s. 6 is not the same as the test under s. 16(2), to which we shall refer later. This fundamental misapprehension has fatally flawed the course of the judge's reasoning and he has throughout his judgment confused the two tests.

The second criticism relates to the first test, whether it is in the child's best interests that she should be adopted. Having set out very briefly some of the relevant facts and considered access to the mother and her present position in somewhat more detail the judge said:

> 'What I have to decide is not whether it is in K's interests in the near or foreseeable future or perhaps the long-term future that she should remain with the prospective adopters, but whether it is in K's interests, at this time and at this age, that her right of contact with her mother and with her half-sister should be terminated. Notwithstanding the present careful reports to the contrary, I find it difficult to hold that it is in her best interests that contact should cease. Access is taking place, she enjoys it and it is causing no ill-effects.'

[Counsel] has argued with considerable cogency that the judge never addressed the underlying question of the welfare of the child, nor did he analyse objectively the value of access to the child. That value in turn depended upon the quality of the relationship between the mother and the child. How strong was the bond between them? ... There was no evidence of any real bond between the mother and child, not surprisingly with the history of interrupted care throughout her short life, and some evidence of rejection by the mother during each of the two periods when K was returned to the mother's care. She had a period of one year between October 1985 and October 1986 with her mother, followed by a gap of 9 months away from her. She returned in July 1987 for 7 months and thereafter, in the subsequent 16 months had seen her mother, at most, five or six times. The evidence of the social worker was that she was indifferent to access. It was a time for her to play with toys. She was happy there and happy to say goodbye. The social worker also said that she did not believe that there was a meaningful relationship between the mother and the child and that she would not suffer from the cessation of access by her mother. None of that evidence was referred to by the judge. Further, although he referred to the reports, he did not refer specifically to the report of the child's guardian ad litem, who found a lack of sustained commitment by the mother to access over the year up to the hearing and gave careful reasons on behalf of the child why he recommended adoption.

The judge also failed to make a finding as to whether the child was likely to return to the mother in the foreseeable future. This was a matter of importance in applying both the first and second tests. The undisputed evidence before him was that the child would remain with the prospective adopters whatever the outcome of the application, even if they had to be redesignated long-term foster parents. The local authority had a full care order and unless the mother succeeded in revoking it, an application for which was not in prospect, the child would not be likely to return home. The purpose of access, therefore, had to be considered: was it to create a greater bond between them which might lead to a change of heart by the local authority; or was it to be contact access for a few times a year to keep alive the child's knowledge of her mother? ... Reasons for continuing the second type of access were given to the judge by junior counsel then appearing for the mother, as he informed us. But it is unclear which sort of access the judge had in mind and whether he believed that a return to the mother was feasible. If rehabilitation was not feasible, the realities of the situation of access as the child grew older and became more settled with long-term foster parents did not appear to have been considered by the judge.

For all these reasons we are satisfied that the judge failed to look beneath the surface and did not look at all the circumstances. He gave what he thought was the desirability of access continuing at this time predominant weight over all other factors. He did not give sufficient consideration to the child's long-term welfare throughout her childhood and did not correctly apply the test under s. 6. In our judgment he erred in law in his approach to the first stage.

We now turn to the second stage. The test under s. 16(2) as to whether a parent is withholding his or her agreement unreasonably is entirely different from that under s. 6. ...

From *Re W (An Infant)* [p. 666, above] and subsequent speeches in the House of Lords and judgments of this court it is clear that reasonableness is to be judged by an objective and not a subjective test. Would a reasonable parent have refused consent? (per Lord Reid in *O'Connor v A and B* [1971] 1 WLR 1227,1229). This involves considerations of how a parent in the actual circumstances of this mother, but (hypothetically) endowed with a mind and temperament capable of making reasonable decisions, would approach a complex question involving a judgment as to the present and the future and the probable impact upon the child (per Lord Reid in *Re D* [1977] AC 602, 625). There has become a greater emphasis upon the welfare of the child as one of the factors (but not the overriding one), and the chances of a successful reintroduction to or continuance of contact with the natural parent is a critical factor in assessing the reaction of that hypothetical reasonable parent (per Purchas LJ in *Re H: Re W (Adoption: Parental Agreement)* (1983) 4 FLR 614, 625). This test is to be applied at the time of the hearing and the court is not entitled simply to substitute its own view for that of the parent (*Re W (An Infant)* (above) at p. 667).

In his judgment, the judge said:

> 'Miss D looks forward to the eventual reunification of K and S with her and Mr B. Although Miss D has not really explained all of the past, on the evidence I have heard from her I do not consider her aspiration eventually to have K back to be an unreasonable one. She has not said precisely how she expects this to come about. She is after all in the hands of the local authority, but I do not regard her aspiration as being unreasonable.'

Since the judge in considering the first test had never decided whether such an aspiration was objectively reasonable, the criticism of [counsel] that this was a subjective approach of the judge is, in our judgment, well-founded. The judge went on to say:

> 'Apart from eventual reunification there is access continuing and I do not see how I can say that she is being unreasonable to want it to continue as she thinks it is for the benefit of K and S. Especially when it is going on with no ill-effect to K.'

Again, since there was, as we have already set out under the first test, no finding as to the purpose or long-term benefit of access to K, [counsel's] criticism applies equally to this passage. ...

The question then arises as to whether this court should substitute its own discretion upon the facts before us or remit the application to the county court for a rehearsing and reassessment of the two tests. ... We are satisfied that in this case this court has sufficient information to enable it to consider the test of welfare and the objective assessment as to whether a hypothetical reasonable parent in the circumstances of this mother ought to have given her consent. On the first test we are entirely satisfied that there is no prospect whatever of this child returning to live with her mother. There is no evidence of a real relationship between the mother and the child. ... Further, the contact of K with her half-sister, S, has been infrequent and at their respective ages and in the circumstances it was not suggested by any one that any relationship at all has developed. We are satisfied that there is ample evidence upon which to answer the first test under s. 6: the adoption would safeguard and promote the welfare of K throughout her childhood.

The second test of consent is more difficult and we keep well in mind the importance of 'the band of decisions within which no court should seek to replace the individual's judgment with its own'.

Looking at the hypothetical reasonable parent in the circumstances of this mother, we see that the factors in her favour are: she is the mother and the child lived with her for two main periods totalling about 18 months: she now has a settled home with a potential step-father and S has returned to live with her and is being cared for satisfactorily – if she were not, no doubt the local authority would have intervened; she desires to reunite the family; she is continuing to have access and the child on one level enjoys it and is having no ill-effects from it.

The contrary factors are: the efforts at rehabilitation have failed in the past, not only because the child was not well cared for and there was suspected non-accidental injury which may have been attributable to the then cohabitee, but also a failure of bonding, and hostility and rejection by the mother; K has not lived with her mother since 19 February 1988, there is no present evidence of any close or warm or effective relationship between them nor any foundation upon which to recreate it; there is no evidence of any relationship between the half-sisters; there is no real possibility of rehabilitation not only in the foreseeable future, but since children cannot wait for ever and will settle where they are, at any time thereafter – consequently the entirely natural aspirations of the mother to have K back and reunite the family are unrealistic; in the absence of eventual rehabilitation and without an adequate existing relationship, the continuance of access in the long term is not likely to be beneficial to the child in any real sense; contact a few times a year without any firm basis of a relationship between the mother and child for a child of 4 and a half years old would at best be entirely superficial and more for the adult than the child, and at worst, as the child settled with the present family and grew older, might be unsettling and upsetting. ...

In our judgment, a reasonable parent in the position of the mother would recognise the overwhelming force of the negative points and the unreasonableness of refusing to agree to the freeing for adoption. We, therefore, hold that the mother has unreasonably withheld her agreement under s. 16(2). We allow the appeal and accede to the application of the local authority to free K for adoption.

Appeal allowed.

Question

In a somewhat similar case, *Re L (a minor) (adoption: statutory criteria)* [1990] 1 FLR 305, Balcombe LJ stated: '[counsel for the mother] submitted that there was a presumption in the case of all children that access by the natural parent was desirable, and the onus ought to be on those who sought to stop access to prove it. It seems to me that that submission is ... misconceived'. But if this presumption applies between separated parents, why should it not apply between birth parents and prospective adopters?

Re B (a minor) (adoption: parental agreement)
[1990] FCR 841, [1990] 2 FLR 383; Court of Appeal

After a history of neglect and inadequate parenting by the mother, care orders were made in respect of two children, N and S. The children were placed with foster parents. N settled well into the foster family but S was unhappy and disruptive. The local authority decided to terminate access for a trial period to see how the children would respond. A compromise was reached between the local authority and the mother whereby access would be restored. When access was reintroduced, there was a marked difference in the attitude between the two children: S wanted access to continue but N was diffident. S was subsequently returned to the mother and the care order in respect of her was revoked. The foster parents decided to apply to adopt N. The judge found that adoption would be in the best interests of N, but that he could not say that the mother's refusal to agree fell outside the band of reasonable parental decisions. Accordingly, he refused to dispense with the mother's agreement. The foster parents appealed.

Butler-Sloss LJ: ... In the careful judgment of the judge, he was satisfied under [s. 6 of the Adoption Act 1976] (1) that the welfare of the child during his childhood would be met by the adoption; and (2) that the boy himself wanted to be adopted. The boy was angry that the adoption proceedings were adjourned and, according to the judge, would be 'devastated if it did not take place,' and he was a very vulnerable child. He saw his sister as a threat in the home and was relieved when she left. He was not close to his sister. He regarded access as an intrusion and his attitude to it was ambivalent. He did not want to see his mother now, although he might wish to see her in the future. The judge was satisfied on the basis of welfare that the balance was in favour of adoption, although not overwhelming; and, from the wishes of the child to be adopted, he was satisfied that adoption was in the best interests of the boy. The only issue was the refusal of the mother to agree.

... The judge correctly set out the objective test that was to be applied. In my judgment, however, he did not go on to consider the effect upon a reasonable mother faced with this situation, a boy of 11, whose view was strongly held, who had lived with the foster family for 7 years at the time of the hearing before the judge and was entirely integrated within that family; a very vulnerable child who would be devastated by the result if the adoption did not take place. ...

The continuing contact between the mother and the son is undoubtedly an important factor, as indeed Purchas LJ said in *Re H; W (Adoption: Parental Agreement)* (1983) 4 FLR 614, at p. 625A:

> 'The chances of a successful reintroduction to, or continuance of contact with, the natural parent is a critical factor in assessing the reaction of a hypothetical, reasonable parent as was recognised in *Re F.*'

This, however, is an unusual case with unusually understanding foster parents said by the judge to be 'quite wonderful and selfless'. They have not sought in the past to prevent contact between the boy and his mother and sister, and there is nothing to indicate that they would do so in the future. ... The judge would not have granted access at this time, if asked, but he took the view that estrangement was not complete; he found it difficult to contemplate that the dialogue would not continue and attached considerable importance to it. The dialogue at that time was telephone calls and cards.

In refusing the adoption the judge referred to the possible effect of a Pyrrhic victory and the possibility that it might bring about the cessation of the very contact that the mother was wishing to have. He does not, however, appear to have considered that aspect of the problem within the situation of the mother and her refusal to consent. At the age of this child, his view of being in touch with his mother with or without an adoption order would carry a great deal of weight with these appellants and with any court who might in future consider whether access should be granted. The mother's position for herself and for her daughter in respect of contact with N is more likely to be secure with adoption than in a situation where the adoption was refused.

The judge was also, in my view, over-influenced by the position of S, which was undoubtedly different from that of the boy, N. She was isolated and alone, whereas he had his foster brother and foster sister. The position appeared to be very different to that in *Re C (A Minor) (Adoption: Conditions)* [1989] AC 1, [1988] 1 All ER 705, [1988] 2 FLR 159 [p. 679, below], where there was a real danger that the girl would lose contact with her brother after adoption and that was seen to be of substantial importance to her. In this case, the contact with his sister is not of great importance to N. The effect upon the sister, which is understandably in the mind of the mother, should not, in my judgment, in the circumstances of this case have assumed great importance in the assessment by a reasonable mother.

The other matter of which the judge took some account is that of the grievance of the mother. In my judgment, he misdirected himself in putting that into the balance, particularly since he found that the grievance was not justified since October 1984. There can, in my view, only be rare instances when a sense of grievance can justifiably have an important effect upon a reasonable parent with a decision to refuse consent, and I find it difficult to envisage when that could occur.

This was a difficult and worrying case in which the judge wanted to make an adoption order, but refused to do so on grounds which, in my judgment, were untenable. This was one of those cases in which the welfare of the child was decisive and a reasonable parent should have come to the conclusion that adoption was in the best long-term interests of this boy. I too would allow this appeal.

Appeal allowed.

Questions

(i) If the court first concludes that adoption is in the best interests of the child, how can it then conclude that the mother is reasonable in objecting?

(ii) How might a mother's *justifiable* sense of grievance be taken into account (see *Re E (minors) (adoption: parental agreement)* [1990] 2 FLR 397)?

(iii) Why were these cases argued under 'unreasonable withholding' rather than one of the other grounds for dispensing with parental agreement?

(iv) Would a different type of order have been appropriate in either of them?

The Review of Adoption Law (1992) had this to say about the grounds for dispensing with agreement:

12.4 Much of the difficulty surrounding this part of the law is associated with the ground used most often for dispensing with parental agreement – that the parent is withholding his agreement unreasonably. The court may dispense with parental agreement if it considers that a hypothetical reasonable parent would agree to the adoption. But it has not been clear how much weight a hypothetical reasonable parent would be expected to place upon the welfare of the child, particularly ... where a significant relationship has developed between the child and prospective adoptive parents. Even where (in freeing applications) the child has not yet been placed with prospective adoptive parents, there has been a tendency to decide that adoption is in a child's best interests and for this reason alone to dispense with parental agreement on the grounds that it is being unreasonably withheld. This has meant that the test has given paramount weight to the child's welfare, which we consider unsatisfactory when dealing with parental wishes and feelings in relation to so important a step as adoption. It is also unsatisfactory that the parent whose agreement is dispensed with on these grounds thereby acquires what may be perceived as the stigma of being an unreasonable parent.
12.5 Most of the other grounds for dispensing with agreement, although seldom used, are unsatisfactory in that they relate exclusively to shortcomings in parental care rather than to the needs of the child. Where there are faults or shortcomings in parental care, this should not imply that adoption is ipso facto a suitable option for a child. Nor in cases where it is decided that adoption is in a child's best interests should this imply that the parents are necessarily at fault. For instance, a mother whose eldest child has been in care for some years may have other children whom she has shown herself capable of looking after: although the child in care is not at risk of significant harm if he returns home, he may no longer consider himself part of that family and may want to make a fresh start with adoptive parents. Responses to the review largely favoured the removal of fault-based grounds for dispensing with agreement.
12.6 We therefore propose that, of the existing grounds in section 16(2) of the 1976 Act, only (*a*) ('the parent cannot be found or is incapable of giving agreement') should be retained. The remaining grounds should be replaced by a single test which should apply in all situations where a parent who is capable of giving agreement can be found and is withholding agreement. This test should:

a. address the question of the advantages of becoming part of a new family and having a new legal status (rather than the question of where the child should reside);
b. focus on the needs of the child rather than any parental shortcomings;
c. require the court to be satisfied that adoption is significantly better than other available options and that parental wishes should therefore be overridden.

It might be expressed in terms of the court being satisfied that the advantages to a child of becoming part of a new family and having a new legal status are so significantly greater than the advantages to the child of any alternative option as to justify overriding the wishes of a parent or guardian. The court should consider not just whether the child should go to live with, or continue to live with, the prospective adoptive parents but whether it is in the child's interests to sever his links with the birth family and become part of a new family. This should of course be considered carefully in any proposed adoption, but it is especially important where a child or a parent does not agree to adoption.

The draft Bill published in *Adoption – A Service for Children* (1996), however, not only makes the child's welfare paramount in decisions about parental consent (see p. 665, above) but words the grounds for dispensing with it in this way:

Parental etc. consent

46. – (2) The court cannot dispense with the consent of any parent or guardian of a child to the making of a placement order or adoption order in respect of that child unless –

(*a*) the parent or guardian cannot be found or is incapable of giving consent, or
(*b*) the court is satisfied that the welfare of the child requires the consent to be dispensed with.

Questions

(i) Is the combined effect of this provision and clause 1(1), (2) and (6) to *require* the court to dispense with consent when the simple balance of advantage to the child lies with adoption?
(ii) Do you think that this would be a good thing?
(iii) Do you think that it is compatible with either the child's or the birth family's right to respect for their family life, protected by Article 8 of the European Convention on Human Rights (see p. 714, below)?

The *Report of the Departmental Committee on the Adoption of Children* (the Houghton Report) (1972) recommended a new procedure:

168. ... There is considerable dissatisfaction with the timing and nature of the present consent procedure. Parental rights and obligations are not terminated at the time the parent signs the consent document. They continue until an adoption order is made some weeks or months later. The argument in favour of this system is that there is never a period when the child is not the legal responsibility of either natural or adoptive parents. But there is evidence that this procedure imposes unnecessary strain and confusion on the mother. Moreover, it may encourage indecisiveness on her part; and by maintaining her legal responsibility for the child until the adoption order is made, it may prevent her from facing the reality of her decision and planning her own future. This period of uncertainty can be considerably prolonged if there is a delay in the adoption arrangements.
169. The disadvantages for the adoptive parents are obvious. The welfare of the child is at risk while his future remains in doubt and there is a possibility that he may be moved. Even though this happens only in a small minority of cases, the knowledge that it is possible may give rise to anxiety on the part of all prospective adopters, who may hesitate to give total commitment to a child whom they may not be allowed to keep.
170. We suggested in our working paper that in agency cases it should be possible for consent to become final before an adoption order was made. ... These rights and obligations are transferred by the court to an adoption agency, and in due course are transferred by the agency to the adopters when an adoption order is made....
...
221. There is known to exist a sizeable number of children in the care of local authorities and voluntary societies for whom no permanent future can be arranged for a variety of reasons, for example, because the parents cannot bring themselves to make a plan, or do not want their child adopted but are unable to look after him themselves. Some of these children may have no contact with their parents and would benefit from adoption, but the parents will not agree to it. In other cases a parent may have her child received into care shortly after birth and then vacillate for months or even years over the question of adoption, thus depriving her child of the security of a settled family home life.
...
223. In some of these cases a court might well consider that there were statutory grounds for dispensing with the parents' consent because they had persistently failed to discharge the obligations of a parent, or were withholding consent unreasonably. Under the present law there is no way of testing this without first placing the child with prospective adopters and awaiting a court decision after at least three months care and possession by them. If the court then decides that there are insufficient grounds for dispensing with the parents' consent the child must be returned to the agency. Moreover, unless the child is in the care of a local authority which has parental rights, or a care order has been made, the parents can frustrate the proceedings by removing the child before the court hearing. Agencies are therefore understandably reluctant to place these children for adoption.
224. We accept the principle that the natural family should be preserved wherever reasonably possible. But where a child is in care with no satisfactory long-term plan in mind, and lacking the possibility of long-term stable relationships, we think that it should be open to a local authority or a registered adoption agency to apply to a court for the parents' consent to be dispensed with on one of the statutory grounds, for parental rights to be transferred to the agency and the child thus freed for placement for adoption. The parents should not be permitted to remove the child from the agency's care without the leave of the court while the application is pending. This procedure would enable a decision to be taken without a child first being placed for adoption.

The hearing would be in the nature of a relinquishment hearing but with the application made by the local authority or agency. Such an application would be made only where there was every prospect of a satisfactory placement for the child, and if it were granted the agency would have parental rights and obligations until an adoption order was made.

The resulting recommendations are contained in ss. 18 to 20 of the Adoption Act 1976:

Freeing child for adoption
18. – (1) Where, on an application by an adoption agency, an authorised court is satisfied in the case of each parent or guardian of the child that

(*a*) he freely, and with full understanding of what is involved, agrees generally and unconditionally to the making of an adoption order, or

(*b*) his agreement to the making of an adoption order should be dispensed with on a ground specified in section 16(2),

the court shall make an order declaring the child free for adoption.

(2) No application shall be made under subsection (1) unless –

(*a*) it is made with the consent of a parent or guardian of a child, or

(*b*) the adoption agency is applying for dispensation under subsection (1)(*b*) of the agreement of each parent or guardian of the child, and the child is in the care of the adoption agency.

(3) No agreement required under subsection (1)(*a*) shall be dispensed with under subsection (1)(*b*) unless the child is already placed for adoption or the court is satisfied that it is likely that the child will be placed for adoption.

.... .

Questions

(i) Freeing transfers parental responsibility for the child's upbringing to the agency (until he is adopted or the freeing order revoked): but is he still related to his birth parents and relatives? Can he succeed to their property?
(ii) In *Re E (a minor: adoption)* [1989] FCR 118, [1989] 1 FLR 126, Balcombe LJ commented: 'So the hypothetical reasonable mother could also take into account – although I doubt whether she could properly place much weight on this factor – that the choice lay between the family unit, with all its known deficiencies, with which [the children] have never lost contact, and a new and untried (though carefully vetted) placement with adopters': why should she not give this great weight, especially if adopters who can handle the child's continuing relationship with his birth family are hard to find?

Research into freeing for adoption in England and Wales (see Lowe, 1990) suggested that it had not lived up to expectations, mainly because of delays and differences in practice. The Review of Adoption Law (1992) voiced some more fundamental criticisms:

14.1 At present, the court fulfils a number of key functions in relation to adoptions which have been arranged by agencies. It scrutinises the report prepared by the agency to confirm that the agency has carried out the duties required of it. It ensures that the child, the parents and other people involved in the adoption are given the opportunity to put their views to the court and that their rights are protected. A court officer confirms that parental agreement has been freely given; where parental agreement is withheld, the court is responsible for deciding whether to dispense with that agreement. And the court confirms that adoption is in a child's interests before granting an adoption order.
14.2 Bearing in mind the new, permanent status that adoption confers on a child and the implications this has for the child, his birth family and the adoptive family, we consider that adoption should continue to be a judicial process with all the safeguards which this entails.

However, we also consider that the court should become involved in the scrutiny of an adoption plan at a stage which is appropriate to the nature of the decisions which it is required to make – this is not always the case under the present adoption process. In all adoption applications and in some freeing applications, the court is given the opportunity to consider the issues only after the child had been living with the prospective adopters for some months and a relationship has developed between them. This may present the court with something approaching a fait accompli, such that it feels unable to do anything other than dispense with parental agreement, if it has been withheld, and grant an adoption order. This is clearly unsatisfactory. ...

Freeing for adoption

14.3 At present, it is possible for an agency to seek the court's judgment on the matter of parental agreement at an earlier date by applying for a freeing order before or at about the same time as the child is placed with prospective adopters. A freeing order transfers the parents' parental responsibility to the adoption agency, pending the making of an adoption order. This procedure was originally designed to enable parents to make an irrevocable decision to give up their child at an early stage in the adoption process. In practice, its more common use has been by care authorities seeking to have the question of parental agreement resolved before – or in the early stages of – an adoption placement, so that the parents cannot contest the later adoption application. But freeing is not mandatory, and some agencies place children who are in care with prospective adopters despite parental opposition and without applying for a freeing order, perhaps in part because the court is felt to be more likely to dispense with parental agreement after the child has lived with the prospective adopters for a time.

14.4 Freeing for adoption has attracted much criticism, mainly on account of the delays which are usually involved. We consider that the difficulties associated with freeing are not just procedural ones. Other problems include:

a. the court is expected to resolve the question of parental agreement without looking at a particular placement (or proposed placement): there is a danger that courts may contrast the readily apparent shortcomings in the care offered or likely to be offered in future by a child's parents with the care likely to be offered by hypothetically perfect adoptive parents;

b. where an order is made prior to the identification of prospective adoptive parents, there is a danger that the child may be left without a family: although the court is not allowed to dispense with parental agreement unless the child is already placed for adoption or the court is satisfied that it is likely that the child will be placed, this is no guarantee that a freed child will be found a suitable adoptive family, and in uncontested cases an order can be made regardless of the likelihood of placing the child;

c. a child may also be left without a family if the placement breaks down before an adoption order is made;

d. although the agency may apply for a freeing order where the question of parental agreement ought to be resolved prior to placement, there is no requirement for the agency to do so, nor any guarantee that the hearing will take place before the placement has been made.

14.5 Freeing for adoption has been perceived to have some advantages. One reason why some agencies still find it helpful is that the application is by the agency, not the prospective adopters: this is felt to reduce the conflict between the birth family and adoptive family and lessen the risk that the child will later regard his adoptive parents as having 'taken him away' from the birth family. However, the distancing of the prospective adopters from the freeing process may not always work to the advantage of the child: it may in fact be that their closer involverment in the process at the stage when parental agreement is examined would encourage the different parties to discuss matters such as contact and share information about the child's background.

The Review's solution was that the child should not be placed with prospective adopters until the court had authorised that placement and in doing so had dealt with the question of parental agreement: thus the parents would not be faced with a fait accompli if the placement had already been made or with a picture of the ideal placement which might be available. The system proposed in the draft Bill (1996), however, is outlined in the accompanying consultation document:

Placement with parental consent

4.4 Provisions continue to allow the placement of children for adoption with the consent of the parent or guardian. There are two forms of parental consent to a placement: consent to the child being placed with named prospective adopters, or general consent to the child being placed with any prospective adopters who may be chosen by the adoption agency. It is expected that most parents or guardians will give general consent.

4.5 Parental consent to a child being placed for adoption is not synonymous with their giving consent to an adoption order; these are two distinct stages, each requiring a separate consent to be given. However, consent to the making of a future adoption order can be given at the same time as consent to the child's placement or subsequently before the application to adopt is made. Consent of the mother to adoption may not be given until the child is at least six weeks old.

4.6 It is considered that before giving parental consent to placement or to the making of a future adoption order a parent or guardian should be counselled. It is also considered that the form of the agreement should be prescribed and should be witnessed. ...

4.7 A parent or guardian does not lose parental responsibility for the child until an adoption order is made, although the exercise of that responsibility is to be limited. Where a parent or guardian consents to placement, he will be required at the same time to agree to parental responsibility being given to prospective adopters while the child is placed with them (and in any case to the adoption agency). The prospective adopters will exercise parental responsibility subject to certain restraints.

Placement orders

4.8 Arrangements for placing a child for adoption introduce a new provision – placement orders. Where the parent or guardian does not consent to the placement for adoption and the adoption agency has considered all available options and is satisfied that adoption is in the child's best interests, the matter is to be put to the court at an early stage to enable the court to make realistic decisions about the child's future. The purpose of a placement order is to enable the court to be involved at an early stage in those cases where the agency considers that adoption is in the child's best interests but the parent or guardian is not prepared to give his consent to placement and while other available options for the child's future can also be considered.

4.9 A placement order authorises the adoption agency to place the child for adoption with suitable prospective adopters. An order will not restrict a placement to named prospective adopters even where they are known to the agency; this is to avoid the agency having to go back to court for a new placement order in the event of the first placement breaking down.

4.10 Once a placement order has been made, parental responsibility is given while the child is placed with prospective adopters, to them. Regulations will provide for the names of the prospective adopters to be notified to the court by the adoption agency. Where the child is removed from that placement and subsequently placed with another set of adopters, the court is to be notified of the change. Parental responsibility reverts to the agency when the child is removed and in due course is given to new prospective adopters.

Placement of children under a care order

4.11 A placement order will be required for a child who is the subject of a care order; once the placement order is made it is to have the effect of suspending the care order for the duration of the placement order. Where a local authority applies to the court for a care order most courts already require them to provide a care plan for the child. Where the recommendation in the care plan is that the child should be adopted, the authority must also apply for a placement order at the same time as they apply for a care order. Should the placement order by revoked, the care order will automatically revive. This means that where placement for adoption turns out not to be the best solution there is no obstacle to revoking the placement order because the child will remain protected.

4.12 Where the care plan did not originally contain a recommendation that the child be placed for adoption but is revised at a later stage to make such a recommendation, an application for a placement order must be made at this stage. This will usually be heard by the same court which made the care order.

Placement generally

4.13 Once a child is placed with prospective adopters whether with the parent's consent or under a placement order, he ceases to be a 'looked after' child under the Children Act. Where the local authority may place a child for adoption, the authority may provide accommodation for him at any time when he is not so placed and during that period he will be a 'looked after' child under that Act.

Removal provisions

4.14 Where placement is by consent, the parent may withdraw that consent and require the return of the child (subject to set procedures) at any time up to the time when an application to adopt is made. After that, leave of the court is required. Where a child is placed under a placement order, the parent will not be able to have the child back unless the placement order is revoked. An application to revoke the order by the parent may only be made where the child is not placed with prospective adopters, at least a year has elapsed since the order was made and the court gives leave, being satisfied that there has been a change in circumstances.

Question

Do you consider that these proposals strike a fair balance between the interests of parents and the interests of children? Which is worse for the parents: the fait accompli or the prospective ideal? Which is better for the child?

5 Adoption: an open or shut case?

We saw in Chapter 11 how the Tomlin committee had disapproved of secrecy in adoption, yet over the years since then the complete segregation of birth and adoptive families had become the norm. But then chinks began to appear, particularly in foster parent adoptions:

Re B (MF) (an infant), Re D (SL) (an infant)
[1972] 1 All ER 898, [1972] 1 WLR 102, Court of Appeal

Two brothers, then aged four and one, were removed from their parents as being in need of care. They were fostered with the appellants, with whom they 'made great strides' and were 'undoubtedly happy and extremely well cared for.' Their natural parents' home was 'nothing like as satisfactory,' they had three other young children and were in 'constant financial difficulties,' partly because of the father's psychiatric difficulties. After three years, the foster parents applied to adopt the boys and the natural parents both consented, but the judge refused to make the order. The foster parents appealed.

Salmon LJ: ... The only other point that I should deal with is the fact that the appellants take the view that Mr and Mrs D, for whom they have much sympathy, should from time to time visit the children, and particularly that these two boys should be kept in touch with their sister Pauline. It is quite true that in law Pauline will cease to be their sister after the adoption order is made, but Pauline will remain their natural sister and no order of any court can alter that fact.

As a rule, it is highly undesirable that after an adoption order is made there should be any contact between the child or children and their natural parents. This is the view which has been taken, and rightly taken, by adoption societies and local authorities as it has been by the courts in dealing with questions of adoption. There is, however, no hard and fast rule that if there is an adoption it can only be on the terms that there should be a complete divorce of the children from their natural parents. ... Although the courts will pay great attention to the general principle to which I have referred, namely, that it is desirable in normal circumstances for there to be a complete break, each case has to be considered on its own particular facts.

The facts of this case are exceptional. Although it may be – I know not – that it would be a good plan if there were a complete break here between Mr and Mrs D and the two boys, the

appellants (who I suspect know a good deal more about the situation than I do) consider that the occasional encounters between Mr and Mrs D and the boys and Pauline [are] for their good.
Appeal allowed.

Re C (a minor) (adoption: conditions)
[1989] AC 1, [1988] 1 All ER 705, [1988] 2 WLR 474, House of Lords

C was taken into care, together with her two older brothers, at a very early age. C became very attached to her brother M during the next seven years, spent mainly in children's homes, and remained in touch with him after her placement with the prospective adopters. C wanted to be adopted, but her mother withheld agreement in case adoption might weaken her relationship with M. The judge thought this should be preserved at all costs. Both the judge and the Court of Appeal refused to dispense with the mother's agreement, being doubtful of the power to make continued contact a condition of the adoption order. The prospective adopters appealed.

Lord Ackner: ... It seems to me essential that, in order to safeguard and promote the welfare of the child throughout his childhood, the court should retain the maximum flexibility given to it by the Act and that unnecessary fetters should not be placed on the exercise of the discretion entrusted to it by Parliament. The cases to which I have referred illustrate circumstances in which it was clearly in the best interests of the child to allow access to a member of the child's natural family. The cases rightly stress that in normal circumstances it is desirable that there should be a complete break, but that each case has to be considered on its own particular facts. No doubt the court will not, except in the most exceptional case, impose terms or conditions as to access to members of the child's natural family to which the adopting parents do not agree. To do so would be to create a potentially frictional situation which would be hardly likely to safeguard or promote the welfare of the child. Where no agreement is forthcoming the court will, with very rare exceptions, have to choose between making an adoption order without terms or conditions as to access, or to refuse to make such an order and seek to safeguard access through some other machinery, such as wardship. To do otherwise would be merely inviting future and almost immediate litigation.

The cases in the Court of Appeal have essentially been concerned with the question of whether provision can properly be made in an adoption order for access to a natural parent or parents. Although it is one of degree, a distinction can properly be drawn between access to natural parents on the one hand and other natural relatives on the other. Other relatives and, in particular, brothers and sisters have no parental rights which by the adoption order are being extinguished and then vested in the adopters. The Court of Appeal was, in my judgment, correct in paying no regard to the suggestions made by the judge that if C were told that M was no longer her brother, she would be bitterly and desperately hurt. Fresh evidence put before the Court of Appeal established that C, when interviewed a little over a year ago, had made it clear that she wanted to be adopted, that to her adoption meant that 'she would then know that no one could ever take her away from her mum and dad' (the appellants). She said she could not see how it would affect her relationship with M or how she felt for him and he for her. Even without this additional evidence, it seems to me that the judge's evaluation of C's reaction to learning that technically M was no longer her *legal* brother was quite unreal.

...

The order which the judge made sacrificed the benefits of adoption in order to provide for an event which might never eventuate, namely the failure of the adopters properly to co-operate in maintaining access between C and M. The fresh evidence put before the Court of Appeal established that there continued to be no obstacles put by the appellants in the way of such access and none were anticipated by M. Indeed, your Lordships have been informed, without objection, that the appellants took C to London twice last year so that she could visit M, and had invited M to come to see his sister in Norfolk. Contact had continued by phone and letter. Moreover, the judge failed to appreciate that, were it to become necessary to enforce access between C and M, to do so through the machinery of wardship was no easier and, indeed, might be more complex, then by seeking to enforce a term or condition of the adoption order.
Appeal allowed.

Questions

(i) But what if the local authority had been unable to find prospective adopters who could recognise and respect the child's relationship with her brother?
(ii) Does the distinction drawn between birth parents and other relatives make sense?

A psychiatrist's view of the advantages and disadvantages of post-adoption contact is given by Jonathan Dare (1995):

The advantages and disadvantages of open adoption and the merits of subsequent contact with the natural parents

It is axiomatic that children in adoptive placements should have a reasonable knowledge of their biological parents and origins. With the gradual increase in age of adoption children increasingly come for adoption with considerable direct knowledge, experience and profound feelings about their biological background. This can be both helpful and unhelpful in the process of their making use of adoptive placement.

In 'open adoption', this knowledge will be augmented and developed, which again can have beneficial as well as detrimental effects on the adoptive child.

The use of the phrase 'natural parents' involves a degree of ambiguity. In particular, its meaning 'in the normal course of events' suggests an attitude and idea which may not be appropriate in the context of a child being placed in an adoptive family. The phrase 'biological' is more neutral and perhaps more appropriate.

CONTACT WITH BIOLOGICAL PARENTS IN OPEN ADOPTION

Advantages	*Disadvantages*
Not cut off from biological roots. Helps establish adult persona.	Confusion – 'where do I belong?' How to make sense of two sets of parent(s)
Provides continuity. 'Best of both worlds', i.e. providing a good parenting experience without losing known background.	Undermine absolute security/stability which is the whole idea of adoption. If see biological parent(s) sufficiently to 'know emotionally', then this can make problems in child committing self to adoptive placement. If see very frequently, contact may become a 'ritual' of little benefit but may still undermine placement. Reduces ability of child to emotionally invest in adoptive placement.
Reduces feeling of guilt and low self-esteem always associated with removal from biological family and placement elsewhere. Enhances self worth through knowledge about self background.	Confusion to child as to whether they belong and have characteristics related to their adoptive or biological family.
Allows view of biological parents in the 'round' i.e. not as all positive or all negative – crucial to developing rounded self-image as child, adolescent and adult.	Confusion caused if gross disparity between attitudes of biological and adoptive family.
Biological parents can promote child to invest in adoptive family and reduce child's wish to return to biological family.	Contact with biological parent(s) almost inevitably leads child to feel that there is possibility of rehabilitation – again undermining investment in adoptive placement.
Help child to make more sense of reason for adoption.	Contact with apparently loving and caring biological parents may make adoptive placement completely inexplicable to child.

With biological parents supporting and promoting placement in adoption, child has clear view of where all important adults feel child should be.	Danger of being in middle of parental 'competition' between adoptive and biological parents. Biologial parents may actively undermine child's commitment to adoptive placement.
Child seeing biological parents may facilitate adoptive parents' care of child.	Conflicts and uncertainties from adoptive parents' viewpoint. Perhaps undermining them in their ability to be 'all round' i.e. both setting firm limits and loving.

It must, however, be remembered that for the large majority of children (especially the older ones) being placed for adoption, these children are suffering from *chronic emotional damage and deprivation*. Thus their ability to make relationships and be able to cope with different sets of parents is almost de facto very significantly less than normal children. Such children have a much greater than normal need for absolute security and stability in order to facilitate them being able to invest emotionally in an adoptive family.

Similarly, the biological parents of such children are also likely to be adults with the type of parental characteristics which would make it difficult for them to facilitate and promote the placement of the child in an adoptive family. They will almost inevitably feel rivalrous and may unconsciously wish for the placement to fail in the adoptive placement in the same way that it failed with the child in their own care.

Question

How far do (*a*) the particular 'pros and cons' and (*b*) the general propositions derived from clinical experience coincide with the more general research evidence discussed earlier (pp. 641–648)?

Despite such misgivings, a more 'open' view of adoption has been developing, particularly for older children who need a secure placement but retain a knowledge of their origins. Open adoption has been pioneered in New Zealand, and the results appear in the *Report of the Adoption Practices Review Committee* (1990):

WHAT IS OPEN ADOPTION?

Open adoption can mean different things to different people and can take different forms. Social work practices differ throughout the country. At one end of the spectrum, it involves nothing more than an exchange of letters and photographs, sometimes through the mediation of the Department. At the other end of the spectrum, it can mean a degree of co-parenting between the birth and adoptive parents. In between, there is a wide range of different styles of contact, co-operation and mutual care. Open adoption may involve not just the parents, but also the families, and we have heard of moving experiences as families get to know each other and share their lives a little.

Whatever the nature of open adoption for particular individuals, it is important to emphasise that everyone should enter upon the process with the right attitude – an attitude of openness, respect and willingness to explore the options in the interests of the child.

POPULARITY OF OPEN ADOPTION

The evidence we have received strongly supports open adoption. This support comes from all quarters – adopted persons, birth parents, adoptive parents, families, social workers, and experts in the field. Although we cannot be sure what effect open adoption will have long-term on adoptive people, given that it is only recently that the practice has begun, we are confident that it provides a more satisfactory basis for the vast majority of permanent placements of children. …

Open adoption appears to be in the best interests of the child for several reasons:

(i) To develop socially, emotionally, physically and intellectually, the child should have a sense of personal identity. Knowledge of genetic inheritance, whakapapa and roots is a component of identity formation. Open adoption is one of several ways of preserving to varying degrees the child's cultural background.

(ii) For a child to be accepted fully in the adoptive family, there is a need for the child's origins to be known and accepted by the whole family …
(iii) There is research and inherited wisdom that children can maintain more than one relationship simultaneously and indeed may benefit from so doing, provided that there is no threat to the permanency of placement with the principal family.

ONGOING SUPPORT
While the endorsement of open adoption is overwhelming, there are points of concern. Open adoption is sometimes presented as if it were the ideal answer and simple to carry through. The reality is that, even in the best of open adoption arrangements, there can be problems, unforeseen issues, tensions, changes of circumstances and changes of heart. These are all perfectly natural, given that we are dealing with human nature. Sometimes they may stem from the different socio-economic backgrounds of the birth and adoptive parents.

It must be recognised that open adoption needs working at, that the parties sometimes need assistance to make it work, and that each relationship is different. Under 'the new adoption', adoption is a process and not an event. It is important therefore that practice does not suddenly end. It is equally as important that the preparation of the parties be realistic, point out the pitfalls as well as the joys, and get people to think long-term about the arrangement that they come to. Sometimes, for example, a birth mother may want minimal contact for the first few years but feel more confident about herself and the relationship with her child later on. The adopted person may not place much store beside contact with birth parents in the first few years of life but feel quite the opposite as the teenage years are lived. It must be remembered that the welfare of the child is the deciding factor, and security and permanency of placement is a principle which we accept.

The idea was taken up by the Review of Adoption Law here. In its discussion paper on *The Nature and Effect of Adoption* (1990), Option A was to retain the existing concepts of adoption and residence orders, but with possible modifications to the former:

97. One of the great benefits of adoption and its essential feature in contrast to other orders is the permanent status it confers on both child and adoptive parents as members of the new family, the security this gives to them all, and the commitment it demands of the adoptive parents. Given the importance with which permanence has been regarded in social work philosophy in recent years, it is not surprising that the irrevocability of adoption has made it attractive to those involved in finding substitute care for children. Furthermore, this new relationship continues into adulthood and throughout the lives of all involved. …

Suggested modifications: openness
98. Given these advantages, would it be better to modify adoption within its existing legal framework, rather than to create new alternatives? One option would be to facilitate greater openness in the form of pre- or post-adoption contact, while leaving the legal effects of adoption essentially unchanged. …

Pre-adoption contact
100. One form of openness would allow greater involvement of the birth parents, usually the mother, in the selection of adopters. Birth parent involvement might range from actual selection, for example from a number of prospective adopters approved by the agency, to exchange of photographs. It is difficult to say to what extent this is happening already; the legislation itself gives no guidance on the issue and is predicated on the assumption that no such involvement takes place. Legally however there is nothing to stop pre-adoption involvement of birth parents and one option would be to leave this to developments in agency practice. The extent of such links would obviously be related to the post-adoption position, as were there to be contact after adoption, pre-adoption meetings would be a natural corollary.

Openness and the legal process
102. A further corollary of increased openness before and after adoption is to move towards less secrecy at the time of the proceedings. Anecdotal evidence suggests that in many cases serial numbers are applied for as a matter of course without necessarily any regard to the particular

circumstances of the child. One option would be to reduce the use of the serial number procedure by making it available only with leave of the court.

Post-adoption contact

103. If the existing approach is retained and adoption continues to effect a transfer should it necessarily sever all of the links with the child's birth family after adoption? Increased openness might make adoption the favoured solution for some children for whom long-term foster care had seemed the only possibility, even though rehabilitation with the birth family was out of the question. This could include children whose parents do not agree to adoption and children needing contact with relatives.

104. Although the Adoption Act 1976 allows conditions to be included in adoption orders the courts have been reluctant to attach access provisions [see p. 679, above]. However, evidence from one research sample of 'special needs' adoptions showed that contact with parents and siblings continued in a small percentage of cases. Thus, while few adoption orders actually include an access clause, access may continue as a result of informal agreement.

105. The Children Act 1989 will allow a contact order to be added to an adoption order and the court to prescribe the type and extent of contact. This might range from staying access at one end to the exchange of cards on birthdays and special occasions at the other. The Act will also allow a contact order to be attached to a freeing order and so for the first time a child could be freed with a condition of access. Adopters would know that in these circumstances there would be less risk of the parents withdrawing their agreement and their acceptance of the access could be explored at an early stage. This would be a major development for the courts which at present regard access as exceptional and are extremely unlikely to grant it without the adopters' agreement. It would also be a major development for agencies.

106. Again, should developments in post-adoption contact be left to practice or is there a need for legislation? Statutory encouragement of the use of contact orders, perhaps in the form of a duty on the court to consider them in every case where an adoption order is made, is one way in which additional flexibility could be achieved whilst retaining the basic status quo. Or should the use of orders to regulate post-adoption contact be restricted, for example to those cases where the parties themselves have reached agreement? What other restrictions, if any, might there be on the use of post-adoption contact orders? The court could of course refuse to make the order, where it was of the view that this would not be in the child's best interests.

108. It would also be possible to make provision for the court to direct the adoption agency to continue to pass on information to birth parents after adoption. The co-operation of the adoptive parents would obviously be necessary for this to work in practice. Another possibility would be to increase the opportunity for birth parents and relatives to obtain information about the adopted person once he or she had grown up.

Questions

(i) Option B was to have two different types of irrevocable order, one transferring the child from one family to another, the other transferring only parental responsibility for bringing the child up: is this really necessary?

(ii) The Children's Legal Centre (1991) would prefer there to be three different types of residence order ('basic', 'midway', and 'permanent'); they argue that 'the concept of adoption reinforces the notion of children as property *par excellence*'. Do you agree?

(iii) The draft Bill (1996) contains nothing which would lead to greater openness in adoption: although an adopted child will still be able to have his original birth certificate, the other avenues for adopted and birth families to trace one another later in life, through the Adoption Contact Register and the court records, are narrowed rather than widened: is this further evidence of a 'two tier' adoption system – one for anonymous placement of young children and another for older children placed through the care system?

(iv) How would you go about being 'open' with a child whose birth parent had seriously abused or neglected him?

One last aspect of the blurring of distinctions between fostering and adoption is the implementation in 1982 of the following recommendation of the Houghton Report (1972):

Should adoption be subsidised?

93. We suggested in our working paper that consideration should be given to the possibility of guardians and adopters being paid regular subsidies in appropriate cases, and we said that we would welcome views on this. While there was considerable support for allowances for guardians ..., many witnesses saw a clear distinction between adoption and guardianship and opposed the idea of any payments to adopters. Some took the view that payment would conflict with the principle that adoption should put the child in precisely the same position as a child born to the adopters. While some agreed with our suggestion that, if allowances were payable, more homes might be found for children with special needs, others said that it would be unfair to the parents of handicapped children if the adopters of these children could get an allowance which was not available to their natural parents. Some said that the law should not forbid agency payments to adopters but that there should be no national system of allowances.

94. We recognise the objection to singling out handicapped adopted children for special payments, and we do not advocate payments for adopters generally. However, we still think that there is a case for allowances in some circumstances, for example, where suitable adopters are available for a family of children who need to be kept together but, for financial reasons, adoption is not possible if an allowance cannot be paid. Although most witnesses were opposed to our suggestion, we should like to see a period of experiment during which evidence could be gathered. But at present even experiment is not possible, because it would contravene the law, and we recommend that the law should be amended so as to enable payments to be made by a few charitable bodies specially authorised by the Secretary of State for this purpose. There may be a number of difficulties, and we suggest pilot schemes which could be reviewed after, say, seven years, although the subsidy would have to be continued to those who had adopted on that basis for as long as they needed it.

6 The cross-cultural dimension

The following story is told by Barbara Tizard in *Adoption: A Second Chance* (1977):

The fifth set of foster parents, a comfortably-off middle-class couple in their 50s, had fostered children, mainly babies, for many years. Mrs E thought of 'David' as one of her own children. He had taken her name, and addressed her as 'Mummy'. There was, however, no possibility of adoption because his mother would not allow it.

She had placed David in care at the age of two months hoping to reclaim him in two years when she had finished her nursing training. Before this time however, she married, had another child and stopped visiting David. Since her husband didn't want to accept David, she planned to send him to her parents in Jamaica. The grandparents, however, had a large family of their own, and were reluctant to take him till he was 7. It was decided to keep him in the children's home, and hope that he would eventually be united with his family. His mother didn't visit him for two years, but when he was 4 she reappeared, and talked of taking him and leaving her husband. Since she did not do so, David was eventually fostered with Mrs E at the age of 5.

From this time, his only contact with his mother was via occasional telephone calls.

> *Foster mother* 'He can't go back to her or even visit her, because the man she's married to just won't have him in the house. And she's got four children by this man. But she won't give David up – she feels that he's still her son, and she thinks that he might return to her when he's older, and stick up for her. But the thing is, he won't know her, he'll have no genuine feeling for her. He'll know that she's his mother, because she's black, but that's about all.'

Mrs E not only acted as a mother to David, but kept in close touch with his mother and gave her a lot of support.

> *Foster mother* 'I'm the shoulder that she cries on. If things get on top of her, or she finds she's pregnant again she rings me up. My husband and I slip over occasionally, if I know that

she's a bit down, and take some toys or clothes for her children. She usually sends David a pound at Xmas, and sometimes she writes to him but she doesn't see him.'

Mrs E tried to help David understand his position.

Foster mother 'I tell him that his Mummy just can't have him, because her husband doesn't want him living there. So he has to stay with us. He wanted to know who his Daddy was, and what he was like – how tall he was – how black he was – where he came from – things like that. So I contacted his Mummy, and then I told him the basics. I've skimmed over the bad side of his father and given him a fair picture of him. One day, when I feel the time is right, I'll tell him his father left his mother in the lurch. I try to keep to the nicer side about his mother too, and make his family background sound as nice as possible. She rings me up and tells me about her parents and grandparents, and I pass it on to David. I think it's important he should have some background of his own.'

Partly because David is very black – both parents were West Indian – Mrs E tried to foster a pride in his colour in him.

Foster mother 'Although he's been brought up white, I think he should never forget he's coloured, that he's got something to be proud of. He'll need this in a white community – He gets "Sambo" and "Nig-nog" at school already – if he's proud of himself it will be easier for him in the long run.'

Although Mrs E was 'only' a foster mother, she seemed to have the same deep commitment to David as if he were her own child.

Foster mother 'When he came to me he was a chronic asthma sufferer. He never ran – if he walked up the stairs he'd have to stop and get his breath back. Now he never sits still – he's out on a bike all day. He had his last attack 16 months ago – it was a very bad one. I never went to bed for three nights. The doctor wanted him to go to hospital, but I said I'd rather nurse him at home – if he were to get worse, then I'd go with him into hospital, I wouldn't leave him.'

. . . .

The issue of adoption did not arise, because Mrs E knew that David's mother would not consider it. Nevertheless, she felt quite secure in her relationship with David because she knew that there was no possibility of his developing a relationship with his mother. In this situation she was able to support his mother, whilst treating David as her own child.

Foster mother 'I think every mother if she's honest, has individual feelings for every child she's got. You feel differently about each of your children. I won't say I feel the same about David as the others – I feel differently about them all – but he's just like my own.'

... None of the foster parents saw this situation, however, as ideal – they would have preferred adoption.

Foster mother 'I'm a firm believer that the mother is the person to have a child. But as far as David is concerned, there could never be a very good relationship, because the man she's married to won't have him – and she's got the other children to look after. That sort of mother is no good to the child, is she?'

Compare that with the following legal case:

Re N (a minor) (adoption)
[1990] 1 FLR 58, [1989] Fam Law 472, Family Division

The child, N, was born in 1984 of Nigerian parents who were not married. The mother placed her with white foster parents, the Ps, two weeks after birth and went to the USA. The father lived there but they did not live together. The father took an interest in the child and sought consistently to have care for her, but there were visa difficulties. In 1987, the foster parents applied to adopt and then to dispense with the mother's agreement. The father, with the mother's support, applied for care and control. He proposed a gradual transition, through a relative or bridging placement.

Bush J: ... The most important question to decide is where does N's future lie. We are all of us parents or potential parents and it is very difficult and sad for us to say that a child should be brought up by someone other than the natural parents. It should of course always be borne in mind that in English law N is a person in her own right and not just an appendage of her parents. …

Not only does the court in this case have to cope with practical difficulties involved in a transfer of N from the Ps to the father in a foreign land where the father will have to work long hours, and Miss F too has to work long hours, but I have also been bombarded by a host of theories and opinions by experts who derive their being from the political approach to race relations in America in the 1960s and 1970s. The British Agencies for Fostering and Adoption forcefully expressed the view that black children should never be placed with white foster parents. That that part of the approach was politically inspired seems clear from reading the summary to a practice note, the date of which is not clear. Nevertheless, it is an approach which due to the zeal of its authors has persuaded most local authorities not to place black children with white foster parents. The summary note reads as follows:

> 'Over and above all these basic needs, children need to develop a positive identity, including a positive racial identity. This is of fundamental importance since ethnicity is a significant component of identity. Ideally such needs are met within the setting of the child's birth family. Historically black people have been victims of racism for centuries. This has manifested and continues to manifest itself in many forms. Racism permeates all areas of British society and is perpetuated through a range of interests and influences, including the media, education and social service policies and practices. Negative and stereotypical images and actions can have a major impact on black children through the internalisation of these images, resulting in self-hate and identity confusion. Black children therefore require the survival skills necessary to develop a positive racial identity. This will enable them to deal with the racism within our predominantly white society.'

As Dr B, an eminent and experienced child psychiatrist … pointed out … there seems little real evidence, save anecdotal, to suggest that black-white fosterings are harmful. Indeed, Dr B says that her experience … indicates to the contrary namely, that the placement of black children with white foster parents works just as well as black foster children with black foster parents, and the real problem, of course, is that black foster parents are in short supply in this country.

…

In my view – and I have no wish to enter into what is clearly a political field – the emphasis on colour rather than cultural upbringing can be mischievous and highly dangerous when you are dealing in practical terms with the welfare of children. Also, the fact remains that this child has been placed with white foster parents and they have been the only real family she has ever known. I do not for one moment think that the father subscribes to this dogma. He does not have to be condescended to because he is black; he has made his way and his children will make their own way in the world because of intelligence and flair. To suggest that he and his children need special help because they are black is, in human terms an insult to them and their abilities. Yet it is to this principle that a whole social work philosophy has been dedicated. I do not need persuading that if at all possible the parents being suitable, a child should be brought up by its natural parents. Nor do I need persuading that experience tells us that particularly during teenage years there is a desire in children who have not been brought up by their natural parents, or who have not been having a regular access to them, to seek them out and that, if the whole of their placement has not been handled responsibly and delicately throughout their childhood, and sometimes even then, there may be psychological problems. There are of course serious psychological problems likely to arise when an effort is made to part a 4 and a half-year-old child from the only carers she has ever known. …

…

There is, of course, a very important question which relates not so much to colour as to national origins. The father and mother are Nigerian. The father is under some pressure from his father, who will be disgraced if it appears that even an illegitimate child has been abandoned. The father is a Roman Catholic, and I accept that he has a genuine desire to bring up his own child. An older illegitimate child of his, a boy, lives with a different mother in Nigeria and visits his father at regular intervals.

The evidence of Mrs B, a consultant social worker, as to Nigerian practice is of use. … She said there is no concept of adoption in Nigerian society. It is the normal cultural pattern for children to be brought up by others, often for most of their minority, and to be aware of their birth parents. Adoption rather than fostering of a West African child has particular difficulties. Adoption is to transfer a child from one family into another permanently and although the adoptive parents strive to inform the child about its origins in adoption it is clear the child is as if it were born to the adopters. In fostering, even long-term carers and the child are aware this is another and different family from a true family. If the child is moved from a white foster home to

Nigerian culture, with his foster parents not wanting the child to go, this can be devastating. Growing up with a set of values, a way of looking at family life, is constant in the same culture. However, to move from a British family with a closeness, autonomy and freedom to express what you want and to do what you want to a place where you cannot can be very distressing long-term. The damage of losing the people you trust at the same time as the trauma can be life-long. ...

... I am satisfied, as are the local authority and the guardian ad litem that N could not be moved without immense harm to her psychological development and her psychiatric health, both now and in the future. The later harm that may arise in her teens when she wished to seek out her cultural roots can best be dealt with by sympathetic understanding and education, upon which the Ps have already embarked, and it can also hopefully be met by the father continuing his interest and having access to N. It can only be helped if the father accepts the situation and enjoys access not on the basis of an expected rehabilitation but on the basis of a contact access designed to keep N in touch with her origins. If the father cannot accept this, then it may be that for N's security access would have to cease.

The Ps want adoption with an access order. The local authority and the guardian ad litem oppose adoption on the ground: (i) that the father has a useful and important part to play in the child's life in the future, particularly when she is nearing adulthood; (ii) that access to which the Ps are to some extent agreeable might very well be imperilled, the fact being that an adoption would result in the father and the whole of his family losing face. The father told me, and I have no reason to disbelieve, in the course of his argument that in his culture adoption is viewed as a restoration of slavery, which would be a deep and hurtful blow to him and his family. The question one has to ask oneself is whether the security that adoption would give to both the Ps and to N is offset by the fact that it clearly would not be in N's interests for her father to feel the shame and distress that in his culture an adoption order would bring. ...

I know all the arguments, I have heard them many times, about the security that an adoption could give and in the main I accept the arguments and have in the past acted upon them, but in the particular circumstances of this case I would not think it right to make an adoption order. Circumstances of course may change in the future. The guardian ad litem is most concerned, as we all are, that what has really become open warfare between the Ps and the father should cease. It is in the interests of N that it should so cease. I accept that the father is bitterly hurt and distressed and feels utterly betrayed by the Ps, and no doubt my decision has distressed him even more. However, the future of N throughout her childhood lies with the Ps and the father is intelligent enough and dedicated enough to his daughter to appreciate that changes of attitude on his part must come about. ...

Accordingly, the order that I make is that the wardship shall continue, that there be care and control to Mr and Mrs P, that there be reasonable access to the father to be agreed. In default of agreement it should be access once a year over a period of one week to begin with and that access to take place in England.

Questions

(i) Rowe (1984) found that 'the 29 black children who were interviewed mostly shrugged off colour differences as being unimportant but a few of the older teenagers were now facing problems because they had grown up in a white world'. Should white families be allowed to foster or adopt black children? What is black for this purpose?

(ii) Do you consider David's case (*a*) a perfect example of 'inclusive' fostering working to the benefit of all; or (*b*) a case in which the additional security of adoption would have benefited both child and foster parents?

(iii) *Re N* was not (*a*), but was it (*b*)?

Issues of race and ethnic origin arise even more acutely when prospective adopters go abroad to find a child. How the international community should respond to this is one of the many questions raised by increasing mobility to which we shall turn briefly in the last chapter.

Chapter 15

Families and frontiers: our international obligations

The world is getting smaller. Families and family members move about from country to country. Countries try to co-operate in handling the consequences. This affects family lawyers on several different levels. On one level are the rules of private international law, governing when our courts have jurisdiction, what law they will apply, and when they will recognise and sometimes enforce the decisions of courts and authorities in other countries; we have no space to deal with these issues here. But on another level are the international treaties which have led to changes in our own domestic law in order to secure co-operation between states in the movement of children. These are the Hague Convention on the Civil Aspects of International Child Abduction and the Hague Convention on Protection of Children and Co-operation in respect of Inter-country Adoption. Then there are international and regional instruments setting out the objectives towards which the contracting states are committed to working. These are principally the United Nations Convention on the Rights of the Child and the European Convention on Human Rights. The latter has the added dimension of a right of individual application to the European Commission and Court of Human Rights if our laws fail to meet its standards.

1 International child abduction

We do not know a great deal about parents who abduct their children, except that it appears to be on the increase. The causes are discussed by the Parliamentary Working Party on Child Abduction in their report, *Home and Away – Child Abduction in the Nineties* (1993):

The evidence, much of it from the USA, suggests that people abduct children in different ways and for quite different reasons. During the abduction, the behaviour of the parent directly concerned varies from the almost harmless to the homicidal. It is easy to draw the obvious conclusion that each child kidnapping depends on its own individual facts. However, this does not provide much assistance to those trying to prevent child-stealing generally or in individual cases. It also provides no indication as to the dispute resolution mechanisms likely to help deal with individual cases. Generalisations, therefore, have to be made.

In 1981, the American author, Agopian [1984], identified four basic reasons why parents kidnap their children:

(i) the belief that the child is likely to be neglected by the other parent;
(ii) a desire to keep a full-time parenting role;
(iii) a wish to punish the parent for the failure of the marriage; and
(iv) to bring about a reconciliation with the other parent.

In a University of Arizona study [Hegar and Greif, 1991] of 368 cases, 77% gave a wish to punish the other parent as a reason for taking a child. Other writers have extended the list to cover mothers fleeing from abuse of themselves or their children. The Hilary Morgan case in the USA was a dramatic example of the latter phenomenon. There, the mother was imprisoned after taking her daughter to New Zealand. Her object was to escape a court order giving access to the father whom she said had abused the child. Some innocent fathers in the Arizona research thought that women had abducted children owing to pressure imposed on them by third parties, notably the mothers' parents, family and friends to regain a mothering role that society expected them to fulfil.

There are plenty of parents who share the beliefs and desires listed above. However, only a tiny proportion actually resort to the extreme step of abducting a child. The difficult question is to know what extreme pressure pushes this small minority over the edge.

A growing body of literature, particularly in North America, is beginning to identify characteristics or likely indicators of child abduction families. One US study found high levels of physical, emotional and substance abuse in families where abductions took place. It also noted that most of the 'innocent' parents had worried about the risk of abduction before it occurred. In 'slightly less than half', the abductor actually threatened to abduct the child in advance.

In Europe, limited studies and anecdotal evidence suggest that differences in cultural background are a major factor in causing child abductions. A Dutch study mentions disagreements about education and religious upbringing as a cause. That investigation also adds psychological disturbance as a common feature of kidnappers. They may see the loss of custody looming and take extreme steps to avoid the further condemnation by society involved in being required to hand over the right to care for their children.

The law with its historical emphasis on winners and losers may exacerbate this. More generally, the adversarial approach of litigation can help cause the types of breakdowns in communication and feelings of desperation that can cause a parent to take the matter into his or her own hands.

While these generalisations provide some useful guidelines, one should be wary of drawing too many conclusions from them. The causes of child abduction will alter with changing social and legal conditions. One example concerns the sex of child abductors. A study of the 1987 US Child Find pilot scheme in Florida shows that only 60% of kidnappers were fathers. **reunite**'s early records indicate that almost 90% of abductors are men although this figure seems to be coming down now. These figures may reflect cultural differences between Britain and the US. It may also reflect the fact that a greater number of North American fathers were obtaining custody of their children in the early and mid-80's than in Britain. Women who had been brought up to believe that on divorce, they would obtain custody, seem to have reacted in the USA to losing such court cases by taking matters into their own hands. As more men in Britain obtain custodial rights, the sex of abductors may follow the US pattern.

One final feature of statistics on child abduction is that groups such as the National Council for Abducted Children (**reunite**) originally set up by women, probably lacked appeal initially to men who may have felt most aggrieved by the 'fairer sex'. As these organisations broaden their base, more men will tend to join. Recently, there has been a notable increase in the number of fathers approaching **reunite** with tales of maternal kidnapping.

Most research into child abduction is of fairly recent origin and studies continue to be carried out, particularly in North America. What they may reveal is both further information about conclusions reached in the earlier studies as the sample sizes increase and perhaps changes over time in the causes of child-kidnapping.

The law has struggled for a long time to reconcile the desire to deter abduction with the court's usual duty to do what is best for the particular child concerned. The 1983 Hague Convention on the Civil Aspects of International Child Abduction, implemented in English law by the Child Abduction and Custody Act 1985, imposes on contracting states reciprocal obligations to return abducted children to the country of their habitual residence almost irrespective of the welfare of the child. The most important articles are these:

Article 3

The removal or the retention of a child is to be considered wrongful where –

(*a*) it is in breach of rights of custody attributed to a person, an institution or any other body, either jointly or alone, under the law of the State in which the child was habitually resident immediately before the removal or retention; and (*b*) at the time of removal or retention those rights were actually exercised, either jointly or alone, or would have been so exercised but for the removal or retention.

The rights of custody mentioned in sub-paragraph (*a*) above may arise in particular by operation of law or by reason of a judicial or administrative decision, or by reason of an agreement having legal effect under the law of that State.

Article 4

The Convention shall apply to any child who was habitually resident in a Contracting State immediately before any breach of custody or access rights. The Convention shall cease to apply when the child attains the age of sixteen years.

Article 5

For the purposes of this Convention –

(*a*) 'rights of custody' shall include rights relating to the care of the person of the child and, in particular, the right to determine the child's place of residence;

(*b*) 'rights of access' shall include the right to take a child for a limited period of time to a place other than the child's habitual residence.

Article 7

Central Authorities shall co-operate with each other and promote co-operation amongst the competent authorities in their respective States to secure the prompt return of children and to achieve the other objects of this Convention.

In particular, either directly or through any intermediary, they shall take all appropriate measures –

(*a*) to discover the whereabouts of a child who has been wrongfully removed or retained;

(*b*) to prevent further harm to the child or prejudice to interested parties by taking or causing to be taken provisional measures;

(*c*) to secure the voluntary return of the child or to bring about an amicable resolution of the issues;

(*d*) to exchange, where desirable, information relating to the social background of the child;

(*e*) to provide information of a general character as to the law of their State in connection with the application of the Convention;

(*f*) to initiate or facilitate the institution of judicial or administrative proceedings with a view to obtaining the return of the child and, in a proper case, to make arrangements for organizing or securing the effective exercise of rights of access;

(*g*) where the circumstances so require, to provide or facilitate the provision of legal aid and advice, including the participation of legal counsel and advisers;

(*h*) to provide such administrative arrangements as may be necessary and appropriate to secure the safe return of the child;

(*i*) to keep each other informed with respect to the operation of this Convention and, as far as possible, to eliminate any obstacles to its application.

Article 12

Where a child has been wrongfully removed or retained in terms of Article 3 and, at the date of the commencement of the proceedings before the judicial or administrative authority of the Contracting State where the child is, a period of less than one year has elapsed from the date of the wrongful removal or retention, the authority concerned shall order the return of the child forthwith.

The judicial or administrative authority, even where the proceedings have been commenced after the expiration of the period of one year referred to in the preceding paragraph, shall also order the return of the child, unless it is demonstrated that the child is now settled in its new environment.

Where the judicial or administrative authority in the requested state has reason to believe that the child has been taken to another State, it may stay the proceedings or dismiss the application for the return of the child.

Article 13

Notwithstanding the provisions of the preceding Article, the judicial or administrative authority of the requested State is not bound to order the return of the child if the person, institution or other body which opposes its return establishes that –

(*a*) the person, institution or other body having the care of the person of the child was not actually exercising the custody rights at the time of removal or retention, or had consented to or subsequently acquiesced in the removal or retention; or

(*b*) there is a grave risk that his or her return would expose the child to physical or psychological harm or otherwise place the child in an intolerable situation.

The judicial or administrative authority may also refuse to order the return of the child if it finds that the child objects to being returned and has attained an age and degree of maturity at which it is appropriate to take account of its views.

In considering the circumstances referred to in this Article, the judicial and administrative authorities shall take into account the information relating to the social background of the child provided by the Central Authority or other competent authority of the child's habitual residence.

Article 19

A decision under this Convention concerning the return of the child shall not be taken to be a determination on the merits of any custody issue.

Article 21

An application to make arrangements for organising or securing the effective exercise of rights of access may be presented to the Central Authorities of the Contracting States in the same way as an application for the return of a child.

The Central Authorities are bound by the obligations of co-operation which are set forth in Article 7 to promote the peaceful enjoyment of access rights and the fulfilment of any conditions to which the exercise of those rights may be subject. The Central Authorities shall take steps to remove, as far as possible, all obstacles to the exercise of such rights. The Central Authorities, either directly or through intermediaries, may initiate or assist in the institution of proceedings with a view to organising or protecting these rights and securing respect for the conditions to which the exercise of these rights may be subject.

This may look simple but it has generated a great deal of law which we can only touch on here. What, for example, is meant by 'habitual residence'? The principles were stated in:

Re J (a minor) (abduction: custody rights)
[1990] 2 AC 562, [1990] 2 All ER 961, House of Lords

The mother and father were both UK citizens who had emigrated to Australia where they met, cohabited and had a child, but never married. The mother's parents visited her from England and she decided to return with them to live here. Without the father's knowledge or consent, she came here with the child. Under the law of Western Australia an unmarried father did not have automatic custody rights, but shortly after this he obtained a declaration that the removal was wrongful and an order for sole custody and guardianship. His application for the return of the child was unsuccessful before the judge and the Court of Appeal. He appealed to the House of Lords.

Lord Brandon of Oakbrook: ... I consider first the question whether the removal of J from Australia to England by the mother was wrongful within the meaning of art. 3 of the Convention. Having regard to the terms of art. 3 the removal could only be wrongful if it was in breach of rights of custody attributed to, i.e. possessed by, the father at the time when it took place. It seems to me, however, that since s. 35 of the Family Law Act 1975–1979 of Western Australia, as amended, gave the mother alone the custody and guardianship of J, and no order of a court to the contrary had been obtained by the father before the removal took place, the father had no custody rights relating to J of which the removal of J by the mother could be a breach. It is no doubt true that, while the mother and father were living together with J in their jointly owned home in Western Australia, the de facto custody of J was exercised by them jointly. So far as legal rights of custody are concerned, however, these belonged to the mother alone, and included in those rights was the right to decide where J should reside. It follows, in my opinion, that the removal of J by the mother was not wrongful within the meaning of art. 3 of the Convention. I recognise that Anderson J thought fit to make a declaration that J had been wrongfully removed from Australia. I pay to his decision the respect which comity requires, but the courts of the UK are not bound by it and for the reasons which I have given I do not consider that it was rightly made.

I consider secondly the question whether the retention of J in England by the mother following his removal was wrongful within the meaning of art. 3 of the Convention. ...

It is not in dispute that, immediately before his removal, J was habitually resident in Western Australia. It was argued for the father that J remained habitually resident in Western Australia despite his removal to and retention in England by the mother with the settled intention that he should reside there with her on a long-term basis. ...

In considering this issue it seems to me to be helpful to deal first with a number of preliminary points. The first point is that the expression 'habitually resident', as used in art. 3 of the Convention, is nowhere defined. It follows, I think, that the expression is not to be treated as a term of art with some special meaning, but is rather to be understood according to the ordinary and natural meaning of the two words which it contains. The second point is that the question whether a person is or is not habitually resident in a specified country is a question of fact to be decided by reference to all the circumstances of any particular case. The third point is that there is a significant difference between a person ceasing to be habitually resident in country A, and his subsequently becoming habitually resident in country B. A person may cease to be habitually resident in country A in a single day if he or she leaves it with a settled intention not to return to it but to take up long-term residence in country B instead. Such a person cannot, however, become habitually resident in country B in a single day. An appreciable period of time and a settled intention will be necessary to enable him or her to become so. During that appreciable period of time the person will have ceased to be habitually resident in country A but not yet have become habitually resident in country B. The fourth point is that, where a child of J's age is in the sole lawful custody of the mother, his situation with regard to habitual residence will necessarily be the same as hers.

In the light of these points the question which has to be posed and answered is not whether, immediately before the continued retention of J became a breach of the father's rights of custody under the order of Anderson J, J had become habitually resident in England. It is rather whether immediately before that time J had already ceased to be habitually resident in Western Australia. To that second question it seems to me that, on the special facts of this particular case, only an affirmative answer can sensibly be given. ...

Appeal dismissed.

Questions

(i) If both parents have parental responsibility (see p. 499, above), can one of them change the child's habitual residence without the agreement of the other? Would the Hague Convention work if they could?

(ii) If both parents live in one country and send the child to live in another country, where is the child habitually resident? Does it depend upon what they agreed? What if one of them changes his or her mind?

Re J also involved the meaning of 'rights of custody' protected under Article 3, which are deliberately distinguished from the 'rights of access' protected only under Article 21. This too is not an easy issue. It arose in the following case, which also considered the extent to which Article 13(*b*) can be used to protect the child's interests:

Re F (abduction: custody rights abroad)
[1995] Fam 224, [1995] 3 All ER 641, Court of Appeal

A US father and a British mother married in Colorado in 1987. Their son was born there in 1990. The whole family lived there until 1994. The mother alleged that the father had been violent towards her, her mother and the child. In June 1994, she obtained a temporary order ousting the father from the home and giving her care and control of the child. In July she brought the child to this country. The expert evidence was that this was not in breach of the law of Colorado. The judge ordered the child's return and the mother appealed.

Butler-Sloss LJ: ... It is the duty of the court to construe the Convention in a purposive way and to make the Convention work. It is repugnant to the philosophy of the Convention for one parent unilaterally, secretly and with full knowledge that it is against the wishes of the other parent who possesses 'rights of custody', to remove the child from the jurisdiction of the child's habitual residence. 'Rights of custody' within the Convention are broader than an order of the court and parents have rights in respect of their children without the need to have them declared by the court or defined by court order. These rights under the Convention have been liberally interpreted in English law. Waite LJ said in *Re B (A Minor) (Abduction)* [1994] 2 FLR 249 at p. 260:

> 'The purposes of the Hague Convention were, in part at least, humanitarian. The objective is to spare children already suffering the effects of breakdown in their parents' relationship the further disruption which is suffered when they are taken arbitrarily by one parent from their settled environment and moved to another country for the sake of finding there a supposedly more sympathetic forum or a more congenial base. The expression "rights of custody" when used in the Convention therefore needs to be construed in the sense that will best accord with that objective. In most cases, that will involve giving the term the widest sense possible.'

Rights of custody
I am satisfied that the father and mother both enjoyed equal and separate rights of custody by Colorado law. Equally by Colorado law in the absence of a court order to the contrary either parent could remove the child from the State and from the USA without violating any principles of Colorado law. It cannot, however, be the case that the lawful removal of the child by one parent destroys the rights of the other parent nor did any of the Colorado lawyers suggest it. The removal of the child by the mother interfered with the rights of the father in that he was prevented from actually exercising them in the USA. Such interference with rights is recognised in the Convention and Art. 3 includes in its definition rights which 'would have been exercised but for the removal'. In my judgment the father continued to enjoy 'rights of custody' subject to the effect of the orders of the Adams County Court.

... In my view the temporary order for care and control was of a limited nature and did not affect the father's 'rights of custody' nor was it suggested by the Colorado lawyers that it did. The answer to the first part of the question is therefore 'Yes'. ...

...

Having found that the father retains rights as a parent by Colorado law which fall within the Convention definition, as I have, equally it is a matter of English law whether the mother is in breach of those 'rights of custody' by her removal of the child. In applying the Convention we are not bound by the mother's right under Colorado law to remove the child from the USA and that information is in my judgment irrelevant to the decision the English court has to take whether the removal from the USA was wrongful. We are concerned with the mother's unilateral decision to remove the child without the consent of the father and with the knowledge that if he knew he would have opposed her removal of the child. By the removal she frustrated and rendered nugatory his equal and separate rights of custody, in particular that the child should reside in the USA. In so doing she was in my judgment in breach of the father's rights of custody under the Convention and the removal was wrongful.

...

Article 13(b)
When a court has found that the removal of the child is wrongful within the meaning of the Convention, Art. 12 requires that the court 'shall order the return of the child forthwith' unless

any of the provisions of Art. 13 is established and the requested State exercises its discretion not to do so. It is asserted by the mother that Art. 13(*b*) is established on the facts before us and that the judge was in error in finding that it was not proved. ...

[Counsel] recognised that a very high standard is required to demonstrate grave risk and an intolerable situation, but he has argued that the Convention envisaged that there would be cases in which the facts would meet that high standard. In the present case the mother and grandmother have made very serious allegations against the father, in particular of his violence towards the child and the extremely serious effect it has had upon him. ...

Admission of oral evidence in Convention cases should be allowed sparingly.

If the issues between the parties cannot be resolved on affidavit the Art. 13(*b*) criteria will not have been established. The child is returned pursuant to Art. 12 and it will be for the court of habitual residence to determine the disputes issues with the opportunity to hear oral evidence and the parties cross-examined. In many cases the absence of evidence from the other parent on the major issues would cause a court to hesitate to find the Art. 13(*b*) threshold reached: see *Re E (A Minor) (Abduction)* [1989] 1 FLR 135. But I agree with the judge that the evidence adduced by the mother should be treated as true, particularly since the allegations affect this child, there was an opportunity to rebut them and the consequences for this child on the evidence before us are potentially very serious. ...

In looking at this evidence I have reminded myself of the difficulties inherent in proving grave risk of physical or psychological harm or of demonstrating that the child would be placed in an intolerable situation if returned to the country of habitual jurisdiction. ...

The child was, like so many other children, present at acts of violence and displays of uncontrollable temper directed at his mother or elsewhere, and at occasions of violence between the parents. These included assaults on his mother and one on his grandmother on 6 June 1994, and destruction of household items such as ripping the fridge door off its hinges. More important in my view was that the child was himself the recipient of the violence by the father. The judge was in error in finding only one occasion which directly affected the child when he suffered a nosebleed caused by the father in a temper throwing a cool box onto the back seat where the child was sitting which hit him in the face. There were other incidents. He destroyed the child's toys by stamping on them and smashing them when the child was present. This happened more than once. On several occasions he pinched the child on the legs causing bruising. One occasion of pinching was witnessed by the maternal grandmother. On 6 June 1994, C was thrown out of the house as well as his mother. On this occasion, which was immediately before the mother made her ex parte application to the county court, the police were called and took his father away. His father in his presence threatened to kill him and his mother. In these incidents the child was not a bystander to matrimonial discord but a victim of it. In addition other aspects of the behaviour of the father towards the child were unusual and inappropriate, such as waking up the child aged under 4 in the early hours of the morning, once to get him to help wash the jeep. In addition after the temporary restraining order was made and the father left the house, the father seems to have engaged in a campaign of intimidation and harassment directed at the mother, including following her about in his car and threatening her with a gun. He also camped in the jeep several doors away from the matrimonial home, which had a very adverse effect upon the child as well as upon the mother.

The child is asthmatic and the effect upon him of this behaviour was serious. He was present when his grandmother, who was recovering from surgery, was forcibly pushed out of the house and thrown against a wall. The child's reaction was to scream and to cry. He started to bedwet regularly and to have nightmares where he screamed out in his sleep. He became unusually aggressive at the child care centre as well as at home. The effect of the father camping nearby in the jeep made him scared and upset. He copied the tantrums, the yelling, the screaming and bad language of his father.

Since leaving the USA he has been living in Wales in his maternal grandfather's house. The misbehaviour, the bedwetting and the nightmares ceased after he settled down. But his mother told him after the start of the present proceedings that he might have to return to Colorado. He has had a disturbing resumption of the bedwetting and nightmares and has begun to wet himself during the day. He has become aggressive towards other children at the nursery school he is attending and towards grown-ups.

The extent to which the child has himself been drawn into the violence between his parents and the clear evidence of the adverse effect on him of his father's violent and intimidating behaviour would not in my view in themselves be sufficient to meet the high standard required in Art. 13(*b*). The matters which I find most telling are:

(1) the actual effect upon the child of the knowledge that he may be returning to Colorado together with the unusual circumstances;

(2) that he would be returning to the very same surroundings and potentially the very same situation as that which has had such a serious effect upon him before he was removed.

There has to be concern as to whether the father would take any notice of future orders of the court or comply with the undertakings he has given to the judge. How is a child of 4 to have any security or stability or from his perception come to terms with a return to his former home? I have come to the conclusion on the unusual facts of this case that the extreme reaction of the child to the marital discord and the requirement by Art. 12 to return him on the facts of this case to the same house with the same attendant risks would create a grave risk that his return would expose him both to psychological harm and would place him in an intolerable situation. ...

Appeal allowed.

Questions

(i) Why was this removal in breach of the father's rights of custody under the law of the child's habitual residence, while the removal in *Re J* was not?
(ii) Should the question of whether the removal is in breach of custody rights be governed by English law or is it, as stated by Professor Carol Bruch (1993), 'the law of the child's habitual residence that controls this question under the Convention, not the law of the court hearing the return question'?
(iii) What if the abducting mother then claims that the father left behind is not in fact the father of the child?
(iv) By virtue of s. 1 of the Child Abduction Act 1984, and s. 13 of the Children Act 1989, it is contrary to English law for a mother to remove the child for more than one month without either the father's consent or the leave of the court, even if the court has ordered that the child is to live with the mother indefinitely and has made no order for contact with the father: is such a removal in breach of the father's 'rights of custody' for the purpose of the Convention?
(v) The whole purpose of the Convention is to secure the return of the child without the wronged parent having to come to the country to which the child has been taken: how can the court decide about allegations of violence without hearing oral evidence?
(vi) Given that the court treated the mother's allegations as true, would you have had the slightest hesitation in finding Article 13(*b*) applied in this case?
(vii) At what age would you think it 'appropriate' to take account of the child's objection to being returned? What is an objection?
(viii) Had it occurred to you that many cases would be brought by fathers who had not been and did not intend to be the child's main carer?
(ix) Would it place the child in an intolerable situation if his main carer either could not or would not return with him?

The English courts have responded to the last problem by extracting or accepting undertakings from the plaintiff. In *Re O (child abduction: undertakings)* [1994] 2 FLR 349, an English mother had removed two children aged six and five from Greece where they had lived in comfortable circumstances all their lives. The following undertakings were given by their Greek father:

(1) Not to remove or seek to remove the children from the care and control of the mother.
(2) To provide a car for the mother and to pay all running costs, including petrol, maintenance and insurance.
(3) To provide as soon as possible for the mother a three bedroomed apartment ... for the sole occupation by her and the children and to pay all the running costs of such property and not to

enter such property and until provision of such property to permit the mother to reside at [the matrimonial home] and not to enter [the matrimonial home].
(4) To pay all school fees including school books for the children and all medical expenses for the mother and children.
(5) To pay all travel costs for the return of the mother and the children ... together with the cost of the return of the mother's and children's personal belongings.
(6) Not to institute nor voluntarily support any proceedings for the punishment or committal of the mother in respect of any criminal or civil wrong which the mother may have committed by reason of the children's removal from Greece and to use his best endeavours to ensure that such proceedings do not happen.
(7) To pay maintenance to the mother at the rate of £1,000 per calendar month.

Questions

(i) Do you think that these two children would have been placed in an intolerable situation if ordered to return to their home, whether in the care of their mother or of their father and his relatives, without all or any of these undertakings?
(ii) The mother returned to Greece with the children, but left a few days later claiming that the father was in breach, in particular, of undertakings (3) and (7); the father denied this, but also claimed that the undertakings had been extracted under duress and went far beyond what the mother could reasonably expect in Greece; Hale J ordered her to return the children once more; what would you have done?
(iii) Do you get a sense that the English courts are bending over backwards to apply the Convention?

The point of it all is, of course, that if we return children who are wrongly abducted to this country, other Convention countries will return our children who have been wrongly abducted there. But what should we do if the other country is not a party to the Convention?

Re S (minors) (abduction)
[1993] 2 FCR 499, [1994] 1 FLR 297, Court of Appeal

The parents were both Muslims born in Pakistan. The mother had lived here from the age of five. They met and married here but then went to live in Pakistan where they had three children. Some years later, without the father's knowledge or consent, the mother brought the two youngest children, a girl of seven and a boy of three, to this country to live with her own mother. He applied for a summary order for their return to Pakistan. Pakistan is not a party to the Hague Convention. The judge made the order and the mother appealed.

Balcombe LJ: ... There is a fair amount of law as to the test to be applied in these circumstances where, as here, the country from which the children came, Pakistan, is not a signatory to the Hague Convention on the abduction of children and this is, therefore, what is nowadays called 'a non-Convention case'.

But even before this country became a subscriber to the Hague Convention ... the problems presented by actions of the type which the mother has taken in this case had long been known to our courts, and the case from which all the relevant modern law derives is the case of *Re L (Minors) (Wardship: Jurisdiction)* [1974] 1 WLR 250. I need not refer to the facts of that case nor to the classic passage from the judgment of Buckley LJ because it is referred to in all the subsequent cases and it will be convenient to refer to the summary of it which Ormrod LJ gave in a subsequent case – again a non-Convention case, in fact a pre-Convention case: *Re R (Minors) (Wardship: Jurisdiction)* (1981) 2 FLR 416. ... After deprecating the use of the term 'kidnap' or 'kidnapping' and referring to them both in inverted commas, he said at p. 425H:

> ' "Kidnapping", like other kinds of unilateral action in relation to children, is to be strongly discouraged, but the discouragement must take the form of a swift, realistic and unsentimental assessment of the best interests of the child, leading, in proper cases, to the prompt return of the child to his or her own country, but *not* the sacrifice of the child's welfare to some other principle of law.'

Then he refers to the passage in the judgment of Buckley LJ in these terms:

> 'The damage to a child's interest which may arise from not making a summary order is conveniently set out by Buckley LJ at p. 264E–H of his judgment in *Re L* ... In a sentence, they are alienation from background, home, schools, friends, relations and, ultimately, from his country and its society and culture. These dangers have to be weighed against the risk to the child of possible, perhaps probable, separation from the mother, of being entrusted to the care of a father whose capabilities and fitness to act as a single parent may be in doubt, in surroundings which may be unfavourable in themselves, and of being subjected to a regime of law under which the provision of their interests may be open to question ...'

So looking at this, as of course we are bound to do, as a matter of what the interests of the children require, it is clear that Ormrod LJ, in considering the balancing exercise which had to be effected by the court, recognised that one of the facts to be taken into account is the regime of law in the country to which the child is to be returned if that is the order which the court is to make. Since then the Hague Convention came into force, it has been adopted by this country in relation to certain signatories, and I have already said that Pakistan is not one of the Convention countries. But twice in this court it has been laid down that in non-Convention cases, the principles behind the Convention are to be taken into account.

In *G v G (Minors) (Abduction)* [1991] 2 FLR 506, which was a case from Kenya, I said that the jurisdictional concept which lay behind the Child Abduction and Custody Act 1985 was that welfare normally required the return of the abducted child to the country whence it had been abducted. That particular passage from my judgment was approved by this court in a further case, *Re F (A Minor) (Abduction: Custody Rights)* [1991] Fam 25 at p. 30, sub nom *Re F (A Minor) (Abduction: Jurisdiction)* [1991] 1 FLR 1 at p. 3 where Lord Donaldson of Lymington MR cited a passage from my judgment in *G v G* with approval:

> '... in enacting the 1985 Act, Parliament was not departing from the fundamental principle that the welfare of the child is paramount. Rather it was giving effect to a belief "that in normal circumstances it is in the interests of children that parents or others should not abduct them from one jurisdiction to another, but that any decision relating to the custody of children is best decided in the jurisdiction in which they have hitherto normally been resident".'

...

So the issue which came before Sir Gervase Sheldon was this. Applying the test that the welfare of the children is paramount, did their interests require that they should go straight back to Pakistan in order that the courts of that country should decide what their welfare required, or should the matter be allowed to go ahead in this country, again so that the courts of this country should decide what their welfare required, with the inevitable delay – though one would hope not lengthy – that that would entail?

...

The position of the mother can best be summarised by the following submissions from the skeleton argument ...:

> 'The question raised by the instant case is ... whether or not the court should order a peremptory return to a jurisdiction (a) which does not apply a similar system of law to that governing decisions over the welfare of children adopted in the courts of England, and/or (b) in which one parent asserts she will not receive a fair trial.'

...

There is evidence before the court in the form of an affidavit from Professor Pearl, who is an expert in Pakistan law, that the law applicable in Pakistan is the Guardians and Wards Act 1890. It is perhaps not irrelevant to note that the Act dates from the time when Pakistan was part of the Indian Empire. Section 17 of that Act states that:

> 'In the event of a dispute involving the physical care of a child, the court shall be guided by what, consistently with the law to which the minor is subject, appears in the circumstances to be for the welfare of the minor.'

Then he goes on to say:

> 'In the Muslim law as applied in Pakistan, the mother retains custody (physical care) until the girl has reached puberty and the boy reaches the age of 7. However, the mother will lose this entitlement to custody if she is deemed to be unsuitable.
>
> In accordance with s. 17 of the 1890 Act, the courts have developed the presumption that the minor's welfare lies in granting custody in accordance with the personal law of the minor. In this case, the personal law is the Muslim law as applied in Pakistan. This means that Muslim law principles will be applied to the case unless there are overriding reasons to the contrary.
>
> According to Muslim law, the mother will lose the entitlement to bring up her children in her own care in the following circumstances: (a) if she concludes a subsequent marriage, or forms a liaison with another man other than a close relative to the children; (b) if the mother is deemed to be unsuitable, for instance if she has a way of life which the court would consider unIslamic; (c) if there is a suggestion that the children would not be brought up as Muslim.'

...

... All the matters of which Buckley LJ and Ormrod LJ spoke are present here. These are Pakistani Muslim children. Their home is in Pakistan. They have been brought up in Pakistan. Their religion is Muslim. They have been wrenched away from all they knew to this country. Prima facie, therefore, it must, within the test to which I have referred, be in their interest that they should go straight back to allow the courts of their own country to decide what their interests require.

The only point is whether the fact that the Pakistan courts apply a test, which I have set out, which is not in all respects the same as that which the English court would apply, is a good reason for not following what would be the obvious course. ... What I am quite clear of in my mind is the test which Lord Donaldson referred to in *Re F* (above) was whether or not the system of law was appropriate. ...

Sir Gervase Sheldon clearly thought that it would be appropriate for the Pakistan courts to exercise their jurisdiction. To put it the other way round: would it be appropriate for this court to deny the Pakistan courts jurisdiction merely because, as Professor Pearl suggested, they would try to give effect to what is the minors' welfare from the Muslim point of view? The judge thought not and in my judgment the manner in which the judge exercised his discretion is one with which this court cannot interfere.

Appeal dismissed.

Questions

(i) How can it be in the paramount interests of the children to return them to a country in which their interests will not be paramount?

(ii) If the children had been living here with their mother and their father had taken them to Pakistan without her knowledge or consent do you think that the courts in Pakistan would have ordered him to return them?

(iii) Do you sympathise with this view expressed by David McClean and Kisch Beevers (1995): 'in a non-Convention case, let the welfare principle have full rein'?

If a child is taken to a Convention country, the procedure should simply be the reverse of what happens when a child is brought here. If a child is taken to a non-Convention country, however, this is all the Government can advise, in their booklet on *Child Abduction*:

Your child has been taken to a non-Convention country

If you cannot reach an amicable settlement your only recourse may be to start legal proceedings in the courts of the country concerned.

It is important to establish from the outset what your parental rights are under local law and what, if any, local customary child care and control practices exist which might influence a court's decision in a child custody case. You should, therefore, consider obtaining legal advice regarding the laws and practice of the country concerned as soon as possible.

The Consular Department of the Foreign & Commonwealth Office can help by providing a list of local lawyers who correspond in English, but neither the Consular Department nor British consular officers abroad can give legal advice or act as your legal representative.

You should also bear in mind that legal proceedings can be both long and expensive and that British legal aid is not available for actions overseas. You may be able to obtain legal aid from the country to which your child has been taken. This should be discussed with the lawyer whom you consult.

Courts abroad cannot pass down judgments which are contrary to their own law. They are not often willing to oppose family, religious or cultural traditions which are customary, even if not obligatory, in their country. In some countries the law is based strictly on such traditions.

In some countries the law may not give equality of parental or individual rights to women and men. Such factors will usually have a bearing on the outcome of a child custody case, especially if one parent is from a different social, cultural or religious background and intends, if granted custody, to remove a child from these traditions.

The Consular Department may, however, be able to help in other ways through British Embassies and Consulates abroad by:

- asking the local authorities for help in tracing your child
- once the child is located, trying to obtain a report on the child's welfare – this can only be obtained with the other parent's consent and at your own cost
- asking the local court to handle the case as quickly as possible.

Once the child has been traced they may be able to pass letters between you and arrange for a room to be provided where you can spend time together privately – but both parents must consent to these facilities being offered.

They may also be able to draw the attention of the local authorities to any United Kingdom court order(s) which you may have obtained, provided the court agrees. Although such an order has no binding force overseas it may be taken into account by the overseas court in reaching a decision.

It must be stressed that consular staff do not have any formal standing in the matter. In many instances, the children involved are also nationals of the country to which they have been taken. In this case the authorities of that country are not obliged to allow consular staff to make any representations about the children at all.

You do not know where your child has been taken

- alert your local police station, first by telephone and then in person. You will be asked to give a statement. Where threat of removal is real and imminent they will circulate the child's name to all UK points of departure. If there are any difficulties ask to speak to the senior officer in charge.

  A court order is not necessary for the police to act. They will only require a statement which gives evidence of your rights/responsibilities in relation to the child and of your objection to the removal of the child.
- contact the Lord Chancellor's Department Child Abduction Unit.

You fear your child may be taken abroad without your consent

- If your legal position with regard to the child is unclear you should seek legal advice.
- If you have parental responsibility for the child or a court order relating to custody/residence, access/contact or guardianship (or if you have applied for such an order) you or your solicitor should take the following steps:
  - alert your local police station, first by telephone and then in person. You will be asked to give a statement. Where threat of removal is real and imminent they will circulate the child's name to all UK points of departure via the Police National Computer and the details will be entered on a regularly updated list. If there are any difficulties ask to speak to the senior officer in charge.

    A court order is not necessary for the police to act. They will only require a statement which gives evidence of your rights/responsibilities in relation to the child and of your objection to the removal of the child.

    However, if a child is aged 16 or 17 then in most cases a court order in respect of that child is needed. The police will need to see a copy of the order, as will the Passport Agency for the procedure below.
  - write to your regional office of the United Kingdom Passport Agency, asking them not to grant passport facilities to the child(ren). They will usually need to see a court order such as a custody/residence, prohibited steps or wardship order. Court orders are not necessary in the case of unmarried mothers wishing to lodge an objection.

You may telephone first if you think that an application for a passport has already been made or soon will be.

N.B. This does not prevent someone obtaining a British Visitors Passport or even a passport from their own Embassy, High Commission or Consulate in this country. If your spouse or ex-spouse is not a British national, you or your solicitors should consider writing a letter to the Embassy or Consulate of his/her country asking those officials not to issue a passport to your child. They are not obliged to comply with your request, but may do so voluntarily.

2 Inter-country adoption

We have already seen in Chapter 11 how inter-country adoptions can offend against, not only the professional approach to adoption within this country, but also the laws against 'trafficking in children'. Some of the international complexities may be gleaned from David Rosettenstein's article on 'Trans-Racial Adoption in the United States and the Impact of Considerations relating to Minority Population Groups on International Adoptions in the United States' (1995):

The political considerations impinging on international adoptions are complex and multi-faceted. At the national level, they reflect the concerns of the foreign country, and of the United States. Not surprisingly, national interests are usually not couched in terms that necessarily reflect the interests of the child. Thus, traditional objections by source countries to these international adoptions are that they reveal or suggest an inability on the part of the foreign country to care for its children and thus undermine national pride, or constitute an insult or are symptomatic of an ailing society. They have also been seen as a vehicle for depriving the country of a future resource – citizens, even though the numbers are really not sufficiently large to constitute a meaningful threat. Foreign countries are also concerned that the financial rewards and incentives for facilitating an international adoption tend to corrupt the social service infrastructure of the source country as well as leading to kidnapping, coercion, baby-selling and fraud. The process is also seen as manifestly a form of neo-colonialist exploitation and inducing colonial values in the welfare delivery system. In some instances, because intercountry adoptions are seen as exploiting poor countries, indulging the wealthy, and reducing the guilt of rich countries, a refusal to allow such adoptions by potential source countries might be seen as aimed at heightening the discomfort of rich countries. In a similar vein, on occasion, the United States has manipulated its approach to intercountry adoptions with a view to discrediting the source country. Of interest to the policies of both the United States and the source country is the fact that the adoption of a child from a crisis area may only serve to disrupt the foreign country further. Sometimes the argument is made that the commercialism invites inattention to the question of whether the child is truly 'available' for adoption, although this concern has to be balanced against the knowledge that where a child is coming from a country where there is war, social disorder or even simply poverty, delays in evaluating the adoptability of the child may involve risks of harm to the child. A further concern of some countries is that intercountry adoptions distract attention away from the needs of domestic programmes in the source country. This may be a particularly difficult issue where the concept of adoption is culturally unknown in the source country. Thus, in a country such as India, where trans-*ethnic* adoption is an alien concept, such a consequence in the context of an intercountry adoption tends to produce suspicions about the adoptees' motives.

Earlier, he had described the objections to trans-racial placement within the United States:

In 1972 the National Association of Black Social Workers (NABSW) stated:

'Black children should be placed only with Black families whether in foster care or adoption. Black children belong physically, psychologically and culturally in Black families in order that they receive the total sense of themselves and develop a sound projection of their future. Human beings are products of their environment and develop their sense of values, attitudes and self concept within their family structures. Black children in white homes are cut [off] from the healthy development of themselves as Black people.

Our position is based on:

1. the necessity of self-determination from birth to death, of all black people.
2. the need of all young ones to begin at birth to identify with all Black people in a Black community.
3. the philosophy that we need our own to build a strong nation.

The socialization process for every child begins at birth. Included in the socialization process is the child's cultural heritage which is an important segment of the total process. This must begin at the earliest moment; otherwise our children will not have the background and knowledge which is necessary to survive in a racist society. This is impossible if the child is placed with white parents in a white environment.'

The impact of this statement on trans-racial adoptions in the United States was dramatic. The best information suggests that the numbers of trans-racial adoptions reached an all time high of 2,574 in 1971, the number of such placements then falling to 831 by 1975. Since that year, comprehensive national figures on adoption, whether same-race or trans-racial, have not been available. Two prominent authors [Simon and Altstein, 1987] in the field have stated that they and others believe that both public and private agencies are placing children trans-racially, but will not admit to doing so, because of political considerations.

He concluded that:

The overall irony of the role of race in adoption placements is that domestically minority children do not get placed because it is feared that trans-racial placement will harm them. As a consequence, adoptive parents are apparently driven to trans-racial adoptions from abroad. In this context, the children will be subjected to the same potential risks the domestic children were being shielded from, at the same time as being exposed to increased risks resulting from the international process.

Question

To what extent do you think that similar considerations would operate here? Is it right to call them political?

The other side of the coin is stated by William Duncan in *Regulating Intercountry Adoption* (1993):

By contrast, the figures for abandoned children in developing countries remain staggering. It is estimated by UNICEF [1991] that about 155 million children under five in the developing countries live in absolute poverty. There are about 100 million abandoned children who 'subsist only by back-breaking work, or turn to petty crime, prostitution or begging' [Ngabonziza, 1991]. Every civil war or civil upheaval seems to add to this tragic picture. In Europe, much attention has been paid in the recent past to Romania where the official estimate of abandoned children is 67,339. But the scale of the problem is far greater in Latin America, Asia and Africa, where the fundamental causes remain poverty and, in some countries, continuing economic deterioration. The same economic conditions hinder the development of child care (including adoption) services in the developing countries, despite the widely accepted view that priority should always be given to placement of abandoned children in families in their own communities – a view eloquently expressed by the Indian Supreme Court in 1984 in *Laxshmi Kant Pandey v Union of India*. The development of adoption services in developing countries will no doubt continue to be a principal theme. It is obviously of great importance for those who come from the wealthier countries to appreciate the problems involved, and to avoid developments, especially in the context of intercountry adoption, which may frustrate efforts to build up local services and encourage domestic placements of children.

The present procedures in this country are explained by the Department of Health in a 1990 Circular on *Adoption of Children from Overseas* (CI(90)17, modified slightly in CI(91)14):

1. The Department's approach to intercountry adoption is influenced by the provisions of the 1986 United Nations Declaration on Social and Legal Principles relating to the Protection and Welfare of Children, with special reference to Foster Placement and Adoption Nationally and Internationally. This provides that:

(*a*) intercountry adoption may be considered as an alternative means of providing a family for a child who cannot be cared for in any suitable manner in his own country;

(*b*) in all matters relating to the placement of a child outside the care of the child's own parents, the best interests of the child should be the paramount consideration;

(*c*) safeguards and standards equivalent to those which apply in national adoption are to be applied in intercountry adoption to protect the welfare of the children concerned.

2. Social Services Departments have a vital role to play in safeguarding the welfare of children who came from overseas for adoption. This includes:

(*a*) advising and counselling those who are considering adopting a child from overseas;

(*b*) assessing the suitability of prospective adopters;

(*c*) supervising placements and making reports and recommendations to the courts when children arrive from overseas for adoption.

...

6. It is for the Home Office to decide whether a child will be admitted to the UK. If the Home Office are satisfied that there are no immigration reasons for refusal and that the proposed adoption involves a genuine transfer of parental responsibility on the grounds of the parents' inability to care for the child, they will look to this Department for advice on welfare aspects of the proposed adoption.

7. In giving advice the Department's central concern is to give first consideration to the welfare of the child. This is the test in section 6 of the Adoption Act 1976 which requires a court hearing a subsequent adoption application to give first consideration to the welfare of the child. The Department needs to be satisfied on the following matters:

(*a*) the reasons for the proposed adoption; evidence of the child's identity and as much information about his circumstances, history and background as can be discovered, including a health report on the BAAF Intercountry Medical Form;

(*b*) evidence that the child is legally available for adoption and that the appropriate authorities support the adoption plans and have authorised the child's departure from the country of origin for the purposes of adoption;

(*c*) there is either a valid parental consent, in a form which is acceptable to a UK court, given freely and with full understanding of the effects of a UK adoption order, or official certification that the child has been genuinely abandoned and the parents cannot be found;

(*d*) the prospective adopters are recommended by their Social Services Department as suitable adopters for the child.

8. The Department relies on reports from the authorities in the child's country of origin, supplemented where necessary by enquiries made by the Entry Clearance Officer in that country, and on information provided by prospective adopters, in order to be satisfied about (*a*), (*b*) and (*c*), above. The Department relies on the prospective adopters' SSD for a report and recommendation on their suitability (or otherwise) as adopters.

This all looks splendid until tested by a couple who went strictly 'by the book':

R v Secretary of State for Health, ex p Luff
[1991] FCR 821, [1992] 1 FLR 59, High Court

The facts

Mr and Mrs Luff who are aged 53 and 37 wish to adopt two Romanian orphans – a boy born in October 1987 and a girl born in May 1988. The Luffs applied to the Home Office for entry clearance in respect of the two children who are presently living in appalling conditions in Romanian orphanages. The London Borough of Bexley's adoption panel approved the Luffs as prospective adopters. However, the Health Department had medical reports on Mr Luff who had had coronary artery bypass graft surgery. The first report had said Mr Luff was suitable as a prospective adopter but the medical officer changed her mind after seeing the opinion of consultant cardiologists. She then advised that because of Mr Luff's limited life expectancy, it was not recommended that he be allowed to adopt young children. The Health Secretary advised the Home Office that 'Mr and Mrs Luff are unable to offer the long-term security throughout childhood and adolescence that is considered necessary in adoption.' The Home Office rejected the application for entry clearance. The Luffs applied for judicial review of the Health Secretary's advice.

The decision

Mr Justice Waite said that the only function of the Health Secretary in the case of foreign adoptions was to advise the Home Secretary who had the ultimate decision. It was conceded that the Health Secretary's advice was susceptible of judicial review, but the court was reminded that in reviewing advice as opposed to decisions, a judge is acting at the extremity of his powers and should confine himself to deciding whether the proposition of law is erroneous and avoid expressing opinions in areas of controversy.

Favourable recommendations had been given in 150 out of 160 foreign adoption applications. It was not realistic nor fair to foist upon the Health Secretary, in the absence of any evidence to support it, an automatic assumption that the only alternative to adoption by the Luffs for these children would be internment until majority in their present orphanages.

It was also said that the Health Secretary had displayed an obsessive preoccupation with speculative medical evidence about Mr Luff's life expectancy so as to exclude other considerations altogether or alternatively to give it undue importance. However, it appeared that the Health Secretary asked himself what the appropriate advice to give was on these facts. That included the ages of the parties and the circumstances in which the medical advice was given. It was wholly a matter for the Health Secretary to decide what weight to give any one factor over another and the weighing process was not one with which the court could interfere.

It was then claimed that the Health Secretary had brushed aside the advice of the Bexley Adoption Panel, notwithstanding that the panel was the 'lynchpin' of the adoption system. His Lordship could not accept the assertion that the Health Secretary, although not bound by the panel, was disabled from rejecting the panel's advice unless it was so demonstrably absurd as to be overturned on judicial review. The panel's advice was an opinion which the Health Secretary was invited to and did take into account.

The principal ground of attack was the irrationality of the Health Secretary's advice. His Lordship said no one disputed that many people, perhaps a majority of concerned, sympathetic and understanding people, would take the view that these two children had pressing needs. The Luffs were admirably suited to undertaking the special care these children required.

There was however another view. It might only appeal to a minority because it proceeded in the cold light of caution rather than the warm glow of hope. But the people to whom it might appeal are people with the same qualities of concern, sympathy and understanding. That view would say of these children that they had already endured physical and emotional suffering which threatened to scar them psychologically for life. Their most pressing need therefore was stability. The risks of future trauma could never be eliminated but they could be reduced to the lowest level that human endeavour could achieve. They should therefore be adopted by people whose health held out at least a reasonable prospect that they would be spared the pain of family bereavement in their teenage years.

Both those views were tenable. Both were supported on grounds of humanity. Both could claim to have the children's best interests at heart. It followed therefore that the advice tendered by the Health Secretary was cogent and rational advice, incapable of being struck down by the process of judicial review.

Questions

(i) If you had been advising the Secretary of State in this case, what would your advice have been?

(ii) Is it consistent with the view you took on the case of *Re K (a minor) (wardship: adoption)* [1991] 1 FLR 57 (p. 654, above)?

(iii) Left to yourself, would you (*a*) ban inter-country adoption altogether, (*b*) set up an agency to arrange placements properly, or (*c*) recognise all foreign adoption orders?

The Government's plans for the future were set out in their White Paper, *Adoption: The Future* (1993):

Background

6.1 The adoption of children from overseas by parents domiciled in the United Kingdom has become significant in scale only in recent years.

6.2 Up to 1990 only about 50 adoptions a year in England and Wales were of children brought here to be adopted and many of those were already related to the adopting parents. A Hague Convention of 1965 attracted ratification from only three countries.

6.3 A number of other countries – mostly those with adoption procedures and safeguards similar to our own, including most Western European countries, the USA, and many Commonwealth countries in Africa, Asia, Australasia and the Caribbean, have been designated under the Adoption Act 1976.

6.4 When a child born in one of these designated countries is adopted by parents domiciled here, there is:

- recognition of the child's adopted status under the law of the child's country of origin (the 'sending country') and UK law; and therefore no need to duplicate in UK courts an adoption order made in the sending country;
- a minimum of emigration and immigration formality.

6.5 Assessment of parents' suitability is required by the designated countries and is normally done by the local social services authority for the area in which the adopting parents live.

The recent expansion in inter-country adoption

6.6 In recent years, however, there has been an increase in the number of couples in the United Kingdom wishing to adopt children from countries whose adoption orders the UK does not recognise. These countries include Romania and other eastern European countries and countries in Central and South America. The interest in adopting children from eastern European countries was stimulated by harrowing reports of orphaned or abandoned children in institutions which emerged after the collapse of their communist regimes. The general decline in the number of babies and very young children now available for adoption in this country also helped to stimulate a general interest in adoption from overseas.

6.7 When a child is adopted from a country with which there is no bilateral arrangement through designation, the process is more complex:

- because there is no mutual recognition of adoption orders, adoptive parents must obtain an adoption order in the UK courts even if an adoption order has already been made in the sending country;
- separate entry clearance for the child is required from the UK immigration authorities, which is sought by the adopting parents through the British Embassy in the sending country;
- an assessment of the applicant parents by their local authority is normally passed by the Department of Health to the London Embassy of the sending country who send it on to the appropriate authorities in that country.

6.8 As well as being more complex for all concerned, and leading to delays and uncertainty in settling the adoptive status of the child, these arrangements have not been wholly successful in preventing the bringing into this country of very young children without proper regularisation of their legal or immigration status here, often without proper regard for legal and childcare processes in their countries of origin.

6.9 Other problems have included the reluctance of some local authorities to give any priority to the assessment of applicant parents' suitability for adoption in overseas cases, and criticism in some cases that their assessments or attitudes may have been affected by inherent objection to the concept of overseas and other transracial or transcultural adoptions. Through the Chief Social Services Inspector, the Government has worked closely with authorities on these issues, and the position is now somewhat better than it was.

The government's objectives in inter-country adoption

6.10 The Government considers that the wishes of parents here to adopt children from overseas should be respected and in all suitable cases supported and facilitated. The Government wishes to see the same principles and safeguards and so far as is realistic the same clarity of procedure introduced for overseas adoption as for domestic adoption. At the same time, the Government intends to increase the safeguards against and the disincentives to the bringing here of babies and children from overseas in circumstances which offer no reasonable child care or immigration safeguards.

...

The Hague Convention of 1993

6.16 The Government considers as a general principle, that *mutual recognition* of adoption orders, practices and procedures is a desirable objective wherever it can realistically and safely be achieved.

6.17 The Government has therefore participated fully and actively in the Hague Convention on Private International Law on Inter-Country Adoption which completed its work in May 1993 by drawing up a Convention on international co-operation in inter-country adoption. ...

6.18 The Convention is consistent with the UN Convention on the Rights of the Child (which the UK ratified in 1991) and the 1986 UN Declaration on Social and Legal Principles relating to the Protection and Welfare of children with special reference to Foster Placement and Adoption Nationally and Internationally.

6.19 The principles underlying the Hague Convention include:

- intercountry adoptions should only take place after the best interests of the child have been properly assessed and in circumstances which protect his fundamental rights;
- birth parents or others responsible for consenting to adoptions should understand what they are consenting to and its implications. They should be objectively counselled, and should not be offered financial or other inducements;
- agencies acting in intercountry adoptions should be suitably staffed and supervised;
- no one should derive improper financial gain from adoption;
- adoptive parents should be carefully and objectively assessed for their suitability.

6.20 The framework it will establish makes the sending country responsible for the assessment of the child's situation, needs and interests and gives it a responsibility to transmit to the receiving country the information necessary to show that this has been done. Receiving countries, where the adoptive parents are domiciled, have the responsibility for arranging their assessment and transmitting its results to the sending country.

6.21 The Convention envisages that adoptions carried out between each ratifying State according to the Articles of the Convention will be known as 'Convention adoptions' and in each State there will be established a 'central authority' and 'accredited bodies'. The central authority should normally be part of the country's central government. ...

6.22 The accredited bodies would be agencies authorised to prepare and arrange adoptions. For the UK, local authorities would be accredited agencies. So too would approved voluntary agencies. Few have so far shown interest in inter-country adoption, but the Government considers that at least one voluntary adoption agency, able to build up skills and experience in this complex field, would be a valuable addition. ...

Convention adoptions

6.23 When countries ratify the 1993 Hague Convention they take on a responsibility for ensuring that their standards and procedures in all inter-country adoptions with other Convention countries conform with the Convention's principles. ... It affects both 'sending' countries, who will have the prime responsibility to the child and his birth parents, and 'receiving' countries in which the adoptive parents live.

6.24 There will in principle be two very significant benefits to all concerned when adoptions occur between two countries which have ratified the Convention.

6.25 First, there will be mutual recognition of adoption orders. This means that there will be no need in the receiving country for adoptive parents to apply to the courts in their own country for a further adoption order if as will usually happen the courts in the child's country of origin have already made one. There will thus be no period of uncertainty over the child's legal status once he or she has come with the new parents to his new country.

6.26 Secondly, immigration procedures will be brought within the adoption process. Home Office entry clearance which allows the child to enter the United Kingdom will form an integral part of the adoption process prior to an adoption order being made in the sending country. The Convention does not allow a sending country to make an adoption order unless it has received confirmation that the child will be permitted to enter and remain in his new country.

6.27 The Convention includes safeguards which can be invoked if there appear to be lapses in standards in the adoption practices of any participating country. ...

6.28 The Government sees the Convention as offering a major opportunity for improving standards and streamlining the process in inter-country adoptions. The Convention, once it has become an established system of co-operation should increase safeguards against child trafficking.

6.29 The Government intends to ratify the Convention. Like many other countries, the UK will need changes in the law governing adoption. The Government intends to seek the necessary legislation through the new Adoption Bill.
6.30 In the meantime, it intends to maintain the system which facilitates adoption with 'designated' countries and to continue to work constructively to improve mutual understanding with others.

Role of local authorities
6.31 Another important change the Government intends through the new legislation is to clarify the role of local authorities in inter-country adoption.
6.32 At present, local authorities have neither any duty nor any explicit power to undertake or arrange for assessment of parents wishing to adopt children from overseas.
6.33 As part of the obligations the UK will assume when it ratifies the Convention, the Government intends to give local social services a statutory duty to provide or arrange for such assessments, and an explicit power to charge for them (but not for any domestic adoption process), as most of them do already.
6.34 The Government will also, in guidance, emphasise the need for balanced and objective assessments consistent with the principles of the Convention and of domestic adoption policy and free from any prejudice against the principle of inter-country adoption.

Sanctions
6.35 The Government intends that in due course, it should become a criminal offence to bring a child to the United Kingdom for adoption without having obtained authorisation to proceed from the relevant Health Department or agency to which this responsibility is delegated. It is essential that the requirements and safeguards designed to protect the welfare of children adopted from abroad are not treated as optional.
6.36 The Government also proposes that people who bring children into the UK without entry clearance should, subject to their means, be made liable for costs if it becomes necessary for the local authority to look after the child.

These proposals are implemented in the draft Bill and proposed regulations, contained in *Adoption – A Service for Children* (1996).

Questions

(i) Woody Allen and Mia Farrow were allowed to adopt a child from overseas although they were not married to one another or living together and Ms Farrow already had several children both natural and adopted: should they have been?
(ii) The White Paper (para 6.10) states that 'the wishes of parents [sic] here to adopt children from overseas should be respected and in all suitable cases supported and facilitated'. What might it be about the Government's philosophy which made it more sympathetic than others to inter-country adoption?

3 The UN Convention on the Rights of the Child

The Convention on the Rights of the Child was adopted by the United Nations General Assembly on 20 November 1989 and came into force on 2 September 1990. It is a statement of children's rights, and over 150 countries are parties to it, although in some instances there are significant reservations. It has three overriding themes: the child's best interests, respect for the child's evolving capacities, and protection against all forms of discrimination. The UK Government ratified the Convention in December 1991. It made reservations as we shall see.

Philip Alston and Stephen Parker in their introductory essay to *Children, Rights and the Law* (1992) point to the extraordinary commitment to the Convention:

No other treaty, particularly in the human rights field, has been ratified by so many states in such an extraordinarily short period of time. The Convention has thus generated an unprecedented degree of formal commitment on the part of Governments and the task confronting children's rights advocates will be to ensure that this commitment is matched by action.

There are 54 Articles in the Convention. The following Articles are four of the most important:

Article 3

1. In all actions concerning children, whether undertaken by public or private social welfare institutions, courts of law, administrative authorities or legislative bodies, the best interests of the child shall be a primary consideration.
2. States Parties undertake to ensure the child such protection and care as is necessary for his or her well-being, taking into account the rights and duties of his or her parents, legal guardians, or other individuals legally responsible for him or her, and, to this end, shall take all appropriate legislative and administrative measures.

...

Article 9

1. States Parties shall ensure that a child shall not be separated from his or her parents against their will, except when competent authorities subject to judicial review determine, in accordance with applicable law and procedures, that such separation is necessary for the best interests of the child. Such determination may be necessary in a particular case such as one involving abuse or neglect of the child by the parents, or one where the parents are living separately and a decision must be made as to the child's place of residence.

...

3. States Parties shall respect the right of the child who is separated from one or both parents to maintain personal relations and direct contact with both parents on a regular basis, except if it is contrary to the child's best interests.

Article 12

1. States Parties shall assure to the child who is capable of forming his or her own views the right to express those views freely in all matters affecting the child, the views of the child being given due weight in accordance with the age and maturity of the child.

Article 18

1. States Parties shall use their best efforts to ensure recognition of the principle that both parents have common responsibilities for the upbringing and development of the child. Parents or, as the case may be, legal guardians, have the primary responsibility for the upbringing and development of the child. The best interests of the child will be their basic concern.

Questions

(i) Look back at the provisions of the Children Act 1989. Do you think that English law falls short of or goes beyond the principles laid down in these Articles?
(ii) Are there any dangers in a project which attempts to set out universal norms, and if so, what do you suppose these dangers to be?

(iii) Bettina Cass (1992) states that the Convention disaggregates the rights of children from the rights of 'families', to constitute children as independent actors with rights vis-à-vis their parents and vis-à-vis the state. She goes on to say that 'the very crux of the conservative ideology of family as unified, private and inviolate is exposed' by the Convention. Is that your view of a conservative ideology of the family? Is the Convention undermining any such ideology?

There is a growing literature about the Convention. Some of this has been labelled 'feminist' and Francis Olsen (1992) discusses four different approaches in this literature. The first view, labelled by her as 'Legal Reformist' focuses on a doctrinal examination of the Convention to determine how it might be interpreted to benefit women. The second approach she calls 'Law as Patriarchy' which she sees as a document in a move toward a fuller, more feminist view of rights. The third approach is the 'Feminist Critical Legal Theory' and the fourth approach is 'Post-Modern Feminism'. These last two share much in common, but the emphasis is different:

LEGAL REFORMIST APPROACHES

Legal reformist is a broad category in which I intend to include probably most feminist lawyers and liberal legal scholars. The important shared view is that the current inequality between men and women could be changed by allowing women to enjoy the privileges currently all too much reserved to men. Some legal reformists would also like to see other societal changes, but the identifying characteristic is that the primary goal is to include women in the existing structure, not wait until some more global change takes place, and not base hopes for improving the role and status of women on any other major changes in values, technology, social systems or economics. Law is valued for its ability to abstract from particularistic situations and provide a relatively neutral playing field on which reason and principle may prevail over the dead hand of tradition and over a wide variety of forms of illegitimate power.

Most of the legal reforms that have improved the role and status of women have taken place within a broad liberal legal reformist perspective. While I believe it is important to be critical of this perspective, it would be foolish not to recognize both its practical value and the widespread perception that liberal reformism is the approach that works 'in the real world'. From such a perspective, rights for children, and specifically the United Nations Convention on the Rights of the Child, can be seen to have both positive and negative potentials.

Positive

Rights for women and children are usually seen as complementary, not as a zero sum game. The patriarchal family is generally understood to have denied rights to both women and children. The problem with the ideology of liberal rights is often seen to be that it is too limited in that it too often provides only for the 'Rights of Man'. The legal and social treatment of women and of children during much of the past two or three centuries has been criticized as 'feudal'. Thus, the extension of rights to children is in one sense simply a more or less logical next step after the extension of rights to women.

Negative

Yet there are also less positive evaluations of the Convention on the Rights of the Child to be made from a feminist liberal reform perspective. One of the most significant of these concerns is whether the Convention may be used to control and confine women. Children, and the expressed interest in their welfare (expressed often by people who show no other interest in children) have often been used to control women.

...

Although the provisions making *both* parents responsible for children would seem to be generally beneficial to women, who otherwise too often wind up solely responsible for children, the provisions may also work against the interests of women as a group. It may well be that the obligations placed 'equally' upon fathers will turn out to be unenforceable as a practical matter, but that the provisions can be used by 'father's rights' groups, composed often of recently-divorced, angry and misogynistic men, to harass the women who are taking care of 'their' children. ...

LAW AS PATRIARCHY

The 'Law as Patriarchy' approach is less familiar to most people than the legal reformist approach and seems to some to make less positive contribution. Nevertheless, it is important to understand this approach and particularly to understand the critique it presents of liberal feminist legal reform. Moderate versions of the 'Law as Patriarchy' approach may play a particularly important role in dealing with children's rights issues. Just as a legal reformist approach is associated with and resonates with liberal feminism, the 'Law as Patriarchy' approach is associated with and resonates with the feminist movement referred to (especially by those who do not consider themselves part of the movement) as 'cultural feminism'.

Cultural feminists criticize legal reformist demands for women's equality with men as settling for too little. Men do not represent an adequate aspiration. The greatest problem with society is not just the suppression of women, but the suppression of the values associated with women. Indeed, the effort to achieve legal and social equality could even contribute to the devaluation and suppression of those values.

... The primary evil of 'paternalistic' behaviour toward adults is really not that it treats an adult with the kind of care and concern that would be proper toward a child. As Onora O'Neill (1992) recognizes, the claim of fatherly concern by those exercising illegitimate power over women, minorities, colonial peoples, or other oppressed groups is generally not made in good faith but is 'highly political rhetoric'. The same kind of negative, bad faith 'paternalism' that oppresses adults is just as oppressive to children.

FEMINIST CRITICAL LEGAL THEORY

A ... dimension of the public/private distinction is the dichotomy between the 'private' family or domestic world, and the 'public' commercial world. A critical examination of this distinction allows us to 'denaturalize' the family, and to recognize the contingent character of family life. The Convention on the Rights of the Child is striking in its ability to bridge over different family forms found throughout the world. Someone whose only knowledge of life on earth came from a careful reading of the Convention would be puzzled by the occasional references to 'traditional practices' and 'those responsible for children' other than parents. Throughout most of the document, one would assume that all children were born into two-parent families that look a lot like the family of my first grade reader – Dick, Jane and Baby Sally, Mom baking cookies at home, Daddy coming home from the office in a nice suit and playing with the children. Although cookie baking is clearly *productive* work, this family displays a sharp split between productive work in the market and affective life at home with the family. The family is the private haven to which Dick and Jane return from the public world of school and Daddy from the public world of work. Baby Sally and Mom stay at home, non-productive. If Sally helps bake the cookies, we all know that this is not child labour.

In the family worlds of many societies, life is not so easy and pleasant. It is not always clear when a child is being allowed to participate in the life of the community, and when the child is being exploited. The radical separation of home from work place is taken for granted, and the separation is assumed to be a good thing. The alternative possibility of making work places healthy and educational environments for children seems never to have been considered.

POST-MODERN FEMINISM

... The distinction between Critical Feminism and Post-Modern Feminism is not a sharp or clear division, but rather more a matter of emphasis. Each challenges both the gendering of life and law, and the claimed differences between men and women. ...

The concerns of post-modern feminism that bear most closely on the Convention on the Rights of the Child include the whole notion of a universal document to deal with all children, throughout the world; the concern that such an effort will almost inevitably result in a western-oriented document that merely purports to be universal; and, more positively, the question of the category 'child' and the status of that category.

Universal standards have serious problems, however. One such problem is that they seem to overlook particular social meanings. The social meaning of a law forbidding abortion for sex selection, for example, is very different in India than in the United States. In the United States where there is no history of gender-specific abortion nor a realistic danger of the practice, such a law serves the purpose of chipping away at the woman's right to abortion by entitling the State to harass a woman with questions regarding why she is choosing to have an abortion. At some point, it may serve to drive women to overseas or back-alley abortions. In India, the meaning is different. There amniocentesis has been used specifically to determine the sex of a foetus and if the sex is female, the pregnancy is in most instances terminated. Moreover, in India the abortion decision is all too often forced upon women by their families.

Question

Olsen ends her discussion of the literature by the remark that the Convention is not a document she would have drafted and chosen to focus her energies upon. Would you have followed Olsen's advice?

In contrast to Olsen, Geraldine Van Bueren is supportive of the Convention. In 'The Challenges for the International Protection of Family Members' Rights as the 21st Century approaches' in Lowe and Douglas (ed) *Frontiers of Family Law* (1996) she develops her theme:

The Convention ... has been criticised because it appears to place duties directly on individuals, thereby confusing the nature of duties and international law. However, such criticism fails to understand that ... family responsibilities and rights are interconnected like a double helix.

She continues:

By incorporating a reference to 'all matters affecting the child' there is no longer a traditional area of exclusive parental or family decision-making. Similarly by referring to two criteria of equal value, the age and maturity of the child, States Parties do not have an unfettered discretion as to when to consider and when to ignore the views of children when children disagree with the traditional family decision-makers. Hence the participation rights of children, which are essential to child empowerment, are consistent with the ideological basis of the Convention on the Rights of the Child which is based upon the principle that children have rights which 'transcend those of the family of which they are part.'

Despite being in force less than five years articles 12 and 13[1] of the Convention on the Rights of the Child have already had a significant impact on domestic family legislative policies. In the United Kingdom, for example, the impact has been both in relation to the provision of information, most recently as recommended in the review of adoption provisions, and in the Children Act 1989 on the participation of children in decisions.

A third approach is taken by Michael King (1994). He suggests that both the detractors and the supporters concentrate their minds on policy and the philosophical aspects of rights for children. He offers a different analysis, known as 'autopoietical theory':

Among all the prevailing images of 'the child', it is the child-as-victim which dominates the Convention. As we move from the national to the international stage, however, it is not evil individuals who are seen as the instigators and perpetuators of crimes against children, but the generalised scourges of injustice, intolerance, inequality and failure to respect fundamental human rights and dignity. The preamble to the Convention asks us to 'bear in mind' that 'the child by reason of his physical and mental immaturity, needs special safeguards and care, including appropriate legal protection' and recognise that 'in all countries of the world there are children living in difficult conditions and such children need special consideration.' It recognises also 'the importance of international cooperation for improving the living conditions in every country, in particular in developing countries.'

What is interesting from a socio-legal perspective is that the Convention is presented to the world, not as a declaration of intent by the governments of the different countries or as a blueprint for action by United Nations agencies such as UNICEF, but as international law. ...

---

1. The child shall have the right to freedom of expression; this right shall include freedom to seek, receive and impart information and ideas of all kinds. ...

... By what authority, one may well ask, have these laws or non-laws been created? Although formally legitimated by its adoption by the United Nations as an international Convention, this authority finds its origins in no court or legislature. Unlike international treaties or accords between states, its evolution owes little to the activities of state governments pursuing national or party interests. It is embedded neither within the legislation of any of the nation-states of the Convention's signatories nor in any international treaties governing political relations between these states. Rather, the Convention is the product of a Working Group of national representatives, set up by the UN Commission on Human Rights. This is not the end of the story, for it is clear that the major influence over its final form was exercised, not so much by the government delegations who were able to exercise an effective power of veto, but by the non-governmental organisations (NGOs) who attended the meetings of the *Ad Hoc* Group on the Drafting of the Convention. According to one writer, from the United Nations Centre for Human Rights in Geneva, 'The Working Group is its ten-year history ... never had a recourse to voting, since all the decisions are reached by consensus.' This meant that there was no practical distinction between those State delegations, who were accountable to their governments, and those NGOs, who were accountable for the most part to no one but themselves. According to another commentator, the *Ad Hoc* Group's influence on the Working Group increased considerably as the drafting process progressed and as its 'influence grew, its activities became more completely integrated into the Working Group process.' What did these NGOs consist of? They appear to have been a collection of 32 supranational organisations as diverse as Amnesty International and the International Association of Juvenile and Family Court Magistrates, the Bahai International Community and the International Federation of Women's Lawyers. While it is true that before it could be treated as law within individual states the Convention had to be ratified, in practice the national governments were presented with a ready-made package which they could either accept, reject or accept with reservations on the application in their territories of certain of the Articles. In the United Kingdom there was certainly no detailed debate on the contents of the Convention in Parliament and one suspects that the same was true of the vast majority of those 151 countries which have now ratified the Convention.

...The phenomenon of the campaign by adults for children's rights may seem, at first sight, a strange one. On a rather simplistic psychological level, it may be explainable by the fact that many adults who have suffered as children wish to prevent future generations from having similar experiences. More sophisticated sociological explanations have pointed to the relatively recent social construction of the parent-child relationship as a combination of strong emotional bonds with due recognition of the child's autonomy. This autonomy is sustained and given a public form through the notion of children's rights. As a philosophical and political phenomenon, the rights perspective owes much to Kantian rationality, social hygienics and liberal theories of justice. It proceeds as if children represent an oppressed group, who are likely to suffer hardship, exploitation and lack of respect for their dignity as human beings and of their capacity for self-determination. Children are, in other words, denied those rights which would, if granted, reduce their suffering and enhance their dignity and allow them to seize some control over their own lives. They have no way of achieving these objectives unless rights are granted to them. As Onora O'Neill (1992) points out, however, the logic that is relevant to the provision of rights for oppressed *adult* groups – that the notion of rights provides the necessary capacity and rhetoric for such groups to exert the necessary 'pressure from below' and so improve their situation – does not apply or applies only to a limited degree of children. 'Childhood,' she explains,

> is a stage of life from which children normally emerge and are helped and urged to emerge by those who have power over them. Those with power over children's lives usually have some interest in ending childish dependence. Oppressors usually have an interest in maintaining the oppression of social groups.

Therefore, she argues, 'The analogy between children's dependence and that of oppressed groups is suspect.' ... The introduction into international law of the 'manifesto rights' or 'dignified statements' about interests of and 'pious hopes' for children is clearly seen by the promoters of the Convention as the first stage in a process of taking children's rights seriously. It is certainly true that the Convention is likely to have the effect of drawing the attention of governments and the mass media of post-industrial Western societies to the needs of children as a weak, vulnerable and sensitive group and to the harms that they may suffer if those needs are not met.

It is no startling conclusion to suggest that at the level of international law the mechanisms do not exist to force governments to comply with the demands which may involve the massive redeployment of resources and major changes in policy. Nor is it particularly surprising if we find that, at the level of individual states, campaigns for substantive rights for children may become obstructed by government inertia, poverty or indifference. What autopoietic theory is able to add, however, is the image of demands for substantive rights for children being reconstructed as legal communications which governments are then able to respond to and operate upon within the closed system of law and so avoid the complexities and, at times, embarrassment that these demands generate.

Reconstructing children's rights as law has the additional advantage for governments and the United Nations of giving the impression that something is being done for the children of the world. In its communications, the legal system provides society with an image of law as capable of providing order and structure in an unruly and disordered world. The United Nations in its Convention on the Rights of the Child offers us a vision of a three-tiered hierarchy consisting of international law at the top, state law in the middle, and those national institutions, agencies and organisations concerned with child protection and welfare at the bottom. In the exhortations to national governments to 'assure,' 'promote,' 'encourage,' 'undertake,' 'provide,' 'respect,' 'use their best efforts' and 'take all appropriate legislative, social and educational measures,' and in the impressive tally of countries that have ratified the Convention, the impression is conveyed of a direct line of command (or at least strong influence), from the United Nations to nation-state to citizen. As we have seen, this impression bears little relation to any realities except those created by law.

Any false hopes generated by the Convention are nobody's fault. One cannot blame those advocates of children's rights, stirred into action by the spectacle of widespread child suffering and the powerlessness of children in the face of adult tyranny, insensitivity of indifference, for being carried away on the magic carpet of excessive optimism. It was not they who misled us into believing that the law was capable of improving children's lives by the imposition of legal order, but law itself. They were themselves misled. Their hopes arose from a genuine misreading of the nature of law and legal operations. To enter into and operate within the communicative world of law is to talk and think like a lawyer, that is to commit oneself increasingly to a belief in law's version of the social universe where political, economic and moral statements are all represented as amenable to direct legal transformation and to enforcement by law. At times when people are reeling from the uncertainties and insecurities created by global political and economic upheavals of enormous proportions law's vision of itself and of society may prove particularly attractive. To see children, the hope for the future, as protected and respected for their human attributes by an all-embracing legal order, which offers them rights, is to give the impression that the rational control of that future is within our grasp, if only we were to take seriously children's rights, now reconstructed by law, by believing in them and their magic.

Question

Which if any of these various approaches do you support? Are they inconsistent with each other?

There are important Articles in the Convention on immigration, refugee children, and juvenile justice.

Article 10

1. In accordance with the obligation of States Parties under article 9, paragraph 1, applications by a child or his or her parents to enter or leave a State Party for the purpose of family reunification shall be dealt with by States Parties in a positive, humane and expeditious manner. States Parties shall further ensure that the submission of such a request shall entail no adverse consequences for the applicants and for the members of their family.

2. A child whose parents reside in different States shall have the right to maintain on a regular basis save in exceptional circumstances personal relations and direct contacts with both parents. Towards that end and in accordance with the obligation of States Parties under article 9, paragraph 1, States Parties shall respect the right of the child and his or her parents to leave any country, including their own, and to enter their own country. The right to leave any country shall be subject only to such restrictions as are prescribed by law and which are necessary to protect the national security, public order (*ordre public*), public health or morals or the rights and freedoms of others and are consistent with the other rights recognized in the present Convention.

Article 22

1. States Parties shall take appropriate measures to ensure that a child who is seeking refugee status or who is considered a refugee in accordance with applicable international or domestic law and procedures shall, whether unaccompanied or accompanied by his or her parents or by any other person, receive appropriate protection and humanitarian assistance in the enjoyment of applicable rights set forth in this Convention and in other international human rights or humanitarian instruments to which the said States are Parties.
2. For this purpose, States Parties shall provide, as they consider appropriate, cooperation in any efforts by the United Nations and other competent intergovernmental organizations or non-governmental organizations co-operating with the United Nations to protect and assist such a child and to trace the parents or other members of the family of any refugee child in order to obtain information necessary for reunification with his or her family. In cases where no parents or other members of the family can be found, the child shall be accorded the same protection as any other child permanently or temporarily deprived of his or her family environment for any reason, as set forth in the present Convention.

Article 40

1. States Parties recognize the right of every child alleged as, accused of, or recognized as having infringed the penal law to be treated in a manner consistent with the promotion of the child's sense of dignity and worth, which reinforces the child's respect for the human rights and fundamental freedoms of others and which takes into account the child's age and the desirability of promoting the child's re-integration and the child's assuming a constructive role in society.
2. To this end, and having regard to the relevant provisions of international instruments, States Parties shall, in particular, ensure that:
   (*a*) No child shall be alleged as, be accused of, or recognized as having infringed the penal law by reason of acts or omissions which were not prohibited by national or international law at the time they were committed;
   (*b*) Every child alleged as or accused of having infringed the penal law has at least the following guarantees:
      (i) to be presumed innocent until proven guilty according to law;
      (ii) to be informed promptly and directly of the charges against him or her, and if appropriate through his or her parents or legal guardian, and to have legal or other appropriate assistance in the preparation and presentation of his or her defence;
      (iii) to have the matter determined without delay by a competent, independent and impartial authority or judicial body in a fair hearing according to law, in the presence of legal or other appropriate assistance and, unless it is considered not to be in the best interest of the child, in particular, taking into account his or her age or situation, his or her parents or legal guardians;
      (iv) not to be compelled to give testimony or to confess guilt; to examine or have examined adverse witnesses and to obtain the participation and examination of witnesses on his or her behalf under conditions of equality;
      (v) if considered to have infringed the penal law, to have this decision and any measures imposed in consequence thereof reviewed by a higher competent, independent and impartial authority or judicial body according to law;
      (vi) to have the free assistance of an interpreter if the child cannot understand or speak the language used;
      (vii) to have his or her privacy fully respected at all stages of the proceedings.
3. States Parties shall seek to promote the establishment of laws, procedures, authorities and institutions specifically applicable to children alleged as, accused of, or recognized as having infringed the penal law, and in particular:
   (*a*) the establishment of a minimum age below which children shall be presumed not to have the capacity to infringe the penal law;
   (*b*) whenever appropriate and desirable, measures for dealing with such children without resorting to judicial proceedings, providing that human rights and legal safeguards are fully respected.
4. A variety of dispositions, such as care, guidance and supervision orders; counselling; probation; foster care; education and vocational training programmes and other alternatives to institutional care shall be available to ensure that children are dealt with in a manner appropriate to their well-being and proportionate both to their circumstances and the offence.

Questions

(i) Does it surprise you to be told that the UK Government has entered reservations to all three of the above articles? Why do you think it has done so?
(ii) The Children's Rights Development Unit has been established to monitor the UK's compliance with the Convention. What are the areas of family law, other than those where there are reservations, which in your opinion most fall short of the principles of the Convention?

4 The European Convention for the Protection of Human Rights and Fundamental Freedoms

Articles 8 and 12 of the European Convention have been considered in Chapters 1 and 11:

Article 8
1. Everyone has the right to respect for his private and family life, his home and his correspondence.
2. There shall be no interference by a public authority with the exercise of this right except such as is in accordance with the law and is necessary in a democratic society in the interests of national security, public safety or the economic well-being of the country, for the prevention of disorder or crime, for the protection of health or morals, or for the protection of the rights and freedoms of others.

This article was considered by the European Court of Human Rights in *Keegan v Ireland* (1994) 18 EHRR 342 and *Kroon v Netherlands* (1994) 19 EHRR 263.

Keegan v Ireland (family life: adoption)
(1994) 18 EHRR 342, European Court of Human Rights

The applicant met his girlfriend in May 1986, and they began living together in February 1987. In February 1988, it was confirmed that she was pregnant. The conception was the result of a deliberate decision, and the couple had planned to marry. Shortly afterwards, however, the relationship broke down and they ceased to cohabit. After the child was born, it was placed for adoption by the mother without the applicant's knowledge or consent. The relevant provisions of the Adoption Act 1952 permitted the adoption of a child born outside marriage without the consent of the natural father. The applicant applied to the Circuit Court, under the Guardianship of Infants Act 1964, to be appointed as the child's guardian, which would have enabled him to challenge the proposed adoption. He was appointed guardian and awarded custody of the child. The decision of the Circuit Court was upheld by the High Court, but on appeal by way of case stated the Supreme Court ruled that the wishes of the natural father should not be considered if the prospective adopters could achieve a quality of welfare which was to an important degree better. The case was remitted to the High Court. On the rehearing a consultant psychiatrist gave evidence that if the placement with the prospective adopters was disturbed after a period of over a year, the child was likely to suffer trauma and to have difficulty in forming relationships of trust. The High Court therefore declined to appoint the applicant as guardian. An adoption order was subsequently made.

Judgment of the court:

A. *Applicability of Article 8*

42. The Government maintained that the sporadic and unstable relationship between the applicant and the mother had come to an end before the birth of the child and did not have the minimal levels of seriousness, depth and commitment to cross the threshold into family life within the meaning of Article 8. Moreover, there was no period during the life of the child in which a recognised family life involving her had been in existence. In their view neither a mere blood link nor a sincere and heartfelt desire for family life were enough to create it.

43. For both the applicant and the Commission, on the other hand, his links with the child were sufficient to establish family life. They stressed that his daughter was the fruit of a planned decision taken in the context of a loving relationship.

44. The Court recalls that the notion of the 'family' in this provision is not confined solely to marriage-based relationships and may encompass other *de facto* 'family' ties where the parties are living together outside of marriage. A child born out of such a relationship is *ipso iure* part of that 'family' unit from the moment of his birth and by the very fact of it. There thus exists between the child and his parents a bond amounting to family life even if at the time of his or her birth the parents are no longer cohabiting or if their relationship has then ended.

45. In the present case, the relationship between the applicant and the child's mother lasted for two years during one of which they cohabited. Moreover, the conception of their child was the result of a deliberate decision and they had also planned to get married. Their relationship at this time had thus the hallmark of family life for the purposes of Article 8. The fact that it subsequently broke down does not alter this conclusion any more than it would for a couple who were lawfully married and in a similar situation. It follows that from the moment of the child's birth there existed between the applicant and his daughter a bond amounting to family life.

...

50. According to the principles set out by the Court in its caselaw, where the existence of a family tie with a child has been established, the State must act in a manner calculated to enable that tie to be developed and legal safeguards must be created that render possible as from the moment of birth the child's integration in his family. In this context reference may be made to the principle laid down in Article 7 of the United Nations Convention on the Rights of the Child of 20 November 1989 that a child has, as far as possible, the right to be cared for by his or her parents. It is, moreover, appropriate to recall that the mutual enjoyment by parent and child of each other's company constitutes a fundamental element of family life even when the relationship between the parents has broken down.

51. In the present case the obligations inherent in Article 8 are closely intertwined, bearing in mind the State's involvement in the adoption process. The fact that Irish law permitted the secret placement of the child for adoption without the applicant's knowledge or consent, leading to the bonding of the child with the proposed adopters and to the subsequent making of an adoption order, amounted to an interference with his right to respect for family life. Such interference is permissible only if the conditions set out in paragraph 2 of Article 8 are satisfied.

Held unanimously:

(i) that it was unnecessary to examine the Goverment's preliminary objection concerning the applicant's standing to complain on behalf of his daughter;
(ii) that the remainder of the Government's preliminary objections should be dismissed;
(iii) that Article 8 applied in the instant case and had been violated;
(iv) that Article 6(1) had been violated;
(v) that it was unnecessary to examine the applicant's complaint under Article 14;
(vi) that Ireland was to pay, within three months, IR£12,000 in respect of non-pecuniary and pecuniary damage, and in respect of costs and expenses, the sums resulting from the calculation to be made in accordance with paragraph 71 of the judgment.

Kroon v Netherlands (non-recognition of paternity) (1994) 19 EHRR 263, European Court of Human Rights

A child was born of a stable relationship between the first and second applicants when the former was still married to another man. Under Dutch law it was impossible to obtain recognition of the biological father's paternity unless the husband denied paternity. The applicants complained that they were victims of a violation of Article 8 of the Convention, both taken alone and in conjunction with Article 14, and claimed compensation for non-pecuniary damage, costs and expenses under Article 50.

Judgment of the court:

B. *General principles*

31. The Court reiterates that the essential object of Article 8 is to protect the individual against arbitrary action by the public authorities. There may in addition be positive obligations inherent in effective 'respect' for family life. However, the boundaries between the State's positive and negative obligations under this provision do not lend themselves to precise definition. The applicable principles are nonetheless similar. In both contexts regard must be had to the fair balance that has to be struck between the competing interests of the individual and of the community as a whole; and in both contexts the State enjoys a certain margin of appreciation.

...

40. In the Court's opinion, 'respect' for 'family life' requires that biological and social reality prevail over a legal presumption which, as in the present case, flies in the face of both established fact and the wishes of those concerned without actually benefiting anyone. Accordingly, the Court concludes that, even having regard to the margin of appreciation left to the State, the Netherlands has failed to secure to the applicants the 'respect' for their family life to which they are entitled under the Convention.

There has accordingly been a violation of Article 8.

Held:

(1) by eight votes to one that Article 8 of the Convention was applicable;
(2) by seven votes to two that there had been a violation of Article 8 of the Convention;
(3) unanimously that no separate issue arose under Article 14 of the Convention in conjunction with Article 8;
(4) unanimously that as regards the claim for non-pecuniary damage the finding of a violation constituted, in itself, sufficient just satisfaction;
(5) by eight votes to one that the respondent State had to pay to the applicants, within three months, H 20,000, less FF 13,855.85 to be converted into Netherlands guilders in accordance with the rate of exchange applicable on the date of delivery of the present judgment, plus any value-added tax that may be payable on the resulting figure, in respect of legal costs and expenses;
(6) unanimously that the remainder of the claim for just satisfaction should be dismissed.

Questions

(i) Do you think that Article 8 creates rights for fathers in stable de facto relationships even in the absence of a s. 4 agreement under the Children Act 1989? (See the decision in *McMichael v United Kingdom* [1995] Fam Law 478 and the article on the case by Chris Barton and Alastair Bissett-Johnson [1995] Fam Law 507.)

(ii) Is the definition of 'family life' developed by the European Court of Human Rights in *Keegan v Ireland* (1994) 18 EHRR 342 and *Kroon v Netherlands* (1994) 19 EHRR 263 different from your own understanding of what is meant by 'family life' and if so, how does it differ?

Article 12
Men and women of marriageable age have the right to marry and to found a family, according to the national laws governing the exercise of this right.

Questions

(i) Reread the material in Chapter 1 on transsexuals and homosexuals and their rights to marry. Do you now believe that English law contravenes Article 12?
(ii) Refer back to Chapter 11. Does Article 12 mean that married couples have a right to be supplied with IVF treatment?

Seventh Protocol (1984)

The member States of the Council of Europe signatory hereto,

Being resolved to take further steps to ensure the collective enforcement of certain rights and freedoms by means of the Convention for the Protection of Human Rights and Fundamental Freedoms signed at Rome on 4 November 1950 (hereinafter referred to as 'the Convention');

Have agreed as follows:

Article 1
1. An alien lawfully resident in the territory of a State shall not be expelled therefrom except in pursuance of a decision reached in accordance with law and shall be allowed:
(*a*) to submit reasons against his expulsion,
(*b*) to have his case reviewed, and
(*c*) to be represented for these purposes before the competent authority or a person or persons designated by that authority.

2. An alien may be expelled before the exercise of his rights under paragraph 1(*a*), (*b*) and (*c*) of this Article, when such expulsion is necessary in the interests of public order or is grounded on reasons of national security.

Article 2
1. Everyone convicted of a criminal offence by a tribunal shall have the right to have conviction or sentence reviewed by a higher tribunal. The exercise of this right, including the grounds on which it may be exercised, shall be governed by law.

2. This right may be subject to exceptions in regard to offences of a minor character, as prescribed by law, or in cases in which the person concerned was tried in the first instance by the highest tribunal or was convicted following an appeal against acquittal.

Article 3
When a person has by a final decision been convicted of a criminal offence and when subsequently his conviction has been reversed, or he has been pardoned, on the ground that a new or newly discovered fact shows conclusively that there has been a miscarriage of justice, the person who has suffered punishment as a result of such conviction shall be compensated according to the law or the practice of the State concerned, unless it is proved that the non-disclosure of the unknown fact in time is wholly or partly attributable to him.

Article 4
1. No one shall be liable to be tried or punished again in criminal proceedings under the jurisdiction of the same State for an offence for which he has already been finally acquitted or convicted in accordance with the law and penal procedure of that State.

2. The provisions of the preceding paragraph shall not prevent the re-opening of the case in accordance with the law and penal procedure of the State concerned, if there is evidence of new or newly discovered facts, or if there has been a fundamental defect in the previous proceedings, which could affect the outcome of the case.

3. No derogation from this Article shall be made under Article 15 of the Convention.

Article 5

1. Spouses shall enjoy equality of rights and responsibilities of a private law character between them, and in their relations with their children, as to marriage, during marriage and in the event of its dissolution. This Article shall not prevent States from taking such measures as are necessary in the interests of the children.

Question

The Seventh Protocol (1984) has not been ratified by the UK. Why do you think this is so? Could it just be something to do with Article 1 of this Protocol?

Article 9

1. Everyone has the right to freedom of thought, conscience and religion; this right includes freedom to change his religion or belief and freedom, either alone or in community with others and in public or private, to manifest his religion or belief, in worship, teaching, practice and observance.
2. Freedom to manifest one's religion or beliefs shall be subject only to such limitations as are prescribed by law and are necessary in a democratic society in the interests of public safety, for the protection of public order, health or morals, or for the protection of the rights and freedoms of others.

Protocol No. 1, Article 2

No person shall be denied the right to education. In the exercise of any functions which it assumes in relation to education and to teaching, the State shall respect the right of parents to ensure such education and teaching in conformity with their own religious and philosophical convictions.

Thus the European Convention of Human Rights seeks to achieve a free and plural society through, among other things, a proper balance between family privacy and the right to learn. Relying on parents to bring up their children is seen as an essential feature of Western democratic society. But is this for the parents', the children's or society's sake? When should a child's interests or wishes prevail over his parents? How much help should the parents be given to perform their task?

Campbell and Cosans v United Kingdom
(1982) 4 EHRR 293, European Court of Human Rights

Mrs Campbell's son, Gordon, attended a primary school in Scotland at which corporal punishment was used for disciplinary purposes, although in fact Gordon was never so punished while he was at that school. Mrs Cosans' son, Jeffrey, attended a secondary school where corporal punishment was also used. On his father's advice, Jeffrey refused to accept corporal punishment for trying to take a prohibited short cut on his way home from school. As a result, he was suspended from school until such time as he was willing to accept the punishment. He remained suspended from September to the following May, when he ceased to be of compulsory school age. Each mother claimed a violation of the second sentence of Article 2, Protocol No. 1, and Mrs Cosans claimed that Jeffrey's suspension violated his right to education under the first sentence of that Article. (They also claimed breach of the prohibition of 'torture' or 'inhuman or degrading treatment or punishment' in Article 3 of the Convention, but the Court found that no such treatment had taken place.)

Judgment of the court: ... in the submission of the Government, the obligation to respect philosophical convictions arises only in relation to the content of, and mode of conveying, information and knowledge and not in relation to all aspects of school administration.

As the Government pointed out, the *Kjeldsen, Busk Madsen and Pedersen* judgment states:

> 'The second sentence of Article 2 implies ... that the State, in fulfilling the functions assumed by it in regard to education and teaching, must take care that information or knowledge included in the curriculum is conveyed in an objective, critical and pluralistic manner. The State is forbidden to pursue an aim of indoctrination that might be considered as not respecting parents' religious and philosophical convictions. That is the limit that must not be exceeded.'

However, that case concerned the content of instruction, whereas the second sentence of Article 2 has a broader scope, as is shown by the generality of its wording. This was confirmed by the Court in the same judgment when it held that the said sentence is binding upon the Contracting States in the exercise, inter alia, of the function 'consisting of the organisation and financing of public education'. ...

The Government also contested the conclusion of the majority of the [European Commission of Human Rights] that the applicants' views on the use of corporal punishment amounted to 'philosophical convictions', arguing, inter alia, that the expression did not extend to opinions on internal school administration, such as discipline, and that, if the majority were correct, there was no reason why objections to other methods of discipline, or simply to discipline in general, should not also amount to 'philosophical convictions'. ...

Having regard to the Convention as a whole ... the expression 'philosophical convictions' in the present context denotes, in the Court's opinion, such convictions as are worthy of respect in a 'democratic society' ... and are not incompatible with human dignity; in addition, they must not conflict with the fundamental right of the child to education, the whole of Article 2 being dominated by its first sentence. ...

The applicants' views relate to a weighty and substantial aspect of human life and behaviour, namely the integrity of the person, the propriety or otherwise of the infliction of corporal punishment and the exclusion of the distress which the risk of such punishment entails. They are views which satisfy the various criteria listed above; it is this that distinguishes them from opinions that might be held on other methods of discipline or on discipline in general. ...

Mrs Campbell and Mrs Cosans have accordingly been victims of a violation of the second sentence of Article 2 of Protocol No. 1. ...

The right to education guaranteed by the first sentence of Article 2 by its very nature calls for regulation by the State, but such regulation must never injure the substance of the right nor conflict with other rights enshrined in the Convention or its Protocols. ...

The suspension of Jeffrey Cosans – which remained in force for nearly a whole school year – was motivated by his and his parents' refusal to accept that he receive or be liable to corporal punishment. ... His return to school could have been secured only if his parents had acted contrary to their convictions, convictions which the United Kingdom is obliged to respect under the second sentence of Article 2. ... A condition of access to an educational establishment that conflicts in this way with another right enshrined in Protocol No. 1 cannot be described as reasonable and in any event falls ouside the State's power of regulation under Article 2.

There has accordingly also been, as regards Jeffrey Cosans, breach of the first sentence of that Article.

Questions

(i) In the *Kjeldsen, Busk Madsen and Pedersen* case (7 December 1976, Series A, No. 23) the court held that compulsory sex education in state schools was *not* a contravention of the duty to respect the parents' religious and philosophical convictions: can you explain why?

(ii) What would have been the position if Jeffrey Cosans had wanted to exercise his right to education, but his parents had prevented him?

(iii) In the event, the Government found it impossible to legislate to allow parents to choose and the Education (No. 2) Act 1986 bans corporal punishment for all state-educated pupils: is this a victory for parents' or children's rights?

The European Convention, as an unincorporated treaty, forms no part of English law. The traditional approach is illustrated by the following case decided by the Court of Appeal in the area of deportation:

Chundawadra v Immigration Appeal Tribunal
[1988] Imm AR 161, Court of Appeal

The facts appear in the judgment of Glidewell LJ.

Glidewell LJ: On 21 March 1984 this appellant, Mr Surendra Jessn Chundawadra, was convicted at Aylesbury Crown Court of being involved in the illegal importation of a controlled drug, namely cannabis, and was sentenced to 30 months imprisonment. That court made no recommendation for his deportation. On 6 February 1985 the Home Secretary gave notice of his intention to make an order for the deportation of the appellant to Tanzania under section 3(5)(*b*) of the Immigration Act 1971, that is to say on the ground that his deportation would be conducive to the public good. The appellant appealed against that decision under section 15 of the 1971 Act. The Immigration Appeal Tribunal heard his appeal on 21 June 1985 and notified their decision dismissing the appeal to him on 5 July of that year. The appellant moved to quash that decision by way of judicial review, namely an order of certiorari. On 28 January 1987, Taylor J refused to quash the decision of the Appeal Tribunal. It is against his decision that the appellant now appeals to this court.

The facts I take from the decision of the tribunal. At the time of their hearing the appellant was aged 27 and he is presumably now aged 29. When he was 17 or 18, in 1976, he came to this country with his parents. His father and mother have since lived here. In August 1979 the lady who is now his wife came to this country from India and they were married on 1 September of that year. A daughter was born to them in August 1980. In February 1983 the appellant and his wife separated after some disagreement, but in February 1984 they were reconciled and the wife returned to live with the appellant at his parents' home. They were still living together at the time of the appeal to the tribunal. Meanwhile, in November 1982, the appellant and another lady, a Miss Patel, came back to this country from India and were arrested at Heathrow Airport in possession of some 10 kg of cannabis resin with an estimated value of some £20,000. It was that which led to the charge which took him to Aylesbury Crown Court and to his subsequent conviction, after pleading not guilty.

I accept that, if a Minister makes a clear statement of Government policy as to how some matter is to be dealt with in the future, that in itself, while not giving rise to any legal rights, may give rise in particular circumstances to an expectation that, until the policy is altered and announced to be altered, it will be followed. But that is a wholly different situation from that which arises here. [Counsel for the appellant] professed to see no distinction between the two situations. With respect to him, to my mind there is a gulf between them. Here there is an international treaty; the Government of the United Kingdom has acceded to it but it is not embodied in our domestic legislation, and indeed, whether it should be is the subject of a good deal of discussion. But it is not, and because it is not it may not be looked at or prayed in aid in relation to matters in these courts save when a question of ambiguity in a statute or other legal text arises. That not being the case here, it may not be looked at all and no expectation that it should be followed can arise. [Counsel for the Secretary of State] put it in these graphic terms: it is not appropriate to introduce the Convention into the law of England by the back door of legitimate expectation when the front door is firmly barred. I respectfully agree. It cannot be implied, in my view, either from section 5 of the 1971 Act or from the relevant paragraphs of HC Paper 169 that the European Convention is intended to be or is in any way a relevant consideration in the circumstances of this case. And, indeed, to put it in another way, if the test derived from article 8 of the Convention is different from that laid down in section 3(5) of the 1971 Act, a matter upon which I find it unnecessary to express any opinion, it is difficult to see how, in the face of the statute, the test derived from the Convention could be relevant to the Appeal Tribunal's determination. The tribunal was obliged to follow the statute.

Often, in my view, the answer to the question 'Is deportation conducive to the public good?' would be the same as would be the answer to the question, 'Is it necessary for the prevention of crime?'; but, if events arise where the two questions produce different answers, then it may be that the European Court of Human Rights will pronounce that a decision made by the domestic

tribunals of this country was made in breach of an article of the Convention. So far as the courts of this country are concerned, we must follow English law. No implication is to be derived from anywhere except the Act and the rules. Accordingly, persuasively though [Counsel for the appellant] advanced his arguments, to my mind they fail and I would dismiss this appeal.
Appeal dismissed.

There is no doubt, however, that the Convention provides a valid aid to construction of ambiguous or unclear statutory provisions. (See *R v Secretary of State for the Home Department, ex p Brind* [1991] 1 AC 696, CA.)

Perhaps of equal importance is the fact that Government materials now often make express reference to the provisions of the European Convention. One example is the documents known as DP/3/96, DP/4/96 and DP/5/96, which provide guidance to immigration officers on cases involving marriage and children in this sensitive area of deportation and illegal entry. To benefit from any presumption against deportation or removal the applicant must have a genuine and subsisting marriage to a person settled in the UK and the couple must have lived together in the UK continuously for two years before the commencement of enforcement action. In addition, the guidance says that it must be unreasonable to expect the settled spouse to accompany the applicant on deportation. Where the person marries after the commencement of the enforcement action it is only in the most exceptional circumstances that removal action should be stopped and the person allowed to stay. Where there are children of the marriage with a right of abode in the UK then this fact is to be taken into account but it is no more than one of many factors. (See *R v Secretary of State for the Home Department, ex p Meftah Zighem* [1996] Imm AR 194.)

Questions

(i) Why do you think that these guidelines only operate in favour of the person subject to deportation procedures if he has married a person *settled in the UK*. Why do you think there is this restriction? Is this restriction in conformity with Article 8?
(ii) Should the guidelines benefit a lesbian or gay couple?
(iii) You are advising a man who has overstayed his leave to remain in the UK and he is liable to deportation. He has a wife who is settled in the UK and there are two young children of the marriage. The marriage is breaking down and there is agreement that the children should live with the father. Would an application for a Residence Order be successful, given the father's immigration status? If a Residence Order were obtained, would this prevent deportation proceedings from being continued? (See *Re T* [1994] Imm AR 368, CA; *Re E* [1995] Imm AR 475.)

Index